A DIGEST

OF

INTERNATIONAL LAW

AS EMBODIED IN

DIPLOMATIC DISCUSSIONS, TREATIES AND
OTHER INTERNATIONAL AGREEMENTS, INTERNATIONAL
AWARDS, THE DECISIONS OF MUNICIPAL COURTS, AND
THE WRITINGS OF JURISTS,

AND ESPECIALLY IN

DOCUMENTS, PUBLISHED AND UNPUBLISHED,
ISSUED BY PRESIDENTS AND SECRETARIES OF STATE OF
THE UNITED STATES,
THE OPINIONS OF THE ATTORNEYS-GENERAL, AND THE
DECISIONS OF COURTS, FEDERAL
AND STATE.

BY

JOHN BASSETT MOORE, LL. D.,

Hamilton Fish Professor of International Law and Diplomacy, Columbia University,
New York; Associate of the Institute of International Law; Sometime
Third Assistant Secretary of State and Assistant Secretary of State of the United States;
Author of a Treatise on Extradition and Interstate Rendition, of American Notes on
the Conflict of Laws, of a History and Digest of International Arbitrations, of an Exposition of the Spirit and Achievements
of American Diplomacy, etc.

IN EIGHT VOLUMES
(THE EIGHTH BEING INDEXICAL).

VOLUME II.

WASHINGTON:
GOVERNMENT PRINTING OFFICE.
1906.

Philip Stein

CONTENTS OF VOLUME II.

Chapter VI.

NATIONAL JURISDICTION: ITS LEGAL EFFECTS.

CHAPTER VII.

EXEMPTIONS FROM TERRITORIAL JURISDICTION.

Chapter VIII.

THE HIGH SEAS.

I. *SUPREMACY OF TERRITORIAL SOVEREIGN.*

1. JURISDICTION.

(1) THE NATION'S ABSOLUTE AND EXCLUSIVE RIGHT.

§ 175.

" The jurisdiction of the nation within its own territory is necessarily exclusive and absolute. It is susceptible of no limitation not imposed by itself. Any restriction upon it, deriving validity from an external source, would imply a diminution of its sovereignty to the extent of the restriction, and an investment of that sovereignty to the same extent in that power which could impose such restriction. All exceptions, therefore, to the full and complete power of a nation within its own territories, must be traced up to the consent of the nation itself. They can flow from no other legitimate source. This consent may be either express or implied."

> Marshall, C. J., Schooner Exchange *v.* McFaddon (1812), 7 Cranch, 116, 136.
>
> Church *v.* Hubbart, 2 Cranch, 187, 234.
>
> " It is a settled principle of international law that a sovereign cannot be permitted to set up one of his own municipal laws as a bar to a claim by a foreign sovereign for a wrong done to the latter's subjects." (Mr. Bayard, Sec. of State, to Mr. King, Oct. 13, 1886, MS. Inst. Colombia, XVII. 568.)
>
> From the supremacy of the territorial sovereign is derived the right to expel aliens and to regulate their immigration, as is hereafter more fully explained in this work.

A seizure within the waters of the United States, by a British cruiser, of a Spanish vessel alleged to be a slaver, is an invasion of the sovereignty of the United States.

> Mr. Clay, Sec. of State, to Mr. Vaughan, Brit. min., Feb. 18, 1828, MS. Notes For. Leg. III. 430.

" The jurisdiction of every independent nation over the merchant vessels of other nations lying within its own harbors " being " absolute and exclusive, nothing but its authority can justify a ship of war belonging to another nation in seizing and detaining a vessel thus situated for any cause or pretext whatever."

> Mr. Buchanan, Sec. of State, to Mr. Wise, min. to Brazil, Sept. 27, 1845, MS. Inst. Brazil, XV. 119. This statement related to the action of Commodore Turner, U. S. S. *Raritan*, in seizing the American vessel *Porpoise* at Rio de Janeiro on suspicion of her being engaged in the

slave trade. It appeared that Commodore Turner in the first instance placed a marine guard on board the vessel, at the instance of the United States consul and with the consent of a Brazilian police officer, until the Brazilian authorities could be apprized of the case, but that he afterwards refused to remove the guard when requested by the local authorities to do so. With reference to this circumstance Mr. Buchanan said: "The moment that these authorities had manifested their desire that the vessel should no longer remain in the custody of the commodore, the guard ought to have been instantly removed. After this decision of the supreme authority, its continuance on board was a violation of the territorial jurisdiction of Brazil."

"When a foreign territorial jurisdiction has been violated in the seizure of an American vessel (by officers of the United States), and process of the United States courts, it has been decided by our Supreme Court, in affirming the condemnation of a vessel so seized, that the offense thereby committed against the foreign power did not invalidate the proceedings against the vessel. (Ship Richmond, 9 Cranch, 102.)"

> Mr. Buchanan, Sec. of State, letter to Committee of Claims, Mar. 4, 1846, MS. Report Book, VI. 172.

The seizure of an American vessel by an American ship-of-war, within the jurisdiction of a foreign government, for an infringement of our revenue or navigation laws, is a violation of the territorial authority of the foreign government, though this is a mater of which such government alone can complain.

> Nelson, At.-Gen. (1843), 4 Op. 285.

"Nations are bound to maintain respectable tribunals, to which the subjects of states at peace may have recourse for the redress of injuries and the maintenance of their rights. If the character of these tribunals be respectable, impartial, and independent, their decisions are to be regarded as conclusive. The United States have carried the principle of acquiesence, in such cases, as far as any nation upon earth, and in respect to the decisions of Spanish tribunals quite as frequently, perhaps, as in respect to the tribunals of any other nation. In almost innumerable cases reclamations sought by citizens of the United States against Spain for alleged captures, seizures, and other wrongs committed by Spanish subjects, the answer has been, that the question has been fairly tried before an impartial Spanish tribunal, having competent jurisdiction, and decided against the claimant; and in the sufficiency of this answer the Government of the United States has acquiesced. If the tribunal be competent, if it be free from unjust influence, if it be impartial and independent, and if it have heard the case fully and fairly, its judgment is to stand as decisive of the matter before it. This principle governs in regard to the decisions of courts of common law, courts of equity, and especially courts of admiralty, where proceedings so often affect the rights and interests of citizens of foreign states and governments."

> Mr. Webster, Sec. of State, to the Chevalier d'Argaïz, Span, min. June 21, 1842, Webster's Works, VI. 399, 403, in relation to the case of the *Amistad*.

" It was a rule of international law in 1861, and is a rule of that law now, that offenses committed in the territorial jurisdiction of a nation may be tried and punished there, according to the definitions and penalties of its municipal law, which becomes for the particular purpose the international law of the case. It matters not what the offense may be termed, if it appear that a violation of the municipal law was committed and punished. The municipal law of Hayti is not alone in defining the slave trade as piracy. It is so denominated by the laws of the United States (Revised Statutes, sec. 5376), and is punishable with death; and if the Government of the United States, like that of Hayti, were to make attempts at slave-trading equivalent to the consummated act and equally punishable therewith, it is not supposed that the rules of international law would thereby be violated."

> Report of Mr. Bayard, Sec. of State, to the President, on the case of Antonio Pelletier, Jan. 20, 1887, For. Rel. 1887, 606.

" Both by our own common law and by the French law a punishable attempt is an intended, unfinished crime. It requires four constituents: First, intent; secondly, incompleteness; thirdly, apparent adaptation of means to end; and fourthly, such progress as to justify the inference that it would be consummated unless interrupted by circumstances independent of the will of the attemptor. Nowhere are these distinctions laid down more authoritatively than by Rossi, Ortolan, and Lelièvre, when commenting on Article I. of the French Penal Code, which declares that '*toute tentative de crime . . . est considérée comme le crime même.*' I cite these high authorities in French jurisprudence because it is important to show that the Haytian courts, when laying down the law in this respect, did so in accordance with the law accepted in Hayti as part of the jurisprudence of France. But I do not cite the numerous cases in which the same law had been laid down in England and the United States. It is enough now to say that it is an accepted principle in our jurisprudence that an attempt, as thus defined, is as indictable in our courts as is the consummated crime of which it was intended to be a part, and that under the indictment for the consummated crime, there may be now, both in England and in most of our States, a conviction of the attempt. . . . It seems a mockery to assert that the guilty parties are to elude Haytian jurisdiction on the pretense that anchoring a slave ship in Haytian waters, with every contrivance to entrap and enslave Haytian citizens, is not disturbing the tranquillity of those waters, even though, on the discovery of the conspiracy, on the eve of its consummation, the slaver, in seeking to escape, fired on its pursuers. Such firing was part of one and the same outrage. I can conceive of no more flagrant disturbance of the tranquillity of territorial waters than these facts disclose.

" The view here maintained of the jurisdiction of the sovereign of territorial waters of offenses committed in such waters, when of a character calculated to disturb the peace of the port, is sustained in the case of Mali v. Keeper of Jail, decided this week by the Supreme Court of the United States. From the opinion in this case of Chief Justice Waite, which I am permitted to cite in advance of publication, occurs the following: ' It is part of the law of civilized nations that when a merchant vessel of one country enters the ports of another for the purpose of trade, it subjects itself to the law of the place to which it goes, unless by treaty or otherwise the two countries have come to some different understanding or agreement; for, as was said by Chief Justice Marshall in The Exchange, 7 Cranch, 144, it would be obviously inconvenient and dangerous to society, and would subject the laws to continual infraction, and the Government to degradation, if such . . . merchants did not owe temporary and local allegiance, and were not amenable to the jurisdiction of the country. United States v. Diekelman, 92 U. S., 520; 1 Phillimore's Int. Law, 3d ed., 483, sec. cccli; Twiss's Law of Nations in Time of Peace, 229, § 159; Creasy's Int. Law, 167, § 176; Halleck's Int. Law, 1st ed., 171. And the English judges have uniformly recognized the rights of the courts of the country of which the port is part to punish crimes committed by one foreigner on another in a foreign merchant ship. Regina v. Cunningham, Bell C. C., 72; S. C., 8 Cox C. C., 104; Regina v. Keyn, 11 Cox. C. C., 198, 204; S. C., L. R., 1 C. C., 161, 165; Regina v. Keyn, 13 Cox C. C., 403, 486, 525; S. C., 2 Ex. Div., 63, 161, 213. As the owner has voluntarily taken his vessel for his own private purposes to a place within the dominion of a Government other than his own, and from which he seeks protection during his stay, he owes that Government such allegiance for the time being as is due for the protection to which he becomes entitled.' "

Report of Mr. Bayard, Sec. of State, to the President, on the case of Antonio Pelletier, Jan. 20, 1887, For. Rel. 1887, 602–604; S. Ex. Doc. 64, 49 Cong. 2 sess.

Mali v. Keeper of Jail, supra, is reported as Wildenhus's Case, 120 U. S. 1.

The United States, having acquiesced in the establishment by Great Britain of a protectorate over the Gilbert Islands, should not undertake to remonstrate against the British regulations of trade with the natives by which all traders, without distinction of nationality,

are prohibited from selling firearms and liquor to the natives, and
from giving them credit.

Mr. Gresham, Sec. of State, to Messrs. Wightman Bros., June 8, 1893,
192 MS. Dom. Let. 283.

The Russian consul-general at New York, having refused to visé
the passport of Mrs. Mannie Lerin, a naturalized citizen of the
United States, born at Odessa, Russia, the Russian minister, in
response to an inquiry of the Department of State as to the cause,
stated that Mrs. Lerin " declared herself to be a Jewess," and that
the consul-general " acted according to the instructions of his Government, interdicting to visé passports of foreign Jews, with the
exception of certain cases, under which Mrs. Lerin can not be placed."[a]
This communication was acknowledged by the Department of State
" under the reserve necessarily imposed upon the Government by its
constitution and laws, and by its just expectation that its certification
of the character of American citizenship will be respected;"[b] and the
minister of the United States at St. Petersburg was instructed to
bring the matter to the attention of the Russian Government in the
following sense: That it was to be inferred, from the statement of
the Russian minister, " that the declaration of Mrs. Lerin's religious
profession was elicited from her by some interrogative process on the
part of the imperial consul-general;" that as it was " not constitutionally within the power of this Government, or of any of its authorities, to apply a religious test in qualification of the equal rights
of all citizens of the United States," it was " impossible to acquiesce
in the application of such a test, within the jurisdiction of the United
States, by the agents of a foreign power, to the impairment of the
rights of any American citizen or in derogation of the certificate of
this Government to the fact of such citizenship;" that the Government
had on several occasions in the past " made temperate but earnest
remonstrance against the examination into the religious faith of
American citizens by the Russian authorities in Russia," but the
" asserted right of territorial sovereignty over all sojourners in the
Empire has, to our deep regret, outweighed our friendly protests;"
and that it could not be expected that the United States would
" acquiesce in the assumption of a religious inquisitorial function
within our own borders, by a foreign agency, in a manner so repugnant to the national sense." [c]

" I am directed by my Government to bring to the attention of
the Imperial Government the refusal of the Russian consul of New

a For. Rel. 1893, 547.   c For. Rel. 1893, 536; also 538.
b For. Rel. 1893, 548.

York to visé passports issued by the United States to its citizens if they are of the Jewish faith.

"As your excellency is aware it has long been a matter of deep regret and concern to the United States that any of its citizens should be discriminated against for religious reasons while peacefully sojourning in this country, or that any such restraint should be imposed upon their coming and going. Painful as this policy toward a class of our citizens is to my Government, repugnant to our constitutional duty to afford them in every possible way equal protection and privileges and to our sense of their treaty rights, yet it is even more repugnant to our laws and the national sense for a foreign official, located within the jurisdiction of the United States, to there apply a religious test to any of our citizens to the impairment of his rights as an American citizen or in derogation of the certificate of our Government to the fact of such citizenship.

" It is not constitutionally within the power of the United States Government, or of any of its authorities, to apply a religious test in qualification of the equal rights of all citizens of the United States, and no law or principle is more warmly cherished by the American people. It is therefore impossible for my Government to acquiesce in any manner in the application of such a test within its jurisdiction by the agents of a foreign power.

" When this mater was the subject of correspondence between my Government and the Imperial representative at Washington, as shown by Prince Cantacuzène's note of February 20/8, 1893, such action by the Russian consul at New York was shown to be ' according to the instructions of his Government.'

" I can sincerely assure you that the continuation of this practice is as embarrassing as it is painful to my Government, especially when it is on the part of a nation for whose Government and people such intimate friendship has so long been manifested by the United States. I am happy that in this spirit I can frankly submit the matter to your excellency with the sincere hope that assurance can be given that such practices will be henceforth interdicted on the part of Russian officials located within the jurisdiction of the United States."

> Mr. Breckinridge, min. to Russia, to Prince Lobanow, min. of for. aff., May 5/17, 1895, For. Rel. 1895, II. 1057.
>
> This note was addressed to Prince Lobanow, under an instruction dated April 15, 1895, in which Mr. Gresham, Secretary of State, called attention to the Department of State's No. 60, of February 28, 1893, to Mr. White, and the latter's reply of April 11, 1893 (For. Rel. 1893, 536, 538), and said that the subject of " the refusal of the Russian consul-general at New York, under instructions from his Government, to visé passports issued by this Department to persons of the Jewish faith, has again come up for consideration." (For. Rel. 1895, II, 1056.)

See, also, dispatch of Mr. Peirce, chargé d'affaires ad interim, June 13, 1895, narrating an interview with Baron Osten-Sacken, to whom all questions in the foreign office relating to Jews were intrusted; and the reply of Mr. Adee, Acting Secretary of State, July 5, 1895. (For. Rel. 1895, II. 1058, 1059.)

President Cleveland, in his annual message of Dec. 2, 1895, referred to the practice of the Russian consuls as "an obnoxious invasion of our territorial jurisdiction." (For. Rel. 1895, I. xxxix.)

"I have not failed to devote the most serious attention to the contents of the note which you have had the goodness to address to me, under date of May 5/17 last, on the subject of the difficulties which the visé of passports, by the Russian consulate-general at New York, of people of Jewish faith under American jurisdiction encounters.

"You are good enough to express the opinion that the refusal interposed by the Russian consular authority to the request for a visé, is contrary to the American Constitution, which does not allow that a citizen of the United States should be deprived of his rights by reason of the faith he professes. I desire first and foremost to make this distinction, that the refusal to visé, which has been given in certain cases by our consular authorities, is in no wise founded on objections properly religious. Indeed, if it was at all the fact of belonging to the Jewish religion which was an obstacle for certain foreigners to be admitted into Russia, the law would extend this interdiction to all the members of that religion.

"Now, on the contrary, it recognizes formally the right of whole categories of Israelites to enter Russia, and the selection which it has made of these very categories proves that it has been guided in this question solely by considerations of an internal administrative character, which has nothing in common with a religious point of view.

"It is not necessary to say to you, Mr. Minister, that the broadest spirit of toleration for all cults forms the very basis of Russian laws; the Jewish religion is no more prohibited in Russia than in the United States; it is even legally recognized here and enjoys here certain privileges.

"But when, for motives of internal order, Russian law raises obstacles to the entrance of certain categories of foreigners upon our territory, the Russian consuls, who can neither be ignorant of nor overlook the law, are in the necessity of refusing the visé to persons who they know belong in these categories.

"I will add even that in forewarning on the spot the persons who address themselves to them to obtain visés, they save them difficulties and dangers which they would encounter later if they had not been advised.

"It is a question, moreover, of a general legislative measure, which applies to certain categories of Israelites of all countries whatsoever.

"As to the American Constitution, I must confess that it seems to me to be here beside the question. The article of the Constitution which you are good enough to mention, and which prescribes that no religion is prohibited in the United States, is, by the very nature of things, placed outside of all prejudice by the consular authority. He has neither to prohibit nor authorize the exercise in America of any cult; and the fact of his visé being accorded or refused does not encroach upon the article in question. The refusal of the visé is not at all an attack upon any established religion; it is the consequence of a foreign law of an administrative character, which only has its effect outside of the territory of the Union.

" I enjoy the hope, Mr. Minister, that the preceding considerations will be accepted by your Government in the spirit which inspires them, and that the just respect which is held in the United States for the precepts of the laws will make it understood that the Russian consular authorities have acted in this matter as they have from necessity. The frank and complete exposition which I have the honor to make of our point of view in this question appears to me to accord the better with the relations of close friendship which exist between the two Governments and the two countries—relations to which in your note, Mr. Minister, you pay a respect so merited, and to which we also, for our part, attach the highest value."

> Prince Lobanow, min. of foreign affairs, to Mr. Breckinridge, min. to Russia, June 26/July 8, 1895, For. Rel. 1895, II. 1064. For a translation of the Russian laws in regard to the admission of foreign Jews, see For. Rel. 1895, II. 1069–1070.

" I have received your No. 116, of the 24th ultimo, giving the correspondence between yourself and the Russian foreign office on the subject of the viséing by Russian consuls in this country of passports issued to American citizens of Jewish faith. Your presentation of this Government's view of that question meets with the approval of this Department.

"Apart from the constitutional objections to the discrimination made by Russian consular officers against American Jews, this Government can never consent that a class embracing many of its most honored and valuable citizens shall within its own territory be subjected to invidious and disparaging distinctions of the character implied in refusing to visé their passports. For, notwithstanding Prince Lobanow's suggestion that his Government's consular regulation upon the subject under consideration does not apply to all Israelites and therefore can not be regarded as a discrimination against them on religious grounds, the fact remains that the interrogatories propounded to applicants for the consular visé relate to religious faith, and upon the response depends the consul's actions.

" Viewed in the light of an invidious discrimination tending to discredit and humiliate American Jews in the eyes of their fellow-citizens, it is plain that the action of Russian consular officers does produce its effect within American territory, and not exclusively in Russian jurisdiction.

" But the Russian discrimination against American Jews is not confined simply to the matter of viséing passports. This Department was informed a few years since by the Russian minister here that Russian consuls in this country would refuse authentication to legal documents for use in Russia when Jews are ascertained to be interested. This is not merely an unjust and invidious discrimination against Jews, but would seem to be plainly a violation of the spirit of Article X. of the treaty of 1832 between this country and Russia in respect of the property rights of American citizens in that country."

> Mr. Adee, Acting Sec. of State, to Mr. Breckinridge, min. to Russia, Aug. 22, 1895, For. Rel. 1895, II. 1067.
>
> In an instruction to Mr. Peirce, chargé, July 5, 1895, before the correspondence between Mr. Breckinridge and Prince Lobanow was received at Washington, Mr. Adee, as Acting Secretary, in illustration of the position of the United States, said : " The customs laws of the United States require the administration of a consular oath to exporters presenting manifests of goods for certification ; but upon the representation of certain European governments, among them Great Britain and Germany, that the administration of such oath by a foreign consul to a subject of the country is an invasion of the judicial independence thereof, our consuls have been enjoined to refrain from the act complained of in all cases affecting a subject of a sovereign of the country where they reside. It might, however, have been deemed entirely competent for the Governments of Great Britain and Germany to insert in the consular exequatur an express inhibition of the obnoxious act." (For. Rel. 1895, II. 1059, 1060. At pp. 1060–1061, of the same volume, a correspondence between the Russian consul-general at New York and a Jewish citizen of the United States, touching the refusal to visé a passport is given.)

" The question is not whether the Russian Government by Imperial order or ministerial regulation has directed its consuls to make such inquiries in respect to the religious faith or business transactions of American citizens, but whether the Imperial Government has any right to make such inquisition in a foreign territory when the effect may be to disregard the Government's certification of the fact of citizenship ; or, assuming for the argument's sake, but not by way of admission, that such a right may technically exist, the question remains whether the assumption to exercise it in face of the temperate but earnest remonstrance of this Government against foreign interference with the private concerns of its citizens is in accordance with those courteous principles of comity which this Government is so anxious to observe in all its relations with foreign States, and which it naturally expects from them in return."

Mr. Uhl, Acting Sec. of State, to Mr. Peirce, chargé, Oct. 23, 1895, For. Rel. 1895, II. 1070, 1071.

Dec. 6, 1895, Mr. Breckinridge addressed to Prince Lobanow another note, embodying the substance of previous instructions, but based, so far as it referred to the question of treaty rights, chiefly upon Mr. Blaine's instruction to Mr. Foster, No. 87, July 29, 1881, For. Rel. 1881, 1030. In communicating to the Department of State a copy of his note to Prince Lobanow, Mr. Breckinridge adverted to the change that had taken place in the form of the controversy as it had progressed, from one "largely colored by the religious feature which seemed to give rise" to it, as in the instruction to Mr. White of Feb. 28, 1893, to the broader question presented in the latest instructions. (For. Rel. 1895, II. 1071–1074.)

" The laws and regulations against which your Government's objections are especially directed are:

"(1) The provisions of the quarantine act of February 15, 1893, and the regulations made in pursuance of it, which require the consular or medical officer of the United States stationed in a foreign port to inspect vessels of all nationalities departing for the United States, and the crews, passengers, and cargoes.

"(2) The provisions of the same act and regulations which empower the consular or medical officer to order the disinfection of such vessels, and in other respects to regulate their internal condition and arrangement, before granting the bill of health required for the entry of the vessel in a port of the United States.

"(3) The provisions of the immigration act of March 3, 1893, which require that the master and surgeon of any vessel carrying immigrants to the United States shall present to the American consular officer at the port of departure descriptive lists of the immigrants, verified by the oaths of the master and surgeon taken before such officer.

" Your Government regards the exercise of these administrative functions by our consular and medical officers in Germany in connection with ships that are not American as unauthorized and in disregard of its sovereignty. . . .

" This Government does not claim that under any treaty or the rules of international law it can authorize its officers to inspect foreign vessels or order their disinfection in German ports, or to administer oaths to officers of foreign ships within the jurisdiction of the German Empire. The operation of the sanitary and immigration system of the United States in a foreign port is conditioned upon the consent of the Government having jurisdiction of the port. Prior to the receipt of your protest the consent of your Government was reasonably assumed, because these provisions were beneficial to your carrying trade and commercial interests. If the Imperial Government is unwilling that consular and medical officers of the United States shall continue to execute these laws and regulations in German ports upon vessels which are not American, steps will be taken to comply with its wishes, leaving foreign vessels coming to the United States from German ports subject to the sanitary provisions in force at the port of arrival and the prescribed consequences.

" I will add for the information of your Government that no medical officers have been stationed in German ports within the last twelve months for the purpose of executing our quarantine and immigration laws and regulations. These duties have been performed by consular officers alone, and they are forbidden to receive any personal compensation whatever for their services. The actual expense of the inspection or disinfection and a moderate official fee, which goes into the Treasury of the United States, form the total of direct expense thus incurred by vessels in foreign ports."

> Mr. Gresham, Sec. of State, to Baron Saurma, German amb. Jan. 26, 1895, For. Rel. 1895, I. 513, 514.
>
> "With respect to your request of the 6th instant to be informed if any difficulty may be expected to arise under treaty stipulations or international law in regard to stationing such officers as are described in the 2nd section of the act of July 2, 1879, entitled 'An act to prevent the introduction of contagious or infectious diseases into the United States,' in the ports of Cuba, for the purposes indicated in the act, I observe that in the opinion of the Department questions might very possibly be raised under existing treaties or international law in the course of the action taken by these officers at the ports and under the act named, but what such questions might be, if any, cannot well be anticipated." (Mr. Evarts, Sec. of State, to Mr. Cabell, Pres. of the National Board of Health, June 10, 1879, 128 MS. Dom. Let. 392.)

The Government of the Netherlands declined to grant the request of the United States for permission to station officers of the United States Public Health and Marine-Hospital Service at Dutch ports to make medical inspections under the act of March 3, 1903, of persons intending to emigrate to the United States.

> For. Rel. 1904, 519–521.

With reference to an Arctic expedition, which visited Greenland in 1894 and narrowly escaped being wrecked near the colony of Sukkertoppen, the Danish Government called attention to the royal ordinance of March 18, 1776, forbidding all persons, whether Danes or foreigners, to touch, except in case of necessity, at any of the ports or places of Greenland or of the adjacent islands without having previously obtained the authority of the royal Government.

> For. Rel. 1894, 202–205. See, in this relation, Art. VI. of the treaty between the United States and Denmark of 1826, excepting Iceland, the Faroe Islands, and Greenland from the operation of the convention.

In 1895 instructions were issued by the Danish Government to the authorities in Greenland, upon the request of the United States, to give all necessary support to the Peary relief expedition. The United States in the correspondence referred to the royal decree which prohibited foreigners from landing at any of the ports of Greenland without first obtaining permission to do so at Copenhagen.

> For. Rel. 1895, I. 207–210.

Advertisements of government or municipal bonds, where prizes, different in amount determinable by chance, in addition to par value of the bonds with interest, are offered the holders, are forbidden by the act of September 19, 1890, to be carried in the mails; and this prohibition applies to advertisements in foreign newspapers of the bonds of foreign governments or foreign municipalities which fall within that category. This rule was held to apply, not only in the case of certain Austrian Government bonds, but also in the case of bonds of the Crédit Foncier and of the city of Paris, into which, although they bore interest, a lottery element was introduced.

> Mr. Gresham, Sec. of State, to Mr. Patenôtre, French min., April 16, 1895, For. Rel. 1896, 116. This note referred to the case of Horner v. United States (1893), 147 U. S. 449. See, also, Mr. Bayard, Sec. of State, to Mr. Garland, At. Gen., April 23, 1887, 163 MS. Dom. Let. 688.
> See Ballock v. State, 73 Md. 1.

By Article XVI. of the Universal Postal Union Convention of July 4, 1891, each signatory government reserves the right to refuse to convey over its territory or to deliver matter contravening the legal enactments or regulations in force in its jurisdiction. With reference to this stipulation, it was held that the exclusion of any journal published in the United States from entrance into or circulation in Turkey contravened no provision of the convention.

> Mr. Olney, Sec. of State, to Mr. Vlasto, June 15, 1895, 202 MS. Dom. Let. 620.

Official contributions to charitable objects do not fall within the range of Congressional or Executive power. But favors may be granted in aid of such objects by special passports, or, in certain cases, by remissions of duty. " Of such a character was the assistance rendered by the Government of the United States for transporting to Ireland the contributions of provisions spontaneously offered by the American people."

> 1 Halleck, Int. Law (by Baker, 1893), 457.

By the act of March 24, 1874, §§ 1960 and 1962, Revised Statutes, in relation to the killing of fur seals on the Pribiloff Islands, were so amended as to authorize the Secretary of the Treasury to designate the months of the year in which seals might be taken for their skins, as well as "the number to be taken." In 1890, pursuant and subject to the laws of the United States, a lease was made to the North American Commercial Company of the exclusive right for twenty years to take seals on the islands, the company agreeing to "abide by any restrictions or limitations upon the right to kill seals that the Secretary of the Treasury shall judge necessary, under the law, for the preservation of the seal fisheries of the United States." In accordance with the stipulations of the *modus vivendi* between the United States and Great Britain, of April 18, 1892, entered into for the purpose of restricting the killing of seals during the arbitration under the convention of February 29, 1892, the number of skins which the company was allowed to take during the season of 1893 was reduced to 7,500. The company claimed damages from the United States for the skins which, as it alleged, it might have taken without unreasonable injury of or diminution of the seal herd, but was prevented by the United States from taking. The court, in denying this claim, observed: "The seal fisheries of the Pribiloff Islands were a branch of commerce and their regulation involved the exercise of power as a sovereign and not as a mere proprietor. Such governmental powers can not be contracted away, and it is absurd to argue that in this instance there was any attempt to do so, or any sheer oppression or wrong inflicted on the lessee by the Government in the effort to protect the fur seal from extinction."

North American Com. Co. *v.* United States (1898), 171 U.S. 110, 137.

(2) DIVISION OF AUTHORITY.

§ 176.

Under the Constitution of the United States a statute of a State enacting that the masters and wardens of a port within it should be entitled to demand and receive, in addition to other fees, the sum of $5, whether called on to perform any service or not, for every vessel arriving in that port, is a tonnage tax, and is unconstitutional and void.

Steamship Company *v.* Port Wardens, 6 Wallace, 31.

It has also been held that while taxes levied by a State upon vessels owned by its citizens as property, and based on a valuation of the same, are not prohibited by the Federal Constitution, yet taxes cannot be imposed on them by the State "at so much per ton of the registered tonnage." Such taxes are within the prohibition of the Constitution that "no State shall, without the consent of Congress, lay any duty of tonnage." Nor is the case varied by the fact that the vessels were not only owned by citizens of the State, but exclusively engaged in trade between places within the State.

> State Tonnage Tax Cases, 12 Wallace, 204.

Any duty, or tax, or burden imposed under the authority of the States, which is in its essence a contribution claimed for the privilege of arriving and departing from a port of the United States, and which is assessed on a vessel according to its carrying capacity, is a tonnage tax within the meaning of the Federal Constitution, and therefore void.

> Cannon v. New Orleans, 20 Wallace, 577.

An offence committed on San Juan Island in 1869, while the island, which was claimed to be a part of Washington Territory, was, pending the settlement of the international boundary, in the joint military occupation of Great Britain and the United States, was not committed at a place within the " sole and exclusive jurisdiction " of the United States, under the crimes act of 1790, but was justiciable in the Territorial courts.

> Watts v. United States, 1 Wash. Ter. Rep., N. S., 288; Wats v. Territory, id. 409.
> As to State jurisdiction over tide-waters, see 3 Harvard Law Review, 346.

" The State of Texas has municipal jurisdiction under the law of nations over the Rio Grande to the middle of the stream, so far as it divides Texas from Mexico. This is subject to such international jurisdiction as the United States may have over such waters under the Constitution of the United States, and to the right of the free use by Mexico of the channel."

> Mr. Bayard, Sec. of State, to Mr. Bowen, June 12, 1886, 160 MS. Dom. Let. 462.

Where the United States acquires, with the consent of the legislature of a State, lands within its borders for the purpose of a military reservation, and the State omits to reserve concurrent jurisdiction over the lands so acquired, the Federal jurisdiction is exclusive. Hence it was advised that the sheriff of the county within which a reservation was situated had no authority to enter upon the land for the purpose of serving the process of a State court.

> Griggs, At. Gen., Sept. 26, 1900, 23 Op. 254.

It was advised that the Postmaster-General of the United States might properly refuse to demand of the insular government of Porto Rico rent for the post-office building at San Juan, which had belonged to the Spanish Government and which came into the possession of the United States with the cession of Porto Rico. It was stated, however, at the same time that the general question whether certain public buildings and structures in Porto Rico were owned by the United States or Porto Rico, and whether various public utilities and functions were to be controlled or exercised by the national or insular government under the treaty with Spain and existing laws, was then under review, to the end that a comprehensive determination of it might be reached. It was added that this question, which fitly required judicial review and decision rather than executive opinion, was not intended to be decided in the present instance.

> Knox, At. Gen., Oct. 29, 1901, 23 Op. 571.

3. SERVITUDES.

§ 177.

" It is usual in works on international law to enumerate a list of servitudes to which the territory of a state may be subjected. Amongst them are the reception of foreign garrisons in fortresses, fishery rights in territorial waters, telegraphic and railway privileges, the use of a port by a foreign power as a coaling station, an obligation not to maintain fortifications in particular places, and other derogations of like kind from the full enforcement of sovereignty over parts of the national territory. These and such like privileges or disabilities must however be set up by treaty or equivalent agreement; they are the creatures not of law but of compact. The only servitudes which have a general or particular customary basis are, the above-mentioned right of innocent use of territorial seas, customary rights over forests, pastures, and waters for the benefit of persons living near a frontier, which seem to exist in some places, and possibly a right to military passage through a foreign state to outlying territory. In their legal aspects there is only one point upon which international servitudes call for notice. They conform to the universal rule applicable to ' jura in re aliena.' Whether they be customary or contractural in their origin, they must be construed strictly. If therefore a dispute occurs between a territorial sovereign and a foreign power as to the extent or nature of rights enjoyed by the latter within the territory of the former, the presumption is against the foreign state, and upon it the burden lies of proving its claim beyond doubt or question."

> Hall, Int. Law, 4th ed. 166.
> See, also, § 219, pp. 623–626.
> In a note to the foregoing passage, Hall says : " It is somewhat more than doubtful whether any instances of a right to military passage have survived the simplification of the map of Central Europe."
> See Fabre (Pierre-Paul), Des Servitudes dans le Droit International Public; Paris, 1901.

(7) NEUTRALIZATION.

§ 178.

Limitations on national jurisdiction have been created by various agreements for the " neutralization " either of whole states or of parts thereof, or of particular bodies or streams of water.

"A state is neutral which chooses to take no part in a war, and persons and property are called neutral which belong to a state occupying this position. The term has in recent times received a larger application. A condition of neutrality, or one resembling it, has been created, as it were, artificially, and the process has been called ' neutralization.'

" I. States have been permanently neutralized by convention. Not only is it preordained that such states are to abstain from taking part in a war into which their neighbors may enter, but it is also prearranged that such states are not to become principals in a war. By way of compensation for this restriction on their freedom of action, their immunity from attack is guaranteed by their neighbors, for whose collective interests such an arrangement is perceived to be on the whole expedient. . . .

" II. When persons, things, and places, though in fact belonging to a belligerent state, are invested with immunities to which, as so belonging, they would not be entitled, they are said to be ' neutralized.' . . .

" III. The term ' neutralization ' was used in a very extended meaning with reference to the Black Sea in the Treaty of Paris [1856]. . . . By Article XI. . . . : ' The Black Sea is neutralized. Its waters and ports, thrown open to the mercantile marine of every nation, are formally and in perpetuity interdicted to the flag of war of either of the powers possessing its coasts, or of any other power.' By Article XIII., ' the Black Sea being thus neutralized,' neither Russia nor Turkey are to establish or maintain upon its coasts any military-maritime arsenal."

> Holland, Studies in Int. Law (1898), 271–275.
>
> With reference to what is stated in the foregoing passage as to the Black Sea, it should be observed that by the treaty of London of March 13, 1871, Articles XI. and XIII. of the treaty of Paris of 1856 were abrogated. It was at the same time declared: " III. The Black Sea remains open, as heretofore, to the mercantile marine of all nations." (Hertslet, Map of Europe by Treaty, III. 1921.)

As to Belgium,[a] the Ionian Islands, Savoy, Switzerland, Luxemburg, the Independent State of the Congo, and formerly Samoa, as

---

[a] See La Neutralité de la Belgique, par Éd. Descamps: Bruxelles et Paris, 1902, pp. x., 639.

examples of neutralized states, see supra, § 12, pp. 26–27. It may be observed that by the treaty of May 3, 1815, the free city of Cracow was declared to be independent and neutral. By the treaty of November 6, 1846, however, between Austria, Prussia, and Russia it was annexed to Austria and its independence and neutrality were suppressed.

As to the neutralization of particular persons, places, or things, it may be observed that it was agreed in the peace of Amiens that Malta should be restored to the order of St. John of Jerusalem and its independence and perpetual neutrality acknowledged under the guarantee of Austria, France, Great Britain, Prussia, Russia, and Spain. This stipulation was not carried into effect and the peace was ended a year later.

Article 26 of the regulations for the free navigation of rivers, forming Annex XVI. to the Vienna Congress treaty of June 9, 1815, provides: " If it should happen (which God forbid) that war should break out among any of the States of the Rhine, the collection of the customs shall continue uninterrupted, without any obstacle being thrown in the way by either party. The vessels and persons employed by the custom-houses shall enjoy all the rights of neutrality. A guard shall be placed over the offices and chests belonging to the customs." [a]

The act for the navigation of the Danube, made in 1865 by the European commission, and confirmed by the conference of the powers at Paris in the following year, declares that the staff and works of the commission are to enjoy the benefit of neutrality. By Article VII. of the treaty of London of March 13, 1871, it is provided that all the works and establishments created by the commission " shall continue to enjoy the same neutrality which has hitherto protected them." [b]

In order to increase the guaranties of the free navigation of the Danube, it was provided by Article LII. of the treaty of Berlin of July 13, 1878, that " all the fortresses and fortifications existing on the course of the river from the Iron Gates to its mouth " should " be razed and no new ones erected." By Articles LIII. and LIV. provision was made for continuing the European commission, which was thenceforth to exercise its functions " as far as Galatz in complete independence of the territorial authorities." [c]

The subject of the closure of the Dardanelles and the Bosphorus against ships of war is discussed under the head of " Straits " in the preceding chapter.[d]

---

[a] Hertslet, Map of Europe by Treaty, I. 86.

[b] Holland, Studies in Int. Law, 273; Hertslet, Map of Europe by Treaty, III. 1922.

[c] Moore, Int. Arbitrations, V. 4853.

[d] Supra, § 134. See also Guizot's Embassy to the Court of St. James, chaps. 6 and 7.

We have given in the preceding chapter the history and provisions of the arrangement between the United States and Great Britain of April 28–29, 1817, limiting armaments on the Great Lakes.[a]

By the treaty between the United States and Great Britain, signed at Washington, April 19, 1850, commonly called the Clayton-Bulwer treaty, the contracting parties agreed to guarantee the " neutrality " of the canal which it was then supposed would soon be built between the Atlantic and Pacific oceans by way of the San Juan River and the lakes of Nicaragua or Managua.   It was further agreed (Art. 8) that the contracting parties, desiring not only " to accomplish a particular object, but also to establish a general principle," would " extend their protection, by treaty stipulations, to any other practicable communications, whether by canal or railway, across the isthmus which connects North and South America, and especially to the interoceanic communications, should the same prove to be practicable, whether by canal or railway, which are now proposed to be established by the way of Tehuantepec or Panama."   Such communications were to be open to all states joining in the guarantee.   The subject is now regulated by the treaty between the same powers, signed at Washington, November 18, 1901, commonly called the Hay-Pauncefote treaty, the object of which is recited to be to facilitate the construction of a ship canal to connect the Atlantic and Pacific oceans, by whatever route may be deemed expedient, under the auspices of the Government of the United States, without impairing the " general principle " of " neutralization established in Article VIII. of the Clayton-Bulwer treaty."   The Clayton-Bulwer treaty is declared to be superseded, and it is agreed that the canal may be constructed " under the auspices of the Government of the United States, either directly at its own cost, or by gift or loan of money to individuals or corporations, or through subscription to or purchase of stock or shares, and that, subject to the provisions of the present treaty, the said Government shall have and enjoy all the rights incident to such construction, as well as the exclusive right of providing for the regulation and management of the canal."   It is then declared (Art. III.) that " the United States adopts, as the basis of the neutralization " of the canal, certain rules which are then expressly set forth and which are textually given elsewhere in the present work.

By the treaty between the United States and Nicaragua, signed June 21, 1867, Nicaragua grants by Article XIV. " to the United States, and to their citizens and property, the right of transit between the Atlantic and Pacific oceans through the territory of that Republic, on any route of communication, natural or artificial, whether by land or by water," on the same terms as it shall be enjoyed by Nicaragua and its citizens, " the Republic of Nicaragua, however, reserving its rights of sovereignty over the same." By the next article, the United States "agree to extend their protection to all such routes of communication as aforesaid, and to guarantee the neutrality and innocent use of the same. They also agree to employ their influence with other nations to induce them to guarantee such neutrality and protection."[a]

The treaty of territorial limits between Costa Rica and Nicaragua, signed April 15, 1858, contains the following stipulation: "Article IX. On no account whatever, not even in case of war, if it should unfortunately occur between the Republics of Nicaragua and Costa Rica, shall any act of hostility be allowed between them in the port of San Juan del Norte, nor on the river of that name, nor on Lake Nicaragua."[b]

By article 35 of the treaty between the United States and New Granada, now the Republic of Colombia, signed December 12, 1846, New Granada guaranteed to the Government of the United States that "the right of way or transit across the Isthmus of Panama upon any modes of communication that now exist, or that may be hereafter constructed, shall be open and free to the Government and citizens of the United States." On the other hand, the United States guarantees "the perfect neutrality" of the Isthmus and "the rights of sovereignty and property" of New Granada thereover.

As to neutralization of canals, further information may be found in the present work in the chapter on "Interoceanic communications."

By Article V. of the treaty of July 23, 1881, between the Argentine Republic and Chile, it is declared: "The Straits of Magellan are neutralized forever, and their free navigation is guaranteed to the flags of all nations. To insure this neutrality and freedom, it is agreed that no fortifications or military defences which might interfere therewith shall be erected."

By a convention between various maritime powers, including the United States on the one part and the Sultan of Morocco on the other, concluded May 31, 1865, the Sultan agreed to construct a light-house at Cape Spartel. With a reservation as to the sovereign rights of the Sultan, it was agreed that the light-house should be managed by representatives of the contracting powers who were to bear the cost of maintaining it. The contracting powers bound themselves "to respect the neutrality of the light-house, and to continue the payment of the contribution intended to uphold it, even in case

---

[a] See the following treaty stipulations: Spain and Nicaragua, July 25, 1850, Art. XIII.; Spain and Costa Rica, May 10, 1850, Art. XIII.; France and Nicaragua, April 11, 1859, Arts. XXVII.–XXXIII.; Italy and Nicaragua, March 6, 1868; Great Britain and Nicaragua, Feb. 11, 1860. The last mentioned treaty expired June 11, 1888, on notice given in conformity with its terms.

[b] 48 Brit. and For. State Papers, 1051.

(which God forbid) hostilities should break out either between them or between one of them and the Empire of Morocco."

By the Geneva Convention of 1864, commonly called the " Red Cross Convention," for the amelioration of the condition of the wounded in the field, surgeons, the wounded, and hospitals and their attendants are " recognized as neutral." The supplementary convention of 1868, which was intended to apply similar stipulations to naval warfare, has not been ratified, but its provisions were observed as a *modus vivendi* between the United States and Spain in 1898.

Proposals have been made for the neutralization of submarine telegraph cables, but the draft convention to that effect, which was prepared at a conference held in Paris in 1882, upon the invitation of the French Government, has not yet been adopted by the powers. The convention signed at Paris March 14, 1884, provides for the protection of submarine cables outside territorial waters, but its operation is by Article XV. limited to time of peace, by an express reservation in favor of the rights of belligerents.[a]

2. Governmental Acts.

§ 179.

Governor Collot, of the French island of Guadeloupe, having arrived in the United States, as a prisoner of war to the British on parole, on his way to France, was arrested and obliged to give bail in a civil action based on his seizure and condemnation of a vessel while acting as governor of the island. He declined to plead to the action, but appealed to the French minister, who, addressing in turn the Government of the United States, asked that the suit, which was pending in a Pennsylvania court, be stopped, on the ground that the wrong complained of was a public act, performed by the governor in the exercise of his official powers. This request was referred to the Attorney-General of the United States, who advised that the defendant was not personally privileged from arrest, and that his defense should be placed before the court. As to the merits of the defense, the Attorney-General said: " I am inclined to think, if the seizure of the vessel is admitted to have been an official act, done by the defendant by virtue, or under color, of the powers vested in him as governor, that it will of itself be a sufficient answer to the plaintiff's action; that the defendant ought not to answer in our courts for any mere *irregularity* in the exercise of his powers; and that the *extent* of his authority can, with propriety or convenience, be determined only by the constituted authorities of his own nation."

---

[a] Holland, Studies in Int. Law, 273; and an article by the same author in the Journal du Droit International Privé (1898), vol. 25, p. 648.

Bradford, At. Gen., June 16, 1794, 1 Op. 45. The plaintiff eventually discontinued his action. (Waters *v.* Collot, 2 Dallas, 247.)

In this relation we may note the following statement: " On the subject of
General Collot, . . . I have to inform you that the friend of the
plaintiff in the suit has assured me that he will immediately withdraw
it, and the General will be discharged from his bail. I can not, however, dismiss this subject without observing, that if the General had
shown to the court that his act which occasioned the injury complained of had been within his lawful powers as governor of Guadeloupe, the court would have discharged him long ago, as they discharged Mr. Peroud, the ordonnateur at Cape François. But the
General refused, as I am informed, to say anything more than that
he was, at the time, the *governor of Guadeloupe*, as though a governor could commit no unlawful act for which he would be personally
responsible." (Mr. Pickering, Sec. of State, to Mr. Letombe, French
consul-general, May 29, 1797, 10 MS. Dom. Let. 51.)

" It is as well settled in the United States as in Great Britain, that
a person acting under a commission from the sovereign of a foreign
nation is not amenable for what he does in pursuance of his commission, to any judiciary tribunal in the United States."

Lee, At. Gen., Dec. 29, 1797, 1 Op. 81, citing Bradford, At. Gen., June 16,
1794, 1 Op. 45.

The opinion of Attorney-General Lee related to two suits pending against
Henry Sinclair, evidently of a civil nature.

In November, 1840, Alexander McLeod was arrested by the authorities of the State of New York and held for trial on a charge of murder committed at the destruction of the steamer *Caroline*, December
29, 1837, within the territorial jurisdiction of that State. On the
13th December, 1840, Mr. Fox, the British minister at Washington,
on his own responsibility asked for his immediate release, on the
ground that the destruction of the *Caroline* was " a public act of
persons in Her Majesty's service, obeying the order of their superior
authorities; " that it could, therefore, " only be the subject of discussion between the two national Governments," and could " not justly
be made the ground of legal proceedings in the United States against
the persons concerned."

Mr. Forsyth, Secretary of State, replied on the 28th of December,
with the declaration that no warrant for the interposition called for
could be found in the powers with which the Federal Executive was
invested, but at the same time denying that the demand was well
founded. On the 12th of March, 1841, Mr. Fox, in behalf of his
Government, presented a formal demand for McLeod's immediate
release, on the ground which he had previously stated. Mr. Webster, who had then become Secretary of State, made answer on the
24th of April, and, while admitting the grounds of the demand,
declared that the Federal Government was unable then to comply

with it. In May McLeod was taken down to the city of New York, and was there brought before a justice of the supreme court of the State on a writ of *habeas corpus*. After a full argument, that tribunal, in July, refused to discharge him; and in the ensuing October, ten months after the first demand and seven months after the second, he was tried at Utica, and acquitted on proof of an *alibi*. This case led to the adoption by Congress, in August, 1842, of an act to provide for the removal of cases involving international relations from the State to the Federal courts.

> For the case of the Caroline, see infra, § 217. For correspondence in relation to the case of McLeod, see message of Dec. 28, 1840, H. Ex. Doc. 33, 26 Cong. 2 sess.; report of Feb. 13, 1841, H. Report 162, 26 Cong. 2 sess.; message of June 1, 1841, S. Doc. 1, 27 Cong. 1 sess.; message of March 8, 1842, H. Ex. Doc. 128, 27 Cong. 2 sess.; message of Aug. 11, 1842, H. Ex. Doc. 2, 27 Cong. 3 sess.; message of Jan. 23, 1843, S. Ex. Doc. 99, 27 Cong. 3 sess.
>
> Correspondence on the subject may also be found in 29 Br. & For. State Pap. 1126, and 30 id. 193.
>
> The judicial proceeding on the application for a writ of habeas corpus are reported in People *v.* McLeod, 25 Wend. 483; and they are reviewed, adversely to the action of the court, by Judge Tallmadge, 26 Wend. 663, Appendix. " Chancellor Kent, Chief Justice Spencer, and other eminent jurists, have expressed their approbation of Mr. Talmadge's ' Review.' " (Webster's Works, VI. 266, note.)
>
> The act of Congress of August 29, 1842, is given, infra.
>
> See, particularly, Mr. Fox, Brit. min., to Mr. Webster, Sec. of State, March 12, 1841, Webster's Works, VI. 247; Mr. Webster, Sec. of State, to Mr. Fox, Brit. min., April 24, 1841, id. 250.
>
> The correspondence between Mr. Forsyth and Mr. Fox may be found in H. Ex. Doc. 33, 26 Cong. 2 sess.

" That an individual, forming part of a public force, and acting under the authority of his Government, is not to be held answerable as a private trespasser or malefactor, is a principle of public law sanctioned by the usages of all civilized nations, and which the Government of the United States has no inclination to dispute. This has no connection whatever with the question, whether, in this case, the attack on the ' Caroline ' was, as the British Government think it, a justifiable employment of force for the purpose of defending the British territory from unprovoked attack, or whether it was a most unjustifiable invasion, in time of peace, of the territory of the United States, as this Government has regarded it. The two questions are essentially distinct and different; and, while acknowledging that an individual may claim immunity from the consequences of acts done by him, by showing that he acted under national authority, this Government is not to be understood as changing the opinions which it has heretofore expressed in regard to the real nature of the transaction which resulted in the destruction of the ' Caroline.' That subject it is not necessary for any purpose connected with this communication now to discuss. The views of this Government in relation to it are known to that of England; and we are expecting the answer of that Government to the communication which has been made to it.

"All that is intended to be said at present is, that, since the attack on the ' Caroline ' is avowed as a national act, which may justify reprisals, or even general war, if the Government of the United States, in the judgment which it shall form of the transaction and of its own duty, should see fit so to decide, yet that it raises a question entirely public and political, a question between independent nations; and that individuals connected in it cannot be arrested and tried before the ordinary tribunals, as for the violation of municipal law. If the attack on the ' Caroline ' was unjustifiable, as this Government has asserted, the law which has been violated is the law of nations; and the redress which is to be sought is the redress authorized, in such cases, by the provisions of that code."

> Mr. Webster, Sec. of State, to Mr. Crittenden, Attorney-General, March 15, 1841, Webster's Works, VI. 262, 264. See, also, Bancroft's Seward, I. 111–116.
>
> See Vattel, Book III. ch. ii. § 187; Rutherforth, Book II. ch. ix. § 18; Burlamaqui, Part IV. ch. iii. §§ 18, 19; Lawrence, Com. Sur. Droit Int. III. 430; 18 Alb. L. J. 506; Hall, Int. Law (4th ed.), 328; Memoirs of J. Q. Adams, XI, 26; 4 Boston Law Rep. 169; Gould, McLeod's Trial, pamph.; Neilson's Choate, 173–184; Am. Law Mag. I. 348.
>
> Halleck says: "As McLeod was *acquitted* on the trial, there was no opportunity to obtain, by appeal to the Federal courts, an opinion of the highest tribunal of the United States on this important question, and the subsequent act of Congress has obviated all danger of the recurrence of a similar case. The opinion of Mr. Justice Cowen, however, seems not to have received the approbation of the best judicial minds of his own State, and to have been very generally condemned in other States and by the political authorities of the Federal Government." And he goes on to say that "among European writers on public law there seems to be a very general unanimity of opinion " sustaining Mr. Webster's view. But the act of Congress which General Halleck cites does not settle the law, but only indicates a way in which such cases may be reached by the Federal courts. (Int. Law, ed. 1861, 305, 306.)
>
> Sir R. Phillimore appears to accept Mr. Webster's conclusions. (3 Int. Law, 3d ed. 1885, 60.)
>
> Hall cites Mr. Webster's conclusions without dissent, and declares that " when a state in the exercise of its right of self-preservation, does acts of violence within the territory of a foreign state, while remaining at peace with it, its agents cannot be tried for the murder of persons killed by them, nor are they liable to a civil action in respect to damages to property which they may have caused."

Mr. Calhoun, June 11, 1841, when the McLeod case was under discussion in the Senate, stated the position of the British Government to be " that where a government authorizes or approves of the act of an individual, it makes it the act of the government, and thereby exempts the individual from all responsibility to the injured country." The position, as thus stated by him, Mr. Calhoun controverted. " The laws of nations," he said, " are but the laws of morals, as applicable to individuals, so far modified, and no further, as reason may make necessary in their application to nations. Now, there can be no doubt that the analogous rule, when applied to individuals, is, that both principal and agents, or, if you will, instruments, are responsible in criminal cases; directly the reverse of the rule on which the demand for the release of McLeod is made. . . . Suppose, then, that the British, or any other government, in contemplation of war, should send out emissaries to blow up the fortifications erected, at such vast expense, for the defense of our great commercial marts, . . . would the production of the most authentic papers, signed by all the authorities of the British Government, make it a public transaction, and exempt the villains from all responsibility to our laws and tribunals? Or would that Government dare make a demand for their immediate release? Or, if made, would ours dare yield to it, and release them? . . . But, setting aside all suppositious cases, I shall take one that actually occurred—that of the notorious Henry, employed by the colonial authority of Canada to tamper with a portion of our people, prior to the late war, with the intention of alienating them from their Government, and effecting a disunion in the event of hostilities. Suppose he had been detected and arrested for his treasonable conduct, and that the British Government had made the like demand for his release, on the ground that he was executing the orders of his Government, and was not, therefore, liable, personally or individually, to our laws and tribunals: I ask, would our Government be bound to comply with the demand? " Mr. Calhoun, after accepting the position taken by Mr. Webster, that the case was not one of war, proceeded to say that the attack on the *Caroline* was an invasion of the territorial sovereignty of the united States not justified by necessity, and that persons concerned in such attack were responsible to the State of New York for the wrong done by them in it.

Calhoun's Works, III. 618. In accord, Benton's Thirty Years' View, II. 434 et seq.; Life and Letters of Francis Lieber, 149.

" Then the violence and bad spirit displayed in America have produced no small consternation here, though everybody goes on saying that a war between the two countries and for so little cause is impossible. It does seem impossible, and the manifest interest of both nations is opposed to it; but when a country is so mob-governed as America, and the Executive is so destitute of power, there must be great danger. However, the general conviction is, that the present

exhibition of violence is attributable to the malignity of the outgoing
party, which is desirous of embarrassing their successors, and casting
on them the perils of a war or the odium of a reconciliation with this
country, and strong hopes are entertained that the new Government
will be too wise to fall into the snare that is laid for them, and strong
enough to check and master the bad spirit which is rife in the Northern States.   The real difficulty arises from the conviction here, that
in the case of McLeod we are in the right, and the equally strong
conviction there that we are not, and the actual doubt on which side
the truth lies.   Senior, whom I met the other day, expressed great
uncertainty, and he proposes and has written to Government on the
subject, that the question of international law shall be submitted to
the decision of a German university—that of Berlin, he thinks, would
be the best.   This idea he submitted to Stevenson, who approved of
it, but the great difficulty would be to agree upon a statement of facts.
Yesterday Lord Lyndhurst was at the council office, talking over the
matter with Sir Herbert Jenner and Justice Littledale, and he said it
was very questionable if the Americans had not right on their side;
and that he thought, in a similar case here, we should be obliged to
try the man, and if convicted, nothing but a pardon could save him.
These opinions, casting such serious doubts on the question of right,
are at least enough to restrain indignation and beget caution."

> Greville's Memoirs, second part, I. March 12, 1841, p. 383.

" Connected with these transactions there have also been circumstances, of which, I believe, it is generally admitted that Great Britain has had just ground to complain.   Individuals have been made
personally liable for acts done under the avowed authority of their
Government; and there are now many brave men exposed to personal
consequences for no other cause than having served their country.
That this is contrary to every principle of international law it is useless for me to insist.   Indeed, it has been admitted by every authority
of your Government; but, owing to a conflict of laws, difficulties
have intervened, much to the regret of those authorities, in giving
practical effect to these principles; and for these difficulties some
remedy has been by all desired.   It is no business of mine to enter
upon the consideration of them, nor have I sufficient information for
the purpose; but I trust you will excuse my addressing to you the
inquiry, whether the Government of the United States is now in a
condition to secure, in effect and in practice, the principle, which has
never been denied in argument, that individuals acting under legitimate authority are not personally responsible for executing the orders
of their government?   That the power, when it exists, will be used on
every fit occasion, I am well assured; and I am bound to admit that,
looking through the voluminous correspondence concerning these

transactions, there appears no indisposition with any of the authorities of the Federal Government, under its several administrations, to do justice in this respect in as far as their means and powers would allow."

Lord Ashburton, British plenipo., to Mr. Webster, Sec. of State, July 28, 1842, Webster's Works, VI. 294, 300.

" This Government has admitted that, for an act committed by the command of his sovereign, *jure belli*, an individual cannot be responsible in the ordinary courts of another state. It would regard it as a high indignity if a citizen of its own, acting under its authority and by its special command, in such cases were held to answer in a municipal tribunal, and to undergo punishment, as if the behest of his government were no defence or protection to him.

" But your lordship is aware that, in regular constitutional governments, persons arrested on charges of high crimes can only be discharged by some judicial proceeding. It is so in England; it is so in the colonies and provinces of England. The forms of judicial proceeding differ in different countries, being more rapid in some and more dilatory in others; and, it may be added, generally more dilatory, or at least more cautious, in cases affecting life, in governments of a strictly limited than in those of a more unlimited character. It was a subject of regret that the release of McLeod was so long delayed. A State court, and that not of the highest jurisdiction, decided that, on summary application, embarrassed, as it would appear, by technical difficulties, he could not be released by that court. His discharge shortly afterward by a jury, to whom he preferred to submit his case, rendered unnecessary the further prosecution of the legal question. It is for the Congress of the United States, whose attention has been called to the subject, to say what further provision ought to be made to expedite proceedings in such cases; and, in answer to your lordship's question toward the close of your note, I have to say that the Government of the United States holds itself, not only fully disposed, but fully competent, to carry into practice every principle which it avows or acknowledges, and to fulfill every duty and obligations which it owes to foreign governments, their citizens or subjects."

Mr. Webster, Sec. of State, to Lord Ashburton, British plen., Aug 6, 1842, Webster's Works, VI. 301, 302–303.

See Mr. Webster's speech in the Senate, April 6 and 7, 1846, Webster's Works, V. 123 et seq.

See, also, Mr. Olney, Sec. of State, to Mr. Thomas, min. to Venezuela, June 25, 1896, directing the latter to urge unofficially the release of the British surveyor, Harris, who had been arrested by the Venezuelan authorities on territory claimed by Venezuela. " He acted under orders," said Mr. Olney ; " any settlement should be between two governments." (MS. Inst. Venez. IV. 425.)

A claim for indemnity, preferred by McLeod before the mixed commission under the treaty of Feb. 8, 1853, was dismissed on the ground that the entire incident was disposed of by the correspondence between Mr. Webster and Lord Ashburton. (Moore, Int. Arbitrations, III. 2419 et seq.)

By the act of Congress approved Aug. 29, 1842, and since embodied in sec. 753, Rev. Stat., the United States courts, in view of the difficulty encountered in the McLeod case, were empowered to issue a writ of habeas corpus, in the case of a prisoner in jail, " where he is in custody under or by color of the authority of the United States, or is committed for trial before some court thereof; or is in custody for an act done or omitted in pursuance of a law of the United States, or of an order, process, or decree of a court or judge thereof; or is in custody in violation of the Constitution or of a law or treaty of the United States; or, being a subject or citizen of a foreign state, and domiciled therein, is in custody for an act done or omitted under any alleged right, title, authority, privilege, protection, or exemption claimed under the commission, or order, or sanction of any foreign state, or under color thereof, the validity and effect whereof depend upon the law of nations."

The obvious effect of this act is to bring the prisoner into the custody of the Federal courts, but it does not prescribe what the decision of those courts upon a particular application may be.

Early in 1892 a revolution was begun in Venezuela, under the lead of General Crespo, against the government of President Palacio. August 8, 1892, an engagement took place at Buena Vista, and on the 13th of the month the victorious revolutionary forces entered Bolivar under the command of General Hernandez, who assumed command of the city as civil and military chief, filling all the local offices which had been vacated by their incumbents. October 6, 1892, the revolutionary forces took possession of Caracas, and on the 23d of the month the government of General Crespo was formally recognized by the United States as the legitimate Government of Venezuela. After the entry of General Hernandez into Bolivar, George F. Underhill, a citizen of the United States, who had constructed and was in charge of the waterworks of the city, besides carrying on a machinery repair business, applied to him as commanding officer for a passport to leave the city. Hernandez refused to grant this request, as well as similar ones subsequently made, until October 18, 1892, when Underhill obtained a passport and left the country. Subsequently Hernandez, being in the State of New York, was sued by Underhill for damages for detention, caused by the refusal of the passport, for alleged confinement in his own house, and for certain alleged arrests and affronts by soldiers of the revolutionary army. On the trial of the case in circuit court of the United States for the eastern district of New York, the court directed a verdict for the defendant on the ground that, " because the acts of defendant were those of a military commander, representing a *de facto* government in the prosecution of a war, he was not civilly responsible therefor." Judgment was rendered for the defendant and on appeal was affirmed by the circuit court of appeals on the ground " that the acts of the defendant were the acts of the Government of Venezuela, and as such are not properly the subject of adjudication in the courts of another government." 26 U. S. Ap. 573. An appeal was then taken to the Supreme Court of the United States. This court, Chief Justice Fuller delivering the opinion, rendered the following decision:

" Every sovereign state is bound to respect the independence of every other sovereign state, and the courts of one country will not sit in judgment on the acts of the government of another done within its own territory. Redress of grievances by reason of such acts must be obtained through the means open to be availed of by sovereign powers as between themselves.

" Nor can the principle be confined to lawful or recognized governments, or to cases where redress can manifestly be had through public channels. The immunity of individuals from suits brought in foreign tribunals for acts done within their own states, in the exercise of governmental authority, whether as civil officers or as military commanders, must necessarily extend to the agents of governments ruling by paramount force as matter of fact. Where a civil war prevails, that is, where the people of a country are divided into two hostile parties, who take up arms and oppose one another by military force, generally speaking foreign nations do not assume to judge of the merits of the quarrel. If the party seeking to dislodge the existing government succeeds, and the independence of the government it has set up is recognized, then the acts of such government from the commencement of its existence are regarded as those of an independent nation. If the political revolt fails of success, still if actual war has been waged, acts of legitimate warfare cannot be made the basis of individual liability. United States *v.* Rice, 4 Wheat. 246; Fleming *v.* Page, 9 How. 603; Thorington *v.* Smith, 8 Wall. 1; Williams *v.* Bruffy, 96 U. S. 176; Ford *v.* Surget, 97 U. S. 594; Dow *v.* Johnson, 100 U. S. 158; and other cases.

" Revolutions or insurrections may inconvenience other nations, but by accommodation to the facts the application of settled rules is readily reached. And where the fact of the existence of war is in issue in the instance of complaint of acts committed within foreign territory, it is not an absolute prerequisite that that fact should be made out by an acknowledgment of belligerency, as other official recognition of its existence may be sufficient proof thereof. The Three Friends, 166 U. S. 1.

" In this case, the archives of the State Department show that civil war was flagrant in Venezuela from the spring of 1892; that the revolution was successful; and that the revolutionary gorvernment was recognized by the United States as the government of the country, it being, to use the language of the Secretary of State in a communication to our minister to Venezuela, ' accepted by the people, in the possession of the power of the nation and fully established.'

" That these were facts of which the court is bound to take judicial notice, and for information as to which it may consult the Department of State, there can be no doubt. Jones *v.* United States, 137 U. S. 202; Mighell *v.* Sultan of Jahore, (1894) 1 Q. B. 149.

" It is idle to argue that the proceedings of those who thus triumphed should be treated as the acts of banditti or mere mobs.

" We entertain no doubt upon the evidence that Hernandez was carrying on military operations in support of the revolutionary party. It may be that adherents of that side of the controversy in the particular locality where Hernandez was the leader of the movement entertained a preference for him as the future executive head of the nation, but that is beside the question. The acts complained of were the acts of a military commander representing the authority of the revolutionary party as a government, which afterwards succeeded and was recognized by the United States. We think the Circuit Court of Appeals was justified in concluding ' that the acts of the defendant were the acts of the Government of Venezuela, and as such are not properly the subject of adjudication in the courts of another government.'

" The decisions cited on plaintiff's behalf are not in point. Cases respecting arrests by military authority in the absence of the prevalence of war; or the validity of contracts between individuals entered into in aid of insurrection; or the right of revolutionary bodies to vex the commerce of the world on its common highway without incurring the penalties denounced on piracy; and the like, do not involve the questions presented here.

" We agree with the Circuit Court of Appeals, that ' the evidence upon the trial indicated that the purpose of the defendant in his treatment of the plaintiff was to coerce the plaintiff to operate his waterworks and his repair works for the benefit of the community and the revolutionary forces,' and that ' it was not sufficient to have warranted a finding by the jury that the defendant was actuated by malice or any personal or private motive; ' and we concur in its disposition of the rulings below. The decree of the Circuit Court is *affirmed.*"

Underhill *v.* Hernandez (1897), 168 U. S. 250, affirming 26 U. S. App. 573, 13 C. C. A. 51, and 65 Fed. Rep. 577.

3. LEGISLATIVE POWER.

(1) RIGHTS OF PROPERTY.

§ 180.

" In my opinion all questions touching the title of lands in this State, or any other State, must be tried and decided in the manner prescribed by the Constitutions and laws of the land."

> Mr. Jay, Sec. for For. Aff., to Mr. de Lotbiniere, Jan. 29, 1789, 4 MS. Am. Let. 81. See the case of William Crooks, Moore, Int. Arbitrations, I. 415.

Whether the authorities of Cuba, in disposing of property in the island, proceeded regularly or irregularly would depend wholly upon the laws in force there.

> Mr. Marcy, Sec. of State, to Mr. Hernandez, March 29, 1856, 45 MS. Dom. Let. 177.

The United States will take no part in the contentions between citizens of the United States in regard to the interoceanic route by way of Nicaragua. " The law of the country must regulate all questions of this nature. If grants are made, its judicial authority in the event of disputed claims must determine the rights of the parties. The United States can only insist, that treaty stipulations be fairly executed, and that good faith be observed toward all those deriving rights from the local government."

> Mr. Cass, Sec. of State, to Mr. Lamar, min. to Central America, Jan. 2, 1858, MS. Inst. American States, XV. 288.

" It is an established principle of international law that every State has the right to regulate the conditions upon which property within its territory, whether real or personal, shall be held and transmitted." It is *prima facie* a question for the courts.

> Mr. Gresham, Sec. of State, to Mr. Hoxtun, December 20, 1893, 194 MS. Dom. Let. 598.

Transactions depending upon the rules of international law are to be decided in accordance with those rules as they existed at the time when the transaction took place.

> Mortimer *v.* N. Y. Elevated Railroad Co. (1889), 6 N. Y. Supp. 898.

(2) INDUSTRIAL PROPERTY.

§ 181.

The Government of the United States cannot with propriety ask the Government of another country to suspend the operation of its laws in order that a citizen of the United States may have further time in which to secure in such country a patent for his invention.

Local regulation.

> Mr. Frelinghuysen, Sec. of State, to Mr. Mann, Dec. 27, 1884, 153 MS. Dom. Let. 515; Mr. Frelinghuysen, Sec. of State, to Mr. Russell, Feb. 7, 1885, 154 MS. Dom. Let. 188.

"Your letter of the 26th ultimo, with the enclosures, has been examined in this Department with the care which your own merits, as well as the importance of the subject deserves.

"The question that arises is, how far the Government of the United States can officially interfere to insist upon a construction given by a British court to a British municipal statute being reversed by the British executive. I feel bound to say at the outset that this Government cannot so interfere. The point in dispute does not arise under a treaty, nor does it fall under the general range of international obligations, as interpreted by ourselves and Great Britain. Were a British subject to lose a suit brought by him before one of our courts for the maintenance of alleged patent rights, we would peremptorily repel any attempt on the part of the British Government to induce this Department to interfere by giving by executive warrant relief which was refused by the court before whom such suit was brought. The only possible cases for such interference are those of torts wrongfully inflicted by the opposing government as an unprovoked assailant; and even in such cases where there is a local independent judiciary to be appealed to, there is no diplomatic interposition unless it should appear that on appealing to such judiciary, justice was denied.

"I cannot see that your case presents these features. No tort was inflicted on you by Great Britain so as to impair rights belonging to you by the law of nations. You went to England voluntarily to obtain privileges which are exclusively the products of British statutes. To obtain such privileges you appealed to the British chancery division of the English high court of justice, by which alone, under British legislation, could the relief you sought be granted.

"The elaborate adverse opinion of Mr. Justice Sterling given on February 23, 1887, has been examined in this Department with care, and I have to inform you that in the judgment of this Department the decision made by Mr. Justice Sterling is not one in which such error can be found as will justify diplomatic intervention. The decision is simply an interpretation of British local legislation by the court, by which that legislation is to be judicially applied, and to which you yourself properly appealed for this purpose.

"Your present method of redress is either the presentation of an amended case, so as to avoid the difficulties stated by Mr. Justice Sterling, or an appeal from the latter's decision to the appellate tribunal appointed in such case."

> Mr. Bayard, Sec. of State, to Mr. Avery, May 4, 1887, 164 MS. Dom. Let. 78.

The rule that the validity of patents in the United States is a question to be determined by the courts is applicable not only to litigation by private parties, but also to litigation in which the Government of the United States is interested. Hence the United States may properly intervene as a party in a suit brought by alien patentees against an American company for the use of a process which is employed by such company in manufacturing, under contract, articles for the use of the Government of the United States.

> Mr. Adee, Acting Sec. of State, to Mr. Patenôtre, French minister, July 23, 1897, For. Rel. 1897, 137–141.
> The Navy Department may withhold its approval of a voucher for the payment to the Carnegie Steel Company of a sum of money which is claimed as royalty for the use of the Harvey process in the manufacture of armor plate for naval vessels till the right of the Harvey Steel Company to collect from the Government a royalty for the use of the process is determined in a suit pending in the Court of Claims. (Griggs, At.-Gen., March 14, 1901, 23 Op. 422. Affirmed by Beck, Acting At.-Gen., Aug. 23, 1901, 23 Op. 495.)

As to the registration of trade-marks in the Argentine Republic, see For. Rel. 1899, 5–6.

In a despatch of January 9, 1894, Mr. Denby, United States minister at Peking, enclosed a copy of a note which he had addressed to the Tsung-li-Yamên, asking that a proclamation be issued reprobating the practices of counterfeiting or fraudulently imitating trade-marks on American piece goods, and directing all officials to arrest and punish persons found guilty of the offense. He communicated to the Yamên a copy of the proclamation then lately issued by the taotai at Tien-tsin, warning all wholesale and retail dealers at that place not to change the trade-marks on American goods.

> For. Rel. 1894, 134.

A patent for a spinning machine granted, by the Chinese Government June 17, 1898, to one of its own subjects, was bought by two American missionaries and an Englishman. The purchasers subsequently complained of the infringement of the patent by another Chinaman, and a complaint was made by the United States legation to the Chinese Government in behalf of the two Americans. The Tsung-li yamên, December 19, 1899, replied that China would permit them " at all the treaty ports, to carry on their business of their own free will and accord, but as to protecting them in their exclusive right and prohibiting others from making machines, as there is no treaty stipulation on the subject, the Yamên still finds no way of taking action."

> Mr. Conger, min. to China, to Mr. Hay, Sec. of State, Dec. 20, 1899, For. Rel. 1899, 178–185.
>
> In reporting this decision Mr. Conger said : " The Chinese look with a degree of suspicion upon the missionaries who engage in any sort of business scheme or enterprise, and possibly this may in some measure account for their decision."

By Art. II., par. 3, of the Japanese trade-marks regulations, trade-marks can not be registered which are " identical with or similar to trade-marks already registered or trade-marks used by others before the application for registration was made, and which are intended to be applied to identical goods," whether the applicant be a Japanese or a foreigner.

> For. Rel. 1898, 464, 469, 471.

" I have the honor to acknowledge the receipt of your letter of the 26th ultimo, commending to this Department's favorable consideration the suggestion of the Commissioner of Patents that such steps be taken as may be necessary to effect an exchange of diplomatic notes between this Government and that of Mexico, to the end that Mexican citizens may be enabled to register their trade-marks in the United States, as contemplated by the act of Congress, approved March 3, 1881.

United States legislation.

" The Commissioner of Patents expresses the opinion that an exchange of diplomatic notes with Mexico this subject would seem to constitute the declaration mentioned in section 3 of the act of March 3, 1881, under which the right can be accorded to citizens of Mexico to register their trade-marks in this country.

" My predecessors, Mr. Gresham and Mr. Olney, in instructions to our minister at Athens (Foreign Relations, 1894, pp. 293–295; and Foreign Relations, 1895, pp. 759–765), took the position that a declaration signed by the minister and the Greek minister for foreign affairs, to the effect that the treaty of 1837 between the United States and Greece conferred upon the citizens of either country in the dominions of the other the same rights as respects trade-marks as such citizens may enjoy in their own, would not accomplish the end desired, but that a formal treaty was necessary.

" I think it is plain that a simple declaration would not bind this Government to grant trade-mark privileges to Mexican citizens, but in view of the Mexican law, which (the Commissioner of Patents states) allows citizens of the United States to register their trade-marks in Mexico, it would appear that Mexicans can *now* obtain registration of their trade-marks here, under the provisions of our law of March 3, 1881.

" Section 1 of the act of 1881 provides that:

" ' Owners of trade-marks used in commerce with foreign nations . . . , provided such owners shall be domiciled in the United States, or located in any foreign country . . . which, by treaty, convention *or law,* affords similar privileges to citizens of the United States, may obtain registration of such trade-marks by complying with the following requirements.'

" Section 3 of the act further provides:

" ' But no alleged trade-mark shall be registered unless the same appear to be lawfully used as such by the applicant in foreign commerce, . . . as mentioned above, *or is within the provision of a treaty convention or declaration with a foreign power.*'

" It will be observed that the provision of section 3 is in the alternative; that in order to entitle a trade-mark to registration, it must appear:

" 1. That it is lawfully used as such by the applicant in foreign commerce, the owner being domiciled in the United States *or located in a foreign country* which, by treaty, convention or by law, affords similar privileges to citizens of the United States; *or*

" 2. That such trade-mark is within the provision of a treaty, convention or declaration with a foreign power.

" While registration could not be claimed by a Mexican under the second alternative, it seems to me that it could properly be claimed under the first.

" I think an exchange of notes with the Mexican Government would be entirely proper to establish the fact that under the Mexican law, citizens of the United States may obtain registration of their trade-marks. This was done with the Netherlands in 1883. (See printed pamphlet herewith.) Such an exchange of notes does not, however, in my opinion, constitute *the declaration* mentioned in section 3 of the act of 1881."

> Mr. Hay, Sec. of State, to Sec. of Interior, Nov. 4, 1898, 232 MS. Dom. Let. 466.
>
> See, also, as to the declaration above referred to, in the case of Greece, Mr. Gresham, Sec. of State, to Sec. of Interior, Feb. 23, 1895, 200 MS. Dom. Let. 645.
>
> As to the protection of trade-marks in Morocco, see For. Rel. 1904, 407.

Porto Rico being an organized Territory of the United States in the sense of sec. 1981, Rev. Stat., and the laws of the United States not locally inapplicable having been extended thereto, its residents are entitled to register their trade-marks in the United States under the act of Congress of March 3, 1881, 21 Stat. 502.

The Philippine Islands not being an organized Territory in the same sense, and perhaps not being embraced in the phrase " United States " in the trade-marks act, the residents of the islands are not as such entitled to the privilege in question.

Cuba being at present governed by the United States, and the law there purporting to give to citizens of the United States trade-mark privileges " similar " to those given by the United States law—a condition which doubtless would be continued since it was itself but a continuation of the arrangement previously existing between the United States and Spain—the residents of the island may be considered as residents of a country with which the United States has a reciprocal arrangement and as entitled to register their trade-marks under the act of 1881.

> Knox, At.-Gen., Feb. 19, 1902, 23 Op. 634.
>
> But rights of property in trade-marks in Cuba and the Philippines are entitled to the protection stipulated for " property of all kinds " in Arts. I. and VIII. of the treaty of peace between the United States and Spain of December 10, 1898 ; and trade-marks registered prior to that time in the international registry at Berne are entitled to the same recognition and protection from the military governments of Cuba and the Philippines as trade-marks registered in the national registry at Madrid or in one of the provincial registries of the islands. (Mr. Magoon, law officer, Division of Insular Affairs, War Department, March 27, 1901, Magoon's Reports, 305.)

The provision in the convention between the United States and
Treaty questions.   Austria-Hungary of Nov. 25, 1871, Art. I., that if a trade-mark has become public property " in the country of its origin " it shall be equally free in the other country, does not prevent the appropriation in the United States of a word that is not the subject of appropriation under the laws of Austria.

> J. & P. Baltz Brewing Co. v. Kaiserbrauerei, Beck & Co., 74 Fed. Rep. 222, 20 C. C. A. 402.

It was held that the name " Hunyadi " having become public property in Hungary, it also became, under the treaty between the United States and Austria-Hungary of November 25, 1871, public property in the United States; that the court could not take notice of the law of Hungary of 1895 reinstating the exclusive right of the person who first used the word as a trade-mark; and that the name having also become public property in the United States his right to an exclusive appropriation of it was lost. It was also held that he had been guilty of laches in vindicating his claim to an exclusive right to the word, if he had any. But it was also decided that the appropriation by other persons of his bottle and label, being without justification or excuse, was an active and continuing fraud on his rights, and that the defense of laches in this particular was not maintained.

Saxlehner *v.* Eisner & Mendelson Co. (1900), 179 U. S. 19.

The agreement between the United States and Brazil, Sept. 24, 1878, provides that the citizens or subjects of each contracting party shall have in the territory of the other the same rights as natives in everything relating to trade-marks. By a law of Brazil of Nov. 14, 1899, the " importation of goods made abroad which carry labels wholly or partly in Portuguese, except when imported from Portugal or when made for factories," was forbidden.[a] The Department of State expressed the opinion that this constituted a violation of the trade-marks agreement.[b] The Commissioner of Patents of the United States, however, afterwards said: "As I understand the Brazilian law from the correspondence, the requirement that the importation of foreign products shall not carry an inscription in the Portuguese language, unless imported from Portugal, applies to the citizens of Brazil as well as to others. This being so, of course our citizens in this particular would be on the same footing under the treaty as Brazilians." He therefore expressed the opinion that the contention that the law violated the treaty could not be sustained. The law subsequently was amended so as to allow importations of manufactures with labels in Portuguese, with the requirement that the country of origin must be indicated.[c]

Under the stipulation of Art. XVII. of the treaty between the United States and the German Empire of Dec. 11, 1871, that the citizens of each country shall enjoy in the other " the same protection as native citizens " in the matter of trade-marks, a German may acquire in the United States a trade-mark in a particular word, although in Germany a word alone, apart from any symbol or design, can not be so appropriated.

J. P. Baltz Brewing Co., 74 Fed. Rep. 222, 20 C. C. A. 402.

For a treaty between Germany and Mexico, signed at the City of Mexico, Aug. 16, 1898, for the protection of trade-marks, see For. Rel. 1899, 502.

---

[a] For. Rel. 1900, 62.

[b] Mr. Hill, Acting Sec. of State, to Mr. Bryan, min. to Brazil, tel., June 1, 1900, For. Rel. 1900, 56; Mr. Hay, Sec. of State, to Mr. Bryan, min. to Brazil, June 1, 1900, For. Rel. 1900, 57.

[c] For. Rel. 1900, 63, 64–65.

" In accordance with instructions which I have received, I have the honor to call your excellency's attention to the following subject:

" In a memorandum handed to the Imperial Government by the United States ambassador at Berlin October 19, 1894, a copy of which is inclosed, the wish is expressed to conclude a special agreement with the Imperial Government to the effect that American citizens be granted the benefit of certain provisions of the German patent law of April 7, 1891, which are not in themselves applicable to aliens.

" The opinion repeatedly expressed therein, that the American patent legislation already grants to German inventors that which is asked of Germany by America, rests, in the judgment of the Imperial Government, upon a not quite correct view of the legal situation. The points to be considered in the matter were communicated to the then United States Secretary of State, Mr. J. W. Foster, in the German note of September 15, 1892. As they were mentioned in the memorandum of October 19, 1894, without a reply being made to them, the Imperial Government thinks itself called upon to refer to them again, and to add that if the three months' limitation were withdrawn from American patent documents in Germany the Americans would obtain an advantage over the Germans which the Germans do not enjoy in America.

" The draft of an agreement for the conclusion of a patent, sample, and trade-mark convention between the United States and Germany, transmitted to your excellency with the German note of November 10, 1893, which, according to the kind note of Acting Secretary of State Uhl of November 30, 1893, was handed to the proper authorities for examination and approbation, contains, in article 3, a provision which, in the opinion of the Imperial Government, is calculated to satisfy fully the wishes of the United States Government. The Imperial Government cherishes the opinion that by the speedy conclusion of a convention upon the basis of the above-mentioned draft the matter would be settled in the most satisfactory manner, and in that most conducive to the interests of both parties."

> Baron Saurma, German amb., to Mr. Gresham, Sec. of State, April 3, 1895, For. Rel. 1895, I. 528.
> For the previous correspondence referred to in the foregoing note, see For. Rel. 1892, 185, 186, 189, 190, 191-197, 200, 214, 217; For. Rel. 1894, 243.

"An American patent may be applied for by a foreign inventor whose invention has been patented abroad at any time during the life of his foreign patent unless his invention has been introduced into public use in the United States for more than two years prior to the application, the American patent, if granted, to expire the same time as the foreign patent.

"All that can be secured for an American inventor under the German law is the right to obtain a patent in Germany if the application be made within three months from the date of the publication of the American patent. This benefit of the German law extends only to those States which warrant reciprocity, according to a publication in the Reichsgesetzblatt. The benefit, then, is not granted until the publication of a notification that such reciprocity exists.

" Now, under American law the German inventor has more than the German law would give an American inventor if it were declared that reciprocity exists; for a German inventor may apply in America for a patent for his invention at any time during the life of his German patent unless he has permitted his invention to be in public use in the United States for more than two years prior to his application, so that he has in any event two years in which to apply, while the American inventor could only get a patent in Germany by applying within three months from the time of getting his American patent.

" The claim that reciprocity does not exist is, according to Baron von Ketteler's note of September 15, 1892, based on two grounds.

" First. That to obtain a patent in the United States the German applicant must swear that he is the inventor, while in Germany patent is granted to the inventor or anyone who has legally come into possession of the invention.

" Second. That the right of caveat is confined to American citizens and not granted to German subjects.

" When this subject was previously under discussion here it was suggested by the Imperial Government that it be left for adjustment under the proposed new treaty between the United States and Germany in regard to patents and trade-marks. That treaty has not yet been agreed upon, and my instructions are to endeavor to reach an understanding with the German Government separately and apart from that treaty (which involves other things) whereby American citizens may enjoy the benefit of the German law before referred to."

Memorandum handed by the American ambassador, at Berlin, to the German Government, Oct. 19, 1894. For. Rel. 1895, I. 529.

" The negotiation of a treaty for the reciprocal protection of patents, trademarks, and designs has been the subject of correspondence between this Government and that of Germany for a number of years past without so far reaching a conclusion satisfactory to both Governments." (Mr. Adee, Second Assist. Sec. of State, to Mr. Brown, Nov. 1, 1897, 222 MS. Dom. Let. 131.)

This was a controversy relating to a trade-mark for protective paint for ship's bottom. The court *held:*

(1) That no valid trade-mark was proved on that part of the Rahtjens Company in connection with paint sent from Germany to their agents in the United States prior to 1873, when they procured a patent in England for their composition;

(2) That no right to a trade-mark which includes the word " patent," and which describes the article as " patented," can arise when there has been no patent;

(3) That a symbol or label claimed as a trade-mark, so constituted or worded as to make or contain a distinct assertion which is false, will not be recognized, and no right to its exclusive use can be maintained;

(4) That of necessity when the right to manufacture became public, the right to use the only word descriptive of the article manufactured became public also;

(5) That no right to the exclusive use in the United States of the words " Rahtjen's Compositions " has been shown.

Holzapfel's Co. v. Rahtjen's Co. (1901), 183 U. S. 1.

March 20, 1883, a convention for the protection of industrial property was concluded at Paris between Belgium, Brazil, France, Guatemala, Italy, the Netherlands, Portugal, Salvador, Spain, and Switzerland. It was subsequently acceded to by the Dominican Republic, Great Britain, Sweden and Norway, the United States, and Tunis, while Salvador withdrew. See, as to the accession of the United States, For. Rel. 1887, 1067.

Industrial property union.

A supplemental convention was signed at Madrid April 15, 1891.

An additional act modifying the convention of March 20, 1883, was signed at Brussels December 14, 1900, the signatory powers being Belgium, Brazil, Denmark, Dominican Republic, France, Great Britain, Italy, Japan, the Netherlands, Portugal, Servia, Spain, Sweden and Norway, Switzerland, the United States, and Tunis.

The convention of 1883 provided (Art. II.) that the citizens or subjects of the contracting states should enjoy in the various states of the union, so far as concerned patents for inventions, trade or commercial marks, and the commercial name, such advantages as the respective laws of those states then accorded or should thereafter accord to citizens or subjects.

The British merchandise-marks act, 1887, designed " to carry out in their complete spirit the principles " of the convention, is printed in For. Rel. 1887, 546.

See, as to certain proposed additional articles to the convention, For. Rel. 1887, 636.

" I have the honor to acknowledge the receipt of your note of the 27th ultimo, enclosing a circular received by you from Her Majesty's principal secretary of state for foreign affairs, enquiring as to the manner in which effect is given in the United States to the stipulations contained in the International Convention for the Protection of Industrial Property of March 20, 1883, and what protection is afforded foreigners in the matter of patents, trade-marks, &c.

" The first question asked by Her Majesty's Government is understood to be in effect whether the convention referred to has immediately force of law by virtue of the accession of this Government, or whether it only becomes of effect, as in England, by virtue of separate legislative enactments.

" In reply it may be said that by virtue of legislative enactments already in existence at the time of the adhesion of the United States to the convention, its general provisions, so far as they are effectual at all, took effect at once. These general provisions are contained in Article II. of the convention, and provide for the reciprocal enjoyment by the subjects and citizens of each of the contracting states of all rights in all the other states, that they accord to their own subjects and citizens, in respect to patents, trade-marks, and other industrial property.

" So far as concerns patents for inventions and designs the United States statutes already extend to every person all the rights which American citizens possess. Sections 4886 and 4929 of the Revised Statutes give the privilege of obtaining patents to ' any person,' no discrimination being made against foreigners.

" With respect to trade-marks, section 1 of the act of Congress of March 3, 1881, provides for the registration of trade-marks whose owners are ' domiciled in the United States or located in any foreign country which by treaty, convention or law affords similar privileges to citizens of the United States.' It should be observed, however, in respect to trade-marks that the constitutional power of the Federal Government to deal with the registration and protection of trademarks and the precise effect of the statutes enacted by Congress upon the subject, are by no means free from doubt; and the representatives of the United States at the Paris conferences of 1880 and 1883, accordingly made certain reservations, which are to be found in the protocols of those conferences. For your information, I enclose herewith, a copy of a note addressed by me on January 11, 1888, to the minister of Switzerland at this capital bearing upon this subject.

" Some of the specific provisions of the convention of 1883 would seem to need further legislation to enable the United States to carry them into effect. Such provisions are found in Articles IX. and X. for the seizure upon importation of merchandise bearing unlawfully a trade or commercial mark or commercial name.

" No machinery exists under the legislation of the United States to enable the seizure of merchandise bearing spurious trade-marks, and it may therefore, be doubted whether these provisions can be carried out without legislation by Congress.

" The second inquiry of Her Majesty's Government is, in substance, how far the legislation of the United States, irrespective of treaties or conventions, gives protection to foreigners in respect to patents, designs, trade-marks, trade-names, &c.

" This subject is dealt with in Chapter LX. of the Revised Statutes
of the United States sections 4883 to 4971, and in subsequent legislation, particularly in the act approved March 3, 1881, in relation to
trade-marks. As already stated this legislation permits inventors
of every nationality without reference to treaties, to apply for
patents on the same footing as citizens of the United States; and
owners of trade-marks used in commerce with foreign nations or with
the Indian tribes may obtain registration ' provided such owners
shall be domiciled in the United States or located in any foreign
country or tribes which by treaty, convention or law give similar
privileges to citizens of the United States.'

" For your further information, I enclose herewith a pamphlet on
the ' History of the International Union for the Protection of Industrial Property, including a discussion of the articles of the union
and their effect upon industrial property of citizens of the United
States,' prepared by the Examiner of Trade-Marks under the direction of the Commissioner of Patents."

> Mr. Bayard, Sec. of State, to Mr. Herbert, Brit. chargé Jan. 18, 1889,
> MS. Notes to Gr. Br. XXI. 38.

> Art. IV. of the convention of 1883 does not require the United States
> to accord to the subjects or citizens of the other members of the
> Industrial Property Union greater privileges than it grants to its
> own citizens. (Mr. Claparede, Swiss min., to Mr. Blaine, Sec. of
> State, April 3, 1891, stating the opinion of the Swiss Government to
> that effect; acknowledged by Mr. Wharton, Act. Sec. of State, April
> 15, 1891, MS. Notes to Switzerland, I. 255.)

(3) INTERNATIONAL COPYRIGHT.

§ 182.

" An international copyright conference was held at Berne in September, on the invitation of the Swiss Government.
The envoy of the United States attended as a delegate,
Berne Convention.
but refrained from committing this Government to the results, even
by signing the recommendatory protocol adopted. The interesting
and important subject of international copyright has been before you
for several years. Action is certainly desirable to effect the object
in view. And while there may be question as to the relative advantage
of treating it by legislation or by specific treaty, the matured views of
the Berne conference cannot fail to aid your consideration of the
subject."

> President Cleveland, annual message, Dec. 8, 1885. (For. Rel. 1885, p.
> xiv.)

> This message referred to the project of an international copyright con-
> vention which was adopted by the conference at Berne, Sept. 18, 1885.

" The drift of sentiment in civilized communities toward full recognition of the rights of property in the creations of the human intellect has brought about the adoption, by many important nations, of an International Copyright Convention, which was signed at Berne on the 18th of September, 1885.

" Inasmuch as the Constitution gives to Congress the power ' to promote the progress of science and useful arts by securing for limited times to authors and inventors the exclusive right to their respective writings and discoveries,' this Government did not feel warranted in becoming a signatory pending the action of Congress upon measures of international copyright now before it, but the right of adhesion to the Berne Convention hereafter, has been reserved. I trust the subject will receive at your hands the attention it deserves, and that the just claims of authors, so urgently pressed, will be duly heeded."

> President Cleveland, annual message, Dec. 6, 1886. (For. Rel. 1886, p. xii.)
>
> The convention here referred to was the project adopted by the conference at Berne on the date mentioned. A new conference met at Berne, Sept. 6, 1886, for the purpose of transforming the project into a definitive diplomatic act. This was done Sept. 9, 1886, the convention being on that day formally signed as an international agreement. A report on the subject may be found in a dispatch of Mr. Winchester, then United States minister at Berne, of Sept. 13, 1886. (For. Rel. 1886, 852.)
>
> The text of the convention is printed in For. Rel. 1886, 855. See, also, For. Rel. 1887, 362, 363.

By an act of Congress approved March 3, 1891, the statutes of the United States were so amended that international copyright might be obtained in the United States on certain conditions. The whole of the existing legislation of the United States on the subject of copyrights may be found in title 60, chapter 3, Revised Statutes, and the acts of March 3, 1891; March 2, 1895, and Jan. 6. 1897.

Act of Congress March 3, 1891.

The international application of the act of March 3, 1891, 26 Stat. 1110, is discussed in a report given below, in which the effect of section 13 is examined. That section reads as follows:

" Sec. 13. That this act shall only apply to a citizen or subject of a foreign state or nation when such foreign state or nation permits to citizens of the United States of America the benefit of copyright on substantially the same basis as its own citizens; or when such foreign state or nation is a party to an international agreement which provides for reciprocity in the granting of copyright, by the terms of which agreement the United States of America may, at its pleasure, become a party to such agreement. The existence of either of the conditions aforesaid shall be determined by the President of the United States by proclamation made from time to time as the purposes of this act may require."

" By the act of March 3, 1891, amending title 60, chapter 3, of the Revised Statutes of the United States, relating to copyrights, the Government of the United States has undertaken to admit the citizens or subjects of foreign states or nations to the privileges of copyright in this country on either of two conditions. These conditions are expressed in section 13 of that act and are alternative, not concurrent.

" The first in order of the conditions stated in section 13 is, that the act shall apply to the citizens or subjects of a foreign state or nation, ' when such foreign state or nation permits to citizens of the United States of America the benefit of copyright on substantially the same basis as its own citizens.'

" The second condition is that the act shall aply to the citizens or subjects of a foreign state or nation ' when such foreign state or nation is a party to an international agreement which provides for reciprocity in the granting of copyright, by the terms of which agreement the United States of America may, at its pleasure, become a party to such agreement.'

" The existence of either of these conditions is to be determined by the President of the United States ' by proclamation made *from time to time, as the purposes of this act may require.*'

" Under this clause it is the duty of the President to withhold, issue, or revoke his proclamation, in accordance with the facts as to the existence or nonexistence of one of the two specified conditions at any particular time.

" The terms of the first condition are clear, and have not as yet presented any difficulty of interpretation.

" The terms of the second condition are less determinate and have given rise to much discussion and to variant interpretations. For convenience, we will consider the second condition first.

" SECOND CONDITION.

" On the 9th of September, 1886, a convention was concluded at Berne, Switzerland, for the establishment of an international union for the protection of literary and artistic works. The parties to this convention were Belgium, Germany, France, Liberia, Spain, Great Britain, Hayti, Italy, Switzerland, and Tunis.

" The minister of the United States at Berne attended the conference which formed this convention, but only in an *ad referendum* capacity, and, as the subject of international copyright was then pending before Congress with a view to legislation, the representative of the United States did not sign the convention. By the eighteenth article of the Berne Convention it is provided that countries which have not joined it, but which, ' by their municipal laws, assure legal protection to the rights' of which the convention treats, 'shall be admitted to accede thereto on their request to that effect.'

" It has been argued that this eighteenth article of the Berne Convention completely satisfies the second condition specified in section 13 of the act of March 3, 1891, and *ipso facto* entitles the contracting parties to a proclamation by the President admitting their citizens or subjects to participation in the benefits of that act, without reference to the question whether the present legislation of the United States would be accepted as satisfying the conditions of accession to the convention.

" This argument gives to the words ' at its pleasure,' in the second condition, a very remarkable extension. It disregards not only the declared purpose of the second condition, which was to secure ' reciprocity in the granting of copyright,' but the terms prescribed in article 18 of the Berne Convention for the accession of countries not parties thereto.

" It was obviously contemplated in the second condition that wherever it was made the ground of extending to the citizens of foreign nations participation in the benefits of our copyright law it should be possible for the United States by its own voluntary act— " at its pleasure "—to secure for its citizens the benefits of the copyright law of such foreign nations; for it is expressly required that this international agreement shall provide for ' reciprocity in the granting of copyright,' and also that by the terms of the agreement the United States ' may, *at its pleasure*, become a party.'

" The argument that the signatories of the Berne Convention are entitled to the benefits of our act merely because that convention. provides for the accession of other powers neglects both the reciprocal feature of the second condition as well as the fact that by article 18 of the Berne Convention a condition of accession is prescribed, namely, that the municipal laws of the countries desiring to accede must ' assure legal protection to the rights whereof this convention treats.'

" The act of March 3, 1891, unquestionably does assure legal protection to the rights of which the Berne Convention treats, but it does so only under certain limitations specified in the act. The most important of these limitations is that found in section 3, which requires that the copies of the book, photograph, chromo, or lithograph deposited to obtain copyright shall be printed from type set within the limits of the United States, or from plates made therefrom, or from negatives or drawings on stone made within the limits of the United States, or from transfers made therefrom.

" The Swiss minister, representing the Government which is the organ of the signatories of the Berne Convention, has applied for the extension of the benefits of our act to the citizens or subjects of the signatories on the ground of their being parties to that convention.

In response to this application, this Government has inquired whether it can become a party to the Berne Convention upon the basis of the present law, including the requirement as to typesetting, etc., in the United States. The assurance that this very important and indeed essential condition of the law would not prove to be an obstacle to our accession has not as yet been received.

" If the United States can not become a party to the convention of Berne upon the basis of the act of March 3, 1891, which is the last and the mature expression of the legislative will and pleasure of this country on the subject of international copyright, can it in any proper sense be maintained that the United States may, ' *at its pleasure,*' become a party to that convention? Or, to put the question in another way, can it be contended that the United States may ' at its pleasure ' become a party to the Berne Convention, if, on making its request for accession under article 18 of that instrument, it is informed that its law does not entitle it to accession?

" The provision as to typesetting, etc., in the United States, was a very weighty one in the deliberations of Congress upon the adoption of the statute; and, in inserting in the body of the statute a provision for the conditional extension of its benefits to the citizens or subjects of foreign states, it could scarcely have been the intention of Congress to put this Government in the position of extending those benefits to the citizens or subjects of foreign states, while our own citizens were denied reciprocal advantages, except on condition of the repeal of very important provisions of our statute. Such a contention would place Congress in the attitude of passing an act to define the conditions of granting copyright, and at the same time inserting a provision which, if we are to secure reciprocal justice to our citizens, requires the immediate and material alteration of the statute. Not only is such an interpretation unreasonable, and therefore to be avoided, if possible, but it is also directly opposed to the language of the act, which, in the condition now under consideration, clearly discloses the object of obtaining the privileges of copyright for our citizens in foreign countries. It was with this end in view that the extension of the benefits of the act to the citizens of foreign states was made conditional. The construction which we have combated, while extending the privileges of our law to the citizens of foreign states, would actually deprive this Government of the power to exact for our citizens the privilege of copyright in those states. According to this construction an international agreement for reciprocity in copyright might be framed with the deliberate design of excluding the United States, unless it materially and even radically changed its law; and yet, if the agreement contained a stipulation that other countries than those signing might accede, it would be the duty of the President at once to proclaim that the second condition of section 13 had been fulfilled in respect to the citizens of the contracting parties, and they would immediately enjoy the benefit of copyright in this country, while our citizens would effectually be debarred from obtaining it in theirs. Unless clearly required, a construction leading to such incongruous results should not be adopted, even if it were not, as in the present instance it is, immediately destructive of the declared purpose of the legislature, which was to make the extension of the act to the citizens of foreign states conditional upon the granting of copyright to our citizens in those states.

" In a note to the Swiss minister of the 8th instant, this Department fully explained its interpretation of the second condition expressed in section 13 of the act of March 3, 1891. If the parties to the Berne Convention shall decide that the legislation of the United States entitles this Government to the privilege of accession, on its request to be permitted to do so, there will probably be no difficulty in determining what should be done; for in that case the citizens or subjects of the signatories of that international agreement would, in the opinion of the undersigned, clearly be entitled to the benefit of our law under the second condition of section 13. The United States could then, ' at its pleasure,' become a party to the convention, which also secures a general reciprocity in the granting of copyright among the states of the literary and artistic union. But, until such a decision shall have been made, applications for the benefit of our law should be presented under the first condition of section 13, which we now proceed to consider.

" FIRST CONDITION.

" The first condition specified in section 13 of the act of March 3, 1891, presents no difficulty. It simply extends the benefits of our law to the citizens of any country that extends the benefits of its law to our citizens on substantially the same basis as to its own. In ascertaining whether this condition is fulfilled, it is entirely irrelevant to inquire whether the foreign law is the same as our own, and grants copyright as freely and fully in every particular. Congress, in acknowledging and protecting the property of the author or artist in the products of his intellect, was not so illiberal as to require that the foreign law should offer a strict reciprocity by containing the same provisions as our own. Such an exaction, involving the assimilation of the laws of all other countries to our own, would have offered a practically impossible condition, incompatible with the purpose of the act and to the last degree restrictive. Congress did not assume such a position. On the contrary, it made the equal participation of our citizens in the benefit of the law of the foreign country, whatever that law might be, the condition of the participation of the citizens of that country in the benefit of our law.

" There are several countries that have applied, in behalf of their citizens, for the benefits of our law under the first condition specified in section 13.

"*Belgium.*—In a note of June 9, 1891, the Belgian minister conveys a copy of the law of his country on the subject of literary and artistic copyrights, and informs the Department that ' foreigners enjoy in Belgium, in the matter of artistic and literary protection, the same rights and privileges as natives.'

" The provisions of the Belgian law are in some respects more liberal than our own, and article 38 of section 7 reads as follows:

" ' Foreigners enjoy in Belgium the rights guaranteed by the present law, but the duration of such rights shall not, in their case, exceed the duration fixed by the Belgian law. Nevertheless, if such rights sooner expire in their own country, they shall cease at the same time in Belgium.'

" The Belgian law clearly falls within the first alternative condition specified in section 13 of the act of March 3, 1891, and the proclamation of the President may accordingly be issued on the 1st of July, 1891, the date at which the act takes effect.

"*France.*—The first country to apply in behalf of its citizens for the benefits of the act of March 3, 1891, was France. Communications on the subject were made both to our legation in Paris and through the French minister at this capital to this Department. France claims to have complied with both of the alternative conditions specified in section 13 of our act. It is, however, only the first that we are now considering. We have been furnished with the French legislation on literary and artistic copyrights, and the French minister, in a note of May 25, 1891, declares that the legislation of his country ' secures to American authors rights that are not only " substantially " equal to, but identical with, those belonging to French authors.'

" In respect to French citizens, the proclamation of the President may issue on the same basis as in the case of Belgian subjects.

"*Great Britain.*—The third country to apply in behalf of its subjects for the benefits of the act of March 3, 1891, was Great Britain.

" In a note to our minister in London of June 16, 1891, Lord Salisbury says:

" ' Her Majesty's Government are advised that under existing English law an alien by first publication in any part of Her Majesty's dominions can obtain the benefit of English copyright, and that contemporaneous publication in a foreign country does not prevent the author from obtaining British copyright; that residence in some part of Her Majesty's dominions is not a necessary condition to an alien obtaining copyright under the English copyright law, and that English law permits to citizens of the United States of America the benefit of copyright on substantially the same basis as to British subjects.'

" By a telegram from our minister in London of June 20, 1891, the Department is informed that Lord Salisbury has substituted for the above assurance the following:

"' Her Majesty's Government are advised that under existing English law an alien by first publication in any part of Her Majesty's dominions can obtain the benefit of English copyright, and that contemporaneous publication in a foreign country does not prevent the author from obtaining English copyright; that residence in some parts of Her Majesty's dominions is not a necessary condition to an alien obtaining copyright under the English copyright law, and that the law of copyright in force in all British possessions permits to citizens of the United States of America the benefit of copyright on substantially the same basis as to British subjects.'

" It will be seen by comparison that the only change made in the phraseology of the note of June 16 by the later statement communicated by telegraph is in the last clause. This clause in the note of June 16 was ' that English law permits to citizens of the United States of America the benefit,' etc.

" In place of this the statement now made by the British Government is ' that the law of copyright in force in all British possessions permits,' etc.

" This assurance is more comprehensive than the first and, as the official statement of the British Government, given in the very language of the first alternative condition of section 13 of the act of March 3, 1891, warrants the inclusion of Great Britain and the British possessions in the proclamation applicable to Belgium and France.

"*Switzerland.*—By a note of the 26th instant, the Swiss minister applies, in behalf of the citizens of Switzerland, for the benefit of our law under the first condition of section 13. To this end he refers us to the law of his country, which contains the following provisions:

"'ARTICLE 10. The provisions of this act are applicable to authors domiciled in Switzerland, as regards all their works, no matter where those works appear or are published; also to authors not domiciled in Switzerland, as regards works that appear or are published in Switzerland.

"'Authors not domiciled in Switzerland enjoy the same rights, as regards works which appear or are published in foreign countries, that are enjoyed by authors of works appearing in Switzerland, provided that the latter receive the same usage in the country concerned as the authors of works published there.

"'ART. 4. Authors domiciled in Switzerland have the right to give such notice (or make such declaration) in the case of all their works, and authors not domiciled in Switzerland; also, authors not domiciled in Switzerland in the case of works published in foreign countries, but only when the authors of works published in Switzerland receive the same usage in the country concerned that is received by the authors of works published there. Foreign authors of the latter class must meet the requirements of this provision, unless some other arrangement has been made by means of an international convention.'

" These provisions, officially presented as constituting a compliance with the first condition of section 13, appear to warrant the inclusion of Switzerland in the proclamation with Belgium, France, and Great Britain.

"Annexed hereto is a copy of the act of March 3, 1891, and a form of proclamation."

> Report of Mr. Moore, Third Assist. Sec. of State, to the President, June 27, 1891, For. Rel. 1892, 261.

By the President of the United States of America.

A PROCLAMATION.

Whereas it is provided by section 13 of the act of Congress of March 3, 1891, entitled "An act to amend title sixty, chapter three, of the Revised Statutes of the United States, relating to copyrights," that said act "shall only apply to a citizen or subject of a foreign state or nation when such foreign state or nation permits to citizens of the United States of America the benefit of copyright on substantially the same basis as its own citizens; or when such foreign state or nation is a party to an international agreement which provides for reciprocity in the granting of copyright, by the terms of which agreement the United States of America may, at its pleasure, become a party to such agreement; "

And whereas it is also provided by said section that " the existence of either of the conditions aforesaid shall be determined by the President of the United States by proclamation made from time to time as the purposes of this act may require ; "

And whereas satisfactory official assurances have been given that in Belgium, France, Great Britain and the British possessions, and Switzerland, the law permits to citizens of the United States the benefit of copyright on substantially the same basis as to the citizens of those countries ;

Now, therefore, I, Benjamin Harrison, President of the United States of America, do declare and proclaim that the first of the conditions specified in section 13 of the act of March 3, 1891, is now fulfilled in respect to the citizens or subjects of Belgium, France, Great Britain, and Switzerland.

In testimony whereof, I have hereunto set my hand and caused the seal of the United States to be affixed.

Done at the city of Washington, this first day of July, one thousand eight hundred and ninety-one, and of the Independence of the United States the one hundred and fifteenth.

[SEAL.]

BENJ. HARRISON.

By the President:

WILLIAM F. WHARTON,
Acting Secretary of State.

For. Rel. 1892, 265.

Proclamations have been issued by the President, under the first condition specified in section 13 of the act of 1891, as follows:

Belgium, France, Great Britain and the British possessions, and Switzerland, July 1, 1891; German Empire, April 15, 1892; Italy, October 31, 1892; Denmark, May 8, 1893; Portugal, July 20, 1893; Spain, July 10, 1895; Mexico, February 27, 1896; Chile, May 25, 1896; Costa Rica, October 19, 1899; the Netherlands, November 20, 1899; Cuba, November 17, 1903; Norway, January 1, 1905.

Correspondence with the Argentine Government in 1893 failed to result in an agreement.[a]

A similarly fruitless correspondence took place with Greece in 1894.[b]

In the course of the correspondence prior to the issuance of the proclamation as to Costa Rica, attention was called to the fact that the first condition of the act of March 3, 1891, required the President " to ascertain the actual existence in the foreign state of law or regulation according to citizens of the United States the benefit of copyright on substantially the same basis as to the citizens of such foreign state. It does not authorize the President to enter into reciprocal or conditional negotiation with such foreign state to the end of establishing equivalence of treatment in the two countries." [c]

" No proclamation has issued under the second condition expressed in the statute, to wit, that the foreign state or nation be a party to an international agreement which provides for reciprocity in the granting of copyright, by the terms of which agreement the United States of America may at its pleasure become a party to such agreement, and, indeed, the greater convenience and simplicity of the first condition seems to make its ascertainment preferable as the basis of an international understanding. . . . In some instances, as in the case of the Spanish negotiation, an agreement was only reached by removing the impression which existed that the statute contemplated a reciprocal identity of the provisions of copyright legislation in the two countries, and by showing that the first of the alternative conditions prescribed by the act of Congress merely required the ascertainment of the fact that citizens of the United States stand in the foreign state on substantially the same footing in regard to the privileges of copyright registration as the citizens or subjects of such state. This being determined to the President's satisfaction, his proclamation issues, giving to the citizen or subject of such foreign state the same privileges of copyright in the United States as are enjoyed by citizens of the United States."

Circular, Mr. Hay, Sec. of State, to U. S. dip. officers, July 25, 1899, MS. Inst. Arg. Rep. XVII. 481.

---

a For. Rel. 1894, 1–3.
b For. Rel. 1894, 291–292.

c For. Rel. 1899, 584, 585, 587.

Circulars in relation to the act of March 3, 1891, were previously sent out by the Department of State, May 7, 1891; May 23, 1893; Feb. 21, 1896, For. Rel. 1892, 261; MS. Inst. Arg. Rep. XVII. 55; XVIII. 161.

" I have to acknowledge the receipt of your letter of the 25th instant, asking whether we are now in copyright relations with Spain.

" In reply I enclose copy of the President's proclamation, of July 10, 1895, issued, in virtue of section 13 of the act of Congress of March 3, 1891, granting the benefits of that act to subjects of Spain, in view of the assurance conveyed to him that the laws of Spain and her colonial possessions granted the benefits of copyright to citizens of the United States on substantially the same basis as to Spanish subjects.

" While the Government of Spain has maintained that all treaties with the United States were terminated by the recent war, it is thought that it would hold that its general laws granting copyright were at the most only suspended, so far as American citizens were concerned, during the period of the existence of the war.

" The Department has no information that any copyright has been refused in Spain to United States citizens."

> Mr. Hay, Sec. of State, to Mr. Johnson, May 29, 1900, 245 MS. Dom. Let. 328.

" The Canadian authorities have steadily declined to permit the registration of copyright in Canada to citizens of the United States, the ground of objection being that the enactment of the Congress of the United States and the President's proclamation of July 1, 1891, extending the benefits of the act of March 3, 1891, to all British subjects, did not constitute ' an international copyright treaty ' within the meaning of the Canadian copyright act, which provides that any person domiciled in Canada or in any part of the British possessions, or being a citizen of any country having an *international copyright treaty* with the United Kingdom, who is the author of any book, map, chart, etc., shall have the sole right of printing, publishing, etc., for a number of years on certain conditions.

" In February 1897, this Government proposed the negotiation of a copyright convention which should expressly meet this allegation of the Canadian government. This proposal the Canadian government declined to entertain."

> Mr. Hill, Assist. Sec. of State, to Messrs. Wilmer and Canfield, March 3, 1899, 235 MS. Dom. Let. 269.
>
> By the English copyright law any person, whether a native or an alien, can obtain copyright throughout the British dominions by the mere fact of first publication there. The British Government, in notes to Mr. Lincoln and Mr. White of June 16, 1891, and November 12,

1892, maintained that the English copyright law ran in Canada as in every part of the British dominions, and that it was open to United States authors to protect their rights in Canada by registering at Stationers' Hall in London. In a note to Mr. Hay, United States ambassador, of April 12, 1898, the British foreign office, while reaffirming this position, stated that the Dominion government would be prepared to accord to United States authors, under the Canadian as distinct from the Imperial law, the privilege of copyright in Canada on publishing only, if a similar favor were conceded to Canadian authors who desired copyright in the United States. (For. Rel. 1898, 365–366. See, also, For. Rel. 1892, 220–223, 225, 227, 240, 266.)

(4) TAXATION.

§ 183.

" I have to acknowledge the receipt of your letter without date, but which reached this Department to-day, in which you present for the consideration of the Department the question as to the right of the Jewish congregation at Munich, under their constitution, and under the laws of Bavaria, to exact from you, as a citizen of the United States of Jewish descent, a tax levied for purposes connected with the Jewish Church and worship.

The power of taxation.

" The question presented appears to be one of internal administration or municipal concern in a foreign government; and is as yet, so far as it relates to yourself, hypothetical, as the demand for the tax has not yet been made upon you. It is the rule of this Department not to express opinions in such cases in advance of occurrences which may be anticipated; but I will in this instance, so far depart from the rule, as to inform you that while this Government stands ready to extend due protection to bona fide citizens, native or naturalized, whose rights or liberties, under the law of nations and the Constitution and laws of the United States, are infringed upon, it would seem to be beyond the proper sphere of its duties to attempt to interfere with such domestic regulations or laws of foreign states as that above indicated."

Mr. Hale, Assist. Sec. of State, to Mr. Netre, April 13, 1872, 93 MS. Dom. Let. 464.

Tangible movables are generally taxable at the place where they are situated. (Pullman's Car Co. v. Pennsylvania, 141 U. S. 18.) But, in many States, all personal property has been held to be taxable at the domicil of the owner. (See Moore's Am. Notes, Dicey's Conflict of Laws, 170–173; Seligman, Essays in Taxation, 112, 113.)

As to death and succession duties in England, see Dicey, Conflict of Laws, 781; in the United States, see Dos Passos, The Law of Collateral Inheritance, Legacy and Succession Taxes; 3 Williams on Executors, 7th Am. ed., Randolph & Talcott's notes, pp. 1–7.

" The assessment and collection of local taxes are entirely the subjects of municipal law and regulations of the government of the country in which the property subjected to such taxes may be situated, and the assessment and collection of taxes by the Spanish authorities in Cuba upon property in that island can not properly be made a subject of interference by this Government."

> Mr. F. W. Seward, Acting Sec. of State, to Mr. Acosta y Foster, April 8, 1878, 122 MS. Dom. Let. 403.
>
> See Mr. Frelinghuysen, Sec. of State, to Mr. Foster, min. to Spain, Dec. 19, 1883, instructing the latter to make an " earnest remonstrance " to the Spanish Government against the exaction by the authorities in Cuba, from an American firm, of certain arrearages, in derogation of a " compromise arrangement " which had been effected, through the efforts of the United States, in respect of an " obnoxious tax " which was considered to be specially injurious to American mercantile interests in the island. (MS. Inst. Spain, XIX. 459.)

" Your despatch of the 4th of October last, (No. 243) in relation to the will and personal effects of Mr. Robert Apple left in Vienna at the time of his death in Italy, has been received.

" Your proceedings in the matter are approved, and your suggestions in regard to the general question have also received attentive consideration. I am disposed to think that there is no substantial difference in the meaning of the words, ' dues, taxes or charges ' used in the treaty of 1829, and the term ' duties ' employed in that of 1848. Like the word ' steuern ' which you give as that used in the German text of the treaty of 1848, the word ' duties ' is a comprehensive term, its meaning in the connection in which it is there used, being ' tax, toll, impost, or customs ' ; and there seems to be no just ground for supposing that it was understood in any other than this comprehensive sense by the negotiators of the treaty in question. Be that as it may, however, the case of Mr. Apple's representatives is not conceived to be one that calls for a discussion of the question. That gentleman's act in making the deposit of his last will, and, as it would appear, of the bulk if not the whole of his estate in an Austrian bank, with certainly no better security than he might have been assured of from a like deposit in San Francisco or New York, seems to have been one of deliberate choice on his part ; and when an American citizen thus chooses to collect his fortune together, take it to a foreign country and there deposit it with his will, disposing of it beyond his own life ; and in the course of distribution after his death, it becomes subject to the taxes and charges incident to such distribution, under the municipal laws of the country where the property may be, that circumstance does not, it is believed, present a question that should deeply concern this Government.

" You will therefore confine your future efforts in behalf of Mr. Apple's representatives, to the exercise of such unofficial good offices as it may be convenient for you to render. The extent to which these unofficial aids may become necessary and proper is also left to your judgment and discretion."

> Mr. Evarts, Sec. of State, to Mr. Kasson, min. to Austria-Hungary, Jan. 17, 1880, MS. Inst. Austria-Hungary, III. 80.

" Citizens of the United States in Colombia are exempted from paying any tax from which the subjects or citizens of another power are exempt, both by the ' favored nation ' clause of our treaty of 1846 with Colombia, and by the general principle of the law of nations which justifies this Government in insisting that there shall be no undue discrimination against citizens of the United States wherever they may be resident."

> Mr. Bayard, Sec. of State, to Mr. Walker, chargé at Bogota, April 28, 1888, For. Rel. 1888, I. 422–423.
> The imposition by Mexico of a tax unduly discriminating against citizens of the United States, if not a breach of the treaty between the United States and Mexico, is an unfriendly act to be noticed by the United States. (Mr. Cass, Sec. of State, to Mr. Forsyth, min. to Mexico, June 23, 1858, MS. Inst. Mex. XVII. 194; same to same, July 15, 1858, id. 199.)

Foreigners " are not bound . . . to work personally on the roads, their obligation in this last respect is limited to the payment of the corresponding road tax. . . . Foreigners are bound to respect the police regulations and orders; to pay the local imposts and the established taxes upon trade, industry, professions, property or possession thereof, as also such imposts and taxes as may be established thereafter, or when those first mentioned shall have been increased or diminished."

> Circular of the Guatemalan ministry of foreign relations, Sept. 13, 1888, For. Rel. 1888, I. 167–168.

" If by the law of Austria the owner of property wrongfully taxed is required to bear the expense of correcting the error of the officials levying the tax, he can not complain unless the law discriminated against him as a foreigner."

> Mr. Gresham, Sec. of State, to Mr. Hill, Aug. 22, 1893, 193 MS. Dom. Let. 219.

The Haitian Chambers having passed a law compelling every foreigner in business to make to the President of the Republic an application for a license on a certain stamped paper and to pay therefor five dollars, the United States objected to the requirement on the ground that under the treaty between the two countries citizens of the United States were entitled to pay no higher taxes in Haiti than Haitians in the same business. The Haitian Government relinquished the claim for the fee, but insisted that the application for license should be made to the President, maintaining that this was a matter which the treaty did not affect. The decision of the Haitian Government on this question was accepted by the United States. The ground, it was said, on which the United States had contested the license fee was that it violated the treaty stipulation that American citizens engaged in business in Haiti should not be obliged to pay "any contributions whatever" other or higher than those paid by natives, and it was held that neither this nor any other provision of the treaty would justify the United States "in contesting the Haitian requirement that American citizens shall make applications for licenses to conduct business."

> Mr. Hill, Acting Sec. of State, to Mr. Terres, chargé, Sept. 21, 1899, For. Rel. 1899, 405.

A stamp tax on a foreign bill of lading is, in substance and effect, equivalent to a tax on the articles included in that bill of lading, and therefore is a tax or duty on exports, and therefore in conflict with Article I., section 9, of the Constitution of the United States, that "No tax or duty shall be laid on articles exported from any State."

An act of Congress is to be accepted as constitutional, unless on examination it clearly appears to be in conflict with provisions of the Federal Constitution.

If the Constitution in its grant of powers is to be able to carry into full effect the powers granted, it is equally imperative that where prohibition or limitation is placed upon the power of Congress, that prohibition or limitation should be enforced in its spirit and to its entirety.

> Fairbank v. United States (1901), 181 U. S., 283.

"Your dispatch No. 25, in relation to the imposition of income-tax upon citizens of the United States residing in Germany, has been received and considered with attention.

Income taxes.

"To your dispatch are annexed communications from Mr. Leo Wolf, Mr. Wierss, and Mr. Appleton, all claiming to be citizens of the United States residing in different parts of Germany, and objecting to the imposition of this tax; added to which is your correspondence on the question with them, and an opinion of Mr. Jansen, at Berlin, as to the legal aspects of the law of the different German States imposing these several taxes. It appears that each of the persons objecting to the tax is admittedly a resident in that part of the German Empire where he is assessed, and not a mere temporary sojourner for pleasure or otherwise.

" Upon examination of the statement of Mr. Jansen, it further appears that taxes on income of aliens appear to be assessed under certain restrictions and within certain limitations upon resident aliens only, although it appears that a person carrying on business is deemed to be a resident immediately upon taking up his residence in any place.

" The real question raised, therefore, by this correspondence, is, whether an income tax may properly be assessed against an alien resident in Germany.

"As a general rule the power to impose taxes is an attribute of sovereignty, and where the person or the property in question is a proper subject of taxation, the species of tax and the amount which should be collected may fairly be left to the state or government exercising this power.

" By the act of March 2, 1867, it was provided—

" ' That there shall be levied, collected, and paid annually upon the gains, profits, and income of every person residing in the United States, or of any citizen of the United States residing abroad, whether derived from any kind of property, rents, interest, dividends, or salaries, or from any profession, trade, employment, or vocation carried on in the United States or elsewhere, or from any other source whatever, a tax,' &c.

" Such provision does not materially differ from the corresponding provision in the previous acts on the same subject. It applies in terms to all persons, aliens as well as citizens residing in the United States, and to all citizens residing beyond the limits of the United States.

" So far as the subjects of taxation are concerned, the income tax referred to in your correspondence does not appear to differ from the income tax imposed by this Government.

" On the ground, therefore, that the parties complaining in these cases are all residents of Germany, and so long as the tax is uniform in its operation and can fairly be deemed a tax and not a confiscation or unfair imposition, it is not believed that any successful or consistent representation can be made to the German Government in their behalf.

" It is true that in some cases a party may be liable to double taxation, but such instances are exceptional, and this fact cannot alter the rule. No income-tax, as such, is at present collected in this country.

" Some of these statements complain of excessive taxation, even under the provisions of the German laws, but such matters would seem more properly to be questions for submission to the German courts.

" The views of the Department are confined to the particular cases presented in your dispatch.

" It is not admitted that an income-tax could be collected from nonresident aliens, nor is the general question of municipal taxation adverted to in the communication of Mr. Kreismann, the consul-general, but concerning which no particulars are given, here considered.

" The general views expressed in your dispatch on this question are concurred in by the Department."

> Mr. Fish, Sec. of State, to Mr. Davis, min. to Germany, Nov. 21, 1874, For. Rel. 1875, I. 488–489. See Mr. Davis' dispatch, id. 479.
> Approved and followed by Mr. Evarts, Sec. of State, to Mr. White, min. to Germany, Oct. 13, 1880, MS. Inst. Germany, XVII. 8.
> Dicey lays it down that under the British law an "income tax is payable on any income arising or accruing to any person whomsoever, from a British source;" that "an income arises from a British source which is derived from property or possessions in the United Kingdom," or "from a trade or profession carried on in the United Kingdom," or "when either it arises from property or possessions the United Kingdom, or it results (e. g. in the case of a trade) from acts done in the United Kingdom." (Dicey, Conflict of Laws, 800.)

In 1887 the city authorities of Frankfort-on-the-Main sought to levy an income tax on Mrs. Samuel R. Honey, the wife of a citizen of the United States. It appeared that Mrs. Honey was making an extended but temporary sojourn at Frankfort with her daughter, who was attending the school of music, and that she received a monthly allowance from her husband to defray her own and her daughter's expenses. Under the circumstances the authorities came to the conclusion that she was not subject to the tax, but proceeded to levy an income tax on Mr. Honey, on the theory that, as his wife and daughter occupied a dwelling there, he had a domicile at Frankfort. It appeared that Mrs. Honey rented furnished rooms, and that all the furniture in them belonged to the landlord. Mr. Honey was a citizen of the United States and was domiciled at Newport, R. I., where he pursued the profession of the law. He stated that the money which he sent to his wife was derived almost exclusively from the proceeds of his professional income, and that she had no income or estate of her own. Mr. Honey had never resided in Germany and had no property, business, or income there. It appeared that in September, 1887, the Prussian authorities also sought to levy a state income tax upon Mr. Honey. These levies were the subject of discussion between the consul-general of the United States at Frankfort-on-the-Main and the local authorities, and the matter was ultimately communicated by the legation of the United States at Berlin to the German foreign office, in order that it might be laid before the

Prussian minister of finance. The Prussian minister of finance subsequently directed that the assessment of the state income tax should be discontinued and the amount already paid refunded. A similar conclusion was reached in regard to the communal tax.

> Mr. Pendleton, min. to Germany, to Mr. Bayard, Sec. of State, March 20, 1888; Mr. Bayard, Sec. of State, to Mr. Pendleton, min. to Germany, April 6, 1888; Mr. Coleman, chargé at Berlin, to Mr. Bayard, Sec. of State, July 2, 1888, Aug. 13, 1888, and Oct. 4, 1888; For. Rel. 1888, I. 623, 630, 642, 650, 655.
>
> "Your wife, being resident in Germany, is subject from the nature of things to any laws which the Government of Germany may impose as to taxes. If such impositions appear to be unjust, the proper course is to pay the amount under protest, taking care that the character of such payment should be so evidenced as to make it the subject of subsequent action. If the enforcement of payment should appear to you to be in violation of international law, you can then present the facts in detail to this Department, which will then consider whether the case is one which will sustain an appeal to the German Government for redress." (Mr. Bayard, Sec. of State, to Mr. Honey, March 21, 1887, For. Rel. 1888, I. 631.)

The minister of the United States at Vienna having reported the case of an American citizen who alleged that he was not properly liable to an income tax in Austria, the Department of State replied that the matter was one which should be tested in the Austrian courts, and that it did not in its present aspect present a subject for diplomatic intervention.

> Mr. Hay, Sec. of State, to Mr. Harris, min. to Austria-Hungary, May 31, 1899, For. Rel. 1899, 50.
> To the same effect, see Mr. Bayard, Sec. of State, to Mr. Honey, March 21, 1887, For. Rel. 1888, I. 631.

" With reference to your instruction No. 141 of December 6, 1889, relating to the income tax imposed in Burmah upon American missionaries residing there, I have the honor to acquaint you . . . that I am now in receipt of a reply from the Marquis of Salisbury, dated the 18th instant, of which a copy (with its original printed enclosures) is also transmitted herewith, from which it will be seen that Lord Salisbury expresses his regret that the government of India, after a full consideration of the case, are unable to make an exception in favor of the missionaries.

" It seems that Mr. Bunker, who addressed you in the matter, complains especially that the tax is charged upon, not only that portion of their salaries paid the missionaries in Burmah, but upon that portion thereof which is arranged to be paid directly to their families remaining in the United States. It would appear that the law requires the tax to be assessed upon ' income or profits accruing and arising or received in British India,' and that the government of India holds that the income of a missionary residing in India accrues or arises there, though it may not be received there. I venture to suggest that the income tax act in India, in this respect, does not seem to be more rigid than was our own act of 1862 (sec. 90, chap. 119, 2d session, 37th Cong.), under which a tax was laid upon the excess over $600 of the annual gains, profits, or income of every person residing in the United States."

> Mr. Lincoln, min. to England, to Mr. Blaine, Sec. of State, March 20, 1890, For. Rel. 1890, 325.
>
> Instruction No. 141 of Dec. 6, 1889, to which Mr. Lincoln referred, expressed the hope that the British Government would " look into this matter, which, as stated, appears to involve hardship and injustice to a most meritorious class of persons engaged in labors which have always received the encouragement and support of both Governments." (Mr. Blaine, Sec. of State, to Mr. Lincoln, min. to England, Dec. 6, 1889, For. Rel. 1890, 321.)

Missionaries in Japan are subject to the payment of an income tax on their salaries, precisely as are native priests.

The Government, however, did not exact the tax from the surgeon and enlisted men of the Marine Corps stationed at the United States naval hospital at Yokohama.

> For. Rel. 1900, 760, 763.

" I acknowledge the receipt of your dispatches Nos. 92 and 93 of February 13th, 1870, with enclosures, relating to a tax recently voted by the legislative authority of Nueva Leon for the purpose of sustaining the existing Government of Mexico against insurrectionary assaults.

War taxes.

" Whether the imposition of such a tax is within the powers of the several States, or is only competent to the Federal Congress, is a question of Mexican constitutional law which must be referred to the judicial tribunals of that country. If the State legislature could not authorize the tax in question, it is to be assumed that the judiciary of the country will furnish adequate protection and redress to those who may be aggrieved. It is vital to the existence of every government that it should have the capacity, through some of its legislative or administrative departments, to levy taxes necessary for its maintenance against rebellion, upon all persons, whether native subjects or foreign residents who enjoy its protection. The particular agency through which this shall be accomplished, is necessarily in the discretion of the government concerned. Citizens of the United States who voluntarily take up their residence in countries exposed to frequent insurrections, must be considered as having elected to take upon themselves the risks and expenses to which such condition exposes them in view of the advantages which in their estimation countervail the security which they would enjoy in the land of their native allegiance.

"There is no objection to your authenticating such protest as any citizen of the United States may be advised to make, to avail for what it shall be worth."

Mr. J. C. B. Davis, Assist. Sec. of State, to Mr. Ulrich, U. S. consul at Monterey, March 21, 1870, 57 MS. Inst. Consuls, 242.

"Your letter of the 23d instant, in relation to a 'war-tax' recently imposed, as you allege, upon your property in Cuba, by the authorities of that island, has been received. You inquire whether you have the right to 'refuse the payment of that tax, and if in so doing you may depend upon the interposition of the Government of the United States, for redress in case of need.' The Spanish Government in common with every other independent power, possesses the exclusive right of imposing taxes upon property situated within the territories and jurisdiction of their own country, and of determining the purposes to which the revenues derived from such taxes shall be devoted. If therefore the tax to which you refer is general and uniform in its operation, upon property situated in Cuba, and makes no discrimination against the property of American citizens, it is not within the province of the Government of the United States to interfere."

Mr. Fish, Sec. of State, to Mr. Bachiller de Toscano, Oct. 28, 1874, 105 MS. Dom. Let. 22.

"Referring to your despatches 630 of October 27, 1875, and 634 of the 29th of the same month, relating to the liability of citizens of the United States resident in Spain, for the payment of special or extraordinary taxes, called war taxes, I have to inform you that the questions treated of therein have been carefully considered.

"The precise question, upon which you ask information and instruction, seems to be, admitting the liability of citizens of the United States resident in Spain for the payment of their fair and just proportions of the general public burdens, whether they are also liable to pay such particular taxes as may be imposed as war taxes *eo nomine*, and which are made necessary by the existing disturbances in Spain.

"It appears that under the subsisting tax laws of Spain an extra tax of one-ninth part of the general tax is imposed, in addition to such general tax, as a war tax; that foreigners, of all nationalities in Spain, while willing to pay ordinary taxes, have resisted payment of this particular amount; and that, in consequence of representations made in behalf of such foreigners, the Spanish Government after having decided at different times in different ways, has at last issued a general order, intended to apply hereafter to all cases of this nature.

" This order provides, that whenever the citizens or subjects of any foreign power are by actual treaty provisions exempted from the imposition of a tax of this nature, they shall be relieved therefrom; that, where by treaty such citizens or subjects are made liable to pay such a tax, the same shall be collected; but that, where either no treaties exist, or where the existing treaties are silent on the question, the authorities of Spain, will exempt the citizens or subjects of such countries as exempt Spaniards resident therein under like circumstances, and will collect such taxes from those citizens or subjects where the countries to which they owe allegiance collect the same from resident Spaniards.

" Your despatch clearly shows the difficulty in dealing with this question, and in claiming for citizens of the United States any positive exemption from such taxes, pursuant to treaty provisions; and your hesitation in addressing the Government of Spain on this question, in compliance with requests from your fellow citizens, was judicious. As a general proposition, it will be conceded that foreigners who have chosen to take up their residence, to purchase property, or to carry on business in a foreign country, thereby place themselves under the jurisdiction of the laws of that country, and may fairly be called upon to bear their fair share of the general public burdens, when properly imposed upon them and other members of the community, alike. As a general proposition, the right to tax includes the power to determine the amount which must be levied, and the objects for which that amount shall be expended. These powers are powers incident to sovereignty, the exercise of which, unless abused, can not, in general, be made the subject of diplomatic remonstrance.

" If, therefore, the system of taxation in practice in Spain had imposed upon these American residents, in common with others, a certain tax, increased in amount, by reason of the disturbances in Spain, it would be impossible to distinguish what portion had been imposed particularly for war purposes, and it would be difficult to found any remonstrance, if the necessities of that government required greater taxation. It is believed that such is the system in this country, and that increased taxation must result from a war, or from any convulsion or cause which requires a large expenditure of money.

" This Government would greatly hesitate to insist upon the exemption of citizens of the United States residing in Spain from such taxes as are referred to by you and as are borne by all Spaniards engaged in the same vocations, and thus perhaps establish a basis for a claim for exemption from such taxes as may hereafter be required by the public necessity in this country, when imposed on or demanded from Spaniards resident or carrying on business in the United States.

"On an examination of the order issued by the Spanish Government in the light of these conclusions, and referring to your question whether reciprocity could be assured to Spaniards resident and engaged here in business from the payment of similar impositions, it is doubtful whether any such reciprocity could be assured, and more than doubtful, in view of the small amounts involved, and the small number of Americans affected thereby, whether such exemption should be demanded.

"I coincide therefore in your opinion as to the inexpediency of presenting this question to the Government of Spain, and have treated of it at some length, as cases not infrequently come before the Department of extraordinary extortions, under the name of taxation, practiced upon citizens of the United States; and while this Government is desirous of assuming no untenable position, it may be necessary to seriously remonstrate against the abuse of the power of taxation, which occurs in Cuba."

Mr. Fish, Sec. of State, to Mr. Cushing, min. to Spain, Jan. 12, 1876, MS. Inst. Spain, XVII. 432.

"The right [of taxation] is admitted, but complaints are based on the fact that opportunity is taken under the cover of a right, to perpetrate wrong and injustice. . . . It is difficult (for instance) to call it a rightful exercise of the sovereign power of taxation, to require an individual owner of an estate to erect a fort, of a particular and specified description, on his estate, at his individual cost, or to require him to construct a particular line of telegraph; and when such things are done by an arbitrary order of a local or a military officer, they have very much the appearance of something very different from what is generally recognized as taxation."

Mr. Fish, Sec. of State, to Mr. Cushing, min. to Spain, May 22, 1876, MS. Inst. Spain, XVII. 528. See note to Mr. Mantilla, Jan. 11, 1876, infra, § 1034.

With reference to extraordinary war taxes levied in Cuba during the Ten Years' War (1868–1878), the Department of State said that, while it was difficult to protest against the exaction of such taxes on well-defined principles, it appeared that many of the taxes were loosely if not unfairly assessed, that they were excessive in amount, and that they not infrequently failed to be applied to the purposes for which they were raised. Besides, exemptions appeared to be sometimes granted, which made the burden all the heavier upon those who still remained liable. All these facts had created dissatisfaction and had called for remonstrance and complaint. The United States expressed the hope that its citizens in Cuba would not be treated in these matters differently from those of other countries, and that they would receive the full benefit of any relief which might be granted.

Mr. Fish, Sec. of State, to Mr. Adee, chargé, No. 484, Dec. 21, 1876, MS. Inst. Spain, XVIII. 63; Mr. Fish, Sec. of State, to Mr. Cushing, min. to Spain, No. 513, Feb. 20, 1877, id. 118; Mr. Evarts, Sec. of State, to Mr. Adee, chargé, No. 532, May 29, 1877, id. 158.

A royalty imposed by a government upon the product of its mines, equally upon foreign and native occupiers and workers, presents no ground for remonstrance. (Mr. Adee, Acting Sec. of State, to Mr. Harrah, Dec. 3, 1897, 223 MS. Dom. Let. 143.)

"Referring to your letter of the 9th of March last, in relation to the repayment by Colombia of forced loans exacted on the Isthmus in July, 1877, I have to inform you that the Department has given the matter attention and has corresponded on the subject with the vice-consul-general at Bogota.

"It is unquestionably true that the repayment now being made by Colombia falls short of the refunding of the sums originally taken, to say nothing of interest. At the same time it may be worth while for those from whom the loans are exacted to consider whether it may not be expedient to accept this partial payment, as the Department is informed that nearly all of them have done.

"The subject of extraordinary exactions in the form of forced loans is not new to the Department, which has been frequently required to act upon the subject, especially in Cuba, and in Mexico. Where a specific provision of treaty can be invoked, the matter can be readily treated; but in the absence of such a provision, grave difficulties have been encountered. So that in 1879 the Department instructed Mr. Foster, United States minister at the City of Mexico, as follows: 'The Department concurs in your belief that further discussion of the question of forced loans must be fruitless unless the Mexican Government can give assurance of its willingness to take up the subject with a view of reaching an international agreement thereon.'

"In the present instance the matter is complicated by the fact that the exaction in question has not been made the subject of correspondence between this Government and that of Colombia, as constituting an international claim."

Mr. Moore, Third Assist. Sec. of State, to Mr. Robinson, June 29, 1889, 173 MS. Dom. Let. 487.

See, generally, as to forced loans, Moore, Int. Arbitrations, IV. 3409, 3411.

(5) CUSTOMS LAWS.

§ 184.

Complaint was made by an American firm against the Government of Guatemala for causing some packages of imported merchandise to be opened. "Though the inconvenience to which those gentlemen may have been subjected by that proceeding may," said the Department of State, "be a subject of regret, it is apprehended that exemp-

tion from it can not be claimed on the principle of international law
which you suppose may be applicable to the case.   In the absence of a
treaty, at least, that Government may carry into effect its municipal
law in regard to importations from abroad in such way as may be
deemed necessary for the protection of its revenue.   The same right
will be exercised here in respect to importations by citizens of Guatemala into the United States."

> Mr. Fish, Sec. of State, to Mr. Williamson, min. to Central America, Feb.
> 15, 1875, MS. Inst. Costa Rica, XVII. 232.
> In a subsequent letter Mr. Fish said: "It is believed that all govern-
> ments exercise the right to open packages of imported merchandise
> when there may be cause to suspect that their contents have been
> misrepresented. This privilege therefore must be allowed to the
> Government of Guatemala. Under these circumstances there do not
> appear, at least for the present, to be grounds for making the case
> referred to an international one." (Mr. Fish, Sec. of State, to Mr.
> Williamson, min. to Central America, March 15, 1875, MS. Inst.
> Costa Rica, XVII. 235.)

May 22, 1883, the Congress of Costa Rica passed a law declaring
Limon to be a free port for 10 years, the law to take effect August
10, 1883.   June 19, 1884, the same Congress, without previous notice
of its intention, repealed this law and reestablished the former tariff
on imports.   It was stated that the publication and execution of the
act of June 19, 1884, were simultaneous, and that protests made on
behalf of foreign interests were disregarded.   The minister of the
United States in Central America was instructed that the subject
was "deemed a proper one to submit, as you have already done, to
the sense of equity and fair dealing of the Government of Costa
Rica."   Should that Government deny responsibility, as of right,
for the losses inflicted, he was directed to transmit to the Department
of State any claims for loss growing out of the act in question, "and
at the same time urge upon the Government of Costa Rica the right
of this Government to be fully indemnified for all losses sustained
by citizens of the United States by reason of the repeal, without reasonable notice, of the law which declared Limon a free port of entry
for a period of ten years."

> Mr. Frelinghuysen, Sec. of State, to Mr. Hall, min. to Central America,
> Aug. 20, 1884, For. Rel. 1884, 41.
> See, also, Mr. Hunter, Acting Sec. of State, to Mr. Hall, min. to Central
> America, Oct. 13, 1884, For. Rel. 1884, 45.
> September 13, 1884, the legation reported that the Costa Rican minister
> for foreign affairs had declined to consider Mr. Hall's protest against
> the immediate application of the decree of revocation, alleging that
> the law of May 22, 1883, merely specified the maximum duration of
> the period during which Limon was to be a free port, and did not
> bind the Congress to maintain the privilege. The legation, however,
> at the same time reported that a decree had been issued by virtue of

which the "principal articles" of trade could be imported free of duty for the use of the district of Limon. November 25, 1884, the legation further reported that no claims of American citizens had reached it, and that the Government seemed to have permitted free importation of all goods that were ordered under the guaranties of the former law, and had thus avoided motive for complaint. (For. Rel. 1884, 42, 45.)

By a decree of June 14, 1882, the Guatemalan Government declared Livingston a free port, and an adjacent strip of territory, lying between the Sarstoon River and Santo Tomas, a free zone, from January 1, 1883. This decree was duly carried out, but in 1888 the Government, without previous notice, issued a decree closing the port of Livingston, transferring the custom-house to Yzabal, and abolishing the free zone. As Yzabal was the former site of the custom-house, its transfer to that place was not expected to cause serious inconvenience, but it appeared that many foreigners, among whom were some Americans, had purchased land and established plantations in the free zone under the guaranties and inducements held out by the decree of 1882. Mr. Hall, then United States minister in Central America, deemed it his duty, under the circumstances "to invite the attention of the Guatemalan Government to these facts; to a consideration of the injuries that those interests are likely to sustain in consequence of the abolition of the free zone, and to suggest that its enforcement, at least, shall be postponed until they shall have been assured against losses." In reporting his action he referred to the correspondence with Costa Rica in 1884, touching the case of Port Limon, supra.

Mr. Hall was advised that his action was approved and that the instructions sent to him in 1884 in the case of Port Limon sufficiently stated the principles by which his conduct should be guided.

He subsequently reported that the Guatemalan Government had reconsidered the matter, and had temporarily suspended the enforcement of that part of the decree which related to the free zone. The custom-house had already been transferred to Yzabal.

> Mr. Hall, min. to Central America, to Mr. Bayard, Sec. of State, July 21, 1888, For. Rel. 1888, I. 159–160; Mr. Bayard, Sec. of State, to Mr. Hall, min. to Central America, Aug. 14, 1888, id. 162; Mr. Hall, min. to Central America, to Mr. Bayard, Sec. of State, Aug. 14, 1888, id. 162–163.

"Mr. Donaghy states that he took a trip to Europe last year, that on landing at Queenstown he was arrested by the British Government for having two revolvers and two boxes of cartridges in his baggage, and that he was fined five pounds and costs, together with forfeiture of the articles in question. . . .

" The right of independent governments to prohibit and punish the introduction of contraband articles is unquestionable. Our own Government exercises the right at its pleasure. It is widely known that the British Government seizes many articles found in the baggage or on the persons of passengers entering its ports, such as firearms and munitions, unauthorized reprints of copyright books, foreign manufactures which contravene the British trade-marks act, tobacco, liquors, and gold or silver plate.

" In some cases the law is satisfied with forfeiture of the contraband articles, in others a penalty is superadded. It is not alleged that the penalty in Mr. Donaghy's case was unusual or excessive. It is not, in fact, thought to be greater than would have been imposed according to the laws of several of our States, had he been found carrying the property concealed. The act of attempted introduction of these articles being itself unlawful, it is not possible to determine what weight is to be attached to Mr. Donaghy's averment that he had them in his possession ' for a perfectly legitimate purpose.'

" So far as the facts appear from Mr. Donaghy's letter, the case does not seem to call for any action by this Department."

Mr. Blaine, Sec. of State, to Mr. Bingham, M. C., Jan. 11, 1890, 176 MS. Dom. Let. 86.

Complaints having been made by Siegfried Koenigsberger, a naturalized citizen of the United States, of the confiscation by Guatemalan authorities of silver belonging to him to the amount of $2,300, the Department of State held that there was no ground for intervention, it appearing that Koenigsberger was attempting to export the silver in violation of Guatemalan law.

For. Rel. 1901, 252–260.

By the treaty of commerce and navigation with Great Britain, concluded at London July 3, 1815, " it was for the first time agreed that no higher or other duties or charges should be imposed in any of the ports of the United States on vessels of another power than those payable in the same ports by vessels of the United States; that the same duties should be paid on the importation into the United States of any articles the growth, produce, or manufacture of a foreign power, whether such importation should be made in vessels of the United States or in vessels of that power, and that in all cases where drawbacks were or might be allowed upon the reexportation of any goods the growth, produce, or manufacture of either country respectively, the amount of the drawback should be the same, whether the goods should have been imported in American vessels or in vessels of the

Discriminating duties.

foreign power. How frequently these principles have since been recognized in treaties of the United States, an examination of the index following these notes will show."

Treaties and Conventions between the United States and Other Powers, 1776–1887, Mr. Bancroft Davis' Notes, 1224.

"There is indeed a principle of still more expansive liberality which may be assumed as the basis of commercial intercourse between nation and nation; it is that of placing the foreigner in regard to all objects of navigation and commerce upon a footing of equal favor with the native citizen, and to that end of abolishing all discriminating duties and charges whatever. This principle is altogether congenial to the spirit of our institutions, and the main obstacle to its adoption consists in this: that the fairness of its operation depends upon its being admitted universally. For while two maritime and commercial nations should bind themselves to it, as a compact, operative only between them, a third power might avail itself of its own restrictive and discriminating regulations to secure advantages to its own people at the expense of both the parties to the treaty. The United States have nevertheless made considerable advances in their proposals to other nations towards the general establishment of this most liberal of all principles of commercial intercourse."

Mr. Adams, Sec. of State, to Mr. Anderson, min. to Colombia, May 27, 1823, MS. Inst. U. States Ministers, IX. 274, 290.

By the act of May 24, 1828, the President, on satisfactory evidence given by the government of any foreign nation that "no discriminating duties of tonnage or impost" were levied in the ports of such nation on vessels wholly belonging to citizens of the United States, or on the produce, manufactures, or merchandise imported in such vessels from the United States or from any foreign country, was authorized to issue his proclamation declaring that the foreign discriminating duties of tonnage and impost within the United States were suspended as to the vessels of such foreign nation and the produce, manufactures, or merchandise therein imported into the United States from such foreign nation or from any other foreign country, such suspension to continue so long as the reciprocal exemption from duties should last.

Act of May 24, 1828, 4 Stat. 308; embodied in Rev. Stat. of the U. S. § 4228.

The reciprocity on which this statute is based has been established or confirmed by various treaties. See Moore's American Diplomacy, 105–130.

For proclamations suspending discriminating duties, see Richardson's Messages and Papers of the Presidents, X. Index, 644.

As to discriminations in Central American ports, in the form of drawbacks on importations by particular lines of steamers, under special
contracts with the various Central American Governments, see For.
Rel. 1887, 98, 125, 126, 128, 131, 133, 136, 137, 138, 142, 144; For. Rel.
1888, I. 90–95, 98, 124, 131, 141, 148, 151, 159, 166.

These discriminations were regarded by the United States as justifying
the application of § 2502, Rev. Stat., which imposes a discriminating
duty of ten per cent. ad valorem on goods, wares and merchandise
imported into the United States in foreign vessels not entitled by
treaty or any act of Congress to be entered on payment of the same
duties as are levied on goods, wares, and merchandise imported in
American vessels.   (For. Rel. 1888, I. 124–125, 127–131, 166.)

The rebates were defended by the minister of foreign relations of Costa
Rica on the ground that, as they were allowed under special contracts
with a particular line or particular lines of steamers in consideration
of reciprocal services to the Government, no national discrimination
was created.   (For. Rel. 1888, I. 127–131.)

For the views of the Mexican Government on this question, see For. Rel.
1887, 668–670, 678, 682, 684–691, 698, 709, 711, 714, 715–719, 723–726,
729–742; For. Rel. 1888, II. 1091, 1094.

As to the application of § 2502 in the case of the Mexican steamer Mon-
serrat, see For. Rel. 1888, II. 1263, 1288, 1291–1292.

The question of the imposition of discriminating tonnage and cargo dues
on Mexican vessels in American ports was again discussed in 1893
and in 1894.   The Government of the United States declined to remove the discriminations, since it appeared that in spite of certain
changes in the Mexican law the Mexican Government still imposed
on foreign sailing vessels a discriminating duty of $1.50 a ton, while
exempting altogether sailing vessels owned by Mexican citizens, the
only foreign vessels that were exempt being those which carried pit
coal.   (For. Rel. 1894, 397–410.)

As to the proclamation of the President, suspending tonnage dues on
Mexican vessels in certain cases, see Mr. Day, Assist. Sec. of State,
to Sec. of Treasury, Nov. 16, 1897, 222 MS. Dom. Let. 471.

As to the question of the importation of American goods into Portuguese
colonies by way of Lisbon, as distinct from direct importations into
such colonies from the United States, and the question of the application of Art. IV. of the treaty between the United States and Portugal, of 1840, see Mr. Bayard, Sec. of State, to Mr. Lewis, min. to Portugal, Dec. 7, 1887, For. Rel. 1888, II. 1381.   In this instruction Mr.
Bayard said: "The question of indirect importations into the colonies of a country is generally *casus omissus* in treaties."   It appeared
that goods imported in American vessels into the colonies by way of
a Portuguese port enjoyed a reduction of 30 per cent of the tariff
duties on cargoes.   The Portuguese Government replied that the
commerce of the metropolis with the province of Cape Verde and with
the other provinces of West Africa was regarded as coasting trade
(*cabotage*), and as such was reserved to the Portuguese flag under
article 1315 of the commercial code; that this reservation was entirely consistent with the treaty of 1840, and that no government had
objected to the principle; that since 1877, however, the reservation
of the coasting trade to the national flag had been gradually abandoned as to the colonies, except within the limits of Cape Verde and

Angola. (Senhor Barros Gomez, min. of for. aff., to Mr. Wilbor, Am. chargé, July 7, 1888, For. Rel. 1888, II. 1386–1388.)

By the act of July 24, 1897, the President is authorized to suspend the operation of §§ 4219, 2502, R. S., so that vessels from a foreign country imposing partial discriminating tonnage duties on American vessels, or partial discriminating import duties on American merchandise, " may enjoy in our ports the identical privileges which the same class of American vessels and merchandise may enjoy in said foreign country." (30 Stat. 214.)

As to a remonstrance against the imposition of discriminating duties on the cargoes of American vessels which had touched at an intermediate port on their voyage to France, see Mr. Rives, min. to France, to Mr. Van Buren, Sec. of State, Nov. 7, 1829, H. Ex. Doc. 147, 22 Cong. 2 sess. 69.

As to "universal reciprocity," see Mr. Clayton, Sec. of State, to Mr. Bancroft, min. to England, No. 65, July 30, 1849, MS. Inst. Gr. Br. XVI. 1.

For a discussion of discriminating duties, see Annals of Congress, Jan. 10, 1803, 7 Cong. 2 sess., vol. 12, p. 347.

As to the discriminating British export tax, first laid in 1798, under the name of " convoy duty," see Mr. Madison, Sec. of State, to Mr. Monroe, March 6, 1805, MS. Inst. U. States Ministers, VI. 271.

A proclamation abolishing discriminating duties on Roman vessels, which was issued by the President June 7, 1827, was inadvertently omitted from the Statutes at Large. (Mr. Marcy, Sec. of State, to Mr. Guthrie, Sec. of Treasury, Sept. 29, 1856, 46 MS. Dom. Let. 45.)

As to the regulations for the enforcement of the Turkish license law, see Mr. Rives, Acting Sec. of State, to Mr. Straus, min. to Turkey, No. 143, Oct. 22, 1888, MS. Inst. Turkey, IV. 699; Mr. Blaine, Sec. of State, to Mr. Hirsch, min. to Turkey, No. 57, Feb. 12, 1890, id. V. 102.

As to an attempted discriminating duty on American flour in Turkey, see President McKinley's annual message of Dec. 5, 1899.

August 9, 1880, the Chinese legation at Washington asked that the screw steamer *Wo Chung*, the first Chinese steamer to enter an American port, might, on her arrival at San Francisco, receive the same privileges as were accorded " to vessels of other nations in treaty relations with the United States."

The Department of State, in reply, August 13, 1880, called attention to §§ 4219 and 4228, Revised Statutes, and, referring to the fact that the treaties between the United States and China did not establish reciprocal exemption from discriminating taxes, stated that the Secretary of the Treasury had directed the collector at San Francisco to impose a tonnage tax on the steamer at alien rates, but had reserved the question of duties on the cargo.

" Referring to your note of the 9th instant relative to the expected arrival of the Chinese steamer Wo Chung at the port of San Francisco, and to my reply thereto of the 13th, I have now the honor to inform you that the reserved question of the customs duties of importation chargeable upon the cargo which the vessel may bring has received careful consideration.

" Like the question of alien tonnage dues, of which my former note treated, the matter of customs duties on cargo entering the ports of the United States from foreign ports is one to be exclusively decided, in the absence of specific and reciprocal exemption by treaty, according to the domestic legislation of the country.

" The existing treaties of commerce between the United States and China do not provide for such reciprocal exemption, but stipulate solely ' that citizens of the United States shall never pay higher duties' [on merchandise entering China] ' than those paid by the most favored nations.' The question is, therefore, remitted to the domestic legislation of the United States. That legislation prescribes, in section 2502 of the Revised Statutes, a discriminating duty of ten per centum ad valorum in addition to the regular duties imposed by law on goods imported in vessels not of the United States; but it also provides that this discriminating duty shall not apply to merchandise imported in alien vessels which are entitled by treaty *or any act of Congress* to enter the United States on the same footing as though imported in vessels of the United States.

"An act of Congress, applicable to the case in point, is found embodied in section 4228 of the Revised Statutes, which empowers the President, upon satisfactory proof being given by the government of any foreign nation that no discriminating duties of tonnage or import are there levied upon United States vessels, or upon merchandise carried thither in American bottoms, to issue a proclamation suspending and discontinuing the discriminating duties aforesaid with respect to the vessels and cargoes coming to the United States under the flag of such foreign nation.

" In order, however, that the discretionary authority conferred by this enactment should be applied in conformity with its entire spirit as well as its letter, it becomes necessary that the satisfactory proof it contemplates shall cover not merely American imports into China, but the flag under which they enter the Empire, on which point the treaty is silent.

" It is found practicable, in this view of the question, to join the question of tonnage dues, treated of in my former note, to the question of customs duties now under consideration between us, inasmuch as both matters are within the competency of the President under the above-mentioned section 4228 of the statutes.

" I have, therefore, the honor to inquire whether you are prepared to support the request contained in your note of the 9th instant, for the accordance of the most favored nation treatment to the Wo Chung, and consequently to Chinese vessels in general which may enter our ports with cargo, by giving, on behalf of your Government, satisfactory proof on the following points:

" First. Are any other or higher tonnage dues exacted in the open ports of China, from the vessels of the United States resorting thereto, than are paid by Chinese vessels or any foreign vessel engaged in like trade therewith?

" Second. Are any other or higher customs duties of impost exacted in China from American citizens importing merchandise thither than are paid by Chinese subjects, or the citizens of the most favored power, importing the like merchandise into China?

" Third. Is there any discriminating or additional customs duty imposed upon merchandise, whether of American or foreign origin, entering the open ports of China in vessels of the United States, which is not imposed upon the like goods entering those ports in Chinese vessels, or in the vessels of any foreign power?

" I have thus presented my inquiries in categorical form, in view of the circumstance that the most favored nation treatment which is sought by your note of the 9th, for the Wo Chung and her cargo, is identical with that which a vessel of the United States and her cargo receive on entering the ports of the United States. I have also, as you will perceive, limited my inquiries to the open ports of China, because a Chinese vessel coming from or trading with a port of the Empire closed to the commerce of non-Chinese vessels would necessarily have no claim to exemption or favor based upon reciprocity of treatment.

" Upon the receipt of your reply to the foregoing inquiries, the Department will be in a position to decide whether and to what extent the case of the Wo Chung and vessels of her class come within the discretionary power of the Presidential proclamation contemplated in section 4228 of the Revised Statutes, both as to tonnage and customs duties."

> Mr. Hay, Acting Sec. of State, to Mr. Chen Lan Pin, Aug. 23, 1880, For. Rel. 1880, 304.
>
> Sept. 4, 1880, the Chinese legation gave explicit assurances that no discriminating duties or taxes were imposed on American vessels or their cargoes in Chinese waters; and on Nov. 23, 1880, the President issued a proclamation exempting Chinese vessels and their cargoes from discriminating duties in the United States. (For. Rel. 1880, 306, 308.)

By section 14 of the act of June 26, 1884, a duty of 3 cents a ton, not to exceed in the aggregate 15 cents a ton in one year, was imposed in lieu of the uniform tax of 30 cents a ton previously levied on vessels which should be entered in any port of the United States from any foreign port or place in North America, Central America, the West Indies, the Bahamas, the Bermudas, the Hawaiian Islands, or Newfoundland; and a duty of 6 cents a ton, not to exceed the old rate of 30 cents a ton per annum, was imposed at each entry on all vessels entered in the United States from any other foreign ports or places. The President, however, was authorized to suspend the collection of so much of the 3 to 15 cents duty on vessels entered from any port in Canada, Newfoundland, the Bahamas, the Bermudas, the West Indies, Mexico, and Central America, down to and including Aspinwall and Panama, as might be in excess of the tonnage and light-house dues, or other equivalent tax or taxes, imposed on American vessels by the government of the foreign country in which such port was situated. In course of time claims were presented by the Governments of Belgium, Denmark, Germany, Italy, Portugal, and Sweden and Norway for the 3 to 15 cents rate. These claims, except in the case of Sweden and Norway, were based on the most-favored-nation clause. The claim of Sweden and Norway was based upon a further stipulation in Article VIII. of the treaty of July 4, 1827. The claims were all denied, though that of Sweden and Norway was eventually admitted, it appearing that the construction given by that Government to Article VIII. of the treaty of 1827 was originally claimed by and conceded to the United States. By the act of June 19, 1886, however, sec. 11 of the act of June 26, 1884, was amended so that the President was directed to suspend the collection of so much of the duties imposed on vessels from any foreign port as might be " in excess of the tonnage and light-house dues, or other equivalent tax or taxes, imposed in said port on American vessels by the government of the foreign country in which such port is situated." Under this provision proclamations for the reciprocal suspension of duties were issued by the President in the case of the Netherlands, Germany, and certain other countries.

Report of Mr. Bayard, Sec. of State, to the President, Jan. 14, 1889, H. Ex. Doc. 74, 50 Cong. 2 sess. ; For. Rel. 1888, II. 1857–1956.

See, further, as to the case of Germany and also Sweden and Norway, For. Rel. 1890, 318, 319, 320.

The proclamation of suspension in the case of Germany, which was issued in 1888, was revoked by President Cleveland by a proclamation of Dec. 3, 1896, on the ground of local duties imposed in German ports. (Report of Mr. Olney, Sec. of State, to the President, Dec. 7, 1896, For. Rel. 1896, lxix.)

In 1903, American merchants complained of a law published by the Haitian Government on August 22, 1903, by which a special license tax was imposed on all foreigners doing business in that country. The United States reaffirmed the position which it had taken in 1876, 1893, and 1897, that all such discriminatory taxes were a violation of Article V. of the treaty of 1864. The Haitian Government raised the point that the article in question applied only to war contributions, but the United States declared that this suggestion was negatived both by the language of the treaty and by uniform precedents. The United States also referred to the decision of the Hon. William R. Day, as arbitrator in the case of Metzger, to the same effect.

> Mr. Adee, Act. Sec. of State, to Mr. Powell, min. to Hayti, No. 579, Oct. 5, 1903, For Rel. 1904, 377; Mr. Hay, Sec. of State, to Mr. Powell, No. 582, Nov. 6, 1903, id. 378; Mr. Hay to Mr. Powell, No. 603, May 9, 1904, id. 388.
>
> In February, 1904, the Haytian Government stated that American citizens should continue to be placed on the same footing as Haytian citizens, but intimated that a proposal would be made to modify the treaty of 1864. Such a proposal was made on May 7, 1904, together with notice of termination of the treaty at the expiration of a year. (For. Rel. 1904, 370, 381.)

(6) MONOPOLIES.

§ 185.

" With regard to the other topic of Mr. Brown's letter, it may be observed that although the grant of the monopoly of importation of ice into Rio to an Italian may not be contrary to the strict letter of the treaty, yet as the manifest tendency of such grants would be to defeat the object of the treaty, which was to establish a perfect reciprocity in trade and navigation between the two countries, you will intimate that the grant is considered incompatible with that object. You will also represent that no similar restriction exists in the United States with respect to any production of Brazil, and that, if no such obstacles to the perfect freedom of commerce between the two countries were in future to be interposed, this Government would deem it an additional proof of the disposition of the Brazilian Government to reciprocate our wish to cultivate the best understanding with that country."

> Mr. Forsyth, Sec. of State, to Mr. Hunter, chargé d'affaires to Brazil, Dec. 17, 1834, MS. Inst. Brazil, XV. 15. As to the case of the Boston Ice Co., in Colombia, see For. Rel. 1888, I. 411, 420, 429. The report of the Colombia minister of foreign affairs, justifying the monopoly in the sale and production of ice in the Department of Panama, accompanies the dispatch of Mr. Abbott, min. to Colombia, to Mr. Blaine, Sec. of State, Aug. 14, 1890. For. Rel. 1890, 258.
>
> The Colombian Government also maintained for a time a monopoly in matches. This monopoly ceased in April, 1900. (Mr. Hill, Assist. Sec. State, to Mr. Moore, April 6, 1900, 244 MS. Dom. Let. 202.)

March 12, 1881, the Government of Guatemala entered into a contract with certain citizens of the United States for the completion of a railroad from Champerico, on the Pacific coast, to a place in the interior. A supplementary contract was made May 30, 1882. By these contracts, which were afterwards duly assigned to a California corporation, the Guatemalan Government agreed that for twenty-five years from the date of the opening of the line for traffic no other rail-road should be operated between the specified terminal points, and that no competing line should be constructed within 15 leagues on either side. The railroad was built in accordance with the contract, and was accepted by the Guatemalan Government September 24, 1884. It was alleged, however, that in 1887 the Guatemalan Government entered into a contract with another company for the construction of a new railway within the prohibited distance throughout the entire length of the existing line. With reference to the exclusive privilege thus put in jeopardy, the Department of State said: " The transaction, as above stated, can not be treated as open to the objections which could be made to a grant of a perpetual monopoly. . . . The petitioners aver that this guaranty against competition is of vital importance to them, and that without it they should not have undertaken the construction of this important work. . . . It is not questioned that a government, when a monopoly becomes oppressive, may give public relief by the grant of privileges to an adverse interest. If, however, it should do so in such a way as to destroy private rights granted by its own express agreement, it would seem but just that compensation should be made to the parties thereby injured. And it may be observed that in the case now in question the exclusive privileges granted to the petitioners' assignors are not only conferred for a limited period, but are so guarded by provisions for prompt and effective service, at rates fixed in the contract itself, as to prevent the possibility of any oppression to the public."

> Mr. Bayard, Sec. of State, to Mr. Hall, min. to Central America, March 27, 1888, For. Rel. 1888, I. 134, 136, 137.
>
> A correspondence having arisen as to an exclusive ferry privilege granted at Port Sarnia, in Canada, it was agreed that cooperative action was desirable as to ferries between the United States and the Dominion of Canada. (For. Rel. 1884, 243, 245, 250, 255, 256.)
>
> For references to various discussions of exclusive privileges, see Martin's Index to Foreign Relations, 555–556.

Though the grant of a monopoly " is inconsistent with American ideas and probably would be prejudicial to American interests, any official protest against it, unless based upon treaty obligations, would necessarily have the appearance of attempting to interfere with the sovereign right of a country to regulate its own export and import trade."

> Mr. Foster, Sec. of State, to Messrs. McKesson & Robbins, Nov. 12, 1892, 189 MS. Dom. Let. 151.
>
> By Arts. XIV. and XXVII. of the French treaty with China of 1860 the augmenting of the number of articles reputed contraband or subjects of monopoly was prohibited. (For. Rel. 1887, 181; For. Rel. 1888, I. 252, relating to a camphor monopoly in Formosa.)

As to a monopoly of cotton manufacture in China, see For. Rel. 1883, 129.
Mr. Abbott, min. to Colombia, to Mr. Blaine, Sec. of State, No. 15, July 31,
1889, S. Ex. Doc. 264, 57 Cong. 1 sess. 235, says it is probable that
diplomatic demands for justice to the Boston Ice Company, whose
business in Colombia had been destroyed by the creation of a monopoly, will continue to be refused, unless the United States should take
some "unusual measures" to obtain a favorable response.

"The mere fact that the Western Union Telegraph Company is
enjoying, under a grant of exclusive right, what amounts to a monopoly is no reason of itself why it should be deprived of its concession.
It is easy to say that monopolies are odious, but there are concessions
which amount to monopolies which are lawful, and cannot be disturbed except by a violation of public faith. The laying and operation of cables, especially a quarter of a century ago, were attended
with great expense and risk, and it was a very common thing for
different nations, including the United States, to grant exclusive
concessions for a term of years to companies that would undertake
to invest the necessary capital and carry on such enterprises. With
the chances of success the concessionaries took also the hazard of failure and loss. If loss ensued, they bore it; if success and profit, it
was deemed proper to secure for a limited period to those who had
risked the venture the enjoyment of the fruits of their enterprise,
and not to allow other competitors who had not shared the risk to
come in and take a share of the benefits. With the wisdom of such
arrangements for exclusive franchises the Executive Departments are
not concerned. The grants are made in this country by Congress,
and in other countries by the constituted sovereign authority. It is
the duty of those who administer the Government to deal with the
conditions as they find them, and to see that legal rights of every
nature are respected."

Griggs, At.-Gen., June 15, 1899, 22 Op. 514, 516.
The opinion contains a list of concessions by various sovereignties of ex-
clusive cable rights, including such grants by the United States,
England, France, Spain, Portugal, Brazil, Peru, Ecuador, Colombia,
Mexico, and Japan.
See also Griggs, At.-Gen., March 18, 1901, 23 Op. 425, 427.

4. LEGAL REMEDIES.

(1) COMPETENCE OF TRIBUNALS.

§ 186.

The courts of the United States have jurisdiction in cases of claims
for salvage even where all the parties are aliens.

Mason v. Blaireau (1804), 2 Cranch, 240, 264

In an action brought on certain promissory notes made in St. Domingo it was held that the courts of the United States have no jurisdiction of cases between aliens.

> Montalet *v.* Murray (1807), 4 Cranch, 46.

" Torts originating within the waters of a foreign power may be the subject of a suit in a domestic court. . . . Had both parties to the libel been foreigners, it might have been within the discretion of the court to decline jurisdiction of the case, though the better opinion is that, even under those circumstances, the court will take cognizance . . . ; at least in the absence of a protest from a foreign consul."

> Panama Railroad Co. *v.* Napier Shipping Co., 166 U. S. 280, 285; citing The Avon, Brown's Adm. 170; Smith *v.* Condry, 1 How. 28; The Maggie Hammond, 9 Wall. 435; The Belgenland, 114 U. S. 355; and other cases.
>
> See, further, as to the jurisdiction of the courts in civil matters, Dicey, Conflict of Laws, 222–237, 361–396; and (the American Notes) 229, 230–232, 268, 283, 330, 397.

The courts of admiralty have jurisdiction of collisions on the high seas between vessels of different nationalities;[a] and of torts committed on the high seas, without reference to the nationality of the vessels or of the parties;[b] but, in the absence of a statute, not of suits in rem for damages for the death of a human being.[c] Jurisdiction of libels for seamen's wages is discretionary.[d] The United States admiralty courts have jurisdiction of a libel in personam against an American corporation for injuries received at its dock by a foreign vessel in a foreign ccountry.[e]

In exercising jurisdiction in admiralty upon libel for wages against a foreign vessel, the court will, through comity, administer the law of the country whose flag the vessel carries, to which law the seamen, by shipping for service on such vessel, subject themselves.

> The Belvidere, 90 Fed. Rep. 106.

The general maritime law, and not the local law, governs the question of the liability of a municipal corporation for an injury negligently done to a vessel by a city fire boat while hastening to put out a fire.

> Workman *v.* New York City, 179 U. S. 552, 21 S. Ct. 212, reversing City of New York *v.* Workman, 67 Fed. Rep. 347, 14 C. C. A. 530.

---

[a] The Belgenland, 114 U. S. 355.

[b] The Noddleburn, 28 Fed. Rep. 855. See The Carolina, 14 Fed. Rep. 424; The Montapedia, 14 Fed. Rep. 427; Bolden *v.* Jensen, 70 Fed. Rep. 505.

[c] The Harrisburg, 119 U. S. 199.

[d] The Karoo, 49 Fed. Rep. 651, and cases there cited; The Belgenland, 114 U. S. 355.

[e] Panama R. R. Co. *v.* Napier Shipping Co., 166 U. S. 280, 17 S. Ct. 572.

A private in the United States Army was held at Havana, in April, 1900, awaiting trial by the civil courts of Cuba on a charge of murder committed in that island, the victim being a teamster in the military service. By art. 58 of the Articles of War it is provided that " in time of war, insurrection, or rebellion . . . murder," when committed by persons in the military service of the United States, shall be punished by sentence of a general court-martial. By art. 59, when an officer or soldier is accused of a capital crime his commanding officer is required, except in time of war, on application by or on behalf of the party injured, to endeavor to deliver him over to a civil magistrate in order that he may be tried. It was advised that in the condition of affairs then existing in Cuba, the island being occupied by the United States in pursuance of the treaty of peace with Spain, the private in question should not be tried either by a court-martial or by a military commission, and that while art. 59 did not require him to be delivered to the Cuban courts it was nevertheless proper to permit such courts to try him.

> Griggs, At.-Gen., May 9, 1900, 23 Op. 120.
>
> The opinion proceeded upon the theory that the President might, as the commander of the American forces then occupying Cuba in time of peace, exempt them from " the laws of the sovereignty of Spain, which he himself has adopted as the laws of the sovereignty of Cuba," but that this power should not be exercised to defeat the chief end and aim of all government, as would result from exempting American soldiers from trial for crime.

" In suppressing an irregular establishment formed by persons who had no legal authority from any government, on a spot in the immediate neighborhood of the United States, and for purposes incompatible with their laws and with public tranquillity, the Government of the United States were bound by no obligation to assume a jurisdiction over those persons for acts previously committed by them on the high seas or within the jurisdiction of a neighboring state. They were required to depart from the island, with their property, which has accordingly been effected."

> Mr. Adams, Sec. of State, to Mr. Hyde de Neuville, French min., March 19, 1818, MS. Notes to For. Legations, II. 316, replying to notes of Mr. de Neuville of February 12 and March 11, 1818, requesting the assistance of the United States for the restoration to their original owners, who were subjects of France, of certain French vessels and cargoes alleged to have been taken and carried into Amelia Island by persons who had lately occupied that place.

" While admitting that the conduct of the captain of the *Camillus*," an American vessel, " in causing several New Granadian citizens, among whom were two commissaries of police, to be cruelly whipped on board the aforesaid vessel, to which they had resorted in the discharge of their duty, for the purpose of obtaining from the captain thereof the compensation due by him to these persons for several days' labor performed in his service," " appears from the testimony furnished to have been of a most reprehensible character, the undersigned does not perceive that there is the slightest ground upon which this Government can be called upon to punish him. The offence in question was committed in New Granadian territory upon citizens of that Republic, and in violation of its peace and laws. The perpetrators of the outrage therefore are amenable, not to the laws of this country, but to those of New Granada. There is no law of the United States which authorizes this Government to enforce the respect due to the local and municipal authorities of other States."

> Mr. Marcy, Sec. of State, to Señor Don V. de Paredes, Sept. 27, 1853, MS. Notes to Colombia, VI. 40.

In March, 1882, the American schooner *Daylight*, being on a voyage from Key West, Fla., to Tampico, in Mexico, was, while lying at anchor during a storm outside the bar, near the harbor of Tampico, waiting to enter that port, run into by the Mexican gunboat *Independencia*, the schooner and cargo becoming a total loss. A claim for compensation having been presented diplomatically, the Mexican Government, though observing that it might be sued under the Mexican law before the proper tribunals, and that this course should be pursued by the claimant, stated that the case might be settled between the two Governments, but that, as the diplomatic channel was available only in the event of a denial of justice, the claimant must himself appear before the Mexican department of war and marine, to which the matter particularly pertained. The United States, on the other hand, contended that as the wrong complained of was suffered at the hands of a high officer of the Mexican navy, and as the Mexican Government was therefore conceived to be justly responsible for it, the claimants, who were not residents of Mexico, should not be required to go to that country to seek redress, but that the case should be dealt with by the two Governments; and that if, by the laws or administrative regulations of Mexico, it was essential that the facts should be first investigated by the ministry of war and marine, the subject should be referred to that department by the minister of foreign affairs. Such a course, it was said, would be pursued by the United States were a similar demand to be made on it by Mexico.

> Mr. Frelinghuysen, Sec. of State, to Mr. Morgan, min. to Mexico, Nov. 15, 1883, and May 17, 1884, For. Rel. 1884, 343, 358; Mr. Morgan, min. to Mexico, to Mr. Frelinghuysen, Sec. of State, Sept. 21, 1883, Jan. 2, 1884, March 25, 1884, and June 26, 1884, For. Rel. 1884, 340, 345, 362, 370.
>
> See also Mr. Bayard, Sec. of State, to Mr. Jackson, min. to Mexico, July 2, 1885, MS. Inst. Mexico, XXI. 317, where the subject is discussed as

that of the entry of a vessel into foreign waters under stress of weather. It seems, however, that, although a storm was prevailing when the schooner was run into she had entered Mexican waters off Tampico because that port was her destination, and was only waiting for an opportunity to cross the bar. The idea of stress may have been derived from a remark by Mr. Frelinghuysen, in his instruction of May 17, 1884, that " at the time of the occurrence which gave rise to the claim the vessel could scarcely be said, with strict propriety, to have been in Mexican waters. She was anchored outside the bar, near the harbor of Tampico, in an exceptionally rough sea, at the close of a severe storm, which rendered it unsafe for her to attempt to cross the bar or enter the harbor." He had previously stated that the schooner, when so lying at anchor, was "on her voyage from Key West, Fla., with a cargo of lumber for Tampico." (For. Rel. 1884, 358, 359.)

The remark that the vessel could "scarcely be said, with strict propriety, to have been in Mexican waters," referred to the contention that the case properly belonged to the jurisdiction of the Mexican courts. Mr. Frelinghuysen took the ground that " the municipal civil laws can only be held applicable to and operative on the rights, property, and persons of the citizens of the country and foreigners who may be either permanently or temporarily residing in the country," and in this relation he said: " The owners of the *Daylight* were never residents of Mexico, either permanent or temporary. They are not known to have ever been in that country. The master of the vessel was not a resident of Mexico, and . . . the vessel could scarcely be said, with strict propriety, to have been in Mexican waters. . . . To insist that those claimants shall go from Maine to Tampico to seek redress in the Mexican tribunals for a grievous wrong suffered at the hands of a high officer of the navy of that Republic, and in such proceedings to be met by the evidence which the commander of the *Independencia* would readily be able to elicit from the ship's crew, would, in the estimation of this Government, be a practical denial of justice." (For. Rel. 1884, 359–360.)

In July, 1885, three seamen of the American schooner *Maggie E. Abbott* were arrested at Port au Prince, on a charge of murdering a Haytian policeman in a drinking house. Two of them were soon discharged, but the third, a Swede named Robinson, was held. As he had gone ashore without leave, he might, said the Department of State, " be reclaimed as a deserter, but this right is subordinated to any claim which the justice of Hayti may have upon him for violation of the laws of Hayti. If so accused, he has no exceptional right as an American seaman, and this would hold true, whether he went ashore with or without leave. If charged with the commission of crime in Haytian jurisdiction, he is amenable to Haytian law therefor."

Mr. Bayard, Sec. of State, to Mr. Thompson, min. to Hayti, July 31, 1885, MS. Inst. Hayti, II. 511. For affirmation of prior decisions in the Goerdeler case, see Mr. Gresham, Sec. of State, to Mrs. Goerdeler, April 26, 1893, 191 MS. Dom. Let. 425.

February 27, 1897, the United States legation at St. Petersburg reported that the Russian Government had refused to pardon the five Americans who were sentenced for illegal sealing on Robben Island, but that, under the operation of the Imperial manifest of May 14 (26), 1896, their sentences expired January 25 (February 6), 1897.

> For. Rel. 1897, 446, referring to correspondence printed in For. Rel. 1896, 495–507.
>
> June 19, 1895, the embassy of the United States at London, cabled that the home secretary would release John Curtin Kent on ticket of leave as soon as his friends should arrange to care for him. (For. Rel. 1895, I. 728.)

It being stated that certain Tyrolese subjects were detained against their will on a steamer at San Francisco, after having been induced to embark for Hawaii, under a contract to labor, by representations as to pay which they had found to be fraudulent, reply was made: " Neither the police authorities of San Francisco, nor the [United States] Commissioner of Immigration, had any legal right or power to release the said Tyrolese from the restraint alleged to have been put upon their liberty. This could only be done by the institution of legal proceedings for a writ of habeas corpus, . . . either by the injured parties themselves or by their friends in their behalf," it not being the legal duty of any Federal or State official to institute proceedings in such cases.

> Mr. Hay, Sec. of State, to Mr. Hengelmuller, Aust. amb., July 27, 1900, MS. Notes to Aust. Leg. IX. 450, referring to previous notes of July 6 and 13, and the ambassador's notes of June 19 and July 21.
>
> The matter was referred to the governors of California and Hawaii, on general grounds, for the purpose of acquainting them with the case and enabling them to give it consideration.

Article XII. of the convention between the United States and France of 1788 provided that " all differences and suits " between French subjects in the United States and United States citizens in France, and particularly all disputes and differences between the officers and crews of vessels, should be " determined by the respective consuls and vice-consuls, either by a reference to arbitrators, or by a summary judgment, and without costs; " that no officer of the country should " interfere therein, or take any part whatever in the matter; " and that " the appeals from the said consular sentences shall be carried before the tribunals of France or of the United States, to whom it may appertain to take cognizance thereof."

Convention with France, 1788.

This convention, after giving rise to many differences, was, together with the other treaties with France, declared by the United States in 1798 to be abrogated.

Did the consular convention with France of 1788 give the French consul cognizance of all differences and suits between Frenchmen, or confine it to the description of cases therein enumerated or other cases not arising from transactions in the United States? The court held that the consular jurisdiction did " not extend generally to all differences and suits between Frenchmen."

> Villeneuve *v.* Barron, U. S. circuit court, Dist. of Mass., May term, 1792, 2 Dallas, 235, note.

Mr. Harrison, United States district attorney at New York, March 6, 1794, stated that, having considered the provisions of the treaty and the act of Congress concerning consuls and vice-consuls, he was of opinion that the United States marshals were " bound by law to execute any sentence of a French consul arising under the said [twelfth] article."

Mr. Bradford, Attorney-General of the United States, March 14, 1794, stated that he perfectly coincided in this opinion.

On the same day these opinions were communicated to the French minister.

> Mr. Randolph, Sec. of State, to M. Fauchet, French min. March 14, 1794, 6 MS. Dom. Let. 121.

" The subject of the French consulate in the United States has again been considered, in reference to the claim of execution of the judicial decrees of the French consuls by the officers of the United States, and the result is the same as formerly. The present Attorney General (the law officer whose constitutional duty it is to investigate all legal questions on which the Executive is to decide) concurs in the opinions of his predecessor and of the Attorney of the District of New York, that neither the consular convention between the United States and France, nor the law enacted by Congress for carrying the convention into effect, render it the duty of any officer of the United States or give him the power to execute such consular decrees. Of the opinion of the Executive of the United States on this point, with some reasons on which it was founded, you are already possessed in my letter of the 16th January last to General Pinckney. You say that the number of American commercial citizens in France vastly surpasses the number of French commercial citizens in the United States, and thence you infer that a mutual acknowledgment or cession of the consular powers you contend for would be proportionally more beneficial to us than to France. But, Sir, the United States desire no extension of the advantages secured to their citizens by the consular convention, and of course readily relinquish all claim to the powers which you say are accorded to the American consuls in France, relative to the authoritative execution of their judicial decrees. If any material inconvenience follows to the citizens of the United States, Congress must provide by law a penalty to be inflicted on such of them as refuse to obey the regular decisions of their consuls in France; in like manner as you informed me the laws of France impose a penalty of 1,400 livres, on any of her citizens, in such case offending."

> Mr. Pickering, Sec. of State, to Mr. Letombe, French consul-general, May 29, 1797, 10 MS. Dom. Let. 51.

The commander of a French privateer, having captured on the high seas the sloop *Betsey*, sent the vessel into Baltimore, where the owners of the vessel and cargo filed a libel in the United States district court for restitution on the ground the property was neutral. The captor pleaded to the jurisdiction of the court. The plea was allowed, and the decree was affirmed by the circuit court, from which an appeal was taken to the Supreme Court of the United States. The general question was raised whether an American court of admiralty had jurisdiction to entertain the libel and decree restitution. The Supreme Court, besides holding that the district court should proceed to determine whether, agreeably to laws and treaties, restitution should be made, declared that, since no foreign power could of right institute or erect any court of judicature in the United States but in pursuance of treaties, the admiralty jurisdiction which had been exercised in the United States by French consuls, not being so warranted, was not of right.

> Glass v. The sloop Betsey (1794), 3 Dallas, 6.
> "The United States and France have, by their consular convention, given mutually to their consuls jurisdiction in certain cases specially enumerated. But that convention gives to neither the power of establishing complete courts of admiralty within the territory of the other, nor even of deciding the particular question of prize or not prize." (Mr. Jefferson, Sec. of State, to Mr. Morris, min. to France, Aug. 16, 1793, Am. State Papers, For. Rel. I. 169.)
> The action of the French consul at Charleston in condemning as prize a British vessel, not being warranted by the law of the land, " is consequently a mere nullity." (Mr. Jefferson, Sec. of State, to the British min., May 17, 1793, 5 MS. Dom. Let. 105.)
> See, also, Moore, Int. Arbitrations, I. 311 et seq.

Suits by foreign sovereigns. The Constitution of the United States gives jurisdiction to the courts of the United States in cases where foreign states are parties, and the judiciary act gives to the circuit courts jurisdiction in all cases between aliens and citizens; but the court refused to inquire, upon a motion, whether Ferdinand VII., King of Spain, could institute this suit, the Government of the United States not having acknowledged him King.

> King of Spain v. Oliver, 2 Wash. C. C. 429.

A suit brought in a court of the United States by a foreign sovereign [Napoleon III.], where the nation he represents is the party substantially aggrieved, as in the case of an injury to a public ship, is not defeated, not does it abate, by a change in the person of the sovereign or by his deposition. Such change may, if necessary, be suggested on the record.

> The Sapphire, 11 Wall. 164.
>
> In this case the court observed that if a special case should arise in which it could be shown that injustice to the other party would ensue from a continuation of proceedings after the death or deposition of a sovereign, the court, in the exercise of its discretionary power, would take such order as the exigency might require to prevent such a result.

A bill was filed by " The Government of the State of Colombia and his Excellency Don Manuel José Hurtado, a citizen of the said State, and minister plenipotentiary from the same to the court of His Britannic Majesty, now residing at No. 33, Baker street, Portman square, . . . in the county of Middlesex."

The vice-chancellor :

"A foreign state is as well entitled, as any individual, to the aid of this court in the assertion of its rights : but it must sue in a form which makes it possible for this court to do justice to the defendants. It must sue in the names of some public officers who are entitled to represent the interests of the state, and upon whom process can be served on the part of the defendants; and who can be called upon to answer the cross bill of the defendants. This general description of ' The Colombian Government ' precludes the defendants from these just rights; and no instance can be stated in which this court has entertained the suit of a foreign state by such a description.

" Demurrer allowed."

> The Colombian Government *v.* Rothschild (1826), 1 Simons, 94, 104.

A foreign sovereign prince, though entitled to sue in the court of chancery in his political capacity, stands in such case on the same footing as ordinary suitors with respect to the rules and practice of the court, and is bound, like them, to answer a cross bill personally and on oath, and can not claim the privilege of putting in an answer by his agent, or without oath or signature.

> The King of Spain *v.* Hullet (1833), 1 Cl. & Fin. 333.
>
> The same principle was enforced in Rothschild *v.* Queen of Portugal, 3 Younge & Collyer, 594, (June 24, 1839,) in which Alderson, B., overruled a demurrer of the Queen to a bill brought by Rothschild for the discovery of certain correspondence relating to the transaction in respect of which she had sued him. The matter was of a public nature.

See, also, the United States *v.* Prioleau, and other cases, *supra,* § 26.

"This principle [that a sovereign is not subject to suit] extends so far that a sovereign state, by coming into court as a suitor, does not thereby abandon its sovereignty and subject itself to an affirmative judgment upon a counterclaim. People *v.* Dennison, 84 N. Y. 272; United States *v.* Eckford, 6 Wall. 490." (Hassard *v.* United States of Mexico (1899), 29 Misc. (N. Y.) 511.)

(2) REGULATION OF PROCEDURE.

§ 187.

When a suitor applies to foreign tribunals for justice, he must submit to the rules by which those tribunals are gov **General principles.** erned.

Bradford, At.-Gen., 1794, 1 Op. 53.

" Citizens of the United States whilst residing in Peru are subject to its laws and the treaties existing between the parties, and are amenable to its courts of justice for any crimes or offenses which they may commit. It is the province of the judiciary to construe and administer the laws; and if this be done promptly and impartially towards American citizens, and with a just regard to their rights, they have no cause of complaint. In such cases they have no right to appeal for redress to the diplomatic representative of their country, nor ought he to regard their complaints. It is only where justice has been denied or unreasonably delayed by the courts of justice of foreign countries, where these are used as instruments to oppress American citizens or deprive them of their just rights, that they are warranted in appealing to their Government to interpose. No such circumstances exist, so far as I understand the question, in the case of Dr. Norris, which was the subject of Mr. Jewett's protest."

Mr. Buchanan, Sec. of State, to Mr. Osma, Peruvian min., Feb. 1, 1848, MS. Notes to Peru, I. 9.

" Complaints of unfounded seizures of property by Mexican authorities on the Rio Grande frontier have recently been addressed to this Department by citizens of the United States. They inveigh against arbitrary acts of the military and corrupt proceedings of the judicial officers of Mexico in that quarter. This Government is not disposed to connive at any infractions of the laws of Mexico by our citizens, but it has a right to expect that if they are charged with a violation of those laws the cases will be fairly and impartially tried and decided. If a contrary course should be adopted it may be difficult to restrain the aggrieved parties from seeking reparation by acts of violence against the property of Mexicans on the southern bank of the Rio Grande."

Mr. Webster, Sec. of State, to Mr. Smith, May 5, 1851, MS. Inst. Mexico, XVI. 258.

" Our citizens who resort to countries where the trial by jury is not known, and who may there be charged with crime, frequently imagine, when the laws of those countries are administered in the forms customary therein, that they are deprived of rights to which they are entitled, and therefore may expect the interference of their own Government. But it must be remembered, in all such cases, that they have of their own free will elected a residence out of their native land, and preferred to live elsewhere, and under another government, and in a country in which different laws prevail.

" They have chosen to settle themselves in a country where jury trials are not known; where representative government does not exist; where the privilege of the writ of *habeas corpus* is unheard of, and where judicial proceedings in criminal cases are brief and summary. Having made this election, they must necessarily abide its consequences. No man can carry the ægis of his national American liberty into a foreign country, and expect to hold it up for his exemption from the dominion and authority of the laws and the sovereign power of that country, unless he be authorized to do so by virtue of treaty stipulations."

> Report of Mr. Webster, Sec. of State, to the President, Dec. 23, 1851, on Thrasher's case, 6 Webster's Works, 521, 528.
> See, also, as to Thrasher's case, Moore, Int. Arbitrations, III. 2701.

" Every nation, whenever its laws are violated by anyone owing obedience to them, whether he be a citizen or a stranger, has a right to inflict the penalties incurred upon the transgressor if found within its jurisdiction. The case is not altered by the character of the laws, unless they are in derogation of the well-established international code. No nation has a right to supervise the municipal code of another nation or claim that its citizens or subjects shall be exempted from the operation of such code, if they have voluntarily placed themselves under it. The character of the municipal laws of one country does not furnish a just ground for other states to interfere with the execution of these laws even upon their own citizens when they have gone into that country and subjected themselves to its jurisdiction. If this country can rightfully claim no such exemption for its native-born or naturalized citizens, it can not claim it for those who have at most but inchoate rights of citizens.

" The above principle, that persons, being citizens or subjects of one state and having violated the laws of another state, may be punished while they remain under or are fairly brought within the jurisdiction of the latter state, is too well established to be made a matter of serious controversy. It is clearly affirmed in, and, indeed, is the basis of, every extradition treaty. Each contracting party agrees to deliver up to the other fugitive offenders,—generally including its own citizens as well as strangers,—for specified offenses, to be dealt with according to the laws of the country demanding the surrender of them. It is true that there are some kinds of offenses which are not, and ought not to be, included in extradition treaties;— such, for instance, as are called political offenses;—yet because one nation will not enter into a compact to deliver such offenders to another, that does not justify the inference that if such offenders go voluntarily within the jurisdiction of the country whose laws they have offended they may not be rightfully punished, or that they can claim exemption from punishment if they were citizens of another country when the offense was committed, or had, after committing it, acquired another nationality.

" The country whose ' protection ' is invoked can not, it is conceived, properly interpose in such a case unless the municipal law, the violation of which is charged, contravenes some right of such country acquired by treaty stipulations or otherwise. The principle does not at all interfere with the right of any state to protect its citizens or those entitled to its protection when abroad from wrongs and injuries, from arbitrary acts of oppression or deprivation of property, as contradistinguished from penalties and punishments, incurred by the infraction of the laws of the country within whose jurisdiction the sufferers have placed themselves."

Mr. Marcy, Sec. of State, to Mr. Jackson, chargé d'affaires, Jan. 10, 1854,
MS. Inst. Austria, I. 89.

" The system of proceedings in criminal cases in the Austrian Government has, undoubtedly, as is the case in most other absolute countries, many harsh features, and is deficient in many safeguards which our laws provide for the security of the accused; but it is not within the competence of one independent power to reform the jurisprudence of others, nor has it the right to regard as an injury the application of the judicial system and established modes of proceedings in foreign countries to its citizens when fairly brought under their operation. All we can ask of Austria, and this we can demand as a right, is, that in her proceedings against American citizens prosecuted for offenses committed within her jurisdiction, she should give them the full and fair benefit of her system, such as it is, and deal with them as she does with her own subjects or those of other foreign powers. She can not be asked to modify her mode of proceedings to suit our views, or to extend to our citizens all the advantages which her subjects would have under our better and more humane system of criminal jurisprudence."

Mr. Marcy, Sec. of State, to Mr. Jackson, chargé d'affaires, Apr. 6, 1855,
MS. Inst. Austria, I. 105.

" It cannot be expected that any government would go so far as to yield to a pretension of a foreign power to revise and review the proceedings of its courts under the claim of an international right to correct errors therein, either in respect to the application of principles of law, or the application of facts as evidence in cases where the citizens of such foreign power have been convicted. It certainly could not be expected that such a claim would be allowed before the party making it had first presented a clear case *prima facie* of wilful denial of justice or a deliberate perversion of judicial forms for the purpose of oppression."

> Mr. Marcy, Sec. of State, to Mr. Jackson, chargé at Vienna, Apr. 6, 1855, MS. Inst. Austria, I. 105.
>
> See, also, McDonald *v.* State, 80 Wis. 407 ; 50 N. W. Rep. 185.

" In France and on the continent of Europe generally, the police authorities have the right and are in the habit of setting on foot proceedings against individuals upon suspicion merely, and not upon probable cause alleged under oath. The power referred to is, no doubt, sometimes abused. Citizens of the United States, however, whether native or naturalized, who, of their own accord, visit countries where it exists, must expect to incur that hazard, unless by treaty stipulation they should be placed upon a more favorable footing than the subjects of the government whose agents may commit the abuse."

> Mr. Marcy, Sec. of State, to Mr. Richter, Feb. 21, 1854, 42 MS. Dom. Let. 231.

Complaint was made as to the action of the police of Valparaiso in searching the house of and arresting a citizen of the United States on suspicion of being concerned in a robbery. On the facts in the case the Department of State thought that the conduct of the police " was certainly censurable," but that the case was " scarcely one the circumstances of which would warrant its being made an international grievance. The Chilean Government, like ours," continued the Department of State, " is sovereign within its own territory, and can not without derogation from its sovereignty allow a foreign government to dictate the form in which judicial proceedings are to be carried on. There may have been some irregularity in the manner in which the search was made of the house of Priest. If, however, his rights were thereby invaded, and there are no means of making the authorities judicially accountable, this is a defect which may work injury to Mr. Priest, but it does not appear to be an intentional and aggravated denial of justice, for the redress of which the peaceful relations between the United States and Chile ought to be disturbed. You are aware that we have no treaty with the Government of that Republic. The rights of citizens of the United States there must accordingly be measured by the municipal laws of Chile. By a respectful and temperate appeal to the justice of the Chilean Government you will be able, I trust, to secure for Mr. Priest a fair compensation for any actual loss he may have sustained from the apparently unwarrantable conduct of its officials."

> Mr. Marcy, Sec. of State, to Mr. Starkweather, min. to Chile, Aug. 24, 1855, MS. Inst. Chile, XV. 124.
> But "an absolute denial of justice in cases arising even under municipal laws may sometimes be considered as an international offence." (Mr. Marcy, Sec. of State, to Mr. Wilson, Aug. 1, 1854, 20 MS. Disp. to Consuls, 1.)

If a citizen of the United States, whether native born or naturalized, commit a crime in Great Britain his citizenship will not protect him from the penalty of his crime; nor can he complain that he is not accorded a right which would be granted to a British subject on trial for crime in the United States.

A person born in Ireland, but naturalized as a citizen of the United States, is not entitled, when arraigned in a British court for the offense of treason-felony, to the privilege of a jury *de medietate;* the reason being that as the right of trial by jury *de medietate* does not exist generally in the United States, we have no right to complain that an American citizen indicted for crime in Great Britain is not entitled to such privilege.

> Stanbery, At.-Gen. 1867, 12 Op. 319.

" It is not within the powers of the executive branch of this Government to interfere in any way with the proceedings of the judiciary in an action instituted by a private citizen," even though such a citizen be a consul for a foreign state.

> Mr. Fish, Sec. of State, to Mr. Catacazy, Russ. min., June 13, 1871, MS. Notes to Russia, VII. 23.

" We are not entitled to claim for our citizens on trial in that Kingdom (Great Britain) privileges which are, 1st, not granted by British law to British subjects; 2d, are not allowed in the United States to aliens of any country in any case, civil or criminal."

> Mr. Fish, Sec. of State, to Mr. Rogers, Jan. 11, 1870, 83 MS. Dom. Let. 55.
> " British subjects, when within the territorial jurisdiction of the United States, are required to respect and obey the laws of the United States, and when held to answer for any offense against these laws in the courts of the country, have the same rights and privileges extended to them that are enjoyed by citizens held to answer for similar offenses. Citizens of the United States, when held to answer in the courts of Great Britain or her colonies, have a right to demand the same privileges extended to British subjects under like circumstances." (Mr. Davis, Acting Sec. of State, to Mr. Austin, July 17, 1873, 99 MS. Dom. Let. 388.)

" When application is made to this Department for redress for the supposed injurious actions of a foreign judicial tribunal, such application can only be sustained on one of two grounds:

" (1) Undue discrimination against the petitioner as a citizen of the United States in breach of treaty obligations; or

" (2) Violation of those rules for the maintenance of justice in judicial inquiries which are sanctioned by international law.

" There is no proof presented in Captain Caleb's case establishing either of these conditions.   It is true that it is alleged that there was a failure of justice, and were this Department sitting as a court of error, it is not improbable that there are points in the proceedings complained of in the Mexican adjudication before us which might call for reversal.   But this Department is not a tribunal for the revision of foreign courts of justice, and it has been uniformly held by us that mistakes of law or even of fact by such tribunals are not ground for our interposition unless they are in conflict, as above stated, either with treaty obligations to citizens of the United States or settled principles of international law in respect to the administration of justice."

> Mr. Bayard, Sec. of State, to Mr. Morrow, Feb. 17, 1886, 159 MS. Dom. Let. 99.
>
> As to the circumstances of the case of Captain Caleb, see For. Rel. 1884, 348, and infra, pp. 324–325.

In 1886 Mr. Phelps, United States minister in London, was instructed to "ask for explanations" in regard to the claim of Francis de Freitas, who complained of the action of a Trinidad (British) court. Subsequently, after conference with Mr. Phelps and a mature consideration of the papers, the Department of State came to the conclusion that the request ought not to be pressed till further proof, in the way of documents or of affidavits from third parties sustaining claimant's main allegations, should be furnished. It was, said the Department of State, a familiar principle of international law, as expressed by Mr. Marcy, Secretary of State, in instructions to Mr. Fay, Nov. 16, 1855, that a citizen of the United States dwelling abroad "is subject to the laws, civil and criminal, of the country within which he is domiciled or resides, and the United States could not make the proceedings against him a ground of complaint unless those laws were contrary to treaty stipulations or were used in bad faith or oppressively to inflict injuries upon him." The " burden," therefore, so the Department declared, was " on the claimant, in cases where judicial injustice is set up by him, to prove such injustice; and this rule applies with peculiar force where the trial complained of is before a British provincial court under safeguards and subject to appellate suspension such as those recognized in similar

cases in the United States. There is no proof, however, of such judicial injustice by the Trinidad court, except that contained in the
affidavit of Mr. de Freitas himself. Under these circumstances the
Department will not be ready to take further action in the premises
until such supplementary proof is received."

> Mr. Bayard, Sec. of State, to Mr. Brook, Jan. 7, 1887, 162 MS. Dom.
> Let. 508.
> In the case of C. Pouble, arrested and imprisoned in Cuba, it was stated
> that no ground had been discovered for attempting "to interfere with
> the course of the law . . . beyond our earnest efforts to hasten the
> proceedings and to have good treatment and proper opportunity of
> defence allowed him." (Mr. Porter, Acting Sec. of State, to Mr.
> Carrasco, Aug. 15, 1885, 156 MS. Dom. Let. 542. See, also, Mr. Rives,
> Assist. Sec. of State, to Mr. Carrasco, June 29, 1888, 169 MS. Dom.
> Let. 29, stating that Mr. Edmunds, Com. on For. Rel., March 24, 1886,
> had reported that there was then no ground for intervention in behalf
> of Pouble.)

"Mr. Blaine instructs Mr. Egan to claim the privilege of reading
the paper which the American sailors have signed in secret, in a
language they did not understand, and without being accompanied by
counsel, and to see that no one from the *Baltimore*, officer or sailor,
is allowed to testify except in the presence of a friend acting as
counsel and in his own language openly and not secretly."

> Mr. Blaine, Sec. of State, to Mr. Egan, min. to Chile, tel., Nov. 1, 1891,
> For. Rel. 1891, 211.

In July, 1895, L. S., a citizen of the United States, was arrested at
Kissengen and held to bail in the sum of 80,000 marks (about
$20,000) on a charge of an insult to and resistance to the authority of
the royal district court assessor, Baron von Thuengen, in the latter's
capacity as substitute bath commissioner, in a dispute concerning the
right of S.'s son to dance in the Kursaal. On August 5, 1895, S., who
had meanwhile written a letter of apology to the Baron, was tried and
convicted of having "resisted the authority of the State, and of having insulted a royal official," and was sentenced to two weeks' imprisonment and to pay a fine of 600 marks. In a note to the German
ambassador at Washington, invoking his intervention in the matter,
the sentence was characterized as severe and out of proportion to the
offense, and the whole proceeding as "gratuitously and undeservedly
onerous from the beginning," especially the sentence of imprisonment,
and the good offices of the ambassador with the Government of Bavaria were requested, to the end that S. might not "unjustly suffer the
personal degradation to which the extraordinary action of the Bava-
rian tribunal has most unwarrantably condemned him."[a] The ambas-

---

[a] Mr. Olney, Sec. of State, to Baron Thielmann, German ambassador, Sept. 26,
1895, For. Rel. 1895, I. 469–470.

sador, besides rejecting as " entirely unjustified" the criticism of the sentence, declined " to see the administration of justice within a state of the German Federal Union, and the right of pardon, which belongs to the princes of the German Federal Union, discussed in this way and treated in the form of a diplomatic claim." [a] The discussion was somewhat continued on similar lines without substantial result.[b] A petition was made by S. for a pardon or a commutation of the sentence of imprisonment by a pecuniary fine. The application was denied, but S., who had meanwhile gone back to the United States, did not return to undergo the imprisonment.[c]

" In reply to your letter of the 27th ultimo, with inclosure from Mr. W. C. Parker, of Comanche, Tex., asking to be supplied, if possible, with a record of the trial of his brother, one Jesse Kittle, who was recently tried at Truxillo, Honduras, I have the honor to inform you that our consul at Tegucigalpa will be instructed to ask for the desired record if the applicant will furnish the money to pay for the copying and other fees.

" The Department has no right to demand the record, and can not assure its procurement even upon offer to pay the usual expense of making the copy."

> Mr. Olney, Sec. of State, to Mr. Chilton, M. C., June 5, 1896, 210 MS. Dom. Let. 496.

In the correspondence between the United States and Great Britain respecting the imprisonment of Messrs. Berger and Ryan for treasonable practices in Ireland, there is a note from Lord Palmerston to Mr. Bancroft, then American minister in London, of Sept. 30, 1848, stating, among other things, that " if there should be any citizens of the United States who have chosen this period of disturbance for visiting Ireland, for innocent purposes, they must not be surprised if, like persons whom curiosity may lead into the midst of a battle, they should be involved into the sweep of measures aimed at men of a different description. But Her Majesty's Government will always lament that mistakes of this kind should happen, by which unoffending travelers may be exposed to inconvenience; and the utmost alacrity will at all times be evinced by the Irish government to rectify such errors."

> 42 British & For. State Papers (1852–1853), 412, 414.
>
> See, also, President Polk's message of Dec. 27, 1848, with a report of Mr. Buchanan, Secretary of State, and accompanying papers, in relation to the imprisonment of American citizens in Ireland, H. Ex. Doc. 19, 30 Cong. 2 sess.

---

[a] Baron Thielmann, German ambassador, to Mr. Olney, Sec. of State, Oct. 1, 1895, For. Rel. 1895, I. 479.

[b] For. Rel. 1895, I. 480, 482, 483–485.

[c] For. Rel. 1895, I. 487–488.

"Referring to my general instruction of the 26th ultimo (No. 166), in relation to the case of Michael P. Boyton, I now inclose to you a copy of a letter of the 30th of the same month from the Hon. Samuel J. Randall, in behalf of Mr. Joseph B. Walsh, a citizen of the United States, who, it appears, was arrested on the 3d of March last, under the provisions of the late act of Parliament, known as the 'protection act.' Mr. Walsh is represented as being imprisoned in Dublin, and it is probable that Kilmainham jail is the place of confinement. His relatives in this country, knowing only of his arrest and imprisonment, are unable to afford the Department any information as to the specific charge, if any, upon which he is held; and it seems quite likely that the prisoner himself is also in ignorance in regard to the particular offense for which he is thus subjected to summary detention and confinement.

"Mr. Walsh has been a citizen of the United States since 1875. His character as a law-abiding and good citizen is vouched for by well known and respectable citizens of Pennsylvania. I inclose a copy of his certificate of naturalization.

"I have already indicated to you in my instruction of the 26th of May, the entire absence of any disposition on the part of this Government to interfere with the administration of the local or general municipal laws of Great Britain. The laws of that country, and especially those that relate to the personal liberty and security of the citizen, have always been so much in harmony with the principles of jurisprudence cherished by Americans as a birthright, that they have never failed to command the respect of the Government and people of the United States. But whatever the necessity may be in the estimation of Her Majesty's Government for the existence and enforcement in Ireland of the exceptional legislative measures recently enacted in respect to that country, this Government cannot view with unconcern the application of the summary proceedings attendant upon the execution of these measures to naturalized citizens of the United States of Irish origin, whose business relations may render necessary their presence in Ireland or any other part of the United Kingdom, or whose filial instincts and love for kindred may have prompted them to revisit their native country.

"If American citizens while within British jurisdiction offend against British laws this Government will not seek to shield them from the legal consequences of their acts, but it must insist upon the application to their cases of those common principles of criminal jurisprudence which in the United States secure to every man who offends against its laws, whether he be an American citizen or a foreign subject, those incidents to a criminal prosecution which afford the best safeguard to personal liberty and the strongest protection against oppression under the forms of law, which might otherwise be practiced through excessive zeal.

" That an accused person shall immediately upon arrest be informed of the specific crime or offense upon which he is held, and that he shall be afforded an opportunity for a speedy trial before an impartial court and jury, are essentials to every criminal prosecution, necessary alike to the protection of innocence and the ascertainment of guilt. You will lose no time in making the necessary inquiries into the cause of Mr. Walsh's arrest and detention, in which it is probable Mr. Barrows, the consul at Dublin, may be able to aid you. And if you shall find that the circumstances of the case, in the light of this and previous instructions, are such as to call for interference on the part of this Government, you will make such temperate but earnest representations as in your judgment will conduce to his speedy trial, or in case there is no specific charge against him, his prompt release from imprisonment."

> Mr. Blaine, Sec. of State, to Mr. Lowell, June 2, 1881, For. Rel. 1881, 532. For the instructions of May 26, 1881, in the case of Boyton, above referred to, see For. Rel. 1881, 530.

Dennis H. O'Connor, a native of Ireland, was naturalized in the United States in 1875. Subsequently he returned to Ireland, and while engaged in business there was arrested under the "Peace Preservation Act." Replying to his appeal for the intervention of the United States, Mr. Blaine, who was then Secretary of State, said that Mr. Lowell, the American minister in London, had been instructed to scrutinize the cases arising under the statute in question, and to do whatever he could to bring about speedy inquiry and trials; that Mr. Lowell had pursued his instructions with great energy and sagacity, and that Mr. O'Connor's case must take the same course as the rest. Continuing, Mr. Blaine said that the act under which the arrests were made was " a law of Great Britain, and it is an elementary principle of public law that in such case the Government of that country, in the exercise of its varied functions, judicial and executive, administers and interprets the law in question. The right of every government in this respect is absolute and sovereign, and every person who voluntarily brings himself within the jurisdiction of the country, whether permanently or temporarily, is subject to the operation of its laws, whether he be a citizen or a mere resident, so long as in the case of the alien resident no treaty stipulation or principle of international law is contravened by the proceedings taken against him."

> Mr. Blaine, Sec. of State, to Mr. O'Connor, Nov. 25, 1881, 139 MS. Dom. Let. 663.
> See, also, For. Rel. 1882, 192–199, 200–241, 284–293.

"I am bound to say that our exertions have been met in a spirit of friendship by Her Majesty's Government; but it assumes as the basis of its action a principle to which the President cannot assent. In his note of the 6th April, to Mr. West, Lord Granville quotes with approval the following extract from a note of the 14th October, 1861, from Mr. Seward to Lord Lyons: ' In every case subjects of Her Majesty residing in the United States and under their protection are treated, during the present troubles, in the same manner and with no greater or less rigor than American citizens.' And he deduces from this the principle that ' no distinction can be made in favor of aliens,' or, as stated to yourself in a note of the 28th June last, that Her Majesty's Government would not admit ' any claim to exemption on behalf of any person, whether alien or citizen, from the operation of the laws which equally affect all persons residing in the domain and under the protection of the Crown.'

"Mr. Seward's statement was rather an allegation of a fact than the enunciation of a principle. But if it can be taken to be the statement of a principle as broad as Lord Granville now lays down, the President cannot but look upon it as an extreme position taken in the heat of conflict, to which the Government of neither Great Britain nor the United States can give adhesion in time of quiet and reflection. . . . He concedes to every sovereign power the right to prescribe its own code of crimes and its own mode of trying offenders, and if it shall choose to adopt a system which gives the citizen fewer guarantees against injustice than prevail in the United States he feels that he cannot complain if it is applied to citizens of the United States who are found where it prevails. But if, when thus applied, it works actual injustice; if it takes possession of an American citizen, and deprives him of his liberty without any allegation of offense; if it leaves him incarcerated without hope of trial or chance of release, it then becomes the duty of the President to inquire why this is done. Her Majesty's Government pursued that course during the civil war. They will see that a self-respecting government must do the same now. . . . The President is gratified to observe that the claim thus to hold American citizens is modified by the following language in Lord Granville's instruction of April 6th to Mr. West:

" ' The Irish government have in many instances released prisoners upon a reasonable belief that it could be done without risk to the public safety, and I need hardly say that Her Majesty's Government are not desirous of detaining unnecessarily in prison any person from whom no danger to the public peace is to be apprehended.

" ' They will therefore be prepared to consider the circumstances of any citizens of the United States now detained who may be willing to engage forthwith to leave the United Kingdom.'

"The President moreover his little doubt that Her Majesty's Government do not intend to insist in practice upon the extreme doctrine that an American citizen against whom there is no charge shall, without trial, remain in prison or leave the United Kingdom. But he believes, by fairly considering each case as it arises, conclusions will be reached satisfactory to both Governments."

> Mr. Frelinghuysen, Sec. of State, to Mr. Lowell, April 25, 1882, For. Rel. 1882, 230, 232–234.
>
> With regard to the prevention of crime (Ireland) act, which revived the alien act as part of the crimes act, Mr. Frelinghuysen observed that the President "cannot contemplate the enforcement of this measure on mere suspicion against American citizens without fears of its having an unhappy influence upon the good feeling" which existed between the two countries. (For. Rel. 1882, 294.)
>
> As to the right of a government to punish seditious acts committed by aliens, see Mr. Bayard, Sec. of State, to Mr. Jackson, min. to Mexico, Aug. 5, 1885, MS. Inst. Mexico, XXI. 355, citing the act of Congress of July 14, 1798, commonly called the sedition act.

In August, 1882, Mr. Henry George, during a visit to Great Britain and Ireland, and while on his way from Dublin to the west of Ireland, was arrested at Loughrea by the constabulary and taken to prison, where he was kept a close prisoner about three hours, his person and baggage searched, and his papers and letters examined. At length a magistrate arrived, who stated that Mr. George was arrested on telegraphic information as a suspicious stranger, and, as nothing suspicious was found upon his person or among his effects, he was discharged. Two days later, at Athenry, within the jurisdiction of the same magistrate, he was again by a subinspector of police placed under arrest, carried to the police barrack, and searched. He protested as before against his treatment, declaring his identity and citizenship and the nature of his journey as a traveler, and demanding to be taken before a magistrate. He was, however, detained from morning till nearly midnight, when he was discharged by the same magistrate, after again being subjected to a long examination. Mr. Frelinghuysen, in calling attention to the case, observed that the acts of the officials, especially the second arrest, seemed to indicate an intention on the part of the officials "to subject Mr. George to unnecessary personal annoyance." It was stated that Mr. George had visited the ruins of Athenry in company with the curate and another gentleman, and that he was seen to enter shops of "suspects;" but Mr. Frelinghuysen thought that his conduct was only such as was natural in a traveler seeking information and amusement, and such as could not fairly subject him to suspicion. Mr. Frelinghuysen added: "While citizens of the United States traveling or resident abroad are subject to the reasonable laws of the country in which they may be sojourning, it is nevertheless their right to be spared such indignity

and mortification as the conduct of the officers at Loughrea and
Athenry seems to have visited upon Mr. George.

"This Government is loath to believe that the current rumors are
true that the behavior of the officers and magistrate was prompted by
a prejudice said to exist among the officials in Ireland against citizens
of the United States.

"In Great Britain, as in the United States, it has been a governmental principle that the right of the individual to exemption from
arrest or search without good reason, and without the observance of
forms calculated to insure that right, should be jealously guarded,
and when unfortunate events have demanded a temporary suspension
or qualification of the right great care has been exerted to avoid
injustice or unnecessary indignity.

"The power given to subordinate officials by the ' prevention-of-
crime act ' is so great and the rights subjected to their discretion are
so important that foreign governments may reasonably require that
so far as their citizens, present in Ireland on legitimate and proper
business, are concerned, the individuals selected to administer that act
should be competent, well-informed, and unprejudiced. And should
it appear that these officials have in the case of such foreign citizens
misused the powers intrusted to them, they should be subjected to such
condemnatory action, and the citizens wronged should receive such
amends as the facts may warrant.

"The President regrets to observe that, so far as he has the facts
before him, the officials at Loughrea and Athenry seem to have fallen
far short of treating the rights of an innocent traveler with that
respect which he cannot doubt Her Majesty's Government exacts of
subordinate officials.

"It is not necessary now to comment upon the law under color of
which these arrests were made.

"As you have already addressed a note to Lord Granville on this
subject, a reply will probably soon be received by you. It is trusted
that the tenor of that reply may prove satisfactory to this Government and also relieve Mr. George from any reproach the arrests are
calculated unjustly to cast upon him. More definite instructions,
therefore, than those herein contained and those heretofore received
by you need not now be given."

> Mr. Frelinghuysen, Sec. of State, to Mr. Lowell, min. to England, Oct. 3,
> 1882, For. Rel. 1882, 296, 298. See, also, For. Rel. 1882, 289, 290, 293,
> 295, 296, 301; and For. Rel. 1885, 483–484.

"This Government has not claimed that citizens of the United
States, who place themselves in a foreign jurisdiction,
carry with them the particular immunities surrounding trials in their own country, nor has it insisted
that peculiar advantages to the accused, such as trial by jury and

Protocol with
Spain, 1877.

the *habeas corpus*, are or must be a part of the jurisprudence of foreign countries.

" But we have claimed that by international law, and by the usages and customs of civilized nations, a trial at law must be conducted without unseemly haste, with certain safeguards to the accused, and in deference to certain recognized rights, in order to mete out justice.

" It was for the purpose of securing to our citizens such well-known rights and privileges that article seven is found among the provisions of our treaty of 1795. . . .

" It certainly can not be said that an accused person has all the benefits of our treaty, where the defender appointed refused to read the defense provided, when the accused was not present at a considerable portion of the trial, and where no counsel was allowed or provided, in the proper sense of the term, as the military officer defending him practically admitted his culpability.

" Moreover, you can not fail to remember that the prisoners of the Virginius reached Santiago de Cuba in the evening of November 1; that the next morning at 9 o'clock a council of war was convened on board the Tornado; that its labors were completed at 4 o'clock in the afternoon; that the consular officer who demanded of General Burriel permission to advise with his countrymen was in a gross manner denied access to them; that the sentences were not confirmed, and the executions were hastened for fear that they would be stopped by superior authority. . . .

" In fine, if trial by military courts, as it has been practiced in Cuba, is to be continued, it is difficult to see how, in cases in which justice and moderation are most required, such form can supply the guarantees to which, in the opinion of this Government, our citizens are entitled, and the absence of which will and must cause frequent and dangerous differences."

> Mr. Fish, Sec. of State, to Mr. Cushing, min. to Spain, Dec. 27, 1875, MS. Inst. Spain, XVII. 396.
>
> As to the treaty with Spain of 1795, above referred to, see Moore, Int. Arbitrations, III. 2777, 3124, 3147; IV. 3252–3255.
>
> Art. XX. of the treaty with Spain of 1795 does not give either Government the right to interfere in the administration of the reasonable municipal laws of the other. (Mr. Frelinghuysen, Sec. of State, to Mr. Valera, Span. min., March 15, 1884, 10 MS. Notes to Spain, 291.)

January 12, 1877, a protocol was signed at Madrid by Mr. Cushing, United States minister, and Señor Calderon y Collantes, Spanish minister of state, for the purpose of terminating amicably all controversy as to the effect of existing treaties in certain matters of judicial procedure. In this protocol Señor Calderon y Collantes declared as follows:

1. No citizen of the United States residing in Spain, her adjacent islands, or her ultramarine possessions, charged with acts of sedition, treason or conspiracy against the institutions, the public security, the integrity of the territory or against the supreme Government, or any other crime whatsoever, shall be subject to trial by any exceptional tribunal, but exclusively by the ordinary jurisdiction, except in the case of being captured with arms in hand.

2. Those who, not coming within this last case, may be arrested or imprisoned, shall be deemed to have been so arrested or imprisoned by order of the civil authority for the effects of the law of April 17, 1821, even though the arrest or imprisonment shall have been effected by armed force.

3. Those who may be taken with arms in hand, and who are therefore comprehended in the exception of the first article, shall be tried by ordinary council of war, in conformity with the second article of the hereinbefore-mentioned law; but even in this case the accused shall enjoy for their defense the guarantees embodied in the aforesaid law of April 17, 1821.

4. In consequence whereof, as well in the cases mentioned in the third paragraph as in those of the second, the parties accused are allowed to name attorneys and advocates, who shall have access to them at suitable times; they shall be furnished in due season with copy of the accusation and a list of witnesses for the prosecution, which latter shall be examined before the presumed criminal, his attorney and advocate, in conformity with the provisions of articles twenty to thirty-one of the said law; they shall have right to compel the witnesses of whom they desire to avail themselves to appear and give testimony or to do it by means of depositions; they shall present such evidence as they may judge proper; and they shall be permitted to be present and to make their defense, in public trial, orally or in writing, by themselves or by means of their counsel.

5. The sentence pronounced shall be referred to the audiencia of the judicial district, or to the Captain-General, according as the trial may have taken place before the ordinary judge or before the council of war, in conformity also with what is prescribed in the above-mentioned law.

Mr. Cushing declared as follows:

1. The Constitution of the United States provides that the trial of all crimes except in cases of impeachment shall be by jury, and such trial shall be held in the State where said crimes shall have been committed, or when not committed within any State the trial will proceed in such place as Congress may direct (Art. III, § 2); that no person shall be held to answer for a capital or otherwise infamous crime unless on presentment of a grand jury except in cases arising in the land and naval forces or in the militia when in actual service, (Amendments to the Constitution, Art. V.); and that in all criminal prosecutions the accused shall enjoy the right to a speedy and public trial, by an impartial jury of the State and district wherein the crime shall have been committed, and to be informed of the nature and cause of the accusation; to be confronted with the witnesses against him; to have compulsory process for obtaining witnesses in his favor; and to have counsel for his defense (Amendments to the Constitution, Art. VI.).

2. The act of Congress of April 30, 1790, chap. 9, sec. 29, reenacted in the Revised Statutes, provides that every person accused of treason shall have a copy of the indictment and a list of the jury, and of the witnesses to be produced at the trial, delivered to him three days before the same, and in all other capital cases two days before that takes place; that in all such cases the accused shall be allowed to make his full defense by counsel learned in the law, who shall have free access

to him at all seasonable hours; that he shall be allowed in his defense to make any proof which he can produce by lawful witnesses, and he shall have due power to compel his witnesses to appear in court.

3. All these provisions of the Constitution and of Acts of Congress are of constant and permanent force, except on occasion of the temporary suspension of the writ of *habeas corpus.*

4. The provisions herein set forth apply in terms to all persons accused of the commission of treason or other capital crimes in the United States, and therefore, as well by the letter of the law as in virtue of existing treaties, the said provisions extend to and comprehend all Spaniards residing or being in the United States.

Señor Calderon y Collantes then declared as follows:

In view of the satisfactory adjustment of this question in a manner so proper for the preservation of the friendly relations between the respective Governments, and in order to afford to the Government of the United States the completest security of the sincerity and good faith of His Majesty's Government in the premises, command will be given by Royal Order for the strict observance of the terms of the present Protocol in all the dominions of Spain and specifically in the island of Cuba.

The protocol was duly " interchangeably signed " by the declarants.

> See United States Treaty Volume (1776–1887), 1030.
>
> Dr. Wharton, in his International Law Digest, declared that this protocol was " to be regarded as simply an opinion by the parties as to the state of the law in this relation in the United States and Spain. As to the United States it has not the force of a law."   (II. 623.)
>
> With reference to the constitutional and legal provisions recited by Mr. Cushing, see Hurtado *v.* California (1883), 110 U. S. 516.
>
> As to the controversy between the United States and Spain concerning judicial procedure, see Moore, Int. Arbitrations, II. 1019–1050.

(3) EXECUTION OF FOREIGN JUDGMENTS.

§ 188.

Bar, in discussing the effect to be given to foreign judgments, mentions, among the theories advanced for their recognition, (1) that the refusal of such recognition would imply an invasion of the jurisdiction of the foreign state; (2) that the sentence of a foreign judge gives rise to a *jus quæsitum;* (3) that a judgment is to be assimilated to a contract, and (4) that comity requires such recognition.   He himself propounds the theory that a judicial sentence is most accurately defined as a *lex specialis*, a law for the particular case which is in dispute, and that " if the law of a particular state rules some particular claim, then the judicial sentence pronounced in that state upon that claim must also be recognized as authoritative."

> Bar, Private Int. Law, 2d ed., Gillespie's translation, 1892, p. 895, citing Wharton, Confl. of Laws, § 671; v. Martens, § 82; Phillimore, § 937; Fiore, Effetti, pp. 11 and 73; Haus, Droit pub. n. 147; Olivi, Rev. gén. de droit, 1887, p. 521; Brocher, Traité Franco-Suisse, p. 6; Calvo, II. § 860.

Lachau, Charles, Project de Traité entre la France et l'Allemagne sur la Compétence judiciaire, sur l'autorité et l'exécution des décisions judiciairies, des sentences arbitrales et des actes authentiques; Paris, 1902. (Extrait du Bulletin de la Société de Législation Comparée, XXI. 328.)

In an early case in the United States it was held that a judgment of a court of the Province of New Brunswick was only *prima facie* evidence as between the parties to it; and a new trial was granted because the trial judge had refused to allow testimony to go to the jury impeaching the judgment for mistake and irregularity.[a] In later decisions, not only upon the ground of comity, but also upon the ground that the judgment of a court of competent jurisdiction should bind the parties to it, it is held that such a judgment was conclusive as to the merits of the controversy, unless it can be shown that the proceeding was tainted by fraud,[b] or unless the judgment affects a matter of local policy.[c] But it was held by the Supreme Court of the United States, June 3, 1895, in an opinion by Mr. Justice Gray (Fuller, C. J., and Harlan, Brewer, and Jackson, J. J., dissenting), that a judgment rendered in France was not conclusive as to the merits of the case, but was only prima facie evidence of the justice of the plaintiff's claim, such being the rule in France as to the effect of foreign judgments, the rule of reciprocity being thus applied.[d] On the same day the court sustained a Canadian judgment, which the defendant sought to attack on the ground that, although he had appeared in the action, he did not appear at the trial, and that the judgment was entered against him in his absence, without a full examination of the merits.[e]

As to judgments of divorce, see Dicey, Confl. of Laws, Am. Notes, 434; Atherton *v.* Atherton (1901), 181 U. S. 155; Bell *v.* Bell (1901), 181 U. S. 175; Streitwolf *v.* Streitwolf (1901), 181 U. S. 179.

As to foreign judgments as to movables, and foreign judgments in admiralty, see Dicey, Confl. of Laws, Am. Notes, 434.

See, generally, as to the effect of foreign judgments, Dicey, Confl. of Laws, 400 et seq.; Minor, Confl. of Laws, 186 et seq.

---

[a] Burnham *v.* Webster, 1 Wood. & M. 172.

[b] McMullen *v.* Ritchie, 41 Fed. Rep. 502; Lazier *v.* Wescott, 26 N. Y. 146; Dunstan *v.* Higgins, 138 N. Y. 70; Rankin *v.* Goddard, 54 Me. 28, 55 Me. 389; Baker *v.* Palmer, 83 Ill. 568; Roth *v.* Roth, 104 Ill. 35, 44 Am. Rep. 81; Hilton *v.* Guyot, 42 Fed. Rep. 249.

[c] Hohner *v.* Gratz, 50 Fed. Rep. 369; De Brimont *v.* Penniman, 10 Blatch. C. C. 436.

[d] Hilton *v.* Guyot, 159 U. S. 113, reversing Hilton *v.* Guyot, 42 Fed. Rep. 249

[e] Ritchie *v.* McMullen, 159 U. S. 235.

(4) LETTERS ROGATORY.

§ 189.

" Letters rogatory for the purpose of taking the testimony of persons residing in the United States, which may be material in suits pending in the courts of foreign countries, are frequently sent to this Department, usually with a note from the minister for foreign affairs of the foreign country or from its diplomatic representative here, requesting that the business may be attended to. It is not, however, the province of the Department of State to dispose of matters of this kind. Frequently witnesses whose testimony is sought reside in places far from this city, rendering it impracticable to have the testimony taken within the time at which it is required in order to make it available.

Law in United States: Civil cases.

" It is, therefore, deemed advisable to issue this circular, to which are appended the provisions of the Revised Statutes of the United States regulating the taking of testimony in such cases. Other information upon the subject, which will be found useful to persons interested, is contained in the following

" *Directions.*—Both circuit and district courts of the United States are held in each of the States at the following points:

In Alabama, at Huntsville, Birmingham, Montgomery, and Mobile; in Arkansas, at Little Rock; in California, at San Francisco and Los Angeles; in Colorado, at Denver, Pueblo, and Del Norte; in Connecticut, at New Haven and Hartford; in Delaware, at Wilmington; in Florida, at Tallahassee, Pensacola, Jacksonville, Key West, and Tampa; in Georgia, at Atlanta, Savannah, and Macon; in Illinois, at Chicago, Springfield, and Cairo; in Indiana, at New Albany, Evansville, Indianapolis, and Fort Wayne; in Iowa, at Dubuque, Fort Dodge, Sioux City, Keokuk, Council Bluffs, and Des Moines; in Kansas, at Fort Scott, Leavenworth, and Topeka; in Kentucky, at Frankfort, Covington, Louisville, and Paducah; in Louisiana, at New Orleans, Opelousas, Alexandria, Shreveport, and Monroe; in Maine, at Portland; in Maryland, at Baltimore; in Massachusetts, at Boston; in Michigan, at Port Huron, Detroit, Grand Rapids, and Marquette; in Minnesota, at St. Paul; in Mississippi, at Aberdeen, Oxford, and Jackson; in Missouri, at St. Louis, Jefferson City, and Kansas City; in Nebraska, at Lincoln and Omaha; in Nevada, at Carson City; in New Hampshire, at Portsmouth and Concord; in New Jersey, at Trenton; in New York, at Canandaigua, Albany, Syracuse, Utica, New York, and Brooklyn; in North Carolina, at Raleigh, Greensborough, Statesville, Asheville, and Charlotte; in Ohio, at Cleveland, Toledo, Cincinnati, and Columbus; in Oregon, at Portland; in Pennsylvania, at Philadelphia, Erie, Pittsburgh, Williamsport, and Scranton; in Rhode Island, at Newport and Providence; in South Carolina, at Charleston and Columbia; in Tennessee, at Knoxville, Chattanooga, Nashville, Jackson, and Memphis; in Texas, at Graham, Dallas, Waco, Galveston, Tyler, Jefferson, Austin, San Antonio, Brownsville, and El Paso; in Vermont, at Burlington, Windsor, and Rutland; in Virginia, at Richmond, Alexandria, Norfolk, Lynchburgh, Abingdon, Harrisonburgh, and Danville; in West Virginia, circuit court at Parkersburgh, district court at Wheeling, Clarksburgh, and Charleston; in Wisconsin, at Milwaukee, Oshkosh, Madison, Eau Claire, and La Crosse.

" In some of the States district courts are held at other points in addition to those above specified.

" The clerks of the courts of the United States are authorized to take depositions, and may be designated as commissioners for that purpose in letters rogatory, which, when returned, are to be used in the courts of foreign countries.

" The letters rogatory may be addressed to the judge of either the circuit court of the United States for the State of ———, or the district court of the United States for the district of ——— (naming the State), praying the judge of that court to name and appoint the commissioner; or such letters may be addressed to the commissioner directly.

" The letter or package should in all cases be directed to the clerk of the district or circuit court to which the letters rogatory are addressed.　The clerk's office is at the place where the court holds its sessions."

Mr. Bayard, Sec. of State, to the dip. and cons. officers of the U. S., Circular No. 21, revised, March 25, 1887, For. Rel. 1888, I. 521.

Sections of the Revised Statutes relating to letters rogatory.

Sec. 4071. The testimony of any witness residing within the United States, to be used in any suit for the recovery of money or property depending in any court in any foreign country with which the United States are at peace, and in which the government of such foreign country shall be a party or shall have an interest, may be obtained, to be used in such suit.　If a commission or letters rogatory to take such testimony, together with specific written interrogatories, accompanying the same, and addressed to such witness, shall have been issued from the court in which such suit is pending, on producing the same before the district judge of any district where the witness resides or shall be found, and on due proof being made to such judge that the testimony of any witness is material to the party desiring the same, such judge shall issue a summons to such witness requiring him to appear before the officer or commissioner named in such commission or letters rogatory, to testify in such suit. And no witness shall be compelled to appear or to testify under this section except for the purpose of answering such interrogatories so issued and accompanying such commission or letters: *Provided*, That when counsel for all the parties attend the examination they may consent that questions in addition to those accompanying the commission or letters rogatory may be put to the witness, unless the commission or letters rogatory exclude such additional interrogatories.　The summons shall specify the time and place at which the witness is required to attend, which place shall be within one hundred miles of the place where the witness resides or shall be served with such summons.

Sec. 4072. No witness shall be required, on such examination or any other under letters rogatory, to make any disclosure or discovery which shall tend to criminate him either under the laws of the State or Territory within which such examination as is had, or any other, or any foreign state.

Sec. 4073. If any person shall refuse or neglect to appear at the time and place mentioned in the summons issued, in accordance with section forty hundred and seventy-one, or if upon his appearance he shall refuse to testify, he shall be liable to the same penalties as would be incurred for a like offense on the trial of a suit in the district court of the United States.

SEC. 4074. Every witness who shall so appear and testify shall be allowed, and shall receive from the party at whose instance he shall have been summoned the same fees and mileage as are allowed to witnesses in suits depending in the district courts of the United States.

SEC. 875. When any commission or letter rogatory, issued to take the testimony of any witness in a foreign country, in any suit in which the United States are parties or have an interest, is executed by the court or the commissioner to whom it is directed, it shall be returned by such court or commissioner to the minister or consul of the United States nearest the place where it is executed. On receiving the same, the said minister or consul shall indorse thereon a certificate, stating when and where the same was received, and that the said deposition is in the same condition as when he received it; and he shall thereupon transmit the said letter or commission, so executed and certified, by mail, to the clerk of the court from which the same issued, in the manner in which his official dispatches are transmitted to the Government. And the testimony of witnesses so taken and returned shall be read as evidence on the trial of the suit in which it was taken, without objection as to the method of returning the same. [When letters rogatory are addressed from any court of a foreign country to any circuit court of the United States, a commissioner of such circuit court designated by said court to make the examination of the witnesses mentioned in said letters, shall have power to compel the witnesses to appear and depose in the same manner as witnesses may be compelled to appear and testify in courts.]

In a dispatch to Mr. Blaine, of Oct. 9, 1889, Mr. Lincoln, United States minister at London, made, in regard to the foregoing circular, the following suggestions (H. Ex. Doc. 281, 51 Cong. 2 sess. 18):

" I have the honor to suggest a reconsideration of the terms of the above-mentioned circular of March 25, 1887, giving directions for the information of those desiring to procure the issuance of letters rogatory to obtain the testimony of persons residing in the United States to be used in suits pending in the courts of foreign countries.

" Whether or not it is required by section 4071 of the Revised Statutes that such letters shall be addressed to the district court of a named district, it would seem that if such letters invoke the aid of a circuit court, it is contemplated by section 875 that they should be addressed to the circuit court of a named circuit, and the directions of the circular suggests the designation of the court by the name of its circuit or district, as the case may be. I beg to point out that those directions give a form of address which, as to eighteen States, would describe no court known under our laws. For example, under the circular, letters to obtain the testimony of a witness residing in Chicago would be moved from a foreign court addressed ' to the judge of the circuit (or district) court of the United States for the State (or district) of Illinois,' although there is actually no court bearing either of those titles. In such a case, at the present time, the letters should be addressed to the judge of the circuit (or district) court of the United States for the northern district of Illinois, in order that the execution of the commission might, upon its return to the foreign court, appear by the seal of the United States court to have been executed under the jurisdiction of the court to which it was directed.

" By reason of the frequency of statutory changes of the territorial limits of the Federal judicial districts, no circular could for more than a short time be safely used without examination as to subsequent legislation, and I think no such circular would be of practical use at any time which did not contain a reprint of chapter 1 of Title XIII of the Revised Statutes (second edition) corrected to show legislative changes made since the Forty-fourth Congress, so that upon the county of residence of the proposed witness being given, the judicial district including it may be found by using, in the case of States having more than one district, a map showing counties. Neither such maps nor our latest statutes are easily found abroad, unless at our legations, and if they were, in the nature of the case, they could hardly be used by a foreigner in connection with a circular, with the feeling of certainty important to the matter in hand.

"The information as to the territorial limits of the Federal judicial districts, which I have suggested as being essential in a useful circular, is already compiled in an American publication, ' Desty's Federal Procedure,' a late edition of which is easily to be had. With that book and the maps and the latest volume of statutes now in the library of this legation, any inquiry made here as to the proper address for letters rogatory in respect to a witness whose postal address in the United States is given could be answered at the legation with little trouble."

The circular of March 5, 1887, and particularly the sections of the Revised Statutes accompanying it, are referred to in Mr. Sherman, Sec. of State, to Mr. Grip, Swedish min., Jan. 21, 1898, MS. Notes to Swedish Leg. VIII. 77; Mr. Adee, Acting Sec. of State, to Señor Pulido, Venez. min., Aug. 21, 1900, MS. Notes to Venez. Leg. II. 49.

" I have the honor to acknowledge the receipt of your note of the 8th instant, accompanied by five Rogatory Commissions addressed by the Civil Tribunal of Valparaiso to the Probate Court of San Francisco, California.

" You request that this Department will take the proper course with these commissions and that, when executed, they may be forwarded to your legation.

" In reply I have the honor to inform you that the commissions will be sent to the attorney of the United States at San Francisco with a letter requesting him to attend to them. As much time would be saved by their sending them directly to Chile, he will also be requested to forward them thither through the United States consulate at Valparaiso.

" It seems, however, expedient that I should take this opportunity to correct an impression which your Government seems to entertain that it is proper and usual for the Executive Government of the United States to receive and cause to have executed Rogatory Commissions from courts of justice in foreign countries. No such duty or authority is by law imposed upon or granted to the Executive Government of this country. Heretofore, as a matter of courtesy, this Department has in some instances, through United States attorneys, caused commissions rogatory to be executed. As this, however, is an irregular proceeding, it is preferred that in future the agency of this Department in the matter be dispensed with, and that courts of justice in foreign countries who may have occasion to have testimony taken here, will pursue the course prescribed by law and usage in such cases."

Mr. Seward, Sec. of State, to Mr. Fontecilla, Chilean min., Oct. 12, 1868, MS. Notes to Chilean Leg. VI. 169.

See, also, Mr. Seward, Sec. of State, to Mr. Gana, March 16, 1867, MS. Notes to Chilean Leg. VI. 153 ; Mr. Fish, Sec. of State, to Mr. Stetson, Nov. 15, 1872, 96 MS. Dom. Let. 300.

" Sections 871 and 874 [Revised Statutes] authorize any Justice of the Supreme Court of the District of Columbia upon the production before him of a commission issued from a foreign Court, or a notice to the same effect according to its rules of practice, to require, under certain conditions the attendance of any witness so named, for the purpose of giving his testimony. Section 875 empowers any of the Circuit Courts of the United States, upon receipt of letters rogatory from any Court of a foreign Country, to designate one of its Commissioners to make the examination mentioned in the letters and requires the attendance of the necessary witnesses in the same manner, as when summoned to the Courts. This system of legislation would seem to afford ample facilities so far as the Government of the United States is concerned, for securing the testimony of any witness residing within its territory where the Courts of a friendly Government signify its wishes in that direction.

"As to the special legislation which the several states of this country may have adopted upon the subject, I am unable to assure you, at present, of an uniform system. In some of them, the pains of perjury are affixed to false responses in proceedings to obtain testimony upon commissions or letters rogatory from foreign Courts, and I apprehend, where no positive enactments exist the State Courts would be found as far as in their power, ever ready to heed and further an application to them of the character specified. At all events the Revised Statutes to which I have referred, would seem in this particular, to offer so extensive methods, as to be equally available independently of state laws throughout the various local governments of this country."

Mr. Frelinghuysen, Sec. of State, to Baron von Schaeffer, Aust. min., March 29, 1883, MS. Notes to Austria, VIII. 384.

As to letters rogatory from abroad to take the testimony of persons in prison in the United States, see Mr. Frelinghuysen, Sec. of State, to Mr. Sargent, min. to Germany, June 27, 1883, MS. Inst. Germany, XVII. 280.

" I have the honor to say that the laws of the State of New York, in regard to letters rogatory, require the letters to be presented to the court, having jurisdiction, by the consul of the Government making the request, and it would, therefore, be necessary for the

Belgian consul at New York, as was pointed out in my note of August 18 last, to take the action required."

> Mr. Uhl, Acting Sec. of State, to Mr. Le Ghait, Belg. min., Feb. 17, 1894, MS. Notes to Belg. Leg. VIII. 28.
>
> To the same effect, Mr. Olney, Sec. of State, to Mr. Andrade, Venezuelan min., Dec. 9, 1895, MS. Notes to Venez. I. 543.

" Referring to your note of June 21st last, in which you ask the intervention of the Department to secure the execution of certain letters rogatory addressed by the senior judge of the Queen's bench division of the high court of justice in England, to the President and judges of the supreme court for the city and county of New York; also to subsequent correspondence on the same subject; I have the honor to inform you that his excellency the governor of New York, in response to my letter requesting information as to what proceedings were necessary to secure the taking of the testimony desired, has transmitted to me a copy of a letter from the presiding justice of the first department of the supreme court at New York City, to whom the matter was referred by the governor. The justice expresses the opinion that the court would have no power to act upon *letters* from the senior judge of the English court, and he doubts the power of the New York court to appoint a commissioner even if a *commission* should be issued attempting to confer that power. He states that the usual practice in such cases is for a *commission* to issue from the *foreign court* in which the testimony is to be used, *under its seal, appointing a commissioner* in this country to take the testimony of the witness. Then our court would have the power to issue a subpœna and compel attendance of the witness. The letters rogatory are returned herewith in order that a new commission may be issued in accordance with the above."

> Mr. Gresham, Sec. of State, to Sir J. Pauncefote, Brit. amb., Aug. 22, 1894, MS. Notes to Great Britain, XXII. 602.

The circuit court will issue letters rogatory for the purpose of obtaining testimony when the Government of the place where the evidence is to be obtained will not permit a commission to be executed.

> Nelson *v.* United States, 1 Pet. C. C. 235. In this case a form of such letters is given.
>
> See also Mexico *v.* De Arangoiz, 5 Duer, 634; Kuehling *v.* Leberman, 9 Phila. 160.

The certificate and seal of the British minister resident in Hanover is not a proper authentication of the proceedings of an officer of that country in taking depositions. It is not in any way connected with the functions of the minister, and his certificate and seal can only authenticate those acts which are appropriate to his office.

> Stein *v.* Bowman, 13 Pet. 209.

A court in Porto Rico issued, on April 16, 1900, an *exhorto*, or letter rogatory, requesting the proper judge, tribunal, or court in the city of New York to cooperate in serving upon two persons living in that city an order to appear as defendants in a suit instituted against them in the Porto Rican tribunal. The papers were accompanied with copies of the complaint in the case, which related to an easement affecting a house in San Juan, Porto Rico. The documents were transmitted to the War Department at Washington by the military authorities of the United States in Porto Rico " for the necessary diplomatic action." The Attorney-General, to whom the matter was referred, advised that there was nothing in the statutes of the United States or of the State of New York which invested either the Federal courts or State courts with jurisdiction to make such an order as was desired.

> Griggs, At.-Gen., May 7, 1900, 23 Op. 112.

A commission was issued by a judge in Cuba to the Spanish consul in New York to take testimony to be used in a criminal prosecution for swindling, and the consul thereupon applied to the district court for a summons to compel the witness to appear and testify. It was ruled that the court had no power to issue the summons asked for, the only provisions made by Congress on the subject of enforcing the giving of testimony in judicial proceedings pending in a foreign country being those found in the acts of 2 March, 1855 (10 Stat., 630), and of 3 March, 1863 (12 Stat., 769; Rev. Stat., 4071), neither of which acts applies to the case proposed.

Criminal cases.

> Matter of the Spanish Consul, 1 Benedict, 225.

"As the letters rogatory which accompany your note contemplate the taking of testimony to be used in a criminal prosecution in Switzerland, it is proper that I should call your attention to the fact that it has been judicially decided that the [Federal] courts have only the power to take testimony to be used in suits for the recovery of money or property as is provided in sec. 1 of the act of March 3, 1863, relating to letters rogatory."

> Mr. Bayard, Sec. of State, to Colonel Frey, Swiss min., March 13, 1888, MS. Notes to Switzerland, I. 180.
> To the same effect, Mr. Adee, Act. Sec. of State, to Baron Fava, Ital. amb., tel., Aug. 13, 1900, MS. Notes to Ital. Leg. IX. 467; and Mr. Gresham, Sec. of State, to Dr. von Holleben, German amb., July 8, 1893, MS. Notes to Germany, XI. 243.

" I have the honor to acknowledge your communication of June 26, transmitting to me a letter from the Secretary of State at Washington, enclosing a note from the minister of Germany and letters rogatory issued by the royal Prussian district court at Konitz, for the purpose of securing the testimony of Theresia Saydack, to be used in the criminal prosecution of Michael Zimmel. Referring to this and to your request that I should advise you upon the matters contained therein, I beg to say: The Pennsylvania statute of April 8, 1833, (P. L. 308—1 Purdon's Digest, page 725, sections 6, 7, 8 and 9), provides that:—

" In all cases where letters rogatory shall be issued out of any court of any one of the several States composing the United States, or out of any court of any Territory of the said United States, requesting any court of common pleas in this Commonwealth, to afford its aid in the examination of any witness or witnesses within the limits of the jurisdiction of such court of common pleas, it shall be competent for such court of common pleas to issue *subpœnas* to such witnesses as may be required by any party concerned, requiring their attendance either before such court of common pleas, or before a commissioner or commissioners, to be by said court of common pleas named, at a certain hour and place therein designated, having regard to the distance of such witness or witnesses, and under a penalty not exceeding one hundred dollars.

" In case of the nonattendance of any such witness or witnesses, it shall and may be lawful for such court of common pleas, on due proof of the service of the *subpœna*, to issue process of attachment against the defaulting witness or witnesses, and thereupon the same proceedings shall be had as are used and allowed in like cases in the courts of record in this Commonwealth.

"Any party injured by such nonattendance shall also be entitled to the same remedies at law, against the person subpœnaed, as are provided where a *subpœna* is issued from a court of record of this Commonwealth, in a cause pending therein.

" If any person subpœnaed under this act shall attend, but refuse to testify, he or she shall be subject and liable to the same proceedings on the part of the said courts of common pleas, as if he or she had refused to testify in a cause pending in any court of record of this Commonwealth.

" It has been held in our State (McKenzie's case, 2 Parsons, 227) that the court will not inquire whether the letters rogatory are issued according to law and the practice of the court from whence they purport to come, and that when letters rogatory are regularly issued, the court will compel the witnesses to testify, and will not examine into the relevancy of the testimony.

" It has also been held in the courts of common pleas of this State, in an opinion rendered by one of the most learned of its judges (Kuehling et al. *v.* Leberman, 9 Phila. 160), ' that there is a very broad distinction between the execution of a commission and the procuring of testimony by the instrumentality of letters rogatory, or letters requisatory, as they are sometimes called. In the former case the rules of procedure are established by the court issuing the commission, and are entirely under its control. In the latter, the methods of procedure must, from the nature of the case, be altogether under the control of the foreign tribunal which is appealed to for assistance in the administration of justice. We can not execute our own laws in a foreign country, nor can we prescribe conditions for the performance of a request which is based entirely upon the comity of nations, and which, if granted, is altogether *ex gratia*.' 'We can not dictate the methods to be pursued by the court whose assistance is invoked. The rules and practice of the foreign court must be the law of procedure in such cases.'

" It seems, therefore, that the statute of 1833, to which reference has been made, is extended to the case of letters rogatory from a foreign tribunal, and that in such cases the courts of common pleas in Pennsylvania will receive them in civil cases and enforce them according to their own prescribed methods of procedure and by their proper and usual processes. It nowhere appears, however, that this statute contemplated the taking of evidence in this way for criminal cases, nor under the direction and by the process of our courts of quarter sessions and oyer and terminer, organized for criminal jurisdiction. The taking of testimony by deposition for criminal cases is unknown to our system of jurisprudence, and section 9 of Article I. of the Declaration of Rights in our Constitution provides that in all criminal prosecutions the accused hath the right to meet the witnesses face to face.

" I am, therefore, of the opinion that the courts of this Commonwealth are not competent to receive these letters rogatory and to enforce the testimony of this witness by deposition or answers to interrogatories, to be used in the criminal cause. I therefore advise you to return them to the honorable the Secretary of State, with this opinion."

Opinion of Mr. Hensel, Attorney-General, to Governor Pattison, of Pennsylvania, June 30, 1893, transmitted by Governor Pattison to the Secretary of State of the United States, July 1, 1893, MS. Misc. Letters; communicated by Mr. Gresham, Sec. of State, to Dr. Von Holleben, German amb., July 8, 1893, MS. Notes to Germany, XI. 243.

" I have the honor to acknowledge the receipt of your note of the 19th ultimo, enclosing letters rogatory of the examining judge of Antwerp in the case of George Bunn, charged with murder, for execution at New York City, Utica, New York, and Hartford, Connecticut.

" I have to say in reply that the execution of letters rogatory is not, except in certain cases, regulated by act of Congress, and does not come within the province of this Department. In many of the States the subject is regulated by local statutes, by which it is provided that such letters are to be presented to the proper court through the consul of the Government making the request. In fact, in a case in which the Department, deviating from its usual course, undertook to secure the execution of letters rogatory by communicating them to the governor of New York, in order that they might be presented to the proper judicial authority, they were returned with the statement that they would have to be presented in accordance with the provisions of the statute, and the Department was thus unable to secure their execution."

> Mr. Gresham, Sec. of State, to Mr. Le Ghait, Belg. min. Aug. 18, 1893, MS. Notes to Belg. Leg. VIII. 1.
>
> The laws of the State of New York require letters rogatory to be presented to the court by the consul of the Government making the request for their execution. (Mr. Uhl, Acting Sec. of State, to Mr. Le Ghait, Belg. min. Feb. 17, 1894, MS. Notes to Belg. Leg. VIII. 28; Mr. Olney, Sec. of State, to Mr. Andrade, Venez. min. Dec. 9, 1895, MS. Notes to Venez. I. 543.)

September 18, 1889, Mr. Blaine, Secretary of State, addressed to the diplomatic and consular officers of the United States an instruction, enclosing copies of the circular of March 25, 1887, and directed them, while bearing in mind the fact that applications for the execution of letters rogatory in the United States were not made through the diplomatic channel, to report upon the method or methods by which such letters might be executed in the countries in which they respectively resided.[a]

Law in foreign countries: Austria and Hungary.

Responding to this instruction, Mr. Grant, minister to Austria-Hungary, February 10, 1890, enclosed a copy of a note from M. Pasetti of January 17, 1890, with reference to the practice in Austria.[b] The statement of M. Pasetti was as follows:

Aside from the rules governing the execution of judgments given by civil courts of justice in foreign countries there are no laws in the kingdoms and countries represented in the Reichsrath by which aid can be secured on requisition made by foreign countries.

Austrian courts of justice, nevertheless, invariably dispose of matters of this kind by granting their intervention for the purpose of giving testimony and other judicial proceedings, on condition of reciprocity; and in case the foreign authorities especially desire it the formalities of taking testimony, as sanctioned by the laws of the country in which the suit is pending, will be strictly observed.

The laws referring to executions of judgments given by foreign courts will be found in the following decrees: No. 16, of May 18, 1792; No. 452, of January 18, 1799; No. 711, of February 15, 1805; No. 159, of June 24, 1860, and finally in paragraph 70 of the imperial patent No. 251, of November 20, 1852.

The ministry of justice, not understanding from the contents of the above-mentioned esteemed note that it was desired to learn the principles applied to this branch of international law, has omitted to dwell at length on the provisions in question.

---

[a] H. Ex. Doc. 281, 51 Cong. 2 sess. 2.
[b] H. Ex. Doc. 281, 51 Cong. 2 sess. 5.

With the same dispatch Mr. Grant enclosed another note from M. Pasetti of February 1, 1890, in relation to the practice in Hungary. In this note M. Pasetti said:

The question of letters rogatory or commission of a foreign court, including those of the United States, to take testimony in Hungary, is regulated by paragraphs 61 to 63 of Article LIV. of the law of 1868, and paragraphs 3, 5, and 20 of Article LX. of the law of 1881.

The practical appliance of the above-mentioned paragraphs of Article LIX. of 1868, on requisitions coming from the courts of the United States, touching the taking of testimony of experts, as well as the taking of oaths, is not subject to any special formality, and it suffices that a requisition is made, through the diplomatic channel, accompanied by a Hungarian translation.

According to Article LX. of the law of 1881, touching execution, such requisitions on the part of United States courts can not be executed in Hungary because no reciprocity exists between the two countries.

The sections of the Hungarian law referred to by M. Pasetti were as follows:

Section 61, of Article LIV., of the law of 1868 : " Official letters rogatory which are to be executed outside of the country, in other countries and provinces of His Majesty, or in other foreign states with which reciprocity exists, are addressed directly to the proper court, or to the authorities and organs designated in the treaty. In default of such reciprocity, application is made indirectly to the courts of foreign states through the Royal Hungarian Ministry of Justice."

Section 62, of Article LIV., of the law of 1868 : " Hungarian courts must act in accordance with these principles, when application is made to them by a foreign court to execute letters rogatory. The procedure, however, is also conducted when foreigners or foreign courts are concerned, according to the provisions of the present regulations concerning judicial practice."

Section 63, of Article LIV., of the law of 1868 : " Evidence of the existence of reciprocity with a foreign state must be furnished, in case of doubt, by the party in whose interest the application is made. With regard to His Majesty's other countries and provinces, such evidence is not necessary.

Section 3, of Article LX., of the law of 1881 : " When execution is ordered in compliance with the requisitions of foreign courts, or on the ground of their executable public documents [records?] having a clause of execution, the existing treaties are to be taken as the principal guide."

If there is no treaty, the order for execution is to be issued only in case of reciprocity, to be granted by the country of the court making the request [section 63 of Article LIV. of the law of 1868] and then only in the following instances :

(a) When a judicial decision that has acquired force of law, or an arrangement made before the court by which the case is to be tried, is taken as the basis of the execution.

(b) When the summonses have been delivered personally, in the country in which the soliciting court is situated, to the Hungarian witnesses whose depositions are wanted, and who have failed to appear, or when the said summonses have [been] served upon such witnesses in due form, in pursuance of a requisition by a Hungarian court.

(c) When in accordance with the provisions of this law, which define the competence of the court, any court of the state in whose territory the decision to be executed was pronounced, or the arrangement to be executed was concluded, was competent ; and, finally, (*d*) When the thing to be secured by the execution does not conflict with any Hungarian law.

In these cases that court which, according to section 18, is competent to grant the requests contained in letters rogatory shall decide concerning the ordering of the execution.

When application is made to several courts for the execution of letters rogatory, the court first named in the requisition decides concerning the ordering of the execution, and when application is made to district courts only the district court first named so decides and notifies the other competent courts of its decision.

Requisitions addressed to incompetent courts are to be transmitted to those which are competent.

Section 5 of Article LX. of the law of 1881: " In questions concerning the personal status of a Hungarian subject, decisions of foreign courts against a Hungarian subject can not be executed in Hungary."

Section 20 of Article LX. of the law of 1881: " The court instructed to execute letters rogatory is obliged to do so *ex officio* only when, in the order directing that the execution take place, the execution is declared to be executable *ex officio;* [and] provided that the applicant for the execution, or his attorney, has not given notice in writing to such court of his withdrawal of his application, or of the suspension of the execution before it has taken place. In the cases in sections 3 and 4 the execution is to take place *ex officio* unless the contrary is clearly stated in the requisition or in the application."

If the execution is not to take place on the spot, the executing court may require payment of the costs in advance. When such requirement is made, due notice thereof shall be given.

A report on the law in Belgium was made by Mr. Terrell, United States minister at Brussels. October 17, 1889. His report was as follows: [a]

Belgium.

" Commissions of this character are brought to the attention of the Belgian Government through the diplomatic channel, and their execution is regulated entirely under the authority of the minister of justice by virtue of article 139 of the law of June 18, 1869. It seems under the Belgian law that the diplomatic channel should be used as constituting a sufficient guaranty of the authenticity of the documents relating to the matter. (See circular letter of the minister of justice, November 20, 1878.) In most of the extradition treaties between Belgium and foreign countries there is a clause especially providing that commissions rogatory, deemed necessary in the penal proceeding, shall be sent through the diplomatic channel.

" Under the general law of March 15, 1874, regulating extradition, it is expressly provided that commissions rogatory, issued by competent foreign authority, leading to domiciliary visits or the seizure of the substance of the offense or of matters of circumstantial evidence, can be executed only when they bear upon such offenses as are enumerated under that law.

---

a H. Ex. Doc. 281, 51 Cong. 2 sess. 7.

" In practice the execution of letters rogatory is in charge of the public prosecutor, acting under the minister of justice, as well in civil as in repressive matters.

" The expenses connected with the execution of rogatory commissions in repressive matters are borne by the Treasury; in civil and commercial matters reimbursement is claimed from the foreign government within the limits fixed by a circular of the minister of justice issued May 14, 1888.

" In this circular it is provided that acts performed on demand of the public prosecutor, and having for an object the execution of commissions rogatory emanating from a foreign tribunal, can be written on unstamped paper, registered free, and are moreover to be exempt from all rights of the clerk's record office.

" The circular above referred to further traces for the Belgian magistrates the course to be pursued in such matters as follows:

" ' The public prosecutor will demand directly of the several jurisdictions, civil and commercial, the execution of rogatory commissions, which are addressed to them through the intermediary of the Department of Justice, without one being obliged hereafter to have recourse to the agency of attorneys or barristers, unless these have been specially designated by the parties to the cause. The witnesses to be heard will be cited upon simple invitation either of the prosecutor or of the judge delegated, and it is only in case they refuse to appear voluntarily that they will be summoned through a sheriff.

" ' The sole expense that can be reclaimed will be the cost of translating the rogatory commission, the cost of experts and interpreters, and such expenses as result from citations made through the sheriff and from the fees allowed witnesses.'

" I beg to say further that Belgian tribunals are not allowed to execute commissions rogatory, issued by foreign authority, relating to political facts. Most of the extradition treaties made between Belgium and foreign countries contain a provision to this effect. There are also some special features in some of these treaties, regulating minor details in the execution of letters rogatory, to which I do not deem a more particular reference necessary.

" What I have given in this report is the general Belgian law applicable where no treaty has made special provisions."

A report on the law of Brazil was made by Mr. Adams, United States minister, November 15, 1889.[a] He enclosed a note of the Brazilian ministry of foreign affairs of November 6, 1889, which was accompanied with a circular dated November 14, 1865. With reference to this circular, the ministry of

Brazil.

---

[a] H. Ex. Doc. 281, 51 Cong. 2 sess. 8. See, as to letters rogatory from a United States court to a Brazilian court, Mr. Cadwalader, Assist. Sec. of State, to Mr. Partridge, min. to Brazil, Aug. 13, 1875, MS. Inst. Brazil, XVII. 18.

foreign affairs said: " Rogatory letters should be presented in a dip-lomatic way through this ministry, where the party interested must pay the stamp and fees for issuing the papers and for the consular firm, otherwise naming a power of attorney to some one to prepare the necessary papers and pay also judicial costs of the court where the residence of the person called to testify or sued may be or where the cause requested is to be judged."

The circular of November 14, 1865, which was issued by the min-istry of justice, directed to the presidents of the various provinces, was as follows:

Rogatory letters.

MINISTRY OF JUSTICE,
Rio de Janeiro, November 14, 1865.

[Circular.]

SIR: His Majesty the Emperor, in view of the necessity of facilitating inter-national relations as well as attending to the principles and usages observed by the greater part of enlightened nations in reference to the rogatory letters or commissions issued by foreign courts, is pleased, without in any way abol-ishing the principles and clauses of the aviso of October 1, 1847, to declare it as follows:

First. That the provisions of the above said aviso from equality of reasons are applicable to all nations.

Second. That the civil proceedings which, according to the aviso of April 29, 1849, the authorities of the Empire may obey independently of the placet of this ministry are not only the summons and judicial inquiries expressly mentioned in the above said aviso of October 1, 1847, but also, and for the same reason, the inspections and examinations of books, valuations, interrogatories, oaths, exhibition of documents and books, the copying, the verifying or delivery of documents, and all other proceedings that are important for the decision of suits at law.

JOSÉ THOMAZ NABUCO DE ARAUJO.

To the President of the Province of ———.

Aviso to which the preceding circular refers.

No. 95. Justice. Aviso of 20th April, 1849.

To the president of the Province of Pernambuco, on sending him a rogatory letter, issued at Lisbon, to be executed by the judge of orphans in accord-ance with the aviso of October 1, 1847, sent to the chief judge of the supreme court at Rio de Janeiro.

MINISTRY OF JUSTICE,
Rio de Janeiro, April 20, 1849.

SIR: His Majesty the Emperor orders me to send you the inclosed rogatory letter, issued at Lisbon, in favor of Anna Joaquina de Miranda e Brito, in order that you may give the necessary orders to the judge of orphans of that capital to have it executed in accordance with the aviso of October 1, 1847, which was sent to the chief justice of the supreme court of this city, a copy of which is herewith inclosed; it is likewise understood that you will hereafter see that the authorities of that province obey rogatory letters referred to in the above said aviso independently of the placet of this ministry.

EUZEBIO DE QUEIROZ CONTINHO M. CAMARA.

To the President of the Province of Pernambuco.

Aviso to which the preceding refers.

MINISTRY OF JUSTICE,
Rio de Janeiro, October 1, 1847.

It having been declared, in the report of the minister of foreign affairs presented to the general legislative assembly at last year's session, that "not having been carried out in Portugal the diplomatic agreement concluded in this city on the 18th of March, 1841, between this Government and that of His Most Faithful Majesty, relative to simple precatory or rogatory letters, issued by the judicial authorities of the two countries, that agreement should be considered as nonexistent," and it appearing, in view of this, that our judicial authorities were not obliged to obey such letters, not even for the purpose of simple summons in regard to civil suits, on the supposition that those issued in this Empire were not executed in that Kingdom; the minister of the above said department has informed me that such a supposition is not true, since it appears from official advices that the Government of His Most Faithful Majesty had not agreed to that part of the convention which made the execution of such precatory letters depend on a placet of the two contracting Governments, but that the authorities should obey them and execute the summons requested, these letters being presented to them *directly.*

As, however, it is necessary to regulate this affair so that neither our judges may deny the observance of simple letters calling for summons in civil questions, nor obey any not conformable to the principles adopted in the above said convention, His Majesty, the Emperor, has ordered me to declare to you, for your knowledge and guidance, and that it may be made known wherever necessary, that all rogatory letters, for the purpose of summons or investigations, issued by foreign judiciary authorities, must be observed, if they contain the following requisites:

First. They must be simply precatory or rogatory, issued by judiciary authorities for the purpose of simple summons or examining of witnesses; all *executory* letters, whether they include final sentence or not, will be refused.

Second. All such letters will be framed in civil and deprecative terms, not in the form or with the expression of an imperative order, being only excepted letters of summons in regard to criminal acts or objects.

Third. All such rogatory letters must be properly legalized by the Brazilian consuls of each respective country in the form and manner prescribed in such cases.

Fourth. Persons interested will be allowed to embargo or bring legal stay to the proceedings in all cases of precatory or rogatory letters, if founded in law and equity, and such stay of proceedings will be received and follow the usual legal process and will be finally admitted to sentence as justice may demand.

NICOLAO PEREIRA DE CAMPOS VERJUEIRO.
To Sr. MANUEL IGNACIO CAVALCANTI DE LACERDA.

Mr. Egan, United States minister at Santiago, February 12, 1890,

Chile.

transmitted a copy of a letter of the 4th of that month from the minister of foreign affairs, conveying a note from the minister of justice. It appears that the minister of justice had laid the subject before the supreme court of justice, which made the following report: [a]

---

[a] H. Ex. Doc. 281, 51 Cong. 2 sess. 10.

"This court has taken cognizance of the note of Mr. Envoy Extraordinary and Minister Plenipotentiary of the United States, transcribed to your honor by Mr. Minister of Foreign Affairs and which your honor has communicated by your note dated on the 16th December last. Mr. Minister Plenipotentiary incloses to his note a circular relating to letters rogatory for taking evidence to persons residing in the United States, in lawsuits pending before foreign courts of justice, and calls attention to the reformed statutes regarding letters requisitorial. The honorable minister above referred to wishes also to know what kind of procedure is observed in Chili regarding letters rogatory. The high court has ordered the above-mentioned circular to be communicated to all the other courts in order that they may bear it in mind when addressing to judicial authorities in the United States.

"As regards to the dispatching of letters requisitorial addressed by judicial authorities of other countries to authorities of the same rank of this Republic, procedure thereof is submitted to the rules contained in supreme decree of May 5, 1873, published in the bulletin of the said year. Every letter rogatory sent by a foreign court and put before the department of foreign affairs is addressed by this department to the supreme court, and this corporation sends it to the corresponding judge in order that it may be duly executed by him. This officer acts of his own authority, if the proceeding asked for relates to a criminal affair. If it refers to a civil one, the person to whom the interested party has entrusted this commission must take charge of seeing that the affair is carried through, paying the corresponding fees to the court officers who may act therein and in the criminal suits between two or more parties. In criminal suits the judge must examine the witnesses personally and in the civil suits he can delegate this commission, except in cases when the interested party may ask the judge to take personally the evidence of witnesses.

"Witnesses can be compelled to render their evidence under the penalty of a fine or an imprisonment should they refuse to give the said evidence. Witnesses are entitled to demand from parties calling them before the court the travelling or transportation expenses they may incur, including those necessary to get back to their own home. All of which this high court has the honor to communicate to your honor in answer to your note of 16th December last."

Mr. Denby, minister to China, on November 6, 1889, made the following report:[a]

China.

"I have to state that no method for this purpose is provided for in Chinese law. The performance of notarial duties is confided to the consuls by divers sections in the consular regulations

---

[a] H. Ex. Doc. 281, 51 Cong. 2 sess. 11.

of 1888, commencing with section 449. Section 451 provides that the consul, when called on by a State or Territorial tribunal, may execute a commission for taking testimony.

"Section 1750 (Rev. S. U. S., 2d Ed., 1878) confers power on all secretaries of legation and consular officers to do all acts that notaries public may ordinarily do. As the United States exercises extraterritorial jurisdiction in China it would seem that no decree from the Imperial Government is necessary, having especial relation to letters rogatory. The means provided by our own Government are ample to accomplish all useful purposes in the way of taking proof.

"It may be said also that under the law proof is often taken in China."

A report in regard to the law in Colombia, by Mr. Abbott, United States minister, November 30, 1889,[a] was as follows:

Colombia. "I beg leave to say that there is no rule or practice in Columbia as to the execution of letters rogatory proceeding from jurisdictions. The foreign office, however, undertakes to execute all such letters rogatory, coming through the diplomatic channel, by passing them to the proper judicial authority of the district in which the witness may reside. Such letters should, therefore, be directed in general terms to 'The judicial authority, authorized to execute letters rogatory, in that district of the Republic of Colombia in which is situated the city (or town) of (place of residence of the witness),' or in similar terms.

"They should then be forwarded through the diplomatic channel. The signature of the authorities taking the testimony would be certified to in the usual form before the depositions are returned to the United States.

"Foreign letters rogatory are practically, and perhaps entirely, unknown in Colombia. But by following the above directions it is believed that their execution can be secured without serious difficulty."

Mr. Carr, minister at Copenhagen, made, on December 23, 1889, the following report:[b]

Denmark. "I transmitted a copy of the circular of March 25, 1887, to the Royal Danish minister for foreign affairs, and requested him in turn to give me similar information upon the same subject, viz, concerning the taking of testimony of persons residing in Denmark, to be used in law cases in other countries.

"To this his excellency the minister replies in substance, as follows:

"'After having corresponded with my colleague, the minister of justice, upon the matter, I have the honor to give you the following statement:

---

[a] H. Ex. Doc. 281, 51 Cong. 2 sess. 12.
[b] Id. 13.

" ' The requisition from a foreign country for examination of witnesses residing in Denmark should be transmitted through the diplomatic channel. It must contain the necessary information concerning the law case; the names of the parties, the names and place of residence of the witnesses to be examined, and finally, the interrogatories to be propounded. Thereupon the Danish Government will take charge of the examination of the witnesses and transmit the evidence in due form, requiring at the same time that the amount of the expense of the proceeding, viz, the fees of the attorneys and the costs of court, etc., shall be advanced.'

" It will be observed in the above that the minister limits his information to testimony taken through the diplomatic channel. In addition to this information I have also the opinion of Mr. Otto Liebe, a reliable, painsaking, and conscientious Danish lawyer, whom I consulted in relation to the matter.

" Mr. Liebe says:

" ' Some days ago you were pleased to put the following question to me, viz, " If, according to the laws of this country, foreigners should be (are) obliged to go through the diplomatic channel in order to obtain the testimony of persons residing here for use in suits pending in the courts of foreign countries."

" ' In reply I have to say, a Danish lawyer is able to take up evidence, especially to examine witnesses, before every court of this country on demand of the person interested in that evidence or of his commissioner (client) abroad, and the court can not prohibit (deny) such production of evidence or examination of witnesses, nor require an official demand from our executive Government simply because the evidence may be material for a lawsuit pending in a foreign country and in a *foreign* court.

" ' But when the evidence must be taken for a foreign law case, the other party in that law case must be duly notified to appear at the examination, and, save in some special kinds of cases, particularly in those concerning commerce and navigation, and save in cases of compromise between the parties about a shorter notice, there must be given the notice of a whole year to the other party residing abroad. This law rule can only be put aside when the ministry of justice is willing to nominate a curator (*tutor in litem*) for the defendant (other party), as then the notice shall be fixed at the residence, not of the party himself, but of his curator, who is always a lawyer residing in the district of the court where the evidence is to be taken. Such a curator is only nominated on demand, and the nomination can never be claimed as a right, but I am quite sure that the ministry always would be willing to admit a demand for that purpose when it comes from a respectable and reliable lawyer on behalf of the plaintiff (his client), who guarantees the costs and fees of the curator the same as if put on in the diplomatic way. In my opinion there is no advantage at all connected with the diplomatic way; that is, of course, much slower.'

" It is perhaps proper for me to add, after giving you the substance of the notes referred to above, that in cases pending in our American courts it is customary to take the testimony of witnesses residing in Denmark before the United States consul here, which, as the country is limited in extent, can be done without great expense, even though the witnesses are obliged to come to Copenhagen from the country."

Mr. Vignaud, chargé at Paris, reported, December 11, 1889, as follows:

France.   " Formerly the French courts of justice accepted letters rogatory issued by American courts only when they came through the diplomatic channel. During Mr. Washburne's and General Noyes's mission papers of this kind, which had been sent directly to French courts, were returned to this legation with the intimation that they should be forwarded through the foreign office. When they were thus transmitted they were executed without charge, but only after a very long delay, and sometimes after the matter had been recalled to the attention of the minister for foreign affairs.

" In February, 1888, the minister for foreign affairs, replying to a communication from this legation with reference to letters of this kind, inquired whether our Government would be in position to have papers of the same character issued by a French court of justice executed by American courts. The answer was that letters rogatory issued in France were assured to be executed in our courts under the provisions of the statutes of the United States as explained in the Department circular of March 25, 1887, copies of which were furnished to the foreign office. It does not appear, however, that this information facilitated matters any, for, if I am correctly informed, the French Government avoids applying directly to American courts on account of the heavy charges which this mode of proceeding involves.

"At present when letters rogatory are sent directly to a French magistrate he refers them to the minister of justice, who in turn sends them to the foreign office, where they may remain for weeks and months without receiving any attention. Sometimes they are returned to the United States through the French minister at Washington. In other instances the legation is asked whether the United States Government is willing to assume the payment of the fees and legal expenses of the case. The answer necessarily is that the United States Government can assume no such responsibility, but when the legation is enabled to add that a French solicitor (avoué), whose name and address are given, is prepared to take charge of the case, to conduct the legal proceedings, and pay all fees, the French foreign office usually requests the minister of justice to allow the execution of the commission, and to my knowledge he has never refused to do so.

" The only practical and speedy way of securing in France the execution of letters rogatory issued by an American court of justice is, therefore, to place them in charge of a French or American lawyer practicing in France who will select a solicitor (avoué) attached to the court which is to execute the commission, and charge him with conducting the legal proceedings and paying the expenses. This avoué will always be able, with the assistance of the legation, if required, to obtain from the minister of justice the necessary authorization.

" This subject has been referred to in Mr. McLane's dispatch No. 549 of February 14, 1888, and in Mr. Reid's No. 55 of August 26."

On December 12, 1889, Mr. Vignaud added a copy of a note from the minister of foreign affairs, in relation to a rogatory commission which had been sent from a court at New York directly to the vice-president of the tribunal of the Seine. The minister of foreign affairs stated that the commission had been forwarded to him by the keeper of the seals, who pointed out that as the United States Government did not undertake to secure the execution of letters rogatory issued by the French tribunals, the French Government could not undertake to secure the execution of American commissions in France, and he requested the legation to inform the interested parties that they must apply to the tribunal of the Seine through the intermediation of a lawyer (avoué).[a]

A report on the law of Germany was made by Mr. Phelps, United States minister at Berlin, July 29, 1890. He stated

German

that letters rogatory had from time to time been sent to the legation by persons in the United States with the request that the legation have them executed through the foreign office. With these requests the legation had complied, meeting with ready cooperation. In some instances, however, the legation had found difficulty in obtaining reimbursement for expenses, although the amounts were small, never having exceeded in any case the sum of $15. With his dispatch Mr. Phelps enclosed a note of Baron Holstein, of the imperial foreign office, which conveyed the following information:

" The practice to be observed in Germany in disposing of applications by foreign authorities for the taking of testimony in actions pending in foreign lands, has not as yet been regulated by imperial legislation. In the majority of the extradition treaties concluded by the Empire with foreign states it is provided that, when in a penal

---

[a] H. Ex. Doc. 281, 51 Cong. 2 sess. 15, 16.   See, also, Mr. Frelinghuysen, Sec. of State, to Mr. Morton, min. to France, Dec. 19, 1884, MS. Inst. France, XXI. 149.

proceeding on account of nonpolitical acts one of the treaty powers considers it necessary that the testimony of witnesses be taken or that any other proceeding of an investigatory character be had within the territory of the other party, an application to that end shall be made through a diplomatic channel, which shall, with the reservation of certain exceptions, be fulfilled in accordance with the laws of the land where the testimony of the witness is to be taken or the proceeding had. Further rules concerning the manner in which such applications are to be disposed of are not contained in the treaties referred to.

" In general, however, the German authorities will gladly respond to the applications of foreign authorities for the taking of proof to be used in civil and penal actions pending in foreign countries in accordance with the principles which obtain in Germany, in so far as the application is made through the diplomatic channel, and reciprocity appears to be assured. It is, therefore, to be recommended that when the courts of the United States of America desire to cause the taking, for actions pending there, of judicial proceedings in Germany, an application to that end be addressed by the appropriate American to the appropriate German court, and that this application be conveyed to this office (the foreign office) through the diplomatic channel, with the request that it be complied with.

" As German courts, in disposing of such applications, do not act by virtue of the instruction of the foreign courts, but by virtue of the judicial authority of their own country, it would appear that the end in view would be best answered, if for the application to be addressed to Germany, not the form of an instruction (commission), but that of the document of application (letter rogatory), should be chosen. In the case of the particular German court whose action is needed not being known in America with certainty, the more exact designation of the same could be omitted. In the event of it being thus designated, it will, nevertheless, be advisable to add to the address the words ' or to the other appropriate authority,' in order that when the lack of jurisdiction of the court first applied to subsequently appears, the application may, without the necessity of any intermediate proceedings, be at once conveyed to the other appropriate authority." [a]

In 1874 a suit was pending in the district court of the United States for the southern district of New York against a German firm having a branch in New York City, to recover penalties for alleged undervaluation in the importation of goods. As both parties desired to obtain the testimony of persons at various places in Europe, the court, on motion of the attorney, made, in conformity with the practice long prevailing in the district, and order designating the United States consuls at the specified places as commissioners to take the desired testi-

---

[a] H. Ex. Doc. 281, 51 Cong. 2 sess. 16, 17, 18.

mony. The order authorized, but did not require, the consuls so to act, and in performing such functions it was understood that they acted as commissioners and not as consuls, their compensation being paid by the litigants, and that they had no power to compel the attendance of witnesses, except with the cooperation of the local authorities, which was sometimes granted and sometimes withheld.[a]

Among the consuls designated to act in the present instance, four were in Germany. The German Government objected to their executing the commissions, on the ground that the taking of the sworn testimony of German subjects in the cities of the Empire was not one of the functions of consuls, and could not be derived from Article IX. of the consular convention between the two countries.[b]

The United States replied that it was not claimed that a United States consul, as such, had, by treaty or convention, the right to take such testimony; that the consul's services in such matters were purely ministerial and entirely voluntary; that the Government was not a party to the proceeding, except so far as it might have, as in the present instance, an interest in the action; and that it was hoped that the German Government would, with these explanations, withdraw its objections and consider it an act of comity to facilitate the taking of the testimony.[c]

The German Government answered that, while the competency of the courts in the United States to appoint commissioners to take testimony was not doubted, yet, if the testimony was to be taken in a foreign country, it could, according to international law, be taken, in the absence of a treaty on the subject, only under the limitations and forms prescribed by the laws there in force; that the objection of the German Government "was not so much to the taking of testimony under oath by American consuls in their official capacity" as to "the taking of testimony by American commissioners within the limits of the German Empire, . . . it being incompatible with the legal system of this country;" that the German courts, however, recognized the duty, under the sanction of German law, of assisting the courts of other countries to do justice, and therefore made it a practice to comply, without treaty obligation, with the requests of foreign courts to obtain testimony, such demands being known in Germany as "requisitions," which were analogous to "letters rogatory" in England and the United States; and that in such proceedings the parties to the liti-

a For. Rel. 1874, 458.

b Mr. Von Bülow, sec. of state for for. aff., to Mr. Bancroft, Am. min., June 24, 1874, For. Rel. 1874, 446.

c Mr. Fish, Sec. of State, to Mr. N. Fish, chargé at Berlin, Aug. 18, 1874, For. Rel. 1874, 456. See, also, Mr. Davis, min. to Germany, to Mr. Fish, Sec. of State, Oct. 30, 1874, For. Rel. 1874, 460; Mr. Fish, Sec. of State, to Mr. Davis, min. to Germany, Nov. 14, 1874, id. 461.

gation were at liberty through their attorneys to exercise a proper influence by putting questions through the judges.[a]

Mr. Lincoln, United States minister at London, made, November 1, 1889, the following report :[b]

Great Britain.   " With further reference to your circular instruction, dated September 18, 1889, directing a report as to the method in which letters rogatory may be executed in this country, I have now the honor to report to you that a method of obtaining the testimony of a witness within British dominions to be used in a suit relating to a civil matter pending in a tribunal of a foreign country is given by the act of Parliament, 19 and 20 Vict., c. 113, of which copies are inclosed.   By a later enactment there was given to this act the title ' Foreign tribunals evidence act, 1856,' for purposes of citation.

" The great changes made in 1873 in the constitution of Her Majesty's superior courts for England and Ireland require that the first part of the sixth section of the act, viz, ' Her Majesty's superior courts of common law at Westminister and in Dublin respectively,' should now be read ' Her Majesty's high court of justice, England (or Ireland), Queen's bench division.'

" Under this act letters rogatory are not required and no particular court or judge or commissioner to take the testimony need be named in the commission of the foreign court.   It is not even clear that a commission from the foreign court is necessary if the application to the British court is supported by the diplomatic or consular certificate provided for in the second section of the act.   I understand, however, that for such an application originating in the United States, in which both in the Federal and State jurisdictions the forms of legal procedure are essentially like those of the British dominions, it would be advisable that the court desiring the testimony of a witness or witnesses should issue a commission for taking it directed generally, such commission to have attached a certificate under the seal of the court, stating that the testimony desired to be taken under the commission is in relation to a civil or commercial matter pending before the court, and that it is a court of competent jurisdiction in the premises.

" In cases where the diplomatic or consular certificate above mentioned might be added without undue trouble, it would be advisable to procure it ; but probably all British courts and judges empowered under the act would proceed upon the certificate of the court alone.

---

[a] Mr. Von Bülow, sec. of state for for. aff., to Mr. Schlözer, min. to United States, Oct. 12, 1874, For. Rel. 1874, 463.   See, also, Mr. Fish, Sec. of State, to Mr. Schlözer, German min., Dec. 9, 1874, For. Rel. 1875, I. 573 ; Mr. Fish, Sec. of State, to Mr. Davis, min. to Germany, April 7, 1875, and June 8, 1875, For. Rel. 1875, I. 537, 562.

[b] H. Ex. Doc. 281, 51 Cong. 2 sess. 19–20.

"In view of the similarity between American and British modes of procedure, it is perhaps unnecessary to add that, for the purpose of presenting the application to a British court and conducting the subsequent proceedings, it would be necessary in every case to employ a local attorney or solicitor.

"After inquiry in several quarters, I am led to believe that the rules and orders contemplated by the last section of the ' Foreign tribunals evidence act, 1856,' have never been framed; but if they do in fact exist, they would, it is thought, be of no interest in this report, as they would, with hardly a doubt, merely regulate the practice upon an application made upon papers conforming to the act."

Anno Decimo Nono & Vicesimo Victoriæ Reginæ.

CAP. CXIII.

An Act to provide for taking Evidence in Her Majesty's Dominions in relation to Civil and Commercial Matters pending before Foreign Tribunals.　[29th *July* 1856.]

Whereas it is expedient that Facilities be afforded for taking Evidence in Her Majesty's Dominions in relation to Civil and Commercial Matters pending before Foreign Tribunals: Be it enacted by the Queen's most Excellent Majesty, by and with the Advice and Consent of the Lords Spiritual and Temporal, and Commons, in this present Parliament assembled, and by the Authority of the same, as follows:

I. Where, upon an Application for this Purpose, it is made to appear to any Court or Judge having Authority under this Act that any Court or Tribunal of competent Jurisdiction in a Foreign Country, before which any Civil or Commercial Matter is pending, is desirous of obtaining the Testimony in relation to such Matter of any Witness or Witnesses within the Jurisdiction of such first-mentioned Court, or of the Court to which such Judge belongs, or of such Judge, it shall be lawful for such Court or Judge to order the Examination upon Oath, upon Interrogatories or otherwise, before any Person or Persons named in such Order, of such Witness or Witnesses accordingly; and it shall be lawful for the said Court or Judge, by the same Order, or for such Court or Judge or any other Judge having Authority under this Act, by any subsequent Order, to command the Attendance of any Person to be named in such Order, for the Purpose of being examined, or the Production of any Writings or other Documents to be mentioned in such Order, and to give all such Directions as to Time, Place, and Manner of such Examination, and all other Matters connected therewith, as may appear reasonable and just; and any such Order may be enforced in like Manner as an Order made by such Court or Judge in a Cause depending in such Court or before such Judge.

II. A Certificate under the Hand of the Ambassador, Minister, or other Diplomatic Agent of any Foreign Power, received as such by Her Majesty, or in case there be no such Diplomatic Agent, then of the Consul General or Consul of any such Foreign Power at London, received and admitted as such by Her Majesty, that any Matter in relation to which an Application is made under this Act is a Civil or Commercial Matter pending before a Court or Tribunal in the Country of which he is the Diplomatic Agent or Consul having Jurisdiction in the Matter so pending, and that such Court or Tribunal is desirous of obtaining the Testimony of the Witness or Witnesses to whom the Application relates, shall be

Evidence of the Matters so certified; but where no such Certificate is produced other Evidence to that Effect shall be admissible.

III. It shall be lawful for every Person authorized to take the Examination of Witnesses by any Order made in pursuance of this Act to take all such Examinations upon the Oath of the Witnesses, or Affirmation in Cases where Affirmation is allowed by Law instead of Oath, to be administered by the Person so authorized; and if upon such Oath or Affirmation any Person making the same wilfully and corruptly give any false Evidence, every Person so offending shall be deemed and taken to be guilty of Perjury.

IV. Provided always, That every Person whose Attendance shall be so required shall be entitled to the like Conduct Money and Payment for Expenses and Loss of Time as upon Attendance at a Trial.

V. Provided also, That every Person examined under any Order made under this Act shall have the like Right to refuse to answer Questions tending to criminate himself, and other Questions, which a Witness in any Cause pending in the Court by which or by a Judge whereof or before the Judge by whom the Order for Examination was made would be entitled to; and that no Person shall be compelled to produce under any such Order as aforesaid any Writing or other Document that he would not be compellable to produce at a Trial of such a Cause.

VI. Her Majesty's Superior Courts of Common Law at *Westminster* and in *Dublin* respectively, the Court of Sessions in *Scotland*, and any Supreme Court in any of Her Majesty's Colonies or Possessions abroad, and any Judge of any such Court, and every Judge in any such Colony or Possession who by any Order of Her Majesty in Council may be appointed for this Purpose, shall respectively be Courts and Judges having Authority under this Act: Provided, that the Lord Chancellor, with the Assistance of two of the Judges of the Courts of Common Law at *Westminster*, shall frame such Rules and Orders as shall be necessary or proper for giving Effect to the Provisions of this Act, and regulating the Procedure under the same.

Mr. Stevens, United States minister at Honolulu, November 4, 1889, reported, on the authority of the Hawaiian minister of foreign affairs, that there was no statute in Hawaii regulating the execution of letters rogatory, but that it had been the practice of the supreme court and its justices, when such letters had been received from the courts of foreign countries, to execute them as a matter of courtesy. Commissions to administer interrogatories and to take testimony had also been received by private parties and executed, there being no law to the contrary.[a]

Hawaii.

Mr. Porter, United States minister at Rome, October 26, 1889, enclosed the following translation of the Italian law regulating the execution of letters rogatory and of foreign judgments:[b]

Italy.

941. Executive force to the judgments of foreign judiciary authority is given to the court of appeals in whose jurisdiction it must be executed, a judgment having preceded in which the court examines:

(1) If the sentence may have been pronounced by a competent judicial authority;

---

[a] H. Ex. Doc. 281, 51 Cong. 2 sess. 21.
[b] Id. 22.

(2) If it may have been pronounced, the parties having been regularly cited;

(3) If the parties may have been legally represented or legally contumacious;

(4) If the judgment contains dispositions contrary to public order or to public right within the Kingdom.

942. The judgment of delibation is promoted with a citation in a summary way of those interested and the public prosecutor must be heard.

The party who promotes it must present the judgment in a form authentic (duly authenticated).

If the execution of the judgment is requested through the diplomatic channels and the party interested has not appointed a procurator who promotes the judgment of delibation the court of appeals, at the instance of the public prosecutor, names officially to the party himself a procurator who may promote it in his name.

943. For the execution in the kingdom of the provisions for sequestration given by foreign judiciary authority, the dispositions are observed of the two preceding articles (sections) in so far as they may be applicable.

944. The executive force to the authenticated acts received in a foreign country, is given by the civil tribunal of the place in which the act must be executed, after a judgment (of delibation) in which the rules must be observed which are established by articles 941 and 942 in so far as they may be applicable.

945. The judgments and provisions of foreign judicial authorities relating to the examination of witnesses, expert testimony, oaths, interrogatories, or other acts of instruction to be made in the kingdom, are rendered executive by a simple decree of the court of appeals of the place in which such acts are to be executed.

If the execution is asked directly by the parties interested, the application is presented by recourse to the court, and there shall be joined with it an authentic copy of the judgment or of the provisions which ordered the acts asked for.

If the execution is asked by the foreign judicial authority itself, the request must be transmitted through the diplomatic channels, without the necessity of joining the copy of the judgment or provisions.

The court, having heard the public prosecutor, deliberates in the chamber of council. If the execution is permitted, it commits the execution of the acts requested to the judicial authority, or to the functionary thereof who has the authority to receive them or to have them executed.

946. When the request is made through the diplomatic channels, and the interested party has selected no procurator to promote the execution of the acts enumerated in the preceding article, the provisions, the citations, and the notifications required to accomplish them are given or ordered officially (*d'ufficio*) by the authority which is proceeding in the matter. If the acts requested require, through special circumstances, the watchful care of the party interested, the said judiciary authority may officially (*d'ufficio*) name a procurator who will represent such party.

If the presence of the parties interested in the acts asked for is necessary or permitted the decree which fixes the day on which the act will be proceeded with to be executed (*in cui si procedera all' atto stesso*) is notified by a simple note handed by the usher to the parties whose residence in the kingdom may be known. A copy of the decree is transmitted through the diplomatic channels to the foreign authority, in order that the other parties may be informed thereof.

947. When it is a question of citations to appear before foreign authorities, or of simple notifications of acts coming from a foreign country, the permission is given by the public prosecutor near to the court or tribunal in whose jurisdiction the citation or notification must be executed.

If the requests have been made through the diplomatic channels, the citations or notifications are committed by the public prosecutor directly to an usher.

948. The fulfillment in the kingdom of the acts indicated in the three preceding articles does not take away the necessity of a judgment of delibation (delibazione) when the question is one of the execution of a definitive judgment.

949. The executive force given according to articles 941, 942, 943, 944, 945, 946, and 947, by a civil tribunal, by a court of appeals, or by the public prosecutor, avails for promoting the execution also in other jurisdictions.

950. The dispositions of this title are subordinate to those of the international conventions (treaties) and of the special laws.

Mr. Ryan, United States minister at Mexico, January 23, 1890, enclosed a translation of a note from Mr. Mariscal, Mexican minister of foreign affairs, of January 22, 1890, which was as follows:[a]

Mexico.

" Referring to the esteemed notes of September 28 of last year and of yesterday's date, I have the honor to inform your excellency that the method generally observed throughout the States and Territories of this Republic for the execution of commissions and letters rogatory to take testimony coming from foreign countries is, to wit, they are admitted, provided always they are presented through the diplomatic representative of the country of issue of same. The said diplomatic representative transmits them to this Department, which in its turn forwards them to the Department of Justice, so that the latter may take care that the judicial authorities to whom the papers come consigned pay requisite attention thereto. The only difference is some of the States require that those documents shall be legalized by the Mexican minister or consul resident in the country of issue, and in default thereof by the minister or consul of a nation having a treaty of friendship with this Republic, and that their translation in Spanish shall accompany such documents, while in other States it suffices for the commission or letters rogatory to be forwarded through the channel of the legation and the Federal Government (as indicated) to take due effect, even without legalization.

" The States and Territories that require the prior legalization are: The Federal District, Territory of Lower California, and States of Coahuila, Durango, Guerrero, Jalisco, Michoacan, Morelos, Sinaloa, Sonora, Vera Cruz, Puebla, and Yucatan.

" Where such legalization is not required are the States of Colima, Guanajuate, Mexico, Nuevo Leon, Tlaxcala, and Tabasco.

" I lack information as to the methods which obtain in the other States. As soon as I receive the information I have sought therefrom, I will have the satisfaction of transmitting it to your excellency, to whom I meanwhile reiterate the assurance of my very distinguished consideration."

---

a H. Ex. Doc. 281, 51 Cong. 2 sess. 24.

Mr. Thayer, United States minister at The Hague, November 29,
Netherlands. 1889, enclosed a note from the ministry of foreign
affairs of that date, in which it was stated that for the
transmission of judicial commissions addressed by the Dutch judicial
authorities to a foreign judicial authorities in civil matters, the diplomatic channel was generally employed, although no regulation
requiring it existed. The employment of the diplomatic channel was,
however, stipulated in the majority of the Dutch extradition conventions in respect of judicial commissions concerning penal matter. It
was stated that the courts of the Netherlands executed letters rogatory in civil cases *ex comitate gentium.*[a]

Mr. Wurts, chargé at St. Petersburg, May 12, 1890, sent to the
Russia. Department of State a translation of a " notice " of
the Russian foreign office concerning the execution of
letters rogatory.[b] This notice was as follows:

" The relations of the tribunals of the Empire with the judicial
institutions of foreign countries are maintained in accordance with
the provisions of article 190 of the Regulations of the Judicial Institutions by the ministry of justice through the mediation of the ministry of foreign affairs.

" Conformably to this law, rogatory commissions addressed by a
foreign state to a Russian tribunal, having in view the examination of
witnesses, the delivery of a summons to appear, requests for information, etc., which are to be executed in Russia, are transmitted through
the diplomatic channel to the imperial Russian ministry of foreign
affairs, whence they are communicated by the ministry of justice to
the competent tribunal.

" The replies of the tribunals appealed to, drawn up after the
execution of the rogatory commissions, follow the same course.

" The tribunals of the Empire are not authorized to correspond
directly with the judicial authorities abroad. As an exception, and
by virtue of special conventions, the tribunals of the judicial districts
of Warsaw are permitted to correspond, without diplomatic intermediation, with the tribunals of the frontier regions of Germany and
Austria.

" The legislation in force contains no disposition on the character of
the rogatory commissions, which may be executed in Russia, nor on
the manner of their execution by the competent Russian tribunals.
These tribunals are obliged to conform in the matter to the general
rules of the codes of criminal and civil procedure.

" The custom of rogatory commissions being generally admitted in
Russia, with the understanding of reciprocity, these commissions

----

a H. Ex. Doc. 281, 51 Cong. 2 sess. 24–25.
b Ibid.

coming from abroad are executed by our tribunals when they are not contrary to the provisions for public order.

" The expenses caused by the execution in Russia of rogatory commissions from foreign tribunals are charged to the State requesting their execution, unless a special convention arranges differently."

Mr. Thomas, United States minister at Stockholm, April 26, 1890, communicated to his Government a translation of a memorandum which had been furnished to him by the foreign office in relation to the execution of letters rogatory in Sweden. He was advised that the law was substantially the same in Norway. The memorandum, which was dated April 26, 1890, reads, translated, as follows: [a]

Sweden and Norway.

" In Swedish law there exists no provision which obliges a Swedish court, upon the request of a foreign court, to take up the examination of witnesses.

" On the other hand there is no statute which forbids the Swedish courts to enter up on such examination, and in practice such assistance is usually not denied.

" As, however, in the administration of Swedish justice the courts never concern themselves with summoning witnesses, it is necessary that an attorney for the foreign suitor should be present and request the Swedish court to appoint a day for a hearing. The attorney will then summon the witnesses for the day so appointed.

" If the hearing concerns a felony, the proceedings should take place in an administrative way (officially), and similar measures should be taken for summoning witnesses.

" The costs of the hearing fall upon the attorney who requests the same. If it has been requested in an administrative way, it is the duty of that Swedish authority that requested the hearing to provide for the payment of costs. Testimony in criminal cases is never taken gratuitously unless this is specially stipulated by treaty still in force.

" It is not to be presumed that witnesses will present themselves without reimbursement, and the courts can not grant them compensation out of the public funds, on account of the law of June 4, 1886.

" The protocol of the hearing is placed at the disposition of the attorney or the authority requesting the same.

" In no other respect does the Swedish law oblige the Swedish courts, upon the request of a foreign court, to lend any assistance; and there are no precedents in such respects that can be cited."

Mr. Washburn, United States minister at Berne, November 26, 1889, enclosed a note of October 19, 1889, from the President of the Swiss Confederation, in which it was stated that there were no legal prescriptions in Switzerland as to how

Switzerland.

---

[a] H. Ex. Doc. 281, 51 Cong. 2 sess. 27.

letters rogatory should be executed. Such letters, it was stated, should therefore be submitted through the diplomatic channel to the Swiss Federal Council, which would not fail to transmit them to the proper authorities of the respective Cantons.[a]

Mr. Scruggs, United States minister at Caracas, October 12, 1889, enclosed a copy and translation of a note from the Venezuelan minister of foreign affairs, of October 7, 1889. This note was as follows:[b]

Venezuela.

" I have the greatest pleasure in answering your excellency's communication of the 1st instant relative to the execution of letters rogatory in this Republic. Here it is likewise a matter specially referred by law to the courts of justice, as will be seen by article 559 of the code of civil proceedings, which says:

" ' The decrees of foreign tribunals relative to the examination of witnesses, procuring affidavits, taking interrogatories, and other mere informatory acts are executed by the simple decree of the judge of first instance having jurisdiction in the place where such acts have to be verified.'

"And article 560, which says:

" ' The provisions of the foregoing article are applicable to citations made to individuals resident in the Republic to appear before foreign authorities, and to notifications of judicial proceedings of foreign countries.'

" Finally, article 561 prescribes that ' the provisions of this title shall be subordinate to those of public treaties and international conventions, and to those of special enactments.' The title here cited is 19, relative to the execution of foreign decrees in Venezuela, with the exceptions therein expressed.

" The honorable envoy extraordinary of the United States is right in saying there is not and has never been any embarrassment relative to the execution of letters rogatory in Venezuela. On the contrary, such execution has been facilitated, even through the diplomatic channel, to the end that reciprocity might be had with friendly governments and countries.

" But since, in sending letters rogatory of the national tribunals to those in foreign countries, some difficulties have sometimes arisen in their execution—owing perhaps to the want of convenient means of defraying costs and of an agency of the parties interested—the Government resolved on the 17th of January, 1883, that, in such cases, the parties should constitute an agent to represent them and provide for the expenses of the same."

---

[a] H. Ex. Doc. 281, 51 Cong. 2 sess. 27–28.
[b] H. Ex. Doc. 281, 51 Cong. 2 sess. 29.

5. POLICE AND OTHER REGULATIONS.

(1) DISPLAY OF FOREIGN FLAGS.

§ 190.

Section 70 of the Consular Regulations of the United States, 1896,
reads: "The arms of the United States should be
placed over the entrance to the consulate or commercial agency, unless prohibited by the laws of the country. . . .
Wherever the custom prevails, the national flag should be hoisted
on such occasions as the consular officer may deem appropriate, or
when it may be required for his protection or as the emblem of his
authority. It is not usually necessary that it should be unfurled
daily. The occasions for its display are within the judgment of the
consular officer; but its use will be suggested on all national holidays
of his own country and whenever it would indicate a becoming respect to the customs, festivals, or public ceremonies of the country
to which he is accredited."

Official display.

Section 73 states: "A consul may place the arms of his Government
over his doors. Permission to display the national flag is not a matter of right, though it is usually accorded, and it is often provided
for by treaty."

Section 86 refers to certain treaty stipulations as to the use of the
national arms and flags.

Section 64 of the Instructions to the Diplomatic Officers of the
United States reads: "A mission is not under the same necessity of
displaying a coat of arms and raising a flag as a consulate; but it is
in most capitals customary to place an official shield above the principal entrance of the diplomatic representative's residence, or the
offices of the mission, when these are separate from his residence,
with a short flagstaff set above the shield, on which to display the
flag of the United States on occasions of special ceremony."

These regulations, consular and diplomatic, should, it is thought,
" suffice for all practical purposes, subject of course to a proper discretion and judgment by the individual officer." Where the flag is
raised on any occasion, it is usual to fly it from sunrise to sunset. It
is not flown during the night.[a]

" Your letter of the 8th of October, in further reference to your
inquiry of September 14th touching the etiquette of displaying the flag
of one's own country in a foreign country, has been received.

" The Department's letter of October 1st whereby you were advised
that such a display of a foreign flag is a matter which would natu-

---

[a] Mr. Hay, Sec. of State, to Mr. Merry, min. to Nicaragua, Jan. 6, 1900, MS
Inst. Cent. Am. XXI. 609.

rally be regulated by the laws of the country of residence, was framed with the knowledge that the laws of certain countries of the American Continent, and in particular those of Mexico, restrict or inhibit the display of a foreign flag upon national soil.

" The Mexican rule is laid down in an Executive order of the President of the United States of Mexico of August 23, 1828, whereby it was prescribed that within the territory of Mexico no flag should be displayed except that of Mexico, and that the representatives of Mexico in foreign parts should by way of reciprocity abstain from displaying the Mexican flag in the country of their residence, even though the privilege were enjoyed by the representatives of other nations. On the 4th of September, 1830, this order was more precisely stated with specific reference to the custom of foreign consuls to display their flags in Mexico. Later the Mexican law of November 26, 1859, regulating and defining the privileges of foreign consuls in Mexico, incorporated this provision in its 30th article, permitting, however, the display of the consular flag when the town of the consul's residence might be besieged or mutiny or sedition arise within it.

"As your letter is written from Monterey, Mexico, and appears to relate to the specific inhibition in that country, rather than to any general proposition, this Department does not feel called upon to express any opinion on the further inquiry you present touching the post of honor and relative positions of national and foreign flags, in cases where both may be displayed."

> Mr. Day, Assist. Sec. of State, to Mr. Barron, October 20, 1897, 221 MS. Dom. Let. 560.

In April, 1864, Gen. James Watson Webb, United States minister to Brazil, issued to the United States consuls in that country a circular prohibiting the flying of the United States flag without his permission, unless by persons in an official capacity. The reason that he gave for his action was that the flag was often used by irresponsible persons, over disreputable places and in improper localities, on payment of a license fee to the local authorities for the privilege; and it appeared that, prior to issuing the order in question, he laid the matter before the Brazilian Government and received its sanction and approval. On the facts his action was approved, the Department of State declaring that the Government of the United States believed itself to be " fully empowered and authorized to prevent the abuse and disgrace of its national emblem both at home and abroad."

Unofficial display.

> Mr. Seward, Sec. of State, to Mr. Rollins, M. C., Feb. 15, 1865, 68 MS. Dom. Let. 198.

"This Government does not mean to insist that citizens of the United States have an absolute right to display the national flag over their buildings and ships in Nicaragua, and on steamers navigating merely inland waters of that country. But the undersigned is now informed that the American Transit Company has heretofore, with the full consent and approval of the Government of Nicaragua, habitually kept the flag of the United States flying over such buildings and vessels as the buildings and waters aforenamed. It seems to the undersigned that if for any reason the Government of Nicaragua had thought it desirable that this indulgence should cease, comity would require in that case that this should have been made known to the Government of the United States or at least its representatives residing in Nicaragua, to the end that the now offending flag might be voluntarily withdrawn.

"The forcible and violent removal of the flag, at so many points, without any previous notice, seems to imply a readiness to offend the just sensibilities of this country, and indeed the allegation is distinctly made that the flag was removed in each case with marked indignity and in a specially insulting manner."

> Mr. Seward, Sec. of State, to Mr. Molina, Sept. 28, 1863, MS. Notes to Cent. Am. I. 240.

In April, 1899, certain citizens of the United States at Bluefields, whose merchandise had been seized in the custom-house by order of Colonel Torres, the "executive delegate," on account of their refusal to pay to the Nicaraguan Government the amount of customs duties which they had previously paid to a de facto revolutionary government which held possession of the town from the 3d to the 25th of the preceding February, closed their stores and hoisted over them the American flag. Señor Sanson, the Nicaraguan minister of foreign affairs, orally requested Mr. Merry, the minister of the United States to Nicaragua, to direct that the flags be hauled down. Mr. Merry, on consideration, replied that in his opinion "such a request to American citizens would only increase the ill feeling which has resulted from the seizure of their property," and added: "The occasional use of the national ensign on the domicile or place of business in foreign countries is a courtesy allowed by all civilized governments, especially among the Republics of the American continent. It can not be properly claimed as a right except over legations and consulates, but long usage has sanctioned the practice. If I make no such request, the incident will attract no attention and will be forgotten in a short time."

The Department of State instructed Mr. Merry as follows:

"The display of the flag, not as denoting extraterritorial jurisdiction, but as indicating the foreign ownership of the property covered thereby, has become so far a usage in countries liable to domestic disturbances as to warrant its convenient continuance. In this view of the matter your action in declining to order the owners to remove the flags is approved by the Department."

> Mr. Hay, Sec. of State, to Mr. Merry, min. to Nicaragua, May 8, 1899,
> For. Rel. 1899, 572, 582; MS. Inst. Cent. Am. XXI. 477.
> See, also, For. Rel. 1899, 571–572.

It appearing that there was no penal law in Belgium prohibiting the use of national flags for advertising purposes, and there being no similar Federal statute in the United States, the opinion was expressed that the question of such use of the United States flag in Belgium (in the particular case to advertise "American stables" at Antwerp) could not be " effectively treated either under international law or as a matter of equitable comity between the two Governments; " nor was it deemed advisable to attempt, as the Belgian Government suggested, a civil suit for damages against the persons so using the flag, there being no precedent for such an action.

> Mr. Sherman, Sec. of State, to Mr. Storer, min. to Belgium, Feb. 7, 1898,
> For. Rel. 1898, 159.
> In the course of the instruction Mr. Sherman said: "A line of steamers plying between England and the United States under the British flag has for some years past used the United States union jack as its house flag. Upon inquiry being made by the ambassador in London the British board of trade intervened, in virtue of its authority in matters of shipping and navigation, and I am just informed that the line in question has been constrained to adopt another distinctive house flag."
> The Belgian constitution of 1831, art. 125, says: " The Belgian nation adopts the colors red, yellow, and black." The Belgian law of July 30, 1831, art. 2, provides: "Whoever shall have maliciously and publicly attacked the obligation of the law (la force obligation des lois), or shall have directly incited disobedience to the law, shall be punished by imprisonment of from six months to three years." On the ground that " the flag represents the country, and the country means the land and the constitutional and legal institutions which govern it, and which form and organize our social life and our nationality," the Belgian tribunals in 1898 convicted and sentenced to six months' imprisonment two Socialists, who, as a part of their political campaign, publicly burnt the Belgian flag at Charleroi and treated the fragments with indignity. (For. Rel. 1898, 161.)

In reply to an inquiry whether in case of " trouble " in Caracas Cubans might hoist the United States flag for protection, the Department of State said: " Flag should only be shown by citizens. You may notify authorities of any menaced Cuban property and use good offices for them."

> Mr. Adee, Acting Sec. of State, to Mr. Russell, chargé at Caracas, tel.,
> Sept. 19, 1899, For. Rel. 1899, 796.

The action of the United States vice-consul at Colon, in Colombia, in refusing to permit Greek subjects to hoist the United States flag over their places of business as a means of protection, was approved. (Mr. Cridler, Third Assist. Sec of State, to Mr. Cobbs, vice-consul at Colon, Dec. 1, 1900, 175 MS. Inst. Consuls, 302.)

With reference to a complaint of the Haytian Government, in 1903, that many aliens usurped the privilege reserved to the diplomatic corps of flying the national flag, with the result that the flag was often abused to cover seditious persons and depots of arms, the chargé d'affaires ad interim of the United States, in a communication to the Haytian Government, stated that it had for many years been the custom of foreigners in times of political disturbance to display their national flag over or before their residences or places of business as a protection of themselves and their property against lawless acts which, although not sanctioned by the Government, it might not for the moment be able to check; that, in no instance known to him during a period of service of twenty-two years, had dwellings or places of business covered by a foreign flag been violated by a mob; and that, as a result of the protective use of foreign flags, the Haytian Government has been saved from many diplomatic complications and claims. In conclusion, he declared that the United States would never sanction the abusive use of its flag, and expressed confidence that the Haytian Government would never have cause to complain that an American citizen had used the flag for any purpose other than that of the protection of life and property. These representations were approved by the United States.

For. Rel. 1903, 596–597.

In May, 1903, the American minister at Rio de Janeiro brought to the notice of the Brazilian Government the fact that a Brazilian line of sailing vessels was using a house flag resembling one of the forms of the national ensign of the United States. The complaint was referred to the navy department of Brazil, and the American minister was subsequently informed that the Brazilian firm owning the ships in question had ordered another flag to be substituted for that which had been in use.

For. Rel. 1904, 101–103.

" I have the honor to acknowledge the receipt of your note of the 19th ultimo, in the matter of the complaint of Mr. Auguste Lelang or Leland, a French resident of Jeannette, Westmoreland County, Pa., against a policeman of that borough, for having torn down and maltreated two French flags which Mr. Lelang had hoisted from the second story of his residence.

" I at once brought the subject to the attention of his excellency Robert E. Pattison, governor of that State, for his information and report, and I have now before me the sworn testimony of the witnesses on both sides of the controversy, which has been furnished by the district attorney of Westmoreland County to Governor Pattison, by whom it has been transmitted to this Department.

" This testimony shows that on the morning of May 30, 1892, in the borough of West Jeannette, Pa., Mr. Auguste Leland (or Lelang), having in his possession two French flags about 4 feet square which he had brought from France, and having purchased an American flag—the largest he could buy, but considerably smaller than the others—placed the three flags in the second story window of his house, intending evidently no disrespect to the American flag, which he placed in the middle, though probably for some reason lower than the others. Certain neighbors of his, deeming that the arrangement of the flags was disrespectful to the United States, prevailed on a policeman, T. A. Spires, to take them down. It does not appear that Mr. Spires injured the flag, but that later some persons unknown and certain children did tear the flag more with a design to preserve (each) a piece than for worse motive.

" To-day I telegraphed Governor Pattison urging his earnest and hearty coöperation to prevent any hostile demonstration against the flag of France or her citizens on the 14th instant—the French national holiday—should they in honor thereof fly the flag.

" It affords me pleasure to say that I have received a reply this afternoon from Governor Pattison saying that he had telegraphed Joseph A. McCurdy, esq., district attorney of Westmoreland County, in the sense of my telegram, adding as follows:

" I want to impress upon you (Mr. McCurdy) the importance of giving this matter your prompt personal attention; confer with the local authorities at Jeannette and see that provisions are made to prevent any hostile manifestations against the flag or the French residents. Communicate with me [Governor Pattison] in regard to your action.

" The occurrence is deeply regretted by myself and the governor of Pennsylvania, and was entirely without the sanction of the authorities thereof, as you can readily understand.

" In a letter which I have addressed to Governor Pattison I have adverted to the fact that although the flag is only a national emblem when displayed by a competent authority, it is also private property which should under no circumstances be wantonly maltreated by a police officer or by any other person in time of peace. I alluded to the time-honored friendship which had so long existed between the Government of the United States and that of France, and to our natural desire that friendly and peaceable relations should at all times prevail between the citizens of this country and those of a friendly foreign power residing within our jurisdiction. These reasons strongly suggested to my mind, as I doubt not they will to Governor Pattison, that all undue manifestations that tend to engender ill feeling or bitter resentment should be avoided or suppressed.

" In this connection it is pleasant to note that Governor Pattison's telegram herein referred to gives assurance that he intended to do everything that is possible to promote good feeling at Jeannette.

" The occurrence of May 30 last can not in anywise be regarded as an insult to the flag of France as a national emblem, since it is possible for like incidents to occur in any country under similar circumstances, and, as I have shown, there was an entire absence of design to offer an insult to the citizens of France or the flag as a national emblem. It was the personal act of a police officer, in which certain other persons, including children of the town of Jeannette, participated, and without the sanction or knowledge of the Pennsylvania State authorities. I have, however, suggested to the governor that some measure of punishment should, if possible, be meted out to the policeman, Thomas A. Spires, and entertain no doubt that he will give the question his further attention to that end."

> Mr. Foster, Sec. of State, to Mr. Patenôtre, French min,, July 13, 1892, For. Rel. 1892, 174.
>
> Mr. Patenôtre's note of June 19 is printed in the same volume, at p. 172. The report on which his representations were based stated that the policeman, Spires, assisted by another person, " pulled down the two French flags, which they afterwards tore and threw into the mud." Mr. Patenôtre's communication was acknowledged June 24, with a statement that a translation of it had been referred to the governor of Pennsylvania.
>
> Aug. 16, 1892, Mr. Foster wrote personally to Mr. Patenôtre that the delay in dealing with the case of the policeman was due to the fact that he was elected by the people and was under the jurisdiction of the court of quarter sessions.
>
> Aug. 26 Mr. Foster stated that he had been dismissed.
>
> Sept. 27, 1892, the French legation expressed the French Government's appreciation of the "satisfaction accorded it in this case by the Federal Government, at the request of Mr. Patenôtre." (For. Rel. 1892, 176.)

July 21, 1897, the Portuguese minister at Washington brought to the attention of the Department of State an alleged insult to the Portuguese flag at Monterey, Cal. It appeared that one Ortins, a naturalized citizen of the United States of Portuguese origin, desiring to celebrate the 4th of July, raised the Portuguese and the American flag on separate poles, upwards of 20 feet apart. During the day the Portuguese flag was hauled down by a boy at the instigation of a certain Captain Seeley, a drillmaster of the Monterey Cadets. Ortins raised the flag again, but in the evening it was cut down by a small boy at the instance of one Harry Morton, and was burned.

The matter was brought by the Department of State to the attention of the governor of California, who caused it to be investigated by the district attorney of Monterey County. The district attorney, in his report, said: " The acts of both Seeley and Morton must not be attributed to the citizens, and the latter surely disavow all blame for the deeds of Captain Seeley, an adventurous drillmaster of unknown and unbegrudged antecedents, and of Harry Morton, an extremist in the imbibing from the flowing bowl." A copy of the district attorney's report was communicated to the Portuguese minister, with an expression of confidence that he would find in it abundant proof that the lawless act of which he had complained " in no wise represented the feelings of the law-abiding portion of the community." The Department of State added: " That no insult to the Portuguese Government could be intended is obvious when it is considered that Mr. Ortins, who displayed the flag, was himself a naturalized citizen of the United States, and as such had no right to fly the flag of the country of his origin for the distinctive purpose of protection or in assertion of any right claimable by him as a Portuguese subject. So far as his individual rights are concerned, he had a remedy at law against the guilty parties, but declined to lodge a complaint. These circumstances, however, do not exclude sincere regret for the occurrence and disavowal of sympathy therewith on the part of the reputable citizens of Monterey, which I have now the pleasure to express to you."

> Mr. Adee, Acting Sec. of State, to Viscount de Santo-Thyrso, Portuguese min., July 28, 1897, For Rel. 1897, 433.
>
> The Portuguese minister expressed the belief that these explanations would be well received by his Government, and a copy of his note was communicated to the governor of California as closing the incident. (For. Rel. 1897, 434.)

" Referring to the informal memorandum handed to the Assistant Secretary on the 25th of September last by Mr. von Mumm, touching the reported action of soldiers from the United States transport *Sheridan* in hauling down a German flag from the Orpheum Hotel, in Honolulu, I have the honor to advise you that I am now in receipt of a report from the Secretary of War, to whom I communicated the memorandum with a view to ascertaining what steps had been taken to discover and appropriately punish the authors of this act.

" From the report of the senior officer in command of the troops on board the *Sheridan* at the time of the occurrences complained of, it appears that a prompt investigation was made by him with a view to severely punishing such soldiers as might have been guilty of the offense charged; but that, notwithstanding all efforts, it was not possible to bring the charges home to the recruits concerned, owing to the inability of the authorities to fix their identity. It is deeply regretted that this untoward result should have defeated the desire and purpose of the responsible commander to inflict condign punishment on the offenders, and the Secretary of War, in communicating to me the report of the commander of the *Sheridan*, is pained that, under the circumstances, he can do no more in this instance than express reprobation of such disgraceful conduct on the part of men wearing the uniform of the United States and give assurance of the determination of the military authorities to severely punish such offenders when it is possible to ascertain their identity."

> Mr. Hay, Sec. of State, to Herr von Holleben, German ambassador, January 25, 1900, MS. Notes to German Leg. XII. 398.
>
> See, also, Mr. Hay, Sec. of State, to Mr. von Mumm, German embassy, Oct. 21 and Oct. 23, 1899, MS. Notes to German Leg. XII. 361, 362.

(2) QUARANTINE.

§ 191.

In a letter to the governor of Pennsylvania, July 8, 1796, Mr. Pickering, referring to the "orders" which had General principles. "been given on the subject of quarantine, agreeably to an act of Congress passed at their last session," enclosed a "copy of a letter from the Secretary of the Treasury showing what instructions have been given to the collectors of the customs, and the copy of a circular letter from the Secretary of War to the officers commanding the forts on the seacoast."

> Mr. Pickering, Sec. of State, to the governor of Pennsylvania, July 8, 1796, 9 MS. Dom. Let. 202.
>
> July 8, 1803, Mr. Madison addressed a communication to the British and French ministers, requesting them to take such measures as they might deem useful to lessen the inconveniences which American vessels might suffer on account of "the vigorous precautions of quarantine" which had at times been exercised against American commerce in France and Great Britain. Mr. Madison observed that "the occasional prevalence of the yellow fever in some of the seaports of the United States" had "sometimes produced abroad apprehensions not justified by the local state and degree of the malady." (Mr. Madison, Sec. of State, to Messrs. Thornton and Pichon, British and French ministers, July 8, 1803, 14 MS. Dom. Let. 169.)

"I have received information that measures, imposing serious restrictions on our navigation and commerce, are taking in the North of Europe, with a view to guard against the disorder called the yellow fever. It is represented that these restrictions are likely to be generally extended in that quarter through the means of a concert, promoted by one of the most influential powers, and it is probable that the —— government may be invited to adopt them. Should it yield to such solicitations, a source of injury will be opened affecting not only ourselves but the interest of . . . , to whom the navigation of the United States, as a neutral nation entitled to and enjoying in a high degree the respect due to its flag, is of the greatest importance, whilst it would prove an unnecessary expedient, as far as respects the United States, for the prevention of the calamity for which it may be calculated.

" In the circular letter from this Department to the consuls and commercial agents of the United States, dated 1st Aug. 1801, the injustice was noticed of indiscriminating prohibitions of intercourse with a country so extensive as the United States on account of the prevalence of this disease in an individual port, and it was also observed that in the winter months it was impossible it could be conveyed from the United States, as that season has been found uniformly to extinguish it. It may be added, that at the utmost a very slight examination by the health officers in the . . . ports would ascertain whether any of our vessels were infected, as the infection could not fail, on account of the distance of the two countries, to manifest on their arrival the most unequivocal appearances, if it existed in them. But it is a fact highly encouraging to the prospect of a final exclusion and extinction of the malady in our ports, that of late years its recurrence has been less frequent, has affected fewer of them, and that its character of malignity and fatality has been mitigated; accordingly no disorder resembling it appeared during the last summer and autumn on any point of the seaboard north of Charleston, S. C., or if there were any such appearance it was too slight to claim attention, and some of the cities where its visitation was most apprehended escaped it the preceding year.

" Copies of the circular referred to and its enclosure are enclosed, and you are requested to lose no time in explaining this subject to . . . ministry. In particular you will furnish them with a copy of the letter of the Secretary of the Treasury respecting it, and assure them that its injunctions have been and will continue to be scrupulously observed."

> Mr. Madison, Sec. of State, to United States ministers at Paris, London, and Madrid, May 13, 1805, MS. Inst. to U. States Ministers, VI. 294.
>
> In the instruction to Gen. Armstrong, minister to France, there was added the following sentence:
>
> "As the Bavarian Government may be in like manner requested to accede to the restrictions in question, you will make similar explanation to its minister at Paris."
>
> Mr. McLane, Secretary of State, in an instruction to Mr. Hammett, United States consul at Naples, May 13, 1834, said that the boards of health in the principal cities of the United States had been advised to open correspondence with the board of health of Naples to induce the latter to abate the severity of its quarantine regulations. (5 MS. Desp. to Consuls, 311.)

"The tabular statement accompanying my report of the 18th ultimo to the Senate contains a notice of French sanitary regulations requiring of all passengers, landing in France, individual bills of health, delivered by the French consul at the port of departure. From a French paper lately received at this Department, I extract the ordinance, of which the enclosed is a translation, and from which it appears that the regulation referred to is repealed. I communicate this information, that the proper correction may be made in the tabular statement from the Department, if it shall be thought necessary." (Mr. Forsyth, Sec. of State, to the Vice-President of the United States, Jan. 3, 1840, 30 MS. Dom. Let. 431.)

"The French passenger steamer *La France*, of Marseilles, on December 30, 1885, entered the bay of Bahia, and being signaled to stop by the national gun-boat for the purpose of undergoing sanitary inspection before proceeding to her anchorage, disregarded the signal, whereupon the gun-boat fired two blank charges at her. This warning likewise receiving no attention, the fort of Gamboa gave her two shots, one of which struck her on the prow, killing a passenger, an Italian. The French Government, on behalf of the owners of *La France*, sent in a claim for damages caused by the cannon ball fired from the fort, and proposed to the Imperial Government that in the future the firing of ball be discontinued, substituting for this fines graded to suit the gravity of the case. It was alleged by the captain of the packet that the first signal was not given; that the two blank shots were supposed to come from a man-of-war at gun practice, and, finally, that his vessel had a clean bill of health, and did not come from an infected port. Brazil replied that the damage done the vessel and the death of the passenger were the result of systematic disobedience of port regulations on the part of commanders of foreign packets, and of utter disregard for the signals from the gun-boat, which were duly given in the case; that the only way to prevent the introduction of disease from foreign ports was to subject vessels coming from those ports to rigid inspection before entering the inner harbor, and the only way to compel them to stop, when they disregarded the signals, was to fire on them with shot. The claim of the Italian Government in behalf of the family of the passenger killed was likewise rejected. Claims made by English companies for firing upon their vessels under circumstances similar to the above were not entertained by the foreign office."

Mr. Trail, chargé at Rio de Janeiro, to Mr. Bayard, Sec. of State, Jan. 21, 1887, For. Rel. 1887, 54, 55.

In 1893 the Italian Government obtained an award of damages, in behalf of an Italian subject, named Lavarello, against the Government of Portugal, for the arbitrary and illegal application of quarantine measures at Cape Verde in August, 1884, while cholera was prevalent in certain European ports. (Moore, Int. Arbitrations, V. 5021 et seq.)

" I have received advices from Messrs. Miller, Bull and Co., of New York, agents of the New York and Porto Rico Steamship Company, that the Spanish consul at the port of New York refuses to clear the steamship *Rannock*, carrying freight only, or any other vessel for the island of Puerto Rico, until twenty days after the last case or suspected case of cholera at New York. The consul states that he thus acts in conformity with cabled instructions from the governor-general of Puerto Rico. The *Rannock*, being laden and ready for sea, has been thus detained for several days.

" The question thus presented goes far beyond that of the onerous quarantine, whether of observation or of sanitary detention, imposed at Mariel upon vessels from any port of the United States to any port of Cuba, which has called forth my recent notes to Señor Sagrario. The action of the governor-general of Porto Rico and of the Spanish consul at New York is in fact a complete inhibition for the time being upon commerce between the port of New York and the island of Puerto Rico. Indeed it may be regarded as going still further and imposing preventive detention at the will of the authorities of Puerto Rico, in a foreign jurisdiction.

" I have already had the honor to apprise your legation of the sanitary condition of the ports of this country, and I now beg to repeat my statements and to request that you will use your good offices with the governor-general of Puerto Rico to remove the wholly needless and exaggerated embargo upon commerce between the United States and that island. To the reasonable enforcement of local observation in the country of destination, and of quarantine when the conditions of the particular vessel and voyage may require it, this Government can have no objection. But the reported measure in respect to Puerto Rico is not quarantine, it is absolute non-intercourse."

Mr. Foster, Sec. of State, to Señor Don Enrique Dupuy de Lome, Span. min., Oct. 1, 1892, MS. Notes to Spain, X. 669.

"A copy of your No. 92, of the 1st ultimo, concerning the entire closure of the Pacific Isthmus ports against vessels coming from Chile, having been inclosed to the Postmaster-General, I now state in substance his views in regard to the question.

" While this is the first instance known to the Post-Office Department of an absolute exclusion of the mails as a sanitary measure, yet it is to be observed that the ordinary precautions of disinfection, etc., have never proved entirely effective as regards cholera, and therefore, despite the inconvenience caused by the action of the Colombian Government, the Postmaster-General is of opinion that we will have no tenable ground of complaint if the ports are opened as soon as the danger of infection ceases.

" This Department is, however, disposed to regard the Colombian measures as extreme and at variance with the usages of civilized nations, not to speak of the transit question involved.

" The mails are, as we are informed, now being sent to Chile via Buenos Ayres."

> Mr. Bayard, Sec. of State, to Mr. Walker, chargé at Bogota, April 17, 1888, For. Rel. 1888, I. 422.
>
> See, to the same effect, Mr. Bayard, Sec. of State, to Mr. Roberts, min. to Chile, April 17, 1888, For. Rel. 1888, I. 194.
>
> See also Mr. Bayard, Sec. of State, to Mr. Maury, min. to Colombia, Jan. 11, 1888, For. Rel. 1888, I. 408; Mr. Bayard, Sec. of State, to the Postmaster-General, April 10, 1888, 168 MS. Dom. Let. 21.

" I have received and duly considered your letter of the 10th instant, invoking, on behalf of the Panama Railroad Company, the further intervention of the Government of the United States with that of Colombia to cause the relaxation of the quarantine regulations of the Department of Panama so as to permit the conveyance in transit of freight from the ' so-called infected ports ' of Europe.

" This Department has gone as far as the proper protection of the national and commercial interests of the United States demanded and warranted in representing the extraordinary hardships inflicted on the commerce of this country by excluding its vessels from entry into the isthmian ports, when nothing in the sanitary condition of the ports of the United States could justify such treatment on the assumption that they were infected with Asiatic cholera. In this it has happily been successful.

"As regards the maritime commerce of the isthmian ports with European countries, this Department has not the same latitude and right of original protest which it possesses in respect to commerce of American origin. The rigid measures imposed in the United States against European communications rested necessarily on the ascertained fact that many of the most important ports of the Continent were infected with epidemic cholera; and we could not urge the Government of Colombia to show less concern at the existence of the disease in such ports as Hamburg and Havre, nor assume the defence of European exporting interests, on the ground that an American corporation comes in for a share of the hardship occasioned by sanitary measures applied to the commerce of those countries. As you state it, the existing restrictions are injurious to the Panama Railroad Company in so far as they prevent the entry into the isthmian ports of vessels bringing freight from ' infected ports.'

" If applied to freight from European ports known to be infected, and so regarded by our own quarantine administrations, this Government could not consistently remonstrate.

" The treaty stipulations between the United States and Colombia relative to the uninterrupted neutrality of the Isthmus of Panama as an avenue of interoceanic transit do not strike one as pertinent to the present aspects of the question.

" There remains the practical suggestion that, under the terms of its contract with Colombia, your company is competent to maintain a local system of quarantine at the ports of the Department of Panama, and to enforce, at its own expense, such sanitary measures as may be adopted in cooperation with the Colombian Government. I have already brought this aspect of the problem to the notice of the Colombian Government in a telegraphic instruction to Mr. Abbott; and if you so desire I shall take pleasure in further supporting it by sending to Consul-General Adamson a copy of your letter and of this reply, and instructing him to intimate the pleasure this Government would feel were the friendly proposals of your corporation found adequate to provide such adequate and usual sanitary measures of local precaution and prevention as would remove the danger of infection through commerce with any cholera ports."

Mr. Wharton, Act. Sec. of State, to Mr. Lauterbach, Oct. 13, 1892, 188 MS. Dom. Let. 492.

Mr. Adamson was afterwards so instructed. (Mr. Wharton, Act. Sec. of State, to Mr. Lauterbach, Oct. 22, 1892, 188 MS. Dom. Let. 604.

See, also, Mr. Cridler, 3rd Assist. Sec. of State, to Mr. Snyder, Oct. 30, 1897, 222 MS. Dom. Let. 115.

" The measures taken by the Government in 1892 to protect the towns on the Atlantic coast from contagion from the Asiatic cholera by the closure of the ports against vessels proceeding from infected or suspicious places, caused the U. S. Government to claim that their vessels should be exempted from such a measure, and claiming, with justice, that the epidemic had not declared itself in any part of the United States.

" The home office having resolved to empower the authorities on the coast to decide each case on its own merits, the press of this capital and of other places declared the closure to have been stopped in favor of the United States on account of the Government at Washington having declared its intention of opening our ports by force. It was evident that this false report tended to diminish the cordiality cultivated by the United States with Colombia, as it made the Government of that country appear to ignore the sovereignty of the Republic in the most flagrant manner; and it was also evident that it made this Republic appear to be insensible to so great an insult, and to tolerate the violation of her most sacred rights. For these reasons it was necessary to rectify these assertions, and to this end a note was passed to the American legation in this city, in which, having explained the causes thereof, it was asked whether the President of the

Union had given any order resembling that which had appeared in the public papers. The representative of the United States certified not only that such orders had not been communicated to the legation, but that having asked the Secretary of State whether any such orders had been transmitted to any agent of their Government, it had received an answer in the negative."

> Report of the Colombian Minister of Foreign Affairs, 1894, For. Rel. 1894, 197.
>
> The laws of South American countries contain very strict provisions against the disinterment, within certain terms, of persons who have died of certain diseases. (Mr. Day, Assist. Sec. of State, to Mr. Wilson, Oct. 22, 1897, 221, MS. Dom. 615.)

In September, 1893, the United States legation at Lisbon was instructed: " Protest earnestly against groundlessness and injustice of decree declaring ports of New York and New Jersey infected. Rigid quarantine exists and general health excellent. Last death at New York quarantine August 12, and last case August 13; no cholera there or elsewhere in the United States."

> Mr. Gresham, Sec. of State, to Mr. Caruth, min. to Portugal, Sept. 19, 1893, MS. Inst. Portugal, XVI. 36.

" I have the honor, by order of my Government, to submit the following for your information:

" The American quarantine and immigration acts of February 15 and March 3 of last year, respectively, and the regulations issued by the Treasury Department for carrying these into effect, contain certain provisions which, in the opinion of the Imperial Government, are not exactly compatible with the sovereign rights of foreign states. This is especially the case—referring only to the salient points—(1) with the provision of the quarantine act whereby the American consul of the port of departure, or the American medical officer specially detailed there for that purpose, shall, before he issues a bill of health, in order to verify that the facts therein stated are true, make an inspection of the crew, passengers, and cargo, etc., before the vessel's departure. The officer making the inspection is further authorized by the quarantine regulations, based upon the quarantine act, to order the disinfection of the vessel and such other sanitary measures on board as he considers necessary.

" By these and similar provisions American consuls and medical officers at European ports of departure are given authority to act officially toward vessels clearing therefrom, for which no foundation exists either in generally recognized international maxims or even— with respect to Germany—in the consular convention of December 11, 1871. Concerning the inspection of vessels and their equipments, the examination of the crew and passengers, and the supervision of measures for disinfection, German regulations exist in German ports, which are most conscientiously carried out by the German authorities.

"While, as is seen from the above statements, the duties of American consuls and medical officers in German ports do not appear to be founded upon international rules, the apprehension, furthermore, is not to be dismissed, that the working, side by side, of the German (official) sanitary authorities with American consuls and physicians might create confusion and apparently unnecessary impediments in intercourse.

"(2) In like manner the provision of the American immigration act does not appear reconcilable with the law of nations where it provides that the lists prescribed, in which a number of dates concerning the emigrants are to be given, must be sworn to by the master or an officer or the physician of the vessel before the American consul at the port of departure. In the opinion of the Imperial Government the administering of oaths is an authoritative act which can not be performed without the sanction of the government of the country in the territory of which the oath is administered by the foreigner.

"An American consul, therefore, except with reference to American citizens, is not deemed authorized to perform such an act without first obtaining the sanction of the German authorities.

"For the above reasons the Imperial Government considers it its duty to enter a protest against the provisions of the American quarantine and immigration acts of February 15 and March 3, 1893, so far as they encroach upon the [rights of] sovereignty of the German Empire. While the Imperial Government at present restricts itself to a defense in principle of its position, it must in the future reserve the right, on befitting occasions, to oppose American consuls and medical officers on German territory with reference to German ships.

"Requesting that your excellency will be good enough to advise me of his views on the subject above set forth, I avail myself also of this occasion," etc.

Baron Saurma, German embassy, to Mr. Gresham, Sec. of State, Dec. 17, 1894, For. Rel. 1895, I. 511.

"I have the honor to acknowledge the receipt of your note of December 17, 1894, calling attention to certain provisions of the quarantine and immigration laws and regulations of the United States which, in the opinion of your Government, are not consistent with the principles of international law, nor with any treaty between this Government and the German Empire. The laws and regulations against which your Government's objections are especially directed are:

"(1) The provisions of the quarantine act of February 15, 1893, and the regulations made in pursuance of it, which require the consular or medical officer of the United States stationed in a foreign port to inspect vessels of all nationalities departing for the United States, and the crews, passengers, and cargoes.

"(2) The provisions of the same act and regulations which empower the consular or medical officer to order the disinfection of such vessels, and in other respects to regulate their internal condition and arrangement, before granting the bill of health required for the entry of the vessel in a port of the United States.

"(3) The provisions of the immigration act of March 3, 1893, which require that the master and surgeon of any vessel carrying immigrants to the United States shall present to the American consular officer at the port of departure descriptive lists of the immigrants, verified by the oaths of the master and surgeon taken before such officer.

" Your Government regards the exercise of these administrative functions by our consular and medical officers in Germany in connection with ships that are not American as unauthorized and in disregard of its sovereignty.

" The United States have an extensive seaboard open on both oceans to the introduction of infectious and contagious diseases from Europe and Asia and Central and South America. To avert this danger a rigid system of maritime sanitation has been provided. It is set forth and explained in a pamphlet published by the Treasury Department. I append a copy for your examination. The regulations to be observed at ports of the United States are printed on pages 24 and following. It will be seen that they provide for the inspection, quarantine, and disinfection of vessels after arrival at American ports, but before entry and discharge of passengers, cargo, and crew.

"All vessels are required to be inspected before entry in order that it may be known on arrival whether or not they are in fit sanitary condition to enter our ports. The conditions which require detention in quarantine are specified. It will be noticed that compliance with the regulations to be observed in foreign ports may, and in practice often does, avert or shorten quarantine at the port of arrival; and the same is true in regard to disinfection.

" The United States have in operation in their own jurisdiction a complete and adequate system of safeguards against the introduction of disease from foreign countries, and are not dependent upon precautions taken abroad; but it has been our policy to effect this purpose of keeping out disease with as little hindrance as possible to commercial intercourse with foreign countries, and with the least inconvenience and expense to incoming ships. To this end provision has been made for taking measures at the port of departure which will enable a vessel to enter our ports with an authentic sanitary record,

and often to escape the more burdensome of our domestic requirements. Failure to comply with these regulations at foreign ports
subjects the vessel on arrival here to the full rigor of our domestic
quarantine system.

" The authority given by the act of March 3, 1893, to consular
officers to administer oaths to the masters and surgeons of vessels carrying immigrants to the United States was intended to serve the
same beneficial purpose by preventing the embarkation of immigrants
prohibited by law from coming to the United States, and by facilitating the examination at the port of arrival of the immigrants, who
are confined at the vessel's expense until their right to land is ascertained. A copy of this act and of the regulations made under it is
inclosed for your perusal.

" The acts of the United States consular and medical officers, of
which your Government now speaks, are performed primarily in the
interest of the vessels, many of which are German, and of foreign
trade. They have been efficiently aided by the shipowners, who avail
themselves of the opportunity offered them to avoid delays and impediments to their business in our ports. This alternative opportunity is offered, and the necessary agencies for taking advantage of
it are provided in a spirit of cooperation and comity which it was
expected would be appreciated, and in furtherance of mutually beneficial commercial intercourse which we, no less earnestly than any
foreign nation, desire to maintain. This Government does not claim
that under any treaty or the rules of international law it can authorize
its officers to inspect foreign vessels or order their disinfection in
German ports, or to administer oaths to officers of foreign ships
within the jurisdiction of the German Empire. The operation of the
sanitary and immigration system of the United States in a foreign
port is conditioned upon the consent of the government having jurisdiction of the port. Prior to the receipt of your protest the consent
of your Government was reasonably assumed, because these provisions
were beneficial to your carrying trade and commercial interests. If
the Imperial Government is unwilling that consular and medical
officers of the United States shall continue to execute these laws and
regulations in German ports upon vessels which are not American,
steps will be taken to comply with its wishes, leaving foreign vessels
coming to the United States from German ports subject to the sanitary provisions in force at the port of arrival and the prescribed
consequences.

" I will add for the information of your Government that no
medical officers have been stationed in German ports within the last
twelve months for the purpose of executing our quarantine and
immigration laws and regulations. These duties have been per-

formed by consular officers alone, and they are forbidden to receive any personal compensation whatever for their services. The actual expense of the inspection or disinfection and a moderate official fee, which goes into the Treasury of the United States, form the total of direct expense thus incurred by vessels in foreign ports."

> Mr. Gresham, Sec. of State, to Baron Saurma, German embassy, Jan. 26, 1895, For. Rel. 1895, I. 512.
>
> The medical officers sent abroad to various European countries by the Marine-Hospital Service, under the act of March 3, 1893, were all withdrawn in December of that year.

November 2, 1895, Mr. Olney, as Secretary of State, referring to a communication of the Secretary of Agriculture to the effect that for a number of years the Canadian government had prohibited the shipment of cattle from the United States across Canadian territory for export from Canadian ports, requested the British ambassador to inquire as to the cause of the prohibition to the end that its revocation might be brought about in conformity with "Article 29 of the existing treaty between the United States and Great Britain of May 18, 1871," by which the privilege of such shipment " appears to be clearly granted." [a] The British ambassador, on the 4th of the following February, replied " that the Dominion government, while admitting to the fullest extent the transit obligations defined in article 29 of the treaty of May 18, 1871, explain that the restrictions of which complaint is made have relation simply to regulations formed under the 'animal contagious diseases act,' and therefore pertain solely to 'health of animals.' " The United States, it was observed, made similar restrictions under the quarantine laws in regard to Canadian animals in transit, and the opinion was expressed that such restrictions were not in contravention of the provisions of the treaty of 1871.[b]

" Referring to your note of the 17th ultimo, requesting that the prohibition of the importation of Swiss cattle into the United States be removed, I have the honor to inform you that I have received a letter from the Acting Secretary of Agriculture dated the 11th instant, stating that it is not the purpose of the Department of Agriculture to criticise either the laws or the administration of the veterinary police regulations in Switzerland, but the fact that a large number of animals have been reported with foot-and-mouth disease, month after month, indicates that prompt measures have not been adopted for the eradication of the disease; that as to the admission of cattle from Holland,

---

[a] For. Rel. 1895, I. 704.

[b] For. Rel. 1895, I. 705. The power of the several States of the United States to protect by suitable quarantine legislation domestic animals from contagious and infectious diseases is upheld in Smith *v.* St. Louis & S. R'y Co. (1901), 181 U. S. 248.

which is referred to in your note, the Department of Agriculture is making an investigation concerning the prevalence of contagious diseases in that country; that in case it finds that contagious diseases prevail there which are dangerous to the domesticated animals of the United States, the entry of cattle from that country will not be allowed; that as a matter of fact no cattle can be imported from any European country without a permit from the Department of Agriculture, and that no permit will be issued for cattle from Holland or any other country if it is known to the Department of Agriculture that foot-and-mouth disease exists in such country.

" The Acting Secretary of Agriculture concludes his letter by stating that in order to demonstrate his friendly feeling toward the Swiss Government, he has issued a permit for the importation of the cattle of Mr. de Wattenryl, concerning which this correspondence originated, on the condition that such cattle shall be quarantined in Holland before shipment.

" It is hoped that this course will relieve all the parties concerned of the embarrassment of a herd of cattle stopped in transit; and, as sufficient notice has now been given of the regulations of this Government, it is thought that all cause for dissatisfaction has been removed."

> Mr. Adee, Act. Sec. of State, to Dr. Vogel, Swiss Leg., Aug. 13, 1896, MS. Notes to Switzerland, I. 412.

In 1898 an order was issued prohibiting the importation under certain circumstances of American fruit into Germany, the object of the prohibition, as declared in the decree, being to prevent the introduction of the San José scale (*Aspidiotus perniciosus*).

> For. Rel. 1898, 307–319, 320, 321–346.

In August, 1900, the minister of the United States at Montevideo was, by request of the Secretary of the Navy, instructed to express to President Cuestas, of Uruguay, the thanks of the Navy Department for his " courtesy " in reducing " the length of quarantine that would otherwise have been imposed upon the *Chicago*, *Montgomery*, and *Wilmington*, arriving at Montevideo from Rio de Janeiro in June last."

> Mr. Adee, Act. Sec. of State, to Sec. of Navy, August 9, 1900, 247 MS. Dom. Let. 87.

Question of National and State control. " Referring to your note of the 8th instant, in regard to the arrival at San Francisco of Ye Wang Yong and Ye Cha Yung, members of the Corean legation at this capital, said to be detained at quarantine at that port, I have now the honor to apprize you of the receipt of a letter from the Secretary of the Treasury dated the 12th instant, informing me of the receipt of a telegram on the 11th instant from the collector of customs at San Francisco, wherein he states that the Department has been misinformed as to the cause of the detention of the Coreans. It appears that no notice or application had been made to the collector's office in their behalf, and that the gentlemen you mention arrived with a number of Chinese on a steamer infected with typhus fever. The steamer and passengers were accordingly, under State law, placed in quarantine. The collector has, however, applied to the board of health for the release of the Coreans."

Mr. Bayard, Sec. of State, to Mr. Ye Ha Yung, Corean Leg. Jan. 15, 1889,
MS. Notes to Corea, I. 11.

" I have the honor to transmit herewith for your information, in connection with my note of the 8th instant, a copy of a letter from his excellency the governor of Texas, of the 15th instant, in respect of the quarantine established by that State against the ports of Vera Cruz, Tuxpan and Tampico.

" It will be observed that Governor Hogg expresses regret that the State of Texas is forced by the apparent inadequacy of the quarantine regulations in Mexico, to resort to vigorous measures for the protection of her own citizens against contagious and infectious diseases originating at the points named. Until the situation is voluntarily altered in Mexico, Governor Hogg believes that he is justified in adhering to the recommendations of his health officer. 'As a solution of the trouble, I beg to suggest,' he adds 'that should the health officers of Vera Cruz, Tuxpan and Tampico be willing to meet those in charge of the quarantine affairs of our State at some convenient point, I shall cheerfully have every measure taken by the Texas authorities to make the conference satisfactory and successful.' "

Mr. Wharton, Act. Sec. of State, to Mr. Romero, Mex. min. Sept. 21,
1891, MS. Notes to Mexico, IX. 576.

The right of the several States to establish quarantine regulations is not limited by any existing treaty between the United States and Sweden and Norway.

Minneapolis, &c. Ry. Co. v. Milner, 57 Fed. Rep. 276.

" The subject of quarantine regulations, inspection, and control was brought suddenly to my attention by the arrival at our ports in August last of vessels infected with cholera. Quarantine regulations should be uniform at all our ports. Under the Constitution they are plainly within the exclusive Federal jurisdiction when and so far as Congress shall legislate. In my opinion the whole subject should be taken into national control, and adequate power given to the Executive to protect our people against plague invasions. On the 1st of

September last I approved regulations establishing a twenty-day quarantine for all vessels bringing immigrants from foreign ports. This order will be continued in force. Some loss and suffering have resulted to passengers, but a due care for the homes of our people justifies in such cases the utmost precaution. There is danger that with the coming of spring cholera will again appear, and a liberal appropriation should be made at this session to enable our quarantine and port officers to exclude the deadly plague.

" But the most careful and stringent quarantine regulations may not be sufficient absolutely to exclude the disease. The progress of medical and sanitary science has been such, however, that if approved precautions are taken at once to put all of our cities and towns in the best sanitary condition, and provision is made for isolating any sporadic cases and for a thorough disinfection, an epidemic can, I am sure, be avoided. This work appertains to the local authorities, and the responsibility and the penalty will be appalling if it is neglected or unduly delayed."

President Harrison, annual message, Dec. 6, 1892, For. Rel. 1892, xxx.–xxxi.

State laws in regard to quarantine belong to that class of legislation which is valid till displaced by Congress, and such legislation has been expressly recognized by the laws of the United States from the beginning of the Government. (Louisiana v. Texas (1900), 176 U. S. 1, 21, citing Morgan Steamship Co. v. Louisiana Board of Health, 118 U. S. 455 ; Compagnie Française v. Board of Health, 186 U. S. 380.)

"A National Board of Health was created by act of Congress, approved March 3, 1879. Another act was approved June 2, 1879, clothing the Board with certain quarantine powers, but this last act was limited to a period of four years, at the expiration of which time Congress declined to renew it. The National Board of Health, therefore, had an active existence from 1879 to 1883. The act establishing the Board, March 3, 1879, remained upon the statute books until February 15, 1893, when it was formally repealed by Congress, but the operations of the Board were confined to the four years above mentioned—1879 to 1883. The principal functions of the National Board of Health are now administered by the Marine Hospital Service." (Public Health Service in the United States, by Surgeon-General Walter Wyman, U. S. Marine Hospital Service, Cleveland Journal of Medicine, February, 1897.)

Jan. 4, 1882, Mr. Frelinghuysen, Secretary of State, transmitted to the consular officers of the United States a set of regulations, revised by the National Board of Health, for securing the best sanitary conditions of vessels, etc., coming to the United States, and certain additional rules to prevent the introduction of smallpox into the United States. The rules, approved by President Arthur, were signed by J. L. Cabell, as president of the National Board of Health. (MS. Circulars, Dept. of State.)

In the Annual Report of the Marine-Hospital Service, 1896, may be found a protest addressed by Surgeon-General Wyman to the Secretary of the Treasury, Dec. 4, 1895, against the conditions existing at Havana, together with the letter of the Secretary of the Treasury forwarding it, the reply of the Secretary of State, Mr. Olney, and the note addressed by Mr. Olney to the Spanish minister at Washington on the subject. The protest of Dr. Wyman is also printed in the Cleveland Journal of Medicine, February, 1897, in his article on the Public Health Service in the United States.

See, also, the report of the Committee on International Quarantine, adopted by the Pan-American Medical Congress, held in the City of Mexico, November 16–19, 1896. (New York Medical Journal, March 6, 1897.)

See Marine-Hospital Service: Maritime Quarantine against Yellow Fever; reprint from Yellow Fever, its Nature, Diagnosis, etc., 1898.

" The recent prevalence of yellow fever in a number of cities and towns throughout the South has resulted in much disturbance of commerce and demonstrated the necessity of such amendments to our quarantine laws as will make the regulations of the national quarantine authorities paramount. The Secretary of the Treasury in the portion of his report relating to the operation of the Marine Hospital Service calls attention to the defects in the present quarantine laws and recommends amendments thereto which will give the Treasury Department the requisite authority to prevent the invasion of epidemic diseases from foreign countries, and in times of emergency like that of the past summer will add to the efficiency of the sanitary measures for the protection of the people and at the same time prevent unnecessary restriction of commerce. I concur in his recommendation."

President McKinley, annual message, Dec. 6, 1897.

For the appeal of the owners of the Norwegian steamship *Nicaragua* to the equitable consideration of the United States Government for losses resulting from being quarantined at Mobile, Ala., in consequence of bringing American citizens from Bluefields as an act of humanity, see S. Doc. 17, 56 Cong. 1 sess.

As to the order of the Secretary of the Treasury of July, 1884, that no rags be received from infected ports, see Mr. Frelinghuysen, Sec. of State, to the consulate-general at Cairo, July 19 and 21, and Aug. 6, 1884; and Mr. J. Davis, Assist. Sec., to same, Sept. 1, 1884, MS. Inst. Egypt, XVI. 383, 384.

May 16, 1900, the Surgeon-General of the United States Marine-Hospital Service instructed the supervising surgeon-general at San Francisco, in case the existence of bubonic plague was officially proclaimed there, to request certain transportation officials to refuse tickets to Chinese and Japanese, without a certificate signed by the marine-hospital officer.[a] May 18 the existence of the plague was officially declared by the board of health.[b] Thereupon the Surgeon-

---

[a] For. Rel. 1900, 743.   [b] For. Rel. 1900, 741.

General, acting under the act of Congress of March 27, 1890, issued an order directing transportation companies to refuse transportation to Asiatics without certificates.[a] Notice of this order was communicated to the Japanese consul-general at San Francisco by the president of the board of health, who stated that the board was actively cooperating with the United States authorities to prevent the exit of Chinese and Japanese who failed to present a certificate that the bearer had been inoculated with the Haffkine prophylactic against bubonic plague.[b] The consul-general protested against this discriminatory treatment of his countrymen, which he maintained was not warranted by existing conditions; and the subject was brought by the Japanese legation at Washington to the notice of the Department of State as a violation of treaty rights.[c] The Surgeon-General of the Marine-Hospital Service stated that no orders had been issued by his Bureau requiring preventive inoculations; that its action was confined to inspections and restraints of travel, as temporary emergency measures, in regard to Asiatics, the plague having been found to exist only among the Chinese in Chinatown, where also dwelt a number of Japanese; and that the representative of the Bureau at San Francisco had been instructed to make no race discrimination.[d] The Japanese legation also complained that the health board of Colorado had imposed a general quarantine against Chinese and Japanese who should be without certificates that they had not been exposed to the plague for the preceding six months.[e]

The Japanese legation subsequently inquired (1) whether the United States Government would give an official assurance that, as it had no intention to discriminate against Japanese subjects, and as the action of the local medical officials had been declared by the Federal district court to have been illegal, the facts might be considered as a sufficient proof that the United States concurred in the views of the Japanese Government on the question of treaty rights; (2) whether the United States Government, in communicating the legation's complaint to the governor of Colorado, intended to suggest to him to refrain from any further action inappropriate to a reasonable solution of the question, and whether he had raised any objection.

The Department of State replied:

1. That the Government of the United States could with pleasure assure the Japanese Government that in the enforcement of the quarantine measures at San Francisco there was no intention to discriminate against Japanese subjects; that the rights of Japanese, as defined in art. 1 of the treaty of 1894, were subject to the proviso of

---

a For. Rel. 1900, 742. c For. Rel. 1900, 737–744.
b For. Rel. 1900, 740. d For. Rel. 1900, 745–746.
e For. Rel. 1900, 746.

art. 2 that the stipulations of the preceding article should "not in any way affect the laws, ordinances, and regulations with regard to trade, the immigration of laborers, police, and public security, which are in force or which may hereafter be enacted in either of the two countries;" that the decision of the Federal district court was based upon the ground that the discrimination against Asiatic races was unconstitutional, and not upon any ground of treaty right, but that, as the reasoning of the decision was in line with the Japanese contention, the course of the United States, unless the Supreme Court should in some future case determine the question differently, would, as regarded its own acts and its representations to State authorities, coincide with the view of the Japanese Government as to the treaty rights of its subjects in the matter under discussion.

2. That it was the intention of the Department to make to the governor of Colorado the suggestion mentioned, and that no case had since arisen requiring his action; and that the United States Government, while for constitutional reasons unable to give guaranties against the recurrence of cases like that in Colorado, would use its efforts to prevent their occurrence there or elsewhere. [a]

" Referring to your note of June 13 last in relation to certain quarantine measures of San Francisco and Colorado, and to the explanatory statement in connection therewith which you handed to me on the 14th instant, I observe that, in view of the explanations heretofore furnished by the Department, there remains apparently only one point on which you ask further satisfactory assurances, namely: That some action may be taken to protect Japanese subjects against the recurrence of discriminatory quarantine measures. This assurance I am happy to be able to give you; not, indeed, in the precise form in which it is requested, but in a way which will substantially and effectually accomplish the end in view.

" It is in the nature of things impossible to prevent by Federal legislation the enactment of improvident and unconstitutional laws by local authorities, whether State or municipal. But it is entirely feasible to afford prompt and complete redress against such regulations whenever their enforcement is sought to the detriment of personal rights. The individual affected may at once avail himself of the writ of habeas corpus before the Federal courts and obtain his deliverance from any illegal imprisonment, confinement, or restraint.

---

[a] Memorandum of Oct. 13, 1900, For. Rel. 1900, 756. "Complaint was made last summer of the discriminatory enforcement of a bubonic quarantine against Japanese on the Pacific coast and of interference with their travel in California and Colorado, under the health laws of those States. The latter restrictions have been adjudged by a Federal court to be unconstitutional. No recurrence of either cause of complaint is apprehended." (President McKinley, annual message, Dec. 3, 1900.)

He may also avail himself in such cases of the writ of injunction to prevent the enforcement of such illegal regulations. This was done in this very affair in the case of Wong Wai *v.* Williamson (103 Fed. Rep., 1) ; and the act of Congress, which was passed in consequence of the exigencies of the McLeod case, was adopted, not with a view to prevent the passage of illegal local legislation and regulations, but to nullify their effects by empowering the Federal courts, on proper application, to deliver and discharge from the operation of such laws all persons injuriously affected by them, thereby nullifying them for all practical purposes. The remedy thus afforded was and is equally applicable in all cases where quarantine regulations restrain personal liberty (including freedom from interference with the right of personal locomotion or the exercise of any restraint upon the person) in breach of constitutional or treaty rights.

" The remedies already afforded are, therefore, complete; and since it is physically impossible by any act of legislation to prevent at all times and in all places illegal action of local authorities, the demands of civil justice and of national good faith are reasonably met when ample and speedy remedies for the redress of such grievances or of wrongs of any kind are afforded by the laws.

" In case, however, of the passage of local regulations alleged to be in violation of a treaty, the Department would, if the same would be brought by you to its attention, cause the matter to be investigated, and if proper would request the Attorney-General to cooperate in taking the necessary legal steps to enforce the due observance of treaty obligations."

> Mr. Hay, Sec. of State, to Mr. Takahira, Japanese leg., Nov. 26, 1901, For. Rel. 1901, 377.
> As to proceedings taken for the adjustment by the Hawaiian authorities of the claims of Japanese subjects, growing out of the burning of certain houses in Honolulu, as an incident of measures adopted by the board of health there to check the spread of the bubonic plague, see Mr. Hill, Act. Sec. of State, to Mr. Takahira, Sept. 11, 1900, and Mr. Adee, Act. Sec. of State, to Mr. Takahira, Sept. 22, 1900, MS. Notes to Jap. Leg. II. 33, 36.

By the second international conference, held at the City of Mexico, it was recommended that all measures relating to international quarantine should be wholly within the control of the national governments; that each government should establish in its ports two kinds of detention, (*a*) that for inspection or observation, and (*b*) that for disinfection; that quarantine regulations be so framed as to interfere no more than may be necessary with travel and commerce; that the several governments endeavor to cooperate with each other to this end; that notice be given by health organizations in each country to the diplomatic and consular representatives of the other countries of the existence of cholera, yellow fever, bubonic plague, smallpox, or any other serious outbreak; and that it should be made a duty of the sanitary authorities in each port to note on the bill of health of each departing vessel the transmissible diseases there existing. A resolution was also adopted looking to the calling at Washington of a general convention of the representatives of the health organizations of the several republics and of the establishment of a permanent international sanitary bureau at Washington.

Second Int. Conf. of Am. States, S. Doc. 330, 57 Cong. 1 sess. 16.

By the act of April 12, 1900, it was provided that quarantine stations should be established at such places in Porto Rico as the Supervising Surgeon-General of the Marine-Hospital Service of the United States should direct, and that the quarantine regulations relating to the importation of diseases from other countries should be under the control of the Government of the United States (31 Stat. 75–80).

(3) PILOTAGE.

§ 192.

The statutes of New York impose compulsory pilotage on foreign vessels inward and outward bound to and from the port of New York by way of Sandy Hook.

Homer Ramsdell Co. v. La Compagnie Générale Trans-Atlantique (1901), 182 U. S. 406.

In the waters of the United States the regulation of pilotage has been left to the legislatures of the several States.

The international code for preventing collisions was first adopted by act of Congress of April 29, 1864, now incorporated in section 4233 of the Revised Statutes, and was made applicable generally to the " vessels of the Navy and of the mercantile marine of the United States." By the act of March 3, 1885, 23 Statutes at Large, 438, Congress adopted the Revised International Regulations and made them applicable to " the navigation of all public and private vessels of the United States upon the high seas and in all coast waters of the United States," except such as are otherwise provided for. By section 2 all inconsistent laws were repealed, *except* as to the navigation of such vessels within the *harbors*, lakes, and inland waters of the United States. Held that Gedney Channel, a dredged passage about 1,100 feet wide, which constitutes the main entrance to New York Harbor, was as much a part of the inland waters of the United States, within the meaning of the act of 1885, as the harbor within the entrance, the intention of Congress being to allow the original code to remain in force, so far as it applied to waters within which it was necessary for safe navigation to have a local pilot.

The Delaware, 161 U. S. 459 (1896).

The court, p. 463, said:

"Counsel upon one, if not both, sides have assumed, upon the authority of The Aurania and The Republic, 29 Fed. Rep. 98, and Singlehurst *v.* Compagnie Transatlantique, 11 U. S. App. 693, that Gedney Channel is within the 'coast waters of the United States,' and therefore that the vessels involved were subject to the Revised International Regulations of March 3, 1885, c. 354, 23 Stat. 438. We think that they are mistaken in this assumption.'

It having been represented that "American vessels of 80 tons and over" were liable at the port of Halifax to compulsory pilotage, while Canadian vessels were "exempt up to 120 tons," the British Government replied that at Halifax all vessels, whether British or foreign, coming from foreign ports and over 80 tons register, were required to pay pilotage dues, and that the exemption as to vessels of not more than 120 tons applied only to vessels registered in the Dominion and engaged in trading or fishing voyages within ports in the Dominion of Canada, Newfoundland, and St. Pierre, Miquelon.

Mr. Lincoln, min. to England, to Mr. Blaine, Sec. of State, Jan. 6, 1890, For. Rel. 1890, 322.

(4) FREEDOM OF SPEECH AND OF THE PRESS.

§ 193.

"In a charge by Chief Justice McKean, in Philadelphia, in 1791, the attention of the grand jury was called to certain publications of Cobbett and others, grossly attacking the King of Spain as the 'supple tool' of the French nation. From this charge, the following passages are extracted:

"'At a time when misunderstandings prevail between the Republic of France and the United States, and when our General Government have appointed public ministers, to endeavor to effect their removal and restore the former harmony, some of the journals or newspapers in the city of Philadelphia have teemed with the most irritating invectives, couched in the most vulgar and opprobrious language, not only against the French nation and their allies, but the very men in power with whom the ministers of our country are sent to negotiate. These publications have an evident tendency, not only to frustrate a reconciliation, but to create a rupture and provoke a war between the sister Republics, and seem calculated to villify—nay, to subvert—all republican governments whatever.

"'Impressed with the duties of my station, I have used some endeavors for checking these evils, by binding over the editor and printer of one of them—licentious and virulent beyond all former example—to his good behavior; but he still perseveres in his nefarious publications. He has ransacked our language for terms of insult and reproach, and for the basest accusations against every ruler and distinguished character in France and Spain with whom we chance to have any intercourse, which it is scarce in nature to forgive—in brief, he braves his recognizance and the laws. It is now with you, gentlemen of the grand jury, to animadvert on his conduct; without your aid it can not be corrected. The Government that will not discountenance, may be thought to adopt it, and be deemed justly chargeable with all the consequences.

" ' Every nation ought to avoid giving any real offense to another. Some medals and dull jests are mentioned and represented as a ground of quarrel between the English and Dutch in 1672, and likewise called Louis the XIV. to make an expedition into the United Provinces of the Netherlands in the same year, and nearly ruined the commonwealth.

" ' We are sorry to find our endeavors in this way have not been attended with all the good effects that were expected from them; however, we are determined to pursue the prevailing vice of the times with zeal and indignation, that crimes may no longer appear less odious for being fashionable, nor the more secure from punishment from being popular.' (See Whart. St. Tr., 325; Whart. Cr. L., § 1612a.)

"The bill against Cobbett was ignored by the grand jury, as, under the circumstances, might have been expected. The party contest between the friends of a French and the friends of an English alliance was then at its height, and never was there a party contest more bitter and more unscrupulous. The prosecution was instituted no doubt by persons in sympathy with the Democratic party, and the bill was signed by Mr. Jared Ingersoll, then the Democratic attorney-general of Pennsylvania, and it was not to be expected that those members of the grand jury who detested France would give it their votes. But while this explains the ignoring of the bill against Cobbett, on the same principle as may be explained the verdict of acquittal in Bernard's case, the result does not in any way affect the authority of Chief Justice McKean's ruling as a matter of law. He was not only a learned, well-trained, and experienced lawyer, but he was thoroughly familiar with the history of our institutions, and with the relation of the States to the Federal Government and to European sovereignties. He had been for seventeen years a member of the Pennsylvania legislature. He was the only member of the Continental Congress who remained in continuous service during the whole Revolutionary war. He was a signer of the Declaration of Independence. He was president of the Congress in 1781. He was Chief Justice of Pennsylvania from 1777 to 1799, and during that long period he was regarded by the bar of Philadelphia, a bar of singular learning and cultivation, as a master in jurisprudence, and as a judge who never permitted himself to be swayed by partisan or personal temper. Nor was there at that time any dissent from the position that if libels on foreign countries were published in the State of Pennsylvania, it was the function of the State of Pennsylvania to prosecute the authors of these libels. Congress, in Mr. Adams's Administration, did not hesitate to pass a statute making ' seditious libels ' indictable in Federal courts, but it limited its action to such libels as attacked the Federal system. Libels on foreign powers were left to the action of the several States, and within the jurisdiction of such States they still remain."

> Dr. Francis Wharton, in 6 Crim. Law Magazine, 176.
>
> It was held in 1794, by Mr. Randolph, when Secretary of State, following the opinion of the Attorney-General, that a libel on the British minister was indictable at common law in the Federal courts. (Mr. Randolph, Sec. of State, to Mr. Harrison, Sept. 18, 1794, 7 MS. Dom. Let. 27.)
>
> It may be observed that at this time it was the prevalent opinion that the Federal courts had common-law jurisdiction of crime; but this opinion was twenty years later set aside by the decision of the Supreme Court in the case of United States v. Hudson.

" I have had the honor to receive your letter of the 23d instant, representing that you had seen published in the journals of the United States the treaty with the Kingdom of the Two Sicilies, and that you consider this publication as impolitic, premature, and not well calculated in the present state of suspense between the two nations.

" It would certainly have been more respectful towards both nations, in the present posture of affairs, had this publication not been made; but from the nature of the institutions of the United States, the General Government is not to be held responsible for the conduct of the public journals. You appear to be sensible that the publication in this instance is unofficial, and when you learn, as I now have the honor to inform you, that it is altogether unauthorized and that the Executive has no knowledge of the means by which a copy of the treaty has been procured for that purpose, it will not appear to you, I hope, to require more particular attention."

> Mr. McLane, Sec. of State, to Mr. Morelli, Sicilian cons. general, July 26, 1833, MS. Notes to For. Leg. V. 135.

Libelous letters addressed in this country by a citizen of the United States to a foreign minister may be the subject of judicial prosecution, but not of diplomatic interference.

> Mr. Hunter, Acting Sec. of State, to Mr. Sartiges, French min., May 22, 1852, MS. Notes to France, VI. 178.
>
> See Mr. Marcy, Sec. of State, to Mr. Sartiges, June 2, 1856, id. 272.

" The Government of the United States have no jurisdiction over the press in the respective States, and if such jurisdiction existed, its exercise with a view to prevent or to inflict punishment for any publication criticising or condemning the course of public measures in other countries or in our own would be an experiment upon the feeble forbearance, little likely to be made, and if made, sure to be defeated."

Mr. Cass, Sec. of State, to Mr. Molina, Nov. 26, 1860, MS. Notes to Central America, I. 177.

" I have the honor to recur to your note of the 12th of January instant, on the subject of the decision of the Turkish Government in the case of the Robert's College.

" In that note you have informed me that you have been affected with deep sorrow in reading discourses which were made on the 8th instant in New York, at a meeting assembled, as was avowed, to come in aid of the insurgent Cretan refugees. . . . You intimate a desire that I will cause it to be understood that those proceedings are disapproved by the Government of the United States.

" I have the honor to inform you in reply, that free discussion by speech and in the press, in public assemblies and in private conversation, of the Cretan insurrection, and of all other political transactions and movements occurring either abroad or at home, is among the rights and liberties guaranteed by the Constitution of the United States to every citizen and even to every stranger who sojourns among us, and is altogether exempt from any censure or inquiry on the part of the Government of the United States. The opponents of Crete and the friends of Turkey exercise very freely the same right. On the other hand, this Government makes no inquiry concerning what is preached, spoken or written in Turkey, or in any other country, by the citizens or subjects thereof, although the matters discussed may be deeply interesting to the American people. The maxim was long since adopted in the United States that even error of opinion may be safely tolerated where reason is left free to combat it. I am therefore so far from being able to accept your suggestions in the matter of the New York meeting that I should rather deem it my duty, if occasion should arise, to commend the liberty of speech, which was exercised in that assembly and of which you complain, to the acceptance of all other nations."

Mr. Seward, Sec. of State, to Blacque Bey, Turkish min., Jan. 20, 1869, MS. Notes to Turkey, I. 29.

Oct. 24, 1868, the Greek Chambers adopted a resolution expressing their appreciation of the sentiments of the American people towards the Greek nation, and of the sympathy expressed by Congress in behalf of the suffering Cretans. A copy of this resolution was communicated to the Government of the United States, and was transmitted by the President to Congress. (Mr. Seward, Sec. of State, to Mr. Rangabe, Jan. 18, 1869, MS. Notes to Turkey and Greece, I. 364.)

" The undersigned, Secretary of State of the United States, duly received the note of the 20th instant, addressed to him by Mr. Roberts, envoy extraordinary and minister plenipotentiary of Spain, occasioned by a paper relative to the affairs of Cuba, which Mr. Roberts stigmatizes as a libel on the Spanish Government and authorities, and expresses his apprehension that its recent publication in New York may tend to disturb the friendly relations existing between the United States and Spain.

" In reply the undersigned has the honor to state that, while duly sympathizing with the wounded sensibilities of Mr. Roberts, as shown in his note, he is persuaded that that gentleman attaches undue importance to the paper referred to and to its publication in the United States, and that it is believed to be impossible that that or any similar publication should lead to the deplorable result apprehended. In this country the press is entirely free. A signal proof of this is that, for years past, newspapers, in foreign languages, owned and managed by aliens, have been published in the city of New York, which have, without stint, criticised the measures of this Government, and the persons entrusted with its administration. Here, anything can be published which does not injure the character or the business of those who may be attacked. When, however, such an injury shall have been committed, the law provides a process and a remedy for the grievance. Whether the law is applicable to the case presented by the note of Mr. Roberts, it is not the province of the undersigned to determine."

> Mr. Fish, Sec. of State, to Mr. Roberts, Span. min., June 1, 1869, MS. Notes to Span. Leg. VIII. 280.
>
> In a note of October 14, 1832, Baron de Sacken, Russian chargé d'affaires, referred to the course of the American journals in republishing misrepresentations of " self-styled Liberals " in Europe concerning the government established by Russia in Poland, while they avoided the publication of answers to those charges. He added that his Government had always treated such warfare with silence and contempt, and had directed its agents in foreign countries to do the same, so long as " these calumnies " against Russia should receive no support from governments to which Russian agents were accredited, and he adverted without specification to articles relating to Russia and Poland which had appeared in the Washington *Globe*. By direction of the President, the chargé d'affaires was informed that no explanations on the subject could be entered into until the imputation that the Government of the United States had directly or indirectly given its support to the " calumnies " in the *Globe* should be withdrawn. (Mr. Livingston, Sec. of State, to Baron de Sacken, Russian chargé d'affaires, Dec. 4, 1832, MS. Notes to For. Legs. V. 73.)

" Your letter of the 11th instant has been received. It requests for the commission the protection of this Department against charges in the Mexican press like one in a Matamoras newspaper which, with a translation, accompanies your communication. In reply, I regret to state that I am at a loss as to the course which might be taken for that purpose with any prospect of success. It is understood that the press in Mexico is not amenable to the Government for its utterances, and it is quite unlikely that there is any law there which would enable that Government to comply with your wishes even were it so disposed. Charges in the newspaper press, especially in the press of a foreign country, against officers of this Government are conceived to be best met by indifference and by that silence which is an indication of it. The dignity and authority of the Government might be put in jeopardy if its agents were to show undue sensitiveness in regard to such accusations by condescending to a denial or refutation of them through the same channel."

> Mr. Fish, Sec. of State, to Mr. Robb, Feb. 25, 1873, 98 MS. Dom. Let. 12.
> Mr. Robb was chairman of a commission sent to Texas, under a joint resolution of Congress of May 7, 1872, to investigate depredations along the border. (H. Ex. Doc. 39, 42 Cong. 3 sess.; H. Report 701, 45 Cong. 2 sess. 95–110.)

The prohibition by the French Government, in 1873, of a course of lectures in France " on the advantages held out by a part of the United States to emigrants," while " one of those acts of illiberality which it is difficult to believe would have been exercised by a pro- fessedly republican government in this age of the world," can not be alleged to have " transcended the limit of power to which an inde- pendent state, if inclined in the direction of the exercise of extreme powers of repression, may go without giving ground for remonstrance on the part of other states whose citizens may thereby be prohibited the exercise of free speech, or the opportunity of diffusing informa- tion tending to the possible melioration of the condition of large numbers of people."

> Mr. Fish, Sec. of State, to Mr. Washburne, Mar. 1, 1873, MSS. Inst. France, XIX. 67.

" I have to acknowledge the receipt of your No. 975, of the 17th October last, in which you enclose a copy of a note which, as dean of the diplomatic corps, you addressed to the Foreign Office, for the purpose of calling attention to a book entitled ' Death-blow to Cor- rupt Doctrines,' which is now circulating in China and which, by reason of the vile and monstrous charges it contains against for- eigners, is likely, as was intended, to arouse popular animosity toward them and to expose them to insult and violence, a result which has actually occurred in one case. This book, it is stated, first appeared in 1870 and was promptly suppressed by the Tsung-li-Yamen, but it has lately been circulated in Han Chow under a slightly changed title, although three years ago the viceroy gave imperative orders for its suppression. The Tsung-li-Yamen is now requested to take steps to suppress the book to the end that commotion and riot and disorder may be avoided.

" In most cases such a request would be a matter of great delicacy and would be inadmissible. But in a country such as China, where the press is controlled by a Government censorship, as a matter of public police, and a publication is circulated which puts in jeopardy the lives and property of foreign residents, a protest and request of the character of that in question, invoking the only method of relief available, is, under the peculiar circumstances of the case, allowable and proper."

> Mr. Blaine, Sec. of State, to Mr. Denby, min. to China, Dec. 3, 1889, MS. Inst. China, IV. 475.

" I have to acknowledge the receipt of your No. 194 of the 9th ultimo, giving an account of your recent audience, accompanied by Mr. Reid, your colleague at Paris, with the Sultan, who took occasion to refer to the reported production in the United States of a play or drama called *Mahomet*, recently suppressed in Paris by order of the Government out of regard for the religious sentiments of friendly Moslem Powers. It seems unnecessary to say to you that in the production of such a play in this country the Federal Government has no power to act in the premises. It is a matter entirely for local control and jurisdiction."

> Mr. Blaine, Sec. of State, to Mr. Hirsch, min. to Turkey, Jan. 7, 1891, MS. Inst. Turkey, V. 194.

" I have received your dispatch No. 134, of the 18th ultimo, reporting the representations made by you to the President of Venezuela, concerning publications in the Spanish press of that country alike mendacious and unfriendly.

" Having in view the constitutional freedom of the press in this country, it is a matter of some delicacy to invoke repressive action in favor of this Government on the part of the authorities of other countries, whose laws may give the local governments greater powers to regulate the press. You appear to have recognized this by mainly directing your remonstrances to the mendacious and dangerous character of the publications to which you refer, and the action taken by the administration of the federal district, under direction of the President of the Republic, appears to be confined to this particular feature of the situation, in that it prescribes the authentication of published news by giving its responsible source. The action so taken was considerate and timely, as well as eminently just to the Vene-

zuelan community itself, and so far as it indicates a friendly disposition of the Venezuelan Government it is cordially appreciated."

Mr. Day, Sec. of State, to Mr. Loomis, min. to Venezuela, June 3, 1898, For.
Rel. 1898, 1133.

In May, 1881, Johann Most was convicted in the central criminal
court, in London, on an indictment containing twelve counts. The
first two counts charged a scandalous libel at common law, and on
these a separate verdict of guilty was taken and no question arose
upon them. The remaining ten counts charged an offence against
24 & 25 Vict. c. 100, s. 4, which provides that " all persons who shall
conspire, confederate, and agree to murder any person, whether he
be a subject of Her Majesty or not, and whether he be within the
Queen's dominions or not, and whosoever shall solicit, encourage,
persuade, or endeavor to persuade, or shall propose to any person
to murder any other person, whether he be a subject of Her Majesty
or not, and whether he be within the Queen's dominions or not," shall
be guilty of a misdemeanor, and upon conviction thereof be liable to
penal servitude for from three to ten years, or to imprisonment for a
term not exceeding two years with or without hard labor. The ten
counts framed under this section charged the prisoner with having
" encouraged " or " endeavored to persuade " persons to " murder
other persons," some named and others not named, who were in all
cases not subjects of Her Majesty nor within the Queen's dominions.
The third count charged that persons were encouraged to murder
" the sovereigns and rulers of Europe; " while in other counts
Emperor Alexander III., of Russia, and Emperor William I., of
Germany, were specified as persons whom the defendant had encouraged or endeavored to persuade others to murder. The evidence on
all the twelve counts was the same and consisted of an article in a
weekly newspaper called the *Freiheit*, written in German and published in London, and enjoying an average circulation of 1,200 copies.
Of this newspaper Most was editor and publisher. The article
lauded the assassination of the Emperor Alexander II., which had,
it was declared, " penetrated into princely palaces where dwell those
crime-beladen abortions of every profligacy who long since have
earned a similar fate a thousandfold."   All rulers " from Constantinople to Washington " were represented as trembling " for their
long since forfeited heads." The " rarity of so-called tyrannicide "
was represented as a proper cause of complaint, and the hope was
expressed that the killing of the Czar might be imitated.

A case having been reserved as to the coviction on the ten statutory
counts, counsel for Most, while conceding that the publication was a
seditious libel at common law, argued that it did not come within
the act of 24 and 25 Vict. It was admitted that before that act per-

sons might be indicted in England for libels on foreign sovereigns, as in the case of Peltier for the libel on Napoleon I.

The court held that the conviction was proper. The jury, said Lord Chief Justice Coleridge, had found, and rightly found, that the article was naturally and reasonably intended to incite and encourage and to persuade or to endeavor to persuade persons who should read it to the murder either of the Emperor Alexander or the Emperor William, or in the alternative of the crowned and uncrowned heads of other states; and an endeavor to persuade or an encouragement was none the less so because it was not personally addressed to one or more individuals. It was therefore decided that the court below was correct in charging the jury that they should find the prisoner guilty under the statute if they thought that by the publication of the article in question he intended to and did encourage or endeavor to persuade any person to murder any other person, whether a subject of Her Majesty or not, and whether within the Queen's dominions or not, and that such encouragement was the natural and reasonable effect of the article. The conviction was unanimously affirmed.

Regina v. Most (1881), 14 Cox. C. C. 583.

See Mr. Frelinghuysen, Sec. of State, to Mr. Edmunds, U. S. Sen. Feb. 3, 1885, 154 MS. Dom. Let. 145.

See, as to the case of Bernard, one of the Orsini conspirators, Lewis on Foreign Jurisdiction, 58–62.

" R. v. Bernard, 1 F. & F. 240, which was for participation in the Orsini conspiracy, was under a statute; but Lord Campbell, who tried the case, while holding the statute covered the offence, did not hesitate in the House of Lords to declare that the offence was indictable at common law. As the defendant was acquitted, the question did not receive final judicial revision.

(" During the civil war in the United States the British Government frequently asserted the jurisdiction of its courts to punish persons engaged on British soil in conspiracies to commit crimes in the United States. This was held in reference to the 'Greek fire' attempts in Canada, and to the alleged attempts to send infected clothing from Bermuda to New York. See North Am. Rev. for June, 1884 (p. 527), and Crim. Law Mag. March, 1885. . . . In accordance with the views of the text, persons sending from one of our States dynamite to injure property or life in England, would be indictable in the State from which the dynamite is sent. See Crim. Law Mag. March, 1885. As to libel on foreign sovereign, see infra, § 1612a. As to perjury to take effect abroad, see Philippi v. Bowen, 2 Barr, 20." (Wharton's Crim. Law (9th ed.), I. 318, note.)

As to the announcement in the press of one country of a determination, real or pretended, on the part of persons within the jurisdiction of another country, there to commit an unlawful act, see Mr. Frelinghuysen, Sec. of State, to Mr. West, Brit. min., April 14, 1883, and Feb. 24, 1885, MS. Notes to Brit. Leg. XIX. 284, 636; Mr. Frelinghuysen, Sec. of State, to Mr. Lowell, min. to England, Dec. 4, 1883, and Nov. 24, 1884, MS. Inst. Gr. Britain, XXVII. 69, 349.

" This Government and people feel nothing but detestation for such publications [prompting assassination and arson in England]. The question whether a journal making publications of the character of those referred to could or could not by process of law be suppressed, as calculated to lead to an infraction of our treaty engagements, or whether Congress could properly legislate on the subject, does not now demand the expression of an opinion. The Government of the United States knows the effect of the publications in question, and how to treat them. We have a large population of Irish people, and of those directly descended from them. They are attached to this country, obedient to its laws, and for the most part citizens of this Republic. They naturally have a friendship for their kinsmen in the United Kingdom, and perhaps a passive sympathy with them in the agitations in Ireland, but as their sympathy does not manifest itself in overt acts, we think it would not be wise by any governmental action to excite in them hostility towards a nation with which we are at peace, and thus disturb the cordiality which it is both the pleasure and the interest of this Republic to maintain with Her Majesty's Government. These considerations have weight and influence; but what is conclusive on the subject is that this Government cannot consent, by its official notice, to emphasize, dignify, and give prominence to articles of the character complained of, which, while unnoticed, are impotent. Her Majesty's Government should, if satisfied with the friendly purpose of this Government, accord to it the right when it thinks its own interests are involved, of shaping its policy according to its own discretion. This right the Government of the United States must exercise."

> Mr. Frelinghuysen, Sec. of State, to Mr. Lowell, Dec. 4, 1883, MS. Inst. Great Britain, XXVII. 69.

" This Government is as deeply sensible as any other of the danger to all government and society from lawless combinations which may secretly plot assassination and destruction of life and property. At the same time it can only proceed against offenders, or suspected offenders, in accordance with law; and it is at least doubtful whether any law is now in existence in this country by which the publishers of the paper or papers in question can be called to account. I am not aware that such a law exists in any country. It is but recently that any law for the punishment of incitement to the commission of murder in foreign countries was placed on the British statute book.

" The present laws of the United States only aim to meet the cases of actual overt acts of hostility against a friendly nation when such acts are committed within the territory of the United States. So far as I remember, this is the full extent to which other nations have gone in this direction."

Mr. Frelinghuysen, Sec. of State, to Mr. Lowell, Nov. 24, 1884, MS. Inst. Great Britain, XXVII. 349.

The publications referred to by Mr. Frelinghuysen in the two foregoing passages were not direct incitements to assassination or arson, but were announcements, in the form of news reports, of the alleged intention of persons in British jurisdiction to commit such unlawful acts.

(5) RELIGIOUS FREEDOM.

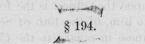

§ 194.

" I greatly regret that I do not feel myself at liberty to comply with the request contained in your letter of the 15th instant. I would to God that the governments of all countries, like that of our own happy land, might permit knowledge of all kinds to circulate freely among the people. It is our glory that all men within the United States enjoy the inestimable right of worshipping God according to the dictates of their own conscience. In Sardinia, however, the case is unhappily far different. There they have a state religion and a strict censorship of the press; and they exclude all books of every kind, except such as are in accordance with their own faith and principles. They have their system and we have ours; and it has ever been the policy of this Government not to interfere with the internal regulations of foreign governments, more especially in questions of religion. From the jealous character of the Sardinian Government it is almost certain that our interposition would be unavailing; and the attempt might injure instead of proving beneficial to the Waldenses themselves.

" Your information in respect to the Baptist missionary who was imprisoned at Hamburg is not correct. This you will perceive from a copy of Mr. Forsyth's letter to our consul at Hamburg, which I enclose to you. The missionary had been released before Mr. Forsyth's letter reached Hamburg. Had he been an American citizen, it would have been the duty of this Government to interpose its good offices for the purpose of relieving him from imprisonment. The case of requesting permission to introduce books into a country, prohibited by the state religion and the state policy is far different.

" I have had a conversation on this subject with our excellent friend, Walter Lowrie, esq., who entirely concurs with me in opinion, that we ought not to interfere, and, if we should, that our interference would prove unavailing. Such is also the judgment of the President.

" It is with sincere pain that I feel myself constrained to deny your benevolent request."

Mr. Buchanan, Sec. of State, to the Rev. Mr. Baird, Oct. 22, 1845, 35 MS. Dom. Let. 299.

" The President has referred to this Department the memorial of the 13th instant, over your signature and that of other clergymen of your denomination, asking a renewal of supposed instructions of my predecessor, William L. Marcy, to the United States representative in Japan, for the purpose of inducing the Government of that Empire to repeal the laws which make the profession of Christianity penal. In reply I have to state that the only passage in the instructions to Mr. Townsend Harris upon the subject is the following, contained in a letter of Mr. Marcy to him, of the 13th of September, 1856: ' The intolerance of the Japanese in regard to the Christian religion forbids us to hope that they would consent to any stipulation by which missionaries would be allowed to enter that Empire, or Christian worship,' according to the form of any sect, would be permitted.' Hence it appears that you are under a misapprehension in regard to the instructions referred to. It is evident from Mr. Marcy's language that he was familiar with the antecedents of Christianity in Japan. You yourselves are no doubt aware that our religion was in a flourishing state there about two centuries ago, that large numbers of Japanese had become converted to it; that consequently the priests of other religions became alarmed at its progress, when, owing to the imprudence or as some suppose the arrogance of the Christian divines, the Japanese rulers, lay and clerical, caused them and their converts to be attacked and massacred, whereby Christianity was at once as it were extirpated. The same penal laws against it to which you refer were then enacted and remain in force to this day. The occasion and policy which dictated them may be presumed to be still fresh in the memories of the many cultivated people in that quarter. Some of the prejudices against Christians may have been softened by the intercourse with them which has taken place since that country was reopened by us to foreign trade. It is to be feared however, that any attempt to induce them to change their policy in respect to our religion would be premature. Still this Department will instruct Mr. Van Valkenburgh, the United States minister in Japan, to make inquiries upon the subject, and, if he should find the prospect at all favorable at the present time, to cooperate with Her Britannic Majesty's representative, if as you intimate that functionary should also be instructed to endeavor to have the disabilities against Christians in Japan removed."

> Mr. Seward, Sec. of State, to the Rt. Rev. Horatio Potter, Nov. 23, 1866,
> 74 MS. Dom. Let. 417.

" Your No. 10, under date of April 27th, submitting a statement of facts furnished by the Rev. Henry Schauffler, who has requested the interposition of your legation in his behalf, has been received.

" Mr Schauffler, who represents himself to be a citizen of the United States residing at Brunn, in Moravia, complains that while his family and some invited friends were in the habit of occasionally assembling at his private house for devotional exercises, he had been interdicted by the authorities from holding such meetings, and judicial proceedings against him had been instituted. On this account he has claimed the interposition of your legation, and you informed him in reply that you must decline to take any official action without the instructions of this Department.

"A statement, a copy of which you transmit to the Department, has been prepared by him to obtain such instructions.

" The Department approves your refusal to address the Austrian Government on this question without instructions in reference thereto. I have carefully examined your dispatch and the statement of Mr. Schauffler enclosed therewith. Mr. Schauffler states that, having moved to Brunn to further the dissemination of the Scriptures through colporteurs, and the understanding of the Bible through private exposition in his own dwelling, in the circle of his invited friends and by public lectures, he commenced holding Bible exposition meetings at his home, in the summer of 1874. Although these meetings are denominated private and domestic, the attendance increased until ninety or one hundred persons were present.

" In January he began to hold public Bible lectures in a hired hall, obtained for the purpose. Soon afterwards he was charged with ' enticing ' children into these meetings, and with violations of the law in having distributed tracts to children, and was forbidden to hold further meetings. Various proceedings followed, during which he appealed to the stadtholder of Moravia, who rejected his appeal, and after efforts on his part to procure a revocation of the order he was finally refused the right to hold private meetings, because his meetings had been too large; or to hold public ones, on account of the police prohibition.

" Under all these circumstances, and as he intends to appeal to the ministry to reverse these proceedings, he has appealed to you for your intervention.

" It does not appear that Mr. Schauffler claims the right to carry on his work, or to hold these meetings under any treaty obligation, or under any other authority than the laws of the country; but he insists that, while charged with the violation of the law, he has not in reality been guilty thereof; and that he therefore should be allowed to continue to hold his meetings. It does not, moreover, appear that he has been punished for any violation of law, nor does any such punishment seem to be feared or expected. The question, therefore, which he has presented, seems to be whether under the laws of Austria he is entitled to hold these meetings.

" To address the Government of Austria-Hungary on his behalf under these circumstances would require a complete understanding of the Austrian law, and clear proof that the authorities have improperly construed the law against him.

" It is a delicate task for this Government to assume to enter upon an examination of a question depending solely on foreign law, and to express to the Government of Austria-Hungary the opinion that its authorities have improperly or unfairly refused what is claimed merely as a privilege pursuant to its laws. If this were competent in any case, it might be said in this case with force that it is not easy to distinguish between a public meeting and a meeting of some ninety or one hundred persons, gathered for whatever purpose, or between ' giving tracts to children ' and ' lending them ' to those who have asked for them.

" It appears, moreover, that Mr. Schauffler has not exhausted his appeal to the courts, or authorities of the country. The Department is not in possession of the text of these laws, or of sufficient evidence to warrant an expression of opinion that Mr. Schauffler has been un- fairly dealt with. Without therefore passing upon the correctness of the position assumed by him, and with every disposition to aid him in any proper work, I do not see, under the circumstances of the case as presented or with the information now furnished, that it is com- petent for this Government to direct its representative to make an appeal of the nature asked for. You are, however, authorized to use your unofficial good offices, if requested, that Mr. Schauffler may have an opportunity for a fair hearing and presentation of his case in such quarter as may be desired.

" I am aware of the many sacrifices and the unselfish labors of many gentlemen of his profession, and it is a source of regret that the Department is not always enabled to afford such active assistance in foreign countries, as they may desire."

> Mr. Fish, Sec. of State, to Mr. Delaplaine, chargé at Vienna, June 2, 1875,
> MS. Inst. Austria, II. 352.

" I have to acknowledge the receipt of your No. 190, relating to the case of Mr. H. A. Schauffler.

" It is understood that Mr. Schauffler desires merely to receive the treatment which any foreigner under similar circumstances would be entitled to receive under Austrian laws; and that being the case, it is desirable that such action may be taken as will be most likely to bring about that result. It was the design of the Department, in its com- munication to you of the 13th March last (No. 95), to have procured (informally or otherwise as you might think proper) from the foreign office the legal provisions therein referred to. It was thought by the Department that if, on the receipt of the laws in question, it should be found that Mr. Schauffler's case admitted of amelioration, or would seem to do so, under a fair interpretation of the laws, the matter could be brought to the attention of the foreign office with great assurance of success, the application being fortified already by the material previously obtained from that source.

" The Department does not consider an attempt to put Mr. Schauffler on the same footing in Austria, in respect to the conduct of his meetings, as are other foreigners, similarly situated, as in anywise interfering with or complaining of the legal internal or domestic administration of His Majesty's Government or the laws of Austria-Hungary; nor would the Department act otherwise in the matter, were Mr. Schauffler a propagandist of any other school. The question is one of equal rights and privileges in a given case, for a citizen of the United States, to those accorded other foreigners under the actual laws of the Empire.

"As your No. 190 has failed to advance the interests of Mr. Schauffler and leaves the official statement of the laws yet unobtained, I will thank you to proceed in the matter as indicated in instruction No. 95."

Mr. Evarts, Sec. of State, to Mr. Kasson, min. to Austria-Hungary, May 19, 1879, MS. Inst. Austria-Hungary, III. 13.

"With reference to your remark that the Government cannot consent that the power of a state shall anywhere be exercised against our people who are adherents of the Christian religion because of their religion, or that they shall be subjected to abuse for this reason, you are understood of course to confine your statement to the maintenance of religious views, and not to contemplate the obtrusive presentation of certain views in violation of the laws of a country in which the parties voluntarily have entered."

Mr. Fish, Sec. of State, to Mr. Seward, min. to China, May 2, 1876, MS. Inst. China, II. 385.

" Upon the 23d of November, Sir Edward Thornton called upon me and stated that he was instructed by Lord Derby to read to me, and if I desired it to leave with me a copy of an instruction bearing date October 28, which had been addressed to Mr. Layard, Her Majesty's minister at Madrid, touching religious toleration in Spain, and that Lord Derby expressed the hope that the Government of the United States might instruct its representative at Madrid to make representations in a similar sense to the Government of the King. I transmit, herewith, a copy of this instruction, which was given me by Sir Edward Thornton.

" You will perceive its guarded character, and while Lord Derby states that Her Majesty's Government have learned with great regret that the Spanish Government had placed upon the XIth article of the constitution an interpretation so much at variance with the spirit of toleration now so universal in civilized states, and with the more enlightened policy which has been followed in Spain since the year 1869, without apparent ill consequences, and while Her Majesty's Government would gladly learn that the recent orders have been rescinded or relaxed, he has not thought it advisable to instruct Mr. Layard to make any formal or official application to the Government of Spain in that sense. Lord Derby, however, expresses the hope entertained by Her Majesty's Government that the steps lately taken by the Spanish Government with regard to religious freedom may not be followed by others of a still more retrograde character, and its expectation that the rights enumerated in the instruction, which Señor Calderon y Collantes, the minister of state, admits are secured to Protestants by the XIth article of the constitution, will be scrupulously respected, with its reliance upon the good faith of the Spanish Government to act promptly and energetically in repressing any attempt on the part of the local authorities to infringe upon these rights. Mr. Layard is instructed to speak in this sense to the Spanish minister of foreign affairs and to lose no opportunity for impressing upon the Spanish Government the deep interest with which the question of religious liberty in Spain is regarded by Her Majesty's Government and by all classes of Her Majesty's subjects.

" The question had been presented to this Government before Sir Edward's interview with me, and I have appreciated the delicacy of making representations to a foreign state concerning religious freedom within its own borders, as Lord Derby appears to have done. While, therefore, it is not deemed advisable to instruct you to make any remonstrances, or to prefer any formal or official application concerning the steps that have lately been taken in Spain on the question, you are instructed to act in concert with Mr. Layard, Her Majesty's minister, in the sense in which he is instructed by Lord Derby, and to take occasion to speak in a similar sense to the minister of state, impressing upon him the deep interest which the question of religious liberty in Spain excites in the United States, and the strong hope that the steps lately taken by the Spanish Government with reference to religious freedom and toleration may not be followed by others of a more retrograde character, and that the rights which the minister of state admits are secured to Protestants by the XIth article of the constitution may be entirely respected, and that the United States rely upon the good faith of the Spanish Government to promptly and firmly suppress any attempt from any quarter to infringe upon these rights."

Mr. Fish, Sec. of State, to Mr. Adee, chargé at Madrid, Dec. 8, 1876, MS. Inst. Spain, XVIII. 52.

As to the threatened sale of the American college at Rome, under the
decision as to the real estate of the Propoganda, and the "prompt
and friendly action" of the Italian Government, see Mr. Frelinghuysen, Sec. of State, to Mr. Astor, min. to Italy, March 4, 5, and 29,
1884, MS. Inst. Italy, 263, 267.

For an inquiry as to rights of religion under the constitution of Portugal,
see Mr. Hay, Sec. of State, to Mr. Irwin, Feb. 28, 1900, MS. Inst.
Portugal, XVI. 198.

"In a letter dated the 8th Feb./27 Jan'y 1883 you informed
me that the American Bible Society, and their agent at Constantinople, Dr. Bliss, desired permission to import into Caucasia the publications of that society, in the modern Armenian language, as approved
and recommended by the foreign church authorities.

"According to the Russian law, Bibles in the Armenian tongue can
only be imported with the permission of the patriarch of the Catholic
Armenian Church, or by that of the Armenian Georgian Synod.

"The prohibition was promulgated not only in consequence of the
incompleteness of the sample submitted to these authorities by Dr.
Bliss in 1872, but also because it distorted the doctrines of the Armenian as well as the whole Eastern Church.

"Having received a petition from Dr. Bliss in 1881, together with
a copy of the Bible in the Armenian tongue, as distributed without
hindrance by the British Bible Society, of which fact I have no
cognizance, I deemed it my duty to refer Dr. Bliss's petition and the
accompanying Bible to the Synod; and I am unable either to announce
their decision in advance, or to rescind the aforementioned prohibition."

Note of Count D. Tolstoi, Russian min. of the interior, to Mr. Hunt, min.
to Russia, March 3, 1883, accompanying Mr. Hunt's No. 43 of March
23, 1883, 37 MS. Desp. Russia.

"This Department is informed by a dispatch No. 109 of the 10th of
June last, from Mr. Doty, consul of this Government at Tahiti, that
certain American citizens, members of the so-called Mormon Church,
or Church of Latter Day Saints, as sometimes styled, laboring
as missionaries in the Society Islands, have been forbidden to hold
and conduct their religious services without a special license from
the President of the French Republic.

"I presume they have made their application in the proper quarter
for such license. So long as polygamy was maintained as a doctrine
and practiced as a fact by the Mormon Society, this Government
refused to intervene in any way to protect them against hostile
regulations or legislation of countries where they might be located. But
it is asserted that they have now entirely abandoned polygamy. They
profess to inculcate doctrines of the highest morality and promotive
of good citizenship and loyalty to established government. The doc-

trine of entire freedom of religious belief and practice, prevailing both in the United States and in France, should, in the opinion of the Department, entitle these people to the same rights as any other religious society, provided they have actually renounced their polygamous tenets, and do in fact practice and promote principles of morality and virtue.

" Assuming this to be true of them, it is hoped that the license desired by them may be granted by the French authorities."

> Mr. Adee, Act. Sec. of State, to Mr. Eustis, amb. to France, July 29, 1895, MS. Inst. France, XXIII. 139.

" I have received your No. 179, of the 3d ultimo, reporting the cause of the imprisonment of the Reverend Francis Penzotti, the business agent of the American Bible Society.

" As Mr. Penzotti was cognizant of the laws of Peru which forbid the importation of books or preaching which may tend to disturb the established religion of the land, and as our only ground for friendly intervention in the case was the fact that he represented an American society, he being an Italian subject, the Department has at present no further instructions to give in regard to the matter.

" The use of your good offices in Mr. Penzotti's behalf is commended."

> Mr. Blaine, Sec. of State, to Mr. Hicks, min. to Peru, Dec. 5, 1890, MS. Inst. Peru, XVII. 440.
>
> "Department informed that Penzotti acquitted, but still confined pending appeal by prosecution to higher court. Use good offices to urge speedy decision or prisoner's provisional release." (Mr. Blaine, Sec. of State, to Mr. Hicks, min. to Peru, tel., Jan. 15, 1891, MS. Inst. Peru, XVII. 448.)

" I have to acknowledge the receipt of your letter of the 28th ultimo, in which, on behalf of the Evangelical Alliance for the United States, it is urged that this Government consider the propriety of instructing the representatives of the United States in South America with a view to securing—

" 1. Religious liberty for missionaries working in States of South America.

" 2. Religious liberty for native Christians who dissent from the Roman Catholic faith.

" 3. The fullest civil liberty for foreigners and native-born Protestants, especially by the legalization of marriages performed by others than the Roman Catholic clergy.

" The standing instructions of the Department to the representatives in that quarter, supplemented by special instructions from time to time as cases arise, have been directed to securing for American citizens the same right to pursue their vocation of preaching and teaching, if such practices are lawful in the country of their residence, as any other American professional men or merchants have to pursue their calling. On the whole the success of the efforts of our diplomatic and consular officers in this direction has been gratifying.

"As respects your second point, the Department would overstep a long-established rule were it to instruct its ministers abroad regarding the civil and religious rights of citizens of the countries where they reside.

"As respects the legalization of marriages performed by others than the Roman Catholic clergy, the Department has for several years past given much attention to the question in Peru, where the laws declared non-Catholic marriages invalid, and after persistent effort, in which the United States minister was aided by the British representative, whose countrymen were in the same case as ours, the passage of a law was brought about by which civil marriages are made valid as well as the civil registry of non-Catholic marriages heretofore performed in that country. The Department does not recall any special complaints on this score by American citizens in Ecuador and Bolivia, but should any such cases be reported the same efforts will be made as in Peru, and with the slight advantage of the Peruvian precedent in favor of such representations as may be made."

> Mr. Day, Sec. of State, to the Rev. Mr. Strong, June 3, 1898, 229 MS. Dom. Let. 113.

" This Government, practicing as it does at home the largest principles of freedom of thought and belief, is naturally desirous to see its citizens enjoy in other countries a reasonable freedom from restrictions or disabilities imposed by reason of religious faith. While recognizing that the determination of the internal policy of a nation is an attribute of its sovereignty, the United States have not hesitated to express this desire, in considerate and friendly ways, as in the instance of the marriage laws of Peru, to the end that the law-abiding citizens of the United States sojourning in lands to which our country is bound by ties of amity and similarity of representative institutions may be relieved from discriminations affecting their individual life, liberties, and domestic relations in a manner at variance with the tendencies of this liberal age. . . .

" You are requested to examine and report upon the present condition of the legislation of Bolivia in regard to the liberty of conscience and teaching enjoyed by foreigners and as respects the status of aliens contracting marriage according to other rites and codes than those of the established church.

" If in the course of your examination you shall deem the ascertained facts to warrant you in so doing, you are authorized to make such discreet representations in the proper quarters, by way of friendly but earnest suggestion, as may conduce to the desired end. You will, however, be cautious in such case to avoid wounding the sensibilities of a generous people or appearing to advocate any unduly exceptional treatment of the natives of the country."

> Mr. Hay, Sec. of State, to Mr. Bridgman, min. to Bolivia, Sept. 1, 1899, For. Rel. 1899, 112.
>
> With the foregoing instruction there was enclosed for Mr. Bridgman's perusal a copy of a letter addressed to President McKinley by the Rev. John Lee, chairman of a committee appointed by the Chicago Methodist Ministers' Meeting to make efforts to bring about larger religious liberty in Bolivia, Ecuador, and Peru. In this letter Mr. Lee said: "While the committee rejoices that Peru has already adopted 'a marriage law more consonant with the general practice of modern nations,' it would be more than pleased if the kindly offices of the United States Government would be exercised in securing in Bolivia, and especially in Ecuador, what has already been secured in Peru. . . . The committee aims at the accomplishment of three things: (1) To secure religious liberty for missionaries working in the Republics of Peru, Ecuador, and Bolivia; (2) to secure religious liberty for native Christians who dissent from the Roman Catholic faith; (3) to secure in these South American republics the fullest civil liberty for American citizens and native-born Protestants, especially by the legalization of marriages performed by others than clergy of the Roman Catholic Church."
>
> An instruction similar to that to Mr. Bridgman was sent on the same day to Mr. Sampson, minister to Ecuador. (Mr. Hay, Sec. of State, to Mr. Sampson, min. to Ecuador, Sept. 1, 1899, MS. Inst. Ecuador, II. 2.)
>
> A similar instruction was also sent to the United States legation at Lima. (Mr. Hay, Sec. of State, to Mr. Dudley, min. to Peru, Sept. 1, 1899. MS. Inst. Peru, XVIII. 176.)
>
> "You will lose no suitable occasion to impress (without appearing to trench upon the prerogatives of a sovereign state) upon the Peruvian Government the great gratification it would give the United States, were Peru to advance in the path of tolerance which is trodden by modern states." (Mr. Hill, Act. Sec. of State, to Mr. Dudley, min. to Peru, Sept. 7, 1900, MS. Inst. Peru, XVIII. 201.)

In March, 1899, the minister of the United States at Quito called upon the Ecuadorian Government to correct the conduct of certain Roman Catholic priests, who had, by inflammatory utterances in the pulpit against certain Protestant missionaries, who were citizens of the United States, put their lives in jeopardy. The Ecuadorian Government instructed the ecclesiastical authorities " to put a stop to such irregularities," and ordered the police authorities to inflict punishment upon persons who had sought to do bodily injury to the missionaries. The Department of State, referring to the incident, said: " The Department is gratified that your representations were effective in securing proper police protection for the lives and property of American citizens. The reported utterances of the ecclesiastics of the Roman Church seem to have gone far beyond the liberty of speech which exists in republican communities, and, inasmuch as the church in Ecuador is a state institution, it was proper to call the attention of the responsible government to the incendiary provocations of the clergy. The Ecuadorian Government appears to admit and accept its disciplinary function in the premises."

> Mr. Hay, Sec. of State, to Mr. Sampson, min. to Ecuador, April 10, 1899, For. Rel. 1899, 260.

> Among the inflammatory utterances of the priests in question there was the following: "If the Virgin Mary does not convert them it is necessary that they (missionaries) be taken out of the city, and if not, they must be destroyed."

(6) LEARNED PROFESSIONS.

§ 195.

The practice of medicine in the United States is regulated by the laws of the various States and Territories, and is not under Federal control.

> Mr. Day, Sec. of State, to Senhor Manoel de Oliveira Lima, May 31, 1898, MS. Notes to Brazilian Leg. VII. 176.

The French law requires, as a condition of practicing medicine in France, the possession of a diploma issued by one of the French schools of medicine. This law is strictly enforced against all foreign physicians. The French Government, it is true, has the right to grant by decree the privilege of practicing medicine in France; but this is done only in exceptional cases where one has reached some eminence or distinction, or where there are special reasons for departing from the rule. The possession, however, of a diploma issued by a reputable foreign medical institution may facilitate the obtaining of the French degree, since it may be accepted as a sufficient ground for dispensing with some of the certificates of studies, "inscriptions," and public examinations ordinarily required.

> Mr. Bayard, Sec. of State, to Mr. Chase, Aug. 3, 1886, 161 MS. Dom. Let. 134, quoting from Mr. Morton's No. 298 of February 7, 1883.

> For the conditions of admission of foreigners to French medical schools, see Mr. Vignaud, Sec. of Embassy at Paris, to Mr. Olney, Sec. of State, July 24, 1896, For. Rel. 1896, 140.

As to the question of enrolling the United States on the list of countries recognized under the British medical act of 1866, see the report of Mr. James R. Roosevelt, secretary of the American embassy in London, of April 16, 1894. For. Rel. 1894, 281–284.

As to the grant to two native women, graduates of a medical school in the United States, of the privilege of practicing medicine in Japan, see For. Rel. 1898, 434–438.

"I have to acknowledge the receipt of your letter of the 13th instant, in which you ask to be apprised of the steps to be taken to enable you to practice medicine in Mexico.

"In reply I have to inform you that if you will transmit hither your diploma, certified under the seal of the State in which the issuing college is located, the proper authentication by this Department and the Mexican legation will be attached thereto, without charge. You will be entitled under this diploma to practice medicine in Mexico, but under the law as set forth by our minister there in a despatch numbered 587 of April 1, 1891, you will not be permitted to sign death certificates until you shall have presented a thesis to the Mexican National College of Medicine. Should this thesis not prove satisfactory, a second may be presented six months later."

> Mr. Gresham, Sec. of State, to Mr. Westmoreland, April 18, 1895, 201
> MS. Dom. Let. 560.
> To the same effect is Mr. Olney, Sec. of State, to Mr. Kellogg, Dec. 23,
> 1895, 206 MS. Dom. Let. 569.

"Your communication of the 29th of June last, addressed to Mr. Hunter, has been received. In his absence I respond to the inquiries you make respecting the status of medical practitioners in Morocco who possess diplomas issued in the United States.

"Every country has the right to prescribe the formalities which shall be observed by physicians to entitle them to practice within its jurisdiction. In nearly all, the simple *visé* and recognition of a diploma known to be genuine and issued by a college in good standing is sufficient. In some countries an examination is necessary also. The Department presumes that medical men, who obtain their titles at the excellent institutions of the United States; and thereafter seek a field of practice in foreign ports, will conform to all reasonable requirements which the local law may impose, without discrimination, upon graduates of any foreign college. You would only be justified in intervening if an unfair discrimination should be made against the holder of a genuine American diploma. . . .

"While the Department is willing in case it be asked by a foreign government to obtain from the State authorities an attestation of the genuineness of any diploma presented, it cannot undertake to do so in the case of the diplomas issued by Buchanan and his associates."

> Mr. John Davis, Acting Sec. of State, to Mr. Mathews, consul at Tangier,
> Aug. 11, 1883, 108 MS. Inst. Consuls, 82.
> The reference to "Buchanan" relates to John Buchanan, "dean" of a
> so-called "university," who was convicted in Philadelphia of fraud-
> ulently issuing medical diplomas. (For. Rel. 1880, 397, 398; For.
> Rel. 1881, 451.)

" This Government is disposed to admit that every country has the right to prescribe the mode of recognition of medical practitioners within its borders. While granting this, it is only reasonable to expect, therefore, that any regulations governing in such cases should be fair and impartial and not discriminate in favor of any one nationality. All that is demanded in the interest of our citizens is that the rule adopted shall be uniform and without any practical discrimination against duly graduated American practitioners."

> Mr. Frelinghuysen, Sec. of State, to Mr. Wallace, min. to Turkey, March 27, 1884, For. Rel. 1884, 553.
>
> This instruction related to the question of recognizing medical degrees granted by the American college at Beirut.
>
> See, also, Mr. Frelinghuysen, Sec. of State, to Mr. Wallace, min. to Turkey, June 25, 1883, MS. Inst. Turkey, IV. 34.

" When the applicant to practice his profession in this Empire produces a diploma of a State institution, where the State guaranties, as it were, by a *staats examen*, as in Germany, the sufficiency of the studies pursued and the examination, then such applicant, upon making proof of the fact that the diploma has been conferred upon him and submitting to a mere formal colloquium or medical conversation, is granted a certificate permitting him to practice his profession in this Empire.

" On the other hand, if the applicant produces a diploma that is not of the grade above specified, that is to say, if the diploma is not from a State or Government institution, as above specified, then the applicant, in order to have the right to practice his profession in the Empire, must undergo a thorough examination, as is prescribed, to entitle him to a diploma from the medical college here.

" This subject it seems presented itself in 1878, when the Porte first attempted to enforce with some degree of system the general law regulating the practice of medicine (see Legislation Ottomane. Vol. III, page 105.)

" The matter was referred by the consul-general to the Department, and in its instruction to the consul-general No. 50, of 29th April, 1878, it incloses a report from the Commissioner of Education, which says:

" ' The United States Government formally recognizes the diplomas of no medical school of this country or any other as affording any evidence of medical capacity, but surgeons of the United States Army and Navy, Marine Hospital Service, etc., are subject to a rigid examination before appointment.' "

> Mr. Straus, min. to Turkey, to Mr. Bayard, Sec. of State, Jan. 10, 1889, For. Rel. 1889, 707, 708, enclosing a report of the council of the administration of civil medicine relating to the conditions of practice, and particularly to the refusal of the Imperial Medical College to license a graduate of the Bellevue Hospital Medical College unless he should submit to an examination, which he refused to do.

Mr. Straus was advised that the Department of State then had no further instruction to give him in the matter. (Mr. Bayard, Sec. of State, to Mr. Straus, min. to Turkey, Jan. 31, 1889, For. Rel. 1889, 712, 713.) See, further, as to the practice of medicine in Turkey, For. Rel. 1898, 1101. As to the question of recognizing degrees granted by the American college at Beirut, see Mr. Freylinghuysen, Sec. of State, to Mr. Wallace, min. to Turkey, March 27, 1884, For. Rel. 1884, 553, 561.

In 1891 the Department of State disapproved a suggestion that the American minister at Constantinople might, in the exercise of his extraterritorial powers, issue licenses to practice medicine in Turkey. (Mr. Blaine, Sec. of State, to Mr. Hirsch, min. to Turkey, Jan. 23, 1891, MS. Inst. Turkey, V. 204.

In 1893 the minister of the United States at Constantinople reported that a vizierial order issued five years before, prohibiting women from practicing as licensed physicians, had been relaxed in the case of Miss Mary Pierson Eddy, M. D., a licensed physician in New York, to whom permission had been granted to appear for examination, and that a vizierial order had been prepared to permit all women, who who were duly qualified, to practice medicine. (Mr. Terrell, min. to Turkey, to Mr. Gresham, Sec. of State, Nov. 8, 1893, For. Rel. 1893, 702; see, also, id. 638, 650, 704, 707.)

As membership of the bar in the several States of the Union is under local and not under Federal control, the practice of the law in the United States is a subject that cannot properly be regulated by international convention.

Mr. Day, Sec. of State, to Senhor Manoel de Oliveira Lima, Brazilian chargé, May 31, 1898, MS. Notes to Brazilian Leg. VII. 176.

" It is understood to be the usual custom of the courts of the United States and the several States near the border to permit the gentlemen of the Canadian bar to appear as counsel for British subjects; but this is an act of courtesy and comity, not an admission of a right, and if the courts of Manitoba do not extend the same courtesy to the bar of the United States, we can only regret their decision, but cannot officially complain of it."

Mr. J. C. B. Davis, Act. Sec. of State, to Governor Austin, of Minnesota, July 17, 1873, 99 MS. Dom. Let. 388.

The second international American conference, held at the city of Mexico, in 1901–2, adopted a project of a convention in relation to the practice of the learned professions. It followed the lines of the plan adopted by the congress of Montevideo.

Second Int. Conf. of Am, States, S. Doc. 330, 57 Cong. 1 sess. 7, 22, 23, 24, 195.

6. MARTIAL LAW.

§ 196.

In the present section the distinction between martial law and military law should be carefully borne in mind. Military law signifies, primarily, the law for the government of military forces. Thus it has been held that persons in the military and naval service of the United States are at all times subject to trial by court-martial under military law.[a]

Military law.

July 16, 1875, the British minister at Washington said in a note that he had been instructed by Lord Derby to make inquiries as to statements made in England by the parents of one John Winstone, lately a soldier in the United States Army, to a member of the British Parliament. The statements represented that Winstone, an Englishman by birth, was killed by a kick from a comrade named Hawie; that Hawie was tried by court-martial and sentenced to be confined in the guardhouse for three months and to forfeit the sum of $30 out of his pay; that the court-martial struck out a charge that Hawie inflicted upon Winstone kicks from which the latter died, and tried him only for the trivial military offence of "fighting in quarters." It was represented that the parents of the deceased thought the punishment of Hawie inadequate to the offence committed by him, and desired that the crime might be brought under the jurisdiction of the civil courts. The Department of State, in replying to the note, observed that it was not alleged that Winstone was at the time of his death a British subject, while it did appear that he was enlisted in the United States Army, as was also Hawie, so that they both "were subject to the military laws of the United States and to trial for an offence such as that alleged," an offence committed within the limits of a military post by one soldier upon another and "properly triable by a court-martial." The Department added that the statements of the parents of the deceased, which were merely hearsay, did not afford "sufficient grounds on which to arraign the judgment of a court competent for the trial in question, or to rest a demand for an executive reversal or repudiation of a judicial judgment and the subjection of the party to a second trial;" and that it was not deemed advisable or proper to present an inquiry to the War Department on the subject.

> Mr. Fish, Sec. of State, to Sir Edward Thornton, British min., July 16, 1875, MS. Notes to Great Britain, XVI. 591.

---

[a] Johnson *v.* Sayre, 158 U. S. 109, 15 S. Ct. 773. So, persons in military prisons are liable to trial by court-martial for offences committed while in confinement, though they be under sentence to be discharged from the service. (In re Craig, 70 Fed. Rep. 969.)

Mr. Fish, in concluding his reply, observed that the parents of the deceased probably were " not aware of the legal difficulties which might attend an attempt to subject a man who had been once tried and punished for an offence to a second trial, or of the grave questions which might be raised under the existing circumstances in an effort to prosecute in civil courts for an offence committed by one soldier upon another within the limits of a military post and the jurisdiction of military courts."

In another part of the note Mr. Fish said : " The United States have inherited from their mother country a sensitiveness to any attempt by other powers to review the judicial decisions of their constituted courts."

Civil tribunals will not revise the proceedings of courts-martial except for the purpose of ascertaining whether they had jurisdiction of the person and the subject-matter, and whether although they had such jurisdiction they had exceeded their powers in the sentence pronounced. (Carter v. McClaughry (1902), 183 U. S. 365.)

See, also, In re Vidal (1900), 179 U. S. 126; Swaim v. United States (1897), 165 U. S. 553.

The term martial law refers to the exceptional measures adopted,
Martial law. whether by the military or the civil authorities, in times of war or of domestic disturbance, for the preservation of order and the maintenance of the public authority. To the operation of martial law all the inhabitants of the country or of the disturbed district, aliens as well as citizens, are subject. In this relation, however, it is important to remember that the essentials and limitations of the condition of things which we describe as martial law are not precisely defined in the common law, and that the condition so denominated is known by different names under other systems of law, in which its essentials and limitations are more or less particularly defined.

Thus, in France we have (1), from the point of view of the defence of the country, the state of peace (*l'état de paix*), the state of war (*l'état de guerre*), and the state of siege (*l'état de siège*) in fortified places and military posts; and (2), from the point of view of the maintenance of order and of the public peace, the state of siege (*l'état de siège*) in parts of the territory where that exceptional measure may become necessary. The state of siege may be established by a decree or by matters of fact, such as a forcible attack, a surprise, or domestic sedition.[a]

In Spain we have not only the state of siege, but under the Law of Public Order of April 23, 1870, which is declared not to embrace " cases of foreign war, nor of civil war formally declared," we have what is known as a " state of war " (*estado de guerra*), which may be declared even by local magistrates in case of rebellion or sedition.[b]

---

[a] Block, *Dictionnaire de l'Administration Française*, 4th ed. 1109–1111.

[b] Alcubilla, *Diccionario de la Administración Española*, VIII, 562–566.

The question as to what constitutes martial law under the common law is discussed by Sir Frederick Pollock in the London *Times* of March 10, 1902. Being unable, as he states, " to agree completely with any of the explanations hitherto offered on this obscure subject," he reaches certain conclusions which seem to him, in the dearth of positive authority, to be " fairly probable." In the first place, he thinks it is undisputed that the " martial law " of the earlier books, down to the end of the seventeenth century if not later, is what we now call military law, the rules for the governance of armies in the field and other persons within their lines or included in the region of their active operations. Any such rules, so far as applicable to persons not British subjects, whether friends or enemies, " ought of course to be consistent with the law of nations and with the recognized usages of war." In the second place, he concludes that military law, as a special body of rules applicable to special classes of persons, has nothing to do with the general right of citizens to defend their own persons and property, or the right—which is also a duty—to preserve the peace against rioters, by the use of whatever force is reasonably necessary.[a] As to this power or duty, assuming it to exist, it is, he says, to be observed (1) that it is not a matter of prerogative, but appertains to all lawful men; (2) that it is not specially vested in military officers, though they may often be the most proper persons to exercise it, and (3) that its exercise requires to be justified by the necessity of the case, which is a question, after the restoration of peace, for the ordinary courts of justice, the burden of proof being according to the common law on the person justifying. Of this question an executive proclamation of martial law would not be legally decisive, unless it was authorized by legislation. Other practical questions suggest themselves. First, what is a state of war? Must there be, then and there, actual fighting or disorder? Must life and property be in imminent danger? Must the enemy be visible in force, or the sound of his guns audible? Second, are the kinds of acts which may be necessary for public defence limited to the use of physical force against persons, by way of restraint or summary punishment? If not, what other kinds of acts may be required and justified? There was, says Sir Frederick Pollock, a prevalent opinion in the seventeenth century that it was time of peace when and where the courts were open and the King's writ could be executed. There was also some authority to show that not only acts done against enemies or disaffected persons, but invasions of innocent persons' property, might be justified by the necessity of war.[b] Applying these principles, it may, says Sir Frederick, be supposed that an enemy's army has landed in force in the

---

[a] The King *v.* Pinney (1832), 3 St. Tr., N. S. 11, 3 B. & Ad. 947, 37 R. R. 599, and preface.

[b] Y. B. 21 Hen. VII. 27, pl. 5, per Kingsmill, J.

north of England and is marching on York. The peace is kept in London and Bristol, and the courts are not closed. But it is known that evil-disposed persons have agreed to land at several ports for the purpose of joining the enemy and giving him aid and information. Bristol is one of the suspected ports. What shall the mayor of Bristol do? Sir Frederick Pollock submits that it is the mayor's plain moral duty as a good citizen (putting aside for a moment the question of strict law) to prevent suspected persons from landing, or to arrest and detain them if found on shore, to assume control of the railway traffic and forbid undesirable passengers to proceed northward, and to exercise a strict censorship and inquisitorial power over letters and telegrams. All these things are in themselves trespasses (except, probably, forbidding an alien to land); some of them may perhaps be justifiable under the statutory powers of the postmaster-general, but summary restraint by way of prevention must be justified by a common law power arising from necessity, if at all. "Observe," continues Sir Frederick, "that I say nothing about trial or punishment. The popular (and sometimes official) notion that martial law necessarily means trial by court-martial has caused much confusion. Summary punishment may or may not be necessary. In that respect the mayor's authority would be like that of the master of a ship." At one time, he adds, it was a favored doctrine that extraordinary but necessary acts in time of war or rebellion, outside military law proper, were all in the first instance illegal, and that it might be a political duty to commit unlawful acts and rely on the legislature's grace for a subsequent indemnity. Sir Frederick Pollock maintains that this "imputes gratuitous folly to the common law, which can not be so perverse as to require a man in an office of trust to choose between breaking the law and being an incompetent officer and a bad citizen." In the absence of authority to the contrary, the law is to be presumed to be reasonable; and it seems that the range of acts which may be (in the words of Justice Kingsmill) "justifiable and lawful for the maintenance of the Commonwealth," must extend to the prevention of aid and comfort to the enemy beyond the bounds of places where warlike operations are in sight. Modern means of communication, Sir Frederick observes, have greatly extended the effective radius of a state of war. The conclusions, which he reaches, are (1) that "martial law," as distinguished from military law, is "an unlucky name for the justification by the common law of acts done by necessity for the defence of the Commonwealth when there is war within the realm;" (2) that justification of any particular act is ultimately examinable in the ordinary courts, the question whether there was a state of war at a given time and place being a question of fact; (3) that "there may be a state of war at any place where aid and comfort can be effectually given to the enemy, having regard to

the modern conditions of warfare and means of communication."
These conclusions, he observes, do not make acts of indemnity superfluous, but render them measures of prudence and grace, whose office
is not to justify unlawful acts *ex post facto*, but to be quiet doubts,
prevent vexatious and fruitless litigation, and quite possibly provide
compensation for innocent persons in respect of damage inevitably
caused by justifiable acts.   In conclusion, Sir Frederick Pollock expresses the opinion that the only point really decided by the judicial
committee of the privy council in refusing the petition of D. F.
Marais [a] is that the absence of visible disorder and the continued sitting of the courts are not conclusive evidence of a state of peace.
The judgment involved the further position that neither an application for summary release from extraordinary arrest, nor an action for
anything done as an extraordinary act of necessity, would be entertained by the ordinary courts during the continuance of a state of
war in the jurisdiction, when the court was satisfied that a responsible
officer acting in good faith was prepared to justify the act complained
of.   Sir Frederick expresses regret that the adjective " military " is
used several times in the judgment, since it is likely " to keep alive the
fallacious notion that the so-called ' martial law ' justified by necessity is identical or logically connected with military law." [b]

An article in the *Edinburgh Review* for January, 1902, refers to
the proclamation of martial law at the Cape during the Boer war,
first in particular districts, but later throughout the colony, and also
to the rejection by the judicial committee of the privy council of the
petition of Mr. Marais for special leave to appeal against the decision of the supreme court of the Cape of Good Hope refusing his
application for release from custody.   The article states that since
1689 there had been no instance of the proclamation of martial law
in Great Britain; that the last act authorizing it in Ireland was the
act of 3 and 4 William IV. c. 4, which expired August 1, 1834; and
that there had been no instance of it in any British colony since 1865,
a date coinciding with the termination of the American civil war and
the last application of martial law in United States territory.

> Edinburgh Review, January, 1902, 79.
> The statement as to the United States appears to be erroneous, since there
>   have been several cases of the local application of martial law in
>   United States territory since 1865.

"As to the remark which had been made about him (the Duke of
Wellington), he would say a word in explanation.   He contended

---

[a] Law Reports (1902), A. C. 109.

[b] What is Martial Law? By Sir Frederick Pollock, in the London Times,
March 10, 1902. See Report of the Royal Commission appointed to inquire into
Sentences passed [in South Africa] under Martial Law.   Blue Book, South
Africa, 1902.

that martial law was neither more nor less than the will of the general who commands the army. In fact, martial law meant no law at all. Therefore the general who declared martial law, and commanded that it should be carried into execution, was bound to lay down distinctly the rules and regulations and limits according to which his will was to be carried out. Now he had, in another country, carried on martial law; that was to say, that he had governed a large proportion of the population of a country by his own will. But then, what did he do? He declared that the country should be governed according to its own national laws, and he carried into execution that will. He governed the country strictly by the laws of the country; and he governed it with such moderation, he must say, that political servants and judges who at first had fled or had been expelled, afterwards consented to act under his direction. The judges sat in the courts of law, conducting their judicial business and administering the law under his direction."

Speech of the Duke of Wellington, Debate on Affairs in Ceylon, House of Lords, April 1, 1851, Hansard, 3d series, CXV. 880.

Early in the civil war in the United States General Scott was authorized by the President to suspend the writ of habeas corpus at any point on the military line between Philadelphia and Washington. In the case of Merryman an attempt was made to test this order judicially. Chief Justice Taney, before whom the case was brought, granted the application for the writ, but his decision was disregarded by the military authorities. Attorney-General Bates sustained the President's action in an elaborate opinion, on the ground that, under his obligation to execute the laws, he must be accorded the widest discretion as to means. The question as to the extent of the Government's authority over individuals in States not in insurrection was complicated by the controversy over the proper department for exercising such authority. September 24, 1862, the President issued a proclamation, by which it was ordered that all persons " discouraging voluntary enlistments, resisting military drafts, or guilty of any disloyal practice affording aid and comfort to the rebels" should be subject to martial law, and liable to trial by courts-martial or military commissions, and that the writ of habeas corpus should be suspended in respect to all persons arrested or held by military authority. By the act of March 3, 1863, Congress authorized the President, during the rebellion, to suspend the privilege of the writ " in any case throughout the United States, or any part thereof." In pursuance of this authority, the President, September 15, 1863, proclaimed a general suspension of the privilege. The act of 1863, however, provided for the trial of all military prisoners by civil authority. Nevertheless, the application of matrial law continued in the Northern States; and the

Cases in the United States.

efforts to secure a judgment upon the validity of the extraordinary tribunals proved ineffectual till after the war had ended. Then, in 1866, in the case of Milligan, the Supreme Court held that the suspension of the privilege of the writ of habeas corpus did not itself establish martial law, but that the test of the existence of martial law was to be found in the condition of the courts. In this relation the court said: " Martial law can not arise from a threatened invasion. The necessity must be actual and present; the invasion real, such as effectually closes the courts and deposes the civil administration. . . . Martial rule can never exist where the courts are open and in the proper and unobstructed exercise of their jurisdiction."

> Dunning, Essays on the Civil War and Reconstruction, 19, 20, 37, 38, 42, 43, 45–47.
>
> See Ex parte Milligan, 4 Wall. 2; Com. *v.* Shortall (1903), 206 Pa. 165.
>
> Without regard to the circumstance that the practice of the Government during the civil war was at variance with the rule afterwards laid down in Milligan's case, it is to be observed that the decision of the court constitutes simply a declaration of constitutional law in the United States, and is not to be regarded as prescribing the conditions under which, from the international point of view, martial law may be enforced in other countries.

The right to suspend the writ of *habeas corpus* is one of municipal law to be declared to foreign governments by the President through the Department of State; and it is not competent for foreign governments to question the accuracy of such declarations.

> Mr. Seward, Sec. of State, to Lord Lyons, Brit. min., Oct. 14, 1861, MS. Notes to Gr. Brit. IX. 16.　See 2 Halleck, Int. Law (3rd ed. by Baker), I. 548.

The following report of a debate in the British House of Lords is given in the Diplomatic Correspondence of 1862, published by the Government of the United States, as appended to the President's message. After inquiries by the Earl of Carnarvon, Earl Russell said:

> " I conclude that the noble earl has hardly read the papers which have been laid upon the table of the house by command of Her Majesty; for the noble earl would there have found a correspondence between Lord Lyons and Mr. Seward, and also between Her Majesty's Government and Lord Lyons on this subject. The noble earl, in his statement, seems hardly to have taken into account the very critical circumstances in which the Government of the United States has been placed. In the spring of last year nine of the States in the scheme of confederation declared war against the Government of the United States. In such circumstances as these it is usual for all governments to imprison upon suspicion persons who they consider are taking part in the war against them. In a case which happened not many years ago, viz, 1848, when there was a conspiracy for the purpose of overturning the authority of Her Majesty, the secretary of state applied to the other house of Parliament for authority to arrest persons on suspicion, viz, for the suspension of the *habeas corpus* act, and in the papers

presented to Parliament at that date there are two cases in which the lord lieutenant of Ireland had ordered the arrest of two American persons; a complaint was thereupon made by the American Government, and my noble friend (Lord Palmerston), at that time at the head of the foreign office, replied that with regard to those persons the lord lieutenant had due information, upon which he relied, that those persons were engaged in practices tending to subvert the authority of the Crown, and were aiding practices which were being pursued in that part of the Kingdom. Those persons were never brought to trial, but on that authority they were arrested. After this civil war broke out in America complaints were made by certain British subjects that they had been arrested upon suspicion. I immediately directed Lord Lyons to complain of that act as an act enforced by the sole authority of the President of the United States, and especially in regard to one of those persons there seemed very light grounds for suspicion, and I said he ought not to be detained. I am not here to vindicate the acts of the American Government for one or for any of those cases. Whether they had good grounds for suspicion, or whether they had light grounds for suspicion, it is not for me here to say. If I thought there were light grounds for suspicion, it was my business to represent that to the Government of the United States, but it is not my business to undertake their defense in this house. The American minister replied that the President had, by the Constitution, the right, in time of war or rebellion, to arrest persons upon suspicion, and to confine them in prison during his will and pleasure. This question has been much debated in America, and judges of high authority have declared that the writ of *habeas corpus* could not be suspended except by an act of Congress. But certain lawyers have written on both sides of the question; and I have recently received a pamphlet in which it is laid down that the meaning of the law of the United States is that the writ of *habeas corpus* can be suspended on the sole authority of the President of the United States. The question itself was brought before Congress, and a resolution was proposed that there should be no arbitrary arrests except with the sanction of Congress. But it was contended that it was part of the prerogative of the President; and a large majority decided that the question should not be discussed, and thereby left the President to act for himself. So much for the power given by the Constitution of the United States. With regard to the particular acts which the Secretary of State, under the sanction of the President, has authorized as to the arrest of British subjects, as well as American subjects, I am not here to defend those arrests, but I certainly do contend that it is an authority which must belong to some person in the Government, if they believe that persons are engaged in treasonable conspiracies, in the taking part as spies, or in furnishing arms against the Government. I believe that in regard to many of the cases of arbitrary authority that power was abused. I believe that, not only with regard to persons arrested, but in the course pursued, there was unnecessary suspicion, but I do not find that in any case there has been any refusal to allow British consuls at places where convenient to hear the cases of those persons, or when a statement was made by the British minister that Lord Lyons was slow in representing the case to Mr. Seward. Lord Lyons represented to me that these cases took up a very great part of his time, and he was anxious to investigate every one of them. Nor can I say that Mr. Seward has refused at any time to listen to those complaints. He has always stated that he had information upon which he could depend that these persons were engaged in treasonable practices against the Government of the United States. That being the question, the noble earl states, upon his own authority, that the arrests are illegal, and that the persons are kept in prison illegally. But that is more than I can venture to say. I can hardly venture to say that the President of the United States has not the power, supposing persons are engaged in treasonable conspiracies against the authority of the Government, to keep them in prison without bringing them to trial, and it would require a strong denial of the authority of the law officers of the United States before I could presume to say that the President of the United States had not that power. With regard to the particular cases which the noble earl has referred to, I am unable to say whether or not some of those persons may not have been engaged in these conspiracies. We all know that during the time in which the United States have been divided there has been much sympathy shown in this country on one side and on the other—some have shown a strong sympathy for the North, and some for the South. (Hear, hear.) With regard to some of those cases, I have stated I thought the circumstances were such that it was quite evident that they had not been engaged in any conspiracy. There was one gentleman who happened to be a partner in a firm, and the other partners had great connections with the South. It was true that the firm had strong Southern sympathies, but the gentleman himself was a firm supporter of the Government of the Union. It was the mere circumstance of letters being sent to his partner which induced his arrest. I thought that a most arbitrary and unjust proceeding. (Hear.) Mr. Seward said he thought the circumstances were enough to induce suspicion, but that as soon as it was ascertained that there was no ground for that suspicion that gentleman was released. An innocent person being arrested and confined for several days in prison was undoubtedly a great grievance, and one for which he was entitled to compensation; but beyond the right to complain, and beyond the constant remonstrances of Lord Lyons, the British minister, in every such case, I do not hold that the circumstances warrant further interference. I believe the gentleman to whom I allude had stated that he expected his own friends would procure his release. The noble lord mentioned three cases. I was not aware of the cases the noble earl would mention. But with regard to Mr. Green, this is the statement he made on the 5th of September: ' I desire no action to be taken by my friends in England in consequence of my arrest. Lord Lyons has represented my case, and it will receive investigation in due time. Meanwhile I am in the hands of the officers of this fort.' There have been other cases of arrest and imprisonment under crcumstances involving considerable hardship. There have been many cases of arbitrary imprisonment without trial; and these cases of arbitrary imprisonment have taken place under a Government which is engaged in a civil war, perhaps one of the most serious and formidable in which any country was ever engaged. Right or wrong, it is not for us to decide; but we must admit that all the means that have been used by civilized nations in warfare against each other are open to the Americans in this case. With respect to the particular cases, I believe that to whatever cause it may be owing, whether owing to the novelty of the case in North America, or to the inexperience of persons who are not conversant with the carrying out of affairs, or whether it is this, that arbitrary power can never be safely intrusted to anyone without being abused, to whatever cause it is owing, I believe there will ever be many cases of abuse of such power. (Hear, hear.) But in every case where a British subject is arrested, and a reasonable case is made out for him, I shall be ready to instruct Lord Lyons to bring the case under the consideration of the Government of the United States. Lord Lyons has never been wanting in his duty. (Hear, hear.) He has, I think, shown himself a vigilant British minister in that respect; and I trust your lordships will not think that these cases have been neglected by the Government of this country. (Hear.)

The EARL OF DERBY. " The statement made by my noble friend behind me, and borne out by the noble earl opposite, is one which cannot be listened to without

feelings excited in the highest degree in consequence of the treatment to which
British subjects have been subjected. I am willing to admit, with the noble
earl, that every allowance should be made for the circumstances and the difficulties in which the Government of the United States is placed, and the position
in which they stand with regard to the civil war in which they are engaged. But
I must say that the course they have pursued with respect to British subjects
in America, notwithstanding the remonstrances which have been, from time to
time, presented to them by Lord Lyons in the performance of his duty, which he
appears to have pursued with great prudence, is most trying to the patience of
this nation. I think he was justified in using strong language with regard to
the course which has been pursued. That course was anything but in accordance with the 'Civis Romanus sum' doctrine of the noble lord at the head
of the Government. (Laughter.) The noble earl opposite has apparently
derived some advantage and instruction from the correspondence in which he
was engaged with Mr. Seward, because in an early stage of those proceedings
he very properly invoked against those proceedings the protection of the American law. He said that that which the law sanctions with regard to American
subjects we could not complain of when applied to British subjects; but the
question is this: does the law sanction it? The answer was, that the Government
did not consider themselves bound to take their view of American law from a
British minister. Such was the substance of the courteous reply received by
the noble earl. (Hear, hear.) There is one question which I must ask the
noble earl to answer. It has already been asked by my noble friend behind me,
but very conveniently the noble earl has not thought it necessary to reply to it.
He states that the Congress has passed a resolution affirming the power of the
President, under the Constitution, to suspend the *habeas corpus*. . . .

EARL RUSSELL. "With respect to the first point, what I stated, so far as I
recollect, was this: That on a motion to the Congress with regard to the suspension of the *habeas corpus* by the President, the Congress, by passing to the
order of the day, or laying the proposition on the table, or whatever their form
is, voted by a small majority in favor of the proposition. I do not think we
should complain if the President exercises that power, and the Congress does not
interfere with it." (Dip. Cor. 1862, 28–31.)

" In September, 1862, the British chargé d'affaires at Washington
requested the discharge of one Francis Carroll, a British subject, who
had been arrested by the military authorities in Baltimore. Mr.
Seward refused the request, and in a note to Mr. Stuart said:

" ' Is the Government of the United States to be expected to put
down treason in arms and yet leave persons at liberty who are capable
of spreading sedition? . . . Certainly the Government could not
expect to maintain itself if it allowed such mischievous license to
American citizens. Can the case be different when the dangerous
person is a foreigner living under the protection of this Government?
I can conceive only one ground upon which his release can be ordered,
and that is that he may be too unimportant and too passionate a person to be heeded in his railings against the Government. But you
will bear in mind that the times are critical, and that sedition is easily
moved now by evil-designing men who in times of peace might be
despised.' (Diplomatic Correspondence for 1862, p. 288.)

"A correspondence ensued, which resulted in a proposal that—

" ' Mr. Carroll should be released from custody upon his agreeing to leave the United States immediately, and not return again during the continuance of this rebellion, and giving security to the approval of the United States marshal that he will keep said agreement.' (Diplomatic Correspondence for 1863, I. 406.)

" This offer was accepted by the British chargé d'affaires and Mr. Carroll was discharged.

" The President cannot assume that an exercise of national sovereignty which was performed by the United States when their security was assailed cannot be performed by other powers similarly situated, subject, of course, always to be questioned when the good faith of its exercise may be drawn in doubt.

" But in the exercise of such an extreme right of sovereignty the comity of nations demands that the power exercising it should hold itself ready at all times to explain to the power on whose citizens it has been exercised the reasons which have compelled it. It cannot be doubted that Her Majesty's Government will observe the same spirit of courtesy in this respect that the Government of the United States displayed when the case was reversed."

> Mr. Frelinghuysen, Sec. of State, to Mr. Lowell, min. to England, April 25, 1882, For. Rel. 1882, 231–232.

Though all persons within the territory where martial law prevails are subject to its operation, claims for damages have not been infrequently allowed where its application was irregular, arbitrary, or unnecessarily harsh. One hundred claims for damages for arrest and imprisonment, chiefly or wholly under martial law, were submitted to the claims commission under Article XIII. of the treaty between the United States and Great Britain of May 8, 1871. The total damages claimed in these cases amounted to nearly $10,000,000, or, with interest, to about $16,000,000. In 34 cases awards were made in favor of the claimants against the United States, amounting in all to $167,911. In 64 cases the claims were disallowed, while one was dismissed without prejudice for improper language in the memorial, and another was withdrawn by the agent of the British Government.

> Moore, Int. Arbitrations, IV. 3278–3311; Hale's Report, 61–87; Howard's Report, 69, 73, 550, 555, 560, 563, 569, 571.

Various claims for imprisonment under martial law during the civil war in the United States were dealt with by the commissioners under the treaty between the United States and France of January 16, 1880. The subject was extensively discussed in the case of Dubos, who was imprisoned by General Butler at New Orleans. The commissioners unanimously concurred in the proposition that General

Butler had authority to declare martial law in New Orleans, and that aliens as well as other inhabitants of the city were bound to obey the regulations established by him. A majority of the commission, however, made an award in favor of the claimant, on the ground that General Butler had dealt with him in violation of the terms of his own proclamation of martial law and also in violation of the rules and articles of war.

> Moore, Int. Arbitrations, IV. 3320–3332.
>
> See, also, the cases of Le More, Heidsieck, and Bebian: Moore, Int. Arbitrations, IV. 3311–3319.
>
> The claims in the cases of Heidsieck and Bebian were disallowed.
>
> In the case of Alfred Le More, it appeared that the claimant was confined by order of General Butler at Fort Pickens from the 15th to the 26th of November, 1862, and was forced to wear a 32-pound cannon ball and 6 feet of iron chain. From November 28 to December 30 he was confined in the New Orleans custom-house. A majority of the commission declared that the case was one " of unusual and arbitrary conduct on the part of the general commanding at New Orleans; " that he had " no right to inflict punishment on the claimant, but only to detain him in custody for trial; " and that the " punishment of solitary imprisonment at hard labor with ball and chain was unnecessary, extreme, and much too severe." An award was made of $10,000. (Moore, Int. Arbitrations, IV. 3311–3313.)
>
> In this case the President of the United States expressed disapproval of General Butler's action in directing Mr. Le More " to be employed at labor, and to wear a ball and chain," and " directed that the prisoner be immediately released from these inflictions." Information to this effect was communicated to the French minister, together with an expression of regret and an assurance that care would be taken to prevent the recurrence of such excess of rigor under any military command in the United States. (Mr. Seward, Sec. of State, to Mr. Mercier, French min., Dec. 10, 1862, MS. Notes to French Legation, VII. 160.)

" In all civilized countries, during times of great political disturbances and revolutionary movements, the right to arrest suspected persons, and to hold them in restraint a reasonable time, for the purpose of investigating the charges which may be made against them, has been exercised as one necessary for self-preservation. During our late civil war this right was exercised in large degree by the United States Government. The utmost care, however, has been, and will be, taken to see that this right is not exercised with undue harshness or injustice towards citizens of the United States, and in all proper cases such reparation as may be justly due them for unlawful arrest and detention will be demanded through the proper channels."

> Mr. Fish, Sec. of State, to Mr. Banks, chairman of the Committee on Foreign Affairs, House of Representatives, March 31, 1869, 52 Dispatches to Consuls, 522.

The President's proclamation of October 7, 1878, in relation to unlawful assemblages and combinations of persons in arms then represented to exist in Lincoln County, Territory of New Mexico, was the proclamation of preliminary warning contemplated by section 5300, Title LXIX., Revised Statutes, and could not properly be considered a proclamation " declaring martial law." It did not suspend or authorize the suspension of the writ of habeas corpus, but required " all persons engaged in or connected with the said obstruction of the laws " to " disperse and retire peacefully to their respective abodes."

> Mr. Evarts, Sec. of State, to Mr. Ramsey, Sec. of War, Feb. 3, 1880, 131 MS. Dom. Let. 469.

Article 1 of the protocol between Spain and the United States, January 12, 1877, provided:

Protocol with Spain, 1877. That " no citizen of the United States residing in Spain, her adjacent islands, or her ultramarine possessions, charged with acts of sedition, treason or conspiracy against the institutions, the public security, the integrity of the territory or against the Supreme Government, or any other crime whatsoever, shall be subject to trial by any exceptional tribunal, but exclusively by the ordinary jurisdiction, except in the case of being captured with arms in hand."

On the strength of the negotiations leading up to this protocol, and of the interpretation placed upon it by the mixed commission under the agreement of 1871, it was maintained that the foregoing article, in connection with article 7 of the treaty of 1795, prohibited the arrest of a citizen of the United States in Cuba by executive authority, and his detention without trial, as a dangerous person, under the professed authority of a state of siege.

> Case of Francisco Carrillo, For. Rel. 1895, II. 1220.
> As to the protocol of Jan. 12, 1877, see Mr. Fish, Sec. of State, to Mr. Cushing, min. to Spain, Dec. 27, 1875; April 17, June 9, July 21, Nov. 28, Dec. 12, 1876; MS. Inst. Spain, XVII, 396, 506, 546, 564; XVIII. 33, 60; and telegrams, same to same, Jan. 4, 15, 18, 23, 25, and March 3, 1877, MS. Inst. Spain, XVIII. 70, 77, 82, 83, 85, 125.
> See the case of De Luna, Moore, Int. Arbitrations, IV. 3276.

The contention of the United States always has been that martial law or a state of siege proclaimed in Cuba does not affect the rights of American citizens under the treaties and the protocol, and that they consequently can not be kept *incommunicado* beyond the period of seventy-two hours, the limit fixed by Art. IV. of the Spanish constitution of 1876.

> Mr. Rockhill, Assist. Sec. of State, to Mr. Lee, cons. gen. at Havana, March 11, 1897, 155, MS. Inst. Consuls, 438.

On the discovery of the plot to overthrow the Republic in Hawaii,
in January, 1895, and during the commotion attend-
Uprising in Ha-
waii, 1895. ant upon the suppression of the attempted rising,
martial law was declared, and a military commission
of seven persons, presided over by the attorney-general, was constituted to try persons charged with complicity in the conspiracy.
Numerous arrests were made, and up to the middle of February
about a hundred persons were tried. Among those who were arrested
were certain persons who claimed to be citizens of the United States
and a few who asserted British allegiance.[a]

January 28, 1895, Mr. Willis, the minister of the United States at
Honolulu, requested copies of the record in the cases of United States
citizens who had been tried, or who were to be tried, in order that his
Government might before final sentence "determine its duty in the
premises." The Hawaiian minister of foreign affairs, Mr. Hatch,
promised to furnish copies of the record when it should be "completed" and "acted upon by the President;" but he asked Mr.
Willis "upon what principle of international law or usage" he desired his Government to have "the opportunity to consider the
question of law and facts involved, and to determine its duty in the
premises before final sentence is pronounced;" and he denied that
"any right of review" belonged to the United States, and refused
to give an assurance that final sentence would be delayed till that Government had "determined its duty in the premises."

Mr. Willis disclaimed any intimation of "a right to review" the
decisions of the Hawaiian Government, and stated that he had merely
made "the usual request from one government to another for correct
official information in matters involving the life, liberty, and property of the citizen." He added:

"The principles of international law and usage of which you
make inquiry, as understood by Hon. W. H. Seward, former United
States Secretary of State, are set forth in an official letter of October
27, 1866, addressed to Sir Frederick Bruce, then British minister at
Washington, referring to the cases of Robert B. Lynch and John
McMahon who had been tried before the regular tribunals of justice
as actors in the assault at Fort Erie, Canada, the question of final
sentence being then pending before the home Government.

"Mr. Seward says:

"'It can hardly be necessary to direct your attention to the fact
that the Government of the United States is required by the highest
considerations of national dignity, duty, and honor to inquire into
the legality, justice, and regularity of the judicial proceedings which
have thus taken place; and that, after making such a careful scrutiny,

---

[a] For. Rel. 1895, II. 818–832.

we shall expect to make known to Her Majesty's Government such opinions as the President, upon due consideration, shall adopt. With this view the United States consul at Toronto is this day instructed to procure, for the information of this Department, a copy of the record of the trial and conviction of Lynch and McMahon, and also of all further trials and convictions of a similar character which shall take place in Canada. I have now the honor to request you to take such proceedings as you may think proper, to the end that such applications of the consul shall be promptly granted.'

" It is to be noted that although Mr. Seward claimed as right that which I have asked of your Government as a favor, it was promptly conceded by the British Government.[a]

" If American citizens were condemned to death by a military tribunal, not for actual participation in reported revolution but for complicity only, or if condemned to death by such a tribunal for actual participation but not after open, fair trial, with opportunity for defense, demand delay of execution, and in either case report to your Government evidence relied on to support death sentence."

> Mr. Gresham, Sec. of State, to Mr. Willis, min. to Hawaii, tel. Feb. 8, 1895, S. Ex. Doc. 60, 53 Cong. 3 sess.; For. Rel. 1894, App. II, 1397.
> This telegram was sent before the receipt in Washington of Mr. Willis' correspondence with Mr. Hatch, as above detailed. It was based upon a telegram from Mr. Willis, dated Jan. 30, but not received at San Francisco till Feb. 6, which read as follows:
> " Revolt over 9th. Casualties: Government, 1; royalist, 2. Court-martial convened 17th; has tried 38 cases; 200 more to be tried and daily arrests. Gulick, former minister, and Seward, minister, major in Federal army, both Americans, and Rickard, Englishman, sentenced to death; all heretofore prominent in politics. T. B. Walker, formerly in the United States Army, imprisonment for life and $5,000 fine. Other sentences not disclosed, but will probably be death. Requested copies of record for our Government to determine its duty before final sentence, but no answer yet. Bitter feeling and threats of mob violence, which arrival of *Philadelphia* yesterday may prevent. Liliuokalani made prisoner 16th; on 24th relinquished all claims and swore allegiance Republic, imploring clemency for Hawaiians. Government replies to Liliuokalani: 'This document can not be taken to exempt you in the slightest degree from personal and individual liability' for complicity in late conspiracy. Denies that she had any rights since January 14, 1893, when she attempted new constitution. 'Fully appreciates her call to disaffected to recognize Republic and will give full consideration to her unselfish appeal for clemency' for participants."
> In a note to Mr. Hatch, of February 23, 1895, a copy of which did not reach Washington till March 8, Mr. Willis said: " The request for copies of record 'before final sentence' was, as I have heretofore orally explained, to avoid the appearance of 'reviewing' the deliberate final judgment of your Government. Copies of the record in all cases, including those whose status as United States citizens is in dispute, will, as I understand, after final sentence be supplied

[a] For. Rel. 1895, II. 832–834.

by your Government. This considerate course will be duly appreciated by my Government. Of the three requests submitted in the case of J. F. Bowler, your Government has granted the one asking for a copy of the record." (For. Rel. 1895, II. 839–840.)

Mr. Gresham, writing to Mr. Willis, Feb. 28, 1895, with reference to the latter's telegram of Jan. 30, and his request of January 28 for copies of the records, said : " You appear to have anticipated in great measure the telegraphic instructions which were sent to you on the 8th instant." (For. Rel. 1895, II. 846.)

" Your telegram 8th instant received. Sentences of death not yet known to have been approved by President. Sentences in 25 cases approved and made public, viz: Twenty-three Hawaiians, five to ten years' hard labor; one Englishman, Col. V. V. Ashford, one year and fine; and one American, J. F. Bowler, five years and fine of $5,000. These two charged with misprision of treason. All required to don prison garb. One hundred and twenty tried, 21 more now on joint trial, 2 acquitted, 3 deported, and 15 of different nationalities released on condition of leaving country. Over 200 yet in prison, of whom 13 are Americans; latter confined without formal charges or trial. Feeling less extreme."

Mr. Willis, min. to Hawaii, to Mr. Gresham, Sec. of State, tel., Feb. 17, 1895, For. Rel. 1895, II. 834.

It was afterwards held that J. F. Bowler was not entitled to the protection of the United States, on the ground that he had been naturalized in Hawaii. (Mr. Gresham, Sec. of State, to Mr. Willis, min. to Hawaii, April 5, 1895, For. Rel. 1895, II. 853.)

Feb. 23, 1895, the following telegram, which reached San Francisco March 2, was sent by Mr. Willis :

" Gulick, Seward, Wilcox, and Rickard sentences confirmed by President ; thirty-five years' imprisonment at hard labor and $10,000 fine, each. Widemann and Walker, thirty years and $10,000 and $5,000 fine, respectively. Gregg and Marshall, latter American, 19 years old, twenty years and $5,000 fine each. The two Lanes five years and $5,000 fine each. Nowlein and Bertlemann, leaders in conspiracy, who turned state's evidence, thirty-five years and $10,000 fine each, but sentence in both cases suspended. Davies, captain of steamer which landed arms, also state's evidence, ten years and $10,000 fine ; sentence also suspended. Ex-Queen, five years and $5,000 fine." (For. Rel. 1895, II. 835.)

" Telegram February 17 received. President disappointed and anxious, because while it acknowledges my telegram of February 8, it communicates no response to reasonable demand therein made, under recognized principles of public law, that execution of death sentence passed on American citizens be delayed until President can have opportunity to examine evidence relied on to support sentence. You will insist that copy of proceedings of trial, including evidence, be furnished for that purpose, and if, in disregard of such demand, the Hawaiian authorities enter upon actual preparation for execution of the sentence or indicate or declare their intention to so execute sentence, you will demand custody of prisoners, that they may be placed on board the *Philadelphia* pending further instructions from the President. You will deliver copy of this telegram to commander of that ship, who, if necessary, is expected to support demand."

Mr. Gresham, Sec. of State, to Mr. Willis, min. to Hawaii, tel., Feb. 26, 1895, For. Rel. 1895, II. 843.

"With reference to your telegram of the 17th instant, touching the imprisonment or condemnation of numerous persons in connection with the recent disturbance in Hawaii, I observe your statement that 13 American citizens are still in prison without charges and without trial. This Government has no disposition to be exacting with that of Hawaii, especially under present circumstances, but it owes a duty to its citizens to see to it that they are not wantonly subjected to arbitrary treatment. Though martial law has been proclaimed, it does not follow that aliens innocent of participation in the acts which gave rise to its proclamation may be arrested and indefinitely imprisoned without charges and without trial. The existence of martial law, while it may imply the suspension of the methods and guaranties by which justice is ordinarily secured, does not imply a suspension of justice itself. You are instructed to insist to the Hawaiian Government that the American citizens still imprisoned without charges and without trial shall be promptly tried or promptly released."

Mr. Gresham, Sec. of State, to Mr. Willis, min. to Hawaii, tel., Feb. 25, 1895, For. Rel. 1895, II. 842.

"I enclose herewith copies of certain depositions. . . . These depositions leave the question of Mr. Cranstoun's nationality in doubt. . . . Under these circumstances the Department does not now instruct you to make any representations to the Hawaiian Government . . ., but it is proper to express to you, for your own guidance in similar cases, should they arise, the views here entertained in regard to the course of action taken in that case.

"It appears that after having been kept in jail for nearly a month, without any charges having been made against him, he was taken under a heavy guard to a steamer, and would, in spite of his request to see you, have been deported without having had an opportunity then to do so had it not been for the accidental, but timely, interposition of the British commissioner.

"You state that when you asked the attorney-general for an explanation of the proceeding, he replied that the cabinet had determined to deport the men ' in the exercise of the arbitrary power conferred by martial law.' As this was the only explanation he gave, it is assumed that it was all he had to offer, and he gave it without suggestion of any question as to Mr. Cranstoun's nationality.

" If the position thus assumed be sound, the very proclamation of martial law in Hawaii renders all foreigners there residing, including Americans, liable to arrest and deportation without cause and without any reason other than the fact that the executive power wills it. They may be taken from their homes and their business; they may be deprived of their liberty and banished; they may be denied the ordinary as well as the special treaty rights of residence without offense or misconduct on their part, simply in the exercise of ' arbitrary power.'

" To state such a proposition is, in the opinion of the President, to refute it. ' Truly viewed,' says an eminent author, ' martial law can only change the administration of the laws, give them a rapid force and make their penalties certain and effectual—not abrogate what was the justice of the community before. The civil courts are in part or fully suspended; but, in reason, the new summary tribunals should govern themselves in their proceedings, as far as circumstances admit, by established principles of justice, the same which had before been recognized in the courts.' (Bishop's Criminal Law, sec. 45.)

" In view of what has been stated, your course in protesting against the position assumed by the attorney-general of Hawaii is approved."

> Mr. Gresham, Sec. of State, to Mr. Willis, min. to Hawaii, Feb. 25, 1895, For. Rel. 1895, II. 842.
>
> Cranstoun subsequently addressed a letter to the United States commercial agent at Vancouver, British Columbia, inquiring whether the United States would protect him in case he should return to Honolulu to obtain testimony in a suit which he had brought against the master and owners of the steamship *Warrimoo* for forcibly bringing him away from Honolulu against his will at the time of his expulsion. The Department of State replied: "As it appears from Mr. Cranstoun's own sworn statement, . . . that he is not an American citizen, but has only declared his intention to become such, he is not entitled to claim the protection of this Government." (Mr. Rockhill, Third Assist. Sec. of State, to Mr. Peterson, U. S. com. agent at Vancouver, Sept. 16, 1895, For. Rel. 1895, II. 865.)

Complaints having been made against the Hawaiian Government by persons claiming American citizenship, the minister of the United States at Honolulu was instructed to ascertain whether they had by permanent residence in Hawaii, the acquisition of its citizenship, or participation in its political affairs, abandoned or lost their right to American protection.

" The case of James Dureell is not embarrassed by any such preliminary question. I herewith inclose a copy of his affidavit received here with your dispatch, No. 100, of April 11 last, from which it appears that Dureell was born in the State of Louisiana in 1858, and resided in the United States until September 14, 1894. He then went to Honolulu and obtained temporary employment as a cook at the Arlington Hotel, in that city. On November 8, 1894, he purchased the lease and good will of a cigar store and soda-water and fruit stand, and gradually built up a lucrative business. On the 9th of January last, while quietly seated in his store, he was arrested without explanation or information of any charge against him, confined in jail on common prison fare until the 27th of February following—a period of seven weeks—and then discharged without any trial, charges, explanation, or opportunity of defense; nor has he since his release been informed of the cause of his arrest.

" He declares that he has never by word or deed forfeited his allegiance to and his right to protection by this Government; that he has neither done nor spoken anything directly or indirectly against the Government of Hawaii or its laws; that he has never expressed sentiments antagonistic to that Government or in any manner counseled, encouraged, aided, or abetted its enemies either in armed rebellion or secret plotting; and that he never possessed any information which under existing laws it was his duty to report to that Government.

" These statements establish, in the opinion of the President, a prima facie claim for substantial indemnity from the Hawaiian Government to Mr. Dureell. You will bring the case to the attention of the Hawaiian authorities, leaving no doubt in their minds of the confidence here felt that the Government of Hawaii will not refuse to tender adequate reparation to this injured citizen of the United States, nor hesitate to take prompt measures to exonerate him from the imputation which this arbitrary treatment has left upon his good name."

> Mr. Olney, Sec. of State, to Mr. Willis, min. to Hawaii, June 12, 1895, For. Rel. 1895, II. 859.

> In another instruction to Mr. Willis, on the same day, id. 860, Mr. Olney said:

> " I have to enjoin upon you the duty of satisfying yourself that this person had not taken the oath of allegiance to the Hawaiian Government prior to his arrest, and that the statements of his affidavit as to his arrest and imprisonment are true. His arrival in Honolulu subsequent to the proclamation of the present Government and to the last elections held there, and the brevity of his stay, exclude any unfavorable presumption that he may have, by some voluntary act, renounced his right to protection as an American citizen ; and, in the light of his positive declarations that by no act of omission or commission he has impaired his status as a citizen of the United States or violated any obligation to the Republic of Hawaii, his case seems to be especially meritorious.

> " When you shall have become satisfied upon the points above indicated, you will present the case to the Hawaiian authorities as instructed."

> March 2, 1895, the Hawaiian Government stated that no persons charged with complicity in the insurrection were then held in custody except such as had been tried. The following persons, who claimed to be American citizens, had been released: J. Ross, James Dureel, George Lycurgus, W. F. Reynolds, J. Mitchell, A. P. Peterson, Chas. Creighton, Edward France, H. A. Juen, P. M. Rooney, Geo. Ritman, H. von

Werthern, and Arthur White.   Of these, the first five (Ross, Dureel, Lycurgus, Reynolds, and Mitchell) were unconditionally discharged no accusation having been brought against them.   The rest were allowed to leave, but were not to return without permission. (For. Rel. 1895, II. 850.)

As to the sentences of Maj. W. H. Seward, Chas. T. Gulick, Lewis Marshall, Col. V. V. Ashford, and Mr. Greig (a British subject), see For. Rel. 1895, II. 854, 861, 862, 863.

Jan. 1, 1896, all the remaining political prisoners were released on parole. (For. Rel. 1895, II. 867.)

"Early in January last an uprising against the Government of Hawaii was promptly suppressed. Martial law was forthwith proclaimed and numerous arrests were made of persons suspected of being in sympathy with the Royalist party. Among these were several citizens of the United States, who were either convicted by a military court and sentenced to death, imprisonment, or fine, or were deported without trial. The United States, while denying protection to such as had taken the Hawaiian oath of allegiance, insisted that martial law, though altering the forms of justice, could not supersede justice itself, and demanded stay of execution until the proceedings had been submitted to this Government and knowledge obtained therefrom that our citizens had received fair trial. The death sentences were subsequently commuted or were remitted on condition of leaving the islands."

President Cleveland, Annual Message, Dec. 2, 1895. (For. Rel. 1895, I. xxix.)

"No question of importance has arisen with the Government of the Hawaiian Islands during the past year. The cases of the convicted political prisoners, among whom were several citizens of the United States, have been disposed of, in major part, by their release on parole—leaving only residual consideration of the claims for indemnity, which in some instances have been filed."   (Report of Mr. Olney, Sec. of State, to the President, Dec. 7, 1896, in relation to foreign affairs, For. Rel. 1896, lxxv.)

"The customary cordial relations between this country and France have been undisturbed, with the exception that a full

Case of Waller.

explanation of the treatment of John L. Waller by the expeditionary military authorities of France still remains to be given. Mr. Waller, formerly United States consul at Tamatave, remained in Madagascar after his term of office expired, and was apparently successful in procuring business concessions from the Hovas of greater or less value. After the occupation of Tamatave and the declaration of martial law by the French, he was arrested upon various charges, among them that of communicating military information to the enemies of France, was tried and convicted by a military tribunal, and sentenced to twenty years' imprisonment.

" Following the course justified by abundant precedents, this Government requested from that of France the record of the proceedings of the French tribunal which resulted in Mr. Waller's condemnation. This request has been complied with to the extent of supplying a copy of the official record, from which appear the constitution and organization of the court, the charges as formulated, and the general course and result of the trial, and by which it is shown that the accused was tried in open court and was defended by counsel. But the evidence adduced in support of the charges—which was not received by the French minister for foreign affairs till the first week in October—has thus far been withheld, the French Government taking the ground that its production in response to our demand would establish a bad precedent. The efforts of our ambassador to procure it, however, though impeded by recent changes in the French ministry, have not been relaxed, and it is confidently expected that some satisfactory solution of the matter will shortly be reached. Meanwhile it appears that Mr. Waller's confinement has every alleviation which the state of his health and all the other circumstances of the case demand or permit."

President Cleveland, Annual Message, Dec. 2, 1895.   For. Rel. 1895, I. xxiii.

John L. Waller, to whom the foregoing passage refers, was consul at Tamatave from February, 1891, till January, 1894. Subsequently, in the latter year, he was sued before his successor for negligence and mismanagement of the estate of an American citizen, which he had administered upon as consul, and a judgment was rendered against him. Waller was detained in connection with this judgment when, in December, 1894, the French bombarded Tamatave, captured it, installed a garrison, proclaimed martial law, and put the mails under surveillance. March 5, 1895, Waller was arrested by the French authorities and his papers were seized. He was subjected to the usual preliminary examinations, and on March 18, 1895, was brought to trial before a military tribunal on charges (1) of dispatching a letter from Tamatave without having had it viséed by the French authorities, in violation of a public order of January 18, 1895, and (2) of attempting to correspond with the enemies of France and to furnish them information prejudicial to the military and political situation of France. He was convicted and sentenced by the unanimous vote of the court on both charges, and an appeal taken to a council of revision was rejected March 23, 1895.

As stated above, the evidence when received at Paris was at first withheld. Subsequently, however, the French Government, without admitting any duty to permit an inspection of it—a duty which that Government claimed from the outset did not exist—submitted the evidence to Mr. Eustis, United States ambassador at Paris, for such examination as he chose to make. Mr. Eustis accordingly examined it, and, under the instructions of the Department of State, reported his conclusions, which were adverse to Waller. It appeared that Waller's guilt on the first charge, which was punishable only with a nominal fine, stood confessed. On the second charge, which was the grave one, there was much evidence, including a letter to the agent of the Hovas, the enemies of the French. This letter conveyed information which invited an attack on the garrison, besides making allegations against the French which tended to inflame the feelings of the natives against them. In another letter, which was addressed to his wife, then at Antananarivo, besides giving information of interest to the Hovas, he denounced " D. and P." (who were supposed to be two American citizens, named Duder and Poupard, against whom he had a grudge) as French spies, thus exposing them to the Hovas's vengeance.

" On all the evidence, and in view particularly of his own letters, Waller was unquestionably guilty of an offense against the French Government of a serious character, and fully justifying severe punishment. It will be seen, however, that at a time when it seemed uncertain whether or not an inspection of the evidence in Waller's case would be permitted, Mr. Eustis, by direction of the Department, submitted the record of the charges, procedure, sentence, etc., to an eminent French lawyer, M. Eduard Clunet, and asked his opinion upon the validity of the proceedings as thus shown. The opinion, given in writing, is annexed to this report. It points out that a proclamation of martial law was the basis of the jurisdiction of the court, and that the record is defective in not showing the issuance of such a proclamation. But as there is no doubt that such a proclamation was issued—Waller himself so states—the defect would seem to be of a technical rather than a substantial nature, and easily curable by an amendment of the record.

" The opinion also sets forth certain other peculiarities of the proceedings, which are treated by M. Clunet rather as irregularities than as matters touching the jurisdiction. His conclusion upon the whole case, however, is that there is no mode by which the Waller judgment could be successfully challenged through the courts, and that any relief from his sentence must be sought through an application for clemency. If the evidence had not been produced and the substantial merits of the case thus disclosed, it might have been the duty of this Government to test the accuracy of M. Clunet's findings by appropriate legal proceedings or otherwise. But the evidence having been exhibited and Waller having been thus satisfactorily shown to have given the French Government grave cause of complaint and to be guilty of the offenses charged against him, an attack upon the proceedings of the Tamatave court for alleged irregularities—even if attended with the most successful result—could not do more for Waller than accomplish his release.

"So far as compensation by damages for any illegal arrest or detention is concerned, this could only be sought later, either through the action of the United States or by suit by Waller himself in the French courts. But in view of Waller's willful and culpable attempt against the French authority in Madagascar, it is manifest that no claim for damages on Waller's account could be properly pressed by the United States, or could be expected to be entertained by the French Government. An international reclamation, the rejection of which may justify reprisals or even be treated as a *casus belli*, ought not to rest on pure technicalities when the facts and evidence are against the claim. It should be founded upon something more than the mere nonobservance of legal formalities—upon something more than irregularities originating in ignorance or inadvertence rather than in intention, and not necessarily nor actually working any substantial wrong or injustice.

"The rule laid down by the Supreme Court of the United States (110 U. S., p. 74) in relation to claims before an international tribunal of arbitration a fortiori applies to a claim made by one Government upon another direct.

"'International arbitration must always proceed on the highest principles of national honor and integrity. Claims presented and evidence submitted to such a tribunal must necessarily bear the impress of the entire good faith of the Government from which they come, and it is not to be presumed that any Government will for a moment allow itself knowingly to be made the instrument of wrong in any such proceeding. No technical rules of pleading as applied in municipal courts ought ever to be allowed to stand in the way of the national power to do what is right under all the circumstances. Every citizen who asks the intervention of his own Government against another for the redress of his personal grievances must necessarily subject himself and his claim to these requirements of international comity.'

"Hence, in accordance with this rule, notwithstanding the appearance of omissions and irregularities in the record and proceedings of the tribunal, it can not be said that substantial injustice has resulted therefrom, since upon the facts and the evidence of Waller's own letters the result must have been the same if every technical requirement had been observed. So, though Waller has been deprived by the French of his liberty for nine or ten months, it can not be said that the penalty to which he has been subjected has been disproportionate to his offense. On the contrary, the penalty regarded as the outcome of a lawful proceeding would universally be regarded as an exceedingly moderate one. In short, the production of the evidence in

Waller's case showed him to have been guilty of a grave offense, though perhaps the strictly legal formalities and procedure necessary to make his trial unquestionably regular were not complied with.

" In any event it became quite clear that any objections to the legal proceedings in the case were either technical and formal, and so not necessarily fatal to them, or, if more serious because jurisdictional or substantial, they might be met by the French Government by remanding Waller for a new trial, which upon the undisputed facts could not be expected to result any differently from the first trial.

" In these circumstances, after urgent representations by this Government, an offer was made by the French Government to release Waller from further imprisonment and pardon his offense upon the condition that the affair be thereby terminated as between the two Governments and that the United States should make no claim in behalf of the prisoner based upon his arrest, conviction, or imprisonment. The acceptance of this offer seemed to be so favorable to Waller, and in view of all the facts so considerate toward our Government, that under the direction of the President our ambassador to France has been instructed to give notice of such acceptance on our part and to exchange the notes necessary to carry out the arrangement.

" Waller has not consented to this adjustment and still insists that he should receive compensation from the French Government.

" The fact has not been overlooked that Waller is reported to have at one time declared that on the voyage to Marseilles from Tamatave he was subjected to gross personal indignity and abuse. In view, however, of the intrinsic improbability of the charge, of its never having been repeated even by Waller himself, of there being no allusion to it in the narratives of his wife and stepson, of the alleged maltreatment forming no part of Waller's formal specification of his injuries and claims for damages as communicated to Mr. Eustis, and of the proven unreliability and malice of Waller's assertions in other connections, it is impossible not to regard Waller's complaint of cruelty practiced upon him on shipboard as either wholly unfounded or at the best grossly exaggerated.

" It is further discredited by the fact that the treatment of Waller since his arrival in France has been exceptionally considerate and humane. Reaching Marseilles in delicate health, he was at once provided with competent medical advice and attention, and soon after, upon the suggestion of the physician in charge, was removed to a different locality better adapted to his physical condition, and where he has since greatly improved. Nevertheless, that no possible injustice might be done to him, Waller's complaint of ill-treatment on his journey to France was specially called to the attention of the French Government. That Government at once disavowed the cruelties charged and insisted that they could never have been inflicted, but undertook, at the request of this Government, to investigate and to punish any persons found guilty of them.

" It at the same time declared, however, that even if the complaint should prove to be well founded, it could not entertain any claim of damages for Waller preferred by the United States, because the French tribunals were open to him and he could pursue his remedies there either against the Government or private individuals in the same manner and with the same effect as could any French citizen under the like circumstances. This position of the French Government—that claims of aliens cognizable by the courts of a foreign country can not be made the subject of diplomatic intervention unless there has been a palpable failure of justice after all local judicial remedies have been exhausted—is one upon which this Government has often insisted and of which it has often availed itself.

" Its applicability to the case of Waller was confirmed by the opinion of the eminent French lawyer already referred to, by whom it was pointed out that in respect of remedies in the French tribunals an alien was in all respects on the same footing as a Frenchman except that the alien must furnish security for costs. As our ambassador at Paris, under instructions from this Department, could easily arrange to furnish such security should Waller desire to resort to the French courts, there seemed to be nothing in Waller's charges of ill-treatment while on his way to France which ought to stand in the way of an acceptance of the offer of the French Government for his immediate release.

"Accordingly, upon the request of Waller, our ambassador at Paris will be instructed to arrange for furnishing security for the costs of any suit before the French tribunals which Waller may be advised the facts of his case will warrant. Mr. Eustis has already been instructed to supply him with the means of transportation to the United States, should he desire to come here. It may be added as part of the history of the case, that the family of Waller being left in destitute circumstances, the Department instructed its representatives to provide for their present necessities and to furnish them the means of getting to the United States. That relief was accordingly extended to them, the charges to which this Government has thus far been put amounting to $1,317.14."

> Report of Mr. Olney, Sec. of State, to the President, Feb. 5, 1896, For. Rel. 1895, I. 251, 257–259; also H. Doc. 225, 54 Cong. 1 sess.
>
> President Cleveland, in his message to the House of Representatives, communicating the foregoing report and accompanying documents, Feb. 11, 1896, said: " Upon a fair and just consideration of all the facts and circumstances as presented, and especially in view of Mr. Waller's own letters, the conclusions set forth in the report of the Secretary of State do not appear to admit of any reasonable doubt, nor to leave open to the Executive any other course of action than that adopted

and acted upon as therein stated." (H. Doc. 225, 54 Cong. 1 sess.; For. Rel. 1895, I. 251.)

Mr. Clunet's opinion on the question of the jurisdiction of the court-martial at Tamatave is as follows:

" The undersigned, Edouard Clunet, advocate of the court of Paris, consulted by the ambassador of the United States at Paris on the questions hereinafter enumerated, having seen the affidavit of John Waller, dated August 25, 1895, at the prison of Clairvaux (Auge) ; having seen the official copy of the judgment of the first permanent court-martial, sitting at Tamatave, dated March 18, 1895, has delivered the following opinion:

" I. *Jurisdiction of the first permanent court-martial of Tamatave in respect of John Waller.*

" The question of the jurisdiction of the court-martial in the question of John Waller is a delicate one, by reason of the somewhat vaguely defined political and international position of France at Tamatave before the occupation of Antananarivo by French forces on the 1st of October, 1895, the consequences of which will directly modify the antecedent territorial sovereignty.

" France has occupied Tamatave for several years. She had even instituted a French tribunal there, composed of judges by profession, with civil, commercial, and correctional jurisdiction (see treaty of December 17, 1883, and the law of judicial organization of April 8, 1891, Clunet's Journal of 1891, p. 356). But herself restricting the powers of the delegates of her sovereignty by the decree of August 24, 1892, she limited the extent of that jurisdiction to Frenchmen solely, so that foreigners and Malagasy might avoid it (see Le Garrec, advocate at Tamatave, on the working of the French courts in Madagascar in dealings with French citizens, natives, and aliens, Clunet's Journal, 1895, p. 259).

" John Waller, formerly vice-consul of the United States at Madagascar, had been relieved of his post. He was in March, 1895, no more than an ordinary citizen, a foreigner residing at Tamatave.

"As such he was not subject to the jurisdiction of the French common-law tribunal at Tamatave, no new decree having as yet extended to the subjects of any power the effect of the decree of August 24, 1892 (see text in Clunet's Journal, 1892, p. 1084), as was nevertheless provided in the second paragraph of the said decree.

" Nor was he subjected to any native or foreign jurisdiction, since as far back as January, 1895, the military campaign against the Hova Government had already begun, Majunga being occupied by a battalion of marines in January, 1895, and because, in fact, the French authorities alone ruled at Tamatave.

" Supposing Waller, or any other foreigner not in the army or assimilated thereto, guilty of a crime against the external safety of the French state, would he have been subject to the exceptional jurisdiction of a court-martial?

" If the court-martial at Tamatave had been constituted as a ' court-martial in the expeditionary forces,' its jurisdiction as regards a civilian would have been based upon texts of law. Article 84 of the code of maritime justice lays down the limits of jurisdiction of such courts-martial, placed in exceptional and perilous circumstances ; it permits them to apply articles 62 to 69, 71, and 75 of the code of military justice, which code gives direct jurisdiction ' to courts-martial in the armies and in the territorial conscriptions in a state of war ' in respect of foreigners having committed crimes of the nature of that charged against Waller. But the judgment of the court-martial of Tamatave does not mention either that article 84 nor those quoted from the code of military justice to which the said article refers, because the court did not rely upon them.

" In point of fact, the court-martial of Tamatave is, as it styles itself, a ' permanent court-martial,' as provided by the code of maritime justice for a state of peace, and in a normal condition of things. It existed prior to the armed conflict of France with the Hova Government; it was a normal court, the jurisdiction of which is prescribed by articles 76 to 83 of the code of maritime justice (title 1, jurisdiction of maritime courts sitting upon land; chap. 1, sec. 1, jurisdiction of permanent courts-martial in maritime districts). These courts have jurisdiction only over individuals belonging to the naval forces of those assimilated thereto. John Waller did not belong to that category.

" In support of this jurisdiction the court-martial of Tamatave relies solely upon article 104 of the code of maritime justice.

" This article does not apply to the case. It is taken from Title III of Book II, entitled ' Jurisdiction in case of complicity,' and it provides that all prisoners, without distinction, shall be brought before the court-martial when the crime has been committed in part by persons who are ordinarily subject to its jurisdiction, and in part by others who are not personally subject thereto. In the present case, Waller was not prosecuted as accessory or as joint author of the crime, but as sole author thereof. Article 104, which is peculiar to cases of complicity, does not cover his case. Waller does not fall into the category of individuals dealt with in article 104 of the code of maritime justice.

" One circumstance alone would have given jurisdiction to the ' permanent court-martial ' of Tamatave in regard to even civilian delinquents—that is to say, the lawful proclamation, prior to the proceedings, of a state of siege.

" The declaration of a state of siege and its effects are regulated by the law of August 3, 1849, by the law of April 3, 1878, and for places in a state of war by a decree of October 4, 1891, rendered in consequence of the two preceding laws.

" Tamatave in March, 1895, might have been considered as a place in a state of war.

" By virtue of article 189 of the decree of October 4, 1891, the military commander may declare a state of siege in case of investment of the place, of attack, of internal sedition, and of armed gatherings within a radius of 10 kilometers.

" In proclaiming a state of siege the military commander makes known that all offenses, which he does not consider it his duty to submit to the ordinary tribunals, shall be tried by the military tribunals, whatever be the status of the delinquents.

" What did the military authorities do at Tamatave? Did they proclaim a state of siege? At what period did they proclaim it? Was such declaration made in the circumstances provided by the law and in the prescribed forms?

" It may be doubted whether such was the case in view of the laconic tenor of the judgment of March 18, 1895.

" This judgment, in fact, only mentions upon page 2, and in quite an incidental manner, that Tamatave is ' in a state of siege.'

" Now, from the point of view of the jurisdiction of the ' permanent court-martial ' in respect of a civilian, this was a circumstance of capital importance, as it alone could give jurisdiction over him. Nevertheless, the judgment does not mention either the law of 1849, nor the law of 1878, nor the decree of 1891, while, in order to fulfill article 170 of the code of maritime justice, it reproduces all the articles of law upon which it rests its jurisdiction and justifies the sentence.

" Even if no court of common law or an exceptional jurisdiction existed or was competent at Tamatave to take cognizance of the crime charged against John Waller or any other civilian, it does not follow that they would remain unpunished. Accused of a criminal offense perpetrated within the territory where French sovereignty was de facto exercised, and finding no judges there to judge them, the delinquents should have been removed to the nearest portion of French territory (to the island of Réunion, for example), where all the organs of French justice were performing their regular functions, and should have been brought before a court of common law, having jurisdiction over them, in accordance with the rules of the code of criminal. procedure. The crime charged against Waller (article 78 of the Penal Code) belonged to the jurisdiction of the criminal jury (court of assizes).

" In order to understand the actual facts, it must be remembered that at Tamatave at that period the French army was in a condition of open war with the Hovas, and that in particular at Tamatave it was in presence of the enemy, for at a short distance the Malagasy troops occupied the Fort of Farafata.

" In such a situation a military post, established even before hostilities were begun, easily assumes the characteristics of an army of occupation. Now, armies at such a junction are authorized by the law of nations and the practice of nations to secure their own protection by exceptional methods.

" We may consult upon this point an authoritative article on the jurisdiction of armies of occupation in regard to offenses committed by aliens, etc. (Clunet's Journal, 1882, p. 511, and following). Among the quotations may be remarked that of the American Instructions of 1863, and prepared for the armies in the field by the eminent Professor Lieber, revised by a commission of officers, and ratified by President Lincoln :

" 'ART. 7. Martial law extends to property and persons, without distinction between the subjects of the enemy and other foreigners.

" 'ART. 16. The consuls of the American and European nations are not considered as diplomatic agents. Nevertheless, their chanceries and their persons shall not be subjected to martial law except in cases of necessity. Any offense which they shall commit against the military government shall be punished as if it had been committed by an ordinary citizen, and such offense can not give rise to any international claim.'

"*Conclusion.*—The first permanent court-martial sitting at Tamatave had jurisdiction over John Waller, who was neither a military man nor a person assimilated thereto, if Tamatave had been, prior to the proceedings, declared in a state of siege, under the conditions laid down by the laws of August 3, 1849, April 3, 1878, and the decree of October 4, 1891.

" In any case, there is a serious omission in the judgment of March 18, 1895, consisting in its not having stated the grounds of the exceptional jurisdiction, in its not having cited the laws and decrees which justify such jurisdiction, and in its not having reproduced in fine the text of the declaration of the state of siege, the basis of its exceptional common-law jurisdiction in regard to a civilian, as it reproduces the text (without date, however) of the warrant of the delegate of the chief of the naval division relating to the transmission of correspondence."

The second part of the opinion relates to the regularity of the judgment of the court. This subject is discussed fully and minutely, with the result that various irregularities were disclosed ; but it appeared that the periods of appeal having elapsed, they could no longer be made the subject of judicial appeal. The irregularities related to (1) dates in the judgment, (2) the constitution of the court, (3) the formal description of the advocate, (4) the absence from the record of the evidence taken in the preparatory investigation and certain informalities and defects in the evidence taken at the trial, and (5) defects in procedure and sentence. (H. Doc. 225, 54 Cong. 1 sess. ; For. Rel. 1895, I. 304–306, 306–309.)

II. *TERRITORIAL OPERATION OF LAWS.*

1. MUNICIPAL LEGISLATION.

§ 197.

The municipal laws of one nation do not extend, in their operation, beyond its own territory, except as regards its own citizens or
subjects.

> The Apollon, 9 Wheat. 362.
> See Report on Extraterritorial Crime (Washington: Government Print-
> ing Office, 1887).

As a general proposition the laws of one country have in themselves no extraterritorial force, and whatever force they are permitted
to have in foreign countries depends upon the comity of nations, regulated by a sense of their own interests and public convenience.

> Le Roy *v.* Crowninshield, 2 Mason, 151.

The existence of a foreign law being a question of fact, the Attorney-General can not give an opinion upon the law of a foreign nation.

> Harmon, Atty.-Gen., July 2, 1896, 21 Op. 377.

Municipal laws "have no controlling operation beyond the territorial limits of the countries enacting them." Hence, in questions
between two independent nations, "neither has the right to appeal
to its own municipal laws for the rules to settle the matter in dispute,
which occurred within the jurisdiction of a third independent power."

> Mr. Marcy, Sec. of State, to Mr. Hülsemann, Austrian chargé d'affaires,
> Sept. 26, 1853, H. Ex. Doc. 1, 33 Cong. 1, sess. 33; 44 Br. and For.
> State Papers (1853–1854), 984, 987–988.

A law providing for the succession of nonresident aliens to real
estate confers a right to be enjoyed within the state, and is not a law
having an extraterritorial operation.

> State *v.* Smith, 70 Cal. 153, 12 Pac. Rep. 121; Blythe *v.* Hinckley, 127
> Cal. 431, 59 Pac. Rep. 787.

The provisions in the Constitution of the United States relating to
writs of habeas corpus, bills of attainder, *ex post facto* laws, trial by
jury, and generally to the fundamental guarantees of life, liberty,
and property, have no relation to crimes committed outside the jurisdiction of the United States and against the laws of a foreign country; and an act of Congress therefore is not unconstitutional because
it fails to secure to persons whose extradition it authorizes to a for-

eign country such rights, privileges, and immunities as are secured
to persons charged with crime in the United States.

> Neely v. Henkel (1901), 180 U. S. 109, 122–123.
> See, also, In re Ross, 140 U. S. 453; Ex parte Ortiz, 100 Fed..Rep. 955.

Where an attempt was made to hold a British subject personally
liable for the conversion of a vessel which he had captured under a
commission from the Queen of Portugal, on the ground that in accepting the commission he violated the British foreign enlistment act,
judgment was rendered for the defendant, the court saying that no
one could dispute " the right of the Queen of Portugal, to appoint
in her own dominions, the defendant or any other person she may
think proper to select, as her officer or servant, to seize a vessel which
is afterwards condemned as a prize."

> Dobree v. Napier (1836), 2 Bingham's New Cases, 781, 796.

In 1858, William Lesley, master of a British ship, entered into a
contract with the Chilean Government to convey to Liverpool certain
citizens of Chile who had been ordered to be banished. The persons
in question were brought by force, guarded by soldiers, on board
the ship at Valparaiso. After her arrival in England, Lesley was
indicted on a charge of assaulting, falsely imprisoning, and detaining
the Chileans on the high seas, and was convicted. One of the Chileans testified that, after the ship had reached the high seas, they
requested Lesley to take them to Peru, offering him as much money
as the Chilean Government was paying, but that he replied that his
contract required him to take them to England. The same witness
also stated that the ship called at the Azores, and that he there saw
the carpenter making holes in the boats, in order to prevent their
escape. It was not alleged, however, that they made any request to
be allowed to land at the Azores. On the contrary, the witness stated
that, when the master refused to take them to Peru, " we then resolved
to submit to our fate, hoping that our wrongs would be satisfied in
England." The same witness stated that no protest was made to the
master when they were received on board at Valparaiso, nor was he
sure that he would have desired to be handed back to the officers who
brought him on board. Lesley was convicted; and on a case reserved
the conviction was sustained. The court, however, expressly declared
that the conviction could not be sustained for what was done in
Chilean waters.

" We assume," said the court, " that in Chile the act of the Government towards its subjects was lawful; and, although an English ship
in some respects carries with her the laws of her country in the territorial waters of a foreign state, yet in other respects she is subject to

the laws of that state as to acts done to the subjects thereof. We assume that the Government could justify all that it did within its own territory, and we think it follows that the defendant can justify all that he did there as agent for the Government, and under its authority." But the court held that the defendant was indictable for what was done outside of Chilean waters, on the ground " that an English ship on the high sea, out of any foreign territory, is subject to the laws of England; and persons, whether foreign or English, on board such ship, are as much amenable to English law as they would be on English soil." On this ground the court decided that, although the master was justified in first receiving the prosecutors in Chile, yet that justification ceased when he passed the line of Chilean jurisdiction, after which " it was a wrong . . . intentionally planned and executed in pursuance of the contract, amounting in law to a false imprisonment. It may be that transportation to England is lawful by the law of Chile, and that a Chilean ship might so lawfully trans- port Chilean subjects; but for an English ship the laws of Chile, out of the state, are powerless, and the lawfulness of the acts must be tried by English law."

> Regina v. Lesley (1860), Bell's C. C. 220, 8 Cox C. C. 269.
>
> It is not improper to suggest a doubt as to whether the principle on which this case was decided is sufficient for the purposes of such a transaction or of analogous transactions. It may be suggested that, as the transportation of the prosecutors within Chilean jurisdiction was admitted to have been lawful, their subsequent detention, after the vessel reached the high sea, was properly to be regarded as the natural and legitimate consequence of that lawful act. Had the pros- ecutors sought to go ashore at the Azores, another question would have been presented; but they neither desired nor asked to be allowed to do so. It seems to follow from the decision of the court that even a fugi- tive from justice may not be transported from one national jurisdic- tion to another in a vessel flying the flag of a third country. Such transportation is a matter of common occurrence, the prisoner usually being in the custody of an officer of the demanding govern- ment; but we are not acquainted with any case in which an action for false imprisonment has subsequently been brought, or in which the government of the country to which the vessel belonged has demanded his release on the ground of a violation of its national jurisdiction. If the doctrine of the court be correct and sufficient, it would seem that either or both of these courses might be taken, certainly by, or within the jurisdiction of, governments such as Great Britain and the United States, which hold that the extradition of criminals is not obligatory in the absence of a law or a treaty.

By the act of March 3, 1885, 23 Stat. 362, 376, an appropriation was made for the investigation of certain Indian depredation claims. The act evidently referred to claims for property destroyed within the limits of the United States. Under it the Secretary of the Interior made an investigation and reported its results to Congress. By an act of March 3, 1891, 26 Stat. 851, jurisdiction was conferred on the Court of Claims to adjudicate all such claims for property taken or destroyed by Indians in amity with the United States as were covered by previous legislation. In 1894 a petition was filed in the Court of Claims by a New York corporation doing business in Mexico for property taken from it in that country in 1881 and 1882, and stolen and carried off by the Apache Indians, then in amity with the United States, and brought from Mexico into the United States. The objection having been made that the court had no jurisdiction of the suit because of the situation of the place where the depredation was alleged to have occurred, it was held that the United States was not responsible for the loss, since it took place within the territorial jurisdiction of Mexico.

> Corralitos Co. v. United States (1900), 178 U. S. 280, affirming the judgment of the Court of Claims, 33 C. Cl. 342.

A power to seize for a violation of the laws of the country is an attribute of sovereignty, and is to be exercised within the limits which circumscribe the sovereign power from which it is derived. And while the rights of war may be exercised on the high seas, a seizure beyond the limits of territorial jurisdiction for a breach of a municipal regulation is not warranted by international law.

> Rose v. Himely, 4 Cranch, 241.

" From the best information which the Department is able to obtain it is believed that the capture of the vessel [*Haytian Republic*] took place about 6 miles from the nearest point of land. It is unnecessary to comment further than to say that if the capture was made outside the territorial waters of Hayti the inadmissibility of a trial for an offense against the municipal law of Hayti would be obvious."

> Mr. Bayard, Sec. of State, to Mr. Preston, Haytian min., Nov. 28, 1888, For. Rel. 1888, I. 1001, 1004.

One country will not execute the penal laws of another.

> The Antelope, 10 Wheat. 66.

The maxim stated by Chief Justice Marshall, in the case of The Antelope, 10 Wheat. 66, 123, that " the courts of no country execute the penal laws of another," is discussed by the Supreme Court in Huntington v. Attrill, where the question related to a statute making the officers of a corporation, who sign and record a false certificate of the amount of its capital stock, liable for all its debts, Fuller, C. J., dissenting. Gray, J., delivering the opinion of the court, held that the statute was not penal, saying: " Penal laws, strictly and properly, are those imposing punishment for an offence committed against the state." Again: " The test whether a law is penal, in the strict and primary sense, is whether the wrong sought to be redressed is a wrong to the public, or a wrong to the individual." Again: The question whether a statute, " which is some aspects may be called penal, is a penal law in the international sense, so that it can not be enforced in the courts of another state, depends upon the question whether its purpose is to punish an offence against the public justice of the state, or to afford a private remedy to a person injured by the wrongful act."

> Huntington v. Attrill, 146 U. S. 657, 667, 668, 673, 674, Fuller, C. J., dissenting.

An American vessel, having been embargoed in a port of Brazil by competent authority, was unlawfully taken away by her master, without the payment of the required charges, and brought to New York. It was advised that, as the act of the master did not violate any statute of the United States, the request of Brazil that measures be taken against him by this Government could not be complied with.

> Devens, At.-Gen., March 13, 1879, 16 Op. 281.

The violation, by the master of an American vessel at a port in Jamaica, of the British revenue laws, is not punishable by any statute of the United States.

> Devens, At.-Gen., March 13, 1879, 16 Op. 283.

2. JUDICIAL DECISIONS.

§ 198.

Whatever may be the municipal law under which a tribunal acts, if it exercise a jurisdiction which its sovereign is not allowed by the laws of nations to confer, its decrees must be disregarded out of the dominions of the sovereign.

> Rose v. Himely, 4 Cranch, 241. But see Hudson v. Guestier, 6 id. 283.
> See, as to the effect of foreign judgments in England, Dicey's Conflict of Laws, 400; in the United States, id., Am. Notes, 433.

The presumptions indulged in support of judgments of superior courts of general jurisdiction are limited to jurisdiction over persons within their territorial limits; persons who can be reached by their process.

> Galpin v. Page, 18 Wallace, 350.
> See, also, McEwan v. Zimmer, 38 Mich. 765.

Under the statute law of France, which provides that a father-in-law and mother-in-law must make allowance to a son-in-law who is in need, so long as a child of the marriage is living, a son-in-law, a French citizen, obtained a decree in the French courts for an allowance against his father-in-law and mother-in-law who were American citizens, all the parties then residing in France. The son-in-law subsequently brought an action of debt on the decree in the courts of the United States to recover the amount of the decreed payment, which had not been paid. It was ruled:

(1) That the suit could not be maintained. The laws of France, upon which such decrees were made, are local in their nature and operation. They are designed to regulate the domestic relations of those who reside there and to protect the public against pauperism. They have no extraterritorial significance, but must be executed upon persons and property within their jurisdiction.

(2) Adjudications of the French tribunals under these laws are in the nature of local police regulations, like orders of filiation and orders made under local statutes to guard against pauperism, and are not of extraterritorial operation, like judgments for claims founded upon contracts or other private rights everywhere recognized.

De Brimont v. Penniman, 10 Blatchf. 436.

"A citizen and resident of this country, who has his principal place of business here, but has an agent in a foreign country, and is accustomed to purchase and store large quantities of goods there, and, in a suit brought against him by a citizen and in a court of that country, appears and defends with the sole object of preventing his property within the jurisdiction, but not in the custody of that court, from being taken in satisfaction of any judgment that may be recovered against him there, can not, in an action brought against him in this country upon such a judgment, impeach it for want of jurisdiction of his person.

" The admission, at the trial in a court of a foreign country, according to its law and practice, of testimony not under oath and without opportunity of cross-examination, and of documents with which the defendant had no connection and which by our law would not be admissible against him, is not of itself a sufficient ground for impeaching the judgment of that court in an action brought upon it in this country.

" When an action is brought in a court of this country, by a citizen of a foreign country against one of our own citizens, to recover a sum of money adjudged by a court of that country to be due from the defendant to the plaintiff, and the foreign judgment appears to have been rendered by a competent court, having jurisdiction of the cause and of the parties, and upon due allegations and proofs, and opportunity to defend against them, and its proceedings are according to the course of a civilized jurisprudence, and are stated in a clear and formal record, the judgment is *prima facie* evidence, at least, of the truth of the matter adjudged; and the judgment is conclusive upon the merits tried in the foreign court, unless some special ground is shown for impeaching it, as by showing that it was affected by fraud or prejudice, or that by the principles of international law, and by the comity of our own country, it is not entitled to full credit and effect.

"A judgment for a sum of money, rendered by a court of a foreign country, having jurisdiction of the cause and of the parties, in a suit brought by one of its citizens against one of ours, is *prima facie* evidence only, and not conclusive of the merits of the claim, in an action brought here upon the judgment, if by the law of the foreign country, as in France, judgments of our own courts are not recognized as conclusive."

Syl., Hilton *v.* Guyot (1895), 159 U. S. 113.   See Dicey, Conflict of Laws, Am. Notes, 433, 434.

"In an action upon a foreign judgment, an answer admitting that 'certain attorneys entered, or undertook to enter, the appearance of the defendant' in the action in the foreign court; and alleging that the judgment was entered without his knowledge, in his absence, and without any hearing; but not alleging that the attorneys were not authorized to enter his appearance in that action, or that he appeared and answered under compulsion, or for any other purpose than to contest his personal liability, is insufficient to show that the foreign court had no jurisdiction of his person.

"Averments, in an answer to an action upon a foreign judgment, that it was 'an irregular and void judgment,' and 'without any jurisdiction or authority on the part of the court to enter such a judgment upon the facts and upon the pleadings,' are mere averments of legal conclusions, and are insufficient to impeach the judgment, without specifying the grounds upon which it is supposed to be irregular and void, or without jurisdiction or authority.

"To warrant the impeaching of a foreign judgment because procured by fraud, fraud must be distinctly alleged and charged.

"A judgment rendered by a court having jurisdiction of the cause and of the parties, upon regular proceedings and due notice or appearance, and not procured by fraud, in a foreign country, by the law of which, as in England and in Canada, a judgment of one of our own courts, under like circumstances, is held conclusive of the merits, is conclusive, as between the parties, in an action brought upon it in this country, as to all matters pleaded and which might have been tried in the foreign court."

Syl., Ritchie *v.* McMullen (1895), 159 U. S. 235.

"No sovereignty can extend its process beyond its own territorial limits so as to subject either persons or property to its judicial decisions, and every exertion of authority of its sort beyond its limits is a mere nullity, and incapable of binding such persons or property in any other tribunals."

> Halleck Int. Law, cited by Mr. Frelinghuysen, Sec. of State, to Mr. Morgan, min. to Mexico, May 17, 1884, For. Rel. 1884, 358, 359.

"It is a well-settled principle that judgments duly entered in a competent court having jurisdiction, duly certified to be such by the executive, are ubiquitous in their effect; and eminently is this the case with judgments of naturalization, which are bound up so intimately with national honor and polity."

> Mr. Bayard, Sec. of State, to Mr. McLane, min. to France, Feb. 15, 1888. For. Rel. 1888, I. 510, 511.

A judgment was rendered by a court in Allegheny County, Pa., between two Croatians who were domiciled there. Judgment was rendered for the plaintiff, who afterwards applied to a Croatian court to give effect to it in order that it might be levied upon certain real estate belonging to the defendant in Croatia. An inquiry was then made by the Austrian minister in the United States as to how far the judgments of Croatian courts would be enforced in Pennsylvania, since the Croatian courts acted in such matter upon the principle of reciprocity. The governor of Pennsylvania, in response to an inquiry, stated that under the laws of that State the judgment of a Croatian court of competent jurisdiction, when proved to have been given on due notice to the defendant according to the laws of Croatia, might be sued on in Pennsylvania and would be accepted as conclusive of the rights adjudicated between the parties in the country in which it was rendered, so that the defendant would have the right to defend only as to matters arising since the rendition of the judgment, such as payment made or a release.

> For. Rel. 1897, 7–8.

"Mr. Butler's despatch No. 36, of July 20, 1895, replying to Mr. Uhl's instruction No. 21 of June 7, 1895 in regard to the Oberlander and Messenger claims has been received and its enclosures considered.

"The United States in behalf of Charles Oberlander and Mrs. Barbara M. Messenger, has claimed indemnity from the Mexican Government for injuries done to those citizens of the United States by certain Mexican citizens on the ground that the latter violently and unlawfully entered the house in which Mrs. Messenger dwelt, within the territory and jurisdiction of the United States, and took therefrom with force and violence the said Oberlander and carried him away into the territory of Mexico where he was imprisoned and cruelly used until released by order of a Mexican judicial officer—all of which has been fully set forth in the previous correspondence with your legation on the subject.

" The Mexican Government admits the arrest and imprisonment of Oberlander, but denies that he was taken in Mrs. Messenger's house or on United States territory. In support of this contention, and as conclusive proof of it, Mr. Mariscal, the Mexican minister for foreign affairs, presents a report of a criminal prosecution against the Mexican citizens charged by Oberlander in his memorial with kidnapping him in the United States, which report shows that the accused persons were found not guilty and were acquitted of the offence for which they were tried, and further that no appeal was taken from that judicial finding.

" ' From the moment,' says Mr. Mariscal, ' in which this sentence assumed the character of *res judicata*, the legal fact was established of the nonexistence of the kidnapping on which Oberlander and Messenger founded their claim. This conclusion is unanswerable not only in accordance with the laws of this Republic, but also in accordance with the principles of international law which are recognized by all civilized nations.' ' I believe,' he adds, ' it is a well established legal precept in the United States that a government must not be held responsible in any case whatever, with respect to another government, even when error is alleged to have taken place in a judicial sentence that works to the prejudice of a subject or citizen of the latter, if the complainant neglected to procure, it being in his power to do so, the redress of the injustice which he is supposed to have received, before the court of last instance which could revoke the sentence.'

" The judicial proceedings to which Mr. Mariscal refers and upon which he relies as a bar to the claims of Oberlander and Messenger, were instituted by the Mexican judge who examined into the case against Oberlander and released him. Of his own motion, this judicial officer held the persons concerned in the arrest and imprisonment of Oberlander to await criminal prosecution under section 1090 of the Mexican Criminal Code, which provides (as translated in Mr. Butler's despatch No. 392, of December 24, last) that ' any Mexican who by acts not authorized nor approved by the Government provokes a foreign war against Mexico or gives motive for the declaration of such war, or exposes the Mexicans to suffer injury or reprisals, shall be punished with four years imprisonment.'

" The parties to this proceeding were, on the one side, the Mexican people and Government, and, on the other side, certain Mexican citizens who were charged with having committed a penal offence, not against Oberlander or Mrs. Messenger, but against the peace and welfare of the Republic of Mexico and the interests of their countrymen. The prosecution was conducted, after the manner of criminal proceedings, by an officer of the Mexican Government and was controlled by him and by the court. If the officials charged with the vindication of the peace and dignity of the Mexican Republic in this proceeding were satisfied with the result of the trial, it was their privilege to acquiesce in it without appeal. No one else, so far as the report furnished the United States shows, had the right of appeal. Certainly Oberlander and Mrs. Messenger had no control of the proceedings nor connection with them. The object of the prosecution was not to determine their rights. The questions of fact upon which their claims are based were only incidentally and partially involved, and only to the extent that these facts evidenced a violation of the Mexican neutrality laws by Mexican citizens. The judgment of the court in this prosecution ought to have no legal effect upon the right to indemnity presented by the United States in behalf of Oberlander and Mrs. Messenger. The judgment extended only to the fact that the defendants were not guilty of violating the statute under which they were prosecuted. The evidence and other considerations which induced the judgment are not a part of it, and do not extend its legal consequences.

"The authorities (Wheaton, Wharton and Story) cited by Mr. Mariscal in support of his contention relate to the international effect of judgments in civil cases as they affect the rights of parties duly summoned and afforded opportunity to be heard respecting the precise matter in question, and to judgments in criminal proceedings as they affect the rights and liberties of the defendants therein. The judgment in a civil case may be admitted to be in general conclusive upon the *parties* as to the *issues* involved in the suit, but no further. In respect of criminal cases, the authorities seem not to be in perfect accord. Mr. Mariscal quotes the following from Wheaton: 'A valid sentence, whether of conviction or acquittal, pronounced in one state, may have certain indirect and collateral effects in other states. If pronounced under the municipal law in the state where the supposed crime was committed, or to which the supposed offender owed allegiance, the sentence, either of conviction or acquittal, would, of course, be an effectual bar (*exceptio rei judicatae*) to a prosecution in any other state.' Wharton (Conflict of Laws, sec. 828, note 1) quotes this proposition of Wheaton's and says of it: ' Mr. Wheaton on this point speaks without his usual precision.' Wharton says (section 828) that ' while a judgment of a court *delicti commissi* would be final, to the effect that the act in question was not penal in that country, *no extra-territorial force can be assigned to a decision of the judex domicilii unless he has international jurisdiction. The judgment in such a case could not be regarded as barring a prosecution in the forum delicti commissi.*' Again he says (section 833) : ' We have already seen that penal laws have no extra-territorial force. The same limitation applies to foreign penal judgments, since otherwise all that would be necessary to give ubiquitous effect to a penal law would be to put it in the shape of a judgment.' Brocher (Droit Int. Privé, 103, as quoted by Wharton) says ' Les jugements rendus in matière penale ne depassent généralement pas les frontières.' The eminent authority on private international law, Bar (1st edition, section 143, page 685), says: ' A judgment of acquittal is a declaration of the court which administers the criminal authority of the State to this effect, that no sentence against the accused can be justified, either because his guilt was not proved, or because the act in question could not be punished. The *lex specialis* implied in a judgment of this kind must have the same, but no greater effect upon the criminal jurisdiction of the other country than a *lex generalis* to the same effect. In so far, then, as a deliverance by the law of the place where the deed was done excludes punishment in the domicil of the accused, it will be excluded by such a judgment, whereas a judgment of this kind pronounced at the domicil of the accused does not by any means exclude a prosecution by the state in whose territory the deed was done.' Even if the doctrine quoted from Wheaton be accepted, its only effect in application to the facts of this case would be to bar a prosecution in the United States of the persons acquitted by the Mexican court for the identical offence of which they were acquitted; that is the offence of committing acts tending to bring war upon Mexico or to subject Mexican citizens to reprisals. In California where the principal injury of which Oberlander complains was done, the acts charged by him upon these persons constitute the common law offences of assault and battery with kidnapping. Should these persons, therefore, cross the boundary line into the jurisdiction of the State of California they would be liable to indictment and trial for the offences against the laws of California involved in the acts attributed to them; and the plea of acquittal in Mexico of the charge upon which they were there tried would not be a bar to such prosecution. ' It is a fundamental principle of international law,' says Wharton (section 813), ' that each state is primarily authorized to punish offences against itself. Of course it cannot invade the territory or the ships of another country in order to arrest the offender. But the arrest may certainly be made whenever the offender is found in the territory of the offended sovereign.' "

Mr. Olney, Sec. of State, to Mr. Ransom, min. to Mexico, Nov. 30, 1895, MS. Inst. Mexico, XXIV. 25.

For further correspondence in relation to this case, see For. Rel. 1897, 370–388.

The case having been submitted to arbitration, on a claim for indemnity, the arbitrator, Señor Don Vicente G. Quesada, Argentine minister at Madrid, dismissed the claim on the ground that the claimants " did not bring the criminal and civil actions which they had a right to bring before the courts of the country [Mexico], but had recourse to diplomacy without any good cause to do so."   (For. Rel. 1897, 387.)

"A certificate of discharge from a court in bankruptcy can have no validity in a foreign country as against a foreign creditor representing a debt contracted in a foreign country unless he has brought his claim within the jurisdiction of the courts of the United States by proving it, and thus putting himself in a position to share in the dividends.   Whether, in case he does so prove it, such certificate will have weight in a foreign country will depend upon the local laws in such country, whose courts will undoubtedly act with due regard to the comity of nations."

> Mr. Fish, Sec. of State, to Mr. Riger, October 21, 1869, 82 MS. Dom.
> Let. 224.   See Wharton, Confl. of Laws, §§ 531, 804 ; Dicey, Confl.
> of Laws, Moore's Am. Notes, 467.

3. Questions of International Right.

§ 199.

" I now acknowledge your several letters of Feb'y 8, Mch. 17, April 8, June 20, July 13 & 26.

" If the Spanish Government meant to assert the doctrine that the decisions of its tribunals on questions affecting the rights of other nations under Treaties and the Law of Nations were definitively binding on other nations, it has taken a ground which its own reflections must abandon.   Every sovereign is answerable for the conduct of the instrumental authority in relation to other sovereigns.   A certain degree of confidence is due to the ordinary agencies by which the national obligations are fulfilled, but an appeal always lies from them to the supreme authority, where this right has not been mutually relinquished by treaty.   No such relinquishment can be pretended against the United States in favor of the Spanish tribunals.   They have therefore the clearest right to disown the illegal decrees of those tribunals, and to require from the Government of Spain the fulfillment of the treaty violated by them.   The like doctrine was advanced before the Board of Commissioners under the 7th article of the British treaty of 1794.   It was rejected by that joint tribunal, and decisions of the British Admiralty Courts, not excepting that of the highest resort, were reversed in favor of American claims.   The case is indeed too plain to need argument, or to admit of perseverance in error by a government which respects its reputation either for justice or intelligence."

> Mr. Madison, Sec. of State, to Mr. Erving, chargé at Madrid, Oct. 18, 1807,
> MS. Inst. U. States Ministers, VI. 440.
> For numerous decisions on this subject, see Moore, Int. Arbitrations, III.
> 3160–3234.
> See, also, supra, § 1, vol. 1, p. 6.

III. *EXTRATERRITORIAL CRIME.*

I. MISCELLANEOUS CASES AND OPINIONS.

§ 200.

" No act committed in one country, however criminal, according to its laws, is criminal according to the laws of the other. Crimes, in a legal sense, are local, and are so only because the acts constituting them are declared to be so by the laws of the country where they are perpetrated. Great Britain can not by her laws make an act committed within the jurisdiction of the United States criminal within her territories, however immoral of itself, and *vice versa.* The proposition is too clear to require illustration or to be contested ; but, if that be admitted, it must also be admitted that the criminality referred to in the proviso is to be judged of by the laws of the place within whose jurisdiction the act was charged to have been perpetrated, and not where the fugitive is found."

> Mr. Calhoun, Sec. of State, to Mr. Everett, August 7, 1844, MS. Inst. Great Britain, XV. 211.

" We hold that the criminal jurisdiction of a nation is limited to its own dominions and to vessels under its flag on the high seas, and that it can not extend it to acts committed within the dominion of another without violating its sovereignty and independence. Standing on this well-established and unquestioned principle, we can not permit Great Britain or any other nation, be its object or motive what it may, to infringe our sovereignty and independence by extending its criminal jurisdiction to acts committed within the limits of the United States, be they perpetrated by whom they may. All therein are subject to their jurisdiction, entitled to their protection, and amenable exclusively to their laws."

> Mr. Calhoun, Sec. of State, to Mr. Everett, September 25, 1844, MS. Inst. Great Britain, XV. 23.
>
> The courts of the United States do not execute the penal laws of another country. (Berrien, At.-Gen. (1830), 2 Op. 365.)

" The conflicting laws on the subject of allegiance are of a municipal character, and have no controlling operation beyond the territorial limits of the countries enacting them. All uncertainty as well as confusion on this subject is avoided by giving due consideration to the fact, that the parties to the question now under consideration are two independent nations, and that neither has the right to appeal to its own municipal laws for the rules to settle the matter in dispute, which occurred within the jurisdiction of a third independent power."

> Mr. Marcy, Sec. of State, to Mr. Hulsemann, Austrian chargé, Sept. 26, 1853, H. Ex. Doc. 1, 33 Cong. 1 sess. 33, in relation to the Koszta case.

" By the law of nations every independent state possesses the exclusive right of police over all persons within its jurisdiction, whether upon its soil or in its vessels upon the ocean, and this national prerogative can only be interfered with in cases where acts of piracy are committed, which, by the public law of the world, are cognizable by any power seizing the vessel, thus excluded from the common rights of the ocean."

> Mr. Cass, Sec. of State, to Mr. Dallas, Feb. 23, 1859, MS. Instr. Great Britain, XVII. 150.

The question of extraterritorial jurisdiction was discussed in Congress in the cases of Warren and Costello, two naturalized American citizens, who were tried and sentenced in Dublin, in 1867, for treason felony, on account of participation in the "Jacmel" (Fenian) expedition. It was proved that they had come over to Ireland in that vessel, and had cruised along the coast for the purpose of effecting a landing of men and arms in order to raise an insurrection. At the trial, in order to connect them with the Fenian conspiracy that existed at Dublin and to show their *animus* in cruising along the Irish coast, evidence was introduced of certain acts and declarations of the prisoners in the United States. It was ultimately shown that this evidence was introduced merely in proof of the criminal design with which the prisoners entered the British jurisdiction and of the criminal object of their acts there. But, while still under the impression that the acts and declarations in the United States were being made the foundation of a criminal prosecution in Dublin, the House of Representatives, on the 15th of June, 1868, adopted a resolution requesting the President to take such measures as should seem " proper to secure the release from imprisonment of Messrs. Warren and Costello, convicted and sentenced in Great Britain for words and acts spoken and done in this country," &c.

> Dip. Cor. 1868, I. 21, 49, 50, 309.
> For the resolution of the House of Representatives, see Mr. Seward, Sec. of State, to Mr. Moran, chargé at London, June 22, 1868, id. 318–319.

" Your despatch, No. 322, of the 20th ultimo, has been received. It represents that the British Government, pursuant to the opinion of the law officers of the Crown, has instructed its minister to inform the Government of Brazil that it will not acquiesce in the application of the Brazilian law, to which you refer, to acts done by British subjects outside of the jurisdiction of Brazil. This decision may be regarded as obviously sound, and is entirely concurred in by this Government.

" If, therefore, there should be occasion, you will inform the minister of foreign affairs that we can not consent to the prosecution or punishment of a citizen of the United States pursuant to the objectionable statute adverted to."

> Mr. Fish, Sec. of State, to Mr. Partridge, min. to Brazil, May 26, 1876,
> For. Rel. 1876, 26.

In March, 1880, Richard Braeg, a native of Germany, who had been naturalized in the United States, returned to Europe and settled on an estate in Switzerland, near the German frontier, conducting, however, a coal business at Constance, near by on the German side of the line. Not long afterwards he was charged in Germany with having made insulting remarks about the German Emperor and the Grand Duke of Baden at a place called Tivoli, in Switzerland, near the Baden frontier. He was tried at Constance, and was acquitted on the ground that the offense was committed on foreign soil and was not committed by a German. The state's attorney took an appeal to the supreme court at Leipsic, which reversed the decision on the ground that it appeared that the defendant, who had lived in Europe from June, 1874, till April, 1879, was not naturalized in conformity with the treaty between the United States and the North German Union of February 22, 1868, and therefore had not lost his German nationality. It seems that the defendant avoided the consequences of proceedings against him under the supreme court's decision by remaining on the Swiss side of the frontier.

> Mr. White, min. to Germany, to Mr. Blaine, Sec. of State, July 30, 1881,
> 29 MS. Desp. Germany.

" Your letters of the 26th ultimo and 1st instant in regard to the case of Cirilo Pouble, an American citizen imprisoned in Cuba, have been received. In reply I have to say that further instructions have been addressed to the consul-general at Havana stating that if the specific crime or offence for which he is confined consists of membership in this country in a society maintaining speculative opinions which, however distasteful to the Cuban authorities, are yet simply opinions and unaccompanied by acts tending to the perpetration of a crime to take effect in Spanish territory, this Government would maintain that such membership is not recognized internationally as a crime, and that the attempt to punish Pouble for it in Cuba is a breach of international law. He has been further instructed to communicate to the Department the ground upon which Pouble is held for trial."

> Mr. Porter, Assist. Sec. of State, to Mr. Beraza, April 9, 1885, 155 MS.
> Dom. Let. 29.
> " The general proposition has been acceded to by the Government of
> Spain that no citizen of the United States can be tried by a council
> of war in his absence, for acts committed elsewhere." (Mr. Fish,
> Sec. of State, to Mr. Cushing, min. to Spain, May 17, 1876, MS. Inst.
> Spain, XVII. 520.

" I have to acknowledge the receipt of your letter of the 9th instant, in which you ask the advice of the Department on a proposition to print in various newspapers the facts you have learned in the case of Mr. C. Pouble now imprisoned in Havana.

" The Department cannot assume to advise you in the matter and is unable to see that anything more could be done than has been and is being done in Pouble's behalf. Pouble having voluntarily gone within Spanish jurisdiction was arrested there and it is now alleged that seditious publications and papers were found in his baggage. If this be so, the alleged offense would appear to have been actually within Spanish jurisdiction, and it is for him to disprove the charge, by showing that the papers were not knowingly in his possession at the time of landing, or that they are not of the unlawful character alleged. The consul-general is instructed to continue to use all endeavors towards a speedy, open and impartial investigation of the charge according to the rules of judicial procedure to which American citizens in Cuba are entitled."

> Mr. Bayard, Sec. of State, to Mr. Carasco, June 16, 1885, 156 MS. Dom. Let. 11.

" The points upon which you rely to prove that Mr. Pouble has been convicted in contravention of the law of nations have been repeatedly advanced and considered during the progress of the trial and subsequent appeal. The facts do not bear out the theory that the offence with which he stood charged was committed wholly within the jurisdiction of the United States. It was proved that upon persons taken in Cuba in the acts of rebellion and sedition were found commissions, signed by Mr. Pouble, purporting to empower and authorize the commission of such acts. It is shown that Mr. Pouble thereafter voluntarily placed himself within Spanish jurisdiction. The offence charged belongs therefore to a class abundantly recognized by international law where a crime concocted within one jurisdiction takes effect designedly within another jurisdiction."

> Mr. Bayard, Sec of State, to Mr. Wallace, September 12, 1888, 169 MS. Dom. Let. 650.
>
> See S. Rep. 275, 49 Cong. 1 sess.

2. CUTTING'S CASE.

§ 201.

"After reading the telegrams and dispatches (copies of which I inclose for your information) of Mr. J. Harvey Brigham, United States consul at El Paso, Mexico, and also your No. 266, dated the 8th instant, relating to the case of Mr. A. K. Cutting, I telegraphed you on the 19th instant as follows:

" You are instructed to demand of the Mexican Government the instant release of A. K. Cutting, a citizen of the United States, now unlawfully imprisoned at Paso del Norte.

" By the documents before me the following facts appear:

" On June 18 last A. K. Cutting, a citizen of the United States, who for the preceding eighteen months had been a resident, ' off and on,' of Paso del Norte, Mexico, and as to whose character for respectability strong evidence has been adduced, published in a newspaper of El Paso, Tex., a card commenting on certain proceedings of Emigdio Medina, a citizen of Mexico, with whom Mr. Cutting has been in controversy. For this publication Mr. Cutting was imprisoned on the 22d of June last, at El Paso del Norte, in Mexico. Such a publication would not, even had it been made in Mexico, be the subject of criminal prosecution in that country, according to the Roman common law there in force, nor of any adverse governmental action, unless, perhaps, for the single purpose of requiring security in some small sum to keep the peace. But the paper was not published in Mexico, and the proposition that Mexico can take jurisdiction of its author on account of its publication in Texas is wholly inadmissible and is peremptorily denied by this Government. It is equivalent to asserting that Mexico can take jurisdiction over the authors of the various criticisms of Mexican business operations which appear in the newspapers of the United States. If Mr. Cutting can be tried and imprisoned in Mexico for publishing in the United States a criticism on a Mexican business transaction in which he was concerned, there is not an editor or publisher of a newspaper in the United States who could not, were he found in Mexico, be subjected to like indignities and injuries on the same ground. To an assumption of such jurisdiction by Mexico neither the Government of the United States nor the governments of our several States will submit. They will each mete out due justice to all offenses committed in their respective jurisdictions. They will not permit that this prerogative shall in any degree be usurped by Mexico, nor, aside from the fact of the exclusiveness of their jurisdiction over acts done within their own boundaries, will they permit a citizen of the United States to be called to account by Mexico for acts done by them within the boundaries of the United States. On this ground, therefore, you will demand Mr. Cutting's release.

" But there is another ground on which this demand may with equal positiveness be based. By the law of nations no punishment can be inflicted by a sovereign on citizens of other countries unless in conformity with those sanctions of justice which all civilized nations hold in common.

"Among these sanctions are the right of having the facts on which the charge of guilt was made examined by an impartial court, the explanation to the accused of these facts, the opportunity granted to him of counsel, such delay as is necessary to prepare his case, permission in all cases not capital to go at large on bail till trial, the due

production under oath of all evidence prejudicing the accused, giving
him the right to cross-examination, the right to produce his own evidence in exculpation, release even from temporary imprisonment in
all cases where the charge is simply one of threatened breach of the
peace, and where due security to keep the peace is tendered. All
these sanctions were violated in the present case. Mr. Cutting was
summarily imprisoned by a tribunal whose partiality and incompetency were alike shown by its proceedings. He was refused counsel; he was refused an interpreter to explain to him the nature of
the charges brought against him; if there was evidence against him
it was not produced under oath, with an opportunity given him for
cross-examination; bail was refused to him; and after a trial, if it
can be called such, violating, in its way, the fundamental sanctions of
civilized justice, he was cast into a ' loathsome and filthy ' cell, where,
according to one of the affidavits attached to Mr. Brigham's report,
' there are from six to eight other prisoners, and when the door is
locked there are no other means of ventilation '—an adobe house,
almost air-tight, with a ' dirt floor '; he was allowed about ' 8½ cents
American money for his subsistence '; he was ' not furnished with
any bedding, not even a blanket.' In this wretched cell, subjected to
pains and deprivations which no civilized Government should permit
to be inflicted on those detained in its prisons, he still languishes,
and this for an act committed in the United States, and in itself
not subject to prosecution in any humane system of jurisprudence,
and after a trial violating the chief sanctions of criminal procedure.

"These circumstances you will state as giving an additional basis,
a basis which if it be established this Government will not permit to
be questioned for the demand for Mr. Cutting's immediate release."

> Mr. Bayard, Sec. of State, to Mr. Jackson, min. to Mexico, July 20, 1886,
> For. Rel. 1886, 700.
> See, also, Mr. Bayard, Sec. of State, to Mr. Jackson, min. to Mexico, July
> 27, 1886, For. Rel. 1886, 706; report of Mr. Bayard, Sec. of State, to
> the President, Aug. 2, 1886, S. Ex. Doc. 224, 49 Cong. 1 sess.

July 24, 1886, Mr. Romero, Mexican minister at Washington,
handed to Mr. Bayard a copy of article 186 of the Mexican Penal
Code, on which the proceedings against Mr. Cutting were taken.
The article, translated, reads as follows:

"Penal offenses committed in a foreign country by a Mexican against Mexicans or foreigners, or by a foreigner against Mexicans, may be punished in the
Republic (Mexico) and according to its laws, subject to the following conditions:

"I. That the accused be in the Republic, whether he has come voluntarily or
has been brought by extradition proceedings.

"II. That, if the offended party be a foreigner, he shall have made proper
legal complaint.

" III. That the accused shall not have been definitively tried in the country where the offense was committed, or if tried, that he shall not have been acquitted, included in an amnesty, or pardoned.

" IV. That the breach of law of which he is accused shall have the character of a penal offense, both in the country in which it was committed and in the Republic.

" V. That by the laws of the Republic the offense shall be subject to a severer penalty than that of ' arresto mayor.' "

Arresto mayor, it may be stated, is detention from one to eleven months, as distinguished from arresto menor, which lasts from three to sixty days.

The words " penal offences," in the translation of article 186, are intended as the equivalent of the Spanish word *delito*.

For correspondence between Mr. Bayard and Mr. Romero, see For. Rel. 1887, 849–867.

" In compliance with a resolution of the Senate, I communicated to that body on August 2d last, and also to the House of Representatives, the correspondence in the case of A. K. Cutting, an American citizen, then imprisoned in Mexico, charged with the commission of a penal offense in Texas, of which a Mexican citizen was the object.

"After demand had been made for his release the charge against him was amended so as to include a violation of Mexican law within Mexican territory.

" This joinder of alleged offenses, one within and the other exterior to Mexico, induced me to order a special investigation of the case— pending which Mr. Cutting was released.

" The incident has, however, disclosed a claim of jurisdiction by Mexico, novel in our history, whereby any offense, committed anywhere by a foreigner, penal in the place of its commission, and of which a Mexican is the object, may, if the offender be found in Mexico, be there tried and punished in conformity with Mexican laws.

" This jurisdiction was sustained by the courts of Mexico in the Cutting case, and approved by the executive branch of that government, upon the authority of a Mexican statute. The appellate court, in releasing Mr. Cutting, decided that the abandonment of the complaint by the Mexican citizen aggrieved by the alleged crime (a libelous publication), removed the basis of further prosecution, and also declared justice to have been satisfied by the enforcement of a small part of the original sentence.

" The admission of such a pretension would be attended with serious results, invasive of the jurisdiction of this Government, and highly dangerous to our citizens in foreign lands; therefore I have denied it, and protested against its attempted exercise, as unwarranted by the principles of law and international usages.

"A sovereign has jurisdiction of offenses which take effect within his territory, although concocted or commenced outside of it; but the right is denied of any foreign sovereign to punish a citizen of the United States for an offense consummated on our soil in violation of our laws, even though the offense be against a subject or citizen of such sovereign. The Mexican statute in question makes the claim broadly, and the principle, if conceded, would create a dual responsibility in the citizen, and lead to inextricable confusion, destructive of that certainty in the law which is an essential of liberty.

" When citizens of the United States voluntarily go into a foreign country they must abide by the laws there in force, and will not be protected by their own Government from the consequences of an offense against those laws committed in such foreign country; but watchful care and interest of this Government over its citizens are not relinquished because they have gone abroad; and if charged with crime committed in the foreign land a fair and open trial, conducted with decent regard for justice and humanity, will be demanded for them. With less than that this Government will not be content when the life or liberty of its citizens is at stake.

" Whatever the degree to which extraterritorial criminal jurisdiction may have been formerly allowed by consent and reciprocal agreement among certain of the European states, no such doctrine or practice was ever known to the laws of this country or of that from which our institutions have mainly been derived.

" In the case of Mexico there are reasons especially strong for perfect harmony in the mutual exercise of jurisdiction. Nature has made us irrevocably neighbors, and wisdom and kind feeling should make us friends.

" The overflow of capital and enterprise from the United States is a potent factor in assisting the development of the resources of Mexico, and in building up the prosperity of both countries.

" To assist this good work all grounds of apprehension for the security of person and property should be removed; and I trust that in the interests of good neighborhood the statute referred to will be so modified as to eliminate the present possibilities of danger to the peace of the two countries."

> President Cleveland, Annual Message, Dec. 6, 1886. (For. Rel. 1886, vii.)
> The message to the Senate of Aug. 2, 1886, will be found in S. Ex. Doc.
> 224, 49 Cong. 1 sess.

" On the 19th of July, 1886, the minister of the United States at the City of Mexico was instructed to demand of the Mexican Government the release of A. K. Cutting, a citizen of the United States, then imprisoned at Paso del Norte, where he had been incarcerated since the 23d of the preceding month on a charge of libel alleged to have been published by him in Texas.

" The case was first brought to the notice of the Department by Mr. Brigham, consul of the United States at Paso del Norte, who, in a dispatch dated the 1st July, 1886, reported that Mr. Cutting had been arrested and imprisoned for the publication in Texas, in the United States, of an alleged libel against a citizen of Mexico. Accompanying the consul's dispatch were affidavits substantiating his statements. It was also set forth that when Mr. Cutting was arrested and brought before the court, he was refused counsel and an interpreter, both of which he asked for, and that bail was refused him, which he was prepared to give in any reasonable amount. It was further stated that there was great cruelty in the manner of the prisoner's confinement, and that the physical suffering which he was compelled to undergo could not be borne without permanent injury to his health.

"On the 17th of July a telegram was received at this Department from Mr. Brigham saying that Mr. Cutting was still in prison and that nothing had been done by the local authorities to alleviate his condition.

"It is unnecessary to set forth in this communication a detailed account of the case, the facts of which are fully reviewed and copious extracts from the correspondence given in a report made in this Department on the subject of extraterritorial crime, with a special reference to the case in question, and a copy of which is herewith inclosed for your information. It is sufficient here to state, as was set forth at the time of the demand, that the ground upon which Mr. Cutting's release was demanded was that the judicial tribunals of Mexico were not competent under the rules of international law to try a citizen of the United States for an offense committed and consummated in his own country, merely because the person offended happened to be a Mexican. This was coupled with another ground, namely, that, by the law of nations, no punishment can be inflicted by a sovereign on citizens of other countries 'unless in conformity with those sanctions of justice which all civilized nations hold in common.' 'Among these sanctions,' it was stated, 'are the right of having the facts on which the charge of guilt was made examined by an impartial court; the explanation to the accused of these facts; the opportunity granted to him of counsel; such delay as is necessary to prepare his case, permission in all cases, not capital, to go at large on bail till trial; the due production, under oath, of all evidence prejudicing the accused; giving him the right to cross-examination; the right to produce his own evidence in exculpation; release even from temporary imprisonment in all cases where the charge is simply one of threatened breach of the peace, and where due security to keep the peace is tendered.'

"From the facts before the Department it appeared that all these sanctions had been violated in the case of Mr. Cutting by the judge before whom he was brought. The importance of this second ground upon which Mr. Cutting's release was demanded is not to be underestimated, although, in the course of time, it was overshadowed by the jurisdictional question raised by the claim of the Mexican Government of a right to try and punish a citizen of the United States for an offense committed by him in his own country against a Mexican. Not only was this claim, which is defined in Article 186 of the Mexican penal code, defended and enforced by Judge Zubia, before whom the case of Mr. Cutting was tried, and whose decision was affirmed by the supreme court of Chihuahua (translations of both of which decisions are given in the inclosed report above referred to), but the claim was defended and justified by the Mexican Government in communications to this Department, emanating both from the Mexican minister at this capital and from the department of foreign affairs in the City of Mexico.

"The statement of the consul at Paso del Norte that Mr. Cutting was arrested on the charge of the publication in Texas of an alleged libel against a Mexican is fully sustained by the opinion of Judge Zubia. Under the head of ' It appears 6,' in that decision, it is stated that on the 22d of June, 1886, ' the plaintiff enlarged the accusation, stating that although the newspaper, the El Paso Sunday Herald, is published in Texas, Mr. Cutting had had circulated a great number in this town (Paso del Norte) and in the interior of the Republic, it having been read by more than three persons, for which reason an order had been issued to seize the copies which were still in the office of the said Cutting.' The conclusive inference from this statement is that the charge upon which the warrant of arrest was issued was the publication of the alleged libel in Texas. It matters not whether such publication was originally treated by the court as a breach of a conciliation previously entered into between Cutting and Medina, the Mexican plaintiff, or whether it was treated as a distinct and original offense. In either case the assumption of the Mexican tribunal, under the law of Mexico, to punish a citizen of the United States for an offense wholly committed and consummated in his own country against its laws was an invasion of the independence of this Government. To say that a conciliation in Mexico which operates as a stay of criminal proceedings there binds a citizen of the United States in his own country, is simply to assert that the Mexican penal law is binding upon citizens of the United States in their own country. It appears, however, under ' Considering 6,' in Judge Zubia's decision, that the claim made in Article 186 of the Mexican penal code was actually enforced in the case in question as a distinct and original ground of prosecution. The decision of Judge Zubia was framed in the alternative, and it was held that, even supposing the defamation arose solely from the publication of the alleged libel in the El Paso (Texas) Sunday Herald, Article 186 of the Mexican penal code provided for punishment in that case; Judge Zubia saying that it did not belong to the judge to examine the principle laid down in that article but to apply it fully, it being the law in force in the State of Chihuahua. It nowhere appears that the Texas publication was ever circulated in Mexico so as to constitute the crime of defamation under the Mexican law. As has been seen, this was not a part of the original charge on which the warrant for Mr. Cutting's arrest was issued; and while it is stated in Judge Zubia's decision that an order was issued for the seizure of copies of the Texas paper which might be found in the office of Mr. Cutting in Paso del Norte, it nowhere appears from that decision that any copies were actually found in that place or elsewhere in Mexico.

"But, however this may be, this Government is still compelled to deny what it denied on the 19th of July, 1886, and what the Mexican Government has since executively and judicially maintained, that a citizen of the United States can be held under the rules of international law to answer in Mexico for an offense committed in the United States, simply because the object of that offense happens to be a citizen of Mexico. The Government of Mexico has endeavored to sustain this pretension on two grounds: First, that such a claim is justified by the rules of international law and the positive legislation of various countries; and, secondly, on the ground that such a claim being made in the legislation of Mexico the question is one solely for the decision of the Mexican tribunals. In respect of the latter ground it is only necessary to say, that if a Government could set up its own municipal laws as the final test of its international rights and obligations, then the rules of international law would be but the shadow of a name and would afford no protection either to States or to individuals. It has been constantly maintained and also admitted by the Government of the United States that a government can not appeal to its municipal regulations as an answer to demands for the fulfillment of international duties. Such regulations may either exceed or fall short of the requirements of international law, and in either case that law furnishes the test of the nation's liability and not its own municipal rules. This proposition seems now to be so well understood and so generally accepted, that it is not deemed necessary to make citations or to adduce precedents in its support.

"I turn now to the consideration of the Mexican jurisdictional claim in connection with the principles of international law. It is not now, and has not been contended, by this Government, as seems to have been assumed in some of the arguments put forth in behalf of the Mexican Government, that if Mr. Cutting had actually circulated in Mexico a libel printed in Texas, in such manner as to constitute a publication of the libel in Mexico within the terms of the Mexican law, he could not have been tried and punished for this offense in Mexico. Oftentimes, the question where a libel may actually have been printed is a matter of small moment, the real offense being the publication or circulation. I shall, therefore, pass this question by as having nothing to do with the present case.

"As to the question of international law, I am unable to discover any principle upon which the assumption of jurisdiction made in Article 186 of the Mexican penal code can be justified. There is no principle better settled than that the penal laws of a country have no extraterritorial force. Each state may, it is true, provide for the punishment of its own citizens for acts committed by them outside of its territory; but this makes the penal law a personal statute, and while it may give rise to inconvenience and injustice in many cases, it is a matter in which no other Government has the right to interfere. To say, however, that the penal laws of a country can bind foreigners and regulate their conduct, either in their own or any other foreign country, is to assert a jurisdiction over such countries and to impair their independence. Such is the consensus of opinion of the leading authorities on international law at the present day, from whom ample quotations are made in the report accompanying this instruction. There being then no principle of international law which justifies such a pretension, any assertion of it must rest, as an exception to the rule, either upon the general concurrence of nations or upon express conventions. Such a concurrence in respect to the claim made in Article 186 of the Mexican penal code can not be found in the legislation of the present day. Though formerly asserted by a number of minor states, it has now been generally abandoned, and may be regarded as almost obsolete.

" The only assertion I have found in the legislation of Europe of a general jurisdiction by one state of offenses committed abroad by foreigners against subjects is in the cases of Greece and Russia. The legislation of these countries gives to the judicial tribunals general jurisdiction over such offenses. In Sweden and Norway their punishment is discretionary, and depends upon the King ordering the prosecution. In Austria felonies, but not misdemeanors (the charge against Mr. Cutting of libel is only a misdemeanor, not only under the Mexican law, but under that of Texas), committed by foreigners abroad are punished, but only (except in crimes against the safety of the state and against the national seals and moneys, etc.) after an offer of surrender of the accused person has first been made to the state in which the crime was committed, and has been refused by it. The law is substantially the same in Hungary and in Italy; but criminal offenses committed outside the state by foreigners against its citizens or subjects are not punished under any circumstances or conditions by France, Germany, Belgium, Denmark, Great Britain, Luxembourg, The Netherlands, Portugal, Spain, and Switzerland.

" It is thus seen that Russia and Greece are the only European countries whose claim of extraterritorial jurisdiction is as extensive and absolute as that of Mexico; for it was held by Judge Zubia, whose decision was affirmed by the supreme court of Chihuahua, that it did not belong to the judicial tribunals of Mexico to examine the principle laid down in Article 186, but to apply it in all force, it being the law of the State of Chihuahua, and Mr. Mariscal disclaimed any power on the part of the Mexican Executive to interfere with the execution of the law by the judicial tribunals. Thus the Mexican claim is absolute, and exceeds that made by Sweden and Norway, where the prosecution can only take place if the King order it.

"An appeal has been made in the Mexican arguments to the law of France as sustaining Article 186. The error of this is apparent when we observe that the French code authorizes the prosecution of foreigners for offenses outside of the territory of France, only in the exceptional cases of crimes against the safety of the state, and of counterfeiting the seal of the state, national moneys having circulation, national papers or bank bills authorized by law. Not only is the law thus clear, but it was decided by the court of cassation of France in 1873, in a case which is fully set forth in the report above referred to, that, with the exception of the crimes above mentioned, the French tribunals are without power to judge foreigners for acts committed by them in a foreign country; that their incompetence in this regard is absolute and permanent; that it can be waived neither by the silence nor by the consent of the accused; that the right to punish emanates from the right of sovereignty, which does not extend beyond the limits of the territory, and that the incompetence of the French tribunals, as above stated, exists always and to the same degree in every stage of the proceedings.

" Neither is Article 186 sustained by the legislation of the Spanish-American Republics. Neither in the Argentine Republic, nor in Chili, nor in Peru, nor in Colombia, nor in Costa Rica, is there any law, so far as known to this Department, that authorizes the punishment of foreigners for offenses committed abroad against citizens of those countries. Indeed, such a pretension is incompatible with those free and friendly relations which it is so important for Governments mutually to promote.

" It has constantly been laid down in the United States as a rule of action, that citizens of the United States can not be held answerable in foreign countries for offenses which were wholly committed and consummated either in their own country or in other countries not subject to the jurisdiction of the punishing state. When a citizen of the United States commits in his own country a violation of its laws, it is his right to be tried under and in accordance with those laws, and in accordance with the fundamental guaranties of the Federal Constitution in respect to criminal trials in every part of the United States.

" To say that he may be tried in another country for his offense, simply because its object happens to be a citizen of that country, would be to assert that foreigners coming to the United States bring hither the penal laws of the country from which they come, and thus subject citizens of the United States in their own country to an indefinite criminal responsibility. Such a pretension can never be admitted by this Government.

" It has been seen that Article 186 of the Mexican penal code requires that the offenses included in the article must be also punishable in the place of their commission; and the proceedings before Judge Zubia, as set forth in his decision, show that the Texas penal code was introduced in the trial to prove that Mr. Cutting had committed the offense of libel in Texas. With this code before him, Judge Zubia held that its provision had been violated. Thus, sitting as a Mexican magistrate, he did what no Texas judge could have done had Mr. Cutting been on trial in that State for the alleged offense against its laws. By the Texas code (sec. 2291), ' It is no offense to publish statements of fact as to the qualification of any person for any occupation, profession, or trade.' But this is not all. By the fundamental law of the State no judge can convict any person of libel; for section 6, Article 1, of the constitution, of Texas provides that ' in all indictments for libels the *jury* shall have the right to determine the law and the facts under the direction of the court, as in other cases.'

" The provisions render it wholly unwarrantable for any judge, domestic or foreign, alone to decide that a person has committed a libel under the law in Texas. Nor is it shown that Judge Zubia even attempted to inquire as to the truth of Mr. Cutting's alleged libelous statements.

" You are therefore instructed to say to the Mexican Government, not only that an indemnity should be paid to Mr. Cutting for his arrest and detention in Mexico on the charge of publishing a libel in the United States against a Mexican, but also, in the interests of good neighborhood and future amity, that the statute proposing to confer such extraterritorial jurisdiction should, as containing a claim invasive of the independent sovereignty of a neighboring and friendly state, be repealed. It would surely be highly honorable to the Mexican Government to follow in this regard the example of the Government of France, which, in 1852, withdrew an objectionable measure similar to Article 186 of the Mexican penal code in the interest of maintaining friendly relations with the Government of Great Britain. It appears that a draft of a law conferring upon the courts of France jurisdiction over offenses committed by foreigners against Frenchmen outside of France was adopted on the 10th of June, 1852, by the Corps Legislatif by a vote of 191 to 5. The measure then went to the Senate, but was subsequently withdrawn by the Government because of representations made by the Government of Great Britain; and when this action of the French Government was announced in the British House of Lords the Marquis of Normanby, formerly British embassador at Paris, expressing his satisfaction, said that during the whole period in which he had labored to maintain amicable relations between the two countries, he had seldom listened to any statement with greater pleasure than that of the manner in which the French Government had acted in respect to the withdrawal of the *projet de loi* above referred to. Sincerely desirous of maintaining with the Government of Mexico the most cordial and friendly relations, I can not think that that end could be more signally promoted than by that Government following the highly honorable example of France in removing from the amicable relations of the two countries a law which stands as a constant menace to their continuance.

" Nor is a change of municipal law to meet the exigencies of international intercourse without precedent in the United States. In the case of McLeod, in 1842, when, in reply to the demand of the British Government for the release of the prisoner, who was in the custody of the authorities of the State of New York, this Government was compelled to return a reply not dissimilar to that made by Mr. Mariscal to the demand for the release of Mr. Cutting, namely, the inability of the Federal authorities to interfere, Congress amended the law regulating the issuance of writs of habeas corpus so as to facilitate the performance by the Government of the United States of its international obligations. So that nothing is suggested to the Government of Mexico in this relation which has not been put in practice by the Government of the United States.

" The importance of the harmonious exercise of jurisdictional powers by the Governments of the United States and Mexico, and the desire of this Government to maintain the closest and most friendly relations between these two neighboring countries, were so impressively stated by the President in his last annual message to Congress, that it is proper to quote from it the following pertinent passage:

" ' In the case of Mexico there are reasons especially strong for perfect harmony in the mutual exercise of jurisdiction. Nature has made us irrevocably neighbors, and wisdom and kind feeling should make us friends.

" ' The overflow of capital and enterprise from the United States is a potent factor in assisting the development of the resources of Mexico and in building up the prosperity of both countries.

" ' To assist this good work all grounds of apprehension for the security of person and property should be removed; and I trust that in the interests of good neighborhood the statute referred to will be so modified as to eliminate the present possibilities of danger to the peace of the two countries.'

" I have not burdened this instruction with citations of authorities and quotations from the works of publicists, which may be found in the elaborate report which accompanies this paper, and of which you are instructed to communicate a copy to Mr. Mariscal."

> Mr. Bayard, Sec. of State, to Mr. Connery, chargé to Mexico, Nov. 1, 1887, For. Rel. 1887, 751.
> For the reply of the Mexican Government, see Mr. Mariscal, min. of for. aff., to Mr. Connery, chargé, Feb. 10, 1888, For. Rel. 1888, II. 1114.

" I have to acknowledge the receipt of Mr. Connery's dispatch of the 21st of February last, numbered 306, inclosing a translation of a note from Mr. Mariscal of the 10th of the same month, in relation to the case of A. K. Cutting.

" It is regretted that the representations of this Government, especially in regard to their chief object—to secure the modification by Mexico of her claim of criminal jurisdiction over the territory of the United States—have not received more favorable consideration from Mr. Mariscal. In my instruction to Mr. Connery the question of compensation to Mr. Cutting was subordinated to that vastly more important issue, and was not, in view of his general course of conduct and of his early discharge by the supreme court of Chihuahua, intended to be bound up with it. Mr. Connery was instructed to say to the Mexican Government ' not only that an indemnity should be paid to Mr. Cutting for his arrest and detention in Mexico on the charge of publishing a libel in the United States against a Mexican; but also in the interests of good neighborhood and future amity, that the statute proposing to confer such jurisdiction should, as containing a claim invasive of the independent sovereignty of a neighboring and friendly state, be repealed.'

" I then proceeded to show that there were important precedents, in view of which it would be highly honorable to Mexico to make such modification of her law.

" The question of pecuniary indemnity was not urged as a necessary incident or consequence thereof, nor was it deemed desirable that it should be suffered to interfere with the consideration of the more important question of jurisdiction by being presented in connection with it.

" The consideration of Mr. Cutting's personal merits or of the general features of his conduct cannot be regarded as affecting in any way the essential principle of international right and independent sovereignty which his case involved, and which it is so obviously the interest of the United States and Mexico to have settled.

"At the close of his note Mr. Mariscal sums up the results of his arguments in various propositions, of which the eighth is as follows:

" The right which every nation has to impose national conditions upon the entry of foreigners upon its own territory conveys with it the right within the limits of legislation to hold such foreigners responsible for acts they may commit abroad against that nation, or against any of its citizens or subjects.

"The fallacy of the last clause of the proposition cannot be more clearly shown than by referring to that part of the same note in which Mr. Mariscal endeavors to show that Fiore, notwithstanding the express declarations quoted by this Department from his works, does not antagonize or condemn the punishment by a state of a foreigner when he offends one of its citizens in a foreign country. To prove this, Mr. Mariscal quotes from section 66 of Fiore's 'Droit Pénal International,' in which the learned author admits the right of the state 'to punish every individual without distinction, be he foreigner or native, when he, by acts committed abroad, may have transgressed the laws that sustain our institutions, or may have violated the rights either of a state *or those of persons protected by our laws.*'

"This passage, which Mr. Mariscal has quoted to sustain his contention, seems to me to be fatal to it. If it could be contended that a Mexican or any other foreigner is protected in the United States by the municipal law of his own country, then the passage quoted from Fiore might be held to contradict his explicit declaration that he 'cannot admit' the doctrine that 'the extraterritoriality of penal law ought to depend on the quality of the person to the prejudice of whom the offense has been committed;' and his further declaration that he cannot admit 'that a rule of action may be violated which was not obligatory in the place where the offense was committed.'

"But it cannot be contended that foreigners are protected in the United States by their national laws. Fiore himself says that 'no sovereign can exercise his repressive power on territory under the dominion of another sovereign.' (Droit Pénal International, Paris, 1880, p. 94.) Nor am I acquainted with the works of any author, ancient or modern, who holds an opposite opinion.

"Hence, when Fiore limits penal jurisdiction to the punishment of infractions of the rights of a state or of persons protected by its laws, he clearly and unmistakably negatives the claim of extraterritorial jurisdiction, against which this Government protested in the case of Mr. Cutting. No sovereign state can admit that its citizens are subject in their own country to the control of a foreign municipal law. And so must every sovereign state equally repudiate the correlative proposition that foreigners within its territory are protected by the municipal law of their own country or countries against the acts of citizens of such state. Such a doctrine would carry the extraterritoriality of penal law even beyond the limits set in the conventions between Christian and non-Christian countries, under which the citizens of the former are exempt from the local law, and would produce a confusion and conflict of jurisdictions which could only lead to dangerous and frequent disputes. It is not denied that a state may impose 'rational conditions upon the entry of foreigners upon its own territory,' as Mr. Mariscal contends, but in the opinion of this Department no condition can be regarded as rational, or as consistent with those amicable relations which nations should seek to cultivate and foster, that derogates from the sovereignty and exclusive jurisdiction of foreign states over their own territory.

" In view of these circumstances, it is hoped that the Government of Mexico will yet see its way to a modification of article 186.

" In regard to Mr. Mariscal's reference to the codes of New York and Texas, and his expression of surprise that they are not noticed in the report on extraterritorial crime, it should be observed that they are both discussed on page 25 of that document, and shown to rest, as to the provisions cited by Mr. Mariscal, on a principle precisely opposite to that which he has defended in article 186 of the Mexican penal code.

" You are authorized to state the views herein expressed to Mr. Mariscal and to leave him a copy of this instruction should he desire it."

> Mr. Bayard, Sec. of State, to Mr. Bragg, min. to Mexico, May 4, 1888, For. Rel. 1888, II. 1189.

Article III. of the treaty of extradition between the United States and Mexico, concluded February 22, 1899, contains the following stipulation: " 4. When the extradition is demanded on account of a crime or offense for which the person demanded is undergoing or has undergone punishment in the country from which the extradition is demanded, or in case he or she shall have been prosecuted therein on the same charge and acquitted thereof; provided that, with the exception of the offenses included in clause 13 Article 2, of this convention, each contracting party agrees not to assume jurisdiction in the punishment of crimes committed exclusively within the territory of the other."

Clause 13 of Article II. of the treaty provides for the extradition of persons charged with or convicted of " embezzlement or criminal malversation of public funds committed within the jurisdiction of either party by public officers or depositaries."

3. Legislation and Judicial Decisions.

§ 202.

" The various theories of criminal jurisdiction discussed in the

Moore's Report: Theories of criminal jurisdiction. books may conveniently be arranged as follows:

" I. TERRITORIAL.

" 1. *Actual*—

" *a.* Subjective: As to offenses committed by persons on the territory, except diplomatic officers.

" *b.* Objective: As to offenses committed within the territory by persons outside; *e. g.*, a shot fired on one side of the boundary and taking effect on the other; infernal machine, swindling letter, poisonous food, counterfeit money, &c., sent into country by person outside.

" 2. *Constructive.*—Over offenses committed on vessels of country.

" II. NON-TERRITORIAL.

" 1. *Personal, over citizens:*

" *a.* generally; *b.* in particular places, *e. g.*, barbarous lands; *c.* as to particular acts.

" 2. *As to particular offenses*, whether by citizens or foreigners.

" *a.* Piracy.

" *b.* Where two countries by convention agree to punish the citizens of each other, *e. g.*, conventions for suppression of slave trade.

" *c.* Against safety of state; counterfeiting or forging national seals, papers, moneys, bank bills authorized by law.

" 3. Offenses committed abroad by foreigners against citizens.

" 4. All offenses, wherever and by whomsoever committed.

" It is unnecessary for our present purpose to discuss in detail all the theories of criminal jurisdiction which are stated in the foregoing synopsis. The right of every nation, in the exercise of its sovereignty, to punish acts committed on its soil and in violation of its laws by persons within its territory, may be conceded. The right of a nation to punish offenses committed on its vessels, national or private, which for jurisdictional purposes are considered as part of the national territory, is also admitted. Such offenses, it has been held, may be punished by the vessel's sovereign even when they were committed on a merchant vessel in the ports of another sovereign, provided the latter did not take jurisdiction. And it may also be granted that a nation may, under proper limitations, punish offenses committed within its territory by persons corporeally outside.

" It is true that in the case of an offense committed within the territory of one state by a person corporeally within the territory of another state, there may sometimes be concurrent jurisdiction—the former state having jurisdiction by reason of the locality of the act, the latter by reason of the locality of the actor.[a] In such case the latter state may punish the perpetrator, or may give him up to the other state; or, if it see fit, may decline to do either. But the fact that a state may be unable to obtain jurisdiction of the offender is not a test of its jurisdiction over the offense, for such inability may exist where the person who committed the offense was, at the time of its commission, within the territory, but subsequently fled to the jurisdiction of another country.

"The principle that a man who outside of a country wilfully puts Causal connection, in motion a force to take effect in it is answerable at and construct- the place where the evil is done, is recognized in the ive presence. criminal jurisprudence of all countries. And the methods which modern invention has furnished for the performance of criminal acts in that manner has made this principle one of constantly growing importance and of increasing frequency of application.

"Its logical soundness and necessity received early recognition in the common law. Thus it was held that a man who erected a nuisance in one county which took effect in another was criminally liable in the county in which the injury was done. (Bulwer's case, 7 Co. 2 b. 3 b.; Com. Dig. Action, N. 3, 11.) So, if a man, being in one place, circulates a libel in another, he is answerable at the latter place. (Seven Bishops' Case, 12 State Trials, p. 331; Rex v. Johnson, 7 East, 65.) The same rule applies to obtaining money or goods by false pretences; but it must appear that the false pretences were actually made at the place where the prisoner is held, and not merely that the pretences, which were made elsewhere, resulted in defrauding some one at the place of trial. (Reg. v. Garrett, 6 Cox C. C. 260.) So, if persons outside of a country procure therein the making and engraving of a plate for purposes of forgery, they are indictable there. (Queen v. Bull & Schmidt, 1 Cox C. C. 281.) Likewise, for cheating by false papers. (King v. Brisac & Scott, 4 East, 164.)

"The same principle obtains in the United States. Thus a man may be convicted of subornation of perjury in the State in which, through the agency of a person there resident, the offense was committed, though he was himself in another State. (Com. v. Smith, 11 Allen, 243.) So, where a citizen and resident of Ohio obtained money in the State of New York by a fictitious receipt signed by him in Ohio, but sent to the city of New York to be fraudulently used, it was held

---

[a] State v. Williford, 91 N. C. 529. Adjacent States of the Union and adjacent countries sometimes exercise concurrent jurisdiction of offences committed within a certain distance of the boundary. (Jackson v. State, 90 Ala. 590, 8 So. 862; State v. George, 60 Minn. 503, 63 N. W. 100; State v. Rockwell (Iowa), 48 N. W. 721.

For a discussion as to the locality of the offence, see State v. Morrill, 68 Vt. 60, 54 Am. St. Rep. 870.

that, being in that State, he was liable to trial and punishment; and the court observed—

"'It is not necessary to notice the peculiar relation which a citizen of one of the United States sustains to the other States; for if a subject of the British Crown, while standing on British soil in Canada, should kill a man in this State, by shooting or other means, I entertain no doubt that he would be subject to punishment here whenever our courts could get jurisdiction over his person. . . . If our courts cannot get jurisdiction over his person they cannot try him. But that is no more than happens when a citizen, who has committed an offense within the State, escapes, and cannot be found. Jurisdiction of the offense or subject-matter and jurisdiction to try the offender are very different things. The first exists whenever the offense was committed within this State, and the second when the offender is brought into court, and not before.' (Bronson, J., in Adams *v.* The People; Comstock's R. (N. Y.), 173, 179.)[a]

"The same principle has also been held to apply as to nuisances. (Stillman & Co. *v.* White Rock Mfg. Co. et al., 3 Woodbury & Minot, C. C. Rep. 538.) So if a person forge notes in one place and utter them in another, using for that purpose the mails, he is answerable in the latter place for the utterance of the forged papers. (The People *v.* Rathbun, 21 Wend. 509; Supreme court of New York.) But where, under a statute providing that 'every person who shall sell or in any manner transfer the services of any black, who shall have been forcibly taken, inveigled or kidnapped from this State (New York) to any other State, place, or country, shall, upon conviction, be punished,' a person was indicted not only for inveigling a free negro from the State of New York with intent to sell him, but also for the *actual sale* of him in another State, it was held that the counts in the indictment relating to the latter charge were bad, the court saying: 'It cannot be pretended or assumed that a State has jurisdiction over crimes committed beyond its territorial limits.' (People *v.* Merrill, 2 Parker's Crim. Rep. 590.)

"It has been held by the supreme court of Connecticut that where an inhabitant of Massachusetts sent some paupers into Connecticut in charge of his son, who, by direction of his father, left them there, in contravention of the statute of Connecticut forbidding the bringing of paupers into the State, under penalty of a fine, the father was answerable under the statute. (Barkhamsted *v.* Parsons, 3 Conn. 1.) The same principle was applied in the case of the State *v.* Grady, 34 Conn. 118, the court at the same time saying:

"'It is undoubtedly true, as claimed, that the courts of this State can take no cognizance of an offense *committed* in another State. Such was the decision in Gilbert *v.* Steadman, 1 Root, 403. But it

---

[a] Obtaining property by false pretences is punishable at the place where the property is delivered. (State *v.* House, 55 Iowa, 466; State *v.* Dennis, 80 Mo. 589; State *v.* Shaeffer, 89 Mo. 271, 1 S. W. 293.)

is true, and universally conceded, that if an offense is *committed* in this State by the procuration of a resident of another State, who does not himself personally come here to assist in the offense, . . . such non-resident offender can be punished for the offense by the courts if jurisdiction can be obtained of his person.'

" On the principle of causal connection it is provided in the Penal Code of New York of 1881, that if a person without the State commits an act which affects persons or property within the State, or the public health, morals, or decency of the State, he is punishable therefor in the State of New York. On this principle also rest the provisions of the Texas code for the punishment of persons who, outside of that State, forge titles to land within the State.[a]

---

[a] So it has been held by the Texas courts. In the case of Hanks *v.* The State (13 Tex. Appeal, 289, decided in 1882), the question was fully discussed, and I quote from the opinion of the court the following passages, which speak for themselves :

"Appellant and one P. F. Dillman were jointly indicted in the district court of Travis County (Texas) for the forgery of a transfer of a land certificate for a league and labor of land in the State of Texas. It is alleged in the indictment that the acts constituting the forgery were all committed in Caddo Parish, in the State of Louisiana. No act or thing connected with the execution of the forgery is charged to have been done in Texas; but the crime and injury, so far as this State is concerned, are averred to consist in the fact that the said forgery in Louisiana ' did then and there relate to and affect an interest in land in the State of Texas, . . . and would, if the same were true and genuine, have transferred and affected certain property, to wit, a certain land certificate, number 222, for one league and labor of land in the State of Texas,' &c.

" This indictment was brought under article 451 of the Penal Code.

" By article 454 of the code it is declared that ' persons out of the State may commit and be liable to indictment and conviction for committing any of the offenses enumerated in this chapter *which do not in their commission necessarily require a personal presence in this State*, the object of this chapter being to reach and punish all persons offending against its provisions, whether within or without this State,' &c.

" It was made a ground both in the motion to quash the indictment and in arrest of judgment, and is again urgently insisted upon in the able brief of counsel for appellant, that the facts alleged, if true, would constitute an offense against the sovereign State of Louisiana alone, and one of which the courts of this State would have no jurisdiction.

" If the position thus assumed in behalf of the appellant be correct, then the legislature had no authority to pass the act quoted, and the same is an absolute nullity. . . . We can see no valid reason why the legislature of the State of Texas could not assert, as it has done in article 454 *supra* her jurisdiction over wrongs and crimes with regard to the land titles of the State, no matter whether the perpetrator of the crime was at the time of its consummation within or without her territorial limits. Such acts are offenses against the State of Texas and her citizens only, and can properly be tried only in her courts. It may in fact be no crime against the State in which it is perpetrated; and if it is, under such circumstances we are considering, that other State would have no interest in punishing it, and would rarely, if ever, do so. When this forgery was committed in Louisiana, *eo instanti* a crime was committed against, and injury done to the State of Texas, because it affected title to lands within her sovereignty."

See, also, Rogers *v.* State, 11 Tex. App. 608.

"The principle of the liability of persons outside of a State for acts caused by them within the State was early established in Pennsylvania by the decision of the supreme court in the case of the Commonwealth *v.* Gillespie et al., 7 Sergeant and Rawle, 469, decided in 1822. The facts in this case, which came up on a motion for a new trial, were that a lottery office was kept in Philadelphia in a house rented by *Gillespie,* one of the defendants and a resident of New York; that a lad named *Gregory,* the other defendant, kept the office and sold lottery tickets there as the agent of Gillespie, who occasionally visited the place; and that, in this capacity, Gregory sold at the office a New York lottery ticket, endorsed in the name of Gillespie and not authorized by the laws of Pennsylvania. The prisoners being indicted jointly as participants or conspirators in the crime, the court at the trial did not instruct the jury that Gillespie was criminally answerable for the act of his agent or servant, but left it to them to say whether, from the whole of the evidence, he was concerned in the sale of the ticket. The jury found that he was, and the supreme court sustained the verdict. This court said:

"'It makes no difference where Gillespie resided; if he conspired to sell New York lottery tickets in Pennsylvania, with his agent, and his agent effected the act, the object of unlawful conspiracy, he is answerable criminally to our laws. . . . It must be recollected, the conspiracy is a matter of inference, deducible from the acts of the parties accused, done in pursuance of an apparent criminal purpose, in common between them, and which rarely are confined to one place: and if the parties are linked in one community of design, and of interest, there can be no good reason why both may not be tried, where one distinct overt act is committed.' *a*

"This doctrine has, since Gillespie's case, been applied again in Pennsylvania to an indictment for a conspiracy to cheat and defraud, which was executed in that State, in the case of the Commonwealth *v.* Corliss et al., 3 Brewster's Rep. 575, decided in 1869.

"These Pennsylvania cases were decided in accordance with the rule of the common law that where two or more persons conspire to do an unlawful act, each conspirator is responsible in any place where any overt act by any of his co-conspirators is done, as well as in the place where the crime is concocted and started. *b* (Wharton's Crim. Law, 9th ed., Book 1, § 287.) So careful, however, have courts been to keep within what they deemed proper jurisdictional limits, that

---

a A State may punish the sale within its limits of the tickets of a lottery lawfully organized in another State. (People *v.* Noelke, 94 N. Y. 137, 46 Am. Rep. 128.)

b Hatfield *v.* Com. (Ky.), 12 S. W. 309; Thompson *v.* State, 17 So. Rep. 512; People *v.* Arnold, 46 Mich. 268; Archer *v.* State, 106 Ind. 426; Ex parte Rogers, 10 Tex. App. 655, 38 Am. Rep. 654.

where, in the case of a felony, a person was guilty only as an accessory *before the fact*, as, for example, where a person counseled a felony to be committed, but was not present at its commission, it was held that he could be tried only in the place where his guilty act of accessory-ship took place. This limitation never applied to treason and mis-demeanors, in which all participants before or at the commission of the offense were regarded as principals. By statute in several of the United States the accessory before the fact may be tried in the place having jurisdiction of the principal act, and by statutes still more recent, making all accessories before the fact principals, the accessory before the fact, or instigator, is triable in the place where the crime is perpetrated. But, where no statute on the subject exists, it is still held that an accessory before the fact can be tried only in the place of his accessoryship. Thus it has been held in Indiana that a person who, in the State of Ohio, counseled with and encouraged two per-sons to come into Indiana and commit larceny, could not be held in that State, there being no statute abolishing the distinction in such case between principals and accessories. (Johns *v.* The State, 19 Ind. 421.) So, where several persons entered into a conspiracy in Ohio to burn a steamboat, and the crime was executed in Arkansas, it was held by the supreme court of the latter State that one of the confed-erates, who remained in Ohio, was, by the law of Arkansas, merely an accessory before the fact, and could not be tried in that State. (State *v.* Chapin, 17 Ark. 561.)

" The same rule was held to exist in New Jersey, in the case of The State *v.* Wyckoff (2 Vroom's Rep. 65), decided by the supreme court of that State in 1864. The defendant made arrangements in New York with one Kelly to go into New Jersey and steal certain articles, which he did, afterwards delivering them to the defendant in New York. Wyckoff never came into New Jersey, and it was held that as his offense merely constituted the crime of accessoryship before the fact, and this in New York, he could not be tried in New Jersey. Nevertheless the court said that it was a firmly established rule ' that where the crime is committed by a person absent from the country in which the act is done, through the means of a merely ma-terial agency or by a sentient agent who is innocent, in such cases the offender is punishable where the act is done. The law implies a constructive presence from the necessity of the case; otherwise the anomaly would exist of a crime but no responsible criminal.'[a]

" The decision just quoted speaks of an *innocent agent*, and implies that if a person outside of a State commits an act within it, through an agent who is cognizant of the character of the act which, as such agent, he performed, the principal can not be held. This opinion

---

[a]Acc., Lindsey *v.* State, 38 Ohio State, 507.

rests on the doctrine of accessoryship, which, as has been seen, the New Jersey court recognized; the theory being that if the agent had a guilty knowledge of the character of his performance he became the principal offender in the place where he committed the act, and that the person for whom he acted was merely an accessory before the fact, and as such punishable only in the place of his accessoryship. But, as has been shown, the doctrine of assessoryship has been abolished by statute in many jurisdictions in which it formerly prevailed, and is condemned by many writers as unnecessary and unsound. Referring to accessories before the fact, Mr. Bishop says:

" ' The distinction between such accessory and a principal rests solely in authority, being without foundation either in natural reason or in the ordinary doctrines of the law. The general rule of the law is, that what one does through another's agency is to be regarded as done by himself.'

"And on this point he cites Broom's Legal Maxims, 2 ed., p. 643; Co. Lit. 258*a;* and the opinion of Hosmer, C. J., in Barkhamsted *v.* Parsons, 3 Conn., 1, that ' the principle of common law, *Qui facit per alium, facit per se*, is of universal application, both in criminal and civil cases.'

"Another jurisdictional question worthy of notice is that of the offense of larceny, where goods are stolen in one State or country and brought into another. It was held in England, and the decision has been widely followed in the United States, that in such a case an indictment will not lie for larceny in the country into which the goods were brought. These decisions rest on the ground that a person committing a larceny in one country can not be punished for it in another jurisdiction. This may be regarded as sound, so far as it goes. But in some of the United States it has been provided by statute, as well as decided by the courts, that a person bringing stolen goods from one State into another may be indicted for larceny in the latter.*a* And by a recent statute the same rule is in force in Canada in respect to persons bringing stolen goods into Canada from foreign jurisdictions.

" This rule appears to rest on solid jurisdictional grounds. It does not imply a right to punish the offender for the taking in the foreign State, but only for his felonious act of holding in his custody in the punishing State with an intent to convert to his own use goods which he knows to be the property of another.*b* This completely constitutes the crime of larceny in the latter State. For a clear and forcible

---

a Mack *v.* People, 82 N. Y. 235; Dixon *v.* State, 15 Tex. App. 480; McKenzie *v.* State, 32 Tex. Cr. R. 568, 25 S. W. 426; Powell *v.* State, 52 Wis. 217; State *v.* Johnson, 38 Ark. 568.

b Embezzlement may be punished where the goods are received. (Cohen *v.* State, 20 Tex. App. 224.)

exposition of the jurisdiction in such a case I quote from Bishop on Criminal Law, § 140, vol. 1, 7th ed., the following passage:

" ' Though our courts are not permitted to recognize a foreign larceny and punish it, they can take cognizance of a foreign civil trespass to personal goods; and, if they obtain jurisdiction over the parties, they will redress the wrong done in the foreign country. The method under the common law procedure is by the familiar transitory action of trespass. Now, in every larceny there is a civil trespass as well as a criminal one. This civil trespass, when committed abroad, our courts can recognize, and practically enforce rights growing out of it to the same extent as if done on our own soil. So much is settled doctrine, about which there is no dispute. It is equally settled doctrine in larceny, that if one has taken another's goods by a mere civil trespass, even though it was unintended, then, if finding them in his possession, the intent to steal them comes over him, and with such intent he deals with them contrary to his duty, this is larceny. Applying these two plain doctrines to the present case we have the result, that where a thief brings goods from a foreign State into ours our courts are required to look upon him as a trespasser; and, when he commits any asportation of them here, such as he necessarily did in bringing them across the territorial line, the intent to steal inpelling him, they should regard him as a felon under our laws.'

"An interesting case of the constructive presence and consequent criminal liability of an absent confederate in the commission of a crime, is that of the State of Nevada v. Hamilton et al., 13 Nevada, 386, decided by the Supreme Court of that State in 1878.[a] The circumstances of the case were that a plan was concocted between certain persons to rob the treasure box of a stage on the road from Eureka, in Eureka County, Nevada, to Nye County, in the same State; that one of the confederates was to ascertain when the stage left Eureka, and to make a signal to his confederates in Nye County, thirty or forty miles distant, by building a fire on the top of a mountain in Eureka County, all of which he did. The question being whether this confederate could be held in Nye County for an attempt to rob there, he having been corporeally in Eureka County when his confederates attacked the stage, it was decided that he was properly so held, the court adopting from Bishop's Criminal Law, sec. 650, vol. 1, the declaration that ' where several persons confederate together for

---

[a] A person who, while an offence is committed in one State, stands in another, near enough to give active aid in case of need, and intending to give it, is punishable in the latter State. (Hatfield v. Com. (Ky.), 12 S. W. 309.

Where the acts constituting a crime are committed partly in one place and partly in another, the offence may be punishable where any of the overt acts was committed. (In re McFarland, 59 Hun. 304, 13 N. Y. Supp. 22; Prestwood v. State, 87 Ala. 147, 6 So. 392; State v. Smith (Iowa), 48 N. W. 727.)

the purpose of committing a crime which is to be accomplished in pursuance of a common plan, all who do any act which contributes to the accomplishment of their design are principals, whether actually present at its consummation or not. They are deemed to be constructively present though in fact they may be absent.'

"A question which has given rise to much contrariety of opinion Cases of murder is that of the proper jurisdiction of the offense of and manslaugh- murder, where the injury is inflicted in one place or ter. state, and the victim dies in another place or state. In England it was once held that where a blow was struck in one county and death ensued in another county, the criminal could be tried in neither. To remedy this defect, the statute of 2 and 3 Edw. VI, chap. 24, A. D. 1549, was passed, after which it was held that the criminal could be tried in either county.[a] But as this statute was adopted merely to remedy a defect in the common law procedure, by enabling juries in one county of the realm to take cognizance to a certain extent of facts that occurred in another county of the kingdom, it has frequently been asserted in the United States, and is definitively settled in England, that where a blow is struck outside of the boundaries and jurisdiction of an independent state by a foreigner, the mere death of the victim, who subsequently to his injury has come or been brought into the state, does not give it jurisdiction of the crime. The decision of this question depends upon the view the court may take of the relation of the death to the infliction of the injury. The question was settled in England in the case of the Queen v. Lewis, 7 Cox C. C. 277, decided by the court of criminal appeal in 1857. The prisoner, who was a Frenchman by birth, and a naturalized citizen of the United States, shipped at New York in December, 1856, as a seaman on board of an American ship, on a voyage from thence to Liverpool. On board of the vessel, and shipped for the same voyage, was a seaman named George, towards whom the prisoner, soon after the commencement of the voyage, began to exercise acts of cruelty. The last act proved was committed four days before the vessel arrived at Liverpool, and when she was on the high seas west of Cape Clear, Ireland. The vessel arrived in the Mersey on the morning of January 12, 1857, and George died at a hospital in Liverpool on the afternoon of the same day, in consequence of the cruelty and violence committed upon him by the prisoner during the voyage. The indictment was for manslaughter.

" It was conceded by the counsel for the prosecution that by the common law the English courts would have had no jurisdiction, but he contended that it was conferred on them by the statutes of 2 Geo. II. c. 21, and 9 Geo. IV. c. 31. The former act provided that where

---

[a] State v. Sweat, 16 S. C. 624.

any person, at any time after the 24th June, 1729, should be feloniously stricken or poisoned upon the sea, or at any place out of
England, and should die of the same stroke or poisoning within
England, or where any person should be feloniously stricken or
poisoned within England and should die of the same stroke or poisoning upon the sea, or at any place out of England—in either of the
said cases an indictment thereof found by the jurors of the county in
England in which such death, stroke, or poisoning should happen,
respectively, should be as good and sufficient as if such felonious
stroke or poisoning, death thereby ensuing, had happened in the same
county where the indictment was found. The statute 9 Geo. IV.
c. 31, § 8, provided 'that where any person, being feloniously
stricken, poisoned, or otherwise hurt upon the sea, or at any place out
of England, shall die of such stroke, etc., in England, etc., every
offense committed in respect of any such case, etc., may be dealt with,
inquired of, tried, determined, and punished in the county or place
in England in which such death, etc., shall happen, in the same manner, in all respects, as if such offense had been wholly committed in
that county or place.'

" Notwithstanding the general words, especially of the latter act,
the court of appeal held that the British courts had no jurisdiction,
and said that 'that section (§ 8, 9 Geo. IV. c. 31) ought not, therefore, to be construed as making homicide cognizable in the courts of
this country by reason of the death occurring here, unless it would
have been so cognizable at the place where the blow was given; and
the homicide in this particular case would have been by the 7th section so cognizable if the offender had been a British subject, but not
otherwise.' [a]

"An opposite view of the relation of the death to the mortal injury
has been taken in the United States in the case of the Commonwealth
v. Macloon et al., 101 Mass., 1, decided by the supreme judicial court
of the State of Massachusetts in 1869. The defendants, one a citizen
of the State of Maine and the other a British subject, were convicted
in the superior court of Suffolk County, Massachusetts, of the manslaughter of a man who died in that county, in consequence of injuries
inflicted on him by the defendants in a British merchant ship on the
high seas.

" The statute of Massachusetts under which the defendants were
tried and convicted provides that 'If a mortal wound is given, or
other violence on injury inflicted, or poison administered, on the
high seas, or on land either within or without the limits of this State,
by means whereof death ensues in any county thereof, such offense

---

a See also Hoong v. The Queen, 7 Cox C. C. 489.

may be prosecuted and punished in the county where the death happens.' (Gen. Stats., c. 171, par. 19.)

"The decision of the Supreme Court, which was delivered by Gray, J., stated that the principal question in the case was 'that of jurisdiction, which touches the sovereign power of the Commonwealth to bring to justice the murderers of those who die within its borders.' It was not pretended that a foreigner could be punished in Massachusets for an act done by him elsewhere. But it was held that where a mortal blow was given outside and death ensued within the State the offender committed a murder there. The court said 'Criminal homicide consistes in the unlawful taking by one human being of the life of another in such manner that he dies within a year and a day from the time of the giving of the mortal wound. If committed with malice, express or implied by law, it is murder; if without malice, it is manslaughter. . . . The unlawful intent with which the wound is made or the poison administered attends and qualifies the act until its final result. No repentance or change of purpose, after inflicting the injury or setting in motion the force by means of which it is inflicted, will excuse the criminal. If his unlawful act is the efficient cause of the mortal injury, his personal presence at the time of its beginning, its continuance, or its result is not essential.'

"The same view of the crime of murder, and consequently of jurisdiction in a case where death occurs in an independent state from an injury committed outside, was taken by the supreme court of Michigan, in the case of Tyler v. The People, 8 Mich., 320, decided in 1860. Tyler was indicted under a statute of that State, which is substantially identical with the Massachusetts statute referred to in the case of Macloon; and it was held that although the mortal wound was given in Canada, the person inflicting the blow was indictable in Michigan, where the death occurred, notwithstanding that it did not appear by the evidence that he was a citizen of that State.[a] Manning, J., delivering the opinion of the majority of the court, said: 'The shooting itself, and the wound which was its immediate consequence, did not constitute the offense of which the prisoner is convicted. Had death not ensued, he would have been guilty of an assault and battery, not murder; *and would have been criminally accountable to the laws of Canada only*. But the consequences of the shooting were not confined to Canada. They followed Jones [the

[a] Tyler was, in fact, a U. S. marshal. His extradition was demanded by the British Government under the treaty of 1842, for murder committed within British jurisdiction. But after his trial and conviction, the demand was permitted to rest. See Clarke upon Extradition, p. 68 *et seq.*

victim] into Michigan, where they continued to operate until the crime was consummated in his death.'

"Campbell, J., delivered a dissenting opinion of much force, in which he argued that the coming into the State was the act not of the wrongdoer but of the injured person, and therefore should not subject the former to the jurisdiction of Michigan merely because the latter happened to die there. This argument was adverted to in the case of Macloon, and the answer made by the Massachusetts court was that 'it is the nature and the right of every man to move about at his pleasure, except so far as restrained by law; and whoever gives him a mortal blow assumes the risk of this, and in the view of the law, as in that of morals, takes his life wherever he happens to die of that wound.' (See Com. v. Macloon, ante.)

"In New Jersey, however, the contrary view was taken by the Supreme Court in the case of The State v. Carter (3 Dutcher, 499), decided in 1859. The defendant, who was assumed to be a citizen of New York, was indicted for homicide, by inflicting on the deceased in that State mortal wounds of which he afterwards died in New Jersey. The statute under which the indictment was found provided that 'where any person shall be feloniously stricken or poisoned upon the sea, or at any place out of the jurisdiction of this State, and shall die of the same stroke or poisoning within the jurisdiction of this State, . . . an indictment thereof found by jurors of the county within the jurisdiction of this State, in which such death, etc., shall happen, etc., shall be as good and effectual in the law, etc., as if such felonious stroke and death thereby ensuing, or poisoning and death thereby ensuing, etc., had happened in the same county where such indictment shall be found.' (Nixon's Dig., N. J., p. 184.)

"Green, J., delivering the opinion of the court, said: 'Nothing was done by the defendant in this State. When the blow was given both parties were out of its jurisdiction, and within the jurisdiction of the State of New York. The only fact connected with the offense alleged to have taken place within our jurisdiction is, that after the injury the deceased came into and died in this State. . . . Here no act is done in this State by the defendant. . . . The coming of the party injured into this State afterwards was his own voluntary act, and in no way the act of the defendant.'

"It was consequently held that the offender not being a citizen of New Jersey, the courts of that State were incompetent to try him, notwithstanding the general language of the act under which the indictment was found.

"The preponderance of decisions of the American courts unquestionably sustains the doctrine that in murder the crime is committed where the blow is struck.[a]   It is not, however, my purpose to discuss here the soundness or unsoundness of these opposing views. My object in the preceding discussion of the English and American cases has been, in the first place, to show that in no case has an English or an American court assumed jurisdiction, even under statutes couched in the most general language, to try and sentence a foreigner for acts done by him abroad, unless they were brought, either by an immediate effect or by direct and continuance causal relationship, within the territorial jurisdiction of the court.[b]   In the second place, I have sought to illustrate the various phases of this principle for the purpose of dissipating the notion that it in some way sustains the doctrine of Article 186 of the Mexican Penal Code. The mere existence of the English and American cases negatives the claim made in that article. If a nation has jurisdiction of offenses committed and consummated by a foreigner outside of its actual or constructive territory, then all argument as to the place where his acts took effect is useless and irrelevant. It is only because such a pretension is denied and repudiated not only in England, but also in the United States, and as between the several States of the United States, united as they are by a supreme Federal Constitution, that the courts have inquired so constantly as to the locality of the crime.

" Taking up the theories classified as non-territorial, we may first notice that which proposes the punishment by the State of its own citizens for acts done abroad.

Nonterritorial theories.

" This theory has been separated into three subdivisions, as follows:

" (a) The punishment by the State of all acts of its citizens abroad, which, if committed within its territory, would constitute violations of its criminal law. This proposition makes the penal law of the State a personal statute binding upon its citizens everywhere.

" (b) The punishment by the state of all acts of its citizens which may be committed in particular places, and which, if committed within its territory, would constitute violations of its criminal law.

" (c) The punishment by the state of particular acts of its citizens abroad, which, if committed within its territory, would constitute

---

[a] Wharton's Cr. Law, § 292; Bishop's Cr. Law, § 113, vol. 1; Riley v. State, 9 Humph. (Tenn.), 646; State v. Kelly, 76 Maine, 331; Kelly v. United States, 27 Fed. Rep. 616. See, also, Weller v. State, 16 Tex. App. 200; Hernandez v. State, 19 Tex. App. 408; Hall v. State, 115 N. C. 811, 19 S. E. 602; Lovelace v. State, 12 Lea (Tenn.), 721; Foute v. State, 15 Lea (Tenn.), 712; Ex parte Carr, 28 Kan. 1; State v. Smith, 82 Iowa, 423; State v. Morrow (S. C.), 18 S. E. 853; United States v. Guiteau, 1 Mackey (D. C.), 498; Green v. State, 66 Ala. 40, 41 Am. Rep. 744; Binfield v. State, 15 Neb. 484.

[b] General words in a criminal statute are to be interpreted as applying only to places within the jurisdiction of the legislature. (MacLeod v. Attorney-General of New South Wales (1891), App. Cas. 455.)

violations of its criminal law, and which, by reason of their gravity, or the fact that, as is the case with political crimes, the foreign state may not punish them, it is the duty of the state, not only to mankind but to itself, to punish.

" It is not to be doubted that each state may, in the exercise of its sovereignty, punish its own citizens for such acts and in such manner as it may deem proper.

" For the exercise of this right each state is responsible to itself alone, no other state being competent to intervene. Nevertheless, the subject has presented to publicists and legislators so many grave doubts on the score of expediency and justice, that few countries have attempted to require of their citizens a general observance of their criminal law outside of the national territory, except in particular places.

" These exceptions are barbarous lands, in which local law does not exist, and to which the doctrine of the sovereignty of each nation over all persons within its territory does not completely apply; and Mohammedan and other non-Christian countries, in which the citizens of many states enjoy a conventional immunity from the local law. In such places it is not only proper but necessary for each state to subject its citizens to its own regulations. The argument of expediency may also be applied to the punishment of citizens for offenses of a high grade, such as murder, wherever committed. But, to quote the language of Sir George Cornewall Lewis,[a] ' the system of tying the entire criminal law of a country round the neck of a subject, and of making him liable to its operation, in whatever part of the world he may be, converts the criminal law into a personal statute, and puts it on the same footing as the law respecting civil *status*.'

" The objection to this, as he states it, is that ' the personal statute of one country, in civil matters, is recognized by another, so that there is no conflict of laws. But if the criminal law were a personal statute a foreigner would at the same time be subject to two criminal laws— the criminal law of his own state and that of the state of his domicile. No text writer and no state disputes the rule that all foreigners in a country are subject to its criminal law.'

" It is no answer to this cogent reasoning to say that the punishment of a citizen by the country in which the crime was committed would be a bar to his punishment at home for the same offense; for it may be very differently regarded by the two countries. The law of the sovereign of allegiance might punish it much more severely than the law of the country in which the offense was committed; and, were the case reversed, the punishment of the criminal in his own country would either guarantee him immunity from a greater penalty justly

---

[a] Foreign Jurisdiction and the Extradition of Criminals.

incurred in the state where the offense was committed, should he return thereto, or, assuming that the former prosecution could not be set up as a bar in the latter country, would leave him liable on such return to a second punishment for the same offense. I am aware that it has been proposed by some writers, and adopted as a rule in some codes, to apply to offenses committed outside of the state either the penalty attached to the act by the law of the place where it was committed, or that imposed by the law of the place of trial, whichever may be the less severe. But the general and more consistent rule is to apply the penalty prescribed by the law of the punishing state; for, as it is a universal principle that one state will not enforce the penal laws and judgments of another state,[a] it seems to be illogical to apply to a criminal act, although committed abroad, the penalty prescribed by a foreign law.

" In addition to the inharmonious and conflicting results already noticed of the proposition generally to extend the operation of criminal law to citizens when abroad, it is obvious that if such a rule were enforced the trial of persons at a place far away from the *locus delicti* would often be productive of great hardships and injustice; and, if the law were not enforced, its inutility and the capriciousness of its enforcement would render its existence inexpedient and improper.

" The second subdivision of non-territorial jurisdiction in our synopsis includes, first, the single crime of piracy. This offense has been placed by itself, because it is *sui generis*. The scene of the pirate's operations being the high seas, which it is not the special duty or right of any nation to police, and his crime being treated as a renunciation of the protection of the flag which he may carry, he is regarded as a complete outlaw, and may be punished by any nation that captures him. Such an exercise of jurisdiction is both logical and necessary, and is recognized by all nations as a common duty and a common advantage. It scarcely need be said that the exercise, as in the case of conventions for the suppression of the slave trade (non-territorial, 2, *b*.), of criminal jurisdiction by one country over the citizens of another, under a special treaty between the two countries, presents no conflict of jurisdictions, and is simply a question of expediency to be considered by the parties to the agreement. The punishment by a nation of extraterritorial offenses against the safety of the state, and the counterfeiting or forging of national seals, papers, moneys, and bank bills authorized by law (non-territorial, 2, *c*.) is, as will hereafter be seen, regarded as an exception to the general principles of criminal jurisprudence, and is placed by those who maintain and defend it upon the high ground of necessity and self-defense.

---

[a] Foelix, Droit International Privé, tom. ii, tit. ix, chap. iv.

"Our fourth subdivision of non-territorial jurisdiction proposes the punishment by each state of all offenses, wherever and by whomsoever committed. It is unnecessary to discuss this theory specifically, because, in the first place, it is so rhapsodical and cosmopolitan in its character, and, while intended to be benevolent, is so impracticable and intrusive, that it has never assumed a legislative guise; and, in the second place, its character will necessarily be disclosed in the consideration, immediately to follow, of our third subdivision of non-territorial jurisdiction, which proposes the punishment, by the state, of offenses committed abroad by foreigners against citizens, and which is found in article 186 of the Mexican Penal Code. [Here follows an examination of penal legislations in Europe and in America touching offences committed outside the national jurisdiction.]

"The importance in the present discussion of the preceding examination of the laws of different states touching offenses committed on foreign territory may best be apprehended in a tabular statement showing to what extent such jurisdiction over foreigners is actually claimed. It is unnecessary to tabulate the legislation respecting citizens, because that is merely a question of expediency which each state may determine for itself, and not a matter of international right, concerning which other nations may have to be consulted. It is, however, to be observed that while in some of the codes that have been quoted the provisions respecting offenses committed abroad by citizens are general and sweeping in their character, in no case is a claim put forth to punish a foreigner for such offenses, save under exceptional circumstances and in exceptional cases, which are supposed to justify the pretension.

"Foreigners are punished who, outside of the national territory and jurisdiction, commit offenses—

"1. *Against the safety of the state:* (*a*) By France, Germany, Austria, Belgium, Hungary, Italy, Luxembourg, the Netherlands, Norway, Russia, Sweden, Greece, Brazil, Spain, Switzerland; (*b*) *not punished* by Denmark, Great Britain, Portugal.

Legislation of various countries.

"2. *Counterfeiting seals of the state, national moneys having circulation, national papers, or bank bills authorized by law:* (*a*) *Punished* by France, Germany, Austria, Belgium, Hungary, Italy, Luxembourg, the Netherlands, Norway, Sweden, Greece, Brazil, Spain, Switzerland; (*b*) *not punished* by Denmark, Great Britain, Portugal.[a]

---

[a] See, in this relation, U. S. *v.* Arjona, 120 U. S. 479, in which the Supreme Court, at its October term, 1886, held that the counterfeiting of foreign securities, whether national or corporate, which have been put out under the sanction of public authority at home, especially the counterfeiting of bank notes and bank bills, is an offense against the law of nations; and that, con-

" 3. *Other offenses:* (*a*) General jurisdiction of offenses committed abroad by foreigners against subjects is claimed by Greece and Russia; (*b*) such offenses are punished by Sweden and Norway, if the king orders the prosecution; (*c*) *crimes*, but not *délits*, committed by foreigners in another state are punished by Austria, provided that (except in the case of *crimes* specified under 1 and 2) an offer of surrender of the accused person has first been made to the state in which the *crime* has been committed, and has been refused by it; (*d*) criminal offenses committed abroad by foreigners are punished by Hungary, if the minister of justice orders the prosecution, provided that the act is punishable at the place of commission, that it has not ceased to be punishable there, and that the competent authority does not undertake to punish it; (*e*) criminal offenses committed by foreigners against Italians in another state are punished by Italy, but only when (except in the cases under 1 and 2) an offer of surrender of the person accused has been made to the state in which the *crime* was committed, and has been refused by it, unless the offense was committed within three miles of the frontier, or stolen property has been brought into the Kingdom; (*f*) non-bailable offenses committed abroad by foreigners are punished by Brazil, if the prosecution is authorized by the Government, and the laws of the criminal's country punish foreigners in like cases; (*g*) criminal offenses committed outside of the state by foreigners against citizens or subjects are not punished under any conditions by France, Germany, Belgium, Denmark, Great Britain, Luxembourg, the Netherlands, Portugal, Spain, or Switzerland.

" It is thus seen that among all the countries whose legislation has been examined, Russia and Greece are the only ones whose assertion of extraterritorial jurisdiction is as extensive and absolute in form as that of Mexico. For the question we are now considering is not that of the punishment of extraterritorial crimes against the safety of the state, or of coinage felonies, but of offenses, both *crimes* and *délits* (or felonies and misdemeanors,) committed outside of a country by foreigners against a citizen. The only limitation imposed by

---

sequently, the Congress of the United States has authority, under its constitutional power to provide for the punishment of offenses against the law of nations, to enact laws to punish the counterfeiting of foreign securities in the United States.

Referring to accusations brought, in connection with transactions in Colombia, against a person who claimed citizenship of the United States, the Colombian minister of foreign affairs, in his annual report, said that the acts in question, " as they affected the national interests, would be under the jurisdiction of the Republic, even if they were committed in a foreign country, as the Colombian criminal law considers every person whose delinquency may cause loss to the national treasury, subject to the sovereignty of this country." (For. Rel. 1894, 195.)

article 186 upon the jurisdiction of the Mexican tribunals over offenses of this character, is that they must be punishable with a severer penalty than 'arresto mayor' by the law of Mexico, and as penal offenses by the law of the country in which they were committed. Thus offenses which by the law of Mexico are merely *délits* and by the law of the United States merely *misdemeanors*, may be punished under article 186. Not only is this the language of the law, but such was its interpretation by the Mexican court in the case in question; and by the law of Texas libel is not a felony, but only a misdemeanor. (Smith *v.* The State, 32 Texas, 594.)

"The claim of Mexico is not only thus extensive, but it is also absolute. We have seen that it was held by Judge Zubia, whose decision was affirmed by the supreme court of Chihuahua, that according to the rule, '*Judex non de legibus sed secundum leges debet judicare,*' it did not belong to the judge to examine the principle laid down in article 186, but to apply it in all force, it being the law of the State of Chihuahua. And we have further seen that Mr. Mariscal disclaimed any power to interfere with the execution of the law by the judicial tribunals. Thus the Mexican claim is absolute. In this respect it goes beyond the jurisdictional lines laid down by Sweden and Norway, whose claims of jurisdiction are, after those of Russia and Greece, the most extensive of any that have been examined. In Sweden and Norway the foreigner may be punished for an offense committed in a foreign country against a Swedish or Norwegian subject, *if the King orders the prosecution.* This makes the prosecution discretionary and enables the Government to meet any diplomatic question that may be raised in relation to the international right involved. The same thing may be said of the law of Hungary, where, in the case supposed, the prosecution must be ordered by the minister of justice. Austria punishes only *crimes*, not *délits* or misdemeanors, and then, except in the case of *crimes* against the safety of the state, or coinage felonies, only after an offer of surrender of the accused person has been made to the state in which the *crime* was committed, and has been refused by it. The same principle is found in the law of Italy, with almost the same definition of jurisdiction. Brazil makes the assertion of extraterritorial jurisdiction over foreigners in similar cases depend upon the assertion of a like jurisdiction by the criminal's country.

"I have said that crimes committed outside of the national territory by foreigners against citizens or subjects are not punished under any circumstances or conditions by France, Germany, Belgium, Denmark, Great Britain, Luxembourg, the Netherlands, Portugal, Spain, or Switzerland. Before showing this, I pronounced the Mexican contention, that the claim to punish foreigners for offenses committed against Mexicans outside of the national territory was sustained by the French Code, to be wholly unfounded. I shall now show that such a claim has been pronounced by the highest judicial tribunal in France to be unwarranted by the principles of international law.

" I refer to the case of *Raymond Fornage*, decided by the court of cassation, or supreme court, of France, at Paris in 1873, and reported in the *Journal du Palais* (p. 299 *et seq.*) for that year. This court being the highest judicial tribunal in France, its decisions in respect to the French law are not to be questioned. The circumstances of the case of Fornage are as follows: The prisoner was indicted by the ' *Chambre des mises en accusation* ' (grand jury) of the court of appeal of Chambéry for the crime of larceny, which was described in the indictment as having been committed in the Canton of Vaud, Switzerland; and the case was referred for trial before a jury to the court of assizes (composed, in departments where there are courts of appeal, of three judges of that court) sitting at Haute-Savoie. The prisoner did not take an appeal, as he had a legal right to do, from the judgment of reference, but proposed before the court of assizes an exception to the competency of that court, based on the ground that, having the quality of a foreigner, the French tribunals could not try him for a crime committed in a foreign country. But the court of assizes, regarding itself as irrevocably clothed with jurisdiction by the judgment of reference from the court of appeal, which had not been attacked, declared that the exception of the accused was not receivable. Upon these facts the case was argued at length before the court of cassation by M. Réquier, a counsellor and reporter of the court, and M. Bédarrides, advocate-general, both of whom, while admitting that the rule was settled that a court of assizes could not declare itself incompetent to take cognizance of a case of which it had been possessed by a judgment of reference from which no appeal was taken within the periods established by law, nevertheless argued that there were considerations of a higher order in the case of Fornage, which ought to make it an exception to the general rule. In this relation I quote from the argument of M. Réquier, the following passage:

" ' The right to punish has no foundation except the right of sovereignty, which expires at the frontier. If the French law permits the prosecution of Frenchmen for crimes or misdemeanors committed abroad, it is because the criminal law has something of the character at the same time of a personal statute and of a territorial statute. A Frenchman, when he has reached a foreign country, does not remain the less a citizen of his own country; and, as such, subject to the French law, which holds him again when he reënters France. *But the law can not give to the French tribunals the power to judge foreigners for crimes or misdemeanors committed outside of the territory of France; that exorbitant jurisdiction, which would be founded neither on the personal statute nor on the territorial statute, would constitute a violation of international law and an attempt against the sovereignty of neighboring nations.* There exists a single exception to that rule of the law of nations. When a foreigner has committed, even outside of the territory, a *crime* against the safety of the state, he can be prosecuted, judged and punished in France. But, save that exception, founded on the right of legitimate self-defense, foreigners are justiciable only by the tribunals of their own country for acts done by them outside of the territory. The French tribunals, in punishing an act of that nature, would commit a veritable usurpation of sovereignty, which might disturb the good relations of France with neighboring nations. . . . When a crime has been committed outside of the territory by a foreigner the culprit is not subjected by that act to the French law; the French tribunals have no jurisdiction over him; the incompetence is radical and absolute. The criminal court, in punishing the act, would commit an abuse of powers; it would usurp a right of sovereignty appertaining to a foreign power. Would it not be contrary to all the principles of justice to oblige the magistrates to render themselves guilty of an arbitrary act, of a violation of international law ? '

" Not only did the court of cassation adopt this view, but in its judgment (the full text of which is given herewith as Exhibit B) the rule of international law, as laid down by the Government of the United States in the Cutting case, is expressed in terms which, for force, precision, and freedom from doubt or qualification, have not been surpassed. Translated, the material parts of the judgment are as follows:

" ' Whereas, if, as a general principle, the courts of assizes, possessed of a case by a judgment of the chamber of indictments not attached within the times fixed by article 296 of the Code of Criminal Procedure, cannot declare themselves incompetent, . . . this rule is founded on this, that the courts of assizes, being invested with full jurisdiction in criminal matters, can, without committing any excess of power and without transgressing the limits of their attributes, take cognizance of all acts punished by the French law; *but this jurisdiction, however general it may be, cannot extend to offenses committed outside of the territory by foreigners*, who, by reason of such acts, are not justiciable by the French tribunals;— seeing that, indeed, *the right to punish emanates from the right of sovereignty, which does not extend beyond the limits of the territory;* that, except in the cases specified by article 7 of the Code of Criminal Procedure, the provision of which is founded on the right of legitimate defense, *the French tribunals are without power to judge foreigners for acts committed by them in a foreign country; that their*

*incompetence in this regard is absolute and permanent; that it can
be waived, neither by the silence nor by the consent of the accused;*
that it exists always the same, at every stage of the proceedings
. . . ; whereas, indeed, Raymond Fornage was brought before the
court of assizes of Haute Savoie, accused of larceny committed in the
canton of Vaud, Switzerland; . . . and, in ordering the trial to
proceed, without passing upon the question of nationality raised by
the accused, it (the court) violated article 408 of the code, and disregarded the rights of the defense.

" 'Annul, etc.' *a*

" This judgment may be regarded as finally and conclusively
answering the contention that a precedent for article 186 may be
found in the French Code."

" In the United States the territorial principle is the basis of criminal jurisprudence, and the place of the commission
of an offense is generally recognized as the proper
and only place for its punishment.*b* . . .

**Principles of
American law.**

" The earliest bestowal by Congress upon the Federal courts of
jurisdiction over offences committed outside of the territory, actual or
constructive, of the United States, was in the crimes act of 1790,
which, as read in the text, has sometimes been supposed by writers
to have conferred a far more extensive jurisdiction on the courts
of the United States than the decisions of those tribunals have
attributed to it. [Here follows an examination of United States *v.*
Palmer (1818), 3 Wheaton, 610; United States *v.* Klintock (1820),
5 Wheat. 144; United States *v.* Pirates (1820), 5 Wheat. 184; United
States *v.* Holmes (1820), 5 Wheat. 412; United States *v.* Howard
(1818), 3 Wash. C. C. 340.]

" It may, therefore, be said that in respect to offenses committed
on the high seas, the jurisdiction exercised by the judicial tribunals
of the United States, under the legislation of Congress and the decisions of the Supreme Court, does not exceed, if, indeed, in the case
of citizens of the United States, it reaches, the limitations of criminal jurisdiction over the high seas as defined by Wheaton, who, in
his ' Elements of International Law,' lays down the following rules:

" ' § 124. Pirates being the common enemies of all mankind, and all
nations having an equal interest in their apprehension and punishment, they may be lawfully captured on the high seas by the armed
vessels of any particular state, and brought within its territorial
jurisdiction, for trial in its tribunals.

---

a See, also, case of Jacques Trottet, court of cassation, 1864, Journal du
Palais, 1864, p. 404.

b As to Art. III., sec. 2, of the Constitution, concerning the trial of crimes by
Federal courts, see Ex part Pritchard, 43 Fed. Rep. 915.

" ' This proposition, however, must be confined to piracy as defined by the law of nations, and cannot be extended to offenses which are made piracy by municipal legislation. Piracy, under the law of nations, may be tried and punished in the courts of justice of any nation, by whomsoever and wheresoever committed; but piracy created by municipal statute can only be tried by that state within whose territorial jurisdiction, and on board of whose vessels, the offense thus created was committed. There are certain acts which are considered piracy by the internal laws of a state, to which the law of nations does not attach the same signification. It is not by force of the international law that those who commit these acts are tried and punished, but in consequence of special laws which assimilate them to pirates, and which can only be applied by the State *to its own subjects, and in places within its own jurisdiction.* The crimes of murder and robbery, committed by foreigners on board of a foreign vessel, on the high seas, are not justiciable in the tribunals of another country than that to which the vessel belongs; but if committed on board of a vessel not at the time belonging, in fact as well as right, to any foreign power or its subject, but in possession of a crew acting in defiance of all law, and acknowledging obedience to no flag whatsoever, these crimes may be punished as piracy under the law of nations, in the courts of any nation having custody of the offenders.' *a*

" Mr. Dana, in a note citing these and other cases, states the following conclusion :

" ' If an act of robbery or murder were committed upon one of the passengers or crew by another in a vessel at sea, the vessel being at the time and continuing under lawful authority, and the offender were secured and confined by the master of the vessel, to be taken home for trial,—this state of things would not authorize seizure and trial by any nation that chose to interfere, or within whose limits the offender might afterwards be found.'

" In 1799 an act was passed by Congress, the provisions of which are now substantially embodied in section 5335 of the Revised Statutes, which reads as follows:

" ' SEC. 5335. Every citizen of the United States, whether actually resident or abiding within the same, or in any foreign country, who, without the permission or authority of the Government, directly or indirectly, commences or carries on any verbal or written correspondence or intercourse with any foreign government, or any officer or agent thereof, with an intent to influence the measures or conduct of any foreign government, or of any officer or agent thereof, in relation to any disputes or controversies with the United States, or to defeat

---

a Dana's edition, p. 193 et seq., Wheaton cites, as sustaining his views, the cases of United States *v.* Klintock and United States *v.* Pirates.

the measures of the Government of the United States; and every person, being a citizen of, or resident within, the United States, and not duly authorized, who counsels, advises, or assists in any such correspondence, with such intent, shall be punished by a fine of not more than five thousand dollars, and by an imprisonment during a term not less than six months, nor more than three years; but nothing in this section shall be construed to abridge the right of a citizen to apply, himself or his agent, to any foreign government or the agents thereof for redress of any injury which he may have sustained from such government, or any of its agents or subjects.'

" The act of 1799, commonly called the ' Logan ' statute, after the person by whose informal diplomatic enterprises its enactment was suggested,[a] applied in terms, as does the section above quoted, only to citizens of the United States. It raises, therefore, no question of jurisdiction as between nations, and is of no importance in the present discussion.

" The same observation may be made on the laws passed by Congress in pursuance of treaties with China, Japan, Siam, Egypt, and Madagascar, to confer on the minister and consuls of the United States in those countries, or in any other countries with which the United States has similar treaties, jurisdiction ' to arraign and try, in the manner herein provided, all citizens of the United States charged with offenses against law, committed in such countries.' (Sec. 4084 R. S.) Neither, as has heretofore been stated, is any international question raised by another provision of the law (sec. 4088 R. S.) conferring a similar jurisdiction over citizens of the United States upon ' consuls and commercial agents of the United States at islands and in countries not inhabited by any civilized people, or recognized by any treaty with the United States.' In such places there being no system of law, or courts of justice, to which foreigners may be held answerable, it is admitted that they must remain subject to the laws and authorities of their respective governments.[b]

" There is still another law, the act of Congress of August 18, 1856, section 24, now substantially embodied in section 1750 of the Revised Statutes, to which reference should be made. By this section secretaries of legations and consular officers of the United States in foreign lands are authorized, at their respective posts or places, ' to administer to or take from any person an oath, affirmation, affidavit, or deposition, and to perform any notarial act which any notary public is required or authorized by law to do within the United States.'

" It is provided further that ' every such oath, affirmation, affidavit, deposition and notarial act administered, sworn, affirmed, taken, had,

---

[a] See Lawrence's Wheaton, ed. 1863, p. 1003; Wharton's Int. Law Digest, § 109, and same author's State Trials, pp. 20, 21.

[b] See Lewis on Foreign Jurisdiction, p. 11.

or done, by or before any such officer, when certified under his hand and seal of office, shall be as valid, and of like force and effect within the United States, to all intents and purposes, as if administered, sworn, affirmed, taken, had, or done, by or before any other (*sic*) person within the United States duly authorized and competent thereto.'

"And it is finally provided that ' if any person shall wilfully and corruptly commit perjury, or by any means procure any person to commit perjury in any such oath, affirmation, affidavit, or deposition, within the intent and meaning of any act of Congress now or hereafter made, such offender may be charged, proceeded against, tried, convicted, and dealt with in any district of the United States, in the same manner, in all respects, as if such offense had been committed in the United States, before any officer duly authorized therein to administer or take such oath, affirmation, affidavit, or deposition, and shall be subject to the same punishment and disability therefor as are or shall be prescribed by any such act for such offense; and any document purporting to have affixed, impressed, or subscribed thereto or thereon the seal and signature of the officer administering or taking the same in testimony thereof, shall be admitted in evidence without proof of any such seal or signature being genuine or of the official character of such person; and if any person shall forge any such seal or signature, or shall tender in evidence any such document with a false or counterfeit seal or signature thereto, knowing the same to be false or counterfeit, he shall be deemed and taken to be guilty of a misdemeanor, and on conviction shall be imprisoned not exceeding three years nor less than one year, and fined in a sum not to exceed three thousand dollars, and may be charged, proceeded against, tried, convicted, and dealt with, therefor, in the district where he may be arrested or in custody.'

" I am not aware that any case has ever arisen to require a judicial construction of this act, but, as it is generally understood,[a] it is not confined in its operation to citizens of the United States, but applies as well to aliens committing the designated offenses; and it has sometimes been referred to as an instance of the assertion by the United States of a general international right to try and punish aliens for acts done in a foreign country. It is not difficult to show that such a view of the statute is not warranted either by its terms or by the scope or results of its operation. It is not even necessary to its justification, upon principles of international law, to adopt the reasoning of Attorney-General Williams (14 Op. 285), who, referring to the law in question, affirmed its international validity on the ground that ' according to international law, the domicile of an embassador, minister extraordinary, or consul is a part of the territory he represents for many pur-

---

[a] Wharton's Cr. Law, § 276; Williams, Attorney-General, 14 Op. 285.

poses.' . . . But the international validity of the act of 1856 does not, in my judgment, rest solely, nor even in the main, on that ground.

" It is to be observed that the act relates solely to certain officers, known to international law, who, upon the recognition and with the consent of the governments of foreign countries, discharge there the functions of official representatives of the Government of the United States. One of those functions is the performance of the official acts enumerated in the statute of 1856, namely, the taking of oaths, etc., and the performance of notarial acts, for use in the United States. And as these acts are performed under the laws of the United States, not only does the person who appears before a secretary of legation or a consular officer for any of the purposes enumerated in the act of 1856 submit himself to the laws of the United States to that extent, but if he swears falsely or does any other thing in contravention of the act, he violates a law to whose execution in its territory the foreign government has consented. The act contains, therefore, neither an assertion of a general right to punish aliens for acts done by them outside of the United States, nor even an assertion of such a right to punish them for acts so done against the Government of the United States, to say nothing of acts merely against its citizens.[a]

" The general rule that the laws of a nation have no binding force, except as to citizens, outside of the national territory, actual or constructive, was again laid down by the Supreme Court in 1824, in the case of the Apollon, 9 Wheaton, 362. In that case, Mr. Justice Story, speaking for the court, said :

" ' The laws of no nation can justly extend beyond its own territories, except so far as regards its own citizens. They can have no force to control the sovereignty or rights of any other nation, within its own jurisdiction. And, however general and comprehensive the phrases used in our municipal laws may be, they must always be restricted, in construction, to places and persons upon whom the legislature have authority and jurisdiction.'

" In a still later case heard before him in the circuit court of the United States at Boston,[b] Mr. Justice Story again had occasion to consider and decide the question of jurisdiction over offenses committed outside of the national territory. In this case the defendant, the master of an American whale ship, was indicted for manslaughter, by shooting at and killing a man on board of another and foreign vessel in the Society Islands. It appeared that the shot was fired by the defendant from his own vessel, and took effect as above described. Taking the view that, although the shot was fired from

[a] The statutes of the United States do provide for the punishment of consular officers who commit criminal acts abroad. (Mr. Day, Assist. Sec. of State, to Mr. Hinton, Nov. 17, 1897, 222 MS. Dom. Let. 480.)

[b] United States v. Davis (1837), 2 Sumner C. C. 482.

the American vessel, the crime was, in contemplation of law, committed ' where the shot took effect,' the learned judge said:

" ' Of offenses committed on the high seas on board of foreign vessels not being a piratical vessel, but belonging to persons under the acknowledged government of a foreign country, this court has no jurisdiction under the act of 1790, ch. 36, § 12. That was the doctrine of the Supreme Court in United States *v.* Palmer, (3 Wheat. R. '610), and United States *v.* Klintock (5 Wheat. 144), and United States *v.* Holmes (5 Wheaton, 412); applied, it is true, to another class of cases; but in its scope embracing the present. *We lay no stress on the fact that the deceased was a foreigner. Our judgment would be the same if he had been an American citizen.* We decide the case wholly on the ground that the schooner was a foreign vessel, belonging to foreigners, and at the time under the ackknowledged jurisdiction of a foreign government.'

" It would be useless to attempt to collect all the declarations and applications by the State courts of the principle that penal laws have no extraterritorial force; and I shall quote the language of only a few cases, to mark the uniform current."

> John B. Moore, Report on Extraterritorial Crime, 22–37, 51–57, 63–68; also, For. Rel. 1887, 770–781, 790–793, 798–801. Following the passages above quoted are citations of Gilbert *v.* Stedman (Conn. 1792), 1 Root 403; State *v.* Grady (1867), 34 Conn. 118; People *v.* Wright (New York, 1804), 2 Caine's Rep. 213; Charles *v.* People (1848), 1 Comstock, 180; People *v.* Noelke (1883), 94 N. Y. 137; Green *v.* State (1880), 66 Ala. 40; State *v.* Knight (North Carolina, 1799), Taylor's Rep. 65; State *v.* Carter (N. J., 1859), 3 Dutcher, 499; Johns *v.* State (1862), 19 Ind. 421; State *v.* Chapin (1856), 17 Ark. 561; Haven *v.* Foster (Mass.), 9 Pick. 112; State *v.* Moore (N. H.), 6 Foster 448; In re Carr, 28 Kan. 1. See also Simpson *v.* State (Ga.), 17 S. E. 984, 22 L. R. A. 248; State *v.* Morrow (S. C.), 18 S. E. 853; State *v.* Bailey, 50 Ohio St. 636, 31 Ohio L. J. 106, 36 N. E. 233; State *v.* Hall, 114 N. C. 909, 19 S. E. 602; Field *v.* Bennett, London Times, July 27 and Dec. 16, 1886; In re Trufort, London Times, July 27, 1887; Castrique *v.* Imrie, L. R. 4 H. L. 414; Godard *v.* Gray, L. R. 6 Q. B. 139.

> An examination is also made of the proceedings of the Institut de Droit International, as found in the Revue de Droit Int. IX. 461 et seq.; XI. 308 et seq.; Annuaire de l'Institut (1880), 50 et seq.; and of the following publicists: Fiore, Droit Int. Privé (Paris, 1885), I. 408; Fiore, Droit Pénal Int. (Paris, 1880), 94; Phillimore, IV. 707; Wheaton (Dana's ed.), 180; Hall, Int. Law (2nd ed.), 190; Story, Confl. of Laws (5th ed.), 984; Bar, Int. Law (Edinburgh, 1883), 626; Field, Int. Code, §§ 643, 644; Wharton, Confl. of Laws (2nd ed.), § 809; Woolsey, Int. Law, §§ 20*a*, 20*b*, 76, 77; Lewis, For. Juris. 29; Heffter, Int. Law, § 36; Heffter, Criminalrecht, §§ 25–27; M. Faustin Hélie, Traité de l'Instruction Criminelle, II. §§ 127, 128; Pradier-Fodéré, Traité de Droit Int. III. § 1840.

> See also Attorney-General *v.* Kwok-a-Sing (1873), L. R. 5 P. C. 179; Case of Carl Vogt, Moore on Extradition, I. 135.

See L'Affaire Cutting, by M. Albéric Rolin, Rev. de Droit Int. (1888), XX.
559; A Continental Review of the Cutting Case, Am. Law Rev. (May–
June, 1889), XXIII. 329; L'Affaire Cutting, by Señor José M. Gamboa,
of Mexico, Rev. de Droit Int. XXII. 234.

IV. *JURISDICTION OVER PORTS.*

1. Entrance of Foreign Vessels.

§ 203.

" It is consistent with the just principles, as it is with the interests, of the United States to receive the vessels of all countries into their ports, to whatever party belonging, and under whatever flag sailing, pirates excepted, requiring of them only the payment of the duties, and obedience to the laws while under their jurisdiction, without adverting to the question whether they had committed any violation of the allegiance or laws obligatory on them in the countries to which they belonged, either in assuming such flag, or in any other respect."

> Mr. Monroe, Sec. of State, to Chev. de Onis, Span. min., Jan. 19, 1816, Am. State Pap. For. Rel. IV. 424, 426.

" You will state that this Government does not question the right of every nation to prescribe the conditions on which the vessels of other nations may be admitted into her ports.   That, nevertheless, those conditions ought not to conflict with the received usages which regulate the commercial intercourse between civilized nations.   That those usages are well known and long established, and no nation can disregard them without giving just cause of complaint to all other nations whose interests would be affected by their violation.

" That the circumstance of an officer of a vessel having published, in his own country, matters offensive to a foreign government does not, according to those usages, furnish a sufficient cause for excluding such vessel from the ports of the latter. . . .

" That the steamers employed in transporting the mail from this country to Havana, being in the employment of Government, and placed by law, to a certain extent, under its control, partake, in some degree, of the character of public vessels."

> Mr. Conrad, Acting Sec. of State, to Mr. Barringer, Oct. 28, 1852, MS. Inst. Spain, XIV. 369.

" I have received your No. 77 of the 13th ultimo, in which you inclose a copy of a note from the Haitian minister of foreign affairs complaining of the presence of two American schooners at Grand-Gosier, a port of the Republic of Haiti not open to foreign commerce.

" The general tenor of your reply, a copy of which you inclose, is approved.

" If the presence of the vessels in question in a port not open to trade was not due to stress of weather or some other of the exceptional circumstances provided for in the treaty of 1864 between the United States and Haiti, and was therefore not privileged, the enforcement of the revenue laws of the latter Government would seem to be incumbent upon its authorities.

" The Government of the United States and its representatives in Haiti can have no responsibility for unlawful acts of American vessels committed beyond its jurisdiction and within that of another sovereign power; our only concern is to see that any proceedings against such offenders are conducted in accordance with law and conformably with such treaty stipulations as may be in force."

> Mr. Blaine, Sec. of State, to Mr. Douglass, minister to Hayti, July 2, 1890,
> For. Rel. 1890, 530.
> The correspondence of Mr. Douglass with the Haytian minister of foreign
> affairs is printed in the same volume, p. 528 et seq.

While it was permissible, under the law of nations, for China, during the French-Chinese war, to sink obstructions in Canton River for the purpose of preventing the access of French men-of-war to Canton, such obstructions can only be retained as long as needed for belligerent purposes. Their removal after peace is required, not merely by the treaties entered into by China making Canton an open port, but by the law of nations.

> See infra, § 1286.

Unless closed by local law the ports of a friendly nation are considered as open to the public ships of all powers with whom it is at peace, and they are supposed to enter such ports, and to remain in them while allowed to remain, under the protection of the government of the place. The implied license under which such vessel enters a friendly port may reasonably be construed, and, it seems to the court, ought to be construed, as containing an exemption from the jurisdiction of the sovereign within whose territory she claims the rights of hospitality.

> The Exchange v. McFaddon, 7 Cranch, 116.

The hospitality of the ports of the United States, when a neutral, is extended equally to the vessels of each belligerent when visiting for purposes of convenience, or when driven to take refuge from storms or a superior naval force.

> Mr. Clay, Sec. of State, to Mr. Tacon, Oct. 29, 1827, MS. Notes to For.
> Leg. III. 394; Mr. Clay to Mr. Rebello, Apr. 8, 1828, id. IV. 7.

" I have the honor to acknowledge the receipt of your notes of the 6th and 7th instant, in further reference to the approaching visit of the United States vessels in the Mediterranean to the Turkish ports of the Levant.

"As was stated to you by Mr. Gresham on the 5th, and as I had the pleasure to say to you on the 6th instant, the intended visit of our ships is without any unfriendly purpose.   Their presence at the ports of the Syrian, Aleppan, and Adanan coasts will, however, afford an opportunity to learn whether there is just ground for the apprehensions of insecurity of life and property which our citizens in that region have expressed, and which have called forth the positive assurances of the Porte that full safety will be guaranteed them, with enjoyment of all their residential and professional rights, in which sense I am informed instructions have been telegraphed by the Porte to the valis of the several Levantine provinces as well as in the interior of Asia Minor."

> Mr. Uhl, Acting Sec. of State, to Mavroyeni Bey, Turkish min., April 8, 1895, For. Rel. 1895, II. 1250.

" I have the honor to acknowledge the receipt of your excellency's note of the 8th instant and to communicate to you the substance of a dispatch I have just received from His Excellency Saïd Pasha, according to which the visit of the American squadron in Ottoman waters can naturally only be considered by the Sublime Porte in the same light as those which the ships of war of the other Powers are in the habit of making annually to Ottoman ports.   His excellency adds that the fears of want of security alleged by some American citizens have no foundation in fact, and that these groundless fears are the work of those who are endeavoring, for certain subversive objects, to show to the world an abnormal situation which does not exist in reality."

> Mavroyeni Bey, Turkish min., to Mr. Gresham, Sec. of State, April 30, 1895, For. Rel. 1895, II. 1250.

" You announce the view of His Excellency Saïd Pasha, that this visit ' can naturally only be considered by the Sublime Porte in the same light as those which the ships of war of the other Powers are in the habit of making annually to Ottoman ports,' and communicate his excellency's further declaration that the security of American citizens in the Turkish dominions is not threatened.

" I do not understand that the position of the United States naval vessels in Turkish waters is to be defined by the especial relations or functions of ships of war of European Powers under their existing treaty obligations with regard to Turkish affairs.   Abstaining from intermixture in the internal matters of other states, this Government employs its naval agencies abroad only for keeping up the usual courtesies of friendly intercourse and for the protection of American citizens and American interests in other countries.   Performance of this latter function is alike the right and duty of every sovereign state. The state so acting can alone be the judge of the occasion therefor, and may not be called upon to account for the course it may consider wise or necessary."

> Mr. Uhl, Acting Sec. of State, to Mavroyeni Bey, Turkish min., June 6, 1895, For. Rel. 1895, II. 1251.

2. JURISDICTION OVER MERCHANT VESSELS.

(1) APPLICATION OF LOCAL LAW.

§ 204.

" The jurisdiction of every independent nation over the merchant vessels of other nations lying within its own harbors is absolute and exclusive."

> Mr. Buchanan, Sec. of State, to Mr. Wise, min. to Brazil, Sept. 27, 1845, MS. Inst. Brazil, XV. 119.
>
> May 6, 1891, the minister of the United States at Santiago was instructed to ask the Chilean Government to give all proper consideration to a request of the Central and South American Telegraph Company that their repair steamer Relay might be as far as possible exempted from entry and clearance, the certification of papers, and other formalities useless in her case, but productive of delay.   (For. Rel. 1891, 120.)
>
> As to the subjection of merchant vessels, their officers, crew, and passengers, in foreign ports, to the local jurisdiction, see Alex. Porter Morse, 42 Alb. L. J. 345.

In the case of William Bush, steward of the American barque *Childe Harold*, who was arrested on board that vessel, at Havana, on a charge of having delivered various packages of papers calculated to create an insurrectionary spirit among the inhabitants of Cuba, the Department of State said: " The American masters in the port of Havana . . . are entirely mistaken in supposing that it would be a violation of the national flag, and national honor, to arrest one of the crew of a merchant vessel, which had voluntarily entered that port, for a crime committed within the local jurisdiction."

> Mr. Buchanan, Sec. of State, to Mr. Campbell, consul at Havana, Nov. 1, 1848, 10 MS. Disp. to Consuls, 493, citing Schooner Exchange *v.* McFaddon, 7 Cranch, 144, 156, and adding : " In the United States we should be in a sad condition . . . if all crimes committed on board of foreign merchant vessels in our numerous ports should pass unpunished and all criminals who could make their escape on board such vessels should be protected from arrest."
>
> The arrest of an American citizen on an American vessel in foreign territorial waters, on process issuing from a competent court, presents no ground for a demand for redress.   (Mr. Buchanan, Sec. of State, to Mr. Jordan, Jan. 23, 1849, 37 MS. Dom. Let. 98.)

In the case of the alleged abduction of certain seamen from the American whale ship *Addison* by the marine governor at Valparaiso, which was reported by Mr. Peyton, American minister to Chile, Mr. Webster stated that, while no opinion could be formed of the case sufficiently definite in all particulars, the proceeding on the part of the Chilean authorities seemed to be arbitrary and not justified by any apparent necessity. It was stated by the Chilean Government that the seamen in question, who had been shipped in Chile, being discontented with the treatment they received on board the *Addison*, invoked the intervention of the marine governor, who had first sought to prevail upon them to remain with the ship, but, as they insisted on leaving it, did not allow them to go ashore, but transferred them to the national frigate *Chile*. It was alleged that the Chilean Government, being in need of men for its navy, for that reason impressed the men into its service; but this the Chilean Government denied. With reference to the allegation in question, Mr. Webster said: "Those governments which assert a right to the services of their subjects, who may be seamen on board of the vessels of other nations, do not often exercise this right by taking them from such vessels in time of peace. The Department, however, was not aware that Chile claimed the right even in time of war. The sudden use of the power, even in her own waters, at a period of profound peace, and without justifiable necessity, would be an act at variance with the comity of nations for which her Government may justly be held responsible. It is presumed that the impressment was not authorized by any law of Chile, and that the sailors had not offended against any law of that Republic. If, however, the circumstance that two of the seamen were Chileans might afford some palliation for the proceding, the fact that one of them was a Frenchman heightens its arbitrary character. If we were quietly to submit to this, we could not remonstrate if the many English sailors on board our merchant vessels at Havana, or Rio de Janeiro, were to be removed from them to gratify the caprices of Spanish or Brazilian officers, or to make up any alleged deficiency in the crews of vessels under their command. Such acts would embarrass commercial enterprise, and engender a feeling in this country at variance with that good understanding with foreign governments which we wish to preserve, so far as the most patient moderation and forbearance compatible with a just regard for our interests will allow."

> Mr. Webster, Sec. of State, to Mr. Peyton, min. to Chile, July 2, 1851, S. Ex. Doc. 27, 34 Cong. 1 sess. 100 ; MS. Inst. Chile, XV. 90.

Merchant vessels in port are subject to the police law of the port.

> Mr. Everett, Sec. of State, to Mr. Ingersoll, Feb. 17, 1853, MS. Inst. Great Britain, XVI. 192.

See an article on " Jurisdiction over Foreign Ships in Territorial Waters,"
by Charles Noble Gregory, Michigan Law Review (Feb. 1904), vol. 2,
No. 5.

"A copy of your dispatch in relation to the sailor Francis Boyle,
under date of August 5th, addressed to the Hon. D. D. Bernard, late
minister plenipotentiary and envoy extraordinary, has been transmitted by him to this Department.

" It appears, so far as the facts have been presented to the Department, that Francis Boyle, the sailor above mentioned, belonged to the
crew of the ship *Talleyrand*, an American vessel, commanded by Captain Young, lying on the 2d of August in the port of the free city of
Hamburg; that, on this day, the Hamburg police went on board the
said vessel, during the absence of the captain, and, under pretence of
his having been concerned in a riot on shore, arrested Francis Boyle,
who held at the time a protection as a citizen of the United States, and
who was so designated on the crew list; that the cause assigned for
the arrest was merely a pretence, since, in point of fact, it was done at
the instigation of the Prussian authorities of Stettin who forwarded
a requisition for the sailor, as being a Prussian by birth, and as such
liable to military service; that it was alleged by the Prussian minister,
and the chief of the police at Hamburg, that his ' protection ' could not
shield him, as it was assumed by them that the said Boyle, not having
been five years in the United States, could not be a citizen thereof;
and, finally, that the chief of police, after declaring that he must
surrender the man to the Prussian authorities, having been deterred
from so doing by the energetic remonstrances of yourself and of Captain Young, referred the matter to the syndicus, in charge of foreign
affairs, by whom the sailor, after a detention of three days, was
liberated and sent back on board his vessel.

" These facts, as they are thus presented, exhibit a case of so gross
a violation of the rights of an American sailor, that I deem it unnecessary at this time to do more than to assure you that your active
exertions to prevent the consummation of a high-handed outrage
deserve and have received the strong approbation of the President.

" It is for the authorities of the so-called ' Republic and Free Hanseatic City of Hamburg ' to determine how it may affect the commerce of that flourishing state, to permit their police officers to become the instruments of foreign nations in acts of violence and oppression, and upholding them in their entry, under a false pretext, on
board of an American vessel, lying peacefully at their wharves
engaged in commercial transactions under the sanction of solemn
treaty stipulations, and arrest one of its crew, shipped as an American sailor, holding an American protection and relying upon it, and
upon the flag, which floated over him, as his safeguards from all
illegal acts.

" It is for the Government of the United States to determine what steps it will take to vindicate its sovereignty, violated in the person of one under its protection, and to make known its determination to protect those who place themselves under the banner of the Republic.

" I do not deem it necessary at the present time to enter into any argument as to the question whether Francis Boyle was or was not a native-born citizen of the United States, whether he had been naturalized or had not resided five years in the United States, as contended by the Prussian authorities. The principles heretofore laid down, and acted upon by this Government, in regard to the citizenship of *seamen* are plain and well settled and require no elaborate vindication. The various questions which have arisen in respect to the protection to be extended to those who have taken the incipient steps to become American citizens, do not apply to them.

" The rule laid down by the distinguished person who first held the office of Secretary of State, Mr. Jefferson, was, ' that the vessel being American shall be evidence that the seamen on board are such,' and fifty years afterwards it was restated, with no less precision by one of the most eminent of American statesmen, one of my predecessors, that ' in every regularly documented merchant vessel the crew who navigate it will find their protection in the flag which is over them.'

" This is the principle which will hereafter, certainly not less than heretofore, be maintained, in its fullest extent, by the Government of the United States."

> Mr. Marcy, Sec. of State, to Mr. Bromberg, consul at Hamburg, Sept. 1, 1853, 17 MS. Desp. to Consuls, 70.

"As to the jurisdiction over offenses committed on board of a merchant vessel by the officers or company of the vessel, towards each other, while in the harbor or waters of a foreign power, there is considerable diversity of opinions. Some nations yield the jurisdiction in such cases, and some assert it.

" If the United States claim jurisdiction over all offenses committed on board of foreign private vessels in their harbors or waters, they cannot, with consistency, assert the right to have their citizens exempt from the jurisdiction of the local authorities when they commit similar offenses in foreign ports.

" This question of jurisdiction has been under the consideration of the Supreme Court of the United States. The views expressed by that court are those which this Government approves, and is disposed to abide by in its intercourse with foreign nations.

"As a general rule, the jurisdiction of a nation is exclusive and absolute within its own territories, of which harbors and littoral waters are as clearly a part as the land. Restrictions may be imposed upon it by treaties and a few have been yielded by common consent, and thus have come to be regarded as rules of international law.

" There is nothing in our treaty with Peru which debars her from taking cognizance of such an offense as is imputed to Captain Adams. Our right to withdraw him from her general jurisdiction over offenses committed within her territories must be derived, if we have such a right, from the law of nations."

> Mr. Marcy, Sec. of State, to Mr. Clay, Aug. 31, 1855, MS. Inst. Peru, XV. 175.
>
> In the course of the same instruction, Mr. Marcy said :
>
> " We should undoubtedly deny the right of any foreign power to demand the exemption from trial and punishment by our courts, of one of its subjects, who had committed a crime on board of a foreign trading vessel in one of our harbors, though the offense should be one which only affected the officers, crew, or company of that vessel. Circumstances might render it proper to forego the exercise of the right to try such an offender, but still the right would exist, and it would be at our option to yield or enforce the exercise of it.
>
> " This being our position towards all nations where treaty stipulations do not interfere, they can hold the same position towards us without our being able to gainsay it." •
>
> Where there has been no concession by treaty or otherwise a government possesses jurisdiction over merchant vessels in its waters. (Mr. Marcy, Sec. of State, to Mr. Dobbin, Sec. of Navy, April 21, 1856, 45 MS. Dom. Let. 212.)

The jurisdictional rights of consuls in Brazil were regulated by a decree of November 8, 1851, which conceded to them a certain civil and criminal cognizance of matters arising between members of the crews of vessels of their respective countries, but provided (art. 15) : " When a foreign merchant vessel shall be lying within any of the ports of Brazil the criminal and police jurisdiction of the respective consular agents shall not extend to high crimes or to those that may in any manner disturb public tranquillity or particularly affect any inhabitant of the country."   It was held that the United States consul at Rio de Janeiro possessed under this decree no jurisdiction over an offense committed on the American vessel *Nestorian* against two persons named Davis and Barbosa, who were neither members of the crew nor citizens of the United States.

> Mr. Marcy, Sec. of State, to Mr. Trousdale, min. to Brazil, Oct. 11, 1856, MS. Inst. Brazil, XV. 254.

A deserter from the British army, who embarked on board the American vessel *American Eagle*, at Malta, was, on her arrival at Palermo, taken from her by the local police.   He was subsequently released under orders from the Italian and British Governments. The American minister at Rome having suggested that the question of the right of search was involved in the matter, the Department of State replied : " It is understood that the vessel was within Italian jurisdiction, when the deserter was removed from her.   The right of the Italian authorities to search a vessel in their ports for a person charged with crime is entire, unless it shall have been surrendered by treaty, which was not the fact in this instance."

> Mr. Fish, Sec. of State, to Mr. Marsh, min. to Italy, No. 517, May 2, 1876, MS. Inst. Italy, I. 527.
>
> Mr. Fish further said: "Though the deserter did not prove to be amenable to the jurisdiction of the local authorities, as he was arrested by them at the instance of the British consul, they may have supposed that they were only discharging their duty in the matter. The release of the man by the command of their superior has undeceived them on that point and a repetition of the proceeding at that place is not probable."
>
> In a prior instruction, written in a reply to a dispatch in which the arrest of the person in question was first reported, Mr. Fish said: "The conduct of Mr. Fraser, the consul, in sending a written request to the master to allow search to be made for the deserter deserves reprehension. Your view of the case, as far as it has gone, seems to have been correct. There is not only no treaty between the United States and Great Britain providing for the surrender of military deserters, but the Department is not aware that there is any such treaty between Italy and that power. If there should be none, the act of the police of Palermo in taking the man from the vessel was supererogatory and illegal. As such, you will make it a subject of complaint to the Italian Government. You will also demand that the man be restored to the vessel if she should still be in Palermo, or that he be set at liberty." (Mr. Fish, Sec. of State, to Mr. Marsh, min. to Italy, No. 516, May 2, 1876, MS. Inst. Italy, I. 526.)

"The bark and her master being within the jurisdictional limits of the State of Georgia, the master undertook to resist by force civil process of the State issued against him and the owners of the vessel. For this offense against the State a criminal proceeding was instituted, and the captain was arrested. He then gave bond in the civil suit and the criminal prosecution was abandoned. There can, I presume, be no doubt that for the purposes of these legal proceedings the vessel and her master were at the time subject to the jurisdiction of Georgia, and he was bound to submit to the execution of process issued by her regular constituted authorities. I am, therefore, unable to see in the case any ground for complaint by the Spanish Government against the United States."

> Opinion of the Attorney-General quoted by Mr. Evarts, Sec. of State, in note to Mr. Mendez, Dec. 27, 1879, MS. Notes to Spain, X. 60.

"Referring to Mr. Drummond's note of the 4th ultimo, submitting for examination an extract from the 'Merchant Seamen (Payment of Wages and Rating) Act' 1880, 43 & 44 Victoria, chapter 16, which enacts certain penalties against unauthorized persons who without a permit go on board a vessel arriving at the end of her voyage, or who shall remain on such vessel after legal notice to leave; and referring also to the reply of this Department, dated the 16th ultimo, to the above-mentioned note, I now have the honor to inform you, that I have received a letter from my colleague, the Secretary of the Treasury, dated the 11th instant, in which he states that there is no provision of law in force in this country similar to that contained in the extract submitted by Mr. Drummond's note, and that therefore, in his opinion, this Government can on no reasonable ground ask that the provisions of the above-mentioned act should be extended to American vessels arriving in British waters."

> Mr. Evarts, Sec. of State, to Sir E. Thornton, Brit. min., Dec. 16, 1880, MS. Notes to Gr. Br. XVIII. 412.

One E. Menez, a native of Cuba, who had made a declaration of intention to become a citizen of the United States but had not been naturalized, went to Cuba as a member of the crew of an American merchant vessel. It was said that he had previously asked permission to revisit Cuba, which had been refused. While the vessel on which he was serving was lying at Sagua la Grande, the chief of police of the city applied to the United States consul for authority to take him from the vessel on charges of crime previously committed in Cuba. The consul communicated with the consul-general at Havana, who authorized the surrender if the charges were not political. The consul at Sagua inquired into the matter, and, coming to the conclusion that the charges, which comprised allegations of assassination and robbery as a bandit, were not political, authorized the master of the vessel to surrender him. With reference to these circumstances, the Department of State said: "A merchant vessel in port is within the jurisdiction of the country owning the port, with reference to offenses committed on shore or by any member of the crew on board when the peace of the port is disturbed. In the United States police officers have frequently gone on board vessels of foreign nations in harbor and arrested persons accused of crimes under our laws for whose arrest proper warrants were issued. A case of this kind with which you perhaps are familiar was decided by a Philadelphia court about a year ago which arose from the arrest of the master of an Austrian vessel."

> Mr. Frelinghuysen, Sec. of State, to Mr. Randall, M. C., March 14, 1884, 150 MS. Dom. Let. 276.
>
> For the case in Philadelphia above referred to, see For. Rel. 1883, 9–11; and infra, § 206, under the discussion of the treaty with Austria-Hungary of July 11, 1870, Art. XI.

" It may be safely affirmed that when a merchant vessel of one country visits the ports of another for the purposes of trade, it owes temporary allegiance and is amenable to the jurisdiction of that country, and is subject to the laws which govern the port it visits so long as it remains, unless it is otherwise provided by treaty.

"Any exemption or immunity from local jurisdiction must be derived from the consent of that country."

> Mr. Bayard, Sec. of State, to Mr. Hall, min to Central America, March 12, 1885, For. Rel. 1885, 82, 83.

" Replying to your telegram in relation to Lieut. Bell's application for permission to board British steamer *Berlin* and arrest seamen alleged to be deserters from U. S. Navy, and to your inquiry whether he should not obtain a warrant of arrest from civil authorities, I beg to say that no civil officer in the United States is authorized to issue a warrant under the circumstances. Lieut. Bell will, however, be directed by the Navy Department to invoke the aid of the police in making the arrest."

> Mr. Gresham, Sec. of State, to Sir J. Pauncefote, Sept. 9, 1893, MS. Notes to Gr. Br. XXII. 390.

Where a vessel registered in a foreign country and flying its flag becomes involved there in litigation, it can not, by a transfer to the American flag, under § 313 of the Consular Regulations, be withdrawn from the local jurisdiction for acts previously committed.

> Mr. Uhl, Acting Sec. of State, to Mr. Bartleman, chargé at Caracas, June 6, 1894, For. Rel. 1894, 793, 794.

The Turkish Government having expressed a wish that the diplomatic representative of the United States at Constantinople be instructed to direct the authorities within his jurisdiction to lend their aid and give necessary facilities to enable the Turkish authorities to watch incoming steamers, in order to prevent the landing at Constantinople of "Armenian anarchists, as well as dynamite, infernal machines, and explosives," the United States, while remarking that no steamers or other commercial vessels under the flag of the United States were known to ply between foreign ports and those of Turkey, carrying passengers or arriving under circumstances likely to give rise to the abuses complained of, said: " It is understood, however, that the Ottoman Government elaborately regulates the entry of persons and merchandise into the territory of the Empire, and if any attempt were made to clandestinely land men or munitions from a vessel under our flag, the officers of the United States would certainly interpose no obstacle to the due execution of the laws of Turkey by Turkish agents, or intervene further than to secure for any implicated citizen of the United States all rights and privileges to which he may be entitled in virtue of such citizenship, precisely the same as they would intervene to safeguard the interests of any American citizen found on board a vessel of another flag than ours and accused under like circumstances."

> Mr. Olney, Sec. of State, to Moustapha Bey, Turkish min., Nov. 11, 1896,
> For. Rel. 1896, 926–927.

Where a detention of a Prussian vessel in the port of New Orleans, during the late civil war, was caused by her resistance to the orders of the properly constituted authorities, whom she was bound to obey, she preferred such detention to a clearance upon the conditions imposed, it was ruled that her owner, a subject of Prussia, was not entitled to any damages against the United States under the law of nations or the treaty with that power of 1799.

> United States v. Diekelman, 92 U. S. 520.
> That a merchant vessel, unless by treaty stipulation, is not exempt from
> the local jurisdiction, see Taft, At. Gen., 1876, 15 Op. 178.

The rule, as laid down in the United States Navy Regulations, that a neutral vessel, captured as prize, is to wear her national flag till she is condemned, applies "*a fortiori* . . . in cases of customs seizures, where fines only are imposed and where no belligerency whatever exists. In the port of New York, and other of the countless harbors of the United States, are merchant vessels to-day flying the British flag which from time to time are liable to penalties for violations of customs laws and regulations. But I have yet to learn that any official, assuming, directly or indirectly, to represent the Government of the United States, would under such circumstances order down or forcibly haul down the British flag from a vessel charged with such irregularity; and I now assert that if such act were committed, this Government, after being informed of it, would not wait for a complaint from Great Britain, but would at once promptly reprimand the parties concerned in such misconduct and would cause proper expression of regret to be made."

> Mr. Bayard, Sec. of State, to Mr. Phelps, min. to England, Nov. 6, 1886,
> For. Rel. 1886, 362, 370.
> See, also, Mr. Bayard, Sec. of State, to Mr. West, Brit. min., Nov. 11, 1886,
> For. Rel. 1886, 425, 426.
> For the act in this case of hauling down the flag of a fishing vessel seized
> for breach of port rules an apology was made in a letter from the
> Canadian authorities forwarded by the British Government. See Sir
> L. West to Mr. Bayard, Dec. 7, 1886, For. Rel. 1886, 491.

May 29, 1897, Mr. Sherman, Secretary of State, in a note to the Spanish minister at Washington, requested an instant investigation of the complaint of the American mail steamship *Valencia*, chartered by the Ward Line of New York, that the vessel, when leaving Guantánamo Bay, was fired upon by the Spanish man-of-war *Reina Mer-*

cedes, then about two miles distant from the *Valencia,* first with a blank shot, and then with a solid shot which fell about 80 yards astern. The Spanish minister in reply explained that the *Valencia* was not at the time flying her flag, although the Spanish warship had one hoisted, and that the latter, " following the practice of all navies, confirmed her flag by firing a gun, and after the regular interval had passed she fired another shot." The minister referred to " repeated breaches of courtesy " by the steamers of the line in question, and asked that the attention of the owners be called to the subject in order that such incidents might be avoided. The master of the *Valencia* declared that when the man-of-war was sighted its ensign was not visible from the *Valencia's* position and that, as no signal was seen and as the vessels were not passing each other, the cruiser being abaft the beam of the *Valencia* on the port quarter, the master did not believe himself required to salute the cruiser with his flag, as he would have done had he met her on the usual course. Hence, when the first shot was fired, although it was heard on the *Valencia,* it was not supposed to be a call for colors; but when the second shot, within two minutes afterwards, was heard and was seen to fall so near, the master of the *Valencia,* realizing that the shots were intended for him, immediately hoisted his national flag, although no flag or signal even then was visible on the cruiser, which was, however, recognized by the master of the *Valencia.* Under these circumstances Mr. Sherman expressed the opinion that no discourtesy was intended by the captain of the *Valencia,* and that if he erred at all it was an excusable error of judgment. Mr. Sherman added: " However this may be, I am prepared to admit, in all frankness, that during the continuance of a civil war such as is now flagrant in the Island of Cuba, it would be extremely convenient, and perhaps a prudent precaution, for American ships legitimately resorting to Cuban waters to show their flag when sighting a Spanish cruiser within the 3-mile limit, even if a formal salute be not called for by the ordinary code of maritime ceremonial, and I shall so advise Messrs. James E. Ward & Co.

" With this statement the incident may be dismissed, but I can not refrain from commenting upon the recklessness of the Spanish commander's action. Upon your own showing, knowing the vessel to be the *Valencia* and in the temporary service of the Ward Line, and apparently moved by feeling toward that line because of supposed discourtesies suffered from other of its ships in the past, he fired upon the *Valencia* for no other purpose than to make her show her flag. How far this confessedly careless act comports with the interests and dignity of two great and friendly nations it is not necessary to consider, but the fact remains that the falling of a solid shot near the stern of an American ship under such circumstances imports wanton and unjustifiable peril to the citizens and property of a friendly state.

This Government has never admitted that life and property may be unnecessarily jeopardized by superior force, even when an offense against the revenue or other formal laws may have been committed by an American ship within a foreign jurisdiction, and it can not be expected to admit that one of its ships or those on board may be endangered because of a friendly foreign commander's ideas as to maritime punctilio. I must therefore repeat the hope expressed in my note of the 29th ultimo that such disagreeable incidents as this be not suffered to recur."

> Mr. Sherman, Sec. of State, to Mr. Dupuy de Lôme, Span. min. June 21, 1897, For. Rel. 1897, 504, 505–506.
>
> In a note of June 29, 1897, Mr. Dupuy de Lôme stated that at the time of the firing the cruiser was not aware of the indentity of the *Valencia*, and repelled any inference that the firing was caused from "a mere capricious point of honor." (For. Rel. 1897, 506.)

September 28, 1876, Sir Edward Thornton, British minister at Washington, communicated to the Department of State a copy of the merchant shipping act, 1876, and called attention to the clause with respect to the overloading and improper loading of foreign ships in the United Kingdom, and particularly to section 24, imposing certain penalties in case of the arrival of a ship, whether British or foreign, between the last day of October and the 6th of April, at any port of the United Kingdom from any port out of the United Kingdom, carrying deck cargo in violation of the act; and in subsequent notes of January 22 and 29, 1877, Sir Edward transmitted reports made by officers of the board of trade with reference to the alleged infraction of section 24 by certain American vessels.

The Department of State replied that, as attention was thus particularly called to the questions under section 24, it seemed proper to state that the right to impose penalties on the master or owner of an American vessel, sailing from a port of the United States, for the manner in which the cargo was laden or stored, was of so doubtful a character that, however wise or beneficent the intent of the act might be, the Government of the United States "cannot but invite the attention of Her Majesty's Government particularly thereto, before further steps are taken in Great Britain to enforce obedience to the law in these particular cases, and before any steps be taken toward the enforcement of fines in these or similar cases." [a]

The representations of the United States "appear to have received the careful attention of the Government of Great Britain, and toward

The Plimsoll act.

---

[a] Mr. Fish, Sec. of State, to Sir Edward Thornton, Brit. min., Feb. 10, 1877, MS. notes to Gr. Br. XVII. 331; Mr. Fish, Sec. of State, to Mr. Pierrepont, min. to England, Feb. 26, 1877, MS. Inst. Gr. Br. XXIV. 510; Mr. F. W. Seward, Act. Sec. of State, to Mr. Pierrepont, April 10, 1877, id. 543.

the close of the year 1877, the minister of the United States at London
received a note from Lord Derby, justifying the provisions of the act
adverted to, which had been specially made the subject of complaint,
as not inconsistent with the principles of international law, or with
the practice of nations in such matters," and expressing the hope that
the United States would " yield the provisions of the act mentioned
a friendly support, by enjoining its observance on the part of American shippers and owners of vessels, in the interest of humanity."
The subject thereafter " failed to become one of special action on the
part of the United States." [a]

In 1886, the British minister having reported the arrival of an
American vessel in London with a deck cargo of heavy wood in contravention of section 24, he was advised that the Secretary of the
Treasury had called the attention of collectors of customs to the law,
with a view to notifying masters of vessels sailing from the United
States of its provisions. It was observed, however, that it was not
to be understood that the notification would reach all such masters,
and that therefore the action of Her Majesty's Government in such
cases arising in the future should not be based on the supposition that
the masters of all American vessels were acquainted with the law.[b]

By section 1 of the act of February 13, 1893, 27 Stat. 445, known
as the Harter Act, it was declared to be unlawful for
Shipping contracts. the representative or owner of any vessel transporting
merchandise " from or between ports of the United States and foreign
ports " to insert in any bill of lading any clause for relief from
liability for damage arising from negligence in the proper loading,
stowage, custody, care, or delivery of property so transported. It
was held in the case of a British vessel trading between New York
and ports in the West Indies and South America, in respect to certain
merchandise shipped from Buenos Ayres to New York, that the provisions of the act overrode and nullified any such stipulation in a
bill of lading.

---

[a] Mr. Evarts, Sec. of State, to Count Lewenhaupt, Swedish & Nor. min. Jan.
20, 1880, MS. Notes to Sw. & Nor. VII. 187.

[b] Mr. Bayard, Sec. of State, to Mr. West, Brit. min., April 26, 1886, MS. Notes
to Gr. Br. XX. 243. See, also, Mr. Bayard to Mr. West, April 9, 1886, id. 223.

As to the validity of legislation requiring all vessels sailing from the ports of
a country to carry a certain equipment for the safety of passengers in case of
shipwreck, see Mr. Fish, Sec. of State, to Gen. Schenck, min. to England, Jan. 6,
1855, 10 Stat. 715, secs. 1, 3, and 15, and the case of the Swedish brig *Neura*, 19
How. 92 ; to the British Merchant Shipping Act, 1854, 17 and 18 Vic. sec. 292 ;
and to the Passengers, Harbors, and Navigation Act, 1865, of the Colony of Victoria. See, also, as to complaints concerning the last-named act, Mr. Fish, Sec.
of State, to Mr. Pierrepont, min. to England, Feb. 26, 1877, and Mr. F. W.
Seward, Act. Sec. of State, to Mr. Pierrepont, April 10, 1877, MS. Inst. Gr. Br.
XXIV. 510, 543.

Knott *v.* Botany Mills (1900), 179 U. S. 69

"Before the act of Congress of February 13, 1893, c. 105 (27 Stat. 445), known as the Harter Act, it was the settled law of this country, as declared by this court, that common carriers, by land or sea, could not by any form of contract exempt themselves from responsibility for loss or damage arising from negligence of their servants, and that any stipulation for such exemption was void as against public policy; although the courts in England and in some of the States held otherwise. Railroad Co. *v.* Lockwood, 17 Wall. 357; Liverpool Steam Co. *v.* Phoenix Ins. Co., 129 U. S. 397; Compania La Flecha *v.* Brauer, 168 U. S. 104, 117, 118. In many lower courts of the United States it has been held, independently of the Harter Act, that a stipulation that a contract should be governed by the law of England in this respect was void, and could not be enforced in a court of the United States; but the point has not been decided by this court. Nor is it necessary for us now to decide that point, because these bills of lading were issued since the Harter Act, and we are of opinion that the case is governed by the express provisions of that act." (Id. 71–72.)

The courts of the United States will not uphold exemptions from liability stipulated in shipping contracts where such exemptions violate a rule of public policy.

The Kensington (1902), 183 U. S. 263; The Germanic (1905), 196 id. 589.

In December, 1893, the Department of State, in a note to the French embassy, drew attention to the fact that changes in French legislation as to the rules of admeasuring merchant vessels, made since the exchange of notes in 1888–1889, whereby it was agreed to accept as evidence of the fact the tonnage-measurement certificates issued by the respective Governments, a serious discrepancy had arisen between the French and American rules. The Department of State said that in view of this discrepancy, the arrangement of 1888–1889 could not be regarded as effectively continuing. The French Government offered to enter into an arrangement based on the reciprocal acceptance of special certificates of admeasurement issued by the proper authorities of either country according to the rules in force in the other. The United States replied that as by its legislation the tonnage of a vessel, not a vessel of the United States, was required to be ascertained in the manner provided by law for the measurement of vessels of the United States, it was impracticable to accept admeasurements made by French officers, since the law required admeasurement by an officer of the United States.

Admeasurement of vessels.

For. Rel. 1894, 215, 217.

For an arrangement in regard to the admeasurement of Norwegian vessels, see For. Rel. 1894, 636–645.

" The Secretary of the Treasury has referred to this Department your note to the Commissioner of Navigation (not dated) in which your request to be informed with regard to the views of the Government of the United States relative to the proposition of the London International Statistical Institute for convening an international commission for the establishment of uniform rules for the admeasurement of seagoing vessels.

"A similar inquiry was made of the Secretary of the Treasury by this Department in January last, and on the 30th of that month that official replied as follows:

" ' While the Government of the United States recognizes the utility of uniformity among commercial nations in the methods of admeasuring vessels and is willing to cooperate in any practical measure to establish such uniformity, at the present time it is disposed to believe that some more rapid progress toward the desired end can be effected through correspondence and the concentration of efforts in the lawmaking branches of the governments of the commercial nations interested than through the convocation of an international conference.

" ' It is confirmed in its belief by a review of the parliamentary history of the establishment of the regulations for admeasurement in vogue in the various countries subsequent to and based upon the adoption of the Moorsom system by Great Brltain in 1854.

" ' It deems applicable in part to the proposition for an international tonnage conference the conclusions of the international maritime conference of 1889 concerning the proposed establishment of a permanent international maritime commission. Those conclusions, to which the delegates from Belgium, Chile, France, Germany, Great Britain, Sweden, and the United States assented, were: " It seems to your committee that such a consulting body of experts would not serve the purpose for which it is intended to be created, viz, that of facilitating the introduction of reforms in maritime legislation, because the advice given by such a commission would not in any way enable the governments of the maritime nations to dispense with the necessity of considering the subjects laid before them, and laying the proposals made to them, if adopted, before the legislative bodies of the different states.

" ' " The consequence of instituting a body like that in question, on the contrary, would, it appears, be this: That merely another investigation of any scheme proposed with a view to reforming international maritime laws would have to be gone through before the opinions of the governments could be taken, and thus the course of procedure as it is now—by correspondence between the different governments—would be made more complicated instead of being simplified." '

" The Secretary of the Treasury concludes by observing that, so far as his Department is aware, the British Government has taken no steps to carry out the recommendations of the London International Statistical Institute."

> Mr. Gresham, Sec. of State, to Mr. Tavera, Austrian min., March 7, 1894, For. Rel. 1894, 48.
>
> See, in the same sense, Mr. Gresham, Sec. of State, to Mr. Le Ghait, Belg. min., Feb. 5, 1894, For. Rel. 1894, 53.

(2) QUESTIONS OF INTERNAL ORDER AND DISCIPLINE.

§ 205.

Consular jurisdiction depends on the general law of nations, existing treaties between the two governments affected by it, and upon the obligatory force and activity of the rule of reciprocity. French consular jurisdiction in an American port depends on the correct interpretation of the treaties existing between France and the United States, which limit it to the exercise of police over French vessels, and jurisdiction in civil matters in all disputes which may arise; and provide that such police shall be confined to the interior of the vessels, and shall not interfere with the police of our ports where the vessels shall be. They also provide that in cases of crimes and breaches of the peace the offenders shall be amenable to the judges of the country. The claim of the French envoy for the exercise of judicial power by the consul of his Government in the port of Savannah is not warranted by any existing treaties, nor by a rule of reciprocity which the Executive has power to permit to be exercised. " The principles of international law, as they are recognized in Europe, afford no warrant for the exercise of judicial power by consuls; and that the rights and duties of these functionaries depends, both for their authority and extent, upon the treaties subsisting between the governments respectively interchanging this species of commercial agents."

> Berrien, At.-Gen., 1830, 2 Op. 381.
>
> The opinion of Mr. Berrien related to the case of an officer of the French ship *Venus*, who was ordered by a justice of the peace at Savannah, Georgia, to be arrested on a complaint made by a seaman of assault and battery, committed on board the ship while she lay at anchor in the roadstead. The justice also took measures to compel the attendance of seven other members of the crew as witnesses. The master of the ship, in order to avoid the interruption of his voyage, paid a sum of money for the withdrawal of the suit and defrayed all costs. M. Roux de Rochelle, the French minister, complained of the proceeding, on the ground that, as the alleged offence took place on board the vessel and the peace of the port was not endangered, the generally admitted principles of consular jurisdiction were infringed by the local authorities; and he contended that "upon this ground, and

upon that of the uniform and authoritative practice in France in analogous cases, affecting American vessels and their crews in the ports of that country," the owners of the *Venus* had a good claim to reimbursement of expenses, and to demurrage for the detention of the vessel, by reason of the proceedings in question. (Mr. Brent, Acting Sec. of State, to Mr. Berrien, At. Gen., Sept. 3, 1830, 23 MS. Dom. Let. 454.)

A copy of Mr. Berrien's opinion was communicated to M. Roux, with the statement that it was not within the competency of the Executive to admit his claim. The only treaty between the two countries, it was observed, that could give any countenance to it was the convention of 1788, which had long since expired. It was added, however, that the United States would be willing to conclude a suitable arrangement on the subject. (Mr. Van Buren, Sec. of State, to M. Roux de Rochelle, French min., Jan. 27, 1831, MS. notes to For. Leg. IV. 354.)

" In the letter of Mr. Webster to Lord Ashburton, of the 1st August, 1842, the principles of the law of nations which apply to the subject were discussed with great clearness and ability. To that letter I refer you. It will be perceived that Mr. Webster does not ' propose the introduction of any new principle into the law of nations.' He contends that ' a vessel on the high seas, beyond the distance of a marine league from the shore, is regarded as part of the territory of the nation to which she belongs, and subjected exclusively to the jurisdiction of that nation; and consequently, if those who have charge of her endeavor, in good faith, to keep her at sea, that is, within that exclusive jurisdiction, and if, contrary to their will, she be forced within another jurisdiction by stress of weather, by violence, or other necessity, she does not cease to be within the jurisdiction of her own country.' In this case, however, such jurisdiction is not *exclusive* to all purposes. ' For any unlawful acts done by her while thus lying in port, and for all contracts entered into while there, by her master and owners, she and they must doubtless be answerable to the laws of the place.'

" Mr. Webster further contends that ' by the comity of the law of nations, and the practice of modern times, merchant vessels entering open ports of other nations for the purpose of trade, are presumed to be allowed to bring with them and to retain, for their protection and government, the jurisdiction and laws of their own country.' These, of course, extend both over persons and things, subject always to the laws of the place, in cases of crimes, contracts, &c., as above mentioned. The right here claimed is not in derogation of the sovereignty of the place where the vessels may be, but is presumed to be allowed by that sovereignty."

Mr. Upshur, Sec. of State, to Mr. Everett, Nov. 28, 1843, MS. Inst. Great Britain, XV. 177.

The letter of Mr. Webster, cited by Mr. Upshur, related to the case of the *Creole*.

" The difficulty which has arisen between you and the British authorities at Hong Kong has been duly considered and I am directed by the President to communicate to you his views thereon. . . .

" Most of the unpleasant occurrences which you have presented to the Department seem to have had their origin in the conflicting opinions between you and the British authorities as to your powers and rights as consul. You appear to have placed much reliance on the remarks of Mr. Webster in his letter to Lord Ashburton of August 1st 1842. The case he was discussing differed in an essential feature from that of the *Reindeer*. The *Creole* was taken forcibly by mutineers into a British port, and Mr. Webster seems to have considered her in a different situation from that she would have been in, had she voluntarily visited such port. If he meant to give a more general application to the rules he laid down, the authorities against him are so many and so strong as to render it impossible to sustain him. . . .

" Throughout the elaborate decision of the court in the case of the schooner *Exchange*, it is assumed that the jurisdiction of the country extends over a foreign merchant vessel in its harbors. There are several other cases, which announce and sustain the same principle, as to the jurisdiction of a country over a foreign merchant or private vessel in its harbor, . . . and the doctrine is approved by elementary writers. . . .

" There is in my mind no doubt that the State and Federal courts of this country, could if they chose to do so, and would, on any proper occasion, exercise jurisdiction over any foreign merchant vessel and its company in any of our ports, even in regard to transactions which might take place within our territory between the members of that company, and they would not yield to the claim of a foreign consul to surrender that jurisdiction as a matter of right. . . .

" It is true that France has, in this respect, made some liberal concessions in favor of private ships, but we must look to British concessions to justify the claim you asserted in the case of the *Reindeer*, as the transaction took place in a British port, and I have looked in vain for them. It is desirable, I think, that they should exist, particularly in remote countries, where annoyances to trade are more likely to occur by the interference of civil courts, but questions which you have raised must be settled upon the law as it is, rather than on what it ought to be. I am, however, disposed to think that the State governments of this Union would be unwilling to have the immunities of exterritoriality given to all the private or merchant ships, and their crews, which visit our numerous harbors, and we could not with propriety ask from other nations, in this respect, what we would not in turn grant to them. . . .

"The manner of conducting the prosecution was apparently exceptionable, and afforded an ostensible ground of complaint. Though there is a dispute about many of the facts with respect to this point in the case, it is not denied that officers of the police went on board of the *Reindeer*, and, without a written warrant, took John Madison from the vessel who had shipped as carpenter, and was there confined. Unusual as this proceeding appears, it is alleged that it was authorized by an existing law or ordinance, to which a particular reference was made, but a copy of it is not found among the papers sent to this Department, and I am not, therefore, able to say that it is not, in effect, what it is alleged to be.

"Having sovereign dominion over the place, British authority would be competent to make an ordinance conferring on police officers the right to enter a vessel in a British port and make an arrest of a person charged with an offence on board without any written process for that purpose.

"The proceedings, in this respect, appear to have been extraordinary, yet I am not able to pronounce them illegal.

"If obliged to yield the point, as I think we are, that the *Reindeer* and her crew, while in the harbor of Hong Kong, were subject to the civil authority of the place, we cannot question its right to take cognizance of the charge of Madison against Captain Nichols for the alleged battery and false imprisonment. I do not, therefore, perceive upon what ground the objection, which was taken in his behalf, to the jurisdiction of the court, can be sustained.

"It is to be regretted that Captain Nichols did not recognize the authority of the court and present to its consideration his defence. Had he taken that course and shown, as probably he could, that he had in his treatment of Madison done nothing more than proper discipline required, all subsequent unpleasant occurrences might have been avoided. . . .

"In the foregoing remarks I have considered the questions raised in this case with reference to strict international rights, for in this light only could they be properly regarded when made the subject of a national grievance for which redress is to be demanded.

"Though the strict right of the civil authority at Hong Kong to entertain Madison's complaint and investigate the charge against Captain Nichols cannot be successfully questioned, yet inasmuch as the affair related to the discipline on board of a foreign vessel, and the offence, if any there were, was an abuse of the captain's power, courtesy and national comity should have led the authorities at Hong Kong to decline to act in the case, referring the matter to the government to which the vessel belonged. Whether Captain Nichols had or had not exceeded the limits of the powers with which he was invested, as captain of the *Reindeer*, over the crew, in his treatment of Madison, might with great propriety have been left to the determination of the courts of the United States. Had the case been put on this ground, it is to be inferred from the letter of W. T. Mercer, esq., colonial secretary, of the 25th of October last, that the object you had in view might have been attained, but your denial of the jurisdiction of the civil court at Hong Kong brought up the question of strict right, and it appears to the President that the decision cannot be regarded as erroneous, though the consequences which have resulted from the interposition of the court are regretted."

> Mr. Marcy, Sec. of State, to Mr. Keenan, consul at Hong Kong, April 14, 1856, 21 Disp. to Consuls, 567, citing Schooner Exchange *v.* McFaddon, 7 Cranch, 135; Story, Conflict of Laws; Ortolan, Diplomatie de la Mer; Phillimore, Int. Law.

" This Government does not apply the doctrine of extraterritoriality to its private or merchant ships in foreign ports, except in cases where it has been conceded by treaty or established usage, and it does not pretend that it has been so conceded in criminal cases to American merchant vessels in British ports. . . .

" While each country can unquestionably exercise jurisdiction in its own ports over the private or merchant vessels of the other, it is presumed there is a mutual disposition on both sides not to exert it in a way which will interfere with the proper discipline of the ships of either nation. If every complaint of any individual of the crew of a vessel against the officers for ill-treatment is to be taken up by the civil authorities on shore, and these officers prosecuted as criminals, commercial intercourse will be subjected to very great annoyance and serious detriment."

> Mr. Marcy, Sec. of State, to Mr. Crampton, Brit. min., Apr. 19, 1856, MS. Notes to Great Britain, VII. 524.

In 1856 the American merchant vessel *Atalanta*, while on a voyage from Marseilles to New York, was obliged by the mutiny of her crew to put back to the former port. The revolt took place on the high seas outside the municipal jurisdiction of any government. On the return of the vessel to Marseilles the seamen were, on application of the United States consul, imprisoned by the local authorities on shore. Some of them were afterwards released with the assent of the consul, while six were, on his application, restored to the vessel for conveyance to the United States. Subsequently, in spite of the consul's remonstrances, the local authorities went on board the vessel, resumed possession of the prisoners, and replaced them in confinement on shore. The nationality of these prisoners does not certainly appear, but the tenor of the correspondence indicates that they were not citizens either of the United States or of France. It was agreed that the case did not come within the consular convention between the two countries, which was not construed as conferring on the consuls of either nation jurisdiction of crimes; nor was it claimed that merchant vessels of one nation enjoyed in the ports of other nations the privilege of extraterritoriality. The question in controversy was whether, when a crime had been committed on an American vessel on the high seas, the " crime being of the sole competency of the United States, and the ship is compelled by her contract of destination, by stress of weather, or by the crime itself, to touch at a French port, . . . the criminal may be forcibly withdrawn from the ship by the local authorities or by the order of the government." It was advised that the local authority, even if it might refuse to aid, could not lawfully interpose to defeat, the lawful confinement of members of the crew by the master, on board the ship, with the advice and approbation of the consul.

> Cushing, At. Gen., Sept. 6, 1856, 8 Op. 73. See, also, Lawrence's Wheaton (1863), 207, 1001 ; Mr. Marcy, Sec. of State, to Mr. Mason, min. to France, Sept. 8, 1856, MS. Inst. France, XV. 344.
>
> In accord, opinion of Mr. Grundy, At. Gen., in the case of the *Amistad*, Nov. 1839, 3 Op. 484.

" I can not account for the omission of my immediate predecessor to authorize you to give to the French Government an assurance that the same construction which was placed by it upon the 8th article of the consular convention between the United States and France of 1853, in adjusting the case of the mutineers of the *Atalanta*, would be given to that article by this Government if a similar case should occur with reference to a French vessel while within the ports of the United States. It may, however, be ascribed to the pressure of business consequent upon the close of the last session of Congress. The decision of the French Government in that case is in conformity with the opinion of the Attorney-General of the United States upon the subject, which opinion has been approved by this Government. Under these circumstances you are consequently authorized to give to Count Walenski on behalf of this Government the assurance above referred to, in conformity with the suggestion made in your No. 182 of the 27th of November last."

> Mr. Cass, Sec. of State, to Mr. Mason, min. to France, April 14, 1857, MS. Inst. France, XV. 359.
>
> It appears by this instruction that, although Art. VIII. of the consular convention, as Mr. Cushing stated, does not give consuls jurisdiction of crimes, the two Governments ultimately agreed to treat the detention of persons charged with crime on vessels of the two countries at sea, as coming within its spirit. By the terms of the article, consular officers have " exclusive charge of the internal order of the merchant vessels of their nation," and can alone take cognizance of " differences " arising, in port or at sea, between the officers and crews, particularly as to wages and contracts.

The local port authority has jurisdiction of acts committed on board of a foreign merchant ship while in port, provided those acts affect the peace of the port, but not otherwise; and its jurisdiction does not extend to acts internal to the ship, or occurring on the high seas.

The local authority has right to enter on board a foreign merchantman in port for the purpose of inquiry universally, but for the purpose of arrest only in matters within its ascertained jurisdiction.

> Cushing, At. Gen., 1856, 8 Op. 73.
>
> For an account of the cases of the Newton and the Sally, involving the question of the jurisdiction of United States consuls over crimes committed on board United States vessels in French ports, see 1 Phillimore Int. Law (3 ed.), 484.

" There is no doubt of the jurisdiction of our officers and tribunals to interfere in the way of prevention or of punishment in breaches of the peace occurring in American waters upon foreign vessels. There is no reason why our police, civil or naval, should hesitate to board a British vessel for the purpose of quelling a mutiny, attended with assaults upon the officers or violent resistance to the exercise of their legitimate authority—or subjecting refractory seamen to temporary confinement. The difficulty, however, is supposed to arise in cases where seamen simply refuse to work, and where confinement of them would reduce the vessel to a floating jail, without the power of motion. The remedy that is supposed to be wanted is a compulsion upon the men to do their duty; in other words, to enforce a specific obligation of their contract. No officer or tribunal of the United States has the capacity to apply such a remedy, except in execution of a treaty or convention, which seems necessary as the basis of laws of Congress regulating the mode of proceeding. A treaty is also necessary to justify the detention here of a foreign seaman upon the order of his consul, or otherwise than as a criminal offender.

"For any intervention beyond the limit thus indicated an agreement between the two Governments would seem to be requisite. I have to remark, however, that the question which I have discussed is purely a legal one, upon which I ought to reserve myself for consultation with the Attorney-General."

> Mr. Seward, Sec. of State, to Sir F. Bruce, Brit. min., Mar. 16, 1866, Dip. Cor. 1866, I. 231.
>
> This note referred to the case of the British bark Campsie, which, while on her way to sea, came to anchor in the Chesapeake Bay, about ninety miles below Baltimore. Next morning the men refused to weigh the anchors and declared that they would not proceed on the voyage. The captain, with the aid of a steamer, returned to Baltimore in order to secure the assistance of the British consul in putting the men in irons and getting to sea. The consul applied to the United States marshal, who, after consulting the district attorney, decided

that he could not interfere; and the municipal police would give no aid, as the matter was out of their jurisdiction. Subsequently, however, a United States revenue cutter put an armed boat's crew on board the bark, by whom she was taken to Norfolk, where the nine mutineers were put in jail. It was stated that Judge Underhill, of the United States district court at Norfolk, was of opinion that he could not put the men on trial; and the bark, after lying at Norfolk several days, sailed for Ireland, four of the mutineers having returned to duty. The remaining five were left behind and were set at liberty. It was stated that a few days later one of them acted as ringleader in a similar mutiny on the British bark *Kathleen*, fifteen miles below Baltimore, there being, as it appeared, an organized gang who pursued the practice of " bounty jumping," by shipping as sailors, getting advance pay, and then deserting or refusing to work. In the case of the *Kathleen* legal redress was again refused, but the master, besides shipping a new crew, was able to put some of the worst of the mutineers in irons and take them to England. (Sir F. Bruce, Brit. min., to Mr. Seward, Sec. of State, March 7, 1866, Dip. Cor. 1866, I. 228.)

" Referring to the case of Albert Allen Gardner, master of the American ship *Anna Camp*, tried in the county court at Liverpool, in May last, copies of certain papers relating to which were forwarded to you by General Badeau, I desire to call your attention to the claim of jurisdiction put forth by the local common-law courts of Great Britain in this and other similar cases.

" It seems to be claimed by the courts in question that their jurisdiction extends to the hearing and determining of causes arising upon complaints between masters and mariners of vessels of the United States, not only when the occurrences upon which the complaint may be founded took place within British ports or waters, but also when the offense which is made the ground of the action was committed on board the vessel on the high seas.

" The exercise of this jurisdiction by the local common-law courts at Liverpool has already been the cause of much annoyance and, in some instances, serious inconvenience to masters and owners of American vessels, and if persisted in may affect injuriously the interests of American shipping.

" The courts of the United States, even those possessing admiralty jurisdiction, have repeatedly declined to take cognizance of cases of this nature when the parties to the action were seamen and masters of foreign vessels. The reasons assigned by the courts of the United States for refusing to entertain jurisdiction of such cases are believed to be in accord with the general practice of other maritime powers and supported by the principles of international maritime law, as understood and interpreted by the highest judicial authority of maritime nations.

" In a case of controversy between the crew and the master of the British ship *Reliance*, sought to be prosecuted before the district court of the United States in the city of New York, the master and crew in question being British subjects, the court, in declining to entertain the case, says: ' The admiralty courts of the United States will decline jurisdiction of controversies arising between foreign masters and owners unless the voyage has been broken up or the seamen unlawfully discharged. It is expected,' continues the same judge, ' that a foreign seaman seeking to prosecute an action of this description in the courts of this country will procure the official sanction of the commercial or political representative of the country to which he belongs, or that good reasons will be shown for allowing his suit in the absence of such refusal. This court,' adds the learned judge, ' has repeatedly discountenanced actions by foreign seamen against foreign vessels not terminating their voyages at this port as being calculated to embarrass commercial transactions and relations between this country and others in friendly relations with it.'

" The justice and wisdom of those observations of the court will be at once obvious. The laws of the United States, and the instructions of this Department to its consular officers resident in foreign countries, provide with more than ordinary care for the adjustment of all questions of controversy which may arise between the masters and crews of American vessels growing out of the relations of such masters and seamen on board the vessel while on the high seas or in the ports of foreign powers; and where offenses are committed by either master or mariner, or other questions of dispute between them arise which are beyond the province of the consul to determine, ample provision is made by law for the trial and punishment of such offenses and the settlement of those questions by the courts of the United States. These provisions of the law and consular regulations of this country are believed, moreover, to be in general harmony with existing laws and regulations of Great Britain on this subject.

" This Department, as you are aware, has repeatedly brought to the attention of Her Majesty's government the necessity of a consular convention between the two countries, the existence of which would do much to obviate in future occurrences such as that now complained of. It is not designed in this connection to renew any discussion of that subject now, as you are fully informed that this Government is now, as it has been heretofore, ready to enter into a convention on that subject.

" You will avail yourself of the earliest opportunity to bring the question involved in the case of Captain Gardner to the attention of Her Majesty's government, with the expression of the hope indulged by the Government of the United States that measures will be adopted to prevent in future the exercise of jurisdiction by the local common-law courts of Great Britain in controversies arising between the masters and seamen of vessels of the United States growing out of occurrences on board their vessels on the high seas."

Mr. Fish, Sec. of State, to Mr. Schenck, Nov. 8, 1873, MS. Inst. Great Britain, XVIII. 431; For. Rel. 1874, 490.

" Referring to my instruction of the 8th of November, 1873, (No. 476,) in relation to jurisdiction assumed by the local common-law courts of Great Britain, in cases of disputes arising between the masters and crews of merchant vessels of the United States, I now transmit to you a copy of a dispatch recently received by the Department from the United States vice-consul at Hongkong, together with a copy of its inclosures, relating to a case between Joseph D. Ellis, the steward of the American ship *Lathley Rich*, and Thomas Mitchell, the master of that vessel, in which the jurisdiction complained of, was assumed and exercised by the local courts of that colony. Complaints have also recently reached the Department from Melbourne and Singapore of a similar assumption of jurisdiction by the local courts of these colonies.

" The laws of the United States make ample provision for the regulation and protection of the seamen of the United States, and for the settlement of all disputes which may arise between the masters and crews of American vessels before the consuls of the United States resident in the ports of foreign countries, carefully reserving, at the same time, to the parties all the rights and remedies that are secured to them by law through the courts of the United States.

" Regulations similar in character for the government and police of their merchant marine are established by the government of Great Britain, and, indeed, by the governments of most, if not all, commercial nations, and this Government has never failed to recognize the effective beneficence of such domestic regulations in promoting discipline, order, and good government on vessels engaged in the merchant service. They rest upon principles of convenience, international comity, and well-settled rules of public law. The claim of jurisdiction made by the local common-law courts of Great Britain, and particularly by the colonial tribunals, is conceived to be in contravention of those principles; and the exercise of it, moreover, calculated to work serious injury to the commerce of the United States, in those ports where it obtains, and to the interests of the vessels which, from time to time, become the subjects of such unauthorized interference.

" Acting in the spirit of these views, this Government has on several occasions, when interference of a similar character by local courts or magistrates of this country, in the case of British vessels, has been brought to its notice by Her Majesty's government, promptly made such complaints the subject of inquiry and correction.

"On the 19th of February, 1873, Her Majesty's minister at this capital brought to the attention of the Department a case, occurring at Galveston, Texas, in which the master of the British ship *Bucephalus* had been arraigned before a local State magistrate, who happened, also, to be a United States commissioner, upon the complaint of one Thomas Moffit, a seaman of that vessel, for an alleged assault, commenced while the ship was at sea and continued after her arrival at that port. The case was referred by this Department to the Attorney-General, and that officer instituted an immediate investigation. It was found, upon inquiry, that the magistrate in question had instituted the proceedings in his capacity of justice of the peace, an office which he held under the laws of the State of Texas, and not as United States commissioner, and that upon being advised by the United States district attorney for that district that it was not a matter of which either the authorities of the United States or of the State should take cognizance, the master being amenable to the laws of the nation to which his vessel belonged, the complaint was at once dismissed by the magistrate. In the same note the British minister complained of certain proceedings of two United States commissioners at New Orleans with reference to the discharge of seamen from a British vessel at that port, the seamen in question being citizens of the United States and claiming the interposition of the local authorities on that ground. These officers were also instructed that such interference with the police regulations established by Great Britain for the government of their merchant-vessels was contrary to the policy of this Government, and that even in cases where the right of the local magistrates to assert the jurisdiction was undoubted, its exercise should be avoided. These instructions have been adhered to, and there has since been no recurrence at that port of the interference then complained of.

"In another case, which occurred at Charleston, S. C., and which was brought to the attention of the Department by Sir Edward Thornton in a note of the 6th of May, 1874, in which it appeared that John Bogan, a seaman of the British ship *Amelie*, complained before a United States commissioner of ill treatment received at the hands of the captain of that vessel. It turned out, upon inquiry, that the commissioner was not advised of the nationality of the vessel when he issued his warrant of arrest, and, that as soon as the fact was disclosed to him that the occurrences complained of took place upon a British vessel, he promptly advised the United States district attorney of that circumstance, and, upon the advice of the latter officer, immediately dismissed the complaint.

" In these several cases, occurring in the United States, it must also be noticed that the proceedings were taken by petty or inferior magistrates, who may not reasonably be supposed to be learned in the law, while in the case of the *Lathley Rich*, at Hong-Kong, the proceedings were commenced before a *nisi prius* court, and ultimately heard and determined on appeal before the supreme court of the colony, and the same is true of some cases which occurred at Melbourne.

" The instances thus given, taken in connection with the practice and doctrine laid down by Mr. Justice Betts in the United States court for New York, sitting in admiralty, to which I adverted in my No. 476 to you, serves to show the uniform regard in which these principles of international comity and convenience have been held by the Government of the United States.

" It is therefore with regret that I notice the absence of a reciprocal respect for these principles in the administration of the local courts of Great Britain, and particularly in Her Majesty's colonies, in their proceedings towards American merchant-vessels.

" Bearing in mind the views expressed in my former instruction, (No. 476,) it is desired that you will take the earliest favorable opportunity of bringing to the attention of Her Majesty's Government the case of the *Lathley Rich*, now transmitted in connection with the general question of the jurisdiction referred to, and you will represent to Earl Derby the interest felt by this Government in the adoption of such measures by that of Great Britain as will prevent a recurrence of such cases, and be effective, especially as regards the colonial courts, in putting a stop to this exercise of jurisdiction, at once injurious to the interests of the vessels which may be the subjects of it, and the possible cause of international inconvenience to two nations so largely interested in the commerce of the world as are those of the United States and Great Britain."

> Mr. Fish, Sec. of State, to Mr. Schenck, March 12, 1875, For. Rel. 1875, I. 592.

" The state of international law on the subject of private vessels in foreign ports . . . may be said to be this: So far as regards acts done at sea before her arrival in port, and acts done on board in port, by members of the crew to one another, and so far as regards the general regulation of the rights and duties of those belonging on board, the vessel is exempt from local jurisdiction; but, if the acts done on board affect the peace of the country in whose port she lies, or the persons or property of its subjects, to that extent that state has jurisdiction. The local authorities have a right to visit all such vessels, to ascertain the nature of any alleged occurrence on board. Of course, no exemption is ever claimed for injuries done by the vessel to property or persons in port, or for acts of her company not done on board the vessel, or for their personal contracts or civil obligations or duties relating to persons not of the ship's company."

Dana's Wheaton, § 95, note 58.

(3) AUTHORITY OF CONSULS.

§ 206.

By various treaties between the United States and other powers, exclusive jurisdiction is conferred upon consuls over disputes between the masters, officers, and crews of vessels of their respective nations, including questions of wages. To this jurisdiction an express exception is usually made as to offences that disturb the peace or tranquillity of the port.[a]

Treaties and leg-
islation.

In June, 1844, the crew of the Prussian ship *Borussia*, while at New Bedford, Massachusetts, refused to obey the master. July 7, 1845, the Prussian minister at Washington, complained that the judicial authorities of the United States in Massachusetts, when appealed to for assistance in enforcing the decision of the Prussian consul-general, pursuant to Art. X. of the treaty with Prussia of 1828, had failed to interfere on the ground that no law had been passed by Congress to give effect to the article. The Department of State on inquiry found that " the late Judge Story had arrived at the conclusion that he did not possess the power to give effect to the 10th article of the treaty, without an act of Congress; " and the Department, " although by no means satisfied with the correctness of this opinion," stated that it perceived " no other means of obviating this evil, and of giving full effect to like decisions of His Prussian Majesty's consuls . . . but the passage of a law framed for this express purpose." It was further stated that the whole subject would be submitted to Congress at its next session.[b]

Article 10 of the treaty with Prussia of 1828 provides that the consuls, vice-consuls, and commercial agents of each party " shall have the right, as such, to sit as judges and arbitrators in such differences as may arise between the captains and crews of the vessels belonging to the nation whose interests are committed to their charge, without the interference of the local authorities," subject to the right of the contending parties " to resort, on their return, to the judicial authority of their country," and to the right of the consuls, vice-consuls, and

[a] The authority of consuls under these stipulations is ministerial only, not judicial. (Cushing, At. Gen. 1857, 8 Op. 380.)

[b] Mr. Buchanan, Sec. of State, to Baron von Gerolt, Prussian min., Nov. 4, 1845, MS. Notes to German States, VI. 121.)

commercial agents to require the assistance of the local authorities " to cause their decisions to be carried into effect or supported." The crew of a Prussian vessel sued *in rem*, in admiralty, in the district court, to recover wages alleged to be due to them. The master of the vessel answered, denying the debt, invoking the protection of said treaty, denying the jurisdiction of the court, and averring that the claim for wages had already been adjudicated by the Prussian consul at New York. The consul also protested formally to the court against the exercise of its jurisdiction. The case was tried in the district court, and it appeared that the consul had adjudicated on the claim for wages. The district court decreed in favor of the libellants. It was held that the district court had no jurisdiction of the case.

> The Elwine Kreplin, 9 Blatch. 438.
>
> As to the general effect of similar treaty stipulations in the United States, see Williams *v*. Welhaven, 55 Fed. Rep. 80.
>
> As to jurisdiction of offences affecting the peace or tranquillity of the port, see the cases given below in connection with particular treaty stipulations, and particularly Wildenhus's case, 120 U. S. 1, under the treaty with Belgium, infra, p. 303.

" The act to enforce treaty provisions respecting disputes between masters and crews was approved June 11, 1864. It is not to take effect as to the ships or vessels of any nation, unless the President shall have been satisfied that similar provisions have been made by the other contracting party for the execution of the treaty, and shall have issued his proclamation to that effect. On the 10th of February, 1870, proclamation was made under this act as to the treaties with France, Prussia, and the other States of the North German Union, and Italy; and on the 11th of May, 1872, as to the treaty with Sweden and Norway.

" This statute authorizes any court of record of the United States, or any judge thereof, or any commissioner appointed under the laws of the United States to take bail or affidavits, or for other judicial purposes whatsoever, to receive the application of the consular officer, to issue process against the person complained of, and if it shall appear, on his being returned before the magistrate, that he is not a citizen of the United States, and if a *prima facie* case shall be made out that the matter concerns only the internal order and discipline or the foreign vessel, and does not affect directly the laws of the United States or the rights and duties of any citizen, then the magistrate shall commit the seaman to prison to abide the lawful order or control of the master: provided the expenses of the proceedings shall be paid by the consular officer, and the seaman shall not be detained for more than two months after his arrest."

> Mr. J. C. B. Davis, Treaty Notes, Treaty Vol. (1778–1887), 1279.
>
> For the act of June 11, 1864, see 13 Stat. 121.

For the proclamation of Feb. 10, 1870, see 16 Stat. 1130; proclamation of
May 11, 1872, 17 id. 955.

The Department of State declined to issue a proclamation in the case of
the Netherlands, in the absence of an appropriate treaty stipulation,
such as was afterwards made in Art. XI. of the convention of May 23,
1878.   (Mr. Fish, Sec. of State, to Mr. Mazel, Oct. 9, 1869, MS. Notes to
Netherlands Leg. VII. 130.   See, however, Mr. Fish, Sec. of State, to
Mr. Westenberg, May 22, 1872, id. 238.)

" Whatever embarrassment this [the absence of a proclamation
under the act of June 11, 1864, supra,] might create in the way of
affirmative action, such as ordering the arrest of a deserter, it is suggested that the operation [of Art. X.] of the treaty " with Prussia, of
1828, would, " without the aid of any statute," forbid the interference
of the local authorities in differences between masters and crews.
" The treaty being the supreme law of the land executes itself, for
this restraining purpose."

Mr. E. Peshine Smith, Solicitor of Department of State, to Mr. Cadwalader, July 2, 1869, 81 MS. Dom. Let. 349.

" There has never been the slightest doubt as to the entire legality
of extraterritorial jurisdiction when acquired in foreign ports by
treaty.   The first treaties creating such rights were concluded in
1787 and 1788, almost simultaneously with the adoption of the Constitution, and were understood by the framers of the Constitution as
compatible therewith.   In the next sixty years several other extraterritorial treaties were concluded, but no law was even deemed
necessary to the execution of those treaties until 1848, and then the
statute aimed simply to codify the treaty rights acquired in a convenient form; it could not create them.   And finally the circuit
courts of the United States have fully sustained the constitutionality
of the existing statutes."

Mr. Frelinghuysen, Sec. of State, to Mr. Gardiner, Mar. 16, 1883, 146 MS.
Dom. Let. 164.

" Generally speaking, the consul has jurisdiction of all disputes on
shipboard, not affecting the peace of the port, but as this right is not
specially conceded by treaty, it could only be claimed and exercised
by comity, and in the absence of any competent claim of jurisdiction
by the local courts, unless indeed the right may spring from Art.
XXXIII. of said treaty [of 1864 with Hayti], the most favored
nation clause."

Mr. Bayard, Sec. of State, to Mr. Thompson, min. to Hayti, July 31, 1885,
MS. Inst. Hayti, II, 511, referring to the case of an American
man who had been arrested at Port au Prince on a charge of murdering a Haytian policeman in a drinking house.

The Austrian chargé d'affaires having claimed, under the most-favored-
nation clause, the benefit of the provisions of the treaties between

the United States and Russia and certain other countries, conferring
jurisdiction on consuls in regard to questions arising between the
masters and crews of merchant vessels, the Government of the
United States replied: "Seeing that the right now under consideration . . . is, in every such instance, given in exchange for the
very same right conferred in terms equally express upon the consuls
of the United States, it cannot be expected that it will be considered
as established by the operation of a general provision, which, if it
were allowed so to operate, would destroy all reciprocity in this
regard, leaving the United States without that equivalent in favor
of their consuls, which is the consideration received by them for the
grant of this right wherever expressly granted." (Mr. Buchanan,
Sec. of State, to Chev. Hülsemann, Austrian chargé d'affaires, May 18,
1846, MS. Notes to German States, VI. 130.)

It was advised by Attorney-General Speed, in 1866, that the United States
might claim consular jurisdiction of disputes among American citizens belonging to the crews of American vessels in the Hawaiian
Islands, under the most-favored-nation clause in the treaty with that
country, which secured to the "consuls" of the contracting parties
"the same privileges and powers" as to "those of the most favored
nation," such jurisdiction having been conceded by treaty by Hawaii
to France. (11 Op. 508.)

"I have the honor to acknowledge the receipt of your note of the
9th instant, in relation to the cases of the captains
of the Hungarian merchant vessels *Ararat* and *Mimi
P.*, in which you request, on behalf of your Government, to be put in possession of the views of the Government of the
United States on the question of local jurisdiction involved in the
case referred to.

Treaties; Austria-Hungary, July 11, 1870, Art. XI.

"I inclose herewith a copy of an opinion of the Attorney-General
of the 9th July last, in response to the request I made of that functionary on the 27th of June of the same year, and of which I had
the honor to inform Count Lippe-Weissenfeld.

"Your contention rests on the eleventh article of the consular convention concluded between the United States and the Austro-Hungarian monarchy on the 11th July, 1870. The article referred to is
in the following words, namely:

"Consuls, vice-consuls, or consular agents shall have exclusive charge of the
internal order of the merchant vessels of their nation. They shall have, therefore, the exclusive power to take cognizance of and to settle all differences
which may arise at sea or in port between captains, officers, and crew in reference to wages and the execution of mutual contracts, subject in each case to
the laws of their own nation.

"The local authorities shall in no way interfere, except in cases where the
differences on board ship are of a nature to disturb the peace and public order
in port or on shore, or when persons other than the officers and crew of the
vessel are parties to the disturbance. Except as aforesaid, the local authorities
shall confine themselves to the rendering of forcible assistance if required by
the consuls, vice-consuls, or consular agents, and shall cause the arrest, tempo-

rary imprisonment, and removal on board his own vessel of every person whose name is found on the muster-rolls or register of the ship or list of the crew.

" I find no difficulty in agreeing with your statement, that by the general principles of international law private or merchant vessels entering the ports of another nation than their own are subject to the local jurisdiction; and I also recognize at once the convenience and desirability of the rule you suggest as that adopted by France, and followed by some other nations, that local courts should decline to take jurisdiction of cases involving acts of mere interior discipline of the vessel. Such, indeed, has been the course recommended by the executive branch of this Government to the courts, and it gives me pleasure to be able to add that both the Federal and State courts have as a general rule conformed their proceedings in such cases to that suggestion. These tribunals, however, are bound under the Constitution and laws of the United States to entertain every complaint in which is presented a *prima facie* case of violation of the local laws, and it consequently becomes necessary in such cases that the judge should hear the evidence before he is able to determine whether the case is one of mere discipline connected with the ship, or whether it is of such a nature as to involve a disturbance of the public order in port or on shore; and bound by the same constitutional and statutory provisions the executive branch of the Government must refrain from all interference with the judicial tribunals in regard to cases or questions that may be pending before such tribunals. No doubt is entertained, however, but that the declarations of the courts will always be had, and their decisions be always rendered with a due regard for the obligations of the Government under its treaty stipulations with foreign powers.

" The President, I need scarcely add, will ever deem it his duty to give full effect, in spirit and in letter, to the provisions of the convention of July, 1870, between this Government and that of Austria-Hungary, which you so worthily represent."

> Mr. Frelinghuysen, Sec. of State, to Baron Schaeffer, Aust. min., Nov. 13, 1883, For. Rel. 1883, 30.
>
> In For. Rel. for 1883, 17 *ff*, is given a full report of the trial of Com. *v.* Ferlan, Philadelphia, 1883, referred to above.

Article XI. of the convention with Austria-Hungary of July 11, 1870, having invested consular officers with " power to take cognizance of and to setttle all differences . . . between captains, officers and crews in reference to wages and the execution of mutual contracts," and there being no consular officer of Austria-Hungary at Savannah, Ga., the minister of Austria-Hungary authorized Mr. Cosulich, a ship agent, to act as consular agent specially to settle a difference as to wages between the master and crew of the Austrian vessel *Celestina*, then lying at that port, the Department of State at the same time requesting the Secretary of the Treasury to telegraph the officers of his Department at Savannah provisionally to recognize Mr. Cosulich in the capacity mentioned.

> Mr. Frelinghuysen, Sec. of State, to Mr. McCulloch, Sec. of Treas., Jan. 17, 1885, 153 MS. Dom. Let. 694.

W., a Belgian subject, in October, 1886, stabbed and killed F., another Belgian subject, on a Belgian steamship then moored at a dock in Jersey City in the State of New Jersey. Both W. and F. were members of the crew of the steamship; the affair began and ended wholly below deck; and the only witnesses present were other members of the crew. W. was arrested and imprisoned by the local authorities under the laws of the State of New Jersey on a charge of felonious homicide.

Belgium, March 9, 1880, Art. XI.

By articles 8, 9, and 10, of the royal decree of March 11, 1857, Belgian consuls were invested with " the right of discipline on Belgian merchant vessels " in their various districts and were authorized in the matter of offenses or crimes to hold examinations conformably to the provisions of the disciplinary and penal code of the merchant service; and they were directed, except where the peace of the port should have been compromised, to protest against every attempt of the local authority to take cognizance of crimes or offenses committed on board of a Belgian vessel by one of the ship's company against a person belonging either to the same crew or to the crew of another Belgian vessel, to the end that the offender might ultimately be tried according to the laws of Belgium. Where the crime or offense was committed outside the ship, or even on board of it but against a person not of the company, the consul was directed, in case the local authorities should arrest or prosecute the offender, to see that he was treated with humanity, defended, and impartially tried.

By Article XI. of the convention between the United States and Belgium " concerning the rights, immunities, and privileges of consular officers," concluded March 9, 1880, it was provided as follows:

The respective Consuls-General, Consuls, Vice-Consuls, and Consular Agents shall have exclusive charge of the internal order of the merchant vessels of their nation, and shall alone take cognizance of all differences which may arise, either at sea or in port, between the captains, officers and crews, without exception, particularly in reference to the adjustment of wages and the execution of contracts. The local authorities shall not interfere except when the disorder that has arisen is of such a nature as to disturb tranquillity and public order on shore, or in the port, or when a person of the country or not belonging to the crew shall be concerned therein.

In all other cases, the aforesaid authorities shall confine themselves to lending aid to the Consuls and Vice-Consuls or Consular Agents, if they are requested by them to do so, in causing the arrest and imprisonment of any person whose name is inscribed on the crew-list, whenever, for any cause, the said officers shall think proper.

An application for the discharge of W. on habeas corpus was made by the Belgian consul at Jersey City, who contended that both by the law of nations and the provisions of the treaty the offense with which W. was charged was " solely cognizable by the authority of the laws of the Kingdom of Belgium," and that the State of New Jersey had no jurisdiction in the matter.

It was held (1) that, by the law of civilized nations, " when a merchant vessel of one country enters the ports of another for the purposes of trade, it subjects itself to the law of the place to which it goes, unless by treaty or otherwise the two countries have come to some different understanding or agreement; " (2) that it had come to be generally understood among civilized nations, however, that matters of discipline and other things done on board which affected only the vessel or those belonging to it should be left to be dealt with by the authorities of the nation to which the vessel belonged, while crimes committed on board of a character to disturb the peace and tranquillity of the port should be dealt with by the local tribunals if they should see fit to assert their authority; (3) that the provisions of the convention between the United States and Belgium, by which the conduct of the two Governments towards each other must in the pending matter be governed, embodied, and were intended to give effect to this general distinction; (4) that, this being the case, the only question to be determined was whether the disorder in question was of a nature to disturb the public peace or public repose of the people who looked to the State of New Jersey for protection. It was held that the disorder was of this nature; and the judgment of the court below remanding the prisoner to the custody of the authorities of the State of New Jersey was affirmed.

In the course of its opinion, the court said:

" If the thing done—' the disorder,' as it is called in the treaty—is of a character to affect those on shore or in the port when it becomes known, the fact that only those on the ship saw it when it was done is a matter of no moment. Those who are not on the vessel pay no special attention to the mere disputes or quarrels of the seamen while on board, whether they occur under deck or above. Neither do they as a rule care for anything done on board which relates only to the discipline of the ship, or to the preservation of order and authority. Not so, however, with crimes which from their gravity awaken a public interest as soon as they become known, and especially those of a character which every civilized nation considers itself bound to provide a severe punishment for when committed within its own jurisdiction. In such cases inquiry is certain to be instituted at once to ascertain how or why the thing was done, and the popular excitement rises or falls as the news spreads and the facts become known. It is not alone the publicity of the act, or the noise and clamor which attends it, that fixes the nature of the crime, but the act itself. If that is of a character to awaken public interest when it becomes known, it is a ' disorder ' the nature of which is to affect the community at large, and consequently to invoke the power of the local government whose people have been disturbed by what was done. The very nature of such an act is to disturb the quiet of a peaceful community, and to create, in the language of the treaty, a ' disorder ' which will ' disturb tranquillity and public order on shore or in the port.' The principle which governs the whole matter is this: Disorders which disturb only the peace of the ship or those on board are to be dealt with exclusively by the sovereignty of the home of the ship, but those which disturb the public peace may be suppressed, and, if need be, the offenders punished by the proper authorities of the local jurisdiction. It may not be easy at all times to determine to which of the two jurisdictions a particular act of disorder belongs. Much will undoubtedly depend on the attending circumstances of the particular case, but all must concede that felonious homicide is a subject for the local jurisdiction, and that if the proper authorities are proceeding with the case in a regular way, the consul has no right to interfere to prevent it. That, according to the petition for the *habeas corpus*, is this case."

Wildenhus's case (1887), 120 U. S. 1.

In 1886, in consequence of difficulties between the master and crew, a libel was filed against the Russian ship *Nautilus* in the United States district court at Mobile, Alabama, and a prosecution for assault and battery was instituted against the master and mate before the city court. The district court decided against the vessel, while the city court acquitted the mate but fined the master $100. On the advice of the United States district attorney, who had appeared and excepted to the jurisdiction, the Russian consul furnished an appeal bond in the criminal case; but while the question of an appeal in the maritime case was still under advisement, the master of the ship, declining to wait longer, settled both cases of his own accord and sailed away. (Mr. Bayard, Sec. of State, to Baron Rosen, Russian chargé, July 29, 1886, MS. Notes to Russia, VII. 493. See, also, Mr. de Struve, Russ. min., to Mr. Bayard, Sec. of State, June 5, 1886, MS. Notes from Russia; Mr. Bayard, Sec. of State, to Mr. Garland, At.-Gen., June 15, 1886, 160 MS. Dom. Let. 485, asking that "proper instructions" might be sent to the United States district attorney.)

" By a circular dated 20th August, 1884, the Department of State requested this legation to inform the French consuls
France, 1853, Art. VIII. at the ports of the United States of the provisions of the tenth section of the law voted by Congress the 26th June, 1884, under the name of the ' shipping act.'

" The Government of the Republic, to which these provisions were likewise communicated, highly appreciated the humane object of the principal provisions of the shipping act. At the same time certain questions of detail have suggested to the minister of foreign affairs and to the minister of marine of the Republic some considerations which I have been charged to call to the attention of the Department of State.

" Section 10 of the shipping act forbids captains of ships, under pain of fine and imprisonment, from giving to the crew of the vessel any kind of advance on their wages at the moment of embarking. It declares, also, illegal the transfer of wages to a third party, though authorizing reservations of part of the pay in favor of the families of sailors; it stipulates, finally, that the different provisions are equally applicable to foreign ships, which would be refused permission to leave any port of the United States if they contravened them.

" It appears to the above-mentioned ministers that, on account of the general character of its terms, this provision cannot be reconciled with the stipulations of Article VIII of the Franco-American consular convention. It appears to them, moreover, to infringe the rights of the different nations to determine, according to their own legislation, the duties and obligations of their merchant captains towards their crews on the merchant vessels of their own nation.

" The Government of the United States has the incontestable right to forbid American captains in the ports of the Union and foreign countries from making any payment in advance to their crews. But can this right be legally extended to French captains who enlist French sailors in the ports of the United States?

"As to what concerns American sailors, Mr. de Freycinet and Admiral Galiber agree in recognizing that the Federal authorities, preserving their jurisdiction over their citizens when they engage themselves in their own ports on foreign vessels, claim, in that case justly, from French captains an observance of the provisions of the shipping act, as far as it relates to American sailors.

" The objection then reduces itself, as you see, Mr. Secretary, to the question of the rights of French captains over French sailors, rights concerning which the very general terms of the final provision of section 10 might raise difficulties between the Federal authorities and the consuls. If you share with my Government this manner of looking at the question, you will perhaps consider that a circular from your Department might decide the scope of these general provisions, without infringing the legislative sovereignty of each nation with regard to its subjects.

" I should add, in order to completely eliminate the question of humanity, that the French laws and regulations have already protected with efficient guarantees the advances made by captains to the crews during the voyage or at the moment of embarkation. These advances to be recognized as available must have been authorized by a French consul. Finally, as regards the sailors who disembark in foreign countries, the consuls can only give them the half of the sums deposited in their name at the (consular) chancery by the captains, unless this advance exceeds 150 francs, or about $30. The rest of the amount is transmitted to France and deposited in the Mariners' Deposit Bank, to be remitted to the claimant on his return to his district of enrollment.

" I hope, Mr. Secretary of State, that these explanations will be of a nature to convince you that it is possible to harmonize the dictates of humanity in this question with the free exercise of the rights of our respective Governments over their own citizens."

Mr. Roustan, French min., to Mr. Bayard, Sec. of State, July 31, 1885, For. Rel. 1885, 384.

" The views expressed in your note are apparently not only based upon a conception not sufficiently broad of the power of this Government to affect by its legislation foreign merchant ships when within its territorial jurisdiction, but also upon a misconception, it is apprehended, of the scope and operation of the statutory provision prohibiting the payment of advance wages to seamen to which you refer.

" That provision is from its subject-matter of the nature of a commercial regulation. Commerce, in its simplest signification, means an exchange of goods, but, in the advancement of society, labor, transportation, intelligence, care, and various mediums of exchange, become commodities and enter into commerce; the subject, the vehicle, the agent, and their various operations, become the objects of commercial regulation. (9 Wheaton, 229.) The officers and crew of a merchant vessel are as much the instruments of commerce as the ship. (7 Howard, 408.)

" The immediate purpose of the provision of section 10 of the act in question is to protect the interests and promote the welfare of merchant seamen while sojourning at American ports, persons whose occupation is indispensable to maritime commerce, and who are objects of solicitude and care in the codes of all commercial nations. They are characterized as usually a heedless and ignorant but most useful class of men, exposed to constant hardships, perils, and oppression, and in port the ready victims of temptation and fraud (3 Kent Com., 176), as notoriously and proverbially reckless and improvident, and on all accounts requiring protection against themselves (Sh. Minerva, 1 Hagg., 355), as credulous, complying, and easily overreached, and requiring to be treated in reference to their bargains as courts of equity treat young heirs in dealing with their expectancies, wards with their guardians, *cestuis que trusts* with their trustees (Harden *vs.* Gordon, 2 Mason, 556). Legislation for their security and protection when employed in the merchant service was early adopted by Congress (act of July 20, 1790, chap. 29), and has been enacted from time to time down to the present, containing many wise and wholesome provisions directed to that end. (See Revised Statutes, Title LIII.)

"The provision now under consideration deals with the subject of the wages of those seamen *who are hired in American ports*, and those only. It is thereby made unlawful to pay advance wages to the seamen himself before he leaves *the port at which he is engaged*, or to pay the same (*i. e.*, advance wages of such seaman) to any person; and this by the express terms of the statute applies to foreign as well as to American vessels. The power of Congress to regulate the employment or hire of merchant seamen within the ports of the United States can not be questioned. There is no principle of international law which forbids the application of such legislation to foreign ships.

"Marshall, C. J., observes in The Exchange, 7 Cr., 136:

'The jurisdiction of the nation is necessarily exclusive and absolute. It is susceptible of no limitation not imposed by itself. Any restriction upon it, deriving validity from an external source, would imply a diminution of its sovereignty to the extent of the restriction and an investment of that sovereignty to the same extent in that power which could impose such restriction. All exceptions, therefore, to the full and complete power of a nation within its own teritories must be traced up to the consent of the nation itself. They can flow from no other legitimate source.'

"Hence, a foreign merchant vessel going into the port of a foreign state subjects herself to the laws of that state and is bound to conform to its commercial as well as to its police and other regulations during the period of her stay there. ' She is as much a *subditus temporaneus*,' remarks Sir R. Phillimore with reference to such a case, in The Queen *vs.* Keyn, 2 Ex. D., 82, ' as the individual who visits the interior of the country for the purposes of pleasure or business.'

"From this doctrine it follows that in extending the provision adverted to so as to make it applicable to foreign merchant ships within our ports the same as to American vessels, Congress has not assumed to deal with any rights of such ships with which on principles of international law it is not entitled to interfere, nor has it exceeded the proper limits of its jurisdiction, having regard to the rights of other nations. Therefore, unless exempted from the operation of the provision by virtue of some treaty or statute having that effect, no nation has any valid ground to claim for its merchant shipping, in any case or under any circumstances, immunity from observance thereof. Whether the seaman hired or engaged in one of our ports by a foreign ship is or is not of the same nationality as the vessel is wholly immaterial, the language of the provision being general and including (as it may properly do) all merchant seamen who are there hired or engaged by such ship, irrespective of their nationality.

" In regard to the supposed conflict between the statutory provision and Article VIII. of the convention of February 23, 1853, between this country and France, this Government holds that the subject-matter of the one is entirely distinct from that of the other, and that no collision necessarily arises.

" By that said article of the treaty the respective consuls—

' Shall have exclusive charge of the *internal order* of the merchant vessels of their nation, and shall alone take cognizance of differences which may arise, either at sea or in port, *between the captain, officers and crew* without exception, particularly in reference to the *adjustment of wages and the execution of contracts.*'

" The word ' execution ' is obviously used here in the sense of performance.

" This provision accords the consular officer—

"(1) A limited *police jurisdiction* over the merchant vessels of his nation, embracing only those acts which relate to the interior discipline of the vessel, and which do not disturb the peace and good order of the port. With respect to that jurisdiction the scope of the provision is precisely determined by the word ' internal.'

"(2) A limited cognizance of civil controversies between the officers and the crews of such vessels, particularly those relating to the performance of contracts of service and the adjustment of wages thereunder.

" It seems very plain to this Government that a public law of the port which prohibits the payment of advance wages to seamen, hired at that port, before the vessel sails, does not concern the ' internal order ' of such vessel in contemplation of the above provision; and it is difficult to see wherein the law could become a subject of ' difference ' between the officers and crew of the vessel. In hiring a seaman at an American port, the master of a ship can make no valid agreement to pay advance wages before leaving the port, for the reason that such payment is prohibited by the public law of the place. Should he do so, and fail to pay the advance, this might give rise to a ' difference ' between him and the seaman, but it would be a difference manifestly involving no conflict between the law and the treaty. On the other hand, should the master pay the seaman advance wages, the enforcement of the law against the former could not, in any point of view, be deemed an interference in a ' difference ' between the two individuals.

" This Government holds that the provisions of section 10 of the act of June 26, 1884, are designed to regulate dealings with seamen who are commorant in the ports of the United States and with whom shipping agreements are there entered into. They do not apply to dealings with the seamen under such agreements made elsewhere. Obligations arising out of the latter agreements are unaffected by the statute; the former can give rise to no obligation the performance of which involves an infraction of its provisions.

"In brief, the conclusions reached by this Government upon the points presented by your note are as follows:

"(1) That the provisions of the act of June 26, 1884, respecting the payment of advance wages, in so far as they apply to foreign shipping, are not in conflict with the stipulations of Article VIII. of the convention of February 23, 1853, between this country and France.

"(2) That the provisions of said act infringe upon no principles of international law which other nations are entitled to exercise within American ports as regards their merchant vessels.

"(3) That therefore those provisions can legally extend to French captains who hire French sailors in American ports, and that in extending, as they do to them, they violate or prejudice no right of such captains in the premises."

> Mr. Bayard, Sec. of State, to Mr. Roustan, French min., Aug. 26, 1885,
> For. Rel. 1885, 386.

February 9, 1901, the German ambassador at Washington represented that the United States marshal at Philadelphia had libelled the German steamship *Assyria*, without giving the previous advice required by par. 2, Art. XII. of the Consular Convention of December 11, 1871.[a]

Germany, Dec. 11, 1871, Art. XII.

March 1, 1901, Mr. Hay replied that the Attorney-General, whom he had consulted, thought that the previous notice required by Article XIX. to be given to the consular officers of the respective nations related "only to an examination or search of merchant vessels by judicial authorities or custom-house officials, and to the taxing of the depositions or statements of officers or persons belonging to the crew of a vessel of the respective nations, to be made or used in judicial proceedings. In his judgment, therefore, the service of a writ of attachment upon a vessel is not within the language or intent of said Article XII.; and as immediate service of such a writ is often the very essence of the claimant's or creditor's right, as showing due diligence, especially where preferences are concerned, he thinks the reasons are obvious why the service of an ordinary attachment was not intended to be, and was not in fact embraced, in the proceedings which require previous notice under Article XII. of the treaty aforesaid."[b]

The German Government stated that it was unable to concur in

---

[a] For. Rel. 1901, 161.

[b] Mr. Hay, Sec. of State, to Mr. Von Holleben, German ambassador, March 1, 1901, MS. Notes to German Leg. XII. 558; For. Rel. 1901, 162.

this view, the Imperial Government having always adhered to the position "that the obligation of notifying the imperial consular officers concerned extends, if not to all official proceedings of American local authorities on board German merchant vessels, at least to all such as affect the interests of the vessel or its service." Various precedents were referred to in which the United States had, it was maintained, admitted that the provisions of the treaty governed the case of an attachment. The Imperial Government, it was said, conceded that an attachment must in most cases be executed without delay, but this was not thought to lend support to the opinion of the Attorney-General, since in the opinion of the Imperial Government "a notification given immediately after entering upon" the execution of an official proceeding would be deemed sufficient where loss of time in giving previous notice would defeat the object of the process. The concurrence of the United States in this view was requested.[a]

The Department of State again consulted the Attorney-General, who adhered to the previous opinion of his Department.[b]

" I have the honor to state that I have given careful consideration to your letter of November 19 and to the note from the German embassy which you inclose, with its accompanying papers, relative to the construction of Article XII. of the convention of 1871 between the United States and Germany. The language of that article is that ' the judicial authorities and custom-house officials shall in no case proceed to the examination or search of merchant vessels without having given previous notice to the consular officers of the nation to which the said vessels belong, in order to enable the said consular officers to be present.' The concluding paragraph of the article provides for giving such notice when statements by officers or members of a crew are to be made in court or before a magistrate, in order to prevent error or false interpretation which might impede the correct administration of justice.

" The view of Mr. Griggs (letter of February 26, 1901), to which the embassy's note refers, was that the service of a writ of attachment upon a vessel is not within the language or the intent of this article of the treaty, especially since immediate service of such writ is often the very essence of the right of a claimant or creditor. The note of the German embassy, while claiming that the service of attachments is covered by the language of Article XII., concedes generally that when the object of the proceedings can otherwise not be attained, or be attained but partially, the obligation to give previous notice is so far qualified, and that the proximity of a vessel's departure justifies the

---

[a] Count Von Quadt, German chargé, to Mr. Hay, Sec. of State, Nov. 8, 1901, For. Rel. 1901, 163.

[b] Mr. Hay, Sec. of State, to Mr. von Holleben, German ambassador, Jan. 6, 1902, For. Rel. 1901, 164.

failure to notify before the attachment is effected, provided due notice is subsequently given.

" On review of the entire subject, I concur in the conclusion announced in my predecessor's letter of February 26, 1901, viz, ' that the reasons are obvious why the service of an ordinary attachment was not intended to be and was not in fact embraced in the proceedings which require previous notice under Article XII of the treaty.' "

> Mr. Knox, At. Gen., to Mr. Hay, Sec. of State, Dec. 28, 1901, For. Rel. 1901, 165.

> See Mr. Adee, Acting Sec. of State, to the governor of Virginia, Nov. 2, 1897, 222 MS. Dom. Let. 177 ; Mr. Adee, Act. Sec. of State, to Baron von Richenau, Nov. 2, 1897, MS. Notes to German Leg. XII. 97 ; Mr. Sherman, Sec. of State, to Baron von Richenau, Nov. 9, 1897, MS. Notes to German Leg. XII. 98.

By section 24 of the act of December 21, 1898, touching advance
Germany, Dec. 11, 1871, Art. XIII. wages and allotment of wages to seamen, the provisions were declared to be applicable to foreign as well as to American vessels, and like penalties were imposed in both cases. A reservation, however, was made with regard to the conflicting stipulations of treaties. The German Government took the ground that the application of the section to German vessels would conflict with Article XIII. of the treaty of December 11, 1871.

> Mr. Adee, Act. Sec. of State, to Sec. of Treasury, Oct. 12, 1899, 240 MS. Dom. Let. 492, enclosing copy of a note from the German embassy of Oct. 6, 1899.

> See, supra, the correspondence with France, in 1885, as to Art. VIII. of the consular convention of 1853.

A seaman of an Italian bark at Savannah, Ga., applied to a justice
Italy, May 8, 1878, Art. XI. of the peace to obtain payment of wages and a discharge, under sections 4546 and 4547 of the Revised Statutes of the United States, alleging as the ground on which his discharge was asked that he had been assaulted on board ship by the master. A summons was issued, but the master declined to appear, on the strength of Article XI. of the consular convention between the United States and Italy of September 18, 1878, which confers upon the consular officers of the contracting parties exclusive cognizance of " questions of whatever kind that may arise, both at sea and in port, between the captain, officers, and seamen, without exception," on merchant vessels of their respective nations. The justice of the peace then issued his certificate to the clerk of the United States district court, under section 4547, Revised Statutes, but the clerk, on the ground of the provisions of the treaty, declined to issue any process. Subsequently the seaman also filed a libel in the United States district court for the recovery of his wages.

The court likewise refused to issue any process. In so holding, however, the court intimated an opinion that if the libel, instead of being confined to the question of wages, had contained a prayer for the discharge of the seaman on account of assault, the decision might have been different, it being doubted whether the consular jurisdiction under the treaty applied to "an unjustifiable assault by the master upon the seaman on board ship, an assault which would indicate settled hostility and probable repetition while in port." The Italian legation called this dictum to the attention of the Department of State and suggested that it be corrected in order to prevent any "unlawful interpretation" of the treaty. The Department of State replied that, as the jurisdiction of the consul was sustained, the decision of the court brought the dispute to an end, but that if the case had been otherwise, the only mode of obtaining a correction of the court's judgment would have been by appeal.

> Mr. Bayard, Sec. of State, to Mr. Ferrara, Italian chargé, Jan. 10, 1887, For. Rel. 1887, 646, citing For. Rel. 1883, 9–31. The opinion of the court is printed in For. Rel. 1887, 643–646.
>
> The Italian chargé enclosed with his note a copy of a letter of the district attorney at New York, Sept. 4, 1882, to the Italian consul-general in that city, in relation to the case of an Italian seaman who had been committed by a local magistrate for an assault on another seaman on an Italian vessel. The district attorney stated that the magistrate had been advised that the State courts had no jurisdiction in the matter, and that the offender should be handed over to the consulate. (For. Rel. 1887, 642, 643.)
>
> See, however, New York Daily Register, March 13, 1875, cited in For. Rel. 1887, 645.
>
> That questions of jurisdiction are primarily of judicial cognizance, see Mr. Marcy, Sec. of State, to Mr. Clay, min. to Peru, July 18, 1855, MS. Inst. Peru, XV. 171.

Questions having arisen as to the interpretation of Article XI. of the convention with Italy of May 8, 1878, a supplementary article was concluded February 24, 1881, by which it was provided that "in case any disorder should happen on board of vessels of either party, in the territorial waters of the other," the local tribunals should not "on any pretext interfere except when the said disorders are of such a nature as to cause or be likely to cause a breach of the peace or serious trouble in the port or on shore; or when, in such trouble or breach of the peace, a person or persons shall be implicated, not forming a part of the crew."

In 1900 the courts of Florida took cognizance of the crime of murder committed by a seaman on the Italian brigantine *Pieta*, while at anchor in Pensacola Bay. The Italian ambassador protested against the action of the Florida authorities, the Italian consular agent reporting that the tranquillity of the port was not disturbed by the crime. The Department of State declined to accept this interpretation of the treaty, and referred to Wildenhus's case, 120 U. S. 1.

> Mr. Hay, Sec. of State, to Baron Fava, Ital. amb., July 19, 1900, MS. Notes to Ital. Leg., IX. 440.
>
> In 1879 the Attorney-General was requested to take such steps as might be necessary to secure to subjects of Italy their rights under Art. XI. of the convention of May 8, 1878, against a suit brought in the marine court of New York City by seamen of the Italian bark Carmela against the master for wages. The magistrate subsequently suspended the proceedings. (Mr. Evarts, Sec. of State, to Mr. Devens, At. Gen., July 24, 1879, and Mr. F. W. Seward, Acting Sec. of State, to Mr. Devens, At. Gen., Aug. 13, 1879, 129 MS. Dom. Let. 206, 411.)

"A question has recently arisen between this Government and that **Feb. 8, 1868, and** of Italy in regard to the proper construction of **May 8, 1878,** Article X. of the convention of February 8th, 1868, **Art. X.** between the United States and Italy. The question may best be stated by a brief synopsis of the case out of which it arose.

" The American bark *C. H. Foster*, while on a voyage from New York to Pozzuoli, loaded with petroleum, was obliged by stress of weather to cast overboard a part of the cargo in order to save the vessel and remaining freight. On her arrival at Pozzuoli, the captain went before the United States consul at Naples and extended his protest in accordance with the facts. A copy of this document was duly forwarded by the consul to the customs authorities and was at first received without any objection. When the vessel was ready to sail, however, it was insisted by the local officers that this mode of proof was not competent in cases of jettison, and the question having been brought to the notice of the Department, correspondence ensued between the two Governments as to the true interpretation of the article in question. This correspondence has resulted in a concurrence of views between this Department and the Italian council of state, the Government of Italy conceding that the construction of the article contended for by this Government is the correct one. The Italian minister for foreign affairs in a note of the 3d of February 1879 to the minister of this Government at Rome, says: ' The council of state to which the question was submitted has expressed the opinion that Article X. of the consular convention between Italy and the American Union should be broadly interpreted, that is to say, in the sense that the evidence of captains and crews given before their consuls and the written depositions relating thereto be accepted by the custom-house as legal proof of damage, until evidence to the contrary before the judicial authority, as is practiced in the case of depositions taken before presidents of tribunals of commerce and pretors.'

"Article X. of the consular convention of May 8th 1878 is similar in its provisions to Article X. in the convention of February 8th, 1868, upon which the foregoing construction was given.

" It is deemed proper to bring the conclusion thus arrived at to your notice in order that it may serve as a guide to your official conduct in any similar cases that may arise within the jurisdiction of your consulate."

> Mr. Hunter, Second Assist. Sec. of State, to U. S. consuls in Italy, circular, May 14, 1880, MS. Circulars, II. 482.

The right " to sit as judges and arbitrators in such differences as may arise between the captains and crews," given to consular officers by article 13 of the treaty with Sweden and Norway of 1827, is expressly qualified by the clause " unless the conduct of the crews or of the captain should disturb the order or tranquillity of the country," which includes all acts amounting to actual breaches of the public peace.

Sweden and Norway, 1827, Art. XIII.

It seems that a more enlarged jurisdiction is conferred upon consuls by some other treaties; *e. g.*, with France, February 23, 1853; with the German Empire, December 11, 1871; with Italy, February 8, 1868.

> Taft, At.-Gen., 1876, 15 Op. 178.

There is nothing in the treaty between the United States and Sweden and Norway which precludes the courts of Philadelphia County from taking jurisdiction of an indictment for assault and battery committed on board a Norwegian bark lying in the port of Philadelphia.

> Com. *v.* Luckness, 14 Phila. (Pa.) 363.

" Referring to your note of the 13th of February last, in regard to the case of Jacob Jacobsen, a seaman of the Norwegian bark *Livingstone*, at Philadelphia, to mine of the 19th of April and to subsequent conversation on the subject, I have the honor to state that I have given the matter careful consideration in connection with the views and suggestions of your note and the provisions of the XIIIth article of the treaty of 1827, between the United States and Sweden and Norway. The stipulations contained in the last clause of that article . . . are those under which it is contended by you that jurisdiction is conferred on the consular officers, not only in regard to such differences of a civil nature growing out of the contract or engagement of the seaman, but also as to disputes and controversies resulting from personal violence and involving offences for which the party may be held amenable under the local criminal law.

" This Government does not view the article in question as susceptible of this broad interpretation. The jurisdiction conferred upon the consuls is conceived to be limited to their right to sit as judges or arbitrators in such differences as may arise between the captains and crews of the vessels, where such differences do not involve on the part of the captain or crew, a disturbance of the order or tranquillity of the country. When, however, a complaint is made to a local magistrate, either by the captain or one or more of the crew of the vessel, involving the disturbance of the order or tranquillity of the country, it is competent for such magistrate to take cognizance of the matter in pursuance of the local laws; and under such circumstances in the United States, it becomes a public duty which the judge or magistrate is not at liberty voluntarily to forego. In all such cases it must necessarily be left to the local judicial authorities whether the procedure shall take place in the United States or in Sweden, to determine if in fact there has been such disturbance of the local order or tranquillity; and, if the complaint is supported by such proof as results in the conviction of the party accused, to visit upon the offender such punishment as may be denounced against the offence by the municipal law of the place. This is all that the judicial authorities at Philadelphia appear to have done, and I note with satisfaction from the report of my colleague, the Attorney-General, that Judge Pierce of the criminal court of Philadelphia County, before whom the case was finally tried, afforded every facility consistent with law, to the vice-consul of Sweden and Norway, to render effective such measures as that officer deemed it proper to inaugurate in the interest of the accused mate, and expressed his willingness to allow the vice-consul to take the case before the United States district court, if he so desired.

" The trial appears to have been in every respect fair and impartial towards Mr. Lickness, the accused mate; and the punishment inflicted it must be admitted was very moderate. I need scarcely observe to you that in the United States, as in Sweden and Norway, a personal assault and battery involves a breach of the public peace and is held to be a disturbance of the order and tranquillity of the country.

" In all cases in which it may become necessary and proper for the consular officers of Sweden and Norway to sit as judges or arbitrators in differences that may arise between the captain and crews of the vessels of their nation, this Government will cheerfully recognize such jurisdiction and will also find satisfaction in affording such aid, through its judicial and other officers, as may be necessary to cause their decisions to be supported and carried into effect."

Mr. Evarts, Sec. of State, to Count Lewenhaupt, Swed. & Nor. min., July 30, 1880, MS. Notes to Swed. & Nor. VII. 204.

Art. XIII. of the treaty of 1827, in excluding the interference of the local authorities, makes the qualification " unless the conduct of the crews or of the captain should disturb the order or tranquillity of the country."

In the case of two mates of the Swedish bark Fredrika and Carolina, who were fined by a justice of the peace at Galveston, Texas, on account of a "quarrel" that took place on board the vessel, the United States district attorney was instructed to take the necessary steps to have the proceedings dismissed, and the aid of the governor of Texas was invoked with a view "to guard against a repetition of similar proceedings." (Mr. Fish, Sec. of State, to Mr. Grip, Swed. & Nor. chargé, May 6, 1876; Mr. F. W. Seward, Act. Sec. of State, to Count Lewenhaupt, Swed. & Nor. min., May 17, 1877, MS. Notes to Sw. & Nor. VII. 92, 122.)

As to the case of Captain Sorensen, of the Swedish or Norwegian ship *Carl Angell*, before the marine court of New York City, and to the opinion in Petersen *v.* Brockelmann, affirmed on appeal by the supreme court of New York, general term, see Mr. Evarts, Sec. of State, to Count Lewenhaupt, Oct. 25, 1877, MS. Notes to Sw. & Nor. VII. 134.

The right of consular officers under the treaty with Sweden and Norway of July 4, 1827, to "sit as judges and arbitrators in such differences as may arise between the captains and crews of the vessels belonging to the nation whose interests are committed to their charge, without the interference of the local authorities" (Art. XIII.), applies to disputes as to wages.

Mr. Foster, Sec. of State, to the governor of Massachusetts, Aug. 20, 1892, 187 MS. Dom. Let. 624, acknowledging the latter's letter of Aug. 13; Mr. Uhl, Act. Sec. of State, to gov. of Mass., May 3, 1894, 196 MS. Dom. Let. 586; Mr. Uhl, Act. Sec. of State, to Attorney-General, Jan. 9, 1895, 200 MS. Dom. Let. 186.

This correspondence related to the arrest, at Boston, of Captain Tellefsen, of the Norwegian steamer *Albert*, by constable, who went on board the vessel to serve a summons issued by the municipal court of that city in a suit instituted by some of the seamen for wages. The captain having refused to accept the service, the constable forcibly arrested him. The captain, to secure his liberty, paid the claim, amounting to about $23, and also about $10 in costs, but afterwards sued the constable in the supreme court of the State, apparently for false imprisonment, and the jury, under instructions from the court, found for the defendant. The minister of Sweden and Norway then presented to the United States a claim for indemnity, amounting to about $130. The Department of State, in transmitting it to the governor of Massachusetts, said: "This language [of Art. XIII.] seems clearly to give jurisdiction of controversies about wages between captains and crews of Norwegian vessels to the Norwegian consul, and to exclude the jurisdiction of the local authorities over such controversies. Since treaties in this country are laws binding on all the courts, I can not but think that this treaty was not brought to the notice either of the municipal court . . . or of the judge who presided at the subsequent trial. I infer from the instructions given at the trial, of which the Norwegian minister has sent a copy to this Department, that the judge's attention was directed merely to the general question of local jurisdiction over foreign merchant ships in our ports. Viewed in this general light the instruction was undoubtedly correct, but I scarcely think the judge can have considered the question in the special light of the treaty." (Mr. Uhl, Act. Sec. of State, to governor of Mass., May 3, 1894, 196 MS. Dom. Let. 586.)

It seems that an appeal was afterwards taken from the verdict in favor of the constable. The Department of State requested the Attorney-General if practicable to take such action as might be proper to protect the rights of jurisdiction conferred by the treaty. (Mr. Uhl, Act. Sec. of State, to Attorney-General, Jan. 9, 1895, 200 MS. Dom. Let. 186, enclosing copies of notes from the minister of Sweden and Norway of March 15 and 22, April 28, and May 22, 1894.)

In the same communication the Department of State referred to another claim for indemnity in the case of the Swedish vessel *Adele*, whose master was arrested in December, 1893, at Brunswick, Georgia, on a warrant issued by a justice of the peace, based on his detention of certain bags of clothing belonging to some seamen who had deserted because of the nonpayment of wages demanded by them. It seems that, although the provisions of the treaty were brought to the justice's attention, he ordered the master to be imprisoned till he should surrender the property. The decision of the justice was afterwards reversed by the superior court of Glynn County. (Mr. Adee, Act. Sec. of State, to governor of Georgia, Sept. 4, 1895, 204 MS. Dom. Let. 431.)

The claim for indemnity, amounting to $295.64, was transmitted to the governor of Georgia. (Mr. Adee, Act. Sec. of State, to governor of Georgia, Sept. 4, 1895, 204 MS. Dom. Let. 431; Mr. Olney, Sec. of State, to governor of Georgia, Oct. 19, 1895, 205 MS. Dom. Let. 405, referring to a previous letter to the governor of Oct. 7.)

The proceedings against the master of the Norwegian vessel *Vestfold* in 1884, on a complaint made by three seamen before a justice of the peace at Mobile, Alabama, in a dispute about wages, were, in view of the provisions of the treaty, "evidently void *ab initio*," and it was asked that such aid as might be proper be given to the Swedish and Norwegian vice-consul in having the judgment against the master vacated. (Mr. Frelinghuysen, Sec. of State, to the Attorney-General, Dec. 30, 1884, 153 MS. Dom. Let. 532; Mr. Frelinghuysen, Sec. of State, to governor of Alabama, Dec. 30, 1884, id. 528.)

Under Article XIII. of the treaty of 1827, between the United States and Sweden and Norway, providing that consuls shall have the right to sit as judges in differences between captains and crews of vessels belonging to their respective nations without interference of local authorities, the consul of Sweden and Norway, residing in Boston, has exclusive jurisdiction of a controversy as to wages between the captain of a Norwegian vessel lying within the territorial jurisdiction of the municipal court of said city and one of the crew, also a Norwegian, who has left the ship because his term has expired.

Telefsen *v.* Fee (Mass.), 46 N. E 562.

3. PROTESTS AGAINST ONEROUS EXACTIONS

§ 207.

Fines, taxes, and seizures. In 1873 complaint was made to the Spanish Government of the onerous burdens to which the trade of the United States was subjected by reason of the system of fines imposed by the customs authorities of Cuba. The same subject had been presented to the Spanish Government in 1870 and 1872.

Complaint was made of the fines imposed on vessels for any variance between manifest and cargo, either in the weight or contents of packages, while the goods escaped all responsibility, as well as of fines imposed on vessels for want of a statement of the specific class of goods, although the generic class was stated in the manifest in conformity with the requirements of the Spanish laws, and the manifests were accepted and certified by the Spanish consul at the port of shipment. Complaint was also made of differences in the construction of the laws at the various ports in Cuba, of the onerous conditions imposed on appeals, and of the losses occasioned by the detention of vessels.

> Mr. Fish, Sec. of State, to Gen. Sickles, min. to Spain, March 21, 1873, For. Rel. 1873, II. 932; MS. Inst. Spain, XVI. 409.
>
> See, also, Mr. Fish, Sec. of State, to Gen. Schenck, March 22, 1873, MS. Inst. Gr. Britain, XXIII. 307.
>
> See Gen. Sickles, min. to Spain, to Mr. Fish, Sec. of State, June 1, 1873, reporting his action. (For. Rel. 1873, II. 989–999; also 1036–1044.)
>
> See, further, as to fines imposed on vessels in Cuba, Mr. Frelinghuysen, Sec. of State, to Mr. Hamlin, min. to Spain, Feb. 15, 1882, For. Rel. 1882, 460.
>
> As to the fines imposed on the American bark Masonic, at Manila, in 1879, and the award of Baron Blanc, as arbitrator, in favor of the United States, see Moore, Int. Arbitrations, II. 1055–1069.

In 1882 and 1883, a long correspondence took place between the United States and Spain in regard to the latter's consular tariff, and particularly to a tax of 40 cents a head imposed by Spanish consuls at Key West on cattle shipped to Cuba and Porto Rico, in addition to the usual consular fees for clearance and certification of papers. The United States protested against it as being virtually an export tax levied in the United States by Spain. Spain ultimately ordered the return of so much of the tax collected as was in excess of 10 per cent.

> Mr. J. Davis, Act. Sec. of State, to Mr. Hamlin, min. to Spain, Sept. 4, 1882, For. Rel. 1882, 478; Mr. Foster, min. to Spain, to Mr. Frelinghuysen, Sec. of State, Jan. 23, 1884, For. Rel. 1884, 474.

See, for further discussion as to the Spanish consular tariff, and as to other Spanish charges, For. Rel. 1882, 455–459, 461, 463, 467, 470, 480, 486; For. Rel. 1883, 764, 771, 779, 791–795.

"A controversy on a similar subject [to the cattle tax] took place a few years since between this Government and that of Hayti. A copy of the two principal instructions in regard to the subject from Mr. Evarts to the minister of the United States in that country is transmitted for your information.

"The Haytian Government ultimately repealed the obnoxious tax."   (Mr. Frelinghuysen, Sec. of State, to Mr. Hamlin, min. to Spain, Sept. 22, 1882, For. Rel. 1882, 480.)

" I have alluded in my previous messages to the injurious and vexatious restrictions suffered by our trade in the Spanish West Indies. Brazil, whose natural outlet for its great national staple, coffee, is in and through the United States, imposes a heavy export duty upon that product. Our petroleum exports are hampered in Turkey and in other Eastern ports by restrictions as to storage and by onerous taxation. For these mischiefs adequate relief is not always afforded by reciprocity treaties like that with Hawaii or that lately negotiated with Mexico and now awaiting the action of the Senate. Is it not advisable to provide some measure of equitable retaliation in our relations with governments which discriminate against our own? If, for example, the Executive were empowered to apply to Spanish vessels and cargoes from Cuba and Puerto Rico the same rules of treatment and scale of penalties for technical faults which are applied to our vessels and cargoes in the Antilles, a resort to that course might not be barren of good results."

President Arthur, third annual message, 1883.

See annual message of President Cleveland of Dec. 3, 1894, saying, among other things: " Unreasonable and unjust fines imposed by Spain on the vessels and commerce of the United States have demanded from time to time during the last twenty years earnest remonstrance on the part of our Government."

See, also, for further correspondence in relation to fines imposed on American vessels in Cuba and Porto Rico, For. Rel. 1889, 658–682.

Fraud, when essential to sustain a custom-house confiscation, is only to be held to exist when plainly to be inferred from the facts.

Mr. Frelinghuysen, Sec. of State, to Mr. Foster, min. to Spain, Feb. 25, 1884; Mr. Bayard, Sec. of State, to Mr. Foster, min. to Spain, July 25, 1885. MS. Inst. Spain, XIX. 490; XX. 75.

" The undersigned, Secretary of State of the United States, has the honor to acknowledge the receipt of the note of Mr. Preston, envoy extraordinary and minister plenipotentiary of Hayti, of the 16th instant.

" It states that his government has thought proper to transfer to its legation in this country the discussion which has heretofore been carried on with the legation of the United States at Port au Prince, relative to the act of the Haytian Congress of the 23d of August, 1877, authorizing certain charges by the consuls of that republic abroad on exportations from foreign countries to Hayti. With a view to show that those charges are not incompatible with the treaty between the United States and that republic, Mr. Preston quotes several articles of that instrument. These, however, are general in their terms and appear to have no special reference to the question at issue.

"According to the preamble, one of the main objects of the treaty was to place the commercial relations between the two countries upon the most liberal basis.

" The act of the Haytian legislature referred to cannot be regarded as in conformity with that stipulation. It authorizes the consuls of that republic to charge exorbitant fees on exportations from the United States; among others, one per cent. on the value of cargo of the vessel. This, besides being illiberal in its character, is tantamount to an export duty, acquiescence in which by this government would be a concession to that of Hayti of an authority in ports of the United States which has not been conferred on this government by the Constitution.

" There is, however, a clause in the thirteenth article of the treaty, one of those cited by Mr. Preston, which seems to have a direct application to the point in dispute.

" If the Haytian consular charges in the United States are so considerable as virtually to be an export tax, this would in effect contravene the stipulation which declares that no higher duties or charges shall be imposed in the United States on the exportation of any article to Hayti than such as shall be payable on the exportation of the like article to any foreign country. This clause is unconditional, and not only forbids this government from levying any such tax, but also a consul of Hayti at a port of the United States.

" The preamble to the Haytian law in question expressly acknowledges that one of its objects was to benefit the treasury of that republic. Several of the other charges which it authorizes appear to be excessive. Such charges may not be uniform as prescribed by the laws of different countries. It is believed, however, that no other than Hayti has authorized them to such an extravagant amount as that provided for by the law referred to, or has required an export tax on merchandise. This Department had hoped that the remonstrances on the subject which had been addressed to that government through the United States legation in Hayti would ere this have led to a repeal or modification of that statute. This hope has, however, been disappointed, but as the charges complained of are believed to work a serious discouragement to trade, it is hoped that, as the Haytian Government is understood to be adverse to a policy lead-ing to such a result, it will no longer delay removing the cause of the grievance.

"It is believed that Mr. Preston is mistaken in saying that the United States is the only government which has complained of the effect of the statute referred to. According to reports from the lega-tion of this country in Hayti, representatives of other governments have also pointedly complained to the same effect."

> Mr. Evarts, Sec. of State, to Mr. Preston, Haytian min., Jan. 22, 1879, For. Rel. 1879, 586.
>
> See, also, Mr. Preston to Mr. Evarts, Feb. 4 and April 4, 1879, For. Rel. 1879, 587, 591; Mr. Evarts to Mr. Preston, April 19 and June 13, 1879, id. 593, 595; Mr. Langston, min. to Hayti, to Mr. Evarts, Sec. of State, Jan. 24, 1879, For. Rel. 1879, 546–550; Mr. Evarts, Sec. of State, to Mr. Langston, min. to Hayti, Nov. 7, 1877, and April 12, 1878, For. Rel. 1878, 410, 445; and dispatches from Mr. Langston, min. to Hayti, to Mr. Evarts, Sec. of State, Dec. 6 and 22, 1877, and Jan. 9 and 24, 1878, For. Rel. 1878, 415, 416, 427, 428.

"Referring to your note of the 9th of May last, and my acknowl-edgment thereof on the 13th of the same month, in relation to the Haytian tariff of consular fees under the decree of August 23, 1877, and to the protests of the representatives at Port au Prince of the United States, Great Britain, Germany, and France, and the reply of the Haytain Government thereto, I have now the honor to com-municate to you, in conformity with the desire expressed by the Marquis of Salisbury, the views of this government in relation to that question.

"The Government of Hayti, prior to the reply of the 6th of March last to the foreign representatives named, had seen fit on the 4th of February to transfer the discussion of the question to Washington, so far as this government was concerned, by a very full and argu-mentative note, addressed to me by Mr. Stephen Preston, the Haytian minister in this country. Although much more extended, the note of Mr. Preston in the main merely repeats and reaffirms the reasoning and conclusions of the communications made to the foreign representatives by M. Ethéart, and, like those, they appeared to this government, as well as to that of Her Majesty, as appears from your note, to be alto-gether unsatisfactory, and reply was so made to Mr. Preston on the 13th ultimo. In that reply the Haytian minister was informed, with with respect to that portion of his note which related to the authenti-cation by the consular officers of Hayti in this country of the invoices of the cargoes of vessels bound to the ports of that country, that the charge of one per cent. on values for that proceeding is, after the most deliberate consideration, believed to be unduly exorbitant, and tanta-mount to an export tax, which it does not comport with the dignity of this government to allow to be exacted by any foreign authority within the jurisdiction of the United States. It was asserted that, even if the exaction in the form in which it is imposed were moderate and unobjectionable as to amount, still, if it were once acquiesced in, this would be a bar to any objection which this government might make if the consular fee were afterward to be much augmented. The inexpediency of subjecting exports from this country to Hayti to a tax of the kind was further illustrated by the consideration that, owing to the dangers of the sea and other causes, many cargoes do not reach their destination.

" The Government of the United States being, by its Constitution, expressly prohibited from levying an export tax, it can not allow any foreign power to exercise here, in substance or in form, a right of sovereignty denied to itself. No denial was made of the right of the Haytian Government, at its discretion, so far as this may not have been limited by treaty, to impose duties on the cargoes of vessels from this country arriving in Haytian ports, but it was complained most positively that the present grievance of a consular fee of this character exacted in our ports is, in its form, derogatory to the sovereignty of the United States, and that this character was not removed from it by the Haytian citation of the axioms of political economy that all duties are ultimately paid by the consumer. In view of all this, it was hoped that the Haytian Government would see the expediency of changing its regulations upon that subject without any unnecessary delay."

> Mr. Evarts, Sec. of State, to Sir E. Thornton, Brit. min., July 14, 1879, For. Rel. 1879, 501.
>
> "The Haytian Government ultimately repealed the obnoxious tax." (Mr. Frelinghuysen, Sec. of State to Mr. Hamlin, min. to Spain, Sept. 22, 1882, For. Rel. 1882, 480.)
>
> See Mr. Langston, min. to Hayti, to Mr. Blaine, Sec. of State, reporting the passage of the law abolishing the charge in question owing to the joint efforts of the American and British ministers. (For. Rel. 1881, 646.)
>
> For correspondence in relation to the detention of sailing vessels in Haytian ports after the discharge of their cargoes till duties were paid, see For. Rel. 1891, 650–657.

" The frequent recurrence of these arbitrary seizures of American vessels by the Mexican customs officers in the Gulf and Pacific ports of that Republic is becoming a matter of serious anxiety to this Government in view of the possible effect such proceedings may ultimately have on the commerce of both nations. The similarity of institutions, the close neighborhood, and the community of interests of the peoples of the two great North American Republics, no less than the permanent and abiding friendship that exists between both Governments, renders it most desirable that every obstacle and impediment to the growth and progress of this commerce, which this Government, in common with that of Mexico, is at the moment so earnestly engaged in fostering, should be as far as practicable removed. In most instances these arbitrary and irregular proceedings are directed against small vessels, and often in their results involve losses far beyond the pecuniary value of the vessel. The masters are driven to the courts for redress, often by appeal to the Supreme Court, at great expense; and the instances are few, if, indeed, any can be found, where the courts have sustained the action of the customs officers. In bringing the present claim to the attention of the minister for foreign affairs, which you will do with as little delay as convenient, you will also submit to the minister, for the consideration of the Government, these general suggestions which I have felt it my duty to offer."

> Mr. Frelinghuysen, Sec. of State, to Mr. Morgan, min. to Mexico, Jan. 31, 1883, MS. Inst. Mexico, XX, 568.

" Your conclusion accords with that of this Department, that the case, on the admitted statements, presents certain grave features.

" 1. The refusal of the Mexican authorities to allow Captain Caleb to have access to the consul when arrested, or when called upon to plead.

" 2. Their action in requiring Captain Caleb to sign certain declarations while *incommunicado* and without knowledge of their purport, especially as it appears that these so-called declarations may be relied upon to establish the Mexican claim that Captain Caleb admits a violation of the criminal law of Mexico. That Captain Caleb signed the papers in question under bodily fear or constraint is not yet fully established. If it were, it would lend an exceptional gravity to the case.

" 3. The refusal of the collector to permit the consul to visit the vessel.

" It is of course impossible to judge fully of the case until the text of the so-called declarations of Captain Caleb is known. . . .

" If you have not already done so, you will now address Señor Mariscal, asking an examination, and requesting copies of the *declarations* signed by Captain Caleb. You will intimate to the minister that the manner in which Captain Caleb alleges he was constrained to sign papers of the contents of which he was ignorant, and while deprived of the assistance of the consul for his intelligent protection against any misunderstanding on his part, is regarded as an irregularity which, in the judgment of this Government, will deprive those declarations of any moral weight if they be trusted to sustain the charge of smuggling brought against the captain. And you will further intimate that the whole course of the proceedings appears to be so inconsistent with the principles recognized in the intercourse of maritime states that persistence in the prosecution of Captain Caleb on those premises could not fail to call forth the most earnest remonstrance of this Government.

" It is not the desire or purpose of this Government to screen any of its citizens who may have willfully violated foreign law.   But it is its plain duty to endeavor by every legitimate means to secure for its citizens under accusation of wrong-doing such justice and impartiality of treatment and such safeguards for their defense as shall entitle the judgment reached to the respect which judicial proceedings should everywhere command.

" If the rules of international justice shall appear to have been in any way infringed, it is the undeniable right and obligation of this Government to interpose its diplomatic offices to insure a fair trial."

> Mr. Frelinghuysen, Sec. of State, to Mr. Morgan, min. to Mexico, Feb. 20, 1883, For. Rel. 1883, 625.
>
> This instruction related to the proceedings taken at La Paz, Mexico, against the American vessel Adriana, and her master, Captain George Caleb, on a charge of smuggling. They resulted in the condemnation and sale of the vessel and a sentence against Captain Caleb of 5 years' imprisonment. He afterwards petitioned for a pardon, but his petition, which admitted that he had transferred effects from his vessel while in the bay of Pulmo to Los Frailes in Lower California, was refused.   (For. Rel. 1884, 348, 350, 351.)
>
> June 12, 1884, the United States consul at La Paz reported that Captain Caleb had on the 11th of May " deserted the private house wherein he was confined, committing a breach of parole, under which custody he had been kept before and after he was sentenced," and had gone to San Francisco.   (For. Rel. 1884, 371, 372.)   See supra, p. 92.

" Referring to Mr. Bartleman's No. 375, of the 5th ultimo, inclosing a copy of a decree issued by the Venezuelan Government on December 30, 1892, imposing, on and after March 1, next, a differential duty of 30 per cent on merchandise from the United States and Europe destined for the western ports of the Republic, but transshipped at Curaçao, I desire to call your attention to the correspondence exchanged between this Department and the legation at Caracas in 1881, 1882, and 1883, and published in the volumes of Foreign Relations for the years 1882 and 1883.

" This correspondence related to the act of the Congress of Venezuela of May 27, 1881, imposing a similar differential duty of 30 per cent on all merchandise imported into the Republic which had been transshipped at any of the ports of the West India islands.

" The act in question was found to be prejudicial to the interests of this country, and upon the representations of our minister was modified by executive decree of January 26, 1883, in a manner satisfactory to our business interests.   (See Foreign Relations, 1883, pp. 897–900.)

" You are instructed to make similar representations against the present decree, which, though more limited in its operations, is none the less objectionable."

> Mr. Foster, Sec. of State, to Mr. Partridge, min. to Venezuela, Feb. 8, 1893, For. Rel. 1893, 718. Mr. Bartleman's dispatch and the text of decrees of Dec. 30, 1892, and Jan. 5, 1893, are printed on p. 717, of the same volume. See Mr. Partridge's full report of March 8, 1893, For. Rel. 1893, 718.
>
> May 25, 1893, Mr. Partridge reported that the Venezuelan Government, by a decree of the 22nd inst., copy and translation of which he inclosed, had restored the privilege of transshipping freight at Curaçao. (For. Rel. 1893, 725, 726.)
>
> See, also, Mr. Partridge's dispatches of July 22 and July 25, 1893, in relation to decrees of July 7 and July 21, 1893, respectively conferring on the postal steamers of the General French Transatlantic Company and the American Red D Line preferential facilities for loading and discharging cargo. (For. Rel. 1893, 733, 734.)
>
> In 1887 the Government of Venezuela threatened to close its ports against the island of Curaçao, in consequence of the refusal of the Dutch authorities to expel certain Venezuelan revolutionists. Two of them were afterwards expelled, and the difficulty was adjusted. The United States minister at Caracas was instructed to protest against the enforcement of such a measure as that proposed, which, by preventing transshipment at Curaçao, would seriously affect American commerce. The subject was deemed to be of such importance that the views of the United States upon it were submitted to Venezuela, notwithstanding the settlement of her difficulty with the Dutch authorities. (For. Rel. 1888, II. 1637, 1639, 1640.)

" The question of the *Lorine*, as laid before this Department in your despatches Nos. 237 and 238, has received care-

Custody of ship's papers.

ful consideration. The despatch of Señor Ramirez, of April 25th last, with its enclosed supplement to the *Gaceta de Panamá* of the same date, has also been considered in the same relation. . . .

" The conflict of the Colombian statute, known as the 60th law of 1875, with the treaty obligations of Colombia in regard to the freedom of the ports of Colon and Panama and the isthmian transit, was formerly recognized by the Colombian Government in the diplomatic agreement of 1876, as stated in the note addressed by Señor Ancizar on the 27th of July of that year to the representatives of Great Britain, Germany, the United States, and France. That note set forth the inconvenience of the law, in that, by its 3d and 5th articles, it prescribed the unusual procedure of delivering the registers of foreign vessels in all Colombian ports, without specifying to what officer they were to be delivered, and it was agreed that until the law should be modified by the Colombian Congress, the registers of such vessels should be deposited with the consul of the respective nation, or, in the absence of such consul, then with the consul of a friendly power.

" This diplomatic understanding is not known to have been derogated from by any subsequent international agreement, or by any act of the supreme Government of the United States of Colombia. Even were it annulled this Government could not freely assent to the delivery of the registers of its vessels to the keeping of the local authorities of another nation, in the free ports of Panama and Colon, or indeed in any port where there may be a consular representative of the United States, duly acknowledged under the consular convention with Colombia. The practice of all commercial nations is opposed to such a course, which is moreover deemed to be not merely totally unnecessary as a preventive measure, but to directly trench upon the fundamental principle of consular control over foreign vessels as laid down by the law of nations.

" It is trusted, however, that, as the matter now stands, the enforcement of the vague, unnecessary, improvident and unusual requirements of the 3d and 5th articles of the 60th law of 1875 will not be attempted in contravention of the diplomatic agreement of 1876; and that the firm and energetic action of his excellency the President of the State of Panama, as summed up in his executive resolution of April 22d last, will receive from the Federal Government of Colombia the support due to his zealous desire to uphold the international obligations of his country in the face of the conflicting orders of its Government.

" The course of the local officer of the Colombian treasury, although founded on the instructions of his superior officer at Bogota, is believed to have been unnecessarily peremptory and arbitrary. Such acts and such employment of force to support his excessive demands, as are attributed to him, done against the vessels of friendly nations in a free port like that of Colon, cannot but be regarded as censurable.

" Your proceedings in the matter of the *Lorine* are, in view of all the facts, approved by the Department; and, in the event of a similar case arising, you will insist, firmly but dispassionately, on the observance of the international agreement of July 27, 1876, in so far as relates to the delivery of ship's papers to the consular officer instead of the local revenue authorities."

Mr. Evarts, Sec. of State, to Mr. Thorington, commercial agent at Colon, May 11, 1878, 89 MS. Desp. to Consuls, 187.

See For. Rel. 1879, 260, 266, 280; For. Rel. 1880, 312, 315, 320. A copy of a new Colombian statute, based on §§ 4209, 4211, U. S. Rev. Stats., will be found in For. Rel. 1880, 489.

See, also, Mr. Frelinghuysen, Sec. of State, to Mr. Scruggs, min. to Colombia, March 6, 1883, MS. Inst. Colombia, XVII. 329.

" You have yourself already made known to the President several very convincing reasons why the practice in Venezuela of demanding that the custody of ships' papers while in port be confided to the Venezuelan officers is not in consonance with the practice of nations or with commercial interests. Your grounds were good, as far as they went, but the principles underlying the question are broader, and involve the doctrine of reciprocity under treaty and international maritime laws.

" In the first place, it is proper that the President should be disabused of any impression he may have formed that the matter is brought up as an innovation. It has for more than fifty years been the occasion of discussion and remonstrance with various nations of Spanish America; and if it be now revived in connection with Venezuela, it is because it seems necessary to the best interests of both countries that an anomalous practice should not exist between them in this respect.

" The discussion with Colombia is in point. In 1876 a general movement of the foreign representatives at Bogota was made to secure the abrogation of a law which required the delivery of the papers of foreign vessels to the local port officers. An arrangement then concluded diplomatically set the matter at rest by recognizing the right of the consul of the ship's nationality to have the custody of the ships' papers of their national vessels, and the law has since been repealed.

" I transmit, herewith, for your information, copies of two dispatches from Mr. Dichman, then our minister at Bogota, in which the merits of the demand are forcibly presented. Although the circumstances made the argument somewhat special, as applying to a specific law, and to the peculiar *status* of Colon and Panama as free ports, you will find in these dispatches ample material for fortifying your representations to the Venezuelan Government in the premises. You may, also, profitably consult the remaining correspondence on the subject, found in the volumes of Foreign Relations for 1875, 1879, and 1880, which are, or should be, in the library of your legation.[a]

" It may be convenient to note herein, briefly, a few points to which prominence should be given.

" In the first place, the existing rule in Venezuela is deemed to be in contravention of the spirit of perfect equality and reciprocity of commerce and navigation between the two countries, as stipulated in the abrogated treaty of 1836, and as pervading the existing treaty of 1860. The law of the United States, following the usage of most

---

[a] For. Rel. 1879, 260, 266, 280; For. Rel. 1880, 312, 315, 320. A copy of the new Columbian statute, based on §§ 4209, 4211, U. S. Rev. Stats., will be found in For. Rel. 1880, 489. See, also, Mr. Frelinghuysen, Sec. of State, to Mr. Scruggs, min. to Colombia, March 6, 1883, MS. Inst. Colombia, XVII. 329.

civilized countries, provides that the custody of the papers of foreign ships shall rest with the consuls of their nations, and this because such custody is deemed essential to that consular control over national vessels which is stipulated in all our treaties. It cannot be expected that the United States will unreservedly yield to the authorities of a foreign state a measure of control over our vessels in their ports which is not permitted by our own law to be exercised by our own officers in our own ports, over foreign vessels, except as a retaliatory measure in the absence of reciprocity. In this connection it may be well for you to examine as to the provisions of Venezuelan law touching the custody of the papers of Venezuelan vessels in foreign ports. I make this suggestion because in the discussion of this question with Colombia it was found that the Colombian law was strangely inconsistent in requiring Colombian consuls abroad to take charge of the papers of vessels of their nation, while denying a reciprocal practice to foreign consuls in Colombia. If a like law should be found on the Venezuelan statute books, no stronger argument in our favor could be devised.

" You should also, in this relation, call attention to the twenty-sixth article of the treaty of 1860, and ask how it is expected that an American consul can *exhibit* the register and crew-roll of an American vessel in proceedings for the arrest of deserters, if at no time he is permitted to have possession of those papers.

" In the second place, apart from considerations of reciprocity founded on treaty, the sacredness of the principles of reciprocity as an enduring basis of international intercourse under the law of nations may be forcibly invoked to sustain our position. A vessel, under a civilized flag, on the high seas or in a foreign port, possesses a national life of which its papers are the strongest evidence. They are to all intents a part of the vessel itself. To assume that by the act of entering a friendly port, a vessel is to be stripped of that which is in a large measure essential to the proof of its nationality, and to await the pleasure of a local foreign officer before such part of its life can be restored to it, is inconsistent with international principles and usage. Hence, we find that the custom of nations (with but few exceptions in the Spanish-American ports of South America) recognizes the consul of the vessel's nationality as the sole guardian of all national rights appertaining thereto. The exceptions to which I refer (and which are happily growing fewer as the principles of international intercourse are better understood) rest on no broad principle of comity; they violate comity, on the contrary, by asserting a painful spirit of distrust. It is, as Mr. Dichman aptly expresses it in a dispatch of September 4, 1879 (Foreign Relations, 1880, page 313), much as though it were regarded by the local authorities as a more effective pledge to prevent a ship's leaving a port to have material possession of her register ' than if the rudder had been unshipped.' The form in which this distrust is expressed, moreover, seems to evidence a misapprehension as to the nature and value of a ship's register. As I have said above, the register is the evidence of the ship's nationality, and as such, with the ship itself, are properly within the continuous jurisdiction of the vessel's nation, and, therefore, in a foreign port, within the jurisdiction of the consul of that nation. . . .

" In the next place, a conclusive reason for the custody of a ship's papers by the consul of her nation is found in the necessity of preventing frauds against individuals in connection with marine survey, repairs, bottomry bonds, the right of absent owners, &c., and protection of the rights of seamen. It is for these purposes that the legislation of nations provides that the register of a vessel while in port shall pass out of the control of her commander and into the custody of the consul. It is not at all necessary that these diversified rights should be subservient to the local police surveillance while in a foreign port, and yet the rule existing in Venezuela so subordinates them. Moreover, the exercise of these several rights over a vessel for which the laws of her nation make abundant provision is rendered almost impossible by the passage of the papers out of the control of the nation to which the vessel belongs.

" Finally, in your conversation with General Guzman Blanco, you have set forth the considerations of convenience which should have weight in determining the question. The loss of important ship's papers while in foreign custody has been only too common an occurrence in the countries where this obnoxious regulation obtains. The correspondence with Colombia shows that this was admitted as a powerful objection to the practice, and you can doubtless adduce examples occurring in Venezuela to strengthen your point. I must compliment you, too, on your aptness in meeting General Guzman Blanco's objection that if any feeling of distrust were shown in this matter, it lay in an endeavor to take from the local officers the custody of a foreign vessel's papers. We do not seek to take from Venezuela a recognized right because we distrust its exercise; we simply wish to retain for our own consuls a right which we deem pertains to them as the representatives of our national sovereignty, and one which is claimed and recognized as just among maritime nations.

" I infer from the request of General Guzman Blanco that he is not tenacious of the point, but rather asks for so conclusive a statement of our position as would warrant him in bringing the matter to the consideration of the Venezuelan Congress, with a view to asking such modification of existing law as will put Venezuelan legislation in this respect in harmony with the legislation and usage of maritime countries throughout the world. You will, therefore, in presenting to him

a succinct memorandum founded on this dispatch, set the question
forth on its merits, as aiming to facilitate a needed reform rather
than as aggressively combating an assumed intent to adhere to an
obnoxious system."

> Mr. Frelinghuysen, Sec. of State, to Mr. Baker, min. to Venezuela, No.
> 190, Nov. 29, 1882, For. Rel. 1882, 543.   See, also, Same to Same, No.
> 191, Nov. 29, 1882, MS. Inst. Venez. III. 268.
>
> It appeared that by the Venezuelan law the Venezuelan consuls were
> charged with the custody of ship's papers.   (For. Rel. 1883, 919.)
>
> For dispatches on the subject, of April 19, June 8, and Oct. 31, 1882, see
> For. Rel. 1882, 532, 534, 539.
>
> See, also, Mr. Frelinghuysen, Sec. of State, to Mr. Baker, min. to Vene-
> zuela, May 8, 1882, For. Rel. 1882, 534.
>
> The representations of the United States were supported by Great Britain,
> and the subject was submitted to the Venezuelan Congress and
> referred to a committee.   (For. Rel. 1883, 897, 904, 919, 921, 931.)
>
> The United States continued to urge a modification of the law.   (For.
> Rel. 1885, 902, 912, 914, 916, 928; For. Rel. 1888, II. 1642, 1644, 1646;
> MS. Inst. Venez. IV. 81; For. Rel. 1893, 736, 737; For. Rel. 1899, 779,
> 780, 782, 784, 788, 791.)

June 13, 1899, a revolution being then in progress in Venezuela,
the attention of the legation of the United States at Caracas was
again directed to the question of the custody of ship's papers, in consequence of a complaint of the consul at Maracaibo of the embarrassment caused him by the detention of the papers of American vessels
by the port authorities.[a]

The President of Venezuela admitted, when the matter was laid
before him, that the Venezuelan law was at fault and promised to
bring the matter to the attention of the Congress.[b]

November 7, 1899, Mr. Loomis, then United States minister in
Venezuela, reported that on the arrival of the American mail steamer
Philadelphia at La Guayra, on the first of the month, her register
was received by the commander of the U. S. S. *Detroit*, and by him
placed in the possession of the United States consul, with a view to
the protection of the steamer and avoidance of delays and annoyances, the collector of customs having informed the agent of the line,
in a manner that was deemed offensive, that no steamer would be
cleared for Puerto Cabello, and that the *Philadelphia* would be
obliged to land Puerto Cabello cargo at La Guayra.   This was confirmed by a decree of the Castro government of October 31, 1899,
declaring Puerto Cabello to be closed to commerce, and requiring
merchandise for that port to be landed at La Guayra.   By the same

---

[a] Mr. Hay, Sec. of State, to Mr. Loomis, min. to Venezuela, June 13, 1899,
MS. Inst. Venez. IV. 648; For. Rel. 1899, 779.

[b] Mr. Loomis, min. to Venezuela, to Mr. Hay, Sec. of State, June 30, 1899,
For. Rel. 1899, 780.

decree, which was not promulgated till twelve hours after the register of the *Philadelphia* had been taken by the commander of the *Detroit*, Puerto Cabello was declared to be blockaded. Mr. Loomis subsequently learned that the British minister had arranged with the captain of a British man-of-war at La Guayra to receive and turn over to the British consul the register of a British merchant vessel, for the same reason as in the case of the *Philadelphia*, and that when the vessel was ready to sail she was cleared by the captain of the man-of-war. Mr. Loomis added that the incident of the *Philadelphia* was closed, so far as the Venezuelan Government was concerned, by the collector of customs going aboard the *Philadelphia* as she was leaving for Curaçao, and presenting her with clearance papers with Gen. Castro's compliments. In 1892, under somewhat similar circumstances, she was fined $10,000, which was afterwards remitted. Mr. Loomis cited numerous instances of the arbitrary control exercised over foreign vessels through detention of their papers.[a]

On receiving Mr. Loomis's despatch, the Government of the United States replied: "Insist on ship's papers being delivered to the United States consul, in accordance with practice of modern nations. Invite coincident action by other ministers."[b]

November 20, 1899, Mr. Loomis reported that General Castro had, with the concurrence of his cabinet, decided to amend the law;[c] and on the 28th of November Mr. Loomis enclosed to his Government a decree of the 22nd of the month, which, after referring to article 44, law 16 of the Finance Code, to the complaints of foreign governments, and to the fact that the Venezuelan law required the masters of Venezuelan ships to deposit their papers with the consul, declared that "the supreme chief of the republic, animated by a desire to extend to commerce the greatest facilities," had "seen fit to repeal temporarily said article, so that hereafter the consuls shall take charge of their ships' papers, instead of the chiefs of the custom-houses: *Provided always*, That said papers shall be first presented to the customs authorities." This resolution was to remain in force till the legislative power should consider and definitely dispose of the matters. Mr. Loomis stated that the customs authorities would at no time have the

---

[a] Mr. Loomis, min. to Venezuela, to Mr. Hay, Sec. of State, Nov. 7, 1899, For. Rel. 1899, 784–788. November 14, 1899, Messrs. H. L. Boulton & Company, agents of the Red D Line, to which the *Philadelphia* belonged, reported that Mr. Goldschmidt, United States consul at La Guayra, had that day imposed on Captain Woodrick of the American steamer *Caracas*, belonging to the same line, a fine of $500 for having delivered the register of the ship to the custom-house authorities in compliance with the Venezuelan law. They stated that unless they complied with that law they were not only subject to heavy fines, but that the custom-house authorities denied them legal clearance.

[b] Mr. Hay, Sec. of State, to Mr. Loomis, min. to Venezuela, tel., Nov. 18, 1899, For. Rel. 1899, 791.

[c] For. Rel. 1899, 791.

ships' papers in their custody, but would exercise their right of inspection on board the vessel.[a]

" There has been at times an effort on the part of certain of the South American Republics to require the master of a foreign vessel to deposit the ship's papers with the port authorities, instead of with the consul of his nation. This contention has been uniformly resisted by the United States, as well as by other governments, on the ground of its inconvenience, its inconsistence with the spirit of international law and with the express or implied stipulations of treaties. Colombia and Venezuela both receded from their position. You will find the correspondence with Colombia published in For. Rel. 1879 and 1880; that with Venezuela in For. Rel. 1882 and 1883.

" You will observe from Mr. Buchanan's dispatch that the Government of France is understood to have protested at Rio de Janeiro against the practice of the Brazilian consul-general at Buenos Ayres.

" The Department will be glad to have you present its views on this subject to the Government of Brazil, pointing out the inconvenience, if not the impropriety, of the course pursued by its officer, which it trusts will be abandoned."

> Mr. Adee, Acting Sec. of State, to Mr. Conger, min. to Brazil, Dec. 3, 1897, For. Rel. 1897, 42, referring to the reported refusal of the Brazilian consul-general at Buenos Ayres to furnish an American bark with a bill of health to enable it to clear his vessel for Rio de Janeiro, unless the master presented the original of the ship's articles to him for certification, and to be by him affixed to the manifest.

In reply to your request for an answer to your note of September 8, 1873, in which you informed me that you were

Shipment and discharge of seamen.

instructed to bring certain sections of the British shipping acts to my notice, with a view of learning whether this Government may not be willing that all or some of the provisions in question should be applied to vessels of the United States when in British ports, I have the honor to say that the sections of the British shipping act of 1854, to which you particularly called my attention, seem to provide for the shipment and discharge of seamen, and for other matters connected with the employment of seamen, while at the same time similar acts in force in the United States contain provisions for the same purpose. If, therefore, it were in any view competent to assent that the law of Great Britain should be applied to American vessels, when in the ports of that Kingdom, the fact that the provisions of the British act would be in conflict with the terms of an act of Congress would make it impossible."

> Mr. Fish, Sec. of State, to Sir E. Thornton, Brit. min., Feb. 28, 1877, MS. Notes to Gr. Br. XVII. 350.

---

[a] For. Rel. 1899, 792.

" I transmit a copy of a dispatch from our consul-general at Havana, reporting that whenever any discharged or destitute American sailors are sent home to the United States in American vessels by that consulate-general (in accordance with art. 16, par. 271, Consular Regulations), he is compelled by the local police to obtain, first, the visa of the civil governor of the province to his consular certificate before the consignees of said American vessels will issue passage tickets to his office for the American seamen concerned, and furnishing a statement of such consignees, by which it appears that they act in obedience to Cuban authorities.

" This report illustrates the exceptional and vexatious character of the Cuban passport regulations. By general maritime law, and particularly by the statutes of the United States, the discharge of seamen is under the direct control of the Government of the country under whose flag they ship, and its certificate, duly issued, is the highest evidence of their status as American seamen. To claim that, in addition to such certificate, the seamen must also present a national passport, is an anomalous attempt to assimilate his condition to that of a voluntary traveler. Moreover, in the case of a seaman not a citizen of the United States, but discharged from an American vessel, this rule would seem to require that he should be furnished not only with the lawful certificate of discharge as an American seaman, but also with a passport issued by the authority of the nation of which he is a subject.

" The point to be emphasized is that a discharged American seaman in a foreign port is under the direct charge of the Government of the United States, which assumes the duty of sending him home to the United States. This duty is performed wholly independently of the citizenship of the seaman."

Mr. Bayard, Sec. of State, to Mr. Curry, min. to Spain, May 31, 1887,
For. Rel. 1887, 995.

" I inclose herewith a copy of a dispatch, No. 173 of the 22d ultimo, from the United States consul at St. John, New Brunswick, in relation to the shipment of seamen on American vessels in that port.

" The laws of the United States provide that all seamen shipped on board of American vessels in foreign ports shall sign articles before the United States consular officers there. This provision is enforced with appropriate penalties.

" By section 126 of the Canadian seaman's act of 1876 the requirement of shipment of crews before a Canadian shipping-master is extended to the shipping of seamen on foreign vessels; but there is a saving clause in favor of vessels belonging to countries between which and Great Britain there is a treaty to prevent such extension.

" It is supposed that it has been under this clause and in consideration of the reciprocity existing in our ports that it has not been the practice in Canadian ports to require American vessels to ship seamen before Canadian shipping-masters and upon Canadian articles. If any American master has so shipped seamen he has failed to comply with our law in so doing, and no consul has been warranted in authenticating articles so entered into. The Department, therefore, on recently being informed that the consul at St. John, New Brunswick, had in some instances authenticated articles of shipment entered into and signed by masters and seamen of American vessels before the Canadian shipping-master at that port, directed him to abstain from such a course in the future, since it was unauthorized and illegal.

" Being so instructed the consul on a recent occasion shipped seamen on an American vessel at his consulate in accordance with the laws of the United States; objection was made by the Canadian shipping-master, who claimed the sole right to ship the seamen under Canadian articles, whereupon the consul informed him of the instructions he had received from this Department to abstain in future from authenticating such articles.

"This announcement called forth the letter from the shipping-master to the consul of the 21st ultimo, inclosed in the latter's dispatch of the 22d the same month, in which the shipping-master informs the consul that if hereafter seamen required for American vessels are not shipped in the former's office he shall be obliged to take such legal steps as will enforce compliance with the Canadian act as applied at the port of St. John.

" Under these circumstances and as the subject is one of wide-spreading importance I deem it expedient to bring the matter to the attention of Her Britannic Majesty's Government with a view to secure corrective action in the premises without waiting for a case of controversy to arise.

" It is believed to be an accepted doctrine that the right of a vessel to be governed in repect of her internal discipline by the laws and regulations of her own country is not forfeited by her entrance into the port of a foreign country. The position of the Canadian Government in regard to the shipment of seamen at St. John would not only deprive a vessel of that right while in that port, but would by necessary consequence destroy the right until she had shipped another crew in another port, under the laws and regulations of her own country, for which in the meantime would be substituted the laws and regulations to the Dominion of Canada.

" While under a strict construction of the terms of sections 4511 and 4512 of the Revised Statutes shipments of seamen on foreign vessels in ports of the United States might be required to be made before United States shipping commissioners, yet I am informed by the Treasury Department that the law has never been so applied, and that such shipments have invariably been allowed to be made before the foreign consular officer in accordance with foreign regulations, on the ground that such action was demanded by international comity. This Government, however, expects and requires reciprocal treatment for its vessels in the ports of other countries, and the Treasury Department does not at present recall any instance other than that now under consideration in which such reciprocal treatment is not accorded.

" It is hoped that Her Majesty's Government will take the necessary measures to secure such treatment for American vessels in Canadian ports.

" You will communicate a copy of this instruction to Her Majesty's Government."

> Mr. Bayard, Sec. of State, to Mr. White, chargé at London, March 1, 1889, For. Rel. 1889, 447.
>
> The construction given in the United States to sections 4511 and 4512, Revised Statutes, as referred to by Mr. Bayard, may be found in Mr. Fairchild, Sec. of Treasury, to Mr. Bayard, Sec. of State, Feb. 25, 1889, For. Rel. 1889, 458. While saying that those sections had never been construed as requiring seamen engaged by foreign vessels in the United States to be shipped before United States shipping commissioners, Mr. Fairchild stated that, if the Canadian government should prove to be an exception to the rule, which was understood to be everywhere else observed, that shipments of seamen by foreign vessels were allowed to be made before their consular officers, he should deem it his duty to instruct the officials of the Treasury Department to require all shipments of seamen on British vessels in American ports to be made before United States shipping commissioners. He added that the United States took notice in analogous cases of foreign law, and in exercising jurisdiction administered relief by comity, in accordance with the flag of the vessels. In this relation he cited the Brantford City, 29 Fed. Rep. 373 ; the Olga, 32 Fed. Rep. 330 ; the John Ritsan, 35 Fed. Rep. 663.
>
> See Mr. Lincoln, min. to England, to Lord Salisbury, Sept. 18, 1889, For. Rel. 1889, 461.
>
> October 12, 1889, Sir T. V. Lister, of the British foreign office, communicated to Mr. Lincoln an extract from a report of a committee of the Canadian privy council, bearing date September 20, 1889, by which Mr. Lincoln stated it appeared that the Canadian government had directed " the cessation, for an indefinite period, of the enforcement of the seamen's act as to shipping seamen before shipping masters, so far as American vessels are concerned." (Mr. Lincoln, min. to England, to Mr. Blaine, Sec. of State, For. Rel. 1889, 464.) In the report, however, it was stated that the minister of justice had no doubt as to the right of the government of Canada to enforce the provisions of the act, the object of which was to restrain the evils attendant upon the crimping of seamen and to restrain desertion ; but it was added that the minister, considering the desire of the United States that American vessels should enjoy the benefit of the act, and observing the practice prevailing in United States ports with regard to British ships, recommended that, while the operation of the different clauses of the act, so far as the rights of private per-

sons were concerned, could not be interfered with without an act of Parliament, her Majesty's Government be informed "that instructions will be issued to the collectors of customs and the different shipping officers not to insist upon a compliance with the provisions of the act requiring the shipment of foreign seamen before the shipping master, so far as American vessels are concerned, until further notice." (For. Rel. 1889, 465–466.)

Mr. Lincoln was instructed to express the gratification of the Department of State " that the Canadian Government has directed the nonenforcement, for an indefinite period, of the act of 1886 as to shipping seamen before 'shipping masters,' so far as American vessels are concerned." (Mr. Blaine, Sec. of State, to Mr. Lincoln, min. to England, Oct. 29, 1889, For. Rel. 1889, 467.)

" I enclose for your information copy of correspondence from which it appears that the master of the American vessel *Evie J. Ray* was compelled by the local authorities at Singapore to ship part of his crew at the office of the British master attendant, to pay for the service in question, and to give a bond for each seaman shipped, thereby causing expense and delay to the master.

" The matter having been referred to the Secretary of the Treasury, that officer expresses the opinion that the laws of the United States require that the crews of American vessels shipped in British ports shall be shipped before American consuls, and that, in this respect, the action of the consul appears to have been in accord with the law and regulations.

" The Secretary of the Treasury adds that ' the action of the British authorities at Singapore in demanding that part of the crew be shipped before them and in exacting compensation and a bond from the American master appears to have been based on an Indian act of 1859, not usually enforced hitherto. That act relates to lascars and other native seamen. The men shipped on the *Evie J. Ray*, it appears, were not lascars and they were not native seamen in the sense that they were British subjects. They appear to have been Javanese, subjects of the Netherlands. Though it is contrary to general maritime custom for local authorities to demand that the crew of a foreign vessel shall be shipped before them as well as before the consul of the nation to which the vessel belongs, the Treasury Department does not at this time suggest a protest against this requirement by British authorities in so far as the Asiatic subjects of Great Britain are concerned. The contention of the British master attendant at Singapore that he can control and demand compensation and bonds for the shipment before him for American vessels of seamen who are not British subjects appears to the Treasury Department unprecedented and involves a principle, the recognition of which would be harmful to American navigation interests in Asia.'

" You are instructed to draw the attention of the foreign office to this matter, with a view to having the proper corrective applied."

Mr. Hay, Sec. of State, to Mr. Choate, min. to England, November 20, 1899, No. 248, MS. Inst. Gr. Br. XXXIII. 298, enclosing copy of a dispatch from United States consul-general at Singapore, No. 30, September 13, 1899, and copies of letters from the Secretary of the Treasury, October 26, 1899, and November 6, 1899.

September 2, 1899, one Chambers, a British subject, shipped as a fireman on the British steamship *Kestor*, from Baltimore, in Maryland, to Mexico, Cuba, and Philadelphia, and thereafter on another voyage from Philadelphia to Cuba and to some port in the United States north of Cape Hatteras. He was to receive 1 shilling for the first 20 days, and $30 a month afterwards. He duly entered on his employment and continued in it till he was discharged in Philadelphia, November 19, 1899. He had then received money and supplies amounting to $20.82, and a dispute arose as to the amount he should receive in final settlement of his account. The master of the vessel offered him $36.18, and, when Chambers refused to receive it, deposited it with the British consul at Philadelphia, subject to Chambers's order; and the consul subsequently sent it to the London Board of Trade, pursuant to the British shipping act. Chambers demanded $20 more, basing his claim on section 24 of the act of December 21, 1898 (30 Stat., 755), and section 10 of the act of June 25, 1884 (23 Stat., 53) by which is was, subject to certain exceptions and to the stipulations of any treaties, made unlawful in any case to pay a seaman wages in advance, it being provided that in such case the payment of full wages might afterwards be required. Chambers having libeled the steamer, it was contended that the statutes in question were intended to apply to the prepayment of wages of a British seaman serving on a British vessel, and that, if it was so intended, they were beyond the power of Congress. The court found, in the first place, upon the evidence in the case, that the stipulation for the payment of 1 shilling for the first 20 days was a mere cover for an attempted evasion of the statute, and that the master violated the provisions of the law by paying at Baltimore a part of Chambers's wages in advance. As to the application of the statute, the court held that it applied uniformly to all seamen, of whatever nationality, shipped in American ports on merchant vessels, whether American or foreign, and that it was a constitutional exercise of power by Congress. A decree was therefore entered in favor of the libellant for the sum of $56.18.

Bradford, J., Chambers *v.* Steamship Kestor (1901), 110 Fed. Rep. 432, citing the Eclipse, 53 Fed. Rep. 273; the Case of the Exchange, 7 Cranch, 116; United States *v.* Diekelman, 92 U. S. 520; Wildenhus'

Case, 120 U. S. 1; *Ex parte* Newman, 14 Wall. 152; the Belgenland, 114 U. S. 355; the Topsy, 44 Fed. Rep. 631.

The court dissented from the view that the statute applied only to American seamen, as expressed in United States *v.* Nelson, 100 Fed. Rep. 125. See Patterson *v.* Eudora, 190 U. S. 169.

The court also referred to the State of Maine, 22 Fed. Rep. 734, in which Judge Brown held that section 10 of the act of June 26, 1884, was not applicable to the shipment of seamen in foreign ports, the ground being that the statute had no extraterritorial force.

4. INVOLUNTARY ENTRANCE, AS GROUND OF EXEMPTION.

§ 208.

An American vessel, having been forced by stress of weather into a French port and obliged to land her cargo in order

Judicial decisions. to make repairs, was afterwards prevented from relading the cargo, or from taking away anything in exchange for it but produce of the country, for taking which she was afterwards charged with a violation of the act of nonintercourse with France of June 13, 1798. She was found not guilty, and Marshall, C. J., said: " Even if an actual and general war had existed between this country and France, and the plaintiff had been driven into a French port, a part of his cargo seized, and he had been permitted by the officers of the port to sell the residue, and purchase a new cargo, I am of opinion that it would not have been deemed such a traffic with the enemy as would vitiate the policy upon such new cargo."

Hallet & Bowne *v.* Jenks (1805), 3 Cranch, 210, 219.

Necessity, by reason of being taken and sent in by a belligerent cruiser, excused the entrance into a foreign port while the embargo acts were in force, even though the original crew might have been able to effect a rescue, since such an act would have exposed the vessel to condemnation in case of capture.

Brig Short Staple *v.* United States (1815), 9 Cranch, 55.

A question was raised in argument as to the effect on jurisdiction of an entrance under stress of weather. It does not appear, however, that the necessity was established, and the question is not discussed in the opinion of the court. (The Alerta *v.* Moran (1815), 9 Cranch, 359.)

Where goods are brought by superior force, or by inevitable necessity, into the United States, they are not deemed to be so imported as necessarily to attach the right to duties. If, however, such goods are afterwards sold or consumed in the country, or incorporated in the general mass of its property, they become retroactively liable to the payment of duties.

Brig Concord, 9 Cranch, 387.

A cargo having been libelled for being imported into the United States in violation of the nonintercourse act of March 1, 1809, it was alleged that the entrance of the ship was compelled by stress of weather. Livingston, J., delivering the opinion of the court, held that the allegation was not established, and said : " The necessity must be urgent, and proceed from such a state of things as may be supposed to produce on the mind of a skilful mariner, a well-grounded apprehension of the loss of vessel and cargo, or of the lives of the crew." Johnson, J., who, with Marshall, C. J., and Washington, J., dissented, while not impugning this definition, maintained that the distress was established.

> The New York (Feb. 10, 1818), 3 Wheaton, 59, 68.
>
> It seems to have been admitted that if the vessel with the goods on board was forced in by stress of weather the libel could not be maintained, even though they were originally taken on board with an intent unlawfully to import them.
>
> Mr. Wheaton, in a note to this case, quotes from the opinion of Sir William Scott, in the case of the Eleanor (Edwards, 159, 160), the following passages as to the legal requisites of the plea of necessity : " Real and irresistible distress must be at all times a sufficient passport for human beings under any such application of human laws. But if a party is a false mendicant, if he brings into a port a ship or cargo under a pretence which does not exist, the holding out of such a false cause fixes him with a fraudulent purpose. If he did not come in for the *only* purpose which the law tolerates, he has really come in for one which it prohibits, that of carrying on an interdicted commerce in whole or in part. It is, I presume, an universal rule, that the mere coming into port, though without breaking bulk, is *prima facie* evidence of an importation. At the same time, this presumption may be rebutted ; but it lies on the party to assign the other cause, and if the cause assigned turns out to be false, the first presumption necessarily takes place, and the fraudulent importation is fastened down upon him. The court put the question to the counsel, whether it was meant to be argued, that the bringing a cargo into an interdicted port, under a false pretence, was not a fraudulent importation, and it has not been denied that it is to be so considered. Upon the fact of importation, therefore, there can be no doubt ; and, consequently, the great point to which the case is reduced, is the distress which is alleged to have occasioned it. Now, it must be an urgent distress ; it must be something of grave necessity ; such as is spoken of in our books, where a ship is said to be driven in by stress of weather. It is not sufficient to say it was done to avoid a little bad weather, or in consequence of foul winds ; the danger must be such as to cause apprehension in the mind of an honest and firm man. I do not mean to say that there must be an actual physical necessity existing at the moment ; a moral necessity would justify the act ; where, for instance, the ship had sustained previous damage, so as to render it dangerous to the lives of the persons on board to prosecute the voyage : Such a case, though there might be no existing storm, would be viewed with tenderness ; but there must be at least a moral necessity. Then,

again, where the party justifies the act upon the plea of distress, it
must not be a distress which he has created himself, by putting on
board an insufficient quantity of water or of provisions for such a
voyage; for there the distress is only a part of the mechanism of
the fraud, and cannot be set up in excuse for it; and in the next
place, the distress must be proved by the claimant in a clear and
satisfactory manner.   It is evidence which comes from himself, and
from persons subject to his power, and probably involved in the
fraud, if any fraud there be, and is, therefore, liable to be rigidly
examined."

A vessel and cargo were condemned under the non-importation
laws, during the war between the United States and Great Britain
of 1812.   The defense set up was an entry under stress of weather.
The question was one of fact.   The condemnation was affirmed, Mr.
Justice Johnson dissenting.   Mr. Justice Livingston, delivering the
opinion of the court, said that under the strong circumstances of
suspicion existing in the case, the court would require " the most
satisfactory proof of the necessity " which was urged by the defence.   The ostensible destination of the ship was Havana, but it
appeared that the ship left Liverpool without any chart of Havana
or the adjacent coast, and that, two days after her departure, the
master ordered the supercargo to proceed off the port of Wiscasset,
which was accordingly done.   Her passage was long and boisterous,
but the principal, if not the only, witnesses produced as to the necessity of entrance were the master and supercargo.   No seamen were
examined, nor any person residing at the place where the vessel discharged; and no survey was produced, though the master, in his testimony, said that one had been made.   The court discredited the supercargo's testimony, because of his " incredible " statement that he had
no written instructions, but merely verbal ones.

The Æolus (1818), 3 Wheaton, 392.
That the burden of proof is on the party setting up necessity, see The
    Major Barbour, Blatch. Prize Cases, 167; The Sunbeam, id. 316, 656;
    The Diana, 7 Wall. 354.

Article VIII. of the treaty between the United States and Spain of
1795 provides for cases where ships belonging to the inhabitants of
either country are forced through stress of weather, pursuit of pirates
or enemies, or any other urgent necessity to seek shelter in the ports
of the other.   It was contended that this article was applicable to the
case of the Spanish schooner Amistad, which was taken possession of
in August, 1839, by the U. S. S. Washington, within a mile and a
half of the shore of Long Island, the schooner being then in the possession of negroes, who had killed the captain at sea.   The negroes
were ultimately set free, on the ground that they were kidnapped
Africans and were not slaves under the Spanish law.   The court, in

the course of its opinion, referring to the argument that Art. VIII.
required the restoration of the negroes to the Spanish claimants, said:
" There may well be some doubt entertained, whether the present case,
in its actual circumstances, falls within the purview of this article.
But it does not seem necessary, for reasons hereafter stated, absolutely
to decide it."

> United States *v.* Schooner Amistad, 15 Pet. 518, 592.
> For a history of this case see Moore on Extradition, I. § 389, pp. 588–592.

A Spanish-owned vessel on her way from New York to Havana,
being in distress, put, by leave of the admiral commanding the squadron, into Port Royal, S. C., then in rebellion, and blockaded by a
Government fleet, and was there seized as a prize of war and used by
the Government. She was afterward condemned as prize, but ordered to be restored. She never was restored, damages for her seizure, detention, and value being awarded. It was held that she was
not prize of war, or subject of capture, and that her owners were
entitled to fair indemnity, although it might be well doubted whether
the case was not more properly a subject for diplomatic adjustment
than for determination by the courts.

> The Nuestra Señora de Regla, 17 Wall. 30.
> See further, as to this case, Moore, Int. Arbitration, II. 1016–1018.

On the requisition of the British minister, a British vessel and

Official opinions. cargo which have been wantonly and feloniously
taken into an American port in violation of our reve-
nue laws and there seized by the officers of the port for such violation,
should be restored to an innocent owner. The forfeitures and penalties prescribed by our laws have never been inflicted on owners of
vessels which have been brought within our jurisdiction by others'
crime.

> Wirt, At. Gen. (1821), 1 Op. 509.

"Herewith you will receive a copy of a letter to this Department
from the Messrs. Whitehorne, of Newport, Rhode Island, complaining
of an exaction of transit duties upon the cargo of the ship *Erie*, which
put in Rio de Janeiro, in distress, and asking that you might be
instructed to demand their repayment. If, therefore, you should not
have addressed the Brazilian Government upon the subject before
the receipt of this communication, you will present the claim and urge
its prompt adjustment. Several cases of the kind occurred during
the mission of your predecessor, and the procrastination he experienced in the settlement of them was vexatious in a high degree and
inconsistent with that regard for the United States which has uni-

formly been professed by the Brazilian Government. You will intimate that the President is particularly solicitous for the faithful observance of the tenth article of the treaty, because the position of Rio de Janeiro and the safety and convenience of its harbor, render it a place of resort for those of our vessels that may experience stress of weather on their way to and from the Pacific and Indian oceans, or that may require refreshment or repairs."

> Mr. Forsyth, Sec. of State, to Mr. Hunter, chargé d'affaires to Brazil, June 23, 1835, MS. Inst. Brazil, XV. 22.
>
> See, also, same to same, April 15, 1837, id. 47.
>
> An award in favor of the claimants in this case was made by the commissioner appointed to distribute the Brazilian indemnity under the convention between the United States and Brazil of Jan. 27, 1849. (Moore, Int. Arbitrations, V. 4609, 4623.)

May 20, 1864, the Russian minister at Washington communicated to the Department of State a copy of a decision of the council of the Empire to the effect that vessels putting into Russian ports, not for the purpose of carrying on commercial operations, but under compulsion, such as stress of weather, chase by an enemy, want of provisions or, in case of a steamer, of coal, should be exempt from all navigation dues. He inquired whether a similar law existed in the United States, and in case there should be none, offered to negotiate on the subject. His note was referred to the Treasury Department, and he was afterwards advised "that a similar exemption from navigation dues is extended by existing law to all foreign vessels in the ports of the United States."

> Mr. Seward, Sec. of State, to Mr. Stoeckl, Russ. min., June 4 and June 13, 1864, MS. Notes to Russ. Leg. VI. 156, 157.
>
> See U. S. Rev. Stats. §§ 2891, 2892, 2893, 2894; Treasury Regulations, 1884, Art. 177.

"Were there no treaty relations whatever between the United States and Great Britain, were the United States fishermen without any other right to visit those coasts than are possessed by the fishing craft of any foreign country simply as such, the arrest and boarding of the *Grimes*, as above detailed, followed by forcing her into the port of Shelburne, there subjecting her to fine for not reporting, and detaining her until her bait and ice were spoiled, are wrongs which I am sure Her Majesty's Government will be prompt to redress. No Governments have been more earnest and resolute in insisting that vessels driven by stress of weather into foreign harbors should not be subject to port exactions than the Governments of Great Britain and the United States. So far has this solicitude been carried that both Governments, from motives of humanity, as well as of interest as leading maritime powers, have adopted many measures by which foreigners as well as citizens or subjects arriving within their territorial waters may be protected from the perils of the sea. For this purpose not merely light-houses and light-ships are placed by us at points of danger, but an elaborate life-saving service, well equipped with men, boats, and appliances for relief, studs our seaboard in order to render aid to vessels in distress, without regard to their nationality. Other benevolent organizations are sanctioned by Government which bestow rewards on those who hazard their lives in the protection of life and property in vessels seeking in our waters refuge from storms. Acting in this spirit the Government of the United States has been zealous, not merely in opening its ports freely, without charges, to vessels seeking them in storm, but in insisting that its own vessels, seeking foreign ports under such circumstances, and exclusively for such shelter, are not under the law of nations subject to custom-house exactions.

" ' In cases of vessels carried into British ports by violence or stress of weather [said Mr. Webster in instructions to Mr. Everett, June 28, 1842] we insist that there shall be no interference from the land with the relation or personal condition of those on board, according to the laws of their own country; that vessels under such circumstances shall enjoy the common laws of hospitality, subjected to no force, entitled to have their immediate wants and necessities relieved, and to pursue their voyage without molestation.'

" In this case, that of the *Creole*, Mr. Wheaton, in the Revue Française et Étrangère (ix, 345), and Mr. Legaré (4 Op., 98), both eminent publicists, gave opinions that a vessel carried by stress of weather or forced into a foreign port is not subject to the law of such port; and this was sustained by Mr. Bates, the umpire of the commission to whom the claim was referred (Rep. Com. of 1853, 244, 245) :

" ' The municipal law of England [so he said] can not authorize a magistrate to violate the law of nations by invading with an armed force the vessel of a friendly nation that has committed no offense, and forcibly dissolving the relations which, by the laws of his country, the captain is bound to preserve and enforce on board. These rights, sanctioned by the law of nations, viz, the right to navigate the ocean and to seek shelter in case of distress or other unavoidable circumstances, and to retain over the ship, her cargo, and passengers, the law of her country, must be respected by all nations, for no independent nation would submit to their violation.'

" It is proper to state that Lord Ashburton, who conducted the controversy in its diplomatic stage on the British side, did not deny as a general rule the propositions of Mr. Webster. He merely questioned the applicability of the rule to the case of the *Creole*. Nor has the principle ever been doubted by either Her Majesty's Government or the Government of the United States; while, in cases of vessels driven by storm on inhospitable coasts, both Governments have asserted it, sometimes by extreme measures of redress, to secure indemnity for vessels suffering under such circumstances from port exactions, or from injuries inflicted from the shore.

" It would be hard to conceive of anything more in conflict with the humane policy of Great Britain in this respect, as well as with the law of nations, than was the conduct of Captain Quigley towards the vessel in question on the morning of October 8th.

" In such coasts, at early dawn, after a stormy night, it is not unusual for boats, on errands of relief, to visit vessels which have been struggling with storm during the night. But in no such errand of mercy was Captain Quigley engaged. The *Marion Grimes*, having found shelter during the night's storm, was about to depart on her voyage, losing no time while her bait was fresh and her ice lasted, when she was boarded by an armed crew, forced to go seven miles out of her way to the port, and was there under pressure of Captain Quigley, against the opinion originally expressed of the collector, subjected to a fine of $400 with costs, and detained there, as I shall notice hereafter, until her voyage was substantially broken up. I am confident Her Majesty's Government will concur with me in the opinion that, as a question of international law, aside from treaty and other rights, the arrest and detention under the circumstances of Captain Landry and of his vessel were in violation of the law of nations as well as the law of humanity, and that on this ground alone the fine and the costs should be refunded and the parties suffering be indemnified for their losses thereby incurred.

> Mr. Bayard, Sec. of State, to Mr. Phelps, Nov. 6, 1886, For. Rel. 1886, 362, 364–365.

" The *Rebecca*, an American schooner, cleared at Morgan City, La., on the 30th January, 1884, with a cargo of lumber for Tampico, Mexico, and having also on board six cases of merchandise to be left on the way at Brazos Santiago, Tex., and which were not on the manifest of the cargo for Tampico. While on her voyage, and off the bar at Brazos, a storm arose, which increased in violence until the vessel, which was then awaiting a favorable opportunity to enter the port of Brazos, was driven a considerable distance to the southward, and so seriously damaged by the storm that the captain, deeming it unsafe to attempt to return to Brazos Santiago, made for the port of Tampico, which he entered with his vessel, in a leaking and seriously disabled condition.

" When the *Rebecca* began to leak at sea the six cases of merchandise intended to be landed at Brazos Santiago, and which had been reached by the water, were broken open, and the packages, thirty in number, contained in the cases, were so stored as to be protected from damage by the sea. On the arrival of the vessel at Tampico, the master immediately noted a protest of distress with the United Stated consul. On the following day the Mexican customs officials seized the thirty pack-ages in question, which were not on the manifest of cargo for Tampico, on the ground that they had been brought into port in violation of the Mexican law requiring all goods entered in a Mexican port from a foreign country to be manifested, and arrested the master of the vessel on the charge of attempting to smuggle. This charge was not sustained, and the master was released; but he was subsequently arrested and required to give bond to answer the charge of bringing goods into a Mexican port without proper papers. In due time this charge was heard before the district court for the south and center of Tamaulipas, sitting at Tampico, and it was adjudged by the court that the goods should pay triple duty. The master refused to comply with this sentence, and thereupon the goods and vessel were sold by order of the court.

" This Department has taken the ground that as the *Rebecca* was driven by stress of weather from her intended course and entered the port of Tampico in distress, making no attempt to conceal the unmani-fested merchandise, and without any intention on the part of the master or owners to violate the port regulations or tariff laws of Mexico, the vessel was not liable to penal prosecution either for 'smuggling' or for 'bringing goods into port without proper papers'; and that the seizure and sale of the vessel, under the circumstances above stated, was a gross breach of comity and hospitality peculiarly unreasonable and unjust.

" The Mexican Government, while denying that the entrance of the *Rebecca* into Tampico was enforced by stress of weather, has taken the position that the judgment of its courts, ordering the sale of the vessel, is final and conclusive, especially as the master and owners failed to take an appeal from the judgment so rendered to another court, as it is contended might have been done.

" This Department has contested and denied the doctrine that a Government may set up the judgment of one of its own courts as a bar to an international claim, when such judgment is shown to have been unjust or in violation of the principles of international law; and has further maintained that, under the circumstances of the case and in view of the fact that the prior proceedings had been so palpably arbitrary and unjust, the master and owners were not bound to attempt further judicial remedies in the local tribunals."

> Report of Mr. Bayard, Sec. of State, Feb. 26, 1887, S. Ex. Doc. 109, 49 Cong. 2 sess.
>
> The case referred to in the foregoing report formed the subject of an instruction to the minister of the United States in Mexico of April 7, 1884. In that instruction Mr. Frelinghuysen, who was then Secre-tary of State, said that the aspect of the case which gave the United States concern was the question how far it was " compatible with comity, or humanity even, to enforce against the vessels and ship-masters of a friendly state penalties due for proven and intentional

violation of law, when in fact the vessels, under stress of the elements, may have been forced to deviate from the exact conditions of the voyage prescribed by the ship's papers." Mr. Frelinghuysen added that the case of the *Rebecca* was "one of a number which have lately happened in various parts of the world, under Spanish or Spanish-American law. From Manila, from Spain, from Cuba, from Venezuela, from Mexico, the same story comes, of vessels driven by stress of weather to deviate in some measure from the plan of their voyage, and punished by heavy fines or even confiscation, because the documents or cargo did not conform to the rules laid down for regular direct importations." (Mr. Frelinghuysen, Sec. of State, to Mr. Morgan, min. to Mexico, April 7, 1884, H. Ex. Doc. 328, 21 Cong. 1 sess. 4.)

See, also, Mr. Frelinghuysen, Sec. of State, to Mr. Morgan, min. to Mexico, May 16, 1884, H. Ex. Doc. 328, 51 Cong. 1 sess. 12; Mr. Porter, Act. Sec. of State, to Mr. Jackson, min. to Mexico, Sept. 14, 1885, H. Ex. Doc. 328, 51 Cong. 1 sess. 15.

Mr. Mariscal, Mexican minister of foreign affairs, in a note to Mr. Jackson, United States minister, of October 31, 1885, enclosing a copy of the sentence of the court in the case, stated that the Executive could take no action in the matter, since it was evident that the captain of the Rebecca had violated the fiscal laws of the country, although he was well acquainted with them, as he had traded with Mexican ports for many years past; that, "although he sought to excuse his fault, attributing it to bad weather through which the vessel had passed, giving one to understand that he arrived at Tampico by force of circumstances, in the sentences of the district judge it is shown that the *Rebecca* had cleared for the very port of Tampico, and that if bad weather had retarded the arrival of the ship this did not prevent the latter from arriving at the port for which she was destined." (H. Ex. Doc. 328, 51 Cong. 1 sess. 27.)

December 5, 1885, Mr. Bayard stated that, in view of the decision of the Mexican Government, it did not seem hopeful to press the case further, but called attention to the point made in the Mexican answer "that the *Rebecca* could not be deemed to have entered Tampico in distress." It never was asserted, said Mr. Bayard, that she did. The position of the United States was that a storm prevented her from making Brazos, and caused her to abandon the attempt to enter that port and to sail for Tampico, carrying on board the packages destined to Brazos. Stress of weather, therefore, was the legitimate cause of the "variation" of her course for which the fine was technically imposed. (Mr. Bayard, Sec. of State, to Mr. Jackson, min. to Mexico, Dec. 5, 1885, H. Doc. 328, 51 Cong. 1 sess. 33.)

In a note of February 9, 1886, written in reply to certain representations of the American minister, Mr. Mariscal stated that, as was shown by the documents previously communicated by him, the captain of the *Rebecca*, though duly advised of his right to appeal, had not availed himself of his opportunity to oppose the execution of the sentence, and that the matter must therefore be considered as having been finally determined judicially, and as not being subject to revision by the Executive. He further stated that, had the documents subsequently communicated to the Mexican Government been known to the court, they would perhaps have modified the sentence pronounced by it; but that, if they were not taken into consideration,

" nobody is to blame for it but [Captain] Dujay himself, who, imitating the bad example of some foreigners who treat with disdain the tribunals of the country, omitted to make use of the recourses which our laws granted him on an equality with the natives, and waived the presentation of such proofs before the court, failing to appeal from its decision, as the laws freely allowed him to do, presuming that he could remedy everything afterwards by means of a diplomatic claim. . . . It is not within his [the President's] power to destroy what was done by virtue of a sentence pronounced with the legal requisites, and which was carried into effect because the party in interest interposed no recourse against it." (Mr. Mariscal, min. of for. aff., to Mr. Jackson, U. S. min., Feb. 9, 1886, H. Ex. Doc. 328, 51 Cong., 1 sess. 36.)

March 9, 1886, Mr. Bayard, referring to Mr. Jackson's reply to the foregoing note, suggested that the discussion might be diverted " into the broader field of equitable consideration as between sovereigns who are and must be jealous of the judicial independence." (Mr. Bayard, Sec. of State, to Mr. Jackson, min. to Mexico, March 9, 1886, H. Ex. Doc. 328, 51 Cong., 1 sess. 40.)

In a note of April 2, 1886, written in reply to a note of Mr. Jackson of February 25, Mr. Mariscal reiterated and argued at length, with citations of authorities, the position that the case had been finally disposed of by judicial action. (Mr. Mariscal, min. of for. aff., to Mr. Morgan, chargé, April 2, 1886, H. Ex. Doc. 328, 51 Cong., 1 sess. 41–47.)

With reference to this note, Mr. Bayard stated that " there would seem to be no reason to hope for any more favorable result by reviewing the case," though he expressed regret that the Mexican Government " did not recognize that its course in this case had been harsh and oppressive, and hasten to make prompt and satisfactory amends therefor as it was hoped its sense of justice would have led it to do." (Mr. Bayard, Sec. of State, to Mr. Morgan, chargé, April 27, 1886, H. Ex. Doc. 328, 51 Cong., 1 sess. 47.)

(" The records of the Department show that no action has been taken by this Government in relation to the claim [in the case of the Rebecca] since April 15, 1890, the date of the message of President Harrison, transmitting copies of correspondence in the case in response to a resolution of the House of Representatives. It is customary to suspend the prosecution of a claim against a foreign government when either House calls for the papers with a view to consideration of the subject." (Mr. Hay, Sec. of State, to Mr. Allison, Oct. 26, 1900, 248 MS. Dom. Let. 535.)

As to penalties imposed in Venezuela on a vessel seeking port in distress, see Mr. Frelinghuysen, Sec. of State, to Mr. Baker, min. to Venezuela, February 18, 1884, and April 1, 1884, MS. Inst. Venezuela, III. 333, 342.

The case at Manila, referred to by Mr. Frelinghuysen in his instruction of April 7, 1884, *supra*, was that of the American bark *Masonic*. This case was afterwards submitted to arbitration, and an award was made in favor of the United States for $51,674.07. For a full report of the case, see Moore, International Arbitrations, II. 1055–1069.

See, for other cases of vessels in distress, decided by international tribunals, Moore, Int. Arbitrations, IV. 4346–4348, 4379.

In February, 1891, the minister of the United States at Buenos Ayres was instructed to investigate a complaint that heavy charges were imposed on vessels putting into that port in distress, and if he should find it to be well founded to endeavor to induce the Argentine Government to remedy it. The Argentine ministry of finance stated that no such taxes had been imposed except in the case of ships " loading or unloading in the ordinary conditions;" that the custom-house ordinances provided that ships in case of forced entry should be exempt from all port charges, unless they discharged as at their final destination; and that if charges had in any case of distress been otherwise exacted they would be reimbursed.

> Mr. Blaine, Sec. of State, to Mr. Pitkin, min. to Arg. Rep., Feb. 13, 1891, For. Rel. 1891, 4; Mr. Pitkin, min. to Arg. Rep., to Mr. Blaine, Sec. of State, May 27, July 7, 1891, id. 10–12.
>
> A similar complaint was made in regard to Montevideo.

In 1894 the customs authorities at Cape Haytien fined the American schooner *John I. Snow* for entering the port after 6 o'clock p. m. without a pilot, although she was forced in by want of water, all drinking water on board having been salted during a storm. The United States asked for the return of the fine, particularly under Art. XV. of the treaty of 1864, requiring hospitality to be exercised where refuge is sought " through stress of weather, pursuit of pirates or enemies, or want of provisions or water." The fine was returned.

> Mr. Uhl, Act. Sec. of State, to Mr. Smythe, min. to Hayti, May 3, 1894, MS. Inst. Hayti, III. 398; Mr. Olney, Sec. of State, to Mr. Smythe, min. to Hayti, Jan. 30, 1896, id. 474.
>
> On the other hand, where the master of the American schooner Lucy Holmes was arrested in Hayti for taking part in an affray on shore, and he maintained that he was in fact endeavoring to quell the disturbance, the Department of State said: " The accountability of the Haytian Government for the arrest and imprisonment of the captain and the consequent detention of the vessel, will depend upon whether there was probable cause for those proceedings under the municipal law of the country." (Mr. J. C. B. Davis, Act. Sec. of State, to Mr. Bassett, min. to Hayti, Dec. 23, 1873, MS. Inst. Hayti, II. 17.)

" It is a well-settled principle of international law that the ships and subjects of a neutral nation, which are driven by superior force into prohibited ports or waters of a belligerent, draw upon themselves no penal consequences therefor, but must be allowed freely to depart therefrom."

> Report of Mr. Davis, Com. on For. Rel., July 14, 1897, on case of Alfredo Laborde and others, *Competitor* prisoners, S. Rep. 377, 55 Cong. 1 sess. 5.

In 1831 the American brig *Comet*, while on a voyage from Alex-
Cases of "Comet" andria, then in the District of Columbia, to New
and "Enco- Orleans, with a cargo of slaves, the property of
mium." American citizens, was wrecked on the Bahama
Banks. The slaves were saved and carried to the island of New
Providence, where they were libeled for forfeiture under the British
acts prohibiting the slave trade. The libel was dismissed by the court,
but the governor on his own authority declared the slaves to be free,
and refused to permit the owners to take them from the island. Mr.
Van Buren, who was then minister to England, was instructed to
lay the case before the British Government, with a strong expression of confidence that the action of the governor would be disavowed.
On February 25, 1832, Mr. Van Buren presented the case to Lord
Palmerston, and asked that the slaves be ordered to be restored and
that a reasonable indemnity be paid for their detention. The case
was referred to the law officers for their opinion, but though often
urged to do so the British Government failed to reply to Mr. Van
Buren's note. In February, 1833, the American brig *Encomium*,
while on a voyage from Charleston to New Orleans, with 45 slaves
on board, was wrecked at nearly the same place as the *Comet*. The
slaves were saved and taken to Nassau, where they were liberated by
the police magistrate, against the protest of the United States consul.
On the 2d of August, 1834, Mr. Vail, who was then chargé d'affaires
of the United States in London, was instructed by Mr. Forsyth, then
Secretary of State, to press for an answer to Mr. Van Buren's note
in the case of the *Comet*, and also to call attention to the case of the
Encomium.

On the 11th of May 1835, no answer in these cases having been
Cases of the "En- received, Mr. Vail renewed the subject, and also
terprise" and presented the case of the brig *Enterprise*, which,
the "Hermosa." while on a voyage from Alexandria to Charleston in
1835, with 73 slaves on board, was driven from her course by stress
of weather and compelled by lack of provisions to put into the port
of Hamilton, in Bermuda, where, some time after her arrival, a writ
of habeas corpus was served on the master, requiring him to produce
the slaves, who on disembarking were taken from his custody and
set at liberty. Mr. Vail, in bringing the occurrence to the notice
of the British Government, said it was the third case " of an American vessel, pursuing a voyage recognized as lawful by the legislation of the United States, and by all the principles of public law,
forced, by the act of God, to seek, in a British port, a refuge from the
tempest, relief from starvation for her crew and passengers, and that
aid, protection, and hospitality " which were due to the distressed
mariner and the property in his charge, and which were in these
cases denied. On November 13, 1835, Lord Palmerston stated that it

had been decided to refer the whole subject to the judicial committee of the privy council. In 1836 Mr. Stevenson, who had become the diplomatic representative of the United States in England, twice pressed for a decision, his second note bearing date of December 13. On the 7th of February, 1837,* the Senate of the United States adopted a resolution, which was offered by Mr. Calhoun, asking the President for the correspondence " in relation to the outrage committed on our flag and the rights of our citizens, by the authorities of Bermuda and New Providence, in seizing the slaves on board of the brigs *Encomium* and *Enterprise*, engaged in the coasting trade, but which were forced by shipwreck and stress of weather into the ports of those islands." To this resolution the President replied on the 13th of the same month, transmitting the correspondence.[a] In 1840 the Senate adopted a resolution declaring that, where a vessel on the high seas, in time of peace, engaged in a lawful voyage, was forced by stress of weather or other unavoidable circumstance into the port of a friendly power, the country to which she belonged lost " none of the rights appertaining to her on the high seas, either over the vessel or the personal relations of those on board."

On the 19th of October, 1840, the American schooner *Hermosa*, bound for Richmond, Va., to New Orleans, with a cargo of 38 slaves belonging to a citizen of the United States, was wrecked on the key of Abaco. Wreckers came alongside and took off the master and crew and the slaves, and against the wishes of the master, who desired to go to a port in the United States, proceeded to Nassau, where certain magistrates in uniform, who represented themselves as officers acting under the orders of the civil and military authorities, and who were accompanied by armed soldiery, came out to the vessel, and taking forcible possession of the slaves transported them in boats to the shore, where, after some judicial proceedings, they were set free, against the remonstrance of the master of the *Hermosa* and of the American consul.

The excitement created by these incidents culminated in the case of the brig *Creole*, which sailed from Hampton Roads
Case of the "Creole." for New Orleans on the 27th of October, 1841, having
on board 135 slaves. On the night of the 7th of November a portion of the slaves revolted, wounded the master, chief mate, and two of the crew, and murdered one of the passengers, and having secured possession of the vessel, ordered the mate, under pain of death, to steer for Nassau, where the brig arrived on the 9th of November. The slaves were afterwards liberated, under circumstances disclosed below in the opinion of Mr. Bates, umpire of the mixed commission under the treaty between the United States and

---

[a] S. Ex. Doc. 174, 24 Cong. 2 sess.

Great Britain of 1853, to which commission the cases of the *Enterprise*, *Hermosa*, and *Creole* were ultimately submitted, on claims for damages.

In the cases of the *Comet* and *Encomium*, which respectively occurred in 1831 and February, 1833, Great Britain in the latter part of President Van Buren's Administration paid an indemnity of $116,179.62.[a] But in the cases of the *Enterprise*, *Hermosa*, and *Creole*, which occurred after August 1, 1834, when the act of Parliament of August 28, 1833,[b] for the abolition of slavery in the British colonies took effect, the British Government refused to acknowledge any liability on the ground that the slaves on entering British jurisdiction became free. The United States, on the other hand, maintained that if a vessel were driven by necessity to enter the port of another nation the local law could not operate so as to affect existing rights of property as between persons on board, or their personal obligations or relations under the law of the country to which the vessel belonged. In the case of the *Creole* this argument was emphasized by the fact that the vessel was brought into British jurisdiction by means of a crime against the law of the flag. The case gave rise to animated discussions in the British Parliament as well as in the Congress of the United States, and came near breaking up the negotiations between Mr. Webster and Lord Ashburton in 1842.

> See Curtis, Life of Webster, II. 53, 54, 61, 62, 64, 69, 85, 99, 104, 119, 120–122; Benton, Thirty Years' View, II. 409; Phillimore, Int. Law, IV. 14; Legaré, At. Gen. (1842), 4 Op. 98; Brit. & For. State Papers (1841. 1842), XXX. 181; Calvo, Droit Int. (3d ed.), II. 269; Abdy's Kent (1878), 149; Woolsey, Int. Law. § 70; Snow, Cases on Int. Law, 136.

Where a coasting vessel, bound from one port to another in the United States, is carried by mutineers into a foreign port, the officers of such vessel are entitled to aid from the local authorities in recovering control; nor is the cargo subject to confiscation or disposal in such port because it may consist of articles which are there held not to be the subject of property.

> Mr. Webster, Sec. of State, to Mr. Everett, min. to England, Jan. 29, 1842, MS. Inst. Gr. Br. XV. 38. See, also, same to same, Feb. 24, 1842, id. 50.

" In cases of vessels carried into British ports by violence or stress of weather, we insist that there shall be no interference from the land, with the relation or personal condition of those on board, according to the laws of their own country; that vessels under such circumstances shall enjoy the common laws of hospitality, subjected to no force,

---

[a] H. Ex. Doc. 242, 27 Cong. 2 sess.; Act of Feb. 18, 1843, 5 Stats. at L. 601.
[b] 3 and 4 William IV. ch. 73.

entitled to have their immediate wants and necessities relieved, and to pursue their voyage without molestation."

> Mr. Webster to Mr. Everett, June 28, 1842, Curtis's Life of Webster, II. 106.
>
> "'ship or vessel, on the high seas, in time of peace, and engaged in a lawful voyage, is, by the law of nations, under the exclusive jurisdiction of the state to which her flag belongs; and . . . if forced by stress of weather, or other unavoidable cause, into a port of a friendly power, she would lose none of the rights appertaining to her on the high seas; but, on the contrary, she, with her cargo and persons on board, including their property and all the rights belonging to their personal relations, would be placed under the protection which the law of nations extends to the unfortunate in such cases." (Speech of Mr. Calhoun, March 13, 1840, 3 Calhoun's Works (by Crallé), 465.)
>
> "Mr. Wheaton wrote an article upon this subject in the Revue Française et Étrangère, ix, 345, in which he took the ground that the Creole never passed under British jurisdiction so as to affect the legal relations of persons and things on board, or to give the British Government such jurisdiction over the persons on board as to make the case one of extradition; and that the master, with such aid as he could obtain from the consul or otherwise, was entitled, not only to carry to the United States all the persons on board, whether held as slaves or criminals, without molestation from the authorities, but to receive the assistance of those authorities to regain and hold possession of his vessel." (Dana's Wheaton, § 103, note 62.)

"A vessel on the high seas, beyond the distance of a marine league from the shore, is regarded as part of the territory of the nation to which she belongs, and subjected exclusively to the jurisdiction of that nation. If, against the will of her master or owner, she be driven or carried nearer to the land, or even into port, those who have, or ought to have, control over her struggling all the while to keep her upon the high seas, and so within the exclusive jurisdiction of her own government, what reason or justice is there in creating a distinction between her rights and immunities in a position thus the result of absolute necessity, and the same rights and immunities before superior power had forced her out of her voluntary course?

"But, my Lord, the rule of law, and the comity and practice of nations, go much further than these cases of necessity, and allow even to a merchant vessel, coming into any open port of another country voluntarily, for the purposes of lawful trade, to bring with her and keep over her, to a very considerable extent, the jurisdiction and authority of the laws of her own country, excluding to this extent, by consequence, the jurisdiction of the local law. A ship, say the publicists, though at anchor in a foreign harbor, preserves its jurisdiction and its laws. It is natural to consider the vessels of a nation as parts of its territory, though at sea, as the state retains its jurisdiction over them; and, according to the commonly received custom, this jurisdiction is preserved over the vessels, even in parts of the sea subject to a foreign dominion.

" This is the doctrine of the law of nations, clearly laid down by writers of received authority, and entirely conformable, as it is supposed, with the practice of modern nations.

" If a murder be committed on board of an American vessel by one of the crew upon another or upon a passenger, or by a passenger on one of the crew or another passenger, while such vessel is lying in a port within the jurisdiction of a foreign state or sovereignty, the offense is cognizable and punishable by the proper court of the United tSates, in the same manner as if such offense had been committed on board the vessel on the high seas. The law of England is supposed to be the same.

" It is true that the jurisdiction of a nation over a vessel belonging to it, while lying in the port of another, is not necessarily wholly exclusive. We do not so consider or so assert it. For any unlawful acts done by her while thus lying in port, and for all contracts entered into while there, by her master or owners, she and they must, doubtless, be answerable to the laws of the place. Nor, if her master or crew, while on board in such port, break the peace of the community by the commission of crimes, can exemption be claimed for them. But, nevertheless, the law of nations, as I have stated it, and the statutes of governments founded on that law, as I have referred to them, show that enlightened nations, in modern times, do clearly hold that the jurisdiction and laws of a nation accompany her ships not only over the high seas, but into ports and harbors, or wheresoever else they may be water-borne, for the general purpose of governing and regulating the rights, duties, and obligations of those on board thereof, and that, to the extent of the exercise of this jurisdiction, they are considered as parts of the territory of the nation herself.

" If a vessel be driven by weather into the ports of another nation, it would hardly be alleged by anyone, that, by the mere force of such arrival within the waters of the state, the law of that state would so attach to the vessel as to affect existing rights of property between persons on board, whether arising from contract or otherwise. The local law would not operate to make the goods of one man to become the goods of another man. Nor ought it to affect their personal obligations, or existing relations between themselves; nor was it ever supposed to have such effect, until the delicate and exciting question which has caused these interferences in the British islands arose. The local law in these cases dissolves no obligations or relation lawfully entered into or lawfully existing according to the laws of the ship's country."

Mr. Webster, Sec. of State, to Lord Ashburton, British plenipotentiary, Aug. 1, 1842, Webster's Works, VI. 303, 306.

" Upon the great general principles affecting this case we do not differ.

You admit that if slaves, the property of American citizens, escape into British territories, it is not expected that they will be restored; . . . the present state of British law is in this respect too well known to require repetition; nor need I remind you that it is exactly the same with the laws of every part of the United States where a state of slavery is not recognized; and that the slave put on shore at Nassau would be dealt with exactly as would a foreign slave landed, under any circumstances whatever, at Boston. But what constitutes the being within British dominion, from which these consequences are to follow? Is a vessel passing through the Bahama Channel, and forced involuntarily, either from storm or mutiny, into British waters, to be so considered? What power have the authorities of those islands to take cognizance of persons or property in such vessels? These are questions which you, Sir, have discussed at great length, and with evident ability. Although you have advanced some propositions which rather surprise and startle me, I do not pretend to judge them; but what is very clear is, that great principles are involved in a discussion which it would ill become me lightly to enter upon; . . . Our object is rather to look to the means of future prevention of such occurrences [as those that had given rise to the discussions]. That this may be obtained I have little doubt, although we may not be able immediately to agree on the precise stipulations of a treaty. . . . In the meantime I can engage that instructions shall be given to the governors of Her Majesty's colonies on the southern borders of the United States to execute their own laws with careful attention to the wish of their government to maintain good neighborhood, and that there shall be no officious interference with American vessels driven by accident or by violence into those ports. The laws and duties of hospitality shall be executed; and these seem neither to require nor to justify any further inquisition into the state of persons or things on board of vessels so situated than may be indispensable to enforce the observance of the municipal law of the colony, and the proper regulation of its harbors and waters." (Lord Ashburton, British plenipotentiary, to Mr. Webster, Sec. of State, Aug. 6, 1842, Webster's Works, VI. 313, 314–316.)

" The *Creole* was taken forcibly by mutineers into a British port, and Mr. Webster seems to have considered her in a different situation from that she would have been in had she voluntarily visited such port. If he meant to give a more general application to the rules he laid down, the authorities against him are so many and so strong as to render it impossible to sustain him." (Mr. Marcy, Sec. of State, to Mr. Keenan, consul at Hongkong, April 14, 1856, 21 Disp. to Consuls, 567.)

The views of Mr. Webster are examined, and to some extent adversely criticised, in Hall, Int. Law (4th ed.), 209, note.

" This claim is presented on behalf of the Charleston Marine Insurance Company of South Carolina, and of the Augusta Insurance Company in Georgia, for the recovery of the value of seventy-two slaves, forcibly taken from the brig *Enterprize*, Elliot Smith, master, on the 20th of February, 1835, in the harbor of Hamilton, Bermuda. The following are the

Decision in the case of the "Enterprize."

facts and circumstances of the case: The American brig *Enterprize*, Smith, master, sailed from Alexandria, in the District of Columbia, in the United States, on the 22d of January, 1835, bound for Charleston, South Carolina. After encountering head winds and gales, and finding their provisions and water running short, it was deemed best by the master to put into Hamilton, in the island of Bermuda, for supplies. She arrived there on the 11th of February, having taken in the supplies required, and having completed the repair of the sails, she was ready for sea on the 19th with the pilot on board. During the repairs, no one from the shore was allowed to communicate with the slaves. The vessel was kept at anchor in the harbor and was not brought to the wharf. Being thus ready for sea, Captain Smith proceeded, with his agent, to the custom-house to clear his vessel outward. The collector stated that he had received a verbal order from the council to detain the brig's papers until the governor's pleasure could be known.

" The comptroller, and a Mr. Tucker, then went to the other public offices, and on their return to the custom-house, the comptroller, after consulting for a few minutes with the collector, declared that he would not give up the papers that evening, but would report the vessel out the next morning, as early as the captain might choose to call for the papers.

" In consequence of this decision, the captain immediately noted his protest in the secretary's office against the collector and comptroller for the detention of his ship's papers, and informed the officer of the customs he should hold them responsible; that he (the captain) feared the colored people of Hamilton would come on board his vessel at night and rescue the slaves, as they had threatened to do.

" The collector then replied there was no danger to be apprehended, that the colored people would not do anything without the advice of the whites, and they knew the laws too well to disturb Captain Smith. At 20 minutes to 6 o'clock, p. m., the chief justice sent a writ of habeas corpus on board, and afterwards, a file of black soldiers armed, ordering the captain to bring all the slaves before him, the chief justice, which Captain Smith was obliged to do. On the slaves being informed by the chief justice that they were free persons, seventy-two of them declared they would remain on shore, which they did, and only six of them returned on board to proceed on the voyage.

" This is believed to be a faithful sketch of the case, from which it appears, that the American brig *Enterprize* was bound on a voyage, from one port in the United States to another port of the same country, which was lawful according to the laws of her country and the law of nations. She entered the port of Hamilton in distress for provisions and water. No offence was permitted against the munici-

pal laws of Great Britain or her colonies, and there was no attempt
to land or to establish slavery in Bermuda in violation of the laws.

" It was well known that slavery had been conditionally abolished
in nearly all the British dominions about six months before, and that
the owners of slaves had received compensation, and that six years'
apprenticeship was to precede the complete emancipation; during
which time apprentices were to be bought and sold as property, and
were to be liable to attachment for debt.

" No one can deny that slavery is contrary to the principles of justice and humanity, and can only be established in any country by
law. At the time of the transaction on which this claim is founded,
slavery existed by law in several countries, and was not wholly
abolished in the British dominions; it could not then be contrary
to the law of nations, and the *Enterprize* was as much entitled to
protection as though her cargo consisted of any other description of
property. The conduct of the authorities at Bermuda, was a violation of the laws of nations, and of those laws of hospitality which
should prompt every nation to afford protection and succor to the
vessels of a friendly neighbor that may enter their ports in distress.

" The owners of the slaves on board the *Enterprize* are therefore
entitled to compensation; and I award to the Augusta Insurance and
Banking Company, or their legal representatives, the sum of sixteen
thousand dollars, and to the Charleston Marine Insurance Company,
or their legal representatives, the sum of thirty-three thousand dollars, on the fifteenth of January, 1855."

> Bates, umpire, case of the *Enterprize*, convention between the United
> States and Great Britain of February 8, 1853. (S. Ex. Doc. 103, 34
> Cong. 1 sess. 187, 236–237.
>
> For the arguments of counsel and the opinions of the commissioners in
> this case, see Moore, Int. Arbitrations, IV. 4349–4372.
>
> The cases of the *Hermosa* and *Creole* were submitted by the commis-
> sioners to the umpire on their opinions in the case of the *Enterprize*.

" The umpire appointed agreeably to the provisions of the conven-
Decision in the tion entered into between Great Britain and the
case of the United States, on the 8th of February, 1853, for the
"Hermosa." adjustment of claims by a mixed commission, having
been duly notified by the commissioners under the said convention,
that they had been unable to agree upon the decision to be given
with reference to the claim of H. N. Templeman against the government of Great Britain; and having carefully examined and considered the papers and evidence produced on the hearing of the said
claim; and having conferred with the said commissioners thereon,
hereby reports that the schooner *Hermosa*, Chattin, master, bound
from Richmond, in Virginia, to New Orleans, having thirty-eight

slaves on board, belonging to H. N. Templeman, was wrecked on the 19th October, 1840, on the Spanish key, *Abaco*.

" Wreckers came alongside, and took off the captain and crew, and the thirty-eight slaves, and contrary to the wishes of the master of the *Hermosa*, who urged the captain of the wrecker to conduct the crew, passengers, and slaves to a port in the United States, they were taken to Nassau, New Providence, where Captain Chattin carefully abstained from causing or permitting said slaves to be landed, or to be put in communication with any person on shore, while he proceeded to consult with the American consul, and to make arrangements for procuring a vessel to take the crew and passengers and the slaves to some port in the United States.

" While the vessel in which they were brought to Nassau was lying at a distance from the wharves, in the harbor, certain magistrates wearing uniform, who stated themselves to be officers of the British government, and acting under the orders of the civil and military authorities of the island, supported by soldiery wearing the British uniform, and carrying muskets and bayonets, took forcible possession of said vessels, and the slaves were transported in boats from said vessel to the shore, and thence under guard of a file of soldiers, marched to the office of said magistrates, where, after some judicial proceedings, they were set free, against the urgent remonstrances of the master of the *Hermosa* and of the American consul.

" In this case there was no attempt to violate the municipal laws of the British colonies. All that the master of the *Hermosa* required was that aid and assistance which was due from one friendly nation to the citizens or subjects of another friendly nation, engaged in a business lawful in their own country, and not contrary to the law of nations.

" Making allowance, therefore, for a reasonable salvage to the wreckers, had a proper conduct on the part of the authorities at Nassau been observed, I award to the Louisiana State Marine and Fire Insurance Company, and the New Orleans Insurance Company, (to which institutions this claim has been transferred by H. N. Templeman,) or their legal representatives, the sum of sixteen thousand dollars, on the fifteenth January, 1885, viz: eight thousand dollars to each company."

> Bates, umpire, case of the Hermosa, convention between the United States and Great Britain of February 8, 1853. (S. Ex. Doc. 103, 34 Cong. 1 sess. pp. 239–240.)

" This case having been submitted to the umpire for his decision, he hereby reports that the claim has grown out of the following circumstances:

Decision in the case of the "Creole."

" The American brig *Creole*, Captain Ensor, sailed from Hampton Roads, in the State of Virginia, on the 27th October,

1841, having on board one hundred and thirty-five slaves, bound for New Orleans. On the 7th November, at nine o'clock in the evening, a portion of the slaves rose against the officers, crew, and passengers, wounding severely the captain, the chief mate, and two of the crew, and murdering one of the passengers; the mutiners, having got complete possession of the vessel, ordered the mate, under threat of instant death should he disobey or deceive them, to steer for Nassau, in the island of New Providence, where the brig arrived on the 9th November, 1841.

" The American consul was apprised of the situation of the vessel, and requested the governor to take measures to prevent the escape of the slaves, and to have the murderers secured. The consul received reply from the governor, stating that under the circumstances he would comply with the request.

" The consul went on board the brig, placed the mate in command in place of the disabled master, and found the slaves all quiet.

"About noon twenty African soldiers, with an African sergeant and corporal, commanded by a white officer, came on board. The officer was introduced by the consul to the mate as commanding officer of the vessel.

" The consul, on returning to the shore, was summoned to attend the governor and council, who were in session, who informed the consul that they had come to the following decision :

" ' 1st. That the courts of law have no jurisdiction over the alleged offenses.

" ' 2d. That, as an information had been lodged before the governor, charging that the crime of murder had been committed on board said vessel while on the high seas, it was expedient that the parties, implicated in so grave a charge, should not be allowed to go at large, and that an investigation ought therefore to be made into the charges, and examinations taken on oath; when, if it should appear that the original information was correct, and that a murder had actually been committed, that all parties implicated in such crime, or other acts of violence, should be detained here until reference could be made to the Secretary of State to ascertain whether the parties should be delivered over to the United States government; if not, how otherwise to dispose of them.

" ' 3d. That as soon as such examinations should be taken, all persons on board the *Creole*, not implicated in any of the offences alleged to have been committed on board the vessel, must be released from further restraint.'

" Then two magistrates were sent on board. The American consul went also. The examination was commenced on Tuesday, the 9th, and was continued on Wednesday, the 10th, and then postponed until

Friday, on account of the illness of Captain Ensor. On Friday morning it was abruptly, and without any explanation, terminated.

" On the same day, a large number of boats assembled near the *Creole*, filled with colored persons armed with bludgeons. They were under the immediate command of the pilot who took the vessel into the port, who was an officer of the government, and a colored man. A sloop or larger launch was also towed from the shore and anchored near the brig. The sloop was filled with men armed with clubs, and clubs were passed from her to the persons in the boats. A vast concourse of people were collected on shore opposite the brig.

" During the whole time the officers of the government were on board they encouraged the insubordination of the slaves.

" The Americans in port determined to unite and furnish the necessary aid to forward the vessel and negroes to New Orleans. The consul and the officers and crews of two other American vessels had, in fact, united with the officers, men, and passengers of the *Creole* to effect this. They were to conduct her first to Indian quay, Florida, where there was a vessel of war of the United States.

" On Friday morning, the consul was informed that attempts would be made to liberate the slaves by force, and from the mate he received information of the threatening state of things. The result was, that the attorney-general and other officers went on board the *Creole*. The slaves, identified as on board the vessel concerned in the mutiny, were sent on shore, and the residue of the slaves were called on deck by direction of the attorney-general, who addressed them in the following terms: ' My friends,' or ' my men, you have been detained a short time on board the *Creole* for the purpose of ascertaining what individuals were concerned in the murder. They have been identified, and will be detained. The rest of you are free, and at liberty to go on shore, and wherever you please.'

" The liberated slaves, assisted by the magistrates, were then taken on board the boats, and when landed were conducted by a vast assemblage to the superintendent of police, by whom their names were registered. They were thus forcibly taken from the custody of the master of the *Creole*, and lost to the claimants.

" I need not refer to authorities to show that slavery, however odious and contrary to the principles of justice and humanity, may be established by law in any country; and, having been so established in many countries, it can not be contrary to the law of nations.

" The *Creole* was on a voyage, sanctioned and protected by the laws of the United States, and by the law of nations. Her right to navigate the ocean could not be questioned, and as growing out of that right, the right to seek shelter or enter the ports of a friendly power in case of distress or any unavoidable necessity.

"A vessel navigating the ocean carries with her the laws of her own country, so far as relates to the persons and property on board, and to a certain extent, retains those rights even in the ports of the foreign nations she may visit. Now, this being the state of the law of nations, what were the duties of the authorities at Nassau in regard to the *Creole?* It is submitted the mutineers could not be tried by the courts of that island, the crime having been committed on the high seas. All that the authorities could lawfully do, was to comply with the request of the American consul, and keep the mutineers in custody until a conveyance could be found for sending them to the United States.

" The other slaves, being perfectly quiet, and under the command of the captain and owners, and on board an American ship, the authorities should have seen that they were protected by the law of nations; their rights under which can not be abrogated or varied, either by the emancipation act or any other act of the British Parliament.

" Blackstone, 4th volume, speaking of the law of nations, states: ' Whenever any question arises, which is properly the object of its jurisdiction, such law is here adopted in its full extent by the common law.'

" The municipal law of England can not authorize a magistrate to violate the law of nations by invading with an armed force the vessel of a friendly nation that has committed no offense, and forcibly dissolving the relations which by the laws of his country the captain is bound to preserve and enforce on board.

" These rights, sanctioned by the law of nations—viz: the right to navigate the ocean, and to seek shelter in case of distress or other unavoidable circumstances, and to retain over the ship, her cargo, and passengers, the laws of her own country—must be respected by all nations; for no independent nation would submit to their violation.

" Having read all the authorities referred to in the arguments on both sides, I have come to the conclusion that the conduct of the authorities at Nassau was in violation of the established law of nations, and that the claimants are justly entitled to compensation for their losses. I therefore award to the undermentioned parties, their assigns, or legal representatives, the sums set opposite their names, due on the 15th of January, 1855."

> Bates, umpire, case of the *Creole,* convention between the United States and Great Britain of February 8, 1853. (S. Ex. Doc. 103, 34 Cong. 1 sess. pp. 242–245.) The total amount awarded was $110,330.
> This decision is to a certain extent adversely criticised by Dana, in his edition of Wheaton, note 62, § 103, pp. 165–167.

The British ship *York*, while stranded on the coast of North Carolina, having been driven ashore by stress of weather
Case of the "York." while proceeding in ballast from Valencia, Spain, to
Lewes, Delaware, was destroyed by two United States cruisers to
prevent her from falling into the possession of the enemy. An award
was unanimously made of $11,935 in gold, based on the value of the
wreck at the time of its destruction.

> American and British Claims Commission, treaty of May 8, 1871, Article
> XII. Hale's Report, 51. See also Howard's Report, 148.

V. *INVIOLABILITY OF TERRITORY.*

1. RULE OF INVIOLABILITY.

§ 209.

A sovereign, according to modern international law, can not exercise the prerogatives of sovereignty in any dominions but his own.

> Mr. Jefferson, Sec. of State, to Mr. Ternant, French min., May 15, 1793,
> Am. State Papers, For. Rel. I. 147.
>
> This principle applies to the commission of unneutral acts, such as the
> enlistment of troops by one sovereign in the territory of another,
> without the latter's consent. See, in this relation, the case of Mr.
> Crampton, Cushing, At.-Gen., 1855, 7 Op. 367; 48 Br. and For. State
> Papers (1857, 1858), 190 et seq.; S. Ex. Doc. 35, 34 Cong. 1 sess.
> See, also, the case of Genet, Moore, Int. Arbitrations, I. 310 et seq.

" No principle is better established than that no government has a
right to pursue offenders against its laws, or deserters from its service
into the dominions of another: that such persons can be recovered
by application only to the government within whose jurisdiction they
take shelter, and in obedience to its laws and treaties applicable to
such a case. A departure from this principle being a violation of sovereignty, seldom fails to produce disagreeable consequences."

> Mr. Monroe, Sec. of State, to Mr. Anthony St. John Baker, Dec. 6, 1815,
> MS. Notes to Foreign Legations, II. 113.

" In the late war with the Regency of Algiers, it is represented that
an Algerine sloop of war was captured on the coast of Spain, within
a marine league thereof. . . . Should it finally appear that the
jurisdiction of Spain has been infringed, it will be a circumstance of
regret on the part of this Government. This declaration, it can not be
doubted, will be satisfactory to His Catholic Majesty, and that the
brig will be no longer detained on that account. As by an arrangement on the part of the United States with the Dey of Algiers, the
brig is to be restored to them, you will see at once, that by enabling
this Government to comply with that engagement, all difficulties with

Algiers will be precluded as well on the part of Spain, as of the United States. In making this communication I have full confidence that your early representation to your Government will promote the object of it."

Mr. Monroe, Sec. of State, to the Chev. de Onis, Span. min., Feb. 7, 1816, MS. Notes to For. Leg. II. 128.

"An armed force in the service of the Republic of Texas, under the command of General Rusk, has crossed the acknowledged boundary between the United States and that country and has encamped on our soil for the avowed purpose of punishing certain Indians of the Caddo tribe for alleged depredations within the limits of Texas. Against this insult and outrage you will promptly and in strong terms remonstrate, demand satisfactory explanations on the subject and inform the Texian Government that it is expected adequate measures will be adopted by it to prevent a recurrence of such acts, which if repeated, would inevitably lead to collisions between the troops of the two countries which there would be great reason to deplore."

Mr. Forsyth, Sec. of State, to Mr. La Branche, chargé d'affaires to Texas, Jan. 8, 1839, MS. Inst. Texas, I. 15.

" Current newspaper reports, which, of course, may not be altogether reliable, give some reason for believing that the United States Steamer, *Adirondack*, has lately continued the chase of the British vessel the *Herald*, understood to be engaged in violating the blockade, even within the line of maritime jurisdiction that is to say, within a marine league of the shore of the Island of New Providence. The President desires that you ascertain the truth of this fact, with as little delay as possible, since, if it be true, the commander of the *Adirondack* has committed an inexcusable violation of the Law of Nations, for which acknowledgment and reparation ought to be promptly made. To guard against any such occurrences hereafter, the President desires that you at once give notice to all commanders of American vessels of war, that this Government adheres to, recognizes, and insists upon the principle that the maritime jurisdiction of any nation covers a full marine league from its coast, and that acts of hostility or of authority within a marine league of any foreign country, by naval officers of the United States, are strictly prohibited, and will bring upon such officers the displeasure of this Government."

Mr. Seward, Sec. of State, to Mr. Welles, Sec. of Navy, Aug. 4, 1862, 58 MS. Dom. Let. 15.

" You will exercise constant vigilance to prevent supplies of arms, munitions, and contraband of war from being conveyed to the insurgents, but . . . under no circumstances will you seize any vessel within the waters of a friendly nation."

> Mr. Welles, Sec. of Navy, to U. S. Naval Officers, Aug. 18, 1862, Official Records of the Union and Confederate Navies, Ser. I., vol. 1, p. 417. These instructions were based on a letter of Mr. Seward, Sec. of State, to Mr. Welles, Sec. of Navy, Aug. 8, 1862, 58 MS. Dom. Let. 34; Blue Book, North America, No. 5 (1863).

In view of the fact that steps were being taken for the survey at an early day, by the United States Coast and Geodetic Survey, of the boundary line between the United States and Canada near Burnt Island, Michigan, in Lake Huron, and that in order to perform the work it would be requisite to erect temporary signals on Canadian soil or in Canadian waters, the British minister at Washington was requested to communicate the facts to the Canadian government, with a view to obtain its permission for the erection by an officer of the Coast Survey " of such temporary signals on the adjacent islands or in the adjacent waters in the locality in question as may be deemed requisite to the speedy or convenient prosecution of the contemplated survey."

> Mr. Bayard, Sec. of State, to Sir L. S. S. West, Brit. min., March 27, 1888, MS. Notes to Great Britain, XX. 618.

The seizure by a naval vessel of the United States of an American merchant vessel, within the jurisdiction of a friendly foreign power, for a violation of the nonintercourse act of June 28, 1809, " is certainly an offense against that power, which must be adjusted between the two governments. This court can take no cognizance of it; and the majority of the court is of opinion that the law does not connect that trespass, if it be one, with the subsequent seizure by the civil authority, under the process of the district court, so as to annul the proceedings of that court against the vessel." In this case the violation of territory was set up by the claimant, not by the foreign Government.

> Ship Richmond v. United States (1815), 9 Cranch, 102, 104.

A seizure for the breach of the municipal laws of one nation can not be made within the territory of another.

> The Apollon, 9 Wheaton, 362.

Where an officer of the Navy, without instructions from his Government, seized property in the Falkland Islands, claimed by citizens of the United States, which, it was alleged, had been piratically taken by a person pretending to be governor of the islands, it was held that such officer had no right, without express direction from his

Government, to enter the territory of a country at peace with the United States and seize property found there claimed by citizens of the United States. Application for redress should have been made to the judicial tribunals of the country.

> Davison *v.* Seal-skins, 2 Paine, 324.
> See, however, as to the circumstances of this case, and the position of the United States regarding them, supra, §§ 89, 171.

The seizure by a ship-of-war of the United States of a vessel within the jurisdiction of a foreign government, for an infringement of our revenue or navigation laws, is a violation of the territorial authority of such government.

> Nelson, At.-Gen. 1843, 4 Op. 285.

The United States Government can not purchase a grant of land in, or concession of right of way over, the territories of another nation, as could an individual or private corporation, since, by the law of nations, one government can not enter upon the territories of another, or claim any right whatever therein.

> Black, At.-Gen. 1859, 9 Op. 286.
> This opinion appears to have been based upon a misconception as to the power of a government to exercise proprietary as well as strictly political rights.

2. Breaches by Military and Naval Authorities.

§ 210.

" During the war of 1812–15 between the United States and Great Britain, the United States frigate Essex was attacked and compelled to surrender, while at anchor, dismasted, in Valparaiso, by the British frigate Phœbe and sloop-of-war Cherub. The sloop-of-war Levant, a recent prize to the United States frigate Constitution, was chased into Port Praya, and captured while at anchor there by vessels from the British fleet. The United States privateer General Armstrong, lying in the harbor of Fayal, was destroyed by vessels from the British fleet. The demand upon Portugal, by the United States, for indemnification, was ultimately left to the arbitration of Louis Napoleon, then President of the French Republic. He recognized the attack as a violation of neutral rights, but decided against indemnification, on the ground that the privateer did not demand protection from the Portuguese authorities at the time, but resisted by battle the unjust attack of the British vessels, instead of relying upon the neutral protection. This decision was not satisfactory to the United States, as they did not consider the fact on which it rested as established in proof. The principle of the decision must certainly be

confined to cases where the vessel attacked has reason to believe that
effectual protection can be seasonably afforded by the neutral, and
makes a fair choice to take the chances of a combat rather than to
appeal to neutral protection. Ex. Doc., 32d Cong., Senate, No. 24."

> Dana's Wheaton, § 429, note 208.
>
> See, further, as to the case of the *General Armstrong*, Moore, Int. Arbitrations, II. 1071.

In December, 1863, the United States merchant steamer *Chesapeake*
was seized on the high seas by certain persons who had taken passage
on her from New York to Portland, Maine, and who, in making the
seizure, represented themselves as acting for the Confederate States.
Several United States men-of-war were sent in pursuit of her. One
of them, the *Ella and Annie*, under the command of Captain Nichols,
found the *Chesapeake* in Sambro Harbor, Nova Scotia, abandoned
by all but three of the persons who had seized her, and flying a flag
of distress. Captain Nichols took charge of the vessel and of the
persons whom he found on board of her, placing the three captors in
irons, and brought them all into Halifax, and delivered them over to
the British authorities. The *Chesapeake* was turned over by the
authorities to the vice-admirality court, but the three prisoners, in view
of the irregularity of their seizure by a foreign man-of-war in British
waters, were released, although their arrest with a view to extradition to the United States was requested by the American consul.
When Mr. Seward was informed of the seizure of the vessel, and of
the fugitives found on board of her, in Sabro Harbor, he at once
wrote to Lord Lyons, the British minister, as follows: "Assuming
this statement of facts to be true, I am not aware that the naval
officers have, in any respect, violated the sovereignty of jurisdiction
of Great Britain. It is possible, however, that the case may not yet
have been fully made known to this government. To guard, therefore, against any possible misapprehension, I have now by the President's directions to inform your lordship that this government has
not authorized, nor does it propose to justify, any exercise whatever
of authority, by its agents, within the waters or on the soil of Nova
Scotia. If any such authority has been assumed, this government
will at once express its profound regret; and it stands ready, in that
case, to make amends which shall be entirely satisfactory."

This note bore date December 18, 1863. On the same day Lord
Lyons replied, saying: "I accept with entire satisfaction the disavowal you so promptly make of any assumption of authority by officers of the United States within the territorial jurisdiction of Her
Majesty's Province of Nova Scotia."

> Mr. Seward, Sec. of State, to Lord Lyons, Brit. min., Dec. 18, 1863, Dip. Cor. 1864, II. 404; Lord Lyons to Mr. Seward, Dec. 18, 1863, id. 405.
>
> Before the vice-admirality court at Halifax, no appearance was entered for

the captors, and they were pronounced in default. Claims were
made by British owners of parts of the cargo and allowed. The
vessel was claimed by her American owners and was ordered to be
delivered to them on payment of costs. (Dip. Cor. 1864, I. 196–200.)
See Calvo, 3d ed. III. 481; Dana's Wheaton, § 428, note 207.

The seizure of the Confederate cruiser *Florida*, by the Federal
cruiser *Wachusett*, in the port of Bahia, Brazil, in October, 1864, was
conceded by the United States Government to be an invasion of Brazilian territorial waters. The act was disavowed by the United
States, and in a note of December 26, 1864, to Mr. Barbosa da Silva,
Brazilian minister at Washington, Mr. Seward announced the proposed trial by court-marital of the captain of the *Wachusett*, the dismissal of the United States consul at Bahia, who advised the attack,
the release of the parties on the *Florida*, and a salute to the Brazilian
flag. Mr. Seward proceeded to mention that the *Florida*, while at
anchor in Hampton Roads, had, by an unavoidable casualty, foun-
dered. To fulfill the engagement of saluting the Brazilian flag, the
United States Government, in 1866, sent to Bahia a United States
vessel of war for the announced purpose of delivering a solemn salute
to the Brazilian flag on the spot where Brazilian neutrality had been
invaded.

> See Dana's Wheaton, § 430, note, 209; Calvo, 3d ed., III. 486, and infra,
> § 1334, where the case is given in detail.
> The papers connected with the seizure of the schooner Greyhound, in
> Boston Harbor, in August, 1793, by orders of the French vice-consul
> in Boston, are given in Am. State Papers, For. Rel. I. 178.

In October, 1864, when the town of St. Albans, Vermont, was
raided and pillaged by a band of men who, although claiming to act
as soldiers of the Confederate States, proceeded from Canada as the
base of their operations, General Dix, when advised of the affair,
telegraphed an order to the officer of the United States in command
at Burlington, Vermont, to send all his efficient force to St. Albans,
and to try to arrest the marauders; and, in case they were not found
in the United States, to pursue them into Canada, if necessary, and
destroy them. The text of the order was as follows:

[General Orders, No. 97.]

HEADQUARTERS DEPARTMENT OF THE EAST,
New York City, December 14, 1864.

Information having been received at these headquarters that the rebel marauders who were guilty of murder and robbery at Saint Albans have been discharged from arrest, and that other enterprises of a like character are actually
in preparation in Canada, the commanding general deems it due to the people
of the frontier towns to adopt the most prompt and efficient measures for the
security of their lives and property.

All military commanders on the frontiers are therefore instructed, in case further acts of depredation and murder are attempted, whether by marauders or persons acting under commissions from the rebel authorities at Richmond, to shoot down the perpetrators, if possible, while in the commission of their crimes; or, if it be necessary, with a view to their capture, to cross the boundary between the United States and Canada, said commanders are hereby directed to pursue them wherever they may take refuge, and if captured they are under no circumstances to be surrendered, but are to be sent to these headquarters for trial and punishment by martial law.

The major-general commanding the department will not hesitate to exercise to the fullest extent the authority he possesses, under the rules of law recognized by all civilized states, in regard to persons organizing hostile expeditions within neutral territory and fleeing to it for an asylum after committing acts of depredation within our own, such an exercise of authority having become indispensable to protect our cities and towns from incendiarism and our people from robbery and murder.

It is earnestly hoped that the inhabitants of our frontier districts will abstain from all acts of retaliation on account of the outrages committed by rebel marauders, and that the proper measures of redress will be left to the action of the public authorities.

By command of Major-General Dix:

> D. T. VAN BUREN,
> *Colonel and Assistant Adjutant-General.*

Official:

> WRIGHT RIVES, *Aid-de-Camp.*

This order having been disapproved, it was revoked, and in its place the following modified order was issued:

[General Orders, No. 100.]

HEADQUARTERS DEPARTMENT OF THE EAST,
New York City, December 17, 1864.

The President of the United States having disapproved of that portion of department General Orders, No. 97, current series, which instructs all military commanders on the frontier, in certain cases therein specified, to cross the boundary line between the United States and Canada, and directs pursuit into neutral territory, the said instruction is hereby revoked.

In case, therefore, of any future marauding expedition into our territory from Canada, military commanders on the frontiers will report to these headquarters for orders before crossing the boundary line in pursuit of the guilty parties.

By command of Major-General Dix:

> D. T. VAN BUREN,
> *Colonel and Assistant Adjutant-General.*

Official:

> G. VON EIKSTEDT, *Aid-de-Camp.*

The foregoing orders are discussed in Bernard's Neutrality of Great Britain, 465; in Dix's Memoirs, II. 110 et seq.; and in Dip. Cor. 1865, I. 50.

See, also, as to the pursuit of deserters in Canada, 51 Br. & For. State Papers (1860–1861).

" I transmit to Congress an extract of a dispatch from Mr. Livingston, the minister of the United States at Paris, dated the 7th ultimo, and the copy of a communication made to him by Captain Ballard, commander of the frigate *United States*, by which it appears that on firing a national salute from that ship, at Toulon, in honor of the birthday of the King of the French, two men were killed and four others wounded on board the French ship of war *Suffren*. Suitable explanations were immediately made to the French admiral; and the officers and crew of the American frigate, with that generosity which distinguishes their profession, promptly contributed, by a liberal subscription, towards providing for the families of the unfortunate sufferers. I am sure, however, that I should not do justice to the feelings of the American people on this occasion, if I did not invite Congress to assume, on their part, this melancholy duty. I propose, therefore, that the same provision be made, by law, for these French seamen and their families as would be made for American seamen killed or wounded in battle. This proceeding will show the deep sensibility with which the disastrous accident is viewed by the United States, and their readiness to alleviate those consequences which cannot be remedied."

> President Jackson, special message to Congress, June 18, 1834, H. Ex.
> Doc. 492, 23 Cong. 1 sess.

> " It is to be observed that the suggested action was supplémentary to
> the humane and benevolent course of the officers of the frigate United
> States, who, as appears from Captain Ballard's letter to the French
> admiral, contributed on the very day of the accident 5,000 francs
> for the relief of the sufferers . . . The recommendation was
> promptly acted upon, and on the 28th June, 1834, the President approved an act ' to enable the President to make an arrangement with
> the Government of France in relation to certain French seamen
> killed or wounded at Toulon and their families ' (Statutes at Large,
> vol. 4, p. 761) under which life pensions were paid through this
> Department to the families and survivors, between 1835 and 1857,
> to the aggregate amount of $9,600." (Mr. Rives, Act. Sec. of State,
> to Sec. of Navy, Oct. 20, 1888, 170 MS. Dom. Let. 305.)

March 4, 1887, while the U. S. S. *Omaha* was engaged in target practice near the island of Ikesima, in Japan, certain Japanese subjects were accidentally killed or injured by the explosion of shells. By an act of Congress, approved February 26, 1889, the sum of $15,000 was appropriated for distribution among the families of the persons so killed or injured. This sum was paid to the Japanese minister at Washington, March 27, 1889.

> For. Rel. 1889, 547–549.
> See Mr. Adee, Act. Sec. of State, to Mr. Whitney, Sec. of Navy, April 16,
> 1887, 163 MS. Dom. Let. 628; Mr. Blaine, Sec. of State, to Mr. Windom, Sec. of Treasury, March 29, 1889, 172 MS. Dom. Let. 334.

> See, also, dispatch from Mr. Hubbard, min. at Tokio, No. 308, March 18, 1887, MSS. Dept. of State.
>
> Mr. Rives, Act. Sec. of State, to Sec. of Navy, Oct. 20, 1888, enclosed copy of a note of Count Okuma, Japanese minister of foreign affairs, to Mr. Mutsu, Japanese minister at Washington, of Sept. 6, 1888, suggesting that the United States make spontaneous and generous provision for the families of the killed and injured persons, and referring to the case of the French seamen, killed or injured at Toulon, in 1834, by the frigate United States. Mr. Rives suggested that, instead of paying pensions, as was done in the Toulon case, a lump sum should be appropriated. (170 MS. Dom. Let. 305.)

In April, 1893, the Mexican minister at Washington presented a complaint from the collector of customs at Camargo, Tamaulipas, that a colored soldier of the United States Army, on two different days, fired several times on the sentry box of the custom-house. Early in June he complained that the offence had been repeated. The military authorities of the United States investigated the case, but were unable to discover the identity of the men who did the firing. Instructions were given to the commanding officer at Fort Ringgold, Texas, to take measures to prevent a like occurrence in the future. Subsequently two of the soldiers were identified and arrested, and were held for court-martial. The court found that the firing was not malicious, but the offenders were convicted and sentenced each to confinement at hard labor for six months and to forfeit a certain amount of pay for the same period. The commanding officer expressed his regret for the occurrence and adopted measures to prevent its recurrence. In his expression of regret the Government of the United States joined.

> For. Rel. 1893, 448, 449, 450, 452, 453.

" I have carefully examined the report of John A. Haddock, captain commanding Company E, 35th regiment of New York Volunteers, concerning his arrest of Ebenezer Tyler, a deserter from the forces of the United States within unquestioned Canadian territories of Great Britain. The violation of the sovereignty of a friendly state was doubtless committed under the influence of an earnest zeal for the interests of the United States, but that motive can not diminish the wrongfulness of the act or furnish excuse for this Government to that of Great Britain. Having submitted the matter to the President, I am instructed by him to disavow with regret the proceeding of Captain Haddock, and to inform the British Government that the captain will be dismissed from the public service and that the deserter Ebenezer Tyler will be discharged from his enlistment in the volunteer forces of the United States."

> Mr. Seward, Sec. of State, to Mr. Stanton, Sec. of War, April 15, 1863, 60 MS. Dom. Let. 231.

" I have received your No. 23, of the 14th instant, touching the invasion of American territory at Eagle Pass, Texas, by Mexican troops from Piedras Negras. It appears that the Mexican Government laments the incident, has ordered the arrest and trial by court-martial of the persons concerned in the affair and promises that full justice shall be administered in the case.

" This preliminary action on the part of Mexico is viewed with satisfaction as is also the further promise of Mr. Mariscal that the ' questions related to this case will receive merited consideration from the Government of Mexico.' "

> Mr. Bayard, Sec. of State, to Mr. Bragg, min. to Mexico, April 26, 1888, MS. Inst. Mexico, XXII. 189.

On March 3, 1888, a squad of Mexican soldiers, under the command of a lieutenant, who was evidently acting under the orders of his superior officer, made, without the assent of the Government of the United States, an incursion from Mexico into the city of Eagle Pass, Maverick County, Tex., for the purpose of seizing one Antanicio Luis, who was alleged to be a deserter from the Mexican army, but who was at the time engaged in lawful labor at Eagle Pass. The soldiers seized Luis and were in the act of beating him, when they were observed by Shadrack White, deputy sheriff of Maverick County, who, in the exercise of his powers, commanded them to desist and notified them that he would arrest them. They resisted arrest and inflicted upon White serious wounds, from which his right hand was permanently disabled. The Mexican Government expressed regret at the incident and stated that it had ordered the arrest and trial by court-martial of the offending parties. The United States argued not only that the offenders should be punished, but also that an indemnity should be paid for the injuries to White. The Mexican Government subsequently stated that the officers concerned in the affair had been punished and expressed readiness to confer on the question of indemnity. It was agreed that White should be examined by a joint commission of surgeons, and upon their report the Government of Mexico settled the claim for the sum of $7,000.

> For. Rel. 1889, 591, 605, 607, 608, 611; For. Rel. 1890, 632, 635, 642; For. Rel. 1894, 418.

3. Breaches by Civil Authorities.

§ 211.

Peter Martin, a naturalized citizen of the United States, was tried at Laketon, British Columbia, for an assault on an officer in the execution of his duty, prison breach, and escape from custody; and, having been found guilty, was sentenced to fifteen months imprisonment at Victoria,

Case of Peter Martin.

in the same Province, there being no jail or secure place of confinement at Laketon. He was accordingly placed in the custody of constables to be conveyed to Victoria. A part of the route taken lay through Alaska, and was traversed by canoe, via the Stickine River, near the mouth of which, and within the Territory of Alaska, the party made a landing for the purpose of cooking food. While they were thus engaged the prisoner obtained possession of a loaded gun and made a deadly assault on one of the constables, but was overpowered and conveyed to Wrangle Harbor, from whence he was taken by steamer to Victoria.

It having been reported that Martin would be tried at Victoria for this assault, Mr. Fish, on the 2d of November, 1876, wrote to the British minister at Washington, Sir Edward Thornton, and after reciting the facts substantially as above stated, said:

" It further appears from what has been intimated to the consul [of the United States, at Victoria] that Martin will be fully committed for this assault, and that his case will be given to the grand jury, where a true bill will most likely be found against him, and that the case then will come up in the supreme court some time during the present month.

" From the facts presented in the case, it is suggested that the person in question should not be tried for the offense with which he is charged, it having been committed, as is reported, within the jurisdiction of the United States, and that, such being the case, he should be set at liberty.

" I will, therefore, thank you, at your earliest convenience, to call the attention of Her Majesty's proper authorities to the matter, in order that a thorough examination of the facts in the case may be made." [a]

On the 10th of January, 1877, Mr. Fish addressed another note to Sir Edward Thornton, informing him that a despatch had been received from the consul at Victoria, stating that Martin had been tried there before the Hon. P. P. Crease, a justice of the supreme court of the Province for the assault committed on the Stickine River, and had been found guilty and sentenced to one year and nine months imprisonment at hard labor, to take effect after the expiration of the term of fifteen months to which he was sentenced at Laketon. The consul's despatch further stated that as the evidence at the trial was conflicting as to the precise distance of the scene of the assault from the mouth of the Stickine, and as the boundary line between the British and American territory was not definitely marked the judge charged the jury that, under these circumstances, the court had either jurisdiction or concurrent jurisdiction, and that the proceedings were

[a] Mr. Fish, Sec. of State, to Sir Edward Thornton, Brit. min., Nov. 2, 1876, For. Rel. 1877, 266.

just and proper. To this line of argument Mr. Fish answered, first, that if the colonial officers, in transporting Martin from Laketon to Victoria conducted him at any time within and through the unquestioned territory of the United States, they committed, in so doing, a violation of the sovereignty of the United States, which rendered his further detention unjustifiable. And in respect to the question of jurisdiction of the assault he said:

" I must not allow this question to pass without entering an explicit dissent from the doctrine which seems to be advanced by the learned judge who presided at the trial of Martin, that jurisdiction or concurrent jurisdiction vests in her Her Majesty's colonial authorities or courts over offenses committed within any part of the territory of Alaska, even though so near to the treaty-line that uncertainty or doubt may exist on which side of such line the offense is committed. It cannot, I think, be necessary to argue this point, or to do more than record this dissent and denial of a doctrine which, I have no doubt, Her Majesty's Government agrees with me in repudiating." [a]

On the 25th of September, 1877, the British *chargé d'affaires* at Washington addressed a note to Mr. F. W. Seward, Acting Secretary of State, saying:

" I have the honor to inform you that I have just learned from the deputy governor of Canada that the Dominion Government has concluded the inquiry into the circumstances of the case, and has decided upon setting Peter Martin at liberty without further delay." [b]

" I transmit herewith copies of papers received by this Department, in relation to the kidnapping of Francisco Arresures, **Case of Arresures.** in Texas, on the evening of the 26th of July last, and his forcible transportation to Mexico, where he was killed on the morning of the 28th of the same month by Mexican officials in whose custody he had been placed.

" It is unnecessary to make, at the present time, a critical analysis of all the statements contained in the annexed papers. Such an attempt would not only consume time uselessly, but would involve the discussion of impertinent matters and obscure the main issue of the case.

" It is admitted on all hands that Arresures was arrested in Eagle Pass, Texas, on the 26th of July last, without authority of law. At that time, as the evidence shows, he had been residing in Eagle Pass, with his family, between three and four months, and had been in the employ of Mr. John O. Williamson, as driver of a stage, for about

---

[a] Mr. Fish, Sec. of State, to Sir Edward Thornton, Brit. min., Jan. 10, 1877, For. Rel. 1877, 268.

[b] For. Rel. 1877, 271. The correspondence in the case of Martin is also printed in 68 Brit. & For. State Papers, 1223.

six weeks. On the day named, near the hour of eight o'clock in the morning, he was seized by three deputy sheriffs of Maverick County, Texas, named, respectively, Diaz, Van, and Latimer, on an order of extradition issued by Judge Hoffstetter, a judge of the court of that county. It is conceded that this order, which appears to have been based on statements of a Mexican police officer, named Mondragon, was improperly and irregularly obtained.

"Immediately after his arrest, Arresures was taken over the Rio Grande and into Mexico, and was left in the custody of Mondragon, above referred to, he being an officer of the force of public security of the district of Rio Grande, State of Coahuila. Whether the delivery of the prisoner to Mondragon was in Texas or in Mexico is uncertain. The three deputy sheriffs state that Mondragon and another Mexican came over into Texas. On the other hand, Mr. John O. Williamson states that Diaz, one of those deputies, told him that Mondragon had promised to come over, but failed to do so, and that Arresures was taken over to Piedras Negras, Mexico, and delivered to Mondragon at his house in that town. This statement is confirmed by the appeal of Arresures to Mr. Linn, U. S. consul at Piedras Negras, for his intervention, in the first of which Arresures said: 'I was taken from my work by armed men who crossed me to this side, and delivered me to the captain of the rangers,' meaning Mondragon.

"It is not disputed that at least two of the Texan deputies went over with Arresures into Mexico. But, in the view that the Department takes of the case, it is not conceived to be material whether the Texan officials who were parties to the kidnapping went over with their prisoner into Mexico, or whether the Mexican officials who were parties to the same transaction came over the Rio Grande into Texas to receive him.

"On the 27th of July, the day following the kidnapping, Arresures appealed to Mr. Linn, U. S. consul at Piedras Negras, for protection, and Mr. Williamson, Arresures' employer, who had come over to look after the case, joined in the application. Mr. Linn, accompanied by Mr. Williamson and a Mr. Schuhardt, then called on Mondragon and asked for Arresures' release. This request Mondragon refused, saying that the case had been placed in the hands of the Zaragoza district court.

"Intending to apply to this court for the prisoner's release, Mr. Linn learned, early the next morning that Arresures had been killed by members of Mondragon's force.

"This fact is undisputed, and, while the circumstances of the killing have been differently stated, there are the strongest reasons to believe that Arresures' violent death was brought about by Mondragon's orders. The plea of the Mexican authorities, stated in Mr. Linn's despatch of September 3, 1886, that the guards acted in self-defense, is incompatible with many of the circumstances. Unarmed, as the prisoner certainly was, and in charge of three armed men, it scarcely seems possible that there was necessity for resort to the extreme measure of homicide to control him. The hurried burial, the condition of the body when exhumed, the enmity of Mondragon towards Arresures, as evidenced by his own statements, by the fears expressed by Arresures, in his appeal to Mr. Linn, as well as by the conspiracy to kidnap, in which, as the papers before the Department show, Mondragon was the prime mover, all lead to the grave conclusion that the violent killing of Arresures was premeditated.

"The question yet to be considered is that of Mexico's liability.

"The Department holds it to be clear that Arresures was, at the time of his forcible removal to Mexico, under the protection of the United States. He had declared his intention to become a citizen of the United States; and the reasonable inference from the evidence is that when kidnapped he was domiciled in Texas, where his family resided and continue to reside. But, admitting that he was not so domiciled, and that he had not declared his intention to become a citizen of the United States, the fact that he was, at the time of his arrest and abduction, residing on the soil of the United States, would entitle this Government to call upon Mexico for redress. Had the case been presented to this Department in time, it is not doubted that Mexico would have admitted the right of this Government to ask for the prisoner's return; and as that has become impossible, it may be reasonably expected that she will not now deny the only reparation that may be made.

"It is no palliation of Mondragon's guilt that his co-conspirators in the abduction were officials of Texas, who wrongfully used the process of that State to effect the abduction. It may be said that in the case of a person regularly extradited, the demanding Government is held bound to exercise the utmost care and good faith. So anxious have Governments been to ensure to those who come within their jurisdiction, even when they are fugitives from justice, the protection of the laws, that it is not uncommon to find in treaties of extradition a provision that persons extradited thereunder shall not be tried for any other offense than that for which the surrender was made.

"In respect to the custody of persons surrendered, it is never expressly provided, because it is always assumed, that they will be treated humanely and protected from violence. No stipulation is needed to enforce this obligation, which is fundamental and self-evident.

"It can not be maintained that this obligation is less binding where the person held has been obtained not in accordance with, but in fraud of existing treaties, as was the case with Arresures. In such case maltreatment of the prisoner but adds another wrong, and makes it more incumbent upon the government whose protection has been defrauded and abused, to maintain its rights.

"You are instructed to bring this case to the attention of the Mexican Government, and impress upon it the importance of the issues herein presented, and its obligation to redress the wrongs complained of and make pecuniary reparation to the family of the murdered man."

> Mr. Bayard, Sec. of State, to Mr. Manning, min. to Mexico, Feb. 26, 1887, MS. Inst. Mexico, XXI. 646.
>
> For previous correspondence in this case, see For. Rel. 1886, 708–722.
>
> "The attention of your legation is called to instruction No. 54, of February 26, 1887, relative to the case of Francisco Arresures, kidnapped in Texas, July 26, 1886, and to the despatches of the legation Nos. 88 and 92 of March 15th and 19th, 1887. Please state what reply has since been received; and if none, again bring the case to the notice of the Mexican Government." (Mr. Wharton, Act. Sec. of State, to Mr. Ryan, min. to Mexico, March 16, 1892, MS. Inst. Mex. XXIII. 196.)
>
> As to the case of Oberlander and Messenger, see For. Rel. 1897, 370–388; Mr. Wharton, Act. Sec. of State, to Mr. Ryan, min. to Mexico, May 24, 1892, MS. Inst. Mex. XXIII. 228; Mr. Foster, Sec. of State, to Mr. Ryan, June 30, 1892, id. 244.

In March, 1887, a Mexican lieutenant named Gutierrez, belonging *Nogales case, 1887.* to a small force garrisoned at the town of Nogales, which lies partly on the Mexican and partly on the American side of the international boundary, committed an offense on the American side of the line and was arrested by the local police. Forthwith a Mexican colonel named Arvizú and two soldiers who had crossed over with him rescued Gutierrez by force and retreated with him to Mexican territory.[a] The Government of the United States, when advised of the incident, instructed its minister that Mexico should at once restore the rescued prisoner "to the United States jurisdiction, and should either inflict prompt punishment on the Mexicans who effected the rescue or deliver them up to the United States."[b] Subsequently, as the result of negotiations at Washington, the Mexican Government received the impression that the United States had given it the option of delivering up the offenders, including Gutierrez, to the American authorities for punishment or of inflicting upon them adequate pun-

---

[a] For. Rel. 1887, 702.

[b] Mr. Bayard, Sec. of State, to Mr. Manning, min. to Mexico, tel., March 7, 1887; For. Rel. 1887, 692.

ishment itself.[a] The United States corrected this impression, saying that, whether the person rescued was or was not a Mexican, nothing could satisfy the United States except his delivery to the American authorities from whose custody he was forcibly taken, and that the alternative offered related only to the Mexicans who effected the rescue.[b]

This position was amplified in the following communication:

" No such option was created or tendered by me to the Mexican Government as to the punishment of the prisoner or prisoners who had been rescued from the jurisdiction of the Uuited States authorities. Having in mind the provision of our extradition treaty, which relieves either party from the obligation to extradite its own citizens, I refrained from formal demand for the surrender of those Mexican soldiers who had invaded our territory and forcibly rescued a prisoner there in legal custody, and intimated that if Mexico did not herself assert the right she claims in respect of punishing her own citizens, the extradition of the rescuers might reasonably be expected. As to the prisoners rescued from the custody of the United States officials in Arizona, no such alternative was contemplated or suggested by me. Armed invasion of our territory and rescue of a prisoner from our lawful jurisdiction could confer upon the rescued person no asylum in Mexico, nor bring him within the formalities of extradition. It becomes, under such circumstances, the simple international duty of the Mexican Government to undo the wrong committed by its own soldiery, by restoring the rescued prisoners to the jurisdiction from which they had been wrongfully taken." [c]

On the assurance, however, of the Mexican Government that it had no desire to avoid a full and friendly compliance with the duties prescribed by the law of nations, the United States, deferring to the earnest request of that Government, which stated that the military law of Mexico prescribed a severer penalty than would be inflicted under the American law, agreed, as the right to the return of the rescued prisoner was acknowledged, to suspend the demand for his restoration to American jurisdiction and await the result of his trial by the Mexican military court.[d]

Responding to this amicable compliance with its request, the Mexican Government said:

" I also willingly accede that your excellency's Government has had

[a] For. Rel. 1887, 693–694.

[b] Mr. Bayard, Sec. of State, to Mr. Manning, min. to Mexico, tel., March 17, 1887 ; For. Rel. 1887, 695.

[c] Mr. Bayard, Sec. of State, to Mr. Manning, min. to Mexico, March 19, 1887 ; For. Rel. 1887, 696.

[d] Mr. Bayard, Sec. of State, to Mr. Manning, min. to Mexico, tel., April 8, 1887 ; For. Rel. 1887, 710.

a *certain* right to request that matters should be restored to their *status quo* by returning Gutierrez to the power of the Arizona authorities who held him a prisoner, for it is not a question of a Mexican fugitive from foreign justice, but of one who was forcibly rescued by Mexican soldiers who entered the neighboring territory armed, without any legal pretense or excuse of any kind, and certainly without order or warrant on the part of the Mexican Government.

" Still, with the same frankness with which I admit the foregoing, I should state that I confidently trust in the good sense and friendly disposition of the Government so worthily represented by your excellency that the suspension of the demand referred to pending the proceeding against Gutierrez does not imply the possible contingency of a renewal thereof after the said party has been judged and duly punished. I can not imagine such a contingency; hence I abstain from all reasoning thereupon. Rather, inclosing this note, I take pleasure in expressing the sincere conviction that touching the unfortunate events at Nogales the honorable Mr. Bayard and your excellency as well have exhibited a spirit of friendly conciliation worthy of notice and of eulogy." [a]

The trial by the Mexican military court having resulted in a sentence of death upon Gutierrez, and also upon Colonel Arvizú and another officer, the American minister was informed that the Government of the United States " would view with deep regret the imposition of a penalty so extreme," and was instructed to say that a mitigation would be regarded with favor.[b] An appeal to the supreme military court resulted in the affirmation of the death sentence as to Gutierrez and Arvizú.[c] This sentence was commuted to twenty years' imprisonment, Señor Mariscal stating that President Diaz had considered it advisable "to follow the humane suggestions" of the United States, and thus to afford " a proof of friendly deference." With the decision thus conveyed the United States expressed gratification.[d]

In March, 1888, certain citizens of the United States entered Mexican territory in pursuit of bandits who had attacked a train on the Southern Pacific Railway. While conducting the pursuit, they were arrested by the Mexican authorities and disarmed, and their horses detained. They were subsequently released, and the Government of

---

[a] Mr. Mariscal, Mex. min. of for. aff., to Mr. Manning, U. S. min., April 14, 1887; For. Rel., 1887, 714. See also same to same, May 21, 1887, id. 728.

[b] For. Rel. 1887, 719, 723, 726, 728, 742. See also Mr. Bayard, Sec. of State, to Mr. Bragg, min. to Mexico, tel., April 23, 1888, MS. Inst. Mex. XXII. 188, saying that a reiteration of the request for clemency might be regarded by the Mexican Government as an interference with its discretion.

[c] For. Rel. 1888, II. 1187.

[d] For. Rel. 1888, II. 1191.

the United States was informed that the arms and horses would be delivered to the person whom it might designate to receive them, and that one of the horses, which had died in detention, would be paid for, if its death should appear to be due to neglect or ill-treatment on the part of those who had had it in charge. This arrangement was accepted, and the collector of customs at El Paso, Texas, was instructed to admit the property to free entry.

> For. Rel. 1888, II. 1293–1294, 1301.

The Mexican minister, in August, 1893, complained that on the 30th of the preceding June, six armed men from Texas, under the command of Capt. Frank C. Jones, invaded Mexican territory in pursuit of Jesus Holguin, who took refuge in the house of his brother Antonio, in the town of Tres Jacales, State of Chihuahua. His son Severo was also in the house. Captain Jones took possession of the houses adjoining that of Holguin, and in the fight Jesus and Severo Holguin were wounded and Captain Jones killed. During the following night, another party from Texas, consisting of about sixty men, took hostile possession of a point opposite Tres Jacales, but withdrew on seeing a body of men, who had been organized for the purpose of supporting the authorities. Concerning these acts, the Mexican minister by direction of his Government presented a formal remonstrance, asking that the invaders be punished and that the United States issue instructions " to prevent the future repetition of acts no less disagreeable than offensive to the sovereignty of the United States of Mexico." An investigation of the case by the governor of Texas was requested. The governor's report showed, in substance, that at the particular point where Captain Jones was killed, the Rio Grande in 1854 changed its course about 6 miles, leaving between the old course and the new a tract of several thousand acres, commonly called an island, which formed a convenient resort for persons in both countries who wished to act in defiance of either Government; that the old river bed had become filled up and so obliterated that it was practically impossible to recognize it; that Captain Jones, if he passed beyond the old river bed in pursuit of criminals, did so ignorantly, to a point only a few hundred yards on the Mexican side, where he was ambushed and murdered by the fugitive criminals; and that he committed no assault on Mexican citizens and no intentional invasion of Mexican territory.

> For. Rel. 1893, 455, 456, 462, 466, 467.
> See, as to the robbery of the custom-house at Las Palomas by bandits who afterwards took refuge in the United States, For. Rel. 1893, 467, 468, 471.

As to an alleged intended incursion into Mexico from Silver City, N. M., see For. Rel. 1893, 467, 471.

For an investigation of reports as to preparations at San Elizario, Texas, for a raid into Mexico, and the adoption of measures to prevent it, see For. Rel. 1893, 468–471.

As to the case of the Garza bandits, from Mexico, see For. Rel. 1893, 424, 425, 426–447, 448, 456.

In September, 1893,[a] the Mexican minister presented a formal complaint of a violation of Mexican territory at Nogales, Mexico, on the 23rd of July. He stated that on that day John Roberts, deputy sheriff at Nogales, Arizona, accompanied by Alfonso Bachelier, a citizen of the United States, crossed over into Mexican territory for the purpose of arresting Jesus Garcia, a Mexican citizen, who had had a fight with Celedonio Carrillo, also a Mexican, in the former place. Bachelier knocked Garcia down, and then he and Roberts, with the assistance of William Mehan, a citizen of the United States, dragged him by the feet into American jurisdiction. On the next day Roberts obtained from a justice of the peace a warrant for the arrest of Garcia, who was tried and sentenced to fine and imprisonment, although several witnesses testified that he was seized in the State of Sonora. The minister asked that the deputy sheriff and his accomplices be punished, and that suitable indemnity be paid to Garcia. The case was referred to the governor of Arizona for investigation.

A careful investigation by the United States showed that Roberts, who had been sitting on the Mexican side of the street, ran over to the American side to arrest Garcia; that the latter then ran toward the Mexican side, and, when perhaps a yard or two over, collided with a person who was running from the Mexican side to intercept him, and fell; that, as he thus lay, most of his body being on the American side, while his head and possibly a small part of his body rested on the Mexican, he was arrested by Roberts, who was then on the American side. On these facts the United States maintained (1) that Garcia was arrested on American soil; but (2) that if Mexico should be disposed to take the view that his being thrown back, by the collision in question, upon the soil of the United States and within reach of the officer, was part of the arrest, no indemnity should be claimed for him, in view of his record as a lawbreaker on both sides of the line, who had at the time of his arrest, as the evidence indicated, deliberately gone upon American territory with intent to violate the law. It further appeared that Garcia, after sentence was passed upon him, was, with a view to strengthen good feeling, handed over to the Mexican

Nogales case, 1893.

---

[a] For. Rel. 1893, 457, 462.

authorities, on the understanding, approved by the governor of Sonora, that the matter was to end. Under the circumstances the United States, while declaring that it had been " anxious to make amends if any violation of Mexican sovereignty " occurred in effecting the arrest, expressed the conviction that it was " not a case which demands the intervention of the Government of Mexico for the protection of its sovereignty or of the rights of one of its citizens from lawless invasion." [a] The Mexican Government accepted this view and terminated the discussion.[b]

Complaint having been made, on the one hand, of the seizure by Mexican officials of a number of sheep and two American citizens on American soil bordering on the Rio Grande near Reynosa, and, on the other hand, of the arrest by American officials of certain Mexicans on soil that was alleged to be Mexican, it was agreed that the Mexican Government should release the two American prisoners and return the sheep, and that the United States should release the Mexican prisoners, reserving the question of violation of territory to be settled by the International Boundary Commission or otherwise.

> Mr. Gresham, Sec. of State, to Mr. Gray, min. to Mexico, Sept. 6, 1893, Sept. 10, 1893, Sept. 14, 1893, and Sept. 19, 1893, MS. Inst. Mexico, XXIII. 416, 418, 420, 422.
>
> As to the alleged arrest by two Arizona deputy sheriffs, in Mexico, of one Dimas Lerma, who had escaped from their custody, see Mr. Rockhill, Act. Sec. of State, to governor of Arizona, Sept. 29, 1896, 213 MS. Dom. Let. 1.

" I have the honor to acknowledge the receipt of your note of the 5th instant, enclosing a memorandum from the minister of justice of Canada, in relation to the case of Thomas Meagher.

"After due consideration of this case, I take pleasure in saying that your request will be granted and the said Meagher will be discharged from the arrest made and from the bail given by him for his appearance. This will relieve him from the necessity of any further action on his part, as it leaves him at liberty.

" In reference to the other suggestion made in regard to Mr. Avery, I beg to say that, as this Government is advised, the facts are not precisely stated in the memorandum of the Canadian minister of justice; that this Government is persuaded that even on the facts stated in the memorandum there was no felonious intent on the part of Mr. Avery, the deputy collector of customs; and if he did the act complained of, yet, as this Government understands the facts, he did not commit any intentional violation of British sovereignty,

[a] Mr. Olney, Sec. of State, to Mr. Romero, Mex. ambassador, Dec. 1, 1896, For. Rel. 1896, 446–448.

[b] For. Rel. 1896, 454.

and if such violation was committed, it was done involuntarily and unintentionally in the endeavor of the deputy to effect an arrest which, in his judgment, he had a right to make and which he believed was undertaken within the territory of the United States.

"This Government disavows any act of force, if any was executed, against Meagher in Canadian territory and regrets the unfortunate occurrence; and in view of the sentiments of friendship existing between the two Governments, it is hoped that these explanations of regret will be accepted as a satisfactory conclusion of the incident."

> Mr. Hay, Sec. of State, to Sir Julian Pauncefote, British amb., January 21, 1899, MS. Notes to British Leg. XXIV. 427.
>
> It is to be observed, as will be seen in the chapter on extradition, that when the alleged criminal is brought within the jurisdiction by irregular extradition process or by kidnapping, he can not set up the illegality of the mode of his recovery as a defense, but can avail himself of it to effect his release only in case the government whose jurisdiction has been violated duly interposes.
>
> That the seizure of Koszta in Turkey by Austrian agents was treated by the United States as a violation of international law, see, infra, the chapter on Domicil.

4. Breaches by Private Persons.

§ 212.

In January, 1797, the Spanish minister complained that the territorial rights of Spain in Florida had been violated by certain persons residing in the United States. The Attorney-General, to whom the matter was referred, advised that it was an offence against the laws of nations for any persons, whether citizens or foreigners, living in the United States, to go into the territory of Spain with intent to recover their property by their own strength or in any other manner than the laws there in force authorized and permitted.

> Lee, At.-Gen., March 26, 1797, 1 Op. 68; cited in Mr. Foster, Sec. of State, to Mr. Washburn, min. to Switzerland, July 27, 1892, For. Rel. 1894, 650.

In a case in 1822 where a slave concealed himself in an American vessel lying at Ste. Croix, and was brought to New York, the Danish minister having demanded his restoration, the Attorney-General advised that he was "of the opinion that it is due to the sovereignty of Denmark, and to our own character as a nation, to restore this slave to the condition from which he has been taken by a ship carrying our flag and belonging to our citizens; and that the policy of our own laws conspires to enforce the performance of this duty."

> Wirt, At.-Gen., Sept. 27, 1822, 1 Op. 566, 569; cited in Mr. Blaine, Sec. of State, to Mr. Washburn, min. to Switzerland, March 1, 1892. For. Rel. 1894, 646, 647.

" Referring to your letter of the 14th ultimo, suggesting a reciprocal arrangement between this country and Mexico permitting the cattlemen of either country to enter the territory of the other for the purpose of rounding up any such cattle belonging to them as may have strayed across the border, I have to inform you that the Department is in receipt of a despatch from the United States ambassador to Mexico, dated the 13th instant, reporting the requirements imposed by the Mexican treasury on American cattlemen desiring to avail themselves of the arrangement on the subject made some four or five years ago between the customs authorities of the two Governments along the border.

" According to the Mexican requirements an American stockman desiring to cross the frontier to make round-ups must make verbal petition to a Mexican custom-house or to the fiscal police, accompanied by the declaration of some known person that the petitioner is really a stockman, and furnish a bond, with stamps to the amount of $3.00, to guarantee the payment of duties on such effects as may not be re-exported.

" These requisites being complied with, the custom-house or fiscal police issues a permit, with a twenty-five cent stamp, good for ten days, renewable up to thirty days, by two successive permits of ten days each.

" It appears that the stamps are affixed officially by the Mexican authorities, and cost the party interested nothing."

Mr. Adee, Second Assist. Sec. of State, to Mr. Marteny, October 22, 1900, 248 MS. Dom. Let. 473.

" I have to acknowledge the receipt of your letter of the 27th instant, in reference to a son of Thomas Golding, alleged to have been stolen and to be now in Ireland, and asking what proceedings can be taken for his restoration to his parents. In reply I have to state that the case as presented in your letter is apparently one in which the employment of legal counsel should be sought, and in which the Department can take no official steps nor offer any efficient interposition.

" The name of the consul at Dublin is Mr. Wilson King. There is no objection to your addressing him, and it is believed that he will not hesitate to use his good offices on the case being presented to him; but it should be understood that he is not authorized to interest himself in it in an official capacity, but only as an individual whose local position makes him available for the service."

Mr. Cadwalader, Assist. Sec. of State, to Mr. Roden, Sept. 30, 1875, 110 MS. Dom. Let. 157.

" I have not been able to see what steps can be taken by Federal authorities in aid of Mr. Hyldahl, mentioned in yours of the 27th ultimo and 23d instant.

"The case which he presents is that of a female child of some 10 years of age abducted by Mormons from (and perhaps by connivance of) her mother, still living provisionally in Denmark, the father (Mr. H.) being now resident in Chicago, but yet a Danish subject. The child has been carried to Utah, and is now there.

"Mr. Hyldahl's redress at law is that which is common to all the citizens of this country—and none of them have more—viz, application by habeas corpus, made within the jurisdiction where the child is detained. At certain stages, in case local authorities refused to execute the law, there may be an interference by Federal officials, but the kind and extent of that can be better defined when circumstances shall have arisen to warrant it."

> Mr. Brewster, At.-Gen., to Mr. Frelinghuysen, Sec. of State, Nov. 27, 1883.
> A copy of this opinion was communicated to the Danish minister, with a personal note, stating that, in partial answer to an inquiry prosecuted by the Department of State, it had been found that Elsinore, Utah, where the child (Gertrude Marie Hyldahl) was said to be, was an isolated place, where the approach of an officer would prove the signal for her secretion; and that the Department's informant was endeavoring to find a suitable person to make an investigation. (Mr. Frelinghuysen, Sec. of State, to Mr. de Bille, Dec. 22, 1883, MS. Notes to Denmark, VII. 158.)
> In a later personal note, it was stated that, as appeared by a letter from the United States marshal in Utah, the child was at Elsinore; and the name and address of the marshal were given to the minister. (Mr. Frelinghuysen to Mr. de Bille, Feb. 20, 1884, MS. Notes to Denmark, VII. 163.)

"Your letter of the 7th instant, stating that Mr. A. von Schade's wife recently carried off their three children to Germany against the husband's wishes, where she detains them, and inquiring whether this Department can aid him in regaining the custody of his children, has been received.

"I regret to say that the case of Mr. von Schade is one in which this Government can not interfere. As the children are with their mother in Germany, the question as to who is their lawful custodian must be decided by German municipal law as administered by German courts. To these courts alone, under the circumstances as stated by you, can an appeal for the surrender of the children be made, by the employment of private counsel in Germany."

> Mr. Bayard, Sec. of State, to Mr. Galvin, December 13, 1886, 162 MS. Dom. Let. 349.

In 1883 Carrie A. Turner, a citizen of the United States, and Albert His, a citizen of Switzerland, both then residing in the city of New York, intermarried. July 23, 1887, there was born to them a child named Constance Madeline. In the following autumn His returned to

Case of Constance Madeline His.

Switzerland, intending permanently to enter into business there. His wife refused to accompany or to join him, and in September, 1889, he began in the district court of Zofingen an action for divorce for malicious desertion. The wife, when served with process in New York, immediately proceeded to Switzerland and, intervening in the judicial proceedings, demanded a divorce on the ground of unconquerable repugnance of the parties to each other. Previously to the trial, the parties agreed upon and presented to the court a form of a decree which provided (1) that the court should dissolve the marriage, and (2) that the child should be given to the mother to be reared and educated, with the understanding that the father should at all times have the right to visit her, and that, in case of the death of the mother, the right and duty to care for and educate her should belong to him. By an outside contract, which was made a part of the record, His engaged to pay the wife a certain amount per annum. The decree of the court was rendered January 22, 1890, in accordance with the terms agreed upon. In the spring of 1891 His returned to New York, and on May 25, 1891, he abducted the child and returned with her to Switzerland. An indictment for abduction was afterwards found against him in New York. Mrs. His employed counsel and presented a petition to the court of Zofingen, in order to regain the custody of the child. His, on the other hand, petitioned for an amendment of the decree of divorce, so as to leave the child in his care. An order was made by the court on the petition of Mrs. His, restraining His from removing the child from the Canton of Aargau till she should be given back to her mother or till it should be otherwise decided by a competent court; but, in view of His's petition, she subsequently applied in writing to the director of justice of the Canton, asking for the execution of the decree of divorce. The director replied that the matter was pending in court; that the executive officials had no right to interfere with the action of a civil tribunal; and that when a valid judicial decree was rendered, then, according to the constitutional procedure, the sheriff would execute it. Subsequently, the district court issued an order restraining Mrs. His from removing the child pending the decision on His's petition for an amendment of the decree of divorce, and this action of the court was confirmed on appeal by the superior court of the Canton. On an appeal taken by Mrs. His to the high federal court, the decision of the cantonal court was approved. Prior to the decision of the high federal court, however, the case was taken up by the Government of the United States, on the ground (1) that the abduction of the child by His was a criminal offence against the laws of New York; (2) that it also was in contempt of the authority and orders of the Swiss courts, the child being, according to the Swiss decree of divorce, lawfully in the custody of its mother; and (3) that the abduction of the child under these circumstances constituted a violation of the territorial sovereignty of the United States, which entitled the United States to demand her return to its jurisdiction.[a] The Swiss Government, on the other hand, took the ground that according to the law of Switzerland the act of His could not be looked upon as an offence; that, as the father of the child, he enjoyed "imprescriptible rights over her, as well as over the mother; " that the fact that the education of the child was entrusted to the mother only in consequence of an agreement of the parties, the pecuniary charge being borne by the father, necessarily implied the right on his part to see to it that she received proper care and education; that by taking the child away he had merely broken the agreement entered into by his wife and himself with the sanction of the court; that for this act redress might be sought in the courts before which the case was actually pending; and that, not only were the courts competent to deal with the case, but that the executive was not competent to interfere with them.[b]

The position of the United States was adhered to in several instructions.[c] The Swiss courts, it was affirmed, had, by keeping the child in the custody of the father, allowed him to take advantage of the crime committed in New York and thus profit by his own wrong, in contravention of principles of law and of morals.[d] The Swiss Government, on the other hand, considered "the action of Mr. His as not a crime, but simply a violation of the arrangements concluded between the husband and wife and sanctioned by the tribunals of Aargau, an offence for which His may be pursued before a competent tribunal, but would not justify, by any means, an administrative intervention.[e]

August 11, 1893, the district court of Zofingen entered a decree by which the custody and education of the child were taken from the mother and entrusted to the father, the original decree of divorce being to this extent modified. This decree was confirmed October 21, 1893, by the court of appeals of the Canton of Aargau. By the

---

[a] Mr. Blaine, Sec. of State, to Mr. Washburn, min. to Switzerland, March 1, 1892, For. Rel. 1894, 646, citing opinions of the Attorney-General, March 26, 1797, 1 Op. 68, and Sept. 27, 1822, 1 Op. 566.

[b] Swiss Federal Council to Mr. Washburn, min. of the U. S., May 6, 1892, For Rel. 1894, 648–649.

[c] Mr. Foster, Sec. of State, to Mr. Washburn, min. to Switzerland, July 27, 1892, For. Rel. 1894, 649 ; Mr. Foster, Sec. of State, to Mr. Cheney, chargé, Jan. 13, 1893, id. 650.

[d] Mr. Wharton, Act. Sec. of State, to Mr. Cheney, chargé, Feb. 17, 1893, For. Rel. 1894, 652.

[e] Mr. Lachenal, min. of foreign affairs, to Mr. Cheney, chargé, May 9, 1893, For. Rel. 1894, 655.

judgment of the court of appeals it appears that His had asked for a modification of the decree of divorce on the ground that the child was not well taken care of. Mrs. His maintained that the district court of Zofingen, in granting the divorce, had exhausted its powers to act in the cause and was not competent to modify the decree; that His's petition for a modification of the decree was to be considered as the beginning of a new action, in respect of which Mrs. His, an American citizen residing in New York, was not within the jurisdiction of any Swiss court. The court of appeals of Aargau held that the district court of Zofingen, having pronounced the decree, was competent to deal with its consequences in respect of the care and education of the child, and cited in support of this opinion decisions of the high federal court.[a] An appeal from the judgment of the court of appeals of Aargau was taken to the federal tribunal, and was rejected by that tribunal on March 1, 1894. The judgment awarding the custody and education of the child to the father thus became executory. "Under these circumstances," said the Swiss Government, "the Federal Council must declare that it considers that this affair has received its regular solution. It regrets to say that it is no longer possible to enter further on the matter of reclamations, which might be addressed to it on the subject, and hopes that the Government of the Union will be pleased to share this manner of viewing it.[b]

The United States replied that, as regarded the right of the mother to the custody of the child, it did not dissent from this view, since she seemed to be precluded by the action of the courts from making any further claim on the basis of her own private rights, but that it dissented from the view expressed by the Swiss Government as to the " political and international questions involved." Those questions, upon the answer to which depended " the more immediate question " whether the United States or Switzerland was entitled to the custody of the child, could not be decided by the Swiss tribunals so as to bind the United States. If the Swiss Government took the position that one of its citizens might " enter the territory of the United States in defiance of their sovereignty and authority, and by stealth or force take from their jurisdiction a citizen or even an alien having a lawful domicil " there, the United States " must emphatically record its dissent from a proposition so subversive of the fundamental principles of sovereignty." In order, therefore, that the case might not in future be cited as a precedent against the United States, the United States minister was instructed to demand of the Swiss Government

---

[a] For. Rel. 1894, 670–673.

[b] Mr. Lachenal, min. of foreign affairs, to Mr. Broadhead, min. to Switzerland, May 9, 1894, For. Rel. 1894, 670.

" such action on its part as will comport with the dignity and sovereignty of the United States." [a]

" The Department has . . . been informed that the Swiss supreme court has confirmed the decrees of the lower courts giving Albert His, the father, the custody of the child. The mother's rights are, in the view of the case taken by the Department, concluded by that adjudication. The other question of the violation of the sovereignty of the United States by Albert His is one in which the mother has no greater right to intervene than any other citizen of the United States."

> Mr. Olney, Sec. of State, to Mr. Southwick, May 22, 1896, 210 MS. Dom. Let. 281, referring to Mr. Gresham's instruction to Mr. Broadhead, of Oct. 31, 1894, supra.

" In its former letter the Department explained to you that the international question was reduced to the simple one of violation of sovereignty in which the mother's right to the child was not involved. You wish to know now, whether in the adjustment of that question between the two Governments the restoration of the child to its mother will not be necessary, and whether there is not some means by which the mother may obtain custody of the child.

" If, in the adjustment of the single international question arising out of the case, the Swiss Government should restore the child to the jurisdiction of the United States, it would by no means follow that the parental control and custody of the child, now vested by the adjudication of a competent court, the jurisdiction of which both the mother and the father acknowledge, would be affected thereby. The mother might, in case the child should be returned to New York, sue in the courts of that State for the custody of it, but she would be at the disadvantage of contending against an adverse judgment rendered by a foreign court in a suit to which she was a party.

" I know of no means by which the mother having been defeated in a suit for the custody of the child can now obtain it. I am not prepared to say at this time whether this Government will insist on the restoration of the child to United States jurisdiction as a reparation of the breach of sovereignty committed in abducting it. Switzerland has disavowed this act of His and acknowledges that it is a violation of law for which His is liable to punishment should he come again within reach of our laws. The offence not being extraditable under the treaty with Switzerland, there is no way of bringing His back to the United States for trial."

> Mr. Olney, Sec. of State, to Mr. Southwick, May 29, 1896, 210 MS. Dom. Let. 418.

---

[a] Mr. Gresham, Sec. of State, to Mr. Broadhead, min. to Switzerland, Oct. 31, 1894, For. Rel. 1894, 674.

" In a despatch No. 72, of June 14, 1895, our minister to Switzerland communicated a note from the Swiss minister for foreign affairs in which it was stated that the Swiss Federal Council repudiated very emphatically any intention to deny or question the sovereignty and jurisdiction of the United States over its territory, but maintained, in effect, that the judicial tribunals of Switzerland of competent jurisdiction in the premises in a controversy between the father and mother having held that the father was entitled to the custody of the child by a modification of the original decree of divorce in that respect, it therefore followed that the father had never been deprived of his paternal power or authority and that it was no invasion of the territorial sovereignty of the United States for him in the exercise of that paternal power to take charge of his child wherever he might find her.

" There is no later correspondence on the subject and the Department is not advised that Mrs. His recovered the child since that date."

> Mr. Adee, Acting Secretary of State, to Mr. Johnson, November 1, 1897, 222 MS. Dom. Let. 136.

5. PERMISSION FOR PASSAGE OF FOREIGN FORCES.

§ 213.

August 27, 1790, Washington having put the question to Adams, Jefferson, and Hamilton, " What then should be the answer of the Executive of the United States to Lord Dorchester in case he should apply for permission to march troops through the territory of the said States, from Detriot to the Mississippi," Adams advised a refusal of such request (8 J. Adams's Works, 497). Jefferson was disposed to grant it (Writings, Washington's ed. VII, 508–510). Hamilton argued earnestly and at length for the granting of the request, even though the object of the movement of troops should be the attack on New Orleans and the Spanish possessions on the Mississippi. [4 Hamilt. Works (ed. 1885), 20.]

Circumstances of necessity or convenience.

> Jefferson's opinion against the policy of permitting British troops to be transported over the territory of the United States, from Detroit to the Mississippi, is given in 7 Jeff. Works, 508.
>
> No belligerent army has the right of passage through, or entry into, neutral territory without the consent of its sovereign. (Cushing, At.-Gen., 7 Op. 122.)
>
> If, during war, by inadvertence or otherwise, belligerent troops cross the frontier, they should be driven back. They may also be received, by virtue of the right of asylum, but they should then be arrested, disarmed, and detained in such manner as to render it impossible for them to return to the theatre of war. (Rivier, Principes du Droit des Gens, II. 396.)

The right of the United States to send troops across the Isthmus of Panama is guaranteed by the treaty with New Granada of 1846.

> Mr. Marcy, Sec. of State, to Mr. Paredes, June 20, 1853, MS. Notes to Colombia, VI. 35; same to same, Oct. 12, 1853, id. 43.
>
> This right was explicitly recognized by the Colombian Government in a communication to the authorities of the State of Panama, of May 15, 1865; and it was also conceded to extend to the transportation of fugitives of justice who should be on the way to the United States in custody. (Moore on Extradition, I. 713–718; For. Rel. 1878, 151–155; For. Rel. 1879, 251–254, 271, 273–277, 284; For. Rel. 1880, 319.)
>
> See infra, § 344.

" Your excellency's letter of the 13th instant has been received. It submits to me an order of the senate of the State of Maine. This order recites a statement that a dispatch has been received from the Secretary of State of the United States addressed to the marshal of the United States, and all Federal officers in Portland, directing that the agents of the British Government shall have all proper facilities for landing and carrying to Canada or elsewhere troops and munitions of war of every kind, without exception. The order then requests you to communicate to the senate of Maine, if compatible with the public interest, all information you may have, if any, in relation to the passage of British troops as so recited, and whether any steps have been taken to prevent such use of American soil within the limits of the State of Maine. After referring me to the senate's order, your excellency asks me to advise you whether such permission has been given, and if such is the fact, then for any information concerning it which I may think proper to communicate. I cheerfully answer these inquiries.

" On the 4th of January instant, this Department was advised by a telegraphic dispatch from Portland, in the State of Maine, that the steamship *Bohemian*, due there on the 7th instant, was telegraphed off Cape Race with troops for Canada, and inquiring whether, in case they came to Portland, any different course was to be taken than what has been heretofore pursued, and asking instructions in that contingency by telegraph. Upon this information, I replied by the telegraph, giving such direction as the order of the senate of Maine recites. The immediate grounds for this proceeding were, that it was supposed that a passage of the troops and munitions named, across the territory of the United States, by the Grand Trunk Railroad would save the persons concerned from risks and sufferings which might be feared if they were left to make their way in an inclement season, through the ice and snow of a northerly Canadian passage. The principle upon which this concession was made to Great Britain is, that, when humanity or even convenience renders it desirable for one nation to have a passage for its troops and munitions through the territory of another, it is a customary act of comity to grant it, if it can be done consistently with its own safety and welfare. It is on this principle that the United States continually enjoy the right of the passage of troops upon the Panama Railroad, across the territories of the Republic of New Granada. The United States claim and enjoy, by the concession of all friendly nations, the kindly comity of entering their ports with ships and munitions of war, and they have conceded a reciprocal comity to the naval marine of Great Britain, France and indeed all other friendly nations. In withholding this customary comity from Great Britain in the present case, this Government must necessarily act upon either a conviction that the passage of the troops and munitions through our territory would be injurious or prejudicial to the public safety or welfare, or else it must capriciously refuse to that power what would be granted cheerfully to any other, or refuse to grant to Great Britain now what would have been cheerfully accorded at any other time and under some different circumstances. No foreign nation, inimical to Great Britain, is likely to complain of the United States for extending such courtesy to that power. If therefore there be any danger to be apprehended from it, it must come in the form of direct hostility on the part of the British Government against the United States. The United States have not only practised the most perfect justice in their intercourse with Great Britain, but they have also cultivated on their part a spirit of friendship towards her, as a kindred nation, bound by peculiar ties of commerce. The Grand Trunk Railroad, a British highway, extending through the territories of the United States to perhaps the finest seaport of our country, is a monument of this friendly disposition. The reciprocity treaty, favoring the productions of British North America in the markets of the United States, is a similar monument of the same wise and benevolent policy. I shall not affect ignorance of the fact that popular asperities have recently appeared in that portion of the British Empire, as well as in the British Islands, which have seemed to indicate a growing alienation of sentiment among portions of the British people. But the Government of Great Britain has nevertheless during all this time held towards us its customary language of respect. This Government practicing entire frankness yields its full faith to these assurances of Great Britain. The public asperities to which I have alluded are believed to have had their origin in accidental misapprehensions of a temporary character. While the policy of this Government has been to fortify its territories, so as to be able to resist all foreign as well as domestic enemies if such enemies must come, it has been equally careful at the same time to secure even greater strength by showing itself courteous in all things, scrupulously just, and if possible magnanimous towards all other nations. It was not supposed, when the directions in question were given, that the State of Maine would feel herself aggrieved by them. At the same time the Federal Government is fully sensible that in all its proceedings it owes to each of the States the most exact respect of her rights and interests. The State of Maine has been so eminently loyal and patriotic in the present emergency that the President would not feel himself at liberty to wound any sensibility that she might feel upon the subject. If therefore you shall advise me that the directions in questions are likely to have that effect, they will be cheerfully modified."

> Mr. Seward, Sec. of State, to Governor Washburne, of Maine, Jan. 17, 1862, 56 Dom. Let. 211.
>
> See Lawrence's Wheaton (1863), 195; Lawrence, Com. sur Droit Int. III. 434.

In 1875 permission was granted to the government of Canada by the Government of the United States to transport " through its territory certain supplies, designed for the use of three divisions of Canadian mounted police force."

> Mr. Fish, Sec. of State, to Sir E. Thornton, Brit. min., May 5, 1875, MS. Notes to Great Brit. XVI. 553.

" I have the honor to enclose the copy of a translation of a note of yesterday, addressed to this Department from Philadelphia, by Don Eleuterio Avila, the acting chargé d'affaires of Mexico, asking permission for the landing at Brazos Santiago, in Texas, of a small body of the troops of that Republic, supposed to be intended to aid in the defence of Matamoras. Having made known to the President the request adverted to, I have been authorized by him to inform Mr. Avila that no objection is entertained to a compliance therewith. This Department has consequently advised Mr. Avila to that effect, but has also told him that it is expected the force will not stay unnecessarily long within United States jurisdiction; and that his Government will be held accountable for any injuries which they may commit upon persons and property during their stay, and on their way to Mexico. I will consequently thank you to cause the proper military commander in that quarter to be informed accordingly, both by wire and by letter."

> Mr. Cadwalader, Acting Sec. of State, to Mr. Cameron, Sec. of War, Oct. 20, 1876, 115 MS. Dom. Let. 502, enclosing copy of a note from Mr. Avila of Oct. 19, 1876.
>
> As to the permission granted by the Mexican Congress, in August, 1861, for the transit of troops across Mexican territory, see Dip. Cor. 1865, III. 538–541.
>
> As to conditional permission for the transit of military supplies, see Dip. Cor. 1867, II. 453, 480.

In April, 1885, the Government of the United States, at the request of the commanding general of the Department of Texas sought permission from the Mexican Government for the passage of his troops across Mexican territory, in consequence of an overflow of the Rio Grande having obstructed their conveyance in the United States. The permission was asked for " with the express condition that none but an absolutely peaceful transfer devoid of any military object affecting the peace of any State was intended by the movement." It was granted as desired.

> Mr. Bayard, Sec. of State, to Sec. of War, April 16, 1885, 155 MS. Dom. Let.
> 120; same to same, April 18, 1885, id. 145, enclosing copy of a note
> from Mr. Romero, Mexican minister at Washington, of April 17, 1885.
> A permission to a foreign government to transport its troops over the ter-
> ritory of the United States will be granted only in case of peaceful
> transfer devoid of any military object affecting the peace of any third
> state. (Mr. Bayard, Sec. of State, to Mr. Morgan, min. to Mex., April
> 25, 1885, MS. Inst. Mex. XXI. 280.)

" I have the honor to acknowledge your letter of the 17th instant, and to apprise you of the receipt of a note from the minister of Mexico here, of the 21st ultimo, asking by direction of his Government that permission be accorded one hundred Mexican infantry, in charge of a captain, to pass through United States territory on their way to Ensenada, Lower California. These troops will enter the United States at El Paso Texas, and will travel by the Southern Pacific Railroad to San Diego, California from which point they will embark for Ensenada.

" The necessary permission for these troops to cross the confines of the States of California and Texas, and of the Territories of Arizona and New Mexico, has been granted by the executive of each.

" The Secretary of the Treasury has also instructed the collectors of customs at El Paso and San Diego to afford the troops in question every proper courtesy and assistance."

> Mr. Blaine, Sec. of State, to Sec. of War, April 18, 1889, 172 MS. Dom. Let.
> 529.

By an act of December 18, 1897, Congress appropriated $200,000 for the purchase of subsistence stores to relieve people who were in the Yukon River country or other mining regions of Alaska and for the transportation and distribution of such stores; and it was provided that with the consent of the Canadian government the relief might be extended into Canadian territory. As it was necessary to cross Canadian territory in order to reach the Yukon River country with the stores in question, permission was sought for that purpose, as well as for the extension of the relief into Canadian territory, with the necessary military escort in both cases.

The Canadian government granted permission for "the entry to the Yukon district, free of duty, of convoys of provisions for gratuitous distribution to distressed persons," as well as for the convoys to be accompanied " by such reasonable escort " as the United States might desire to provide for them, each convoy to be " likewise accompanied by a Canadian officer, the expenses of such Canadian officers being borne by the Dominion government."

> Mr. Sherman, Sec. of State, to Sir J. Pauncefote, Brit. amb., Dec. 20, 1897, For. Rel. 1897, 325; For. Rel. 1898, 358; Sir J. Pauncefote, Brit. amb., to Mr. Sherman, Sec. of State, Dec. 27, 1897, For. Rel. 1897, 326; For. Rel. 1898, 360.

Subsequently, an inquiry was made as to the grounds of the United States request, which was, it was affirmed, contrary to the " unofficial understanding " then recently arrived at between the United States Secretary of War and the Canadian minister of the interior to the effect that " the Dominion Government should furnish escort for the expedition after reaching the summit of the pass, beyond which point no United States armed force should proceed." This inquiry was made by direction of Lord Salisbury.[a]

The United States replied that an armed force to accompany the expedition was necessary for its protection against disorderly persons in Alaska after it had passed through Canadian territory into the territory of the United States, and for this reason permission was desired for a detachment of 55 soldiers and the necessary officers to pass through the Canadian territory. Without this armed escort it would be hazardous for the expedition to start by the proposed route, and it might become necessary to select a route entirely within the United States territory, which would in part defeat the object of the expedition.[b]

The British Government answered that the Dominion government was willing that the United States troops necessary for the protection of the relief expedition should pass through Canadian territory under the same regulations which governed the passage of Canadian mounted police through United States territory, namely, that the men should not be under arms, and that arms and munitions of war should go through Canadian territory as baggage, but that an escort of Dominion police would be furnished for the expedition during its passage through Canadian territory.[c]

---

[a] Sir Julian Pauncefote, British ambassador, to Mr. Sherman, Sec. of State, Feb. 4, 1898, For. Rel. 1898, 360.

[b] Mr. Day, Acting Sec. of State, to Sir Julian Pauncefote, British ambassador, February 16, 1898, For. Rel. 1898, 361.

[c] Sir Julian Pauncefote, British ambassador, to Mr. Sherman, Sec. of State, February 17, 1898, For. Rel. 1898, 361.

This arrangement was declared to be " entirely satisfactory to the War Department," and it was added that " the courtesies so kindly extended to facilitate the expedition " were fully appreciated by the United States.[a]

On the request of the United States, the Japanese Government granted permission for the landing of United States army horses bound for the Philippines at Nagasaki or Yokohama or Kobe for pasture and rest.

> For. Rel. 1899, 478–481.

January 13, 1900, the Japanese Government by courtesy permitted a United States regiment on its way to Manila to hold a parade and drill in one of the public squares of Yokohama.

> For. Rel. 1900, 757.

" The Department is in receipt of a request from the minister of France that permission be granted his Government to send a certain number of French seamen to guard the exhibition which the citizens of France propose making at the World's Fair.　It is proposed to convey these seamen to Chicago in a small national vessel.

International exhibitions.

" The minister has been informed that the request would be referred to the executive of Illinois, which in such matters has primary jurisdiction.

" Should it appear to your excellency advisable to accede to this request, the Department would suggest that, in view of the probability of similar requests being preferred by other governments represented in the exhibition, it should be generally empowered to reply, in the name of the State of Illinois, granting such permission, thereby avoiding special correspondence in each instance.

" I may add that the request is a usual one in the case of international exhibitions and in the present instance finds an exact precedent in the request made by this Government and cordially granted by the Government of the French Republic to permit the exhibits of the United States at the Paris Exhibition of 1889 to be guarded by a detachment of United States marines."

> Mr. Foster, Sec. of State, to the gov. of Illinois July 5, 1892, 187 MS. Dom. Let. 142.

" I have the honor to acknowledge the receipt of your note of the 13th instant, in which you ask that the authorization of the Federal Government be given for the presence of a detachment of thirty

---

[a] Mr. Day, Acting Sec. of State, to Sir Julian Pauncefote, British ambassador, Feb. 21, 1898, For. Rel. 1898, 362.

French sailors at the World's Columbian Exposition as a guard for the protection of the French section.

" In reply I beg to state that under date of June 27 last, you addressed a note to this Department asking that permission be granted for a national vessel of small tonnage, containing a guard of 30 sailors for the French exhibit, to enter and sojourn in the waters of Lake Michigan during the World's Fair.

" This Department replied on the 5th of the following month that such permission as it was in the power of the Federal Government to grant would be most cordially extended, but that it would be necessary to obtain the consent of the executives of the various States through which the detachment was to pass. The governor of Illinois was at once communicated with upon the subject, and on July 15 last you were informed that permission had been granted for the entry and sojourn in that State of the sailors in question.

"As these sailors must necessarily pass within the jurisdiction of other States on their way to Chicago, I shall take pleasure in making request to the respective governors for the required permission upon being apprised of the route which they are to follow. The port of their entry into the United States should be stated in order that the necessary instructions may be given for their admission.

" I take this occasion to again express to you a sense of the willingness with which the Government of the United States, under whose jurisdiction the waters of Lake Michigan rest, accords permission for the sojourn of a French vessel in those waters during the exposition."

Mr. Foster, Sec. of State, to Mr. Patenotre, French min., Dec. 17. 1892, MS. notes to France, X. 263.

" I have to acknowledge the receipt of your letter of the 8th instant, stating that the Mexican Government intends to send to the Pan-American Exposition, 1901, one hundred men from different grades of its army, including sixty-two members of a mounted band.

" You request that permission be granted by the Federal Government for the entry of these troops into the United States, and that permission be obtained from the authorities of the States through which they may pass on their way to Buffalo, authorizing them to make the transit.

" In reply I have to inform you that the proper procedure would be for the Mexican Government to apply through the Mexican ambassador at Washington for permission for the troops to enter the United States with their arms, horses and accoutrements, stating at the same time the point where they will enter and the States through which they will pass.

" The Department will then have the proper customs officials suitably instructed and will obtain the consent of the governors for the [passage of the] detachment through their respective States.

" It is thought probable that this detachment is the same as that for which the Mexican ambassador, on October 25 last, requested permission to enter the United States. In that case he was informed, October 30, that this Government would have no objection to the entry of the band and the detachment, but that it should be informed of the different States through which they would pass.

" This information has not yet been furnished by the ambassador.'

> Mr. Hill, Assist. Sec. of State, to Mr. Buchanan, president of the Pan-American Exposition, Jan. 14, 1901, 250 MS. Dom. Let. 217.

Permission was given in February, 1881, by the Government of Canada for the passage of the " Spaulding Guards," **Social occasions.** of Buffalo, armed and equipped, over the Canada Southern Railway from Buffalo to Detroit.

> Mr. Hay, Asst. Sec. of State, to Mr. Sherman, February 24, 1881, 136 MS. Dom. Let. 360.

" By a note of the 13th of December last, you were pleased to express the desire of obtaining for the volunteer ' Gate City Guards ' of Atlanta, the authorization to wear their uniforms, and to carry their arms during their stay in France, which they propose to visit in the summer of 1887.

"After having taken the advice of the ministers of the interior and of war, I am happy to advise you that the application of this organization meets with no objection on the part of the Government of the Republic. I shall be obliged to you to kindly inform me, when the time comes, of the exact date of the arrival of the ' Gate City Guards ' of Atlanta."

> Mr. Flourens, French min. of for. aff., to Mr. McLane, U. S. min., Jan. 6. 1887, For. Rel. 1887, 283.
> A similar permission was accorded to the Gate City Guards in Belgium, by the Government of that country, on the request of the Government of the United States, preferred through its minister at Brussels. (For. Rel. 1887, 25, 29.)

" Referring to your note of the 18th ultimo, asking permission for the Honorable Artillery Company of London to enter the United States in uniform with arms, and to the subsequent correspondence, I now have the honor to inform you that the necessary orders in the premises have been issued by the respective governors of the States of New York, Connecticut, Rhode Island and Massachusetts.

" Enclosing copies of special orders issued by the respective adjutants-general of Connecticut and Rhode Island relative to the matter, addressed to yourself and the commanding officer of the Honorable Artillery Company of London, I have, &c."

> Mr. Bayard, Sec. of State, to Sir L. West, Brit. min., May 4, 1888, U. S. Notes to Great Britain, XX. 640.

> The course of the correspondence to which the foregoing note relates was as follows:

> April 9, 1888, Mr. Henry Walker, of the Honorable and Ancient Artillery Company of Massachusetts, addressed to the Secretary of State a letter requesting permission for a delegation of 25 members of the Honorable Artillery Company of London, the parent of the Massachusetts organization, to enter the United States in uniform and bearing arms, in order to participate in the 250th anniversary of the Massachusetts company. Mr. Rives, Assistant Secretary, April 14, 1888, replied: "Applications for the admission into the United States of an armed body of men, part of the military organization of a foreign power, must necessarily be made by the foreign government to whom they owe allegiance, through its representative at this capital." (168 MS. Dom. Let. 81.)

> April 21, 1888, Mr. Bayard, Secretary of State, informed the Secretary of the Treasury that he had received from the British minister in Washington a request of the Ancient and Honorable Artillery Company of Massachusetts, on behalf of the Honorable Artillery Company of London, and asked that orders be "issued to the collector of customs at New York for the free entry of the delegation in question, with their arms and equipments." (168 MS. Dom. Let. 168.)

> At the same time Mr. Bayard addressed to the British minister the following note:

> "I have the honor to acknowledge the receipt of your note dated the 18th inst. transmitting the request of the Ancient and Honorable Artillery Company of Massachusetts, on behalf of the Honorable Artillery Company of London, that a delegation of the latter company may receive permission to enter the United States in uniform and with arms, and this you submit for such action as I may see fit to take.

> "By your becoming the avenue of communication for a request of an armed and uniformed body of British artillery to enter the United States, I assume that the permission so to enter is desired by your Government and have the pleasure to announce that orders will be issued by the Secretary of the Treasury for the free entry of the delegation with their arms and equipments.

> "If you could indicate the vessel by which the delegation is expected to arrive in New York, it would assist in giving definiteness to the orders.

> "Moreover, application should be made to the respective governors of the States of New York, Connecticut, and Massachusetts for permission to pass through their several jurisdictions. As the delegation is intended to visit Boston, the transit from New York is made necessary, and I shall have pleasure in applying for such permission." (Mr. Bayard, Sec. of State, to the Hon. Sir L. S. S. West, Brit. min., April 21, 1888, MS. Notes to Gr. Brit. XX. 632.)

In June, 1889, the British Government granted permission for the Massachusetts Volunteer Militia Rifle Team to enter England bearing arms.

> Mr. Blaine, Sec. of State, to Gov. Ames, June 13, 1889, 173 MS. Dom. Let. 372.

" Canadian Government has granted permission to the Thirteenth Regiment of National Guard of the State of New York to visit Hamilton, Canada, uniformed and armed."

> Mr. Wharton, Acting Sec. of State, to Mr. Hill, tel., Aug. 19, 1889, 174 MS. Dom. Let. 181.

The sovereign who, although he had not expressly waived his jurisdiction, should attempt to exercise it over a foreign military force to which he had granted a right of passage through his dominions, " would certainly be considered as violating his faith. By exercising it, the purpose for which the free passage was granted would be defeated, and a portion of the military force of a foreign independent nation would be diverted from those national objects and duties to which it was applicable, and would be withdrawn from the control of the sovereign whose power and whose safety might greatly depend on retaining the exclusive command and disposition of this force. The grant of a free passage, therefore, implies a waiver of all jurisdiction over the troops during their passage, and permits the foreign general to use that discipline, and to inflict those punishments which the government of his army may require."

Questions of control.

> Marshall, C. J., schooner Exchange v. McFaddon, 7 Cranch, 116, 139, cited in Tucker v. Alexandroff, 183 U. S. 424, 432.

The court, after citing the cases given in Wharton's Int. Law Digest, sec. 13, of the entrance of foreign troops into the United States by permission, referred to the parading of the forces of foreign men-or-war, under their various commanders, at the Columbian celebration in New York in 1893; to the permission granted by the Secretary of the Treasury for the admission of Canadian troops to join in the Dewey parade, and to the presence of Mexican troops at the Buffalo Exposition, and said: " In none of these cases, however, did a question arise with respect to the immunity of foreign troops from the territorial jurisdiction, or the power of their officers over them, or the right of the latter to call upon the local officers for the arrest of deserters. While no act of Congress authorizes the executive department to permit the introduction of foreign troops, the power to give such permission without legislative assent was probably assumed to exist from the authority of the President as commander-in-chief of the military and naval forces of the United States. It may be doubted, however, whether such power could be extended to the apprehension of deserters in the absence of positive legislation to that effect."

> Tucker *v.* Alexandroff (1902), 183 U. S. 424, 435. This case related to a detail of Russian marines who had, with the concurrence of the Government of the United States, been admitted into the country to man a Russian cruiser building at the Cramp shipyard in Philadelphia.

" On rare occasions the consent of a foreign government is asked, through diplomatic channels, for the passage of small bodies of troops, or for permission to do other acts which might otherwise be a violation of territory; but in such cases, as the offense would be against the sovereignty of the Government only, permission at times is accorded. It is seriously doubted, however, whether it is in the province of an officer of the Army, in command on a distant station, to permit or sanction such violation. It is also extremely doubtful whether it is in any aspect competent to assume to permit a foreign power to transport persons in custody through the territory of the United States, maintaining over them while *in transitu* any authority or power. In such a case the rights of the individual are also involved."

> Mr. Fish, Sec. of State, to Mr. Cameron, Sec. of War, December 7, 1876, 116 MS. Dom. Let. 166. For the case of Peter Martin, who in 1876 was transported across Alaskan territory in custody of Canadian officials on a charge of crime, without the permission of the United States, and who was afterwards set at liberty on the representations of the United States, see For. Rel. 1887, 837–839.
>
> See, generally, as to the transit of fugitive criminals in custody across the territory of third states, Moore on Extradition, I., §§ 381, 382, 452, 460, 461, 466, 467, 468, 469, 484, 485, 488, 497, 503, 504, 507, 508, 509, 510, 512, 515.

6. LANDING OF FORCES FOR PROTECTION AGAINST VIOLENCE.

§ 214.

In the unsettled state of affairs in Mexico, when the government of Juarez was established at Vera Cruz and the Miramon government occupied the capital, Mr. McLane, who was accredited as minister of the United States to the Juarez government, was directed, in case a hostile force should approach Vera Cruz and he should consider the American citizens there to be in danger from its operations, to request the commanding officer of the United States vessel of war upon the coast to land such forces as might be needed and as could be spared from indispensable duties, and to employ them for the protection of American citizens whose persons or property he might believe to be in danger.

> Mr. Toucey, Sec. of Navy, to Capt. Jarvis, U. S. S. *Savannah*, March 13, 1860, S. Ex. Doc. 29, 36 Cong. 1 sess.

" On several occasions since the establishment of our legation in Korea the presence at Seoul of an armed United States force to protect our legation and the American citizens at that place has been considered necessary, and while the Department does not wish to in any way forbid you calling on the commander of the United States naval force on the Asiatic station for protection when in your judgment such is imperatively demanded, it does wish to discourage, so far as possible, such practice, and you should insist on the Korean Government affording at all times that full protection from all insult and injury of any sort, not only to our diplomatic and consular representatives in the Kingdom, but to all our citizens, which it has promised to extend to them in Article IV. of our treaty of 1882. You are directed before the departure of the guard now on duty at the legation to inform the Korean foreign office of the purpose of the present instruction."

> Mr. Adee, Act. Sec. of State, to Mr. Sill, min. to Corea, July 8, 1895, MS. Inst. Korea, I. 537.

February 27, 1899, Mr. Merry, United States minister to Nicaragua, telegraphed to his Government that Bluefields, which had been in the hands of insurgents, had been captured by the Government of Nicaragua, and that United States and English forces had been landed temporarily.

> For. Rel. 1899, 554.

" In view of disturbances in the populous provinces of northern China, where are many of our citizens, and of the imminence of disorder near the capital and toward the seaboard, a guard of marines was landed from the *Boston* and stationed during last winter in the legation compound at Peking. With the restoration of order this protection was withdrawn."

> President McKinley, annual message, Dec. 5, 1899, For. Rel. 1899, XVIII.

" As for the question of military or naval landing at any point in China, (whether a treaty port or not, or whether there is an American ' concession ' there or not,) such action, while it may be one of actual necessity, is not therefore necessarily a hostile act.

" In our reply of August 11 to Mr. Wu's communication *re* British landing at Shanghai, we said :

" ' The question whether any power should land troops at Shanghai for the protection of its citizens and interests in that part of China is one which each power must determine for itself. If we considered it necessary for the protection of our citizens at Shanghai to land troops there, we should do so, as we have done at Taku; and we can not question the right of any other power having treaty rights at that port to do the same.'

"Although in this reply it was convenient to limit the memorandum to the occasion of landing at a treaty port, it was not designed to forego the right which this Government has always held, and which on occasion it has exercised, in China and in other countries, to land forces and adopt all necessary measures to protect the life and property of our citizens, whenever menaced by lawless acts which the general or local authority is unwilling or impotent to prevent."

> Mr. Hill, Act. Sec. of State, to Sec. of Navy, Sept. 11, 1900, 247 MS. Dom. Let. 597.
>
> For the reply of Mr. Wu of August 11, see memorandum of Mr. Adee, Act. Sec. of State, of Aug. 12, 1900, MS. Notes to Chinese Leg. II. 80.

7. PLEA OF NECESSARY SELF-DEFENSE.

(1) INVASIONS OF WEST FLORIDA.

§ 215.

In 1814, during the war between the United States and Great Britain, General Jackson, having destroyed the power of the Creek Indians, determined to reoccupy Mobile, which had been occupied by the United States during the war and then abandoned, and to seize Pensacola, which had been the principal source of supplies of the Creeks in their hostilities with the United States. In this design he was confirmed by the fact that the waters of the Gulf of Mexico were becoming the theater of active military demonstrations on the part of the British. Early in July, 1814, he gave orders for the reoccupation of Mobile Point. In the following month Major Nicholls, an Irish officer, with a force of marines seized Fort Barrancas, six miles below Pensacola, and began to collect a force of Creeks, at the same time proclaiming his intention to invade Louisiana; and in September a British force attempted to reduce Fort Bowyer, which had been established by the United States at the entrance of Pensacola Bay in 1813. The attempt failed, and early in November, 1814, Jackson marched to Pensacola and took possession of the place—a step which led to the imediate evacuation of Fort Barrancas by the British.

Invasion of west Florida in 1814.

> Am. State Pap., Mil. Aff. I. 698-708; H. Report 99, 20 Cong. 2 sess.; Adams, Hist. of the United States, VIII. 317-330.
>
> In his dispatches General Jackson praised the correct conduct of his troops, but the march of a considerable military force, only a part of which was composed of regulars, and of which a portion was made up of friendly Indians, was naturally attended with some depredations on private property. Claims for indemnity for the losses thus occasioned were ultimately disallowed. (Moore, Int. Arbitrations, V. 4528.)

December 26, 1817, Mr. Calhoun, who was then Secretary of War,
West Florida and the Seminole war. ordered General Jackson to Fort Scott, Georgia, to take command of the forces of the United States against the hostile Seminole Indians. General Jackson reached Fort Scott on the 9th of March, and on the following day assumed command. On the 25th of March, writing to Mr. Calhoun, he reported that "the Indians had demanded arms, ammunition, and provisions, or the possession of the garrison of St. Marks of the commandant," and that the governor of Pensacola had said he "presumed possession would be given from inability to defend it." "The Spanish Government is bound by treaty," said General Jackson, commenting on this situation, "to keep her Indians at peace with us. They have acknowledged their incompetency to do this, and are consequently bound, by the law of nations, to yield us all facilities to reduce them. Under this consideration, should I be able, I shall take possession of the garrison as a depot for my supplies, should it be found in the hands of the Spaniards, they having supplied the Indians; but if in the hands of the enemy I will possess it, for the benefit of the United States, as a necessary position for me to hold, to give peace and security to this frontier, and put a final end to Indian warfare in the South." General Jackson also stated that he had ordered supplies for Fort Crawford by water, and had written to the governor of Pensacola that if he interrupted their passage he should "view it as aiding our enemy, and treat it as an act of hostility." Immediately after writing this letter, General Jackson began an active movement against the Indians, whom he attacked and drove before him; and, believing that some of the hostiles had fled to St. Marks, he directed his march to that fortress. "As advised," he said, "I found that the Indians and negroes combined had demanded a surrender of that work; the Spanish garrison was too weak to defend it, and there were circumstances reported producing a strong conviction in my mind, that, if not instigated by the Spanish authorities, the Indians had received the means of carrying on the war from that quarter; foreign agents, who have been long practicing their intrigues and villanies in this country, had free access into the fort; St. Marks was necessary, as a depot, to insure success to my operations. These considerations determined me to occupy it with an American force." The fortress was accordingly occupied; and General Jackson, having heard that the Indians at war with the United States had free access to Pensacola, determined to make a movement west of the Appalachicola and, if the report proved to be correct, occupy Pensacola. On the 21st of May he entered and occupied the fort of St. Michael commanding the town; but the fort made only a show of resistance. The governor of Pensacola had pre-

viously retired to Fort Carlos de Baranças; and General Jackson now demanded of him the surrender both of this fortress and of the town. The demand was refused, and on the 25th of May the fortress was besieged. It surrendered on the evening of the 27th after having made a spirited resistance. In August, 1818, the United States ordered St. Marks and Pensacola, with the Baranças, to be restored to Spanish authority. During these operations of the United States forces against the Seminoles much property of Spanish subjects was plundered and destroyed. Spain protested against General Jackson's course, and demanded indemnity. The United States, while ordering the captured places to be evacuated, assumed responsibility for his acts.

> Am. State Papers, Mil. Aff. I. 690, 698, 700; Am. State Papers, For. Rel. IV. 496, 776–808.
>
> Among the persons found in the fortress of St. Marks was an Englishman namer Arbuthnot, who, with another Englishman named Ambrister, captured near "Bowlegs town," was, by order of General Jackson, tried by a court-martial and executed for exciting "savage and negro war." (Parton's Life of Andrew Jackson, ch. 36; Am. State Papers, Mil. Aff. I. 681, et seq.)
>
> By Art. IX. of the treaty with Spain of Feb. 22, 1819, the United States agreed to "cause satisfaction to be made for the injuries, if any, which, by process of law, shall be established to have been suffered by the Spanish officers, and individual Spanish inhabitants, by the late operations of the American Army in Florida."
>
> For the execution of this article, see Moore, Int. Arbitrations, V. chap. D. 4519, 4524 et seq.
>
> See Memoirs of J. Q. Adams, IV. 113.

" In authorizing Major-General Jackson to enter Florida, in pursuit of the Seminoles, care was taken not to encroach on the rights of Spain. I regret to have to add, that, in executing this order, facts were disclosed, respecting the conduct of the officers of Spain in authority there, in encouraging the war, furnishing munitions of war and other supplies to carry it on, and in other acts not less marked, which evinced their participation in the hostile purposes of that combination, and justified the confidence with which it inspired the savages, that by those officers they would be protected. A conduct so incompatible with the friendly relations existing between the two countries, particularly with the positive obligation of the fifth article of the treaty of 1795, by which Spain was bound to restrain, even by force, those savages from acts of hostility against the United States, could not fail to excite surprise. The commanding general was convinced that he should fail in his object, that he should in effect accomplish nothing, if he did not deprive those savages of the resource on which they had calculated, and of the protection on which they had relied in making the war. As all the documents relating

to this occurrence will be laid before Congress, it is not necessary to
enter into further detail respecting it.

"Although the reasons which induced Major-General Jackson to
take these posts were duly appreciated, there was, nevertheless, no hesitation in deciding on the course which it became the Government to
pursue. As there was reason to believe that the commanders of these
posts had violated their instructions, there was no disposition to
impute to their Government a conduct so unprovoked and hostile.
An order was, in consequence, issued to the general in command there
to deliver the posts—Pensacola, unconditionally, to any person duly
authorized to receive it; and Saint Mark's, which is in the heart of
the Indian country, on the arrival of a competent force to defend it
against those savages and their associates."

> President Monroe's Second Annual Message, Nov. 16, 1818, Am. State
> Papers, For. Rel. IV. 215.
>
> See President Monroe to Mr. Madison, July 20, 1818, Madison MSS.,
> Library of Congress.
>
> " I could adopt no other way to ' *put an end to the war* ' but by possess-
> ing myself of the stronghold that was a refuge to the enemy, and
> afforded them the means of offense." (Letter of General Jackson to
> the Sec. of War, quoted in Parton's Jackson, II. 500. See also id.
> 451.)
>
> " When they (European powers) know the whole of the affair of Pensa-
> cola, I have no doubt they will withdraw all idea of intermeddling
> between Spain and us. I trust we shall be able to avoid entangle-
> ments with the European alliance. We may let them alone, for they
> can not conquer the South Americans." (Mr. Jefferson to Mr. Mon-
> roe, President, Sept. 17, 1818; MS. Monroe Papers, Library of Con-
> gress.)
>
> See Schouler's Hist. of the United States, III. 74; Mr. Gallatin, min. to
> France, to Mr. Adams, Sec. of State, Gallatin's Writings, II. 69;
> Benton's Thirty Years' View, I. 167.

" After a full and deliberate examination of these proofs, the President deems them irresistibly conclusive that the horrible combination
of robbery, murder, and war, with which the frontier of the United
States bordering upon Florida has for several years past been visited,
is ascribable altogether to the total and lamentable failure of Spain
to fulfill the fifth article of the treaty of 1795, by which she stipulated to restrain, by force, her Indians from hostilities against the citizens of the United States. . . . It is therefore to the conduct of her
own commanding officers that Spain must impute the necessity under
which General Jackson found himself of occupying the places of their
command."

> Mr. Adams, Sec. of State, to Don Luis de Onis, Span. min., Nov. 30, 1818,
> Am. State Papers, For. Rel. IV. 545, 546.)
>
> See a still more extended discussion of the subject in the instruction of
> Mr. Adams, Sec. of State, to Mr. Erving, min. to Spain, Nov. 28,
> 1818, in which Mr. Adams says: " He [General Jackson] took pos-

session, therefore, of Pensacola and of the fort of Barrancas, as he had done of St. Mark, not in a spirit of hostility to Spain, but as a necessary measure of self-defense; giving notice that they should be restored whenever Spain should place commanders and a force there able and willing to fulfill the engagements of Spain towards the United States, or of restraining by force the Florida Indians from hostilities against their citizens." (Am. State Papers, For. Rel. IV. 539, 541.)

(2) AMELIA ISLAND.

§ 216.

" You will have been informed through the channel of the public prints of the manner in which Amelia Island has in the course of the last summer been occupied by an assemblage of adventurers under various commanders, and with commissioners, real or pretended, from several of the South American insurgent governments. You must have heard also of the feeble and ineffectual attempt made by the Spanish commanding authorities in East Florida to recover possession of the island. A similar band of desperate characters from various nations, and presumably impelled by motives of plunder alone, have formed a lodgment at Galveston, which we consider within the limits of the United States. These places have not only been consequently made receptacles for privateers illegally fitted out from our ports, but the means of every species of illicit traffic, and especially of introducing slaves illegally into the United States. The President has therefore determined to break up those settlements, which are presumed to have been made without proper authority from any government; and which if authorized by any government, have assumed an attitude too pernicious to the peace and prosperity of this Union and of its citizens to be tolerated. The orders for breaking them up have been given, and are in a train of execution. Possession will be taken of Galveston as within the limits of the United States, and perhaps of Amelia Island, to prevent its being taken again by similar adventurers for the same purposes, Spain being notoriously unable either to retain possession of it against them or to recover it from them."

> Mr. Adams, Sec. of State, to Mr. Erving, min. to Spain, Nov. 11, 1817, MS. Inst. United States ministers, VIII. 169.
> The occupation subsequently taken of Amelia Island under these orders should not be confused with the occupation of the island and of other parts of East Florida in 1812 by troops and other persons acting under the command of or in concert with Governor Matthews, as special commissioner of the United States. Governor Matthews's measures were disavowed and his commission revoked, and claims growing out of his proceedings were afterwards paid. (Moore, Int. Arbitrations, V. 4519–4522, 4528.)
> "The executive government have ordered, and, as I conceive, very properly, Amelia Island to be taken possession of. This order ought to be carried into execution at all hazards, and simultaneously the

whole of East Florida seized and held as indemnity for the outrages
of Spain upon the property of our citizens. . . . The order being
given for the possession of Amelia Island, it ought to be executed,
or our enemies, internal and external, will use it to the disadvantage
of the Government. If our troops enter the territory of Spain in
pursuit of our Indian enemy, all opposition that they meet with must
be put down, or we will be involved in danger and disgrace." (General Jackson to Mr. Monroe, Jan. 6, 1818, Parton's Jackson, II. 434.)

"In the summer of the present year, an expedition was set on foot
against East Florida by persons claiming to act under the authority of
some of the colonies, who took possession of Amelia Island, at the mouth
of St. Mary's river, near the boundary of the State of Georgia. As the
province lies eastward of the Mississippi, and is bounded by the United
States and the ocean on every side, and has been a subject of negotia-
ation with the Government of Spain as an indemnity for losses by
spoliation, or in exchange for territory of equal value westward of the
Mississippi, (a fact well known to the world,) it excited surprise that
any countenance should be given to this measure by any of the colonies.
As it would be difficult to reconcile it with the friendly relations existing between the United States and the colonies, a doubt was entertained whether it had been authorized by them, or any of them. This
doubt has gained strength, by the circumstances which have unfolded
themselves in the prosecution of the enterprise, which have marked it
as a mere private, unauthorized adventure. Projected and commenced
with an incompetent force, reliance seems to have been placed on what
might be drawn, in defiance of our laws, from within our limits; and
of late, as their resources have failed, it has assumed a more marked
character of unfriendliness to us; the island being made a channel for
the illicit introduction of slaves from Africa into the United States,
an asylum for fugitive slaves from the neighboring States, and a port
for smuggling of every kind.

"A similar establishment was made, at an earlier period, by persons
of the same description in the Gulf of Mexico, at a place called Gal-
vezton, within the limits of the United States, as we contend, under the
cession of Louisiana. This enterprise has been marked, in a more signal manner, by all the objectionable circumstances which characterized
the other, and more particularly by the equipment of privateers
which have annoyed our commerce, and by smuggling. These establishments, if ever sanctioned by any authority whatever, which is not
believed, have abused their trust, and forfeited all claim to consideration. A just regard for the rights and interests of the United States
required that they should be suppressed, and orders have been accordingly issued to that effect. The imperious considerations which produced this measure will be explained to the parties whom it may in
any degree concern."

President Monroe's First Annual Message, Dec. 2, 1817, Am. State Papers, For. Rel. IV. 130.

On the same topic, see report of House Com. on For. Rel. Jan. 10, 1818, Am. State Pap. For. Rel. IV. 132.

As to the occupation of the island by McGregor, professedly in the name of Buenos Ayres and Venezuela, and his expeditions which the United States took steps to suppress, see Parton's Life of Jackson, II. 421 et seq.

See, particularly, President Monroe's special message of Jan. 13, 1818, announcing that "the establishment at Amelia Island has been suppressed, and without effusion of blood," and further explaining the motives of the United States. He described McGregor's followers as "adventurers from different countries, with very few, if any, of the native inhabitants of the Spanish colonies;" referred to their claim to the whole of the Floridas; and declared that their course in regard to slaves and contraband trade had been of "the most odious and dangerous character," and that their claim to exercise sovereignty and to grant commissions to privateers entailed the most serious consequences. (Richardson, Messages, II. 23.)

See, also, President Monroe's special message of March 26, 1818, his annual message of Nov. 16, 1818, and his special message of Jan. 30, 1819. (Richardson, Messages, II. 32, 40, 51.)

See, also, Wait's Am. State Papers, XI. 343, 395; XII. 388; Am. State Pap. For Rel. IV. 183, 184, 292, 450, 463, 464, 478.

The Chev. de Onis, Spanish minister at Washington, protested against the occupation of the island by the United States. (Am. St. Pap. For. Rel. IV. 183–184, 463.) A protest against the occupation was addressed to the House of Representatives by Señor Vicente Pazos, who claimed to represent Venezuela, New Granada, and Mexico. His protest was tabled. (Supra. § 29, pp. 76–77.)

"No dissatisfaction has been expressed here at our occupation of Amelia Island." (Mr. Rush, min. at London, to Mr. Adams, Sec. of State, March 2, 1818, MS. Disp. England.)

"When an island is occupied by a nest of pirates, harassing the commerce of the United States, they may be pursued and driven from it, by authority of the United States, even though such island were nominally under the jurisdiction of Spain, Spain not exercising over it any control."

Mr. Adams, Sec. of State, to Mr. Hyde De Neuville, French min., Jan. 27, 1818, MS. Notes to For. Leg.

See President Monroe, confidential, to Mr. Madison, Nov. 24, Dec. 22, 1817, Madison MSS., Library of Congress.

The possession taken by the United States of Amelia Island, in Florida, gave it a possessory title, for which it was accountable only to Spain.

Mr. Gallatin, minister to France, to Baron Pasquier, French minister of foreign affairs, June 28, 1821, 2 Gallatin's writings, 187.

(3) DESTRUCTION OF THE "CAROLINE."

§ 217.

During the insurrection in Canada in 1837 sympathic commotions occurred at various places in the United States, especially along the Canadian border. The Government of the United States adopted active measures for the enforcement of the neutrality laws, but the difficulties of the situation were increased by the course of the insurgents, who, when defeated, sought refuge in the United States, where they endeavored to recruit their forces. In December, 1837, meetings were held in Buffalo, in the State of New York, by McKenzie and Rolfe, the leaders in the insurrection, who made a public appeal for arms, ammunition, and volunteers. On the 28th of the month, the United States marshal for the northern district of New York, who had proceeded to Buffalo for the purpose of suppressing violations of neutrality, reported that he had found 200 or 300 men, mostly from the American side of the Niagara River, encamped on Navy Island, in Upper Canada, armed and under the command of "General" Van Rensselaer, of Albany, and that the encampment had received accessions till it numbered about 1,000 men, well armed. This expedition had been organized at Buffalo after McKenzie's arrival, and warrants had been issued for the arrest of the men, but could not be served. There was also an encampment at Black Rock.

On the 29th of December occurred the destruction of the *Caroline*. This vessel was a small steamer employed by the men at Black Rock and on Navy Island in communicating with the mainland. According to the deposition of the master, the *Caroline* left Buffalo on the 29th of December for the port of Schlosser, which was also in New York. On the way he caused a landing to be made at Black Rock and the American flag to be run up. After the steamer left Black Rock a volley of musketry was fired at her from the Canadian side, but without injuring her. She then landed "a number of passengers" at Navy Island, and arrived at Schlosser about 3 o'clock p. m. Subsequently, in the same afternoon, she made two more trips to Navy Island, and returned finally to Schlosser about 6 o'clock p. m. During the evening about 23 persons, all citizens of the United States, came on board and asked to be permitted to "remain on board all night." At midnight about 70 or 80 armed men boarded the steamer and attacked the persons on board with muskets, swords, and cutlasses. The "passengers and crew," of whom there were in all 33, merely endeavored to escape. After this attack the assailing force set the steamer on fire, cut her loose, and set her adrift over the Niagara Falls. Only 21 of the persons on board had since been found, and one of these, Amos Durfee, was killed on the dock by a musket ball. Several others were wounded. Twelve were missing. After the *Caroline* was set adrift beacon lights were seen on the Canadian side, and cheering was heard, and it was not doubted that the assailants belonged to the British force at Chippewa. Such was the statement made by the master. It was generally reported and believed at the time that the men said to be missing lay wounded in the steamer, and were sent with her over the falls. It was subsequently ascertained, however, on further investigation that of the persons on board the only ones missing were Durfee and the cabin boy, Johnson, popularly known as "Little Billy," both of whom were shot as they were leaving the steamer; that Van Rensselaer's forces had made some use of Grand Island, and had fired some shots into Canada while the main forces lay at Navy Island and before the *Caroline* went to Schlosser; that two persons from the *Caroline* were carried by the attacking force into Canada, but were afterward set at liberty, and that that force acted under the command of Col. A. N. McNab, of Chippewa, who was acting under the orders of his superior officer.

On receiving information as to this occurrence, Mr. Forsyth, who was then Secretary of State, addressed a note to Mr. Fox, the British minister at Washington, saying that the destruction of property and assassination of citizens of the United States on the soil of New York, when the President was endeavoring to allay excitement and prevent any unfortunate occurrence on the frontier, had produced " the most painful emotions of surprise and regret," and that the incident would be made the " subject of a demand for redress." General Scott was sent to the frontier, with letters to the governors of New York and Vermont, requesting them to call out the militia. On the 6th of February, Mr. Fox communicated to Mr. Forsyth a letter from Governor Head, and while avowing that the force that destroyed the *Caroline* was under the command of Colonel McNab, declared that the piratical character of the *Caroline* seemed to be fully established; that the ordinary laws of the United States were not at the time enforced along the frontier, but were openly overborne; and that the destruction of the *Caroline* was an act of necessary self-defense. On the 22d of May, 1838, Mr. Stevenson, then minister of the United States at London, presented a demand for reparation. Its receipt was acknowledged by Lord Palmerston on the 6th of June, with a promise of consideration.

In March, 1841, a sudden turn was given to the discussion by the arrest and imprisonment on a charge of murder, in the State of New York, of Alexander McLeod, who had, as it appears, while under the influence of liquor, boasted of having taken an effective part in the destruction of the *Caroline*. Lord Palmerston then avowed responsibility, on the part of Her Majesty's Government, for the destruction of the steamer, as a public act of force, in self-defense, by persons in Her Majesty's service, and on this ground demanded McLeod's release. McLeod was ultimately tried, and was acquitted on proof of an alibi.

The case was finally disposed of by Mr. Webster and Lord Ashburton, in the course of their negotiations in 1842, Mr. Webster admitting that the employment of force might have been justified by the necessity of self-defense, but denying that such necessity existed, while Lord Ashburton, although he maintained that the circumstances afforded excuse for what was done, apologized for the invasion of United States territory.

> H. Ex. Doc. 64, 25 Cong. 2 sess.; H. Ex. Doc. 74, 25 Cong. 2 sess.; message of April 4, 1838, H. Ex. Doc. 302, 25 Cong. 2 sess.; message of Feb. 5, 1839, H. Ex. Doc. 183, 25 Cong. 3 sess.; message of Dec. 28, 1840, H. Ex. Doc. 33, 26 Cong. 2 sess.; H. Report 162, 26 Cong. 2 sess.; message of March 8, 1842, H. Ex. Doc. 128, 27 Cong. 2 sess.; message of Jan. 23, 1843, S. Ex. Doc. 99, 27 Cong. 3 sess., enclosing final correspondence. Some of the correspondence may be found in 26 Br. & For. State Papers, 1373; 29 id. 1126; 30 id. 193.
> See autobiography of Lieutenant-General Scott, I. 307–317.
> The case is discussed in Phillimore, Int. Law, 3d ed. I. 315, III. 60; in Hall, Int. Law, 4th ed. 283; in Abdy's Kent, Int. Law, ed. 1878, 148; in Lawrence, Com. sur Droit Int. III. 430.

"Although it is believed that a candid and impartial consideration of the whole history of this unfortunate event will lead to the conclusion that there were grounds of justification as strong as were ever presented in such cases, and, above all, that no slight of the authority of the United States was ever intended, yet it must be admitted that there was, in the hurried execution of this necessary service, a violation of territory; and I am instructed to assure you that her Majesty's government consider this as a most serious fact, and that, far from thinking that an event of this kind should be lightly risked, they would unfeignedly deprecate its recurrence. Looking back to what passed at this distance of time, what is, perhaps, most to be regretted is, that some explanation and apology for this occurrence was not immediately made; this, with a frank explanation of the necessity of the case, might, and probably would, have prevented much of the exasperation, and of the subsequent complaints and recriminations to which it gave rise.

" There are possible cases in the relations of nations, as of individuals, where necessity, which controls all other laws, may be pleaded; but it is neither easy nor safe to attempt to define the rights or limits properly assignable to such a plea. This must always be a subject of much delicacy, and should be considered by friendly nations with great candor and forbearance. The intentions of the parties must mainly be looked to; and can it for a moment be supposed that Great Britain would intentionally and wantonly provoke a great and powerful neighbor? "

Lord Ashburton, British plenipo., to Mr. Webster, Sec. of State, July 28, 1842, Webster's Works, VI. 294, 299–300.

" The President sees with pleasure that your Lordship fully admits those great principles of public law, applicable to cases of this kind, which this government has expressed; and that on your part, as on ours, respect for the inviolable character of the territory of independent states is the most essential foundation of civilization. And while it is admitted on both sides that there are exceptions to this rule, he is gratified to find that your Lordship admits that such exceptions must come within the limitations stated and the terms used in a former communication from this department to the British plenipotentiary here. Undoubtedly it is just, that, while it is admitted that exceptions growing out of the great law of self-defence do exist, those exceptions should be confined to cases in which the ' necessity of that self-defence is instant, overwhelming, and leaving no choice of means, and no moment for deliberation.'

" Understanding these principles alike, the difference between the two governments is only whether the facts in the case of the *Caroline* make out a case of such necessity for the purpose of self-defence. Seeing that the transaction is not recent, having happened in the time of one of his predecessors, seeing that your Lordship, in the name of your government, solemnly declares that no slight or disrespect was intended to the sovereign authority of the United States; seeing that it is acknowledged that, whether justifiable or not, there was yet a violation of the territory of the United States, and that you are instructed to say that your government consider that as a most serious occurrence; seeing, finally, that it is now admitted that an explanation and apology for this violation was due at the time; the President is content to receive these acknowledgments and assurances in the conciliatory spirit which marks your Lordship's letter, and will make this subject, as a complaint of violation of territory, the topic of no further discussion between the two governments."

Mr. Webster, Sec. of State, to Lord Ashburton, British plen., Aug. 6, 1842, Webster's Works, VI. 301–302.

The previous communication of the Department of State, referred to by Mr. Webster in the foregoing extract, was his note to Mr. Fox, British minister at Washington, of April 24, 1841, where the quoted definition of the exceptional circumstances constituting necessity may be found. (Webster's Works, VI. 250, 261.)

See, also, Mr. Webster's speech in defence of the treaty of Aug. 9, 1842, Webster's Works, V. 116 et seq.

" The letter of the British minister, while he attempts to justify that violation upon the ground of a pressing and overruling necessity, admitting, nevertheless, that, even if justifiable, an apology was due for it, and accompanying this acknowledgment with assurances of the sacred regard of his Government for the inviolability of national territory, has seemed to me sufficient to warrant forbearance from any further remonstrance against what took place, as an aggression on the soil and territory of the country."

> Message of President Tyler, Aug. 11, 1842, transmitting to the Senate the treaty of Aug. 9, 1842.   (H. Ex. Doc. 2, 27 Cong. 3 sess.; Webster's Works, VI. 347, 355.)
>
> For the rejection of a claim of McLeod for indemnity, by the Commission under the treaty with Great Britain of Feb. 13, 1853, on the ground that the case was *res judicata*, see Moore, Int. Arbitrations, III. 2419.

" I take it that the late affair of the *Caroline* was in hostile array against the British government, and that the parties concerned in it were employed in acts of war against it: and I do not subscribe to the very learned opinion of the chief justice of the State of New York (not, I hear, the chief justice, but a judge of the Supreme Court of that State) that there was no act of war committed.   Nor do I subscribe to it that every nation goes to war only on issuing a declaration or proclamation of war.   This is not the fact.   Nations often wage war for years, without issuing any declaration of war.   The question is not here upon a declaration of war, but acts of war.   And I say that in the judgment of all impartial men of other nations, *we* shall be held as a nation responsible; that the *Caroline*, there, was in a state of war against Great Britain; for purposes of war, and the worst kind of war—to sustain an insurrection; I will not say rebellion, because rebellion is a crime, and because I have heard them talked of as patriots."

> Mr. John Quincy Adams, in the House of Representatives, quoted by Benton, Thirty Years' View, II. 289.

" The war ground they [Mr. Adams and Mr. Cushing] assumed could only apply between Great Britain and the insurgents: she had no war with the United States: the attack on the *Caroline* was an invasion of the territory of a neutral power—at peace with the invader. That is a liberty not allowed by the laws of nations—not allowed by the concern which any nation, even the most inconsiderable, feels for its own safety, and its own self-respect . . .   No power allows it. That we have seen in our own day, in the case of the Poles, in their last insurrection, driven across the Austrian frontier by the Russians; and the pursuers stopped at the line, and the fugitive Poles protected the instant they had crossed it: and in the case of the late Hungarian revolt, in which the fugitive Hungarians driven across the Turkish frontier, were protected from pursuit."

Benton, Thirty Years' View, II. 290, commenting inter alia on the foregoing extract from Mr. Adams' speech.
See, also, Calhoun's Works, III. 618.

"The affair of the *Caroline* was much more difficult. Even Lord Grey told me he thought we were quite wrong in what we had done. But assuming the facts that the *Caroline* had been engaged, and when seized by us was still engaged, in carrying supplies and military stores from the American side of the river to the rebels in Navy Island, part of the British territory; that this was permitted, and could not be prevented, by the American authorities, I was clearly of opinion that, although she lay on the American side of the river when she was seized, we had a clear right to seize and destroy her, just as we might have taken a battery erected by the rebels on the American shore, the guns of which were fired against the Queen's troops in Navy Island. I wrote a long justification of our Government, and thus supplied the arguments used by our foreign secretary, till the Ashburton treaty hushed up the dispute."

Autobiography of Lord Campbell, Life, 2d ed. 1881, 19.

(41) BOMBARDMENT OF GREYTOWN.

§ 218.

May 1, 1852, the Mosquito authorities surrendered their functions at San Juan del Norte, or Greytown, to a government formed by the people of the town, under a proclamation issued in the preceding March, in behalf of the Mosquito authorities, by the British consul. A controversy soon broke out between the new authorities and the Accessory Transit Company, an organization of citizens of the United States who held a charter from the Government of Nicaragua, as to the occupation by the company of a piece of land at Punta Arenas, over which jurisdiction was claimed by the municipality. The United States, considering Greytown to be within the limits of Nicaragua, never recognized the Mosquito king nor the independence of the town, though American naval officers were instructed to respect the police regulations of any de facto authorities, and not to disturb such author-ities unless they should assail the rights of American citizens. The United States, however, denied that the jurisdiction of the municipal-ity extended in any respect to Punta Arenas.

In February, 1853, the city council ordered the Accessory Transit Company within a certain time to remove certain buildings at Punta Arenas, on the allegation that the land was needed for public uses, and, as the order was not complied with, sent a force of armed men, who, under the joint command of a member of the council and of " Major " Lyons, a colored resident, demolished the structures in question. A few days later the superintendent of the company, who had gone to Greytown to invoke the protection of a British man-of-war, was arrested and detained. March 10, 1853, Captain Hollins, of the U. S. S. *Cyane*, arived at Greytown, and he promptly placed a marine guard at Punta Arenas in order to protect the company's remaining property there, which the authorities of the town directed to be removed, and which, as their direction had not been heeded, they were then threatening to destroy. Captain Hollins also gave public notice of his intention to protect the persons and property of American citizens against molestation; and his proceedings were approved by the Secretary of the Navy.

In May, 1853, new difficulties arose in consequence of the arrest by the Greytown authorities of officials of the company while the latter were pursuing certain employees who were running off with some of its property. Disputes also existed as to dues and port charges which the steamers of the company refused to pay.

May 16, 1854, a more serious cause of difference arose, Captain Hollins having then left Greytown. On that day a body of armed men from the town attempted forcibly to arrest Captain Smith, of the company's steamer *Northern Light*, then lying at Punta Arenas, on the charge of having murdered a native boatman. The attempt was frustrated, mainly by the intervention of Mr. Borland, United States minister to Central America, who happened to be on board. Later in the day Mr. Borland went to Greytown to call upon the United States commercial agent there, when a semiriotous attempt was made to arrest him, during which he was wounded in the face by a broken bottle thrown at him by some one in the crowd. Subsequently armed men posted themselves between the consulate and the harbor, challenging all who attempted to pass and preventing boats from landing or leaving the shore, and thus kept Mr. Borland a prisoner all night. The next morning he took advantage of a temporary lull in the excitement to return to the steamer.

The population of Greytown then numbered about 300 persons, consisting of a few Englishmen, Frenchmen, Germans, and men from the United States, but chiefly of negroes from Jamaica and some natives of the Mosquito shore.

June 10, 1854, Captain Hollins was instructed to return to Greytown in the *Cyane*, and to obtain reparation for the company's losses as well as for the indignity to Mr. Borland. The Government of the United States, it was said, was embarrassed by the rumor that the pretended political authority of the place had dissolved; but if there should be no organized body on which a demand for redress could be made, it was declared that the individuals who had participated in the infliction of the wrongs could not escape responsibility resulting from the acts of the late political organization.

Demands for an apology and an indemnity were duly made upon the local de facto authorities, but they were not answered, the place being virtually in control of those who had been the chief actors in the incidents narrated; and on July 13, 1854, Captain Hollins, after public proclamation of his intention, bombarded and destroyed the town.

His course was upheld by his Government, President Pierce, in his annual message of Dec. 4, 1854, maintaining that the community in question, being well provided with arms, possessed the power and had shown a propensity to do mischief; that, " not standing before the world in the attitude of an organized political society, being neither competent to exercise the rights nor to discharge the obligations of a government, it was, in fact, a marauding establishment too dangerous to be disregarded and too guilty to pass unpunished, and yet incapable of being treated in any other way than as a piratical resort of outlaws or a camp of savages depredating on emigrant trains or caravans and the frontier settlements of civilized states."

See 46 British and For. State Papers, 859, 866–872, 875, 877, 878; 47 id. 1012–1018; Messages and Papers of the Presidents, V. 282. See, also, note of Mr. Marcy, Sec. of State, to the Count Sartiges, French min., Feb. 26, 1857, S. Ex. Doc. 9, 35 Cong. 1 sess.; Lawrence's Wheaton (1863), 173, note 59. In this note, the text of which is given infra, § 1040, the United States declined to pay the claims of French subjects growing out of losses of property by the bombardment. The British Government withheld the similar claims of its subjects.

See, as to the political situation at San Juan del Norte, Mr. Webster, Sec. of State, to Mr. Graham, Sec. of Navy, March 18, 1852, 40 MS. Dom. Let. 26.

As to Punta Arenas, see Mr. Marcy, Sec. of State, to Mr. White, April 7 and Aug. 9, 1853, 41 MS. Dom. Let. 333, 489.

" I have the honor to acknowledge the receipt of your note of the 28th ultimo, in which, referring to the recent destruction of San Juan de Nicaragua by the United States ship *Cyane*, you present in general terms a demand for reparation to those respectable citizens of Nicaragua who suffered, as it is alleged, grievous losses of property by the bombardment, and also to the Government of Nicaragua for the total destruction of her only Atlantic port.

" In reply, I beg to submit that it is scarcely credible, as your note seems to imply, that any considerable number of respectable citizens of the Republic of Nicaragua had taken up their residence or placed their property among those whom you properly characterize as ' the pseudo sovereigns,' ' the authors of all the scandalous excesses that have been consummated at that port '—San Juan—a place, as you admit, held by usurpation against the sovereign authority of their own Government. These citizens for whom you make reclamation must have lived in treasonable association with the open and avowed enemies of your country, and if engaged there in business they must have been incorporated with that community which you describe in such severe but probably just terms. They knew, for notice has repeatedly been given, that the town would be punished for its misdeeds, and they had every opportunity to withdraw from it or to communicate to Captain Hollins after his arrival their claim to be separated from the guilty if they were not implicated with them, but they took no step to have their lot distinguished from that of the abandoned and lawless dwellers at that place. It is unreasonable now to complain of Captain Hollins for not making the separation which they refused to make for themselves, or to furnish him with the means of making the discrimination. They deliberately united their fortunes with men who you admit deserved the chastisement which they received, and consequently involved themselves knowingly and necessarily with their criminal associates. All the circumstances considered, I cannot believe that the Nicaraguan Government will so far forget what is due to itself, and must be evident to its clear sense of justice, as to urge any claims in behalf of those who associated themselves with the usurpers of its territory. Nicaragua may think herself kindly treated if she is not held responsible for the acts of those who were permitted by her to occupy her territory and perpetrate deeds injurious to friendly powers while within her jurisdiction. She owed it alike to herself and to these powers to have driven the band of marauders settled at San Juan from her acknowledged soil. If she has the indiscretion to open an account with the United States upon this matter, this Government will be at liberty to make her responsible for all the injuries its citizens have suffered from those occupying her territory. Having neglected to expel these intruders and regarding at least a part of the persons at San Juan under her protection, she is answerable by the well-established principles of international law for the injuries other nations have suffered by their misconduct.

" If Nicaragua chooses to maintain the position you assume in your note to me, that her citizens who incorporated themselves with the community at San Juan are still in friendly relations with her and entitled to her protection, then she approves by an implication which she is not at liberty to deny [the acts] of that political establishment planted on her own soil and becomes responsible for the mischiefs it has done to American citizens. It would be a strange inconsistency for Nicaragua to regard the organization at San Juan as a hostile establishment on her territory and at the same time claim the right to clothe with her nationality its members.

"Assuming, as it is respectful to do, that you have duly appreciated the consequences of the step you have taken, I infer that the Government of Nicaragua, by claiming the right of protection over the persons at San Juan, will not hesitate to acknowledge her responsibility to other states for the conduct of the people which she has permitted to occupy that part of her territory.

" I take the liberty to ask you to furnish this Government with the views of that of Nicaragua upon the subject of its responsibility for the conduct of the people at San Juan de Nicaragua."

> Mr. Marcy, Sec. of State, to Mr. Marcoleta, Nicaraguan min., Aug. 2, 1854, MS. notes to Cent. Am. I. 62.

> That the Government of Nicaragua has declined to enter into a convention for the settlement of the claims of citizens of the United States, unless it shall include the claims of citizens of Nicaragua growing out of Walker's filibustering expeditions and the bombardment of Greytown, see memorandum of the Diplomatic Bureau, Aug. 15, 1894, MSS. Department of State, and this digest, chapter on relations with various countries, title " Nicaragua," infra, § 794.

(5) PURSUIT OF PREDATORY INDIANS AND OTHER MARAUDERS.

§ 219.

In a memorandum to Mr. Gorostiza, Mexican minister, April 21, 1836, Mr. Forsyth, as Secretary of State, referring to the contest in Texas and to apprehended Indian hostilities, and to the intention to send General Gaines to the frontier for the purpose of protecting United States territory as well as the surveyors of the two countries who might be engaged in running the boundary, said: " Should the troops, in the performance of their duty, be advanced beyond the point Mexico might suppose was within the territory of the United States, the occupation of the position was not to be taken as an indication of any hostile feeling, or of a desire to establish a possession or claim not justified by the treaty of limits," but only as " precautionary and provisional," to be " abandoned whenever (the line being run and the true limits marked) the disturbances in that region should cease, they being the only motive for it."

April 23 Mr. Gorostiza made an extended reply, in which he maintained that the taking by General Gaines of any position " beyond the known limits of the United States " would " not only affect the rights of Mexico as an independent nation, but also injure its interests," and that the holding of " the position taken, even though it be included within the assigned limits of Mexico, until the disturbances in Texas should cease, would be equal to a real military occupation of a part of the territory of Mexico, and to indirect intervention in its domestic affairs."

Mr. Forsyth, April 26, answered that his notice " was not intended to express the intention to occupy a post within the acknowledged, known limits of Mexico, but to apprise Mexico that if General Gaines should occupy a position supposed by each Government to be within its limits, that occupation would not be used either as the foundation of a claim or to strengthen a claim—the sole purpose being to enable this Government to do its duty to itself and to Mexico."

April 28 Mr. Gorostiza expressed satisfaction that Mr. Forsyth's opinion, as he understood it, coincided with his own "on this capital point, . . . that General Gaines's troops will not take a position on any ground known to be beyond the limits of the United States; and as a natural consequence . . . that such position can in no case be on ground previously possessed by Mexico, and, of course, within its known limits."

Mr. Forsyth, May 3, 1836, replied: " Except in case of necessity, General Gaines will not occupy ground not indisputably within the limits of the United States. In case of necessity, whether the possession of the ground he may occupy is now or has heretofore been claimed by Mexico cannot be made a question by that officer; he will take it to perform his duties to the United States, and to fulfill the obligations of the United States to Mexico. The just and friendly purpose for which he does occupy it (if he should do so), being beforehand explained to Mexico, it is expected will prevent either belief or suspicion of any hostile or equivocal design on his part. It is not intended to be the assertion of a right of property or possession."

Mr. Gorostiza expressed his regret, and stated that he would send copies of the correspondence to his Government, to the end that such orders might be given to the commander of the Mexican army in Texas as would prevent difficulty. On May 9, however, Mr. Gorostiza, having learned that General Gaines was authorized, in case of necessity, to advance his troops to Nacogdoches, which his instructions declared to be within the limits claimed by the United States, protested against the order as involving a possible violation of Mexican territory.

In a reply, May 10, Mr. Forsyth said: " General Gaines is not authorized to advance to Nacogdoches, but he is ordered not to go beyond that point. . . . The terms used limit the authority given, and were chosen with the express intention to avoid misconstruction of the motive of the advance. To effect one of the great objects for which General Gaines is sent to the frontier, i. e., to fulfill our treaty with Mexico by protecting its territory against the Indians within the United States, the troops of the United States might justly be sent into the heart of Mexico; and their presence, instead of being

complained of, would be the strongest evidence of fidelity to engagements and friendship to Mexico. Nor could the good faith and
friendship of the act be doubted if troops of the United States were
sent into the Mexican territory to prevent embodied Mexican Indians,
justly suspected of such design, from assailing the frontier settlements
of the United States."

> 25 Br. & For. State Papers, 1089, 1092, 1093, 1094, 1095, 1096, 1097, 1098,
> 1099; S. Ex. Doc. 1, 24 Cong. 2 sess.; H. Ex. Doc. 256, 24 Cong. 1 sess.
> See Moore, Int. Arbitrations, II. 1212–1214.
> The treaty obligation above referred to is that which was embodied in
> Art. XXXIII. of the treaty of April 5, 1831, which bound the United
> States and Mexico to restrain hostilities and incursions on the part
> of Indians living in their respective territories.
> See Moore, Int. Arbitrations, III. 2430 et seq.

" You will perceive that Mr. Gorostiza, in his conference with me,
distinctly admitted our right, in the event of hostility to the United
States by Mexican Indians, to invade the territory of Texas, either
to prevent intended injury or to punish actual depredation. In a
note written subsequently he seeks to avoid the force of that admission, by confounding the principle upon which it obviously rests with
the right of making war for a violation of treaty engagement. You
will find no difficulty in showing to the Mexican Government that it
rests upon principles of the law of nations, entirely distinct from
those on which war is justified—upon the immutable principles of
self-defence—upon the principles which justify decisive measures of
percaution to prevent irreparable evil to our own or to a neighboring people.

" The grossness of the error of placing it on the right of war, as
also the folly of relying upon that mode of redress, you can render
obvious, by supposing that hostilities were, under present circumstances on the frontier, about to begin. Our fellow-citizens, of all
ages and classes, are to be exposed to massacre, their property to
destruction, and the whole frontier to be laid waste by those savages
Mexico was bound to control. Until these evils happen, on Mr.
Gorostiza's theory, we have no right to take a position which will
enable us to act with effect; and before we do act, according to our
promises under Article XXXIII. of the treaty, after the frontier
has been desolated, we must demand redress of Mexico, wait for it to
be refused, and then make war upon Mexico. We are quietly to
suffer injuries we might prevent in the expectation of redress—redress from irreparable injuries from Mexico, who did not inflict them,
but who was, from circumstances, without the power to prevent, as
she would be after they were inflicted, without the power to redress
them. To make war upon Mexico for this involuntary failure to

comply with her obligations, would be equivalent to an attempt to convert her misfortunes into crimes—her inability into guilt."

> Mr. Forsyth, Sec. of State, to Mr. Ellis, min. to Mexico, Dec. 10, 1836, 26 Br. & For. St. Pap. 1419.

A company of Texan rangers having pursued into Mexico a band of Mexican Indians who had made an incursion into Texas, Mr. Marcy said: " If Indians whom the United States are bound to restrain shall, under the same circumstances, make a hostile incursion into Mexico, this Government will not complain if the Mexican forces who may be sent to repel them shall cross to this side of the line for that purpose, provided that in so doing they abstain from injuring the persons and property of citizens of the United States."

> Mr. Marcy, Sec. of State, to Mr. Almonte, Mexican min., Feb. 4, 1856, MS. Notes to Mex. VII. 62.
> In his annual message of Dec. 6, 1858, President Buchanan, referring to the lawless conditions existing along the Mexican frontier, conditions which he described as constituting " a state of anarchy and violence," recommended that the United States " assume a temporary protectorate over the northern portions of Chihuahua and Sonora and to establish military posts within the same," this " protection " to be " withdrawn as soon as local governments shall be established in these Mexican States capable of performing their duties to the United States, restraining the lawless, and preserving peace along the border." (Richardson, Messages, v. 514.)

An incursion into the territory of Mexico for the purpose of dispersing a band of Indians marauders is, if necessary, not a violation of the law of nations.

> Mr. Fish, Sec. of State, to Mr. Belknap, Sec. of War, Jan. 22, 1874, 101 MS. Dom. Let. 373.   See Mr. Fish to Mr. Belknap, Aug 31, 1874, 104 id, 94.
> See Reports of the Committee of Investigation, sent in 1873 by the Mexican Government to the frontier of Texas: New York, 1875, pp. viii, 443.

" The report of W. M. Shafter, lieutenant-colonel Twenty-fourth Infantry, commanding the district of Nueces, Texas, concerning recent raids by Mexicans and Indians from Mexico into Texas for marauding purposes, with your indorsement of the 29th ultimo, has been submitted to the President, and has, together with numerous other reports and documents relating to the same subject, been duly considered.

" The President desires that the utmost vigilance on the part of the military forces in Texas be exercised for the suppression of these raids. It is very desirable that efforts to this end, in so far at least as they necessarily involve operations on both sides of the border, be made with the cooperation of the Mexican authorities; and you will

instruct General Ord, commanding in Texas, to invite such cooperation on the part of the local Mexican authorities, and to inform them
that while the President is anxious to avoid giving offense to Mexico,
he is nevertheless convinced that the invasion of our territory by
armed and organized bodies of thieves and robbers to prey upon our
citizens should not be longer endured.

" General Ord will at once notify the Mexican authorities along
the Texas border, of the great desire of the President to unite with
them in efforts to suppress this long continued lawlessness. At the
same time he will inform those authorities that if the Government of
Mexico shall continue to neglect the duty of suppressing these outrages, that duty will devolve upon this government, and will be performed, even if its performance should render necessary the occasional crossing of the border by our troops. You will, therefore,
direct General Ord that in case the lawless incursions continue
he will be at liberty, in the use of his own discretion, when in pursuit
of a band of the marauders, and when his troops are either in sight
of them or upon a fresh trail, to follow them across the Rio Grande,
and to overtake and punish them, as well as retake stolen property
taken from our citizens and found in their hands on the Mexican
side of the line."

> Mr. McCrary, Sec. of War, to Gen. Sherman, June 1, 1877, House Report
> 701, 45 Cong. 2 sess. 241 ; also, H. Ex. Doc. 13, 45 Cong. 1 sess.
>
> The report of Col. Shafter, referred to in the foregoing order, was dated
> at Fort Clark, Texas, March 9, 1877. It stated that since Oct. 1, 1876,
> seventeen men had been killed by Indians, who had been followed to
> the Rio Grande, taking with them the arms and horses of the mur-
> dered men, which they had openly offered for sale at Saragossa,
> Mexico ; that since Dec. 30, 1876, two large droves of horses, about
> 100 in all, and at least 300 head of cattle, had been taken in two raids
> from within ten miles of Fort Clark ; and that, as the Indians con-
> stantly crossed and recrossed the river, finding both a place of refuge
> and a market for their plunder in the Mexican towns, where no
> attempt was made by the authorities to control them, it was almost
> impossible to head them off. In conclusion Col. Shafter stated (1)
> that it would be necessary to scout for the Indians in Mexico, and
> (2) that it was only by giving authority to the troops to operate in
> Mexico that life and property could be made secure on the frontier.
> (H. Report 701, 45 Cong. 2 sess. 235. See also supra, § 51.)
>
> See, particularly as to conditions on the frontier, Mr. Foster, min. to
> Mexico, to Mr. Evarts, Sec. of State, April 24, 1877, For. Rel. 1877,
> 401.
>
> June 20, 1877, Mr. Foster reported an interview with the Mexican min-
> ister of foreign affairs concerning the order of June 1, supra. (For.
> Rel. 1877, 410.)
>
> General Treviño was sent by the Mexican Government to the border, with
> orders, dated June 18, 1877, to pursue evil-doers and to cooperate
> with the United States authorities, but to inform the commander of
> the American forces that Mexico could not allow a foreign force to

enter the national territory without the consent of the National Congress, and much less to exercise acts of jurisdiction; and he was instructed to "repel force by force, should the invasion take place." (For. Rel. 1877, 416–418.)

Mr. Foster protested against this order, as the Mexican minister at Washington had done against the order of June 1; but as the Mexican Government had previously promised to send a president-general to the frontier with an adequate force and instructions to cooperate with General Ord, the latter was directed to meet the order cordially, "and not to be hasty in pursuit across the border, except in an aggravated case." (For. Rel. 1877, 418, 419.)

General Ord reported that he had reached a good understanding with General Treviño on the basis of cooperation; but it seems that General Treviño declined a proposal for a reciprocal right of passage of the frontier in pursuit of outlaws. (For. Rel. 1877, 419–423.)

December 14, 1877, Señor Cuellar, Mexican minister at Washington, protested against an entry into Mexico by Colonel Shafter and Lieutenant Bullis for the purpose of attacking some Lipan Indians. There was a difference as to the circumstances of the case. (For. Rel. 1878, 536, 664.)

See the Foster-Mata correspondence, July, 1878, as to the crossing of the frontier by American troops under Colonel Mackenzie. (For. Rel. 1878, 555–559, 570.)

"The first duty of a government is to protect life and property. This is a paramount obligation. For this governments are instituted, and governments neglecting or failing to perform it become worse than useless. This duty the Government of the United States has determined to perform to the extent of its power toward its citizens on the border. It is not solicitous, it never has been, about the methods or ways in which that protection shall be accomplished, whether by formal treaty stipulation or by informal convention; whether by the action of judicial tribunals or that of military forces. Protection *in fact* to American lives and property is the sole point upon which the United States are tenacious. In securing it they have a right to ask the co-operation of their sister Republic. So far, the authorities of Mexico, military and civil, in the vicinity of the border appear not only to take no steps to effectively check the raids or punish the raiders, but demur and object to steps taken by the United States. . . .

"I am not unmindful of the fact that, as you have repeatedly reported, there is reason to believe that the Mexican Government really desires to check these disorders. According to the views you have presented, its statesmen are believed to be sagacious and patriotic, and well disposed to comply with all international obligations. But, as you represent, they encounter, or apprehend that they may encounter, a hostile public feeling adverse to the United States, especially in these border localities, thwarting their best intentions and efforts. It is greatly to be regretted that such a state of perverted public feeling should exist. But its existence does not exonerate the Mexican Government from any obligation under international law. Still less does it relieve this government from its duties to guard the welfare of the American people. The United States Government cannot allow marauding bands to establish themselves upon its borders with liberty to invade and plunder United States territory with impunity, and then, when pursued, to take refuge across the Rio Grande under protection of the plea of the integrity of the soil of the Mexican Republic."

> Mr. Evarts, Sec. of State, to Mr. Foster, min. to Mexico, Aug. 13, 1878,
>   For. Rel. 1878, 572, 573, 574.
> See For. Rel. 1879, 754, 773, 801; For. Rel. 1880, 726, 735, 756, 768, 784,
>   785, 786, 788.

" In my last annual message I expressed the hope that the prevalence of quiet on the border between this country and Mexico would soon become so assured as to justify the modification of the orders, then in force, to our military commanders in regard to crossing the frontier, without encouraging such disturbances as would endanger the peace of the two countries. Events moved in accordance with these expectations, and the orders were accordingly withdrawn, to the entire satisfaction of our own citizens and the Mexican Government. Subsequently the peace of the border was again disturbed by a savage foray, under the command of the Chief Victorio, but, by the combined and harmonious action of the military forces of both countries, his band has been broken up and substantially destroyed."

> President Hayes, annual message, Dec. 6, 1880, For. Rel. 1880, p. xii.
> The so-called " Ord " order was withdrawn by an order of the Secretary
>   of War of Feb. 24, 1880.   (For. Rel. 1880, 735.)
> The withdrawal was communicated to the Mexican Government. (For.
>   Rel. 1880, 735, 744, 781, 782.)

" A recent agreement with Mexico provides for the crossing of the frontier by the armed forces of either country in pursuit of hostile Indians. In my message of last year I called attention to the prevalent lawlessness upon the borders and to the necessity of legislation for its suppression. I again invite the attention of Congress to the subject.

" A partial relief from these mischiefs has been sought in a convention, which now awaits the approval of the Senate, as does also another touching the establishment of the international boundary between the United States and Mexico."

> President Arthur, annual message, Dec. 4, 1882, For. Rel. 1882, vi.
> The text of the agreement above referred to, dated July 29, 1882, for
>   crossing the frontier, is printed in For. Rel. 1882, 396, 404–405. For
>   correspondence concerning it, see For. Rel. 1882, 388, 390, 392, 396,
>   404.

President Arthur, in his annual message of Dec. 4, 1883, announced the prolongation of the agreement for another year. For. Rel. 1883, vi. See also similar agreements of June 25, 1890; Nov. 25, 1892; June 4, 1896.

As to the killing of Captain Crawford, while in pursuit of Chiricahua Indians, at Teopar, Mex., see For. Rel. 1886, 570–691, 724–732. It was decided, on the strength of a communication from the War Department, conveying the views of Gen. Sheridan, in November, 1887, that the killing was due to accident, and that a demand for indemnity therefore should not be made. (Mr. Blaine, Sec. of State, to Mr. Bingham, March 7, 1891, 181 MS. Dom. Let. 166.)

By an agreement between the United States and Mexico, concluded June 4, 1896, the Federal troops of the two countries were permitted to cross the international boundary in pursuit of Kid's band of hostile Indians, in the uninhabited and desert parts of the line, which were defined to be " all points that are at least ten kilometers distant from any encampment or town of either country." It was expressly stipulated that no such crossing should take place between the Mexican town of Capitan Leal, 52 miles above Piedras Negras, and the mouth of the Rio Grande. There were various other provisions, requiring notice of crossing, if possible, to be given, and permitting the chastisement of other hostiles concerned with Kid's band whom the troops might chance to meet with.

For. Rel. 1896, 438.

" Since June, 1890, when a provisional agreement was entered into by the United States and Mexico defining and regulating their reciprocal right to pursue hostile Indians across the boundary line, the two Governments have by successive renewals and amendments continued the practice so established. The last agreement in this regard was signed June 4, 1896, having particular reference to the mutual pursuit of the notorious and dangerous hostiles led by the Apache Kid, the extermination or complete subjugation of these Indians having become an imperative duty toward the inhabitants on either side of the border line." (Report of Mr. Olney, Sec. of State, to the President, Dec. 7, 1896, For. Rel. 1896, lxxvii.)

See, also, Mr. Olney, Sec. of State, to Sec. of War, June 5, 1896, 210 MS. Dom. Let. 518, communicating a certified copy of the agreement of June 4, 1896.

8. STATE-AIDED AND COMPULSORY EMIGRATION.

§ 220.

" Congress, at its last session, passed laws which authorized the President to aid the colonization of persons of certain classes of African derivation, with their consent, in some tropical country, first obtaining the consent of the government of such country to receive such settlements and protect them in all the rights of freemen. The execution of these laws was devolved by the President upon the honorable the Secretary of the Interior. That officer is understood to have recognized the honorable Mr. Pomeroy as an agent for persons belonging to the specified classes, to aid and direct them in the choice of their locations and establishing their settlements. The general instructions which were given to him by the Secretary of the Interior expressly inhibited Mr. Pomeroy from attempting to make such location and settlement in any country whatever, without first having obtained the consent of the government of such country to protect the proposed settlement of such persons there with all the rights and privileges of freemen.

" About the time when those instructions were in course of preparation, his excellency Señor Antonio José de Yrisarri, minister plenipotentiary of the republics of Guatemala and Salvador near the United States, gave notice to this Department that those two states were averse to receiving any such settlements; and for that reason the instructions of the Secretary of the Interior to Mr. Pomeroy were modified. He was informed that the President accepted Mr. Yrisarri's communication as a definitive declination of the two governments which he represented to receive and protect a colony of the class proposed in their respective countries. Whereupon Mr. Pomeroy was expressly directed not to proceed with such colony to any part of the territories of either of the said republics of Guatemala and Salvador.

" In your note, which is now under consideration, you protest, in behalf of the republics of Costa Rica, Nicaragua, and Honduras, against the introduction of any colony of the kind proposed within the territory of either of those republics. You also inform this Department that a portion of the region called Chiriqui, which is claimed by Mr. Ambrose W. Thompson, and which he offers as a site for such a colony, lies unquestionably within the territory of Costa Rica, while another portion lies within the unquestioned territory of New Granada, and still a third part is in dispute between the government of Costa Rica and New Granada; and you extend your protest so as to make it cover not only the unquestioned territory of Costa Rica, but also that portion of Chiriqui which is claimed by Costa Rica.

" I have now to inform your excellency that the acts of Congress, under which the colonization in question is proposed to be made, do not warrant the attempt to establish such a colony in any country without the previous consent of the government thereof, and that your protest is accepted by the President as a denial of such consent on the part of the three states you so worthily represent."

Mr. Seward, Sec. of State, to Mr. Molina, min. of Costa Rica, Nicaragua, and Honduras, Sept. 24, 1862, Dip. Cor. 1862, 903.

The transport of paupers from Cuba to the United States is in violation of United States laws and of international comity.

> Mr. Fish, Sec. of State, to Mr. Bernabé, Span. min., May 16, 1872, MS. Notes to Spain, IX. 92.

It having been reported that the authorities of the Swiss Canton of Zug had granted the release of a prisoner named Binzegger, a confirmed incendiary, on condition of his emigrating to the United States, the Department of State approved the action of the American minister at Berne in protesting against their action, and expressed the hope that the Swiss Federal Government would " prevent the consummation of the design to land this criminal on our shores, as a violation of the comity which should obtain between the two Governments."

> Mr. Frelinghuysen, Sec. of State, to Mr. Cramer, min. to Switzerland, Dec. 11, 1884, For. Rel. 1885, 793.
>
> Mr. Frelinghuysen referred to instruction to Mr. Cramer, No. 16, of Dec. 3, 1881, and especially to the President's message of Feb. 28, 1881, S. Ex. Doc. 62, 46 Cong. 3 sess., as to the deportation of criminals, paupers, and insane persons by local authorities in Europe.
>
> The Swiss Government stated that it had done all in its power to prevent the emigration of persons who, by the laws of foreign countries, were not permitted to land, and that it was advised that Binzegger, who had manifested an intention to emigrate, not to the United States, but to the Argentine Republic, had been simply pardoned and set at liberty without any restrictive condition. (For. Rel. 1885, 794.)
>
> As to instructions given to American consuls in India to cooperate with the British authorities in preventing the emigration of Mormon recruits from India to the United States, see Mr. Frelinghuysen, Sec. of State, to Mr. Lowell, min. to England, Jan. 7, 1885, For. Rel. 1885, 445.
>
> The British Government stated that proper steps had been taken to give effect to the wishes expressed by the United States in the circular of the Department of State of Dec. 27, 1884, in reference to pauper emigration from European countries to the United States. (Mr. Lowell, min. to England, to Mr. Frelinghuysen, Sec. of State, Jan. 29, 1885, For. Rel. 1885, 445, enclosing a note of Lord Granville, of Jan. 27, 1885.)

April 25, 1887, the British minister at Washington inquired whether under the existing law Irish emigrants sent out at the public cost, and having friends in the United States " able to help and support them," would be allowed to land.

In reply, Mr. Bayard, May 7, 1887, referred to section 2 of the act of August 31, 1882, prohibiting the landing of any person " unable to take care of himself or herself without becoming a public charge." The duty of ascertaining the facts was committed to the immigration officers at the various ports, and therefore no general assurance in advance could be given.   But, going further, Mr. Bayard, adverting to previous discussions in regard to immigration, said that the Government of the United States, in view if its policy and its laws, could not fail " to look with disfavor and concern upon the sending to this country, by foreign governmental agencies and at the public cost, of persons not only unlikely to develop qualities of thrift and self-support, but sent here because it is assumed that they have ' friends ' in this country able to ' help and support ' them." The exportation of such persons to the United States by a foreign government, in order to get rid of the burden of their support, could, he declared, " scarcely be regarded as a friendly act, or in harmony with existing laws."

May 17, 1887, the British minister stated that he had learned that the intending emigrants were not paupers, but crofters, whose passages were only partly paid from public funds, and he inquired whether this would in any way affect the tenor of the reply previously given.

Mr. Bayard, May 20, replied: " For the reasons stated in my note of the 7th instant, the Department is unable to give any assurances that any particular class of immigrants will be permitted to land.   The provisions of the law look to the actual condition of each person, and are impartial in their operation."

> Sir L. West, British min., to Mr. Bayard, Sec. of State, April 25, 1887;
> Mr. Bayard to Sir L. West, May 7, 1887; Sir L. West to Mr. Bayard,
> May 17, 1887; Mr. Bayard to Sir L. West, May 20, 1887: For. Rel.
> 1887, 520, 539.

VI. DUTY TO RESTRAIN INJURIOUS AGENCIES.

1. Repression of Criminal or Hostile Acts.

§ 221.

The right to accord hospitality to political refugees is well established, and is exercised by all free governments.   Among the cases in which such hospitality has been extended by the United States, that of Kossuth and his compatriots is one of the most conspicuous.[a]   The right of hospitality is formally recognized in the rule, which, if not expressly affirmed or expressly denied, is implied in all extradition treaties, namely, that a nation is not bound to deliver up political offenders.   Such persons share, however, the general duty of obedience to the laws, and are subject to such measures as the government may lawfully adopt to prevent the national territory from being used by any persons as a base for criminal or hostile enterprises.

---

[a] Supra, § 72.

" PHILADELPHIA, *November 23, 1795.*

" My Dear Sir: Inclosed are letters for Mr. de la Fayette and his tutor. I leave them open for your perusal; and notwithstanding the request in my letter of the 18th, I shall cheerfully acquiesce in any measures respecting them which you (and others with whom you may be disposed to consult) may deem most eligible.

"As there can be no doubt that the feelings of both are alive to everything which may have the semblance of neglect or slight, and, indeed, expectant as they must have been (without adverting perhaps to the impediments) of an invitation to fly to me without delay, and distressing and forlorn as the situation of one of them is, it is necessary that every assurance and consolation should be administered to them. For these reasons I pray you to send my letters to them by express, the expense of which I will repay with thankfulness.

" The doubt which you have expressed of the propriety of an open and avowed conduct in me towards the son of Mr. de la Fayette, and the subject it might afford to malignancy to misinterpret the cause, has so much weight that I am distrustful of my own judgment in deciding on this business lest my feelings should carry me further [than] prudence (while I am a public character) will warrant. It has, however, like many other things in which I have been involved, two edges, neither of which can be avoided without falling on the other. On one side, I may be charged with countenancing those who have been denounced the enemies of France; on the other, with *not* countenancing the son of a man who is dear to America.

" When I wrote to you last I had resolved to take both the pupil and tutor into my own family, supposing it would be most agreeable to the young gentleman, and congenial with friendship—at the same time that it would have given me more command over him—been more convenient and less expensive to myself than to board them out. But now, as I have intimated before, I confide the matter entirely to your decision, after seeing and conversing with them.

" Mr. Adet has been indirectly sounded on the coming over of the family of Fayette *generally,* but not as to the *exact* point. His answer was, that as France did not make war upon women and children he did not suppose that their emigration could excite any notice. The case, however, might be different, if one of them (with his tutor, whose character, conduct, and principles may, for aught I know to the contrary, be very obnoxious) was brought into my family, and, of course, into the company that visited it. But as all these things will be taken into consideration by you I shall not dwell upon them, and only add that

" With esteem, regard, and sincere affection, I am ever yours,

" Go. Washington.

" P. S.—I have no doubt but that young Fayette and his tutor might be boarded at Germantown, or in the vicinity of this city, and would be at hand to receive assistance and advice as occasion might require although he might not be a resident under my roof.

" Colonel HAMILTON."

> 4 Hamilton MSS., Dept. of State. See also Washington to Hamilton, May 6, 1794, 10 Washington's Writings (Sparks's ed.), 411.

As all official intercourse between a State and foreign nations is prevented by the Constitution and exclusive authority for that purpose given to the United States, the National Government is responsible to foreign nations for all violations by the United States of their international obligations, and for this reason Congress is expressly authorized " to define and punish . . . offenses against the law of nations."

> United States v. Arjona (1887), 120 U. S. 479, 483. See for a fuller statement of this case, supra, § 23, p. 66.

Field, in his International Code, says that " one who uses his asylum for promoting hostilities against a foreign country, may be proceeded against under the law of the nation of his asylum, or may be surrendered to the nation aggrieved."

> Field, Int. Code, § 207, p. 86.
>
> In saying that the person " may be surrendered to the nation aggrieved," Mr. Field seems to go beyond most writers, who limit themselves to the proposition that the person in question should be prosecuted or expelled. (See Reg. v. Most, cited in Whart. Crim. Law, § 179.)
>
> Field, in a note to the section above quoted, collects the following authorities :
>
> Bluntschli (§ 398) states that, where the refugee abuses his asylum, the nation is bound either to end his sojourn in its territory or to place him under such restrictions as will do away with all danger from him. To the same effect is Phillimore, Int. Law, I. 415.
>
> In 1799 certain English subjects were prosecuted for publishing a libel upon Paul I., Emperor of Russia. They were convicted and punished by fine and imprisonment. (State Trials (Howell), Vol. XXVII. 627–630.)
>
> In 1803 Jean Peltier, a French refugee, was prosecuted for a libel on Napoleon Bonaparte, then first consul of the French Republic. He was convicted, but no judgment was entered in consequence of the breaking out of war. (State Trials (Howell), Vol. XXVIII. 530–619.)
>
> "A nation has a right to harbor political refugees, and will do so, unless weakness or political sympathy lead it to a contrary course. But such persons may not, consistently with the obligation of friendship between states, be allowed to plot against the person of the sovereign, or against the institutions of their native country. Such acts are crimes, for the trial and punishment of which the laws of the land ought to provide, but do not require that the accused be remanded for trial to his native country." (Woolsey, § 79. See also Wildman's International Law, 59 ; Law, Lib., Vol. LII. 42.)

After the attempt to assassinate the Emperor of the French, on the 14th of January, 1858, the French minister of foreign affairs represented that plots to assassinate the Emperor had been formed in England, and asked that England should provide for the punishment of such offenses. In accordance with the request, Lord Palmerston, being prime minister, on the 8th of February introduced a bill for the punishment of conspiracies formed in England to commit murder beyond Her Majesty's dominions; but the bill was rejected, and the ministry immediately resigned. The bill was opposed by some from an unwillingness to interfere in any way with the right of asylum; but the controlling reason evidently was a feeling that the French Government had used too dictatorial a tone in demanding the passage of such a law. (Annual Register (1858), 5, 33, 202; Annuaire des deux Mondes (1857, 1858), 32, 110, 420, cited in Lawrence's Wheaton, 246, note. Whart. Crim. Law, 9th ed. §§ 220, 287, 1397, and discussion in 6 Crim. Law Mag. 155, March, 1885.)

The same application was made to Sardinia, and a law was passed there making it a special offense to conspire against the lives of sovereigns, although the punishment originally proposed in the bill as introduced by the ministers was mitigated by the chambers. M. Cavour sustained the measure, both on political grounds and because he deemed it important that Sardinia, under the circumstances in which she was placed, should not act in opposition to the views of France. (Annuaire des deux Mondes (1857, 1858), 216.)

A government can not be held responsible for the secret transmission of money by individuals within its jurisdiction to individuals in a foreign country to promote the commission of crime there.

Mr. Frelinghuysen, Sec. of State, to Mr. West, Brit. min., April 14, 1883, MS. Notes to Gr. Br. XIX. 284. See, also, Mr. Frelinghuysen, Sec. of State, to Mr. Lowell, min. to England, Dec. 4, 1883, and Nov. 24, 1884, MS. Inst. Gr. Br. XXVII. 69, 349.

The laws of the United States make it a penal offence for any explosive to be transported from the United States to any other country, unless it be done openly and according to certain specific rules.

Mr. Frelinghuysen, Sec. of State, to Mr. Lowell, min. to England, Nov. 24, 1884, MS. Inst. Gr. Br. XXVII. 349.

" Your communication of the 22d ultimo, in which you ask the attention of this Department to the question whether participating in the Irish National League, an organization to promote insurrectionary movements in Ireland, is not an offence against the ' sedition statutes ' of the United States, has been received.

" In reply to your enquiry, I have to say that treasons and seditions made punishable under those statutes are treason and sedition against the United States, and they do not make punishable treason and sedition against foreign sovereigns.

" I may add, however, that if any persons in the State of Pennsylvania take measures to perpetrate a crime in a foreign land, such an attempt, coupled with preparations to effectuate it, though not cognizable in the Federal courts, is cognizable in the courts of the State of Pennsylvania. It is only necessary to obtain legal action in such prosecution that an oath specifying the offence be made before a State magistrate, and the State prosecuting attorney having jurisdiction of the locality notified of the initiation of the proceedings."

> Mr. Bayard, Sec. of State, to Mr. Harris, April 2, 1885, 154 MS. Dom. Let.
> 649.
> In December, 1864, the minister of the United States in London was
> instructed to lay before the British Government certain papers in
> relation to " the alleged manufacture of Greek fire at Windsor,
> Canada, to be used by rebel emissaries in attempts to burn certain
> cities of the United States," with a view to " the adoption of such
> preventive measures as may be practicable." (Dip. Cor. 1865, I. 36.)

In 1894 certain citizens of Louisiana addressed to the President, the Secretary of State, and the Congress of the United States, a petition on the subject of lotteries, praying among other things that the Government of the United States would point out to that of Honduras that the corporation known as the Louisiana Lottery Company proposed to change its base to the Republic of Honduras. The Department of State enclosed a copy of the petition, together with copies of the United States antilottery statutes, to the diplomatic representative of the United States in Honduras, and said : " Should it be true that such an enterprise, made unlawful by our law, is seeking to make use of a foreign territory from which to operate upon our citizens, it would seem to be a subject of which the neighboring and offended state would take notice. It is proper to bring the subject to the notice of the Government of Honduras, through its minister for foreign affairs, in order that it may be advised of the views of the United States and of its legislation in this regard."

> Mr. Adee, Act. Sec. of State, to Mr. Pringle, chargé in Guatemala and
> Honduras, March 22, 1894, For. Rel. 1894, 315.

" The assassination of President McKinley, together with the anarchistic crimes and attempts upon the lives of chief magistrates committed in recent years, have rendered it terribly evident that a struggle against the menace of anarchy is an urgent necessity for all governments and a duty whose performance can not be postponed.

" It is evident that concerted action on the part of the governments interested can not be really successful unless the uniform and strict enforcement of the measures that may be adopted against the anarchists can be secured by an international understanding. It would be preferable, it seems, to attain that end by an exchange of views among the governments rather than by convoking a new conference.

" The Imperial Government of Germany and the Imperial Government of Russia have consequently agreed to propose such common action to the powers as will tend to the adoption of uniform measures in order to check the anarchistic movement.

" The resolutions of the conference held at Rome in 1898, only a very small part of which has been put in practice, might serve as a basis for the projected understanding. It would be desirable that the governments, agreeably to the decisions of that conference, should agree to adopt uniform administrative measures having for their object the establishment of a rigorous surveillance of the anarchists by the creation of central bureaus in the various countries, by the exchange of information, and by international regulations relative to the expulsion of anarchists from all countries of which they are not subjects. The projected understanding should, so far as this may be possible, not confine itself to the measures above referred to, but should comprise various legislative measures tending to strengthen and complete the provisions of the penal code against the anarchists, against the combined effects of their common action, and against the subversive press. It would, furthermore, be well to introduce into legislation a more complete and precise definition of anarchistic crime in all its aspects.

" The Governments of Germany and Russia express the hope that the United States Government will not refuse to recognize the necessity of energetically resisting the development of the anarchistic movement. The representatives of the two Governments, therefore, beg the United States Government to inform them as speedily as possible whether it is disposed in principle to cooperate with the German and Russian Governments in establishing an exchange of views that may lead to common action based, either in whole or in part, upon the propositions set forth.

" In case of an affirmative reply, the details regarding the enforcing of the measures in question might be subsequently elaborated."

> Memorandum handed to the Secretary of State by the German and Russian ambassadors at Washington, Dec. 12, 1901, For. Rel. 1901, 196.

" In reply to the memorandum handed me by the ambassadors of Germany and of Russia, I am directed by the President to express his cordial sympathy with the views and the purposes therein set forth.

" The President in his message of the 3d of December earnestly recommended to the Congress that ' in the exercise of its wise discretion it should take into consideration the coming to this country of anarchists or persons professing principles hostile to all government and justifying the murder of those placed in authority.' ' Such individuals,' the President said, ' as those who not long ago gathered in open meeting to glorify the murder of King Humbert of Italy perpetrate a crime, and the law should insure their rigorous punishment. They and those like them should be kept out of this country; and if found here they should be promptly deported to the country whence they came, and far-reaching provision should be made for the punishment of those who stay. No matter calls more urgently for the wisest thought of the Congress.'

" The President further recommended that ' The Federal courts should be given jurisdiction over any man who kills or attempts to kill the President or any man who by the Constitution or by law is in line of succession for the Presidency, while the punishment for an unsuccessful attempt should be proportioned to the enormity of the offense against our institutions.' He also recommended that anarchy should be declared an offense against the law of nations through treaties among all civilized powers.

" These extracts from the President's message, it is believed, will assure all governments of civilized peoples of the President's earnest desire to adopt every practicable means to eradicate this deadly growth from our body politic. The President will be glad to adopt such administrative measures as are within his constitutional power to cooperate with other governments to this end.

" So far as concerns the legislative action which may be necessary, the large number of bills which have been introduced in both Houses of Congress during the present session sufficiently show the trend of public sentiment in the same direction. The President will take all proper means to urge upon Congress the adoption of such measures for the suppression of anarchy as may be found acceptable to the National Legislature and which may enable the Executive to act in the matter with greater effectiveness in concert with other powers."

> Memorandum sent by Mr. Hay, Dec. 16, 1901, in reply to the memorandum submitted by the German and Russian ambassadors, For. Rel. 1901, 197.
>
> See Mr. Hay, Sec. of State, to governor of New Jersey, Aug. 1, 1900, 246 MS. Dom. Let. 648.

2. INDIANS, AND OTHER MARAUDERS.

(1) INDIANS.

§ 222.

The United States and Mexico, by the treaty of April 5, 1831, fol-
Mexican frontier. lowing the example of Article V. of the treaty between the United States and Spain of October 27, 1795, agreed (Art. XXXIII.) each to use all the means in their power to preserve peace among the Indians within their borders, and to

restrain them by force from making incursions into each others' territories.

By Article XI. of the treaty of February 2, 1848, the United States, considering that much of the territory which it was acquiring was inhabited by savage tribes, who would thenceforth be under its exclusive control, agreed to restrain them, and to pass such laws as the nature of the subject might require.

Complaints by Mexico that the United States had failed to fulfill these stipulations gave rise to an acrimonious correspondence. By Article II., however, of the treaty of December 30, 1853, Mexico released the United States " from all liability on account of the obligations contained in the eleventh article of the treaty of Guadalupe Hidalgo;" and that article, and Article XXXIII. of the treaty of 1831, were declared to be abrogated. In consideration of these stipulations, and of a certain cession of territory, the United States agreed to pay to Mexico $10,000,000.

> See, as to the Indian depredation claims of Mexico against the United
> States, and their dismissal by the umpire of the mixed commission
> under the treaty of July 4, 1868, Moore, Int. Arbitrations, III. 2430.

With reference to the frequency of Indian raids from Mexico into Texas, the serious losses thereby occasioned, and the impunity of their perpetrators, the minister of the United States in Mexico was instructed in June, 1871, to say unofficially that it might become the duty of the United States " at least to weigh the expediency of pursuing the hostile Indians into Mexico, without the consent of that Government, if it shall not adopt measures toward checking the robberies referred to."

> Mr. Fish, Sec. of State, to Mr. Nelson, min. to Mexico, June 26, 1871, For.
> Rel. 1871, 644; H. Report 701, 45 Cong. 2 sess. 204. See, also, J. C. B.
> Davis, Act. Sec. of State, to Mr. Nelson, min. to Mexico, Aug. 7, 1871,
> For. Rel. 1871, 647; H. Report 701, 45 Cong. 2 sess. 204.
>
> See Mr. Mariscal, min. of for. af., to Mr. Nelson, min. to Mexico, April 23,
> 1872, For. Rel. 1872, 420–421; H. Report 701, 45 Cong. 2 sess. 211.
>
> For the second report, June 30, 1873, of the United States commissioners
> for inquiring into the depredations committed on the Texas frontier,
> see H. Ex. Doc. 257, 43 Cong. 1 sess.; H. Report 701, 45 Cong. 2
> sess. 217.

It was intimated in 1877 that, although for " a heavy pecuniary consideration " the Mexican Government had " released the United States from the obligations in respect to predatory incursions of Indians from this country into Mexico, the obligations of that Government in respect to similar marauders from that country into the United States are entire, as provided for both by public law and by treaty."[a] The Department of State, however, had previously said: " The treaty stipulations between the United States and Mexico, by which the parties engaged to restrain savages from attacking each other's possessions, were repealed by the second article of the Gadsden treaty. Still, the obligation to that end, under the law of nations, remains in full force, as it is presumed Mexico will acknowledge." [b]

June 1, 1877, orders were given to the military authorities of the United States to cross the border, if necessary, in pursuit of lawless raiders.[c] Against these orders the Mexican Government protested.[d] The United States, however, justified them as being necessary under the conditions then existing on the border.[e] February 24, 1880, the orders of June 1, 1877, were declared to be no longer operative, it appearing that the Mexican Government was then in a position to insure the full protection of life and property on the borders.[f]

For some time afterwards raids continued on both sides of the boundary.[g] July 29, 1882, an agreement was concluded providing for the reciprocal crossing of the international boundary by troops of the two countries in pursuit of savage Indians in the unpopulated and desert parts of the line.[h] This agreement was subsequently extended.[i]

Certain Papago Indians having made an attack, apparently from the United States, on the Mexican town of El Plomo, twenty-five of them were afterwards arrested in the United States by the American authorities. A complaint was entered against the four chief insti-gators of the attack, and they were held for trial, while the rest were

---

[a] Mr. Evarts, Sec. of State, to Mr. Foster, min. to Mexico, May 22, 1877; H. Ex. Doc. 13, 45 Cong. 1 sess. 12; H. Report 701, 45 Cong. 2 sess. 239.

[b] Mr. Hunter, Act. Sec. of State, to Mr. Nelson, min. to Mexico, Nov. 7, 1871, For. Rel. 1872, 350; H. Rep. 701, 45 Cong. 2 sess. 207.

[c] H. Ex. Doc. 13, 45 Cong. 1 sess. 14; H. Report 701, 45 Cong. 2 sess. 241. See supra, § 219.

[d] H. Ex. Doc. 13, 45 Cong. 1 sess. 18–28; H. Report 701, 45 Cong. 2 sess. 242–254.

[e] Mr. Evarts, Sec. of State, to Mr. Foster, min. to Mexico, Aug. 13, 1878, For. Rel. 1878, 572. See, also, Mr. Foster, min. to Mexico, to Mr. Evarts, Sec. of State, Dec. 14, 1878, For. Rel. 1879, 754; same to same, Dec. 27, 1879, For. Rel. 1880, 726.

[f] Mr. Evarts, Sec. of State, to Mr. Foster, min. to Mexico, March 1, 1880, For. Rel. 1880, 735. See, also, For. Rel. 1880, 781, and supra, § 219.

[g] For. Rel. 1881, 756, 759, 803, 817, 819, 821, 823, 826, 827, 829, 831, 833–838, 841–846; For. Rel. 1882, 388, 390.

[h] For. Rel. 1882, 396.

[i] For. Rel. 1883, 662. See, also, For. Rel. 1883, 654, 655, 657, 658, 660, 680–701. See, as to a further extension of the agreement to Nov. 1, 1886, Mr. Bayard, Sec. of State, to Mr. Jackson, min. to Mexico, Oct. 5 and 6, 1885, MS. Inst. Mexico, XXI. 382, 383; Mr. Jackson, min. to Mexico, to Mr. Bayard, Sec. of State, Oct. 17, 1885, 86 MS. Desp. from Mexico.

detained to await the orders of the Secretary of the Interior. The Department of State expressed the opinion that the Indians in question, no matter what may have been their motive, " committed an offence which was international in character, upon the assumption that the Indians, who were formerly Mexican, had become American Indians or were subject to American control;" and that it was therefore " the international duty of the United States toward Mexico to see that the Indians are properly dealt with and punished." [a]

March 21, 1867, the minister of the United States in London was instructed to propose to the British Government an **Canadian frontier.** arrangement whereby United States troops, when pursuing Indians who might have committed hostile acts within the jurisdiction of the United States, in the country lying between the Red River settlements in the east and the Rocky Mountains in the west, should be allowed to follow them for a reasonable distance in the uninhabited portions of British America. He was directed " distinctly " to " admit " that the United States did " not claim as a right that its armed forces shall in any case cross the frontier," and that the concession if made would be subject to such restraints and guarantees as to prevent any possible abuse. If the request should be declined, the United States would consider any other plan that might be proposed to secure the desired result by some other course of procedure.

> Mr. Seward, Sec. of State, to Mr. Adams, min. to England, March 21, 1867, MS. Inst. Gr. Brit. XXI, 173.

In February, 1878, the British minister at Washington communicated to the Department of State a copy of a dispatch from the Governor-General of Canada relating to the supposed intention of Sitting Bull to enter the United States for hostile purposes, and setting forth the precautions taken by the Canadian government in the matter.[b] In the following March, it being reported that Sitting Bull was near the border and camped on the British side with about 2,500 armed and hostile Indians, the facts were communicated to the British minister with an expression of the hope that all necessary precautions might be promptly taken to avert the consequences arising from the possible outbreak of an Indian war.[c] The Canadian government stated that the Indians in question were driven into Canadian territory after having been worsted by United States troops, and it was

---

[a] Mr. Day, Sec. of State, to Sec. of Interior, June 6, 1898, 229 MS. Dom. Let. 163.

[b] Sir Edward Thornton, British min., to Mr. Evarts, Sec. of State, Feb. 19, 1878, For. Rel. 1878, 344.

[c] Mr. Evarts, Sec. of State, to Sir Edward Thornton, British min., March 15, 1879, For. Rel. 1879, 488.

suggested that measures be taken to induce them " to return to their proper allegiance and their own country." [a]

> See, as to the action of H. B. M. S. *Osprey*, in cooperating with the United States authorities to prevent an Indian outbreak near Sitka, Mr. Evarts, Sec. of State, to Sir Edward Thornton, British min., April 10, 1879, For. Rel. 1879, 490 ; Sir Edward Thornton, British min., to Mr. Evarts, Sec. of State, May 15, 1879, For. Rel. 1879, 492.

It was subsequently reported that companies of hostile Indians from Sitting Bull's camp were scattered about in the Indian reservation in the northern part of Montana, driving and scattering the buffalo and other game and stealing the property of the peaceable resident Indians; that Sitting Bull himself had camped south of the boundary, but had afterwards returned with his chief lodges of warriors to British territory. Under these circumstances it was stated that the United States conceived that it had " a perfect right to regard as a menace to domestic peace and tranquillity the presence within its border of a warlike body of disaffected Indians, who have explicitly defied its jurisdiction and by their own act embraced the protection of another power;" and that, should the Government decide to compel the submission of any of those Indians appearing on the southern side of the line, " it would look upon a new recourse for asylum across the line as calling for prompt and efficient action by the British Government to repulse them, or to disarm, disable, and sequestrate them under a due responsibility for them as a component part of the territorial population of the British-American dominion." As they had sought British protection, and Her Majesty's authorities had done nothing toward denying it, " and still less toward enforcement upon them of submission to the authority of the United States, or of subjecting them to the treatment usually observed toward revolted aliens on the territory of a friendly power," the United States conceived that it was " bound now to regard the Indians of Sitting Bull's command as British Indians." If, therefore, they should make incursions of a hostile character and threaten the property, the domain, or the means of subsistence of the friendly Indian tribes in the United States, or if active military operations on the part of the United States against them should become for any cause inevitable, the hope was expressed that Her Majesty's Government would " recognize the importance of being prepared on the frontier with a sufficient force either to compel their surrender to our forces as prisoners of war, or to disarm and disable them from further hostilities, and subject them to such constraints of surveillance and subjection as will preclude any further disturbance of the peace on the

------

[a] For. Rel. 1879, 488, 490.

·frontier." [a] The Canadian government, on the other hand, renewed its suggestion that the United States should endeavor to induce the Indians to return peaceably to American jurisdiction, representing that the chief difficulty in dealing with the Indians grew out of the dimunition of the natural food supply on both sides of the line.[b] Complaint was subsequently made of an attack on Canadian Indians by Indians from the United States.[c] In the course of 1880, partly through cooperation of the officials on both sides of the line, the situation improved; but the question as to Sitting Bull and his immediate following remained pending, and the opinion was expressed that the British Government, " in the fulfillment of its obligations of neighborly comity and good will, should repel any new attempt on the part of Sitting Bull and his unsubmissive adherents to cross the border into British territory in evasion of pursuit, or should take such active and effective steps as will prevent his recrossing into the territory of the United States, and domicile him as a British Indian, under due restraint of surveillance and subjection." [d] The British minister at Washington expressed the conviction that the government of the Dominion would use its influence to the utmost to prevent predatory incursions into the United States by British Indinas. "At the same time," he said, ": the Government of the United States can fully appreciate the difficulty of preventing such incursions across so extended a frontier, for the forces of the United States were unable about four years ago to prevent Sitting Bull and his followers from crossing the frontier and taking refuge in British territory, although I am confident that this Government earnestly desired that they should not be allowed to do so." He added that the only means which the government of the Dominion had found to prevent depredations by American Indians fleeing to Canada had been by furnishing them with subsistence, which it had done at great cost; but that the Indians had

[a] Mr. Evarts, Sec. of State, to Sir Edward Thornton, British min., May 27, 1879, For. Rel. 1879, 496. See, also, Mr. F. W. Seward, Act. Sec. of State, to Sir Edward Thornton, British min., July 3, 1879, For. Rel. 1879, 500; Sir Edward Thornton, British min., to Mr. Evarts, Sec of State, July 14, 1879, For. Rel. 1879, 502; Sir Edward Thornton, Brit. min., to Mr. F. W. Seward, Act. Sec. Sept. 8, 1879, For. Rel. 1879, 508.

[b] Sir Edward Thornton, British min., to Mr. Hunter, Act. Sec. of State, Sept. 9, 1879, For. Rel. 1879, 508; Sir Edward Thornton, British min., to Mr. Evarts, Sec. of State, Sept. 30, 1879, For. Rel. 1879, 510. See, also, For. Rel. 1880, 491, 497, 498, 507.

[c] Sir Edward Thornton, British min., to Mr. Evarts, Sec. of State, Nov. 23, 1880, For. Rel. 1881, 570. See, also, For. Rel. 1881, 574, 576.

[d] Mr. Evarts, Sec. of State, to Sir Edward Thornton, British min., Feb. 5, 1881, For. Rel. 1881, 577. See, also, Mr. Blaine, Sec. of State, to Sir Edward Thornton, British min., May 10, May 14, and May 26, 1881, For. Rel. 1881, 587, 588.

also consumed a great number of buffalo, thus diminishing the supply and creating discontent among the British Indians.[a] The United States subsequently complained of the incursion of a large body of Canadian Indians into the Indian reservation in Montana for the purpose of driving away buffalo.[b] The Canadian government stated in reply that it had for many years been the habit of the Indians on both sides of the line to cross in pursuit of game, but that whenever depredations had been committed by Canadian Indians upon settlers or Indians in the United States, and the facts had been duly reported, no efforts had been spared by the government of Canada to arrest and punish the offenders; and that instructions had been sent in the present instance to the mounted police to exercise special diligence in finding out and punishing the Indians who had been guilty of the act complained of. A suggestion was renewed that concerted action should be taken by the two governments to restrain the Indians from crossing the border even in pursuit of game.[c] In 1883 a copy of the agreement with Mexico for the reciprocal pursuit of Indians across the boundary line was submitted to the Canadian government for its consideration, with a view to effecting a similar arrangement between the United States and Canada.[d] In June, 1883, a copy of certain correspondence was communicated to the British legation at Washington " as illustrating the good understanding prevailing between the American commanding officers on the frontier and the British commander at Fort Walsh, by which they are enabled to act in concert in repressing the marauding excursions of the Indians on either side of the line."[e] The Canadian government stated that it knew of no circumstances which would warrant the adoption of such an exceptional measure as the agreement between the United States and Mexico, especially in view of the improved situation along the Canadian frontier; but it was suggested that an arrangement should be made between the British and American Governments by which Indians on either side of the line should, on complaint under oath charging them with felonies or serious outrages against property, be arrested and surrendered for trial in the country where the offenses

---

[a] Sir Edward Thornton, British min., to Mr. Blaine, Sec. of State, May 27, 1881, For. Rel. 1881, 589.

[b] Mr. Blaine, Sec. of State, to Mr. Drummond, British chargé, Aug. 25, 1881, For. Rel. 1881, 593.

[c] Mr. Drummond, British chargé, to Mr. Blaine, Sec. of State, Sept. 26, 1881, For. Rel. 1881, 594–596. See, further, For. Rel. 1882, 314–316, 319–322, 323–324.

[d] Mr. Frelinghuysen, Sec. of State, to Mr. West, British min., April 17, 1883, For. Rel. 1883, 496.

[e] Mr. Frelinghuysen, Sec. of State, to Mr. West, British min., June 16, 1883, For. Rel. 1883, 503. See, further, For. Rel. 1883, 506–508, 509–526.

were committed, although such offenses might not come within the provisions of existing extradition treaties.[a]

In December, 1883, the Canadian government proposed that certain Sioux Indians, a remnant of the band of Sitting Bull, should be returned to the United States, with the understanding that they should not be punished for any offenses which they might have committed in American territory, the Indians being willing to submit and go back on those terms.[b]

This suggestion was taken into consideration, and it was afterwards submitted to the appropriate committee of Congress, the Interior Department being unable to take the suggested action till an appropriation should have been made for the care and support of the Indians in question.[c]

President Cleveland, in his annual message of December 7, 1896, said: " With the exception of delicate duties in the suppression of slight Indian disturbances along our southwestern boundary, in which the Mexican troops cooperated, and the compulsory but peaceful return, with the consent of Great Britain, of a band of Cree Indians from Montana to the British possessions, no active operations have been required of the Army during the year past."

" The Secretary of the Treasury has referred to this Department for appropriate action a letter from the collector of customs at Great Falls, Mont., enclosing a letter from United States Immigration Inspector D. J. Tallant, dated August 5 last, in which he states that most, if not all, of the Cree Indians who were returned to Canada from Montana, in 1896, in pursuance of an understanding between the Government of the United States and that of Canada, have returned to that State, where the majority of them congregate about the towns and cities, picking over the garbage barrels, begging, and stealing small articles that they can conceal, destroying fish and game, killing cattle and sheep, and in other ways injuring and annoying the people among whom they dwell.

" Mr. Tallant states that the number of these Indians is variously estimated at from five hundred to three thousand. His own estimate is from two thousand to twenty-two hundred.

---

[a] Mr. West, British min., to Mr. Frelinghuysen, Sec. of State, Aug. 5, 1883, For. Rel. 1883, 527. See, also, For. Rel. 1883, 529, 532–534.

[b] Mr. West, British min., to Mr. Frelinghuysen, Sec. of State, Dec. 12, 1883, For. Rel. 1884, 234.

[c] Mr. Frelinghuysen, Sec. of State, to Mr. West, British min., Feb. 18, 1884, For. Rel. 1884, 239.

For a report of Mr. Seward, Sec. of State, of Jan. 29, 1864, as to the proposed pursuit of Indians into the Hudson's Bay territories, see S. Ex. Doc. 13, 38 Cong. 1 sess.

See H. Ex. Doc. 237, 43 Cong. 1 sess.; H. Report 343, 44 Cong. 1 sess.; H. Mis. Doc. 37, 44 Cong. 1 sess.

" The governor of Montana, in a letter dated the 6th instant, corroborates what Mr. Tallant says, except as to numbers. He says that ' certainly not less than eight hundred or one thousand, that were removed to Canada by the War Department, several years ago, are now roaming all over Montana, living by begging and stealing.'

" I have the honor to request that you will lay these facts before the Canadian government with the request for an expression of its views as to the most practical way to make effective the understanding of 1896 for the return of these Indians to Canada."

Mr. Hay, Sec. of State, to Mr. Tower, British chargé, October 25, 1899,
MS. Notes to British Legation, XXIV. 654.

(2) OTHER MARAUDERS.

§ 223.

" The accountability of the Mexican Government for the losses sustained by citizens of the United States from the robbery and exactions committed at Guaymas, in May last, by the armed force under the command of Fortino Viscaino, seems to be unquestionable. That person was a subordinate of Placido Vega, as appears by the orders of the latter to him, dated at Teacapan the 18th of May. Those orders directed Viscaino to proceed in the vessel (meaning the *Forward*) and perpetrate the very acts complained of. The orders were fulfilled. It is true that Mr. Sisson, the United States consular agent at Mazatlan, in his letter to you of the 13th of June, represents that since the evacuation of Mexico by the French the Government of that Republic had had no other authority in the canton of Tepic, where the expedition of the *Forward* was organized and whence it proceeded, than that connived at by one Manuel Lozada, of whom Placido Vega is supposed to have been an instrument. Mr. Sisson, however, acknowledges that the General Government had appointed a collector and other officers in that quarter, but adds that they are creatures of Lozada. He also says that he had been informed by General Davalos, the commander at Mazatlan, and by Mr. Sessalveda, the inspector of the customs there, that the General Government had directed that its troops must not invade the territory of Lozada. Whether this be a fact or not, that Government, so long as it shall claim jurisdiction over that territory, must be held responsible for any injuries to citizens of the United States, there or elsewhere, by any force which may have proceeded from the same territory.

" In times of peace redress for such injuries may, in the first instance at least, be sought through the judicial tribunals of the country where they may have been committed. When, however, they are silenced or overawed by the force of arms, it seems a mockery to be referred to them, especially if there should be any ground for the charge that the Mexican Government has willfully connived at a defiance of its authority in the canton of Tepic."

> Mr. Fish, Sec. of State, to Mr. Nelson, min. to Mexico, Nov. 16, 1870, For. Rel. 1871, 607. As to depredations on cattle in Texas by armed parties coming from Mexico, see Mr. J. C. B. Davis, Act. Sec. of State, to Mr. Nelson, min. to Mexico, Sept. 6, 1871, For. Rel. 1871, 657. See, also, For. Rel. 1871, 661; For. Rel. 1872, 338, 344, 377, 383, 398, 405, 411, 412, 414, 420–421, 448–450, 456; For. Rel. 1873, I. 633, 634, 661, 666, 707.
>
> Report of the Committee of Investigation sent in 1873 by the Mexican Government to the Frontier of Texas: New York, 1875.
>
> See, also, For. Rel. 1874, 746.

" Your dispatch No. 279, of the 4th instant, relative to Mexican raids in Texas, has been received. The assurances of a disposition on the part of that Government to check them, which have been given to you by Mr. Lafragua, are satisfactory, so far as they go. Those maraudings, however, have of late been so frequent, bold, and destructive, that they have occasioned much excitement in the public on this side the river, which will probably lead to an expectation that acts on the part of that Government will show the sincerity of its professions. We are informed that a few of the raiders have been arrested on the Mexican side, and that probably they are on the way to the capital for trial. It is hoped that, if the proof should warrant their conviction, they will receive a full measure of punishment according to law, so that their fate may serve as an example for deterring imitators.

" I am aware of no purpose here of acquiring an extension of territory on that frontier. If, however, as has been suggested to us, that Government is embarrassed by the risk of desertions in sending a regular force to that quarter, it might not be indisposed to allow United States troops to cross and temporarily occupy the territory whence the raiders are in the habit of coming. The tract for such occupation might be embraced in a line drawn from Matamoras to Laredo. You will consequently sound the minister for foreign affairs on this point, and report the result.

" It may be regarded as frivolous to seek to justify the hostile incursions into our territory on the ground of retaliation for similar excursions from this side. There have been none such, and proof of the contrary is challenged. Indeed, the charge is improbable on its face, from the fact that Mexico, near the border, holds out no temptation to plunderers from this side, while the reverse is the case in respect to baits in Texas for Mexicans."

> Mr. Fish, Sec. of State, to Mr. Foster, min. to Mexico, May 20, 1875, For. Rel. 1875, II. 924. See, also, Mr. Fish to Mr. Foster, May 4, 1875, MS. Inst. Mex. XIX. 190.

For the assurances given by Mr. Lafragua, see For. Rel. 1875, II. 909, 912.

This correspondence related, particularly, to the robbery and burning of the post-office at Nueces, Texas, by marauders from Mexico. See, in addition to the two foregoing citations, For. Rel. 1875, II. 890, 891, 899, 900, 916.

As to the course of the partisans of General Lerdo, in obtaining asylum in the United States, see For. Rel. 1877, 405, 413, 416, 419, 424; For. Rel. 1878, 675–682.

See, as to other border disturbances, For. Rel. 1878, 534, 535, 536, 539, 555, 570, 580, 592, 608, 623, 664, 675–682.

As to the raids of the citizens of Ximenes, under the lead of one Areola, into Texas, the stealing of cattle, and the arrest of Areola, see For. Rel. 1878, 612, 622; For. Rel. 1879, 730, 754, 771, 773.

As to expenses incurred by Texas in repelling invasions, see message of Jan. 22, 1878, S. Ex. Doc. 19, 45 Cong. 2 sess. See, also, as to losses and claims of indemnity, H. Mis. Docs. 37 and 185, 44 Cong. 1 sess.; H. Report 343, 44 Cong. 1 sess.; H. Mis. Doc. 64, 45 Cong. 2 sess.

" The feasibility of adopting specific measures for the prevention of lawless incursions upon either side of the Rio Grande is a subject, I beg to assure you, which has not failed of earnest attention by this Government as well as by the authorities of the State of Texas and the adjacent Territories; and while any proposition for summary Government action which contemplates individual restraint for precautionary rather than penal cause must encounter objections of serious weight, such objections have no place in the established or suggested systems, which, aiming at regular defined and ascertained offenses, seek indirectly to deter from other and more grievous crime.

" Hence, upon the presentation of the subject by Mr. Romero's note of January 20 and April 11 last, the Department took means to ascertain more accurately the extent to which the purpose of preventing these too frequent expeditions was represented in the enactments governing the districts upon this side of the border, and I am gratified now to be able to communicate the general character of the information obtained.

" It has long been manifest that plunder was a principal motive for the excursions which have emanated either from Mexico or the United States, and, recognizing the impracticability of restraining completely the departure or return of evil-minded persons across a border of such considerable extent, the efforts of the legislature have been to so increase the difficulties of realizing profits from unlawfully acquired property that the attempts to obtain such property would lessen.

"Accordingly, and auxiliary to proceedings against the actual offender, the legislatures of the two Territories have made ample and exceptional provisions affecting the receivers or sellers of stolen property. In Arizona these withdraw from the possessor, though innocent, any security of title against the original owner, and if the latter follows his property with reasonable proof he can thus always recover it by judicial assistance. So, too, these statutes are particularly considerate of the safety of all live property, which is peculiarly a subject of plunder, and by heavy penalties require the branding system and guard against any but notable and formal alteration of the marks; and by many severe restrictions tend to render difficult and improbable any but open and lawful dealings in this important species of property.

" In New Mexico the larceny of a branded animal is a felony, without reference to its value, and in Arizona such offense is grand larceny, as may be that of the receivers. In neither is it considered that these and other provisions would be inapplicable in the case of property stolen in Mexico and brought across the border.

" I am uninformed as to whether the neighboring States of Mexico have enactments of equal extent, but presume that the similarity of occupations, interests, and necessity have prompted measures in this direction, and while existing facilities in this country may prove not entirely adequate to preventing the evils in question, they seem a vigorous attempt, and if individual instances under these laws were resolutely prosecuted, with the aid of those wronged, the hazard of theft should constantly increase and in that proportion would its attempts be avoided. As illustrating the readiness and desire of the people of this country to make use of any new expedient seemingly adapted to the repression of this organized plundering, I beg to refer to a letter recently submitted here from the acting governor of Arizona.

" In counseling upon the subject he remarks: ' I think a mounted police or military force should be posted in such manner as to guard the passes between the mountains on the border through which stolen cattle are driven and through which smugglers and raiding Indian bands pass to and from Mexico,' and adds that this opinion, which is shared by all intelligent men of the Territory, had expression in a bill introduced at the late session of the legislature, but too late for final action.

" Should it prove possible for the frontier States to supplement their existing laws with direct measures of the above nature, it might confidently be expected, in conjunction with a similar system in Mexico, that conditions which have so long and persistently threatened the population of both countries would be speedily and favorably affected."

> Mr. Frelinghuysen, Sec. of State, to Mr. Romero, Mex. min., Sept. 15, 1883, For. Rel. 1883, 698.
>
> See, also, Mr. Blaine, Sec. of State, to Mr. Zamacona, Mex. min., Aug. 29, 1881, For. Rel. 1881, 845.
>
> As to the duty of Mexico either to extradite or to punish the marauders, in the case of the raid on the Rio Grande City jail, see For. Rel. 1878, 534, 535, 539.

As to the reported attack of a band of armed men, said to have been organized in Arizona, on the custom-house and town hall at Nogales, State of Sonora, Mexico, see Mr. Rockhill, Act. Sec. of State, to the Attorney-General, Sept. 17, 1896, 212 MS. Dom. Let. 529, enclosing copy of a note of Mr. Romero, Mexican minister, of Aug. 27, 1896.

3. UNNEUTRAL ACTS.

§ 224.

From the supremacy and exclusiveness of the territorial jurisdiction, it follows that it is the duty of a state, within the bounds of legal responsibility, to prevent its territory and territorial waters from being used to the injury of another state. We have seen that this duty has been held to embrace the prevention of the counterfeiting of the moneys of foreign governments.[a] It also extends to the prevention of acts the performance or toleration of which the law of neutrality forbids, such as the use of territorial waters as a base of belligerent operations. The attempt to do these acts constitutes, on the other hand, a violation of the national jurisdiction, of which the offended sovereign may justly complain.

With regard to the proceeding of the Citizen Genet, French minister, in fitting out cruisers and granting military commissions in the United States, Mr. Jefferson stated that the President had reexamined the subject, and the result appeared to be that it was " the *right* of every nation to prohibit acts of sovereignty from being exercised by any other within its limits, and the *duty* of a neutral nation to prohibit such as would injure one of the warring powers;" that "the granting military commissions, within the United States, by any other authority than their own " was " an infringement on their sovereignty, and particularly so when granted to their own citizens, to lead them to commit acts contrary to the duties they owe their own country;" and that it was not doubted that the vessels which had been illegally equipped would be " permitted to give no further umbrage by their presence in the ports of the United States."

> Mr. Jefferson, Sec. of State, to Mr. Genet, French min., June 5, 1793, Am. State Papers, For. Rel. I. 150. See, also, Moore, Int. Arbitrations, I. 311 et seq.

While a neutral state is not bound to forbid its inhabitants to go abroad and enlist in the service of a foreign belligerent, yet it is not lawful for such belligerent, without the consent of the neutral government, to recruit its forces in the latter's territory, either by enlisting men there or by retaining them to go abroad and enlist.

> Cushing, At.-Gen., 1855, 7 Op. 367.

---

[a] United States *v.* Arjona, 120 U. S. 479; supra, § 23.

" One other subject of disscussion between the United States and Great Britain has grown out of the attempt, which the exigencies of the war in which she is engaged with Russia induced her to make, to draw recruits from the United States.

" It is the traditional and settled policy of the United States to maintain impartial neutrality during the wars which from time to time occur among the great powers of the world.　Performing all the duties of neutrality toward the respective belligerent states, we may reasonably expect them not to interfere with our lawful enjoyment of its benefits.　Notwithstanding the existence of such hostilities, our citizens retain the individual right to continue all their accustomed pursuits, by land or by sea, at home or abroad, subject only to such restrictions in this relation as the laws of war, the usage of nations, or special treaties may impose; and it is our sovereign right that our territory and jurisdiction shall not be invaded by either of the belligerent parties for the transit of their armies, the operations of their fleets, the levy of troops for their service, the fitting out of cruisers by or against either, or any other act or incident of war.　And these undeniable rights of neutrality, individual and national, the United States will under no circumstances surrender."

> President Pierce, annual message, December 31, 1855, Messages and Papers of the Presidents, V. 327, 331.

" In authorizing a plan of recruitment, which was to be carried out in part within our territory, the British Government seems to have forgotten that the United States had sovereign rights as well as municipal laws which were entitled to its respect.　For very obvious reasons the officers employed by Her Majesty's Government in raising recruits from the United States would, of course, be cautioned to avoid exposing themselves to the penalties prescribed by our laws, but the United States had a right to expect something more than precautions to avoid those penalties.　They had a right to expect that the Government and officers of Great Britain would regard the policy indicated by these laws, and respect our sovereign rights as an independent and friendly power."

> Mr. Marcy, Sec. of State, to Mr. Crampton, September 5, 1855, MS. Notes, Great Britain, VII. 489.

" This Government does not contest Lord Clarendon's two propositions in respect to the sovereign rights of the United States—first, that in the absence of municipal law Great Britain may enlist, hire, or engage as soldiers within the British territory persons who have left the United States for that purpose; (this proposition is, however, to be understood as not applying to persons who have been enticed away from this country by tempting offers of reward, such as commissions in the British army, high wages, liberal bounties, pensions, and portions of the royal domain, urged on them while within the United States by the officers and agents of Her Majesty's Government) ; and, secondly, no foreign power has a right to enlist and organize and train men as British soldiers within the United States. The right to do this Lord Clarendon does not claim for his Government; and whether the British officers have done so or not is, as he appears to understand the case, the only question at issue, so far as international rights are involved, between the two countries.

" In his view of the question as to the rights of territory, irrespective of municipal law, Lord Clarendon is understood to maintain that Her Majesty's Government may do anything within the United States short of enlisting and organizing and training men as soldiers for the British army with perfect respect to the sovereign rights of this country.

" This proposition is exactly the reverse of that maintained by this Government, which holds that no foreign power whatever has the right to do either of the specified acts without its consent. No foreign power can, by its agents or officers, lawfully enter the territory of another to enlist soldiers for its service or organize or train them therein, or even entice persons away in order to be enlisted without express permission."

> Mr. Marcy, Sec. of State, to Mr. Buchanan, December 28, 1855, MS. Inst. Great Britain, XVI. 419. See discussion by Sir H. L. Bulwer, 99 Quar. Rev. (June 1856) 272 et seq.

The following is part of the award of the Geneva arbitrators on September 14, 1872:

"And whereas the judicial acquittal of the *Oreto* at Nassau cannot relieve Great Britain from the responsibility incurred by her under the principles of international law: * * * the tribunal, by a majority of four voices to one, is of opinion—That Great Britain has in this case failed, by omission, to fulfill the duties prescribed in the first, in the second, and in the third of the rules established by Article VI. of the treaty of Washington."

> Papers relating to the Treaty of Washington, IV. 51–52.

" It is true that the vice-admiralty court of the Bahamas, by its judgment, which is given at page 521 of the fifth volume of the Appendix to the American Case, acquitted the *Florida* of every charge; but, while respecting the authority of the *res judicata*, I ask whether it is possible to deduce from this an argument on which to found a moral conviction that the English government is released from its responsibility under the rules laid down in Article VI of the treaty of Washington? I abstain from repeating the considerations into which my honorable colleagues who have preceded me have entered on this subject.

" It is not the question of special legal responsibility with which we have here to deal, but rather that of the responsibility which results from the principles of international law, and the moral conviction at which we have arrived in consequence of the acts imputed to the *Florida*.

" This conviction is strengthened by a consideration of the terms of the conclusion of the judgment of the vice-admiralty court, where it is said, ' that all the circumstances of the case taken together seem sufficient to justify strong suspicion that an attempt was being made to infringe that neutrality so wisely determined upon by Her Majesty's government.

" The decision of the vice-admiralty court may then be considered as conclusive, even if not perfectly correct, as between those who claimed the vessel and the British government, which claimed its confiscation under the clauses of the foreign-enlistment act; but I do not think it is sufficient to bar the claim of the United States against Great Britain. The United States were not parties to the suit; everything relating to it is for them *res inter alios actâ*."

> Count Sclopis, opinion in Geneva Tribunal, in 1872, Papers relating to the Treaty of Washington, IV. 92–93.

" The objection that the judicial decision at Nassau relieves Great Britain of all responsibility cannot be maintained. As regards the internal (or municipal) law, the judgment is valid; but as far as international law is concerned, it does not alter the position of Great Britain."

> Mr. Staempli, opinion in the Geneva Tribunal, in 1872, id. IV. 112.

The courts of the United States would have authority, in the absence of any act of Congress, to decree restitution of property captured in violation of their neutrality.

The right of adjudicating on all captures and questions of prize belongs exclusively to the courts of the nation to which the captor belongs and from which his commission issues; but if a captured vessel be brought or voluntarily comes *infra præsidia* of a neutral power, the latter may inquire whether its neutrality has been violated by the capture, and, if any violation be shown, should decree restitution.

> The Estrella, 4 Wheat. 298; La Amistad de Rues, 5 Wheat. 385.

4. UNAUTHORIZED OR COUNTERFEIT MONEY.

§ 225.

A suit was brought in England by the Emperor of Austria, as King of Hungary, for an injunction against certain persons who had manufactured a large quantity of printed paper to serve as the public paper money of the Kingdom of Hungary in order to use it when opportunity should occur for purposes hostile to the sovereign ruling power of that Kingdom.   The defendants were ordered to deliver up the paper, to be canceled, and were restrained by perpetual injunction from manufacturing such paper, the court declaring that the law of nations was part of the common law of England, and that, money being the medium of commerce, a foreign sovereign at peace with the Crown of England might, by suit in the court of chancery, protect his prerogative right of issuing coin or paper money.

> Emperor of Austria *v.* Day and Kossuth (1861), 2 Giffard, 628.
> See, particularly, United States *v.* Arjona, 120 U. S. 479, holding that the United States statute punishing the counterfeiting of foreign money is a valid exercise by Congress of its constitutional power to define and punish offences against the law of nations. This case is given supra, § 23, I. 61.

" Representations have been also made to this Department that a person has been arrested at New Orleans, upon whom a quantity of counterfeit Mexican dollars have been found, and he [the Mexican minister] has reason to believe that a manufactory of them is established at St. Louis for the purpose of exporting them to Mexico.   If you find, from the examinations, on the trial of this person, that there is any reasonable ground to suspect, you are requested to communicate with the district attorney of the United States for the State of Missouri on the subject, giving him all the information in your power to enable him to arrest the offenders under the law of the United States, if the coin counterfeited be any such as is made current by law in the United States; and, if it be of any other description, that information is given to this Department of the extent of such operations, as it is intended to propose a law, making it an offence to make or export any such base coin for the purpose of giving it currency in a foreign country."

> Mr. Livingston, Sec. of State, to Mr. Slidell, U. S. attorney at New Orleans, April 16, 1832, 25 MS. Dom. Let. 75.

The United States having brought to the attention of the Belgian Government the counterfeiting in that country of certain stamps and coins of the United States, it was found that no law existed in

Belgium for the punishment of such acts, but a *project* of a law on the subject was then introduced in the parliament.

> Mr. Tree, min. to Belgium, to Mr. Bayard, Sec. of State, March 30, 1888, and May 11, 1888, For. Rel. 1888, I. 41, 42.

5. QUESTION AS TO RUNNING WATER.

§ 226.

For a discussion of this question, in the case of the Rio Grande and the Rio Colorado, see supra, §132.

A party doing an injury in one State of the United States to a water power running into another State, may be proceeded against in civil suit in either State in which he may be served with process; though proceedings *in rem*, by way of injunction or indictment to compel abatement, can only be brought in the jurisdiction in which the nuisance exists.

> See 6 Crim. Law Mag. 169; Stillman *v.* Man. Co., 3 Wood. and M. 538; Foot *v.* Edwards, 2 Blatch. 310; Miss. and Mo. R. R. *v.* Ward, 2 Black, 485; Wooster *v.* Man. Co., 31 Me. 246; In re Eldred, 46 Wis. 530; Thayer *v.* Brooks, 17 Ohio, 489; Armendiaz *v.* Stillman, 54 Tex. 623.

April 12, 1895, the Secretary of the Interior communicated to the Department of State certain papers concerning the reported intention of a dyke company, which afterwards became known in the correspondence as the Alberta and British Columbia Exploration Company, a corporation of British Columbia, to dam Boundary Creek where it crosses the boundary line, the result of which would be the overflow and washing away of the lands and improvement of settlers in the State of Idaho. The papers were communicated to the British ambassador April 17, 1895, with a request that if on investigation the facts were found to be as stated, suitable measures might be taken to avert the threatened injury. Jan. 19, 1897, other papers were communicated to the ambassador, showing that the apprehended injury had been done; the course of the creek having been so changed as to overflow all the low-lying portion of township 65 north range, West Boise meridian, causing destruction of pasturage, hay, improvements, and cattle, and compelling settlers to abandon their homesteads. A request for an investigation was again made, in order that, if the facts were found to be as stated, prompt measures might be taken for the removal of the obstruction in the creek, and the payment of proper indemnity to those who had been injured by the proceedings of the company. The subject was again brought to the ambassador's attention June 9, 1897. It appears that the Canadian government sent an officer to make an investigation, and that for a time work on the dyke was stopped; but the company afterwards resumed operations, raising and strengthening the dyke. This condition of things was brought to the notice of the British embassy Aug. 10, 1897. The embassy, Oct. 1, 1897, stated that the authorities of British Columbia would be instructed to make full and proper inquiry into the complaint of the landowners, but that Her Majesty's Government were advised that the complainants had a right of action in the courts of British Columbia, and that they would be entitled to sue for damages and for an injunction against the continuance of the mischief. The settlers, it seems, engaged a lawyer, who found that " it was impossible to do anything for them individually, as the land damaged belonged to the United States; " and they therefore asked the United States Government to take up the matter for them in the British Columbian courts.

> Mr. Sherman, Sec. of State, to Sec. of Interior, Jan. 31, 1898, 225 MS. Dom. Let. 77.

VII. *LANDING OF SUBMARINE CABLES.*

§ 227.

" On May 4, 1897, the French ambassador submitted to your Department the application of the French Company of Telegraphic Cables (the successor of ' La Compagnie Française du Télégraphe de Paris à New-York ') for permission to land a cable supplementary to that which it has between Brest and Cape Cod, upon the same terms and conditions as those which were imposed by the President in 1879, when the original cable was landed.

Regulation of landing.

" On May 11, 1897, your Department replied to this request, saying:

" ' The present Executive does not regard himself as clothed, in the absence of legislative enactment, with the requisite authority to take any action upon the application which you present. A bill was introduced in the last Congress giving the President of the United States express authority to authorize the landing of submarine cables on the shore of the United States subject to conditions therein specified, but it failed to become a law. Until Congress shall see fit to clothe the President with power to act in matters of this kind, he will be compelled to refrain from doing so.'

" On June 4, 1897, your Department addressed a note to the French ambassador, calling his attention to the fact that it had been represented to the Department that a steamer from France had arrived at Cape Cod with the avowed purpose of laying the shore end of the new cable, and saying:

" ' It is the expectation of the Federal Government that that company (the French Cable Company) will take no steps toward laying its proposed cable from Cape Cod without express authorization of the President or of Congress, before which, as I have observed to you, a bill was introduced at the last session, but which has not yet been enacted into law. If that company should, however, take action in the manner proposed, it is proper to say that it would do so at its peril.'

" On June 5, 1897, another note was sent, informing the French ambassador of advices received to the effect that about 1,000 feet of the new French cable had been laid at Cape Cod the day before, and saying:

" ' Before taking any further action in the matter, I request that you will promptly instruct the proper authorities of the French Telegraph Company, in case the Department's information should be correct, to immediately desist from its work, pending the necessary authorization of the President or of Congress.

" The French ambassador's notes, two of the 5th and one each of the 6th and 8th of June, disclose the fact that, although the Department's notes of the 4th and 5th of June had been promptly forwarded to the company's agent, the work of landing the cable had been completed before their receipt.

" In view of the situation outlined, and the fact that Congress has not acted upon the matter, you request an official expression of my views as to the power of the President, in the absence of legislative enactment, to control the landing of foreign telegraphic cables.

" What the President can do and ought to do in the case of projected cables may possibly be ascertained from what he has done; at any rate, a recurrence to the history of the landing of certain existing cables may prove of service in considering the question you propound.

" The first cable from a foreign country landed upon the shores of the United States was one connecting the island of Cuba with the State of Florida, and was landed in 1867, under supposed authority of the act of Congress of May 5, 1866 (14 Stat., 44), granting to the International Ocean Telegraph Company, a New York corporation, the sole privilege, for fourteen years, of laying and operating telegraphic cables from the shores of Florida to Cuba, the Bahamas, and other West India islands, upon these conditions, namely, the United States to have the free use of the cable for military, naval, and diplomatic purposes; the company to keep all its lines open to the public for the daily publication of market and commercial reports and intelligence; all messages to be forwarded in the order received; no charge to exceed $3.50 for messages of ten words, and Congress to have the power to alter and determine the rates. (Forty-ninth Congress, second session, Senate Doc. No. 122, p. 63; letter of Mr. Freylinghuysen to the President, January 27, 1885.)

" In 1869 a concession was granted by the French Government to a company which proposed to lay a cable from the shores of France to the United States. One of the provisions of this concession gave to the company for a long period the exclusive right of telegraphic communication by submarine cable between France and the United States. President Grant resisted the landing of the cable unless this offensive monopoly feature should be abandoned. The French company accordingly renounced the exclusive privilege, and the President's objection was withdrawn. The cable was laid in July, 1869; it ran from Brest, France, to St. Pierre, a French island off the southern coast of Newfoundland, thence to Duxbury, Mass., and was known as the ' First French Cable.' It soon passed, however, into the control of the Anglo-American Company, controlling the cables connecting Great Britain with this continent. (Senate Doc. No. 122, pp. 63, 71.)[a]

" In a note respecting this cable, dated July 10, 1869, and addressed to the French and British ministers, Mr. Fish said:

" ' It is not doubted by this Government that the complete control of the whole subject, both of the permission and the regulation of this mode of foreign intercourse, is with the Government of the United States, and that, however suitable certain legislation on the part of a State of the Union may become, in respect to its proprietary rights, in aid of such enterprises, the entire question of the allowance or prohibition of such means of foreign intercourse, commercial and political, and of the terms and conditions and its allowance, is under the control of the Government of the United States.' (Sen. Doc. No. 122, p. 65.)

" In his annual message of December, 1875, President Grant recounts his action respecting the French cable of 1869, and says:

" ' The right to control the conditions for the laying of a cable within the jurisdictional waters of the United States, to connect our shores with those of any foreign state, pertains exclusively to the Government of the United States, under such limitations and conditions as Congress may impose. In the absence of legislation by Congress, I was unwilling, on the one hand, to yield to a foreign state the right to say that its grantees might land on our shores while it denied a similar right to our people to land on its shore; and, on the other hand, I was reluctant to deny to the great interests of the world and of civilization the facilities of such communication as were proposed. I therefore withheld any resistance to the landing of the cable, on condition that the offensive monopoly feature of

a See also H. Ex. Doc. 46, 47th Cong. 2 sess., parts 1 and 2 ; S. Ex. Doc. 51, 48th Cong. 2 sess ; 22 Stat. 173, 371.

the concession be abandoned, and that the right of any cable which may be established by authority of this Government to land upon French territory and to connect with French land lines, and enjoy all the necessary facilities or privileges incident to the use thereof upon as favorable terms as any other company, be conceded.' (Senate Doc. No. 122, p. 70.)

" After adverting to the need of new cables in order to provide competition and reduce rates, President Grant continues:

" ' As these cable-telegraph lines connect separate states, there are questions as to their organization and control which probably can be best, if not solely, settled by conventions between the respective states. In the absence, however, of international conventions on the subject, municipal legislation may secure many points which appear to me important, if not indispensable, for the protection of the public against the extortions which may result from a monopoly of the right of operating cable telegrams, or from a combination between several lines:

" 'I. No line should be allowed to land on the shores of the United States under the concession from another power which does not admit the right of any other line or lines formed in the United States to land and freely connect with and operate through its land lines.

" ' II. No line should be allowed to land on the shores of the United States which is not, by treaty stipulation with the Government from whose shores it proceeds, or by prohibition in its charter, or otherwise to the satisfaction of this Government, prohibited from consolidating or amalgamating with any other cable-telegraph line, or combining therewith for the purpose of regulating and maintaining the cost of telegraphing.

" ' III. All lines should be bound to give precedence in the transmission of the official messages of the Governments of the two countries between which it may be laid.

" ' IV. A power should be reserved to the two Governments, either conjointly or to each, as regards the messages dispatched from its shores, to fix a limit to the charges to be demanded for the transmission of messages.

" ' I present this subject to the earnest consideration of Congress.

" ' In the meantime, and unless Congress otherwise direct, I shall not oppose the landing of any telegraphic cable which complies with and assents to the points above enumerated, but will feel it my duty to prevent the landing of any which does not conform to the first and second points as stated, and which will not stipulate to concede to this Government the precedence in the transmission of its official messages, and will not enter into a satisfactory arrangement with regard to its charges.' (Senate Doc. No. 122, pp. 71-72.)

" It will be observed that President Grant rested his authority to annex conditions to the landing of a foreign cable upon his power to prevent its landing altogether, if deemed by him inimical to the interests of this Government, its people, or their business. The right to prevent carried with it the right to control.

" The Direct United States Cable Company completed its line in 1875 from Ballinskellings Bay, Ireland, to Rye Beach, New Hampshire, by way of Torbay, Nova Scotia. This cable was laid under the act of March 29, 1867 (15 Stat. 10), conferring upon the American Atlantic Cable Telegraph Company the privilege for twenty years to land a submarine telegraph cable at any place on the Atlantic coast except the coast of Florida, and to operate the same, the Government to have the preference in its use, on terms to be agreed upon between the Postmaster-General and the company, Congress reserving the right to alter, amend, or repeal the act. Application was made to the Department of State for the privilege of landing, accompanied by the voluntary assurance of the company that no amalgamation should take place with any other company for the purpose of controlling rates.

" In view of these assurances, the landing of the cable was acquiesced in by the President, Mr. Fish, in his letter to Mr. Eckert of January 2, 1877, saying:

" ' On receiving such assurances from the promoters of the company, the President decided to withold resistance to the landing of their cable.

" ' The President adheres to the views which he expressed to Congress in December, 1875, that no line should be allowed to land on the shores of the United States which is not, by prohibition in its charter, or otherwise to the satisfaction of the Government, prohibited from consolidating or amalgamating with any other cable-telegraph line, or combining therewith for the purpose of regulating and maintaining the cost of telegraphing.

" ' These views are understood to have met the approval of Congress and of the people of the United States, indicated by the tacit acquiescence of the Congress, and by the expressed approval of individual members of that body, and the general approval of the public press of the country. In the same message the President announced that the right to control the conditions for the laying of a cable within the jurisdictional waters of the United States, to connect our shores with those of any foreign state, pertains exclusively to the Government of the United States, under such limitations and conditions as Congress may impose. And he further stated that, unless Congress otherwise direct, he would feel it his duty to prevent the landing of any telegraphic cable which does not conform (among others) to the point above referred to,

" ' The President is of the opinion that the control of the United States over its jurisdictional waters extends to the right of discontinuing and preventing their use by a cable whose proprietors may violate any of the conditions on which the Government by acquiescence or silent permission allowed its landing, as well as to the resistance and prohibition of an original landing.' (Senate Doc. No. 122, pp. 11, 12.)

" The so-called ' Second French Cable ' was laid by Compagnie Française du Télégraphe de Paris à New-York in 1879, from Brest to St. Pierre, and thence to Cape Cod. The company applied, through the French minister, to your Department for permission to land the cable, and the privilege was granted upon substantially the conditions formulated in President Grant's message of 1875, Mr. Evarts, in his letter of November 10, 1879, to Mr. Outrey, saying:

" ' I have, without delay, brought the subject, together with the information conveyed by your note, to the attention of the President, and he authorizes me to say that, in view of the assurances thus received from the French Government that reciprocal privileges of landing will be granted by France to any company which may be formed by citizens of the United States upon the same terms that these privileges are granted to the present or any future company of French citizens that may apply for such landing privilege; and landing will be granted by France to any company which may be formed by citizens of the United States upon the same terms that these privileges are granted to the present or any future company of French citizens that may apply for such landing privilege: and having also received the acceptance by the directors of the " Compagnie Française du Télégraphe de Paris à New-York " of the conditions prescribed by this Government, the Executive permission of the Government of the United States will be granted to that company to land its cable at Cape Cod, in the State of Massachusetts. It is proper for me to add, however, that this Executive permission is to be accepted and understood by the company as being subject to any future action of Congress in relation to the whole subject of submarine telegraphy as explained in my note to you of the 27th ultimo.' (Senate Doc. No. 122, p. 76.)

" The Mackay-Bennett commercial cable was laid in 1884 from the coast of Europe to the United States, by permission of the President, upon substantially the conditions outlined in President Grant's message to Congress in 1875. Mr. Frelinghuysen, in his letter of December 5, 1883, describes the attitude of the Government thus:

" ' This Government regards with favorable consideration all efforts to extend the facilities for telegraphic communication between the United States and other nations, and in pursuance of this sentiment the President is desirous of extending every facility in his power to promote the laying of the cables. While there is no special statute authorizing the Executive to grant permission to land a cable on the coast of the United States, neither is there any statute prohibiting such action; and I find on examination of the records of this Department that in 1875 conditional authority was given to land a French cable at Rye Beach, N. H., and that in 1879 permission was given to land a cable at Cape Cod.

" ' These precedents seem to justify a similar concession to the promoters of the present enterprise, which there is the less hesitation in according as they are citizens of the United States.' (Senate Doc. No. 122, p. 84.)

" On October 18, 1889, the Compagnie Française du Télégraphe de Paris à New-York applied to your Department for permission to lay a cable from San Domingo to the United States. To this request Mr. Blaine replied, December 21, 1889:

" ' While the authority of the President to grant the permission you desire must be accepted subject, of course, to the future ratification by Congress, yet there are certain conditions which he regards as absolutely essential before such provisional permission can be accorded.'

" These conditions are as follows:

" ' (1) That neither the company, its successors or assigns, nor any cable with which it connects, shall receive from any foreign government exclusive privileges which would prevent the establishment and operation of a cable of an American company in the jurisdiction of such foreign government.

" ' (2) That the company shall not consolidate or amalgamate with any other line or combine therewith for the purpose of regulating rates.

" ' (3) That the charges to the Government of the United States shall not be greater than those to any other government, and the general charges shall be reasonable.

" ' (4) That the Government of the United States shall be entitled to the same or similar privileges as may by law, regulation, or agreement be granted to any other government.

" ' (5) That a citizen of the United States shall stand on the same footing as regards privileges with citizens of San Domingo.

" ' (6) That messages shall have precedence in the following order: (a) Government messages and official messages to the Government; (b) telegraphic business; (c) general business.

" ' (7) That the line shall be kept open for daily business, and all messages, in the above order, be transmitted according to the time of receipt.

" ' Conditions similar to these were required of your company in 1879 in reply to its application for authority to land one or more of its cables on the Atlantic coast of this country, and assented to by the company's order November 5, 1879. And it would seem needless to add that similar conditions have been imposed upon all cable companies desiring to land their cables from foreign countries upon the shores of the United States. It will be observed, however, that the first condition has been modified to meet a case which did not arise in 1879, of the cable for which the privilege of landing is sought being used as a link in a longer line of communication. Such a case is believed now to exist in respect to the proposed cable between the United States and San Domingo, which is understood to be only a link in a line between the United States and South America. The spirit and purpose of the first condition imposed in 1879 require that American cable companies should not now be excluded from operating and establishing lines between the United States and South America, either directly or by way of San Domingo.

" ' The President, therefore, directs me to say that if the foregoing conditions are satisfactory to your company, and it will first file in this Department a duly authenticated copy of the concession granted by the Dominican Government to land its cable at Puerto Plata, together with a like certified copy of the conditions imposed by this Government, he will be willing to grant the necessary permission to your company to land its cable at Charleston, S. C., subject to the future action of Congress.' (House of Representatives, Fifty-second Congress, first session, Report No. 964.)

" The cable company took no steps to comply with these requirements. Nearly two years later, on December 2, 1891, the French Cable Company, through its attorney, Mr. Jefferson Chandler, renewed its application for permission to land a cable. Meantime, on December 1, 1891, the company, through the same attorney, obtained from the legislature of South Carolina a joint resolution purporting to authorize it to land a cable on the coast of that State, and, in January, 1892, from the legislature of Virginia, an act purporting to authorize it to land a cable on the shore of that State. On March 10, 1892, a joint resolution was introduced into Congress to confirm these grants. This resolution was referred to a committee, of which Mr. Wise was chairman, and to him was addressed the letter of Acting Secretary Wharton of March 22, 1892, published in House Report No. 964, Fifty-second Congress, first session. After receiving this communication the committee reported a substitute granting the landing privilege upon the conditions prescribed by Mr. Blaine. Thereupon, for the time being, the attempt of the company to obtain the consent of Congress ceased.

" On June 21, 1893, the same company, through the same attorney, applied again to the Department of State, ostensibly for permission to land a cable on the shore of Virginia, but the application was accompanied by a written argument to show that the President had no power to act in the matter, the concluding paragraph of this argument and application being:

" ' I respectfully request, therefore, on behalf of the applicant, that the honorable Secretary of State will decide this application on its merits, and will declare that under the law the States may freely land cables, and that the Executive has no jurisdiction nor dispostion to prevent the landing and operation of a submarine cable from the shores of Virginia to any point permitted by the State, and that the authority of the State of Virginia to so permit cable companies to land and establish themselves on its coast is complete; and, further, that no action is required or permitted by any of the executive officers of the Government as the law now is.' (Fifty-third Congress, second session, Senate Doc. No. 14; letter to Mr. Gresham.)

" In response to this argument, Mr. Gresham, changing the attitude of the Government as established by the Presidents and their Secretaries of State from President Grant's time down, declined to act on the application, saying in his communication of August 15, 1893:

" ' There is no Federal legislation conferring authority upon the President to grant such permission, and in the absence of such legislation, Executive action of the character desired would have no binding force.' [a] (Fifty-third Congress, second session, Senate Doc. No. 14; letter of Mr. Gresham.)

" October 2, 1895, Mr. Olney addressed a letter to Mr. Scrymser, president of the Central and South American Telegraph Company, in which, in answer to his letter of September 25, 1895, he stated that La Compagnie Française des Cables Télégraphiques had not made application for permission to land its cables on the coast of the United States, and added:

" ' Furthermore, in the absence of Federal legislation conferring authority upon the Executive to grant such permission, this Department has no power to act in the matter.'

" On the 24th of October, 1895, Mr. Scrymser laid before your Department certain information concerning an agreement for laying and maintaining submarine cables between France, North America, and the Antilles, to which the Government of France was a party, and suggested that the French minister be officially informed as to the policy of the Government of the United States in the matter of cable-landing privileges on our shores. Replying to this communication, on October 28, 1895, Mr. Olney referred to his former letter, and said:

" ' There is no Federal statute conferring authority upon the Executive to grant or withhold permission to land cables on the shores of

---

[a] See, to the same effect, Mr. Gresham, Sec. of State, to Mr. Mackey, Nov. 2, 1894, 199 MS. Dom. Let. 310; Mr. Gresham, Sec. of State, to Mr. Ingersoll, April 13, 1895, 201 MS. Dom. Let. 493; Mr. Uhl, Acting Sec. of State, to Mr. Wilson, May 22, 1895, 202 MS. Dom. Let. 304.

the United States. This Department has, therefore, no power to act in the matter, and I am unable to comply with your request.'

" As a natural sequence of the attitude taken by your Department under Mr. Gresham and Mr. Olney, La Compagnie Française des Cables Télégraphiques, acting in connection with the United States and Haiti Telegraph and Cable Company and the United States and Haiti Cable Company, in 1896, landed a cable, extending from Haiti to this country, at Coney Island, New York, without permission of the Government. This Department, acting through the Attorney-General and the United States attorney, brought an injunction suit against the companies named to prevent the landing and operation of the cable, but in view of the fact that the cable had been landed, the motion for an injunction against its operation was refused. At the same time Judge Lacombe said (77 Fed. Rep. 496) :

" ' It is thought that the main proposition advanced by complainant's counsel is a sound one, and that, without the consent of the General Government, no one, alien or native, has any right to establish a physical connection between the shores of this country and that of any foreign nation. Such consent may be implied as well as expressed, and whether it shall be granted or refused is a political question, and in the absence of Congressional action would seem to fall within the province of the Executive to decide. As was intimated upon the argument, it is further thought that the Executive may effectually enforce its decision without the aid of the courts.'

" It thus appears that from 1869 to August, 1893, during the terms of Grant, Hayes, Garfield, Arthur, Cleveland (first term), and Harrison, it was held by the Presidents and their Secretaries of State that the Executive has the power, in the absence of legislation by Congress, to control the landing, and, incidentally, regulate the operation of foreign submarine cables in the protection of the interests of this Government and its citizens. Against this established rule, supported by the opinion of the only United States judge who has passed upon the question, stands opposed the refusal to act of Mr. Gresham, followed by the dictum of Mr. Olney. The attitude taken by your Department under Mr. Gresham has resulted in the landing of two foreign cables upon our shores without permission of this Government and subject to no limitations or restrictions whatever. Must this condition continue? Is the President powerless to act until Congress legislates?

" A foreign submarine cable which lands upon our shores in its location enjoys rights upon our territory, and in its operation provides a means of international communication, public and private, political and commercial.

" The jurisdiction of this nation within its own territory is necessarily exclusive and absolute. It is susceptible of no limitation not imposed by itself. (Mr. Chief Justice Marshall, The Exchange,

7 Cranch, 116, 136.)   No one has a right to land a foreign cable upon our shores and establish a physical connection between our territory and that of a foreign state without the consent of the Government of the United States.

"The preservation of our territorial integrity and the protection of our foreign interests is intrusted, in the first instance, to the President. The Constitution, established by the people of the United States as the fundamental law of the land, has conferred upon the President the executive power; has made him the commander in chief of the Army and Navy; has authorized him, by and with the consent of the Senate, to make treaties, and to appoint ambassadors, public ministers, and consuls; and has made it his duty to take care that the laws be faithfully executed. In the protection of these fundamental rights, which are based upon the Constitution and grow out of the jurisdiction of this nation over its own territory and its international rights and obligations as a distinct sovereignty, the President is not limited to the enforcement of specific acts of Congress. He takes a solemn oath to faithfully execute the office of President, and to preserve, protect, and defend the Constitution of the United States. To do this, he must preserve, protect, and defend those fundamental rights which flow from the Constitution itself and belong to the sovereignty it created. (Mr. Justice Miller, In re Neagle, 135 U. S. 1, 63, 64; Mr. Justice Field, The Chinese Exclusion Case, 130 U. S. 581, 606; Mr. Justice Gray, Fong Yue Ting v. United States, 149 U. S. 698, 711; Mr. Justice Brewer, In re Debs, 158 U. S. 564, 582.)

"The President has charge of our relations with foreign powers. It is his duty to see that, in the exchange of comities among nations, we get as much as we give. He ought not to stand by and permit a cable to land on our shores under a concession from a foreign power which does not permit our cables to land on its shores and enjoy *their* facilities equal to those accorded its cable *here*. For this reason President Grant insisted on the first point in his message of 1875.

"The President is not only the head of the diplomatic service, but commander in chief of the Army and Navy. A submarine cable is of inestimable service to the Government in communicating with its officers in the diplomatic and consular service, and in the Army and Navy when abroad. The President should, therefore, demand that the Government have precedence in the use of the line, and this was done by President Grant in the third point of his message.

"Treating a cable simply as an instrument of commerce, it is the duty of the President, pending legislation by Congress, to impose such restrictions as will forbid unjust discriminations, prevent monopolies, promote competition, and secure reasonable rates. These were the objects of the second and fourth points in President Grant's message.

" The Executive permission to land a cable is, of course, subject to subsequent Congressional action. The President's authority to control the landing of a foreign cable does not flow from his right to permit it in the sense of granting a franchise, but from his power to prohibit it should he deem it an encroachment on our rights or prejudicial to our interests. The unconditional landing of a foreign cable might be both, and therefore to be prohibited, but a landing under judicious restrictions and conditions might be neither, and therefore to be permitted in the promotion of international intercourse.

" I am of the opinion, therefore, that the President has the power, in the absence of legislative enactment, to control the landing of foreign submarine cables. He may either prevent the landing, if the rights intrusted to his care so demand, or permit it on conditions which will protect the interests of this Government and its citizens; and if a landing has been effected without the consent or against the protest of this Governmnet, respect for its rights and compliance with its terms may be enforced by applying the prohibition to the operation of the line unless the necessary conditions are accepted and observed."

> Mr. Richards, Acting Attorney-General, to Mr. Sherman, Sec. of State, Jan. 18, 1898, 22 Op. 13 ; For. Rel. 1897, 166.
> Affirmed by Griggs, At. Gen., March 25, 1899, 22 Op. 408.
> June 11, 1898, the United States and Haiti Telegraph and Cable Company, in order to secure the dismissal of the suit against it, referred to in the opinion of Acting Attorney-General Richards, supra, adopted, by its board of directors, a resolution accepting the condition to which the French company objected in 1889, viz, that neither the company, " nor any cable with which it connects," shall receive from any foreign government exclusive privileges which would prevent the establishment and operation of a cable of an American company in the jurisdiction of such foreign government. (Mr. Day, Sec. of State, to the Attorney-General, June 13, 1898, 229 MS. Dom. Let. 311. See, also, same to same, May 24, 1898, 227 MS. Dom. Let. 592.)
> See Mr. Foster, Sec. of State, to Mr. Conger, min. to Brazil, July 13, 1892, explaining the position of the United States in opposing the creation of a monopolistic line between the United States and Brazil. (For. Rel. 1892, 16.) See, also, Mr. Uhl, Act. Sec., to Mr. Thompson, April 24, 1894, MS. Inst. Brazil, XVIII. 47.
> See Mr. Partridge, min. to Venezuela, to Mr. Gresham, Sec. of State, March 10, 1893, as to a proposed line from Venezuela to the United States. (For. Rel. 1893, 720.)
> " The President has the power to grant or withhold, in his discretion, permission to land a foreign cable on the shores of the United States, and to impose whatever conditions thereon he may deem proper in the public interest, subject to whatever action Congress may take thereon." (Mr. Bayard, Sec. of State, to Mr. Scrymser, March 7, 1886, 159 MS. Dom. Let. 258.)
> See, to the same effect, Mr. Davis, Acting Sec. of State, to Mr. Thompson, Oct. 10, 1882, 144 MS. Dom. Let. 124.

> As to international telegraph lines through Central America and along the northern Pacific shores, see circular of Mr. Seward, Sec. of State, August 18, 1864, MS. Inst. Am. States, XVI. 456.

September 14, 1897, Mr. Sherman, Secretary of State, informed the British embassy at Washington that the President gave his consent to the construction by the Canadian government of a telegraphic line from the head of winter navigation on the Lynn canal, for a distance of about eighty miles across the summit of the mountains, without prejudice to the boundary or other claims of either Government, and with the reservation that the right of the United States to revoke the license at any time should be admitted.

> For. Rel. 1897, 327–329.

March 29, 1899, the German ambassador at Washington presented a petition of the German-Atlantic Telegraphic Company to land in the United States a submarine cable, in order to establish direct telegraphic communication between Germany and the United States, touching the Azores.[a]

April 10, 1899, the Department of State conveyed to the ambassador the consent of the President, which was to become operative when the company should file in the Department its formal written acceptance of certain terms and conditions.[b]

These terms and conditions, which the company accepted, its acceptance being filed under date of May 13, 1899, were as follows:

I. That neither the said company, its successors or assigns, nor any cable with which it connects shall receive from any foreign government exclusive privilege which would prevent the establishment and operation of a cable of an American company in the jurisdiction of such foreign government.

II. That the company has received no exclusive concession from any government which would exclude any other company or association which may be formed in the United States of America from obtaining a like privilege for landing its cable or cables on the shores of Germany, and connecting such cable or cables with the inland telegraphic systems of said country.

III. That the said company shall not consolidate or amalgamate with any other line or combine therewith for the purpose of regulating rates.

IV. That the company will, in the transmission of official messages, give precedence to messages from and to the Government of the United States of America and of other governments.

V. That the rates charged to the Government of the United States shall not be greater than those to any other Government, and the said rates and those charged to the general public shall never exceed the present telegraphic rates between the said countries, and shall be reasonable.

VI. That the Government of the United States shall be entitled to the same or similar privileges as may by law, regulation, or agreement be granted by said company or its successors or assigns to any other government.

---

[a] For. Rel. 1899, 310.

[b] For. Rel. 1899, 311; MS. Notes to German Leg. XII. 288.

VII. That the citizens of the United States shall stand on an equal footing as regards the transmission of messages over said company's lines with citizens or subjects of Germany or any other country with which the said cable may connect.

VIII. That messages shall have precedence in the following order:

(*a*) Government messages and official messages to the Government.

(*b*) Service messages.

(*c*) General telegraphic messages.

IX. The said line shall be kept open for daily business, and all messages, in the order above, be transmitted according to the time of receipt.

X. That no liability shall be assumed by the Government of the United States by virtue of any censorship which it may exercise over said line in the event of war or civil disturbance.

XI. That the consent hereby granted shall be subject to any future action by the Congress or by the President, affirming, revoking, or modifying, wholly or in part, the said conditions and terms on which said permission is given.

The undersigned company at the same time most respectfully begs to express its best thanks for the granting of said consent, and awaits with pleasure the final document from the Department of State.

We have, etc.,

DEUTSCH ATLANTISCHE TELEGRAPHENGESELLSCHAFT.
C. W. GUILLEAUME, *No. 36764, Rep.*

The undersigned, a notary public for the district of the royal oberlande court at Colonge, residing at Colonge-on-the-Rhine, counselor of justice, Franz Friedrich Wilhelm Goecke, hereby attests under his official seal the genuineness of the above signature, written in his presence by Carl Wilhelm Guilleaume, whose name, occupation, and place of residence are known to him. The said Carl Wilhelm Guilleaume being a merchant, residing at Cologne, and a member of the board of directors of the stock company known as the German Atlantic Telegraph Company (Deutsch Atlantische Telegraphengesellschaft), located at Cologne.

Cologne, May 15, 1899.

[L. S.]   GOECKE,
                             Royal Notary and Counselor of Justice.

The foregoing signature of the royal notary, counselor of justice, Goecke, of Cologne, is hereby authenticated. It is further certified that the notary was authorized to give the above certificate, and that the said certificate is in conformity with the legal provisions enforced here.

Cologne, May 15, 1899.

[SEAL.]   LUTZELER,
                       Chief Justice of the Provincial Court,
                       Superior Privy Counselor of Justice.

CONSULATE OF THE UNITED STATES OF AMERICA AT COLOGNE, GERMANY, *ss:*

I, John A. Barnes, consul of the United States of America at Cologne, Germany, do hereby certify that Lutzeler, whose name is subscribed to the annexed instrument of writing, was, at the time of subscribing the same, Royal Prussian president of the land court of justice, duly commissioned, and that full faith and credit are due to his acts as such.

Given under my hand and seal of office this 15th day of May, A. D. 1899.

[SEAL.]   JOHN A. BARNES,
                       Consul of the United States of America,

No. 138.

This is to certify that the foregoing document is executed and properly legalized according to the requirements of the German law.

Washington, D. C., May 26, 1899.

[SEAL.]

HOLLEBEN,
Imperial German Ambassador.

August 30, 1900, telegrams were exchanged between the German Emperor and the President of the United States on the opening of the cable.

For. Rel. 1899, 314–315

September 19, 1899, the minister of the United States at Tokyo, acting under instructions of his Government, drew attention to the desirability of direct telegraphic communication between Japan and the United States under American auspices, and stated that it would be agreeable to the United States if the Pacific Cable Company of New York should be authorized to establish cable communications between the two countries.

The Japanese Government exhibited a favorable attitude toward the project, and a draft of proposed conditions for the laying and working of the cable was informally handed to the American minister. These conditions provided that the cable should be laid within five years after the date of the Japanese concession; that the Japanese Government should grant an annual subsidy of 150,000 yen, during a term of twenty years after the opening of the cable; that the rate for private telegrams should not exceed two yen per word, and that the rate per word for Japanese Government telegrams should be half the amount collected from the general public for ordinary telegrams; that during the term of twenty years the Japanese Government should not authorize the laying of another cable between America and Japan, either with or without intermediate stations, with the reservation, however, of the right to grant a concession for another cable if it should be important to do so, and if the company, after having had an offer of the first chance to lay it, should decline to accept such offer.

For. Rel. 1899, 481–483.

VIII. *INTERNATIONAL COOPERATION.*

1. PREVENTION OF THE SLAVE TRADE.

§ 228.

As each nation's sphere of action is circumscribed by jurisdictional limits, it is obvious that there are interests common to all for the preservation of which international cooperation is essential. Such cooperation is secured by international agreements, whereby measures beyond the ordinary scope of national authority are mutually permitted and regulated.

The effort by international arrangement and concerted action to put an end to the African slave trade has formed the subject of many treaty stipulations and international regulations. An obstacle in the way of the accomplishment of this object has been the natural unwillingness to do anything that might lead to the revival of the practice of visitation and search on the high seas.

By a convention between the United States and Great Britain, signed at Washington April 7, 1862, for the suppression of the African slave trade, it was agreed, in order to facilitate the adjudication of vessels which might be detained under the treaty, to establish three mixed courts, to be composed of an equal number of individuals of the two nations, and to sit at Sierra Leone, Cape of Good Hope, and New York. The formal proposal for this convention came from the United States.[a] The members of the courts were duly appointed.[b] It was stated in March, 1868, that no vessels were known to have been condemned in the mixed courts.[c] By an additional convention of June 3, 1870, these courts were abolished. The additional convention went into effect August 10, 1870, the day on which the ratifications were exchanged, none of the courts then having any unfinished causes before it.[d]

July 2, 1890, a general act was concluded in a conference at Brussels, under which a plan of joint action in certain seas adjacent to a specified part of the coast of Africa has been put into effect. The parties to this convention are Austria-Hungary, Belgium, Denmark, France, Germany, Great Britain, Italy, the Independent State of the Kongo, the Netherlands, Persia, Portugal, Russia, Sweden and Norway, Turkey, the United States, and Zanzibar. See, infra, § 310.

---

[a] Mr. Seward, Sec. of State, to Lord Lyons, Brit. min., March 22, 1862, MS. Notes to Great Britain, IX. 140. See, also, same to same, March 26 and March 31, 1862, MS. Notes to Great Britain, IX, 144, 145.

[b] Mr. Seward, Sec. of State, to Mr. Stuart, Brit. chargé, Oct. 14, 1862, MS. Notes to Great Britain, IX. 306 ; Mr. Seward, Sec. of State, to Lord Lyons, Brit. min., July 1, 1863, X. 128 ; Mr. F. W. Seward, Assist. Sec. of State, to Mr. Haven, March 28, 1865, 68 MS. Dom. Let. 522.

[c] Mr. F. W. Seward, Act. Sec. of State, to Mr. Morgan, M. C., March 13, 1868, 78 MS. Dom. Let. 189.

[d] Mr. Fish, Sec. of State, to Mr. Boutwell, Sec. of Treasury, July 27, 1871, 90 MS. Dom. Let. 218.

RESTRICTIONS OF TRAFFIC IN FIREARMS AND LIQUOR.

§ 229.

By a note of August 11, 1884, the British minister at Washington proposed that an international understanding should be entered into for the protection of the natives of the islands of the Pacific Ocean by prohibiting the supply to them of arms, ammunition, explosives, and liquors. A similar proposal was made by Great Britain to the Governments of Austria-Hungary, France, Germany, Italy, and Russia, and subsequently Hawaii.[a] Mr. Frelinghuysen, who was then Secretary of State, replying for the United States, stated in a note of August 22, 1884, that his Government looked " with favor upon any humanitarian work, and would like more information as to the scope and form of the proposed agreement." [b] April 6, 1885, the British minister wrote that all the other governments had given a general assent to the suggestion of an international agreement, and requested an early communication of the views of the United States. Mr. Bayard, who had then become Secretary of State, replied, April 11, that, " Whilst recognizing and highly approving the moral force and general propriety of the proposed regulations, and the responsibility of conducting such traffic under proper and careful restrictions," the Government of the United States did " not feel entirely prepared to join in the international understanding proposed," and would " therefore for the present restrain its action to the employment, in the direction outlined by the suggested arrangement, of a sound discretion in permitting traffic between its own citizens in the articles referred to and the natives of the Western Pacific islands." [c]

In a note of July 4, 1892, the British legation recurred to the subject. It stated that the trade in question was already prohibited to British subjects throughout the western Pacific, and was strictly regulated in the German possessions in that region; that it was prohibited under severe penalties in the French colony of New Caledonia, and was " strictly regulated in the Navigator's [Samoan] Islands by the provisions of the final act of the Samoan Conference, to which Great Britain, Germany, and the United States " were parties; but that Her Majesty's Government continued to receive frequent representations as to the prevalence of the demoralizing traffic, showing that some more general action was required to put a stop to it entirely. A draft of the declaration was therefore submitted prohibit-

---

[a] For. Rel. 1884, 253; id. 1892, 287, 320.

[b] For. Rel. 1884, 254; id. 1892, 320.

[c] Mr. Bayard, Sec. of State, to Mr. West, Brit. min., April 11, 1885, MS. Notes to Gr. Br. XIX. 669.

ing the trade altogether. By article 5 of the draft it was provided
that any person charged with an offense against the declaration
might, if difficulty or delay was likely to arise in delivering him over
for trial to the authorities of his own country in the Pacific islands,
be tried summarily, either before a magistrate or other judicial officer
of any of the contracting powers having jurisdiction to try crimes
or offenses in a summary manner, or before the commander of a ship
of war of any of those powers. By section 11 it was stipulated that
the contracting powers would severally take measures to procure such
legislation as might be necessary to give full effect to the declaration.[a]

Mr. Foster, Secretary of State, replied:

" While the sentiments and convictions of this Government indorse
the effective restriction of deleterious commerce with the native
Pacific islanders, the method of giving expressions thereto is necessarily influenced by the disparity of policy and interests between the
United States and the great European states in the Pacific Ocean.
The disparity has become even greater since the present proposal was
first put forth in 1884.

" Nearly all of Polynesia has now passed under European jurisdiction. Were the United States a colonizing power, expanding its
jurisdiction in the same way as the other great powers among the
islands of the Western Pacific, question might legitimately arise as to
the share of responsibility that properly should fall to us in the police
control of those regions. As it is, the Government of the United
States is without colonial interest of any kind in that quarter of the
globe, and its administrative responsibilities are remotely confined
to participation in the encouragement of good government and autonomy in the Samoan group. To the colonizing or protecting powers
the question at issue becomes largely a matter of local municipal government; to the United States it is one of moral influence and cordial
cooperation within the just limits of domestic and international
rights. Although its responsibilities in the matter are not so great,
this Government is none the less interested in the humanitarian purposes of the proposed convention, and I am happy to express, by
direction of the President, his assent to its general scope, provided
paragraph 5 be so amended, with respect to American citizens, at
least, that they shall be handed over to the authorities of their own
Government when arrested for offenses against the declaration.
Were it thought to be strictly permissible under our system of government to confer criminal jurisdiction over American citizens upon
alien magistrates and officers, in practice it would not be likely to
meet with favor. . . .

---

[a] For. Rel. 1892, 287.

" It is proper that I should add that the character of the proposed declaration is such as to make its acceptance subject to the approval of the Senate, and in so far as any further legislation should be necessary in order to give it full effect, as contemplated in paragraph 11, contingent to that extent upon the future action of Congress. This Government will be glad to be advised in due time of the views upon this project of other governments whose adhesion to it has been solicited, and to give attentive consideration to the exact form which it is eventually proposed to have it take."[a]

A copy of this note was communicated by Mr. Foster, with a circular of November 18, 1892, to the diplomatic representatives of the United States at the capitals of the principal powers, in order that they might be enabled to respond to any friendly inquiries respecting the views of their governments on the subject.[b]

By an act of Congress approved February 14, 1902, it is provided that " any person subject to the authority of the United States who shall give, sell, or otherwise supply any arms, ammunition, explosive substance, intoxicating liquor, or opium to any aboriginal native of any of the Pacific islands lying within the twentieth parallel of north latitude and the fortieth parallel of south latitude and the one hundred and twentieth meridian of longitude west and one hundred and twentieth meridian of longitude east of Greenwich, not being in the possession or under the protection of any civilized power, shall be punishable by imprisonment not exceeding three months, with or without hard labor, or a fine not exceeding fifty dollars, or both." [c] Besides, any articles in the offender's possession similar to those in respect of which he was convicted may be forfeited. If opium, wine, or spirits has been given in good faith for medicinal purposes, the charge may be dismissed. Offenses against the act committed on the islands or on the waters in question are to be deemed to have been committed on a merchant vessel of the United States on the high seas and are to be subject to the jurisdiction of the United States courts accordingly.[d]

" Circumstances have prevented an earlier reply to the note you were pleased to address to the late Secretary of State on the 11th ultimo, communicating a copy of the circular dispatch of his excellency the Italian minister for foreign affairs, under date of April 20 last, touching the provisions of the general act of Brussels

---

[a] For. Rel. 1892, 320.

[b] For. Rel. 1892, 198.

[c] 32 Stat. 33.

[d] Treasury Department Circular, No. 18, Feb. 21, 1902. For a compilation of treaties and laws for the protection of native races against intoxicants and firearms, and for other documents on the same subject, see S. Doc. 200, 57 Cong. 1 sess.

of 1890 so far as the same inhibits dealing in slaves and in arms and ammunition in Ethiopia and the neighboring Italian dependencies.

" The question of the extent of the obligations incumbent upon the United States, which have no territorial interests in the regions covered by the said general act, and the steps to be taken in view thereof, has on previous occasions had the attention of this Government; and I have the honor to recite the following passage in the annual message of the President to the Congress of the United States, dated December 4, 1893:

" ' By Article XII. of the general act of Brussels signed July 2, 1890, for the suppression of the slave trade and the restriction of certain injurious commerce in the Independent State of the Congo and in the adjacent zone of central Africa, the United States and the other signatory powers agreed to adopt appropriate means for the punishment of persons selling arms and ammunition to the natives and for the confiscation of the inhibited articles. It being the plain duty of this Government to aid in suppressing the nefarious traffic, impairing, as it does, the praiseworthy and civilizing efforts now in progress in that region, I recommend that an act be passed prohibiting the sale of arms and intoxicants to natives in the regulated zone by our citizens.'

" That recommendation has not yet been acted upon by Congress.

" Prior to this suggestion by the President, the Government of Belgium addressed this Government on the subject, advancing the proposition that the provisions of Article XII. of the general act of 1890 are obligatory upon all of the signatory powers, without distinction whether they have or have not possessions or protectorates in Africa, and that they are consequently constrained to adopt the measures contemplated by said article for the punishment of persons unlawfully trafficking in arms and ammunition.

" In response to this proposition, the minister of Belgium at this capital was informed on the 6th of February, 1893, that there was then pending a proposal made by the British Government to the several powers interested in the Western Pacific and trading therewith looking to the adoption, by international accord, of measures restrictive of the traffic in spirituous liquors, firearms, and ammunition in that region; that the Government of the United States had given its assent to the principle of that proposal; that the consummation of such an arrangement with the participation of the United States would call for some general legislation by Congress regulating and penalizing such traffic when engaged in by citizens of the United States, and that in such event the needful legislation might conveniently be made broad enough to cover not only that arrangement, but generally any obligation which this Government may have under the

Brussels general act as regards similar traffic on the African continent.

" The Western Pacific project, in which our philanthropic citizens are deeply interested because concerning uncivilized regions and communities with which citizens of the United States carry on extensive trade, has not, however, as yet assumed international proportions, and no general legislation on the subject has been had.

" In the absence of appropriate statutory provisions, this Government is without judicial or other machinery to punish, in Ethiopia or any part of the African territory under Italian control or influence, infractions by American citizens of the general act of Berlin as regards traffic in firearms and ammunition. So far as is known, no commerce is carried on by citizens of the United States in those quarters, and no practical application of the considerations advanced by his excellency the minister for foreign affairs is thought to be likely."

> Mr. Olney, Sec. of State, to Baron Fava, Italian ambass., June 20, 1895, For. Rel. 1895, II. 964.
> See the note of Baron Fava, May 11, 1895, id. 960.

" I have to acknowledge the receipt of your letter of January 31st, inquiring when an international conference was held for the purpose of agreeing that no rum should be exported to African Congo; whether the United States, as reported, refused to sign such treaty; and if so was it because, as also reported, international complications were feared as a result.

" Your letter belongs to a numerous class which the Department has received from time to time for several years past, indicating unfamiliarity with the course of the Congo negotiations since 1885, and misapprehension as to the attitude of the United States in regard thereto.

" The first African conference was held at Berlin in 1884–1885, fourteen countries being represented—all European except the United States, which sent two delegates. In the opening session, November 15, the Italian delegates suggested the regulation of foreign trade in arms and liquors with the natives of the Congo and Niger basins. In the fourth session, December 1st, Great Britain adopted this proposition with reference to the transit of spirits in the lower Niger valley. This limited project was discussed in the fifth session, December 18th, and the American representative advocated general control of the liquor traffic through the whole treaty area. The Dutch, German, and French representatives all concurred in principle; but for commercial reasons the conference incorporated no restrictive measures in the general act of the 26th of February, 1885, and confined itself to a sentimental declaration of a wish that the powers might eventually find some way of reconciling the rights of commerce with the interests of humanity. Our representative protested against this declaration as being inadequate. His attitude was strongly in favor of regulation and restriction of the injurious traffic, and under date of January 26, 1885, the National Temperance Society of the United States addressed the minister a letter of thanks for advocacy of this measure by the representatives of the United States. The general act of 1885 was signed by the United States delegates as plenipotentiaries, under an erroneous impression touching their powers, their instructions having merely contemplated report of propositions to be considered by this Government. Consequently the treaty was not submitted to the Senate and the United States has not since become an adhering party to its obligations, which in several political aspects involved a departure from the established principle of nonintervention in foreign administrative concerns.

" The provisions of the general act of Berlin, being mainly political and commercial and dealing imperfectly with existing abuses injurious to the natives of the unappropriated regions of central Africa, a second conference for the purpose of dealing explicitly with the slave trade and providing international remedies, was convoked at Brussels in 1890, this Government being one of the first to respond to the invitation. The United States representative from the outset contended for practical restriction, and in some localities prohibition, of the liquor traffic and proposed an amendment to that end. Articles in that sense were incorporated in the draft of the general act agreed upon by the conference. After this had been done, Mr. Blaine insisted that the tariff regulations for the Congo and central Africa, then under discussion, should impose prohibitive duties upon spirits. This demand nearly wrecked the negotiations and, upon the United States insisting upon their position, the other powers framed a separate tariff convention which our representatives did not sign. There were consequently two general acts of Brussels, to one of which the United States became a party, while the other binds only the signatories of the general act of Berlin. The United States subsequently negotiated a special treaty with the Congo State covering questions of commerce and navigation, in which the liquor question was not the subject of stipulations between the two contracting parties, the subject having been already covered by articles 90 to 95 of the general act of July 2, 1890. That act was ratified by the United States and proclaimed April 2, 1892. A copy is enclosed for your information.

" You will thus observe that both in the conference of Berlin of 1884–85 and the conferences of Brussels, in 1890, the United States went beyond the other powers in advocating repressive measures in regard to foreign liquor traffic with the interior of Africa; that their representations were ineffectual as to the first general act of 1885, to which the United States did not become a ratifying party; and that the more effective provisions included in the general act of Brussels of 1890 were due in great measure to the initiative and insistence of this Government, although as finally adopted not fully responding to our demands."

> Mr. Olney, Sec. of State, to Editor of The Voice, February 10, 1896, 207 MS. Dom. Let. 625.

By a convention between various powers, including the United States, signed at Brussels, June 8, 1899, and proclaimed by the President of the United States, February 6, 1901, provision is made for the regulation of the importation of spirituous liquors into certain regions of Africa. It is recited in the preamble that the contracting parties wish to provide for the execution of article 92 of the general act of Brussels of July 2, 1890, which prescribed the revision of the regulations concerning the importation of spirituous liquors into the regions in question.

3. GENEVA AND HAGUE CONVENTIONS.

§ 230.

Another international arrangement, benevolent in its object, is that which was concluded at Geneva in 1864, for the amelioration of the condition of the wounded in the field. Substantially all civilized powers have become parties to this convention, which provides for protection to ambulances and military hospitals, and to those employed in and about them, and for succor to the wounded, and contains various stipulations designed to secure the ends of humanity. Additional articles, adopted at the conference at Geneva in 1868, for the purpose of extending the advantages of the convention to naval forces, have not become internationally effective, but they were provisionally adopted by the United States and Spain as a modus vivendi during the war in 1898.

Certainly one of the most striking examples of an effort to accomplish objects of philanthropy by international action is that afforded by the Congress at the Hague in 1899, whose acts in relation to the pacific settlement of international disputes and the laws and rules of war are given elsewhere in this work.

4. RULES OF NAVIGATION.

§ 231.

By an act of Congress approved July 9, 1888, the President was authorized to invite all maritime nations to send delegates to confer at Washington upon the practicability of devising uniform rules and regulations for the greater security of life and property at sea.[a]

---

[a] President Cleveland, annual message, Dec. 3, 1888.

The conference met in Washington in the autumn of 1889, twenty-six nations being represented.[a] Rules were adopted for the prevention of collisions at sea,[b] and by an act of Congress of August 19, 1890, they were adopted by the United States, subject to the action of the other powers. Protracted negotiations ensued, and, with certain modifications, the rules were put into operation July 1, 1897.[c]

5. PROTECTION OF SUBMARINE CABLES.

§ 232.

Protection of cables.
" The President thinks the present moment favorable for the negotiation of a joint convention by the maritime powers of the world for the protection of submarine cables.

" The United States have peculiar interest in fostering the construction of these indispensable avenues of intelligence, and in protecting them against wanton injury. Its domains extend from ocean to ocean, and its commerce plies at regular intervals alike from the ports of the Atlantic and of the Pacific to the ports of Europe and of Asia. Its citizens on the shores of both oceans are in constant communication with each other across the continent both by rail and the telegraph. This central position in the commerce of the world entitles the United States to initiate this movement for the common benefit of the commerce and civilization of all.

" The features which the President desires to incorporate into the proposed convention are:

" 1st. Suitable provisions for the protection of such cable lines in time of peace and war against wilful or wanton destruction or injury. We have seen, during the present year, the submarine cable connecting Cuba with the United States severed, and communication through it interrupted. The President proposes to prevent similar destruction and injury hereafter by a joint declaration that such acts shall be deemed to be acts of piracy and punished as such.

" 2d. Suitable provisions to encourage the future construction of such lines. Experience has already shown that the assumption, by one nation, to control the connections with the shores of another, will lead to complications that may, unless arranged, result in preventing all direct telegraphic communication between the two countries. The President deems that this can be best prevented in the future, by providing that hereafter no exclusive concession shall be made, without

---

[a] President Harrison, annual message, Dec. 3, 1889.

[b] S. Ex. Doc. 75, 53 Cong. 3 sess.

[c] See acts of May 28, 1894, and Feb. 23, 1895; see, also, For. Rel. 1894, 217, 219, 261, 262–270, 270–275; For. Rel. 1895, I. 683–686; report of Mr. Olney, Sec. of State, to the President, Dec. 7, 1896, For. Rel. 1896, lxxiv.

the joint action of the two governments whose shores are to be connected. In this way the capital of both countries will be enlisted, and at the same time possible causes of difference will be removed.

" 3d. Provisions against scrutiny of messages by government officials. The President thinks that the right to establish such a scrutiny in favor of the power controlling either end of the cable is calculated to lead to trouble, and had therefore better be prevented.

" A draft of a convention embodying these points has been prepared and is herewith enclosed. It will be understood, however, that this is submitted simply as a basis for future discussion, should the leading powers concur with the United States in considering the subject one for international consideration and jurisdiction.

" The President desires that the representatives at Washington of Great Britain, France, Portugal, Spain, Italy, North Germany, Austria, Russia, Belgium, Holland, Sweden and Norway, Denmark, Turkey, Greece, Venezuela, Brazil, the Argentine Confederation, Colombia, Bolivia, Peru, Ecuador, Mexico and Chile, may be empowered to enter jointly and simultaneously into negotiations with the United States, and with each other with a view of concluding a joint convention for the purpose hereinbefore referred to, and instructions identical with these are issued to the representative of the United States at each of those powers. You will upon the receipt of this, propose to the cabinet of Great Britain to give to its minister at Washington, powers to enter into such negotiations with the United States and with the representatives of such other powers as may be empowered for that purpose, and to conclude with them such a joint convention, and you are at liberty, in your discretion, to furnish to the minister for foreign affairs a copy of these instructions and their enclosure."

Mr. Fish, Sec. of State, to Mr. Motley, min. to England, Nov. 23, 1869, MS. Inst. Great Britain, XXII. 122.

The same instruction was sent, mutatis mutandis, to other diplomatic representatives of the United States. (Circulars, I. 376.)

See Mr. Fish, Sec. of State, to Mr. Bancroft, min. to Germany, March 17, 1870, acknowledging the latter's dispatches, Nos. 67 and 68, of Feb. 14, communicating the views of the North German Union. (MS. Inst. Prussia, XV. 111.)

As to the cutting of the cable connecting Cuba with the United States, see Mr. Fish, Sec. of State, to Mr. Sanford, Oct. 13, 1869, enclosing copy of a letter of the Secretary of War of Oct. 9, 1869, together with a copy of a communication from the United States military commander at Key West, of Oct. 8, 1869, stating that one of the cables seemed " to have been ruptured in some way beyond four (4) miles out." (82 MS. Dom. Let. 194 ; MS. Misc. Let., Oct. 8, 1869.)

" Afford such protection as may be in your power to American interests in cable at Chorillos and land line thence to Lima said to be threatened, and if disregarded enter protest." (Mr. Frelinghuysen, Sec. of

State, to Mr. Phelps, min. to Peru, tel., Aug. 9, 1884, MS. Inst. Peru, XVII. 67.)

Mr. Bayard, Secretary of State, in a letter to Mr. Scrymser, March 16, 1885, stated that instructions had been sent to the United States legation in Guatemala holding that Republic responsible for injuries done by its authority or with its connivance to cables or other interests of United States citizens in Central America, and that the U. S. S. Wachusett, thence en route to La Union, would be duly instructed. (154 MS. Dom. Let. 489.)

Mr. Blaine, Sec. of State, in a telegram to Mr. Hicks, min. to Peru, Jan. 10, 1891, stated that the Central and South American Telegraph Co. represented that the extension of its cable from Chorillos southward to Iquique and Valparaiso, under concessions guaranteed by the Governments of Peru and Chile, was obstructed by the municipal authorities of Chorillos, who forbade the company to connect its north and south cables by a land line, although it was authorized to do so by its national concessions. Mr. Hicks was directed to see the minister of foreign affairs and " discreetly represent importance of completion of cable as a means of international communication." (MS. Inst. Peru, XVII. 446.) The difficulty was amicably adjusted, the company's agent in Peru expressing his appreciation of the legation's good offices. (Mr. Blaine, Sec. of State, to Mr. Hicks, min. to Peru, March 10, 1891, MS. Inst. Peru, XVII. 459, acknowledging receipt of Mr. Hicks's No. 226, of Feb. 13, 1891.)

Subsequently, in consequence of the civil war in Chile, the company was prevented by the Congressional party, who occupied Iquique, from working the cable south of that point, at which it touched. (For. Rel. 1891, 144.) Under these circumstances the company, which was desirous of securing a concession for a line overland from Valparaiso to Argentina, arranged with the Balmaceda government, which was anxious to open communication to the north, to cut the cable and join the ends off Iquique in the open sea. July 10, 1891, Mr. C. H. Baker, superintendent of the company, wrote to Admiral McCann, U. S. S. *Baltimore*, saying: " I am directed by the Government of Washington, through my President, to inform you of any interference that may take place during cable operations outside of territorial waters." (H. Ex. Doc. 91, 52 Cong. 1 sess. 276.) This letter evidently referred to the following telegram: " If your repair ship being under flag of United States is interfered with in doing work on cable outside of territorial waters of Chile, report fully to Admiral McCann at Callao." (Tel. of Department of State to Mr. Scrymser, pres. of Central and South American Telegraph Co., July 9, 1891, quoted in Mr. Wharton, Act. Sec. of State, to Mr. Scrymser, Oct. 21, 1891, 183 MS. Dom. Let. 601.) It seems that the connection was made by the company's repair steamer *Relay* under the protection of the U. S. S. *Baltimore*, on or about July 20, 1891. (See H. Ex. Doc. 91, 52 Cong. 1 sess. 276–278, and Mr. Wharton, Act. Sec. of State, to Mr. Scrymser, Oct. 21, 1891, 183 MS. Dom. Let. 601.) In his special message to Congress of Jan. 25, 1892, President Harrison mentioned " the cable incident " as one of the probable causes of the feeling which led to the attack upon the sailors of the Baltimore at Valparaiso. It seems that the Congressional authorities received an erroneous impression to the effect that the company was constrained to act and join its cable outside Iquique by an arrangement between the Government of the United States and the Balmaceda government. (Mr. Wharton, Oct. 21, 1891, 183 MS. Dom. Let. 601; same to same, Nov. 7, 1891, 184 id. 55.)

For a request that "such special privileges as may be permissible" might be granted to the Central and South American Telegraph Co.'s repair steamer Relay in the ports of Chile, Colombia, Ecuador, Mexico, Nicaragua, Peru, and Salvador, see instructions of May 6, 1891, H. Ex. Doc. 91, 52 Cong. 1 sess. 31; For. Rel. 1891, 120.

See Mr. Gresham, Sec. of State, to Mr. McKenzie, min. to Peru, Sept. 25, 1894, expressing gratification that he had succeeded in securing such privileges in the ports of that country. (MS. Inst. Peru, XVII. 629, referring to Mr. McKenzie's No. 155, of Sept. 3, 1894.)

The subject of the international protection of submarine cables was considered at various European conferences, and at length, on March 14, 1884, a convention was signed at Paris by the representatives of twenty-five powers, including the United States, for the protection outside territorial waters of all legally established submarine cables landed in the territories of one or more of the contracting parties. The ratifications of seventeen of the signatory powers were exchanged at Paris April 16, 1885. By a protocol signed at Paris July 7, 1887, it was agreed that the convention should go into effect May 1, 1888. By an act of Congress approved February 29, 1888, the United States adopted legislation for carrying the convention into effect.

Mr. Bayard, Sec. of State, to Mr. McLane, min. to France, March 1, 1888, For. Rel. 1888, I. 518.

For the text of the convention, see Treaties and Conventions between the United States and Other Powers (1776–1887), 1176–1185.

Article XV. of the convention of March 14, 1884, reads: " It is understood that the stipulations of this Convention shall in no wise affect the liberty of action of belligerents."

It appears that during the Franco-German war, the war between Chile and Peru, and the civil war in Chile cables were cut both within the territorial waters of the belligerents and in waters outside those limits. The same thing took place in the war between the United States and Spain, in which the United States exercised the right of cutting cables connecting the Spanish West Indies and the Philippines with the outer world. The right was exercised in this instance both within and outside of territorial waters.

See an article entitled " Submarine Telegraph Cables in Time of War," by Commander C. H. Stockton, U. S. N., Proceedings of the United States Naval Institute, XXV. 452. Commander Stockton cites Dr. Macdonell, Journal Royal United Service Institute, No. 246, p. 916; Perels, Manuel de Droit Maritime International, pp. 75, 77, 217; Fiore, Nouveau Droit International Public, 22; Owen's Declaration of War, 182, 382; Ferguson, Manual of Int. Law, secs. 123, 124.

See, also, " Submarine Telegraph Cables in Their International Relations," being lectures delivered at the Naval War College, Newport,

Aug., 1901, by George Grafton Wilson, Ph. D. (Washington: Government Printing Office, 1901).

Also, Naval Operations of the War with Spain, 176, 186, 208, 209, 210, 211, 244, 255; and International Situations, Naval War College, 1901, pp. 177–178.

See, further, Mr. Blaine, Sec. of State, to Mr. Pacheco, min. to Cent. Am., Feb. 20, 1891, For. Rel. 1891, 57.

"I have found occasion to approach the Argentine Government with a view to removing differences of rate charges imposed upon the cables of an American corporation in the transmission between Buenos Aires and the cities of Uruguay and Brazil of through messages passing from and to the United States. Although the matter is complicated by exclusive concessions by Uruguay and Brazil to foreign companies, there is strong hope that a good understanding will be reached and that the important channels of commercial communication between the United States and the Atlantic cities of South America may be freed from an almost prohibitory discrimination.

"In this relation, I may be permitted to express my sense of the fitness of an international agreement whereby the interchange of messages over connecting cables may be regulated on a fair basis of uniformity. The world has seen the postal system developed from a congeries of independent and exclusive services into a well-ordered union, of which all countries enjoy the manifold benefits. It would be strange were the nations not in time brought to realize that modern civilization, which owes so much of its progress to the annihilation of space by the electric force, demands that this all-important means of communication be a heritage of all peoples, to be administered and regulated in their common behoof. A step in this direction was taken when the International Convention of 1884 for the protection of submarine cables was signed, and the day is, I trust, not far distant when this medium for the transmission of thought from land to land may be brought within the domain of international concert as completely as is the material carriage of commerce and correspondence upon the face of the waters that divide them."

President McKinley, annual message, Dec. 5, 1898. (For. Rel. 1898, lxviii.)

See Mr. Adee, Act. Sec. of State, to Mr. Scrymser, Nov. 1, 1897, 222 MS. Dom. Let. 132.

See, also, Mr. Bayard, Sec. of State, to Mr. Scrymser, July 7, 1885, and Feb. 25, 1886, 156 MS. Dom. Let. 193; 159 id. 162.

6. OTHER SUBJECTS OF COOPERATION.

§ 233.

The results of international cooperation for the preservation of rights of property are illustrated in the conventions establishing an international union for the protection of industrial property in various conventions and agreements for the protection of copyrights, and in the convention for the protection of submarine cables outside of territorial waters.

Numerous conventions have been entered into in recent times for the regulation of the fisheries on the high seas, both in respect of food fishes and of fur-bearing animals whose habitat is the sea.

International monetary conferences were held at Paris in 1867 and 1878, and at Brussels in 1892.

Conferences looking to the abolition of sugar bounties were held at London in 1887 and at Brussels in 1900.[a]

The several conferences of American States, including the two international American conferences, have sought to regulate various matters falling within the domain of private as well as of public international law.

Various unofficial bodies, international in membership, exist for the accomplishment of similar objects. Among such bodies may be mentioned Institut de Droit International and the International Law Association, formally styled the Association for the Reform and Codification of the Law of Nations.

IX. *MARRIAGE.*

1. AS AN INSTITUTION.

§ 234.

Marriage is something more than a contract; it is an institution, and as understood in Christendom may be defined as " the voluntary union for life of one man and one woman, to the exclusion of all others."

> Lord Penzance, Hyde *v.* Hyde and Woodmansee (1866), L. R. 1 P. and D. 130, 133.
> See Studies in Private International Law, by Émile Stocquart, D. C. L., Avocat à la Cour d'Appel de Bruxelles: Bruxelles, 1900. This

---

[a]As to a Russian proposal for the international regulation of the price of wheat, see Mr. Hay, Sec. of State, to Mr. Stevens, M. C., Oct. 9, 1900, 248 MS. Dom. Let. 287.

interesting and learned monograph is chiefly devoted to the subject of marriage, which is discussed with reference to the law in Spain, France, Belgium, Holland, Italy, Germany, Austria, Hungary, and Switzerland. It also includes disquisitions on divorce under the French law, and the new code of the German Empire. Some or all of the papers embraced in the monograph may be found in French in Clunet's Journal du Droit Int. Privé, and other journals.

See, also, Stocquart's Le Marriage en Droit Ecossais, Journal du Droit Int. Privé, 1902, pp. 746, 988.

On June 12, 1902, three conventions were signed at The Hague, by plenipotentiaries of Austria, Belgium, France, Germany, Hungary, Italy, Luxemburg, the Netherlands, Portugal, Roumania, Sweden, and Switzerland, and were afterwards ratified by all the signatories except Austria and Hungary, Portugal, and Sweden, for the purpose of regulating (1) differences in the laws of marriage, (2) differences in the laws of divorce and separation, and (3) the guardianship of minors.

For an English version of the conventions, see For. Rel. 1904, 526 et seq.

See, also, as to these conventions, Mitteilungen der Internationalen Vereinigung für vergleichende Rechtwissenschaft und Volkswirtschaftslehre, Oct. 1902, 53–55, 55–60.

For reports on the laws of marriage and divorce in various countries, see Parliamentary Papers, Miscellaneous No. 2 (1894), and Miscellaneous No. 2 (1903).

Since it is requisite to a valid marriage, viewed as an institution of civilization, that the union should be "exclusive and for life," the Department of State held that cohabitation of a citizen of the United States with a Samoan woman "fa'a Samoa" was not a sufficient contract of marriage, it appearing, by a consular report of 1874, that, according to the custom of the country, men practiced polygamy, although when a new wife was taken it was usual to send back the first one to her people.

With regard to this ruling, the consul-general of the United States at Apia stated that in recent years polygamy had "steadily decreased," so that "consensual marriages exclusive and for life" were "far more common" than "the marriages purely fa'a Samoa, which were polygamous alliances;" and that this change had "necessarily affected the customs of foreigners who have native wives."

The Department replied that the question was "not one of the intention of the parties in this regard. It is whether by the law of the place the union is compulsory and not at the will of the parties. If by the Samoan law or custom a man and woman who cohabit with the intention of living together in exclusive union for life may, nevertheless, at any time freely separate and treat the union as at an end, the law or custom which permits this does not constitute such a marriage as is recognized by the laws of this country. Whatever may be the intention of the parties, such a union is, from a legal point of view, merely cohabitation at will and not of that permanent and exclusive character which American law demands."

> Mr. Rives, Assist. Sec. of State, to Mr. Sewall, cons. gen. at Apia, April 26 and July 19, 1888, S. Ex. Doc. 31, 50 Cong. 2d sess. 55, 102. See Mr. Sewall to Mr. Rives, June 18, 1888, id. 88.

The question of the existence of a marriage between members of an Indian tribe is to be determined by the laws and customs of the tribe.

> Earl v. Godley, 42 Minn. 361, 44 N. W. 254.

Where an Indian woman, then in the city of Chihuahua, Mexico, did not wish to return to her husband in the United States, it was stated that if they were married according to the laws of the United States the husband " could demand his wife through the medium of the courts of Mexico."

> Mr. Bayard, Sec. of State, to Mr. Endicott, Sec. of War, June 5, 1886, 160 MS. Dom. Let. 409, enclosing copy of dispatch No. 232, May 26, 1886, from the chargé d'affaires *ad interim* at Mexico.

2. MATRIMONIAL CAPACITY.

§ 235.

"As a general rule, matrimonial capacity is determined by the law of the place of domicil of the party in question."

> Section 180, Instructions to the Diplomatic Officers of the United States, 1897.
>
> Wharton, in his Int. Law Digest, § 263, says: "Three distinct theories have been advanced as to the law which is to determine matrimonial capacity. The first is the law of the place of solemnization. This undoubtedly holds good as to merely formal conditions, but cannot be regarded as having force when appealed to in a state where the competency of the parties rests on grounds of morality or public policy. The second is that of the law of the domicil of the parties, to which the same objection would apply, while to both of these tests the objection of uncertainty extends. (See Whart. Confl. of Laws, § 164.) A third, and better theory, is that which maintains the prevalence in such cases of the national policy of the country in which the parties assert their marital rights. No civilized nation will regard persons living within its borders as married when by its laws or policy the union is incestuous, polygamous, or otherwise immoral or antagonistic to national policy. (See Reynolds v. U. S., 98 U. S., 145; Whart. Confl. of Laws, §§ 131, 165.)"

Wharton, referring to his treatise on the Conflict of Laws, § 169 et seq., suggests: " Immigrants marrying at a port of embarkation, in view of settling in the United States, may be so far regarded as domi-

ciled in that one of the United States to which they are bound as to
bring them under the shelter of local laws which make marriages solemnized in accordance with the law of the domicil valid."

See Wharton's Int. Law Digest, II. 734, § 261.

Where persons, domiciled in a particular State, contracted a marriage on an American vessel, on the high seas, with a view to evade
the laws of the State to which they immediately returned and in which
they continued to reside, it was held that the validity of the marriage
must be determined by the State laws.

Norman v. Norman (Cal.), 54 Pac. Rep. 143.

3. SOLEMNIZATION.

(1) CONSENSUAL MARRIAGES.

§ 236.

By the common law in the United States, no particular ceremony
is requisite to the validity of a marriage; but the relation is established by the present agreement of the parties to be man and wife.
Such, it has been held, was the law of the Spanish as well as the
English colonies in America. Cohabitation is but one of the many
incidents of the marriage relation; it is not essential to it. The
declarations and the admissions of the parties, and the fact that they
lived together as husband and wife, and held themselves out to the
world as such, are all circumstances from which the existence of marriage may be inferred.

Murphy v. Ramsey, 114 U. S. 42; Miles v. United States, 103 U. S. 304;
    Meistar v. Moore, 96 U. S. 76; Blackburn v. Crawford, 3 Wall. 175;
    Hallett v. Collins, 10 Howard, 174; Patterson v. Gaines, 6 Howard,
    550; Hutchins v. Collins, 31 Mich. 126; Caryolle v. Ferrie, 26 Barb.
    177; Rose v. Clark, 8 Paige, 574; Com. v. Stump, 53 Pa. St. 132;
    Case v. Case, 17 Cal. 598; United States v. Simpson, 4 Utah, 277;
    Wharton, Confl. of Laws, §§ 171–174; W. B. Lawrence, 11 Alb. Law
    J. 33.

By the common law of the United States, and apart from special
rules adopted by individual States, " consensual marriages are valid."

Mr. Rives, Assist. Sec. of State, to Mr. Sewall, consul gen. at Apia, April
    26, 1888, S. Ex. Doc. 31, 50 Cong. 2 sess. 55.

(2) LAW OF PLACE GENERALLY GOVERNS.

§ 237.

" Marriages are frequently celebrated in one country in a manner not lawful or valid in another; but did anybody ever doubt that marriages are valid all over the civilized world, if valid in the country in which they took place? "

Opinions of Mr. Webster.

> Mr. Webster, Sec. of State, to Lord Ashburton, Brit. plenipo., Aug. 1, 1842, Webster's Works, VI. 303, 307–308.

" I transmit a copy of a letter, under date the 20th inst., addressed to the Department by Mr. J. B. Sutherland, of Philadelphia, requesting the interposition of the Government for the purpose of preventing the forcible separation of Doctor Grayson M. Prevost from his wife, a Mexican lady to whom he was married at Brownsville, in Texas, and with whom he is now residing at Zacatecas, in Mexico. It is presumed that the Mexican ecclesiastical authorities found their proceedings upon the fact that the clergyman to whom the parties applied at Matamoras refused to perform the ceremony, and that, as they repaired to Brownsville and were married there in consequence of that refusal, the marriage was illegal according to the Mexican laws, and therefore that the church authorities have a right and are under the obligation to annul it and separate the parties. It appears that Dr. Prevost had himself addressed a letter to you upon the subject, and it is hoped that it will have reached you in season to enable you to prevent the result which he apprehended. It may be that the local clergymen concerned have proceeded in conformity to the laws of the Republic and the rules of the Catholic Church as established in Mexico, and therefore that any official application to the Mexican Executive would be premature, if not improper. The case, however, seems to be so urgent and the execution by the priests at Zacatecas of their threats would so certainly excite bad feeling in the United States, that it is deemed advisable for you to hold direct communication upon the subject with the head of the church at the City of Mexico. You will accordingly request him to instruct the subordinate clergymen in Zacatecas to suspend and if possible discontinue their proceedings, and express a hope that the rules of the church may be so altered as to prevent a recurrence of such cases. From the proximity of the two countries the intercourse between them and the likelihood of frequent intermarriages between their respective citizens, it is desirable that the rule upon this subject should be uniform in the United States and in Mexico. In this country, in England, and in most nations on the continent of Europe, a marriage is valid if it has been contracted according to the laws of the place where the ceremony was performed. This may be said to be the almost universal rule. It has been firmly established in England after elaborate discussion and investigation. In one of the principal cases upon the subject, the opinion of the celebrated Spanish jurist Sanchez, in favor of the rule, seems to have been much relied upon. His words are quoted below and ought certainly to be respected by the Mexican church. You may refer the Mexican archbishop to the passage and also to the character of Sanchez and of his treatise '*de matrimonio*,' expressed by Pope Clement VIII., also quoted below. Marriages between Protestants and Catholics are frequent in this country. Although the clergy of that persuasion may in general suppose that this may in some degree conflict with the welfare of their church, it is believed that they seldom if ever seriously oppose such marriages, though some of them may object to perform the ceremony if a Protestant clergyman is also to have an agency therein. It is an unquestionable fact, however, that many marriages take place between Catholics and Protestants in which the ceremony is performed by clergymen of both denominations. Although all Christian sects are equal before the law in this country, it is believed that the Catholics themselves do not object to this. Offices of honor and trust are open [in the United States] to them [Catholics] equally with Protestants, although the latter constitute a large majority of the population. The fact that the Chief Justice of the United States is a Catholic, is a signal instance of this. If the Mexican clergy or the Government and people of that country should not be prepared to adopt the system of religious toleration which prevails in the United States, it is hoped that they will relax the rule which forbids a priest from marrying a Protestant to a Catholic and makes it obligatory upon the clerical and other authorities to disavow and annul such marriage when it has taken place in the United States. In your communications with the archbishop upon this topic, you will be frank and conciliatory, and you will particularly endeavor to avoid leaving an impression that we desire anything inconsistent with the prosperity or even substantial supremacy of his church in Mexico. On the contrary, we are actuated by the belief that, if the rule is rigidly enforced there, it will tend to produce an excitement in this country hazardous to its peace and perhaps prejudicial to the interests of Catholics in the United States."

Mr. Webster, Sec. of State, to Mr. Letcher, min. to Mexico, Jan. 29, 1851, MS. Inst. Mex. XVI. 244.

The general principle in the United States is that the validity of a marriage is to be determined by the law of the place where it is celebrated. But there is an exception to this rule, when parties are sojourning in a foreign country where the law is such that it is impossible for them to contract a marriage under it. Such is the case, where, as in some foreign countries, the local law recognizes a marriage as valid when contracted according to the law of domicile, and where the law of the country goes with the parties, as in the case of an invading army and its followers.

Opinion of Mr. Cushing.

> Cushing, At.-Gen. (1854), 7 Op. 18.

"The general rule of our law in this particular, as stated in the opinion of the Attorney-General of the United States of November 4, 1854, is to ascribe validity to marriages when they are valid at the place of celebration. According to the laws of some of the States of the United States, as you are no doubt aware, the ceremony of marriage can not be legally performed unless certain requirements, the obtaining of a license, etc., shall have been duly fulfilled. But these laws, of course, have no effect outside of the jurisdiction of the respective States in which they exist, and I am not aware that the laws of any State of the United States render the consent of its authorities previously obtained necessary to establish the validity of a marriage of one of its citizens celebrated in a foreign country."

Opinion of Mr. Cass.

> Mr. Cass, Sec. of State, to Mr. Hülsemann, Austrian chargé d'affaires, Feb. 2, 1860, MS. Notes to Austria, VII. 104.

"Your despatch of the 8th of August last (No. 395) transmitting copies of your correspondence with Mr. Goundie, consul of the United States at Zurich, respecting the marriage of Mr. Wislicemus, was duly received at this Department, and I have now to communicate to you such remarks upon the subject as appear to me to be called for. . . .

"I suppose that upon principles of general legislation the validity of a marriage, or of any other contract, depends upon the law of the place where such marriage or other contract is entered into. And I suppose also that if there is no special legislation to the contrary the effect of such marriage is legally the same in every country as if celebrated therein. But the validity of a marriage and the consequences to result from it to persons or property are very different questions and depend upon different principles. It is competent for every nation to provide by its own laws that marriages, wherever they take place, unless celebrated in a particular manner, or under particular circumstances, shall be ineffectual to secure to parties claiming under them the rights they would have been entitled to had no such disabling legislation existed.

" This is a subject of internal policy, wholly dependent upon local considerations. But the validity of the marriage itself is quite another matter which can not justly be thus dealt with. Not only is it binding upon the parties *in foro conscientiæ*, but it is beyond the reach of any rightful legislation.

" Exceptions may be found in the exercise of a power in some countries to regulate the condition of the marriage of their citizens abroad, but it finds no support in the institutions of the United States. The degree of consanguinity, the necessary age, the parental assent, and other personal circumstances are questions not to be determined by home legislation, but by the laws of the country where the parties are found; and there can be no doubt but that the mutual declaration of marriage, which is recognized as sufficient by the law of Scotland, would, if made in that country, be considered as obligatory in this. Nor that a marriage, when either of the parties was a French citizen and under the age of twenty-five years, the age prescribed by the law of France within which a marriage can not be contracted without the consent of the father or mother, if living, would be adjudged by our courts to be valid, if celebrated in either of the States of this Union, agreeably to its laws.

" But there is another point connected with this subject and arising out of our peculiar form of government, which is too important to be overlooked, and that is, Where does the authority exist which possesses the power to legislate upon the subject of marriage? There is a want of precision in portions of Mr. Goundie's correspondence which, if not adverted to, might lead to erroneous conclusions. The laws of the United States respecting marriage are spoken of as though the whole question was to be determined by the laws of the General Government. This is a grave error. Congress has nothing to do with the validity or effect of marriages, nor with the marriage contract indeed, except in places subject to its exclusive jurisdiction. These are questions which in the several States are regulated by their respective laws, each exercising the power within its own boundaries. When, therefore, the enquiry is made in Europe how a marriage must be celebrated there, not only to be valid but to carry with it its proper rights in the United States, no general answer can be given to the question. The answer must embrace not only the provisions of the laws of the United States, so far as regards the places governed by those laws, but must embrace also the laws of thirty-three States, besides five Territories. It is obvious that a satisfactory reply, under such circumstances, is a subject which may present some difficulty, and our foreign ministers and consuls should be cautious respecting the information they give, lest unfortunate consequences might result to the parties seeking it."

> Mr. Cass, Sec. of State, to Mr. Fay, min. to Switzerland, Nov. 12, 1860, MS. Inst. Switz. I. 85.

Opinions of Mr. Fish. " Our law regards every marriage as valid if valid at the place where it was contracted, and would not even deem it invalid in the United States if it was celebrated in accordance with the few and simple requisites of our law, though it lacked some of the formalities which are made essential by the law of the place where the marriage took place."

> Mr. Fish, Sec. of State, to Mr. Jay, min. to Austria-Hungary, July 27, 1871, MS. Inst. Austria, II. 29.
>
> Wharton comments upon this statement as follows : " This extension of the rule can not now be sustained. A marriage which is invalid from defect of form in the place of solemnization is invalid everywhere, unless (1) the local law adopts in such cases the *lex domicilii*, or (2) the form omitted was one the parties could not conscientiously adopt, or (3) it was impossible of adoption, or (4) the marriage was solemnized in a barbarous or semicivilized land." (2 Wharton's Int. Law Dig. 734, § 261.)

" You are believed to be mistaken in saying that the 48th section of the new instructions of the Department expresses doubt as to whether marriage can be legally celebrated at all between citizens of the United States in a foreign country, unless it be solemnized in conformity with the laws of such country. Your mistake upon this point will, it is believed, be clear to you upon a further examination of the paragraph referred to. The Department has been careful not to express an opinion as to the validity of any marriage under particular circumstances. Its object has been merely to warn, so as to lessen, as far as might be practicable, the peril of contracting a marriage which in any case might be declared to be invalid. It is not the province of an executive department to decide the question.

" The provisions of our act of 1860 upon the subject of marriages abroad are not supposed to have been influenced by the legislation of any other country. They are understood to have been in the main designed to correct a practice which prevailed at some points of marriages by consuls without reference to the local law. . . .

" The competency of this Government to provide generally for the marriage of citizens of the United States abroad has not been called in question, nor has any opinion upon that point been expressed.

" You seem to have overlooked section 24 of the act of Congress of the 18th of August, 1856, which confers upon secretaries of legation authority to act as notaries in certain cases.

" When the consequences of marriage in respect to property in possession, or which may be acquired by gift, purchase, or inheritance

to the offspring of the parties, or to the peace of mind or good name
of the latter, are duly considered, the weight of the responsibility
which an officer of this Government abroad may incur by in any way
countenancing a rash contract of that kind may become apparent."

> Mr. Fish, Sec. of State, to Mr. Marsh, min. to Italy, Jan. 19, 1875, For.
> Rel. 1875, II. 761, 762.   See also Mr. Fish to Mr. Washburn, Nov. 14,
> 1874, For. Rel. 1875, I. 445.
> See Mr. Marsh to Mr. Fish, Oct. 12, 1874, For. Rel. 1875. II. 755.

Wharton, citing his Conflict of Laws, § 180, says " Persons domiciled in a State in which certain formalities of marriage are prescribed
can marry without such formalities in another jurisdiction where no
such formalities are exacted, unless in such jurisdiction the forms of
the place of domicil are held to be obligatory."

> Wharton's Int. Law Dig., II. 743.

"The conclusion, which cannot be too strongly impressed, is that
when a marriage is solemnized by citizens of the
Opinions of Mr. Bayard. United States in a foreign civilized country, the form
of solemnization must be in accordance with that pre-
scribed by the local civil law.   If the mode of solemnization is good
by this law, it is good everywhere; if it is bad by this law, it is bad in
all countries which do not specially validate it by statute.   It is true
that there are certain exceptions to this rule, in respect to local forms
which are oppressive or which are impossible, or which militate
against the rational religious convictions of the parties; but these
exceptions are so rare that it is not necessary here to notice them, or
to regard them as in any way diminishing the force of the rule that
the mode of solemnization must be in accordance with the law of the
place of solemnization.

" It is true, also, that in some European countries the law is that it
is sufficient to validate the marriages of foreigners within their boundaries that the law of the domicil of the parties be observed.   But
this is only an application of the rule that the law of the place of
solemnization must in such cases be supreme.   When it says, ' You
can follow the law of your domicil,' it gives effect to the law of such
domicil only because it itself chooses so to ordain.

" In conclusion, the importance of the maintenance in this respect
of the supremacy of the law of the place of solemnization cannot be
too highly estimated, nor can our consular and diplomatic representatives impress too strongly this rule upon those who come to them for
advice.   Any variation from this rule may lead to the annulling of
marriages entered into in good faith, and in the bastardizing of the
issue of such marriages.

" It is proper to add that the object of this instruction is not to
determine as to the validity of any particular marriages that have

taken place or may hereafter take place. Questions of this class are for the judicial tribunals. The function of this Department is simply to instruct its diplomatic representatives in civilized countries what advice to give citizens of the United States applying to them for information as to the proper mode of solemnizing marriages, and the answer must be that the ceremonial prescribed by the law of the place of the ceremony must be adopted. They should also be advised that the act of Congress above referred to cannot operate outside of the District of Columbia and the Territories, and that even to persons domiciled in the latter jurisdictions it is a matter of doubt, which can only be settled in each case by judicial decision, whether the act would be regarded by foreign courts as changing, so far as concerns their action, the rule of international law above stated."

> Mr. Bayard, Sec. of State, to Mr. Winchester, Aug. 15, 1885; For. Rel. 1885, 807, 808–809.

" It is a principle of international law that the law of the place of solemnization shall, whenever this is practicable, determine the mode of solemnization. When consuls are requested to act as official witnesses of marriages, they should see that the requirements of the law of the place of celebration have been, as far as practicable, complied with. It is not intended, however, in these instructions, in any way to question or modify the principle of international law that, while the form of solemnizing marriage is determined ordinarily by the law of the place of solemnization, exceptions are recognized: (*a*) When it is impossible to use such form; (*b*) when it is repugnant to the religious convictions of the parties; (*c*) when it is not imposed on foreigners by the sovereign prescribing it; (*d*) when the ceremony is performed in a non-Christian or semicivilized country."

Standing instructions.

> 7 Op. At. Gen., 18.

" In Massachusetts, where the ceremony must be performed by a licensed minister or a justice of the peace, a statute has been adopted validating marriages before foreign consuls and in foreign legations. This may be the case with other States.

" Solemnization by a clergyman or magistrate is not necessary to the validity of the marriage in most jurisdictions in this country."

> Sec. 421, Consular Regulations of the United States, 1896; section 179, Instructions to the Diplomatic Officers of the United States, 1897.
>
> The instructions to Diplomatic Agents of the United States, 1885, stated that the Massachusetts statute validated marriages "by a consul or diplomatic agent of the United States." This evidently is what is meant by the phrase "before foreign consuls and in foreign legations," in the instructions of 1897. The Massachusetts

statute obviously was not intended to validate marriages by the consuls and in the legations of foreign powers in the United States, which are the only "foreign consuls" and "foreign legations" known to our law.

Mr. Hay, Secretary of State, in a letter to the governor of Hawaii of Dec. 27, 1900, speaks of "the well-known principle that a marriage valid at the place of celebration is valid everywhere." (249 MS. Dom. Let. 665.)

In 1872 the United States consul at Rio de Janeiro reported that W.,

Marriage on a man-of-war. who claimed to be an American citizen, and who desired to contract a marriage, had sought advice as to the proper course to be taken. The consul suggested that the ceremony be performed by a certain American Protestant clergyman, then residing at Rio de Janeiro, who was authorized by the laws of Brazil to solemnize marriages, W. having expressed a preference for a minister of that faith. W., however, did not follow the consul's advice, but was married on board the U. S. S. *Lancaster*, then in Brazilian waters, by the chaplain of the ship. W. invited the consul to be present, but the consul declined, and he also refused to give a consular certificate of the marriage. The Department of State said that it could not give its "unqualified sanction" to the consul's course. As the *Lancaster*, being a national ship of war, was "in contemplation of international law United States territory," the marriage was "constructively" solemnized within the United States; and a marriage solemnized by the chaplain, he being "a priest or minister of the gospel," would "be recognized as valid in all the States of the United States." Under such circumstances it might be held that a consular certificate was unnecessary, and that the consul could not be required to be present and give it; but, as the consul "should make himself as useful as he can to his fellow-citizens without giving offence to the government which gives him his exequatur," [a] it "would be proper for the consul (in Christian countries) to give to American citizens desirous to contract marriage, and against whose marriage no reason exists, especially if they be such as would be authorized to marry if residing in the District of Columbia, the benefit of his presence and his certificate when they desire to have the marriage solemnized on board of a national ship of the United States, lying at the time within his consular jurisdiction, if that marriage is to be solemnized by a chaplain in the Navy of the United States, being a priest or minister of the gospel." In such case the certificate need not state that the person solemnizing the marriage was authorized to perform such ceremonies by the laws of the country from which the consul received his exequatur. "It should state the name and character of the vessel, . . . where she is lying at the time, and, if the consul adds to the name

---

[a] Consular Regulations, 1870, p. 303.

of the chaplain his official designation, the certificate would carry on its face the evidence of authority by which the party performed the ceremony. Should the marriage be performed at the consulate or elsewhere on shore, it must be solemnized by a person authorized by the laws of the country to perform the ceremony, and the consul's certificate must so state."

> Mr. Fish, Sec. of State, to Mr. Hinds, consul at Rio de Janeiro, Nov. 19, 1872, 71 MS. Disp. to Consuls, 102.
>
> In the course of the instruction, Mr. Fish says : " Your dispatch is silent as to the nationality of the bride; it is not, however, deemed material."
>
> It is evident that the instruction ascribes to the principle of "extraterritoriality" very extensive effects. It is true that a man-of-war enjoys exemption from the ordinary jurisdiction of foreign courts, but it by no means follows that the local law is inoperative as to all acts done on board by persons not belonging to the ship. A diplomatic residence is exempt from the ordinary processes of the local courts, but it is well settled that acts done within it by persons not entitled to diplomatic privileges are subject to the operation of the local law, no matter what may be the nationality of such persons. In considering the exemption which is accorded, under the title of "extraterritoriality," to persons, places, or things, it is necessary always to bear in mind the distinction between freedom from the operation of the local law and the exercise of jurisdiction in derogation of that law. The admitted purpose of the extraterritoriality of men-of-war is to prevent national objects from being defeated by foreign interference with the nation's armed forces. (Marshall, C. J., Schooner Exchange v. McFaddon, 7 Cranch, 116.) Evidently, it is not essential to this design that all transactions on board, even between persons residing within the local jurisdiction, should be withdrawn from the cognizance of the local sovereign. As to marriage, it involves questions of capacity as well as of ceremony ; and it has repeatedly been laid down by the Department of State that matrimonial capacity is governed by the law of the domicil of the parties. Moreover, the object to be attained is, if possible, to secure a marriage that shall be recognized as valid everywhere, and not merely in the United States.

(3) QUESTION OF EXTRATERRITORIALITY.

§ 238.

" The rule as to prevalence of local forms does not apply to non-Christian or semi-civilized countries where consular courts are established. In those countries the consular officer will have to determine, so far as concerns persons domiciled in the District of Columbia or in the Territories, whether the parties would be authorized to marry if residing in the District of Columbia or in one of the Territories. His duty, so far as concerns persons domiciled in a State, is to inquire whether they are authorized to marry in such State."

Section 181, Instructions to Diplomatic Officers of the United States, 1897. The printed personal Instructions to the Diplomatic Agents of the United States, 1885, contained, in addition to the foregoing, the following: "It is held, also, in respect to a Consular Officer *in such countries* that the right to perform marriage is incident to the judicial office, and consequently that he may solemnize the ceremony if it is the wish of the parties that he should do so. It is deemed preferable, however, in such cases, where there is a duly qualified minister of a religious denomination whose services can be obtained, that the ceremony should be performed by him, and that the Consular Officer should confine himself to granting the certificate before mentioned." By section 417 of the Consular Regulations of 1896, however, consuls are " forbidden to solemnize marriages in any case."

" Your dispatch No. 110 under date of 19th August has been received.

" It is necessary to bring to your attention that you have misconceived the meaning of the word ' exterritoriality ' as used in paragraph 278 of the Consular Regulations.

" The consulate at Carlsruhe has never had and cannot have ' the privilege of exterritoriality ' in the sense in which that phrase is used in that paragraph of the Consular Regulations. The character of exterritoriality to which allusion is there made attaches only to some of our consulates in what are sometimes called semicivilized countries where it follows from express provisions of treaty, or in others where it follows from the custom of the native inhabitants in their dealings with foreigners of Christain countries.

" The custom of solemnizing marriages in the consulate at Carlsruhe does not give to the consulate the character of exterritoriality; nor does the circumstance mentioned in your dispatch, that during the war some courtesies were extended to the consulate of a character similar to those sometimes granted to diplomatic rather than consular agents, operate to give you any other powers with regard to marriages than those lawfully attaching to the office of *consul*, which is the office you hold by the commission of the President. Even if you were commissioned as a diplomatic agent, it is at least doubtful whether the ' fiction of exterritoriality,' as it is styled by Wheaton, would give you the right to solemnize marriages, or to give validity to marriages by your presence at the ceremony, unless authorized to do so by the laws of Baden or Germany.

" Without pursuing a subject which, as Mr. Dana remarks in his note to Wheaton, ' has been obscured by the use of the phrase " extraterritoriality," ' it gives me pleasure to add that the particular circumstances of the marriage of 18 November 1870, now for the first time reported to the Department, and the fact stated in your dispatch that the marriage of that date ' was subsequently referred to the Badish judicial authorities and pronounced valid ' go very far to relieve the apprehensions of the Department with regard to your part in those proceedings. You have moreover now supplied your previous omission to transmit to the Department a certificate of the marriage, as required by paragraph 276 of the Consular Regulations, a provision which it is of the utmost importance that consuls should not neglect.

" While your dispatch is to this degree satisfactory, it would be wrong to leave you under the impression that you may safely continue the practice or custom which you report has grown up at your consulate with reference to solemnizing or witnessing marriages, unless it can be made clearly to appear that this practice is authorized by the laws of the country in which you reside. Paragraph 23 of the Consular Regulations must no longer be understood as superseding in any respect the positive provisions of Article XXI."

> Mr. Hale, Act. Sec. of State, to Mr. Young, consul at Carlsruhe, Sept. 14, 1872, 68 MS. Disp. to Consuls, 104.
>
> Par. 23 of the Consular Regulations of 1870, above referred to, directed consuls to claim all the rights and privileges which had been allowed to their predecessors, unless they had been withdrawn by formal notice; and also all the immunities allowed to the consuls of other countries, unless in the case of extraordinary immunities secured by special treaty stipulations. Art. XXI. related to marriage and various other subjects, the subject of marriage being embraced in paragraphs 275–278.

" By the common law of Christendom, brought with them to this country by its European colonists and built upon as the basis of its political institutions, it is essential to

China.

marriage that it should be a ' voluntary union for life of one man and one woman to the exclusion of all others;' and it is by such marriages alone that the family is constituted as an integer of the State. Such being the case, it is not within the province of this Department to admit extraterritorial validity for any foreign legislation which does not give a similar definition, and make such exclusiveness an essential element of marriage.

" The Department, therefore, can not regard the status of citizens of the United States, though resident in China, as in any way affected by such legislation; and if by the Chinese law controlling marriage such exclusiveness, as it is generally understood, is not imposed, this Department cannot take any steps toward recognizing as marriages such sexual unions as are based on such polygamous law. At the same time the Department will interpose no objection to police regulations requiring notice to Chinese authorities of all consensual marriages in China of citizens of the United States.

" It is proper to add that the matrimonial status of a person who is a citizen of and domiciled in a particular State of the American

Union is determinable by the law of such State and not by the laws of
the Federal Government of the United States."

Memorandum, communicated by Mr. Bayard, Sec. of State, to Count Arco,
German min., Aug. 17, 1888, For. Rel. 1888, I. 683–684.

" I have the honor to report that the question of the issuing of
marriage certificates by diplomatic officers abroad has finally reached
China.

" The Department has always most correctly recognized questions
relating to the validity of marriages as being of grave importance.   I
therefore report for your information the latest phase of this question
which has arisen here.

" Mr. J. B. Thompson is a missionary of the American board, located in Shensi.   He is a subject of Great Britain, born in Newfoundland.   He made a contract of marriage with Miss Vetter, who is a
citizen of the United States, having her home in the State of Missouri.
She is a missionary of the same society.   Some weeks ago Mr. Thompson arrived here from Shensi.   Miss Vetter also arrived a few days
ago from the United States.   The parties desire to return to their
station before the winter sets in.   They are anxious for an immediate
marriage.

" Under the British statutes a delay of thirty days' residence in
China is necessary.   Banns are also to be published twenty-one days
before the marriage can be solemnized by a consul.   Some officials
contend that the time may run concurrently.   My opinion is that the
thirty days must expire before publication of the banns.   For the
reasons stated the parties wish to escape the delay.

" Under the direction of Her British Majesty's minister a marriage
under certain circumstances can take place at the British legation
without delay.

" Mr. Thompson consulted me.   I represented to him that for the
tranquillity and safety of the lady the marriage should take place at
the British legation.   Under the statutes of Great Britain a marriage
solemnized at a legation of that country is valid everywhere in the
Queen's dominions.

" I did not myself doubt that such a marriage would be held valid
in the United States; but I did doubt whether the marriage of a male
British subject to an American woman at the United States consulate
would be held valid in Great Britain.

"At all events, in a matter of such grave importance I desired to be
on the safe side, and would therefore in no manner intervene to assist
the parties to be married by or before the American consul unless the
marriage were to be followed by another marriage between the same
parties at the British legation and according to British law.

" I advised him to apply to Sir John Walsham for permission to be married at the British legation.   Sir John promptly replied verbally that he would direct the marriage to be solemnized at the British chapel if I, as minister of the United States, would certify that the mixed marriage which it is proposed to celebrate at the British legation, will, of itself and without any preliminary or other ceremony be recognized as legal and binding in the United States.

" In an interview with Sir John, in which the whole matter was discussed, I showed him your circular (No. 699, F. R. 1887, p. 1133). This satisfied him that I had no authority to issue such a certificate. But I suggested to him that if his Government insisted on a certificate from me and my Government ordered me not to issue such a certificate, the marriage was evidently blocked and prevented, and we should pursue our investigations further, in the hope that we could find a solution of the difficulty.

" I proposed to him that the parties should first be married before the American consul, and afterwards at his legation, if that were possible.   After further consideration an agreement was arrived at. . . .

" If the American consul shall perform the marriage ceremony between those persons I shall certainly ' recognize ' the validity of the marriage.   The marriage at the English legation will follow, and I am entirely certain that the double marriage will be firm and effectual in the United States and Great Britain, and I believe everywhere in all the world.

" This understanding between Sir John Walsham and myself makes this marriage possible, and does not, in my opinion, in any wise controvert the principles enunciated in the circular cited.

" There is a vast difference between ' recognizing ' the validity of a marriage had before an American consul and giving the certificate which is prohibited in Foreign Relations, 1887, page 1133.   The prohibited certificate goes to the validity of the marriage which is solemnized in a foreign jurisdiction, and not to the validity of marriages solemnized before our own consuls.   I give no certificate whatever. The consul furnishes the usual marriage certificate, Form No. 87, Consular Regulations, 1888.   On the faith of that certificate and of my verbal statement, recognizing the validity of the consular marriage only, the second marriage ceremony will be performed in the British legation according to British law.

" I trust that this solution of a grave difficulty, which has made two lovers happy, will be approved by both the governments which are interested therein.

" It may not be inappropriate to submit a few observations on the general subject as affecting China.

" You have repeatedly enunciated the general doctrine to be that
the *lex loci* governs questions involving the validity of marriage.
You have, however, in your memorandum attached to your dispatch
to me, No. 343, of August 18, 1888, limited this principle to the laws
of those countries which recognize monogamous marriages, and not
polygamous marriages. It is apparent, therefore, that the *lex loci* in
China can not have any controlling effect, because polygamous marriages are recognized as valid here.

" The doctrine of ex-territoriality under which, except as to real
estate, the laws of each nationality accompany its citizens or subjects
in China, also tends to do away with the effect of the local law marriage laws, as far as foreigners are concerned.

" For reasons, therefore, more influential in China than in Europe, it
is proper to substitute for a marriage governed by a '*lex loci*,' a form
of marriage recognized as binding in the United States. It is to be
remarked further that, as far at least as I can find, there is nothing in
the Consular Regulations relating to mixed marriages. Under section 383, Consular Regulations, 1888, marriages between persons
domiciled in the Territories or the District of Columbia, are authorized. Under section 386 persons domiciled in any State may be married by the consul, if the State laws are complied with.

" Compliance in China with bare legal forms, as required by State
laws, is clearly impossible. Licenses can not be procured; banns can
not be published. There is little difficulty in holding that the penalties imposed for failure to comply with these statutory requisites do
not affect the validity of marriages in China. Nor is there any
trouble in holding that a consul who may lawfully unite in marriage
two Americans, may also lawfully unite in marriage one American
and one foreigner. The American is bound by the laws of his country, the foreigner by his voluntary submission to the laws then and
there complied with, and by his civil contract. I do not doubt that,
generally, in the States of the Union, this conclusion of law would be
arrived at. But it can not be claimed that the binding force of such
marriages would be universally sustained in other countries.

" It seems to be important that, so far as possible, these questions should be set at rest by instructions to representatives of the
Government abroad. A regulation defining the power of consuls to
solemnize marriage, where the contracting parties are an American
and a foreigner, would greatly simplify the subject. Until some such
regulation is formulated I shall, out of abundance of caution, in cases
of mixed marriages, adhere to the decision herein reported,—unless
disapproved by you,—that two marriage ceremonies be performed—
one before the American and one before the foreign consul.

" Should, in this particular case, there be other delays or obstacles, I will report them."

Mr. Denby, min. to China, to Mr. Bayard, Sec. of State, Oct. 19, 1888, For. Rel. 1889, 75.

" I have to acknowledge the receipt of your dispatch No. 737, of October 19, 1888, which has been considered with the care and interest which its importance and the ability shown in it call for. In it you state that a marriage being in contemplation in China between Mr. J. B. Thompson, a subject of Great Britain, and Miss Vetter, a citizen of the United States, both missionaries of the American board of commissioners of foreign missions, and it appearing desirable that the marriage should be celebrated at the chapel of the British legation at Peking, you were informed by the British minister that in order, in case of a mixed marriage, to enable the ceremony to be there performed, it would be requisite for you, as minister of the United States, to certify that the mixed marriage in question so proposed to be celebrated at the British legation ' will of itself, and without any preliminary or other ceremony, be recognized as legal and binding in the United States.' This certificate you inform me, you declined to give. Your action in this respect was proper and is approved.

" You proceed in your dispatch to refer to recent instructions from the British foreign office, a fair construction of which you state to be, that ' the British minister may allow a mixed marriage to be solemnized at the legation, if a form of marriage that is recognized as legal and binding by the law of the nation to which the foreigner belongs has previously taken place; in which event the certificate above referred to is dispensed with, and a " recognition " of the validity of the previous marriage by the officials of the foreigner's nation is all that is required.'

" You then state that ' if the American consul shall perform the marriage ceremony between these persons I shall certainly " recognize " the validity of the marriage.'

" I am at a loss to understand why you should use the term ' perform the ceremony ' in connection with the consul. The act of Congress of June 22, 1860, refers only to marriages in the presence of a consul; and it affects, as you have already been instructed, only persons domiciled in the District of Columbia or the Territories. If, however, you should ' recognize ' as valid consensual marriages in China, such marriages being exclusive sexual unions for life, you would be acting in conformity with the great body of juridical authority in the United States. This, I presume, is what you virtually proposed to do.

" The marriage to which you refer was to be unquestionably of the class stated, and while to make it valid it is not necessary that the ceremony should be performed by the consul, yet the fact that the consul is able to attest the fact that the marriage took place will add to the solemnity of the proof by which it is hereafter to be sustained. If the consul's ' officiating ' at the ceremony tends to relieve any difficulties as to the future British solemnization, there is no reason why he should not so officiate; and though neither under the act of Congress nor by the principles of international law is his officiating essential, yet you would be right as a matter of abundant caution to approve of his taking this course.

" You are entirely correct in saying that it is the position of this Department that the rule of the ubiquity of the *lex loci celebrationis* in marriage applies only to countries in which marriages are by law monogamous. But great difficulties lie in the way of compliance with your suggestion that instructions should be issued by this Department ' defining the power of consuls to solemnize marriage where the contracting parties are an American and a foreigner.' To this I have to reply that the marriage of citizens of particular States being, under the Constitution of the United States, exclusively under the control of the States in which they are domiciled, no act of Congress and, *a fortiori*, no instruction of this Department can operate to effect such marriage. That the British foreign office has taken the ground that legislation of this character, even when it rests on the alleged extra-territoriality of embassies in which such marriages are solemnized, has not necessarily any effect on the subjects of foreign states, you correctly state; and the cases to which you refer in which in France and Switzerland the ubiquitous validity of such ceremonies had been denied have been already brought to the notice of this Department. The attitude assumed in France and Switzerland towards British legislation of this character bears equally on similar legislation or diplomatic regulation coming from the United States. For the Department to advise marriages which might thus be declared invalid would be to expose citizens of the United States to peril in the most sacred as well as the most important relations.

" You will remember, also, that the difficulties which beset questions of this class do not relate merely to the marriage ceremonial. They involve the question of matrimonial capacity; as, for instance, whether to the validity of a marriage family consent is essential. On this topic there is a conflict between local jurisprudences which it is not within the province of this Department to determine. By the common law of Christendom, brought with them to this country by its European settlers, want of family consent did not by itself invalidate a marriage, however much it might expose the parties concerned in the marriage to ecclesiastical censure. But since the time when this common law was thus accepted in this country as the basis of our system several leading European Governments have made family consent essential to the validity of the marriage of minors; and by the Governments this disability is held to adhere to their minor subjects wherever they may travel. As to the disability attached to a prior marriage alleged to have been dissolved by divorce, the diversity of legislation is even greater, and the permanency of disabilities of this class has been maintained with peculiar rigor by those sovereigns by whom it is imposed. Nor, to revert to the disability caused by the want of permission of home local authorities, can we forget that statutes of this class are imposed by several European states as matters of high domestic polity, and that the position taken by them is that this polity would be overridden if their subjects, by crossing a boundary line, could bind themselves and their country by marriages solemnized in evasion of its laws. We may deplore this conflict of jurisprudences in a matter of so great importance and interest as marriage. But it exists; and no instructions issued by this Department can validate, in a European country, marriages in China by domiciled subjects of such European country when such marriages are by its municipal law invalid.

"I am far from retracting the opinion expressed by me in the personal instructions issued shortly after I assumed my present duties that, to the general rule that the *lex loci* prevails in determining the form of marriage, marriages in barbarous or semi-barbarous or Mohammedan lands form an exception, and that consensual marriages in the last-named countries by citizens of the United States, or by Europeans, will, if duly authenticated, be regarded as everywhere valid. But to this opinion two important qualifications are to be attached. The first is that these views are expressed as a matter of executive advice and not of judicial decision. The second is that the question of form of marriage is to be separated from that of capacity to marry, as to which the prevalent view is that the *lex domicilii* prevails. It is not for me to predict what may be the future judicial rulings on this difficult question of the law regulating matrimonial capacity in cases of mixed marriages in China or in Mohammedan countries. My duty is to point to the questions arising as to such marriages, and to instruct our diplomatic and consular representatives to advise Americans who desire to contract such marriages to take such precautions as may secure the marriage from impeachment in the country in which is domiciled the party whom such American proposes to marry."

Mr. Bayard, Sec. of State, to Mr. Denby, min. to China, Dec. 5, 1888, For. Rel. 1889, 82.

Mr. Denby, Feb. 6, 1889, made the following reply:

"In your dispatch, No. 375, of December 5, 1888, relating to the question of marriage in China, you say: 'I am at a loss to understand why you should use the term "perform the ceremony" in connection with the consul.'

"I have the honor to state that my authority for this statement will be found in section 386 of the Consular Regulations of 1888. The language is this: 'It is held also that, in respect to a consular officer in such countries [meaning the East] the right to perform marriage is incidental to the judicial office, and consequently that he may solemnize the ceremony if it is the wish of the parties that he should do so.'

"The tenor of my dispatch, No. 737, of October 19, 1888, is clearly to the effect that in the case stated I was not to make any official 'recognition' whatever, but was simply to express my opinion that the marriage had before the United States consul was a valid marriage, so far as the American party was concerned.

"You agree with me that the validity of such a marriage 'being exclusive sexual union for life' would be 'in conformity with the great body of judicial authority in the United States.'

"I thoroughly apprehend the difficulty which, under our form of government, attends the certain determination of questions affecting the validity of marriages. But it is a 'condition and not a theory that confronts us' in China. A well-informed lawyer would know generally what the law governing marriages was. Certainly he could acquire all the information necessary to enable him to determine, in almost every case, whether the parties were competent to marry. Assuming that the conditions authorizing the marriage existed, the question of how to perform the ceremony would alone remain.

"As far as the marriage of Americans is concerned, there is no difficulty whatever. There is in China a large American resident population, and marriages between them are frequent. Usually, in the presence of the consul, the ceremony is performed by a minister of the Gospel, and no one has ever questioned its validity, and no court, I think, ever could, unless some common law or statutory disabilities existed.

"Questions affecting mixed marriages are different, because the laws of two jurisdictions must be complied with. The only mode of satisfying the consciences of both parties is the one suggested by me, that is, a double marriage.

"While the executive can not determine legal questions, it can properly control the conduct of its own officials in matter of procedure relating to marriages as to all other subjects. Without defining the power of consuls, it occurred to me that it would be proper to suggest to consuls that in case they were satisfied that two parties, one of American nationality and one foreign, were competent to marry, they might authorize the ceremony to be performed, provided that the consuls of both nationalities joined in the performance thereof.

"In the particular case stated, the parties started to Tientsin to be married, but finally agreed to disagree, and my work was 'love's labor lost.'" (For. Rel. 1889, 97.)

As is seen elsewhere (supra, p. 493), the provision of section 386 of the Consular Regulations of 1888, referred to by Mr. Denby, is supplanted by section 417 of the Consular Regulations of 1896, forbidding consular officers to solemnize marriages in any case.

" I deem it proper to report to you my recent action on a question of the mode of solemnizing marriages in China between Americans there resident.

" In the case in hand the contracting parties were Dr. B. C. Atterbury and Miss M. T. Lowrie, both citizens of the State of New York and now residents of Peking engaged in mission work.

" It was supposed by Dr. Atterbury that my presence was all that was necessary to give ' legality,' as he said, to the proposed marriage. Under article 387 of the Consular Regulations, I deemed it my duty to say to him that my presence at the ceremony would have no legal effect. I showed to him that under article 389, Consular Regulations, the minister is not authorized to perform the ceremony, or to witness it officially, and under article 390 he could give no certificate whatever. I pointed out that under article 386, Consular Regulations, a consul might perform the ceremony, or it might be performed in his presence, and he could then issue the certificate that the Consular Regulations provide for.

" As a result of this friendly and nonofficial interview, the wedding was postponed, and the parties journeyed to Tien-Tsin, to be there married by or before the consul.

" My action provoked some comment. Several cases have occurred in China wherein the parties were married by a clergyman with no Government official present. Other cases were cited in which one of my predecessors attended marriages that were thus solemnized. It is on this account, and because marriage questions are of the highest importance, that I bring the matter to your consideration. It seems plain to me that as a wise precaution, and in order to avoid any possible future trouble, marriages between Americans in China should be performed in the presence of the nearest consul.

" While entertaining this view, I do not pretend to say that the courts might not hold a marriage valid when the ceremony had been performed by a clergyman, or even in cases where there was no ceremony at all, if cohabitation and public recognition of the conjugal status existed; nor do I pretend that I have any official right to dictate to parties how they shall be married; but the minister must be careful that parties are not misled by his silence or his presence at the ceremony of marriage."

> Mr. Denby, minister to China, to Mr. Blaine, Sec. of State, August 16, 1890, For. Rel. 1890, 197.

" I have to acknowledge the receipt of your No. 1150 of the 16th of August last, in relation to the subject of your presence at the marriages of Americans in China as affecting the validity of such marriages.

" Your views on the subject are approved. The statutes of the United States do not provide for the performance of the marriage ceremony, either by a minister or by a consul. It is provided that in certain cases the ceremony may be performed in the presence of the consul; but it is expressly stated in section 383 of the Consular Regulations that the statute does not authorize the consular officer to perform the ceremony. The minister is not clothed with any functions in the matter.

" Such are the statutory provisions. But it has been held by the Attorney-General of the United States (7 Op., 18) that in non-Christian or semicivilized countries, in which consular courts are established, the right to celebrate marriage is incident to the judicial office; and, consequently, that consuls in such countries may solemnize the ceremony if it is the wish of the parties that they should do so.

" It is, however, stated in section 386 of the Consular Regulations that even in such cases it is deemed preferable, where there is a duly qualified minister of a religious denomination whose services can be obtained, that the ceremony should be performed by him, and that the consular officer should confine himself to granting the certificate elsewhere provided for.

" The pertinent provisions in regard to this certificate are found in section 389 of the Consular Regulations, and in this section it is stated that the statute ' does not authorize a diplomatic officer to witness or certify to a marriage ceremony performed before him.'

" Your advice to the parties who applied to you was in accordance with the rules above stated, which should be observed as far as practicable."

> Mr. Blaine, Sec. of State, to Mr. Denby, minister to China, December 16, 1890, For. Rel. 1890, 209.
> As seen hereafter, infra, § 240, the Consular Regulations of 1896, section 417, forbid consuls " to solemnize marriages in any case."

In non-Christian or semicivilized countries " the marriage contract between citizens of the United States is governed by the law of the domicil of the parties. Under the Constitution of the United States, the States have the exclusive power of determining the conditions of marriage and divorce as to persons domiciled within their borders. There is no general Federal statute relating to marriage except R. S. 4082, which covers only marriages by persons domiciled in the District of Columbia or in the Territories. . . . This law does not exclude modes of solemnization other than that in the presence of a consular officer."

> Mr. Day, Assist. Sec. of State, to Mr. Craffs, Feb. 25, 1898, 226 MS. Dom. Let. 9.
> Replying to an inquiry whether when a marriage had been solemnized in the interior of China by a duly authorized minister of the gospel and

before a number of competent witnesses, and their certificate of such marriage was sent to the United States consul, the consul could record in his book "either the marriage or marriage certificate," the Department of State replied that it would not be competent for the consul to "*record a marriage;* that is, to officially declare in his books that a marriage has taken place, where the marriage was not performed in his presence," but that he might, if requested so to do, record a certificate of marriage sent him by an American citizen in his consular district, and that subsequently, upon request, "properly certify that such document had been recorded in the consulate, or give a certified copy thereof, under the seal of the consulate. This, of course, does not involve the certification of the validity of the marriage." (Mr. Cridler, Third Assist. Sec. of State, to Mr. Sims, Jan. 27, 1900, 242 MS. Dom. Let. 428.)

In a dispatch, No. 160, of Dec. 24, 1873, the consular-general of the
United States at Cairo reported that the vice and
deputy consul-general had solemnized a marriage

Egypt.

between a British subject and an American woman at Alexandria, a similar ceremony having previously been performed at the British consulate, in accordance with the requirements of British law. The consul-general promptly disapproved the action of the vice and deputy consul-general, and of this disapproval the Department of State expressed its " unqualified sanction." " It is unnecessary to discuss," added the Department of State, " in the present instance, the nature or privileges of the exterritorial character that attaches to the consulate-general of the United States in Egypt, whatever these may be. You are right in concluding that in a matter of so grave importance as a contract of marriage, involving as it may the political, social, and moral interests of the parties to the contract, and their offspring, the functions of the principal officer should not be assumed by a deputy. . . . The custom which you allege to have been heretofore observed by the consul-general at Alexandria of having the ceremony performed in the presence of the consul by one of the resident American clergymen, he being a priest or minister of the gospel, who would be authorized to solemnize marriages in the District of Columbia, meets with the approval of the Department, and is moreover in harmony with the general usage of the Christian world in relation to the sacred character of the ceremony itself."

Mr. Fish, Sec. of State, to Mr. Beardsley, consul-general at Cairo, Jan. 30, 1874, MS. Inst. Barbary Powers, XV. 171.

" The marriage to which you refer was certainly not legally contracted, as you will perceive from the 278th article of the Consular Regulations, which it is to be regretted you should have overlooked. The parties must again be married either in Egypt or elsewhere pursuant to the law of the land, if it should in any event become necessary to show the validity of the contract." (Mr. Fish, Sec. of State, to Mr. Butler, consul at Alexandria, Oct. 5, 1871, MS. Inst. Barbary Powers, XV. 62, acknowledging Mr. Butler's No. 86, of Sept. 15, 1871. Article 278, Cons. Reg. 1870, read: "This act [of 1860] does not authorize the consul to perform the ceremony. The consul is forbidden to perform such ceremony unless he performs it within the precincts of a legation of the United States, or of a consulate which has by treaty or custom the privilege of exterritoriality; or unless he is expressly authorized to do so by the laws of the country in which he resides.")

" Your No. 96, of September 6, has been received. In this dispatch you ask the opinion of the Department on your action in the case of the marriage of Joseph Amil, a naturalized citizen of the United States, now residing in Alexandria.

" It has recently been decided by this Department that the act of Congress of June 22, 1860 (R. S. 4082), as to the mode of solemnization of marriage in foreign lands, applies only to persons domiciled in the District of Columbia or in the Territories. You are no doubt aware that the forms of solemnization of marriage will as a rule be held internationally valid, if in accordance with the law of the place of solemnization; though the converse of this rule, that compliance with the local law is essential to the validity of the solemnization, does not hold in semicivilized countries where the law imposes conditions repugnant to the religious convictions of the parties. These positions, however, it is your function to state merely by way of advice, and not to impose judicially on the parties. Under these circumstances the Department approves your advice to the parties of whom you speak to have their marriage solemnized according to the civil law in force in Egypt. Whether or no any other form of marriage might not be internationally valid, it is not necessary for the Department to decide in advance."

Mr. Porter, Act. Sec. of State, to Mr. Cardwell, agent and consul-general at Cairo, Oct. 2, 1886, 119 MS. Inst. Consuls, 250.

The rule that a marriage, celebrated according to the requirements of the law of the place where the ceremony is performed, is to be recognized as valid, " completely applies only to the countries of Christendom. In Mohammedan and other non-Christian countries in which Christians enjoy extraterritoriality, or in uncivilized lands like Samoa, where certain foreign nationalities enjoy the same exemption by treaty, the privileged foreign residents carry with them their local law, and are subject solely to the jurisdiction of tribunals established by their own Governments.

" It follows from this that the custom of Samoa in regard to the lawful cohabitation of men and women can not be accepted as a rule by which to determine the character of the cohabitation of an American citizen with any woman, whether native or foreign. The character of such cohabitation must be decided by the law of the United States."

Mr. Rives, Assist. Sec. of State, to Mr. Sewall, consul-gen. at Apia, April 26, 1888, S. Ex. Doc. 31, 50 Cong. 2 sess. 55.

The opinion that in countries where the privilege of extraterritoriality prevails "a valid contract of marriage [of an American citizen] may be solemnized and the contract authenticated not only by an embassador, but by a consul of the United States," points out "one way in which the contract may be evidenced, and while the Department is far from saying that it might not be otherwise proved, yet it is desirable that this mode of authentication should be observed as far as possible" in the countries in question.

Mr. Rives, Assist. Sec. of State, to Mr. Sewall, cons. gen. at Apia, April 26, 1888, S. Ex. Doc. 31, 50 Cong., 2 sess. 55, citing opinion of Cushing, At.-Gen., Nov. 4, 1854, 7 Op. 30.

(4) LIMITATIONS OF DIPLOMATIC PRIVILEGE.

§ 239.

" Your 246 requests the views of this Department in regard to the right of diplomatic agents of the United States to celebrate marriages between citizens of this Union in foreign countries.

" The laws of the several States as applicable to the *civil* contract of marriage are in many instances so diverse that the Department could not with propriety express an opinion upon this subject which would bear the test of law in all the States.

" Regarding the question in the light of a civil contract consummated before a high functionary of this Government, and within its jurisdiction,—looking to the exterritoriality of the legations,—and bearing in mind that the practice referred to obtains in the French and British legations in foreign countries, the Department does not hesitate to regard the exercise of this function as most expedient, and in many cases perhaps desirable, when circumstances seem to require the solemnization of marriage between Americans residing abroad.

" The validity of such a marriage would in the United States depend upon the enactments of the particular State in which the question might arise.

" The subject is deemed of sufficient importance to demand further consideration from the Department, with reference especially to the propriety of presenting it to Congress for the purpose of obtaining such a law as will be of general application within the jurisdiction of the United States."

Mr. Marcy, Sec. of State, to Mr. Clay, min. to Peru, March 30, 1855, MS. Inst. Peru, XV. 156.

" The question with regard to foreign ministers is somewhat different, as in the consideration of it it has been maintained that this
power is a consequence of the right of extraterritoriality. But, while
this principle of exemption from the jurisdiction of the country where
a foreign minister is accredited protects his person and his domicil
&c. from all interruption, I do not consider that it necessarily carries with it the power to exercise any authority, civil or criminal.
I do not consider that an obligation contracted at the residence of
the minister of the United States at Paris, contrary to the laws of
France, can become valid when the parties are found in the United
States. The utmost extent to which this principle of extraterritoriality can properly be carried, cannot confer upon a foreign minister an authority not necessarily incident to his official position or
which is not granted to him by some law of his own country. It
will scarcely be maintained that the laws of each of the States and
Territories of this Union are operative in the residences of all our ministers abroad, whatever may be taken with respect to the laws of the
United States, or to any portion of them. If this be so, it is difficult
to perceive whence a foreign minister derives the power to celebrate
a marriage which shall not only be valid in each of the States, but
which shall be free from any doubts as to the rights conferred by it,
whatever State legislation may exist upon the subject; nor why his
power of interference with marriages stops at their celebration and
does not extend to the dissolution, legislation in both cases being
equally wanting.

" The expression of these views concerning the power of foreign
ministers is intended to be cautionary and not directory. They are
my personal opinions, and are not to be received as the decision of the
Department.

" They are communicated because the course they naturally suggest
may prevent difficulties hereafter. Under the circumstances it will
be obviously expedient to advise parties applying for information, to
have the marriage ceremony performed in the manner, if possible,
required by the law of the country, and thus avoid questions which
may be fraught with serious trouble."

> Mr. Cass, Sec. of State, to Mr. Fay, min. to Switzerland, Nov. 12, 1860,
> MS. Inst. Switz. I. 85.
> See Certificates of Law, infra, § 241.

The minister of the United States at St. Petersburg having reported the marriage at the legation, in his presence, of a citizen of
the United States with a lady whose nationality is not stated, the
ceremony being preformed by the pastor of the British and American
Congregational Church, Mr. Fish said: " It is desired now to call
your attention to the fact that this marriage was not solemnized in

accordance with the requirements of the laws of the United States in relation to such marriages. [Here follows a quotation of the act of June 22, 1860, validating marriages ' in presence of ' consular officers.] A marriage solemnized in accordance with the provisions of this statute and of the instructions thereunder [Consular Regulations, 1870, Art. XXII. paragraphs 275, 276, 277, 278] will avoid all doubt as to its recognition in the United States.

" It is not the intention of this instruction to raise any question as to the validity of ———'s marriage. Upon that question the Department carefully avoids the expression of any opinion.

" I transmit herewith for your information and future guidance extracts from an instruction of my predecessor, General Cass, in 1860, to Mr. Fay, then minister resident of the United States at Berne."

> Mr. Fish, Sec. of State, to Mr. Jewell, min. to Russia, June 10, 1874, MS. Inst. Russia, XV. 455.

A marriage solemnized by the minister of the United States at Denmark, who was also a minister of the gospel, in his " capacity as minister of the gospel," of parties who " would be legally entitled to marry in the District of Columbia had they been residing there," was held to be " not solemnized in accordance with the laws of the United States in relation to such marriages," though no opinion was expressed as to whether the marriage was in itself valid.

> Mr. Fish, Sec. of State, to Mr. Cramer, June 19, 1874, MS. Inst. Denmark, XV. 103. The " laws of the United States " meant the act of June 22, 1860, R. S. § 4082, with reference to marriages " in presence of " consular officers.

" Your despatch No. 88, of the 2d ultimo, has been received. In compliance with the wish which it expresses, a full copy of the instructions of General Cass to Mr. Fay, of the 12th of November, 1860, is herewith transmitted. That instruction, however, is, as you will see, in the main confined to remarks upon the legality of a marriage by a consul in Switzerland. It also contains observations upon the right of a diplomatic agent in a foreign country to perform that ceremony. This question, however, had not been raised by the despatch of Mr. Fay to which the instruction is intended as an answer. The matter at issue was merely the legality or illegality of a marriage which the consul had performed. No doubt as to its illegality could be entertained after the passage of the act of Congress of the 22d of June, 1860. Formerly unmarried emigrants to the United States about to embark at Hamburg or Bremen were in the habit of having that ceremony performed for them by the consul. As this was not in accordance with the local law, the practice was complained of by the German Government, and those consuls were directed to desist from it. The act of 1860 accordingly only authorizes mar-riages to take place in the *presence* of consuls, who are officially to attest the fact. The act confers no authority on a diplomatic agent to perform that ceremony, and the Department is of the opinion that he can not lawfully exercise it unless it shall be expressly granted. In forming this opinion, however, the Department has not been governed by the reasoning of General Cass, to the effect that, as a diplomatic agent confessedly has no authority to annul a marriage, he has as little to celebrate it. This expression appears to overlook the fact that marriage is a contract between the parties, and that the magistrate or clergyman who may perform the ceremony, so called, is in point of fact substantially a witness to the contract, whose duty, however, it is to see that the parties are competent to enter into it.

" But though the Department believes that, without the authority of law, a diplomatic agent has no authority himself to perform the ceremony of marriage, it is clearly of opinion that the ceremony may be legally performed between citizens of the United States in the dwelling or office of such agent by a person competent for such purpose.

" The statutes of most of the States of the Union appear to be silent as to marriages of their citizens in foreign countries.

" There is a law of Massachusetts, however, which expressly provides that marriages in a foreign country by a consul or diplomatic agent of the United States shall be valid in that State, and that a copy of the record or a certificate from such consul or agent shall be presumptive evidence of such marriage.[a] As consuls and diplomatic agents, however, are subject to the acts of Congress and the instructions of this Department, they can not be expected, in such a matter, to conform to the requirements of the legislature of any particular State. Indeed the Department is under the impression that as citizens of the respective States when abroad are known as citizens of the United States only, Congress alone has competent authority to legislate in regard to their marriage in foreign countries so far as such legislation may be compatible with the local laws.

" By inclining to the opinion that a marriage may lawfully, and independently of the local law, be solemnized between citizens of the United States in a legation of the United States in a foreign country, the Department would, however, expect the diplomatic agent so far to exercise supervision over the contract as not to allow it there to be entered into by persons whose incompetency for the purpose is generally recognized, and in particular that he would not countenance the marriage of a minor without the consent of his or her parent or guardian.

---

[a]General Statutes, 1869, sec. 23, p. 531.

" In your despatch No. 62, of the 9th of April last, you say that you had appointed a clergyman chaplain to your legation, that he might solemnize the marriage to which that despatch relates. If, however, the ecclesiastic had authority to celebrate a marriage anywhere, a special one for the occasion adverted to was not necessary. Indeed, your competency to make such an appointment is at least questionable. Not only is no officer with that title allowed to a legation by act of Congress, but the appointment of such an officer, even for a temporary purpose, may be regarded as forbidden by the 33d section of the act of the 18th of August, 1856.

" It must be allowed that you are correct in your criticism of the 278th paragraph of the Consular Regulations. A consul has, legally, no more authority to perform the marriage ceremony in a legation of the United States than he has to perform it in his own office."

> Mr. Fish, Sec. of State, to Mr. Logan, min. to Chile, Aug. 19, 1874, MS. Inst. Chile, XVI. 126.

" Marriage at legations without regard to the law of the country, on the ground of extraterritoriality, as it is called, is at best a questionable proceeding, which it may be apprehended would scarcely be sanctioned by the courts of the nation where they were solemnized. The tendency of opinion is believed to be towards narrowing the immunities of diplomatic officers and their places of abode to those limits only which may be indispensable to enable them to discharge their official duties without molestation or restraint.

" The use of the legation for the marriage of persons, even of the nationality of the country to which it belongs, can not be said to be necessary or even convenient for diplomatic purposes."

> Mr. Fish, Sec. of State, to Mr. Marsh, min. to Italy, Jan. 19, 1875, For. Rel. 1875, II. 761, 762.
> This subject is more fully discussed in an instruction to Mr. Washburne, minister to France, of Nov. 14, 1874, in which Mr. Fish refers to two cases in which marriages at legations in Paris, without compliance with the local law, were held by the French courts to be invalid. It was pointed out that while, in these cases, one of the parties to the marriage was of the same nationality as the legation, the other was French; but Mr. Fish declined to accept the conclusion, which was somewhat pressed upon him, that the validity of the marriage would have been sustained if both the parties had been aliens, and of the same nationality as the legation. (Mr. Fish, Sec. of State, to Mr. Washburne, min. to France, For. Rel. 1875, I. 445.)

" The act of June 22, 1860, now incorporated in the Revised Statutes (§ 4082), neither expresses nor implies that a minister shall have like powers with a consul as regards the authentication of a marriage, and the performance of a marriage ceremony within the precincts of a legation would require the presence of the consul to fulfill the law. (Personal Instructions, XLVIII.)

" Unless, therefore, a minister of the United States be required or authorized by the *lex loci* where he officially resides to perform the marriage ceremony he cannot lawfully do so."

> Mr. Evarts, Sec. of State, to Mr. Logan, June 8, 1880, MS. Inst. Cent. Am. XIX. 91.

" By the law of nations the forms of solemnization of a marriage must be in accordance with the law of the place of solemnization, and the only exceptions are when those forms are such as the parties can not conscientiously comply with, or when the solemnization is in a barbarous or semicivilized land. It is true that it is said by some authorities that a marriage in a foreign legation is governed only by the laws of the country such legation represents, but this is so much a matter of doubt that the British foreign office has instructed its diplomatic agents that although such marriages, performed in British legations, are valid in Great Britain by statute, their validity elsewhere can not be assumed. . . . Under these circumstances you very properly declined to sanction the solemnization of the marriage in question until you have information that it would be solemnized in conformity with Belgian law. Whether the marriage as actually solemnized is valid it is not the province of this Department to decide.

" Questions of private international law as to the past are for the judiciary; it is as to the future, and this only by way of caution, that this Department in such matters speaks."

> Mr. Bayard, Sec. of State, to Mr. Tree, June 5, 1886, MS. Inst. Belgium, II. 429.
>
> See, also, as to the instructions of the British foreign office, Mr. Bayard, Sec. of State, to Mr. Winchester, min. to Switzerland, Aug. 15, 1885; For. Rel. 1885, 807.

In response to a question whether the marriage of American citizens at the house of the American legation in Antwerp or Berlin, " according to home form," would be valid, it was stated that the marriage, if not solemnized in conformity with the law of the place of celebration, would not be validated, so far as concerned its effect in places where there was not a statute validating it, by the mere fact of its having been solemnized at the legation of the country to which the parties belonged and in accordance with the form held valid in such country.

> Mr. Bayard, Sec. of State, to Mr. Ketcham, M. C., July 2, 1888, For. Rel. 1888, I. 646.
>
> Mr. Bayard added that the question submitted was one ultimately to be determined by courts of justice under the circumstances of each particular case, and that it was not his duty to predict what would

be the action of the courts, but to give such cautions as might induce American citizens proposing to be married abroad to take every step to give validity to the marriage.

"I have the honor to acknowledge the receipt to-day of your instruction No. 333 of the 7th instant, inclosing a correspondence between the Hon. J. H. Ketcham, of the House of Representatives, and yourself, relative to the validity attaching under certain specified conditions to marriages of American citizens in foreign countries . . .

"In your reply you state: 'So far, however, as concerns foreign countries, e. g., Belgium or Germany, the question of the validity of the solemnization would depend upon their own law, and that law is understood to incorporate the general principle above stated, that a solemnization of marriage to be valid must be in conformity with the law of the place of celebration.'

"The principle stated in the above passage is in entire conformity, as far as this country is concerned, with statutory provisions, the law declaring that a marriage within the German Empire can only be validly concluded before the designated civil official, the 'Standesbeamter,' and imposing a penalty upon any clergyman or other minister of religion who solemnizes a marriage before it has been proven to him that the marriage has been concluded before the civil official.

"In order to supply to the Department, in a form convenient for reference, the pertinent provisions of German law, I transmit herewith the copies and carefully prepared translations of the statutory declarations above referred to."

> Mr. Coleman, chargé at Berlin, to Mr. Bayard, Sec. of State, July 23, 1888, For. Rel. 1888, I. 649.

Imperial law of February 6, 1875, concerning the authentication of personal status and the conclusion of marriage.

SEC. 41. Within the domain of the German Empire a marriage can only be validly concluded before the "Standesbeamter" (civil registrar).

SEC. 67. A clergyman or any other minister of religion who undertakes the religious solemnization of marriage before it has been proven to him that the marriage has been concluded before the "Standesbeamter" (civil registrar) is punishable by fine not exceeding 300 marks, or by imprisonment of not more than three months.

"It appears that a circular had been issued from the British foreign office, July 31, 1886, to the effect that two cases of mixed marriages between British and Swiss citizens, duly celebrated at her Britannic Majesty's embassy at Paris, wherein the customary procedure had been followed to the letter, were declared null and void in Switzerland.

"The procedure hitherto followed was to obtain, from the representative of the foreigner's country, a certificate that the marriage at the British embassy should be deemed valid by the laws of his nation.

" The ground on which the said marriages were declared null and void was that the validity of mixed marriages celebrated at the British embassy at Paris was not recognized by French law. To meet this objection, before authorizing any mixed marriage at any legation, the minister is to require that a previous marriage shall take place according to the *lex loci*, and that a certificate, under the hand of the representative of the foreigner's nation, shall be obtained, that such a marriage is recognized as legal and binding by the laws of his country.

" In a circular of the British foreign office, dated July 14, 1887, the stipulation that a marriage according to the *lex loci* shall previously be celebrated, is modified for a form of marriage that is recognized as legal and binding by the law of the nation to which the foreigner belongs.

" If, however, the minister is satisfied that such previous marriage is impracticable, he may, at discretion, dispense with it, on being furnished with a certificate, under the hand of the representative of the foreigner's nation, that the mixed marriage, which it is proposed to celebrate at the British legation, will, of itself, and without any preliminary or other ceremony, be recognized as legal and binding by the laws of such nation.

"A fair construction of these instructions is that the British minister may allow a mixed marriage to be solemnized at the legation, if a form of marriage, that is recognized as legal and binding by the law of the nation to which the foreigner belongs has previously taken place. In that event the certificate is dispensed with, and ' a recognition ' of the validity of the previous marriage by the officials of the foreigner's nation is all that is required."

> Mr. Denby, min. to China, to Mr. Bayard, Sec. of State, Oct. 19, 1888, reporting an interview with Sir John Walsham, British minister at Peking. (For. Rel. 1889, 75, 76–77.)
>
> "A marriage solemnized in the legation of the United States at London should conform in form to the British law." (Mr. Wharton, Assist. Sec. of State, to Mr. Southworth, Jan. 26, 1893, 190 MS. Dom. Let. 139.)

Two citizens of the United States applied to the American minister in Nicaragua to marry them on the ground that they were both Protestants, and that there was no resident of the country authorized to perform the ceremony except a Catholic clergyman. The Department of State declined to authorize the minister to act in the matter, instructing him that it was essential that marriages of American citizens abroad should be celebrated in accordance with the laws of the country where the ceremony was performed. Reference was made to the circular of February 8, 1887, For. Rel. 1887, 1133.

> Mr. Uhl, Act. Sec. of State, to Mr. Baker, min. to Nicaragua, Feb. 24, 1894; For. Rel. 1894, 447.

" 177. Statutory provisions relate only to consuls.—The laws of the United States do not confer on diplomatic officers any power to celebrate marriages, to act as official witnesses of the ceremony of marriage, or to grant certificates of marriage. The statutory provisions relating to the celebration abroad of marriages of citizens of the United States refer only to consuls. (See Consular Regulations of 1896, paragraphs 417–422.)"

> Instructions to Diplomatic Officers (1897), 69.

" 182. Ceremony in a legation.—It is not unusual for Americans abroad to ask permission to have a marriage ceremony performed in the embassy or legation and in the presence of the diplomatic representative. There is no reason why a diplomatic representative should not comply with this request. But it is proper, at the same time, to inform the parties making the application that, in the opinion of the Department of State, a ceremony of marriage performed within the precincts of a legation should, with the above limitations, comply with the requirements of the laws of the country within which the legation is situated.

" 183. Preliminary inquiries.—Whenever an application is made for the use of a legation for such a purpose, it will be the duty of the diplomatic representative to inquire whether the parties may lawfully marry according to the laws of the country in which the legation is situated; and whether the proper steps have been taken to enable the marriage ceremony to be legally performed according to such laws. If either of these inquiries should be answered in the negative, or if the case does not fall within one of the exceptions above stated (paragraph 179), it will be his duty to inform the applicants that he can not permit the ceremony to be performed at the legation, as there may be grave doubts respecting its validity.

" If it is desired in such cases by citizens of the District of Columbia or of the Territories to avail themselves of the provisions of the statute (R. S., sec. 4082), then the diplomatic representative should inform them that under the laws of the United States it will be necessary to have the nearest consular officer of the United States present; and he should give them an opportunity to have such officer present, if they desire it."

> Instructions to Diplomatic Officers of the United States, 1897.
> The same provisions, with only slight verbal differences, may be found in the Printed Personal Instructions to Diplomatic Agents of the United States, 1885.

(5) FUNCTIONS OF CONSULS.

§ 240.

Prohibited to perform ceremony.

" In relation to the celebration of the rites of matrimony between citizens of the United States residing in California, respecting which you ask for instructions, I have to inform you that there is no law in existence which authorizes consuls of the United States to perform the marriage ceremony. The contract of matrimony is local in its nature, and the manner in which it shall be entered into is regulated by the laws of the place. The general principle on this subject, as laid down by Chancellor Kent, is that ' the *lex loci contractus* prevails over the *le domicilii*, as being the safer rule and one dictated by just and enlightened views of international jurisprudence.' He adds, ' as the law of marriage is a part of the *jus gentium*, the general rule undoubtedly is that a marriage valid by the laws of the place where it is celebrated is valid everywhere.' (Kent's Commentaries, vol. 2, pp. 91 & 92.) "

<blockquote>Mr. Buchanan, Sec. of State, to Mr. Larkin, consul at Montery, July 14, 1846, 11 MS. Dispatches to Consuls, 478.</blockquote>

" I desire particularly to call your attention, before entering upon the discharge of your consular duties, to a practice which I have learned with great surprise has been countenanced by your predecessor of performing the marriage ceremony between German emigrants about to embark for the United States, or of furnishing parties desiring them with certificates purporting that it is their intention to emigrate as man and wife.

" The attention of the Department was called to this subject by Mr. King in his dispatch No. 13, to which you will please refer. That communication was accompanied by a form of certificate of which he desired the approval of the Department. He was immediately informed that there was no law in existence which authorized consuls of the United States to perform the marriage ceremony; that the contract of matrimony is local in its nature, and the manner in which it shall be entered into regulated by the laws of the place; that the general principle on this subject is that the lex loci contractus prevails over the lex domicilii; and that, as the law of marriage is a part of the *jus gentium*, the general rule undoubtedly is that a marriage valid by the law of the place where it is celebrated is valid everywhere. From the principles here stated it was made clear to him that the marriage ceremony as solemnized by him was without validity, and must inevitably lead to a great immorality and licentiousness, as well as to lay the foundation for vexatious litigation.

" Since the arrival in this country of Mr. R. Schleiden, the minister resident from Bremen, I have learned from him that Mr. King, notwithstanding the positive instructions which he had received from Mr. Webster, continued the practice of solemnizing marriages, or of giving what was considered by the emigrants as equivalent thereto, the certificates above named. Such a procedure on the part of an officer of this Government merits its severest censure, and had it been known to the Department at an earlier period it would have recommended Mr. King's immediate removal.

" I have been thus particular in making known to you the views of the Department on this subject that you may have no difficulty as to your own course in reference to any application that may be made to you by Germans or others for certificates of marriage or intention of marriage.

" If Mr. King has not left Bremen when you receive this dispatch, you are at liberty to read it to him."

> Mr. Marcy, Sec. of State, to Mr. Hildebrand, consul at Bremen, July 22, 1853, 17 MS. Dispatches to Consuls, 28.
>
> "In the statement of fees accompanying your No. 44, I observe several charges for ' certificates of marriage.' You will explain without delay the nature and object of these certificates, whether the parties applying for them have been legally married according to the laws of Hamburg, and desire to obtain from you, as a United States officer, an authentication of that fact; or, whether the consular certificate is obtained for the purpose of evading the laws of Hamburg, or those of any of the United States. You are doubtless aware that United States consuls are not authorized to perform the marriage rite unless in accordance with the laws of the country in which they reside, and consequently any act of theirs purporting to be a solemnization of that contract is without validity, and will lead most probably to great immorality as well as vexatious litigation." (Mr. Marcy, Sec. of State, to Mr. Bromberg, consul at Hamburg, Oct. 25, 1853, 17 MS. Disp. to Consuls, 128.)

Marriages celebrated by a consul of the United States in any foreign country of Christendom, between citizens of the United States, would have no legal effect here, save in one of the exceptional cases of its being impossible for the parties to marry by the *lex loci*. American consuls have no such power given them by act of Congress, nor by the common law of marriage as understood in the several States. And marriage, in the United States, is not a Federal question (save as to places under the absolute legislative jurisdiction of the United States), but one to be determined by the several States.

> Cushing, At. Gen. (1854), 7 Op., 18.
> The foregoing opinion was given in response to the following letter:
> "I have the honor to enclose herewith several despatches with various documents accompanying them relating to a practice which prevails

to some extent among the United States consuls abroad of marrying parties, either American citizens or foreigners, who call upon them for that purpose.

" No regard is paid by the consuls to the forms or the laws relating to marriage of the country in which they reside. In a recent case at Havana, the consul read the Episcopal service; among the documents annexed are forms which have been used at Bremen and elsewhere. I will thank you to inform me if, in your opinion, the contracts of marriage made under such circumstances would be recognized by the courts of the United States, and if the issue of parties thus married could inherit any property, either in this country or abroad, belonging to their parents.

" It was stated some time since in the public prints that titles to property have been contested in consequence of the alleged illegality of the marriage of one of the parties by a United States consul." (Mr. Marcy, Sec. of State, to Mr. Cushing, At. Gen., Nov. 3, 1854, 43 MS. Dom. Let. 198.)

A consul can not, as consul, solemnize a marriage, whether he be or not a subject of the foreign government. (Cushing, At. Gen. (1855), 7 Op. 342.)

" With respect to the validity of the marriage celebrated by Mr. Goundie [United States consul at Zurich] . . . , it is a question upon which this Department can pronounce no authoritative opinion, so far as the rights of the parties may be involved. When, in matters of administration, it becomes necessary for a Department to issue instructions or to establish regulations with a view to ensure the correct and uniform execution of duties which are enjoined by law, this must be done with reference to the subject under consideration. The Department necessarily forms and makes known its opinion upon the various points connected with its action and prescribes the limitations to be observed or the mode in which the duties required are to be performed. But there its right of interference ceases. It is confined to the proceedings of the officer responsible to such Department. But important subjects of controversy may arise between parties involving the legality or effect of such instructions or regulations, and which the Department issuing them has no power to adjust and ought not to attempt it, nor to interfere in any manner with the prosecution of the claims of persons arising out of the exercise of disputed power. Such cases become the subject of judicial and not of administrative action, and the questions involved can only be authoratively settled by the judicial tribunals. Rights claimed under alleged marriages may be there investigated, upon the demand of any person interested, and the decision, if involving the validity of the marriage, settles that question.

" I make these remarks in consequence of the opinion communicated by you to the Federal council upon its application, that the marriage ceremony performed by the American consul in the case of Mr. ———— and Miss ———— was invalid. From the views presented in this despatch, it is obvious that this Department fully concurs with you in the opinion. But it may be that a question may arise, under that marriage, calling for the decision of courts of justice in order to determine the rights of the parties. It is desirable therefore that the Swiss Government should understand the position occupied by this Department; that, although it may incidentally judge of the legality of a marriage so far as the conduct of our diplomatic or consular functionaries is connected with its celebration, still its views can have no effect whatever, when the rights of parties, under such marriage, are in controversy. The whole subject then passes from the administrative authorities to the judicial tribunals. And therefore, in the event of the institution of proceedings, either at home or abroad, to test the validity of this marriage, the opinion of this Department can have no effect whatever.

" It affords me pleasure to inform you that I think the advice given in your note of August 4, 1860, to Mr. ————, to have the marriage again celebrated and agreeably to the law of the place, in order to obviate difficulty, was wise, and that the course indicated was the proper one to adopt."

> Mr. Cass, Sec. of State, to Mr. Fay, min. to Switz., Nov. 12, 1860, MS.
> Inst. Switz. I. 85.

"A consular officer of the United States is not authorized to perform the marriage ceremony in a foreign country of which he is a resident, unless it is performed within the precincts of a legation of the United States, or of a consulate, which has by treaty or custom the privilege of exterritoriality, or unless he is expressly authorized to do so by the laws of the country in which he resides; nor are such officers invested by the laws of the United States with any of the functions or duties pertaining to ministers of the Gospel."

> Mr. Fish, Sec. of State, to Mr. Christensen, Dec. 10, 1872, MS. Notes to
> Danish Leg. VI. 331.
> A "deputy consul-general" is not a "consular officer" whose action validates a marriage under the act of June 22, 1860, R. S. § 4082. (Mr. Fish, Sec. of State, to Mr. Beardsley, Jan. 30, 1874, MS. Inst. Barbary powers, XV. 171.)
> An American citizen, residing in the United States, can not contract marriage before an American consul in Italy through power of attorney. (Mr. Cridler, Third Assist. Sec. of State, to Mr. Giallorenzi, Jan. 15, 1901, 250 MS. Dom. Let. 229.)

" No doubt as to its illegality [of a marriage ceremony performed by a consul] could be entertained after the passage of the act of Congress of the 22nd of June, 1860. Formerly unmarried emigrants to the United States about to embark at Hamburg or Bremen were in the habit of having that ceremony performed for them by the consul. As this was not in accordance with the local law, the practice was complained of by the German Government, and those consuls were directed to desist from it. The act of 1860 accordingly only authorizes marriage to take place in the *presence* of consuls, who are officially to attest the fact."

> Mr. Fish, Sec. of State, to Mr. Logan, min. to Chile, Aug. 19, 1874, MS. Inst. Chile, XVI. 126.

"A United States consul has no authority, under the laws of the United States, to solemnize marriages, and even if he had such authority it would have to be exercised in obedience to the laws of the country in which he is resident as such consul. Consuls do not possess any extraterritorial privileges in regard to private matters between individuals. The law provides that a United States consul may be present and witness the ceremony, and may give to the parties a certificate of the fact under the consular seal and make a record of it in the archives of the consulate. A marriage thus celebrated between American citizens in a foreign country, and not in contravention of the laws of such foreign country, if performed by a minister of the gospel or other person who by the laws of the country in which it takes place is authorized to solemnize marriages, and between persons who would be competent to marry in the District of Columbia, is held by the laws of the United States to be valid in the United States."

> Mr. Frelinghuysen, Sec. of State, to Mr. Kohnstamm, Dec. 20, 1883, 149 MS. Dom. Let. 201.

" In your despatch No 126, after stating the laws of Ecuador on the subject of marriage, you ask whether a marriage solemnized by you as consul-general, under the circumstances narrated, would be valid in the United States and other countries than Ecuador. The quotation you give from instructions of this Department of November 20, 1885, to Mr. Hodges exhibits the view of the law in this relation, which the Department continues to maintain. ' When the law of the place of celebration,' I again affirm, ' imposes conditions . . . repugnant to the conscience of the parties,' then the law of the place of celebration does not necessarily prevail so as to invalidate everywhere a marriage not solemnized in conformity with such conditions. This has been held in England to be the case with regard to marriages of Protestants at Rome, solemnized by Protestant clergymen, and of marriages in France by Protestant clergymen, at a time when the local law required celebration by Catholics. In the present case there is not only this conscientious objection which may be entertained by Protestants to a Catholic ceremonial, but the still more serious objection which might be made by a Protestant to baptism by a Catholic priest, which it seems is in Ecuador a prerequisite to an Ecuadorian marriage.

"Such being the case, it would probably be held by the courts of this country and of England that a consensual marriage in Ecuador by two citizens of the United States would be valid here, though its validity might be denied in Ecuador. But the marriage of the parties as described, they not being domiciled in the District of Columbia or in one of the Territories, would derive no force from your officiating at it as consul-general, though your presence and attestation as a witness might hereafter be of value as attesting the fact of consent. And it is my duty also to inform you that the Department in giving these views does not and can not speak judicially. Parties marrying abroad must do so at their own risk, remembering that the law, especially in such a question as you now put, is still open to doubts which can be solved only by judicial action in the concrete case. It is proper at the same time that you should advise Mr. ―――― and Miss ―――― that if they should live together as man and wife in Ecuador without a ceremonial marriage in conformity to Ecuadorian law, they might possibly be subjected to prosecution, civil or ecclesiastical, and that in such case it might not be within the range of the powers of this Department to interfere for their relief."

Mr. Rives, Assist. Sec. of State, to Mr. McGarr, cons. gen. at Guayaquil,
Jan. 7, 1888, 123 MS. Inst. Consuls, 550.

"I have before me your despatch No. 3, written at Quito on April 13th, 1888, asking whether the Department would disapprove of your officiating at the marriage of two American citizens, in Ecuador, the reason given being that they cannot conscientiously be married in Ecuador in conformity with Ecuadorian law, such law prescribing a Roman Catholic ceremony and prior baptism by a Catholic priest. As to the validity of a consensual marriage by American citizens in Ecuador, such marriage not being in conformity with Ecuadorian law, I have already expressed my views in my instruction of January 7, 1888, No. 48, which I now reaffirm.

"As to your present specific request I now say that the Department cannot express its approval of your 'officiating' as consul general at a 'consensual' marriage of the parties in question. Aside from the objection that your so 'officiating' as 'consul general' would put you, in your official capacity, more or less in collision with the local law of Ecuador, there is nothing in the legislative specification of the functions of consuls, or in the Consular Regulations, which would authorize such official action on your part. In the only statute which touches this question—a statute which in any view applies only to persons domiciled in the Territories or in the District of Columbia— the idea of conveyance of power to 'officiate' is excluded by the limitation of the act to marriages ' in the presence of ' any consular officer of the United States.

"Under these conditions the Department can issue no instructions which might be held to recognize in its consular officers any distinctive power of ' officiating ' at marriages."

> Mr. Rives, Assist. Sec. of State, to Mr. McGarr, consul-general at Guayaquil, May 8, 1888, 125 MS. Inst. Consuls, 248.

"417. Consuls not to celebrate.—A consular officer of the United States has no power to celebrate marriages in a Christian country between citizens of the United States unless specially authorized by the laws of the country to do so. In non-Christian countries his authority to perform this rite is not sufficiently well established and defined in the jurisprudence of the United States to justify action upon it. It is deemed safer to forbid consular officers, and they are hereby forbidden, to solemnize marriages in any case. (7 Op. Att. Gen., 23, 30, 31, 342, 346; 1 Halleck, Ch. XI., sec. 14; 1 Bishop, Marriage and Divorce, 298.)

"418. May act as witnesses.—A consular officer may, when requested, be an official witness of the ceremony of marriage where one of the contracting parties is a citizen of the United States. In all cases of marriage in the presence of a consular officer he shall give to each of the parties a certificate of such marriage, and shall also send forthwith a certificate thereof to the Department of State.

"419. Certificate.—This certificate must be under the official seal of the consulate, and must give the names of the parties, their ages, places of birth and residence, the date and place of the marriage, and must certify that the marriage took place in the presence of the consular officer giving the certificate. (Form No. 87.)"

> Consular Regulations of the United States, 1896.

The act of June 22, 1860 (Rev. Stat., § 4082), provides that "marriages in presence of any consular officer of the United States in a foreign country, between persons who would be authorized to marry if residing in the District of Columbia, shall be valid to all intents and purposes, and shall have the same effect as if solemnized within the United States. And such consular officers shall, in all cases, give to the parties married before them a certificate of such marriage, and shall send another certificate thereof to the Department of State, there to be kept; such certificates shall specify the names of the parties, their ages, places of birth, and residence."

Act of 1860, R. S. 4280.

> See "An act to regulate marriages in the District of Columbia," approved May 13, 1896, 29 Stat. 118. By this statute the consent of parents or of guardians is required in the case of a male person under twenty-

one years of age, and of a female under eighteen years of age who has not been previously married. Marriages may be celebrated by the judge of a court of record or a justice of the peace, or by duly ordained and authorized ministers; and, where the parties belong to a religious society having no ordained minister, the marriage may be solemnized by the person appointed and in the manner prescribed by and practiced in such society. Licenses to marry are required; but it is forbidden to issue any to a citizen of a foreign country "until a minister or consul representing such foreign country in the United States shall certify that the conditions to the validity of the marriage of the laws of such country shall have been complied with."

As to the form of such a certificate, see Mr. Rockhill, Acting Sec. of State, to Viscount Gough, British chargé, Sept. 23, 1896, MS. Notes to Great Britain, XXIII. 461.

" As to the validity of a marriage, celebrated without regard to the laws of the place, by ministers or consuls of the United States by virtue of their official functions, I have very decided opinions in opposition to the existence of any such power; yet I am aware that there are important considerations in favor of its exercise by foreign ministers, which are not applicable to consuls. There is no law, State or Federal, conferring such authority upon either, and it must therefore be deduced from general considerations and not from positive legislation. With respect to consuls, the question is not only clear upon general principles but it has been settled, so far as it is competent to settle it by the authority of this Department, as may be seen by reference to the 618th section of the Consular Regulations, promulgated November 10th, 1856. It is presumable that when Mr. Goundie assumed this power he could not have been aware that its existence had been thus officially denied.

" There is no subsequent legislation which confers this jurisdiction. I consider that the 31st section of the act of Congress, passed at its last session, giving certain judicial powers to ministers and consuls of the United States in foreign countries, and which declares that marriages celebrated therein in presence of any consular officer, between persons who would be authorized to marry in the District of Columbia, shall have the same force and effect, and shall be valid to all intents and purposes, as if the said marriage had been solemnized within the United States, provides only for the presence of a consular officer upon such an occasion. And the provision is no doubt a wise one, not only because it furnishes security against fraud, but because it renders more easy the authentication of such marriages in the United States. But it does not withdraw the celebration of such marriages from the authority of the country where they take place, nor does it give any power to the consular officer himself to perform the ceremony. And that part of the same section which declares that such marriages shall have the same effect as if they had been cele-

brated in the United States must in my opinion be limited to places
and districts over which Congress possesses the power of exclusive
jurisdiction and cannot operate in the respective States."

> Mr. Cass, Sec. of State, to Mr. Fay, min. to Switzerland, Nov. 12, 1860,
> MS. Inst. Switz. I. 85.

" The purpose of Congress in requiring the presence of a consul
at a marriage may have been to secure the testimony of an official
witness of our own to the act, a witness, too, who would be bound
to record the transaction in the archives of his consulate and attest
it under his official seal.

" Though unofficial witnesses might be held competent to testify,
their testimony might not be held available when required. The
parties to the marriage, however, could always produce the consul's
certificate when occasion might call therefor. . . .

" The provisions of our act of 1860 upon the subject of marriages
abroad are not supposed to have been influenced by the legislation of
any other country. They are understood to have been in the main
designed to correct a practice which prevailed at some points of
marriages by consuls without reference to the local law."

> Mr. Fish, Sec. of State, to Mr. Marsh, min. to Italy, Jan. 19, 1875, For.
> Rel. 1875, II. 761. See, also, Mr. Fish to Mr. Washburn, Nov. 14,
> 1874, For. Rel. 1875, I. 445.
> See Mr. Marsh to Mr. Fish, Oct. 12, 1874, For Rel. 1875, II. 755.

" (1) In the opinion of the Secretary the act of Congress to which
you refer does not affect marriage of persons domiciled in the particular States of the Union. Each of these States is supreme in
its legislation as to all matters relating to the conditions of marriage,
as well as of divorce, within its limits.

" (2) Even to marriage abroad of persons domiciled in the District
of Columbia or in the Territories over which Congress has jurisdiction, the presence and attestation of a consular officer is not,
under the act of Congress, necessary. Such marriages, if otherwise
valid in the District of Columbia or in the Territories, would be
valid, although not solemnized before a consular officer. Nor does
the presence of a consular officer by itself give validity to marriages
otherwise invalid.

" (3) It is very questionable whether, even as to marriages of
persons domiciled in the District of Columbia and in the Territories,
the act of Congress has any effect out of those jurisdictions. It
is a principle of international law that the forms of solemnizing marriages must conform to the rules established by the law of the place
of solemnization. No particular sovereign can withdraw from the
operation of that principle the marriages of his subjects when sol-

emnized abroad. He may say, ' In my own dominions these marriages shall be valid,' but he cannot by such a decree change the rule of international law in this respect, which is accepted by foreign nations. In other words, the general position is, that a local law cannot extraterritorially affect the law of nations. We have applied this rule to cases where foreign sovereigns have attempted by local decrees to vary international law in respect to blockade and to piracy. There is no reason why the same rule should not be applied in respect to marriage, and the British Government in its instructions to its diplomatic agents has been careful to make this distinction. It has told them that while marriages of British subjects abroad in ambassadors' residences would be valid in the British dominions, they are, in the opinion of the crown officers, ' not necessarily valid without the dominions of Her Majesty.' (See Lord Stanley's letter of February 8, 1867, cited in 2 Fraser on Husband and Wife, 2d ed., (Edinburgh, 1878), 1312.)

"(4) There is no reason, however, why a consul should not permit marriages of American citizens, no matter what may be their domicil, to be solemnized in his presence whenever they desire it. While he can not either make or unmake such marriage, he gives in his certificate a memorandum which will enable him, when living, to refresh his memory when called as a witness to the fact of the marriage, and, after his death, such a memorandum may be admissible as documentary proof of the marriage. The fact, also, that the marriage took place in his presence would lead to the inference that it was entered into advisedly."

> Mr. Bayard, Sec of State, to Mr. Winchester, min. to Switzerland, Aug. 15, 1885, For. Rel. 1885, 807, 808.

> Whether a marriage solemnized abroad in the presence of a consular officer of the United States is validated, so far as concerns this country, under the act of Congress of June 22, 1860, by the fact of the presence of the consul, depends upon whether the parties are domiciled in the District of Columbia, or in one of the Territories of the United States. If they are domiciled in one of the States of the Union the question, so far as concerns such State, would depend upon its local law. (Mr. Bayard, Sec. of State, to Mr. Ketcham, M. C., July 2, 1888, For. Rel. 1888, I. 646.)

" 420. Effect of marriage in presence of consul.—It it provided by statute that ' Marriages in presence of any consular officer of the United States in a foreign country, between persons who would be authorized to marry if residing in the District of Columbia, shall be valid to all intents and purposes, and shall have the same effect as if solemnized within the United States.' (R. S. sec. 4082.) The statute does not exclude modes of solemnization other than that in presence of a consular officer. Marriages abroad, when not in the presence of a consular officer, if otherwise valid, are not invalidated by the above statute. The statute does not authorize the consular officer to perform the ceremony, but simply prescribes the legal effect which will be given to a marriage performed in his presence. In view of the exclusive authority of the States in such matters, this statute would probably not be operative outside of the District of Columbia and the Territories."

> Consular Regulations of the United States, 1896.
>
> This section of the Consular Regulations, 1896, forms section 178 of Instructions to the Diplomatic Officers of the United States, 1897. It may also be found in the printed Personal Instructions to the Diplomatic Agents of the United States, 1885, the last sentence of which, however, reads: "As under the Constitution of the United States the States have exclusive power of determining the conditions of marriage and divorce as to persons domiciled within their borders, this statute only covers marriages by persons domiciled in the District of Columbia or in the Territories."
>
> "This statute [of June 22, 1860, R. S. 4082] is now held in this Department to be unconstitutional, except so far as concerns the District of Columbia and the Territories." (Mr. Bayard, Sec. of State, to Mr. Garland, At. Gen., May 16, 1885, 155 MS. Dom. Let. 405.)
>
> "It is now held by the Department that the statute in question [R. S. sec. 4082] operates only as to persons domiciled in the District of Columbia or in the Territories." (Mr. Wharton, Assist. Sec. of State, to Mr. Southworth, Jan. 26, 1893, 190 MS. Dom. Let. 139.)

(6) CERTIFICATES OF LAW.

§ 241.

"Information has reached the Department that it is the practice with some of its diplomatic and consular representatives to issue, at the request of American citizens proposing to marry abroad, certificates as to the freedom of such parties from matrimonial disabilities, and as to the law in the United States regulating the mode of solemnizing marriage.

Order of Feb. 8, 1887.

"Waiving other objections to certificates of this class, it is enough now to say that the practice of issuing them is objectionable, because they may contain erroneous statements which may be productive of difficulty.

"Diplomatic and consular agents can ordinarily certify in respect to the matrimonial disabilities of individuals (*e. g.*, as to prior marriage, or parental control) upon hearsay only, and therefore unreliably.

"In certificates as to the laws in the United States regulating the solemnization of marriage the possibilities of error are great and manifest. Of these laws no accurate or reliable summary could be given. It is essential, for instance, to the validity of a marriage solemnized in Massachusetts and other New England States, that it should be solemnized by a local clergyman or magistrate after a license taken out in the office of the town clerk, which is virtually a publication. In other States [it is alleged] it is necessary to the ceremony that it should be solemnized by a minister of the Gospel. In most States a marriage by consent, so far as concerns ceremonial form, is valid; but even in these States law is frequently undergoing alteration.

" Serious consequences may ensue from errors made in this relation in diplomatic or consular certificates. A foreign local official may solemnize a marriage on such a certificate, but when a question involving the validity of the marriage arises in a superior court of law, it may well be decided that such certificate can not prove matters of fact, nor the law in that particular State, Territory, or District of the United States in which the parties were domiciled.

" The issue of these certificates is not authorized by statute nor by the instructions to diplomatic agents or consuls.

" The withholding of such certificates may prevent serious disaster. If citizens of the United States desire to be married before a foreign officer who requires information as to their individual status and the laws of their domicil, the information can be obtained from persons familiar with the facts, or from experts acquainted with the laws of such domicil; and in matters involving the validity of marriages and the legitimacy of children, too great trouble in this respect can not be taken.

" To the position that it is not competent for diplomatic or consular officers to state the law of the United States as to marriage, there is, however, one important exception to which your attention has been heretofore directed. Throughout the United States is recognized the principle of international law that a solemnization of marriage valid by the law of the place of solemnization will be regarded as valid everywhere. Hence, where persons domiciled in any part of the United States propose to be married in a foreign land, the forms of solemnization prescribed by the law of the domicil are of consequence only when the law of such foreign land adopts those forms as sufficient.

" Nothing in this order is intended to preclude a chief diplomatic representative of the United States, having obtained permission of the Department for that purpose, from certifying as to the law of any particular jurisdiction in the United States when called upon by a judicial tribunal, or a consul, who is an expert as to such law, from testifying thereto when called upon in a court of justice, or from certifying thereto when excused from testifying in such court."

Mr. Bayard, Sec. of State, circular to diplomatic and consular officers, Feb. 8, 1887, For. Rel. 1887, 1133.

" ORDERED BY THE SECRETARY.

" It is not competent, without the special authority of this Department, for diplomatic agents, consuls, or consular agents, to certify officially as to the *status* of persons domiciled in the United States and proposing to be married abroad, or as to the law in the United States, or in any part thereof, relating to the solemnization of marriages.

" T. F. BAYARD."

" I have before me your No. 462, of date of the 18th ultimo, and note your comment upon a circular order lately issued by this Department, that ' it is not competent, without special authority of this Department, for diplomatic agents, consuls, or consular agents to certify officially as to the *status* of persons domiciled in the United States, and proposing to be married abroad, or as to the law of the United States, or any part thereof, relating to the solemnization of marriages.'

"Among the causes which induced this order were statements made to this Department that not only had the law as to marriage in the United States been erroneously certified to by its representatives abroad, but that for such certificates excessive fees had been exacted. Printed certificates had also been issued by certain United States consuls in Europe, which stated, without qualification, that in no part of the United States are banns, or prior publication, or the assent of parents, or the presence of any particular civic or ecclesiastical official essential to the due celebration of marriage. I need scarcely say that such certificates are on their face erroneous.

" Your remark that the practice of granting certificates as to both *status* and marriage laws ' has existed at this [your] consulate for many years past,' and, after saying that you recognize ' the propriety ' of the Department carefully inquiring ' into the competency of a consular officer authorized to give certificates of this character,' you proceed to give reasons why you, from your prior experience and knowledge, and from the books at your command, are to be considered as ' competent ' to give such certificates.

" It is evident that you have misapprehended the meaning and application of the word ' competent,' as used in the circular order. It had no bearing upon the individual qualifications of the parties addressed, nor their capacity as legal experts, but related solely to the extent of their *official* functions and their *official* capacity or competency to perform certain acts. No reflection was implied or intended upon your professional attainments as a lawyer nor your ability to give reliable opinions in the line of that profession.

" But, as it is not within the competence of any officer of the executive branch of this Government to create new law or in any degree to exercise legislative powers, it is equally outside of executive duty or power to invade judicial functions and to certify *construction* of laws. The *status* of the parties to a projected marriage may be a matter of contestable fact, and equally the legal requisites of marriage in a particular jurisdiction may be a matter of contestable law. To neither of these is a consul of the United States legally competent to certify.

" It is proper for this Department and its representatives to advise citizens of the United States proposing to marry in foreign countries to comply in all respects with the *lex loci* of the solemnization, but it can not authorize its representatives to certify to disputed or disputable facts, nor as to the condition of law throughout the United States. Certificates of such a character having no legal authority could have no effect whatever on the judiciary before whom such questions of law or fact would necessarily come for decision. Many illustrations could be given of the danger of exposing marriages contracted abroad in reliance upon such official certificates to being invalidated by the subsequent judgments of courts having jurisdiction of the parties and the contract.

" The order in question is intended to restrain the official action of consuls, but in no degree to prohibit unofficial advice and counsel to individuals, or giving personal opinions or testimony as to laws or facts with which the consuls themselves may be familiar. The inhibition applies only to official certification of facts or law outside the scope and function of official duties and power."

> Mr. Bayard, Sec. of State, to Mr. Walker, Apr. 7, 1887, For. Rel. 1887, 359.
> Mr. Walker's No. 462 is printed in the same volume, p. 356.
>
> "This Department has never made any publication, in the nature of a report or otherwise, of the requisites of a valid marriage in the various states of Europe. The course of this Department has been to advise citizens of the United States desiring to be married abroad to comply with the law of the place of the performance of the marriage with reference to its celebration. Marriages so celebrated are generally recognized as valid everywhere. To this rule, however, requiring the ceremony to be performed according to the law of the place where the marriage occurs, there are certain exceptions; as where the marriage is performed in a barbarous land, or the law of the place of celebration imposes conditions impossible of performance or repugnant to the conscience of the parties. But the general rule applicable to civilized countries is that the ceremony must be performed according to the law of the place of performance." (Mr. Bayard, Sec. of State, to Mr. Hodges, Nov. 20, 1885, 58 MS. Dom. Let. 6.)

" I have received your No. 370, of the 2d ultimo, in which you request that this Department reconsider, so far as the legation of the United States in France is concerned, the recent circular of February 8 last, instructing the diplomatic agents, consuls, and consular agents of the United States to refrain from certifying officially, without the special authority of this Department, as to the status of persons domiciled in the United States and proposing to be married abroad, or as to the law in the United States, or in any part thereof, relating to the solemnization of marriages.

" The question to which the circular relates being one of very grave importance, the Department has given it the most careful consideration before and since the issuance of the circular, and has found no reason to change the conclusions therein stated. Whilst always solicitous to aid in every proper way and by all legitimate means citizens of the United States in foreign lands, the Department is of opinion that in respect to marriage there are more important considerations than that of the mere convenience of the contracting parties.

As was said in the circular, ' if citizens of the United States desire to be married before a foreign officer who requires information as to their individual status and the laws of their domicil, the information can be obtained from persons familiar with the facts, or from experts acquainted with the laws of such domicil; and in matters involving the validity of marriage and the legitimacy of children, too great trouble in this respect can not be taken.'

" It appears, however, from your dispatches, as well as from other sources, that in recent years a practice has sprung up in France and certain other countries, of diplomatic and consular officers of the United States giving official certificates not only as to the personal status of Americans desiring to be married abroad, but as to the law of their supposed domicil in respect to the forms of solemnization of marriage.

This arose in France (as you state in your No. 370) from the fact that it was deemed necessary, under the law, ' for an American desiring to be married in France to produce an official document showing when and where he was born, and to furnish evidence that if he is above age he can marry in the United States without the consent of his parents, and that publication of banns is only necessary where the marriage is solemnized.'

" But all these requisites could, it is supposed, be proved, and before the practice in question sprang up must have been proved by other evidence than the official certificate of a consular or diplomatic officer of the United States; and although such certification may be the most convenient form of proof, there are, in the opinion of the Department, serious objections to its use for the purpose indicated. Aside from the impropriety of consular or diplomatic officers certifying generally as to the law in different parts of the United States, such certification as you describe requires a judgment upon matters of fact. It is obvious that such a judgment, while it may expedite the performance of a marriage ceremony, is not conclusive as to the validity of that ceremony, and is not known to be receivable as evidence by judicial tribunals before whom the marriage might be called in question.

Neither is it known to be receivable under the laws of France by the French magistrates; and this doubt is increased by the statements in your No. 334 that, when the practice of issuing the certificates in question began, they were frequently rejected by the French mayors; that 'gradually, however, the practice established itself, and the Duke Decazes, minister of foreign affairs, having countenanced and recommended it, although unofficially, it was respected by the French authorities; but that even now occasionally a new mayor or an unreasonable subordinate refuses one or more of these papers and compels thereby the legation to ask the interposition of the higher authorities.'

"These statements suggest two conclusions: (1) That there is no law that makes those papers competent evidence in France of what they purport to prove; (2) that their reception is a matter of grace, brought about or aided by the unofficial advice of the French minister of foreign affairs, acting, it may be presumed, on the assurance of the minister of the United States, that the marriages of Americans upon such certificates would be valid in the United States.

"It is, as stated in Department's circular of February 8, a principle of international law, recognized throughout the United States, that a solemnization of marriage, valid by the law of the place of solemnization, will be regarded as valid everywhere.

"This rule is the principal safeguard of persons marrying abroad, and when it is relaxed in favor of the law of the domicil of the parties it is important that the greatest care should be taken to ascertain what that law is, in order that the ceremony may be not only performed, but performed validly. The Department is not, however, aware that the law of France in respect to marriage makes any difference between citizens and foreigners. It was declared at the time of the preparation of the French codes, in answer to the question of the First Consul with respect to marriages of foreigners in France: 'Foreigners residing in France are subject to French laws.' (See article on the international law of marriage, by the late W. B. Lawrence, 11 Albany Law Journal, 33.) It is true that the French law may, as to certain elements of personal capacity, employ the law of the domicil as the test of such capacity, but the Department is not informed that under the French law the requirements of a valid marriage between foreigners are in any other respect different from those of a marriage between citizens.

"Now, as to the personal status or capacity of the parties to a projected marriage, there may be both questions of contested or contestable law and of contested or contestable fact; and to neither of these is a diplomatic or consular officer of the United States competent to certify officially. In an instruction to Mr. Fay, minister of the

United States to Switzerland, under date of November 12, 1860, Mr.
Cass said that when ' the inquiry is made in Europe how a marriage
must be celebrated there, not only to be valid but to carry with it its
proper rights in the United States, no general answer can be given to
the question. The answer must embrace not only the provisions of
the laws of the United States so far as regards the places governed by
those laws, but must embrace also the laws of thirty-three States,
beside the Territories.'

" It may be observed that Mr. Cass, while Secretary of State, gave
special attention to the subject of foreign marriages, and it was by his
instruction, which has never been revoked, that an end was put to
the practice of performing marriage ceremonies in legations, in supposed conformity with the law of the place of the American domicil
of the parties. So decided was he in the opinion that the *lex loci
celebrationis* should be followed, that on the occasion of the marriage of his own daughter, while he was minister of the United
States at Paris, to the American secretary of legation, he did not
consider the marriage of the parties at his hotel as sufficient, notwithstanding their extraterritorial immunities, and after taking the
advice of the most eminent French lawyers, obliged the parties to
be married at the mayoralty and to fulfill all the formalities required
of a French citizen by the Code Napoléon. (11 Alb. L. J. 34.)

" In your No. 334, of December 31 last, you inclosed blank forms
of the certificates which the legation has of late years been issuing.
The first of these states generally that proof having been made to
the legation of certain facts as to the birth of a certain person, it
is given to take the place of an extract from the register of the civil
state. The second certificate states that according to the terms of
the American laws the consent of parents is not necessary to a marriage of persons twenty-one years of age. The third form states
that, according to the American laws, the publications of the marriages of Americans, celebrated in a foreign country, is not required
at the domicil of the parties in the United States.

" The second of these certificates is regarded as the least open to
objection, and may indeed be regarded in the light of a *certificat
de coutume*, twenty-one years being the age of majority and emancipation from parental and other control all over the United States.

" The first is open to the serious criticism that, while it takes
the form of an official judgment upon questions of fact, it is not
authorized by any law, and while it may expedite the performance
of a marriage ceremony, would not, as has already been remarked,
necessarily be received by any judicial tribunal before whom the marriage might be called in question, as evidence of the facts stated.
The third form of certificate states a general conclusion of law,
which the Department is not competent to authorize. Publication

of banns is a matter under the regulation of the different States and Territories, and this Department certainly is not competent to declare what the law in this relation of those States and Territories either is or may be ascertained by their judicial courts to be. The danger of such an attempt is shown by Circular No. 39, to which you refer as furnishing reliable information. The requisites of a valid marriage in the different States and Territories are sometimes matters of judicial ascertainment, as well as of statutory enactment. For example, Circular No. 39, in giving the requisites of a valid marriage in Massachusetts, wholly omits to state what has since been decided by the supreme judicial court of that Commonwealth, that a consensual marriage, without the presence of an officiating clergyman or magistrate, and to which neither party was a Friend or Quaker, is invalid (Com. *v.* Munson, 127 Mass. 459). It has also recently been held in the District of Columbia that a marriage in the District by consent, without some religious ceremony, is not sufficient to make a valid marriage by the law there existing.

" In a general note to Circular No. 39 it is stated that in ' the several States and Territories penalties are imposed by the statutes for a failure to comply with the requirements as to license or return of the certificate; . . . but in none of the States or Territories is the marriage null and void because of a non-compliance with the requirements of the statute.'

" It is, however, understood that by an old statute of North Carolina marriages solemnized without a license first had are null and void, and the same rule has been held to exist in Tennessee, where the statute of North Carolina was in force. (Wharton, Conflict of Laws, § 173, note 1, 2d ed., 1881.) Whether the same rule would be held to be in force in other places in the United States under the special provision of statutes, it is not within the province of this Department to declare, and can only be conjectured.

" It is important to observe that in recent years the tendency of the courts in the United States has been to require a stricter compliance than formerly with forms and ceremonies in the solemnization of marriages. As population has increased, and the difficulty of complying with forms has been diminished, considerations of convenience have been given less and less weight. And, on the other hand, there has been a growing tendency, both in legislation and in judicial decisions, to place some check on inconsiderate and informal alliances.

" Under these circumstances it would be highly inexpedient for this Department to undertake to declare in advance what may be the decisions of the judicial branch with whom the sole power to decide in these important matters rests. The function of delivering judgments, whether orally or in the form of certificates, is wholly judicial, and is not under our system confided to the executive branch. The authentication of a statute, or other matter of record, may be the duty of an executive officer, but not to declare its effect.

" Holding these views, it would be a breach of duty in this Department to authorize its diplomatic or consular agents to issue, in matters which from the nature of things are uncertain, certificates which, if erroneous, would be productive of consequences so disastrous as the illegitimation of marriages, however innocently solemnized, on the faith of such certificates, and the bastardizing of the issue of such marriages.

"All these serious responsibilities and dangers are avoided by the parties conforming to the *lex loci celebrationis*."

> Mr. Bayard, Sec. of State, to Mr. McLane, May 9, 1887, For. Rel, 1887, 295. Mr. McLane's No. 370 is printed in For. Rel. 1887, 287. In his No. 334, of Dec. 31, 1886, Mr. McLane said : " The conditions required by the French laws for a marriage in France are substantially as follows : Each party desiring to marry must produce—
>
> "(1°) A certificate of birth, issued by some civil authority, written or translated into French. A certificate of baptism or any paper issued by a church is not accepted.
>
> "(2°) The written consent of parents or guardian, or a certificate of their death.
>
> " (3°) Evidence of six months' residence in the commune or ward in which the marriage is to take place, from at least one of the two parties.
>
> "(4°) Publication of bans on two Sundays, and at least during eleven days at the mayoralty of that commune, and if one of the two parties has not there the residence required, publication also at the mayoralty of his previous residence.
>
> " Very few Americans being able to comply literally with these conditions, the legation sought to relieve them of the embarrassment by issuing papers which might be accepted as substitutes for those required by the French authorities.
>
> " With this view three forms of certificates were prepared in French, copies of which are herewith inclosed.
>
> " Form No. 1, which is printed because very frequently applied for, is a certificate of birth. It is given upon evidence satisfactory to the legation ; some family record, a certificate of baptism, or, occasionally, the statement under oath of the parties.
>
> " Form No. 2 is a statement that in the United States the consent of the parents is not necessary for the marriage of their children when they are over age.
>
> " Form No. 3 certifies that publication of bans at the domicile in the United States of an American marrying abroad is not required.
>
> " In the beginning these substitutes were frequently rejected by the French mayors, and many of our countrymen who had made arrangements to marry in France had to proceed to England or to Switzerland, where the laws are less exacting, to have their marriage solemnized. Gradually, however, the practice established itself and the Duke Decazes, minister of foreign affairs, having at

the time countenanced and recommended it, although unofficially, it was respected by the French authorities and became general. It happens, nevertheless, that occasionally a new mayor or an unreasonable subordinate refuses one or more of these papers and compels thereby the legation to ask the interposition of the higher authorities. It is an instance of this kind which gives occasion to the present dispatch.

"Originally the certificates above mentioned were issued only by this legation and being given simply to accommodate our countrymen, they were and are still issued without charge. Later on the consulate also issued certificates of this kind, sometimes in the identical form prepared and adopted by this legation, sometimes in another form, and generally made some pecuniary charge for them. As those who were unwilling or unable to pay for these papers could obtain them gratuitously at the legation, I did not think it advisable to question either the right of the consulate to issue such papers or the legality and propriety of charging for them, as my predecessors had not done so. Recently the practice has created trouble and embarrassment, which obliges me to interfere," (For Rel. 1887, 279, 280 et seq.)

The certificates referred to were in the following form :

FORM No. 1.

| Acte de ——
No. ——. Paris —— 188—.
Acte de ——
de ——
Père —— ——
Mère —— ——
le ——
à ——
État —— États-Unis d'Amérique. | LÉGATION DES ÉTATS-UNIS D'AMÉRIQUE. | LÉGATION DES ÉTATS-UNIS D'AMÉRIQUE.
[Extrait des Registres de l'État Civil.]
No. ——.   Paris, ce ——, 188—.
Preuve ayant été faite à cette Chancellerie que F —— légitime de —— est —— le —— 188—, à ——, État de ——, États-Unis d'Amérique; le présent certificat a été délivré pour tenir lieu d'extrait des registres de l'État Civil.
L'Envoyé Extraordinaire et Ministre Plénipotentiaire des États-Unis (or the Secretary):
—— ——. |

FORM No. 2.

LÉGATION DES ÉTATS-UNIS D'AMÉRIQUE.

Paris, ——, 188—.

A la prière de M. ——, citoyen américain demeurant temporairement en France, No. ——, rue ——, il est certifié par la présente qu'aux termes des lois américaines le consetement des père et mère n'est point nécessaire pour le mariage des personnes âgées de vingt et un ans accomplis.

(Signed by the minister or the secretary.)

Form No. 3.

Légation des États-Unis d'Amérique,
Paris, ———, 188–.

A la prière de M. ———, citoyen des États-Unis demeurant temporairement à Paris rue ———, No. ———, il est certifié qu'aux termes des lois américaines la publication des mariages des américains célébrés à l'étranger n'est point requise au domicile originel aux États-Unis.

(Signed by the minister or the secretary.)

" Your No. 408, of the 15th ultimo, has been received. You therein examine the various rulings of the Department, so far as accessible to you, touching the regularity or propriety of permitting consuls to certify to, or state for the information of whom it may concern, the announcement found in Mr. Bayard's circular instruction to diplomatic and consular officers of February 8, 1887, that 'throughout the United States is recognized the principle of international law that a solemnization of marriage valid by the law of the place of solemnization will be regarded as valid everywhere.'

" The language of this instruction appears to be guardedly confined to the question of the form and manner in which a marriage may be solemnized under the laws of the State where it is performed. It does not touch the question of the status of the individuals as a condition to the validity of the marriage, as to which important exceptions are found in the legislation of many countries. Consequently your suggestion is confined merely to certifying to the fact that if parties, citizens of a State or States of this Union, are competent under the laws thereof to contract matrimony, their marriage abroad according to the laws of the country of their temporary sojourn would be held valid as to form in the State or States of which they are citizens.

" The value of such a conditional certification may be doubtful, as it leaves untouched the essential factor of the question, namely, the lawful ability of the parties to contract matrimony according to the statutes of the State or States of their residence. As to this latter point the rule of the Department prohibiting certification is clear and necessary.

" There is another reason why a diplomatic or consular officer should decline to certify as to the legal requisites of marriage in the United States. The power to make such a certificate is not conferred on him by the laws of the United States, nor by international law, and he has no official powers which are not derived from one of these sources. Therefore, whatever private knowledge a diplomatic or consular officer may have respecting the laws of marriage, he is not authorized to certify them upon that knowledge. It is not a question of individual knowledge, but of official competency.

"I have pleasure, therefore, in approving your judgment that it was proper to decline to advise the making of a certificate, even in the quoted language of Mr. Bayard's circular instruction of February 8, 1887."

> Mr. Olney, Sec. of State, to Mr. Runyon, amb. to Germany, Dec. 9, 1895, For. Rel. 1895, I. 538.
>
> Section 390, Consular Regulations, 1888, provided: "It is not competent, without special authority from the Department, for diplomatic agents, consuls, or consular agents to certify officially as to the status of persons domiciled in the United States and proposing to be married abroad, or as to the law in the United States or any part thereof relating to the solemnization of marriage."
>
> The commercial agent of the United States at Freiburg, in Baden, having certified "that according to the laws of the United States there is no impediment to the marriage" of a certain citizen of the United States, and "that especially he does not need the consent of his parents, and that the proclamation of the banns of his marriage in Cleveland is not necessary," Cleveland apparently being considered the American home of the individual in question, attention was called to the consul's "violation of the Department's rules," in certifying as to things "none of which was within his official cognizance;" and particular reference was made to the instruction to Mr. Runyon of Dec. 9, 1895. (Mr. Olney, Sec. of State, to Mr. Uhl, amb. to Germany, Nov. 20, 1896, MS. Inst. Germany, XIX. 684.)

"Consular officers are not competent to certify officially as to the status and ability to marry of persons domiciled in the United States and proposing to be married abroad; nor as to the laws of the United States, or of the States or Territories, touching capacity for marriage or the solemnization thereof. The power to make a certificate as to the legal requisites in the United States for a valid marriage abroad is not conferred on consular officers by the laws of the United States nor by international law, and they have no official powers which are not derived from any of these sources. Whatever private knowledge a consular officer may have respecting the laws of marriage, he is not authorized to certify the same officially."

> Sec. 422, Consular Regulations of the United States, 1896.
>
> The word "ability" in the first sentence of this section evidently refers to the capacity of the parties to contract a marriage.

It is not competent for a diplomatic agent of the United States abroad to give an authoritative certificate as to the effect of a divorce granted in the country of his legation.

> Mr. Frelinghuysen, Sec. of State, to Mr. Cramer, Jan. 10, 1883, MS. Inst. Switz. II. 161.

"Mr. Eustis's dispatch No. 500 of the 21st of May last, in relation to the certification by the embassy or consul-general of the opinions of American counsel on points of the law of the United States or

of the several States of the Union, has been carefully considered
with a view to meeting, as far as might be practicable, the inconveniences which, as the enclosures to Mr. Eustis's dispatch show,
would be occasioned to American citizens residing or being in France
were the custom of giving such certificates suspended.

"A somewhat similar despatch on the same subject, No. 141 of May
22, has also been received from Consul-General Morss.

" In the practice of the French courts in regard to proof of foreign law in cases brought before them, as stated by Mr. Leopold
Goirand in the affidavit attached to Mr. Eustis's dispatch, it appears
to suffice when ' a legal practitioner, duly qualified as such in the
country whose law is to be proved, gives a written opinion thereon.
To this opinion must be subjoined a declaration of the ambassador
or consul of his country, stating that the said practitioner is duly
qualified, according to the law of his country, and that consequently
he is competent to deliver the opinion which precedes such certificate.'

" The form of certificate heretofore employed in the consulate
general, and presumed to be identical with that employed in the
embassy, appears to meet these requirements with two exceptions.
It is not clearly stated that the qualification of the counsel to deliver
an opinion or attestation in question flows from and is solely a
consequence of his membership of a stated bar, but the certificate
appears to be an independent certification of such qualification.
Furthermore, the certificate adds that ' faith is due ' to the counsel's
attestation of the law, which involves virtually, if not in fact, an
independent certification of the embassy or consulate-general that
the counsel's certificate of opinion imports a verity. In none of the
enclosures with Mr. Eustis's dispatch does it appear that this supplementary certification is required.

" An attestation by the competent representative of the United
States that the counsel is a member of a bar and as such qualified to
render the opinion to which his name is signed necessarily carries
with it an assumption that the paper is given by him in good faith,
and as such entitled to credence as the testimony of an expert. It is,
of course, beyond the official competence of our representatives to
attest the verity of his statements.

" It is furthermore noted that the form of authentication heretofore used describes the attested paper as ' a certificate,' a term usually
applied to the attestation of a fact, while in practice the paper is
an opinion of counsel, and may and frequently does involve the construction and application of the law to the case in point. It cannot
well be regarded as a simple attested copy of the text of the law,
and it might also be open to question, inasmuch as under our system a
practitioner at the bar is not legally competent to give a certified copy

of the law of any State as evidence of record before a court, he not being a certifying officer of the State. The same consideration holds good as regards Federal laws.

"The Department has not been able to ascertain definitely, either from the correspondence or from text-books, what are the requirements in French judicial procedure when the application of foreign law becomes necessary, nor in what character ' proofs of foreign law ' are received and viewed by the courts. There are indications, however, that foreign law is not considered purely as a fact to be proved by the party who relies upon it as any other facts supporting his case, but that, when a case turns upon a rule of foreign law, the foreign law is judicially recognized and administered as, for the particular case, a part of the law of the land. In such circumstances, the maxim which rules in native law—*Jura novit curia*—cannot of course be assumed, and the court is entitled to the aid of the parties in obtaining requisite knowledge of the foreign law which is to be applied. In this view, the so-called ' certificates of law ' which have been the subject of this correspondence may be considered, not as evidence proving a fact, but as sources of information to the court, designed to relieve the judge from laborious inquiry and to protect him from error which might result from his unaided investigations. If it be true that foreign laws are not required in France to be proved as substantive facts, but are required to be made known to the court for its information and enlightenment merely, the court being the final judge of what is the law, and at liberty to extend its investigations beyond the statement or ' proof ' of the law furnished by the parties, an *opinion* upon any matter of American law, by a person qualified to render such an opinion, would seem to be as properly admissible in the courts and as valuable in the way of information as the ' *certificate of law* ' which has been the subject of the Department's objection.

"Being satisfied of the necessity of continuing in some practicable and legitimate form the custom of attestation of the testimony and opinions of counsel which has so long prevailed in France, this Department, upon reconsideration of the matter, is prepared to authorize the use of an amended form of certificate, of which copies in French and English are appended hereto. You will ascertain whether this draft form is acceptable to the French judicial authorities, and if it be it may be forthwith substituted for that heretofore used. If, however, an amendment or alteration be suggested to conform to the French requirements or usage, you will report the same to the Department for its further consideration. It is hoped, however, that the form now given will suffice, as it appears to meet all the essential conditions described in the enclosures to Mr. Eustis's dispatch.

" Unless the Department is mistaken in its conception of the French law, as above given, the proposed form of certificate is more consistent with what the French courts require than the certificate heretofore in use, but it must be remembered that the Department has no reliable information as to what is the French requirement, and must leave the question of the sufficiency of the proposed form to be settled by submission to the proper authorities.

" A similar instruction will be sent to the consul-general in answer to his later representations on the subject. When the adoption of an amended form in this or some other equally acceptable shape is decided upon, you will advise Mr. Morss thereof in order that it may be forthwith adopted in the business of the consulate-general.

" I note Mr. Eustis's suggestion that this matter of certification of the opinions of counsel might be left wholly to the consulate-general, but I do not see the necessity for such a course, or that there is any objection to the attestation of the embassy being given in the proper cases when requested by the parties in interest."

> Mr. Olney, Sec. of State, to Mr. Vignaud, chargé at Paris, July 13, 1896, MS. Inst. France, XXIII. 311.

Form of certificate, in French and English.

Je soussigné certifie et atteste que Mr. ——— est membre du barreau de la cour Supreme de l'Etat de ——— et qu 'á ce titre il a qualité pour delivrer la consultation ci-dessus.

Paris, le ——— 18—.

(Signature and official title.)

I, the undersigned, certify and attest that A. B. is a member of the bar of the supreme court of the State of ——— and that, as such, he is legally qualified to give the preceding opinion.

(Signature and official title.)

" Referring to the Department's instruction to you of the 13th ultimo, authorizing the use by your embassy and by the consul-general of an amended form of ' certificates of law,' I have to acknowledge the receipt of your despatch No. 551, of the 10th instant, stating that the French Government is willing to accept the form proposed with the single substitution of the word ' attestation' or ' declaration ' for the word ' consultation.'

" In reply I have to inform you that this Government accepts the amendment ' la declaration,' so that the certificate will read in French as follows:

" Je soussigné certifie et atteste que Mr. ——— est membre du barreau de la cour Supreme de l'Etat de ——— et qu 'á ce titre il a qualité pour delivrer la declaration ci-dessus.

" Paris, le ——— 18—.

" L. S.   (Signature and official seal.)

" The form in the English language will remain unchanged as follows :

" I, the undersigned, certify and attest that A. B. is a member of the bar of the supreme court of the State of ——— and that, as such, he is legally qualified to give the preceding opinion.

"Paris, ———, 18—.

"L. S.   (Signature and official title.)"

" You are instructed to take the necessary steps to have the amended form adopted at once."

> Mr. Adee, Act. Sec. of State, to Mr. Vignaud, chargé at Paris, Aug. 27, 1896, MS. Inst. France, XXIII, 334.

4. LAWS OF VARIOUS COUNTRIES.

(1) ARGENTINE REPUBLIC.

§ 242.

"As a number of vexatious delays and embarrassments have occurred here recently among citizens of the United States in reference to rights of marriage I have deemed it advisable, for personal information, to transmit to the Department duplicate copies of the law of matrimony which went into effect in this country April 1, 1889, together with translations of the same, also in duplicate.

" By article 19 of this law, it is provided that the parties intending to contract matrimony, at the time of expressing their consent as required by article 14 of the law, must produce before the public officer having charge of the respective civil registry the following papers:

" (1) Certificate of birth or baptism.

" (2) In case of previous marriage, certificate of death of former spouse.

" (3) A duly legalized copy of the decree annulling any previous marriage of either party.

" (4) The authentic declaration of the person whose consent is required by the law. Also, in case the original domicile of either party is not in the Argentine Republic, such party must produce a certificate of his or her civil status in that domicile.

" In case of the non-existence of the certificates required by the above article 19, the facts may be shown under article 21 by other modes of proof permitted by the Argentine civil code."

> Mr. Hanna, min. to Arg. Rep., to Mr. Blaine, Sec. of State, May 20, 1889, For. Rel. 1889, 7. The translation of the law, which was passed Nov. 12, 1888, is printed with the dispatch.
>
> Art. 14 reads : " The consent of the contracting parties expressed before the public officer in charge of the civil register is indispensable for the existence of matrimony. The act in which any of these requisites shall be wanting shall not produce any civil effects, even if the parties acted in good faith."

The provisions of article 19 are given above, in the dispatch.

Article 21 reads: "In case of the non-existence of the certificates [required by article 19], or when the inscription on the register shall have been made under false names or as of parents unknown, these facts may be proved by the other modes of proof admitted in this code."

"Referring to Minister Hanna's No. 235, May 20, 1889, reciting certain embarrassments to citizens of the United States contemplating marriage here and inclosing translation of the civil marriage law of this country of November 12, 1888, I have the honor to invite your attention to a new enactment herewith inclosed on the subject-matter, involving certain repeals and amendments whereby it will be seen that a certificate of birth or baptism, and in case of previous marriage a certificate of death, are no longer required and that a certificate of civil status is likewise dispensed with."

> Mr. Pitkin, min. to Arg. Rep., to Mr. Blaine, Sec. of State, Nov. 20, 1889, For. Rel. 1889, 18.
>
> A translation of the new law is printed with the dispatch. Article 1 annuls clauses (1), (2), and (4) of article 19, and also article 21, of the law of Nov. 12, 1888, supra.

(2) BELGIUM.

§ 243.

"I have the honor to acknowledge the receipt of your unnumbered instruction of February 8 last, addressed to the diplomatic and consular officers of the United States, on the subject of issuing certificates, at the request of American citizens proposing to marry abroad, as to the freedom of such parties from matrimonial disabilities, and as to the law of the United States regulating the mode of solemnizing marriage. I have carefully read the instruction and will strictly guide my official conduct by it.

"It is, perhaps, not irrelevant in this connection to also refer to marriages which sometimes take place in the United States between Belgians and Americans, without observing the provisions of the Belgian law, the restrictions of which, as in the case of the French law, attach to the Belgian citizen even in a foreign country. This is especially so with regard to obtaining the consent of the parents, where the Belgian is under twenty-five years of age.

"Several cases have already come under my observation since my residence here, where the marriage has been repudiated by one of the parties, it is always the man, because of noncompliance with the Belgian law in obtaining consent of parents. In one of these cases the marriage has been already declared void, and other cases are now pending in the courts."

> Mr. Tree, min. to Belgium, to Mr. Bayard, Sec. of State, April 7, 1887, For. Rel. 1887, 36.

A correspondent stated that, in order to enable him to marry an Illinois lady, who was residing in Belgium, the Belgian authorities demanded an official statement that the statutes of Illinois did not require the consent of parents where the parties to a marriage had reached their majority, nor the publication of banns. The Department of State replied that the power to certify as to legal requisites in the United States of a marriage celebrated abroad was not conferred on diplomatic or consular officers, either by the laws of the United States or by international law, and that such officers possessed no powers not derived from those sources. " Whatever private knowledge a diplomatic or consular officer may have respecting the laws of marriage, he is not authorized to certify the same officially."

> Mr Day, Assist. Sec of State, to Mr. Reed, March 16, 1898, 226 MS. Dom. Let. 468.

(3) FRANCE.

§ 244.

For the law of France, see Certificates of Law, supra, § 241.

(4) GERMANY.

§ 245.

By article 43 of the Prussian law for the execution of the civil code, which went into effect Jan. 1, 1900, aliens desiring to marry in Prussia must present a certificate from a competent magistrate of the country to which they belong that he does not know of any impediment under its laws to their marriage, the competency of such magistrate to issue the certificate to be attested by a diplomatic or consular officer of the German Empire.

The Department of State informed the German ambassador at Washington that it was not advised of any Federal, State, or Territorial law that provided for the issuance by any magistrate of such a certificate.

> Mr. Hay, Sec. of State, to Mr. von Holleben, German amb., Feb. 21, 1900, For. Rel. 1900, 522.

April 20, 1900, the Department of State addressed to the governors of the various States and Territories a circular letter inquiring whether the courts issued certificates of competency such as are required by sec. 2 of the German imperial marriage code which went into effect throughout the Empire January 1, 1900, and which provides that persons desiring to be married in Germany shall produce a certificate from the proper authorities of their native or home state to the effect that such authorities know of no just cause why the marriage should not take place. Replies received from more than half of the States and Territories were to the effect that the courts did not issue such certificates. Among the States so replying were Connecticut, New York, New Jersey, and Montana.

> Mr. Hay, Sec. of State, to the governor of New York, April 20, 1900, 244 MS. Dom. Let. 410; Mr. Cridler, Third Assist. Sec. of State, to Mr. Mason, consul-gen. at Berlin, April 23, 1900, 172 MS. Inst. Consuls, 137; Mr. Cridler, Third Assist. Sec. of State, to Mr. Chester, June 1, 1900, 172 MS. Inst. Consuls, 555.
>
> It appears that a similar provision is found in the Hungarian marriage laws. (Mr. Cridler, Third Assist. Sec of State, to Mr. Chester, June 1, 1900, 172 MS. Inst. Consuls, 555.)

(5) ITALY.

§ 246.

" You remark that you had only recently become aware that consuls of the United States in Italy had been in the habit of issuing certificates to meet the requirements of section 103 of the Italian civil code, which requires a declaration from competent authority that there are no impediments to a proposed marriage. It is probable, however, that the practice of issuing such certificates has long prevailed, and the Department sees no objection to them if due inquiry be made as to the facts before they are issued."

> Mr. Fish, Sec. of State, to Mr. Marsh, min. to Italy, Jan. 19, 1875, For. Rel. 1875, II. 761.

" Your dispatch No. 538, of the 19th ultimo, has been received. It states, in its closing paragraph, that in a case of marriage between American citizens in Italy, you might advise that a blank in the consular certificate should be filled with the words ' laws of the United States.' This, however, would, it is apprehended, not be a judicious course, and it might prove to be judicially untennable. The only law of the United States on the subject of marriage is that which provides that all marriages celebrated in the presence of a consular officer in a foreign country between persons who would be authorized to marry if residing in the District of Columbia are valid to all intents and purposes as if said marriage had been solemnized in the United States. The phrase ' laws of the United States ' might therefore be deemed to imply laws of the several States. Now, as the laws of the several States on the subject of marriage are various, if the certificate were to say that the marriage was performed according to the ' laws of the United States,' it might be held to be vague and inaccurate.

" The United States statute on the subject of marriages above referred to (Rev. Stat., § 4082) defines those who may be married under its provisions, namely, ' persons who would be authorized to marry if residing in the District of Columbia,' but is silent as to the persons who may perform the ceremony.   When, however, it speaks of ' marriage in a foreign country,' it is but reasonable to hold that to be a marriage, it must be solemnized (in the absence of authority given by the laws of the United States to any other person) by some person authorized, by the law of the country where the marriage takes place, to perform that ceremony, or in some mode recognized by such law.

" In this view it is believed that the blank indicated by you in form of certificate No. 87, in Consular Regulations of September 1, 1874, should be filled with the name of the country in which the marriage takes place, and not refer to the authority of the party performing the ceremony, as derived from the laws of the United States, which do not give authority to any person to solemnize marriages.   It is not supposed that actual statutory enactments are essential to give the authority, but such authority as would seem to exist in Italy for the performance of the marriage ceremony by a Protestant priest, as is inferred from the statement in your dispatch, that ' while there is no express provision on the point in the Italian code,' you are assured that such a marriage ' between Americans would be held legal ' in Italy.

" Possibly it would be well to use the word ' law,' which will cover unwritten as well as statute law, instead of the word ' laws.' "

> Mr. Cadwalader, Acting Sec. of State, to Mr. Marsh, min. to Italy, Apr. 15, 1875, For. Rel. 1875, II. 764.
>
> Mr. Marsh's No. 538 is printed in For. Rel. 1875, II. 764.

" I inclose herewith copy of a dispatch dated June 1 last, from Consul-General Alden, touching the obstacles encountered by citizens of the United States desiring to be married in Italy, growing out of the refusal of the authorities there to perform the ceremony without an official certificate from a consul of the United States that no objection exists to the projected marriage under the laws of the American domicile of the parties.

" The case to which the above-mentioned dispatch of the consul-general refers was reported in his No. 139, of the 4th of May last, copy of which is also inclosed.   It appears from this dispatch that a Miss ———, from Boston, Mass., but for a long time resident in Rome, desired to be married there, and that the authorities refused to permit the ceremony to be performed without an official certificate from the consul-general that ' there is nothing in the laws or customs of the United States that would render the marriage invalid,' and the consul-general requested that he should be authorized by telegraph to give such a certificate. To this request the Department replied by telegraph as follows:

" ' Certificate suggested by you inadmissible. There is no general law or custom in United States respecting marriage, and consuls can not certify officially as to State laws. No objection to your examination as expert.'

" In reply to this the consul-general informs the Department that there is no provision in the Italian law for his examination as an expert; that the authorities require a certificate of ' *nulla osta* ' from a consular authority; and that as the Department has forbidden the general issue of official certificates by consuls of American status and domiciliary law of American citizens in respect to marriage, it will be impossible for any American citizen hereafter to be married in Italy, unless the Italian law is changed or the order of the Department modified.

" In view of so serious a complication, it is important to know precisely what are the requirements of the Italian law in respect to the subject under consideration.

" As the Department is informed, there is not any express provision of Italian law that requires a consular certificate in marriage cases. There must be proof of the capacity of the parties under their personal law, and the certificate of a consul is accepted as sufficient proof, so far as the celebration of the marriage is concerned, of the nonexistence of any obstacle to the marriage under that law. But the Department had not supposed that the consular certificate was the only proof admitted for that purpose, and that the personal law of foreigners in respect to marriage could not be proved in the same way as any other matter of foreign law.

" I will thank you to make inquiry concerning this question and report thereon to the Department. And I herewith inclose for your information, and in explanation of the views of the Department on the general subject of the issuance by ministers and consuls of the United States of official certificates as to the law in this country respecting marriage, copies of certain correspondence which has lately taken place."

Mr. Bayard, Sec. of State, to Mr. Stallo, min. to Italy, July 6, 1887, For. Rel. 1887, 637.

" I have the honor to acknowledge the receipt of your communication of the 6th instant. . . .

" Long before the receipt of your communication I had occasion to examine the questions therein discussed, and found that the Italian law (section 103 of the civil code) not only did not require the consular certificate which our consuls have been in the habit of issuing, but in terms required the certificate of ' the competent authority of the place where the foreigner intending to contract marriage here is domiciled,' to the effect that there is no legal obstacle to the marriage in question. I called the attention of several Italian lawyers, who came to consult me in behalf of American ladies about to contract marriage in Italy, to the clear terms of the law, and told them that the Italian practice of substituting consular certificates for the certificates called for by the law was founded on a total misapprehension of the relation of consular officers of the United States to the several States whose legislation and judicial action determined the matters to be covered by the certificates. One of these lawyers has recently brought the question before the courts, and it has been decided that in lieu of the former consular certificate the Italian authorities must receive the certificate of the competent officer of the State where the party desiring to be married is domiciled, and, if there be no officer charged with the duty of issuing such a certificate, or, if the highest executive officer of the State refuse, on the ground of incompetency, to issue or cause to be issued such certificate, a certified copy of the law of the State may be received instead. And I have no doubt that, if necessary, the courts will go further and decide that proof of the law on the subject of marriages in any American State may be made by experts or in any other manner in which matters of foreign law are usually proved.

" It is, perhaps, not improper to add that the reasons assigned by the Department for its recent action seem to me conclusive, and that the practice, hitherto prevalent in several European states of issuing consular certificates as to the state of the law in any given American State was an abuse which it was eminently proper to abolish."

Mr. Stallo, min. to Italy, to Mr. Bayard, Sec. of State, July 30, 1887, For. Rel. 1887, 639.

" Referring to your No. 149, of the 30th of July last, in which you informed the Department that the law of Italy in relation to the marriage of foreigners in that country requires as evidence of the capacity of the parties—not a consular certificate—but either a certificate of the competent authority of the State in which the foreigner proposing to marry in Italy is domiciled, or else a certified copy of the law of such domicile, I inclose herewith, for your information, a copy of a dispatch just received from the consul-general at Rome, in which it is stated that the civil tribunal there has lately decided the proper evidence of matrimonial capacity of foreigners to be such as you describe.

" It is supposed that this is the decision to which your dispatch referred, and which, as you say, fully sustains the views of this Department as to the impropriety of consular and diplomatic officers

of the United States issuing such certificates in relation to matrimonial capacity as are inhibited by the recent order of the Department."

Mr. Bayard, Sec. of State, to Mr. Stallo, min. to Italy, Oct. 22, 1887, For.
Rel. 1887, 640.

"I have the honor to acknowledge the receipt from the Department
of State of an instruction numbered 43 and dated July 6, 1887, inclosing a copy of a letter dated July 1, 1887, from the Hon. T. F. Bayard,
Secretary of State, to the Hon. E. D. Hayden, showing the Department's views as to the issuance by consular officers of certificates of
matrimonial status.

"Referring to my dispatch No. 143, dated June 1, 1887, I beg to
say that although for many years it has been the custom of the Italian
authorities to require the consular certificate if '*nulla osta*' as a condition precedent to marriage of an American citizen in Italy, and
although the chief officer of the '*stato civile*'—the bureau of the
Roman municipal government having charge of the matters relating
to marriages—repeatedly assured me that the Italian law required
the issuance of such certificate of 'nulla osta' 'by a consular officer,'
and that he therefore had no discretion in the matter and could not
waive the requirement of such certificate; and although the same
statement was, as I am informed, repeatedly made by the officer of
the *stato civile* to several American citizens during the past winter
and spring, it has now been decided by the civil tribunal of Rome
that as section 103 of the Italian civil code specifies that as a condition precedent to the marriage of an American citizen in Italy such
citizen must present a certificate of 'nulla osta' from the 'competent
authority of the place where the foreigner intending to contract marriage here (*i. e.*, in Italy) is domiciled,' the *stato civile* has been mistaken in its claim that a consul is 'the competent authority' referred
to in the civil code, and that an American or other foreigner, desiring
to be married in Italy, must present a consular certificate of 'nulla
osta.' As no court will sustain a rule adopted by any municipal
authority which rule is in conflict with the civil code, it follows that
the rule of the *stato civile*, which has hitherto required a consular
certificate of '*nulla osta*,' can no longer be enforced here.

"The civil tribunal has further decided that when an American
citizen desires to be married in Italy, such citizens must furnish a
certificate of '*nulla osta*' from the proper officer of the State where
such citizen is domiciled; and that in case no such certificate can be
procured, either because there is no state officer whose province it is
to issue such certificates or because the chief executive officer of such
State declines to issue such certificate on the ground that he is not
legally competent to do so, then a certified copy of the laws of such

State relating to the matter in hand may be accepted by the *stato civile* in place of a certificate of ' *nulla osta.*' "

> Mr. Alden, consul-general at Rome, to Mr. Porter, Assist. Sec. of State, Sept. 27, 1887, being the dispatch accompanying Mr. Bayard's instruction to Mr. Stallo of Oct. 22, 1887, supra. (For. Rel. 1887, 640, 641.)

(6) PERU.

§ 247.

By a circular of July 31, 1840, the Peruvian Government prohibited the authorities of the country to permit marriages to take place between alien men and Peruvian women unless such aliens should inscribe themselves in the civil register, in conformity with the sixth article of the constitution, touching the acquisition of Peruvian citizenship. The British chargé d'affaires in Peru, acting under instructions, made representations in relation to the circular. By a circular of the ministry of foreign affairs of November 10, 1841, the prohibition was suspended, subject to the action of Congress. The object of the prohibition, as stated in the circular of 1841, was to secure observance of the principle that children born in Peru were Peruvians for all the purposes specified in the fifth article of the constitution. This principle, the circular observed, was not inconsistent with the privilege, which belonged to the children of aliens, on attaining their majority, " of claiming the citizenship of their fathers, being considered Peruvians in the meantime for all purposes whatever." It was stated in the circular that the British chargé d'affaires admitted in his representations the principle " that the authorities of Peru have a right to dictate the laws that they may deem proper relative to the marriage of Peruvians with foreigners," and that his remonstrance against the prohibition of 1840 was based on considerations of morality and policy. The circular of 1841 directed the authorities to issue the usual licenses for the marriage of aliens, provided that they should declare in their petitions that they would not contest the principle of the law of nations by virtue of which their children born in Peru would be " considered Peruvians by birth for all purposes whatever," until on attaining their majority they should claim the nationality of their fathers.

> MSS. Department of State.

" Referring to Department's instruction of July 29th last, No. 175, and to your despatch of October 26th, No. 334, concerning the registration of the marriage of foreigners in Peru, I enclose herewith copy of a letter from the Honorable R. R. Hitt in further relation to the subject.

"As you are aware, this Department is interested in seeing, if possible, the adoption of a marriage law in Peru more consonant with the general practice of modern nations than that which now prevails, and is particularly concerned lest the civil rights of American citizens in that quarter, as in the case alluded to in the enclosed letter, may be impaired through the deficiency of the existing law. This Government would be glad to learn that the subject will be revived at the next session of the Legislature, during the present year, and satisfactorily disposed of."

> Mr. Sherman, Sec. of State, to Mr. McKenzie, min. to Peru, March 31, 1897, MS. Inst. Peru, XVIII. 23, enclosing copy of a letter from Mr. Hitt, of March 27, 1897.
>
> See Mr. Adee, Act. Sec. of State, to Mr. Hitt, M. C., Dec. 4, 1897, 223 MS. Dom. Let. 687, referring to a civil marriages bill which had passed the Peruvian Congress, and which then awaited the approval of the President.

The Government of Peru issued, May 9, 1899, a decree prescribing a mode of legal proof to be followed by those desiring to marry outside the Roman Catholic Church, by availing themselves of the provisions of the civil marriage law of the 23rd of December, 1897. The law in question legalizes civil marriage when both parties to the contract are non-Catholics, and when, only one of the parties being of that church, the ecclesiastical authority refused to perform the ceremony.

> Mr. Dudley, min. to Peru, to Mr. Hay, Sec. of State, May 24, 1899, For. Rel. 1899, 590.
>
> The text of the decree is printed with Mr. Dudley's dispatch.
>
> "Our representative has been instructed to use all permissible friendly endeavors to induce the Government of Bolivia to amend its marriage laws so as to give legal status to the non-Catholic and civil marriages of aliens within its jurisdiction, and strong hopes are entertained that the Bolivian law in this regard will be brought, as was that of Peru some years ago, into harmony with the general practice of modern states." (President McKinley, annual message, Dec. 5, 1899, For. Rel. 1899, xv.)
>
> In order to satisfy the law of 1897, the mayor may authorize the marriage if either of the contracting parties declares that he or she never belonged to the Catholic communion or had separated from it. (For. Rel. 1903, 694.)
>
> As to a decree requiring diplomatic or consular certificates of celibacy and its revocation, see For. Rel. 1904, 687–692.

(7) RUSSIA.

§ 248.

Mr. Breckinridge, United States minister at St. Petersburg, transmitted to the Department of State, with his dispatch, No. 373, of August 27, 1896, an extract sent him by the Russian foreign office from the Russian Civil Code, containing the law of that country relating to marriage. The extract was as follows:

Extrait du Code Civil de Russie (T. X, 1re p.)

ART. 1. Les personnes professant la religion orthodoxe grecque, quelle que soit leur condition civile, peuvent contracter mariage sans demander l'autorisation spéciale de l'autorité ou le permis des corporations et communautés, dont elles font partie. Aux mêmes conditions est soumis le mariage d'un étranger de religion orthodoxe grecque avec une sujette russe du même culte.

ART. 12. Le mariage ne peut être valablement contracté sans le consentement libre et mutuel des parties; en conséquence il est défendu aux parents et tuteur de contraindre leurs enfants et mineurs, se trouvant sous tutelle, à contracter un mariage contre leur vouloir.

ART. 25. Celui qui désire contracter mariage doit donner par écrit ou verbalement au Prêtre de sa paroisse, ses noms, prénoms, qualités ou condition, ainsi que les noms, prénoms et condition de la future.

ART. 26. Après cette communication, il sera procédé á l'église à la publication des bans trois dimanches ou jours de fêtes consécutifs après la messe; ensuite s'effectue l'enquête préalable ordonnée suivant les règles prescrites par l'autorité ecclésiastique et dans les formes voulues.

ART. 27. A la suite de la publication des bans, tous ceux qui auraient connaissance de quelques empêchements au mariage sont tenus d'en informer le Prêtre verbalement ou par écrit immédiatement ou au plus tard lors de la dernière des trois publications précitées.

ART. 31. Le mariage entre particuliers doit être (conjointement avec les fiançailles) célébré à l'église en présence des contractants aux jours et heures pour cela fixés, devant deux ou trois témoins—le tout conformément aux règles et rites de l'église orthodoxe grecque. Chaque union est portée sur les livres de la paroisse.

ART. 61. Il est permis aux personnes professant les diverses communions chrétiennes de contracter en Russie mariage d'après les règles et rites de leurs églises, sans requerir au préalable le consentement de l'autorité civile, sauf à observer les prescriptions des lois russes relatives au culte de leur religion.

ART. 65. Dans tout les cultes chrétiens les mariages sont célébrés d'après le rite de l'église à laquelle appartiennent les contractants et par l'ecclésiastique competent. Néanmoins ces mariages seront valables s'ils ont été célébrés par le prêtre greco-russe à défaut du curé ou du ministre de la communion des contractants; dans ce dernier cas, la célébration ainsi que la dissolution du mariage ne pourra avoir lieu que d'après les prescriptions et les rites de l'église orthodoxe grecque.

ART. 90. Dans chaque tribu et peuplade sans en excepter les païens, le mariage peut êtré contracté d'après le culte et les coutumes des contractants, sans intervention de l'autorité administrative ou ecclésiastique de l'un des cultes chrétiens.

ART. 102. La femme mariée à un étranger qui n'est ni au service de Russie ni naturalisé sujet russe, suit la condition et acquiert le domicile du mari. (49 MS. Desp. from Russia.)

Jewish marriages and divorces, performed and granted by Jewish rabbis in Russia, are recognized by the Russian law.

For. Rel. 1903, 715.

(8) SWITZERLAND.

§ 249.

" Your dispatch of the 9th of February, No. 50, has been received. In that communication you set forth the following facts, namely : that Anna Maria Suter, a native of the canton of Aargau, in Switzerland, emigrated to the United States, and was married at Philadelphia on the 2d of January, 1855, to John Hürlimann, a citizen of the United States, residing in that city; that she bore a son on the 15th of March, 1857, who was baptized John, and that she died on the 29th of March, 1861; that afterwards the father of the said Anna Maria Suter died in the canton of Aargau, leaving a fortune, a portion of which would have fallen to the said Anna Maria, as one of the heirs of the father, if she were living, or to her legitimate issue if she were dead; that proceedings at law have been instituted in Switzerland by John Hürlimann, the father of the afore-named child, John, son of the said Anna Maria, to recover the portion of the estate before mentioned; and that the legitimacy of the child is denied under law of the canton of Aargau, upon the ground that the marriage in the United States was celebrated without a compliance with the preliminaries prescribed by the laws of the canton. The attorney for the child requests your intervention, and you solicit instructions on the subject. . . .

" The law of Switzerland, and in general those of continental Europe, while admitting that the law of the place controls as to the form of marriage, nevertheless holds that in respect to the capacity of the person to contract marriage the law of the domicil travels with him, and invalidates the union wherever contracted, if it be against the law of his domicil.

" It may, however, I think, be successfully maintained that, even under the European jurisdiction in relation to the capacity of the person to contract marriage, the *bona fide* establishment of a new domicil with the intention of a permanent residence therein, relieves the emigrant from the bonds of his native law."

> Mr. Seward, Sec. of State, to Mr. Harrington, min. to Switzerland, Mar. 21, 1868, Dip. Cor. 1868, II. 192.
>
> The President of the Federal Council addressed to Mr. Harrington, July 14, 1868, the following note: " The federal council announces that it has considered the report of the authorities of the canton of Aargau, dated 29th ultimo, on this affair, and now informs said authorities that it concurs in their decision, that John Hürlimann, senior, was a citizen of the United States; that his marriage with Anna Maria Suter was in accordance with the laws of the United States, and that the male issue of that marriage is considered as the legitimate descendant of an American citizen; therefore no Swiss authority can decide the civil status of an American citizen, be-

cause the laws of the United States, and not those of the canton of
Aargau are to obtain in this matter. The federal council also observes, that, by virtue of an international treaty still in force
between Switzerland and the United States of America, an American
citizen has the right, in case of successions, to be treated as a Swiss ;
and, therefore, John Hürlimann, junior, must be treated in the same
manner as if he were the issue of a lawful marriage of Aargovien
citizens. From the above, the federal council judges the refusal
of the communal council of Entfelden to be contrary to the treaty,
and that it ought to be reversed, inasmuch as no civil suit for the
succession is intended to be prosecuted. The federal council has
instructed the authorities of Aargau to make this known to the
heirs, for their guidance, and to report the result of its intervention
in the affair." (Dip. Cor. 1868, II. 197.)

" The authorities of Switzerland have recognized the validity of the
marriage in Philadelphia of a Swiss female to a citizen of the
United States, although such marriage might, according to the law of
Switzerland, have been deemed void for want of the consent of the
authorities of her native canton." (Mr. Fish, Sec. of State, to Mrs.
Sistmayer, April 21, 1870, 84 MS. Dom. Let. 280.)

Mr. Fish again refers, in the same sense, to the case of Hürlimann in
an instruction to Mr. Jay, minister to Austria-Hungary, July 27,
1871, MS. Inst. Austria, II. 29.

" In my dispatch No. 62, 8th of June, 1886, the Department was
advised that the officers of the *état civil* in Switzerland declined to
accept the circular prepared and issued by this legation, by and with
the advice and consent of the Department, concerning marriages of
citizens of the United States in Switzerland as satisfactorily meeting
the requirements of the Swiss law of December, 1874, concerning
the social state, in that it fails to declare the publication of the bans,
as required under the Swiss law, is not demanded by the laws of the
country of origin (citizenship) of the parties. The object of the
circular was to explain the impossibility of there being a literal compliance with that provision of the law concerning the publication
of the bans, owing to the status of the question of marriage in the
United States, and to persuade the officers of the *état civil* that such
literal and technical compliance as to American citizens was not
necessary to insure the substantial intent and purpose of the law, the
unquestioned recognition and validity of the solemnization, if otherwise according to the law of the country. The whole difficulty
resulted from the confusion of conflicting circulars upon the question
issued by this legation. Mr. Fish cited section 4082, Revised Statutes of the United States, as determining the conditions of marriage
of all citizens of the United States in foreign countries, and gave the
law of the District of Columbia fixing matrimonial capacity. Mr.
Cramer confined his circular to the simple statement ' that a previous
publication in the United States or any State or Territory thereof
of a proposed marriage is not required by the laws thereof,' and

'that a marriage performed in accordance with the Swiss federal law of 1874, *if performed in the presence of a consular officer of the United States*, will be valid to all intent,' etc. Having serious doubt as to the correctness of the view taken of the question by Mr. Fish or Mr. Cramer in their respective circulars, even before the receipt of instructions from the Department, I had made material modification of the statements I found to be in use by the legation, and referred the matter to the better judgment of the Department, and a form of circular was agreed upon which, it was thought, would subserve every purpose. It failed to do so, as stated in my dispatch of June, 1886. Not feeling justified to make any additional statement, the consuls were instructed that in every case where the *état civil* exacted the declaration that the publication of the bans was not necessary under the law of the place of citizenship, this statement should be made only after communicating with the proper officer of the State whereof the parties claimed citizenship; and being thus officially advised of the law, I was not entirely satisfied on the point of a consular officer certifying to the law of a given State, even under the conditions above named, and this doubt was largely due to general views of the main question contained in previous dispatches from the Department. Therefore my dispatch of June, 1886, desired the decision of the Department as to the right or the propriety of a consul giving the certificate indicated. To this no answer has been received, and the consuls continue to pursue the course named. Thinking that an appeal to the high federal council might secure a solution of the trouble, on the 18th of June, 1886, a note was addressed to that body, setting forth fully the case and respectfully urging such modification of the law as might be found practicable. To this note an answer has been received of date February 1, 1887. A copy of the circular issued by the legation and heretofore approved by the Department is inclosed.

" The federal council indicates a willingness to instruct the cantonal officers to grant the exemptions desired from the provision as to publication of bans, when assured by the Department of State as to the exact scope and extent of section 4082, Revised Statutes, and that the publication of the bans is not required except in a few States, and that the failure to publish the bans by citizens of said States, married outside of said States or in foreign countries, would not invalidate the solemnization when complying with the law of the place of celebration. It is earnestly hoped the Department may see its way to satisfy the request of the federal council and put at rest this vexed question. In dispatch No. 23, November 14, 1885, the Department indicated Pennsylvania and Connecticut as requiring previous publication of bans. The secretary of the former State has advised this legation that it is not necessary."

Mr. Winchester, min. to Switzerland, to Mr. Bayard, Sec. of State, Feb. 4, 1887, For. Rel. 1887, 1057.

The circular issued by Mr. Winchester, and referred to by him in the foregoing dispatch, was as follows:

"Applications are frequently made to this legation by the cantonal or communal authorities, as well as by private individuals, for certificates as to the validity of marriages of citizens of the United States in Switzerland, and these applications are generally coupled with a request that the legation should certify that the marriage is valid according to the laws of the United States, and that it will be recognized as valid by the laws of the State or Territory from which such citizen comes.

"It is not within the province of this legation either to certify officially as to the laws of the different jurisdictions in the United States, or to decide judicially whether any particular marriage is valid or not. The duty of this legation is confined to giving advice.

"It is enacted by a statute of the United States that 'marriages in presence of any consular officer of the United States, in a foreign country, between persons who would be authorized to marry if residing in the District of Columbia, shall be valid to all intents and purposes, and shall have the same effect as if solemnized within the United States.' As, under the Constitution of the United States, the States have exclusive power of determining the conditions of marriage and divorce as to persons domiciled within their borders, this statute only covers marriages by persons domiciled in the District of Columbia or in the Territories. The general rule of law in the United States, as well as in European countries, is that a marriage solemnized in a foreign country according to the laws of that country is valid. This is the rule as to the ceremony. Matrimonial capacity is generally determined by the law of the place of domicile of the party in question. From what has been said it appears that a marriage solemnized under and in accordance with the Swiss federal law, *concernant l'état-civil, la tenue des registres qui s'y rapportent et le mariage*, of December 24, 1874, would generally be valid to all intents and purposes in the United States. By way, however, of precaution, it would be well to have a consular officer of the United States present at the ceremony.

"This legation can not undertake to procure certificates as to the laws of the different States and Territories. Persons desiring such certificates should apply to the proper officials of such States or Territories, either directly, or, in the case of Swiss citizens, though the officials of their own country."

This circular, it will be perceived, was based on the provisions of the Printed Personal Instructions to Diplomatic Agents of the United States, 1885. Its form was communicated to Mr. Winchester by the Department of State. (Mr. Adee, Act. Sec. of State, to Mr. Winchester, min. to Switz., Jan. 30, 1886, MS. Inst. Switz. II. 300.)

"Your dispatch No. 97, of the 4th ultimo, in regard to the marriage of American citizens in Switzerland, has been received.

"The questions you ask are answered by the Department circular of the 8th ultimo, as to marriage certificates by consuls. The obstacles which the rules of the Department may put in the way of marriages by American citizens in Switzerland may be regretted; but immeasurably more disastrous would it be to countenance the issuing of certificates which might lead to the solemnization of marriages by Swiss officials which might afterwards be declared invalid by the court having jurisdiction."

> Mr. Bayard, Sec. of State, to Mr. Winchester, min. to Switz., March 1, 1887, For. Rel. 1887, 1059.

> "This Department does not regard the circular [respecting marriages, issued by the legation at Berne prior to 1851] as a proper one to be sent out, because it does not correctly state the law." (Mr. Bayard, Sec. of State, to Mr. Winchester, min. to Switz., Dec. 8, 1885, MS. Inst. Switz. II. 291. A copy of the circular in question accompanied Mr. Winchester's No. 22, Oct. 26, 1885.)

by American citizens in Switzerland may be regretted; but impor-
...

CHAPTER VII.

EXEMPTIONS FROM TERRITORIAL JURISDICTION.

III. QUESTIONS OF ASYLUM—Continued.

I. *FOREIGN SOVEREIGNS.*

1. THEIR PERSONS.

§ 250.

" This perfect equality and absolute independence of sovereigns, and this common interest impelling them to mutual intercourse and an interchange of good offices with each other, have given rise to a class of cases in which every sovereign is understood to waive the exercise of a part of that complete, exclusive territorial jurisdiction which has been stated to be the attribute of every nation.

" First. One of these is admitted to be the exemption of the person of the sovereign from arrest or detention within a foreign territory. . . .

" Second. A second case, standing in the same principles with the first, is the immunity which all civilized nations allow to foreign ministers. . . .

" Third. A third case in which a sovereign is understood to cede a portion of his territorial jurisdiction is, where he allows the troops of a foreign prince to pass through his dominions."

> Marshall, C. J., Schooner Exchange *v.* McFaddon, 7 Cranch, 137, 138, 139.
> See Twiss, Law of Nations (ed. 1861), I. § 158, pp. 228–229; Hall, Int. Law (4th ed.), 175.
> As to the incapacity of the courts of one country to take jurisdiction of the official acts of the government of another country, see Underhill *v.* Hernandez, 168 U. S. 250, and supra, § 179.
> The subject of the immunities of foreign ministers is discussed hereafter.

The Sultan of Johore came to England *incognito*, and lived in London under the name of Albert Baker. An action was subsequently brought against him for breach of promise of marriage, the plaintiff alleging that she had known him as Albert Baker, and believed that that was his name, and that he had promised to marry her and had afterwards broken his promise. A motion was made in behalf of the defendant to stay all proceedings in the action, on the ground that he was the sovereign of an independent state in the Malay Peninsula, and that the courts therefore had no jurisdiction over him. As evidence of his sovereign character there was a letter written and signed on behalf of the secretary of state for the colonies, stating, in answer to an inquiry made by the court, that Johore was an independent state, and that the defendant was the sovereign ruler of it. The court held that this letter, sent by the secretary of state in his official capacity, was in effect a certificate from the Queen and rendered further inquiry as to the sovereign character of the defendant unnecessary. The character of the defendant as a sovereign prince being thus established, the court held that he had not forfeited the privilege of exemption from judicial process by coming to England and living there under a false name. The judges all concurred in the view that a foreign sovereign could not be subjected to the jurisdiction of the court, unless he voluntarily submitted to it, and that he was not required to elect whether he would submit to the jurisdiction till the court sought to subject him to its process.

> Mighell v. Sultan of Johore, Court of Appeal, L. R. 1894, Q. B. D., I. 149; L. J. 1894, N. S., LXIII. 593.

The provision of section 6 of the act of March 3, 1891, which makes the decree of the circuit court of appeals final where the jurisdiction depends on " the opposite parties " to the suit " being aliens and citizens of the United States or citizens of different States," does not apply to the case of a foreign sovereign who submits his case to the courts, such sovereign not being an " alien " or " foreign citizen " within the meaning of the statute.

> Colombia v. Cauca Co. (1903), 190 U. S. 524.

2. MILITARY FORCES.

§ 251.

" Military forces enter the territory of a state in amity with that to which they belong, either when crossing to and fro between the main part of their country and an isolated piece of it, or as allies passing through for the purposes of a campaign, or furnishing garrisons for protection. In cases of the former kind, the passage of soldiers being frequent, it is usual to conclude conventions, specifying the line of road to be followed by them, and regulating their transit so as to make it as little onerous as possible to the population among whom they are. Under such conventions offenses committed by sol-

diers against the inhabitants are dealt with by the military authorities of the state to which the former belong; and as their general
object in other respects is simply regulatory of details, it is not necessary to look upon them as intended in any respect to modify the rights
of jurisdiction possessed by the parties to them respectively. There
can be no question that the concession of jurisdiction over passing
troops to the local authorities would be extremely inconvenient; and
it is believed that the commanders, not only of forces in transit
through a friendly country with which no convention exists, but also
of forces stationed there, assert exclusive jurisdiction in principle in
respect of offenses committed by persons under their command,
though they may be willing as a matter of concession to hand over culprits to the civil power when they have confidence in the courts, and
when their stay is likely to be long enough to allow of the case being
watched. The existence of a double jurisdiction in a foreign country
being scarcely compatible with the discipline of an army, it is evident
that there would be some difficulty in carrying out any other arrangement."

> Hall, Int. Law (4th ed.), § 56, p. 206.
>
> As examples of conventions, Hall cites those between Prussia and Hanover
>   in 1816, and between Prussia and Brunswick in 1835, De Martens,
>   Nouv. Rec. IV. 321, and Nouv. Rec. Gén. VII. i. 60. See, also, Bar,
>   Private Int. Law, § 145; Fiore, Droit Int. §§ 513–514; Rivier, Prin-
>   cipes, I. 333.
>
> These authorities, it may be observed, refer to organized forces exercising
>   a right of passage or of sojourn, and not to individuals merely pos-
>   sessing a military character.
>
> See Tucker v. Alexandroff (1902), 183 U. S. 424; Schooner Exchange v.
>   McFaddon, 7 Cranch, 139.

A question as to the protection due to a military officer of a foreign government was raised in the case of the well-
**Individual officers
and men.** known Austrian commander, Marshal Haynau.
September 4, 1850, that officer, accompanied by two
other persons, paid a visit of inspection to the brewery of Barclay,
Perkins & Co., in London. Marshal Haynau had been the object
of much execration in some of the English journals on account of
his course as commander of the Austrian forces in Hungary, and
when it became known that he was present, nearly all the laborers
and draymen ran out with brooms and dirt, shouting " Down with
the Austrian butcher," and uttering other alarming epithets. The
marshal was soon covered with dirt, and, perceiving some of the
men about to attack him, he ran into the street to Bankside, chased
by a mob and belabored with all sorts of weapons. He finally took
refuge in a public house, where he was rescued by the police.[a] Next

_a_ Annual Register, 1850, p. 110.

day Baron Köller, the Austrian chargé d'affaires, brought the incident to the notice of the British Government, and he subsequently reenforced his representations under instructions from Prince Schwartzenberg, asking for an investigation of the affair, and the punishment of the guilty parties by a punishment which would mark their violation of the country's hospitality. Lord Palmerston expressed regret that an Austrian officer should have been exposed " to such outrageous violence and insult," and referred the case to the home secretary. It appears that Marshal Haynau refused personally to institute criminal proceedings against the offenders, and immediately left England. The home secretary declared that this forbearance threw " insuperable difficulties " in the way of the prosecution, since the offenders could not be prosecuted with " a reasonable prospect of success, in the voluntary absence of the only person injured, whose testimony is expected in such cases both by the court and the jury." The Government therefore declined to institute any prosecution.

In 1864 the sergeant of the military guard on board an American vessel, from San Francisco to Panama, while he was ashore at the latter place, got into an altercation with one of the privates of the guard, in which the latter was killed. As they both were enlisted soldiers in the United States Army, the Department of State, at the solicitation of friends of the sergeant, who was held by the local authorities at Panama for trial, requested the Colombian minister in the United States to use his good offices with the government of Panama, with a view to the surrender of the culprit to the United States military authorities in California, to be tried there by court martial. " I am well aware," said Mr. Seward, " that no obligation rests upon the authorities of Panama, or upon those of the United States of Colombia, to comply with this request; nevertheless, if the matter can be so disposed of, this Government will esteem it a mark of courtesy on the part of Colombia. . . . In the event, however, that the governor of Panama should consider it incompatible with his attributes and prerogatives to grant the above request, I will thank you to urge upon him the speedy trial of the accused, whose friends allege in his defense that he was acting in the discharge of his official duty, at the time the unfortunate occurrence took place."

Mr. Seward, Sec. of State, to Gen. Salgar, Colombian min., March 30, 1865, MS. Notes to Colombia, VI. 182.

H. Doc. 551—vol 2——36

3. Vessels of War.

(1) their public character, and its proof.

§ 252.

The firm of Cramp & Sons, of Philadelphia, entered into a contract with the Russian Government for the construction of a man-of-war. She was to be paid for in instalments as the construction proceeded, but a percentage of each instalment was to be withheld, and final payment was not to be made till the vessel had been accepted by the Russian Government, which was at liberty, unless certain requirements as to draught and speed were met, to reject her. The materials to be used in her construction were, however, when brought upon the premises of the contractors, immediately to become the exclusive property of the Russian ministry of marine. During her construction she was to be inspected by officials of the Russian Government; and it was stipulated that the Russian flag should be hoisted on the ship, whenever desired by the board of inspection, as evidence of the Government's exclusive property, and that the Russian ministry of marine might at any time appoint an officer to take possession of the ship or materials, whether finished or unfinished, subject to the contractor's lien for any part of the value remaining unpaid. With reference to the legal position of the vessel after she was launched, but while she was still lying in the stream under construction, and before the Russian flag had ever been hoisted upon her, the opinion was expressed *obiter* that she was then subject to the local jurisdiction, and that if any crime had been committed on board of her, it would have been cognizable in the local courts. But it was intimated that if proceedings had been taken against her under the mechanic's lien law of the State, or if a material man had filed a libel in admiralty against her for coal furnished in testing her engines, or if upon her trial trip she had negligently come into collision with another vessel, whose owner had instituted a suit against her, the Emperor of Russia might have claimed for her an immunity from local jurisdiction on the ground that she was the property of a foreign sovereign.

> Tucker *v.* Alexandroff (1902), 183 U. S. 424, 440, citing The Constitution, 4 P. D. 39, and the Parlement Belge, 4 P. D. 129.
>
> It was held in Tucker *v.* Alexandroff that the vessel in question at the time referred to was a Russian ship of war within the letter and spirit of the treaty between the United States and Russia of 1832, Art. IX., relating to the recovery of deserters from " ships of war and merchant vessels."
>
> See the case of Chilean gunboat *Pilcomayo*, infra, § 604.

A Russian cruiser, manned by a crew in the pay of the Russian Government, and in command of an officer of the Russian navy, is a war vessel, within the seal-fishery act, and a protocol of examination of an offending ship by such cruiser, signed by the officer in command, is admissible in evidence in an action for condemnation under that act.

The Minnie *v.* Reg., 23 Canada Sup. Ct. 478.

"Mr. Hall, in his treatise upon international law, discussing foreign ships as nonterritorial property of a state (section 44), says that the commission under which a commander acts is conclusive of the public character of a vessel, although such character is usually evidenced by the flag and pendant which she carries, and if necessary by firing a gun. 'When in the absence of, or notwithstanding, these proofs any doubt is entertained as to the legitimateness of her claim, the statement of the commander on his word of honor that the vessel is public is often accepted, but the admission of such statements as proof is a matter of courtesy,' and 'though attestation by a government that a ship belongs to it is final, it does not follow that denial of public character is equally final; assumption and repudiation of responsibility stand upon a different footing.' . . . But it is pertinent to notice here that he is speaking of immunities of public vessels from local jurisdiction, and not of the property of a foreign government in such vessels."

Tucker *v.* Alexandroff (1902), 183 U. S. 424, 441–442.
As to the effect of a commission, in cases of neutrality, see Moore, Int. Arbitrations, I. 612, 655; IV. 4135–4144.

(2) ENTRANCE INTO FRIENDLY PORTS.

§ 253.

If there be no prohibition, the ports of a friendly nation are considered as open to the public ships of powers with whom it is at peace; and those vessels are supposed to enter such ports and remain in them under the protection of the government of the place.

Schooner Exchange *v.* McFaddon, 7 Cranch, 116, 145.

By section 6 of the act of March 3, 1805, 2 Stat. 339, 342, the President was empowered by proclamation to forbid the entrance within the United States of any officer of a foreign armed vessel or of the vessel itself on satisfactory proof that he had committed on the high seas any trespass or tort, or any spoliation on board any vessel of the United States, or any unlawful interruption or vexation of trading vessels actually coming to or going from the United States; and such officer was declared to be liable to arrest and punishment and expulsion thereafter if at any time after a proclamation thus made he should be found within the United States. The existence of the act was limited to two years.

Chief Justice Marshall, in the Schooner Exchange *v.* McFaddon, 7 Cranch, 116, states that the implied license under which men-of-war enter friendly ports may be withdrawn or qualified. An example of its limitation may be found in the act of Congress of May 15, 1820, by which foreign armed vessels were for a period of two years, beginning July 1, 1820, forbidden to enter any harbor in the United States except Portland, Boston, New London, New York, Philadelphia, Norfolk, Smithville (N. C.), Charleston, and Mobile, unless by reason of stress of weather or pursuit of an enemy they were unable to make one of those ports. In case of entering a port not declared to be open, the commanding officer of the man-of-war was required immediately to report his vessel to the collector of the district, stating the object or causes of his entrance, to take such a position in the harbor as the collector should assign to him, and to conform himself to such regulations as the President might have prescribed.[a] By various nations the conditions under which foreign men-of-war are permitted to enter and remain in their ports are expressly defined. An example of such a regulation may be seen in the Austrian ordinance of June 14, 1866.[b] By section 2791 of the Revised Statutes of the United States it is provided that " it shall not be necessary for the master of any vessel of war, or of any vessel employed by any prince, or state, as a public packet for the conveyance of letters and dispatches, and not permitted by the laws of such prince or state to be employed in the transportation of merchandise, in the way of trade, to make report and entry."

In 1835, during the excitement concerning the nonexecution of the treaty between the United States and France of 1831, in relation to the payment of claims, a French man-of-war arrived at New York. On its subsequently being represented by the French chargé d'affaires that certain officers of the ship had been insulted by a crowd in the street, the United States district attorney was instructed to request the mayor of the city to " exercise all the authority he possesses to prevent any injury or further offence from being committed against the officers or crew of the vessel alluded to, and to secure to them while they remain within the limits of the United States the hospitable treatment to which they are entitled, and which the American people are wont to show." Besides, as the chargé d'affaires apprehended that popular excitement might lead to an attempt against the vessel herself, the President, while considering such apprehensions to be groundless, caused orders to be given to the commandant of the Brooklyn Navy-Yard to afford the same protection as if the ship belonged to the United States; and it was suggested that if

---

[a] 3 Stats. at L. 597.
[b] 63 British and Foreign State Papers, 1073.

there should be " the slightest indication of a meditated attack " she
should anchor near the yard, " where the United States have exclusive
jurisdiction and competent force."

> Mr. Forsyth, Sec. of State, to Mr. Price, U. S. dist. attorney at New York,
> Feb. 25, 1835, 27 MS. Dom. Let. 237.

" Section 2791 of the Revised Statutes provides that it shall not be
necessary for the master of any (foreign) vessel of war to make
report and entry on arriving in a harbor of the United States; and
Section 5288 of the statutes authorizes the President to employ such
force as may be necessary to compel any foreign vessel to depart the
United States in all cases in which by the law of nations or the treaties of the United States she might not remain within the United
States.

" These are believed to be the only provisions of municipal law, in
this country, on the subject."

> Mr. Evarts, Sec. of State, to Mr. Comacho, Venezuelan min., Dec. 9, 1880,
> MS. Notes to Venez. I. 210.
> For Austrian regulations concerning foreign men-of-war, see 63 Br. &
> For. State Papers, 1073.
> Mr. Wallace, consul-general at Melbourne, with his No. 81, July 3, 1891,
> enclosed a copy of a proclamation issued by the governor of South
> Australia June 18, 1891, in relation to the navigation of the waters
> of South Australia by foreign transports and armed vessels. The
> proclamation was communicated to the Navy Department, Aug. 14,
> 1891. (183 MS. Dom. Let. 57.)
> For German regulations, see dispatch of Mr. Kasson, min. to Germany,
> No. 12, Sept. 17, 1884, 33 MS. Desp. from Germany.
> For Netherlands regulations, see dispatch of Mr. Thayer, min at The
> Hague, No. 398, April 19, 1893, 33 MS. Desp. from the Netherlands.
> Aug. 9, 1884, Mr. Frelinghuysen sent out a circular to the diplomatic
> representatives of the United States, instructing them to procure, for
> the use of the Navy Department, the regulations adopted by the
> governments to which they were accredited in relation to the
> " entry of foreign ships of war into their ports, together with any
> rules in force as to the stay of such vessels in port, their anchorage,
> their relations with the customs and quarantine officers, the imposi-
> tion upon them of port or other charges, and the employment by them
> of local pilots." (MS. Circulars, III. 157.)

February 9, 1901, Señor Blanco, Venezuelan minister of foreign
affairs, addressed to Mr. Loomis, United States minister at Caracas, the following note:

**Incident in Vene-
zuela, 1901.**

" The law of May 15, 1882, numbered 2419 in the national compilation, gives to the head of the Government the power to grant or
not, in his judgment, permission to foreign men-of-war to enter,
for scientific purposes, ports that are not open. Every time that a
war vessel of the United States has made a request of this nature
it has been granted without any difficulty, and not long ago United

States war vessels were engaged in scientific work in the Caño of San Juan and at the bar at the mouth of the Orinoco, but these vessels had gone through with the legal formality above mentioned, and this formality can not be dispensed with, except in violation of the well-established principles of international law.

"By direction of the Supreme Chief of the Republic, I call your excellency's attention to the aforementioned law for the reason that this Government has been disagreeably surprised to learn that a war vessel called *Scorpion*, flying the flag of the United States, had entered the harbor of Santa Catalina, a port that is not open, and situated in the Dalla Costa district of the State of Guayana; that an officer in uniform went ashore from said war vessel and returned on board accompanied by a gentleman called Boynton, an employee of the company which has its agency at said port, and that no explanation was given for this flagrant violation of the usual formalities.

"The grave nature of this act, violating, as it does, the very principles on which national sovereignty is based, compels the Supreme Chief of the Republic to respectfully call the attention of the Government of the United States to this delicate question, and to protest in the most solemn manner against the action of the man-of-war *Scorpion* as opposed to the principles of international law and a violation of the laws of this Republic." [a]

On receiving this note Mr. Loomis cabled to his Government that the Venezuelan Government protested "most strongly against the presence of the U. S. S. *Scorpion* in the Orinoco River without having asked permission to enter, declaring such presence to be in violation of Venezuelan as well as international laws," and requested instructions as to a reply. [b]

With reference to this telegram, Mr. Long, Secretary of the Navy, made the following memorandum:

"The records of the Department show that naval vessels have visited the Orinoco River on a number of occasions. When no survey has been undertaken these visits have been without previous notice, so far as the Department's records show. Two recent cases of visits to the Orinoco are the visit of the *Kearsarge* Noveember 7, 1892, and the visit of the *Wilmington*, January 23, 1899. The *Kearsarge* carried on a running survey, without, however, erecting shore stations. There is no record of any protest or objection from the Venezuelan Government on the occasion of either of these visits.

"The Navy Department understands the status of the Orinoco River, in regard to navigation, to be in all respects similar to that of the Mississippi River. Foreign war vessels pass freely up the Mississippi River without previous notice to this Government. Our

---

[a] For. Rel. 1901, 543.
[b] Id. 541.

war vessels have done the same in the Orinoco River. In the Amazon, for instance, the case is understood to be different. This river, though open to commercial navigation, is not open to war vessels except on special notice and permission.

"It may be that the minister to Venezuela on his own account, in the case of the visit of the *Wilmington*, asked permission or notified the Government of what was contemplated. If so, this is unknown to the Navy Department.

"On the occasion of the visit of the *Wilmington* the Venezuelan Government marked its acquiescence and gratification in that visit by desiring to decorate the commanding officer of the vessel with the Order of Bolivar." [a]

The Department of State, replying to Mr. Loomis's telegram, stated that the object of the *Scorpion's* visit to the Orinoco was to obtain information; that the visit was in accordance with numerous precedents and without offensive intention, and that the vessel was ordered to La Guaira, touching at Cumana, Carupano, and Barcelona.[b]

On February 16, 1901, Mr. Loomis addressed to Señor Blanco the following note:

"I have the honor to acknowledge receipt of your note of February 9 in which you state that an American war vessel, the *Scorpion*, had been seen in the Orinoco River at Santa Catalina and that her presence there was not in conformity with certain sections of the law of Venezuela, which, as I gather from your note, provides that foreign men-of-war shall not enter the Orinoco River for scientific purposes without first having asked permission of the Chief of the Venezuelan Government. I was not aware that there was a law in force closing the Orinoco River to the public vessels of a friendly nation bent on the peaceful and inoffensive mission of seeking information from its nationals engaged in lawful business on the banks of that stream. It is true that when it was desired to do certain scientific work for the benefit of navigation and the shipping of all nations at the bars of the Orinoco and San Juan rivers, the formal permission of the Venezuelan Government was asked; but in these cases it was deemed necessary to keep a war vessel in Venezuelan waters for many weeks, and the officers and men on these scientific expeditions were at work in small boats taking many observations and measurements, so it was only natural that their presence for a long period, and their activity, should be explained in the form of asking permission for the performance of the task in question.

---

[a] Mem. of Feb. 13, 1901, For. Rel. 1901, 542.

[b] Mr. Hill, Acting Sec. of State, to Mr. Loomis, min. to Venezuela, tel., Feb. 13, 1901, For. Rel. 1901, 541.

" The *Scorpion*, as I understand it, recently made a very quick trip to Santa Catalina and immediately returned to the coast. Her visit was of course wholly inoffensive in character and devoid of significance in any other sense than the one I have the honor to indicate, and, as your excellency knows, there are precedents for the informal visits on the part of war vessels of a friendly nation.

" I should esteem it a favor if you would be kind enough to furnish me with a list of the Venezuelan ports, streams, and harbors, concerning which there is a special provision of law respecting the entry of foreign men-of-war." [a]

In communicating to his Government, Feb. 23, 1901, a copy of the foregoing note, Mr. Loomis said : " In this connection it may be of interest to the Department to know that when the British gunboat *Alert* went to Ciudad Bolivar last summer to inquire into the facts concerning the killing of the British consular clerk at that port, Mr. Grant-Duff, the British chargé d'affaires here asked permission from the Venezuelan Government for the gunboat to go to Ciudad Bolivar. He reported his action to the foreign office in London and was promptly informed that what he had done was not at all necessary, and that in the future permission for English war vessels to navigate the Orinoco River was not to be asked." [b]

February 26, 1901, Señor Blanco made to the foregoing note the following answer :

" Referring to your excellency's note of the 16th of the present month, I am sorry that I did not succeed in explaining with sufficient clearness in my note of the 9th, No. 208, the spirit of the law of the 15th of May, 1882, regarding the entrance of foreign men-of-war in the ports of the Republic. I stated that the above-mentioned law ' gives to the head of the Government the power to grant or not, in his judgment, permission to foreign men-of-war to enter, for scientific purposes, ports that are not open.' I could not refer in a general sense to the Orinoco, as Ciudad Bolivar, situated on one of its banks, is a port open to foreign commerce, in accordance with the provisions of Law XIV. of the finance code.

" The *Scorpion* entered Santa Catalina, a port not open to foreign commerce, which constituted a distinct violation of the law, and of which I spoke to you in the name of the Supreme Chief of the Republic.

" In a communication of July 1, 1882, the law in question was made known to all the diplomatic corps resident in Caracas soon after it was passed by the Congress of the Republic. Said law is the same one cited by one of my predecessors to your legation in notes of January

---

[a] For. Rel. 1901, 543.
[b] Id. 542.

14 and April 20, 1899, and the same law that another of my predecessors referred to in notes of December 19 and December 23, 1899.

" So that when, in the note protesting against the act of the *Scorpion*, mention was made of the law of 1882, it was done with the idea that attention was being called to a well-known public act, an act that had been made known to foreign governments, inserted in the official compilation of laws, and referred to frequently in the correspondence with the representatives of friendly nations. The existence of said law, and the knowledge of its existence on the part of other governments, fully justifies and makes obligatory in the name of the sovereignty of the Republic, the protest contained in my note of the 9th of the present month, and which I hereby confirm by order of the Chief of the Venezuelan Government.

" In regard to the list of the ports, rivers, and harbors which your excellency asks for I need only refer to Law XIV. of the finance code, which specifies the points open to foreign commerce, and these are the only ones in which foreign men-of-war may enter; and article 3 of said law establishes the only exception, which can only be made effective by means of a special permit from the Chief of the Republic." [a]

The law of May 15 (or May 11), 1882, referred to by Señor Blanco, was published in the Official Gazette of April 30, 1901, as a law still in force. It provides:

" ARTICLE 1. The ports where foreign men-of-war can enter are only those open to foreign commerce.

"ART. 2. Foreign men-of-war can not enter the above-mentioned ports except to the number of three or four, at most, nor can they remain longer than thirty days.

"ART. 3. When for any good reason foreign men-of-war are obliged to enter a port in a greater number than above mentioned, or prolong their stay for more than thirty days, or visit for scientific purposes ports that are not open, they must ask special permission from the President of the Republic, who may grant it or not, in his judgment.

"ART. 4. Foreign men-of-war are subject to all police regulations of the ports, such as health laws, anchorage regulations, etc.

"ART. 5. In case of any infraction of the foregoing articles the local authorities shall not take any measures against the men-of-war, out of regard for their extraterritoriality, but the Chief of the National Executive shall be immediately informed and he will proceed in accordance with international usages.

"Given in the Federal palace of the legislative body, at Caracas, May 11, 1882, nineteenth year of the Law and twenty-fourth of the Federation." (For. Rel. 1901, 546.)

The following memorandum by Mr. Long, Secretary of the Navy, of March 13, 1901, refers to the notes of Señor Blanco and Mr. Loomis, of Feb. 9 and Feb. 16, supra:

---

[a] For. Rel. 1901, 544.

"In the practice of this Department there is a distinct and well-recognized difference between the visit of a man-of-war and a visit for 'scientific purposes,' such scientific purposes being usually hydrographic and occasionally topographic examination of territorial waters or shores of a foreign country.

"The Department would ordinarily not order one of its vessels to any port of any country having a recognized government to conduct surveys or examinations, without having first not only notified that government of its wish, but having obtained explicit permission for conducting the survey upon the occasion of the visit.

"On the other hand, it would neither send notice nor request permission in case the visit was not undertaken for the purposes of conducting such survey or other similar purpose, unless the waters proposed to be visited were expressly denied to passage of men-of-war by national decree, as in the case of the Amazon." [a]

In June, 1901, Mr. Russell, chargé at Caracas, reported that the President of Venezuela had made and had "menacingly" repeated a request for an explanation of the entrance of the U. S. S. *Mayflower* into a closed port in the island of Margarita. [b]

The Department of State replied that the visit of the *Mayflower* was in accordance with custom, and that the request made by the United States to be furnished with a list of closed Venezuelan ports had not been complied with. [c]

It seems that a list of the open ports had been furnished to the legation, but had not at the time reached Washington. By this list the open ports were La Guaira, Puerto Cabello, Maracaibo, Ciudad Bolivar, and Carúpano. [d]

"Having submitted the question thus raised to the President of the United States, I have now to express to you my regret

Case of military occupation.

at the conclusion at which the Spanish Government has arrived. It seems to me, in effect, to set up, although unconsciously, a claim that a Spanish ship of war, admitted by courtesy into a place actually held in military occupation by the forces of this Government, may disregard existing military orders, which are issued with a view to the military situation of that place. This seems, in effect, nothing less than a claim of Spanish sovereignty over American citizens on board a Spanish ship, not merely within the civil jurisdiction, but even within the military lines of the United States, in their own territories. The claim

---

[a] For. Rel. 1901, 545, 546.

[b] For. Rel. 1901, 547.

[c] Mr. Hay, Sec. of State, to Mr. Russell, chargé at Caracas, June 22, 1901, For. Rel. 1901, 548.

[d] For. Rel. 1901, 549–550.

thus understood cannot be conceded. I am, therefore, to inform you that the Government adheres to its former declaration that no ship of war, of whatever nation, will be expected to carry into or out from any port of the United States, which is either occupied by their forces, or is in possession of the insurgents, any person who does not actually belong to the civil, military, or naval service of the country whose flag that vessel carries, and especially that such ships of war shall not, without express leave of the military authorities, carry into or out of such ports any citizen of the United States. It can be only on an expected compliance with these terms that any foreign ship of war can enter ports of the classes I have designated during the continuance of the present civil war."

> Mr. Seward, Sec. of State, to Mr. Tassara, Span. min., July 2, 1863, Dip. Cor. 1863, II. 915, 916.
>
> As to the entrance of neutral men-of-war into blockaded ports, see the subject of Blockade.

(3) EXEMPTIONS FROM LOCAL AUTHORITY.

§ 254.

In discussing the status of a foreign man-of-war in a friendly port, the publicists generally confine themselves to the question of exemption from the local jurisdiction; and, while they agree that such exemption exists, they are not altogether in accord as to its extent. In reality the subject has been somewhat confused by the use of metaphorical expressions and needless analogies.

Opinions of publicists.

Cauchy,[a] after observing that an armed squadron is " the immediate and living representative of sovereignty in that which concerns war," says: " This character follows it in all places: wherever a vessel of war is stationed, the sovereign is present by his delegates. There is something here that resembles the inviolability of ambassadors, the principle of which is derived not from territorial jurisdiction, but from a sacred pact, tacitly concluded between all the civilized peoples of the world."

Calvo,[b] while affirming the exemption of a foreign man-of-war from the local jurisdiction, says that the commander of a public ship may in a sense be assimilated to a diplomatic agent accredited to a foreign court; the commander, and the crew placed under his orders, to the official and nonofficial personnel of a mission; and the ship itself to the house of an embassy or legation; and that of this assimilation the first result is that the naval vessel and her personnel as a whole are covered by the fiction of extraterritoriality. In this

---

[a] Droit Maritime International, edition 1862, vol. 2, p. 157.
[b] Le Droit International, 4th ed., vol. 3, sec. 1550.

statement, however, he seems to have in mind the case of a ship with her crew on board, and especially the case of such a ship on the high seas.

Testa (Le Droit Public International Maritime, traduct. par Boutiron, 1886, p. 83 et seq.) says:

" Ships of war, . . . being the property of the state and armed by it for its own defense, are an emanation of it.   Their commanders and officers are also functionaries of the country, delegates of its sovereignty, agents of its executive power and, up to a certain point, of its judicial power.   On board of a ship of war, everything is subject to the rules and codes of the country to which the ship belongs, and it is for that reason that it partakes fully of the independence of the sovereignty which has authorized it and of which it is the delegation.

" A difference so marked in its character and objects as that of ships of war and ships of commerce brings as its consequence:

" 1. That the manner and means of proving their nationality are different;

" 2. That the privileges and immunities of each are also different. . . .

" Armed and authorized by the government of an independent power, commanded by officers, public functionaries who represent, with the whole crew, the public force, ships of war are, in their personification, like an emanation of the state and a continuation of its territory.   From this it follows that no individual foreign to the government has the right to interfere in what goes on on board and still less to penetrate there by main force.

" It is usual to describe, theoretically, this collection of circumstances by the axiom that the ship of war is a portion of the territory of the nation to which it belongs, enjoying, by consequence, all the immunities attached to territorial independence.   It is this that we are wont to express by the word extraterritoriality, the actual meaning of which is not truly applicable, but peculiarly describes the conjunction of privileges, immunities, and rights.

" To justify the use of this expression, it suffices to consider that every ship is a floating habitation, bearing a population placed under the protection and submitted to the laws and government of the state. In the special case of a ship of war, we can add that it is a military place, a mobile fortress which contains a fraction of the state to which it belongs, governed by the functionaries, the military and administrative agents, delegated by the same state. . . .

" It is a constant rule that, for ships of war, the principle of exterritoriality is always absolute even in the ports and territorial waters of another country, and that such ships remain, as to their interior and exterior control, subject only to the laws of the state to which they belong. With the state in whose waters they may happen to be, they simply maintain international relations, through the intermediary of the competent functionaries of the locality. . . .

" It is no less certain that the local sovereign may forbid the entrance and mooring of a ship of war and may also exercise surveillance over the ship when he has reason to think its presence dangerous, or when some legitimate precaution requires or justifies such a measure. In such case, in order to avoid all difficulty, explanations ought to be given to the government to which the ship belongs.

" Moreover, the immunity of ships of war does not exempt them from responsibility for acts of aggression, of violence or of discourtesy which they may commit in the waters of a foreign nation. That nation always reserves the right of legitimate self-defense against such acts. Such ships are not exempt from the observance of sanitary regulations of the ports which they may wish to enter; . . . The public and official character of ships of war imposes on them the obligation to be first in giving an example of the most scrupulous respect for the ordinances of maritime police, the rules of the port, and all provisions for the common interest."

Phillimore (International Law, vol. 1, sec. 341), after stating that ships of war enjoy the privilege of extraterritoriality, says that this privilege " is extended, by the reason of the thing, to boats, tenders, and all appurtenances of a ship of war, but it does not cover offenses against the territorial law committed upon *shore*, though the commanders of vessels are entitled to be apprised of the circumstances attending and causes justifying the arrest of any one of their crew, and to secure to them, through the agency of diplomatic or consular ministers, the administration of justice."

Hall, a publicist of preeminent merit, in the fourth edition of his treatise on International Law, page 202, states that a public vessel is exempt from the local jurisdiction, but that her crew and other persons on board are subject to the local law, at least for acts done outside of her. The ship must, however, respect the administrative rules of the port, such as quarantine regulations. At page 205 he says:

" The immunities of a vessel of war belong to her as a complete instrument, made up of vessel and crew, and intended to be used by the state for specific purposes; the elements of which she is composed are not capable of separate use for those purposes; they consequently are not exempted from the local jurisdiction. If a ship of war is abandoned by her crew, she is merely property; if members of her crew go outside the ship or her tenders or boats, they are liable in every respect to the territorial jurisdiction. Even the captain is not considered to be individually exempt in respect of acts not done in his capacity of agent of his state."

A writ of habeas corpus may be awarded to bring up an "American
Development of doctrine. subject" unlawfully detained on board a foreign
man-of-war, the commander being amenable to the
usual jurisdiction of the state where he happens to be,
and not entitled to claim the extraterritoriality which is annexed to a
foreign minister and his domicile.

> Bradford, At. Gen., June, 1794, 1 Op. 47.
> See Moore, Int. Arbitrations, IV. 4364; Phillimore, Int. Law, I. § cccxlvi.;
> Hall, Int. Law (4th ed.), 196.
> In the case referred to by Attorney-General Bradford, the authorities at
> Newport, R. I., refused to permit the captain of a British sloop of war
> to obtain provisions till he had discharged six American citizens who
> were detained on board. The captain had previously permitted a
> deputation sent by the State legislature to go on board the vessel and
> make an investigation. It was alleged that the permission was
> obtained by constraint upon the captain while on shore. The British
> minister protested against the proceeding as an "unparalleled"
> insult. (Hall, § 54, p. 195.)

A ship of war when in a foreign friendly port is ordinarily
exempt from the jurisdiction of such port.

> Mr. Randolph, Sec. of State, to Mr. Hammond, Brit. min., July 23, 1794,
> 7 MS. Dom. Let. 55.
> See Mr. Frelinghuysen, Sec. of State, to Mr. Romero, May 25, 1882, MS.
> Notes to Mexico, VIII. 320.

"The President highly disapproves that a public vessel of war,
belonging to a foreign nation, should be searched by officers of the customs upon a suspicion of illicit commerce. The propriety of representing such a suspicion to the consul of that nation, or the commander of the vessel, will not be controverted, this being a course
respectful and customary. A general instruction will be therefore
given to pursue this course, with the view that if it should be ineffectual the Government of the United States may adopt those measures
which the necessity of the case and their rights may require."

> Mr. Randolph, Sec. of State, to Mr. Fauchet, French min., Nov. 17, 1794,
> 7 MS. Dom. Let. 403, cited in letter of same to same, June 13, 1795,
> 8 MS. Dom. Let. 262.

It was advised that criminal and civil process might be served on
board a British man-of-war lying within the waters of the United
States. In this relation, reference was made to Art. XXIII. of the
Jay treaty, which provided that "the ships of war of each of the contracting parties shall at all times be hospitably received in the ports
of the other, their officers and crews paying due respect to the laws
and government of the country." The Attorney-General observed
that this stipulation was "conceived to be declaratory of the usage of

nations," and that " hospitality, which includes protection," was " to
be enjoyed upon condition that the laws and government of the country are respected."

Lee, At.-Gen., 1799, 1 Op. 87. See Hall, Int. Law (4th ed.), 196.

By section 1 of the act of March 3, 1805, 2 Stat. 339, the judges or
justices of the courts of the United States were empowered to issue
warrants for the arrest of persons charged with treason, felony, mis-
prison of treason or of felony, misdemeanor, breach of the peace or
of the revenue laws of the United States, committed within the
United States, who should be on board of any foreign armed vessel
in United States waters. The warrants were to be directed to the
United States marshals, who were, upon the order of the judges or
justices, to have the aid of any military force in the vicinity if the
posse comitatus should be insufficient to insure the execution of the
process. Commanders of regular troops or of armed vessels of the
United States were also authorized to give aid to the State authorities in similar cases arising under the State laws. By section 7 the
President was required to issue instructions for carrying the act into
effect. Such instructions were issued May 29, 1805, to the United
States marshals, who were directed previously to the execution of
any warrant to make known to the commanding officer of the foreign
vessel of war having the offender on board the nature of the process
with which they were charged, with a request that the offender be
delivered up. If this request should not be complied with they were
to proceed with as much respect and delicacy as the case would admit
of to serve the process in the usual manner and to take the offender
into custody. If opposed by force, they were to report the case to
the Department of State, and unless special grounds existed for sus-
pecting an escape of the offender by the departure of the vessel of
war, or his removal beyond the reach of the warrant, were to take no
steps toward applying the extraordinary force authorized by the law
until they should receive such further directions as the President
should, on the strength of their report, think proper to give. A full
report of their action on each occasion was to be made to the Department of State. A copy of the circular was communicated to the
governor of each of the several States.

Circulars, Dept. of State, vol. I. pp. 3, 4.

The leading case, in which the principle of the extraterritoriality
of foreign men-of-war was first formally established,
Case of the   is that of the schooner *Exchange*, in 1812. The
"Exchange."   opinion in this case was delivered by Chief Justice
Marshall, and in preparing it he was, as he declared, compelled to
explore " an unbeaten path, with few, if any, aids from precedents

or written law." The facts were that the American schooner *Exchange*, having been captured and confiscated by the French under the Rambouillet decree, which decree both the Executive and the Congress of the United States had declared to constitute a violation of the law of nations, was converted by the French Government into a man-of-war, and commissioned under the name of the *Balaou*. In this character the vessel came into a port of the United States, where she was libeled by the original American owners for restitution. In this suit a suggestion was made by the United States, setting forth the national character of the vessel, and invoking judgment upon the question whether she was subject to the local jurisdiction. This question, having come in due course before the Supreme Court of the United States, it was held:

1. That as the jurisdiction of a nation within its own territory is exclusive and absolute, any restriction upon such jurisdiction must be derived from the nation's consent.

2. That such consent may be either express or implied, and " may, in some instances, be tested by common usage, and by common opinion, growing out of that usage."

3. That the equality and independence of sovereigns, and the common interest impelling them to mutual intercourse and an interchange of good offices, had given rise to a class of cases in which every sovereign was understood to waive the exercise of a part of his complete territorial jurisdiction: e. g. (*a*) the exemption of the person of a sovereign from arrest and detention within a foreign territory; (*b*) the immunity allowed to foreign ministers; (*c*) the immunity conceded to the troops of a foreign prince which a nation allows to pass through its territories.

4. That, in the absence of any prohibition, " the ports of a friendly nation are considered as open to the public ships of all powers with whom it is at peace, and they are supposed to enter such ports and to remain in them while allowed to remain, under the protection of the government of the place."

5. That there is, however, a " clear distinction " to be " drawn between the rights accorded to private individuals or private trading vessels, and those accorded to public armed ships which constitute a part of the military force of the nation; " and that, while it is necessary that the former should be subject to the local jurisdiction, the situation of a public armed ship is in all respects different. " She constitutes a part of the military force of her nation; acts under the immediate and direct command of the sovereign; is employed by him in national objects. He has many and powerful motives for preventing those objects from being defeated by the interference of a foreign state. Such interference cannot take place without affecting his power and his dignity. The implied license therefore

under which such vessel enters a friendly port may reasonably be construed, and it seems to the court ought to be construed, as containing an exemption from the jurisdiction of the sovereign within whose territory she claims the rites of hospitality. . . . Without doubt, the sovereign of the place is capable of destroying this implication. He may claim and exercise jurisdiction either by employing force, or by subjecting such vessels to the ordinary tribunals. But until such power be exerted in a manner not to be misunderstood, the sovereign cannot be considered as having imparted to the ordinary tribunals a jurisdiction which it would be a breach of faith to exercise. Those general statutory provisions therefore which are descriptive of the ordinary jurisdiction of the judicial tribunals, which give an individual whose property has been wrested from him a right to claim that property in the courts of the country in which it is found, ought not, in the opinion of this court, to be so construed as to give them jurisdiction in a case in which the sovereign power has impliedly consented to waive its jurisdiction."

> Marshall, C. J., Schooner Exchange *v.* McFaddon (1812), 7 Cranch, 112.
> See the Pizarro *v.* Matthias, 10 N. Y. Leg. Observer, 97.
> See, also, Twiss (ed. 1861), I. § 158; Bluntschli, § 321; Wharton, Com. on Am. Law, § 190.
> In the case of the British steamer *Tartar*, chartered by the United States and employed as a transport in the military service, the position was taken that she was entitled while so employed to be treated in British ports as the troop-ship of a friendly power and as such exempt from local port regulations affecting the number of passengers which vessels might carry. (Mr. Adee, Acting Sec. of State, to Mr. Choate, tel., Sept. 13, 1899, MS. Inst. Gr. Br. XXXIII. 248.)

Foreign armed vessels, adopting the character of merchant ships by carrying merchandise, render themselves subject to the revenue laws.

> Wirt, At.-Gen., 1820, 1 Op. 337.

" Lord Stowell, on being consulted by his Government in 1820, with reference to the case of an Englishman who took refuge on board a man-of-war at Callao after escaping from prison, into which he had been thrown for political reasons, answered the question, ' whether any British subject coming on board one of His Majesty's ships of war in a foreign port escaping from civil or criminal process in such port, and from the jurisdiction of the state within whose territory such port may be situated, is entitled to the protection of the British flag, and to be deemed as within the Kingdom of Great Britain and Ireland,' by saying that he had ' no hesitation in declaring that he knew of no such right of protection belonging to the British flag, and that he thought such a pretension unfounded in point of principle, injurious to the rights of other countries, and inconsistent with those of our own;' and added that ' the Spaniards would not have been chargeable with illegal violence if they had thought proper to employ force in taking ' the person whose case was under discussion ' out of the British vessel.' "

> Hall, Int. Law (4th ed.), 197, citing Report of Commission on Fugitive Slaves, p. lxxvi.

In a suit against certain British naval officers for refusing to restore some slaves who had escaped in 1815 from the mainland of Florida to their ships, Best, J., in discussing the question of liability, said: " I am decidedly of opinion that they were then no longer slaves. The moment they put their feet on board of a British man-of-war, not lying within the waters of East Florida (where, undoubtedly, the laws of that country would prevail), those persons who before had been slaves, were free."

> Forbes v. Cochrane (1824) 2 B. & C. 448.
> In Seagrove v. Parks (1891), L. R., 1 Q. B. 551, it was held that leave to serve a writ out of the jurisdiction should not be granted in the case of a naval officer on a British man-of-war which was at the time of the application on the high seas, the court saying that " as long as the defendant is on board his ship, he is within the jurisdiction."

" To national armed ships in the harbor of a foreign power the doctrine of exterritoriality undoubtedly applies."

> Mr. Marcy, Sec. of State, to Mr. Dobbin, Sec. of Navy, April 21, 1856, 45 MS. Dom. Let. 212.

Ships of war enjoy full rights of extraterritoriality in foreign ports and territorial waters.

Therefore a ship of war, or any prize of hers, in command of a public officer, possesses, in the ports of the United States, the right of extraterritoriality and is exempt from the local jurisdiction.

A prisoner of war on board such a foreign ship of war, or of her prize, can not be released by *habeas corpus* issuing from courts of the United States or of a particular State. " So long as they (the prisoners) remained on board that ship, they were in the territory and jurisdiction of her sovereign. There, the neutral has no right to meddle with them." Should they be taken on shore, they become subject to the local jurisdiction, or not, according as it may be agreed between the political authorities of the belligerent and neutral power.

> Opinions of Cushing, At. Gen., April 28, 1855, and Sept. 6, 1856, 7 Op. 122, 131, and 8 Op. 73.
> " During the war in which Russia was a party on the one side, and England, France and other powers on the other, questions relating to this

subject arose, some of which were referred by my predecessor, Mr. William L. Marcy, to Caleb Cushing, esq., then Attorney-General. An elaborate opinion of the latter relative to belligerent asylum, bears date the 28th of April, 1855. One of its conclusions is that a foreign ship of war, or any prize of hers in command of a public officer, possesses in the ports of the United States the rights of extra-territoriality, and is not subject to local jurisdiction. This view was repeated in another opinion of Mr. Cushing of the 8th of September, 1856, which declared that ships of war enjoy the full rights of extra-territoriality in foreign ports and territorial waters." (Mr. Evarts, Sec. of State, to Mr. Comacho, Venezuelan min., Dec. 9, 1880, MS. Notes to Venez., I. 210.)

In 1871 Rear-Admiral Boggs, U. S. Navy, commanding the European fleet, refused to give up certain persons on board who were charged by the Italian authorities with larceny. Mr. Fish, while observing that any person attached to a foreign man-of-war was liable to arrest on shore for an offense there committed, said: " In the event that a person on board the foreign ship should be charged with a crime, for the commission of which he would be liable to be given up, pursuant to an extradition treaty, the commander of the vessel may give him up if such proof of the charge should be produced as the treaty may require. In such case, however, it would always be advisable to consult the nearest minister of the United States. This was done in this instance, and the decision of Mr. Marsh that the persons demanded were not liable to be given up, pursuant to the treaty with Italy, is approved by the Department."

Mr. Fish, Sec. of State, to Commodore Case, Jan. 27, 1872, 92 MS. Dom. Let. 322.

January 17, 1879, the United States frigate *Constitution* went ashore on the English coast, having on board at the time a cargo of machinery belonging to private individuals and intended for the Paris exhibition. She was pulled off by tugs, the owners of one of which, being dissatisfied with the amount of remuneration offered him, brought an action for salvage, and applied for warrants for the arrest of the ship and cargo. The court refused to issue the warrants, Sir Robert Phillimore, who rendered the decision, saying that " ships of war belonging to a nation with whom this country is at peace are exempt from the civil jurisdiction."

The Constitution, L. R. 4 P. D. 39, 45, January 29, 1879.

It has been held that while a ship, belonging to a foreign sovereign, cannot be arrested as a defendant in an action, yet she may, as plaintiff in an action for damages against another ship for a collision, be compelled to give security for damages on a counterclaim set up by the defendant.

The Newbattle, L. R. 10 P. D. 33, January 13, 1885.

" Both by the law of nations, and the treaty with France, if a

Question as to un-
neutral acts. French privateer brings an enemy's ship into our ports, which she has taken as prize on the high seas, the United States, as a nation, have no right to detain her, or make any inquiry into the circumstances of the capture. But this exemption from inquiry by our courts of justice in this respect only belongs to a *French privateer, lawfully commissioned*, and therefore, if a vessel claims that exemption, but does not appear to be duly entitled to it, it is the express duty of the court, upon application, to make inquiry, *whether she is the vessel she pretends to be*, since her title to such exemption depends *on that very fact.*" Otherwise a vessel fraudulently pretending to be French might defy all inquiry merely by keeping out of a French port.

Talbot *v.* Janson (1795), 3 Dallas, 133, 159, opinion of Mr. Justice Iredell.

In June, 1810, a Spanish brig with a cargo of slaves was captured on the high seas by a French privateer named *L'Epine.* The brig and cargo were brought to New Orleans, where the Spanish owner libelled them for restitution on the ground that the *L'Epine*, even if duly commissioned, was armed and equipped at New Orleans, and manned by American citizens, contrary to the law of nations. Held, Washington, J., delivering the opinion of the court, that the brig and cargo must be restored. It appeared that, prior to the capture of the brig, the *L'Epine* enlisted a crew at New Orleans, in violation of the act of Congress of June, 1794. Her papers showed that certain persons, whom she was permitted to take on board as passengers, were in fact entered on her crew list, with the number of prize shares to which they were entitled opposite their names, and that advances were there made to them, agreeably to the ordinances of France.

The Alerta *v.* Moran (1815), 9 Cranch, 359.

" The general rule is undeniable that the trial of captures made on the high seas, *jure belli*, by a duly commissioned vessel of war, whether from an enemy or a neutral, belongs exclusively to the courts of that nation to which the captor belongs. To this rule there are exceptions which are as firmly established as the rule itself. If the capture be made within the territorial limits of a neutral country into which the prize is brought, or by a privateer which had been illegally equipped in such neutral country, the prize courts of such neutral country not only possess the power, but it is their duty, to restore the property so illegally captured to the owner. This is necessary to the vindication of their own neutrality."

Washington, J., The Alerta *v.* Moran (March 10, 1815), 9 Cranch, 359, 364.

The cases of the *Cassius*, 3 Dallas, 121, and the *Invincible*, 1 Wheaton, 238, decide that neither a public vessel of another nation, nor its officers, are liable to answer in our courts for a capture on the high seas, but do not touch the question of jurisdiction over her prizes lying in our ports, which extends to libels *in rem* for restitution of such prizes made in violation of our neutrality.

> The Santissima Trinidad, 7 Wheat. 283.
>
> See, also, The Gran Para, 7 Wheat. 471; and Moore, Int. Arbitrations, I. 576–578.

The Geneva tribunal, in its award of September 14, 1872, declared: "The privilege of exterritoriality accorded to vessels of war has been admitted into the law of nations, not as an absolute right, but solely as a proceeding founded on the principle of courtesy and mutual deference between different nations, and therefore can never be appealed to for the protection of acts done in violation of neutrality."

> Moore, Int. Arbitrations, I. 655.
>
> Mr. Bancroft Davis, in his notes to the treaties of the United States, says: "This is in accordance with the settled practice of the United States." He cites the opinion of Attorney-General Lee, 1 Op. 87, (Treaty Volume, 1776–1887, p. 1288.)
>
> Wharton, in his Int. Law Digest, I. § 37, referring to Mr. Davis's statement, says: "But this pretension was resisted and resented by the United States when the *Chesapeake* was 'visited' and searched by the *Leopard* in 1809, and was withdrawn by the British Government. See criticism in Creasy's Int. Law, 177 et seq."
>
> It appears, however, that the case of the *Chesapeake* was one of the attempted visit and search and hostile attack, within the territorial waters of the United States, or on the high seas just beyond, of an American man-of-war by a British man-of-war, on the ground that the former had among her crew persons who had deserted from the British fleet, at Norfolk, Virginia.

Supplies. "As I am informed by the Secretary of the Treasury, 'the practice in exempting from duty supplies, etc., for foreign vessels of war, is governed by section 2982 of the Revised Statutes, and the privilege is only extended to vessels of war of such nations as reciprocate towards vessels of war of the United States while in the ports of such nations.'"

> Mr. Bayard, Sec. of State, to Viscount das Nogueiras, Portuguese min., Oct. 21, 1887, For. Rel 1888, II. 1388–1389. See, to the same effect, Mr. Cadwalader, Act. Sec. of State, to Mr. Washburn, min. to France, Oct. 14, 1876, MS. Inst. France, XIX. 393.

The privilege granted to foreign men-of-war under section 2982, Revised Statutes, of purchasing supplies from the public warehouses duty free when that privilege is reciprocated in the ports of the nation to which the vessel belongs, is limited to purchasing in the bonded warehouses supplies deposited therein pending withdrawal for consumption. The duty referred to from which the supplies so purchased shall be free is the import duty.

> Griggs, At.-Gen., March 9, 1901, 23 Op. 418.

The Peruvian minister of foreign affairs, his attention having been called to the examination by custom-house employees at Callao of packages of naval stores received " for the use of the American squadron anchored in the bay," expressed regret at the occurrence, and stated that he had referred the matter to the minister of hacienda, " for the prevention of a similar abuse and to avoid its repetition in the future."

> Mr. Davis, Act. Sec. of State, to Mr. Chandler, Sec. of Navy, Nov. 18, 1884, 153 MS. Dom. Let. 232.

" The remission of customs duties on the property of foreign governments, as in the case of transshipped or bonded naval stores, materials of equipment and repair, consular supplies and the like, is a matter of usage and good understanding, and this Government, while always ready to promote the freest reciprocity in such regard, can not complain if, as is actually the case, other governments should not concede an equal measure of privilege. It is gratifying to see that the Mexican practice is much the same as our own, and it is trusted that the late incident may emphasize such friendly understanding."

> Mr. Bayard, Sec. of State, to Mr. Bragg, min. to Mexico, June 21, 1888, MS. Inst. Mex. XXII. 235. This instruction related to the transshipment of stores for the U. S. S. Omaha, at Acapulco. It refers to a previous instruction, No. 67, of June 9, 1888.
>
> In May, 1885, boilers were admitted free into the United States for the Mexican gunboat Independencia. The rule in the United States is general, and " includes all supplies and stores." (Mr. Bayard, Sec. of State, to Mr. Bragg, min. to Mexico, tel., June 8, 1888, MS. Inst. Mex. XXII. 223.)

(4) POLICE REGULATIONS.

§ 255.

By a circular of June 14, 1866, in relation to the admission of friendly foreign men-of-war into Austrian waters, it is declared that such vessels " are bound to observe the existing port, sanitary, and financial regulations in Austrian ports, the same as the Imperial-Royal war ships, and to comply with the requisitions of the competent authorities in these matters."

> 63 Br. & For. State Papers, 1073.

The German regulations touching the treatment of foreign men-of-war in German ports were sent to the Department of State by Mr. Kasson, min. to Germany, in his No. 12, Sept. 17, 1884, and were communicated to the Navy Department. (35 MS. Desp. from Germany.)

"Art. 11. That foreign ships and vessels of war shall respect the existing police, sanitary and fiscal laws and regulations, and shall further submit to all the rules and regulations of the port, in both cases to the same extent as is demanded of the national ships and vessels of war."

Royal decree of Feb. 2, 1893, concerning the admission of foreign ships of war into the waters of the Netherlands, enclosed with the dispatch of Mr. Thayer, min. to the Netherlands, to Mr. Gresham, Sec. of State, No. 398, April 19, 1893, 31 MS. Desp. from the Netherlands.

By art. 12 it is provided that any foreign ship or vessel infringing the regulations may be required to withdraw, and that force may if necessary be used for the purpose; and by art. 13 it is provided that the regulations shall be communicated to the Netherlands pilots, who are to give all necessary information concerning them to the commanders of vessels of war which they are piloting.

" In regard to the payment of the charges for pilotage at Tahiti, this Government overrules the objections which were made by Captain Stanley of the ' Tuscarora,' and accepts the instruction of the authorities of Tahiti."

Mr. Seward, Sec. of State, to Mr. Berthemy, French min., Nov. 19, 1867, MS. Notes to French Leg. VIII. 327.

With reference to the United States Fish Commission vessel *Grampus*, it was stated by the British minister, in a note of Sept. 15, 1887, that by the regulations then in force in Newfoundland the public vessels of foreign governments were liable to compulsory pilotage dues, but that the authorities were considering a proposal to amend the regulations so as to require the payment of dues only when the services of pilots were requested.

Mr. Bayard, Sec. of State, to Sir L. West, Brit. min., Sept. 22, 1887, MS. Notes to Gr. Br. XX. 545, acknowledging the receipt of the latter's note of Sept. 15, 1887, with a copy of the regulations then in force.

See, also, Mr. Bayard, Sec. of State, to Mr. Whitney, Sec. of Navy, Sept. 22, 1887, 165 MS. Dom. Let. 433, with copies of correspondence.

" I have the honor to acknowledge the receipt of the letter from your Department, dated the 9th of August last, enclosing for an expression of this Department's views in the matter, a copy of a letter from the chief of the Bureau of Navigation of the Navy Department, with enclosures, relative to the propriety and feasibility of issuing an order to naval vessels directing that when pilots are not employed, local foreign laws requiring the employment of pilots are not to be held to compel the payment of pilotage by public vessels.

" In reply I have the honor to say that the laws of some of our States require the payment of pilotage fees, when pilots are not employed, and these laws, by their terms, apply to all vessels.

" The doctrine of international law is that all vessels are subject to the revenue and police regulations, including those in regard to pilotage, of the territorial waters which such vessels may enter. In the statement of the doctrine no exception is made in favor of public vessels.

" In Secretary Chandler's letter of July 12, 1884, enclosed in yours, the statement is made that certain exemptions are allowed by international law to public vessels; and in Secretary Frelinghuysen's letter, also enclosed with yours, the same statement is made. No authorities are cited in support of the proposition, while the doctrine above mentioned is stated in Lawrence, International Law, pages 223 and 226; Hall, International Law, page 192; Pradier-Fodéré, International Law, section 2379.

" The latter says that ' the ports, the roadsteads, the harbors form a dependency of the national public domain and the ships of foreign nations are under the obligation to observe rigorously the general and special regulations in force in the harbors, roadsteads, and ports.'

" In view of the foregoing the Department could not advise the adoption of the rule suggested."

> Mr. Hill, Acting Sec. of State, to Sec. of the Navy, Oct. 6, 1899, 240 MS. Dom. Let. 399.
>
> " I have the honor to enclose herewith copy of a note dated the 22d instant, received from the British chargé d'affaires at this capital, in regard to a claim for $45 presented to Captain Macalister, of Her Majesty's ship Partridge, by the Charleston Pilots' Association. The Partridge being a public vessel of a foreign nation is, according to universally recognized principles of international law, exempt, even in our own ports, from the operations of the laws either of the United States or of any of the States, and the Department ventures to express the hope that the Charleston Pilots' Association, on being reminded of this fact, will withdraw its claim for pilotage fees against the vessel in question." (Mr. Gresham, Sec. of State, to the Governor of South Carolina, Oct. 25, 1894, 199 MS. Dom. Let. 244.)
>
> " In response to the inquiry whether the statement that ' there are no regulations or restrictions respecting the entrance of men-of-war into ports of the United States ' is still correct, I have to state that, with the exception of local rules of navigation, and quarantine regulations, which are equally applicable to men-of-war and merchant vessels, the statement referred to is still correct. In this connection your attention is invited to the Department's letter of July 12, 1884, to the honorable the Secretary of State (Executive Letter Book No. 37, page 284, et seq.)." (Mem. of Mr. S. C. Lemly, Judge-Advocate-General, U. S. N., communicated by Mr. Soley, Assist. Sec. of Navy, to Mr. Moore, Third Assist. Sec. of State, July 6, 1891.)

In October, 1898, the German embassy at Washington was advised, on the strength of a letter from the Treasury Department, that a German man-of-war, coming to New Orleans, La., from Hamburg, which was not an infected port, would not be detained at quarantine nor disinfected; but that " the *Geier,* coming from Vera Cruz, which is a yellow fever infected port, will in all probability be disinfected and detained by the Louisiana quarantine authorities, the New Orleans quarantine being a State establishment and not under the direct management of the Federal Government. The governor of Louisiana has been advised of the facts by this Department and requested to extend all possible consideration to the *Geier.*"

> Mr. Hay, Sec. of State, to Baron Speck von Sternburg, Oct. 15, 1898, MS. Notes to German Embassy, XII. 206.

(5) OFFICERS AND CREWS.

§ 256.

The officers of a vessel of war belonging to a friendly foreign nation can not set up extraterritoriality when unofficially on shore in a port in whose harbor their vessel is temporarily moored.

> Mr. Randolph, Sec. of State, to Mr. Hammond, July 23, 1794, 7 MS. Dom. Let. 55.

" At the time when I had the honor of receiving your letter of 16 October last, concerning a transaction in the port of Marseilles, in which Captain Gamble of the sloop-of-war *Erie,* a public ship in the service of the United States, was summoned before the tribunal of commerce at that port for damage asserted to have been done to the cable of an English vessel called the *Herald,* and was alleged to have prevented the execution of the citation upon him, on board of his own vessel, that officer being absent from the United States it was thought due to justice, before I should answer your letter, to wait for his report upon the circumstances of the case. That report was expected to be shortly received, having been already required of him, upon a complaint which had been received at this Department from the British minister, Mr. Bagot, in behalf of Captain Snowden, the master of the British vessel, the cable of which was stated to have been damaged. Captain Gamble's report has accordingly been received; from which it appears that the place occupied by the *Erie,* at the time when the accident happened, had been assigned to Captain Gamble, at the time of his arrival in the harbor, by the proper officer of the port, and without any objection from the master of the English vessel; that the damage done to the cable was altogether accidental, without any intention or fault of Captain Gamble; that the conduct of the master of the *Herald* was rude and offensive towards him, and that, in declining to receive the citation of the tribunal of commerce, he had reason to believe that it would be received by the consul of the United States.

" I am directed to assure you, Sir, that the President has a deep sense of the respect due by the officers, commanding vessels of war, to the institutions and authorities of the foreign ports into which they are received. He is persuaded at the same time that your Government will duly appreciate the feelings and the sense of duty to his own flag, of an officer commanding a public vessel of his nation in a foreign port. The British minister has been informed that the damages awarded by the decision of the tribunal of commerce to the master of the *Herald*, together with the charges of the suit, will be paid by this Government, and it is not doubted that this manifestation of respect to the decision of the tribunal of commerce of Marseilles will be received by your Sovereign as an evidence of the spirit of amity and of good harmony which the United States will be on all occasions earnestly desirous of cultivating with his Government."

Mr. Adams, Sec. of State, to Mr. Hyde de Neuville, French min., Jan. 22,
1818, MS. Notes to For. Legs. II. 276.

" The declaration made by Mr. Lisboa in his note, dated on the 21st January last, was not equivalent, as his excellency supposes, ' to a renunciation of the right of the authorities of Brazil ' to try and punish ' crimes and infractions of their police regulations,' committed within its territory by the sailors, citizens, or subjects of any nation. That note contains no expression from which such an inference can be drawn. The Government of the United States never has denied or disputed this sovereign right of Brazil. On the contrary, its existence was cheerfully acknowledged by me in the conferences with Mr. Lisboa which preceded his note.

" It is true that Mr. Wise, in his correspondence with Baron Cayru, did not at first admit, in its just extent, this established principle of public law; but in his last note to that gentleman, of the 10th November, he has recognized it in the clearest and most explicit manner. In it he declares, 'that in respect to the man who drew his knife on his fellow sailor whilst on shore, he [Mr. Wise] admits to the fullest extent the jurisdiction of Brazil.'

" The question is, therefore, at once relieved from the misapprehension which pervades a great part of the instructions to you, that this Government has denied to that of Brazil the sovereign jurisdiction over all persons of whatever nation within its territory."

Mr. Buchanan, Sec. of State, to Mr. Leal, Brazilian chargé, August 30,
1847, S. Ex. Doc. 35, 30 Cong. 1 sess. 29, referring to the arrest at
Rio de Janeiro of a lieutenant and three sailors of the U. S. S.
Saratoga.

"A young officer of the French navy committed an act of disorder in the house of a public woman, which he entered forcibly, against her will; and, having been arrested by the police, his commander, through the medium of the chargé d'affaires of France, before the prosecution was begun, solicited his delivery, with the assurance that he would be corrected on board of his ship. He was immediately given up, and the chargé d'affaires himself thanked the Imperial Government for this act of kindness. A few years since, a marine of the English squadron was seized by the custom-house guards at Bahia, in a boat of the brig of war to which he belonged, coming from a merchant ship, to which he had gone without license from the custom-house; and, agreeably to the law, he was confined in a custom-house vessel, to be kept there until he should have paid the fine incurred by him. The commander of the brig went on board the vessel and took him away; but the English commodore, on being informed of the circumstances, immediately caused the marine to be sent back to the custom-house vessel, and despatched his next officer, in full uniform, to make an apology to the inspector of the custom-house, alleging that their officers were ignorant of the provision of the law, and offering to pay the fine; this ample apology was received, and the fine was remitted. In 1842, two midshipmen of the squadron of Admiral Hugon fought a duel at Naples, in a room of a hotel, and were seized and tried. The French ambassador requested their discharge; the King refused, and the admiral weighed anchor and prepared to go to sea. The King, however, still refused to deliver them up, and they were tried and condemned; after which he pardoned them, and ordered them given up to the admiral." (Mr. de Souza e Olieveira, Brazilian min. of for. aff., to Mr. Leal, Brazilian chargé at Washington, May 31, 1847, S. Ex. Doc. 35, 30 Cong. 1 sess. 9–10.)

June 22, 1862, three officers of the British man-of-war *Forte*—the chaplain, the lieutenant, and a midshipman—were

Case of the "Forte."

subjected by the guard at Tijuca Hill, near Rio de Janeiro, to what Admiral Warren, of Her Britannic Majesty's navy, denounced as a "most brutal outrage." There was, however, some dispute as to the facts. While it was admitted that the officers in question were arrested and confined over night in the guardhouse, then for some hours in the city lockup, and then in a military prison, there was a dispute as to whether their rank was at first known, and as to whether they were conducting themselves in an orderly manner when arrested. The British Government demanded that the ensign of the guard be "dismissed," that the sentry at Tijuca Hill be "adequately punished," that "an apology be made by the Brazilian Government" for the "outrage on British naval officers," and that the chief of police and the official at the Rio police station should "receive a public censure." The Brazilian Government refused all these demands, and the case was afterwards coupled by Great Britain with that of the plundering of the British bark *Prince of Wales* on the coast of Rio Grande do Sul as a justification for reprisals. But in the end the case of the *Prince of Wales* was directly settled and the case of the *Forte* was submitted to the arbitration of King Leopold, of Belgium. The arbitrator rendered, June 18, 1863, an award in which he held that it was not shown that in the origin of the affair the Brazilian agents had no provocation; that as the officers in question were not at the time of their arrest wearing the insignia of their rank, and therefore could not, in a port frequented by so many foreigners, expect their bare declaration to be accepted, they could not at the time of their arrest demand a different treatment from other persons similarly situated; that though their treatment might seem severe, measures were taken, when the English vice-consul declared their position, to assure them proper respect, and that they were afterwards set at liberty; that the functionary who released them had them set at liberty as soon as possible, and that in so doing he was moved " by the desire to spare these officers the unpleasant consequences which according to the terms of the laws would have necessarily followed any further prosecution of the affair; " and that, " in the manner in which the laws of Brazil were applied to the English officers, there was neither premediation of offence nor any offence toward the British marine." After this decision the British Government sent Mr. Edward Thornton on a special mission to Brazil to renew diplomatic intercourse.

> Moore, Int. Arbitrations, V. 4925–4928, citing 53 Br. & For. State Papers, 150; 54 id. 579, etc.

Though the commander of a foreign man-of-war is not bound to give up anyone on board, yet " any person . . . attached to such a man-of-war, charged with an offence on shore, is liable to arrest therefor in the country where the offence may have been committed."

> Mr. Fish, Sec. of State, to Commodore Case, Jan. 27, 1872, 92 MS. Dom. Let. 322.

In the case of Ramsey, a seaman on an American man-of-war, who **Ramsey's case.** was arrested in a Peruvian port, the United States demanded the prisoner's release, because the authorities had failed to observe the provision of the treaty requiring American citizens to be brought before a magistrate or other legal authority for examination within twenty-four hours after their arrest, and if not so examined to be forthwith discharged. In Ramsey's case judicial proceedings were instituted five days after his arrest without examination. But, while demanding Ramsey's release, the United States declared that its object was not to shield him " from lawful prosecution, but to preserve treaty rights," and that after his release his rearrest on the same charge and prosecution in accordance with law and the treaty would not be opposed.

> Mr. Sherman, Sec. of State, to Mr. McKenzie, min. to Peru, tel., April 2, 1897, MS. Inst. Peru, XVIII. 24.

January 26, 1884, Mr. Perez, Colombian minister of foreign affairs, addressed to Mr. Scruggs, then minister of the United States at Bogota, a note in which he stated that a legal process was pending before the judge of the district and Department of Panama, on account of damages caused to the seeded lands of a resident of the island of Toboquilla by the crew of the U. S. S. *Wachusett*, January 15, 1881. In order that this process might follow its legal course, the minister of foreign affairs, at the instance of the judicial authorities, requested the name of the commander of the *Wachusett* and the names of the members of her crew at the time in question. January 29, Mr. Scruggs in reply stated that he would bring the matter to the attention of his Government, but at the same time remarked that he was at a loss to understand why the state authorities of Panama should assume jurisdiction of the commander and crew of a public vessel of war of a friendly power, adding that the immunity of such vessels from the exercise of any civil or criminal jurisdiction, but that of the sovereign power to which they belonged, was uniformly asserted and conceded. He suggested that the better course would be to present a complaint through diplomatic channels. Mr. Scruggs's note was approved by the Department of State, which said that the local tribunals might investigate the facts with a view to asking redress through the international channel, but that the government to which a public ship belonged, though it should not withhold consideration of any charge of wrong-doing brought against the vessel by another government, " may not consent that the foreign courts shall assert any manner of jurisdiction over the individuals concerned." Mr. Scruggs was instructed to say that the United States would consider any duly substantiated charges against the *Wachusett* for injury to the property or persons of citizens or residents of Colombia, but " that it must courteously decline to take any step, such as furnishing a list of the officers and crew of the vessel, which might in advance import a readiness to commit to the courts of Colombia any jurisdiction over the acts of its individual servants." (Mr. Frelinghuysen, Sec. of State, to Mr. Scruggs, min. to Colombia, March 4, 1884, MS. Inst. Colombia, XVII. 384, acknowledging the receipt of Mr. Scruggs's No. 135, of Jan. 29, 1884.)

See Mr. Evarts, Sec. of State, to Mr. Christiancy, min. to Peru, March 16, 1880, MS. Inst. Peru, XVI. 444.

" In the ports of all countries where foreign men-of-war resort, when sailors go ashore, become intoxicated and violate police regulations by quarreling with brother sailors—especially where they have insulted or injured none of the citizens of the country—their officers are always permitted to seize them and take them on board without obstruction, unless they have been first apprehended by the police. This is the custom, founded on courtesy, among all nations."

Mr. Buchanan, Sec. of State, to Mr. Leal, Brazilian chargé, Aug. 30, 1847, S. Ex. Doc. 35, 30 Cong. 1 sess. 28, 32. This statement was made in the course of a discussion, growing out of the attempt of Lieutenant Davis, U. S. S. *Saratoga*, to take back to the ship some deserters at Rio de Janeiro and the subsequent arrest and imprisonment of the lieutenant and the sailor by the local authorities. The circumstances of the case were much controverted.

A midshipman of the U. S. S. *Mohican*, who had gone ashore at the port of St. Louis, in Maranham, Brazil, was arrested and taken before the chief of police for having fired five shots from his pistol in the streets of the city at one of his boatmen who attempted to desert. On learning his national and official character, the chief of police discharged him, but in so doing remarked that "he had acted very roughly in attempting to shoot a man in the street of Maranham, showing a disregard for the laws of the country, and he (the chief of police) trusted that it would not occur again." The commander of the *Mohican* requested the United States consul at the port to make a complaint to the president of Maranham against the chief of police, on the ground that the latter's words constituted a reprimand and indignity, offensive to the midshipman and to the United States flag. The president of Maranham called upon the chief of police for an explanation, and the chief denied having used the language complained of. The consul then presented the case to the United States minister at Rio, who declined to bring it to the attention of the Brazilian Government, but submitted it to the Department of State. The Department replied that the act of the midshipman "in firing a pistol at a deserter in a street of Maranham was a breach of the peace, offensive to the dignity of Brazil, which the Government of that country may well expect the United States to disallow and censure. The complaint of a reprimand, even if it were sustained in point of fact, is groundless and trivial. The United States are not looking out for causes of complaint against foreign states. The Secretary of the Navy will give instructions in this sense to the commander. You will make these views known to the Government of Brazil."

> Mr. Seward, Sec. of State, to Mr. Webb, Jan. 23, 1867, MS. Inst. Brazil, XVI. 162.

While intimating an opinion that if the members of a foreign military force, to which permission had been given to enter the United States, or the members of the crew of a foreign man-of-war, should "actually desert and scatter themselves through the country," their officers would not, in the absence of a treaty, be authorized to call upon the local authorities for their reclamation, the court observed: "We have no doubt that, under the case above cited, the foreign officer may exercise his accustomed authority for the maintenance of discipline, and perhaps arrest a deserter *dum fervet opus*, and to that extent this country waives its jurisdiction over the foreign crew or command."

> Tucker *v.* Alexandroff (1902), 183 U. S. 424, 433.

4. OTHER PUBLIC VESSELS.

§ 257.

In a case involving the question of jurisdiction of a civil action against a Belgian mail packet which had been assimilated, by a special treaty stipulation, to a man-of-war, the English court of appeals said:

"As a consequence of the absolute independence of every sovereign authority and of the international comity which induces every sovereign state to respect the independence of every other sovereign state, each and every one declines to exercise by means of any of its courts, any of its territorial jurisdiction over the person of any sovereign or ambassador of any other state, or over the public property of any state which is destined to its public use, or over the property of any ambassador, though such sovereign, ambassador or property, be within its territory, and therefore, but for the common agreement, subject to its jurisdiction."

> The Parlement Belge (Feb. 27, 1880), L. R. 5 P. D. 197, 217. See, also, Briggs v. Light-Boats, 11 Allen, 157; the Pizarro, 10 N. Y. Leg. Obs. 97.

5. OTHER PUBLIC PROPERTY.

§ 258.

The judicial authorities, as thus disclosed, uniformly place the exemption of a foreign man-of-war from the local jurisdiction on the ground of its being the public property of a sovereign, engaged in public business. This principle has been applied to other public property. In 1878 an attempt was made in the English courts to prevent by injunction certain persons in England from putting on board Japanese vessels of war, building in that country, some shells which were manufactured in Germany and which were to be taken to Japan. An injunction having been granted without prejudice to any question that might be raised, an application was made to the court on behalf of the Mikado and his envoy extraordinary in London for permission to remove the shells. This application was allowed. James, L. J., said: "The Mikado of Japan, who is a sovereign prince, bought in Germany a certain quantity of shells, which shells were lawfully made in Germany, although they were, as alleged, made upon the same principle as something which is the subject of a patent in this country. Those shells were bought by the Mikado for the purpose of his Government. He brought them into this country on the way to Japan, and he asks to be allowed to remove them from this country, that is to say, he asks that he shall not, by reason of something which was done between the plaintiff and some other persons, be interfered with in his removal of them to his own country. It seems to me that to refuse him that leave would be a very dangerous proceeding. If a tribunal of any foreign country were to deal with the ammunition of a British man-of-war under those circumstances, or to refuse to permit the captain of a British man-of-war to remove his ammunition and shells, or anything else, I think that our country would consider it a very serious matter, and possibly demand reparation." Brett, L. J., said: "The Mikado has a perfect right to have these goods; no court in this country can properly prevent him from having goods which are the public property of his own country." Cotton, L. J., said: "This court has no jurisdiction, and, in my opinion, none of the courts in this country have any jurisdiction, to interfere with the property of a foreign sovereign, more especially with what we call the public property of the state of which he is sovereign as distinguished from that which may be his own private property."

Vavasseur v. Krupp, L. R. 9 Ch. Div. 351, 354, 359, 360, July 3, 1878.

An attachment was obtained against the United States of Mexico, in the courts of the State of New York, in respect of certain movable property of the Mexican Government, with a view to secure by that means satisfaction for certain claims. Under instructions of the Attorney-General of the United States, the United States district attorney at New York appeared, and, calling attention as amicus curiæ to the court's want of jurisdiction, moved that the attachment be vacated. The motion was granted, the court saying that a foreign state could not be sued without its consent, and that, so far as jurisdiction was concerned, there was no difference between the sovereign and his property.

Hassard v. United States of Mexico (1899), 61 N. Y. S. 939, 29 Misc. Rep. 511, 46 App. Div. 623.

A copy of this opinion was communicated by Mr. Hay, Sec. of State, to Mr. Aspiroz, Mex. amb., Nov. 22, 1899, MS. Notes to Mex. Leg. X. 503.

It seems that in this case the attachment was served on Messrs. J. P. Morgan & Co., July 20, 1899, and that they gave a certificate to the sheriff that there were no assets in their hands. (Griggs, At. Gen., to Sec. of State, Oct. 31, 1899, MS. Misc. Let. Dec. 1899, Part 3; Mr. Hamilton, county clerk, to Mr. Moore, Nov. 7, 1902, MS.)

That no suit can be maintained against the United States or their property in a State court, see Stanley v. Schwalby, 162 U. S. 255, 16 S. Ct. 754.

"So far as jurisdiction is concerned, there is no difference between suits against a sovereign directly and suits against its property." (Hassard v. United States of Mexico, 29 Misc. 511, 512, citing Stanley v. Schwalby, 147 U. S. 508; United States v. Lee, 106 U. S. 196; Schooner Exchange v. McFaddon, 7 Cranch, 116; Manning v. State of Nicaragua, 14 How. Pr. 517; Beers v. State of Arkansas, 20 How. 527.)

"This principle [of the exemption of the sovereign] extends so far that a sovereign state, by coming into court as a suitor, does not thereby abandon its sovereignty and subject itself to an affirmative judgment upon a counter claim. People *v.* Dennison, 84 N. Y. 272; United States *v.* Eckford, 6 Wall. 490." (Hassard *v.* United States of Mexico, 29 Misc. 511, 512.)

See Valarino *v.* Thompson, 7 N. Y. 576, holding, as cited in Hassard *v.* United States of Mexico, 29 Misc. 511, that the exemption, since it is the sovereign's, cannot be waived by his representative, without the former's assent.

It was suggested that money deposited by a coal dealer in New York, with the Italian consul-general there, as security for the fulfillment of a contract to supply the Italian squadron with coal, was not liable to attachment in the consul-general's hands, at the suit of any private creditor of the depositor, "so long as the contract remains unfulfilled, or at least so long as Italy chooses to assert any rights in respect to it." Reference was also made to the provision in the treaty with Italy, touching the inviolability of consulates. (Mr. Gresham, Sec. of State, to Mr. Nicoll, June 19, 1893, 192 MS. Dom. Let. 385.)

II. *EXTRATERRITORIAL JURISDICTION.*

1. GENERAL PRINCIPLES.

§ 259.

Owing to diversities in law, custom, and social habits, the citizens and subjects of nations possessing European civilization enjoy in countries of non-European civilization, chiefly in the East, an extensive exemption from the operation of the local law. This exemption is termed "extraterritoriality." It is generally secured by treaties and in some instances is altogether based upon them, and its exercise is usually regulated by the legislation of the countries to whose citizens or subjects the privilege belongs. Under this system jurisdiction is exercised by foreign officials, most frequently the diplomatic and consular officers, over persons of their own nationality.

See United States Consular Regulations (1896), §§ 612–653; Instructions to Diplomatic Officers of the United States (1897), 82–93, §§ 200–240.

"By treaties with those countries, consuls have judicial power in civil or criminal cases, or both, in Borneo, China, Japan, Korea, Madagascar, Muscat, Morocco, Persia, Samoan Islands, Siam, Tripoli, Tunis, and Turkey." (Cons. Reg. § 93.)

Since the foregoing section of the Consular Regulations was written, extraterritorial jurisdiction has been abolished by treaty in Japan. It has ceased in Madagascar, by reason of the annexation of the island by France. The Samoan Islands have been divided between the United States and Germany. See, as to Tunis, For. Rel. 1883, 483; as to Egypt, Richardson, Messages, VII. 238, 277, 390, 403; VIII. 172.

Oct. 30, 1896, Mr. Olney asked that an estimate be submitted to Congress of $3,000 for the salary of a consul-general at Apia, Samoa, and

Nukualofa, Tonga, it being desired to extend the jurisdiction of this officer over the Tonga Islands, in order that he might, at stated intervals, hold court there, in the exercise of the jurisdiction given by the treaty between the United States and Tonga, proclaimed Sept. 18, 1888. This jurisdiction, said Mr. Olney, had never been exercised, and the failure to exercise it had caused great inconvenience to American citizens and much annoyance to the Tongan authorities. (Mr. Olney, Sec. of State, to Sec. of Treasury, Oct. 30, 1896, 213 MS. Dom. Let. 501.)

As to consular jurisdiction in Corea, see Mr. Adee, Acting Sec. of State, to Mr. Heard, min. to Corea, Oct. 27, 1890, MS. Inst. Corea, I. 353.

For a treaty between the East India Company and the Sultan of Sulu, Jan. 28, 1761, see 73 Br. & For. State Papers, 1056.

For a collection of treaty provisions of the United States in regard to extraterritorial jurisdiction, see Moore on Extradition, I. 100, note 5.

See Fiore, Droit Int. Public, I. 326–7, 408, 418.

"The treaty also confides unusual powers to the consuls, they being made the exclusive judges of disputes among American citizens. This power is to be considered rather of a mediatory than of an authoritative character. It is only to be exercised in cases which will not admit of being delayed until the return of the parties to the United States, or in cases in which upon such return the courts of the United States could not exercise jurisdiction; and even in such cases it is to be exercised to no greater extent than the occasion may absolutely require. In all cases where you may be called upon under the treaty to decide disputes, you will, with the consent of the parties, endeavor to obtain the aid of some of your countrymen, if any suitable persons of that description are within your consulate. In your proceedings on such occasions, you will take as your guide the manner of proceedings in like cases in the United States, as far as circumstances permit. You will also observe those principles upon which our judicial institutions are founded; and will follow the laws of the United States and the decisions of our courts as far as they may be known to you. You will make a proper record of your proceedings and will report them to this Department."

Mr. Forsyth, Sec. of State, to Mr. Waters, consul for Zanzibar, Muscat, April 7, 1836, 8 MS. Desp. to Consuls, 94, referring to Art. IX. of the treaty with Muscat, Sept. 21, 1833, which read as follows:

"The President of the United States may appoint consuls to reside in the ports of the Sultan where the principal commerce shall be carried on, which consuls shall be the exclusive judges of all disputes or suits wherein American citizens shall be engaged with each other. They shall have power to receive the property of any American citizen dying within the kingdom, and to send the same to his heirs, first paying all his debts due to the subjects of the Sultan. The said consuls shall not be arrested, nor shall their property be seized, nor shall any of their household be arrested, but their persons and prop-

erty and their houses shall be inviolate. Should any consul, however, commit any offence against the laws of the kingdom, complaint
shall be made to the President, who will immediately displace him."

It is to be observed that the foregoing instruction antedates by
twelve years the statute of 1848, by which the judicial character of
the consular jurisdiction was expressed and defined.

The judicial functions of ministers and consuls of the United
States, so far as they exercise such functions, are primarily regulated
by treaties and statutes. The provisions of those treaties and
statutes comprehend the territorial jurisdiction of the countries to
which they apply, including their ports and navigable waters as
well as their lands. The system thus established for the exercise
of jurisdiction over American citizens, by methods different from
those that are prescribed in the United States, is constitutional.

In re Ross (1891), 140 U. S. 453.

" Her Majesty's Government have had under their consideration
a question which has arisen with reference to the Government established de facto in the Fijian Islands, namely, whether beyond the
limits of the new state, British subjects, so long as the new state is
not recognized, can be accepted as citizens of it, and exempted from
British jurisdiction in respect of acts done by them or engagements
entered into with them. A reference has been made to the law officers
of the Crown, who have advised Her Majesty's Government that
British subjects beyond the limits of the new state, not yet duly recognized, should not be accepted as citizens of the new state, nor be
held exempted from British jurisdiction for acts done by them on
British territory or on board ships ' which ought to be navigated
under the British flag.' And further that they should not be held
exempt from British jurisdiction for engagements entered into with
them in cases where the validity or construction of such engagements
would properly and in ordinary course be triable before a British
tribunal. They are further of opinion that Her Majesty's Government may interfere with the acts and engagements of British subjects within Fiji, and may declare certain acts and engagements to
be legal or illegal in the case of British subjects within Fiji."

Earl of Kimberly, colonial secretary, to the governors of Australian colonies, Aug. 14, 1872, Parl. Pap. C. 983, April, 1874, 22–23.
See sec. 30, act of June 22, 1860, investing with judicial functions consuls
and commercial agents of the United States at islands or in countries
not inhabited by any civilized people, or recognized by any treaty
with the United States. (12 Stat. 72, 78.)

The consular courts of the United States at Honolulu have the exclusive right of determining disputes occurring among the crew of a

vessel of the United States, under the " favored-nation " clause of the treaty, such a concession having been made to France.

Speed, At. Gen., 1866, 11 Op. 508.

In a note to the Siamese Government of October 31, 1899, Mr. King, United States minister at Bangkok, demanded the return of the revolver and sword of a citizen of the United States which were seized and taken from him by a native constable. In the course of his note Mr. King maintained that the provision in the British treaty that " British subjects, their persons, homes, premises, lands, ships, or property of any kind shall not be seized, injured, or in any way interfered with by the Siamese," applied equally to United States citizens under the most-favored-nation clause, and that the entire jurisdiction over the interests of the United States in Siam belonged excusively to the consulate-general of the United States. As the demand was not at first complied with it was renewed, with the result that the Siamese Government caused the arms to be returned and afterwards wrote a letter of explanation.

Of the action of the minister, the Department of State expressed its general approval.

> For. Rel. 1899, 676–678. See, also, as to jurisdiction in Siam, Mr. Adee, Act. Sec. of State, to Mr. Heard, min. to Corea, Oct. 27, 1890, MS. Inst. Corea, I. 353.
> As to the right of a British subject in Siam to elect a Siamese, as distinguished from a British consular jurisdiction, see London Saturday Review, March 26, 1887, 443.

In dealing with the subject of extraterritorial jurisdiction, the fact should be borne in mind that while the system rests, in the Ottoman dominions, upon ancient custom as well as upon the provisions of treaties or so-called capitulations, it was established in China and in Japan by the treaties with the western powers, the first being that concluded between Great Britain and China, at the end of the opium war, in 1842. The importance of this distinction is obvious. It serves to explain the existence in the Ottoman dominions of practices which were not based upon the stipulations of treaties and which formed no part of the extraterritorial system as it was established in China and Japan. Of these practices the principal one is that of the protection granted by the consuls of treaty powers to the citizens of other treaty powers or to the citizens of nontreaty powers, or even to natives, not by the mere exercise of good offices, but by the assimilation of the person protected to the nationality of the protector.

The question whether foreigners who were not citizens or subjects of treaty powers were entitled to extraterritoriality in Japan, was decided in the case of the Peruvian bark *Maria Luz*, which put into

Kanagawa under stress of weather in 1872 with a cargo of coolies from China to Peru. The Japanese authorities claimed and exercised the power to inquire into the situation and condition of the coolies on board the bark, and released some of them. Against this action the master protested, and the Peruvian Government, though not a treaty power, supported his claims, which were at length referred to the arbitration of the Emperor of Russia. May 17—29, 1875, the Emperor rendered an award, holding that the Japanese Government had acted in good faith and within its rights, and declaring that foreign governments could not, in the absence of formal treaty stipulations, object to the enforcement by Japan of measures which were in conformity with their own legislation.

> Moore, Int. Arbitrations, V. 5034; For. Rel. 1873, I. 524–553.

The consul of the United States at Canton, having exercised jurisdiction over a citizen of New Granada (Colombia) in a criminal matter, the Department of State said that the consul "had no authority whatever to entertain jurisdiction of the case," even with the concurrent consent of the accused and of the Chinese officials; that a consular court, being "a tribunal of limited and inferior jurisdiction," possessed only such powers as were expressly conferred by acts of Congress in conformity with the provisions of existing treaties; that the waiver of their authority by the Chinese officials invested the consul with no additional powers, since he was not an officer of that Government and could not derive from it any authority which would validate an official act not warranted by the laws of the United States or his instructions.

> Mr. Fish, Sec. of State, to Mr. Low, min. to China, Jan. 8, 1873, For. Rel. 1873, I. 139.
> See, also, Mr. Hale, Asst. Sec. of State, to Mr. Jewell, consul at Canton, Jan. 8, 1873, 69 MS. Desp. to Consuls, 81.
> See, as to the jurisdiction of consular courts, Lawrence's Wheaton (1863), notes 73, 74, Lawrence, com. sur droit int., IV. chap. ii; Wharton, Crim. Law (8th ed.), § 273; In re Stupp, 11 Blatch. 124; The William Harris, Ware, 367; Schuyler, Am. Dip. 64 et seq.

During the Chinese-Japanese war the diplomatic and consular representatives of the United States used their good offices for the protection of Japanese in China and of Chinese in Japan. In August, 1894, while the war was in progress, two Japanese subjects were, at the instance of the Chinese authorities, arrested by the French police in the French concession at Shanghai. The French consul-general sent the prisoners, who were charged with being spies, to Mr. Jernigan, the United States consul-general. Mr. Jernigan stated that the rule prevailing at Shanghai was, when a foreigner had no consular representative, that he was tried before the mixed court. He therefore disclaimed any right to try the prisoners, and asked for instructions as to what he should do with them, meanwhile granting them asylum. Instructions were given by Mr. Gresham, Secretary of State, to the effect that lending good offices did not invest Japanese in China with extraterritoriality, and that the legation and consulates should not be made an asylum for Japanese who violated the local laws or committed belligerent acts; that protection was to be exercised unofficially and consistently with neutrality; that the consul-general should not have received the two Japanese and was not authorized to hold them, and that the suggestion which had been made that the United States consuls should act as arbitrators in the matter was not entertained. Reference was also made by Mr. Gresham to the fact that by the Japanese imperial ordinance of August 4, 1894, declaring that a state of war existed between China and Japan, it was declared that Chinese subjects in Japan were wholly subject to the jurisdiction of the Japanese courts, thus abrogating the provisions of Article XIII. of the treaty between China and Japan of September 13, 1871, by which it was provided, in case an offense was committed in the jurisdiction of one of the contracting parties by a subject of the other, that " when arrested and brought up for trial, the offender, if at a port, shall be tried by the local authority and the consul together. In the interior, he shall be tried and dealt with by the local authority, who will officially communicate the facts of the case to the consul." The abrogation of this article had, said Mr. Gresham, necessarily the same effect in China as in Japan, and the United States could not invest Japanese subjects in China or Chinese subjects in Japan with an extraterritoriality which they did not possess as subjects of their own sovereign. In a subsequent instruction Mr. Gresham stated that the decision in the case of the two suspected Japanese was entirely in conformity with the Japanese interpretation of the authority and power of neutral consuls. He stated in conclusion that he would be glad to see an arrangement made between China and other interested powers which should define the jurisdictional rights of the foreign settlement at Shanghai with respect to crimes charged to have been committed therein in time of war, as well as in time of peace. Continuing, he said : " Whether China would be willing to yield her jurisdiction in respect to subjects of a belligerent charged with offenses against the laws of war, may be doubtful. It is not supposed that any of the French subjects to whom the dispatch of our legation refers as having been brought before the Russian consul at Shanghai for hearing, during the Tonquin war, were charged with offenses of that character. However this may be, the consuls of the United States in China, as has been pointed out in prior instructions of the Department, have never been invested with power to exercise jurisdiction over the citizens or subjects of another nation.

" The Department had repeatedly so held, even in respect to citizens of Switzerland, who have for many years been under the protection of our ministers and consuls. It may also be noticed that Hall, in his recent work on Extraterritoriality in the East, adverts to the fact that, while what is known as the doctrine of assimilation has prevailed in Turkey and certain other countries, the British orders in council touching consular jurisdiction in China do not purport to authorize the exercise of such jurisdiction by British consuls except in the case of British subjects."

> Mr. Gresham, Sec. of State, to Mr. Denby, jr., chargé, tel., Aug. 29, 1894; same to same, Sept. 18 and Oct. 30, 1894; and Mr. Gresham, Sec. of State, to Mr. Yang Yü, Chinese legation, Nov. 30, 1894, For. Rel. 1894, 106, 117, 119, 121, 124.
>
> July 25, 1872, the Department of State, in an instruction to the United States minister in China, referring to the protection of Swiss citizens where the Swiss Republic had no diplomatic or consular officers, said: " The protection referred to must necessarily be confined to the personal and unofficial good offices of such functionaries. Although when exercised to this extent merely, this can properly be done only with the consent of the Chinese Government, that consent must not be allowed to imply an obligation on the part of a diplomatic or consular officer of the United States in that country to assume criminal or civil jurisdiction over Swiss citizens, or to make himself or his Government accountable for their acts." (Quoted in Mr. Gresham, Sec. of State, to Mr. Denby, jr., chargé, Aug. 29, 1894, For. Rel. 1894, 106.)

The chief of police of Chinkiang having arrested and punished two Chinese employees of Mr. Emery, an American merchant at that place, " without even notifying the [American] consul or requesting him to have them turned over to the Chinese officials, a proceeding flagrantly violating the practice in such cases which has grown up under the treaties in all the treaty ports," [a] the demand of the consul that the chief of police, who had fled to Soochow, should be required to return to Chinkiang and apologize to the merchant (in whose office one of the employees was arrested), and should be punished and degraded, was approved; and the minister of the United States at Pekin was instructed, in case the matter was not disposed of satisfactorily by the local authorities, to bring it to the attention of the Tsungli Yamen.

> Mr. Hay, Sec. of State, to Mr. Conger, min. to China, Jan. 8, Feb. 10, and Feb. 26, 1900, For. Rel. 1900, 396, 399, 401.
>
> The local authorities had expressed their readiness to degrade the offending official at Soochow, but desired to avoid bringing him to Chinkiang.

---

[a] Mr. Conger, min. to China, to Mr. Hay, Sec. of State, Dec. 20, 1899, For. Rel. 1900, 394.

A native of Comoro, domiciled in Zanzibar, died there in the service of a citizen of the United States, who complained that the vice-consul of the United States at Zanzibar refused to take jurisdiction of the decedent's estate. The Department of State said that if decedent had been a citizen of the United States, domiciled at Zanzibar, it would be " disposed to maintain on the general principles of the law of nations, that the consul had jurisdiction;" but that the fact that decedent was in the employ of an American citizen " did not confer on him such an American *status* as will subject his estate to extraterritorial jurisdiction." It would, however, be the duty of the vice-consul to protect, so far as he could, any interest the citizen in question might have in decedent's estate as a creditor, if that interest should be in jeopardy by reason of the imperfection of the local processes of administration.

> Mr. Rives, Assist. Sec. of State, to Mr. Ropes, April 28, 1888, 168 MS. Dom. Let. 239.
>
> For a discussion, without definite conclusion, of the question of asserting the inviolability of legation's servants, natives of the country, in Corea, the Department of State saying that there was no case before it " which would make it proper to say that it would claim for our envoys in extraterritorial countries a right to judge such natives as the minister may take into his personal service," see Mr. Adee, Act. Sec. of State, to Mr. Dinsmore, min. to Korea, Sept. 16, 1889, MS. Inst. Korea, I. 293.
>
> For a condemnation of the practice of indiscriminate protection which had obtained in Madagascar, see Mr. Uhl, Assist. Sec. of State, to Mr. Wetter, consul at Tamatave, Nov. 19, 1894, 147 MS. Inst. Consuls, 6.

2. NATIONALITY AS A LIMITATION.

§ 260.

Defendants. Under the system of extraterritoriality the exemption of the alien from the operation of the local law is not complete, since he is as a rule dependent upon that law for the redress of injuries, civil or criminal, received at the hands of natives of the country. For such injuries the native must, as a rule, be proceeded against in the courts of his sovereign. The jurisdiction of the ministers and consuls usually is limited to proceedings against persons of their own nationality. In this sense nationality operates as a limitation upon the jurisdiction; and in the same way the nationality of the plaintiff, or even of a witness, may, in certain contingencies, raise an obstacle to the effective exercise of jurisdiction.

On consideration of their contract with the Egyptian government, the opinion was expressed that Col. Cornelius Hunt and certain other citizens of the United States, who had entered the military or naval service of the Khedive, might be parties as plaintiffs or defendants in the United States consular court at Alexandria, but that, if the aid of the Egyptian government should be necessary to carry into effect the decision in such a case, no application for such aid should be made, as it would be at variance with the contracts.

> Mr. Fish, Sec. of State, to Mr. Babbitt, vice-consul-general, Alexandria, Aug. 12, 1873, MS. Inst. Barbary Powers, XV. 155.

February 19, 1868, a collision took place between the British steamer *Osaca* and the Pacific Mail (American) steamer *Herman*, some miles from the Japanese coast.

Plaintiff.

The Pacific Mail Steamship Company was sued before the United States consular court at Kanagawa for damages, and the consul, with three assessors, decided that the ships should bear in equal parts the aggregate loss suffered by both. The Pacific Mail Steamship Company applied to the Department of State to declare the judgment void, on the ground, among others, that the treaty with Japan in terms covered only controversies between citizens of the United States and Japanese. Mr. E. Peshine Smith, examiner of claims of the Department of State, advised that, while this was " in terms " true, yet the treaty " literally construed " was not the only source of jurisdiction. " The custom," he said, " of the western powers, sanctioned by the tacit assent of the non-Christian nations in which they have planted consuls, may be properly regarded as defining and confirming their jurisdiction exercised in cases where there is no express grant by treaty. What in the Levant is called *the custom of the Franks*, established a consular jurisdiction, which treaties rather recognized than conferred. . . . When China and Japan became open to the subjects of the western powers, the latter imported with them the views and practices in respect to exterritoriality which had been matured through ages in the Levant. These were recognized in part by express convention, in part by tacit acquiescence. It was a necessary consequence of the exterritoriality which each western power asserted in behalf of its own subjects, that it excluded the jurisdiction of Japan to administer justice to the subject of one Christian power against the subject of another. . . . If by reason of that citizen and his property being located in Japan we cannot afford that remedy by our domestic tribunals, and will not allow it to be given by those of Japan, it becomes our duty to afford it by the only other means, our consular courts in Japan. It is upon this notion of common obligation that the western powers have practiced, and the Government of Japan has seen and acquiesced in that practice. I think this is enough to support the jurisdiction of our consul against the objection taken by the appellants."

Mr. Smith, however, considered more formidable the objection that the collision occurred on the high seas " beyond the jurisdiction of the

Empire of Japan." The precise situation was uncertain; and he expressed the opinion that, if the place where the collision occurred was
not within the dominions of Japan, an admiralty suit *in rem* could
not be maintained in the consular court. He also expressed the view
that the presence at Kanagawa of an agent of the steamship company
did not make the corporation, which had its legal seat in New York,
an inhabitant or sojourner in the consular district so as to give jurisdiction of an action *in personam*.

Mr. Seward, in transmitting Mr. Smith's report to the President,
stated that none of the treaties of Japan with France, Prussia, Portugal, and other western nations, in terms professed to confer jurisdiction on consuls in suits between their countrymen and foreigners
others than Japanese; but that their effect was to render it impossible for any Christian to obtain justice against another Christian in
Japan, except by the award of the consul of the defendant, so that
" to prevent a failure of justice it was necessary that each of the
treaty powers should allow its consuls to hear and determine suits
brought against its subjects by the subjects of other friendly nations."
Great Britain did this in express terms, by the order in council of
March 3, 1859; and Japan had acquiesced in the exercise of the
jurisdiction.

> Message of President Johnson, Jan. 8, 1869, transmitting to the Senate a
> report of Mr. Seward, Sec. of State, of Jan. 2, 1869, S. Ex. Doc. 20,
> 40 Cong. 3 sess.
>
> With regard to Mr. Smith's statement that " when China and Japan
> became open to the subjects of the western powers, the latter
> imported with them the views and practices in respect to exterri-
> toriality which had been matured through ages in the Levant," it
> may be pointed out, as an historical fact, that the practice of extra-
> territoriality in China and Japan began with and rested upon the
> treaties, and did not originate in custom, as it did in the Ottoman
> dominions. This distinction has important consequences, and should
> not be lost sight of. The exercise of jurisdiction by the foreign
> consul in Japan over one of his nationals, where the plaintiff also
> was an alien but of different nationality, seems to have been a logical
> deduction from the exemption from local jurisdiction expressly
> secured by the treaties. If the American, or other foreigner, was
> expressly exempted from the local jurisdiction where the com-
> plainant was a Japanese, he would seem *a fortiori* to have been ex-
> empt, as Mr. Seward intimated, where the complainant was an
> alien.
>
> " Although neither the treaty [of 1881 with Madagascar] nor the statutes
> expressly confer jurisdiction upon the consular court in case of a
> civil proceeding by a British or other foreign subject against an
> American citizen, yet it is held that, on general principles of inter-
> national comity, our consular courts should entertain such suits.
> You will find the principle upon which they are permitted to
> exercise jurisdiction in these cases very fully discussed by Attorney-
> General Cushing in the 7th volume of Attorney-General's Reports,

in giving an opinion on the subject of United States judicial authority in China."   (Mr. Strobel, Third Asst. Sec. of State, to Messrs. Butler, Stillman & Hubbard, Jan. 16, 1894, 195 MS. Dom. Let. 166.)

By the treaty between the United States and Corea, of May 22, 1882,
Art. IV., jurisdiction is in terms conferred on United States consuls
only where the dispute is between an American and a Corean and
the former is the defendant; but it has been held that, on general
principles, as well as upon the principle that the greater includes
the less, consular jurisdiction extends under the treaty to controversies between citizens of the United States. (Mr. Adee, Acting
Sec. of State, to Mr. Heard, min. to Corea, Oct. 27, 1890, MS. Inst.
Corea, I. 353. In this case Mr. Heard had refused the application
of one citizen of the United States for a warrant for the search of
the premises of another American citizen for private papers which
the former believed that the latter had taken. Mr. Heard's action
was approved, on the ground that the application, by reason of its
incompleteness, did not afford a sufficient ground for the issuance of
the warrant.)

By a British order in council of October 25, 1881, it was provided
that a foreign resident in Japan not of British nationality must, in
order to maintain a civil action in the British consular courts in that
country, first file in the court a written consent of the competent
authority of his own nation to the jurisdiction of the court, and must,
if the court so required, give satisfactory security for the payment of
costs and the performance of the court's decision. The Department of
State held that the requirement of the order was "fair and just."
Objection was, however, subsequently made to the order upon the
ground (1) that the British court might award damages against the
American plaintiff in a claim unconnected with the plaintiff's cause
of action, and (2) that the court might, in case the plaintiff failed to
perform the decision, commit him to a British consular prison. The
Department of State replied that the first objection was met by provision (c) in section 47 of the order, and that, as to the second objection, it gave a forced construction to the order. After observing that,
except for contempt and to enforce specific orders and decrees in
chancery, imprisonment could not properly be an element of procedure in civil actions in English any more than in American courts,
the Department added: "You are quite right, I think, in saying that
British subjects resident in Japan can not, except by comity, sue in an
American consular court; the same, of course, must be admitted as to
an American's status toward a British consular court. Now, on this,
as well as other grounds, and in the light of the broad view which
sound policy dictates should be taken of this extraterritorial judicial
system, . . . it appears to me most desirable that, in its administration, harmony and comity should be cultivated between the different
foreign nationalities, and that niceties and technical views should be

as far as possible ignored, thereby facilitating that justice to foreign residents in those countries which the system was intended to secure."

> Mr. John Davis, Act. Sec. of State, to Mr. Bingham, min. to Japan, Aug. 11, 1882, For. Rel. 1882, 375, 376, citing instruction of Mr. Bancroft Davis, Assist. Sec. of State, to Consul-General Van Buren, May 9, 1882, and the letter of Mr. Frelinghuysen, Sec. of State, to Mr. Windom, chairman Com. on For. Rel., April 29, 1882, S. Mis. Doc. 89, 47 Cong. 1 sess.
>
> With reference to the instruction of Mr. Bancroft Davis, of May 9, 1882, the instruction to Mr. Bingham makes the following statement: "Although the instruction referred to was brief, it was, nevertheless, the result of careful consideration as Mr. Davis was at that moment engaged in examination of the general question of extraterritoriality, and had the whole subject before him."
>
> Provision (c), sec. 47, of the order in council, above referred to, provided: "A counterclaim or cross suit can not be brought or instituted in the court against a plaintiff, being a foreigner, who has submitted to the jurisdiction, by a defendant, except by leave of the court first obtained." (72 Br. & For. State Papers, 1118.)

A suit was brought in the United States consular court at Kanagawa, Japan, by a firm of Dutch merchants against a firm composed of citizens of the United States. The defendants pleaded a set-off, with the result that the consul rendered judgment in favor of the defendants and against the plaintiffs, the Dutch merchants, to the amount of nearly $2,000. It was advised that under the treaty between the United States and Japan of 1858, and the act of Congress of June 22, 1860, 12 Stat. 72, Rev. Stat. sec. 4083, an American consular court in Japan could not render a judgment against a person not a citizen of the United States, and therefore could not entertain the plea of set-off beyond the amount of the claim asserted by the Dutch plaintiffs.

> Speed, At. Gen., April 21, 1866, 11 Op. 474.

The United States consul at Kanagawa having fined for contempt a British subject who, as a witness, refused to answer

Witness.

certain questions, the British consul, to whom application was made for the enforcement of the penalty, refused to require either the payment of the fine or to impose the alternative of imprisonment for nonpayment. It was intimated that if the power to punish the refractory witness did not belong either to the American or to the British consul, it would remain with the authorities of Japan.

> Mr. F. W. Seward, Assist. Sec. of State, to Mr. Fisher, consul at Kanagawa, April 16, 1866, 43 MS. Desp. to Consuls, 169.

3. JURISDICTION OVER SEAMEN.

§ 261.

" I have the honor to acknowledge the receipt of the two notes you did me the honor to address to me under date of the 24th September, and the 6th October, in reference to the expediency of some agreement or understanding to the effect that jurisdiction over persons serving on board of national vessels of war, for offences committed in Japan, should be assumed by the nation in whose service they are engaged, in so far as may be possible.

" I note the substance of your reply, and that Lord Derby has informed Her Majesty's representatives in China, Japan, and Siam that the British authorities in those countries should abstain from interference with British subjects serving on foreign vessels of war; and, while expressing my thanks for this instruction to Her Majesty's representatives, which I am inclined to believe will be of advantage to both countries, I have the honor to inform you that similar instructions will be issued to representatives of the United States in China, Japan and Siam, that the authorities of the United States in those countries should abstain from interference with American citizens in like manner serving on foreign vessels of war."

Mr. Fish, Sec. of State, to Sir Edward Thornton, Brit. min., Oct. 7, 1875, MS. Notes to Great Britain, XVII. 44.

" The attention of this Government on several occasions has been directed to the question of the exercise of jurisdiction over persons committing offences within the territory of China and Japan, who are at the time regularly enrolled and serving on board national vessels of war, or on merchant vessels.

" It is believed that there are no particular provisions in reference to this question in the several treaties between the foreign powers and these countries, and an interchange of views thereon has lately taken place between this Government and that of Great Britain.

" The conclusions at which this Government has arrived are as follows:

" So far as concerns merchant vessels, while in some respects it would be desirable that jurisdiction over such offences committed by seamen serving on American vessels should be exercised by the consuls of the United States, it is not deemed advisable to issue any instructions in relation thereto.

" When, however, such an offender, being a member of the crew of an American vessel, is a subject or citizen of a country having no treaty engagement on this question with China or Japan, or where the consul of the nation to which such person may belong, shall decline to assume jurisdiction over him for the offence charged against him, it is the opinion of this Department that the consular officers of the United States may properly assume jurisdiction in the case.

" In reference to offences committed on shore in China and Japan, by persons enlisted or serving on board national vessels of war, jurisdiction in such cases, in the opinion of this Government, should be remitted to the consuls of the country under whose flag the offender is serving, on the ground, that all persons who have taken service under a power, are, for the time being, under the jurisdiction of that power exclusively and amenable to its tribunals.

" Information has reached this Department that the Government of Great Britain, entertaining these views, has lately issued instructions to its authorities in China, Japan and Siam, to abstain from interference with British subjects serving on United States or other foreign men-of-war, upon the principle above adverted to, and you are instructed in like manner to abstain from interference with citizens of the United States serving on board British or other foreign vessels of war who may be charged with the commission of offences on shore.

" It is proper also to add that, in the opinion of this Department, without questioning the authority of consular officers of the United States to entertain jurisdiction where offences have been committed on shore by those serving on national vessels of the United States, it will be beneficial to the public service that the question of punishment for the smaller offenses, such as overstaying leave, disorderly conduct or drunkenness be remitted to the proper naval authorities, in cases where the offenders can be tried and punished equally well on board the vessels to which they belong, or under naval regulations, and where the proper naval authorities may so desire."

> Mr. Cadwalader, Act. Sec. of State, to Mr. Avery, Nov. 2, 1875, MS. Inst. China, II. 346, MS. Circulars, II. 96.

" Under these provisions [Art. IV. of the treaty with Japan of 1857, and Art. VI. of the treaty of 1858] no difference can arise. Under them, clearly, the test of jurisdiction is nationality. An offense committed anywhere in Japan, except on a foreign man-of-war or within the precincts of a foreign legation, which are extraterritorial, if committed by an English subject resident in Japan is justiciable before the British courts; if committed by an American citizen resident in Japan, is justiciable in the consular courts of the United States.

" But there is a class of people who are not residents of Japan in the ordinary acceptance of the term, and who are not protected by the extraterritorial character of the vessel on which they serve. They are the seamen of the mercantile marine, and they are specially recognized by Article IX. of the treaty of 1858, which provides:

" ' When requested by the American consul, the Japanese authorities will cause the arrest of all deserters and fugitives from justice, receive in jail all persons held as prisoners by the consul, and give to the consul such assistance as may be required to enable him to enforce the observance of the laws by theAmericans who are on land, and to maintain order among the shipping.'

"And in view of this provision, the Government of the United States, which authorizes the enrollment in every American merchant ship of a certain number of seamen who are not citizens, has enacted in the act providing for the execution of this treaty, as follows:

" 'Jurisdiction in both criminal and civil matters, shall, in all cases, be exercised and enforced in conformity with the laws of the United States, which are hereby, so far as is necessary to execute such treaties, respectively, and so far as they are suitable to carry the same into effect, extended *over all citizens of the United States* in those countries, *and over all others* to the extent that the terms of the treaties respectively, justify or require.' (Section 4886, Rev. Stat.)

" The position taken by the Government of the United States in this legislation, under the articles of the treaty, is, that a foreign seaman duly enrolled on an American merchant vessel, is subject to the laws and entitled to the protection of the United States to precisely the same extent that a native-born seaman would be, during the period of his service; that although not an American citizen, he is unquestionably an American seaman. . . .

" When a foreigner enters the mercantile marine of any nation and becomes one of the crew of a vessel having undoubtedly a national character, he asumes a temporary allegiance to the flag under which he serves, and in return for the protection afforded him becomes subject to the laws by which that nation, in the exercise of an unquestioned authority, governs its vessels and seamen. If, therefore, the Government of the United States has, by treaty stipulation with Japan, acquired the privilege of administering its own laws upon its own vessels and in relation to its own seamen in Japanese territory, then every American vessel and every seaman of its crew are subject to the jurisdiction which by such treaty has been transferred to the Government of the United States."

Mr. Blaine, Sec. of State, to Sir E. Thornton, June 3, 1881, MS. Notes, Gr. Brit. XVIII. 543. A copy of this note accompanied the instruction of Mr. Blaine, Sec. of State, to Mr. Bingham, min. to Japan, June 3, 1881, MS. Inst. Japan, III. 53.

See report of Mr. Blaine, Sec. of State, to the President, Dec. 19, 1881, S. Ex. Doc. 21, 47 Cong. 1 sess. 4–5.

See, also, Mr. Evarts, Sec. of State, to Sir E. Thornton, Brit. min., March 7, 1881, MS. Notes to Gr. Br. XVIII. 457.

" The indictment, trial, and conviction in the consular court at Yokohama of John Ross, a merchant seaman on board an American vessel, have made it necessary for the Government to institute a careful examination into the nature and methods of this jurisdiction.

" It appeared that Ross was regularly shipped under the flag of the United States, but was by birth a British subject. My predecessor felt it his duty to maintain the position that, during his service as a regularly shipped seaman on board an American merchant vessel, Ross was subject to the laws of that service, and to the jurisdiction of the United States consular authorities."

President Arthur, first annual message, 1881.

" Your letter of the 21st instant has been received. It relates to the case of J. M. Ross, alleged to be a British subject, who, having in 1880 killed a fellow-seaman named Robert Kelly, on the American ship Bullion, in the harbor of Yokohama, was tried by the United States consular court there, convicted, and sentenced to death, which penalty was later commuted by the President to imprisonment for life in the Albany penitentiary, where Ross is now confined.

" You state that Ross ' wishes to have his case reviewed mainly on the ground that the court had not jurisdiction of his person, he being then and now a British subject.'

" The question of jurisdiction in Ross's case has already had full consideration on two pleas—want of jurisdiction of his person and unconstitutionality of the form and manner of trial. The latter plea, being of municipal competence, was before the circuit court of San Francisco on a writ of habeas corpus, sued out by Ross on reaching that port, on his way from Yokohama to Albany, April 4, 1881, and the court dismissed the writ. The constitutionality of the judicial extraterritorial procedure prescribed by statute under the authority of the treaty is established. This branch of the question can be municipally tested by being brought before the United States courts by habeas corpus.

" The plea that Ross, being an alien, was beyond the jurisdiction of the consular court, was raised by the British Government. . . .

" This Government denied the plea on the admitted doctrine that the sovereign of the flag of a ship has jurisdiction of crimes committed by foreigners on such ship on the high seas or in ports where the courts of the United States have jurisdiction, and that Ross, being a duly articled seaman on an American ship, was within the statutory and treaty jurisdiction of the United States court at Yokohama. If this phase of the question is to be revived, it can only be presented by the British Government through the diplomatic channel." (Mr. Porter, Asst. Sec. of State, to Mr. Stimson, June 28, 1886, 160 MS. Dom. Let. 595.)

Ross's detention was decided to be legal in In re Ross (1891), 140 U. S. 453.

The crime was committed on board ship. (Mr. Evarts, Sec. of State, to Sir E. Thornton, Brit. min., March 7, 1881, MS. Notes to Gr. Br. XVIII. 457.)

It is stated in an instruction of Mr. Bayard, Secretary of State, to Mr. Hubbard, minister to Japan, March 21, 1888, that an effort had lately been made by the Department of State to obtain the text of the decision of Judge Sawyer on the writ of *habeas corpus* at San Francisco, and that it was believed that his opinion was not written, but was merely an oral dismissal of the application for the writ in chambers. (MS. Inst. Japan, III. 517.) It seems that the object of the proceedings being to have the questions at issue passed upon by the Supreme Court, counsel for Ross, acting upon the supposition that no appeal would lie from the decision of the circuit court, decided to withdraw the application for the writ, which was dismissed with his concurrence. (Mr. Evarts, Sec. of State, to Mr. Bingham, min. to Japan, Feb. 7, 1881, MS. Inst. Japan, III. 26; Mr. Blaine, Sec. of State, to Mr. Bingham, min. to Japan, April 23, 1881, MS. Inst. Japan, III. 36.)

In 1894 Count Mutsu intimated that, in case of an offence on a foreign vessel in Japanese waters by a seaman of such vessel, the jurisdiction of the consul would not be recognized if the seaman was a Japanese subject or a foreigner subject to Japanese jurisdiction. The question being hypothetical the United States, with the concurrence of the Japanese Government, declined to discuss it. (Mr. Gresham, Sec. of State, to Mr. Dun, min. to Japan, Nov. 29, 1894, and Dec. 8, 1894, MS. Inst. Japan, IV. 226, 228.)

In the case of Ross, supra, the ship *Bullion,* on which the offence was committed, was a registered vessel of the United States.

In May, 1886, Peter C. Fullert, a German subject, was convicted by the United States consul-general at Yokohama, Japan, of aiding and assisting Paymaster Watkins to escape from the U. S. S. *Ossipee,* at that port. At the time of the offense Fullert was serving as a seaman on board the *Arctic,* a foreign-built vessel owned by a citizen of the United States and flying the American flag, but not registered, Fullert having applied for a pardon, the Department of State submitted to the Attornty-General the question whether he was at the time of the commission of the offence subject as an American seaman to the jurisdiction of the United States consul. In its communication to the Attorney-General the Department stated that this question had been submitted to the Solicitor of the Department, and that he was of opinion that, while the vessel was entitled to fly the United States flag and to receive the protection of the United States, she was not, under the statutes establishing the consular courts, "a vessel of the United States in such a sense as to make foreign sailors in that vessel amenable to consular criminal jurisdiction." The Attorney-General advised that the proceedings against Fullert were unauthorized and that he should be released. This opinion was broadly based upon the fact that " Fullert was, at the time the alleged offense was committed, a German subject," the Attorney-General declaring that the phrase " citizens of the United States," in section

4084, Revised Statutes, was to be understood " in its legal and ordinary signification, there being nothing in the context to show a different intention."

> Garland, At. Gen., Nov. 4, 1886, 18 Op. 498.
>
> This opinion, in so far as it signifies that the question of jurisdiction was determined by the fact that Fullert was a German subject, is superseded by the decision of the Supreme Court in the case of Ross, the British subject, who, on the strength of his being a seaman on the American ship Bullion, was convicted by the United States consul-general at Kanagawa, Japan, of a murder on board that vessel in the harbor of Yokohama. (In re Ross, 140 U. S. 453.)
>
> As to jurisdiction over foreign-built but American-owned vessels, and the seamen thereon, see, for rulings on various questions since Fullert's case, infra, § 324.

" The judicial authority of the consuls of the United States over American citizens extends over all persons duly shipped and enrolled upon the articles of any merchant vessel of the United States, whatever be the nationality of such person.   And all offences which would be justiciable by the consular courts of the United States, where the persons so offending are native-born or naturalized citizens of the United States employed in the merchant service thereof, are equally justiciable by the same consular courts in the case of seamen of foreign nationality.   And so likewise as to seamen serving on board public vessels of the United States who have committed offences on shore."

> United States Consular Regulations (1896), § 629, p. 268, citing In re Ross, 140 U. S. 453.
>
> Acting upon § 72, Cons. Reg. 1888, Mr. Denby, United States minister to China, decided that the consul at Amoy should decline to try John Liscom on a charge of homicide, since Liscom, though an American citizen, was second mate of a British schooner, and his victim, a Chinese subject, was a member of the crew. (Mr. Blaine, Sec. of State, to Mr. Denby, min. to China, Oct. 19, 1889, MS. Inst. China, IV. 471.)
>
> See Mr. Bingham, min. to Japan, to Mr. Frelinghuysen, Sec. of State, Feb. 18, 1885, For. Rel. 1885, 556.

In 1889 the captain of the ship *Sea Swallow*, flying the English flag, was killed on board his vessel in Chinese waters by a member of the crew, a native of the Philippine Islands and a Spanish subject. The victim was an American. The culprit was arrested and taken before an English examining magistrate, the Spanish consul being present at the examination, and was bound over to appear before the British court at Shanghai to answer a charge of manslaughter. The court found an indictment and a jury was convened, when the Spanish consul claimed the sole right to hear the case. The trial was postponed till the question could be submitted to Sir John Walsham, British minister at Peking, and Count Llorente, Spanish chargé d'affaires. The case became the subject of an informal consultation between Sir John and Mr. Denby, the American minister at Peking. They agreed that, had the case arisen between England and the United States, it was settled that the consuls of the two countries would be considered as having jurisdiction of persons duly shipped and enrolled on the merchant vessels of their respective nations; but that, in the case of other countries, between which no such agreement existed, an actual legal basis for the claim of British jurisdiction in the pending case might not be found to exist. It seems that the British minister's law officers afterwards advised him that the extra-territorial jurisdiction allowed by China to foreign powers did not extend to the flag but must be determined by the nationality of the defendant, in all cases where the crime was alleged to have been committed while the ship was in Chinese waters. As there was no convention, tacit or otherwise, between Spain and England on the subject, Sir John surrendered the accused to the Spanish consul for trial.

> Mr. Denby, Min. to China, to Mr. Blaine, Sec. of State, No. 997, Nov. 8, 1889, 86 MS. Desp. from China.
>
> Mr. Denby, in concluding his report of the case, said: " I simply report this case without legal comment thereon. Should such a question arise between the United States and any power but Great Britain, I would immediately request specific instructions as to how I should act." (Ibid.)

"A seaman of the Navy who is convicted in a consular court of a felonious offense (as distinguished from cases of overstaying leave, disorderly conduct, drunkenness, and other comparatively minor offenses of which, under the navy regulation of November 2, 1875, the naval and consular authorities have concurrent jurisdiction) ceases from the date of such conviction to be in the naval service of the United States, and should be dealt with thenceforth as a private individual. Therefore, consular officers should promptly notify the commanding officer of the vessel on which the man served, or the commander in charge of the squadron, when any such conviction occurs, and he in turn will communicate to the consular officer the action subsequently taken by him under orders of the Navy Department."

> United States Consular Regulations, 1896, sec. 630, p. 268.
>
> See circular of Mr. Rives, Assist. Sec. of State, to U. S. consular officers, Aug. 25, 1888, For. Rel. 1888, II. 1665. This circular amended that of Mr. Porter, Assist. Sec. of State, to U. S. consular officers in extra-territorial countries, Aug. 19, 1887, in which it was stated that seamen of the Navy, convicted of " offences subjecting them to imprisonment," ceased to be in the naval service. The Navy Department considered that this phrase, by reason of its generality, contravened the regulation of Nov. 2, 1875, providing for the concurrent jurisdiction

of the naval and consular authorities as to minor naval offences. (See Mr. Bayard, Sec. of State, to Sec. of Navy, July 12 and Aug. 25, 1888, 169 MS. Dom. Let. 146, 479, and Sec. of Navy to Sec. of State, Aug. 8, 1887, MS. Misc. Let.)

An ordinance was passed in 1896 by the municipal council at Apia with regard to the arrest and imprisonment of men-of-war's men. The purport of the proposed ordinance was to place the offending sailor in the custody of the commander of his ship, who should punish all minor infractions of the municipal regulations as he should see fit. The consuls, Sept. 19, 1896, decided to refer the subject to the powers, and meanwhile unanimously requested " that in case of an arrest of a man-of-war's man the president of the municipal council will at once notify the captain of the man-of-war concerned, and inform him that if he sends the necessary guard the prisoner will be handed over."

It seems that the difficulty began with the arrest of two German seamen from a man-of-war on a charge of being drunk and disorderly and damaging property. They were subsequently released by direction of the German consul, who " assumed all responsibility." It seems that in two cases in the preceding seven years the municipal police had arrested sailors from British men-of-war, and that the men were tried, fined, or acquitted by the municipal magistrate. Mr. Olney considered the existing ordinance sufficient and opposed the new ordinance, declaring that he could see no good reason why an offending man-of-war's man should not be tried and punished by the duly constituted municipal magistrate for a breach of the peace, unless a treaty should provide otherwise.

> Mr. Olney, Sec. of State, to Sir J. Pauncefote, Brit. amb., Jan. 16, 1897, MS. Notes to Gr. Br. XXIII. 533. See also For. Rel. 1897, 452–453, 456–459.
>
> The British Government, however, was inclined to concur with the German Government in the matter, and Lord Salisbury suggested that the consuls of the three powers should consult with the new chief justice of Samoa on the subject, with a view to " settle the question in such manner as to avoid disputes, while at the same time securing the maintenance of order and the proper punishment of offenders." The United States accepted this suggestion, declaring that it would " cheerfully assent to any conclusion that may be reached after such conference." (Mr. Sherman, Sec. of State, to Sir J. Pauncefote, Brit. amb., April 3, 1897, For. Rel. 1897, 460.)

4. Exercise of Judicial Functions.

(1) legislation of united states.

§ 262.

The first statute of the United States, by which the judicial functions of ministers and consuls of the United States were regulated and defined, was approved August 11, 1848.[a] A new and more comprehensive act was approved June 22, 1860.[b] Mr. Cass, as Secretary of State, May 16, 1860, addresses a letter to J. M. Mason, chairman of the Committee on Foreign Relations of the Senate, enclosing a draft of a bill to amend the act of August 11, 1848, to carry into effect the provisions of the treaties of the United States with China and the Ottoman Porte, giving certain judicial powers to United States ministers and consuls. " The act of Congress of 1848 . . . is," says Mr. Cass, " a most important and valuable one. A careful study of every one of its provisions has impressed me with a renewed sense of the sagacity and wisdom of the distinguished statesman, Judge Butler, who is reputed to have been its framer." The enclosed bill had been submitted to the Solicitor of the Treasury, and advantage had been taken of the views presented in the opinion of the late Attorney-General, Mr. Cushing, concerning the judicial powers of the United States ministers and consuls in China and Turkey.[c] There are amendatory acts of July 28, 1866;[d] July 1, 1870;[e] March 23, 1874;[f] and Feb. 1, 1876.[g] These enactments are consolidated in the Revised Statutes of the United States, §§ 4083–4130.

The statutes apply to China, Japan, Siam, Egypt, Madagascar, Turkey, Persia, Tripoli, Tunis, Morocco, Muscat, and the Samoan Islands,[h] and to any other country with which an appropriate treaty may be made.[i] They also authorize consuls and commercial agents at islands or in countries not inhabited by any civilized people, or recognized by any treaty with the United States, to hear and determine civil cases where the debt or damages do not exceed $1,000, exclusive of costs, and to try and punish offenders where the fine does not exceed $100 or the imprisonment sixty days.[j]

---

[a] 9 Stat. 276.

[b] 12 Stat. 72.

[c] Sen. Ex. Doc. 43, 36 Cong., 1 sess.

[d] 14 Stat. 322.

[e] 16 Stat. 183.

[f] 18 Stat. 23.

[g] 19 Stat. 2.

[h] R. S. §§ 4083–4130; act of June 14, 1878, 20 Stat. 131.

[i] R. S. § 4129; act of June 14, 1878, 20 Stat. 131; Inst. to Dip. Officers (1897), 82–83.

[j] R. S. § 4088.

By the general provisions of the statutes above mentioned the ministers and consuls are invested, so far as the treaties allow, with "judicial authority."[a] This authority extends in criminal matters to the trial and punishment of offenses committed by citizens of the United States; and in civil matters to "all controversies between citizens of the United States, or others," so far as the treaties provide.[b] The word "minister" means "the person invested with, and exercising the principal diplomatic functions;" the word "consul" means "any person invested by the United States with, and exercising, the functions of consul-general, vice-consul-general, consul, or vice-consul."[c] Where there is no "minister" in either of the countries mentioned, the judicial duties imposed on that official "devolve upon the Secretary of State."[d] The jurisdiction of ministers in civil matters and also in criminal matters, except in capital cases for murder, or insurrection, or for offenses amounting to felony, is appellate only, unless the consular officer is interested either as party or as witness.[e]

Jurisdiction, both civil and criminal, is exercised in conformity (1) with the laws of the United States, and, if they be unsuitable or deficient, (2) with "the common law, and the law of equity and admiralty," and if all these do not furnish "appropriate and sufficient remedies," (3) with "decrees and regulations," having "the force of law," which the "ministers" may make to "supply such defects and deficiencies."[f] The ministers in making decrees and regulations are required to take the advice of such consuls in their respective countries as may be consulted without prejudicial delay or inconvenience. The consuls thus consulted are required to signify their assent or dissent in writing. The minister may then cause the decree or regulation to be published, together with the opinions of his advisers; if he does so, the decree or regulation becomes obligatory till it is annulled or modified by Congress; and he is required, as speedily as may be after publication, to transmit the papers to the Secretary of State "to be laid before Congress for revision."[g]

The consul sitting alone may decide all cases where the fine

---

[a] R. S. § 4083.

[b] R. S. § 4084, 4085.

[c] R. S. § 4130. In the revision of 1873–'4 the words "vice-consul-general" were omitted, but they were restored in the second edition, of 1878. (Mr. Fish, Sec. of State, to Mr. Seward, min. to China, Jan. 19, 1876, MS. Inst. China, II. 363.) See, also, Consular Instructions of 1855, § 275, and Cushing, At. Gen., 7 Op. 511.

[d] R. S. § 4128.

[e] R. S. § 4109.

[f] R. S. § 4086; Cushing, At. Gen., 7 Op. 503.

[g] R. S. §§ 4117–4119.

imposed does not exceed $500, or the term of imprisonment 90 days;[a] he is required so to decide where the fine imposed does not exceed $100 or the imprisonment 60 days.[b] But, if legal perplexities are likely to arise, or if the punishments are likely to exceed those above speci-fied, he must summon from one to four, and in capital cases not less than four, citizens of the United States to sit as associates in the trial.[c] If any of the associates differs from the consul the case is remitted to the minister.[d] "Capital cases for murder or insurrection against the government, . . . or for offenses against the public peace amounting to felony," may be tried by the minister;[e] if tried by a consul, there can be no conviction unless the consul and his associates all concur in it and the minister approves.[f] The minister may also issue writs to "prevent the citizens of the United States from enlisting in the military or naval service . . . to make war upon any foreign power with whom the United States are at peace, or in the service of one portion of the people against any other portion of the same people; and he may carry out this power by a resort to such force belonging to the United States, as may at the time be within his reach."[e]

In civil cases the consul sitting alone may render judgment where the damages demanded do not exceed $500. When the damages exceed that amount, or the case involves legal perplexities, he must summon two or three citizens of the United States, "if such are residing at the port," to sit with him as associates in the trial."[g]

In criminal cases an appeal lies to the minister (1) where the consul sits with associates and one of them differs from him, and (2) where the consul sitting alone imposes a fine of more than $100 or imprison-ment of more than 60 days.[h] From the sentences of the minister to China or Japan, whether original or appellate, an appeal lies to the United States circuit court in California.[i]

In civil cases an appeal lies to the minister where one of the asso-ciates differs from the consul.[j] In China and Japan an appeal lies to the minister where the matter in dispute exceeds $500 but not

---

[a] R. S. § 4089.

[b] R. S. § 4105.

[c] R. S. § 4106. Though this section refers only to consuls, it is customary for the minister to summon associates in cases where he has original jurisdiction. (Inst. to Dip. Officers, 89–90, § 221.)

[d] R. S. § 4106.

[e] R. S. § 4090.

[f] R. S. § 4102.

[g] R. S. § 4107.

[h] R. S. §§ 4089, 4091, 4105, 4106.

[i] R. S. § 4095.

[j] R. S. § 4108.

$2,500; where it exceeds $2,500, an appeal lies to the United States circuit court in California.[a] Where the matter in dispute exceeds $2,500, a similar appeal is allowed from any final judgment of the minister to China or Japan, given in the exercise of original jurisdiction.[b]

One Holcomb, a citizen of the United States, was charged with the arbitrary punishment, by cruel and inhuman tortures, without any legal proceedings, of a boy in the island of Guap, a barbarous or semi-civilized country with which the United States had no treaty and where there was no American consular representative. It was advised that the case came within section 4088, Revised Statutes, and that, as there was no regular representative there, the United States might send out a special commercial agent for the purpose of trying the accused.

> Garland, At. Gen., July 6, 1885, 18 Op. 219.

" It seems to be well understood that a consul can not take jurisdiction of general consular business beyond the limits of his district (par. 30, Consular Regulations), and it is apprehended that the same rule applies to the exercise of judicial functions in the present state of the law."

> Mr. Olney, Sec. of State, to Mr. Denby, min. to China, Feb. 2, 1897, For. Rel. 1897, 80, 81.
> To the same effect is Mr. Bayard, Sec. of State, to Mr. Denby, min. to China, Jan. 25, 1888, MS. Inst. China, IV. 341.

" If cases arise in which it may appear that the power to punish for a violation already accomplished is concurrent, residing as well in your consular court as in the tribunals of this country, you must be governed by your judgment of the exigencies of the case, and the probability that justice may be evaded if not administered in the somewhat unsatisfactory manner which is necessarily incidental to such exceptional modes of adjudication as are authorized in China and other partially civilized countries. The rule should be, as we incline to interpret it, rather to decline jurisdiction, except where it is necessary to prevent a failure of justice."

> Mr. F. W. Seward, Assist. Sec. of State, to Mr. Wingate, consul at Swatow, June 6, 1866, 43 MS. Desp. to Consuls, 221.
> This instruction, which was written in reply to Mr. Wingate's No. 36 of Feb. 23, 1866, related to the act of Congress to prohibit the coolie trade. Mr. Wingate was told that he was correct in believing that the carriage of emigrants between his consulate and Singapore was within the terms and meaning of the act. It was added, however,

---

[a] R. S. § 4093,   [b] R. S. § 4094.

> that his judicial authority was derived from the treaty with China
> and the act of June 22, 1860, and that "neither" of them clothed
> him "with any jurisdiction for the trial of crimes committed upon
> the high seas."

The jurisdiction given to the courts of the United States over offenses committed on the high seas does not exclude a consular court
from trying the same offense committed in a port of the country in
which such consular court is established.

　　In re Ross (1891), 140 U. S. 453.

(2) POWER TO MAKE REGULATIONS.

§ 263.

It was advised by Mr. Cushing that the power to make " decrees
and regulations " enabled the minister in certain respects to *legislate*
for citizens of the United States, and served " to provide for many
cases of criminality, which neither Federal statutes nor the common
law would cover."

　　Opinion of Sept. 19, 1855, 7 Op. 495, 504.

" Referring to Mr. Williams' despatch No. 25 of the 22d of August,
1868, enclosing copies of a regulation made and published by him,
with the assent, nearly unanimous, of our consuls in China, for the
purpose of giving effect to the prohibition by the Chinese Government
of the use of the ' Straw Shoe Channel ' to steamers navigating the
Yangtze River, I have to state that: This regulation, as a notification
to citizens of the United States of the consequences of disregarding
an order of the Chinese Government, made in the exercise of the
police of its internal waters, is reasonable and necessary for the
security of navigation and is approved.

" The 4th section of the act of June 22d, 1860, (12 Stat. 73,) to
which you refer, has for its principal object, to enable our chief diplomatic representative to establish such process, pleadings and practice in the consular courts, as may be necessary to give effect to the
treaties and to the laws of the United States, including the common
law, equity and admiralty. The succeeding section appears to be
intended as an enumeration of the subjects to which the power
granted by the 4th section is applicable. It is certainly judicious to
avoid, as I understand Mr. Williams has avoided, the assertion of a
power in the minister to make that unlawful which was not forbidden
by the laws of the United States or of China. Such a power is legislative, while the act cited purports by its title and the general tenor
of its provisions to confer only judicial power."

　　Mr. Seward, Sec. of State, to Mr. Browne, min. to China, Feb. 6, 1869,
　　MS. Inst. China, II. 46.

By dispatches of September 19 and October 19, 1870, Mr. De Long, minister to Japan, transmitted to the Department of State regulations which he had promulgated, with the assent of the consuls, for the United States consular courts in Japan.[a] Mr. Fish, who was then Secretary of State, in acknowledging the receipt of the dispatches, stated that he should submit the regulations to Congress without assuming for himself the power or the duty of disapproving or amending them; but, while he considered that nearly all the regulations were clearly within the power of the minister to make and to carry into effect, till Congress should indicate its pleasure to the contrary, he said that he considered it his duty to call the attention of Congress to certain provisions which he thought transcended the authority delegated to the minister, or that delegated to the Secretary of State, in the case of countries to which no minister was accredited.

In this relation Mr. Fish entered into a full discussion of the minister's power to make decrees and regulations, under sections 5 and 6 of the act of June 22, 1860. He described it as being " confined to the course of procedure in pursuing judicial remedies, and as not extending to the creation of new rights or duties in citizens of the United States, or to the modification of personal rights and obligations under the existing law;" and, with regard to the diversities in the " common law " arising from the complex Federal system in the United States, he expressed the opinion that " it would be most discreet to allow the anomalous jurisdiction of our consular courts . . . to find its limits and definition from the practical exigencies of administration and the acquiescence of the government within whose territory the jurisdiction is exercised."

Continuing, Mr. Fish said: "A report made to Congress by my predecessor, Mr. Seward (a copy of which is inclosed), shows that it has been the habit of this Department to regard the judicial power of our consular officers in Japan as resting upon the assent of the Government of that Kingdom, whether expressed by formal convention or by tacit acquiescence in the notorious practice of the consular courts. In other words, they were esteemed somewhat in the same light as they would have been if they were constituted by the Mikado with American citizens as judges, and with all the authority with which a Japanese tribunal is invested in respect to the native subjects of Japan, to the extent that our Government will admit a jurisdiction understood to be extremely arbitrary. They were, so to speak, the agents of a despotism, only restrained by such safeguards as our own Government may interpose for the protection of citizens who come within its sway.

---

[a] See S. Mis. Doc. 89, 47 Cong. 1 sess. 134–178.

" Between this view and that which would regard our consular courts as possessing only that authority which has been conferred upon them in express terms by Congress there is a wide margin. Congress, informed by Mr. Seward's report before mentioned of the general views which had obtained in this Department, has not indicated its dissent or concurrence, except by silence. It is possible that some future appeal under the fifth and sixth sections of the act of July 1, 1870, may lead to a judicial determination of the extent of consular jurisdiction. The communication of your regulations may have the effect of bringing the whole subject to the consideration of Congress, and produce a clear expression of its views."

The particular provisions or regulations to which Mr. Fish took exception were: (1) A requirement that all citizens of the United States be enrolled, on penalty of a fine and forfeiture of the right to protection. (2) A provision for the attachment of the property of nonresidents. (3) A regulation establishing certain grounds for divorce. (4) A definition of the cases in which vessels should be subject to liens. (5) A rule allowing the testimony of absent persons to be taken and used in criminal cases. (6) A definition of the degrees of murder, a provision for the perpetual banishment of persons guilty of felony, and a reference to the " common law " for the definition of felonies and misdemeanors.

> Mr. Fish, Sec. of State, to Mr. De Long, min. to Japan, Dec. 20, 1870, MS. Inst. Japan, I. 373.
>
> In connection with the reference to the " common law," Mr. Fish inquired: " Where are we to look for the exposition of the common law? To the courts of Massachusetts, or to those of Georgia, or to those of England?"
>
> Mr. Fish enclosed, as containing Mr. Seward's report, Jan. 2, 1869, S. Ex. Doc. 20, 40 Cong. 3 sess.
>
> Views, similar to those above expressed by him, as to the limitation of the power to make regulations, were again set forth by Mr. Fish in an instruction to Mr. De Long, Feb. 26, 1873, For. Rel. 1873, I. 570.
>
> For the regulations proclaimed by Mr. De Long, in 1870, and thereafter criticised by Mr. Fish, as herein set forth, see letter of Mr. Frelinghuysen, Sec. of State, to Mr. Windom, chm. Com. on For. Rel., April 29, 1882, S. Mis. Doc. 89, 47 Cong. 1 sess. 134–178, where they are given as the " regulations in force in the consular courts of the United States in Japan." It therefore appears that the regulations were not disallowed by Congress.
>
> In the same document may be found translations of the French edict of June, 1778, and the laws of May 28, 1836, and July 8, 1852; the British statute of 6 and 7 Vict. c. 94, and the orders in council of Nov. 30, 1864, and Oct. 25, 1881; the regulations in force in the United States consular courts in China; the land municipal regulations in Shanghai; the provisions of United States treaties relating to extraterritoriality; the draft of an act concerning the exercise of foreign jurisdiction, amendatory of R. S. §§ 4082–4130.

" I have to acknowledge the receipt of your dispatch No. 324, of the 3d ultimo, in which you present some interesting and important questions as to the obligatory character of Rule XV. of the (Chinese) Consular Court Regulations of 1864. That rule is as follows:

" ' Civil actions, based on written promise, contract, or instrument, must be commenced within six years after the cause of action accrues; others, within two.'

"As you correctly state, there are no general statutes of limitations adopted by Congress as affecting all civil proceedings in Federal courts. But it must be remembered that, by section 721 of the Revised Statutes, Federal courts sitting in a particular State must adopt the limitations in force in such State, and in this way any gap in Federal legislation in this respect is filled up. But as the Revised Statutes contain no provision as to limitations in civil suits which applies to our consular courts, we have, in such courts, either to fall back in each case on the general principles of private international law or to adopt in advance, as was done by Mr. Burlingame, a general rule of limitation.

" If we revert to the general principles of private international law, the following distinctions are to be observed:

"As to mode of solemnization of contracts, the rule is, *locus regit actum;*

"As to personal capacity, *lex domicilii* controls;

"As to interpretation, *lex loci contractus;*

"As to process, *lex fori;*

"As to mode of performance, *lex loci solutionis*, or the law of the place of performance.

" In Scudder *v.* Bank (91 U. S. 406), while these distinctions were in the main adopted, it was held that statutes of limitation, being matters of process, are governed by the *lex fori.* If we assume, in the present case, that there are no limitations by the *lex fori*, then assuming, also, that limitations of suit are part of the essence of a claim, we would revert, if the question be as to the time of payment, to the *lex loci solutionis*, or the law of the place of performance.

" But however important these distinctions may be in those of our foreign consular courts in which the question comes up *de novo*, they are of but subordinate interest in China, under the view I take of Rule XV. of the Consular Court Regulations of 1864. I do not, it is true, regard this rule as a statute. Not only had Mr. Burlingame no power to enact a statute, as such, but the language of the rule shows that it cannot be regarded as a statutory enactment. It limits suits on even sealed instruments to six years, and on unwritten engagements, no matter how solemn or how strongly evidenced, to two years. It contains no exception in favor of minors or persons under disability. It must be regarded, therefore, not as a statute covering civil

limitations in all their bearings, but as an assertion that suits in consular courts in China are to be limited as to time, the limitation to be
adapted to the social and business conditions of the period of suit.
In this way we can explain not only the limitation of two years for
unwritten engagements, which in the then immature and unsettled
condition of our business in China may have been eminently proper,
but the omission of the exceptions I have noticed above.

"I hold, therefore, that Rule XV. of the Regulations of 1864, while
not to be regarded as having the authority or the fixedness of a statute, is to be viewed as a rule of court expressing a principle open to
modification by the court that issued it. It stands in the same position as do the equity rules adopted by the Supreme Court of the
United States and courts of the several States, not as a statutory man-
date, to remain in force until expressly repealed or modified, but as a
principle and regulation of practice which it is open to the court to
expand or vary as the purposes of justice may require.

"As to the importance of your adopting such a rule there can be no
question. Were there no such limitation required in China, American merchants in China might be harrassed by old debts and stale
demands outlawed in the United States, and their business much
impeded. Aside from this the principle that the right of suit should
be limited as to time, is as essential to public justice as is the principle
that the right of suit should exist at all."

> Mr. Bayard, Sec. of State, to Mr. Denby, min. to China, Apr. 27, 1887,
> MS. Inst. China, IV. 263.

By art. 21 of the treaty with China of 1844, and §§ 4083, 4086,
4087, 4111, and 4117 of the Revised Statutes of the United States,
"the right to try and punish all citizens of the United States for
crimes committed in China is clearly given by treaty to our ministers
and consuls. Our statute passed to carry the treaty provisions into
effect prescribes how the jurisdiction conferred by the treaty shall
be exercised. It is to be exercised in conformity with (1) the laws
of the United States and (2) the common law.

"It being seen that deficiencies might be found to exist in the laws
of the United States and in the common law, it was wisely provided
(3) that if these laws do not furnish appropriate and sufficient remedies, the ministers shall, by decrees and regulations having the force
of law, supply such defects and deficiencies.

"The power of the minister to make such decrees and regulations
is limited to furnishing 'sufficient and appropriate remedies.'"

> Mr. Olney, Sec. of State, to Mr. Denby, min. to China, Feb. 2, 1897,
> For. Rel. 1897, 80, 81–82, MS. Inst. China, V. 415.
> In this instruction Mr. Olney expressed approval, as falling within the
> power of the minister, of a proposed regulation providing that, where
> a criminal action was pending in any consular district in China

against an American citizen who might be found in another such
district, the consul before whom the action was pending might issue
a warrant for the arrest of the accused anywhere in China, such
warrant to be viséed by the consul of the district in which the
accused was found, and the accused then to be arrested and transported for trial to the consular district in which the prosecution was
pending.

See Moore on Extradition, II. 820–824.

The consul-general of the United States at Apia having proposed
to issue a regulation touching mortgages and bills of sale of chattels,
it was held that consular officers were not empowered to promulgate
such regulations. It was observed that by section 4128, R. S., in countries where there is no minister, the judicial duties imposed by law upon
ministers devolve upon the Secretary of State, and that, as the authority to make regulations was held to be a judicial one, it was believed
that the Secretary of State was the proper officer to exercise it where
there is no minister.

> Mr. Rockhill, Assist. Sec. of State, to Mr. Churchill, consul-general at
> Apia, Oct. 9, 1896, 154 MS. Inst. Consuls, 119.
> This instruction referred to a previous one, No. 41, of Aug. 15, 1895, in
> which it was held that the consul-general of the United States at
> Apia had no power to promulgate a regulation concerning the impor-
> tation and sale of firearms and ammunition in Samoa. (149 MS.
> Inst. Consuls, 266.)

(3) CONDUCT OF PROCEEDINGS.

§ 264.

Replying to the inquiry whether an acting consul can perform
judicial functions in China, the Department of State
said:

Official competency.

" There is no such office known to our law as an acting consul and
there is, of course, no authority whatever for the exercise by such person of any consular position as pointed out in your dispatch. Section
4130 of the Revised Statutes expressly limits the exercise of judicial
functions conferred upon consuls by section 4083 to ' persons invested
with, and exercising the functions of consul-general, vice-consul-
general, consul, or vice-consul.'

"As bearing directly upon this matter, I would call your attention
to the opinion of the Attorney-General, rendered under date of May 7,
1891, in response to the following query of this Department:

" Can a person placed in charge of a consular office by the incumbent of the consulate, but without appointment and qualification as
prescribed by the Constitution and laws of the United States, perform
(1) the regular official duties of the post and (2) notarial and other
unofficial services?

" The Attorney-General replied:

" ' I am unable to see how a person can lawfully execute the duties of a public office of the United States who has not been clothed with authority to do so by the appointing power of the United States. Such a person can not possibly have any virtue in him as a public officer.'

"As to the second question the Attorney-General held that the value of such services depends entirely on the fact that the person rendering them is a consular officer, that the United States would seem to be in duty bound to protect the public, so far as it may be reasonably expected to do so, against the exercise of even merely voluntary consular functions by persons not regularly appointed consuls, and that it therefore clearly concerns the United States that no person shall be permitted to exercise the office of consul of the United States in any way who has not been authorized by Congress to do so."

> Mr. Adee, Acting Sec. of State, to Mr. Denby, chargé d'affaires ad int. at Peking, March 22, 1894, For. Rel. 1894, 140, replying to dispatch No. 1802, Jan. 31, 1894, of Mr. Denby, min. to China, For. Rel. 1894, 139. See, to the same effect, Mr. Marcy, Sec. of State, to Mr. C. W. Bradley, jr., Amoy, Nov. 13, 1854, 19 MS. Desp. to Consuls, 422.

> In 1875 the master of an American ship, who had in an affray shot a Chinese coolie, at Kulung, compromised the matter by paying the friends of the Chinaman, with the consent of or without objection from the United States consular agent there, a pecuniary compensation. Mr. Henderson, United States consul at Amoy, when the consular agent reported the matter to him, doubted the propriety of such a compromise in case of crime, and suggested that, if another such case should occur, it should be reported to himself, in order that the offender might be arrested and tried. To this suggestion objection was made, it being claimed that the consular agent was himself a judicial officer, and as such competent to deal with the case. This claim was disapproved by Mr. G. F. Seward, then minister to China, and Mr. Seward's view was upheld by the Department of State, which ruled that the judicial power in question could be exercised only by " an officer de jure as well as de facto," i. e., an officer authorized by the terms of the law to exercise it. (Mr. Fish, Sec. of State, to Mr. Seward, min. to China, Jan. 19, 1876, MS. Inst. China, II. 363.)

> By the act of June 22, 1860, it was provided that the word " consul," in connection with the exercise of extraterritorial jurisdiction, should include the " consul-general, vice-consul-general, consul, or vice-consul." In the Revised Statutes of 1873, § 4130, the words " vice-consul-general " were omitted. The omission was afterwards corrected by the act of Congress of Feb. 1, 1876. (Mr. Fish, Sec. of State, to Mr. Seward, min. to China, Feb. 9, 1876, MS. Inst. China, II. 368.)

> That, as held by Mr. Fish, supra, judicial functions under Title XLVII. R. S. do not belong to consular agents, see Mr. Evarts, Sec. of State, to Mr. Bingham, min. to Japan, Jan. 3, 1881, MS. Inst. Japan, III. 23.

> Mr. James W. Allen, who was left in charge of the United States consulate at Zanzibar by the former consul, when he vacated his post,

"had no judicial functions and no authority to sign any instrument as 'acting judge of the United States consular court.'" (Mr. Uhl, Acting Sec. of State, to Messrs. Warren & Brandeis, April 26, 1894, 196 MS. Dom. Let. 504.)

By § 4109, R. S., where a " consular officer " is " interested, either as party or witness," the minister has original jurisdiction. This does not apply to a charge of crime made against the marshal of the consular court, since a jailer or marshal is not considered a consular officer within the meaning of the statute.

> See opinion of Mr. Denby, min. to China, May 18, 1892, approved by the Department of State, For. Rel. 1892, 113, 123, 124.
>
> See, also, Mr. Bayard, Sec. of State, to Mr. Denby, min. to China, Jan. 25, 1888, MS. Inst. China, IV. 341.

The guarantees afforded by the Constitution of the United States in respect of indictment by a grand jury and an impartial trial by a petit jury apply only to citizens and others within the United States and do not prohibit procedures of a different kind in consular courts.

Mode of trial.

> In re Ross, 140 U. S. 453, 464 (1891), citing Cook v. United States, 138 U. S. 157, 181. "I deem it expedient that a well-devised measure for the reorganization of the extraterritorial courts in oriental countries should replace the present system, which labors under the disadvantage of combining judicial and executive functions in the same office." (President Cleveland, annual message, Dec. 8, 1885.)
>
> It was stated by Mr. Seward in 1864, with reference to the question of jury trials in China, that the act of August 11, 1848, to carry into effect the treaty with that country, was drafted either by Governor Davis, of Massachusetts, or by Judge Butler, of South Carolina. When, in 1860, it was proposed to amend the law, a draft of the new measure was prepared wholly in the Department of State. This draft was submitted by Mr. Cass, who was then Secretary of State, to Mr. Hilyer, Solicitor of the Treasury. As thus submitted it contained a section providing for trial by jury in China and Japan. Mr. Hilyer doubted the expediency of this provision, expressing the opinion that trial by jury in China and Japan would constitute a violation of the treaties with those countries, which required the trial of citizens of the United States charged with crime to be held by the consul or some other public functionary of the United States. The suggestion of Mr. Hilyer was adopted by the Department of State, and the bill as thus amended was passed by the Senate. In the House of Representatives objection was made by Mr. Phelps to the section in regard to marriage, and by Mr. Branch, of North Carolina, to the absence of a provision for jury trials. Both those gentlemen, however, afterwards withdrew their objections and the bill was passed in the precise form in which it was adopted by the Senate. (Mr. Seward, Sec. of State, to Mr. Seward, consul-general at Shanghai, June 11, 1864, 37 MS. Desp. to consuls, 292.)

The salary of a person appointed marshal of the United States consular court at Shanghai begins from the time of his
entering upon such duties as are preliminary to his
departure for the field of his services after taking
the oath of office and giving the bond prescribed by law.

Employment of marshals.

Bates, At. Gen., 1862, 10 Op. 250.

" With respect to marshals or other officers to execute the decrees
of your consular court as well as the other means for performing your
judicial functions, the act of July 14, 1890, only makes specific appropriation for marshals in China, Japan and Turkey. But the
creation by Congress of judicial authority in foreign countries must
include the means of exercising it, or otherwise justice which it is
sought to secure would fail; and so in countries where no marshal
is provided for by law, it is usual for the consuls in case of necessity
to designate some one to act as a special constable or marshal, reporting the expense to the Department, which is allowable out of its
contingent funds. In extraordinary cases, also, the course of consuls has been approved in applying to the local authorities to assist
them. In some treaties this is secured as a right, and in any case
it would probably be granted as a favor."

Mr. Adee, Act. Sec. of State, to Mr. Heard, min. to Corea, Oct. 27, 1890,
MS. Inst. Corea, I. 353.

Subjects of a foreign nation may be appointed as marshals of consular courts, and when so appointed they need not take the oath prescribed by sec. 1756, or sec. 1757, Rev. Stat., but should take an oath
similar to the one so prescribed, except as to allegiance.

Knox, At. Gen., Jan. 3, 1902, 23 Op. 608.

(4) CIVIL JURISDICTION.

§ 265.

" The probate of wills has been recognized as a proper subject for
the cognizance of the consular courts. This view
is deducible from the act of the 22d of June, 1860
(12 Statutes at Large, page 72), the substance of
which, so far as the present question is involved, you will find embraced in sections 4085 and 4088 of the Revised Statutes.

Particular sub-jects.

" The practice is found to be of great service in facilitating the
consul in his efforts to preserve the effects of the deceased, and has
also the advantage of securing an authentic record of the instrument
which is more or less subject to loss in the course of transmission to
the home of the testator in the United States. The proceedings of
the consul however, are not intended to supersede, nor is it supposed

they can in any degree supersede, the requirements of the laws of the
State of which the testator was a resident or where the bulk of his
property may be situated as it is well known that it is under the latter
laws the estate must be settled."

> Mr. Evarts, Sec. of State, to Mr. Woodward, March 15, 1879, 127 MS. Dom.
> Let. 193.

As to consular jurisdiction in divorce cases, see Mr. Comanos, acting
consul-general at Cairo, to Mr. Frelinghuysen, Secretary of State,
September 10, 1884. This dispatch enclosed a copy of an order
issued by Mr. S. Wolf, consul-general, February 27, 1882, entertaining an action of Habil Naggiar for divorce *a vinculo matrimonii*
from his wife.[a]

The American consular courts in Turkey alone have the right to
decide who are the heirs of a deceased American citizen in that
country, including the question of who was his wife.

> Mr. Leishman, min. to Turkey, to Mr. Hay, Sec. of State, No. 593, Oct. 6,
> 1903, enclosing copy of a note of Tewfik Pasha, Turkish minister of
> foreign affairs of Oct. 5, 1903, stating that the council of ministers
> had decided that it belonged to the jurisdiction of the United
> States consulate to determine who was the wife of Leon Manou-
> kian, a deceased American citizen. A question of inheritance was
> involved. (74 MS. Desp. from Turkey.)

" Your despatch No. 510 of November 12, 1887, has been received
and read with great interest. The novel and important question to
which it relates appears to be completely answered by you, and in
your conclusions the Department entirely concurs. It may be accepted, therefore, as the opinion of this Department that the powers
of the consular courts over lunatics, are, in this respect, analogous to
those of courts of chancery. Those powers extend to the custody of
the persons and estates of lunatics. A court of chancery may appoint
a committee of the person and a committee of the estate, and may give
directions touching the estate of lunatics. A court of chancery may
appoint a committee of the person and a committee of the estate, and
may give directions touching the expenditure of the funds belonging
to the lunatic for the support and maintenance of himself and those
dependent upon him.

" With the care of pauper lunatics, courts of chancery of course
can have nothing to do. That is a matter to be governed by such
regulations as each particular community may see fit to make for the
relief of their poor.

" If, therefore, the case should arise of an American citizen in
China becoming insane and having no funds whatever of his own, the

---

[a] MSS. Dept. of State.

question would not have to be dealt with as one affecting the jurisdiction of the consular courts, but as one relating to the care of an American citizen suffering from a severe bodily disease.

" The Department has in its control no regular fund out of which the expenses for the maintenance of lunatics, or their transportation to the United States, could be paid. No appropriation has ever been made, so far as I am advised, for this purpose, and indeed the question seems never to have been suggested. I think, however, in an extreme case the Department would probably be willing to draw on the emergency fund for necessary expenses in such an extreme and obvious case of humanity; but it is unnecessary to anticipate an event which may never occur. Should the necessity of dealing with such a case arise, consuls must be guided by the facts of the particular case in affording such relief as may be in their power."

> Mr. Bayard, Sec. of State, to Mr. Denby, min. to China, Jan. 10, 1888, MS. Inst. China, IV. 339.

Prior to the conclusion of the treaty with Samoa, it was held that section 30 of the act of June 22, 1860, investing with judicial functions consuls and commercial agents of the United States at islands or in countries not inhabited by any civilized people, or recognized by any treaty with the United States, prescribed and limited the judicial powers of the American consul at Apia. In this relation, the Department of State said: " Questions involving the title to land are not within the jurisdiction of the consul. It is thought, however, that in the case of a right of possession as between landlord and tenant, if such a relation exists there, or when two persons are claiming possession adversely to each other of the same land under a contract or agreement, the consul might exercise jurisdiction."

> Mr. Hunter, Second Assist. Sec. of State, to Mr. Foster, consul at Apia, Sept. 3, 1874, 75 MS. Desp. to Consuls, 89.

Under sections 4085 and 4127, Revised Statutes, United States consuls appointed to reside in Morocco and other Barbary States may entertain civil suits against citizens of the United States there resident in respect of causes of action which arose elsewhere.

> Mr. Adee, Act. Sec. of State, to Mr. Mathews, consul at Tangier, July 8, 1890, 134 MS. Inst. Consuls, 65, citing Cushing, Atty. Gen., Sept. 19, 1854, 7 Op. 509; Scidmore's United States Courts in Japan, 19, 37, and the practice of the French consular courts in the Barbary States, as set forth in S. Misc. Doc. 89, 47 Cong. 1 sess. 3–5.
>
> As to the question of the jurisdiction of the Moorish tribunals in cases relating to legal rights in connection with real property, see Mr. Wharton, Assist. Sec. of State, to Mr. Mathews, consul-general at Tangier, Dec. 12, 1891, 138 MS. Inst. Consuls, 171.

A consular court is a court of limited jurisdiction, and all the
jurisdictional facts must be alleged in the libel or
petition; otherwise it will be insufficient. In cases
of appeal from the consular and ministerial courts
of China and Japan to the circuit court of the United States for the
district of California, the record on appeal must show an allowance
of the appeal. A citation is necessary, unless the appeal is allowed
in open court, though it may be questioned whether a citation is not
always necessary, if the consular court has once adjourned after
rendering a decree, there being no terms of such courts.

Appeals to the United States.

> Steamer Spark *v.* Lee Choi Chum, 1 Sawyer, 713.
> See, also, Forbes *v.* Scannell, 13 Cal. 242.

" I have received your No. 332, of March 11, 1887, in which you
discuss the appellate jurisdiction of the United States minister to
China.

" I concur with you in the opinion that there is no appeal from a
consular court in China to the United States minister in cases where
the matter in dispute exceeds $2,500; but that the appeal in such
cases is to be to the circuit court for the district of California. This
is in my judgment the proper construction of the statutes. As a
matter of judicial practice, the vesting of appeals in such cases in
the circuit court for the district of California has been accepted by
that court. In the case of The Ping-On, before Sawyer and Hoffman, JJ., in March, 1882 (7 Sawyer's Rep. 483), the question was
vigorously contested, and it was claimed that sections 4092, 4093,
4094, and 4109, giving jurisdiction, were in this respect annulled
by section 4107. But this position was rejected by Hoffman, J.,
who thus states the law:

" ' The provisions of sections 4094, 4109 and 4092 clearly indicate
the system Congress intended to adopt.

" ' In suits for $500 or less, the decision of the consular court is
final, unless the consul sees fit to call in associates and they differ
in opinion. In suits for more than $500 and not more than $2,500
an appeal lies to the minister, whose judgment is final. In suits
for more than $2,500 the appeal lies to the circuit court for the dis-
trict of California, and a similar appeal lies from the final judgment
of the minister in the *exercise of original jurisdiction* when the
amount involved exceeds $2,500. But this original jurisdiction is
confined to cases where the consul is interested either as party or
witness. It thus appears that Congress has seen fit to withhold,
both from the consular court and from the minister, final jurisdiction in all cases where the matter in dispute exceeds $2,500, exclusive
of costs, and to provide in such cases for an appeal to the circuit
court for the district of California.'

" I hold, therefore, that the right of appeal from the final judgment of consular courts in all cases where the matter in dispute
exceeds $2,500 is in the circuit court for the district of California,
and is, consequently, not in the United States minister."

> Mr. Bayard, Sec. of State, to Mr. Denby, min. to China, May 4, 1887,
> MS. Inst. China, IV. 267.

In 1868 the Pacific Mail Steamship Company asked the Department of State to set aside and declare null and void the proceedings
of the United States consul at Kanagawa, Japan, who, sitting with
three assessors, had rendered judgment against the company in an
action for damages for collision, brought by the agents for the owner
and master of the British steamer *Osaca*. The company had taken
an appeal upon the merits from the judgment of the consul to the
United States minister in Japan, who disallowed the appeal for
want of jurisdiction on his part. The Department of State, replying
to the company's protest, said that the United States consuls in
Japan, in exercising judicial authority, acted as judges under a
special law of Congress, which did not direct the President to review
their judgments. The question of jurisdiction was one proper to
be raised before the consul, and he was competent to pronounce upon
it; and, had the question been so raised, " it might have been thought
proper for the Department of State, under the direction of the President, to review his decision upon this point and to affirm the same or
set it aside after obtaining such information concerning facts as
might be obtained from collateral inquiries, and such light upon the
law as the Department could procure by reference to the Attorney-
General of the United States."   But, while the act of Congress gave
an appeal in certain cases to the minister in Japan, it made " no other
provision for correcting errors which may be committed by a consular court. If the proceedings of the consul are absolutely null and
void for want of jurisdiction in the consular court, as the respond-
ents contend, then they probably have their remedy by action against
the consul. The interests of commerce and of international peace
require that judicial proceedings of consuls in Eastern countries
should not be arbitrarily set aside or annulled by Executive interference, when there is no ground for a complaint that injustice has been
done, or attempted to be done. The Secretary of State is therefore
of opinion that the petition of the Pacific Mail Steamship Company
in the present case must be disallowed, and the proceedings in the
consular court be allowed to take their regular course."

> Mr. Seward, Sec. of State, to Mr. Irwin, Aug. 18, 1868, 49 MS. Desp. to
> Consuls, 468.
> In October, 1893, the United States consular court at Tamatave, Mada-
> gascar, rendered judgment in favor of the New Oriental Bank Com-

pany, a British corporation, against Mr. George Ropes, an American citizen. The bank, being dissatisfied with the judgment, sought to take an appeal from it under the treaty between the United States and Madagascar of 1881, which provided that appeals might be taken to either of the two contracting Governments, at the option of the party appealing, in the manner provided in section 16, article VI. of the treaty. The Department of State held that the provision for appeal thus referred to related only to the trial of controversies between American citizens or protégés and subjects of Madagascar. The Department added that by section 4091, Revised Statutes, provision was made for an appeal to the minister from a consular judgment, but that, as there was no minister in Madagascar, it was difficult to see what the rights of parties were who were dissatisfied with the decision of the consular court. The Department of State also referred to section 4128, Revised Statutes, providing that where there is no minister in the countries in question, the judicial duties which are imposed upon the minister shall devolve upon the Secretary of State. With reference to this section, the Department of State said: "In only one case has there been any attempt to appeal to the Secretary of State from a consular judgment. There are certainly grave doubts as to the validity of legislation undertaking to confer judicial authority on the Secretary of State, and in the case referred to the Secretary did not undertake to act judicially, but after examination of the record, which disclosed the fact that the real defendants in the case had never been notified of the proceeding, the consul was simply instructed that the whole proceeding was void." (Mr. Strobel, Third Assist. Sec. of State, to Messrs. Butler, Stillman, and Hubbard, January 16, 1894, 195 MS. Dom. Let. 166.)

Mr. Hubbard, United States minister to Tokio, having communicated to the Department of State his opinion, rendered in the ministerial court of the United States of America for Japan, in the case of The People of the United States of America v. John Kernan, charged with murder, the Department of State replied that, as the "case can come before the Department for revision only on application for pardon, and as such an application can not be made until final judgment," the Department, since the case was remanded for a new trial, could do no more than express its satisfaction with the ability with which Mr. Hubbard had discharged his duties.

Mr. Bayard, Sec. of State, to the Atty. Gen., Dec. 2, 1887, 166 MS. Dom. Let. 250, enclosing a copy of Mr. Hubbard's dispatch, No. 398, Oct. 26, 1887.

(5) CRIMINAL JURISDICTION.

§ 266.

Criminal jurisdiction of United States consular courts being expressly restricted by section 4084, Revised Statutes, to offences committed by citizens of the United States in the countries in which the consuls vested with judicial powers are

Its scope.

appointed to reside, the consular court of the United States at Tangier
had no jurisdiction of an offence committed in the United States by
a naturalized citizen who afterwards escaped and went to Morocco.

Mr. Adee, Act. Sec. of State, to Mr. Mathews, consul at Tangier, July 8,
1890, 134 MS. Inst. Consuls, 65.

" I have to acknowledge the receipt of your despatch No. 156 of the
26th ultimo, in which you report that on the fourth conviction, in the
consular court, of Abraham Amselam, a naturalized citizen of the
United States, of the offence of wife beating, you in your capacity of
judge of that court, had Amselam flogged.

" Consular court jurisdiction is required by section 4086 of the
Revised Statutes and paragraph 610 of the Consular Regulations to
be conducted in conformity (1) with the statute law of the United
States, where applicable; (2) with the common law, including equity
and admiralty law; (3) with prescribed regulations supplementing
the statute and common law. These supplemental regulations are
prescribed by the minister of the United States, where there is one
in the country; and in Morocco, among other powers, the authority
to prescribe them is executed, in conformity with the provisions of the
treaties and the laws of the United States, by the consul of the United
States resident there (Revised Statutes, section 4127). It has
always been the custom of the Department to supervise with great
care the framing and adoption of these regulations, and your predecessor was instructed on December 9, 1886, to adopt the regulations
prepared for the consular court in the Ottoman Empire, and to conduct his consular court proceedings according to law and those regulations. All arbitrary and irregular proceedings were forbidden.

" *Wife beating* is not, at common law, a distinctive offence; nor is
it made such by any statute of the United States, or regulation
enforceable in your consular court. By the earlier common-law
authorities, the wife was considered so far under her husband's power
that he might give her moderate correction " *ex causa regiminis et
castigationis*," but that doctrine is repudiated by all the modern
authorities in this country and in England, so that in the present
state of the common law beating a wife is *assault and battery*, in like
manner as the beating of any other person would be. There is no
United States statute specially providing a punishment for *assault
and battery* on an unofficial person. So we must look to the common
law for the punishment of the ordinary offence.

" This punishment is fine, or imprisonment, or both, and the finding
of sureties to keep the peace. (4th Blackstone, 217; 1 Russell on
Crimes, 1031.) Flogging is prescribed as a punishment in certain
countries, and in some of the States of the Union for certain named

offences; but these statutes have no application to offences tried in your court.

" The offence of Amselam was clearly that of *assault and battery*, and the proper punishment was fine or imprisonment, or both, in your discretion, and the requirement of a bond with security to keep the peace and be of good behavior towards the community in general, and towards his wife in particular. Surety to keep the peace and be of good behavior is one of the most potent and effective means of restraining violent and lawless men known to the law. If you had put Amselam under a peace bond as soon as it appeared that he needed some constantly operating restraint on his violent impulses towards his wife, it is thought that the third and fourth repetitions of his offense would have been prevented."

> Mr. Wharton, Act. Sec. of State, to Mr. Lewis, consul at Tangier, Aug. 9, 1889, 131 MS. Inst. Consuls, 31.

Doubt was expressed as to whether the offense of getting up an expedition with a view simply to exhume a dead body in a foreign country for the purpose of private gain was indictable under any law of the United States. This doubt was expressed with reference to the trial of one Jenkins, before the United States consular court at Shanghai, the prisoner having been acquitted. It was added that the evidence on the trial tended to bring the case within section 6 of the neutrality act of 1819, 3 Stat. 449, under which the accused might perhaps have been more successfully prosecuted.

> Mr. Seward, Sec. of State, to Mr. Browne, min. to China, Feb. 5, 1869, MS. Inst. China, II. 45.

" The obligation of a neutral government to prevent its citizens from joining in hostile movements against a foreign state is limited by the extent to which such citizens are under its jurisdiction and by the municipal laws applicable to their actions. Hence, a citizen outside of such jurisdiction may not be controlled in his free acts; but what he does is at his own risk and peril. If he offers his services to a combatant, that is a matter of private contract, which it may be equally improper for his own government to forbid or protect; and such service in legitimate war is not contrary to international law.

" In China, however, foreign powers have an extraterritorial jurisdiction conferred by treaty. This jurisdiction is in nowise arbitrary, but is limited by laws, and is not preventive but punitory. If a citizen of the United States in China commit an offense against the peace of China, it is triable in the consular courts. Section 4102 of the Revised Statutes provides that ' insurrection or rebellion against the Government of either of those countries [*i. e.*, the countries named in section 4083, whereof China is one], with intent to subvert the same, and murder, shall be capital offenses punishable with death,' &c., the consular court and the minister to concur in awarding the penalty. But the simple act of entering into a private contract to serve either combatant in open warfare would not appear to be triable under this section; and, even if it were, this Government would have no rightful power to forbid such service."

> Mr. Bayard, Sec. of State, to Mr. Young, min. to China, March 11, 1885, MS. Inst. China, IV. 9.

With most countries it has been the rule to regard the recovery of their fugitive subjects, charged with ordinary
Extradition. crimes, as an incident of the extraterritorial jurisdiction exercised through their ministers or consuls. The United States, however, has not generally sought to enjoy this privilege, but has, on the other hand, in two cases—those of the Ottoman Empire in 1874 and Japan in 1876—entered into treaties of extradition with the governments of countries in which citizens of the United States were entitled to extraterritoriality. But there are two cases in which American citizens have been brought back to the United States through the enforcement of extraterritorial rights. One of these is that of John H. Surratt, who was charged with complicity in the assassination of President Lincoln, and who was arrested at Alexandria, Egypt, in 1866, and sent to the United States on an American man-of-war by Mr. Hale, then United States consul at that port. His extradition, as Mr. Hale reported, was accepted at Alexandria " as a matter of course." The other case was that of Henry Myers and J. F. Tunstall, two American citizens who were members of the crew of the Confederate steamer *Sumter*. In February, 1862, while the *Sumter* lay at Gibraltar, Myers and Tunstall embarked on the French merchant steamer *Ville de Malaga* for the purpose of proceeding to Cadiz, in order to obtain a supply of coal for the *Sumter*. The *Ville de Malaga* having stopped at Tangier, Morocco, they went ashore, where, with the aid of a Moorish military guard, the United States consul arrested them and put them in irons, keeping them in the consulate till the arrival of the U. S. S. *Ino*, on which he placed them for transportation to the United States. The commander of the *Ino* afterwards transshipped them to an American merchantman, by which they were taken to Boston, where they were committed into military custody in Fort Warren.

> As to the general rule, see Moore on Extradition, I. 100, citing W. B. Lawrence, 15 Alb. L. J. 230; Billot, Traité de l'Extradition, 6, 7.
> For the case of Surratt, see Dip. Cor. 1866, II. 275–277; id. 1867, II. 82.
> As to the case of Myers and Tunstall, see Mr. Seward, Sec. of State, to Mr. McMath, consul at Tangier, April 28, 1862, Dip. Cor. 1862, 873.
> See the case of J. D. Buckley, Moore on Extradition, I. 105.

See Mr. Olney, Sec. of State, to Mr. Denby, min. to China, Feb. 2, 1897,
approving a proposed regulation by the latter for the arrest and
transportation for trial of American citizens who, being charged
with crime in one consular district in China, should be found in
another consular district in that country. (For. Rel. 1897, 80, 81–
82.)   See, in this relation, Moore on Extradition, II. 820–824.

In January, 1880, one Cheers, a British subject, who had shipped at New
York as a seaman on the American merchant vessel *R. Robinson*,
deserted at Yokohama, Japan, and went on board the British man-
of-war *Hornet*, where, on representing himself as a deserter from
the British navy, he was held a prisoner. Subsequently the United
States consul-general issued a warrant for his arrest on the charge
of desertion from the *R. Robinson* and applied to the British consul
to procure his surrender. The British consul refused to comply with
the request on the ground that Cheers had been placed under arrest
in accordance with naval instructions, the commander of the *Hornet*
stating that he had been dealt with in accordance with the naval
discipline act. The case was directed to be brought to the attention
of the British Government. (Mr. Evarts, Sec. of State, to Mr.
Hoppin, chargé at London, April 19, 1880, MS. Inst. Great Britain,
XXV. 618.)

In the absence of any specific appropriation for the object, the
expense of transferring prisoners, held by the authorities of the
United States in China, from Amoy to Hongkong for trial on a
charge of piracy, is a lawful charge upon the judiciary fund, so
called, being the fund appropriated for defraying " the expenses of
prosecutions for offenses committed against the United States, and
for the safe-keeping of prisoners."

Cushing, At. Gen., 1853, 6 Op. 59.

Imprisonment.

It was advised under the act of August 11, 1848, entitled "An act
to carry into effect certain provisions in the treaties
between the United States and China, and the Otto-
man Porte, giving certain judicial powers to ministers and consuls of
the United States in those countries," that as Congress had not designated any particular place for the confinement of persons who should
be arrested on charges of crime, it was left to be regulated under the
5th section of the act, or in the absence of any such regulation, to the
discretion of the acting functionary.

Toucey, At. Gen., Jan. 31, 1849, 5 Op. 67.

A sentence of imprisonment imposed in any of the regular [con-
sular] courts of China may be served out in any portion of China, and
not necessarily within the limits of the consul's ordinary jurisdiction.

Miller, At. Gen., 1892, 20 Op. 391; cited in Mr. Olney, Sec. of State, to
Mr. Denby, min. to China, Feb. 2, 1897, For. Rel. 1897, 80, 81.

Capt. L. de R. du Vergé, an American citizen, was convicted in the United States consular court at Tamatave, Madagascar, of the manslaughter of Victor F. Stanwood, United States consular agent at Andakobe, in the same island. Du Vergé was sentenced to pay a fine and to undergo ten years' imprisonment; and, as there was no American jail in Madagascar, the consul at Tamatave suggested that he be sent to the United States. August 3, 1889, the Department of State submitted the question to the Attorney-General. In so doing, the Department referred to the case of Mirzan, who, after conviction of murder at Alexandria, Egypt, before Mr. Maynard, United States minister to Turkey, was brought to the United States and imprisoned at Albany; and to the case of Dinkelle, who, after conviction of murder by the United States minister in Japan, was also brought to Albany, and was afterwards transferred to an asylum where insane United States prisoners were treated.

Mr. Chapman, Acting Attorney-General, citing with approval the opinion of Attorney-General Williams, of February 4, 1875, 14 Op. 522, advised that, as there was no statute which authorized the imprisonment in the United States of a person convicted by a consular court, the removal of Du Vergé to the United States for that purpose would be unlawful. With reference to the case of Mirzan, who was convicted at Alexandria, June 12, 1880, and was sentenced to be hanged on the 1st of the following October, Mr. Chapman observed that the President, July 29, 1880, pardoned the convict on condition that he be imprisoned for life in the United States consular prison at Smyrna, or in such other prison or prisons in Turkey or the United States as the President might at any time direct. As to the case of Dinkelle, he observed that the President, August 6, 1880, pardoned the convict on condition that he be imprisoned for life in the Albany penitentiary. It had been held that the President might grant a conditional pardon, and that the acceptance of the condition by the convict bound the latter.

> Chapman, Acting Atty. Gen., Aug. 14, 1889, 19 Op. 377.
> On the validity of a conditional pardon, Mr. Chapman cited 18 How. 307.
> For the letter of the Department of State to the Attorney-General, of August 3, 1889, see 174 MS. Dom. Let. 64.
> For a request for permission to confine an American consular prisoner at Tamatave in the French jail, see Mr. Gresham, Sec. of State, to Mr. Patenotre, French amb., Feb. 21, 1895, MS. Notes to France, X. 369.

June 10, 1890, the Secretary of State wrote to the Attorney-General that the consul at Tamatave considered the further imprisonment at that place of Du Vergé to be inexpedient; that it was impossible properly to guard and imprison him there, and that the Hoova government objected to his remaining. The Secretary of State therefore asked for an opinion as to whether Du Vergé could

lawfully be removed to the consular prison at Shanghai or Kanagawa.   The Attorney-General replied: "I think the opinion of
Acting Attorney-General Chapman, rendered to your Department
under date of August 14, covers your question.   The opinion is to
the effect that, in the absence of statutory provision, there is no power
in the Executive to change the place of confinement of a prisoner
after sentence; and that the statutory provisions of section 5446 do
not cover this case.   In the meantime, however, I have called this
matter to the attention of the Senate Judiciary Committee, and
asked that an amendment to section 5546 (sic), giving the Attorney-
General power to change the place of imprisonment in such cases,
be passed."

> Mr. Miller, At. Gen., to Sec. of State, June 17, 1890, MSS. Dept. of State.
> The Consular Regulations, 1896, § 636, say: "Consular courts have no
> power . . . to send them [American convicts] to the United States
> to serve out their terms of imprisonment."   The regulations cite
> 19 Op. 377.

" 225. The statutes provide that in case of a conviction entailing
the death penalty, it shall be the duty of the minister
Clemency. to issue his warrant for the execution of the convict,
appointing the time, place, and manner; but if the minister is satisfied that the ends of public justice demand it, he may from time to
time postpone such execution.   If he finds mitigating circumstances
which authorize it, he may submit the case to the President for pardon.—R. S., sec. 4103.

" 226. As the provision of section 4103 of the Revised Statutes
stands, it appears to make the diplomatic representative the sole
judge of the propriety of extending Executive clemency to the convict.   It was probably not the intent of Congress to bar the exercise
of the President's power of pardon at the discretion of a diplomatic
representative; and it would be manifestly improper, as well as of
doubtful constitutionality, to do so in the possible case of conviction
being had before the officer whose duty it is made to execute the sentence.   In cases coming under this statutory provision, the Department of State deems it advisable that the diplomatic representative
should always regard the ends of public justice as requiring post-
ponement of the execution until the case is reported and copies of the
judgment and testimony are transmitted to the Department of State
and the President's views in the premises have been received."

> Inst. to the Dip. Officers of the United States (1897), 91–92. Mr.
> Blaine, in a report to the President of Dec. 19, 1881, discusses the
> subject of consular jurisdiction in countries in the East, and advo-
> cates the establishment of courts the officers of which shall not
> belong to the diplomatic and consular service.   He seemed to enter-
> tain doubts as to the constitutionality of the procedure under

§§ 4083–4130, R. S., but this question is settled by In re Ross, 140 U. S. 453. In the course of his report he referred to seven cases of persons who had been capitally sentenced in the United States consular courts: David Williams, claiming to be a British subject, convicted by Consul-General Seward, at Shanghai, in 1863, of "piracy and murder;" James White, convicted at Shanghai, Nov. 23, 1863, of murder; John D. Buckley, claiming to be a British subject, convicted at Shanghai, in 1864, of murder; James Webb, convicted at Nagasaki, 1878, of murder; William Dinkelle, convicted at Hiogo, 1880, of murder; John Ross, convicted at Yokohama, 1881, of murder; Stephen Mirzan, convicted at Smyrna, 1880, of murder. Williams, after sentence, committed suicide. White escaped. Buckley was hanged. (Dip. Cor. 1864, III. 392–419.) Webb's sentence was commuted to imprisonment for life; likewise, Dinkelle's. Ross was pardoned on condition of being imprisoned in the United States; and the same course was pursued in the case of Mirzan. (S. Ex. Doc. 21, 47 Cong. 1 sess.)

See, as to the question of appeal, Mr. Evarts, Sec. of State, to Mr. Bingham, min. to Japan, Oct. 7, 1880, MS. Inst. Japan, III. 5.

A prisoner having been condemned to death by a consular court in Japan, the President commuted his sentence to imprisonment for life, on condition that he undergo the imprisonment in the penitentiary at Albany. The condition was accepted, and the prisoner was brought to the United States, but, while imprisoned at Albany, he sought to be released by habeas corpus. It was held that the commutation, or conditional pardon, was valid, and that there was no question as to the binding force of the prisoner's acceptance of it.

In re Ross (1891), 140 U. S. 453, 480.

" The fact that you find no power lodged in the consul to remit any part of a sentence, or to pardon in any case, doubtless will, as it should, admonish you of the necessity of wary consideration in admeasuring the punishment to the offence. Whether the 18th section of the act of 1860 is applicable to criminal cases after judgment, or after conviction when judgment is suspended, is so doubtful that no determination of the question will be hazarded until a necessity shall arise."

Mr. F. W. Seward, Assist. Sec. of State, to Mr. Wingate, consul at Swatow, June 6, 1866, 43 MS. Desp. to Consuls, 221.

5. End, or Suspension, of Privileges.

(1) Change of Sovereignty.

§ 267.

May 4, 1896, the Department of State, at the instance of the French ambassador at Washington, instructed the consul of the United States at Tamatave to " suspend until further instructed exercise

consular judicial functions in all cases where cooperation of an established French court is available for disposition judicial cases affecting American citizens." Instructions were given by the French Government to the French resident-general in Madagascar to give all
facilities to the American consuls for settling the cases brought before
their courts before October 16, 1896, when, according to the statement of the French resident-general, the French courts were to be
opened for business.

> Mr. Olney, Sec. of State, to Mr. Eustis, amb. to France, Dec. 10, 1896;
> Mr. Vignaud, chargé at Paris, to Mr. Olney, Sec. of State, Feb. 18,
> 1897, inclosing a note from Mr. Hanotaux, min. of for. aff., of Feb.
> 14, 1897: For. Rel. 1897, 152–154.

> In 1882 the Department of State expressed the view, with reference to
> the proposal of France to extend French judicial tribunals and pro-
> cedure to Tunis, that the assent of Congress would be necessary to
> enable the United States to renounce its jurisdiction. (Mr. Freling-
> huysen, Sec. of State, to Mr. West, Brit. min., Dec. 23, 1882, For. Rel.
> 1883, 483.)

> Congress authorized the President to accept the jurisdiction of the mixed
> tribunals in Egypt, but this change was merely in the nature of an
> internal reform, to which, so far as it involved treaty rights, the
> assent of the treaty powers was obviously necessary.

By a treaty between the United States and France, signed at Washington, March 15, 1904, the United States renounced for its consuls
and citizens in Tunis the stipulations of the treaties between the
United States and the Bey of Tunis of August, 1797, and February,
1824, and agreed to claim for them only those rights which belonged
to them in virtue of international law or of treaties between the
United States and France.

> For. Rel. 1904, 304.
> See, further, as to Tunis, infra, § 282.

By a convention between the United States and Great Britain of
Feb. 25, 1905, the United States agrees to renounce "in the British
protectorate of Zanzibar, and in that part of the mainland dominions of His Highness the Sultan of Zanzibar which lies within the
protectorate of British East Africa," the extraterritorial rights
secured to the United States by the treaty of Sept. 21, 1833, between
the United States and the Sultan of Muscat, and by the treaty of
July 3, 1886, between the United States and the Sultan of Zanzibar.
The British courts are to exercise the relinquished jurisdiction.

> See, further, as to Muscat and Zanzibar, infra, §§ 864, 895.

§ 268.

After the lease of Kiaochow, Port Arthur, and Weihaiwei, to Germany, Russia, and Great Britain, respectively, the United States consul at Chefoo, within whose district the three ports lay, made inquiry of his Government as to the continuance of his extraterritorial jurisdiction in those places.

Germany occupied Kiaochow on November 14, 1897, and obtained from China a lease of land there extending for 100 li at high tide, on the southern and northern sides of Kiaochow Bay, for 99 years, with the privilege of establishing dock yards and fortifications. It was declared that China retained her "sovereignty" over the territory, but it was to be "governed and administered . . . solely by Germany."

Port Arthur, with Talienwan, was leased as a naval port by Russia from China in 1898 for a term of 25 years, which might be extended by mutual agreement. The lease was not to prejudice China's "sovereignty," but the control of the territory was to be exercised by one high Russian official.

Weihaiwei was leased by Great Britain July 1, 1898, for military purposes so long as Port Arthur should "remain in the occupation of Russia." The lease comprised the island of Liu Kung and all the islands in the Bay of Weihaiwei, and a belt of 10 English miles along its entire coast. Within the leased territory Great Britain was to have "sole jurisdiction." [a]

It appeared that all the members of the diplomatic corps at Peking, except the Japanese minister, took the view that the ports in question, during the lease, passed wholly under the jurisdiction of the three Governments, respectively, and that consuls accredited to China should not attempt to exercise any jurisdiction in them. [b]

" The inclosed memorandum . . . will acquaint you with the view here entertained of the general subject. . . .

"As a corollary to this view, which from your statement appears to be held by all the powers, with the exception of Japan, the ordinary consular functions prescribed and defined in the intercourse of the Christian powers among themselves could obviously not be exercised within the leased territory by a consul of the United States stationed in neighboring Chinese territory without some express recognition of his official character, by exequatur or otherwise, on the part of the

---

a For. Rel. 1900, 382–385.
b For. Rel. 1900, 385–386.

sovereign into whose control the territory has passed by lease for the time being.   This point is not touched upon in your report, and it can only be inferred that the other Western powers will be found to entertain substantially the same view.   If you find them to be of a similar opinion, you will, as by direction of the Secretary of State, inform Mr. Goodnow that, upon investigation made and consideration given to the subject, the United States consuls in districts adjacent to the foreign leased territories are to be instructed that they have no authority to exercise extraterritorial consular jurisdiction or to perform ordinary nonjudicial consular acts within the leased territory under their present Chinese exequaturs."

> Mr. Hay, Sec. of State, to Mr. Conger, min. to China, Feb. 3, 1900, For. Rel. 1900, 386, MS. Inst. China, VI. 50.
>
> The memorandum above referred to, after citing the provisions in the treaties between the United States and China in relation to extraterritorial jurisdiction, said:
>
> " By the leases made by the Chinese Government of Weihaiwei, Kiaochow, and Port Arthur, to Great Britain, Germany, and Russia, respectively, the *jurisdiction* of China over the territories leased is relinquished during the terms of the leases.
>
> " In the case of Weihaiwei, leased to Great Britain, it is expressly provided that ' within the territory leased Great Britain shall have *sole* jurisdiction.'
>
> " In the lease of Kiaochow to Germany, it is provided that China shall have no voice in the government or administration of the leased territory, but that *it shall be governed and administered during the whole term of the lease by Germany;* that Germany is at liberty to enact any regulation she desires for the government of the territory. Chinese subjects are allowed to live in the territory leased, under the protection of the German authorities, and there carry on their business as long as they conduct themselves as law-abiding citizens. Provision is made for the surrender to the Chinese authorities of fugitive Chinese criminals taking refuge in the leased territory. The Chinese authorities are not at liberty to send agents into the leased territory to make arrests. The lease declares that China ' *retains her sovereignty over this territory.*'
>
> " In the lease of Port Arthur to Russia it is provided that the control of all military forces, as well as of the *civil officials* in the territory, shall be vested in one high Russian official ; that all Chinese military forces shall be withdrawn ; that the Chinese inhabitants may remain or go, as they choose ; that if they remain, any Chinese charged with a criminal offense shall be handed over to the nearest Chinese official to be dealt with. (Mr. Conger says that the Russian legation informs him that this last provision is not correctly translated, and that, construing it in connection with article 8 of the treaty of 1860, the Russian Government has the right and does try Chinese for crimes committed against Russians.) This lease is expressly declared on the understanding that it ' *shall not prejudice China's sovereignty over this territory.*'
>
> " As it is expressly stipulated in the leases that China retains *sovereignty* over the territory leased, it could doubtless be asserted that such

territory is still *Chinese territory* and that the provisions of our treaties with China granting consular jurisdiction are still applicable therein. But in view of the express relinquishment of jurisdiction by China, I infer that the reservation of sovereignty is merely intended to cut off possible future claims of the lessees that the sovereignty of the territory is *permanently* vested in them. The intention and effect of these leases appear to me to have been the relinquishment by China, *during the term of the leases*, and the conferring upon the foreign power in each case *of all jurisdiction over the territory.* Such relinquishment would seem, also, to involve the loss by the United States of its right to exercise consular jurisdiction in the territories leased. And, as Mr. Conger suggests, as these territories have practically passed from the control of an uncivilized people to civilized, there would seem to be no substantial reason for continuing to exercise such jurisdiction." (Mem. of Mr. Van Dyne, Assistant Solicitor, For. Rel. 1900, 387, 388–389.)

In a subsequent dispatch Mr. Conger, while observing that the leased territory in every case was small, reported that judicial procedure according to civilized methods had been established there; that the British Government was preparing to establish consulates at Kiaochow and Talienwan; and that he had instructed Mr. Goodnow, the consul-general at Shanghai, " to inform the United States consuls in China that they have no authority to exercise extraterritorial consular jurisdiction, or to perform ordinary nonjudicial consular acts within the leased territory under their present exequaturs."

For. Rel. 1900, 389–390.

The ambassadors of the United States to Germany, Great Britain, and Russia were instructed to arrange with the Governments to which they were accredited for the recognition of the competency of the most available consul to exercise ordinary consular functions in the leased territories.

- Mr. Hay, Sec. of State, to Mr. Conger, min. to China, May 22, 1900, For. Rel. 1900, 390 ; MS. Inst. China, VI. 77.
- Jan. 30, 1903, the Russian Government announced that it would admit foreign consuls to Dalny (Talienwan), but that they would have no rights beyond those accorded to them throughout Russian territory. (For. Rel. 1903, 84–85, 708.)

(3) EFFECT OF MARTIAL LAW.

§ 269.

" I have to acknowledge the receipt of your despatch No. 155, of the 25th of May last, with which you transmit a copy of a law on the state of siege recently passed by the Ottoman Parliament. The law authorizes the Sultan, and, under certain specified circumstances, the military commanders to proclaim a state of siege and prescribes the manner in which it shall be enforced. Under its provisions Constantinople has been proclaimed to be in a state of siege. No official notice has been given to the foreign missions, and nothing has occurred to present any question for practical decision.

" The consul-general in a despatch to you requests your opinion as to how far the law on the state of siege would under the plea of military necessity be allowed to overrule Article IV. of the treaty of 1830, and you refer the question to the Department for decision.

" Martial law is generally supposed to supersede all other law, all statutes and all treaties. The military commander who enforces it is not expected to and does not regard the civil law of his own country when it conflicts with what he is pleased to regard as martial law, and which is simply his own will, and it can not be expected that he will pay much greater respect to the treaties of his Government than to its laws. But every American citizen in a foreign land is entitled at all times to the protection accorded to him by our treaty stipulations with that country in which he may be residing. The fact that that country is at war with another foreign power does not affect his status so long as the United States retains its peaceful relations with the two powers.

" In view of the above state of facts, should any attempt be made to apply any provision of martial law in conflict with any stipulation of our treaty with the Ottoman Empire to an American citizen residing in Turkey, our representatives will be expected to interpose with the proper authorities in favor of their countrymen, and to demand that all treaty stipulations be strictly observed in the consideration and decision of the case. All cases arising under the law will be at once reported to the Department."

> Mr. F. W. Seward, Act. Sec. of State, to Mr. Maynard, June 26, 1877, MS. Inst. Turkey, III. 251.

" Your despatch No. 124, of the 14th June last, has been received. You therein report the bombardment of Tamatave by the French on the 10th of that month, and your subsequent notification by the French naval commander that the occupation of the city by the forces of the Republic has put an end to your functions as the consul of the United States accredited to the Hovas Government. It further appears that the town has been proclaimed in a state of siege under the French law, and that the customs and other public business are administered by the French authorities. In this state of things you ask for instructions as to your duties and the disposition to be made of the archives and property in your care.

" In reply I have to instruct you that while the temporary suspension of Hovas authority in Tamatave and its replacement by French military control may interrupt your relations with the Hovas Government, it does not annul your relations with the United States Government, which maintains you at the port of Tamatave for the representative protection of any interests of citizens of the United States who may be found there. You will, therefore, remain at Tamatave for the present and continue your charge of the archives and property of the consulate without interruption. You will inform the French authorities that under the circumstances in which you are placed you will in conformity with their order suspend the exercise of representative consular functions in Tamatave towards the Hovas Government awaiting the instructions which your own Government may give you after it has fully considered the situation. You will, however, add that the temporary intermission of your relations with the Madagascan authorities in Tamatave does not exempt you from the moral obligation as a representative of the Government of the United States to use your good offices for the protection of American citizens and property within your jurisdictional limits, and that in case anything should occur calling for your intervention you will feel it your duty to address yourself to whatever authority may be in responsible administrative control of the port."

> Mr. Frelinghuysen, Sec. of State, to Mr. Whitney, acting U. S. consul at Tamatave, Aug. 28, 1883, 108 MS. Inst. Consuls, 185.

On a report that the German consul at Apia had declared war against Mataafa, an aspirant to the kingship of Samoa who had been in hostile collision with a squad of German marines, the minister of the United States at Berlin was instructed to say that his Government assumed that " the German officials in Samoa would be instructed carefully to refrain from interference with American citizens and property there, since no declaration of martial law could extend German jurisdiction so as to include control of American citizens in Samoa. Such a pretension could not be recognized or conceded by this Government."

The German Government replied that when war was declared against Mataafa the commander of the German squadron issued a proclamation by which foreigners residing in Samoa were subjected to martial law; that while " international law would, to a certain extent, not prevent such a measure," yet Prince Bismarck thought that the military authority had gone too far in the present instance; and that the commander had been instructed to withdraw the part of his proclamation relating to foreigners.

> Mr. Bayard, Sec. of State, to Mr. Pendleton, min. to Germany, tel., Jan. 31, 1889; Count Arco-Valley, German min., to Mr. Bayard, Sec. of State, Feb. 1, 1889: H. Ex. Doc. 119, 50 Cong. 2 sess. 2, 3.
>
> Smilar assurances were spontaneously given to Great Britain. (London *Times*, March 13, 1889.)

With regard to the foregoing instances, it may be pointed out that the instruction of Mr. F. W. Seward to Mr. Maynard, in 1877, related to the question of a government's assuming within its own territory, by a proclamation of martial law, jurisdiction over the citizens of a friendly government to whom it had by treaty conceded the privilege of extraterritoriality. In the case of Madagascar in 1883, and of Samoa in 1889, where martial law was proclaimed in the extraterritorial country by a civilized power, the opinions of the Department of State appear to be contradictory.

It will be observed that in the well-considered case of John L. Waller, in Madagascar in 1895, the jurisdiction of the French authorities, under their proclamation of martial law, was admitted with regard to the acts with which Waller was charged, which were offences against the laws of war. (See For. Rel. 1895, I. 251; and supra, § 196.)

6. China.

(1) ESTABLISHMENT OF EXTRATERRITORIAL PRIVILEGES.

§ 270.

Mr. Cushing, in a dispatch of Sept. 29, 1844, written by him as commissioner to China, discusses the question of extraterritoriality. After explaining the customary origin of consular jurisdiction in Mohammedan countries, he states that China had asserted complete jurisdiction over all persons within the territory and waters of the Empire. When crimes had been committed there by foreigners other than Portuguese, the Government had never failed to assert its jurisdiction to seize the accused if accessible on land, and to demand his surrender if on board of a ship. The claim of surrender had sometimes been successfully resisted, and sometimes acquiesced in. In 1780 a French seaman, who killed a Portuguese seaman in one of the hongs of Canton, was delivered up to the local authorities, by whom he was tried, convicted, and executed. In 1784 the gunner of an English merchant ship, who, in firing a salute, had killed a Chinese, was given up and executed. Other cases had occurred affecting one European government or another. In only one case of surrender had the United States been involved—in 1821 an Italian named Terranova, a seaman on the American ship *Emily*, who had caused the death of a Chinese boatwoman alongside the vessel at Whampoa, was surrendered and strangled. The Chinese enforced a reluctant submission on the part of the foreign residents in such cases by stopping or threatening to stop all trade. Captain Elliott, of the British navy, however, at an early stage of the controversy between his Government and that of China, refused to give up some English sailors who were charged with homicide.

Mr. Cushing, comr. to China, to Mr. Calhoun, Sec. of State, Sept. 29, 1844, S. Ex. Doc. 58, 28 Cong. 2 sess. 4.

By Art. XIII. of the general regulations established under the treaty of peace between Great Britain and China of Aug. 29, 1842, provision was made for the adjustment of complaints of Chinese against British subjects, and vice versa, and it was stipulated as follows: " Regarding the punishment of English criminals, the English Government will enact the laws necessary to attain that end, and the consul will be empowered to put them in force ; and regarding the punishment of Chinese criminals, these will be tried and punished by their own laws, in the way provided for by the correspondence which took place at Nanking, after the concluding of the peace." (30 Br. & For. State Papers, 389, 393, 398, 401-402.)

The treaty concluded by Mr. Cushing in 1844 secured for citizens of the United States privileges similar to those which Great Britain had thus, as the result of the war, obtained for British subjects. See Articles XXI., XXV., etc.

In his report upon his negotiations, Mr. Cushing stated that in his opinion jurisdiction over citizens of the United States should be allowed only to Christian states, since they alone acknowledge the system of international law ; and that in the second place, he found that Great Britain had stipulated for the exemption of her subjects from Chinese jurisdiction. (Dispatch of Mr. Cushing, Sept. 29, 1844, S. Ex. Doc. 58, 28 Cong. 2 sess. 4.)

As to the question of establishing mixed tribunals in China, for the trial of cases involving Chinese and foreigners, see reports of Mr. Geo. F. Seward, min. to China, For. Rel. 1879, 220, 221, 229 ; For. Rel. 1880, 145, 210, 214, 242, 249, 273.

(2) UNITED STATES TREATIES.

§ 271.

By the treaty between the United States and China, concluded July 3, 1844, it was provided (Art. XXI.) that " citizens of the United States who may commit any crime in China shall be subject to be tried and punished only by the consul, or other public functionary of the United States, thereto authorized, according to the laws of the United States; " and (Art. XXV.) that " all questions in regard to rights, whether of property or person, arising between citizens of the United States in China, shall be subject to the jurisdiction of and regulated by the authorities of their own Government."

Mr. Cushing, the negotiator of the treaty, afterwards advised, as Attorney-General, that, under the articles just quoted, citizens of the United States in China enjoyed complete rights of extraterritoriality, and were answerable to no authortiy but that of the United States.[a] Attorney-General Black, prior to the act of June 22, 1860, advised that the judicial authority of the commissioner was restricted to the five ports mentioned in the treaty of 1844.[b]

---

[a] Cushing, At. Gen., 1855, 7 Op. 495.

[b] Black, At. Gen., 1859, 9. Op. 294.

Before the passage of the act of 1848, the minister of the United States was instructed, in cases of aggravated crimes by citizens of the United States, to send the accused to the United States for trial.[a]

In a civil controversy between a Chinese and an American, the authorities of the two Governments are to have concerted action. Controversies occurring in China between citizens of the United States and subjects of any other (Christian) government, are to be regulated by the treaties existing between the United States and such governments, respectively.

> Cushing, At. Gen., Sept. 19, 1855, 7 Op. 495.

Although not required by the treaty with China, the United States, in 1877, gave a general expression of approval to " the recommendation of the presence of consular officers of their own nationality in the criminal trial of Chinese where the sufferer is a foreigner, and of allowing a Chinese officer to be present at the trial of foreigners where a Chinese is the sufferer."

> Mr. Fish, Sec. of State, to Mr. Seward, min. to China, Feb. 14, 1877, MS. Inst. China, II. 463.

" I have received your Nos. 9 and 15, of October 8 and 16, 1885, relative to the suit of Lo Chin Lu for damages alleged to have been sustained by the sinking of his charcoal boat which collided with a United States vessel the *Annie.*

" So far as concerns the conflicting interpretation of the treaty of 1858, on the subject of the deposit of court fees, as set forth by yourself, the Department concurs with the conclusions reached in your despatch of October 16th last.

"As regards the conflict between the treaty of 1858 and that of 1880, there can be no question that the latter, being more recent, is to prevail. If there be a question between either treaty and subsequent Chinese legislation, the Department's opinion is that, internationally, such legislation cannot affect treaty obligations. I therefore affirm your suggestion that ' in cases in which an American is sued by a Chinese subject, the United States consul shall invite the proper official of the plaintiff's nationality to sit with him at the hearing to watch the proceedings, to present and examine and cross-examine witnesses, and to protest, if he pleases, in detail.' "

> Mr. Bayard, Sec. of State, to Mr. Denby, min. to China, Dec. 12, 1885, MS. Inst. China, IV. 101.

" The prohibition of Art. II. of the treaty of 1880 not only covers the importation, transportation, purchase, or sale of opium by Amer-

---

[a] Mr. Buchanan, Sec. of State, to Mr. A. H. Everett, min. to China, April 15, 1845, MS. Inst. China, I. 27.

ican citizens in China, but extends also to vessels owned by such citizens, whether employed by themselves or by others in the opium trade. . . .   The enforcement of the prohibition, as to American citizens in China, is expressly dependent upon ' appropriate legislation ' on the part of the United States.   It is only such legislation that consuls of the United States in China can enforce judicially. In the absence of such legislation, it is, to say the least, doubtful whether a consul could lawfully interfere to prevent an American citizen from doing an act not in itself contrary to international law or the domestic law of China.   If, however, the contemplated employment of the American-owned premises by a British subject be opposed by China, and the lease sought to be prevented by the authorities of the latter, the consul would be justified in withholding his approval from the sub-lease."

> Mr. Bayard, Sec. of State, to Mr. Denby, min. to China, May 14, 1886, MS.
> Inst. China, IV. 155.
> See, also, same to same, June 7, 1888, For. Rel. 1888, I. 310.

(3) REGULATIONS.

§ 272.

The commissioner to China, having been empowered by the act of 1848 to make, with the advice of the consuls, " regulations " for the carrying into effect of the extraterritorial clauses of the treaty of 1844, action was taken as follows: See messages of the President, Feb. 25, and July 15, 1856, transmitting regulations promulgated by Mr. McLane, S. Ex. Docs. 32 and 92, 34 Cong. 1 sess.; message of Dec. 12, 1856, with regulations by Mr. Parker, S. Ex. Doc. 6 and H. Ex. Doc. 11, 34 Cong. 3 sess.; message of Dec. 10, 1857, with further regulations by Mr. Parker, H. Ex. Doc. 9, 35 Cong. 1 sess.; [a] message of Dec. 27, 1858, with regulations by Mr. Reed, S. Ex. Doc. 11 and H. Ex. Doc. 21, 35 Cong. 2 sess.; dispatch of Mr. Burlingame of Nov. 9, 1864, with further regulations, and Mr. Seward's reply, Dip. Cor. 1865, II. 413, 437; land regulations at Shanghai, 1866, Dip. Cor. 1867, I. 429, and S. Mis. Doc. 89, 47 Cong. 1 sess. 179.

For regulations in force in China in 1882, see S. Mis. Doc. 89, 47 Cong. 1 sess. 69.

For regulations agreed on in 1868 for the joint investigation of customs cases, see S. Ex. Doc. 19, 40 Cong. 3 sess., and Dip. Cor. 1868, I. 527.

---

[a] The Senate passed a resolution to the effect that these regulations needed no revision.   (Cong. Globe, 35 Cong. 1 sess. 1203, 1555.)

(4) SHANGHAI MUNICIPAL ORDINANCES.

§ 273.

" I have received your No. 240 of the 12th of November last, touching the proposed revision of the municipal regulations and by-laws of Shanghai, and offering certain pertinent points for the consideration of the Department.

" It appears that by the municipal charter of Shanghai every foreigner owning land of the value of at least 500 taels, or occupying a house of an assessed rental value of not less than 250 taels, is a member of what is called the ' municipal body,' and is entitled to vote at all municipal elections. The ' municipal body ' elect at stated times a municipal council, consisting of not more than nine members, who have the power to make regulations for the government of the municipality, subject to the approval of the consuls and foreign ministers, or a majority of them, and of the rate payers at a special meeting.

": In the proposed revision it is insisted by the municipality, in respect to any by-law that may hereafter be passed, that ' any such additional or substituted by-law, or alteration or repeal of a by-law, shall be binding when approved by the treaty consuls and the intendant of circuit, or by a majority of them; but the representatives of the treaty powers may, at any time within six months of the date of such approval, annul any such additional or substituted by-law, or alteration or repeal of a by-law.'

" Your opinion as to this proposed ordinance is in entire accord with that of the Department, that it would reverse the proper order of things and be highly inexpedient to put in force, without the approval of the foreign ministers, a by-law which they might, in the exercise of an acknowledged power, subsequently disapprove and disallow. This would be in fact the substitution of a power of annulment for the power of veto which the foreign ministers now possess, and would diminish the extraterritorial immunities which citizens of the United States in Shanghai at present enjoy.

" The question which you suggest as to the authority of the consul-general at Shanghai to enforce the ordinances of the municipality against citizens of the United States is not without difficulty. Under section 4086 of the Revised Statutes of the United States, consuls of the United States in China are empowered to exercise criminal and civil jurisdiction in conformity with the laws of the United States. It is provided, however, that when those laws are not adapted to the object, or are deficient in the provisions necessary to furnish suitable remedies, the common law and the law of equity and admiralty shall be extended to the persons within the consul's jurisdiction; and if neither the common law [nor the law] of equity or admiralty, nor the

statutes of the United States, furnish appropriate remedies the ministers in the countries, respectively, to which the statute applies shall,
by decrees and regulations which shall have the force of law, supply
such defects and deficiencies.

"The last clause, in respect to decrees and regulations, has been construed by the Department to confer upon the ministers in question the
power to regulate the course of procedure and the forms of judicial
remedies rather than any general legislative power for the definition
of offenses and the imposition of penalties for their commission. It
is true that opinion has been divided on this point. Mr. Attorney-
General Cushing held that the power given to the commissioner of
the United States in China to make 'decrees and regulations' which
should have the force of law gave him the power to legislate in certain
respects for citizens of the United States in China, and 'to provide
for many cases of criminality which neither Federal statutes nor the
common law would cover.' (7 Op. 504, 505.) The disposition, however, of this Department has been to restrict the legislative power of
the minister to the regulation of the forms and course of judicial procedure, it not being regarded as desirable or proper to authorize the
exercise of so great a power, while it was so much in doubt, as that
of criminal legislation.

"But the ordinances of the municipality of Shanghai, although dependent for their operation as to citizens of the United States upon
the approval of the minister of this Government in China, are conceived to present in one aspect a different question from that of the
power of the minister of the United States as to criminal legislation.
The municipality of Shanghai is understood to have been organized
by the voluntary action of the foreign residents [of certain nationali-
ties], or such of [those residents] as were owners or renters of land,
for the purpose of exercising such local powers for the preservation
of the order and morals of the community as are usually enjoyed by
municipal bodies. In the United States, where government is reduced
to a legal system, these powers of local police rest on charters granted
by the supreme legislative authority of the State; but it is not difficult to conceive of a case in which a community outside of any general
system of law might organize a government and adopt rules and regulations which would be recognized as valid on the ground of the right
of self-preservation, which is inherent in people everywhere.

"In this light may be regarded the municipal ordinances of Shanghai. The foreign settlement not being subject to the laws of China,
and the legal systems of the respective foreign powers represented
there being not only dissimilar *inter se*, but insufficient to meet the
local needs, it became necessary for the local residents interested in the
preservation of peace and order to supply the deficiency.

" American citizens residing in Shanghai enjoy, in common with other persons composing the foreign settlement, all the rights, privileges, and protection which the municipal government affords; and as they go there voluntarily, and presumptively for the advancement of their personal interests, they may reasonably be held to observe such police regulations as are not inconsistent with their rights under the laws of the United States. It is true that this reasoning is not conclusive as to the strict legal authority of the consul-general of the United States to enforce such regulations; but, taken in connection with the fact that at present American citizens in Shanghai are not subject to any judicial control except that of the consul-general of the United States, it affords a basis upon which his enforcement of the municipal regulations may be justified.

" It is important to observe that the jurisdiction of consuls of the United States in China is very extensive, including not only the administration of the laws of the United States, and the law of equity and admiralty, but also of the common law. The consular courts have, therefore, what the courts of the United States generally have not—common-law jurisdiction in criminal cases. It is true that this jurisdiction is difficult, indeed incapable, of exact definition, but it implies the power to enforce rules which are not to be found on the statute book of the United States, and which can be ascertained only by the application of the general principles of the common law to special cases and conditions. In respect to matters of local police, a fair measure and definition of the law may be found in the regulations adopted by the municipality in aid of and supplementary to the general juridical systems of the foreign powers. Such a process, while maintaining the peace and order of the community, tends to consolidate the local administration of law.

" The Department is, however, of opinion that all difficulties would be removed if the treaty powers would adhere to the plan suggested in your dispatch of organizing a municipal court to administer the regulations of the municipal body. This course would be advantageous, both to the municipality and to the treaty powers. It would relieve the consular representatives of the latter from the performance of an embarrassing duty, and would secure a uniform and equal administration of the municipal laws."

Mr. Bayard, Sec. of State, to Mr. Denby, min. to China, Mar. 7, 1887, MS. Inst. China, IV. 244.

See, also, Mr. Bayard, Sec. of State, to Mr. Denby, min. to China, Sept. 22, 1887, MS. Inst. China, IV. 307; Mr. Rives, Act. Sec. of State, to Mr. Denby, min. to China, Nov. 12, 1888, MS. Inst. China, IV. 407.

§ 274.

By Article II. of the treaty between the United States and China of October 5, 1880, the contracting parties agreed to restrain their citizens and subjects from engaging in the opium trade, and to adopt appropriate legislation to that end. By section 3 of the act of February 23, 1887, passed by Congress to carry this article into effect, provision was made for the forfeiture by the consular courts of the United States, for the benefit of the Emperor of China, of opium dealt in by citizens of the United States in China contrary to the provisions of the section which forbade such citizens to import opium into any of the open ports of China, or to transport it from one open port to another, or to buy or sell it in any such port. The Chinese minister at Washington protested against the provision as to forfeiture on the ground that it constituted " an interference with the regulations of the customs and the right of local self-government of China."

The Government of the United States, recognizing the principle on which the protest was based, held that the act of February 23, 1887, should be so construed as not to violate the distinction which had been established between the punishment of offenses and the administration of the customs. The distinction, said the Department of State, between mere confiscation cases under the revenue laws and penal charges against individuals was fully recognized in the rules of 1868, Diplomatic Correspondence, 1868, I. 527, which provided (rule 6) that, when the act of which a merchant at any port was accused was not one involving the confiscation of ship or cargo, but was one which by treaty or regulation was punishable by fine, the commissioner of customs should report the case to the superintendent of customs and at the same time cause a complaint to be entered in the consular court. The consul was then to fix a day for trial, at which the commissioner was to appear either personally or by deputy and conduct the case for the prosecution. When the treaty or regulations affixed a specific fine for the offense the consul was, on conviction, to give judgment for that amount, the power of mitigating the sentence resting with the superintendent and the commissioner. If the defendant was acquitted and the commissioner did not demur to the decision, the ships or goods, if any were under seizure, were at once to be released, and the circumstances of the case to be communicated to the superintendent. " So far as the act of February 23 relates to the forfeiture of opium, it may," said the Department of State, " be regarded as contemplating a course of procedure not inconsistent with that provided for in the above rule. The right of the Chinese Government to seize and confiscate contraband goods remains unquestioned and unimpaired. When, however, a citizen of the United States is arrested for importing or dealing in opium contrary to the law, he is to be tried for the offense in the proper consular court, and, if convicted, the confiscation of the opium, if any, found in his possession, and illegally imported or dealt in, to the use of the Emperor of China, would be an incident of his sentence; and the confiscated property would accordingly be delivered to the Chinese authorities. But if the defendant should be acquitted, this would not necessarily imply a release of the opium, which might be subject to confiscation, notwithstanding that the person charged with importing, or transporting, or buying or selling it may have been found guiltless of that charge; and in such case, the goods would be dealt with in accordance with the rules in force and heretofore observed by the two Governments in respect to forfeiture of goods for violation of the Chinese customs laws."

> Mr. Bayard, Sec. of State, to Mr. Denby, min. to China, June 25, 1887, For. Rel. 1887, 225–226; same to same, July 1, 1887, id. 231. For the act of Feb. 23, 1887, and the correspondence with the Chinese minister at Washington, see For. Rel. 1887, 237–243.
>
> See, also, Mr. Bayard, Sec. of State, to Mr. Denby, min. to China, June 7, 1888, For. Rel. 1888, I. 310.
>
> As to the British trade with China in opium, see For. Rel. 1887, 182.
>
> For an additional article, concluded at London, July 18, 1885, to the agreement between Great Britain and China, signed at Chefoo, Sept. 13, 1876, relating to the tax on opium in China, see For. Rel 1887, 187.

(6) MIXED COURT AT SHANGHAI.

§ 275.

At Shanghai, according to the custom in time of peace, foreigners who are subjects of a power having no treaty with China, and who therefore do not enjoy the privileges of extraterritoriality, are, when arrested for crime, tried by the "mixed court," that is, by a Chinese magistrate sitting with a foreign "assessor." On the French concession this assessor is always a French consular officer. On the Anglo-American settlement an English assessor sits with the Chinese official on Mondays, Wednesdays, and Fridays; an American assessor on Tuesdays and Thursdays, and a German assessor on Saturdays. Before this tribunal are also brought all Chinese charged with crimes or misdemeanors in the settlement, and sentence is rendered by the Chinese and foreign officials acting together. Precedents on which to found a practice in time of war seem to be lacking; but it appears that during the Franco-Chinese war, when Russia used her good offices for the protection of the French in China, French subjects arrested at Shanghai were actually brought before the Russian consul for hearing.   It is stated that China made no effort to interfere with them.

> Mr. Denby, jr., chargé d'affaires at Peking, to Mr. Gresham, Sec. of State, Sept. 1, 1894, For. Rel. 1894, 108, 109.
>
> When, in 1868, the rules were promulgated by the Chinese Government for the establishment of the mixed court at Shanghai, Mr. Seward said: " That we might not, at some time, have a consul at Shanghai, is not regarded as a contingency probable or a reason satisfactory enough for derogating from the privilege of extraterritoriality secured to us by the treaty.   The third section of the act of Congress of the 22nd of June, 1860, provides for such cases by giving jurisdiction to the consul at the port where or nearest to which the cause of action might arise.
>
> " It is consequently deemed advisable that you should inform the Chinese minister for foreign affairs that this Government can not consent to the trial of a complaint, civil or criminal, otherwise than in the consular courts of the United States.   In cases, however, where a Chinese subject may be plaintiff, we have no objection to the presence of an officer of that Government as an assessor, but the decision must be made by the consul alone, as in the case where the American assessors unite with him in the trial."   (Mr. Seward, Sec. of State, to Mr. Browne, Feb. 18, 1869, MS. Inst. China, II. 50.)

In the practice of the " mixed court " at Shanghai, where foreign assessors sit with native magistrates, extreme severity of punishment, though it should be discountenanced, " may, unhappily, form part of the regular administration of justice in punishment of crime according to the Chinese laws;" but, with respect to the use of torture to extract testimony, " the case is vastly different.   Such methods should not be recognized or sanctioned by any civilized power; and, if they are practiced, no proper means should be spared to check the abuse, through the influence of the foreign assessors, who can not be expected to lend themselves knowingly to the procedure."

> Mr. Hay, Act. Sec. of State, to Mr. Angell, min. to China, Aug. 16, 1880, For. Rel. 1880, 292.
>
> Dr. Wharton, in a note to the foregoing instruction, said: " The question here involved is one of great difficulty.   In England and in the United States a witness who refuses to testify is imprisoned until this refusal is withdrawn, but in China our consular courts have no means of enforcing an order of indefinite imprisonment, and to hand the contumacious witness over to a Chinese prison would be to hand him over to torture, of which Chinese prison discipline largely consists.   Yet, without the power of compelling the giving of testimony, no court of justice can be efficiently conducted.   It must be conceded that a consul can not direct a witness to be tortured, either by his own direct order or through the agency of Chinese officials.   Yet, if he does not exercise such power, whether a witness shall testify at all, or what limit is to be imposed on his testimony, will have to be determined by himself."   (Int. Law Dig. I. § 125, p. 810.)

7. JAPAN.

(1) POLICE POWERS.

§ 276.

" I am not prepared, without further reflection, to assume the broad ground that the Government of Japan is bound to allow our citizens to conduct at the open ports any business which is lawful by the laws of the United States, or even any and every business which may be lawful by the laws of all other civilized nations. A country having what we regard as an imperfect civilization may, for that very reason, find it necessary to establish and maintain police regulations in the interest of internal order touching with more or less severity upon trade of various kinds which this country and the western powers generally deem it safe to leave untrammeled."

> Mr. Fish, Sec. of State, to Mr. De Long, min. to Japan, May 11, 1871, MS. Inst. Japan, I. 424.
> As to distinctive features of the political system of Japan, see Mr. Fish, Sec. of State, to Mr. De Long, May 20, 1871, MS. Inst. Japan, I. 433.

" Foreigners in Japan, as in any other country, are subject to its jurisdiction, except so far as it is limited by express or tacit convention. All that has been sought by the Christian powers is to withdraw their subjects from the operation of such laws as conflict with our ideas of civilization and humanity, and to keep the power of trying and punishing in the hands of their own representatives. It is proper, therefore, for the latter, when they find a Japanese regulation, not found, in our case, in the statutes or the common law, to acquaint their countrymen with the fact of such recognition, and that it will be enforced according to our methods and in our tribunals. This, combining the sanction of the two Governments, avoids, on the one hand, the assertion of the absolute immunity of our citizens from any Japanese regulation, however reasonable and necessary, and, on the other hand, of an unqualified legislative power in our diplomatic and consular representatives—a position which it seems judicious to maintain until Congress shall act on the subject."

> Mr. Fish, Sec. of State, to Mr. De Long, min. to Japan, May 21, 1871, MS. Inst. Japan, I. 443.

" It seems to me within the legitimate police powers of the Government of Japan to prohibit their subjects from assembling to bet upon the prices of staple commodities which the sham seller does not intend to deliver nor the buyer to take into possession. The circumstance that an American citizen presides over the mock auction or furnishes the building where it takes place does not impair that power."

> Mr. Hunter, Acting Sec. of State, to Mr. De Long, min. to Japan, July 1, 1871, MS. Inst. Japan, I. 453.

" Your action reported in your No. 1206 of November 15th last, in answer to an inquiry of the Japanese Government, in view of certain unjustifiable strictures of a portion of the press on that Government, that it had, in your opinion, clearly a right to apply its press laws and to punish all infractions thereof, whether by foreigners or Japanese, is hereby approved."

> Mr. Evarts, Sec. of State, to Mr. Bingham, min. to Japan, Jan. 3, 1881, MS. Inst. Japan, III. 22.

(2) MUNICIPAL OFFICE AT YOKOHAMA.

§ 277.

By an arrangement between the foreign representatives and the Japanese Government in 1867, an office, to be called the municipal office, was formed under the Japanese Government at Yokohama, and placed in charge of a foreign director, who was to be " subordinate to the governor of Kanagawa," under whose authority he was to see to the repair, cleanliness, and efficiency of all the streets and drains in the foreign settlement of Yokohama, and, in the name of the governor of Kanagawa, to prosecute foreigners before their own authorities for nuisances or any infringement of police order. Land rents payable by foreigners were also to be collected by the director on account of the governor of Kanagawa. The foreign consuls agreed to limit the number of licenses issued by them to their respective citizens or subjects for the sale of liquors or the keeping of houses of entertainment in the foreign settlement or within the port of Kanagawa. The Japanese Government agreed to make arrangements for the safe storage at reasonable rates of explosives imported into Kanagawa, and it was stipulated that the necessary steps should be taken to prevent foreigners from using any other places for the storage of such substances. The United States legation observed that in this arrangement "the principle of exterritoriality has been carefully preserved, and that the citizens of the United States are in all cases of offense amenable only to the jurisdiction of our own authorities."

> Mr. Van Valkenburgh, chargé, to Mr. Seward, Sec. of State, Nov. 16, 1867, Dip. Cor. 1867, II. 73.
>
> This arrangement was discussed in the correspondence between Japan and Peru in 1873 in the case of the *Maria Luz*. The Peruvian minister at Tokio cited it as an instance in which foreigners who were not citizens or subjects of treaty powers secured in Japan some measure of exemption from the local law. The Japanese Government denied that the arrangement had such an effect. (For. Rel. 1873, I. 613.)
>
> As to game laws in Japan, see For. Rel. 1871, 586; For. Rel. 1874, 637, 645, 653; For. Rel. 1875, II. 773, 779; For. Rel. 1876, 366.

As to harbor regulations at Yokohama, see For. Rel. 1878, 486.

Concerning land regulations at Nagasaki, see For. Rel. 1875, II. 798, 802.

As to regulations concerning the sale of opium to foreigners, see For. Rel. 1879, 609.

For regulations for the licensing of pilots and their approval by the United States legation, see For. Rel. 1879, 617.

For correspondence concerning quarantine regulations in Japan and their enforcement, see For. Rel. 1879, 657, 665, 670; For. Rel. 1880, 679.

(3) MUNICIPAL ORDINANCES AT NAGASAKI.

§ 278.

A municipal council was formed at Nagasaki, Japan, composed of foreign consuls and prominent foreigners of different nationalities residing in the "foreign quarter." The council owed its existence to the voluntary action of the "land renters" among the foreign population, and regulations or ordinances were made by the council for general police purposes, including the licensing of public houses and places of entertainment. The question was raised by the United States legation in Japan whether actions could be maintained in the United States consuls' courts against American citizens for penalties for nonobservance of these municipal ordinances. Mr. Fish, who was then Secretary of State, while affirming the position he had always taken as to the limitations upon the power of the minister to make regulations (a power not belonging under the statutes to consuls), said that he conceived the question of the municipal ordinances to be different. He likened the ordinances in question to those made by municipal corporations in the United States for the preservation of the peace, morals, and good order of the community. It was true, he observed, that in the United States the municipal authorities acted under charters granted by the supreme legislative power of the State; but instances, he said, were not wanting "in which similar powers have been exercised by inchoate communities suddenly formed within the jurisdiction of the United States, and who, for the time being, finding themselves situated outside of any organized State or Territory, have been led by the dictates of prudence and necessity to form themselves into a voluntary political organization, frame codes of laws for the preservation of order and good government and the protection of the lives and property of the individuals composing such communities, and to establish tribunals for the administration and enforcement of such laws;" and the laws so enacted and administered had, so far as was known, been sanctioned by the Executive and the courts. Whether the ordinances in question were made by the foreign residents in the exercise of a power conferred upon them by the Japanese Government in the concession, or whether, in the absence of such a direct grant, they were tacitly sanctioned by that Government, it would, said Mr. Fish, seem to follow that they should be accepted as " the municipal law of the community," and as such their observance might be enforced by proceedings in the consular courts. American citizens, in common with the other foreign residents, enjoyed, said Mr. Fish, all the rights and privileges of such residents, and shared in the common protection afforded to persons and property resulting from ordinances of the character of those in question, and while they received the benefits of a regulated police they should not be free from charges for its support or from its control.   In conclusion, however, it was observed that, in view of the imperfect information of the Department as to the source and origin of the powers claimed by the municipal council, it was not intended to give definite and final instructions till further information should be obtained.

> Mr. Fish, Sec. of State, to Mr. Bingham, min. to Japan, Jan. 20, 1876,
>   For Rel. 1876, 350 ; S. Mis. Doc. 89, 47 Cong. 1 sess. 197.
> For the municipal regulations in the foreign quarter of Shanghai, China,
>   see S. Mis. Doc. 89, 47 Cong. 1 sess. 188–197.

(4) EXPULSION OF CONVICTS.

§ 279.

" I have to acknowledge the receipt of your dispatch of the 21st of June last, No. 58.

" The seventh article of the treaty with Japan, of 1858 (12 Stat. 1057), provides that certain persons convicted of felony, or twice convicted of misdemeanor, shall lose their right of permanent residence in Japan, and the Japanese authorities may require them to leave the country.   Our consular authorities are to determine a reasonable time for the convict to settle his affairs, not exceeding one year. When that time shall expire, the convict becomes an outlaw, not entitled to any of the benefits of our treaties with Japan.   Such a state of circumstances, however, if known, will be apt to induce the convict to avoid the position in which the treaty between the two countries will have placed him.   If he persists in remaining, the Government can not protect him against the consequences of his own determination.

" Consular courts have arrogated to themselves the power of *banishing* American convicts to the United States, and, as in the instance reported by you, to China.   This is a form of punishment not known to our law, and if it has been overlooked, it has not been approved by this Department.

" The principles upon which we resist the deportation of foreign criminals to the United States, and which may well estop us from sending American criminals to China, do not appear to afford any reason why we should not bring home, for punishment, our citizens who have been guilty of crime upon the high seas, or in countries where we reserve the jurisdiction for trial and punishment to our own tribunals."

> Mr. Fish, Sec. of State, to Mr. De Long, min. to Japan, Sept. 10, 1870, MS. Inst. Japan, I. 354.
>
> "American consuls can in no case refuse jurisdiction over American citizens." (For. Rel. 1894, 377, citing For. Rel. 1879, 698.)
>
> " The Department has consequently disapproved sentences of deportation whenever they have been pronounced by consuls of this Government as being a mode of punishment not recognized in this country." (Mr. Payson, Third Assist. Sec. of State, to Mr. Van Buren, Nov. 23, 1878, For. Rel. 1879, 697.) It appears, however, that the Department of State, in an instruction of April 16, 1873, approved the sentence of the consular court that John Rogers should " be imprisoned at hard labor for the term of one year and that he forfeit his right of residence in Japan." (For. Rel. 1894, 378.)
>
> Where a person expelled by Japan under Art. VII. supra, returned to that country without permission, he remained subject to the consular jurisdiction, both civil and criminal. Japan might again exercise her right under the treaty to expel him, but so long as she refrained from doing so the treaty provisions as to consular jurisdiction applied no less to him than to other American citizens. (Mr. Uhl, Act. Sec. of State, to Mr. Abercrombie, June 22, 1894, For. Rel. 1894, 390.)
>
> " The expulsion [under Art. VII., supra] can neither be decreed nor executed by our consul. . . . I infer from your dispatch that Lake has been arrested and is now confined under your order for refusing to leave the country. . . . Lake's expulsion must be effected by the Japanese authorities and they can not call upon you to assist in accomplishing it. You should therefore release him and abstain from all participation or interference in the proceedings which those authorities may take for his expulsion, except to see that he is not subjected by them to harsh treatment further than may be necessary to compel him to depart." (Mr. Strobel, Third Assist. Sec. of State, to Mr. Abercrombie, consul at Nagasaki, Feb. 16, 1894, 144 MS. Inst. Consuls, 388.)

(5) WAREHOUSE REGULATIONS.

§ 280.

In the summer of 1898 Mr. Edward Lake, a citizen of the United States, complained of the action of the Japanese customs officials at Nagasaki in refusing him the privilege of transshipping 300 sacks of American flour to his vessel, called the *Adventure*. He had sought the privilege under an export entry in which he stated that the destination of the *Adventure* was " uncertain." He subsequently made

another entry in which, in place of the word " uncertain," he inserted
the word " Chefoo and ports." It appeared that the vessel had been
lying at Nagasaki for some years and was used as a storeship under
the cover of export clearances. The Japanese authorities at length
declined to repeat the privilege unless the vessel should actually clear,
maintaining that otherwise the customs regulations would be evaded
and that the Government would be deprived of warehouse charges.
The minister of the United States at Tokio held that the case was not
one for diplomatic interference, unless an intention should be shown
to cause the vessel to sail within a reasonable time and a clearance
should be applied for for that purpose. The Department of State
approved this decision, saying: " The enactment of suitable warehouse regulations by Japan is obviously a right enjoyed in common
with all commercial nations, and its refusal to sanction a proceeding
in clear evasion of such regulations, inasmuch as Lake & Company's
evasion appears to have been to transship to a vessel lying in port
goods with the intention not of clearing or shipping, but of making
use of her as a storeship, does not call for any protest on the part of
this Government."

> Mr. Hay, Sec. of State, to Mr. Buck, min. to Japan, Oct. 8, 1898, For. Rel.
> 1898, 432.

(6) ABOLITION OF EXTRATERRITORIALITY.

§ 281.

By article 24 of the treaty of commerce and navigation between
France and Japan, signed at Paris, August 4, 1896, it was provided
that the treaty should not take effect in less than three years after
its signature. Consequently, the treaty could not become operative
before August 4, 1899, which was eighteen days after the date (July
17) fixed for the going into effect of the American and other
revised treaties. In this way it appeared that French citizens would,
from July 17 to August 4, enjoy by virtue of the most-favored-nation
clause all the rights of other foreigners under the new treaties in
matters of commerce and navigation, and besides extraterritoriality
and freedom from taxation under the old treaties. As article 18
of the treaty between the United States and Japan, of November 22,
1894, provided that on July 17, 1899, consular jurisdiction should
" absolutely and without notice cease and determine," and as articles
2 and 14 of the same treaty guaranteeing most-favored-nation treatment related only to matters of commerce and navigation, the United
States held that a claim for continuance of American consular jurisdiction up to August 4 could not be maintained, but that American
citizens were entitled to all privileges of trade and navigation that
would be enjoyed by French citizens from July 17 to August 4.

Mr. Hay, Sec. of State, to Mr. Herod, chargé d'affaires, April 25, 1899,
For. Rel. 1899, 468.

It appears that the Austro-Hungarian like the French treaty did not go
into operation till August 4, while all the others took effect on
July 17. (Mr. Buck, min. to Japan, to Mr. Hay, Sec. of State,
June 17, 1899, For. Rel. 1899, 468.)

For rescripts and instructions issued by the Emperor of Japan and the
ministers of state respecting the operation of the new treaties,
together with the comments of the vernacular press on the same
subject, see Mr. Buck, min. to Japan, to Mr. Hay, Sec. of State,
July 7, 1899, For. Rel. 1899, 469–476.

For a notification issued by the U. S. legation to American citizens
in Japan on the going into effect of the new treaties, see Mr. Buck,
min. to Japan, to Mr. Hay, Sec. of State, July 11, 1899, For. Rel.
1899, 476.

" The closing year has witnessed a decided strengthening of Japan's
relations to other states. The development of her independent
judicial and administrative functions under the treaties which
took effect July 17, 1899, has proceeded without international fric-
tion, showing the competence of the Japanese to hold a foremost
place among modern peoples." (President McKinley, annual message, Dec. 3, 1900.)

American vessels (of the Pacific Mail S. S. Co.) " are amenable to Japanese law to the same extent that a Japanese merchant vessel
would be amenable to American law in American waters." (Mr.
Cridler, Third Assist. Sec. of State, to Mr. Gowey, Sept. 5, 1899,
169 MS. Inst. Consuls, 185.)

" The treaty of commerce and navigation between the United States
and Japan on November 22, 1894, took effect in accordance with the
terms of its XIXth Article on the 17th of July last, simultaneously
with the enforcement of like treaties with the other powers, except
France, whose convention did not go into operation until August 4th,
the United States being, however, granted up to that date all the privileges and rights accorded to French citizens under the old French
treaty. By this notable conventional reform Japan's position as a
fully independent sovereign power is assured, control being gained of
taxation, customs revenues, judicial administration, coasting trade,
and all other domestic functions of government, and foreign extraterritorial rights being renounced.

" Comprehensive codes of civil and criminal procedure according to
western methods, public instruction, patents and copyrights, municipal administration, including jurisdiction over the former foreign
settlements, customs tariffs and procedure, public health, and other
administrative measures have been proclaimed. The working of the
new system has given rise to no material complaints on the part of the
American citizens or interests, a circumstance which attests the ripe
consideration with which the change has been prepared."

President McKinley, annual message, Dec. 5, 1899.

See, also, President Cleveland, annual messages of 1894 and 1895.

Concerning consular jurisdiction as it formerly existed in Japan, see a
pamphlet entitled "Extraterritoriality," by Eli T. Sheppard, LL.B.,
formerly of the United States consular service in that country.

Mr. Gresham, Secretary of State, in a letter to Mr. Chambers, Dec. 18,
1894, 200 MS. Dom. Let. 9, enclosed, unsealed, for transmission to Mr.
C. P. Huntington, "a letter this day addressed to him in reply to his
of the 12th instant, . . . in regard to the claim of the Japanese Government to assert jurisdiction over foreign seamen for offences committed within the Empire." The letter to Mr. Huntington does not
appear to have been recorded. Referring to the case of two persons
claiming to be American citizens, who, on reports that they were on
their way to China to render important aid to that Government in
its war with Japan, were arrested and forcibly removed from the
French steamer *Sydney* by the Japanese naval authorities at Kobe,
Mr. Gresham said: "Your No. 193 reports that these men were
released on parole on November 12th not to engage in warlike service
against Japan, nor to go to China during the present war, and that
each was presented with yen 500 to pay their expenses to the United
States. The generous treatment of these men by the Japanese Government is regarded as a striking proof of magnanimity no less than
of implied friendliness to the country of which they claimed citizenship." (Mr. Gresham, Sec. of State, to Mr. Dun, min. to Japan, Dec.
20, 1894, MS. Inst. Japan, IV. 231.)

8. MOROCCO AND OTHER BARBARY POWERS.

§ 282.

" By treaties with those countries, consuls have judicial powers in
civil or criminal cases, or both, in . . . Morocco, . . . Tripoli, Tunis."

U. S. Consular Regulations, § 93, p. 36. See, however, as to Tunis, supra,
§ 267, and infra, § 786.

" The provisions of Title XLVII. of the Revised Statutes extend
also to Tripoli, Tunis, Morocco, . . . so far as the same can be exercised under the provisions of the treaties with those countries and in
accordance with the usages of the countries in their intercourse with
the Franks or other Christian nations.—R. S., sec. 4127."

U. S. Consular Regulations, § 615, p. 263.

" In Tunis, Morocco, and Tripoli, citizens of the United States com-
miting murder or homicide upon a subject of those powers are to be
tried by a mixed court, at which the consul is to ' assist.' "

Mr. Bancroft Davis, Notes, Treaty Vol. (1776–1887), 1283.
See Mr. Clayton, Sec. of State, to Mr. McCauley, Sept. 27, 1849, MS. Inst.
Barbary Powers, XIX. 109; Mr. Webster, Sec. of State, to Mr.
Payne, March 20, 1851, MS. Inst. Barbary Powers, XIX. 129.
See, also, Cushing, At.-Gen., Oct. 23, 1855, 7 Op. 565.
As to Morocco, see, particularly, Mr. Seward, Sec. of State, to Mr. McMath,
consul at Tangier, April 28, 1862, Dip. Cor. 1862. 873.

Dec. 19, 1882, the House of Representatives, at the instance of Mr. Frelinghuysen, then Secretary of State, passed a joint resolution to
authorize the President, in case a system for the administration of
justice should be established in Tunis by the French Government,
under which adequate protection would be furnished to citizens of the
United States, to issue a proclamation declaring that the extraterritorial jurisdiction of the United States in that country had terminated. (For. Rel. 1883, 483.) This resolution was afterwards, on
at least one occasion, referred to as the " joint resolution of Congress,
December 19, 1882." (Mr. Uhl, Assist. Sec. of State, to Mr. Chapelie,
vice-consul at Tunis, Nov. 21, 1894, 147 MS. Inst. Consuls, 21.) It
does not appear, however, to have been acted upon by the Senate,
though, after passing the House, it was sent to that body. The
United States vice-consul at Tunis was instructed to report on the
situation there in 1896. (Mr. Rockhill, Assist. Sec. of State, to Mr.
Chapelie, Oct. 10, 1896, 154 MS. Inst. Consuls, 140.)

9. TURKEY.

(1) ORIGIN AND EXTENT OF EXTRATERRITORIALITY.

§ 283.

" The undisputed portion of the fourth article of the treaty of 1830
with the Ottoman Porte provides for the supervision of the American
dragoman in the hearing of all litigations and disputes arising
between the subjects of the Sublime Porte and citizens of the United
States.

" It is not in dispute that the usages observed towards other Franks
are to be observed toward citizens of the United States. These
usages are believed to be the following:

" 1. Turkish tribunals for questions between subjects of the Porte
and foreign Christians.

" 2. Consular courts for the business of each nation of foreign
Christians.

" 3. Trial of questions between foreign Christians of different
nations in the consular court of the defendant's nation.

" 4. Mixed tribunals of Turkish magistrates and foreign Christians at length substituted in part for cases between Turks and foreign
Christians.

" 5. Finally, for causes between foreign Christians, the substitution at length of mixed tribunals in place of the separate courts; this
arrangement introduced at first by the legations of Austria, Great
Britain, France, and Russia, and then tacitly acceded to by the legations of other foreign Christians."

Mr. J. C. B. Davis, Treaty Notes, U. S. Treaty Volume (1776–1887), 1280–
1283; Instructions to the Dip. Officers of the United States (1897),
84–85.

This statement is founded on the opinion of Cushing, At. Gen., Oct. 23, 1855, 7 Op. 565.

Attorney-General Black, in 1859, advised that, under the treaty of 1830 with Turkey and the act of Congress of Aug. 11, 1848, United States consuls in Turkey had judicial powers only in criminal cases. (9 Op. 296.)

See, however, Art. I. of the convention of Feb. 25, 1862, and Dainese v. Hale, 91 U. S. 13.

" Since June 5, 1884, the Ottoman Government has treated the convention of 1862 as no longer operative." (U. S. Treaty Vol. (1776–1887), 1372.) The United States claimed that the treaty was not duly terminated. (Inst. to Dip. Officers of the U. S., § 212, p. 85.)

As to the question whether the consular courts have jurisdiction as to any real estate in Turkey, see Mr. Hunter, Second Assistant Secretary of State, to Mr. Johnson, consul-general at Beirut, Oct. 27, 1868, 52 MS. Desp. to Consuls, 46.

For reports on judicial functions of consuls, see 8 MS. Report Book, Dept. of State, 97, 233, 369, 399, 489.

As to appeals from consular courts, see Mr. Fish, Sec. of State, to Senator Cameron, chm. Com. on For. Rel., April 21, 1874, 11 MS. Report Book, 489, enclosing copy of a despatch from Mr. Bingham, min. to Japan, No. 38, Jan. 8, 1874, 27 MS. Desp. from Japan.

The defendant, when consul-general of the United States in Egypt, in 1864, issued an attachment against the goods of the plaintiff there situate. Plaintiff, and the persons at whose suit the attachment was issued, were citizens of the United States and not residents or sojourners in the Turkish dominions. For this act the plaintiff brought suit in this country to recover the value of the goods attached. The defendant pleaded his official character, and, as incident thereto, claimed jurisdiction to entertain the suit in which the attachment was issued. It was held that the plea was defective for not setting forth the laws or usages of Turkey upon which, by the treaty and act of Congress conferring the jurisdiction, the latter was made to depend, and which alone would show its precise extent, and that it embraced the case in question.

Dainese v. Hale, 91 U. S. 13. The court said that the most-favored-nation clause of the treaty between the United States and Turkey of Feb. 25, 1862, secured to United States consuls in Turkey, even if the treaty of 1830 did not, the same privileges of jurisdiction, civil and criminal, as the consuls of other Christian nations enjoyed, and that the act of Congress of June 22, 1860, established the necessary regulations for the exercise of such jurisdiction; but that, as the consular jurisdiction was, in terms, only such as was allowed by the laws of Turkey, or by its usages in its intercourse with other Christian nations, those laws or usages must be shown in order to prove the precise extent of the jurisdiction. The point of the decision seems to be that it was assumed that the rule that foreign laws must be proved as facts was applicable to the case before the court.

" Citizens of the United States owning real property in Turkey are, under the real estate protocol of 11th of August, 1874, as proclaimed by the President October 29, 1874, and in accordance with the terms of Article II. of the imperial rescript of 7 Sepher, 1284 (June 10, 1867), placed upon terms of equality with Ottoman subjects ' in all things that concern their landed property,' and are expressly excluded from availing ' themselves of their personal nationality except under the reserve of the immunities attached to their persons and their movable goods according to the treaties.'   (U. S. Stats., vol. 18, part 3, p. 853.) "

> Mr. Bayard, Sec. of State, to Mr. Straus, min. to Turkey, March 17, 1888, For. Rel. 1888, II. 1568, 1569.
>
> " In all times, foreigners have always been attended in judicial matters by their consular authorities. This tutelary and indispensable rule has always been applied in an absolute manner.
>
> " In 1866 only, when the Porte granted to foreigners the right to hold real estate, the protocol annexed to the law of the 7th Sepher introduced a slight derogation to that rule. It was a kind of concession that the powers thought well to make to the Ottoman Government. That was an error to be regretted, inasmuch as the law of Sepher did not give any great advantages to foreigners, as it grants equal rights to the Ottomans, as well as foreigners, on all questions concerning real property." (Memorandum of the dragomans to the chiefs of missions, For. Rel. 1892, 545, 546.)

" Another question which has recently occasioned controversy arises from the action of Turkish officials in arbitrarily examining the baggage, personal effects, and correspondence of Americans without any adequate reason or even excuse further than that some sort of conspiracy was supposed to exist among Armenians against the Ottoman rule. The pursuance of such a course under the alleged conditions is clearly unjustifiable. Such a system of investigation could only rationally be carried on when the country or district has by public decree been placed under martial law. Mere suspicions of a conspiracy among native subjects can in no sense form sufficient ground for violating personal privileges and property of foreigners during a time of peace.

" In several recent instances, our citizens peaceably traveling from one point to another, under regular and formal *teskereh* (travel permit), have suffered the indignity of arrest and search, their books and papers being taken from them for so-called ' examination.' It would be a mere quibble, a trifling with the rights of the alien, to pretend, as the local authorities seem in some cases to have attempted, that this is not such a domiciliary search as the capitulations contemplate and permit only on lawful process and after notification to the consul charged with the resident's protection. The rights of domicile spring from and are but a material manifestation of the rights of the individual—the one can not be respected and the other assailed."

Mr. Foster, Sec. of State, to Mr. Thompson, min. to Turkey, Nov. 29, 1892, For. Rel. 1892, 609, 612.
See, specifically, the case of Mr. W. W. Mead, For. Rel. 1892, 601, 613.

December 2, 1894, the Ottoman police, under the protection of the acting governor, entered the residence of Mr. Lee, an American citizen at Marash, searched his house, examined the contents of a box which had come from the United States, and then took the empty box to the government house, although the acting governor had been informed that the box was examined at Alexandretta. The Turkish authorities did not report the search to the nearest American consul, or observe any of the proper legal formalities, nor was the search made for a cause specified in the protocol. It was alleged that this act involved a violation of the right of domicile in at least four particulars; (1) the entrance of the police upon the premises without permission; (2) the remaining of the police on the premises for several hours and until after nightfall; (3) the course of the acting governor who, when Mr. Lee protested, sent other officers to enter the house and examine the box; and (4) the seizure of the box by those officers against Mr. Lee's protest. The minister of the United States at Constantinople on his own motion demanded the removal of the acting governor, and the minister of foreign affairs " dictated a note to the grand vizier " expressing the opinion that this should be done. The action of the American minister was approved. The offending officials were reprimanded and measures were adopted by the Porte to prevent the further molestation of Americans resident at Marash.

For. Rel. 1895, II. 1252–1255.

" Another incident has served to attract notice : On the night of the 4th of August last the premises of Dr. Christie, principal of St. Paul's Institute, at Tarsus, who was spending the summer months at the neighboring village of Namroun, were invaded by an armed mob, obviously collected in pursuance of a preconcerted plan, and an outrageous attack made on a defenseless native servant of Dr. Christie and on some students of the institute who were then at Namroun. The authors of this brutal attack were abundantly identified, and through the prompt intervention of the United States consul at Beirut and the consular agent at Mersine, the nearest port, a number of arrests were made. Notwithstanding the peremptory demands of the United States minister for simple justice, the assailants, when taken before the local judge at Tarsus, were released. So grave did this miscarriage of justice appear that an early occasion was taken to send the *Marblehead* to Mersine to investigate the incident and lend all proper moral aid to the consular representatives of the United States in pressing for due redress. Their efforts to this end were most cordially seconded by the mutessarif (prefect) of Mersine, and on October 28 last the accused, to the number of eight, were brought to trial at Tarsus and convicted upon the evidence, subsequently confessing their guilt. Having established his rights, and in view of the dismissal of the Tarsus judge who had conducted the preliminary inquest, and a promise to degrade the incompetent mudir of Namroun, Dr. Christie interceded with the court for clemency to the individual culprits, upon whom light sentences of imprisonment were passed.

" The signal rebuke administered in high places where responsibility really existed and was abused, coupled with the establishment of the important principle that American domicile in Turkey may not be violated with impunity, renders the conclusion of this incident satisfactory."

> Report of Mr. Olney, Sec. of State, to the President, Dec. 19, 1895, S. Doc. 33, 54 Cong. 1 sess. 4.   Also For. Rel. 1895, II. 1256, 1258, 1271–1292 1352, 1355.
>
> See, also, Mavroyeni Bey, Turkish min., to Mr. Olney, Sec. of State, Dec. 21, 1895, For. Rel. 1895, II. 1413, 1414.

In a dispatch of November 21, 1895, Mr. Terrell, United States minister at Constantinople, expressed the hope that Admiral Selfridge, U. S. Navy, then in Turkish waters, had been instructed to inform the Turkish functionaries with whom he might have official intercourse, that his force would not be used to protect revolutionists bearing American passports in entering Turkey from Cyprus. Mr. Terrell expressed the belief that all his efforts to protect missionaries would be in vain if the Turks should be led to believe that the United States naval force was aiding revolutionary schemes, and added: " I presume that under article 4090, Revised Statutes of the United States, I could call upon the admiral to enforce an order to prevent the entry of our naturalized citizens as armed revolutionists into Turkey if an emergency should arise requiring it."

Mr. Olney, Secretary of State, December 13, 1895, replied: " Admiral has been telegraphed to cooperate heartily with you and enforce all writs issued by you to prevent any entry into Turkey of naturalized citizens as armed revolutionists under provisions of section cited."

> For. Rel. 1895, II. 1344–1345, 1391.

In January, 1895, an American citizen named Stupe, of German birth, was killed in Constantinople by an insane Turk. The assassin was tried and sentenced to death, the dragoman of the consulate-general of the United States being present at the trial. This sentence was reversed by the court of cassation. At this proceeding the dragoman was not present, no notice of it having been communicated to him. The American minister protested against it as a disregard of treaty stipulations, maintaining that the right to have a dragoman present in such cases would be futile unless he should also be in attendance when the case was reexamined in the appellate court. On a new trial the defendant was sentenced to fifteen years imprisonment.

"In view of the gratifying circumstance that His Majesty the Sultan had, of his own initiative and very soon after the killing, accorded a life pension of 1,200 piastres (about $525) to the widow of the murdered man, no occasion for further pressing this particular case was perceived. This Government will, however, insist upon its right to be represented by the presence of its dragoman at every stage of all criminal proceedings against an Ottoman subject where an American citizen has been injured."

> Report of Mr. Olney, Sec. of State, to the President, Dec. 19, 1895, S. Doc. 33, 54 Cong. 1 sess. ; For. Rel. 1895, II. 1256, 1259, 1292–1295.
> See, for comments on the action of the Porte in this case, the note of Mavroyeni Bey, Turkish minister at Washington, to Mr. Olney, Secretary of State, Dec. 21, 1895, For. Rel. 1895, II. 1413, 1414.

"We think, looking at the whole of this case, that so far as the Ottoman Government is concerned, it is sufficiently shown that they have acquiesced in allowing to the British Government a jurisdiction, whatsoever be its peculiar kind, between British subjects and the subjects of other Christian states. It appears to us that the course was this: That at first, from the total difference of religious habits and feelings, it was necessary to withdraw as far as practicable British subjects from the native courts; then in the progress of time commerce increasing, and various nations having the same interest in abstaining from resort to the tribunals of Mussulmans, etc., recourse was had to consular courts; and by degrees the system became general. Of all this the Government of the Ottoman Porte must have been cognizant, and their long acquiescence proves consent. The principles are fully explained in the celebrated judgment of Lord Stowell in the case of ' The Indian Chief ' (3 C. Rob. 28), to which we have very recently referred (Advocate-General of Bengal *v.* Ranee Surnomoye Dossee, 2 Moore's P. C. 22, 60).

"Though the Ottoman Porte could give and has given to the Christian powers of Europe authority to administer justice to their own subjects, according to their own laws, it neither has professed to give nor could give to one such power any jurisdiction over the subjects of another power. But it has left those powers at liberty to deal with each other as they may think fit, and if the subjects of one country desire to resort to the tribunals of another, there can be no objection to their doing so with the consent of their own sovereign and that of the sovereign to whose tribunals they resort. There is no compulsory power in an English court in Turkey over any but English subjects; but a Russian or any other foreigner may, if he pleases, voluntarily resort to it with the consent of his sovereign, and thereby submit himself to its jurisdiction."

> Papayanni *v.* Russian Steam Navigation Co. (1863), 2 Moore's P. C. C., N. S. 161, 182–184. This was a case arising out of damage by a collision between vessels off the island of Marmora. Appellants were British subjects, whose vessel was libelled by the respondent in the British consular court at Constantinople. A counterclaim was made and two judgments were rendered; and from these an appeal was taken, on a protest by the appellants (defendants below), against the jurisdiction of the court.

> See, further, as to the jurisdiction of consular courts, 1 Beale's Cases on the Conflict of Laws, 92–94.

2. ART. IV., TREATY OF 1830.

§ 284.

" Various attempts were made prior to 1830 to negotiate a treay of amity and commerce with the Ottoman Porte.[a]

Notes by Messrs. Davis and Adee.

These efforts began in 1817, before which time American commerce in Turkish dominions had been ' under the protection of the English Levant Company, for whose protection a consulate duty, averaging one and one-fourth per cent. on the value of cargoes inward and outward, was paid.' [b] On the 12th of September, 1829, full power was conferred upon Commodore Biddle, in command of the Mediterranean Squadron, David Offley, consul at Smyrna, and Charles Rhind, of Philadelphia, jointly and severally, to conclude a treaty. They were instructed to make a commercial treaty upon the most-favored-nation basis,[c] and they were referred to previous negotiations by Offley, in which he had been instructed to ' be careful to provide that the translation shall be correct, and such as will be received on both sides as of the same import.' [a]

" Rhind made a great mystery of leaving America. He sailed at night in a packet for Gibraltar, where he joined Biddle, and they proceeded together to Smyrna; but when Offley came on board in that port he informed them that it ' was perfectly well known in Smyrna that they were commissioners.'

---

[a] H. Ex. Doc. 250, Treas. Dept., and 303 State Dept., 22 Cong. 1 sess.

[b] Offley to Van Buren, June 7, 1830, MS. Negotiations with Turkey, 1817–1831.

[c] H. Ex. Doc. 250, Treas. Dept., 22 Cong. 1 sess. 69–73.

[d] Id. 65.

" Rhind expressed his disappointment.   It was then agreed that he
should go alone to Constantinople and commence the negotiations,
while his colleagues waited at Smyrna.   He proceeded there and presented his letters of credence.   After these ceremonies were over he
submitted a draft of a treaty to the Reis Effendi [a] [which appears to
have been in French, in which tongue the negotiation was conducted].
Some days later he was shown the Turkish text of a treaty, and was
told by the Reis Effendi that it was 'drawn up in strict conformity
with the one which I had submitted,' [b] and on the 7th of May the
treaty of 1830 was signed, the Turkish text being signed by the Reis
Effendi, as it had been prepared by him, and the French text being
signed by Rhind after examination and comparing it with the Turkish.   A secret and separate article was also signed at the same time
respecting the building of ships and purchase of ship timber in the
United States.   Rhind then dispatched a special messenger to summon his colleagues to Constantinople.

" When they arrived, and were made acquainted with the separate
article, they disapproved of the latter; but rather than lose the treaty
they signed both the treaty and the separate article in French and informed the Secretary of State of the reasons for their course.[c]   This
caused a great breach between them and Rhind.

" The Senate approved the treaty itself, but rejected the separate
article.   David Porter was then commissioned as chargé d'affaires,
and was empowered to exchange the ratifications of the treaty and to
explain the rejection of the separate article.   When he arrived in
Constantinople he was met with complaints at the rejection of the
separate article by the Senate.   Then he reports that a discussion was
had ' on the return of the translation made at Washington, instead
of the one signed at Constantinople.' [d]   It appears from the archives
of the Department of State that four translations were sent to America—(1) an English translation from the original Turkish, not verified; (2) a French translation from the original Turkish, verified by
Navoni, the American dragoman; (3) a French translation in black
ink, with annotations in red ink, [which from internal evidence
appears to be substantially the original draft text submitted by
Rhind to the Reis Effendi]; (4) another English translation, made
from the French.   The translation which went before the Senate and
was acted on by that body was neither of these.   No French version
appears to have been transmitted to the Senate with the Turkish
text, but a new English version, which, from internal evidence as

---

[a] Id. 89.

[b] Id. 93.

[c] Id. 95; Commodore Biddle to Mr. Van Buren, Sec. of State, May 31 and
June 2, 1830, MS. Negotiations with Turkey, 1817–1831.

[d] Porter's dispatch, No. 22, Sept. 26, 1831, 2 MS. Desp. from Turkey.

well as from the tradition of the Department, may be assumed to have been made in the Department of State, mainly from the French version No. 3. Whether this be so or not, it is certain that the French translation signed by Biddle and his colleagues was not the version which was submitted to the Senate, and which, after ratification, was offered in exchange at Constantinople.

"[There are three English translations of the treaty in the Department of State, each differing slightly from the other, all in the handwriting of two clerks of the office. One is written in a ' large bold hand,' and the other two are written in a smaller style of chirography and by a different clerk. On the 9th of December, 1830, the President sent the treaty to the Senate. In his message transmitting it, which in fact bears the date of the 10th, he says:

" ' The French versions herewith transmitted, and accompanied by copies and English translations of the same, are transcripts of the original translations from the Turkish, signed by the commissioners of the United States, and delivered to the Government of the Sublime Porte. The paper in Turkish is the original, signed by the Turkish plenipotentiary, and delivered by him to the American commissioners: of this, a translation into the English language, made at the Department of State, and believed to be correct, is likewise transmitted.'

" The Senate ordered the papers to be printed in confidence.[a] The confidential document, as printed, consists of the President's message; a French translation of the treaty and of the Separate and Secret Article; and an English translation of the same. The French translation, as printed, conforms to the one verified by Navoni. With the message was transmitted to the Senate a *copy* of the English translation, written in the ' large bold hand,' and this appears in the confidential document as the English translation. This *copy* of the English translation was not acted upon by the Senate, but on the 16th of December the *original* of one of the other two English translations was presented to the Senate unaccompanied by a communication, and printed in confidence.[b] This was the English translation, which received the consideration of the Senate and met with its approval. It was returned to the President with the Turkish text, and this particular paper and the Turkish text form part of the President's ratification, which bears date of February 2, 1831. It must, therefore, be considered the official English translation of the treaty, as no other translation, either in the English or French languages, accompanies that instrument, and it received the approval of the Senate. The act of ratification as signed by the President is written in the ' large bold hand.' The President's proc-

---

[a] S. Conf. Doc., Dec. 9, 1830.
[b] S. Conf. Doc., Dec, 16, 1830.

lamation of the treaty, dated February 4, 1832, is written in the same handwriting as the English translation which is attached to the ratification of the President.]

" Porter met the difficulty by signing a paper in Turkish of which he returned to Washington the following as a translation: ' Some expressions in the French translation of the Turkish instrument exchanged between the plenipotentiaries of the two contracting parties, and which contains the articles of the treaty of commerce concluded between the Sublime Porte and the United States of America, not being perfectly in accordance with the Turkish original, a circumstance purely the effect of translation, and the Government of the United States being satisfied with the Turkish treaty, and having accepted it without the reserve of any word; therefore, on every occasion the above instrument shall be strictly observed, and if, hereafter, any discussion should arise between the contracting parties, the said instrument shall be consulted by me and by my successors to remove doubts.' [a]

"This was received at the Department of State on the 5th of December, 1831, and there is no evidence that the act was disapproved.   An item was inserted in the appropriation bill to enable the President to carry out the provisions of the treaty.   Porter's dispatches were placed at the service of the Committee of Foreign Affairs of the House,[b] the subject of the appropriation was discussed in the House,[c] and the appropriation was passed.[d]

" No question arose respecting the differences between the versions until 1868, when the Turks claimed jurisdiction over two American citizens arrested and imprisoned by the Turkish authorities in Syria, for alleged offenses against the Ottoman Government.   This claim of jurisdiction over American citizens was resisted by E. Joy Morris, the American minister, who referred to that part of the 4th article of the treaty of 1830 which provides that ' even when they may have committed some offense, they shall not be arrested and put in prison by the local authorities; but they shall be tried by their minister or consul, and punished according to their offense.'   The minister for foreign affairs replied that the translation was incorrect; that the words ' they shall be tried by their minister or consul, and punished according to their offense,' and the words ' they are not to be arrested,' were not to be found in the Turkish text; and he cited Porter's declaration in support of his claim that the Turkish text should be accepted as the standard.   Morris then, under instructions, secured, through the Russian ambassador, translations to be made from the

---

a Porter's No. 22, Sept. 26, 1831, 2 MS. Desp. from Turkey.
b H. Ex. Doc. 303, 22 Cong. 1 sess.
c Debates, 2186–2198.
d 4 Stat. 513.

Turkish text in Constantinople by the first dragoman of the Prussian legation, by the first and second dragomans of the Russian embassy, and by two former dragomans of the Russian embassy, and sent them to the Department of State. In no one of these were found the words objected to by the minister for foreign affairs, nor any equivalent, [although all agree in guaranteeing immunity from arrest for crime by the Turkish authorities and the application of punishment through the instrumentality of the minister or consul].

"Mr. Fish then instructed Morris that the President had 'determined to submit the facts to the consideration of the Senate, and await its resolution before inaugurating any diplomatic action.' This was done,[a] [but without modification or authoritative interpretation of the text by that body.]

"[The discussion as to the true meaning of the Turkisk text, assuming it to be the accepted standard, has since continued, and is still pending. The Turkish Government has controverted the assertion of jurisdiction by the United States minister and consuls over Americans charged with crime in Turkey in several cases, notably with regard to the seaman Kelly, who in 1877 was tried by the consul at Smyrna on the charge of murdering a native Turk, and acquitted. The Turkish Government adheres to the allegation that the words defining jurisdictional rights in the premises, which appear in the English version, are 'not to be found' in the Turkish text. Meanwhile, the Department of State has accumulated a number of additional translations from the Turkish, made by high authority in such matters, without encountering one in which some form does not appear of distinct admission of the intervention of the minister or consuls to inflict, administer, or apply the punishment due to the crime proven. It is to be observed in this relation that in 1838 a treaty was concluded between the Ottoman Porte and Belgium, signed in parallel Turkish and French texts, between which no discrepancy is alleged; and that the French text of article 4 of that treaty is identical, as to extraterritorial jurisdiction over citizens, with the disputed text of our treaty with Turkey, concluded eight years earlier. The same provision also occurs in a still later treaty between Turkey and Portugal.]"

Mr. J. C. B. Davis, Treaty Notes, with supplementary notes, denoted by brackets, by Mr. Adee, Second Assistant Secretary of State, Treaty Vol. (1776–1887), 1368–1371.

For the Turkish capitulations, see reports of Edward A. Van Dyck, consular clerk, President's messages of April 6, 1881, S. Ex. Doc. 3, special sess., and Feb. 2, 1882, S. Ex. Doc. 87, 47 Cong. 1 sess.

See D. Démétriadés, Administration of Justice in the Levant, Juridical Review, III. 145.

[a] S. Conf. E, 41 Cong. 2 sess.

As to the policy of the powers in consulting concerning matters touching the capitulations, see circular instruction of Mr. Frelinghuysen, Sec. of State, to United States ministers at Paris, Berlin, London, Rome, St. Petersburg, and Vienna, May 15, 1882, 3 MS. Circulars, 17.

See, also, Mr. Wallace, min. to Turkey, to Mr. Frelinghuysen, Sec. of State, No. 87, April 17, 1882, 38 MS. Desp. from Turkey; Mr. Hoffman, chargé at St. Petersburg, to Mr. Frelinghuysen, Sec. of State, No. 233, June 15, 1882, 36 MS. Desp. from Russia.

February 1, 1852, Mr. F. Dainese, at one time United States consul at Constantinople, communicated to Mr. Webster,
Report of Mr. Dainese, 1852. who was then Secretary of State, a sketch of the administration of justice in the Ottoman Empire. The laws, he said, were administered by a body of judges called "cadis," with whom were connected interpreters of the law called "muftis." Besides the court of the cadi, each district, county, or province had a council called "medsliss," composed of the cadi, mufti, and certain representatives of the people, and presided over by the chief executive officer of the place. The formation of the medsliss dated from 1839. There was another mixed court in the principal commercial towns called the "tidjaret," with exclusively commercial jurisdiction. So far as American citizens were concerned, Mr. Dainese stated that the treaty of 1830, being rather imperfect, merely enabled the United States to invoke the privileges granted to European powers by the express terms of their capitulations, as well as the right of being treated on the most-favored-nation footing. During the last three years of his administration of the consulate at Constantinople, he had met with no difficulty in the application of these two rules. Mr. Dainese further stated that civil cases between Europeans and Turks, tried before either of the courts he had mentioned, when attended by the proper official representative of the foreign party, were definitely decided, and the awards were subject to prompt execution; but that they were of no validity if made in the absence of an official functionary. Commenting further, he said:

"In criminal cases between Turks and foreigners, which are tried before the council of police, if the award be adverse to the latter, they are not subject to its execution in Turkey, but are sent, together with the documents relative to the case, to their respective governments for disposal.

"Civil and criminal cases arising between Europeans of the same or different nationalities residing in Turkey, are out of the jurisdiction of either of the above courts. Civil controversies are either arranged by arbitrators chosen by the parties themselves, or tried before juries appointed by their respective consuls. Coiners of base coin are subject to the local laws, no matter what nation they belong to.

" These juries are composed of three members, and are selected from the mercantile classes. Their awards are submitted to the consuls, and when sanctioned acquire legal vitality.

" This is obviously the worst system ever devised; most of the consuls, in their selection of juries, and in their power of approving or dissenting from their award, possess the power of entirely controlling the case, and the weaker party becomes frequently the victim of the grossest injustice. The French, Greek, Dutch, and some others, have the right of appeal to the courts of their respective countries, if *defendants;* but if claimants, they have no redress, as the juries are always appointed by the consuls of the defendants; of course under such a system a fair and equitable adjustment of litigated cases can not be hoped for.

" Criminal cases among Europeans are only examined before the consuls of the defendants, but no European consul in Turkey has authority to try them; and delinquents, together with the proceedings and proofs of the process, are sent to the country of the offenders, where the matter is tried and the punishment inflicted.

" I am happy to add, that the act of Congress of 1848, conferring criminal jurisdiction on American consuls in the Turkish dominions, has not been called for as yet in Constantinople."

> H. Ex. Doc. 82, 34 Cong. 3 sess. 189, 192–193. It appears by papers in this document that Mr. Dainese had resided many years in Constantinople; that, as early as 1833, he was employed there as a clerk in an English mercantile firm, the head of which was at the time in charge of the American consulate. (195.)

A copy of Mr. Cushing's opinion of Oct. 23, 1855 (7 Op. 565), on
Report of Mr. Brown, 1857. consular jurisdiction in Turkey, having been placed in the hands of Mr. John P. Brown, then United States consul-general at Constantinople, for many years in the service of the United States in Turkey, Mr. Brown proceeded to furnish the information which, as he said, the Attorney-General " seems to have needed " in preparing his opinion. In the course of his dispatch, Mr. Brown said:

" 1st. All treaties between foreign powers and the Sublime Porte grant jurisdiction to the latter in both civil and criminal cases, when either of the parties, plaintiff or defendant, is an Ottoman subject. To meet this it has of late years established a police court for criminal and a board of trade for commercial suits at this capital, the latter composed of Ottoman and foreign merchants, and presided over by the minister of commerce or his assistant. In this board or court the American legation is represented by two members, both merchants, Messrs. A. Azarian, a naturalized United States citizen, and E. Varncla, a protégé of the legation. As the treaty stipulates that all suits tried in Ottoman courts, in which one of the parties is a citizen of the United States 'shall not be heard or judgment pronounced unless the American dragoman be present,' I found it very necessary and useful to have the American interests represented in the board of commerce, and suggested to the minister resident the propriety of appointing the aforementioned merchants. Without the presence of an American in the board, I, as dragoman, not being allowed to act as a member, was often exposed to lose the suit in which I was interested. This court issues judgments against or in favor of all foreigners, but does not put them into execution. All the foreign legations claim the right to execute them upon their own subjects. A code of commerce is now being drawn up for this court, based upon the French code. The dragomen are supposed only to act as the interpreters of the citizens or subjects of their nations, yet they may exercise considerable influence over the members, require an adherence to certain rules of procedure, and even claim the right to arrest their ' judgments ' until they can lay the case before their minister.

" On the occurrence of a civil suit decreed by the minister of foreign affairs for trial before this court, the petition of the Ottoman or ' fakrii ' (official note) of the foreign legation on which it is based, is always given in charge of an employé of his bureau called a ' Mubashir,' whose business it is to cite and accompany the parties at the trial. He calls at the legation or consulate of the foreigner to request it to cite him before the court. This is ' the usage observed towards other Franks ' alluded to in the fourth article of the treaty. If the plaintiff be an Ottoman subject, his petition against the foreigner, which he presents to the minister of foreign affairs, is always conveyed by the ' Mubashir ' to the dragoman, who makes a translation of it for the information of his minister or consul, and the defendant.

" 2d. The honorable Attorney-General was under a misapprehension when he stated in his opinion ' that Americans committing crime in Turkey are to be tried by their minister or consul; ' for all foreigners are tried for the commission of crime, whenever their plaintiffs are Ottoman subjects, by the Ottoman courts only, ' in the presence of the American dragoman.' For this purpose the Sublime Porte has established a police court under the minister of police or his assistant, and there are no foreigners among its members. Its decisions are executed by itself in ordinary cases, yet, in capital ones, or even when the criminal is condemned to a long imprisonment, it makes him over if so required, to his own legation to be sent to his country for punishment.

" The Porte endeavors to extend this system to its large cities and to its provinces generally. In the latter, the ' local government,' as it styles that of its governors, is composed of a medjilis or provincial council, for the trial of both civil and criminal cases, and for the former trials foreign merchants are admitted. There also the 'presence of the American dragoman' is required, who, if the place has an American consul, is generally a native linguist, temporarily employed by the latter.

"3d. Jurisdiction is allowed by the Sublime Porte to the American minister and consuls in all cases, civil and criminal, occurring between citizens of the United States and these and other foreigners. It is wholly averse to the exercise of any interference in these cases, and it refused positively to interfere between the Americans and Austrians, in the serious affair which occurred in Smyrna, respecting Martze Koszta. This usage towards Franks is rigidly observed in all parts of Turkey.

"The exact language of the 4th article of the treaty, to which the honorable Attorney-General alludes, I thus interpret:

"'When suits occur between subjects and rajahs of the Sublime Porte, and subjects of the American Government, these shall not be heard and judged except in the presence of the dragoman (of the latter). Whenever those (occurring in the provinces of the Ottoman empire) amount to as much as 500 piastres they shall be referred to the capital, where they shall be tried according to justice and equity. When American subjects are occupied with their own affairs of trade, and no crime has been proven against them, they shall not causelessly be molested; and even when their guilt has been proven, the judges and executive officers shall not imprison them, but, in the same manner which is observed towards other foreigners, they shall be punished (i. e. the judgment be executed upon them) by their own minister or consul.'

"In the Turkish original the word 'tried' by their minister or consul certainly does not exist, and the language used refers to the carrying into execution of the punishment deemed necessary for the American criminal.

"The treaty states that 'even when they (Americans) may have committed some offence, they shall not be arrested or put in prison by the local authorities.' The correct language of the original as aforeshown, is 'imprisoned' or detained in prison, which is consistent with the practice or usage observed towards all foreigners generally, whom the police arrest and put in prison on a criminal accusation from Ottoman subjects, but give notice of the fact to the proper legation, with the request that one of its dragomen may be present at the trial. I should here add that the police will also always arrest a foreigner who is accused of crime, on the demand of another foreigner, but sends the accused immediately to his own consul for trial.

"I believe I have shown that, forasmuch as the Sublime Porte is concerned, it refuses to exercise any jurisdiction of a civil or criminal nature in suits arising exclusively among foreigners in Turkey It leaves it to foreign governments represented in Turkey, to adopt whatever systems they may deem most expedient for the settlement of suits arising amongst their own subjects. On this point all have the same rights and liberty of choice. Consequently some have adopted codes for the trial of their own subjects, and established consular tribunals, composed only of their own subjects and protégés and presided over by their consuls. Whenever the plaintiff is the subject of another foreign government, the suit, if a civil one, is referred to a 'mixed commission' of arbitration, composed of two members for the defendant and one for the plaintiff. An appeal may be had under some of the consulates or chancellaries to the minister, who generally decrees a retrial before a similar commission of appeal, whilst in others, as in the French, provision is made for an appeal to the 'Court of Aix;' and in the Austrian to a court at Trieste.

"This system of mixed commissions among the foreign legations and consulates in Turkey has become a kind of *lex loci*. I have heretofore conformed to it in the trial of suits between American citizens and protégés, or these and other foreign subjects, and it would be a source of much satisfaction to me to be apprised by an 'opinion' of the Hon. Attorney-General whether or not my conformance to it renders the 'judgment' of the commission approved of by me valid or legal, and whether I could carry it into execution here?

"In connection with the preceding I would respectfully beg your indulgence while I add the following remarks on the results of the exterritoriality thus enjoyed by citizens of the United States in Turkey.

"Not only are American consuls there called upon to carry the sentences of Turkish tribunals into execution on American citizens, but also to execute those of their own finding. The Ottoman Government is averse to allowing foreign criminals to be confined in its prisons where, by the 'usage' observed, they are fed at its expense. I am compelled, on account of there being no American consular prison here, to confine Americans whom I have had to sentence in the wretched prison of the police department, the filthiness of which exposes the criminal to dangerous diseases. There are no public hospitals here in which American citizens can be placed, and I have been compelled to depend upon the goodness of the Prussian hospital for admittance for suffering Americans.

"Most of the foreign legations here possess a prison and a hospital, and some have a house connected with the latter, for boarding distressed seamen or indigent subjects, especially the British, French, and American.

" As the relations between the United States and Turkey are annually being extended, particularly with Constantinople, the former will before many years be compelled to provide a prison, and perhaps a hospital for their citizens. One prison would suffice for the greater part of the empire, to which Americans sentenced by their consuls to an imprisonment of some months' duration might be sent. So much has already been written to the Department on the subject of civil consular jurisdiction in Turkey, that I beg to believe it is only a sense of duty which has induced me to trouble it again."

> Mr. Brown, consul-general at Constantinople, to Mr. Cass, Sec. of State, Aug. 1, 1857, H. Ex. Doc. 68, 35 Cong. 2 sess. 64.
>
> Mr. Brown accompanied Commodore Porter to Constantinople as acting midshipman in 1830. As the United States was then obliged to rely on a foreign interpreter, Mr. Brown, on Commodore Porter's advice, established himself at Constantinople for the purpose of acquiring oriental languages. After five years' study he was appointed dragoman (interpreter) to the United States legation. " In the various grades of dragoman, secretary of legation, and acting consul and chargé d'affaires, he faithfully served the United States from the year 1835 until near the close of 1872, the period of his death." (Mr. Morgan, Com. on For. Aff., Jan. 21, 1873, H. Report 40, 42 Cong. 3 sess.)
>
> Feb. 24, 1858, Mr. Brown made a return of civil and criminal suits in the consulate during 1857, adding: " Besides these, other suits, both civil and criminal, have occurred in 1857 between United States citizens and Ottoman subjects, which, according to the stipulations of the treaty, were tried in my presence as dragoman of the legation, in the police court, and board of trade (Tidjaret)." (H. Ex. Doc. 68, 35 Cong. 2 sess. 69.)
>
> See, also, Mr. Williams, min. to Turkey, to Mr. Cass, Sec. of State, Nov. 17, 1858, H. Ex. Doc. 68, 35 Cong. 2 sess. 69.
>
> Under the act of Congress of 1848, now superseded, to carry into effect certain provisions in the treaties between the United States and Turkey, giving certain judicial powers to ministers and consuls, there being no designation of a particular place for the confinement of prisoners, such place is left for regulation under section five of the act, or to the discretion of the acting functionary. (Toucey, At. Gen., 1849, 5 Op. 67.)

" The Department has duly considered your several despatches, calling attention to the discrepancies alleged to exist between the Turkish text of the treaty with the Sublime Porte of May, 1830, and the English translation thereof, and suggesting the negotiation of a new instrument as the proper means of avoiding the difficulties to which such a variation in the two versions may give rise.

Views of Mr. Cass, 1859.

" Without going into a history of the circumstances that attended the negotiation of the treaty in question, which are no doubt familiar to you, and admitting that the English version is a somewhat imperfect rendering of the Turkish text, I feel constrained upon reflection to express my belief that the true meaning and intent of the instrument may be deduced either from the English text or from its Turkish counterpart, and that any fair attempt to harmonize the two would not necessarily be unsuccessful.

"It would be well therefore to endeavor to obtain from the Turkish Government a formal recognition of the correctnesss of our interpretation of the provisions of the existing treaty. In the event of this not being practicable, the propriety of negotiating a new convention, by which all misunderstanding might be avoided, would appear to be unquestionable.

"It is evident that Mr. Porter, the chargé d'affaires at Constantinople, in agreeing that, to remove doubts in regard to the true meaning of the treaty, the Turkish text should alone be consulted in any discussion which might arise between the contracting parties, did so under the conviction that there was no essential disagreement between the Turkish and French versions—that the difference was in words only, not in substance. The ' codicil ' itself, as it is termed, speaks of the want of accord between them as being ' purely the effect of translation,' and asserts that the Government of the United States is ' fully satisfied with the treaty, and has accepted it, without the reserve of any word.' Mr. Porter was well aware of the construction which had been put upon the treaty by the United States, at the period of its ratification, and it is not likely that the ratifications would have been exchanged by him if he had not had sufficient reasons for believing that the stipulations were fairly conveyed in the English text. Those parts of the treaty respecting the true interpretation of which it was apprehended doubts might arise, were fully dwelt upon in Mr. Porter's instructions, and were no doubt discussed by him with the plenipotentiary of the Porte before the exchange was made.

"Under the circumstances, it is deemed proper that you should call the attention of the Ottoman Government to the discrepancies adverted to in your No. 21, and urge the necessity of a distinct and clear understanding between the two Governments in regard to the terms of the treaty. Should you fail to elicit a satisfactory reply, the Department will, upon the receipt of your despatch communicating the result of your efforts, lose no time in instructing you further upon the subject."

Mr. Cass, Sec. of State, to Mr. Williams, min. to Turkey, July 18, 1859, MS. Inst. Turkey, II. 1.

" The correct meaning of the fourth article of the treaty of 1830, between the United States and Turkey, has for some time past been under consideration here.   The various translations of the Turkish original of that article made at Constantinople and in this country have been carefully compared, and the conclusion arrived at is that the English version, upon the faith of which the treaty was ratified by the Senate and the President of the United States, is erroneous.   According to that version a citizen of the United States who may have committed a misdemeanor or a crime in Turkey against a Turk, or against the Turkish Government, can not be arrested even on *mesne* process, or imprisoned by the local authorities, and if tried therefor, this must be by the United States minister or consul.

" Considering the virtual impunity which such a stipulation as this bestows upon evil-disposed citizens of the United States, in that country, it is unaccountable that no more serious distrust of the accuracy of the translation should have been entertained than the archives of the Department disclose.

" The history of that translation appears to be as follows:

" Mr. Charles Rhind, who as a special agent of the United States, proceeded to Turkey in 1829, for the purpose of negotiating the treaty, employed, on arriving at Constantinople, one Navoni as his dragoman.   A French version of the Turkish by this Navoni, and another in the same language by another hand, accompanied ·the original treaty sent hither by Mr. Rhind.   It is presumed that neither of these versions was entirely satisfactory to Mr. Van Buren, then Secretary of State, for, pursuant to his direction, Mr. William B. Hodgson, then employed in the Department, and afterwards its official translator, made another translation, which purports to have been from the original Turkish.   It is, however, obvious on inspection that Mr. Hodgson's translation is not from the Turkish original, but seems to be compounded from the two French versions above referred to, both of which err, as alleged by the Turkish Government, and as the other translations recently made plainly show.

" If reasonable weight be allowed to the objection of the Turkish Government that it could not have been, and was not their intention to have placed United States citizens, offenders in Turkey, on a more favorable footing than citizens or subjects of other countries, it is obvious that this objection is decidedly at variance with the English version of the 4th article of our treaty as approved by the Senate, and proclaimed by the President of the United States.   The English translation of the 7th article has also been pronounced defective by that Government, as its correspondence with your predecessor, Commodore Porter, will show.

"Ambiguities and inaccuracies of this character respecting such important instruments are to be deplored; every proper effort should be made to avoid them, and when brought to light they should be corrected.

" The President can not take it upon himself to determine whether the Senate would or would not have advised and consented to the ratification of the treaty had it been understood in the sense which we are now satisfied that it bears, nor is he disposed, without the advice of the Senate, either to promulgate a new and correct translation or to ask the Government of Turkey to enter into a new treaty, conforming to the English version which was proclaimed by President Jackson. He has therefore determined to submit the facts to the consideration of the Senate and await its resolution before inaugurating any diplomatic action. You are instructed in the meantime to avoid, and to direct our consular officers to avoid, making any issue the maintaining of which depends upon the English versions of the 4th and 7th articles of the treaty which is contained in our statutes, or drawing in question the construction which the Government of Turkey puts upon the original document."

> Mr. Fish, Sec. of State, to Mr. Morris, Oct. 19, 1869, MS. Inst. Turkey, II. 262.
>
> July 25, 1876, Mr. Farman, agent and consul-general at Cairo, called the attention of the Department of State to the fact that his berat from the Porte contained the following clause: "Citizens of the United States quietly pursuing their commerce and not being charged or convicted with any crime or offense, shall not be molested; and if they have committed any offense they shall be put in prison by the local authorities, but they will be punished with the cooperation of the consul-general, following in that respect the usage in force toward other Franks." No copies of the berats issued to Mr. Farman's predecessors had been sent to the Department of State, and he was informed that whether the attention of Turkey would be called to the clause in question would depend on the practice that had previously prevailed with regard to its insertion. Meanwhile, he was to govern himself by Mr. Fish's instructions to Mr. Morris, supra. (Mr. Cadwalader, Act. Sec. of State, to Mr. Farman, Aug. 25, 1876, MS. Inst. Egypt, XVI. 41.)

In 1877 the United States consul at Smyrna tried and acquitted a seaman named Kelly, of the U. S. S. *Vandalia*, who was charged with the murder of a Turkish subject. This case caused a renewal of the discussion between the United States and Turkey as to the interpretation of Article IV. of the treaty of 1830. In a note of December 8, 1877, to the Turkish minister at Washington, Mr. Evarts stated that, in order that the discussion of the subject might be approached in perfect good faith, he had " no hesitation in confirming the conclusion" reached by Mr. Fish, October 19, 1869, " that the English version,

Case of Kelly, 1877.

upon the faith of which the treaty was ratified by the Senate and the President of the United States, is erroneous." Mr. Evarts maintained, however, that the English version substantially reproduced "the purposes of the American plenipotentiaries," which were concurred in by the Senate and the President, as well as "the original version in the French tongue, signed first by Mr. Rhind, and afterwards by Commodore Biddle and Mr. Offley, and delivered to the Government of the Porte in exchange for the official Turkish version;" and he also contended that there was no just ground to doubt that the English version, as ratified by the Senate and the President, represented "the current usage towards foreigners accused of crime in Turkey."

> Mr. Evarts, Sec. of State, to Aristarchi Bey, Turkish min., Dec. 8, 1877, MS. Notes to Turkey, I. 197, answering a note of Aristachi Bey, of October 10, 1877.

"Referring to the correspondence heretofore exchanged between your legation and the Department of State, and to the conferences which we have held, concerning the case of the seaman Kelly, who was tried by the United States consul at the port of Smyrna, I have now the honor to acquaint you with the sincere desire of this Government to put an end in an amicable manner to the long-pending discussion.

"I am directed in the first place by the President to admit, on the part of the Government of the United States, that the United States are bound by the Turkish text of the treaty of 1830, which was signed in that text alone. I make this admission the more cheerfully in view of your repeated assurances, in the name of your Government, that not only shall the true intent of that text be observed, but also that the citizens of the United States within Ottoman jurisdiction shall have the treatment accorded to the citizens or subjects of the most favored nation either by treaty or by virtue of existing local laws or customs.

"In the next place, with regard to the case of the above mentioned seaman Patrick Kelly, who, being accused of the commission of a homicide at Smyrna, was tried and released by the consul of the United States, I have the honor to state that without admitting any express or implied obligation in the premises, and without presently passing upon the true English equivalent of the Turkish text in the article involved, and upon the assurances tendered by you that the act of Kelly has reduced a Turkish family to penury and distress, the Government of the United States is prepared to spontaneously offer the sum of twelve hundred dollars ($1,200), money of the United States, for the relief of this suffering family.

"Doubting not that your Government will regard all source of difference on this point as ended by such a course, I embrace this gratifying opportunity to renew to you," etc.

> Mr. Evarts, Sec. of State, to Aristarchi Bey, Turkish min., May 14, 1880, MS. Notes to Turkey, I. 251.
>
> See, also, same to same, June 26, 1880, id. I. 253.

The discussion of Article IV. of the treaty of 1830 was continued in the case of Stephen P. Mirzan, an alleged citizen of the United States, who murdered Alexander Dahan, a distinguished lawyer, in the streets of Alexandria, Egypt, July 17, 1879. It appears that Mirzan and Dahan had an altercation in the street and finally came to blows, Mirzan striking Dahan. The latter ran away, fleeing through a bookstore, closely pursued by Mr. Mirzan, who, as Dahan passed out of one of the doors, shot him through the back of the head, the ball coming out through the forehead. Dahan died instantly. He was a subject of Turkey. Mirzan was tried at Alexandria before Mr. Maynard, then United States minister to Turkey, and was convicted June 12, 1880, of murder in the first degree and sentenced to be hanged October 1, 1880.

Mirzan's case, 1879.

President Hayes, July 29, 1880, commuted his sentence to imprisonment for life. (See supra, § 266, p. 635.)

August 3, 1882, President Arthur directed that he be brought to Albany to serve out the remainder of his sentence in the penitentiary at that place.

> Mr. Bayard, Sec. of State, to Mr. Garland, Att. Gen., June 16, 1885, 156 MS. Dom. Let. 15.
>
> For the notification of the commutation of Mirzan's sentence by President Hayes, see Mr. Evarts, Sec. of State, to Mr. Farman, consul-general at Cairo, Sept. 7, 1880, MS. Inst. Egypt, XVI. 200.
>
> The question whether Mirzan should be tried before the consul-general of the United States at Cairo was fully considered by the Department of State. By the last clause of sec. 22 of the act of June 22, 1860, it was provided that if at any time there should be no minister in either of the countries therein mentioned, the judicial duties imposed upon him by the act should devolve upon the consul-general or consul residing at the capital of the country. This provision was not incorporated into the Revised Statutes, and was therefore excluded from consideration. The conclusion was reached that Egypt could not be deemed, for the purposes of the Revised Statutes, secs. 4083–4130, an independent country, but must be held to be a part of the Ottoman Empire, at the capital of which the United States maintained a diplomatic representative. In capital cases the statute, it was observed, invested the minister with original jurisdiction concurrently with the consul, and that when the trial was held in the consular court the defendant had a right of appeal to the minister. In view of the gravity of the offence with which Mirzan stood charged, and the probability that in the case of conviction before the

consular court he would ask for a new trial before the minister, it
was decided that the trial should be held before the minister in the
first instance, and Mr. Maynard was accordingly instructed to proceed
to Alexandria and hold it.   (Mr. Evarts, Sec. of State, to Mr. Farman,
consul-general, March 16, 1880, MS. Inst. Egypt, XVI. 161.)

As to the refusal of the Department of State to issue to Mirzan a passport
in 1890, after his liberation, on finding that he was apparently naturalized in the United States after only three years' residence, see Mr.
Wharton, Acting Sec. of State, to Mr. Mirzan, July 30, 1890, 178 MS.
Dom. Let. 458.

"The Imperial Ottoman legation has repeatedly been under the
necessity of making representations to the Depart-
Correspondence of 1884–1889. ment of State in relation to the jurisdiction which is
assumed by the United States consuls in Turkey over
American citizens who have been guilty of crimes or misdemeanors
committed within the territory of the Empire, to the exclusion of
all intervention on the part of the Ottoman authorities, and that not
only in cases in which the injured party is a foreign subject, but also
in those in which such party in an Ottoman subject.

"The Sublime Porte has always opposed this view of the United
States, which is based upon an erroneous translation of Article IV. of
the treaty of 1830.

"Without wishing, Mr. Secretary of State, to enter upon a minute
discussion of this question, which has already formed the subject of
much correspondence between the two Governments, I will say that
Article IV. of the said treaty does not create an exceptional *régime* in
favor of American citizens.

"The expression found therein 'following the usage observed
towards (other) Franks,' can leave no doubt on this head.

"It clearly shows that *neither more nor less* was granted to American citizens than was granted to the subjects of other powers. I beg,
moreover, to remind you that according to the declaration of Mr.
Porter, then representative of the United States in Turkey (which
declaration has never been disavowed), the Turkish text of the
treaty of 1830 is the only one that is binding, and as that document
says, 'In case any dispute shall arise between the two contracting
parties, the said instrument (*i. e.*, the Turkish text) shall be the only
one according to which the difficulty shall be settled.' It was not
until the year 1868 that Mr. E. Joy Morris, then United States minister at Constantinople, raised this question of jurisdiction, basing
his action on the English translation of the Turkish text of Article
IV. of the treaty of 1830.

"The case in which he did so was that of two Americans, Romer
and Lamar, who had been concerned in an affray in Syria.

"There are in that translation entire phrases which are wanting in
the Turkish text, which is, I repeat, the only one that is binding.

"A long discussion between the two Governments followed, and Mr. Morris, by order of the Department of State, had new translations of Article IV. made at Constantinople, by six dragomans who were attached to various embassies there. According to the admission of the Department of State not one of those translations contains any phrases or words that would grant to the representatives of the United States the right of jurisdiction which we contest. In view of these facts, Mr. Fish, who was at that time Secretary of State, laid the question before- the Senate, as appears from a dispatch addressed by him to Mr. Morris. Sixteen years have elapsed since then, and notwithstanding the reiterated efforts made by the Sublime Porte, both here and at Constantinople, no decision, so far as I am aware, has been reached by that body on this subject.

"The United States Government, yielding to evidence, finally adhered, it is true, in principle, to the view taken of this question by the Sublime Porte. It will be sufficient for me to quote in this connection the declaration made by Mr. Evarts, then Secretary of State, to my predecessor, in the name of His Excellency the President: 'I am directed,' wrote the Hon. Mr. Evarts, May 14, 1880, 'by the President to admit, on the part of the Government of the United States, that the United States are bound by the Turkish text of the treaty of 1830, which was signed in that text above.' [Mr. Evarts's note says *in that text alone.*]

"'I make this admission the more cheerfully in view of your repeated assurances, in the name of your Government, that not only shall the true extent' [Mr. Evarts's note says *intent*] 'of that text be observed, but also that the citizens of the United States, within Ottoman jurisdiction, shall have the treatment accorded to the citizens or subjects of the most favored nations' [Mr. Evarts wrote *nation*] 'either by treaty or by virtue of existing local laws or customs.'

"Aristarchi Bey took note of this declaration, and, in his reply to the honorable Secretary of State, gave the most positive assurances that citizens of the United States should enjoy, in Turkey, the same privileges and immunities as citizens of other countries. Notwithstanding these declarations, which ought to have put an end to the difference existing between the two countries, the Washington Cabinet thought proper once more to remit the examination of this matter to Constantinople, as stated by the Hon. Bancroft Davis, then Acting Secretary of State, to Aristarchi Bey, under date of December 30, 1881. You were also pleased to assure him, Mr. Secretary of State, that the necessary instructions had been forwarded to the representative of the United States in Turkey, to enable him to settle this difference. No settlement has, however, been reached.

" In the meantime, cases of crimes and misdemeanors continue to occur in the Empire, and frequently give rise to differences of opinion and to difficulties between the Ottoman authorities and the American consulates, to the great detriment of the regular course of justice.

" Thus, quite recently, the United States consul at Beirut positively refused to receive and forward to its destination a summons issued by the public prosecutor, which cited an American missionary of Saida to appear, he having been guilty of a violation of law.

" In calling your serious attention, Mr. Secretary of State, to this fact, I beg you, by order of my Government, to be pleased to hasten the settlement of this question of jurisdiction, which has remained so long in abeyance.

" To sum up, the Sublime Porte can not make, in criminal cases, any exception in favor of American citizens; it guarantees to them, however, all privileges and immunities that have been heretofore and that are now enjoyed by the subjects of other powers. I am authorized to give you, on this point, Mr. Secretary of State, the most formal and explicit assurances, without either hesitation or reticence. My Government feels every confidence in the sentiments of equity and justice which actuate the Washington Cabinet, and it hopes that the difference which has for so many years existed between the two countries on this point will, through your conciliatory spirit, be definitely terminated."

Tevfik Pasha, Turkish min., to Mr. Frelinghuysen, Sec. of State, April 26,
1884, For. Rel. 1885, 890.

" I have the honor to acknowledge the receipt of your note of the 26th ultimo concerning the true interpretation of article 4 of the treaty of 1830, between the United States and the Ottoman Porte, in so far as it concerns the treatment of American citizens accused of crime in Turkey.

" It appears to be your desire to avoid the extended discussion of details which has attended this question for several years past, and treat it in its most practical aspects. To that end you confine your representations to certain elementary considerations which, if I rightfully understand your note, you regard as conclusive in themselves and as rightly sufficient to have closed the controversy before now, under the instructions given to the United States minister at Constantinople to examine and settle the facts.

" This Department is equally desirous to avoid traveling anew the path of previous argument. The matter seems to it to be one readily restricted to precise limits within which it might have been determined at any time in the past fifty years if your Government had met the real issue by a positive statement of the precise meaning of the Turkish text of the fourth article in dispute.

" A part of your argument appears to rest, permit me to say, on a fallacious assumption. You go back to Mr. Porter's declaration in 1831, that the Turkish text should be the standard in case of doubt as to the meaning of the treaty, and you next quote (with some verbal inaccuracies) the words of Mr. Evarts in his note of May 14, 1880, as follows: ' I am directed by the President to admit, on the part of the Government of the United States, that the United States are bound by the Turkish text of the treaty of 1830, which was signed in that text alone. I make this admission the more cheerfully in view of your repeated assurances in the name of your Government that not only shall the true intent of that text be observed, but also that the citizens of the United States within Ottoman jurisdiction shall have the treatment accorded to the citizens or subjects of the most favored nation, either by treaty or by virtue of existing local laws or customs,' both of which you take as showing that ' the United States Government, yielding to evidence, finally adhered, it is true, *in principle to the view taken* of this question by the Sublime Porte.' You surely do not wish to be understood as claiming that an admission of the Turkish text as the standard is equivalent to a blind acceptance of the interpretation which the Porte may see fit to give to that text, where the language itself is ambiguous. As Mr. Bancroft Davis, then Acting Secretary of State, had the honor to inform Aristarchi Bey on the 30th of December, 1881—

" ' The President has not intimated a purpose of yielding to the Ottoman construction of the treaty of 1830, or of abandoning in any way what he regards as the just rights of the United States.'

" The simple question is now, and always has been, what was the meaning of the treaty of 1830? In other words, what did it stipulate for American citizens in Turkey in 1830?

" You are doubtless familiar with the precedent correspondence, and will therefore recall without difficulty the many occasions on which this Government has asked that of Turkey to furnish an intelligible paraphrase of the disputed article, and to explain what was the usage toward other Franks in 1830. Not the slightest attempt to enlighten this Government on those two all-important points has been made.

" The treaty was negotiated, as you are aware, in the French tongue. The commissioners agreed upon a text in French, embracing certain stipulations. The reports of the negotiations which accompanied the text showed the occasion for those stipulations and their nature. With regard to the clause in dispute, forbidding the arrest and imprisonment of American citizens by the local judges, and leaving to their ministers or consuls the power to punish them, as in the case of other Franks, the negotiators remarked that this clause was not always strictly observed in the case of other Franks; that the Turkish authorities in 1830 frequently arrested Franks, who were thereupon demanded and obtained with difficulty by the foreign ministers. There seems to have been no doubt in their minds as to the extent of the stipulated privilege. The French text, so agreed upon, was accepted by the Turkish negotiators, and the American negotiators were thereupon furnished by the Turks with a version in the Turkish language, which they were assured was a faithful equivalent of the French text agreed upon.

" If, under these circumstances, the effect of translation was to occasion differences between the two texts, it would seem to be due to translation from French into Turkish. However this may be, they could have been verbal merely, for to suppose that, under the assurance of equivalence, a Turkish text was submitted radically different from the French text agreed upon, would be to impute something very like bad faith to the Turkish negotiators—an imputation which this Government has no desire to make.

" The Turkish Government denies absolutely the existence in the Turkish text of certain phrases found in the English text. It says:

" ' The words " *they shall be tried by their minister or consul and punished according to their offense* " no more exist in the text than the words " *they shall not be arrested.*" '

" Omit these words and the remaining text becomes utterly meaningless. Nothing whatever is stipulated save the usage observed toward other Franks. This must be more than ' merely the effect of translation.'

" This Department possesses twenty or more translations from the original Turkish text, made by eminent scholars and impartial experts. All these versions, without exception, contain phrases closely following those which the Porte says do not exist at all, and all, despite wide verbal differences (merely the effect of translation), agree in stipulating that no American citizen shall be imprisoned in a Turkish prison, but shall be punished through the instrumentality of his minister or consul.

" The inference is irresistible that something of the nature of an extraterritorial privilege was stipulated, and that the words on which your Government lays such stress—' following in this respect the usage observed towards other Franks '—are simply explanatory. They refer merely, by way of illustration, to a well-known state of things existing in 1830, when, as Mr. Rhind shows, all the foreign ministers successfully resisted the occasional mistaken effort of a Turkish officer to arrest Frankish subjects. They do not contain by limitation the whole of the concession.

" Moreover, this explanatory clause as to the treatment of other Franks was clearly not intended, in 1830, to subject American citizens for the future to whatever changes might thereafter supervene in the Turkish treatment of other Franks. The stipulation was meant to rest on a solid basis, not on a delusive quicksand, shifting with each varying provision of Turkish law. This is evident when we remember that in 1830 there were no tribunals to which foreigners were amenable, and that the system of jurisprudence to which the Porte claims that American citizens are to be subjected originated long after the treaty of 1830.

"The Turkish ground as to the judicial treatment of Franks changes every year. One example will suffice. In the past correspondence the Porte and its representative here have repeated with the most solemn asseverations the assurance that the treaty in the Turkish text distinctly reserved to our ministers and consuls the sole right to *imprison* American citizens even in pursuance of a Turkish judgment whose validity we have denied, and yet, recently, an American citizen, Dr. Pflaum, has suffered *imprisonment* in a Turkish prison by virtue of a Turkish judicial sentence.

"I may recognize a desire on the part of the Porte to bring the treatment of all Franks under the provisions of its recent judicial legislation; but this desire is limited in its effects by treaty rights. It would appear to be the intention of the Porte to eliminate from the last part of article 4 of the treaty of 1830 all that enunciates any specific privilege, and leave only a vague favored-nation clause, whereby American citizens shall receive the most favorable treatment which for the time being may be accorded to any other Frank. This is a very narrow result. We are willing to regard the phrase touching the treatment of other Franks as having some of the quality of a most favored-nation clause; that is, if any other Franks have a more favored treatment than that specifically stipulated in our treaty, an American citizen might rightly claim such extension of favor. But it is not in itself a most favored-nation clause, nor does it stand alone, independent of the specific stipulations of the article in which it is found.

"In every aspect of the case there are two vital considerations: First, the true meaning of the text of the treaty, and, secondly, the treatment of Franks in 1830, when the treaty was signed. As to both of these our efforts to obtain a distinct declaration from the Porte have failed. Our last attempt to obtain the needed light on the subject has been completely ignored. An instruction, No. 44, of March 3, 1882, was sent to Mr. Wallace, summarizing the whole situation in the frankest spirit and with the sole desire to put an end to this controversy. On the 29th of October, 1882, Mr. Wallace communicated a copy of that dispatch to his excellency Said Pasha, the Porte's minister for foreign affairs. No answer has been made. As

I infer from your note of April 26, 1884, that you are not even aware of the existence of my communication of March 3, 1882, I send you a copy thereof for your information, omitting the inclosures, which, as you will see, are of record in your legation.

" I write you this from a courteous desire that you may fully comprehend the situation, not with any purpose of transferring the discussion back to Washington for speculative and impractical discussion. As I said in my note to Aristarchi Bey, of August 29, 1882, 'General Wallace is in a position, under the instructions heretofore sent to him, to respond to any proposal or argument which his excellency the minister for foreign affairs may see fit to address to him.' "

> Mr. Frelinghuysen, Sec. of State, to Tevfik Pasha, Turkish min., May 31, 1884, For. Rel. 1885, 892.
>
> See, also, Mr. Frelinghuysen, Sec. of State, to Mr. Heap, May 31, 1884, and Sept. 18, 1884, MS. Inst. Turkey, IV. 143, 176.

" I have had the honor to receive the note which you were pleased to address to me on the 31st of May last relative to the interpretation of Article IV. of the treaty of 1830.

" This question, which has been kept so long in abeyance, has been the subject of so many controversies, both here and at Constantinople, that another detailed examination of it would, as you are pleased to remark, have no practical result, especially since you have decided, as you are pleased to inform me, again to transfer the discussion of this matter to Constantinople. Nevertheless, the regard and the consideration which I entertain for all communications from the distinguished head of the Department of State, compel me to endeavor to reply to some, at least, of the arguments contained in the aforesaid note.

" The whole question on which we are unable to agree is, you say, 'the exact meaning of the treaty of 1830. In other words, what did that treaty stipulate for American citizens in Turkey in 1830?' You add:

" ' Although this Government has repeatedly requested that of Turkey to furnish an intelligible paraphrase of the disputed article, no attempt to enlighten this Government on this all-important point has been made.'

" You will permit me, Mr. Secretary of State, to appeal to your recollection on this subject. As long ago as 1868 Ali Pasha informed Mr. Edward Joy Morris, the representative of the United States at Constantinople, how the Sublime Porte interpreted this article. We have always maintained the same interpretation, as is shown by the voluminous correspondence which has taken place on this subject. Aristarchi Bey, moreover, at the request of one of your predecessors, transmitted to the Department of State a French translation of the article in question, which was made here, and for which he was directly responsible. You will therefore be pleased to admit, Mr. Secretary of State, that the Imperial Government does not deserve the charge that ' it has done nothing to enlighten that of the United States on this all-important point.'

" As to the definition of privileges that were enjoyed in Turkey by the subjects of foreign powers in 1830, which definition you say you have asked us in vain to furnish, I will take the liberty of stating that this is an entirely new requirement, which seems to me to have been formulated for the first time. An examination of the correspondence shows that, in 1880, Mr. Blaine, then Secretary of State, in his negotiations with my predecessor, was disposed to consider as sufficient a declaration on our part to the effect that American citizens should enjoy the usage and privileges granted to other nations. This declaration we did not hesitate to make. You now ask us to specify the nature of the privileges that were granted by us to foreigners in 1830. This request appears to me singularly to complicate the question. By the treaty of 1830 the Sublime Porte simply promised to allow citizens of this Republic to enjoy the privileges granted to other Franks, and to treat them in all respects on the same footing with the latter. Now, the privileges granted to foreigners by the capitulations can not represent an absolute and immutable state of things, and one never susceptible of any variation. The usage may be modified according to the progress of the times, or according to the mutual consent of the parties; from which it is evident that if any change were to take place in the status of foreigners in general, Americans would have to submit to the common law, and could claim no special privilege beyond what was enjoyed by other foreigners. It would therefore be practically useless to inquire, Mr. Secretary of State, as you suggest, what privileges were granted to foreigners in 1830.

" In the instructions given by the United States Government to its plenipotentiaries charged with the negotiation of the treaty of 1830, it is expressly enjoined upon them (see Notes upon the Foreign Treaties of the United States, page 1060, revised edition, 1873,) to conclude a treaty upon the most-favored-nation basis. In other words, the United States instructed their negotiators to secure for American citizens the same usage that was granted by the Sublime Porte to other Franks at that time. The following, Mr. Secretary of State, was the status of Franks in Turkey in respect to criminal matters, according to the text of the capitulations then in force:

" ' If a Frank commit a murder or other crime, the authorities shall take cognizance thereof, but the judges and officers shall not proceed to do so save in the presence of the ambassador, the consuls, or their substitutes.'

"This is the rule by which the Sublime Porte has always been guided in cases of crimes or misdemeanors committed by foreign subjects or citizens residing in Turkey. Americans, I repeat, cannot claim exceptional usage; the expression found in Article IV. of the treaty of 1830, viz, 'following the usage observed towards other Franks,' cannot leave the slightest doubt on this head; it conclusively proves that nothing more was granted to citizens of this Republic than to the subjects of other powers.

"As to the opinion, which is also enunciated for the first time, that the treaty was negotiated in French, and that the Turkish text was but a translation for which the Ottoman ministers were responsible, it is refuted by the American documents themselves. I will take the liberty, Mr. Secretary of State, to quote in support of this assertion, the following passage from the 'Notes upon the Foreign Treaties of the United States,' page 1061:

"'He [Mr. Rhind] submitted a draft of a treaty to the Reis Effendi. Some days later he was shown the Turkish text of a treaty, and was told by the Reis Effendi that it was drawn up in strict conformity with the one which he had submitted, and on the 7th of May the treaty was signed, the Turkish text being signed by the Reis Effendi, as it had been prepared by him, and the French text being signed by Rhind *after examination and comparing it with the Turkish.*'

"Lower down on the same page are found the following words:

"'It appears from the archives of the Department of State that four translations were sent to America: (1) An English translation from the original Turkish, not verified; (2) a French translation from the original Turkish, verified by Navoni, the American dragoman; (3) another French translation in black ink, with annotations in red ink; (4) another English translation, made from the French. No French version appears to have been transmitted to the Senate with the Turkish text.'

"Do not these quotations, the number of which might easily be increased, most clearly prove that the Turkish text is the original, and that the English and French versions are merely translations, which were verified by the American delegates? The imputation, therefore, of a certain degree of bad faith on the part of the Ottoman negotiators, would be, to say the least, undeserved. I am glad to see, moreover, that you are pleased to declare that the United States Government desires to make no such imputation.

"The Department of State has, you say, more than twenty translations of the original Turkish text, made by competent and impartial persons. All these versions, you add, without exception, agree in stipulating, notwithstanding certain differences of expression resulting from translation, that 'no American citizen shall be imprisoned in a Turkish prison, but shall be punished through the instrumentality of his minister or consul.'

" The Sublime Porte has always maintained that the words ' arrested and tried ' are not found in the Turkish text of the fourth article of the treaty of 1830. It is now glad to find that they are not in the translations of that article which the Department of State has caused to be made. Their omission, moreover, does not render the rest of the article ' utterly meaningless.' Your own quotation is the best proof of this.

"As to the assertion that previously to 1830 there were no Ottoman courts to which foreigners were amenable, it seems to me to be a mistake as to fact which you will, I doubt not, Mr. Secretary of State, hasten to admit, when the true state of the case shall be better known to you. Foreigners charged with the commission of any crime were then tried by a cadi, in presence of their consul or his representative, as appears from the very text of the capitulations. That magistrate has now been superseded by a court composed of several judges; but, although the form of the tribunal has changed, its jurisdiction remains the same; that has not deprived foreigners of the privilege of the presence of their consul or dragoman, which is secured to them by the capitulations.

" To sum up, Mr. Secretary of State, the Imperial Government, for the foregoing reasons, can do nothing more than fulfill the promise which it has so often made, viz, to accord to American citizens, in penal cases, the usage, privileges, and guarantees that are enjoyed by other foreigners. The treaty of 1830, if the official and original text in the Turkish language be taken as the standard, stipulated for nothing more in their favor. On this basis alone will the Sublime Porte negotiate the case arising with the United States legation.

" You are pleased to inform me, in conclusion, that you addressed a dispatch to the United States minister at Constantinople on the 3d of March, 1882, giving him the necessary instructions to bring this controversy to a close. On the 29th of October, 1882, General Wallace sent a copy of that dispatch to his excellency Assim Pasha, minister of foreign affairs; to this communication you say that no reply has been received. In this connection you will permit me to inform you that the Sublime Porte, anticipating, as it were, the step about to be taken by the Department of State, addressed a note to the United States legation, July 6, 1882, more than a month before it received General Wallace's communication, stating that it would be glad to discuss the final settlement of this matter with the representative of the United States. As I have reason to suppose, from the note which you did me the honor to address to me on the 31st of May, that you are not aware of the existence of the communication which thus emanated from our ministry of foreign affairs, I herewith transmit to you a copy of it.

" In conclusion, I earnestly beg you, Mr. Secretary of State, by order of my Government, to be pleased to instruct the United States legation at Constantinople to enter without delay into negotiations with the Sublime Porte with a view to the final settlement of this question, which has been a subject of discussion for so many years, and which threatens to last for an indefinite period, to the great detriment of the well-recognized interests of both countries."

> Tevfik Pasha, Turkish min., to Mr. Frelingheysen, Sec. of State, Nov. 26, 1884, For. Rel. 1885, 898.

The inclosure is as follows:

" I am compelled to recur to the disagreement that exists between the Sublime Porte and the United States Government in reference to the interpretation of Article IV. of the treaty of 1830, concluded between the two countries.

" According to the Washington Cabinet, American consuls in the Empire have the right of jurisdiction over American citizens who are guilty of crimes or misdemeanors, to the exclusion of any intervention on the part of the Ottoman authorities, not only in cases in which the victim is a foreign subject, but also in those in which the injured party is an Ottoman subject.

" This intrepretation, which tends to sanction a mode of procedure at variance with the practice observed towards all other foreigners, without exception, can in no wise be accepted.

" It can have arisen from nothing but an error in translation or a misapprehension. The Imperial Government can by no means grant to citizens of the United States a usage different from that which is accorded to other foreigners residing in the Empire.

" This question has been much discussed, both here and at Washington. Aristarchi Bey informed me, shortly before he left Washington, that the Secretary of State had told him that he had sent you instructions to enter into communication with the Sublime Porte with a view to the settlement of this agreement.

" I think it proper for me to notify you that I shall be happy to enter into negotiations for the final settlement of this matter." (Said Pasha, min. of for. aff., to Mr. Wallace, min. to Turkey, July 6, 1882, For. Rel. 1885, 901.)

> See, also, Mr. Bayard, Sec. of State, to Tevfik Pasha, Turkish min., Sept. 18, 1886; Mr. Bayard, Sec. of State, to Mavroyeni Bey, Turkish min., Dec. 29, 1888; same to same, Feb. 28, 1889; Mr. Blaine, Sec. of State, to Mavroyeni Bey, Turkish min., Feb. 25, 1890; same to same, March 15, 1890: MS. Notes to Turkish Leg. I. 461, 490, 492, 522, 528.

" I herewith transmit a copy of a note from the minister of Turkey at this capital, of November 26, 1884, in regard to the disputed interpretation of the fourth article of the treaty of 1830, between the United States and Turkey. I have merely said in reply that a copy of this note would be sent to you for your information in the examination of the matter under the instructions which have already been given to you. What the Department desires now is a full report from you upon the subject. ●

" You will observe from a perusal of Tevfik Pasha's note that the ground is now changed, and that the words ' arrested and tried ' are the only ones which are regarded as wanting in the Turkish text. These are not in juxtaposition in the English text.

' Tevfik's collocation of these words in one phrase is somewhat misleading. The words are in two different clauses :

" ' (*a*) They shall not be arrested and put in prison by the local authorities, and

" ' (*b*) They shall be tried by their minister or consul and punished.'

" It is not denied that the prohibition against imprisonment by the local authorities exists, and it is not logical to insist on the omission of ' arrest ' without which no imprisonment would be possible. And all the versions agree that our citizens are to be punished according to their offense only through the instrumentality of their ministers and consuls. How such instrumentality can award and inflict punishment in accordance with the offense, if the necessary stage of judicial ascertainment is omitted, does not appear.

" The citation by Tevfik Pasha establishes the very fact he attempts to refute, that Rhind's negotiations were in French, and that the Turkish text submitted to him by the Reis Effendi was said to be the exact equivalent of the text agreed upon in French. I may here properly advert, then, to our view that the words ' following in this respect the usage observed towards other Franks ' is merely explanatory of the specific treatment there accorded and defined in the article, and is not to be deemed as the essential clause subjecting the treatment of American citizens to all the changes it might thereafter undergo.

"As for the state of jurisdiction in 1830 Tevfik Pasha's statement is restricted, and not borne out by a historical examination of the facts. The distinguished publicist, Pradier-Fodéré, than whom there is no higher authority, in a paper contributed to the Revue de Droit International et de Législation Comparée in 1869 (tom. I) sums up the procedure under the capitulations as follows (p. 126) :

" ' L'inviolabilité du domicile et dans le cas de flagrant délit, la défense aux autorités locales d'arrêter dans une maison européenne, même un indigène coupable, sans l'assistance d'un officier du consulat ou de l'ambassade; le droit pour les nationaux des pays de l'occident *d' être jugés* par leurs ambassadeurs ou leurs consuls dans toutes leurs contestations civiles ou criminelles, et l'autorisation pour les autorités ottomanes de prêter main-forte aux agents diplomatiques et aux consuls pour assurer l'exécution des sentences rendues.'

" Or in English, as follows :

" ' The inviolability of domicil, and in the case of *flagrante delicto*, the local authorities to be forbidden to make an arrest in a European house even of a guilty native, without the help of an officer of the consulate or embassy; the right of citizens of nations of the West *to be judged* by their ambassadors or consuls in their civil or criminal litigations and the authority to be given to Ottoman officials to assist diplomatic agents and consuls in securing the execution of pronounced sentences.'

" So far as the Turkish position may be inferred from what has been said heretofore, it implies contention for four alternate stages of procedure, viz:

" (*a*) The Turks to *arrest* (which is expressly forbidden by the capitulations).

" (*b*) The minister *to imprison.*

" (*c*) The Turks to *try* the accused in the presence of their minister or consul (but without the latter exercising any of the ' instrumentality ' which the treaty of 1830 admittedly reserves to them) ; and

"(*d*) The minister or consul to ' *punish* ' in accordance with the offense (although all instrumentality in fixing a punishment in accordance with the offense is denied to the minister or consul).

" Nothing could better show the incongruity of the Turkish claim than this formulation of their position after some twenty years of discussion.

" Under the circumstances, therefore, I can only reiterate the oft-repeated assertion of this Government, that it is still without any intelligible and congruous English or French version which the Sublime Porte admits as correctly interpreting the Turkish text. Certainly none can be deduced from Tevfik Pasha's present note.

" Your report is awaited before further instructing you in the premises."

Mr. Frelinghuysen, Sec. of State, to Mr. Wallace, min. to Turkey, Jan. 22, 1885, For Rel. 1885, 827; MS. Inst. Turkey, IV. 205.

In January, 1888, Hercules A. Proios, a naturalized citizen of the United States, was arrested in southern Russia on a request of the Turkish Government for his extradition on the charge of embezzling public moneys. The local consular representative of the United States intervened, and Proios was ultimately sent to the Russian consul-general in Constantinople, who turned him over to the consul-general of the United States, with the statement that charges would be made against him by the Turkish Government. The Turkish Government, however, in consequence of the question as to art. 4 of the treaty of 1830, declined to prosecute the case before the United States consul-general, and Proios was discharged.

Case of Proios.

For. Rel. 1888, II. 1405, 1406, 1573, 1582, 1583, 1588, 1603, 1607.

" I have to acknowledge the receipt of your Nos. 168, 174, 178, and
Gurdjian's case, 186, of the 19th and 28th of October and the 5th and
1890; Mr. 18th of November, respectively, in relation to the
Blaine's offer. arrest, by the Ottoman authorities, of Siropé Gurdjian, a naturalized citizen of the United States of Turkish origin, his
subsequent delivery over to the consul-general of the United States,
and the demands since made by the Porte for his production before
the Turkish tribunals.

" The facts in regard to Mr. Gurdjian, as ascertained by you and
reported in your dispatches, are that he was born at Cæsarea, in Asia
Minor, on the 13th of September, 1848, and in 1865 came to the United
States. From that time until 1872 he resided in the State of New
Hampshire as a student. He then entered Bowdoin College, where,
in 1877, he was graduated. On the 3d of March, 1874, he was admitted to citizenship of the United States before the United States
district court for the district of Massachusetts.

" In 1878 a project was formed in this country for founding a
university near Constantinople, and Mr. Gurdjian was invested with
power by a board, comprising a number of prominent citizens of the
United States, to proceed to Turkey and enter into negotiations for
the purchase of land and the obtainment of an imperial iradé for the
establishment of the school. It is stated that, with a view to facilitate the accomplishment of the plan, Aristarchi Bey, then Turkish
minister at this capital, furnished Mr. Gurdjian with letters to high
Ottoman authorities.

" On reaching Constantinople Mr. Gurdjian was registered at the
United States consulate-general as an American citizen. His passport is No. 10427, issued on November 8, 1878, by Mr. Evarts, then
Secretary of State. After remaining in that city for more than a
year, he returned, in 1880, to this country. In 1881, however, he went
again to Turkey, where he has since resided. The university project
was not successful, and Mr. Gurdjian, who had acquired some knowledge of geology, chemistry, and other sciences, embarked in coal-
mining enterprises and also worked as chemist and photographer in
Turkey.

" At 8 o'clock on the evening of Wednesday, the 15th of October
last, an agent of the secret police of Pera, accompanied by two
gendarmes, presented himself at the house of Mr. Gurdjian and
ordered him to accompany them to the neighboring police station.
Mr. Gurdjian alleged his American nationality, and said that when
they wanted him they should address the American authorities.
The police officer replied that in case he resisted he would be compelled to remove him by force, and Mr. Gurdjian was obliged to submit. It is stated that he was not allowed time to get his boots or

change his clothes, but was forced away, half clad, to the police station, where questions were addressed to him respecting his name, surname, and his past nationality. He again showed his passport, and was then taken to the mutaserifate of Galata Serai.

"The same formalities were gone through with before the mutaserifate, Mr. Gurdjian again exhibiting his passport. He was then sent with two gendarmes, followed by the police agent, to the central police station in Stamboul, where, after submitting to summary interrogation before the superior official, he once more produced his passport. He was then thrown into a dungeon, where he passed the night. At 9 in the morning he was again brought before the superior officer, who, after having made new inquiries as to his nationality, said that those who had arrested him had make a mistake, and directed that he be forthwith escorted to the United States consulate. He was accordingly sent to the consulate. At the same time a citation was, on the 16th of October, addressed to the consul-general for the appearance of Gurdjian, accompanied by the consular dragoman, before the council of police at Stamboul.

"On being informed of these facts, you at once addressed a note, on the 17th of October, to the Turkish minister of foreign affairs, from which may be quoted the following passages:

"'The legation can not see its way to permitting the appearance of an American citizen before the Ottoman police authorities without having first been furnished with a statement of the reasons for which he may be summoned, and in this case, in addition to such statement, ample satisfaction for the conduct of the police is an indispensable preliminary to the appearance of Siropé Gurdjian.

"'Your excellency, I am persuaded, will agree with me that the occurrence of such an event in the capital itself, without being followed by swift and exemplary punishment of those responsible for the arrest and false imprisonment of an American citizen, and in spite of the most sacred clause of the capitulations and treaties, is of itself a fact of exceeding gravity. With all possible good disposition with which this abuse by the police may be considered, a mistake can not be admitted as sufficient excuse, inasmuch as since the conquest of Constantinople it is a fact known to all that the domicile of a foreigner is inviolable and may not be entered save in the presence of his consul or the consul's deputy. Therefore, if those charged with the public security during the night at the stations of Hendek, at the mutaserifate of Galata, and at the central station in Stamboul are not sufficiently instructed in their duties and their rights your excellency will concede that such a state of affairs is indeed to be lamented.

"'The legation is constrained, therefore, to protest in the most vigorous language and in the most formal manner against such intolerable infringement of the primitive civil rights of the individual, and to demand that His Majesty's Government take steps for the immediate punishment of the offenders and for securing reparation to the victim commensurate with the enormity of the injury inflicted upon him.'

" To this note a reply was made on the 22d of the same month. In his reply the minister of foreign affairs expresses regret that the subordinate agent of the police should have effected the arrest without demanding the presence of the consular representatives of the United States, but alleges that this omission arose from the authorities being ignorant that they had to do with an American citizen, and that the name of the person arrested was not of a nature to enlighten them. The minister further said:

" ' Your excellency will nevertheless do us this justice to recognize that as soon as informed of his character (as American citizen) the superior authorities delivered him to his consulate. Measures having been taken to prevent a repetition of similar mistakes, I allow myself to hope that your excellency will, on your part, be pleased to give orders that Seropé Gurdjian may be brought before the police authorities whenever he may be required.'

" On the 28th of October you replied to this note, dissenting from the view that what was done was satisfactorily explained as a mistake, Mr. Gurdjian having exhibited his passport. You further observed that no statement of the reasons why the consulate had been asked to produce Mr. Gurdjian had been furnished. And you informed his excellency that the punishment of those who may have been responsible for the outrage was a matter for consideration before the question of Mr. Gurdjian's further appearance. Replying on the 5th of November, the minister of foreign affairs states that the crime of which Mr. Gurdjian is accused consists in his participating in a revolutionary committee, the seal of which he is charged to have made. With this statement, the minister of foreign affairs renews his request that orders be issued for bringing Gurdjian before the police authorities whenever his presence shall be required. The minister further said: 'As to the agent guilty of having committed the irregular acts referred to by the legation, he will not fail from being punished.'

" In consequence of the demands of the Ottoman authorities for the production of Mr. Gurdjian you telegraphed to the Department to ascertain whether he ought to be produced. The Department replied that it could not authorize you to produce Mr. Gurdjian to the Turkish authorities and instructed you to report the facts fully by mail. It was after the sending of this telegram that your reports of the case were received.

" In your last dispatch, No. 186, of the 18th of November, you inform the Department that on the forenoon of that day the vice-consul-general called on you with a summons from the police authorities requiring him to produce Mr. Gurdjian for examination on the following day. The vice-consul was accompanied by Mr. Dongian, a naturalized citizen of the United States, recently from this country, who stated that he had, at Mr. Gurdjian's request, called on him and prescribed for him; that he found him in a very deplorable state, suffering from heart and spinal trouble and nervous prostration. The doctor expressed the opinion that it would be impossible for Mr. Gurdjian to leave his bed for several weeks, and that, even were he out of Turkey and free from mental anxiety, he would require two months to rally from the shock he had received. You instructed the vice-consul-general not to produce Mr. Gurdjian without further orders from the legation.

" In concluding your last dispatch you observe that you have treated Gurdjian as being innocent of any connection with the proceedings of the Armenian committee, as well as innocent of the charge of cutting the seal. Mr. Gurdjian still maintains his innocence; nevertheless, he now makes an admission that the engraving of the seal was done in his room by another man.

" In a letter written on the 3d of November to the vice-consul-general Mr. Gurdjian, still maintaining ignorance of the real cause of his arrest, suggested that a Masonic design which hung upon his wall may have excited suspicion. In a letter, however, addressed to you on the 13th of November, just ten days later, he makes a full statement as to the engraving of the seal, though professing ignorance as to the character of the seal and the purpose for which it was engraved. But it appears that the seal was actually engraved in his room.

" It is not within the province of the Department, nor would it be proper for the Department under the present circumstances, to comment upon the latest letter of Mr. Gurdjian and express an opinion as to the truth of the various statements on the ground either of consistency or of probability. But while made nearly a month after his arrest, they relate to matters that occurred prior to that time and disclose knowledge which was in his possession from the beginning of his difficulties and of which the legation might at once have been informed.

" In proceeding to the consideration of the legal aspects of the case, the Department desires to express its high appreciation of your conduct throughout the whole transaction. Your representations to the Turkish Government have been characterized by a clear appreciation of the questions at issue and by a just determination to insist upon proper reparation at the hands of the Ottoman authorities. And they have had the effect of obtaining an expression of regret for the wrong done and a promise of punishment of the offenders.

"Apart from the consideration of jurisdiction, your refusal to order the production of Mr. Gurdjian before the Ottoman tribunals is amply justified by his physical condition. Especially is this so when that condition is the result of the illegal and violent action of the Turkish authorities. In view, however, of the probable recovery of Mr. Gurdjian from the effects of the shock he has received, it is necessary to consider what the duty of this Government would be in that event.

"You are aware of the controversy that the Ottoman Porte has raised in regard to the fourth article of the treaty of 1830. According to the English version of that article, as published among the treaties of the United States, the disputed provision reads as follows:

"'Citizens of the United States of America quietly pursuing their commerce, and not being charged or convicted of any crime or offense, shall not be molested, and even when they may have committed some offense they shall not be arrested and put in prison by the local authorities, but they shall be tried by their minister or consul and punished according to their offense, following in this respect the usage observed toward other Franks.'

"This text was proclaimed in 1832, and it stood without objection on the part of the Turkish Government until 1868, a period of more than thirty-five years. In that year the Turkish Government declared, in respect to a case then pending before the minister of the United States in Constantinople, that the English text was not an accurate reproduction of the Turkish, which was admitted to be the standard, and that according to the latter the minister and consuls did not possess the right to try. Thereupon this Government obtained a large number of translations of the Turkish text, by which it appeared that while the English text published by this Government was not an exact literal translation of the Turkish original, it preserved its tenor and substance. The accuracy of these translations not being admitted by the Ottoman Government, the Government of the United States invited it to submit a correct translation, in order that there might, if possible, be an undisputed basis of discussion. Such a translation was never furnished until the 24th of August, 1888, when Mavroyeni Bey, by authority of his Government, presented the following translation in French:

"'Les citoyens Américains vaquant paisiblement aux affaires de leur commerce ne seront point molestés sans motif tant qu'ils n'auront pas commis quelque délit ou quelque faute; même en cas de culpabilité, ils ne seront pas emprisonnés par les juges et les agents de la sûreté, mais ils seront punis par les soins de leur ministre et consul à l'instar de ce qui se pratique à l'égard des autres Francs.'

"'American citizens peaceably attending to matters of commerce shall not be molested without cause so long as they shall not have committed any offense or fault. Even in case of culpability they shall not be imprisoned by the judges and police agents, but they shall be punished through the agency of their ministers and consuls, according to the practice observed in regard to other Franks.'

"After submitting his French translation, Mavroyeni Bey addressed several notes to this Department, in which he advanced the contention that since the treaty did not say 'they shall be tried and punished' instead of 'they shall be punished,' the right to try belonged to the Porte. This Government replied on the 25th of February that the right to try was involved in and incident to the right to punish, and that the English version of the article, which had stood unchallenged for so many years, merely expressed the obvious meaning of the Turkish text of the treaty as officially translated by that Government. As a measure, however, of concession to a friendly power, I offered to yield the right of trial and to accept the treatment accorded to certain European powers, under which the case is tried by local authorities, the dragoman of the legation being present. It was, however, discovered that this contention would settle nothing, since the Turkish minister at once proceeded to contest our right to punish. His position on this subject, as I stated in a note to him of the 25th of February last, was based upon two grounds—one inside the treaty and the other outside of it, which did not appear to be consistent. One was that if the treaty gave the right to punish it granted inadvertently more than was intended to be given. To state this argument seemed to me to answer it, for if the treaty gives the right it is futile to argue that the right does not exist. The minister also argued that the treaty did not give the right, contending that the express concession of it in the words, 'they shall not be imprisoned by the judges and police agents, but they shall be punished through the agency of the minister and consul,' was restricted by the clause, 'according to the practice observed in regard to other Franks.' This contention was based by the minister upon the statement that in 1830 the ministers and consuls of the Franks did not exercise the right to punish unless 'abusively.' The information in the possession of the Department led to the conclusion that at that time they habitually exercised the right to try and punish as a matter of common usage. It was also observed that the provisions both as to trial and punishment in the English version of the treaty with the United States were repeated in later treaties concluded by the Porte with Belgium and Portugal. The French text, however, of these treaties is contested by the Ottoman Government.

" But, apart from the historical questions and conventional provisions which the Turkish Government contested, I pointed out the impossibility of limiting, by an executive interpretation given to a general and subsidiary clause, a clearly expressed and unequivocal stipulation. 'Even in case of culpability,' the stipulation reads, 'they (American citizens) shall not be imprisoned by the judges or police agents, but they shall be punished through the agency of their ministers and consuls;' the right to punish, as thus stated, being at once forbidden to the Porte and secured to the ministers and consuls of the United States. But I proposed, as a means of ending controversy, while expressly conceding the right to try, to permit the rest of the article to stand without interpretation and to be enforced by this Government should occasion arise. This proposition was declined. To my note of the 25th of February the Turkish minister replied on the 28th of the same month. But after careful consideration of his reply, I was unable to perceive that it contributed anything to the solution of the controversy, or that it met the arguments advanced by this Government. The minister inquired whether it was not evident that I must admit, above all and after all, that what the United States secured by the treaty of 1830, even as regarded the right to punish, was not more than was claimed by other Franks at that time. I did not find myself either required or able to make such an admission. The intent of the treaty seemed to me to be so clear and explicit as not to admit of reasonable controversy, and I was consequently compelled to decline to put upon it an interpretation which the language did not admit of, and thus to substitute by executive agreement a new treaty for that which actually exists. The posture into which the negotiation was brought by the extraordinary contentions of the Turkish minister was described in my note to him of the 25th of February as follows:

"'Sincerely, therefore, as I desire to settle the long-pending controversy now under consideration, I find myself wholly unable to meet your views. I could not, even were I so disposed, first yield everything that can be made the subject of comprehensible controversy, and then enter upon a discussion as to whether I shall maintain what can not by any conceivable method of reasoning be denied.'

"To my last note of the 15th of March of the same year no reply was made, probably for the reason that I had clearly indicated that it would be useless to attempt to continue the discussion upon the lines on which the minister had sought to conduct it.

"For the reasons above stated, this Government is unable to comply with the request of the Turkish minister of foreign affairs for the production of Mr. Gurdjian before the Ottoman tribunals.

"It remains therefore to consider what course the Government of the United States, exercising its rights and performing its obligations under the treaty, ought to pursue in disposing of the complaint made against Mr. Gurdjian. In adopting legislation to give effect to the extraterritorial rights of the United States in certain countries

Congress did not fail to provide for the punishment of offenses against the governments of those countries. Such a provision was obviously essential; for, as our citizens were not to be subject to the local jurisdiction, it was necessary for this Government to take cognizance of possible offenses against the local governments. Hence it was provided by the act of June 22, 1860, section 24, which is now embodied in section 4090 of the Revised Statutes, that ' Capital cases for murder and insurrection against the Government of either of the countries hereinbefore mentioned, by citizens of the United States, or for offenses against the public peace amounting to felony under the laws of the United States may be tried before the minister of the United States in the country where the offense is committed, if allowed jurisdiction.'

" By section 15 of the same act, now embodied in section 4102 of the Revised Statutes, it was provided that ' insurrection or rebellion against the Government of either of these countries, with intent to subvert the same, and murder, shall be capital offenses, punishable with death.'

" These provisions sufficiently illustrate the purpose of the legislation of Congress in respect to offenses against the local government. The duty of enforcing this legislation rests upon the Government of the United States, both as a matter of conventional obligation and as a mattter of obedience to our own laws. To have left the punishment of offenses against the local government unprovided for would have left that government exposed and defenseless against the machinations of foreign residents. On the other hand, to have conceded the trial and punishment of such offenses to the local tribunals would have been, in effect, to deprive our citizens, upon the mere allegation of offense and without trial, of their right of extraterritoriality and to abandon them to the local tribunals on charges the most likely to excite passion and prejudice, and therefore most liable to abuse. For these reasons the Government of the United States in the fulfillment of its obligations, assumed the duty of punishing its citizens for offenses against the governments of the countries in which the right of extraterritoriality was exercised.

" Such being the law it will be your duty to receive the complaints of the Turkish Government against Mr. Gurdjian and any evidence that may be submitted in support of these complaints with a view to his trial by you as the minister of the United States, clothed by act of Congress with judicial functions in such cases. While it is the duty of the Department to give you these general instructions in regard to the discharge of your functions, it would be improper for it to undertake to interfere with or influence your judicial judgment. For that reason it has abstained, as you have already perceived, from expressing any opinion as to the effect of the admissions made to you by Mr. Gurdjian in his letter of the 13th of November. For the same reason, as well as for the reason that the information now before it is defective, the Department is unable to give you specific instructions in regard to the formulation of charges, if, upon examination of the evidence submitted to you, you should be of opinion that Mr. Gurdjian ought to be put upon his trial.

" If upon further investigation you should be of opinion that the facts presented do not constitute a violation of any specific statutory provision, but that Mr. Gurdjian has been guilty of culpable acts affecting the Ottoman Government, for the punishment of which our legislation is defective, it will be necessary to inform him that the protection of the United States can not be extended so as to enable him to continue his residence in the Ottoman dominions.

" The policy of the Government of the United States is to deal with other governments fairly and honorably, and to abstain from interference in their domestic politics. It can not countenance a different course of conduct on the part of its citizens. It can not admit that a person who has come to the United States and secured admission to citizenship and then returned to the country of his origin may be permitted to abuse his privileges as an American citizen by taking part in the political affairs or plotting against the government of the country with which he has declared the severance of his political connection.

" These observations are not made upon the supposition that they will be found to be applicable to the case of Mr. Gurdjian. It is hoped that the suspicions that have been raised against him will be found to be destitute of foundation; but it is proper and indeed necessary, in view of the questions which have been created, that this Department should furnish you, as minister of the United States, with clear and precise instructions as to the principles which must guide this Government and its ministers, and control the conduct of its citizens, in countries in which they enjoy the rights of extraterritoriality."

Mr. Blaine, Sec. of State, to Mr. Hirsch, min. to Turkey, No. 142, Dec. 22, 1890, For. Rel. 1900, 915; MS. Inst. Turkey, V. 176. See, also, Mr. Blaine, Sec. of State, to Mavroyeni Bey, Turkish min., Jan. 16, 1891, MS. Notes to Turkey, I. 536.

See Mr. Day, Sec. of State, to Mr. Straus, min. to Turkey, Sept. 13, 1898, MS. Inst. Turkey, VII. 274.

It appears that Mr. Blaine's offer of Feb. 25, 1890, in reality represented the usage toward other Franks, as reported by Mr. Brown in 1857, supra.

"Although the treaty [with Turkey of 1830, Art. IV.] in terms
gives to the ministers and consuls authority and
power to punish American offenders and absolutely
excludes their imprisonment by the Turkish authorities, the Ottoman Government, while admitting to this extent the
English rendering of the treaty, has on frequent occasions assumed
to imprison citizens of the United States on criminal charges and
denied the right of the agents of this Government to effect their
punishment. A fruitful source of such assertion of authority is
found in the case of persons of Armenian origin naturalized in the
United States and returning within the territorial jurisdiction of
Turkey under circumstances suggesting their complicity in the revolutionary schemes alleged to be rife in Asia Minor.

*Report of Mr. Ol-
ney, 1895.*

" Holding, as it must and should, that no distinction can exist
under the statutes of the United States between native and naturalized citizens, so that it is as clearly the right and duty of this Government to extend the full measure of its protection to the one as to
the other, and finding neither in the treaty nor in our jurisdictional
legislation any distinction as to the character of the criminal offense
charged—but on the contrary seeing that by our laws our ministers
and consuls have express jurisdiction over charges of insurrection
and rebellion when committed in the foreign country by American
citizens as well as over lesser offenses of a similar character—this
Government is unable to forego its right in the premises and can
not relinquish jurisdiction over any citizen, even though after naturalization he return to his native land and identify himself with its
political conspirations. The right to try and punish our citizens
committing offenses in Turkey has been so uniformily and ably
upheld by the successive Secretaries of State since contention on the
subject was first broached in 1862, that no diminution of our claim
can be considered at this important juncture. Consequently, the
United States minister at Constantinople has been instructed to claim
all rights under the fourth article of the treaty of 1830, and to offer
to try any American citizen charged with insurrection, rebellion, sedition, or like offense, or, in the event of such offer being refused, to
demand the release of the accused. Inasmuch, however, as this
Government does not contest the paramount right of a sovereign
state to exclude or deport for adequate cause, and in a proper manner,
aliens whose resort to its territories may be pernicious to the safety
of the State, the release of such persons upon condition of their leaving the country is not gainsaid.

" To illustrate the treatment of this class of cases and the results,
three instances of recent date are in point.

" On July 1, 1895, Krekor Arakelian, son of John Arakelian, a
citizen of the United States, residing in Fresno, Cal., was arrested,

in company with some 150 others, at Marsovan, on the ground, as was asserted, of complicity in the assassination of one Garabet Agha Kouyounijan by Armenian revolutionists. Krekor Arakelian was a mere youth, a student in Anatolia College at Marsovan, bearing a passport issued by the United States legation in Turkey, and his imprisonment appeared to be on the merest suspicion. The consul at Sivas intervened in his behalf, and the minister at Constantinople made energetic representations to the Porte against the detention of a citizen of the United States on a criminal charge. On the 21st of August Mr. Terrell telegraphed to the Department that he had been informed by the Porte that Arakelian had been released upon a decree dismissing the charge against him. He went to Constantinople, and, on being notified by the police that his presence in the Empire was objectionable and that the authorities viewed him with suspicion on account of compromising documents which had been found in his possession, he quitted the country early in September.

"On or about September 6, 1895, Mardiros Mooradian, a native of Armenia, naturalized as a citizen of the United States at Lynn, Mass., on December 21, 1894, and bearing a State Department passport issued five days later, was arrested on landing at Constantinople, on suspicion of being a revolutionary emissary. In his possession were forty-one letters and papers in the Armenian language, indicating his representative connection with the Hentzak, or Huntchaguist Society, a secret organization of Armenians in England and the United States. After several days' confinement, Mooradian was released under surveillance, and the incriminating papers were delivered to the United States minister for translation and examination. No offense appeared chargeable against him except on account of his relation to the revolutionary Huntchaguists, and, in the absence of proof of any overt act committed in Turkish territory, the minister demanded his instant liberty on the ground that his imprisonment was unauthorized, whereupon Mooradian was surrendered to the legation, ' to be kept from correspondence ' until he could be sent out of the country. A disposition on the part of the minister for foreign affairs to assert jurisdiction over Mooradian on the plea that he was still an Ottoman subject, because not having obtained the Sultan's consent to his naturalization abroad, was promptly met by Mr. Terrell and was not afterwards insisted upon.

"As the telegraphed conditions of Mooradian's surrender seemed to imply his deportation through the agency of the representative of the United States, the minister was instructed by telegraph that he might send the man away with his free assent, but that otherwise forcible deportation could only be performed by Turkish authority. It was then learned that Mooradian had gladly accepted the opportunity to depart, and had been sent, in company with the cavass of the legation, on board a steamer sailing for Athens on the 9th of September. This action was construed by the Department as merely indicating that the minister thereby sought to satisfy himself of Mooradian's departure in good faith, but without constraint of any kind.

" More protracted discussion than in the two foregoing instances attended the case of Melcoun Guedjian, which assumed importance as a test and precedent.

" In August last 7 men were arrested in the vilayet of Haleb (Aleppo) and taken to the provincial capital charged, it appears, with belonging to a party of 23 armed revolutionists who had lately come from Cyprus, landing by stealth near the mouth of the Orontes. Among them was a young man named Melcoun Guedjian, naturalized in Boston, December 28, 1894, and a resident at the time of Lynn, Mass., who bore a United States passport, issued early in January last, and upon whose person was found a sum of £800 in money, alleged by him to be for the relief of the poor, together with compromising papers. He is said to have admitted more than three years' membership of the Huntchaguist revolutionary society, and the circumstances under which he was arrested were, on his own showing, not entirely free from suspicion. Having clandestinely landed from a touching vessel, at Iskanderoun (Alexandretta), through bribery of a local boatman, he set out for the interior, and shortly afterwards was set upon and robbed by a large band of men. Being on horseback, he escaped to the mountains. A night or two later his horse was stolen, whereupon he made his way to Antioch and lodged a complaint against his assailants, presenting himself as an Englishman. Upon inquiry, in the presence of the British vice-consul, the facts of his case were elicited and his arrest and removal to Aleppo followed, where he was held for trial upon an indictment charging seditious acts. The United States consular agent at Aleppo was denied access to the prisoner, and his application to the vali to inspect Guedjian's passport was refused. On September 12 he was convicted by a Turkish court, no notice having been given to the consular agent, and without the presence of the dragoman of the agency. A sentence of imprisonment for one hundred and one years was imposed.

" Upon learning of this proceeding, the minister demanded the facts in the case in order that he might ascertain whether by any act of armed resistance to Turkish authority Guedjian had forfeited his right to protection as an American citizen. While such a test might, perhaps, be morally applicable to the worthiness of an individual's claim to bona fide conservation of allegiance to the country of adoption and respect to its laws, it could not operate to absolve him from its lawful jurisdiction. Mr. Terrell was accordingly instructed, September 26, 1895, that under our statutes consuls have extraterritorial jurisdiction over citizens accused of insurrection or rebellion against Turkey, or of a less offense of a similar character; that Guedjian's act seemed to have been political conspiracy with enemies of Turkey in England; that his trial by a Turkish court without notice to the consul at Beirut or the consular agent at Aleppo was in violation of international right, and should be annulled; that his transfer to Constantinople should be asked; and that if accused of insurrection or rebellion committed in Turkish dominion, the minister or the consul should insist upon trying him. The minister presented these demands to the Porte on the 28th of September.

" The grand vizier issued repeated orders to the vali of Aleppo to send Guedjian to Constantinople, which the local authority failed to obey, while continuing to deny the consular agents access to the prisoner. Under date of October 28 Mr. Terrell peremptorily demanded that his repeated protests should be answered, and that the offending vali should be dismissed, intimating that in case no favorable response were promptly made he would be under the necessity of reporting to this Government his inability to obtain justice from that of Turkey, and asking authority to demand his passport. A more satisfactory treatment of this and other vexatiously delayed cases ensued and assurances of Guedjian's removal to Constantinople were obtained. The minister, under the Department's reiterated instructions, continued to press for the delivery of Guedjian to him for trial. On December 3 he telegraphed that Guedjian had been delivered to him, and that the vali of Aleppo had been removed from office, thus closing the incident. The Department is not yet advised whether the Porte has consented to Guedjian's trial by our minister, or whether, as in Mooradian's case, it requires him to quit the country."

> Report of Mr. Olney, Sec. of State, to the President, Dec. 19, 1895, S. Doc. 33, 54 Cong. 1 sess. 5; For. Rel. 1895, II. 1256, 1259–1262.
> For correspondence as to the case of Arakelian, see For. Rel. 1895, II. 1295–1300; of Mooradian, id. 1300–1304; of Guedjian, id. 1304 et seq.
> See Mr. Olney, Sec. of State, to Mr. Terrell, min. to Turkey, tel., Feb. 16, 1897, MS. Inst. Turkey, VII. 33.

" Your excellency likewise refers in the aforesaid report to Article IV. of the treaty of 1830. That article has given rise to a controversy which the Sublime Porte is very desirous to settle. Mr. Blaine has thus far been the only Secretary of State who has proposed a method of settlement. By his notes of February 25 and March 15, 1890, he conceded to the Sublime Porte the right to try offenders, provided that the Sublime Porte would concede the right to punish them to the American authorities. Mr. Blaine made this concession to us, as he wrote, ' rather as an act of deference to a friendly Government than because I was convinced of the correctness of its contentions.' The contention of the Sublime Porte is set forth at length in my two notes to Mr. Bayard of January 10, 1889. Mr. Bayard did not reply to those notes until the 28th of February of that year—that is to say, a few days before he was succeeded by Mr. Blaine as Secretary of State. The two notes of March 25, 1889, which I wrote to Mr. Blaine in reply to Mr. Bayard's note of February 28, 1889, have not yet been answered. Still, as I have already remarked, Mr. Blaine made the concession referred to, rather as an act of deference to a friendly Government, as he said, and, as I add, of justice also. The Sublime Porte then reasoned and still reasons as follows: The United States did not secure, and did not even think of securing, more than other Franks in 1830. Now, the only text that is binding upon the two Governments is, according to their solemn admission, the Turkish text of the treaty of 1830. In that text no mention is made of the right to try offenders. Consequently, this right to try belongs to Turkey, for it is a sovereign right which no independent government can abandon otherwise than by an express and formal declaration, such as does not exist in Article IV. of the treaty in question. As, according to the text of the treaty, Turkey has the right to try offenders, she must likewise necessarily have the right to punish them, since one involves the other.

" The last phrase of the Turkish text of Article IV. does, it is true, contain certain words which, taken by themselves, seem to be at variance with this assertion. These words are, however, themselves in flagrant opposition to the following words of the article: ' Following, in this respect, the usage observed toward other Franks.' The necessary consequence is that there is an error, as regards the right to punish, in the wording of the final portion of Article IV. of the treaty of 1830. There is an error because there is a contradiction of terms, and it is this very error that we ask the United States Government to acknowledge. The Sublime Porte is true to its engagements, which consist of granting to you, in connection with this question of jurisdiction, everything that it now grants and that it granted in 1830 to ' other Franks.' There is thus, I still hope, a possibility of a full understanding between the two friendly Governments in relation to a controversy which, stripped of its cumbersome and useless accessories, seems to me, after all, to be free from any insurmountable difficulty."

Mavroyeni Bey, Turkish min., to Mr. Olney, Sec. of State, Dec. 21, 1895,
For. Rel. 1895, II. 1413, 1414.

" The imperial ministry of foreign affairs has the honor once more to draw the attention of the legation of the United States of America to the long-pending question of the prosecution of American citizens guilty of offenses in the Empire against the persons or the property of Ottomans; in other words, to the controversy arising from the interpretation of article 4 of the treaty of 1830.

Correspondence of 1900–1901.

" The imperial ministry does not wish to repeat the arguments it has already adduced to justify its own point of view. It has stated and developed them so many times in the official correspondence already exchanged that it considers it really useless to repeat them here.

" The imperial ministry limits itself to recalling the fact that the Turkish text of the above-mentioned treaty differs very much in its substance from the French draft; that it does full justice to the indisputable sovereign rights of the territorial jurisdictions; that it limits the privileges to be granted to American citizens solely to the most-favored-nation clause, which, moreover, is likewise provided to some extent in the said French text; that finally, after many discussions, it has been acknowledged that the Turkish text alone must be binding, for the reason that it was formally recognized as the only authentic one by the chargé d'affaires of the United States at the time of the exchange of ratifications of the said act of 1830.

" The imperial ministry thinks it its duty to remark as a supplementary 'considering' (preamble) that the Washington Cabinet assented to the Ottoman point of view—that is to say, to the right of the courts of the Empire to try mixed cases between natives and Americans—by signing the protocol annexed to the law of the 7th Sefer 1284, granting to foreigners the right to hold real estate in Turkey.

" This protocol provides, in fact, that ' in localities more distant than nine hours' travel from the residence of the consular agent foreigners shall be tried without the assistance of the consular delegate by the council of elders . . . and by the tribunal of the Caza, both in actions not involving more than 1,000 piasters and for offenses entailing a fine of not more than 500 piasters. Foreigners shall have in every case the right of appeal to the tribunal of the Sandjak against judgments rendered as above stated, and the appeal shall be carried up and tried with the assistance of the consul in conformity with the treaties.'

" This text, by establishing for the localities more than nine hours distant from a consular residence, an exception to the rule of the dragoman's assistance and by expressly prescribing the system of appeal in these suits, admits the competency of the Ottoman jurisdiction over Americans guilty of reprehensible acts toward Ottoman subjects. In fact, if appeals in the case of suits arising at a place more than nine hours distant are to be tried before the Ottoman tribunal with consular assistance, a fortiori, it must be the same for suits to be tried in first instance in places where there is a consulate, with this difference: That the court trying them would be one of the first degree.

" Now, the United States Government signed this protocol without making any reservation, maintaining its claims based upon the interpretation it gives to article 4 of the treaty of 1830. It therefore consented to allowing its citizens to be tried by the territorial authorities in their relations with the natives, and, furthermore, it tacitly admitted that the treaty does not involve a special extension or interpretation, but simply the most-favored-nation clause.

" The imperial ministry remarks with regret that the present controversy has had the effect of causing a serious disturbance of public order in the Empire. Every time that an American citizen commits a crime or offense he is assured of impunity. The consulate claims the right of trying him. The local judicial authorities plead their rights; and the guilty party, taking advantage of this disagreement, remains perfectly at ease, free from uneasiness with regard to the proceedings instituted against him, and this to the great detriment of the public tranquillity and peace. It is but right, then, to inquire if this state of things, so little in harmony with the requirements of justice, is to continue indefinitely for the sole reason that the United States Government does not consent to abandon a view which is not only debatable, but which is seriously and fundamentally controverted.

" If in former times this question was of hardly any importance, by reason of the small number of Americans residing in the Empire, to-day it is quite different, their number having increased to such an extent that the failure to punish their criminal acts can no longer be regarded as an inconvenience that can be overlooked. Complaints are frequently brought to the imperial ministry from the competent authorities of the capital and the provinces tending to show that American culprits escape public prosecution through the refusal of the United States consulates to assist the territorial jurisdictions in the same manner as those of the other powers.

" The Sublime Porte does not need to state at length the inevitable effects of a situation which permits the greatest impunity and free circulation in the Empire to a number of persons charged in the courts with crimes or offenses and which situation of itself is a sufficient reason for denouncing such a defective agreement. The Porte calls attention to the fact that, if it has not made use of its right to expel from the Empire offenders of this kind, it is because it desired and still desires to see this question settled by frank and final agreements between the two Governments.

"Already, in the course of the negotiations going on at Washington, the secretary of state for foreign affairs proposed a compromise by which the right of the Ottoman courts to try cases would be placed beyond dispute, provided the rights of the consulates to inflict the penalty were recognized. This proposition, which is partially in accordance with the Ottoman view as to the prosecution and conviction of American offenders, considerably reduced the scope of the controversy, and the Sublime Porte cherishes the hope that the most-favored-nation treatment, which it wants to apply in the premises to American citizens will be appreciated to its full value by the United States Government, and on this ground the imperial ministry begs the legation to kindly examine this question anew, with due consideration for the territorial rights which are at stake with regard to its citizens enjoying the hospitality of the territory of the Empire, and to help to end a dispute which the Sublime Porte is desirous of settling on an equitable basis, as one of the last messages of the President of the United States likewise appeared to direct."

> Note verbale, Turkish ministry of foreign affairs to the legation of the United States, Dec. 26, 1899, For. Rel. 1900, 909.
>
> The ministry of foreign affairs again drew the attention of the legation to the subject by notes of April 26, 1900, and Jan. 2, 1901, enclosing with the latter a list of twelve American citizens, who, as it was alleged, had escaped prosecution for misdemeanors. (For. Rel. 1900, 911–914.)
>
> The communications of the Porte were answered by the Department of State March 16, 1901, by an instruction given below.

"I have to acknowledge the receipt of your dispatches Nos. 162, 215, and 322, dated, respectively, February 6, 1900, May 29, 1900, and February 13, 1901, on the subject of the controversy between the Government of the United States and the Ottoman Government respecting the true interpretation of Article IV. of the treaty of 1830.

"Inasmuch as the question of the interpretation of that article has been the subject of voluminous correspondence between the two Governments, I inclose herewith a copy of an instruction, No. 142, dated December 22, 1890, from Mr. Blaine to Mr. Hirsch, in which the question is elaborately summed up. There is nothing that has since been adduced by the Porte which is not already fully answered by the facts and arguments developed in the said instruction. It is there shown that the basis on which the argument of the Porte is built is largely characterized by error of fallacious assumption, and that the superstructure of said argument is wanting in solid foundation.

"In addition to the foregoing observations, it has not escaped the attention of the Porte that the extraterritorial right in question also belongs to the United States in virtue of the most-favored-nation clause of the treaty. This right was given, in all the breadth of its assertion by this Government, by the Ottoman Porte to Belgium by Article VIII. of the treaty signed August 3, 1838, and reaffirmed by Article I. of the treaty between those States signed February 1, 1862. The same right was granted to Portugal in Article VIII. of its treaty with the Porte, signed in the French and Portuguese languages at London, March 20, 1843, and fully confirmed by Article I. of the treaty signed in the Portuguese language at Paris, February 23, 1868.

" In the last two treaties there appears to be no question of the reading or interpretation of any Turkish text, and the lucidity of the French text leaves no possible doubt as to the nature and extent of the right conceded, and that that right is adhered to in all its extent by the Governments of Belgium and Portugal the Government of the United States has not the slightest doubt.

" These considerations seem to fortify and render impregnable the position of this Government as stated in Mr. Blaine's instruction to Mr. Hirsch."

> Mr. Hay, Sec. of State, to Mr. Griscom, chargé at Constantinople, March 16, 1901, For. Rel. 1900, 914.

(3) PRACTICE OF EUROPEAN POWERS.

§ 285.

By a circular instruction dated January 14, 1891, Mr. Blaine directed the ministers of the United States at various courts in Europe to ascertain the rules maintained by the governments to which they were respectively accredited in relation to the trial and punishment of their citizens or subjects in Turkey.

Austria-Hungary. Mr. Grant, minister to Austria-Hungary, March 3, 1891,[a] enclosed a memorandum of the Imperial-Royal foreign office of February 10, 1891, which read as follows:

The treaty of commerce and navigation concluded on July 27, 1718, at Passarowitz, with the Ottoman Empire, and the Russo-Turkish treaty of commerce of June 10th, 1783, provide that Austro-Hungary has jurisdiction for criminal acts committed by its subjects in Turkey.

This rule has an exception when a crime has been committed against a Turkish subject, or when Turkish interests have been injured, or when the perpetrators was apprehended *in flagranti* by the Turkish authorities.

In these cases the trial and punishment is left to the Turkish authorities. Otherwise the Austro-Hungarian consular officers decide cases as courts of first instance, and in second and last instance the I. and R. embassy at Constantinople.

---

a 37 MS. Desp. from Austria.

Crimes committed by Austro-Hungarian subjects in Turkey will be investigated at first by the consular officers, and the trial and passing of sentence is part of the competent courts at home.

As far as the material right is concerned, according to which the consular officers will proceed, the *criminal law of 1852* will be applied for subjects of Austria, and the *criminal law of 1878* for subjects of Hungary.

Special legal provisions concerning jurisdiction over Austro-Hungarian subjects in Turkey do not exist.

Mr. Phelps, minister to Berlin, with his No. 238, of February 18, 1891,[a] enclosed copy of a note of Baron von Rotenhan,

Germany. of the German foreign office, of February 13, 1891, reading as follows:

Pursuant to the capitulations, as to which, for Prussia and the German Empire, are to be chiefly considered the provisions of the treaty of amity between Prussia and Turkey of March 22 (old style), 1761, as also, by virtue of the most-favored-nation clause, the other treaties concluded by Turkey, as well as in accordance with the customary rights based on the capitulations, the German consular officials, in common with those of other nations, are entitled to exercise penal jurisdiction over persons enjoying their protection with respect to all punishable acts by which neither the public interest nor a Turkish subject is injuriously affected.

The penal character of the act is determined by the general penal provisions which obtain in Germany and the procedure by paragraphs 21 to 42 of the law, of which a copy is enclosed, of July 10, 1879, concerning consular jurisdiction, and of the instruction of September 10, 1879, issued thereunder, as well as by the code of penal procedure of the German Empire of February 1, 1877 (Imperial Laws, page 253 and following, which is also enclosed.)

Conflicting opinions exist as to the question of jurisdiction when the punishable act is of a generally dangerous character or a Turkish subject is thereby injured. The Prusso-Turkish capitulations contain no expressed provision on this point. Pursuant, however, to the usage which obtains, the Turkish authorities generally conduct the examination and consular jurisdiction intervenes only when the offender is not called to account by the Turkish authorities.

This Turkish penal jurisdiction may not, however, be practiced until after previous notification to, and except with the cooperation of, the German consular representative.

Nor does the right, accorded by custom to the Turkish authorities, of arresting foreigners caught in the act of committing a crime, release the former from the duty of notifying the consular representative.

While the undersigned permits himself to refer, as respects the principle underlying the subject, to the book of F. Martens, concerning consular matters and consular jurisdiction in the Orient, he avails himself, etc.

Mr. Lincoln, minister to England, inclosed with his No. 401, of February 6, 1891,[b] a note from Lord Salisbury of

Great Britain. January 31, 1891, reading as follows:

Her Majesty the Queen (as you are doubtless already aware) possesses extraterritorial jurisdiction over British subjects in the Ottoman dominions. This

---

[a] 51 MS. Desp. from Germany.
[b] 167 MS. Desp. from Great Britain.

jurisdiction is now exercised by Her Majesty under the "foreign jurisdiction act, 1890," a copy of which I have the honour to enclose, as well as under certain orders in council, having reference to the Ottoman dominions, passed under the authority of previous enactments with regard to foreign jurisdiction, specified in the third schedule to the act of 1890, as being repealed by that act, in which, however, their principal provisions have been consolidated.

The principal of these orders in council is the Ottoman order in council of December 12, 1873 (a copy of which is also enclosed), Part XI. of which deals more particularly with criminal authority and procedure.

With regard to the second paragraph of your letter, I have the honour to inform you that (1) all crimes committed by one British subject against another, or all criminal charges brought against one British subject by another in the Ottoman dominions, are exclusively justiciable by Her Majesty's consular authorities in these dominions.

(2) All criminal charges brought by a British subject against a Turkish subject, or by a Turkish subject against a British subject in the Ottoman dominions, are justiciable by the Turkish tribunals and according to Turkish law; but the presence of a dragoman from the British consulate is necessary to the validity of such proceedings, and if (at any rate in Constantinople) the dragoman refuses to sign the sentence, it can only be carried into effect after negotiations between the higher authorities of the two countries.

(3) Criminal charges where foreigners, other than Turkish subjects, are concerned with British subjects are justiciable by the tribunal of the accused's nationality.

There are also certain limitations upon the power of the Turkish police to arrest British subjects without the presence of the British consular authorities; but it appears to me unnecessary for the present purpose to do more than mention the existence of such limitations in practice, as they do not affect the actual incidence of Turkish jurisdiction in the cases mentioned.

The act of Parliament and order in council above referred to are the salient documents with reference to this matter, and their provisions may probably be considered as containing the principal rules and regulations adopted by Her Majesty's Government in respect to the administration of criminal jurisdiction in Turkey.

I have, however, also the honour to forward herewith a copy of a book entitled "British Consular Jurisdiction in the East." The author, Mr. Tarring, is a member of the English bar, who holds the appointment of assistant judge of Her Majesty's supreme consular court for the Levant, and his book contains much valuable supplementary information on the whole question.

Mr. Porter, minister to Italy, enclosed with his No. 192 of May 4, 1891,[a] copy of a pamphlet furnished him by the foreign office on the jurisdiction of Italian consuls in the ports of the Levant. This pamphlet, translated, reads as follows:

Italy.

Italians in Turkey, like all other foreigners, enjoy the privilege of being governed by the laws of their own country. This is due to the old capitulations (the French one of 1740 and the Sardinian one of 1823 being especially memorable) which were granted to the European powers at different times by the Sublime Porte, and which have been maintained in force in all treaties subsequently concluded, in which are confirmed the ancient privileges and immuni-

---

[a] 24 MS. Desp. from Italy.

ties contained in the capitulations and sanctioned by constant custom.a The same capitulations may be invoked by every state for the principle established in the East, that every nation is entitled to be treated as the most favored nation, which principle is expressly recognized in the commercial treaty of July 10th, 1861, between Italy and Turkey.

Royal consuls and consular courts, composed of the consul or the person acting in his stead, who is the presiding officer, and of two judges, chosen at the beginning of each year from among the residents of the consular district, and preferably from among the Italians (arts. 65–69 of the consular law), exercise penal jurisdiction in the East over Italians residing in the consular district, and enforce the laws of Italy, i. e., the penal code and the code of procedure, the consular law of January 28th, 1866, together with the regulations thereunto appended, and the code and the regulations of the merchant marine (October 24th, 1877; November 20th, 1879).

It may be stated, as a general principle, that Italians have the right in the East (1) to be tried by their own consuls either in penal cases pending among them, or in cases in which foreign subjects of another nationality are interested as parties; (2) to have a guarantee of the attendance of the consular dragoman in penal cases for crimes committed against natives, although the judgment is reserved for the local judge.

Coming down to particulars, it is to be observed that, according to the Italian consular law of 1866, it belongs to the consul, as sole judge, to take cognizance of unlawful acts committed by Italians in the district of the consulate, or on board of merchant vessels carrying the Italian flag, to the consular courts (collegial courts) to take cognizance of crimes, . . . to the courts of assize at Genoa and Ancona to take cognizance of crimes . . . (arts. 105, 111, 114 of the aforesaid consular law).

After the provisions contained in the new penal code, which, no longer admitting the division of criminal acts into crimes, misdemeanors, and infractions of law, classifies them as infractions of law and misdemeanors (French *contraventions et délits*), the competence of consuls, of consular courts, and of the courts of assize of Genoa and Ancona must be ulteriorly determined and logically divided. The draft of a modification of articles 112, 113, and 114 of the consular law is still undergoing examination and is couched in the following language, which, most probably, will receive but slight modifications.

The consul is to be the judge:

" I. 1st, of crimes for which the law provides the penalty of imprisonment (reclusion) or detention for a term not exceeding three months, or confinement for a term not exceeding one year, or a fine, either separate or conjointly with one of the aforesaid penalties, not exceeding one thousand lire;

" 2nd, of the infractions of law provided for in the penal code;

" 3d, of infractions of law provided for in special laws, for which is provided

---

a Capitulation of the Republic of Venice, 1454.

Treaty of peace concluded by the Republic of Venice at Passarowitz July 21st, 1718.

Capitulation of the royal court of Naples, 1740.

Treaty of amity and commerce concluded by Sardinia October 25th, 1823.

Treaty of amity and commerce concluded by the Grand Duchy of Tuscany February 12th, 1833.

Treaty of commerce and navigation concluded by the King of Sardinia September 2, 1839.   (Rat. 1840.)

Treaty of commerce and navigation concluded by Italy July 10th, 1861.

a penalty restrictive of personal liberty for not more than two years, or a pecuniary penalty not exceeding two thousand lire.

"II. It would be the duty of the consular court to try offenses not within the competence of the consul and of the court of assizes of Rome.

"III. It would, moreover, be a prerogative of this court to take cognizance of misdemeanors for which the law provides the penalty of imprisonment with hard labor, or some other penalty restrictive of personal liberty for not less than five or more than ten years.

"Should the offense be fraudulent bankruptcy, for which provision is made in art. 861 of the commercial code, the aforesaid court would be competent to take cognizance thereof only in the gravest cases.

"No appeal is allowed from sentences of consuls and consular courts whereby a penalty has been inflicted restrictive of personal liberty for not more than five days, or whereby a fine has been imposed the amount of which does not exceed one hundred and fifty lire.

"Appeals from other sentences of consuls or consular courts shall be taken, respectively, to the tribunals and courts of Genoa and Ancona as provided in art. 105 of the consular law. Yet on this point, also, some modifications must be introduced."

Consular jurisdiction extends: 1st, to all unlawful acts committed by Italians against Italians or other foreigners; 2nd, to those committed on board of merchant vessels carrying the Italian flag (art. 113 of the consular law).

It does not, however, extend to those committed outside of the Ottoman territory by Italians who have taken refuge in Turkey.

As to the other point, it is proper to observe that, if the offenders are of different nationalities, each of them is to be tried by the consular officer of his own nation. If, however, the injured party is a subject of the Sultan, the Ottoman judicial authorities are to try the offender, even though he be a foreigner, but he shall have the privilege of being attended by the dragoman of his consulate.

Some modern capitulations, such as, for instance, the Swedish capitulation of 1737 (art. 8) the Belgian capitulation of 1838 (art. 8) and that concluded with the United States in 1830 (art. 4) are worded in such a manner as to lead to the conclusion that consuls (of those countries) in the Ottoman Empire have the right to try all crimes committed by their countrymen against any subject of that Empire or of another power. But this right, as regards offenses committed against Ottoman subjects, is not, in practice, recognized by the Porte. Nay, a recent circular sought to claim that the local courts were competent even in penal cases between citizens of another nationality.

This claim, however, being in manifest contradiction with the aforesaid capitulations, and also with the practice hitherto observed, has been rejected in toto both by the Government of the King and by those of the other powers interested.

Turkish courts are, however, competent to take cognizance of offenses against the Ottoman State and of those connected with the counterfeiting of coin, no matter what may be the nationality of the guilty parties, who, even in this case, are to enjoy the benefit of the attendance of the dragoman of their consulate.

As to the second point, it is well to bear in mind, the principle that royal (i. e., Italian) vessels, although they are in the territorial waters of the Ottoman Empire, are but a continuation of the territory of the State, and, as such, are governed by the laws of the State.

In accordance with this principle, if the offense is committed on board of a vessel carrying the Italian flag, by a person not belonging to the crew, the guilty party is surrendered to the competent consular officer, or to the local Government, through the agency of the royal consulate, according as he is a foreigner or an Ottoman subject.

If an Italian citizen has committed an offense, and sought refuge on board of a foreign vessel, his surrender must be demanded of the consulate of the nation to which such vessel belongs, and he is to be tried by his consulate or sent to Italy, according as the offense was committed in Ottoman territory or elsewhere.

If an Ottoman subject takes refuge on board of an Italian vessel, he is to be surrendered by the royal consul to the local authorities, after a formal demand has been made diplomatically by the Sublime Porte.

If a person belonging to the crew of an Italian vessel takes refuge on board thereof, after having committed a crime or offense on land, he shall be tried by his own consulate. He is, however, to be surrendered to the local authorities, if an Ottoman subject is concerned.

As to competence in the case of crimes committed in their own country or elsewhere by Italians who have subsequently taken refuge in Turkey, it is proper to remark that the extradition of such persons should, as a matter of strict legality, be solicited from the Ottoman Government. Nevertheless, constant custom and jurisprudence authorize Italian consuls to avail themselves, even in this case, of the privileges granted by the capitulations, and to cause such persons to be arrested and sent back to their own country.

The consular guards (cavasses) make the arrest, assisted, if necessary, by the local police.

For the same reason, however, Italian consuls cannot act in the case of such offenses as refusal to do military duty, desertion, or the printing and publication of objectionable matter, because these offenses are of a political or quasi-political nature, and are consequently not contemplated in extradition treaties, much less in the capitulations.

A consul in the East performs the duties of an examining judge, has the right of high police (art. 72 of the consular law), and, consequently, the right to expel Italians by means of a consular decree, which may be requested by the local Government (Sardinian instructions of 1859; art. 136 of the Sardinian law; art. 172 of the consular law).

It is doubtful whether a consul has the right of admonition.

The domicile of Italian subjects is inviolable, and the local authorities can not enter it unless the consul is present, except in the cases mentioned in the protocol appended to the law of Sefer 7th, 1284 (1867). This protocol, which was accepted by Italy on the 11/23 of March, 1873, grants to foreigners the right to own real estate in Turkey, and contains, with respect to penal matters some modifications as regards the inviolability of the domicile of foreigners in localities distant nine hours or more from the residence of the consular officer, in cases of murder, arson, counterfeiting of coin, etc.

Diplomatic officers enjoy everywhere, and with all the more reason in the Levant, the privilege of exterritoriality, and are, consequently, not subject either to local or consular penal jurisdiction.

Consular officers, moreover, by constant custom, enjoy the same privileges in the East that are enjoyed by diplomatic officers in respect to penal jurisdiction.

Protégés by acquired right and *protégés* by right of office (dragomans, consular guards, etc.) are specified in the Ottoman regulations concerning foreign consulates of Sefer 23d, 1280 (1865) [and] are on the same footing as Italian citizens as regards penal jurisdiction.

It is to be observed, finally, that an Italian citizen who has accepted a governmental office in Turkey, or has enlisted in the Turkish army, with the permission of his Government, is to enjoy all privileges granted by the capitulations, except as regards the performance of his official or military duties.

As to Italian consular jurisdiction in penal cases in other parts of the Levant, outside of Turkey proper, it is to be observed that the principle " *actor sequitur forum rei* " constantly prevailed in Egypt until 1874, in which year a judicial reform was introduced, the provisions of which have been extended every five years up to the present time.

The courts established by the reform in Egypt do not, however, exercise penal jurisdiction, which, except in the case of certain infractions connected with the administration of justice, and of offenses done to the magistrates themselves in their functions or on the occasion thereof, and in the case of police penalties, is still reserved to the consular authorities.

The protocol of February 12, 1873, which was signed by Italy, England, France, and Turkey, extended to *Tripolitania* (Tripoli?), the system which is in force in the other provinces of the Ottoman Empire.

In the regency of Tunis, subsequently to the French occupation in 1881, the Franco-Italian protocol of January 24th, 1884, provided that consular jurisdiction should be suspended, and that jurisdiction should be exercised by the French magistrates. In all other respects, Tunis still remains a country of capitulations, inasmuch as all the rights and privileges granted to Italian citizens by the treaty of 1868 between Tunis and Italy were expressly confirmed and maintained in the said protocol.

It was, moreover, agreed that all immunities and privileges that were expressly guaranteed by the capitulations and existing treaties and by usage, should suffer no restrictions save those that were strictly necessary for the administration of justice.

Italian consuls therefore still retain the right of high police in Tunis, and, as a consequence, the right to expel those under their authority, and to arrest Italian subjects who have committed crimes and taken refuge in the regency.

As to maritime penal jurisdiction, the French court is competent to try offenses committed on board of national vessels, when such offenses have disturbed the tranquillity of the port, whenever local subjects or persons not belonging to the crew are concerned.

In Bosnia, Herzegovina, and in the island of Cyprus, Italian consular jurisdiction must also be considered suspended; in the two first-named provinces in view of their occupation by Austria, and in Cyprus in view of its occupation by Great Britain.

Such is not the case in Bulgaria, where, owing to art. 8 of the treaty of Berlin of 1878, the capitulations are still in force.

In Eastern Roumelia, which forms de facto a part of Bulgaria, and is governed by the organic statute of April 14, 1879, which statute was accepted by the powers that signed the treaty of Berlin, all privileges and immunities that are enjoyed by foreigners in Turkey are still maintained. (Art. 20, org. stat. R. O.)

Mr. Thayer, minister to the Netherlands, enclosed with his No. 218, of March 10, 1891,[a] a translation of a note from the Dutch foreign office, of March 3, 1891, reading as follows:

The Netherlands.

In reply to your favor of January 26th last, I have the honor to state that the power of Dutch consular functionaries in matters criminal in all foreign

---

[a] 29 MS. Desp. from the Netherlands.

countries, including Turkey, is regulated by the law of July 25, 1871, herewith enclosed, together with the modifications of the same, which have been since adopted. (See official report of laws of 1887, No. 138.)

In virtue of Article I. of this law, a copy of which you will find enclosed, jurisdiction in relation to matters that are prohibitive is vested in consular officials, they being specially charged with this duty by royal decree.

Acting thus in a judicial capacity, either alone or aided by two assistants, as the law of the case requires (see arts. 20, 34, 36, and 43), the consular official tries and determines all punishable offences committed in his district by Dutch subjects, or those living under Dutch protection (see art. 9), excepting such cases as are indicated in article 23, which come under the jurisdiction of the legal authorities of Amsterdam or Batavia.

Articles 83 to 153, inclusive, supplemented as far as necessary by those provisions of the Netherlands code, which relate to penal matters, have reference to the mode of prosecution; while arts. 22, 22ᵃ, 22ᵇ, 23, and 27 treat of the penalties and their mode of execution.

Inasmuch as it is not the purpose of the said law to confer jurisdiction, but to regulate its exercise, it follows that consular jurisdiction can only be exercised within the limits of treaties and custom.

In following the precedents established by custom in criminal matters, it is necessary to distinguish whether the offence made punishable is against an Ottoman subject or the Ottoman Empire, or whether it is an offence against a foreigner.

It is in the case of a foreigner only that the consular official has the right of adjudication. In the former case it is agreed that the territorial tribunals are competent.

I take the liberty, Mr. Minister, of enclosing a copy of the " Instructions concerning births, deaths, and marriages, issued to the Dutch consuls in the year 1890," which contains, on pages 148 to 161 of the English rendering, a translation of articles 1 to 47 of the aforementioned law, and on pages 162 to 175 the royal decree promulgated in virtue of Article I. of the said law.

Mr. Batcheller, minister to Portugal, enclosed with his No. 18 of March 3, 1891,ᵃ a translation of a note of the Portuguese foreign office of Feb. 14, 1891, reading as follows:

Portugal.

In reply to the note which V. Sr. was pleased to address to me on the 29th of last month, it is my duty to inform you of what Portuguese legislation prescribes with relation to the trial of the subjects of His Majesty domiciled in Turkey.

The law which establishes the powers of consuls of Portugal is the consular regulation of the 26 November, 1857, and the annexed provisions which are published in a volume of which I have the honor to send you a copy.

As, however, this regulation is deficient, especially in the part relating to the power of consuls to try Portuguese subjects in civil or criminal cases in those countries, the principle has been adopted of following the rules laid down by other nations. adapting them, as far as practicable, to our own laws. This, however, gives rise to obvious evils, and therefore one of my predecessors appointed a commission charged with the revision and codification of the consular legislation. One of the members of said commission at once proceeded to pre-

---

ᵃ 30 MS. Desp. from Portugal.

pare a draft for the regulation of civil and criminal jurisdiction to be exercised by consuls in non-Christian countries, and this draft was distributed among the Portuguese consular officers in said countries, in order that they might suggest such modifications as they might think proper before said regulations were enforced. Having given this explanation, I consider Y. E.'s note is answered, and I have only to add that the subjects of His Most Faithful Majesty are tried by the courts of their own nation, and, when our law is not specific, according to the form of proceedings adopted by other nations in analogous cases.

Mr. Washburn, minister to Switzerland, enclosed with his No. 31, of Jan. 31, 1891,[a] a copy of a note of the federal department of foreign affairs, of Jan. 28, 1891, in which it was stated that, as the relations of Switzerland with the Porte were not regulated by the capitulations, and as Switzerland had no representative in the Ottoman Empire, Swiss citizens were at liberty to place themselves under the protection of other powers, and were considered to be subjects to the jurisdiction, both civil and criminal, of the protecting state.

Switzerland.

With his No. 43, of March 13, 1891,[b] Mr. Washburn enclosed a further note from the department of foreign affairs of the 10th of the month. In this note there was the following statement:

As a general rule, the Swiss inhabiting the seaports of the Levant are placed under the protection of the United States of America, of France or of Germany. France and Germany do not admit, so far as we know, the criminal jurisdiction of the Ottoman courts over their subjects; hence these two powers could not recognize the same in the case of the Swiss whom they protect, the latter being considered in all respects as natives. But should these powers or others who protect the Swiss in Turkey consent to regard as exceptions to this principle cases in which the crime is one committed against a Turk, we could not claim a different treatment for the Swiss protected by them.

(4) MIXED COURTS IN EGYPT.

§ 286.

" The Ottoman Government and that of Egypt have latterly shown a disposition to relieve foreign consuls of the judicial powers which heretofore they have exercised in the Turkish dominions, by organizing other tribunals. As Congress, however, has by law provided for the discharge of judicial functions by consuls of the United States in that quarter under the treaty of 1830, I have not felt at liberty formally to accept the proposed change without the assent of Congress, whose decision upon the subject, at as early a period as may be convenient, is earnestly requested."

President Grant, annual message, Dec. 1, 1873, Richardson's Messages, VII. 238.

---

[a] 27 MS. Desp. from Switzerland.
[b] 28 MS. Desp. from Switzerland.

" In 1876, as the result of negotiations between the Ottoman and Egyptian Governments and the various Christian powers having representatives at Cairo, certain courts were created in Egypt for the trial of mixed civil causes arising between persons of different foreign nationalities and suits of foreigners against natives, the Egyptian Government and members of the Khedival family. These mixed tribunals in civil matters, within their exclusive jurisdiction, superseded the consular courts. A mixed tribunal consists of five judges, three of whom are foreigners and two natives. The foreign judges are appointed by the Khedive on the recommendation of the great powers, each of which is represented by from one to three judges. There are several tribunals of original jurisdiction (first instance) and a court of appeals at Alexandria.[a] The United States is represented in the court of appeals at Alexandria, court of first instance at Cairo, and court of first instance at Alexandria. These judges are appointed for a term of five years and are paid by the Egyptian Government at the rate of 40,000 francs per year, with an allowance of three months' pay for expense of voyage and installation. At the expiration of the five years' service an additional one year's salary is allowed. In case of death one year's salary is allowed to the widow and children, the same allowance being received by any judges who may be incapacitated by sickness.

" I have also the honor to call your attention to the act authorizing ' the President to accept for citizens of the United States the jurisdiction of certain tribunals in the Ottoman dominions and Egypt, established or to be established under the authority of the Sublime Porte and of the Government of Egypt.' (U. S. Statutes at Large, vol. 18, part 3, chap. 62, page 23, and the proclamation of the President issued in conformity therewith; U. S. Statutes at Large, vol. 19, p. 662.)"

Mr. Porter, Assist. Sec. of State, to Mr. Tucker, Feb. 8, 1886, 159 MS. Dom. Let. 11.

The act of Congress above referred to was approved March 23, 1874; the President's proclamation was issued March 27, 1876. (Richardson's Messages, VII. 390.)

For the act constituting the mixed courts, see 66 Br. and For. State Papers, 593.

For a suggestion that provision might be made for referring certain " pending claims " against Egypt to the mixed tribunals, see Mr. Fish, Sec. of State, to Mr. Farman, Jan. 25, 1877, MS. Inst. Egypt, XVI. 58.

Such jurisdiction in bankruptcy as the American consular courts in Egypt exercised under the act of Congress of June 22, 1860, was, by the act of 1874 and the President's proclamation thereunder, trans-

---

[a] There were three courts of first instance, each consisting of four foreign and three native judges. The court of appeal was composed of seven foreign and four native judges. (66 Brit. and For. State Papers, 593.)

ferred to the mixed tribunals. " If, on the other hand, the Egyptian government desires for these tribunals, in matters of bankruptcy, other or further jurisdiction than was vested in the consular courts, it will be necessary to obtain a further act of Congress." (Mr. Fish, Sec. of State, to Farman, agent, &c., at Cairo, Feb. 27, 1877, MS. Inst. Egypt, XVI. 64.)

This view was controverted by Mr. Farman; and the Department of State, while expressing nonagreement with him, said: " The subject will be reserved for such future consideration as may be necessary, and, in the meantime, you will be governed by the instructions heretofore issued." (Mr. Evarts, Sec. of State, to Mr. Farman, July 13, 1877, MS. Inst. Egypt, XVI. 89.)

As to certain proposed changes in the mixed tribunals, see Mr. Hay, Acting Sec. of State, to Mr. Drummond, British chargé, Oct. 26, 1880, For. Rel. 1880, 527.

On the expiration of the first quinquennial period of the mixed tribunals, their existence was prolonged by decrees of Jan. 6, 1881, and Jan. 28, 1882, each of which decreed an extension of a year. The United States assented to these decrees, as well as to a later one declaring a further prolongation till Feb. 1, 1888, " with the same understanding now as on previous occasions, that the representation of the United States on the international courts is to continue undiminished and unaltered during the term of such extension, unless the proposed joint revision of the codes can be sooner carried out." (Mr. Frelinghuysen, Sec. of State, to Mr. Pomeroy, agent, etc., at Cairo, Dec. 13, 1882, MS. Inst. Egypt, XVI. 288.)

See, also, Mr. Freylinghuysen, Sec. of State, to Count d'Arschot, May 16, 1884, MS. Notes to Belgian Leg., VII. 340.

As to further prolongation of the existence of the mixed tribunals, see Mr. Bayard, Sec. of State, to Mr. Cardwell, agent, &c., at Cairo, Jan. 18 and Jan. 30, 1889, 128 MS. Inst. Consuls, 366, 474; Mr. Gresham, Sec. of State, to Mr. Penfield, agent, &c., at Cairo, Nov. 9, 1893, 143 MS. Inst. Consuls, 454, and dispatches from Mr. Harrison, agent, &c., at Cairo, No. 14, Jan. 5, 1898, ; No. 16, Jan. 27, 1898; No. 25, Feb. 11, 1898; No. 33, March 24, 1898: 29 MS. Desp. from Egypt; No. 41, April 23, 1898; No. 44, April 29, 1898: 30 MS. Desp. from Egypt.

As to the appointment and tenure of judges, see Mr. Frelinghuysen, Sec. of State, to Mr. Kinsman, Nov. 8, 1884, 153 MS. Dom. Let. 155; Mr. Bayard, Sec. of State, to Mr. Cardwell, agent, &c., at Cairo, Nov. 20, 1885, MS. Inst. Egypt, XVI. 424; same to same, Jan. 30, 1889, 128 MS. Inst. Consuls, 474. The nomination and choice of judges belong to the Egyptian Government, on condition of employing only persons having the approval and authorization of their Government; and the Egyptian Government reserves to itself the right to designate, according to the necessities of the service, the seats to which the judges will be assigned, conformably to the desire expressed by the court of appeals, in order to place on a footing of equality the three mixed courts of first instance. (Note of Egyptian minister of foreign affairs, Feb. 11, 1894, enclosed with the dispatch of Mr. Penfield, agent, &c., at Cairo, No. 51, Feb. 17, 1894, 28 MS. Desp. from Egypt. See, also, 66 Br. & For. State Papers, 593.)

As to a proposal to create a court of complaints, to decide questions of jurisdiction between the native and the mixed tribunals, see Mr.

Gresham, Sec. of State, to Mr. Penfield, agent, &c., at Cairo, Nov. 9, 1893, 143 MS. Inst. Consuls, 454.

Concerning the regulation of the expropriation of property for public uses, see Mr. Strobel, Third Assist. Sec. of State, to Mr. Penfield, agent, &c., at Cairo, Nov. 22, 1893, 143 MS. Inst. Consuls, 540.

The establishment of the mixed courts was the result of an international commission which met in Cairo in 1869. A similar commission met there in 1884, and upon its recommendation amendments were made to the articles of the mixed codes, relating to mortgages, bills of exchange, promissory notes, and the seizure and sale of real estate to pay judgments on mortgages. A third commission assembled in 1890 and adjourned subject to the call of its president, nothing having resulted from its deliberations. (Letter of Judge S. P. Tuck, Jan. 21, 1898, accompanying the dispatch of Mr. Harrison, agent, &c., at Cairo, No. 16, Jan. 27, 1898, 29 MS. Desp. from Egypt.)

Yet another international commission was constituted in 1898, for the purpose of considering certain amendments, proposed by the Egyptian Government, of articles 11 and 9, Title I. of the regulations. The Egyptian Government, in a circular of Nov. 15, 1897, complained that, under art. 11, the mixed courts had undertaken to decide upon the validity of measures adopted by the Government with the approval of the debt fund, and proposed that the jurisdiction in such matters should be expressly limited to actions brought by the debt fund against the Government for the alleged violation of the international arrangement under which the interests of creditors of Egypt were placed. The circular also maintained that, under art. 9, the competence of the mixed courts was to be determined by the nationality of the plaintiff, and not by the character of the interests represented by him; and in this relation complaint was made that the courts had assumed jurisdiction where the parties were natives, on the ground that some foreign interest was at stake, as in the case of an Egyptian company or corporation in which foreigners were interested, and that they had also held that a native might select a foreigner as his agent to bring an action against another native. It seems that the courts had consistently held themselves competent where a " mixed interest " was involved, or where the rights of some one not an Egyptian would be affected by the decision, and that the custom of a native choosing a foreign agent to bring his suit had arisen out of the preference shown for the mixed tribunals. For discussions of these and other questions brought before the international commission of 1898, see the following MS. dispatches of Mr. Harrison, agent and consul-general at Cairo: No. 14, Jan. 5, 1898; No. 16, Jan. 27, 1898, enclosing letters of Judges Keiley and Tuck; No. 25, Feb. 11, 1898; No. 33, March 24, 1898; No. 41, April 23, 1898; No. 44, April 29, 1898, supra.

As to matters to be dealt with by the mixed tribunals, see also 81 Br. & For. State Papers, 578.

As to the reorganization of native tribunals, see 83 Br. & For. State Papers, 808.

The regulations authorized the use only of the French, Italian, and native languages in the mixed courts. (66 Br. & For. State Papers, 595.)

A proposal having been made in 1883 to extend the jurisdiction of the mixed courts to criminal matters, the Department of State took the ground that the President, having exercised his power under the act of 1874, had exhausted it; and that, " as our right of extraterritorial jurisdiction flows from our treaty engagements with the Ottoman Government, it being set aside so far as Egypt is concerned might require special negotiation with the Sublime Porte, and would certainly require the assent of Congress to enable the President to accept the criminal jurisdiction of the mixed tribunals in like manner as when the civil jurisdiction of those courts was established."[a]

While disclaiming any intention to modify or overrule this decision, the Department of State in 1889, without any action by Congress or Presidential proclamation, assented to the exercise by the mixed tribunals of " simple police " jurisdiction. In explanation of this action, the Solicitor of the Department of State said: " It is true that ' police ' courts sometimes exercise criminal jurisdiction; and that the line between police offences and ' criminal ' offences is one which it is not easy, as a matter of elementary definition, to draw. In view of the prior history of these courts, however, I am of opinion that the words ' simple police,' as here used, are to be interpreted as meaning ' preventive police;' and as excluding such police jurisdiction as carries with it the power to punish crime by fine or imprisonment. This view is to be considered in connection with the fact that the Egyptian ' code civil,' adopted in 1875, contains a provision (in article 10, page 27) that ' Les poursuites pour contraventions de simple police sont soumises à la jurisdiction des nouveaux tribuneaux ' (the prosecutions for violations of simple police are referred to the new tribunals). The word ' simple ' here is to be taken as part of a complete code, in which it is used to distinguish the terms ' contraventions de simple police ' from crimes elsewhere made punishable. The use of the word *contraventions* goes to strengthen this position. In French law, offenses which are the subject of criminal jurisdiction are called ' crimes ' or ' délits.' The avoidance of the words, in the present case, indicates an exclusion of these contraventions from the category of offences subject to criminal jurisdiction. And an additional argument to the same effect is to be drawn from the fact that in the Egyptian system the civil and the criminal codes are distinct, and the provision before us is placed in the *civil code*." A telegram was accordingly sent to the agent and consul-general of the United States at Cairo, accepting the jurisdiction of the mixed tribunals in matters of " simple police," with the declaration that it

---

[a] Mr. Frelinghuysen, Sec. of State, to Mr. Pomeroy, agent, etc., at Cairo, Aug. 20, 1883, MS. Inst. Egypt, XVI. 317. See, also, Mr. Frelinghuysen, Sec. of State, to Baron van Alphen, Sept. 11, 1883, MS. Notes to the Netherlands, VIII. 103; Mr. Frelinghuysen, Sec. of State, to Mr. West, Brit. min., Oct. 23, 1883, MS. Notes to Great Britain, XIX. 362; Mr. Rives, Assist. Sec. of State, to Mr. Cardwell, agent, etc., at Cairo, Jan. 28, 1889, 128 MS. Inst. Consuls, 460.

was understood to mean preventive police jurisdiction, and not to include authority corporally to punish crime. It was conceived that the proclamation of March 27, 1876, vested this right in the mixed tribunals, so that no new proclamation was necessary.[a]

10. PRACTICE OF PROTECTION.

(1) POLICY OF THE UNITED STATES.

§ 287.

" Some misunderstanding having arisen at the consulates on the coast of Africa in relation to the extent of the protection which ought to be afforded to individuals under the flag of the United States, I am instructed by the President to inform you that such protection is to be afforded to none but American citizens, and the persons actually in the service of the consul, and not to them, if they have been guilty of any crime involving a breach of the peace, proved to the satisfaction of the consul, and for which he can not inflict a punishment satisfactory to the Government."

> Mr. Livingston, Sec. of State, to the consuls at Tangier, Tripoli, and Tunis, April 20, 1833, 4 MS. Despatches to Consuls, 50.

" I was well aware of the custom of the representatives of Christian powers in the Barbary States to extend the protection of their flags over many individuals who are not citizens of their respective countries, and who can not be properly considered as officials, such as brokers, interpreters, &c. But whilst I deem it the duty of our consuls to protect American citizens, and necessary and useful official persons connected with their consulates, they ought scrupulously and carefully to abstain from all interference in behalf of individuals who are neither citizens nor have any rightful claim to our protection, and the more especially when such protection is likely to bring the American consul into any kind of conflict with the rights and prerogatives of the representatives of friendly powers."

> Mr. Clayton, Sec. of State, to Mr. McCauley, consul at Alexandria, Jan. 14, 1850, MS. Inst. Barb. Powers, XIV. 115.

---

[a] Mr. Bayard, Sec. of State, to Mr. Cardwell, agent, etc., at Cairo, Jan. 30, 1889, 128 MS. Inst. Consuls, 474, enclosing an opinion of Dr. Wharton, Solicitor, of Jan. 28, 1889. See, also, same to same, Jan. 18, 1889, 128 MS. Inst. Consuls, 366, as to the general question of changes in the organization and jurisdiction of the mixed tribunals, Mr. Bayard saying: " While expressing sympathy with the proposals of the Khedive's government and willingness to join in any reformatory scheme for the organization and control of the mixed courts which may rationally commend itself to the acceptance of all, it becomes proper to reserve a formal and definitive acceptance of the result until the final agreement is before us."

" By the laws of Turkey and other eastern nations, the consulates therein may receive under their protection strangers and sojourners whose religion and social manners do not assimilate with the religion and manners of those countries. The persons thus received become thereby invested with the nationality of the protecting consulate. These consulates, and other European establishments in the East, are in the constant habit of opening their doors for the reception of such inmates, who are received irrespective of the country of their birth or allegiance. It is not uncommon for them to have a large number of such protégés. International law recognizes and sanctions the rights acquiesced [acquired] by this connection. ' In the law of nations as to Europe, the rule is, that men take their national character from the general character of the country in which they reside; and this rule applies equally to America. But in Asia and Africa an immiscible character is kept up, and Europeans trading under the protection of a factory take their national character from the establishment under which they live and trade. . . .   (1 Kents Com. 78–9.)   The Lords of Appeal in the High Court of Admiralty in England decided, in 1784, that a merchant carrying on trade at Smyrna, under the protection of a Dutch consul, was to be considered a Dutchman as to his national character. (Wheaton's Int. Law, 384, 3 Rob. Adm. Reports, 12.)"

> Mr. Marcy, Sec. of State, to Mr. Hulsemann, Austrian chargé, Sept. 26, 1853, in Koszta's case, H. Ex. Doc. 1, 33 Cong. 1 sess. 44–45.

" The practice that has hitherto prevailed among our representatives in the Barbary States of extending their protection to the subjects of the government where they reside or even to foreigners not clothed with our nationality to screen them from prosecution for offences, or to place them beyond the reach of the laws as applicable to others differently situated, is an abuse that, in the judgment of this Department, ought to be corrected.

" The late Consul Macauley was fully instructed on this subject when he went to Egypt, and I refer you to the despatch addressed to him on the 14th of January, 1850. . . .

" That such a custom, so much abused, should ever have existed is a source of regret; because it is the obvious policy of the United States to avoid and to compel its agents abroad to avoid, as far as possible, all connection and interference with the affairs of citizens of other countries. But the evil must be remedied with as little delay as possible. It may not be easy nor politic to get rid of it suddenly, so far as relates to some of the individuals who are now under protection, although not in the service of the consulate, and who may have rendered services to this Government or its agents in Barbary on former occasions. It might be harsh and unjust to withdraw from such persons the protection they have hitherto deservedly enjoyed, so long as they continue to deport themselves with propriety and to furnish no cause of complaint to the authorities of the country. But you will take care that no employés or protégés of this character not entitled to the protection of the United States, be taken into the service in future without the express and special consent and sanction of this Department."

> Mr. Marcy, Sec. of State, to Mr. De Leon, consul at Alexandria, Dec. 23, 1853, MS. Inst. Barbary Powers, XIV. 157. Cited with approval in Mr. Seward, Sec. of State, to Mr. Hale, consul at Alexandria, Dec. 11, 1866, MS. Inst. Barbary Powers, XIV. 332.

" This Government will not consent that its consuls in Turkey shall be denied any privileges in regard to protecting persons not citizens of the United States which may be enjoyed by the consuls of other nations who have no special treaty stipulations on the subject. If custom in Turkey gives to foreign consuls the right of protecting even Ottoman subjects, it is presumed that this right is limited to such persons as may be absolutely necessary for the discharge of the consular functions, and must have originated and be tolerated on account of the difficulty of obtaining persons, not subjects of the Porte, sufficiently acquainted with the oriental languages. It is obvious, however, that it is the duty of the consul to exercise this privilege with discretion, and not to employ any person for the purpose of screening him from prosecution for offenses against the laws of the country or any one known to be reasonably objectionable to the Government."

> Mr. Marcy, Sec. of State, to Mr. De Leon, Aug. 16, 1854, MS. Inst. Barb. Powers, XIV. 165.
> See, also, Mr. Davis, Assist. Sec. of State, to Mr. Beardsley, March 31, 1873, MS. Inst. Barbary Powers, XV. 129.

Soliman Gharbi, who claimed to be a lineal descendant of Ahmet Pacha Caramalli, of Tripoli, addressed to the President of the United States a petition expressing apprehensions as to the safety of his person and property in Alexandria, and asking that the American consul there be instructed to afford him all the protection which could be extended in his behalf. A declaration of intention by the petitioner, dated at New York, July 26, 1858, accompanied the petition. Mr. Cass, in writing to the consul, said: " This Government cannot extend to Mr. Gharbi such protection as it is bound to afford to its own citizens residing under foreign jurisdictions; . . . yet under the circumstances of the case, and especially in view of the position once occupied towards the Government of the United States by his alleged ancestor, it is deemed proper to commend Mr. Gharbi to your good offices, and to request you—after you shall have satisfied yourself that . . . he has given no just cause of complaint to the authori

ties of the viceroyalty—to grant him such protection as may be
authorized by law and by the regulations of the Department. In
this, you will of course be careful not to transcend the authority
given to consular officers of the United States in the East, by the 28th
chapter of the regulations referred to, which prescribes the issuing,
to aliens under consular protection, of a simple certificate ' that the
person to whom it is given is cared for and received under the protection of the Government whose agent has granted it.' You are
aware that this authority to protect aliens has not always been used
with discretion, and that, in consequence of its abuse, the Department
has, without entirely forbidding it, discountenanced its exercise as far
as possible. It is, indeed, questionable whether the regulation which
admits it is consistent with the act of August 18, 1856, in relation to
the granting of passports and certificates. The Department hopes
that you may be able, without committing your Government to a
defence of the rights of Mr. Gharbi in case of their being invaded, to
secure him and his family against further molestation, so long as
their conduct is not justly obnoxious to censure."

> Mr. Cass, Sec. of State, to Mr. De Leon, consul at Alexandria, No. 17,
> Aug. 18, 1858, MS. Inst. Barbary States, XIV. 200.

The practice of protection being " liable to abuse and one that
ought to be abolished," none but citizens of the United States with
passports from the Department of State, or persons who, being citizens, were certainly known to be entitled to receive passports from
the officials of the United States abroad, " have properly any right to
protection from our legations and consulates."

> Mr. Cass, Sec. of State, to Mr. Williams, min. to Turkey, Feb. 20, 1858,
> MS. Inst. Turkey, I. 408.

In 1861 Mr. Seward, replying to an inquiry whether a person,
alien born, but who had taken the initiatory steps towards becoming
a citizen of the United States, could, during a contemplated visit to
Alexandria, Egypt, place himself under the protection of the United
States consul-general there, stated that, in consequence of the abuse of
the practice of extending consular protection to aliens, the consular
officers of the United States in Turkey and other Eastern nations
had of late years been instructed " to exercise their right in this
respect with much caution." The degree of protection, if any, which
it might be proper to afford to the person in question, it would be for
the consul-general to determine without special instructions.

> Mr. Seward, Sec. of State, to Mr. Roelker, Sept. 9, 1861, 55 MS. Dom.
> Let. 53.

" You are therefore instructed to issue no more *tezkerahs*, or certificates of protection, except to the individuals actually and necessarily employed in the consulate, or in your personal service."

> Mr. Hunter, Acting Sec. of State, to Mr. Wippermann, consul at Galatz,
> April 28, 1863, 34 MS. Desp. to Consuls, 196.

In May, 1863, the United States consul at Galatz was instructed to
inform all so-called protégés who had been nominally placed under
American protection within his jurisdiction that it had been done
without proper authority and contrary to the instructions of the
President, and, consequently, that they were not regarded by the
Department of State as American protégés nor as anywise entitled
to American protection. It was added that the number of protégés
must not be extended beyond the persons " absolutely necessary for
the discharge of the consular functions " or in the consul's personal
service.

> Mr. F. W. Seward, Assist. Sec. of State, to M. Wippermann, consul at
> Galatz, May 2, 1863, 34 MS. Desp. to Consuls, 201.

" Henceforward you will grant no protection to any person whomsoever not actually a citizen of the United States by birth or complete
naturalization, or to any other person not actually employed in the
consulate."

> Mr. Seward, Sec. of State, to Mr. Hale, consul-general at Alexandria,
> Oct. 3, 1864, MS. Inst. Barbary Powers, XIV. 287.
>
> Mr. Hale's action, in granting protection to " the blacks brought by Miss
> Finnie from some point on the White Nile," was approved " as
> exceptional, but not to be drawn into precedent." (Mr. Seward,
> Sec. of State, to Mr. Hale, Oct. 31, 1865, MS. Inst. Barbary Powers,
> XIV. 307.)
>
> With regard to a " blind Hungarian boy," whom Mr. Hale had made a
> " temporary exception " to the rule, Mr. Hale was instructed to lay
> the matter before the Austrian consul-general, " and express a hope
> that he will find it expedient to relieve the United States consulate
> from the charge, while securing protection and kindness to the
> orphan." (Mr. Seward, Sec. of State, to Mr. Hale, May 11, 1867,
> MS. Inst. Barbary Powers, XIV. 342.)
>
> In a later instruction Mr. Seward complained of the " want of apprecia-
> tion " shown by Mr. Hale, and the " signal disregard " exhibited by
> some of his predecessors, of the Department's views and instructions
> on the subject of protection, as well as of the difficulty which the
> Department had encountered in obtaining information concerning pro-
> tected persons. Referring to the instruction of Oct. 3, 1864, supra, Mr.
> Seward said: " This direction seems to be too clear and positive to
> require any interpretation, and certainly does not warrant the con-
> tinuance of protection to the forty persons to whom you refer. The
> Department has no information of the names of those persons, the
> length of time during which they have had the protection of the
> consulate, or the reasons for which this was originally granted. You

have mentioned some of these particulars in only one case, that of the son of a Hungarian bandmaster, who, you say, is blind, and to whom one of your predecessors, an American missionary, is a guardian. However strongly such a case may appeal to sympathy, a feeling of that kind should not, in the judgment of the Department, be allowed to decide so important a question of international law and official propriety. The Hungarian is a subject of Austria, and it is the duty of the Austrian consul to take him under his protection, so far as the orders of his own Government may warrant. It does not appear, however, that any application has ever been made to that functionary upon the subject. It is consequently expected that you will carry into full effect the instruction above referred to. The Department would, however, like to be furnished with the details which have been indicated in regard to the persons who are now protected by the consulate. You will communicate the substance of this instruction to the other consulates in Egypt, and inform them that it is expected they will be governed by it. Similar information, however, in regard to the persons whom they have hitherto protected would also be acceptable." (Mr. Seward, Sec. of State, to Mr. Hale, Dec. 11, 1866, MS. Inst. Barbary Powers, XIV. 332.)

"Your dispatch, Number 96, of the 28th ultimo, has been received. The discovery of which it gives information, that the orphan boy hitherto supposed to be Hungarian is, in point of fact, of Polish parentage, is conceived to impart a new aspect to his case. He will, until further instructions shall have been received, be retained under the protection of the United States." (Mr. Seward, Sec. of State, to Mr. Hale, July 23, 1867, MS. Inst. Barbary Powers, XIV. 345.)

The necessity " which usually exists of employing in subordinate positions in the East persons who are acquainted with the languages of that quarter may justify a relaxation of the restriction [as to extending protection to any but citizens of the United States] in their favor, but only so long as they may be so employed."

> Mr. Seward, Sec. of State, to Mr. Hale, consul-general at Alexandria, Dec. 11, 1866, MS. Inst. Barbary Powers, XIV. 332.
>
> Protection of a local dragoman does not extend beyond his term of service. (Mr. Uhl, Act. Sec. of State, to Mrs. Chamlian, April 11, 1895, 201 MS. Dom. Let. 471.)

" Abuses which have heretofore occurred in granting protection from the local authorities in eastern countries, and especially in the Turkish dominions, to persons who, in the opinion of this Department, had no claim thereto, render it advisable that the legations and consulates in that quarter should, once in six months, report the number, names, and occupations of the persons to whom, during the six months preceding, such protection may have been given or by whom it may have been claimed. You will so report accordingly immediately upon the receipt of this circular, in regard to the ——— at ———. Such report will in future be expected to be made at the beginning of every January and July.

"It is believed that sound policy dictates the utmost scrutiny and caution in extending the protection of this Government to any persons abroad who may not be citizens of the United States. Should that policy be adopted and scrupulously adhered to, those to whom protection may really be due may expect it to be efficient."

> Mr. Fish, Sec. of State, Circular No. 8, May 1, 1871, MS. Circulars, I. 439; For. Rel. 1871, 24.

The diplomatic representative of Greece at Constantinople having, by direction of his Government, asked the United States legation that the American consul at Tunis might be authorized to assume the protection of the interests of Greek subjects at Tunis till the Greek Government should definitely appoint a consul there, the United States consul at Tunis was authorized to protect Greek subjects, and in so doing to be governed by the restrictions imposed in circular No. 11, June 16, 1871, in relation to the protection of Swiss citizens.

> Mr. Bancroft Davis, Act. Sec. of State, to Mr. Heap, consul at Tunis, July 11, 1871, MS. Inst. Barbary Powers, XV. 430.
> For the circular of June 16, 1871, see For. Rel. 1871, 28; infra, § 654.

"Your despatch No. 110, of the 25th ultimo, has been received. It is accompanied by a petition of the Cosmopolitan Workingmen's Association of Alexandria, addressed to this Department, requesting the protection of this Government. While we may feel flattered by the complimentary terms in which the petition speaks of the Government of the United States, it is, as you are aware, the policy of that Government to abstain from protecting any others than its own citizens in foreign countries, excepting only such foreigners as may be in its diplomatic or consular service in other than Christian countries. This Department sees no reason to make the case of the association adverted to an exception to the rule. You will, however, make known this decision in a way which may be the least likely to give offence."

> Mr. Fish, Sec. of State, to Mr. Butler, consul at Alexandria, July 22, 1872, MS. Inst. Barbary Powers, XV. 86.

In 1876 the consul of the United States at Tunis reported that two citizens of Switzerland had applied for the protection of the consulate, basing their claim on the instructions given by the United States in 1871 for the protection of citizens of Switzerland by United States diplomatic and consular representatives. The persons in question had previously been under German protection, but the German consul-general had, on account of their bad reputation and questionable proceedings, notified the Tunisian Government that they were no longer under his care. The United States consul refused to take them under his protection, and his action was approved, the character and ante-cedents of the persons in question appearing to justify such refusal.

> Mr. Fish, Sec. of State, to Mr. Cubisol, vice-consul at Tunis, June 27, 1876, MS. Inst. Barbary Powers, XV. 479.
>
> See, however, Mr. Evarts, Sec. of State, to Mr. Heap, vice-consul at Tunis, Oct. 12, 1877, id. 484, where instructions were given for the protection of one of the persons in question, apparently without knowledge or consideration of what had been stated in the correspondence with the previous vice-consul.

The Pasha of Tripoli having objected to the protection by the United States consulate of subjects of Morocco and the Soudan residing in Tripolitan territory, the consul was instructed that the practice had not only not been sanctioned by the Department of State, but that it had " on several occasions been virtually prohibited, especially by the circular No. 8 of the 1st of May, 1871." The Department, after remarking that the practice was " totally at vari-ance with general public law, a canon of which is that a government shall be supreme within its own jurisdiction," stated that the rules and limitations to be observed in attending to the interests of persons not citizens of the United States were set forth in the circulars No. 11, June 16, 1871, and No. 15, Dec. 15, 1871, relative to the protec-tion of Swiss citizens, in which both the request of the Swiss Gov-ernment and the consent of the government of the country in which the Swiss citizens might reside were deemed essential. Both these conditions were wanting in the case of the Africans patronized by the consulate at Tripoli. The consul was, therefore, instructed to inform the Pasha that he was not authorized longer to give the protection of which complaint had been made.

> Mr. Fish, Sec. of State, to Mr. Jones, consul at Tripoli, Nov. 16, 1876, MS. Inst. Barbary Powers, XV. 589. See infra, § 654.
>
> With reference to Mr. Jones' statement that it had been customary, under the capitulations, for consuls in Tripoli to exercise their discretion in protecting others than their own countrymen, Mr. Fish remarked that the treaties of the United States were silent on the subject; that it " was not deemed necessary that equality in the alleged priv-ilege of protecting others than citizens of this country should be secured to the ministers and consuls of the United States in the Ottoman dominions; " and that, when it was considered " what the obligations of this Government would be in case its protection should be violated, prudence obviously dictates that it should not be exer-cised or authorized."
>
> Circular No. 11, June 16, 1871, in relation to Swiss citizens, is given in For. Rel. 1871, 28; Circular No. 15, Dec. 15, 1871, in For. Rel. 1872, 5.

The protection by the United States in Turkey of persons not American citizens " has usually been regarded as inexpedient, except in so far as it may be extended to persons actually in the service of the diplomatic or consular officers of the United States. The Government prefers in these matters to act in accordance with the spirit of the law, which provides that a passport should be issued to a citizen only."

> Mr. Evarts, Sec. of State, to Aristarchi Bey, Turkish min., Feb. 14, 1878, MS. Notes to Turkey, I. 209.
> To the same effect, see Mr. Evarts, Sec. of State, to Mr. Mathews, consul at Tangier, Feb. 27, 1878, MS. Inst. Barbary Powers, XV. 351.

" Foreigners in the employ of the United States consulates and their agencies [in Turkey] have a right to the protection of the United States in all matters pertaining to their office and personal safety, but not in regard to their commercial affairs and private business, for protection in which they must look to the representatives of the nation of which they are citizens."

> Mr. Bayard, Sec. of State, to Mr. Cox, min. to Turkey, Nov. 6, 1885, MS. Inst. Turkey, IV. 305.

L., an alien by birth, was, when six years of age, brought to the United States. He left at the age of seventeen, and after 1854 resided continuously in Jerusalem, with the exception of fifteen days in March, 1890, when he visited the United States for the purpose of obtaining a certificate of naturalization. It was held that his naturalization was fraudulent, and that he was not entitled to be placed on the list of citizen protégés.

> Mr. Adee, Act. Sec. of State, to Mr. Wallace, consul at Jerusalem, July 9, 1895, 149 MS. Inst. Consuls, 26.

" In Eastern countries, and especially in the Turkish dominions, protection, in accordance with local custom, may be given to aliens actually in discharge of official duties under the direction of consular officers or employed in their domestic service. Where consular protection is regulated by treaty, it must conform strictly to the provisions of the treaty. No instrument in the nature of a passport should be issued to aliens thus protected, but when necessary a certificate may be given setting forth their relation and duties in connection with the consulate. Consuls will report to the Department of State on the 1st of January and July of each year the names and occupations of all aliens to whom, during the six months preceding, such protection may have been given, or by whom it may have been claimed."

> U. S. Consular Regulations, 1896, § 173, p. 60.

In February, 1899, instructions were sent to the consulate-general in Siam to transmit to the Department of State a list of all persons registered there, with a statement of the grounds of registration, and thereafter to send such a list on June 30 and December 31 in each year; to restrict servants' certificates of registration to persons actually servants or employees of American citizens; to register no Chinese person claiming to be a citizen of the United States by naturalization; to register no Chinese person claiming to be a citizen of the United States by birth till the evidence of such birth should have been submitted to the Department, and to charge no fee either for the registration of American citizens or for the certificate of registration.

> Mr. Cridler, Third Assist. Sec. of State, to Mr. King, min. resid. and con-
> sul-gen., Feb. 9, 1899, 165 MS. Inst. Consuls, 595.
>
> The minister of the United States at St. Petersburg was instructed in-
> formally to explain, in private conversation with the minister of
> foreign affairs, " the circumstances under which [the] quasi pro-
> tection [extended by the United States minister and consul-general
> in Siam] to a Russian subject was withdrawn, and intimate our
> readiness to use our good offices, if needed, on behalf of any worthy
> Rusian, including " the one in question. (Mr. Frelinghuysen, Sec.
> of State, to Mr. Hunt, min. to Russia, March 29, 1883, MS. Inst.
> Russia, XVI. 341.)

(2) OTTOMAN DOMINIONS.

§ 288.

In reply to an inquiry as to the protection to be given by the United States consulate at Constantinople to citizens of Switzerland there residing, the Department of State said that it understood that the Turkish Government required every citizen of foreign birth residing in Constantinople to be under the nominal protection of the foreign representatives, and that such protection had been afforded by them, both to citizens of their respective countries and to others who had no immediate representative near the Turkish Government. " In conformity to this custom," said the Department of State, " the Department perceives no impropriety in your extending to citizens of the Swiss Republic such friendly offices as you can afford consistently with your duties to the Government by which you are accredited. It is of course understood that the Department can incur no expense for such nominal protection, nor be held responsible for the conduct of those who thus desire its temporary countenance."

General rules.

> Mr. Webster, Sec. of State, to Mr. Dainese, consul at Constantinople,
> April 9, 1852, 14 MS. Desp. to Consuls, 283.

The privilege of protection " may in special cases and for a limited period be extended to foreigners, and even to Turkish subjects who become official ' employees,' so long as they remain attached to the legation and consulates. The custom, it is understood, had its origin in the difficulty of finding American citizens skilled in the languages of the East, and the right should therefore be confined solely to employees indispensably necessary to our representatives. It is to be used with caution in all cases, and does not intend or tolerate the employment of persons in order to shelter them from justice or such as may be justly obnoxious to the government within whose jurisdiction the right is exercised."

> Mr. Cass, Sec. of State, to Mr. Williams, min. to Turkey, Feb. 20, 1858,
> MS. Inst. Turkey, I. 408.

"Upon the policy which leads several of the great European powers to take under their protection certain religious sects in Turkey, I do not deem it necessary to express an opinion, but it is one certainly in which we can never participate. This Government undertakes to protect neither Protestant nor Catholic, neither Greek nor Armenian, but only American citizens; and this Department can not but think that, if the person or the property of any American citizen had been imperiled, you would have occupied higher and stronger ground in appealing for the necessary protection for a citizen of the United States in that character alone, than in confounding him in a general protection afforded to any sect whatever."

> Mr. Cass, Sec. of State, to Mr. Williams, min. to Turkey, Oct. 22, 1860,
> MS. Inst. Turkey, II. 27.

"The President hears with surprise and regret rumors of abuses of the privilege of granting protections committed by persons vicariously exercising consular functions in behalf of this Government within His Imperial Majesty's dominions. Recent improvements of administration present some grounds for believing that that privilege might now be relinquished without serious prejudice to the interests of the United States. It is not supposed, however, that in the event of either a radical change of administration, or of the occurrence of religious or other domestic disturbances in the capital or the provinces, the right of granting protections as heretofore exercised would be found indispensable to the safety of citizens sojourning in Turkey. In view of these opposing considerations the President has determined that you may announce to the minister for foreign affairs that the power of the ministers and of consuls to grant protection will, until further notice, be restricted so as to allow them to issue only to persons in the actual service of the United States. This restriction will not be deemed to have any bearing upon passports to American citizens granted by this Department or other proper authority."

> Mr. Seward, Sec. of State, to Mr. Morris, min. to Turkey, Sept. 19, 1864,
> MS. Inst. Turkey, II. 112.

" You will extend the protection of the United States only to persons who are either native-born or naturalized citizens of the United States. In case of naturalization the proceeding must not consist merely in a preliminary declaration of intention, but must show a judicial process fully complete and ended before the proper courts, and in conformity with the provisions of the laws of the United States. Whenever the naturalization papers presented are either manifestly fraudulent or well suspected of being fraudulent, you will refuse to extend protection upon them until the case shall have been examined here. When the person who demands protection claims it upon the ground simply that he is the child of a person who has been naturalized in the United States, you will look into the circumstances and see whether the claimant has, by relinquishing his residence in the United States, or by returning to Turkey or any other foreign country, practically waived his legally acquired but provisional title as an American citizen. You will in no case interpose in behalf of a person whose objects appear to be immoral or illegal or frivolous or whose title to United States citizenship is not clear and absolute. On the contrary, in such doubtful cases you will refer yourself to this Department for special instructions."

> Mr. Seward, Sec. of State, to Mr. Morris, min. to Turkey, Aug. 21, 1868, MS. Inst. Turkey, II. 223.

The Department of State in 1872 declined to except a Syrian merchant at Beirut from " the rule which for some time past has been adopted, restricting the protection of this Government to persons in the Turkish dominions, other than citizens of the United States, to those foreigners who may be in the actual service of our diplomatic and consular officers in that quarter."

> Mr. Fish, Sec. of State, to Mr. Nichols, May 11, 1872, 94 MS. Dom. Let. 102.

Protection should always be extended to the bona fide property of citizens of the United States in the Ottoman dominions, so far as the treaty and laws will permit. " The Department, however, cannot approve of any protection to the business interests of an Ottoman subject, merely because he may allege that he is the agent or partner of a citizen of the United States. Those interests must be left to the jurisdiction of the Ottoman authorities only."

> Mr. Fish, Sec. of State, to Mr. Boker, min. to Turkey, No. 60, Nov. 15, 1872, MS. Inst. Turkey, II. 447. In this instruction Mr. Fish declared that the opinion, expressed by Philip Francis, British consul-general at Constantinople, that " if a firm trading in Turkey consists of a British subject and an Ottoman subject, it would be properly held that the firm had no right to British protection," should " be adopted as the policy of the United States on the same point."
>
> See, also, Mr. Fish, Sec. of State, to Mr. Boker, min. to Turkey, No. 47, Oct. 4, 1872, MS. Inst. Turkey, II. 427.

" The status of foreigners in Turkey depending, as I have observed, on ancient usage, while not clearly defined, is to a certain extent determined by the capitulations or treaties between the Porte and various nations. The earliest of these, with the Italian Republics, Genoa and Venice, was concluded in 1453. The most important are those concluded by France in 1740 and by England at various times from 1675 to 1809, which are in force at the present day and which have served as a model for the succeding treaties with other nations. As these various capitulations acted rather to recognize and confirm existing rights than to create especial privileges, it was inevitable that in the course of centuries the policy of autonomous extraterritoriality should be expanded, and that rights and privileges, born of the inherent prerogatives of non-Mussulmans and acquiesced in by long and continuous usage, should become vested rights, sanctioned by the Ottoman power and indefeasible by any act of the Turkish sovereign. It may, thus, not always be practicable to point to the origin of any particular privilege in a solemn covenant, or in a special grant or recognition thereof at any particular time. They have become massed into a concrete assemblage of rights, not readily admitting of classification or definition, but constituting a body of laws and customs resting on usage and having for their fundamental principle the incontrovertible inheritance of non-Mussulmans under Mussulman rule to the fullest autonomy in all that separates them from the Moslem faith and code.

" In 1856 the important firman known as the Hatti-Humayoun sought to generalize the concessions of extraterritoriality in the various capitulations and the privileges and rights of aliens which had grown inseparably upon the ancient conventions. Even this broad generalization proving insufficient to cover the whole ground of alien right, a still ampler declaration was embodied in the treaty of Berlin, July 13, 1878, as follows :

" 'ARTICLE LXXII. The Sublime Porte having expressed the intention to maintain the principle of religious liberty and give it the widest scope, the contracting parties take notice of this spontaneous declaration.

" ' In no part of the Ottoman Empire shall difference of religion be alleged against any person as a ground for exclusion or incapacity as regards the discharge of civil and political rights, admission to the public employments, functions and honors, or the exercise of the various professions and industries.

" ' All persons shall be admitted, without distinction of religion, to give evidence before the tribunals.

" ' The freedom and outward exercise of all forms of worship are assured to all, and no hindrance shall be offered either to the hierarchical organizations of the various communions or to their relations with their spiritual chiefs.

" ' Ecclesiastics, pilgrims, and monks of all nationalities traveling in Turkey in Europe, or in Turkey in Asia, shall enjoy the same rights, advantages, and privileges.

" ' The right of official protection by the diplomatic and consular agents of the powers in Turkey is recognized both as regards the above-mentioned persons and their religious, charitable and other establishments in the holy places and elsewhere.'

" The tendency is thus seen to have been toward generalization from the details of the capitulations to a wider recognition of the inaliena-ble rights and prerogatives of non-Mussulmans and aliens in Turkey, as developed by a slow but steady process of accretion and consolida-tion, continuing to the present day, and not, in the nature of things, admitting of arrest or reversal."

> Mr. Foster, Sec. of State, to Mr. Thompson, min. to Turkey, Nov. 29, 1892, For. Rel. 1892, 609, 610, citing Mr. Bayard, Sec of State, to Mr. Straus, April 20, 1887, For. Rel. 1887, 1094, and Mr. Blaine, Sec. of State, to Mr. Hirsch, Dec. 14, 1891, For. Rel. 1892, 527. •
>
> As to a proposal of the Porte to modify the law regulating the procedure to be followed in civil and penal matters toward foreigners living in places distant more than nine hours from a consular residence, see For. Rel. 1892, 545–547, 554.

Proceedings were instituted in the local courts at Jerusalem against Assad Kassas, a native guard employed by the United States consulate, in relation to the pos-session of a house which he occupied and which he claimed to have inherited from his mother. He ignored the sum-mons of the court, and after Mr. Gillam, the United States consul, had refused to comply with a request to order him to vacate, a decree of dispossession was entered and he was forcibly evicted. It was not stated whether the suit was brought before or after Kassas entered the service of the consulate, nor did it appear to have interfered with the performance of his duties. It seemed to have concerned only his status as the owner or claimant of real property under the laws of Turkey. Under the circumstances, the Department of State did " not feel justified in instructing Mr. Gillam that real estate held by Ottoman subjects is taken out of Turkish jurisdiction when they become yassakdjis, or guards, in consulates." But as the case was novel and the precise question did not appear to have been raised before, the legation at Constantinople was instructed to ascertain the position of the Ottoman Government on the subject, as well as what privileges in such matters were conceded to other Frankish powers.

Native employees of consulates.

Mr. Bayard, Sec. of State, to Mr. Straus, min. to Turkey, March 17, 1888, For. Rel. 1888, II. 1568.

In the course of this instruction, Mr. Bayard observed that citizens of the United States in Turkey were, under the real-estate protocol of Aug. 11, 1874, as proclaimed by the President Oct. 29, 1874, and under the terms of imperial rescript of 7 Sefer, 1284 (June 10, 1867), placed on an equal footing with Ottoman subjects " in all things that concern their landed property," and were expressly excluded from availing " themselves of their personal nationality except under the reserve of the immunities attached to their persons and their movable goods according to the treaties." (18 Stats. part 3, p. 853.) The 11th article of the *règlement* of 23 Sefer, 1280 (Aug. 9, 1863), touching foreign consulates, was, as stated in the explanatory circular to the governors-general, intended to prevent the employés of consulates receiving other or greater protection outside of their actual official duties than any other protégés or than foreigners. (Van Dyck's Capitulations, part 1, p. 98.) The United States, said Mr. Bayard, had never been disposed to claim excessive or unusual immunities for natives employed in any capacity in its legations and consulates abroad. (Mr. Seward, Sec. of State, to Mr. Morris, min. to Turkey, Dec. 23, 1867, MS. Inst. Turkey, II. 202.) In several recent instances, where the foreign servant of a legation had been claimed to be liable for military duty, as at Madrid in 1874 and at Berlin in 1879, the ground of complaint had been that the service of the mission was interrupted by the abrupt action of the authorities, rather than any right to withdraw a native from his national subjection. Continuing, Mr. Bayard said:

" The customary usage of Turkey in regard to the withdrawal of Ottoman subjects by foreign service from their national jurisdiction, as set forth in the consular *règlement* of 1863, appears to be in harmony with the foregoing principles. Article I. prescribes the number of privileged native Turkish subjects to be so employed, the number of yassakdjis (cavasses, janissaries, or guards) allowed at a consulate being three, with privilege of increase of the number by mutual understanding.

" 'Art. I. Consuls are to give notice of the appointment of yassakdjis to to the vali, or governor-general of the province, and obtain his recognition. (Art. 4.)'

" The protection of privileged employés is defined as ' individual and attached to their functions.' The service of yassakdjis counts for five years as army service, and they cannot be withdrawn from the consular service for active or reserve military duty. Privileged employés shall enjoy all the immunities accorded by the capitulations, but their estates shall pay the land tax. (Art. 5.)

" The privilege lasts only during ' effective actual service,' and the protégés are shielded from all prosecution, having origin in the services which the consulate may have received from them. They are not to pay, during their protection, any but real-estate tax, or those burdens to which foreigners are subjected. (Art. 11.) Native servants of consuls, not of the enumerated privileged classes, have no right to protection, but even these are not to be proceeded against or arrested save with timely notice to the consul. (Art. 12. See Van Dyck's Capitulations, pt. 1, p. 96.) . . . Article

50 of the French capitulations of 1740 appears to be in point. It provides that—

"'For the security of the dwellings of the consuls, permission is granted to appoint the janissaries solicited by them, and these janissaries shall be protected by the odtobachies and other commandants.'

"So, too, with article 28 of the English capitulations of 1675, which provides that the ambassadors and consuls may take into their service any janissary or interpreter they please."

An action was brought against G. Costa, dragoman of the United States consular agency at Salonica, Turkey, for 11,000 piasters alleged to be due on his endorsement of a promissory note. The Turkish court summoned Mr. Costa through the consular agency, thus recognizing his official relation, and the consular agent, in conformity with law and custom, sent a second dragoman and two assessors to attend the trial. The president of the court, however, refused to permit them to attend. Mr. Costa thereupon withdrew, by way of protest, and judgment was rendered against him in his absence. The consular agent refused to accept the judgment and returned it to the court, with the statement that he should refer the case to the United States legation. When the legation brought the case to the attention of the Turkish Government, the latter at first intimated that as Mr. Costa was an Ottoman subject he was, under art. 9 of the regulations for foreign consulates, under Ottoman jurisdiction in respect of his private affairs, and that the suit in question must therefore be judged without consular intervention. This view the legation controverted. It appears that by art. 1 of the "règlement" of 1863, in relation to foreign consulates, the consulates may have a certain number of natives as privileged employees (employés privilégées), the "privilége" apparently referring to the immunity belonging to the consular suite, and by art. 5 the same immunities are assured to temporary as to permanent employees. These immunities are explained and confirmed by the "circulaire aux gouverneurs-généraux," which is appended to the règlement, and which expressly assures to the temporary protégés a judicial procedure conformable to the ancient treaties, in the presence of the consul or of his representatives (conformément aux anciens traités, en présence du consul ou de son délégué). Such is the right of the "employé privilégée," of which the dragoman is an example. Art. 9 of the "règlement" indeed provides that Ottoman subjects in the service of *foreign subjects* shall be amenable to Ottoman jurisdiction in respect of their private affairs. But this seems only to render clearer the privilege of the dragoman, who is in the service, not of a foreign subject, but of a foreign government.

The Department of State, in acknowledging the report of the discussion, said:

" Upon careful examination of the Ottoman ' règlement ' of 1863 and of the ' circulaire aux gouverneurs-généraux ' referred to by you, the Department concurs in the view taken and most ably presented by you, and approves your action in the case. As you state that you have heard of no further proceedings being instituted against the dragoman it may be inferred that your interpretation of the law is accepted by the Ottoman Government."

> Mr. Day, Sec. of State, to Mr. Angell, min. to Turkey, June 24, 1898, For. Rel. 1898, 1112 ; Mr. Angell, min. to Turkey, to Mr. Day, Sec. of State, May 31, 1898, enclosing copy of a note to Tewfik Pasha, min. of for. aff., April 23, 1898, For. Rel. 1898, 1109, 1110.

December 10, 1899, the Turkish court at Magnesia, a place 30 miles distant from Smyrna, placed under sequestration some licorice root, which was said to be the property of Avedis S. Avedikian, third dragoman to the United States consulate at Smyrna, and which was stored at Magnesia in a building rented by him. The seizure having been made without notice to the consul at Smyrna, the latter requested the governor to order the release of the goods. Subsequently the consul received from the court at Magnesia a summons addressed to Mr. Avedikian, notifying him of the seizure of his property and citing him to appear for trial. Several days later, the governor having declined to give orders to the court, the consul sent to Magnesia his cavass, who broke the seals upon the building in which the licorice root was sequestered and entered into possession. Two days later the cavass was arrested by soldiers acting under the governor's orders, his arms were taken from him, and he was sent back in custody to Smyrna, where, after four hours' further detention, he was released.

The United States legation at Constantinople represented to the Porte—

1. That, Magnesia being easily within the jurisdiction of the consul at Smyrna, the action of the court in proceeding without notice to him to sequester the property of the dragoman was in contravention of established treaty rights.

2. That the forcible entry by Ottoman soldiers of a building leased by the dragoman constituted an unlawful invasion of an American domicile.

3. That the arrest of the cavass was a violation of treaty rights and a grave affront.

The legation therefore demanded—

1. That telegraphic orders be sent for the removal of the sequestration, so that the judicial proceedings, including, if necessary, a

sequestration, might be instituted in the proper way, with the assistance of the consul.

2. That the building leased by Avedikian be evacuated and given over to the lessee.

3. That telegraphic orders be given for the return of the arms of the cavass to the consul.

The Porte assented to these demands, and effect was given to them.

While the foregoing case was pending the consul at Smyrna reported that the court at Magnesia had illegally ordered the seizure of more American goods, that two employees of Avedikian had been arrested, and that Turkish soldiers had been sent into the country to prevent him from purchasing goods. The version of the affair given by the Turkish governor was that Avedikian had attempted to seize licorice root belonging to an English merchant named Forbes; that, the seizure being resisted, Avedikian's employees beat Forbes's workmen, and wounded the mouktar of the village of Elgi; and that, having thus taken possession of the goods by force, they were arrested by order of the subgovernor.

Mr. Griscom, United States chargé d'affaires ad interim at Constantinople, observed, in his report of this incident, the full details of which he did not possess, that the title to the licorice root clearly was a matter for the Turkish courts, and that, if Avedikian had acted in an arbitrary and illegal manner, he would not be protected by the legation; and he added:

" In my dispatch to the Department, No. 144, of the 8th instant, I had the honor to submit to the Department the question of the protection to be given dragomans of consulates in the transaction of their private mercantile business. The incident, reported by Consul Lane, of the arrest of Avedikian's employees is an illustration of the difficulties which will surround the situation should the United States Government determine to protect the dragomans. On the other hand it is perhaps well to point out that if the honorary dragomans attached to the many consulates are deprived of the protection which they are supposed hitherto to have enjoyed, they will in all probability no longer continue to serve the United States Government without pay.

"Assistant Secretary of State Porter, in an instruction, No. 170, of May 8, 1885, to the consul-general at Constantinople, laid it down in a positive manner that the dragomans were not entitled to protection except in the discharge of their official functions and at the place of their consulate. This decision is not known to the dragomans, nor is it a matter of common knowledge throughout the consular service."

Mr. Griscom, chargé at Constantinople, to Mr. Hay, Sec. of State, No. 144, Jan. 8, 1900; No. 148, Jan. 13, 1900; No. 164, Feb. 9, 1900;

For. Rel. 1900, 921, 927, 928–930, 931–932. In submitting, in his
No. 144, the question of the protection to be given to the dragomans
of consulates, Mr. Griscom requested instructions. As new instructions were not sent, his subsequent citation of the instructions of
Mr. Porter, No. 170, May 8, 1885, is specially to be noted.

The Turkish minister of foreign affairs, in a note of February
13, 1890, referring to the provisions of Article V. of the regulations
concerning foreign consulates, stated that the Sublime Porte, acqui-
escing in the desire expressed by most of the foreign missions, had
decided to call for military service only dragomans and cavasses
who might in future enter the service of consulates, thus excusing
from that obligation Mussulmans already employed. Christian employés must, without distinction, pay the exoneration tax which
fell to their share. It was added that, in order to prevent misunderstanding, the provincial authorities had been instructed, whenever
they were notified of the appointment of a cavass, officially to
acquaint the interested consulate with his exact situation in regard
to military service.

Enclosure with Mr. Hirsch, min. to Turkey, to Mr. Blaine, Sec. of State,
Feb. 15, 1890, For. Rel. 1890, 742.
For a discussion, without definite conclusion, as to the right to a mixed
trial in Turkey of a civil suit in which a consular dragoman may
be a party, see Mr. Blaine, Sec. of State, to Mr. Hirsch, min. to
Turkey, March 20, 1890, MS. Inst. Turkey, V. 111, citing Van
Dyck's report on the Ottoman Capitulations, Appendix XV., p. 117.

With reference to the status of native teachers in American
institutions in Turkey, Dr. Herrick, of Anatolia College, in 1892, inquired whether the United States
would accept the college's assurance as to the loyalty
of its teachers and guard it against injustice and injury in their
persons. He made the inquiry with particular reference to the case
of a person who was described as a young Armenian educated in the
United States. The Department of State replied that there was no
way by which the Government of the United States could intervene
as sponsor for the loyalty of an Ottoman subject to his own Government, nor could it ask the Ottoman Government to accept as conclusive the personal assurances of an individual Turkish subject as to
his loyalty. As an individual owing allegiance to the Ottoman
authority, the representatives of the United States could not " interpose to screen him from any charge of violation of law duly preferred
against him." But the Department added that, in the light of the
undoubted right of any legitimate American enterprise in Turkey to
prosecute its work by the usual and lawful channels of native service,
any action by the Turkish authorities aiming to disturb or stop the

Question as to na-
tive teachers.

operations of the institution by harassing its employees might very properly give rise to remonstrance.

Mr. Wharton, Act. Sec. of State, to Mr. Hirsch, min. to Turkey, May 25, 1892, For. Rel. 1892, 576.

Certain native Armenian teachers in the American college at Aintab having been arrested by the Ottoman authorities on a charge of sedition, the minister of the United States at Constantinople, on being advised of the facts, informed the grand vizier that, as the presence of the native teachers was necessary to the success of the colleges in which they were employed, their arrest could be justified only on prima facie proof of guilt, and asked that, before they were imprisoned without bail, the evidence should be submitted to him, in order that he might judge whether a prima facie case against them existed.[a]   The Department of State replied: " While you will protest against capricious or unreasonable arrest of such persons, as occasion requires, you will not insist [that] the Government . . . shall agree in advance that it will not arrest its own subjects for violating its own laws without your consent." [b]   The minister afterwards reported that, in such cases, by order of the Porte, an official representative of the United States would be allowed to be present at each step of the proceedings in order to satisfy himself of their fairness; and that, by this concession, the possibility seemed to be precluded of capricious and groundless arrests of native teachers with a view to hamper or break up the work in the colleges.[c]

" Your dispatch, No. 757, of the 6th of January last, has had due consideration.

" You therein report that a large proportion of the claims filed by the injured missionaries at Marash consists of claims for injury to native students, preachers, and teachers whose nationality is not stated.

" On general principles of international law a government can not be held accountable to a foreign government for injuries suffered by its own citizens or subjects. The relation of native teachers to the administration of the American schools in Turkey has led this Department, on previous occasions, to instruct you that the operations of the schools are not to be wantonly interferred with by molestation of the native instruments they may legitimately employ in their teachings; and that interference with such native teachers on frivolous and vexatious grounds should call for remonstrance and prevention.

a For. Rel. 1894, 742.

b Mr. Gresham, Sec. of State, to Mr. Terrell, min. to Turkey, tel., Oct. 29, 1894, For. Rel. 1894, 745.

c For. Rel. 1894, 745, 746–749.

" Should the destroyed property of native teachers not have been merely personal belongings, but actual and necessary adjuncts to the operation of the American schools in which they were employed, indemnity of that character and to that extent only might be properly asked. It is not, however, thought that any appreciable amount of claims can be due on this limited account, inasmuch as the usual appliances for the educational work conducted by our citizens would necessarily be the property of the missions which direct them.

"As to the native scholars attending the school, the foregoing principle does not seem applicable."

> Mr. Olney, Sec. of State, to Mr. Terrell, min. to Turkey, March 6, 1896, For. Rel. 1896, 882.

(3) MOROCCO.

§ 289.

"All Christian nations refuse to the Government of Morocco any right, power, or control whatever, in any circumstances, over the persons or property of Christians, or Franks, as they are called, visiting or residing in that Empire. . . . Every citizen of the United States is required, when in Morocco, to seek from the consul and have a certificate showing that he is under the consul's protection. Failing to obtain this he has no right by law to remain there."

> Mr. Seward, Sec. of State, to Mr. McMath, April 28, 1862, MS. Inst. Barbary Powers, XIV. 245.
>
> With reference to Hebrews in Morocco who were not citizens of the United States, Mr. Evarts said that they must apply for protection to the representatives of their respective governments, and that no official interposition in behalf of Israelites who were Moorish subjects could be sanctioned, but that there might be cases in which humanity would dictate a disregard of technicalities if the consul's personal influence would shield them from oppression. (Mr. Evarts, Sec. of State, to Mr. Mathews, consul at Tangier, March 20, 1878, MS. Inst. Barbary Powers, XV. 353. See, also, Mr. Bayard, Sec. of State, to Mr. Marcus, March 10, 1885, 154 MS. Dom. Let. 422.)
>
> For a request for an explanation of the protection of persons who were described as " agents of American citizens," see Mr. Evarts, Sec. of State, to Mr. Mathews, consul at Tangier, Dec. 7, 1877, MS. Inst. Barbary Powers, XV. 348.
>
> With regard to Moorish subjects naturalized in the United States, who might return to Morocco, the consul was instructed to claim for them under the treaty of 1836 the same privileges and immunities as might be enjoyed by citizens or subjects of any other power who also might have been natives of Morocco, unless the government to which they owed allegiance should have a treaty of naturalization with the Emperor, the United States having no such treaty. (Mr. Evarts, Sec. of State, to Mr. Mathews, consul at Tangier, Dec. 7, 1877, MS. Inst. Barbary Powers, XV. 348.)

With reference to the suggestion that an exception should be made in Morocco, on grounds of commercial interest, to the rule which restricted the protection of aliens in Mohammedan countries to persons actually in the service of diplomatic and consular officers, Mr. Evarts, in reply, referred to the provision of the statutes of the United States forbidding the granting of passports to persons other than citizens of the United States. He observed that a written protection from the consul would be to all intents and purposes a passport, and suggested that if it should be found expedient to depart from the rule in Morocco, the attention of Congress might be invited to the subject. (Mr. Evarts, Sec. of State, to Mr. Mathews, consul at Tangier, Feb. 27, 1878, MS. Inst. Barbary Powers, XV. 351.)

Subsequently, however, Mr. Evarts took the ground that Moorish agents employed by citizens of the United States in the sea ports of Morocco to do business in the interior might, since their services were essential to such business, be placed under the protection of the United States and granted safe-conducts. (Mr. Evarts, Sec. of State, to Mr. Mathews, consul at Tangier, May 27, 1878, MS. Inst. Barbary Powers, XV. 357.)

With reference to the case of Mr. Benzacar, a Moorish subject, who was duly appointed and recognized as United States consular agent at Saffi, Morocco, Mr. Fish said that the protection of the United States, so far as it might be requisite to enable him to " discharge his official duties," would be given, but that the Department of State could not authorize " any further official interference for the redress of grievances which he may have suffered with reference to his private business or property in Morocco."

> Mr. Fish, Sec. of State, to Mr. Mathews, consul at Tangier, Oct. 2, 1872, MS. Inst. Barbary Powers, XV. 309.

The fact that a fugitive slave in Tangier takes refuge in the house of an American citizen in that place does not entitle him as a right to make any claim on the Government of the United States for protection.

> Mr. Evarts, Sec. of State, to Mr. Mathews, Mar. 15, 1877, MS. Inst. Barb. Powers, XV. 340.

March 10, 1877, a meeting of the foreign representatives at Tangier took place at the house of the Moorish minister for foreign affairs with reference to the question of protection. The British minister at Tangier, in a report on the meeting, stated that the practice of giving protection to Moorish subjects, particularly by exempting them from the payment of taxes, had given rise to grave abuses, and that the evil was a growing one, more especially on the part of foreign officers representing countries which had no trade and few residents in Morocco. The foreign representatives at Tangier seemed generally to concur in this view. Further meetings were held, and the greater part of the demands put forward by the Moorish Government for the reformation of the system were agreed to, but some important questions were left undecided on account of the objections made by France, Italy, Portugal, and Brazil. The Spanish Government subsequently took the initiative in bringing about a conference on the subject at Madrid. The minister of the United States to Spain was authorized to take part in the conference. He was instructed that the United States was cordially in favor of the adoption, by common consent, of an equitable rule which should do away with the excessive and injurious exercise of protection of natives which had grown up under the shadow of treaty stipulations and native usage, and which was represented as burdensome to the Moorish exchequer and unjust to the Government, but that due regard must be paid to the proper maintenance and security of consular establishments and to the necessary employment of natives as guards, interpreters, and servants, and in such capacity as might be essential to the proper representation and protection of foreign commercial interests.

Mr. Evarts, Sec. of State, to Mr. Fairchild, min. to Spain, March 12, 1880, MS. Inst. Spain, XVIII. 441; extracts, For. Rel. 1880, 893.

The conference at Madrid resulted in the conclusion, July 3, 1880, of a convention between the United States, Germany, Austria, Belgium, Denmark, Spain, France, Great Britain, Italy, Morocco, the Netherlands, Portugal, and Sweden and Norway for the establishment of the right of protection in Morocco on a fixed and uniform basis.

By this convention the protected persons, or protégés, are divided into three clases:

1. Native employees of legations and consulates. (Arts. I I.–VII.)

2. Native factors, brokers, or agents (*semsars*, in Arabic) employed by foreign merchants carrying on the import or export trade on a large scale, for their business affairs. (Art. X.)

3. Natives, not exceeding 12 in number, protected for exceptional services to the protecting power. (Art. XVI.)

Unless for exceptional reasons, there is no necessity for issuing certificates of protection to persons falling within the first class, since the names of all official employees of the consulate-general and of the agencies thereunder are required by Art. VII. to be certified to the minister of foreign affairs and to the local authorities, so that their official status is well known and understood.

Art. XIV. provides: " The mediation of interpreters, native secretaries or soldiers of the different legations or consulates, when persons who are not under the protection of the legation or consulate are concerned, shall be admitted only when they are the bearers of a document signed by the head of a mission or by the consular authority."

In the version of this article given in 22 Stat. 823; Consular Regulations, 1888, p. 339; Consular Regulations, 1896, p. 617, and elsewhere, the word "not" is omitted, thus making the article erroneously read "persons who are under the protection," instead of "persons who are not under the protection."

> Mr. Cridler, Third Assist. Sec. of State, to Mr. Partridge, consul-general at Tangier, June 7, 1898, 162 MS. Inst. Consuls, 222, acknowledging the receipt of Mr. Partridge's No. 50, of May 19, 1898, and citing the following papers: Mr. Mathews, consul at Tangier, to the Department of State, No. 407, March 24, 1883, and the Department's reply, No. 235, April 30, 1883, and Mr. Mathews' No. 502, May 28, 1883.
>
> For regulations framed by the Department of State for the guidance of American consular officers in Morocco in the exercise of protection under the convention of 1880, see Mr. Porter, Assist. Sec. of State, to Mr. Mathews, consul at Tangier, Dec. 9, 1886, 119 MS. Inst. Consuls, 688.
>
> As to a conference at Madrid, in 1888, to consider alleged abuses of protection under the existing treaties, see For. Rel. 1888, II. 1049; and as to the conference of 1880, 71 Br. & For. State Papers, 764, 814.
>
> For the agreement between Morocco and France of August 19, 1863, concerning the protection of native brokers, see 66 Br. & For. State Papers, 734.
>
> The mere fact that a person at one time served as a clerk to a United States consulate or consular agency is not held to constitute a signal or exceptional service under Art. XVI. of the convention of 1880. (Mr. Uhl, Assist. Sec. of State, to Mr. Benzaquen, Feb. 11, 1896, 207 MS. Dom. Let. 635.)
>
> Mr. Barclay, consul-general at Tangier, in his No. 94, June 22, 1895, furnished a detailed list of United States protégés and semsars in Morocco, as well as certain information concerning them requested by instruction No. 46, May 21, 1895. (20 Consular Letters from Tangier.)
>
> For a review of this list, with important directions as to the conduct of the consulate in such matters, see Mr. Rockhill, Third Assist. Sec. of State, to Mr. Barclay, consul-general at Tangier, No. 52, Aug. 29, 1895, 149 MS. Inst. Consuls, 384. In the case of a naturalized American resident in Morocco applying for a passport or any other protective document, Mr. Barclay was directed that he "must call not only for the production of his certificate of naturalization, but examine him under oath (oath being taken with the Koran for a Mohammedan and the Sefer for a Jew) as to the facts of his residence in the United States and compliance with all the requirements of our laws; also as to his intention of returning to the country of his adoption, etc."
>
> See, further, as to the persons protected by the consulate, Mr. Uhl, Assist. Sec. of State, to Mr. Barclay, No. 61, Dec. 7, 1895, 150 MS. Inst. Con-

suls, 376 ; Mr. Rockhill, Assist. Sec. of State, to Mr. Burke, consul-
gen. at Tangier, No. 33, Nov. 7, 1896, 154 MS. Inst. Consuls, 334.

" No certificate of protection can . . . be issued by the consul-general [at
Tangier] until the right of the person claiming it has been fully estab-
lished to the satisfaction of the Department, which then instructs the
consul-general to furnish the applicant with a certificate."   (Mr.
Olney, Sec. of State, to Baron Fava, Ital. amb., Jan. 29, 1896, MS.
Notes to Italy, IX. 78.)

" I have to apprise you in connection with the Department's letter to you
of July 14, last, of the receipt of a letter from the Secretary of the
Navy, of the 9th instant, covering copies of the correspondence be-
teween Mr. Felix A. Mathews, United States consul at Tangier, and
Rear-Admiral Earl English, commanding the European Squadron, by
which it appears that Admiral English, on the 20th ultimo, who visited Tangier in his flagship *Lancaster*, made a formal demand upon
the Moorish Government for the immediate release of your two
native agents imprisoned at Fez; the immediate return of all property belonging to your firm and unjustly taken by the governor of
Ducalla, and for the dismissal and punishment of the said governor
for having violated treaty obligations in the person of those agents."
(Mr. Bayard, Sec. of State, to Messrs. Roosevelt and Howland, March
11, 1885, 154 MS. Dom. Let. 439.)

(4) CONSULAR JURISDICTION.

§ 290.

In 1849 Mr. Daniel S. Macauley, United States consul at Alexandria, entertained and decided the case of Fargion against Halfor.
" His proceedings in that case were disapproved on the ground that
he had no rightful jurisdiction because neither of the parties was a
citizen of the United States, though the defendant, Halfor, was nominally what is called a broker to the consulate."

Mr. Seward, Sec. of State, to Mr. Hale, consul-general at Alexandria, Dec.
11, 1866, MS. Inst. Barbary Powers, XIV. 332.

The British minister at Washington having expressed the opinion
that British consular officers were entitled, under the treaty between
Great Britain and Morocco of December 9, 1856, to exercise jurisdiction, both civil and criminal, over Mr. Scott, the interpreter of the
American consulate at Tangier, who was admitted to be a British subject, the Department of State replied that it failed to find in that
treaty any foundation for the claim of such jurisdiction.   The treaty,
it was true, said the Department of State, gave to British consular
officers " ample jurisdiction over British subjects in Morocco generally, but certainly no treaty to which the United States are not a party
can rightfully extend such jurisdiction over any foreigner whom they
may think proper to employ in their consulate.   Furthermore, Mr.
Scott cannot properly be said to be within British jurisdiction, because

he is in the service of an officer of the United States accredited to the Emperor of Morocco, and who, as such, according to the usage of that country, is entitled to privileges of exterritoriality, one of which is the exemption of his servants, including his interpreter, from any other jurisdiction than his own." With the statement that it was likely that the United States, if the case were reversed, would never claim jurisdiction over an American citizen in British service, the Department of State expressed the hope that Her Majesty's Government would, upon further consideration, " acknowledge the reasonableness of our objections to their claim to jurisdiction over Mr. Scott."

> Mr. Fish, Sec. of State, to Sir Edward Thornton, British min., April 5, 1872, MS. Notes to Great Britain, XV. 466, in reply to a note of Sir Edward Thornton of April 3, 1872.

In 1873 the United States consul at Smyrna was instructed that the Department of State, in authorizing the diplomatic and consular officers of the United States, by circulars No. 11, of June 16, and No. 15, of December 15, 1871, to extend protection to Swiss citizens in certain cases, had not contemplated that those citizens were to be registered as entitled to the same protection as citizens of the United States; but that the purpose of the circulars was to allow the good offices of ministers and consuls to be employed in any particular case in which a Swiss citizen might suppose himself to have been aggrieved.

> Mr. Fish, Sec. of State, to Mr. Smithers, consul at Smyrna, Dec. 18, 1873, 72 MS. Desp. to Consuls, 534.
> For the circulars of June 16 and Dec. 15, 1871, above referred to, see For. Rel. 1871, 28; and For. Rel. 1872, 5. See infra, § 654.

In July, 1888, two Swiss citizens, brothers, named Sigmund Benario and Theodor Benario, applied to Mr. Cardwell, United States agent and consul-general at Cairo, for protection. They had previously been under German protection, but withdrew from it on account of misunderstandings with the German consul at Alexandria. Mr. Cardwell gave them a certificate of protection. They were afterwards accused of swindling certain merchants of Germany, and the United States consular agent at Alexandria was requested to issue an order for their arrest. Mr. Cardwell advised the consular agent not to issue such an order till evidence was submitted to him showing the authority of the person making the complaint and also establishing the grounds of it *prima facie*. Mr. Cardwell having sought the instructions of the Department of State, the Department replied that it did not clearly appear what was the nature of the complaint against the Benarios, whether it was sought to punish them criminally for the crime of " swindling," or whether it was desired to obtain substantially a writ of *ne exeat* in a civil suit to recover money. If the proceedings contemplated were civil in their nature, it would seem clear that he had no jurisdiction, since by the act for the organization of mixed courts the jurisdiction of those tribunals extended to suits, in civil and commercial matters, between natives and foreigners and between foreigners of different nationality. But, assuming that a criminal prosecution was intended, the Department observed that two important questions were to be considered, (1) that of the protection accorded in Egypt to foreigners who had no diplomatic or consular representative, and (2) that of the exercise of jurisdiction. As to the first question, the Department referred to the special case of citizens of Switzerland, as explained in Foreign Relations 1887, page 1074, and stated that, as protection had already been granted to the Benarios, the Department would not direct it to be withdrawn. As to the second question, the Department said that it would seem plain that Mr. Cardwell could not properly assume jurisdiction " of a criminal complaint against persons not citizens of the United States without the consent of their government."

> Mr. Rives, Act. Sec. of State, to Mr. Cardwell, agent and consul-general at Cairo, No. 151, Oct. 13, 1888, 127 MS. Inst. Consuls, 246.

After the foregoing instruction in the case of the Benario brothers was sent, a statement of the matter was presented to the Swiss Government. When the answer of that Government was received Mr. Cardwell was instructed that it removed " any objection to exercising criminal jurisdiction over the persons in question," but that any criminal proceedings instituted against them must be conducted in accordance with the rules applied to citizens of the United States. It then seemed probable, however, that the case had been otherwise disposed of.

> Mr. Rives, Assist. Sec. of State, to Mr. Cardwell, No. 167, Feb. 2, 1889, 128 MS. Inst. Consuls, 523, referring to instruction No. 151 of Oct. 13, 1888.
>
> In 1890 the Department of State, while stating that there was no arrangement between the United States and any of the Spanish American states under which the protection of the former was extended to the citizens of the latter in Turkey or in Egypt, and that, if a request for such protection were made by any of those states, the decision of the Government of the United States thereon " would be made known to its agents in those countries [Turkey and Egypt] by appropriate circulars," said : " I am not unaware that the usage of the Government of Turkey and, under its suzerainty, of that of Egypt, following the ancient capitulations, recognize the right of any alien to place himself under whatsoever foreign protection he will, independently of his own natural allegiance, and that when the fact is established, he is regarded as though in fact a citizen or subject of the protecting state. This fact was brought out in the case of the Benario brothers, in 1888, as reported in Mr. Cardwell's dispatches Nos. 245, 246, and 247.

However this doctrine may be viewed by the European states whose rights in the Ottoman dominions flow from their common capitulations, it seems to the Government of the United States that this concession on the part of Turkey cannot constrain us to treat an alien on the footing of our treaties as a citizen, nor constrain the government of the individual to respect his voluntary choice of another protection than that flowing from his natural allegiance." (Mr. Adee, Second Assist. Sec. of State, to Mr. Grant, vice and deputy consul-general at Cairo, No. 56, Oct. 22, 1890, 134 MS. Inst. Consuls, 595.)

" Referring to previous correspondence concerning the case of the Benario brothers in Egypt, I have the honor to acknowledge the receipt of your note of the 3d ultimo, in which you inform me of the action of the Swiss Federal council in delegating to the American consular court in Egypt the right that would belong to the Swiss courts to try the Benario brothers for the acts with which they are charged.

" In reply I have the honor to inform you that the consul of the United States at Cairo has been informed of the removal of the objection to his exercising criminal jurisdiction over the persons in question. The consul has been instructed in the same connection that any proceedings entertained against the Benario brothers must be conducted in accordance with the rules applied to citizens of the United States, and must not assume the form of a vexatious, inquisitorial process."

Mr. Bayard, Sec. of State, to Mr. de Claparede, Swiss min., Feb. 5, 1889, MS. Notes to Switzerland, I. 211.

In 1890 the governor of Cairo, Egypt, requested the United States consulate-general at that place to assume jurisdiction of a charge against Doctor Arciniega of injuring a native while driving in the streets. The governor having described him as " an American," the consulate-general summoned Doctor Arciniega to appear for verification of his papers and registration. On appearing, Doctor Arciniega declared that he was a citizen of Peru, but had been under the protection of the consulate-general for some months. Whether this allegation was borne out by the records was not stated; but the consulate-general informed him that it could give him no protection without the consent of the United States, but would do what it could for him without going beyond the instructions of the Department of State, No. 151, October 13, 1888, in the case of the Benario brothers. The consulate-general therefore took Doctor Arciniega's voluntary statement denying the charge against him and communicated it to the governor of Cairo. The Department of State, in approving the consul's unofficial aid to an unrepresented foreigner, remarked that the case differed from that of the Benarios, " in that the latter, as Swiss citizens, were under a formal protection asked by the Swiss Government, accorded by our own under certain limitations, and recognized by the Khedivial government. . . . The request of the alien's government is necessary in the first instance to validate the protection; but even when this is of record it has been held, as in the case of the Benario brothers, that the express consent of the alien's government is necessary to permit jurisdiction of any crime with which he may be charged. By reference to the Department's instructions, No. 167, to Mr. Cardwell, under date of February 2, 1889, you will see that the Swiss Government, upon being consulted, removed by its reply any objection to the exercise by our agent of criminal jurisdiction over the two Benarios. . . . I have unofficially conferred with the minister of Peru in this city, and he is unable to state the policy of his Government in regard to the friendly protection of Peruvians by the agents of other states, in countries where Peru maintains no representation. . . . The statutes of the United States contemplate the cases of American citizens only; and the authority and provision for the punishment of an alien under an indirect privilege of extraterritoriality is open to grave question. This aspect of the case may, however, be left for consideration should the emergency arise."

> Mr. Adee, Second Assist. Sec. of State, to Mr. Grant, vice and deputy consul-general at Cairo, Oct. 22, 1890, 134 MS. Inst. Consuls, 598.

The Swiss minister of foreign affairs, in a note of January 28, 1891, referring to the subject of jurisdiction over Swiss citizens in criminal matters in Turkey, stated that, as the relations of Switzerland with the Sublime Porte were not regulated by the régime of the capitulations, Switzerland had no representative in the Ottoman Empire, so that Swiss citizens there were entirely at liberty "to choose the power under whose protection they may wish to place themselves. Consequently, we admit, without reserve, that protected Switzers in Turkey are subject to the consular jurisdiction, both civil and criminal, of the state which protects them."

> Mr. Washburn, min. to Switzerland, to Mr. Blaine, Sec. of State, No. 31, January 31, 1891, 27 MS. Desp. from Switzerland, enclosing copy of a note from Mr. Droz, Swiss min. of for. aff., of Jan. 28, 1891.

III. QUESTIONS OF ASYLUM.

1. THE "RIGHT OF ASYLUM."

§ 291.

No legal term in common use is perhaps so lacking in uniformity and accuracy of definition as the "right of asylum." The word asylum has in its legal relations become to a great extent metaphorical.

In its original sense it was highly descriptive. It was applied to privileged places, devoted to special uses, among which was that of shelter for the fugitive. These places were by positive law or by superstition protected from invasion, and in reality they formed sanctuaries. If the fugitive could reach one of them, he was safe from pursuit. He had clothed himself with a right to protection which could not be violated. It was the right of asylum.

This right was the natural product of the conditions under which it arose. The inspiration of the ancient criminal law was the principle of vengeance. Whether pronounced by the head of a family or of a tribe, sitting in judgment upon an injury inflicted on one of its members, or by a priest, as the mouthpiece of an offended deity, the sentence was imposed as an act of revenge. The right of private vengeance was fully recognized. "Whoso sheddeth man's blood, by man shall his blood be shed," was a law that imported at once the expiatory character of punishment and the righteousness of individual retaliation. The slayer was pursued by the avenger of blood, and if overtaken was summarily killed. It is not strange that under systems based so entirely upon the *lex talionis*, sentiments of religion and humanity, as well as of justice, should have suggested means of escape from undiscriminating violence. Hunted by the avenger, the transgressor, as a fugitive and a suppliant, found shelter at the foot of the altar, and oftentimes obtained there remission of his sin. But even if he was not permitted by an act of sacrifice or of supplication to atone for his offence, he was at least entitled to the benefit of mitigating circumstances and to an opportunity to establish their existence. These various motives prompted the institution of places of refuge. From temples of the gods and other places which it was sacrilege to violate, the right of asylum as an obstacle to violence was extended to cities, islands, and other portions of territory.[a] It existed in Egypt, in Greece, and indeed, in all the ancient world. In these places of refuge the foreigner was received as well as the native. "These six cities," reads the law given to the Levites, "shall be a refuge, both for the children of Israel and for the stranger and for the sojourner among them: that every one that killeth any person unawares may flee thither."[b]

As superstition declined and private vengeance was displaced by the regulated action of judicial tribunals, these places of refuge

---

[a] Bernard de l'Extradition, vol. i, p. 11.

[b] Numbers xxxv, 15. By a decree of the council of Toledo, it was declared that immunity should be enjoyed by him who took refuge in the church, and that he who trespassed within a circuit of 30 paces should be excommunicated and also be punished by the King, with whose approval the decree was established. (Padre Florez, España Lagada, 3d Ed. Madrid, 1859, Vol. VI., p. 212, 12th council of Toledo, A. D. 681, Jan. 9, Canon 10.)

ceased to exist; but all the ideas with which the practice of asylum was identified did not perish with them. From having been so long accorded, hospitality and protection had come to be regarded as the fugitive's privilege, and in the end each separate state became a refuge for offenders against the laws of other nations.[a] But the term " right of asylum," though still used in this relation, gradually lost its ancient fitness. As the administration of justice improved, and the distrust of foreigners abated through familiarity of intercourse and the perception of common social interests, nations came to understand their rights and duties better, and the notion that protection was a right belonging to the fugitive disappeared. In its place was established the right of the state either to extradite or to expel any offender who comes within its jurisdiction.[b] In this relation the so-called right of asylum is simply the right of the government either to grant or to withhold the privilege of residence within its territories. But this right is to be exercised by the government in the light of its own interests, and of its obligations as a representative of social order. The right, therefore, is coupled with the duty, amply acknowledged by the multiplication of extradition treaties, to abstain from asserting the sovereign power for the purpose of shielding individuals charged with crime from trial by the competent judicial authorities. The right of sovereignty is conserved in determining the conditions and limitations under which the fugitive is to be delivered up.

In joining legations and consulates in the discussion it is not intended to imply that consulates are commonly invested with the immunities which attach to the residence of a diplomatic officer. Since the immunities of legations are, as will hereafter be maintained, intended to secure the personal independence of public ministers, they do not ordinarily belong to the offices of consuls, who, by the principles of international law, are not exempt from the local jurisdiction. As illustrations of this distinction, I may refer to the consular convention between the United States and New Granada of 1850, the fifth article of which provides that consuls shall not enjoy in either country the immunities granted to public agents accredited in a diplomatic character. They may exercise certain special privileges, such as placing the arms of their country or other insignia of office over the consular door; " but," it is further stipulated, " those insignia shall not be considered as importing a right of asylum, nor as placing the house or its inhabitants beyond the authority of the magistrates who may think proper to search them."

---

[a] Moore on Extradition, vol. i, § 5.

[b] This right has been affirmed in the United States by the highest judicial authority. Ker v. Illinois, 119 U. S. 436; In re Angelo de Giacomo, 12 Blatchford, 391. See, generally, Moore on Extradition, vol. i, §§ 86, 203.

To the same effect is the fourth article of the consular convention of 1855 between the United States and the Netherlands; and article 6 of the convention of May 23, 1878, between the same countries, stipulates for the inviolability of the consular archives, but not for that of the dwelling or office. By the thirty-fifth article of the treaty between the United States and Salvador of December 6, 1870, it is declared that "the contracting Republics recognize no diplomatic character in consuls, for which reason they will not enjoy in either country the immunities granted to public agents accredited in that character."

Nevertheless, consuls, as the representatives of foreign governments, are entitled to special respect and consideration. In some instances they are clothed with a diplomatic character, and are then entitled to diplomatic privileges. In countries where they exercise judicial power, as in barbarous or certain non-Christian lands, they are regarded as endowing with extraterritoriality the place where their flag is planted.[a] Not infrequently consular offices are made inviolable by express agreement. The treaty with the German Empire of December 11, 1871, stipulates that the local authorities shall not on any pretext invade the consular office or dwelling, "except in the case of the pursuit for crime." By the second article of the treaty between the United States and France of November 14, 1788, it was provided that "they [consuls] shall place over the outward door of their house the arms of their sovereign," which according to former usage imported inviolability. By the third article of the treaty between the same countries of February 23, 1853, it is stipulated that "consular offices and dwellings shall be inviolable. The local authorities shall not invade them under any pretext." The same stipulation is found in the treaties of the United States with Belgium of December 5, 1868, and March 9, 1880; with Italy, of February 8, 1868, and May 8, 1878; with Roumania, of June 17, 1881; and with Servia, of October 14, 1881. It is true that in every one of these instances of specific agreement, there is a stipulation, immediately following those just quoted, that "in no case shall those offices or dwellings be used as places of asylum." A distinction is thus clearly marked between the inviolability of the office or dwelling, and its use as a shelter for fugitives from justice. But this distinction is not peculiar to consulates. It merely signifies that the principle of inviolability is not without its limitations and is not incapable of abuse. By the seventh article of the treaty between the United States and Persia of December 13, 1856, it is provided that "the diplomatic agent or consuls of the United States

---

[a] Wharton's Commentaries on Law, § 170; Lawrence's Wheaton, notes 73, 74; 7 Opinions of the Attorney-General, 342, 495; 8 id. 380.

shall not protect, secretly or publicly, the subjects of the Persian
Government." It is also a fact that in countries in which asylum
under foreign flags is practiced, consulates are sometimes used for
that purpose, though not so frequently as legations. Without, therefore, intending to predicate diplomatic immunities of the consular
office or dwelling, it has been thought proper to include even exceptional cases of asylum by referring to consulates as well as to legations; although, in the discussion of the principles that govern the
subject, the argument will be confined to the privileges of diplomatic
agents and the immunities of their offices or dwellings.

2. Early Diplomatic Privileges and their Decadence.

§ 292.

There is every reason to believe that soon after the establishment
of permanent embassies in the fifteenth century the dwellings of
public ministers became resorts for persons fleeing either from
violence or from legal prosecution. The abolition of cities of refuge
and the decline of reverence for sacred places having left the fugitive without a sanctuary, he naturally sought shelter under the immunities of the public minister. At one time those immunities
attained the most exaggerated proportions. They included not only
the extraterritoriality of the minister and his suite, but also that of
his dwelling or hotel and of other buildings over which he placed
the arms of his sovereign.[a] In some instances ambassadors of a
thrifty turn realized enormous profits by hiring and granting their
protection to houses which they then sublet to malefactors.[b] In
various places, as at Madrid, Venice, and Rome, there existed what
was known as the freedom of the ward or quarter (*franchise des
quartiers*, as it was commonly called), by which the immunity
attaching to the minister's house was extended to the quarter of the
city in which the house was situated. At Frankfort-on-the-Main,
where foreigners were not permitted to stay during the election and
coronation of the Emperor, it was customary at such times for
ambassadors, by placing the arms of their sovereigns in conspicuous
places, to take under their protection, as temporary resorts, whole
districts, which were in that manner exempted from the jurisdiction
of the local authorities and even from taxes.[c] Not only were officers
of justice excluded from the exercise of their functions within the
privileged quarters, but it also appears that in some places the am-

a Embassies and Foreign Courts (London, 1885), 336; Martens, Guide Diplomatique, §§ 33, 34.
b Lorimer's Institutes, 250.
c Embassies and Foreign Courts, 337.

bassador's permission was requisite in order that such officers might even traverse these quarters bearing the badges of their authority. Thus, in 1680 the Marquis de Villars, ambassador of France at Madrid, demanded and obtained satisfaction from the Spanish Government because the mayor of the city, accompanied by his bailiffs, traversed his quarter without permission. The Government, however, did not yield to the ambassador's demand without a protest, since nine years previously, in 1671, the King of Spain had declared that he was resolved to treat the ambassadors of each prince as those of Spain were treated at such prince's court; and no freedom of the ward was accorded in Paris.[a] In 1684 the Spanish Government notified all the ambassadors that for the future the exclusion of the local jurisdiction should apply only to their houses.[b]

The immunity allowed to the ambassador's house and the quarter in which it was situated was also extended to his carriage. In 1655 the Marquis de Fontenay, French ambassador at Rome, granted asylum to certain Neapolitan exiles and rebels; but, being unwilling to incur the expense of keeping them, he sought to send them back to Naples by water. As they were proceeding in the coach of the ambassador to the place of embarkation, seventeen of them were captured by the Pope's guard and taken to prison. The ambassador had an audience of the Pope, and demanded the release of the captives and reparation for the affront. In the prolonged controversy that followed, the Pope complained of the protection granted by the ambassador to profligates and whatsoever was criminal in the ecclesiastical state, and contended that the privileges of ambassadors ought not to extend so far. The ambassador answered that it did not appear that he had harbored any of the Pope's subjects, but only some Neapolitans whom he might lawfully protect against the persecutions of the Spaniards. It was finally agreed that the Pope should release those whom the ambassador should name, and that the Papal nuncio at Paris " should regulate with the King the reparation the ambassador demanded *on account of the violence that had been done to his coach.*" Here, as Wicquefort says, "all the advantage was on the ambassador's side, since the Pope, by surrendering the prisoners, tacitly owned he had done better not to have arrested them, and that he had made a noise for nothing." [c]

The gross abuse of the freedom of the quarter as a shelter for criminals of all descriptions resulted in attempts to abolish it. The effort of the King of Spain to suppress it has already been referred to. In the latter part of the seventeenth century Pope Innocent XI. resolved

---

[a] Martens, Causes Célèbres (ed. of 1858), Vol. I. p. 340.

[b] Wildman's Int. Law, 127 et seq.; Bynkershoek, Foro Legatorum, xxi.

[c] Wicquefort's Embassador, Digby's ed. 272, 273.

not to receive any ambassador who would not renounce the privilege.[a]
In consequence it was given up by the Polish ambassador in 1680, by
the Spanish in 1682, and by the English in 1686.[b] Early in the year
1687, the Duc d'Estrées, ambassador of France, having died, the Pope,
before another minister was sent, occupied the Farnese palace, which
was the seat of the French embassy, proclaimed the abolition of the
freedom of the quarter and gave the French court notice of the fact,
as well as of the renunciation of the privilege by other powers.
Louis XIV., however, then King of France, announced with his customary arrogance that his Crown should never be ruled by the
example of others; that God had established it for an example and
guide to others, and that he had resolved, so long as he reigned, never
to let it be deprived of any of its rights. Accordingly he sent another
ambassador, Lavardin, with an armed force of seven hundred men to
maintain the privilege. The Pope answered him by a bull of excom-
munication and the quarrel continued till 1693, when it was adjusted
by a compromise.[c]

Notwithstanding its unreasonable character and pernicious effects,
the *franchise des quartiers* seems to have survived for a long time
in spite of the efforts to suppress it. In 1759 the French minister
at Genoa would not permit the local police to pass his hotel;[d] and
as late as 1822 it was stated that at Rome certain legations, as those
of France and Spain, still enjoyed a certain freedom of the quarter,
which was carried so far that the Spanish ambassador would not
permit police supervision in the neighborhood of his legation, except
by guards attached to the mission.[e]

How, it may be asked, did such an exaggerated privilege come to
prevail? The causes are manifold. It must be remembered that
in the times when the privilege arose, the idea of territorial sovereignty—of the absolute jurisdiction of the state within its dominions—had not been fully realized. During a large part of what we
usually term modern history sovereignty was not associated with
dominion over the earth.[f] Even the fuedal system, which linked
personal duties to the ownership of land, did not establish this
association, though it may have contributed to its growth. But
with the successful termination of the long struggle against the idea
of universal dominion and with the limitation of peoples to definite

---

[a] Martin, Histoire de France, Vol. IX., p. 78.
[b] Embassies and Foreign Courts, 337.
[c] Martens, Causes Célèbres, Vol. I, p. 343 et seq.
[d] Embassies and Foreign Courts, 336 et seq.
[e] Martens, Manuel Diplomatique, § 30.
[f] Maine, Ancient Law, 103.

regions, the conception of territorial sovereignty and exclusive jurisdiction was gradually wrought out. The incompleteness of its reali-
zation in times comparatively recent is abundantly shown by various
international conventions in which states have imposed servitudes
upon their territories. Thus by the treaty of Utrecht of 1713,
fishing rights were reserved to French subjects in territory ceded
under that convention by France to England; and by the treaty of
peace between the United States and Great Britain of 1783, following the precedent set by the treaty of Utrecht, similar rights were
secured to American fishermen in British territory. As a further
result of the imperfect conception of territorial sovereignty, we find
jurisdiction parcelled out into various hands. Besides the courts
under the control of the sovereign prince, there were tribunals administered independently by lesser authorities and by ecclesiastics. These
administrators of law, with the symbols of their authority in their
coat of arms, which they placed above the doors of their palaces,
shared with the monarch the exercise of jurisdiction. Even in insular England there were civil courts and ecclesiastical tribunals that
subtracted something from the supremacy of the general law of the
land.[a]

That the imperfect conception of the state's supreme and exclusive
jurisdiction bears a causal relationship to the enjoyment of inordinate
privileges by diplomatic agents is more than probable. If the freedom of the quarter ever existed in Paris writers on that subject fail
to disclose the fact; and it was in France that the power of the
National Government was first and most completely established over
the ruins of mediæval privilege. The authority of the Crown scarcely
surpassed that of the Parliament of Paris, with its politico-legal
functions, and along with the growth of royal power there was developed a systematic jurisprudence, displacing the prerogatives of the
nobles and the ecclesiastics.[b] But in the general absence of a conviction of the absolute sovereignty of the state within its dominions, it
was an easy thing for persons endowed with exceptional immunities to
exclude the exercise of local jurisdiction; and it is a remarkable fact
that when the inordinate privileges of ambassadors came to be a subject of complaint the ground of objection was not so much that they
infringed upon the rightful authority of the government as that their
exercise had fostered an abuse that menaced the public safety. As
the representative of a sovereign prince or of the sovereign pontiff, the
ambassador or nuncio bore a character at once privileged and inviolable.[c] The coat of arms of his sovereign, which he placed above the

---

[a] Blackstone's Comm., book 1, *117; book 3, *63.

[b] Hallam, Middle Ages, Vol. I, p. 242 et seq.

[c] "It is on this account," says Wicquefort, "that in several courts of Europe
the embassadors set up the arms of their master over the gate of their palace;

portal of his dwelling,[a] not only guaranteed him freedom from molestation, but also imported authority. It was held that the ambassador had a right " to do justice in his own house, upon those who depend on him." [b] In 1603 the Marquis de Rosny, afterward known as the Duc de Sully, who was sent by Henry IV. to England as special ambassador to compliment James I. on his accession to the throne, condemned one of his suite to death for killing an Englishman in a brawl, and invited the mayor of London to send officers to execute the sentence. The mayor took charge of the culprit and was preparing for his execution when the Comte de Beaumont-Harley, ordinary ambassador of France, who opposed the sentence, procured a pardon from James and gave the offender his freedom. But while Henry IV., desiring not to mar the present good feeling, took no action in the matter, his council and all France condemned the irregularity of the ordinary ambassador's procedure. Nor is it at all likely that James would have ventured to interfere if the culprit had not previously been delivered into the custody of an English magistrate.

As has been observed, the first opposition to exaggerated ambassadorial pretensions was occasioned by their abuse. While evidence of this fact is found in the controversy between the Pope and the Marquis de Fontenay, which has already been narrated, further confirmation of it is afforded by a case that occurred still earlier. In 1540 the Venetian Republic sent an ambassador to Constantinople to conclude a peace. The Porte, having discovered what the envoy was authorized to concede, made large demands, a considerable part of which were secured. Subsequently it was found that the ambassador's instructions had been betrayed to the Porte by certain Venetian officials who were in the pay of France. On learning that they had been detected, these officials fled to the palace of the French ambassador, who granted them asylum. The Council of Ten, however, of whom one of the culprits was secretary, holding that there was no asylum for high treason, demanded their surrender, and being unable to obtain it planted two pieces of cannon before the ambassador's palace and compelled their delivery by force. Francis I, then King of France, when he heard of this transaction,

---

and almost everywhere they have a chair of state, which denotes the presence of the master of the house. At the Congress of Westphalia, the houses of the embassadors and plenipotentiaries were known by the arms of the sovereigns whom they represented; not only those of crowned heads, of republics and of the electors, but also those of the princes of Germany and Italy. The embassadors of the United Provinces, writing to the States General, do not fail to date their letters, ' From the House of Their High Mightinesses,' not so much because they defray the expenses of the embassy, and pay the rent of the house, as chiefly because it is their representative that lodges there." (P. 266.)

[a] Martens, Guide Diplomatique (Paris, 1866), § 29, note; Wicquefort, 266.

[b] Wicquefort, 260.

was so incensed that he refused for two months to give audience to the Venetian ambassador. When at last an audience was granted and the King asked the ambassador what he would do if he were treated as had been the ambassador of France, the Venetian replied: "Sire, if rebellious subjects of Your Majesty had sought refuge in my house, I would have delivered them up to the judges; and if I had done otherwise, I should have been severely punished by my Republic." The pertinency of this answer was, under the circumstances, so complete that the King was pacified.[a]

The opposition to exaggerated privileges which grew out of their abuse was strengthened and endowed with purpose by the growth of the idea of territorial sovereignty and the coincident development of a regular and orderly administration of justice, based upon law. This movement is marked by the advent of the publicists—those learned and philosophical writers on the laws of nature and of nations, who endeavored to reduce the intercourse of states to a system founded upon absolute independence and equality. Of these, Grotius, though not the first, is conceded to be the foremost example. His famous work, *De Jure Belli ac Pacis*, published in 1625, is generally regarded as laying the foundation of the modern science of international law, and, if for no other cause, would be entitled to that distinction by virtue of the influence it has exerted. Grotius, arguing upon the reason of the matter, declared that whether the ambassador had jurisdiction over his family and suite, or whether his house was to be an asylum for all who took refuge there, depended upon the concession of the sovereign near whom he resided, since it was not a part of the law of nations.[b] A century later, in 1721, Cornelius von Bynkershoek issued his great treatise, *De Foro Legatorum tam in Causa Civili quam Criminali*, a masterly exposition of the rights of legation, in which he declared that the privilege of asylum was so preposterous that Quintilian himself could not give color to it.[c] The privileges which the law of nations conferred upon ambassadors were, he maintained, founded upon the necessity of protecting them in the exercise of their functions, an end to the attainment of which the obstruction of justice by granting an asylum to criminals was in nowise requisite; and he cited with approval a demand made by the States General for the surrender of an offender who had taken refuge in the house of the English resident.

---

[a] Martens, Causes Célèbres, Vol I, causes diverses, § 1; Blackwood's Magazine, vol. cxvi, p. 349.

[b] Ipse autem legatus an jurisdictionem habeat in familiam suam, et an jus asyli in domo sua pro quibusvis eo confugientibus, ex concessione pendet ejus apud quem agit. Istud enim juris gentium non est. Grotius, II. 18, viii.

[c] Chap. XXI.; cited by Wildman, Int. Law, § 127, and many other publicists.

It should be remembered, however, that these publicists, while their argument goes further, spoke in the presence of the gross abuses which have already been described; and although the justice of the complaint against those abuses was acknowledged, as shown by the partial abatement of the freedom of the quarter and its associated pretensions, nations did not readily abandon the claim of asylum, which in the general estimation was identified with the immunity belonging to the ambassadorial residence.

In 1726 the famous Duke of Ripperda, minister of finance and foreign affairs to Philip V. of Spain, becoming apprehensive as to his security, sought asylum in the house of the British ambassador at Madrid. It appears that Ripperda came uninvited to the British embassy, after having been refused asylum at the Dutch, and that he was permitted to remain at the former only after assuring the British ambassador that he was not in disgrace (he had been dismissed from office on a pension) or charged with crime. Subsequently the ambassador had an audience of the King and was assured that the duke might remain in the embassy, it being understood that he was not to be permitted to escape and that some soldiers would be placed about the embassy as a precaution against any attempts in that direction. The Spanish Government, however, subsequently becoming alarmed at the discovery that the duke had taken with him important papers, submitted to the council of Castile the question whether he might not be seized. The council of Castile answered in the affirmative, holding that it would " operate to the subversion and utter ruin [of sovereigns] if persons who had been intrusted with the finances, the power and the secrets of the state, were, when guilty of violating the duties of their office, allowed to take shelter under a privilege which had been granted to the houses of ambassadors in favor of only ordinary offenders."

In conformity with this view, the Spanish Government sent officers to seize the duke. This was done without previously communicating to the ambassador the resolution of the Council of Castile and demanding Ripperda's surrender. The ambassador submitted to avoid disturbance. The relations between England and Spain were already exceedingly strained, and the seizure of Ripperda, though not the cause of the subsequent hostilities between the two countries, was resented in England. The burden, however, of the British Government's complaint was the summary and forcible termination, without notice, of the asylum to which the King had consented, the Duke of Newcastle, then Secretary of State, expressly saying that, without deciding whether the ambassador had or had not the right to protect Ripperda, an opportunity should under the circumstances have been afforded for his surrender before resort was had to an act of force. Vattel, however, affirms, in respect of the opinion of the Council of Castile, that " nothing could be said on this topic with greater truth and judgment;" and Phillimore declares " that Spain was not guilty of any violation of international law." [a]

In 1747 a merchant named Springer, a native of Russia domiciled in Stockholm, was convicted before a special commission as an accomplice in the crime of high treason. On the evening of the day on which he was to have been sentenced he escaped from prison in disguise and, on pretence of being an English courier, gained admission to the hotel of the English ambassador, Colonel Guideckens. On the refusal of the ambassador to surrender him, the Swedish Government surrounded the hotel with troops, searched all who entered it, and caused the minister's carriage to be followed by a guard. In consequence, Guideckens surrendered the culprit under protest, but subsequently, under instructions of his Government, demanded redress. Failing to obtain it, he left Stockholm suddenly, by order of his King, without taking formal leave; and as the Swedish Government responded by ordering its ambassador away from London in the same manner, diplomatic relations were for the time suspended. [b]

3. SURVIVALS OF ASYLUM IN EUROPE.

§ 293.

By too readily inferring that the views of Grotius and Bynkershoek were immediately admitted in the practice of states and that the more recent cases of invasion of diplomatic asylum to which I have adverted mark its termination, many writers have been led to assert in terms too sweeping and absolute that the right to grant such asylum has long since ceased to be recognized in European countries. [c] It has, indeed, generally disappeared; but there seems to be

---

[a] Vattel, 494 et seq.; Martens, Causes Célèbres, Vol. I., cause vi.; Phillimore, Vol. II. cciv.; London Law Magazine and Review, Nov. 1891, p. 93.

[b] Martens, Causes Célèbres, Vol. II., cause iv. Philimore, Vol. II., ccv., says: " It seems clear that the conduct of Sweden was in accordance with the principles of international law."

[c] The following are examples: " In modern times the ambassadorial right of asylum, which gave rise to so many abuses, is abolished in all European states " (Embassies and Foreign Courts (1855), 338). At the same time the author adds: "A difference is, however, made between offences against the state and private crimes." Hall, Int. Law, 3d ed. 1890, p. 179, says: " In Europe, however, it has been completely established that the house of a diplomatic agent gives no protection either to ordinary criminals, or to persons accused of crimes against the state." But he adds in a footnote that asylum was " revived " in Spain " for a considerable time." Woolsey, Int. Law, 6th ed., § 92, p. 139, goes still further, and says that " the usage, if we are not deceived, was never general throughout Europe, and even where it obtained, as in Rome and Madrid, was sometimes opposed and violated by the government." See Hall, Int. Law, 4th ed., p. 190, note 1.

ample evidence that its decline was slow and not infrequently interrupted. Vattel, who was a diplomatist as well as a publicist, doubtless wrote in reference to existing practices; and in his great treatise,
published in 1758, while inveighing against a minister's taking advantage of his immunities in order " to afford shelter and protection to
the enemies of the prince and to malefactors of every kind, and thus
screen them from the punishments which they have deserved," he
said :

> I grant, indeed, that when there is question only of certain ordinary trans-
> gressions, and these committed by persons who often prove to be rather unfor-
> tunate than criminal, or whose punishment is of no great importance to the
> peace of society, the house of an ambassador may well serve as an asylum for
> such offenders ; and it is better that the sovereign should suffer them to escape,
> than expose the ambassador to frequent molestation under pretense of a search
> after them, and thus involve the state in any difficulty which might arise from
> such proceedings.[a]

G. F. de Martens, the eminent German publicist and councillor, in
his *Précis*, published in Göttingen in 1789, and republished there in
1821, the year of his death, declared (§ 4) that asylum was still
allowed for private crimes, though it was universally admitted that
persons accused of crimes of state might be seized, if not given up.[b]

It was not until 1815 that asylum was abolished at Rome, and then
an exception was made as to persons charged with misdemeanors.[c]

That the decline of asylum was gradual is not strange. Diplomacy is always tenacious of its privileges. But apart from this fact,
the recurrence of conditions resembling those in which the practice
of asylum earlier found its justification has occasioned its revival at
certain times and places, for the purpose of shielding fugitives from
naked violence. In even a broader form than this it has appeared in
Europe in the last half century, though neither public opinion nor
diplomatic usage would now tolerate its systematic employment, as
in former times, for the purpose of obstructing the course of justice
or of fostering political conspiracies.

In the revolution in Greece in 1862 a refuge was granted both in
legations and in consulates to those in danger of their lives.[d] During
the persecution of the Jews in Moldavia, Wallachia, and Servia in
1867, under cover of the laws relating to vagabondage, the British
consul at Galatz made it known that in case of need a refuge could be
found in the British consulate.[e] It is true that both Greece and the
Danubian principalities were more or less under foreign tutelage,

---

[a] Book IV. ch. ix. sec. 118. Also cited by Félice, Leçons (1830), vol. ii,
p. 560 et seq.

[b] Also cited by Polson, Law of Nations, § 32.

[c] Wildman, International Law, § 127, et seq.

[d] 58 British and Foreign State Papers, 1009 et seq.

[e] 62 id. 689.

though surely not so far as to enable foreign powers to control the authorities. But it is in Spain that the practice of asylum in Europe has been most recent and most extensive. For more than a decade prior to 1850 the country was in a chronic state of revolution. In 1841 the Chevalier d'Alborgo, chargé d'affaires of Denmark in Madrid, received into his dwelling the principal persons who had been engaged in a conspiracy to seize the Queen in her palace and overturn the government of General Espartero. In 1843 the Marquis of Casa Irujo, afterward Duke of Sotomayor, who had fallen into disfavor, found shelter under the roof of the same diplomatist: as also did Señor Salamanca, who, it has been alleged, corresponded from his asylum with General Narvaez and provided that officer with funds to pay the insurgent forces under his command. In 1846, when those whom he had served had come into power, M. d'Alborgo was made a Spanish noble with the unequivocal title of Baron del Asilo. On the 26th of March, 1848, a new insurrection broke out, attended with the utmost confusion, to which the extraordinary measures of the Government contributed not a little. All the guarantees of the constitution were suspended; a council of war was substituted for the civil tribunals; promiscuous arrests were made; leading generals of the Progressist party were banished without trial, and the streets of Madrid were made the scene of hostilities.[a] While these events were occurring, the houses of the foreign ministers were filled with refugees. On the 15th of April the Duke of Sotomayor instructed Señor Isturiz, the Spanish minister in London, to ask for the recall of Mr. Bulwer on the ground that he had directed " all his efforts and the influence of his official position " against the Government to which he was accredited. As a convincing proof of this, it was alleged that his house at that moment served as a refuge for men implicated in the attempt against the Government, and that " from that asylum they continue their machinations in concert with those without, in order to disturb anew the public order and tranquillity of this capital." On May 3 this charge was brought by the Duke of Sotomayor to the attention of Sir Henry Bulwer, in the course of a conversation in which, according to the official report of the latter, the duke " confessed it was customary in this country to give asylum to persons pursued for political offences; that all Spanish governments have allowed this and all foreign agents have practiced it, but that this custom had its limits."

[a] Foreigners did not escape violence. Among those who suffered was an inoffensive English Quaker, who was shot down by a soldier because, when challenged, he was unable, from stuttering, instantly to reply. In reporting this case to the Duke of Sotomayor, then minister of foreign affairs, Mr. Henry Bulwer, the British minister, lugubriously observed: "Another Englishman has been killed, simply because he had an impediment in his speech."

Sir Henry denied the charge of protecting conspiracy and declared that he had but one person in his house—" a person," he said, " whom his family had begged me to keep, in order that he might not mix himself up further in revolutionary schemes, which he had given me his word not to do." In concluding his report of the conversation, Sir Henry says: " I then asked him [the duke] whether he would relieve me from the disagreeable position of still retaining in my house the person, whom [*sic*] I had admitted to him was there, by giving me a passport for the said individual. He said he thought he might; but having since told me that he could not furnish the said passport until some further time had elapsed, the gentleman in question, on my communicating to him what had taken place, left my house."

A few days after this conversation the Duke of Sotomayor sent officers out to search for Señor Salamanca, his former partner in asylum, who, in the rapid shiftings of partisanship, had arrayed himself in opposition to the government of his associate in the revolution of 1843. The first house visited was that of M. d'Alborgo, still chargé d'affaires of Denmark, whose Spanish title seems on this occasion to have operated to his disadvantage. For, says Sir Henry Bulwer, " the police, under M. d'Alborgo's protest, enter the house of M. Alborgo, Baron del Asilo, and search every corner in it; in contradiction, I believe, to the immemorial custom in Spain, which has seen no similar instance, save the celebrated one of the Duke of Ripperda, and in contradiction to the recent recognition of an usage which it might have been well to tolerate, but not to reward." As Señor Salamanca was not found in the Danish legation, the search was extended to the dwelling of M. d'Alborgo's neighbor, the chargé d'affaires of Belgium. Here entry was refused to the police, but on receiving a communication from the Duke of Sotomayor, the chargé d'affaires assured the chief of police on his honor that the fugitive was not in the legation. "A strong force, however, of the police of the Ronda have surrounded the Belgian legation all yesterday and to-day," says Sir Henry Bulwer, in concluding his narrative.

On May 17, 1848, the British minister was given his passports, but not because he had assumed to grant asylum. The complaint, not that he had used, but that he had abused that privilege was only one of many, in large measure groundless, employed to cover the fact, which Sir Henry appreciated, that he was being made a scapegoat for Lord Palmerston, by whose direction he had communicated to the Duke of Sotomayor certain officious criticisms and suggestions which the latter indignantly resented. On June 3 the Spanish minister in London communicated to the British Government, from the Duke of Sotomayor, papers containing six different reasons for Sir Henry's

dismissal. One of these was that the latter had afforded protection
" to many of the individuals most conspicuous in the conspiracy of
the 26th, sheltering them in his house, and allowing them to communicate from thence with the enemies of the government." Lord Palmerston, besides denying the truth of the charge, said :

It is admitted by Sir Henry Bulwer that he conformed, on the occasion of
the insurrection of the 26th of March at Madrid, to the custom which has long
been established in that city, and according to which the houses of foreign
ministers have been always open to afford sanctuary to political offenders
until they might be able to find the means of leaving the country. . . . Her
Majesty's Government are quite ready to acknowledge that such a practice is in
itself and in principle objectionable ; but while it continues to exist, a foreign
minister could not without discredit to himself and to his government refuse to
comply with it ; and I must be allowed to remark that Her Majesty's Government scarcely expected to find objections to that practice proceeding from
General Narvaez, the Duke of Sotmayor and yourself. With regard to yourself, I need not remind you that the Earl of Clarendon, then Mr. Villiers, and
British minister at Madrid, was able in 1836 to enjoy the great pleasure and
the heartfelt satisfaction of affording you, when in danger, a temporary
reception under the diplomatic protection of his roof ; and that he was afterwards so fortunate as to contribute to your permanent safety by facilitating
your removal from thence into Portugal.

His lordship also adverted to the protection of the Duke of Sotomayor by the Danish chargé, in 1843, and to the duke's subsequent
recognition of that service ; and, after reviewing the five other
causes of complaint and pronouncing them to be insufficient, he
informed Señor Isturiz that Her Majesty could no longer continue
to receive him, and that he would " probably think it expedient to
return to Madrid,"—a suggestion which the minister immediately
adopted.[a]

Nor was the granting of asylum at Madrid unknown after the
incidents just narrated. In the revolutionary period of 1865–75,
which, in respect of disorder and violence, reproduced the decade
of 1840–50, the practice was resumed. In 1873, after the abdication
of Amadeus, Marshal Serrano, who had taken an active part in
placing that prince on the throne, was hunted by a mob. He fled
from house to house, but at last repaired to the abode of the British
minister, Mr. Layard, who subsequently disguised him and accompanied him by rail to Santander, where he embarked on a steamer
for St. Jean de Luz.[b]

" The right of asylum, by which I now refer to the so-called right
of a political refugee to immunity and protection within a foreign
legation or consulate, is believed to have no good reason for its continuance, to be mischievous in its tendencies, and to tend to political
disorder.

---

a British and Foreign State Papers, vol. 38, pp. 928–1050.
b Annual Register, 1873, p. 226.

" These views have been frequently expressed, and, while this Government is not able of itself to do away with the practice in foreign countries, it has not failed, on appropriate occasion, to deprecate its existence and to instruct its representatives to avoid committing this Government thereto.

" Upon a recent occasion, occurring in the island of Hayti, where, as represented to this Department, the asylum was forced upon the minister, the Department found it necessary to give a renewed and emphatic expression to these views.

" Such being the case, it is deemed fortunate that Mr. Castro was not compelled to avail himself of the offer you had made."

> Mr. Fish, Sec. of State, to Mr. Cushing, min. to Spain, Oct. 1, 1875, MS. Inst. Spain, XVII. 311.

" The frequency of resort in Spain to the legations for refuge, and the fact mentioned by you that nobody there disputes the claim of asylum, but that it has become, as it were, the common law of the land, may be accounted for by the prevalence of ' conspiracy as a means of changing a cabinet or a government,' and the continued tolerance of the usage is an encouragement of this tendency to conspiracy.

" It is an annoyance and embarrassment, probably, to the ministers whose legations are thus used, but certainly to the governments of those ministers, and, as facilitating and encouraging chronic conspiracy and rebellion, it is wrong to the government and to the people where it is practiced—a wrong to the people, even though the ministry of the time may not remonstrate, looking to the possibility of finding a convenient shelter when their own day of reckoning and of flight may come."

> Mr. Fish, Sec. of State, to Mr. Cushing, min. to Spain, Oct. 5, 1875, MS. Inst. Spain, XVII. 317.
> The foregoing instruction related to the case of Colonel Borreguero, who, being "apprehensive of persecution by the authorities on account of his political opinions," sought asylum in the legation, though no charges were at the time pending against him. " In what sense, if in any," said Mr. Fish, " this may make a difference from the case of one already the object of pursuit, it is not necessary now to consider. It is satisfactory to know that the legation is relieved of the presence of a refugee, and it is hoped that the occasion may not again arise when there shall be any necessity of reporting one's presence."
> See Mr. Olney, Sec. of State, to Mr. Taylor, min. to Spain, Feb. 25, 1897, MS. Inst. Spain, XXII. 300, enclosing a copy of a note to the German ambassador at Washington of Feb. 24, 1897.

" Your despatch No. 346 of the 8th ultimo, in relation to the alleged forcible entry of the United States consular agency at Latakia, by a Turkish soldier, has been received and considered. . . .

"I can not see that there was a violation of the sanctity of the consular office or archives by the soldier, or an intention on his part to violate either. The criminal court of first instance at Latakia convicted the soldier and sentenced him to six months' imprisonment, the court of appeals at Damascus reversed that decision and discharged him. On reading the opinion or decision of the latter court, I must say that the reasons given there commend themselves to approval, whether looked at in the light of national justice or viewed from a legal standpoint. The evidence against the soldier fails in my opinion to show any intent to force an entrance into the consulate, much less to violate its sanctity. It is only by a very technical construction of the law that he could be said to have entered in that manner. He followed closely into that building a Turkish subject whom he was commanded to arrest and who was seeking to escape from him; the consular premises are sacred, and when they are violated this Government will be ready to vindicate the consul's right to possess them unmolested, but such premises are never to be made an asylum for offenders fleeing from justice or seeking to avoid arrest, especially when such persons are citizens or subjects of the country in which the consulate is situated. The point that no notice of the appeal was given to the consul is very technical, and it is doubtful whether in this case it is tenable; in most cases when a party gets notice of the initial proceedings—court of first instance in this case—and appears, he is bound to take notice of every succeeding step in the trial. In this case the Latakia court stated, in rendering the judgment, that it was given with right of appeal. Your note verbale to the imperial ministry was, under the circumstances, warranted. Contenting yourself with the general views so well expressed in that note you will not pursue the matter further."

> Mr. Frelinghuysen, Sec. of State, to Mr. Wallace, min. to Turkey, April 10, 1884, MS. Inst. Turkey, IV. 125.
>
> Though the privileges of asylum in Mohammedan states, as well as in South America, are more liberally dispensed than in the leading European states, they should in all cases be carefully guarded. (Mr. Clayton, Sec. of State, to Mr. McCauley, May 31, 1849, MS. Inst. Barbary Powers, XIV. 101; Mr. Clayton, Sec. of State, to Mr. Gaines, Oct. 3, 1849, id. 112; Mr. Marcy, Sec. of State, to Mr. De Leon, Dec. 23, 1853, id. 157.)

"Your attention is drawn to the statement in Mr. Madden's report that Mr. Seferiades had taken refuge in our Smyrna consulate. You should clearly ascertain whether he is held by Mr. Madden in his judicial capacity, or is simply his protected guest in his consular capacity. This Government does not sanction the so-called right of asylum, even as to the admittedly extraterritorial precincts of an envoy's dwelling, and it does not recognize it in respect to a consulate."

Mr. Gresham, Sec. of State, to Mr. Terrell, min. to Turkey, July 11, 1894, For. Rel. 733, 735, referring to the report of Mr. Madden, U. S. consul at Smyrna, Turkey, as to the case of Mr. Seferiades, a naturalized citizen of the United states, who was accused of involuntary manslaughter.

It may have been observed that in the cases which have been found in Europe since the first quarter of the nineteenth century, the claim to grant asylum has assumed a new aspect. Formerly it was in regard to common crimes that the privilege was conceded, while in respect to political offences the right was denounced and violated. Now, asylum for common offenders is no longer heard of; it is for political refugees that it is claimed and tolerated. This fact possesses a manifold significance. It marks, in the first place, the growth of the idea of justice through the administration of law; in the second place, and partly as the result of that growth, it denotes the subsidence of asylum, both in principle and in practice; lastly, it shows an abrasion of former political conceptions. The judicial trial of common crimes having been secured, the obstruction of the ordinary course of law was conceded to be inadmissible. But in politics a new principle appeared, to introduce temporary confusion. The principle of liberty, enforced by the exercise of " the right of revolution," threw society into a violent ferment, in which the political offender, if not extolled as a hero, was regarded as falling within Vattel's category of " persons who often prove to be rather unfortunate than criminal." It was because of this change in popular ideas, and not by a perversion of his language, that political offenders were to some extent accorded the benefit of his opinion that for unfortunates " the house of an ambassador may well serve as an asylum," and that it was better to " suffer them to escape, than expose the ambassador to frequent molestation under pretence of a search after them, and thus involve the state in any difficulty which might arise from such proceedings." If any evidence were needed, in addition to that afforded by state papers, of the effect upon diplomatic asylum, wherever it has survived, of the development of criminal administration and the change in political conceptions, we might refer to the cognate fact that political offenders, who in former times were almost the only persons delivered up, are to-day exempt from the system of extradition that enmeshes the common criminal.[a] Experience, however, has taught that opposition to government may represent the spirit of anarchy rather than of liberty; that revolution can as readily destroy republics as monarchies; that elective magistrates, constitutional

[a] Moore on Extradition, Vol. I. § 205.

rulers, and hereditary despots may alike fall by the hand of the assassin. Though the United States, instructed by its own tragedies, has not been alone in adhering to the principle that persons who murder or attempt to murder the head of the state or members of his family are not to be treated as political offenders,[a] it has shown its repugnance to disorder by condemning, more emphatically perhaps than any other nation, the concession of diplomatic asylum to revolutionists, and by refusing, so far as seemed practicable, to grant it. Its attitude on this subject has been most frequently defined in the case of American nations.

4. DIPLOMATIC ASYLUM IN INTERNATIONAL LAW.

§ 294.

It is universally admitted that the rights and immunities of a public minister are intended to secure his independence in the discharge of his functions as the representative of a foreign government. In order that he may act with perfect freedom, he and his suite are exempt from the local law. This exemption is called extraterritoriality, as if the minister and his suite were in contemplation of law to be regarded as being outside of the territory in which they reside.[b] In order further to insure the freedom and independence of the diplomatic agent, it is held that his domicile is not subject to the visitation of the ordinary officers of the revenue and the police.[c] This exemption constitutes what is called the inviolability of the diplomatic residence. By a confusion of ideas, this inviolability is often referred to as extraterritoriality, and in consequence writers have frequently been led to state that a minister's domicile is foreign territory and in no wise subject to the local law. Among publicists of modern authority Lorimer stands preeminent for the positiveness with which he asserts this theory. "An English ambassador," he declares, " with

---

[a] Moore on Extradition, I. § 208; Treaty with Belgium, June 13, 1882, art. iv; with Luxemburg, Oct. 29, 1883, art. iv. These treaties were concluded while the impression made by the assassination of Garfield was still fresh. After the assassination of Lincoln and the disclosure of the plot to murder his cabinet, the United States applied to foreign governments to give up any of the malefactors who might find refuge within their jurisdictions, and John H. Surratt, one of those charged with complicity, was captured and brought back from Alexandria, Egypt. Moore on Extradition, I. § 208, note 4. See, also, infra, § 604.

[b] Lorimer's Institutes, I. 249. This writer states, however, that if a diplomatic person purchase property or engage in speculation, he becomes in respect to such transactions amenable to the local law. Fiore maintains the exceptional view that a public minister is answerable to the local law for his criminal acts. Droit Int. Pénal, § 22 et seq.

[c] Writers are generally in accord on this point. For a case in the United States, see United States v. Jeffers, 4 Cranch C. C. 704.

his family and his suite, whilst abroad in the public service, is domiciled in England, and his house is English ground." This statement would carry great weight, if the learned author did not reject its consequences by declaring that a legation cannot be used as an asylum, unless for the minister and his family and suite. This, however, can scarcely be called asylum, since the individuals themselves are personally exempt from arrest. But if an English legation be English ground, why is it that it cannot be used as an asylum to the same extent as any other British territory? In reality, when writers have referred to the extraterritoriality of a minister's domicile, they have employed the term loosely and figuratively, and have either expressly or impliedly rejected the theory that such domicile is actually extraterritorial or that it is a part of the territory of the state which the minister represents.

Foelix says that the house of a public minister " enjoys an entire freedom, in that it is not accessible to the officers of justice of the country: It is considered as being outside of the territory, as well as the person of the minister." [a] Nevertheless, he states that nations do not recognize " the right of asylum in the hotel of a foreign minister " or the " freedom of the quarter of the city in which his hotel is " or " the exemption of the latter from taxes which apply to immovable property." [b] Vattel regards " the house of an ambassador " simply as " independent of the ordinary jurisdiction," since " no magistrate, justice of the peace, or other subordinate officer, is in any case entitled to enter it by his own authority, or to send any of his people to enter it, unless on occasions of urgent necessity, when the public welfare is threatened with imminent danger which admits of no delay." The case should, he maintains, rather be submitted to the sovereign of the country, to whom it pertains to decide how far the claims of the ambassador are to be respected. [c] As has been seen, Vattel entirely approved the action of the Spanish Government in the case of Ripperda. The same opinion is expressed by the Spanish jurisconsult, Riquelme,[d] and by Phillimore.[e] Bello also states that if the minister abuses his immunity by affording asylum to the enemies of the government, the sovereign may have the house of the minister surrounded, and may even take the accused by force.[f] In accord with this view

---

[a] Traité du Droit Int. Privé, vol. i, p. 417.

[b] Ibid.

[c] Vattel, Chitty's ed., Bk. IV. ch. ix. p. 495.

[d] Elementos de Derecho Público Internacional (ed. 1875), 480–481.

[e] Phillimore says that on " this valuable and necessary immunity " of the minister's residence from the visitation of " the ordinary officers of justice or revenue," there was " at one time grafted the monstrous and unnecessary abuse of what was called the right of asylum." Vol. II. p. 241, cciv.

[f] Principios de Derecho Internacional (ed. 1883), 332, 381, nota H. H.

are G. F. de Martens,[a] Baron C. F. de Martens,[b] Klüber,[c] Heffter,[d] Pinheiro-Ferreira,[e] Bluntschli,[f] Burlamaqui,[g] Eschbach,[h] Wicquefort,[i] Wildman,[j] Woolsey,[k] Halleck,[l] and Wheaton.[m] Field cities on the question Foelix and Heffter.[n] Twiss refers to the " fiction of extraterritoriality," and says that an ambassador's house cannot be converted into an asylum.[o] He approves Bynkershoek's statement " that all the privileges of ambassadors have one and the same object in view, namely, to enable them to discharge the duties of their office without impediment or restraint." Of the same opinion is Manning, who also speaks of the " fiction " of extraterritoriality.[p] Pradier-Fodéré holds the same view as C. F. de Martens, though he states that the question of asylum is still agitated in South America.[q] Bar maintains that " the rights of extraterritoriality which ambassadors enjoy do not import that their houses are to be treated as if they were really beyond the territory, but merely as protecting the person of the ambassador from the jurisdiction of the state and its criminal law."[r]

Calvo holds that " in the midst of civil disturbances " a minister's dwelling can and ought to offer an assured refuge " to political persons whom danger to life forces on the moment to take refuge there." To this extent he maintains that asylum has been respected in Europe as well as in America, but he does not advocate the theory of extraterritoriality, and he lays down the following limitations of the inviolability of a minister's domicile:

The dwelling of a public minister is inviolable in so far as it affects things indispensabe to his official service and to the free and regular exercise of his functions; but whenever the conduct or the imprudent attitude of a diplomatic agent puts in peril the peace of the state, violates or tends to elude the laws of the country, by converting, for example, the legation into a refuge for criminals or into a habitation of conspiracy against the established government, the privilege of inviolability of domicile disappears, and the offended state is fully war-

---

[a] Cf. Political Science Quarterly for March, 1892, p. 15.
[b] Id., p. 25.
[c] Droit des Gens, § 208.
[d] Droit Int. Public, § 212.
[e] Cours de Droit Public, Vol. II. p. 195.
[f] Droit Int. Codifié, 200.
[g] Principles, etc., Nugents ed., Vol. II. p. 371.
[h] Introduction Générale à l'Étude du Droit, p. 90.
[i] Embassadors, Digby's ed., p. 266.
[j] International Law, 127.
[k] International Law, § 92.
[l] International Law, Vol. I. p. 295.
[m] Elements of International Law, Lawrence's ed., 1863, p. 417.
[n] Int. Code, 143.
[o] Law of Nations, I., Time of Peace, § 218.
[p] Comm. on the Law of Nations, Amos's ed., p. 112.
[q] Cours, etc., pp. 70–76.
[r] Int. Law, § 154.

ranted in refusing to the dwelling of the agent the benefit of an immunity which reason and justice cease to sustain.[a]

As affecting the question of extraterritoriality, it may be observed that it is sometimes stated that a diplomatic agent possesses the power to administer justice upon those attached to his legation or belonging to his suite. Félice thought that an ambassador might exercise such jurisdiction, but not to the extent of executing infamous or capital punishments, which was an attribute of " territorial supremacy." [b] Wheaton and Twiss cite Vattel and the older writers, who state that a minister may exercise criminal as well as civil jurisdiction over those attached to his embassy, but they also say that the modern usage is to send such persons home for trial.[c] Heffter states the law as it exists at the present day, when he says that it is only in Turkey and other non-Christian states that foreign ministers are invested with the right to decide upon disputes among their countrymen or even among the members of their suites. This view is entirely accepted by Lawrence, who, in his invaluable edition of Wheaton, says that the proposition in the latter's text " seems to have been transferred from one elementary treatise to another without due examination." [d]

The inadmissibility of the theory of the extraterritoriality of a diplomatic residence is further shown by the state of the law touching marriages celebrated in such a habitation. The general rule is that the validity of a marriage ceremony is determined by the law of the place at which the ceremony is celebrated—the *lex loci celebrationis*. Since it is often difficult for persons temporarily sojourning in a country to comply with the forms imposed by that law, foreigners have often betaken themselves to their respective legations and procured the performance of the ceremony there in accordance with the forms prevalent in their own country, without observance of the requirements of the law of the country in which they may happen to be. How far such a ceremony may be valid in the country to which the parties belong, is a question determinable by the law of that country. But it is conceded that the international validity of such a ceremony is at least doubtful, and it has been decided in France that foreigners can not evade the law of that country by such an expedient.[e] When Mr. Cass was Secretary of State of the

a Droit International, 4th ed., § 1521.

b Leçons, vol. ii, pp. 555, 556.

c Abdy's Kent, ed. 1866, p. 132.

d Lawrence's Wheaton, ed. 1863, note 133. See also Wharton's Comm. on Law, § 167, where authorities are cited under the proposition that a minister's extraterritoriality " no longer gives, . . . as was once supposed to be the case, the power to execute penal discipline upon his subordinates."

e Lorimer's Institutes, 251, citing Fraser, Husband and Wife, Vol. II. pp. 1312, 1529; Journal du Droit International Privé, 1890, p. 808.

United States he issued instructions, which have never been revoked, inhibiting the performance of marriage ceremonies in legations of the United States.[a] He doubtless was led to take this step by an investigation he made of the subject on the occasion of the marriage of his daughter, while he was minister to France, to the American secretary of legation. After consulting the most eminent French lawyers, Mr. Cass obliged the parties, notwithstanding their personal immunities, to be married at the mayoralty and to fulfil all the requirements of the Code Napoléon.[b]

The unsoundness of the idea of extraterritoriality is further shown by the enforcement of the local law in respect to criminal offences committed by nondiplomatic persons in the hotel of a public minister. When Nitchencoff, a Russian subject, committed a murderous assault on M. de Balsh in the house of the Russian ambassador in Paris, he was tried by the French courts and sentenced to imprisonment for life. The Russian Government having claimed that he should be given up for trial in Russia, the court of cassation decided on appeal that " the fiction of the law of nations, according to which the house of an ambassador is reputed to be a continuation of the territory of his sovereign, only protects diplomatic agents and their servants, and does not exclude the jurisdiction of French courts in case of a crime committed in such a locality by a person not belonging to the embassy, even although he is a subject of the nation from which the ambassador is accredited." [c]

Had Nitchencoff been given up, he could have been tried under the laws of Russia as a Russian subject, without reference to the particular place in which the offence was committed. Let us suppose, however, that the crime had been committed by a citizen of the United States in the British legation at Washington. If that legation be " English ground," the laws of the United States do not extend over it, and, with a few exceptions, they do not provide for the punishment of offences committed by American citizens on foreign soil. Nor could the culprit have been sent to England, since there is no law or treaty to warrant it. He would therefore have been exempt from punishment.

A Frenchman who had been discharged from the service of the Spanish ambassador at Berlin was arrested there on a charge of assault upon another servant of the ambassador. To this charge he made a plea that the assault was committed in a foreign embassy, and that upon the principle of " extraterritoriality " the local courts had no jurisdiction. It was held, however, that the courts had juris-

---

[a] For. Rel. 1887, 279.

[b] Albany Law Journal, XI. 34.

[c] Solic. Journal, X. 56, November 18, 1865.

diction, and the case was proceeded with accordingly. This decision followed the precedent in II. Strafsenat (criminal division) of the Imperial supreme court at Leipzig, November 26, 1880, which is reported in volume 3 (1881) of the "Entscheidungen des Reichsgerichts in Strafsachen." In that case, in which the question was raised as to whether a naturalized American citizen of German origin could be punished by the German authorities for making a false affidavit before the secretary of the American legation in Berlin, it was held that "the house of the envoy accredited to the domestic government was not to be considered foreign territory, and that consequently a crime committed in such a house must be considered as having been committed in the country itself, and the criminal, even when a foreigner, is under German jurisdiction, as, although the house of an envoy is in accordance with international law exterritorial, this fiction in modern interpretation goes no further than is necessary to insure the personal inviolability of the envoy and his suite." [a]

Since the practice of asylum is not sanctioned by international law, it can be defended only on the ground of the consent of the state within whose jurisdiction it is sought to be maintained. This view has been accepted by the Government of the United States in its Instructions to Diplomatic Officers of the United States, which read as follows:

Par. 49. Immunity from local jurisdiction extends to a diplomatic representative's dwelling house and goods and the archives of the mission. These can not be entered, searched, or detained under process of local law or by the local authorities.

Par. 50. The privilege of immunity from local jurisdiction does not embrace the right of asylum for persons outside of a representative's diplomatic or personal household.

Par. 51. In some countries, where frequent insurrections occur and consequent instability of government exists, the practice of extraterritorial asylum has become so firmly established that it is often invoked by unsuccessful insurgents and is practically recognized by the local government, to the extent even of respecting the premises of a consulate in which such fugitives may take refuge. This Government does not sanction the usage, and enjoins upon its representatives in such countries the avoidance of all pretexts for its exercise. While indisposed to direct its representatives to deny temporary shelter to any person whose life may be threatened by mob violence, it deems it proper to instruct them that it will not countenance them in any attempt knowingly to harbor offenders against the laws from the pursuit of the legitimate agents of justice.

" As to asylum, the United States does not claim such a right under international law and discourages the practice even in countries where it has become a local usage, as in certain Spanish-American

[a] Mr. Jackson, chargé, to Mr. Hay, Sec. of State, July 5, 1899, For. Rel. 1899, 318.

States. Nothing in your dispatches suggests that the local usage so exists in respect to other foreign legations and consulates in Persia as to justify, by parity of custom, a resort by your legation to this vicious practice of sheltering an alleged offender against the local laws, if indeed this man be such an offender. You state no political or criminal charges against him; and the action of the authorities in restoring him to possession of his property excludes any supposition that such charges now exist. As far as shown, he seems to be merely a civil litigant appealing to Persian law for recovery of certain private debts. . . . I am . . . indisposed to countenance an exceptional claim of ' asylum; ' and, indeed, I do not regard the term as pertinent to the circumstances you narrate.

" I am unable to see in what way the good understanding which I am glad to believe Persia desires to maintain equally with the United States, is to be subserved by your continuing to shelter this person, especially when assurances have been furnished, unaccompanied by any conditions as to his nationality, that he is permitted and aided to return unmolested to his home, with recognition of his property rights. The sooner you end this anomalous and very objectionable situation, by causing Hajie Seyyah to take up his residence elsewhere than under your official roof, the better it will be from every point of view.

" I am quite unable to sanction your subterfuge of employing him as a nominal servant of the legation. Whatever rights your representative office may possess in regard to the freedom of official dependents from molestation while performing necessary service, must be asserted in good faith to command due respect."

> Mr. Gresham, Sec. of State, to Mr. Sperry, min. to Persia, May 17, 1893, For. Rel. 1893, 498.
>
> Hajie Seyyah sought the protection of the legation as a citizen of the United States. The facts as to his claim of citizenship are fully stated in the foregoing instruction, in the course of which Mr. Gresham said: " All the circumstances of his case suggest a merely colorable acquisition of American citizenship for the purpose of evading the obligations of his original Persian allegiance, and were he an applicant for a passport as a citizen of the United States you would be unhesitatingly instructed to decline its issuance."

" I am in receipt of your No. 113 of the 12th ultimo, inclosing correspondence relating to renewed persecution of Jews at Hamadan and the forcible removal of a man who had taken refuge in the house of the Rev. James Hawkes, an American missionary at that place.

" With regard to the invasion of Mr. Hawkes's premises by the Persian authorities and the forcible arrest of a fugitive therein, it is regretted that this act should have been brought about by an untenable assertion of asylum for a Persian subject. This Government does not claim that its official agents have the right to afford asylum.

" By the seventh article of the treaty of 1856 between the United States and Persia, it is stipulated that—

" The diplomatic agent or consuls of the United States shall not protect, secretly or publicly, the subjects of the Persian Government, and they shall never suffer a departure from the principles here laid down and agreed to by mutual consent.

" The domiciliary rights of citizens of the United States in Persia may not be expanded to embrace the protection by them of Persian subjects, when such protection is explicitly disclaimed by the Government of the United States, and when its assertion by their diplomatic and consular representatives is positively inhibited."

> Mr. Gresham, Sec. of State, to Mr. Tyler, min. to Persia, Aug. 18, 1894,
> For. Rel. 1894, 497.
> See, also, id. 506.

5. ASYLUM IN AMERICA.

In the United States, where the supremacy of the local law is rigorously maintained, diplomatic asylum has never existed. In an opinion given as early as 1794 the Attorney-General remarked that the house of a foreign minister could not be made an asylum for a guilty, nor, it was apprehended, a prison for an innocent one; and that, although the minister's house be exempt from the ordinary jurisdiction of the country, yet, in such cases, " recourse would be had to the interposition of the extraordinary powers of the state." [a] But, with the exception of the United States, it is believed that examples of diplomatic asylum may be found in substantially all independent American states. In the countries that were formerly Spanish colonies, the practice may be said to have been inherited; and in some of them it has been so far extended as to include even persons resting under civil and commercial responsibilities.[b]

(1) BOLIVIA.

§ 295.

In 1874 an attempt at revolution, aided by a mutiny in the army, brought up the question of asylum in Bolivia. As many as thirty Bolivian citizens applied to Mr. Reynolds, minister of the United States, for protection against the action of their Government. To all applicants he replied that " for criminal offences against the laws of the country, the American flag could afford no protection "; and that " for offences purely political," he " felt assured that the Govern-

---

[a] Bradford, At.-Gen., June 24, 1794, 1 Op. 47–48.

[b] Albertini, Derecho Diplomatico en sus Aplicaciones a las Republicas Sud-Americanas, 151–152.

ment and the administration of President Frias would not molest the parties implicated." " It has been," he said, " common for the defeated party in any revolution " in Bolivia to seek " protection under foreign flags," and especially " under the flag " of the legation of the United States. Consequently he had extended protection to only two persons, named Criales and Poso, both of whom had filed statements to the effect that they were " not engaged, directly or indirectly, with arms in the mutiny "; and that they apprehended molestation because of false reports made to the Government by their personal enemies. Subsequently the minister for foreign affairs informed Mr. Reynolds that there were no charges of crime against either of the refugees, but that the Government wished him to know that Poso once before " took refuge under the flag of the United States during the time that Mr. Markbreit was American minister, and at the same time was in conspiracy against the lawful Government of Bolivia "; and that he was again attempting to do the same thing, by "communicating with outside parties to the injury of the Government." Mr. Reynolds responded that if further acts of that character were alleged, he would notify Señor Poso that he could no longer enjoy the protection of the legation. This response the minister for foreign affairs accepted as " completely and highly satisfactory."

> Mr. Reynolds, min. to Bolivia, to Mr. Fish, Sec. of State, Feb. 20, 1875, For. Rel. 1875, I. 82.
>
> On March 20, 1875, Mr. Reynolds reported another attempt at revolution, in which the Government palace at La Paz was partially burned. Recurring to the subject on April 7, he said: " I have refused asylum in this legation to all persons engaged in the burning of the palace building. . . . I was impelled to make this decision from the fact that, had they succeeded in their attempt to completely destroy the building by fire and set match to the magazine of powder, the United States would have had no legation-room in La Paz, if indeed any ' minister resident ' living. The further fact that the Government of Bolivia could rightfully demand them as criminals, to be tried by the courts of the country for incendiarism and murder, was a serious obstacle to my receiving them in asylum." (For. Rel. 1875, I. 84, 89.)

" Your despatch of the 28th of March last, No. 58, has been received. It is accompanied by a correspondence between you and the Bolivian minister for foreign affairs, respecting the entry of soldiers into the house of one Poso, a Bolivian citizen, to whom you had thought proper to grant an asylum in the legation.

"In reply I have to state that, however questionable under the public law and contrary to the policy of this Government may be the making of the legations of the United States abroad shields for political refugees, the right of the government to which ministers may be accredited to cause the private dwellings of such refugees to be examined at its pleasure can still less be objected to. It is consequently regretted that you should have deemed yourself warranted to call that right into question at La Paz, as you appear to have done in your note to Mr. Baptista of the 10th of March last."

Mr. Cadwalader, Act. Sec. of State, to Mr. Reynolds, June 16, 1875, MS. Inst. Bolivia, I. 211.

For Mr. Reynolds's No. 58, of March 28, 1875, see For. Rel. 1875, I. 87.

" Your despatch No. 82, of the 3d ultimo, has been received. In reply I have to state that it is not conceived that the general rule of the law of nations, which forbids a diplomatic representative to extend what is called the right of asylum to persons at the place of his abode, makes any exception in the case of foreigners. The refuge, therefore, which you granted to Mr. D. Poso, who, you say, is a citizen of the Argentine Republic and not of Bolivia, may be regarded as no more countenanced by public law than if he had been a native and citizen of the republic, to the government of which you are accredited."

Mr. Fish, Sec. of State, to Mr. Reynolds, min. to Bolivia, Sept. 15, 1875, MS. Inst. Bolivia, I. 217.

In October, 1875, a Bolivian named Suariz ran into the United States legation at La Paz, and finding that Mr. Reynolds, the minister, was absent, awaited his return. When Mr. Reynolds arrived, Suariz informed him that he desired protection, since there could be no accusation against him of a criminal character, though he might be charged with political offences on the 20th of the preceding March. The police officer knew nothing as to the charges, having received only verbal orders to arrest Suariz and take him to police headquarters. Mr. Reynolds declined to grant asylum, and advised Suariz to respond to any charges against him. Mr. Fish, then Secretary of State, approved the minister's course, saying that it had been " the universal practice " of the United States " to discountenance the granting of asylum by its diplomatic and consular officers." The practice, he said, was " believed to have no good reason for continuance, to be mischievous in its tendencies, and to tend to political disorder;" and the government of the United States, while " not able of itself to do away with the practice," had " not failed on appropriate occasions to deprecate its existence and to instruct its representatives to avoid committing it thereto;" for the practice must necessarily prove " a cause of annoyance and embarrassment to the minister, and tend to bring about questions of a vexatious and troublesome nature," which it was desirable for both Governments to avoid.

Mr. Fish, Sec. of State, to Mr. Reynolds, min. to Bolivia, Dec. 3, 1875, For. Rel. 1876, 18.

In December, 1898, Mr. Bridgman, the minister of the United States at La Paz, drew up a set of rules which were accepted and signed by his Brazilian and French colleagues, in relation to the reception and treatment of refugees seeking asylum at the legations during the insurrection then existing. "The idea in South America is," said Mr. Bridgman, "deeply rooted, among the populace at least, that a foreign legation is legally a refuge for all sorts of criminals, who may remain in safety from lawful or unlawful pursuit."[a] The rules were as follows:

Every person asking asylum must be received first in the outer or waiting room of the legation, and there state his name, official capacity, if any, residence, and reasons for demanding refuge; also if his life is threatened by mob violence or is in active danger from any attack.

If, according to the joint rules laid down by the committee composed of the Brazilian, American, and French ministers, he shall be adjudged eligible for protection, he must subscribe to the following rules in writing:

First. To agree that the authorities shall be at once notified of his place of refuge.

Second. To hold no communication with any outside person, and to receive no visitors except by permission of the authority quoted above.

Third. To agree not to leave the legation without permission of the resident minister.

Fourth. To hold himself as virtually the prisoner-guest of the minister in whose legation he is.

Fifth. To agree to peaceably yield himself to the proper authorities when so demanded by them and requested by his host.

Sixth. To quietly depart when so requested by the minister, should the authorities not demand his person after a reasonable time has elapsed.

EDWARDO LISBOA.
GEORGE H. BRIDGMAN.
C. DE CONTONLY.

LA PAZ, BOLIVIA, *December 21, 1898.*

(2) CENTRAL AMERICAN STATES.

§ 296.

In May, 1870, Mr. Corbett, British minister in Guatemala, gave asylum to one Granadas, who was eluding prosecu-

Guatemala.

tion for rebellion and whom Mr. Hudson, the minister of the United States, had refused to shield. On hearing that Granadas was in the British legation, the minister of foreign relations inquired of Mr. Corbett whether it was true. Mr. Corbett declined to answer, holding that "according to international usages" no one had a right to ask "any explanations" as to what occurred "within the house of Her Britannic Majesty's representatives." The minister of foreign relations, while admitting "the doctrine of

---

[a] Mr. Bridgman, min. to Bolivia, to Mr. Hay, Sec. of State, Dec. 24, 1898, For. Rel. 1898, 171.

immunity, as . . . taught by the practice of enlightened nations,"
declined to accept Mr. Corbett's contention, since it might wholly
defeat the action of justice and " establish the most complete immunity for abuses committed within the habitation of a foreign agent."
Meanwhile, soldiers were stationed about the British minister's
dwelling, with orders to arrest Granadas, if he attempted to escape.
Nor were they withdrawn till, by the acceptance of conditions offered
by the Government, Granadas obtained permission to leave the country. Not long afterward the British minister went away on leave,
and as his going was popularly attributed to the Granadas incident,
the Guatemala Government at his instance pronounced the surmise
to be groundless.

Three months after his departure from the British legation
Granadas and another revolutionist appeared on the Guatemalan
border with five hundred men and stirred up an insurrection which
resulted in the overthrow of the Government. During the attendant
commotion the protection of the legation of the United States was
extended to all parties and all nationalities. " The authorities," said
Mr. Hudson, " have in no instance objected to my action, but approved my course and claimed the protection of the legation. . . .
Humanity called for the part I bore, and where there was so much
to be justly apprehended, I believed my conduct would be excused,
if not fully warranted, in acting in that behalf."

To these representations the Department of State responded:
" The efforts which you have made for the general protection of life
and property, during the recent hostilities in Guatemala, meet with
the approval of this Department."

> Mr. J. C. B. Davis, Acting Sec. of State, to Mr. Hudson, min. to Guatemala, Sept. 6, 1871, For. Rel. 1871, 542.
> See, also, Mr. Hudson, min. to Guatemala, to Mr. Fish, Sec. of State, May 18, 1870, and Aug. 31, 1870, For. Rel. 1870, 443, 446.

" The documents published last month in the Diario Oficial will
have apprised you that as several soldiers were passing in front of the
Mexican legation in Guatemala city in charge of a prisoner the latter
escaped and penetrated into the zaguan of the edifice, whither, without asking permission, his custodians followed him and whence they
forcibly dragged him out. The minister of Mexico, as soon as
informed of the occurrence, lodged a protest, as was his duty, demanding satisfaction for the outrage and the chastisement of the guilty
parties. The Government of Guatemala ordered an investigation and,
without doubt misinformed as to what had transpired, declined at
first to accede to these demands, though expressing regret at the incident. Mindful of the sentiments of fraternity which have always

animated us in our relations with Guatemala, the Government was loath to go to extremes in the manifestations of its displeasure and merely took care to instruct its diplomatic representative to press his demands, seeing that the testimony of various persons who had been eyewitnesses of the occurrence left no doubt that an outrage had been committed. It is gratifying to me to inform you that this conduct, marked by both firmness and prudence, produced the desired result, seeing that the Government of Guatemala gave satisfaction to the Government of Mexico by yielding to its demands, which involved an expression of regret at what had occurred and the punishment of the person who proved to have been directly guilty."

Message of President Diaz to the Mexican Congress, Sept. 16, 1904, For. Rel. 1904, 488.

A consul of the United States in Nicaragua has no right, as such,
Nicaragua. "under the law of nations to make his dwelling an asylum for persons charged with crimes or offenses against that Government."

Mr. Marcy, Sec. of State, to Mr. Wheeler, min. to Nicaragua, May 11, 1855, MS. Inst. Am. States, XV. 236.

"I have received your No. 42 of the 12th ultimo, concerning the report of another revolutionary outbreak at Leon, Nicaragua, and your declination to give asylum to a sympathizer of the revolutionists, one Jesus Hernandez, to whom you announced that the chief aim of your mission in Nicaragua was to look after the interests of American citizens, and next to courteously decline mixing up with the political affairs of any other people.

" The Department cordially approves that sentiment. The views of this Government averse to so-called diplomatic asylum in derogation of the regular and supreme powers of a state are too well known to need repetition, especially as you appear to fully understand your duty in the premises."

Mr. Gresham, Sec. of State, to Mr. Baker, min. to Nicaragua, Aug. 15, 1893, For. Rel. 1893, 212.

In the revolution in Salvador in 1871, the deposed President,
Salvador. Dueñas, found refuge with General Torbert, minister of the United States. The new Government immediately placed a guard about the legation and demanded that the fugitive be surrendered for trial, promising that his life should be spared. General Torbert, " having," as he declared, " due respect for the sovereignty of the state," with the concurrence of Señor Dueñas, accepted the guarantee of his life and delivered him to the agents of the Government. Referring to this transaction, Mr. Fish, then

Secretary of State, sent General Torbert a copy of certain instructions to Mr. Bassett, minister to Hayti, of December 16, 1869, and said: " Having, however, whether for sufficient reasons or otherwise, granted refuge to Mr. Dueñas, you thereby incurred an obligation which, it might be said, more or less implicated the honor of this Government in its exact fulfilment. It appears that Mr. Dueñas assented to his own surrender. This assent, however, may be regarded as so important an element in the case that it would have been preferable if it had been given in writing. This would have made it a matter of record, which might have been used in possible contingencies to refute a charge that the surrender was contrary to the wishes of the refugee."

In April, 1872, charges against Señor Dueñas were presented to the Congress for various malfeasances in office, including the embezzlement and misappropriation of funds, usurpation of office, and nepotism, and for assassination in unlawfully causing ex-President Barrios to be shot. The Senate, after investigation, remitted the charges to the ordinary tribunals, and it was surmised that the trial might end in a death sentence. Mr. Fish, on being so informed, instructed the legation in that event to express to the Government the expectation that the pledge given to General Torbert would be observed. This contingency did not arise. On July 22 the prisoner was sent under guard to La Libertad *en route* for Panama, the Government having taken his bond with five sureties in $10,000 each that he would not return to Salvador within four years without the permission of the authorities, and having required " the hypothecation of all his large estate to abide the result of the civil procedures against him."

> Mr. Fish, Sec. of State, to Mr. Torbert, min. to Salvador, May 18, 1871,
>   For. Rel. 1871, 695; Mr. Fish, Sec. of State, to Mr. Biddle, min. to
>   Salvador, May 24, 1872, For. Rel. 1872, 536.

(3) CHILE.

§ 297.

" The propriety of your granting an asylum to Colonel Arteaga will depend upon circumstances which are at present unknown to the Department. If there should be any precedent showing that the Chilean Government had previously acquiesced in such a proceeding on the part of the diplomatic representative of any foreign nation at Santiago, it could not justly complain of our course, unless formal notice should have previously been given that it would not in future tolerate the exercise of the right. Inasmuch, however, as the right itself is more than doubtful under the public law, and as a formal demand had been made upon you for the offender, if he should still be your guest when this reaches you, it is deemed advisable that you should inform him that your house can no longer screen him from prosecution."

> Mr. Webster, Sec. of State, to Mr. Peyton, min. to Chile, July 2, 1851, MS. Inst. Chile, XV. 90.

" The Department is in receipt this morning of your despatches numbered 37 & 38. . . . The difficulty with Mr. Trevitt, our consul at Valparaiso, is deeply to be regretted. While it is quite true that his house could not rightly be made an asylum for political offenders, it is equally true that the soldiery, who entered it without orders and before any demand for the refugees had been made, deserve reproof and punishment. Their conduct also seems to have been unjustifiably insolent and violent. It is quite probable that, in a frank interview with the minister of foreign affairs, you may be able to arrange this matter satisfactorily. You may give the Chilean Government fully to understand that the consul claims no right and will exercise none to interfere in the local concerns of the country, and as the difficulty at the consul's residence seems to have been somewhat the result of misapprehension or accident, his exequatur may well be restored, and strict inquiry made into the conduct of the Chilean officers in order that they may be properly dealt with. It is not doubted that after mutual explanations in the interview I have suggested a spirit of harmony and compromise will readily lead to a basis of adjustment which will embrace the restoration of Mr. Trevitt's exequatur upon terms perfectly satisfactory to the United States and the Chilean Government."

> Mr. Cass, Sec. of State, to Mr. Bigler, min. to Chile, May 2, 1859, MS. Inst. Chile, XV. 165.

" Since the instruction of 2d May was addressed to you, your communication of 15th April has reached the Department. In that dispatch you state that the English consul at Talcahuano had recently given asylum to a certain number of refugees under circumstances similar to those under which Consul Trevitt acted at Valparaiso, but that the Chilean Government had manifested no dissatisfaction with his conduct, while, on the same grounds, it withdrew the exequatur of our consul. The Department is also informed that the practice on the part of consuls of extending asylum to political refugees is almost generally permitted in the Pacific republics and in none more frequently than in Chile. If this be so, the existence of such an usage, taken in connection with the statement you make in regard to the English consul, would go far to induce this Government to require the restoration of Mr. Trevitt's exequatur. You have doubtless informed yourself with careful accuracy upon this point, and if your information leads to the conviction that our consul has been singled out as a mark for the disapprobation of the Chilean Government for following a precedent generally established, you will express the dissatisfaction of this Government with the course pursued by Chile, and the expectation that Mr. Trevitt's exequatur will be restored to him."

> Mr. Cass, Sec. of State, to Mr. Bigler, min. to Chile, June 17, 1859, MS. Inst. Chile, XV. 167.

" Your despatches to No. 46, inclusive, have been received. In this last dispatch, you inform me that the Chilean Government declines the friendly arrangement in reference to Mr. Trevitt which was proposed in my note of 17 June and refuses to restore to that officer his *exequatur*. The President has heard of this determination with surprise and regret. . . . Surely, the case was not one which required, on the part of Chile, any very stringent adherence to its previous action. . . . It was a case, simply, where a few persons had taken refuge in the house of a consul, and had been afterwards surrendered, upon the demand of the proper authorities. In the first instance, undoubtedly, the house had been rudely and illegally violated, by an officer who had no orders to justify his conduct, and who well deserved to be rebuked and punished. The entrance of a band of soldiers into the domicil of an American consul, without warrant of law, and only by the authority of force, was well calculated to excite the indignation which it did elicit, and to provoke the resistance which it occasioned, on the part of those fearless persons by whom the house was occupied. When, however, a proper demand was afterwards made for the surrender of the refugees, by a legally authorized officer, they were taken from the house without opposition. This is what was fairly to have been expected from an American officer. Resistance to aggression and obedience to law are equally characteristic of citizens of the United States. The Chilean Government had no cause to complain, therefore, of what had occurred. Its authority had been respected, and the refugees had been secured. No reason is perceived, therefore, why it was thought necessary that Mr. Trevitt's *exequatur* should be withdrawn, except the suspicion suggested that he disliked the Chilean Government, and claimed the right to make his house an asylum for political offenders. This suspicion, however, was met by your full assurances that Mr. Trevitt was friendly to the Government and that he made no claim whatever to the right of asylum. Chile, I repeat, therefore, had nothing to complain of. This Government, however, had a right to demand a full investigation into the conduct of the officer (Ramirez) who violated the dwelling of Mr. Trevitt without orders, and a disclaimer of his conduct by the Chilean Government together with the just punishment of the offender. In proposing to waive this right, and consenting that with the return of Mr. Trevitt's *exequatur* the whole transaction should be allowed to rest without further inquiry, the President felt that he was giving renewed evidence of his friendly disposition towards the Government of Chile, from which he confidently anticipated an equally friendly response. In this he has been deeply disappointed. . . .

" You will transmit a copy of this dispatch to the Chilean minister of foreign affairs, and, in thus presenting to him again the case of Mr. Trevitt, you will assure him at the same time of the sincere satisfaction with which this Government would learn that the Government of Chile had found itself at liberty to restore his *exequatur* to that officer. If that Government shall persist, however, in declining to do this, another consul will forthwith be appointed. But, in that event, you will demand an immediate inquiry into the circumstances under which Mr. Trevitt's house was violated on the 2d of March, and will insist upon the prompt punishment of the parties who shall be found to have been guilty of wrong on that occasion."

Mr. Cass, Sec. of State, to Mr. Bigler, min. to Chile, Aug. 16, 1859, MS.
Inst. Chile, XV. 170.

" Altho' the determination of the Chilean Government, communicated in your No. 63 of 30th November last, not to restore Mr. Trevitt's exequatur, has occasioned both surprise and dissatisfaction to the President, in view of the amicable spirit of compromise displayed by this Government in its proposition of the 2d May last, and which was substantially renewed in the despatch to you of 16th August, still, as Chile has an unquestionable right to assume that position, this Government will press its views upon that point no further. We have, however, the right to insist upon the most searching investigation of the conduct of those functionaries whose violence we were willing to overlook, had Chile responded to our request in a becoming spirit. Since she has decided differently we will press our alternative."

Mr. Cass, Sec. of State, to Mr. Bigler, min. to Chile, February 4, 1860, MS.
Inst. Chile, XV. 188.

" In respect to Mr. Trevitt, this Government has yielded, you are aware, to the wishes of Chile, so far as to transfer that officer to Callao, and to supply his place in Valparaiso. There were circumstances, however, attending the entrance of the Chilean soldiers into his dwelling on the 2d March, 1859, and in reference to their conduct on that occasion, which still demand explanation, and this can not be refused by the Chilean authorities without an utter disregard of those friendly relations which now exist between the two countries.

You will, therefore, respectfully insist that a suitable investigation shall be had of this whole subject, in order that the necessary measures may be taken to punish the offenders on that occasion. This is the more necessary because there are some conflicting statements in relation to the occurence."

> Mr. Cass, Sec. of State, to Mr. Bigler, min. to Chile, May 1, 1860, MS. Inst. Chile, XV. 190.

During the summer of 1891, while the civil war growing out of the dispute between President Balmaceda and the Chilean Congress was raging, Mr. Egan, minister of the United States at Santiago, afforded asylum to Señors Augustin Edwards and Eduardo Matte, prominent Congressionalists, on the ground, as he stated, that there was reason to apprehend that their lives were in danger. Subsequently Señor Edwards was given a safe-conduct and went to Callao, leaving Señor Matte in the legation. A few days later an unofficial intimation was conveyed to Mr. Egan through the dean of the diplomatic corps that the President was much annoyed at the granting of asylum to Congressionalists, and that if they did not leave immediately the legations might be searched, that of the United States being particularly mentioned. On hearing of this threat, Mr. Egan called at the ministry of foreign relations and stated that, while he was prepared to discuss the question of asylum in a friendly spirit, his legation could not be searched but by force, and that he would himself shoot the first man who attempted to enter it for that purpose. On the following day he received from the President an assurance that there was no intention to search any of the legations, " and above all that of the United States."

On the 21st of August the army of Balmaceda was routed at Viña del Mar; and the excitement and confusion which that event occasioned in Santiago culminated after the dispersion of his forces at Placillas on the 28th. His resignation on the 29th was followed by the demoralization of the military and police forces, and the houses of some of his prominent partisans were attacked. Towards evening, however, order was restored and all danger of further trouble seemed to vanish. Meanwhile many persons had sought refuge in the houses of the foreign ministers.

> House Ex. Doc. 91, 52 Cong. 1 sess. pt. 1, pp. 64–70.

No trouble occurred till the 22d of September, when the Chilean Government, alleging that the refugees and their friends were abusing the privilege of asylum, began to police the American and the Spanish legation. At that time there were nineteen refugees in the former and five in the latter; and on the first three days of the surveillance many persons were interfered with in entering or in leaving the buildings.   Mr. Egan protested against the course of the Government, contending that its action was without precedent and violative of the rights of the legation.   Señor Matta, the Chilean minister for foreign affairs, declined to consider the protests.   Nevertheless, after September 25 the strictness of the surveillance was relaxed, though for several days in the latter part of December it was again closely enforced, especially about the Spanish legation.

" Mr. Egan states that all officials of the late Government (including the ministers, senators, members of Congress, and judges) would be prosecuted criminally.   This had been resolved by the Government.   Seven ministers and twelve other refugees are in the legation. Intimation has been given Mr. Egan that he was expected to terminate the asylum and send the refugees out to be prosecuted.   To do so would be to sacrifice their lives, and Mr. Egan has taken stand that he will permit them to go out of legation only under proper safe-conduct to neutral territory.   On acount of *Itata*, and other questions, bitter feeling is being fomented by Government supporters against Americans.   Secret police surround the legation with orders to arrest strangers visiting it.   Two of Mr. Egan's servants had been arrested and were now in prison.   Against this disrespect to the legation Mr. Egan addressed a firm protest to the minister for foreign affairs."

> Mr. Egan, min. to Chile, to Mr. Blaine, Sec. of State, tel., Sept. 24, 1891,
> For. Rel. 1891, 166.

" Mr. Egan states that no reply had yet been received to his protest. During the last two days twenty persons, some of whom were Americans, had been arrested for entering the legation, and others had been prevented from entering by warning of the police.   All this is intended to force him to drive out refugees, which, he states, he will not do without instructions.   He has addressed a second note to the minister for foreign affairs requesting [an explanation of] such very extraordinary, unjustifiable, and offensive conduct, which is strongly condemned by a large majority of the serious public men."

> Mr. Egan, min. to Chile, to Mr. Blaine, Sec. of State, tel., Sept. 25, 1891,
> For. Rel. 1891, 166.

" Mr. Wharton instructs Mr. Egan, by direction of the President, to insist firmly that the respect and inviolability due to the minister of the United States and to the legation buildings, including free access, shall be given and observed, fully and promptly, by the Chilean authorities.   The Government of the United States is prepared to consider in a friendly spirit the question as to whether asylum has under the circumstances been properly given to the persons now at the legation when the facts are more fully before it; but it can not allow to pass without a firm protest the evidence of disrespect towards its minister which Mr. Egan reported. It is expected that this protest will be followed by prompt action on the part of the authorities of Chile. The Department expects to be fully advised of the progress of events."

<blockquote>Mr. Wharton, Act. Sec. of State, to Mr. Egan, min. to Chile, tel., Sept. 26, 1891, For. Rel. 1891, 167.</blockquote>

" Mr. Egan is instructed to report to the Department the names of the refugees in his legation and the offices they have filled, the crimes they are accused of, and whether process from any regular tribunal has issued against them. He is also directed to report the conduct of the ministers of other countries, whether persons have taken refuge in their legations, and, if so, the action of the Chilean Government respecting them; and to promptly and fully inform the Department of all facts."

<blockquote>Mr. Wharton, Act. Sec. of State, to Mr. Egan, min. to Chile, tel., Sept. 26, 1891, For. Rel. 1891, 167.</blockquote>

" Mr. Egan states that in a note sent him the minister for foreign affairs refuses safe-conduct or permission to refugees to leave the country, and maintains the correctness of all that has been done by the authorities. The minister for foreign affairs also repeats the unfounded and absurd charges of the refugees conspiring in the United States legation. Since Saturday the trouble to the legation had ceased, and no more arrests had been made."

<blockquote>Mr. Egan, min. to Chile, to Mr. Blaine, Sec. of State, tel., Sept. 30, 1891, For. Rel. 1891, 177.</blockquote>

" Mr. Egan is informed that the President desires to establish and maintain the most friendly relations with Chile, but the right of asylum having been tacitly, if not expressly, allowed to other foreign legations, and having been exercised by our minister with the old Government in the interest and for the safety of the adherents of the party now in power, the President can not but regard the application of another rule, accompanied by acts of disrespect to our legation, as the manifestation of a most unfriendly spirit. Mr. Egan is instructed to furnish a copy of this to the minister for foreign affairs and to take the utmost precaution to prevent any abuse of the privilege of asylum by those to whom he has extended it; their intercourse with outside persons, whether by person or by letter, should be under his supervision and limited to the most necessary and innocent matters. The discussion and adjustment of the matter would probably be much facilitated were there an authorized agent of Chile at Washington."

Mr. Wharton, Act. Sec. of State, to Mr. Egan, min. to Chile, tel., Oct. 1, 1891, For. Rel. 1891, 177.

" Mr. Egan is instructed to inform the Department, by cable, of the essential parts of notes from the foreign office, and to keep it fully advised as to the facts respecting his legation and those of other Governments. He is to report fully by mail (sending copies of all correspondence) all instances of disrespect to the legations and all incidents of arrests of Americans."

Mr. Wharton, Act. Sec. of State, to Mr. Egan, min. to Chile, tel., Oct. 1, 1891, For. Rel. 1891, 178.

" Mr. Egan states that he to-day read to the minister for foreign affairs the Department's telegram of October 1; that the minister replied that his Government fully recognized the views therein expressed, and assured Mr. Egan that there was no intention of disrespect to the legation. The minister claims the right to take measures outside the legation to frustrate conspiracy, or attempts at conspiracy, on the part of the refugees, which he still charges is taking place. He stated that the order to arrest applied only to those against whom there might be legitimate grounds for suspicion, and denied that there could have been any order to arrest all persons visiting legation. The statement of police officers must therefore have been based on misunderstanding. He will investigate this point, and reply in answering Mr. Egan's note of the 1st of October. All correspondence will be forwarded by first mail. Mr. Egan is certain there has not been and will not be any abuse of asylum, and will carry out Department's instructions to prevent any. His desire is to obtain safe-conduct for refugees out of the country."

Mr. Egan, min. to Chile, to Mr. Wharton, Act. Sec. of State, tel., Oct. 3, 1891, For. Rel. 1891, 178.

" Mr. Egan is instructed to furnish to the Department full details as to the number of refugees in other legations now and since the overthrow of Balmaceda, the crimes of which the refugees are or were accused, whether any such refugees have been given safe-conducts, and the treatment by the Chilean authorities of the legations offering asylum."

Mr. Wharton, Act. Sec. of State, to Mr. Egan, min. to Chile, tel., Oct. 26, 1891, For. Rel. 1891, 179.

" Mr. Egan acknowledges receipt of Mr. Wharton's telegram of the 6th instant, and states that 80 persons sought refuge in his legation after the overthrow of the Balmaceda Government; about the same number in the Spanish legation, 8 in the Brazilian, 5 in the French,

several in the Uruguayan, 2 in the German, and 1 in the English.
Balmaceda sought refuge in the Argentine. All these have gone
out except 15 in his own legation, 1 in the German, and 5 in the
Spanish. From the 23d to the 25th September, when the arrests were
made at his legation, several arrests were also made of visitors to
the Spanish legation. No protest, however, was made, owing to the
fact that the new minister having recently arrived had not then been
officially received. The other legations were not molested. Spanish
minister is seeking safe-conduct for refugees in his legation, and will
act in entire harmony with Mr. Egan. All acts of the late Government since the 1st of January last, including the election and proceedings of Congress, have been decreed by the present Government
unconstitutional, and the refugees are charged with crime in having
acted without constitutional authority in their several positions. The
refugee in the English legation, having promised to go home and
remain there, has been permitted to go. Others have been allowed
out on bonds to submit themselves to the tribunal. Those in the
Spanish and United States legations would be subjected to heavy
penalties, and in some cases death. No one has been granted a safe-
conduct to leave the country. The press of Buenos Ayres and Montevideo contain extremely strong articles against the attitude of the
Government towards the supporters of Balmaceda. Mr. Egan's note
of the 1st instant has not yet been replied to by the minister for
foreign affairs."

> Mr. Egan, min. to Chile, to Mr. Blaine, Sec. of State, tel., Oct. 8, 1891, For.
> Rel. 1891, 184.
>
> It appears that, on the subsidence of the first excitement, many of the ref-
> ugees left the legations, some seeking concealment elsewhere and
> others giving bond to appear before the tribunals. Such was the
> course pursued by the refugees in the Brazilian and French legations.
> The refugee in the English legation went out immediately to his own
> house, promising to remain there. Balmaceda committed suicide in
> the Argentine legation on the 19th of September. One refugee, Gen.
> Valesquez, ex-minister of war, remained in the German legation, but,
> encouraged by the German minister, he proposed to give himself up
> as soon as he had recovered from the effects of an accident from
> which he was suffering. In none of these instances was a safe-
> conduct granted. (For. Rel. 1891, 171, 185–188.)
>
> In a dispatch of August 31, 1891, Mr. Egan stated that " the only lega-
> tion which closed its doors and denied asylum was that of England,
> which refused to admit a single person." (For. Rel. 1891, 156.)
> In a telegram of Sept. 27 he stated that two persons entered the
> British legation. (For. Rel. 1891, 168.) In a dispatch of Sept. 29 he
> stated that " one or two " got in " across the roof " of a neighboring
> house that was being searched. (For. Rel. 1891, 171.) In his tele-
> gram of Oct. 8 he stated, as has been seen, that there was one.
> The original statement seems, however, to have been correct, in so far
> as it represented the policy of the British legation. (For. Rel. 1891,
> 184.)

" Mr. Egan states that the foreign office, in its reply to his representations, says that the instructions to the intendente authorized the arrest of no one except upon well-founded suspicion of being agents of illegal attempts on the part of refugees and on the public streets away from the legation, and that access to the legation should have been entirely free. Minister for foreign affairs deplores all errors committed by police agents against any persons not properly subject to suspicion, and avers that no vexation was intended to the legation. He considers that, since a decree was issued on the 14th September by the Provisional Government, submitting supporters of the late Government to the tribunals, it would be an unjustifiable irregularity to grant safe-conduct. Were it possible to do so, he says, without disrespect to the law, the interest of the country, or the prestige of the Government, it would be given as a proof of amity towards the legation. In replying, Mr. Egan will cite important instances in which Chile strongly advocated safe-conduct under similar circumstances."

> Mr. Egan, min. to Chile, to Mr. Blaine, Sec. of State, tel., Oct. 13, 1891,
> For. Rel. 1891, 184.

" Mr. Egan reports that he has again solicited safe-conduct for the refugees in his legation, and had cited in his note to the minister for foreign affairs the case in which the Chilean minister for foreign affairs, in July, 1866, instructed the Chilean minister at Lima to insist upon the safe-conduct of refugees then in the several legations in that city. Those refugees were transported on board ships at Callao under the protection of the foreign ministers. Mr. Egan also cited the case of the approval of the Chilean delegates to the South American Congress held in Montevideo in December, 1888, of a resolution recognizing the right of asylum accompanied by the right of safe-conduct. The decree of September 14, Mr. Egan argues in his note, can not abrogate international usage repeatedly approved by the Chilean Republic, and applies only to persons within the powers of Chilean Government. According to precedent and as a logical consequence of the recognition of the right of asylum, Chilean Government should grant safe-conduct, which it is entirely at liberty to do. A favorable reply is hoped for."

> Mr. Egan, min. to Chile, to Mr. Blaine, Sec. of State, tel., Oct. 17, 1891,
> For. Rel. 1891, 185. See, also, id. 185–188.
>
> In discussing the question of safe-conducts, Mr. Egan and Señor Matta set forth their views as to the legal foundations and limitations of asylum. They both accepted the extraterritoriality of a minister's domicile, but while Señor Matta deduced from that notion merely the right to grant asylum, Mr. Egan pushed it further. Señor Matta argued that safe-conducts might have been and might be given, not in virtue of any right on the part of a legation to demand them, but

"of the courtesy, convenience and will" of the government, and with
due consideration for its own laws and interests; and he maintained
that safe-conducts could not be granted for men who, as was the
case with the refugees in question, had been submitted to the tribunals. Mr. Egan replied that his house was "an integral part of the
United States," and that "without the will and permission" of that
Government, Chile "could not consider" as subject to her "judicial
action" persons "who, from every point of view," were "beyond its
jurisdiction;" and he added that as Señor Matta had recognized that
safe-conducts had been and might be given "as acts of courtesy and
at the spontaneous will of the government," he could not be surprised
if the United States should "interpret as an act of but slight courtesy and consideration" the refusal of the Chilian Government now
to grant them "in accordance with the respect due to the invariable
practice and international policy of Chili."

It is obvious that Mr. Egan's assertion of the privilege of extraterritoriality was very sweeping. If the refugees had actually been within
the territory of the United States they would still have been subject
to the judicial action of Chile, for the escape of an alleged offender
to a foreign country does not affect the right to make charges, issue
warrants, and find indictments against him. Without the exercise of
this right the whole system of extradition would fall to the ground.
A fugitive offender may even be tried *in contumaciam* without let
or hindrance from any quarter. The trial and conviction of General
Boulanger by the Senate of France while he was a fugitive in
England may be cited as one of many examples of such a proceeding.

As to the precedents cited by Mr. Egan to show the "invariable practice and international policy" of Chile, it may be observed that the
first was the instructions given to the Chilean minister at Lima on
July 9, 1866, to the effect that the legation might "concede asylum to
political refugees for the time necessary to enable them to leave the
country," and that "the diplomatic agent should put himself in
accord with the minister of foreign affairs . . . in order to send
the refugees to a foreign country under the necessary guarantees."
While this is far from saying that safe-conducts may be demanded
as of right, Mr. Egan was in error as to the circumstances under
which the instructions were given and employed, since he states
as the "result of the negotiations on that occasion, the refugees in
the several legations were permitted to go out of the country." The
instructions were given in reference to the discussion which was
to take place at Lima, in consequence of the concession of asylum
by the French legation to certain refugees, in 1865. The discussion
took place in January, 1867, and the denunciation of the practice
of asylum by the Peruvian Government, the acquiescent attitude
of the diplomatic corps, and the express repudiation of the practice
by the United States render the occasion conspicuous for the denial
of any legal right to protect political offenders. (Infra, § 303.)

The only other case cited by Mr. Egan as a precedent was the vote cast
by the Chilean delegate in the Montevideo Conference of 1888 in
favor of a resolution to include in a proposed treaty of international
penal law a clause establishing the right to grant asylum to political
offenders, as well as the right to require safe-conducts. The proceedings of the conference show that the resolution was based on
the assumption of the extraterritoriality of a minister's domicile,

and for that reason followed the analogies of extradition; that
it was not adopted as a declaration of subsisting law, but that
it was recommended as a means of avoiding difficulties, by making
that a matter of duty which had formerly been a matter of courtesy.
(Actas de las Sesiones, Buenos Ayres, 1889, pp. 164–166.) The
treaty was subsequently brought before the International American
Conference in Washington, and the committee to which it was referred recommended that it be adopted by the Latin-American
nations. Mr. Alfonso, delegate from Chile, opposed the recommendation on the ground that his Government had rejected the treaty,
and he even voted against the recommendation subsequently adopted
that the Latin-American nations " study " it.

See, further, For. Rel. 1891, 195, 196, 197, 229–230, 235–236.

On January 9, 1892, Mr. Egan escorted two refugees to Valparaiso
and put them on board the United States man-of-war *Yorktown*. On
the 13th he and the Spanish and Italian ministers disposed of seven
refugees in the same manner—five from the American and two from
the Spanish legation. These were all that remained. The refugees
were transported on the *Yorktown* to Callao, Señor Pereira, who had
succeeded Señor Matta in the foreign office, refusing to guarantee
their security on private vessels calling at Chilean ports; and he
expressed displeasure at the ministers' accompanying them, apparently being averse to the display of any sign of diplomatic authority
in the matter. With the departure of the refugees, the police were
removed from about the diplomatic residences.

> Mr. Egan, min. to Chile, to Mr. Blaine, Sec. of State, tel., Jan. 17, 1891,
> H. Ex. Doc. 91, 52 Cong. 1 sess. 191. See, also, pp. 336–337.

April 8, 1893, after unsuccessful attempts at an uprising in the preceding December and January, a renewed attempt was made by Bal-
macedists, at Santiago, to produce a revolution. The leaders in the
movement, ex-Col. Fuentes and Señor Blanlot-Holley, who were also
under prosecution for participation in the previous affairs, were received by Mr. Egan as refugees at the American legation. Mr. Egan
justified their reception on the ground that their lives were in imminent danger, and stated that the Chilean Government regarded his
action as strictly correct; and he asked that Government for a safe-
conduct for the refugees. The Chilean legation at Washington, however, denied that the refugees were entitled to asylum; asserted that
their object was " murder and robbery," and demanded that they be
surrendered. Mr. Egan, in response to a telegraphic request for
information, reported that their delivery had not been demanded of
the legation; that the Government objected to giving them a safe-
conduct only because of their participation in the occurrences of
December and January, and that the indictment against them charged
them with sedition and mutiny and asked for the death penalty in
connection with the events of December. He added that large re-

wards had been offered for their apprehension, and that " if asylum had been refused, almost certain death would have been the conse-quence under the prevailing excitement, the police being, according to positive information, under orders to shoot if the refugees made the slightest offer to resist arrest."   (For. Rel. 1893, 217, 218, 219.)

Mr. Gresham replied : " Mr. Egan is not authorized to protect Chileans against police officers whose duty it is to arrest them for violation of the laws of their country, which his telegrams, as read at the Department, show that he is doing.   He instructs him to cease sheltering them if the Chilean Government demands the refugees on a criminal charge, and if such charge was pending against them before they engaged in the disturbance of the 8th, or in insurrection."[a]

Mr. Egan requested further instructions, saying that " sedition, including riot, mutiny, or insurrection in connection with the attempt made on December 11," was the only charge brought against the refugees prior to the insurrection of the 8th of April, and that there was " no charge against them as common criminals."   He inquired whether he should " withdraw protection if that charge is made the basis of a demand for their surrender, and whether he should not ask, in that event, for guarantees that their lives will be safe and that violence will not be done to them, and put it as a condition that no trial shall take place for their share in the attempted insurrection of the 8th."   He further reported that the refugees had presented to him a petition, setting forth that efforts were being made to compel a military court to proceed with their trial, although it had declared itself incompetent to do so; praying that protection be continued to them " until an impartial trial may be had after a subsidence of public feeling; " and requesting that, in the event of this being denied, they " be restored to the position they were in before coming to the legation, by a withdrawal of the police force from the legation's surroundings, and being freed from surveillance for some four hours or any reasonable length of time." [b]

Mr. Gresham answered that the Chilean chargé d'affaires at Washington had " requested the surrender of the refugees, who will be tried by a civil court, and given assurance that they will, on leaving the legation, be protected against violence;" and instructed Mr. Egan " to require them to leave the legation accordingly, but to give timely notice to the Chilean Government that protection is expected to be afforded as promised before withdrawing the shelter theretofore accorded." [c]

---

[a] Mr. Gresham, Sec. of State, to Mr. Egan, min. to Chile, tel., April 15, 1893, For. Rel. 1893, 219.

[b] For. Rel. 1893, 220.

[c] Mr. Gresham, Sec. of State, to Mr. Egan, min. to Chile, April 18, 1893, For. Rel. 1893, 221.

On receiving these instructions, Mr. Egan acquainted the refugees and the Government with their purport. Three hours later, in the evening, Col. Fuentes was arrested as he left the legation, in company with a lady and disguised by a false beard, although "a second lady and a gentleman who accompanied her were not detained by the police." Mr. Blanlot-Holley escaped. Mr. Egan was at the moment absent from the legation.[a]

"The vexatious question of so-called legation asylum for offenders against the state and its laws was presented anew in Chile by the unauthorized action of the late United States minister in receiving into his official residence two persons who had just failed in an attempt at revolution and against whom criminal charges were pending growing out of a former abortive disturbance. The doctrine of asylum as applied to this case is not sanctioned by the best precedents and, when allowed, tends to encourage sedition and strife. Under no circumstances can the representatives of this Government be permitted, under the ill-defined fiction of extraterritoriality, to interrupt the administration of criminal justice in the countries to which they are accredited. A temperate demand having been made by the Chilean Government for the correction of this conduct in the instance mentioned, the minister was instructed no longer to harbor the offenders."

President Cleveland, annual message, Dec. 4, 1893, For. Rel. 1893, iv.

(4) COLOMBIA.

§ 298.

"Your despatch No. 116, of the 14th ultimo, has been received. The insurrection in the Colombian States, to which it refers, is much to be deplored. Your refusal to accept the invitation of the minister from Venezuela to a conference upon that subject is approved.

"It is noticed that you granted General Salgar temporary asylum in your legation. Though we should much regret any harm which might happen to that gentleman, neither he nor any other person should as a matter of course expect to be received as refugees in the legation of the United States. The right of asylum is denied by public law, and though occasions for claiming it have been frequent in other countries of this hemisphere, it is believed that in no instance has asylum been granted with the approval of this Government."

Mr. Hunter, Act. Sec. of State, to Mr. Scruggs, min. to Colombia, Sept. 11, 1875, MS. Inst. Colombia, XVII. 2.

"Your dispatch, No. 194, of the 23d of February last is received, and your reply of the 21st February to the minister of foreign affairs

---

[a] For. Rel. 1893, 221–222.

on the subject of rights of legations is noticed, inasmuch as in it you
take up certain positions which this Department cannot maintain or
approve.

"It appears that the correspondence between yourself and the
Colombian foreign office arose from the refusal of a certain Señor
Uribe, a wealthy Colombian citizen, to pay his war contributions,
which led to an order for his arrest, and then to his being rescued and
concealed by the minister of the Argentine Republic under the
assumed right of asylum of his legation. This right the Colombian
authorities appear to have respected; but the minister of foreign
affairs addressed a circular note, a copy of which you inclose, to the
representatives of foreign powers, protesting against the right of
asylum of foreign legations for the enemies of the Republic, and intimating that, in spite of past toleration of it, the Government might
feel itself under the necessity of claiming the surrender of individuals
who had taken refuge in the residences of ministers, and ' of whom
the legitimate authority may for any motive whatever be in search.'

"In reply to this you inform the minister of foreign affairs, as you
state, ' upon your own responsibility before having had the opportunity to refer it to your Government,' that a public minister ' is
entitled to all the privileges annexed by the law of nations to his public
character, and among these entire and absolute exemption from local
jurisdiction; also that civil and criminal jurisdiction over those
attached to his legation rests with the minister exclusively, to be exercised by him according to the laws, regulations, and instructions of
his own Government, and above all that his house cannot be invaded
by order of either the civil or military authorities of the local government, no matter how apparent the necessity therefor.' . . .

"These remarks at any time would require to be materially qualified. . . . The works on international law do not sustain the unqualified right of asylum, and the Spanish law forbids it altogether. . . .
The exercise of criminal and civil jurisdiction by a minister is practically a dead custom. . . . There is, it is true, a function of ministerial
and consular extraterritorial jurisdiction attaching to representatives
of Christian powers in certain non-Christian countries, as specified in
section 4083 and following sections of the Revised Statutes, but that
function is derived from treaties *ad hoc*, and is exercised and limited
by means of laws passed to carry those treaties into effect. We cannot
demand from other governments any more privileges for our diplomatic agents than are accorded by us to their agents here; and the
laws of the United States do not confer such jurisdiction as you have
claimed on ministers, as a class, in the absence of a right to do so
acquired by a treaty, and still less could civil and criminal jurisdiction be exercised by a foreign minister in the United States, as you
state, ' under the regulations and instructions of his own Government.'

" In notes 128 and 129 to section 226, Part III., of Wheaton's International Law (Dana's edition, 1866), Mr. Dana discusses the whole subject exhaustively, and very properly remarks that the subject of diplomatic immunity of person and place has been obscured by the use of the phrase ' extraterritoriality; ' that treating this figure of speech as a fact, and reasoning logically from it, have led to results of an unsatisfactory and not practical character; that the phrase should be treated as a figure of speech and not as a fact from which inferences can be drawn.   The whole subject, he says, depends upon the principle—the convenience of nations; nations necessarily agree that the functions of ambassadors must be performed with freedom, and the ultimate test is whether the exercise of the municipal authority in question is an unreasonable interference with that freedom. The Department of State long ago laid down the position of this Government as regards civil or criminal jurisdiction in a letter to Mr. Fay, United States minister at Berne, of the 12th November, 1860; in the above sense and as regards the right of aslyum, in an instruction of Mr. Fish to Mr. Bassett, at Hayti, dated 4th of June, 1875.   (See Foreign Relations for 1875, p. 701.) "

> Mr. Bayard, Sec. of State, to Mr. Scruggs, min. to Colombia, June 16, 1885, For. Rel. 1885, 214.
>
> See, also, Mr. Scruggs, min. to Colombia, to Mr. Bayard, Sec. of State, Sept. 3, 1885, For. Rel. 1885, 218.
>
> It seems that Señor Uribe left the house of the Argentine minister secretly, and went to some place unknown to the public or to the diplomatic corps.

(5) ECUADOR.

§ 299.

" I have received your dispatch No. 29, of the 1st instant, in which you report the collapse of the titular government at Quito and the dispersion of its members in anticipation of the occupation of the capital by the successful revolutionary forces of General Alfaro.

" I note your statement that the family of the late minister of war came to your residence on the 17th of August seeking shelter, and that, at the date you write, they were still inmates of your house.   You add that General Savasti himself joined them on the following night, and still remains your guest, quite ill.   The shelter thus given by you to one of the prominent members of the overturned government, and as it appears similarly granted by other foreign representatives to the families of members of the late government, does not appear up to the time of writing to have been of the nature of asylum, as the word is properly understood by international authorities, there having been apparently no national or municipal government in the capital. Shelter under such circumstances was a mere act of humanity, unaccompanied by any assumption of extraterritorial prerogatives by you, or interference with any rights of legitimate government or sovereignty. This is quite distinct from the so-called right of asylum, which can logically only be exercised in disparagement of the rights of the sovereign power by withdrawing an accused subject from its rightful authority. The practice of this kind of asylum is not a right derived from positive law or custom; it is not sanctioned by international law, and can only find excuse when tacitly invited and consented to by the state within whose jurisdiction it may be practiced.

" The Government of the United States has constantly declined to be bound by such questionable titles to accept its exercise, and has on many occasions and in positive terms condemned the usage and discouraged resort thereto by its representatives. In 1875, to select one among several examples, Mr. Fish instructed Mr. Cushing, then minister to Madrid, that ' The right of asylum, by which I now refer to the so-called right of a political refugee to immunity and protection within a foreign legation or consulate, is believed to have no good reason for its continuance, to be mischievous in its tendencies, and to tend to political disorder. These views have been frequently expressed, and, while this Government is not able of itself to do away with the practice in foreign countries, it has not failed on appropriate occasion to deprecate its existence and to instruct its representatives to avoid committing this Government thereto.'

" In 1884, answering a request of the German Government for the views of the United States as to the propriety of restricting the exercise of asylum in Hayti to the citizens or subjects of the sheltering state, Mr. Frelinghuysen wrote : ' While indisposed from obvious motives of common humanity to direct its agents to deny temporary shelter to any unfortunate threatened with mob violence, it has been deemed proper to instruct them that it (the United States Government) will not countenance them in any attempt to knowingly harbor offenders against the laws from the pursuit of the legitimate agents of justice.'

" Your concluding request for instructions is presumed to relate to this incident of the shelter given by you to General Savasti and family. The foregoing citations will have sufficiently indicated the uniform rule of this Government to discountenance asylum in every form and to enjoin upon its agents the exercise of the utmost care to avoid any imputation of abuse in granting such shelter. It may be tolerated as an act of humanity when the hospitality afforded does not go beyond sheltering the individual from lawlessness. It may not be tolerated should it be sought to remove a subject beyond the reach of the law to the disparagement of the sovereign authority of the state.

" Sections 46, 47, and 48 of the Department's printed personal instructions relate in terms to the extension of asylum to unsuccessful insurgents and conspirators. It seems to be very generally supposed that the case of a member of an overturned titular government is different; and so it may be until the empire of the law is restored and the successful revolution establishes itself in turn as the rightful government competent to administer law and justice in orderly process. Until that happens the humane accordance of shelter from lawlessness may be justifiable; but when the authority of the state is reestablished upon an orderly footing, no disparagement of its powers under the mistaken fiction of extraterritoriality can be countenanced on the part of the representatives of this Government."

> Mr. Olney, Sec. of State, to Mr. Tillman, min. to Ecuador, Sept. 25, 1895, For. Rel. 1895, I. 245.
>
> As to asylum in Ecuador, see dispatches of Mr. Hassaurek, minister to Ecuador, to Mr. Seward, No. 137, July 20, 1864, and No. 164, June 16, 1865, 7 MS. Desp. from Ecuador.

March 9, 1896, Señor Montalvo, Ecuadorian minister for foreign affairs, asked permission of Mr. Tillman, United States minister at Quito, to enter the lower part of the building, in which the latter resided, and arrest a Colonel Hidalgo, who was alleged to be a conspirator against the Government. It appeared that Mr. Tillman rented an apartment on the main floor of the building, but that the rooms below and in the rear, in some of which Colonel Hidalgo lived, formed no part of his quarters, while all the rooms opened on a court, to which there was a common entrance from the street. Mr. Tillman disclaimed any control over the entrance, as well as over the rooms not rented by him; but, when the officers came to make the arrest, he, at the request of Colonel Hidalgo, " tendered " the latter's " surrender " to them, and obtained for him a promise of kind treatment and a fair trial. On being advised of the incident, the Department of State instructed Mr. Tillman that it was not seen how there could have been any occasion for asking his permission to make the arrest, " unless on the absurd assumption that a minister's residential immunities embrace the entire edifice of which he may have rented a part; " that the request for permission to search other parts of the building than those occupied by him, and to pass for that purpose through the common avenue of access, placed him in the false position of a consenting party, a position which was not improved by his " kindly intervention " in the manner above stated; and that it would be proper for him to say to the minister of foreign affairs that he was responsible only for such part of the premises as he actually rented and occupied for residence and offices, and that, while he would neither invite nor tolerate abuse of his individual habitation as a refuge for evil doers cr suspects, he could not permit, even by remote implication, any inference that he was to be regarded as accountable with respect to other parts of the building, or to be called upon to consent to the exercise of legitimate authority therein by the constituted Government.[a]

By a subsequent dispatch it appeared that Colonel Hidalgo, on the evening of his arrest, entered, by permission of a servant, Mr. Tillman's kitchen, and invoked, as a personal favor, Mr. Tillman's good offices to shield him from punishment by " cold baths." Commenting further on the case, Mr. Tillman said: " So general is the misunderstanding of the so-called right of asylum that a thief or a deserter from the army or an assassin considers himself safe if he can secure admission by force or fraud or deception into a building or grounds occupied by a foreign minister, and even lawyers and men of wealth and intelligence regard a refusal to receive them when pursued by Government officials for political offenses as a great discourtesy and contrary to the law of asylum in South America, and this opinion is so general that the Government itself is cautious not to seem to violate public opinion, however ignorant and uninformed and on however little of reason and law it is founded." [b]

January 16, 1899, Mr. Sampson, United States minister at Quito, reported that the revolution then going on in Ecuador had assumed threatening proportions, and that trenches had been dug and barricades thrown up on all streets leading to the palace. Under these circumstances the minister of foreign relations had inquired of him whether, " if the unexpected should happen and the Government should be defeated," he would " give asylum to the Vice-President (acting President in the absence of President Alfaro in Guayaquil) and all the members of the cabinet, with their families, and the chiefs of the army." On Mr. Sampson's giving an affirmative reply, the minister of foreign relations returned thanks and expressed " full confidence " in the " Stars and Stripes." Subsequently, however, the insurgents withdrew and retreated.[c]

In acknowledging the receipt of Mr. Sampson's dispatch, the Department of State called his attention to par. 51 of the Printed Personal Instructions, and to the precedents in Wharton's Digest, vol. 1, sec. 104, " in discouragement of the practice of granting the so-called ' asylum.' " [d]

Mr. Sampson replied that, in promising asylum if need be to the chief officials of the Government, he had consulted par. 51 of the Per-

---

[a] Mr. Olney, Sec. of State, to Mr. Tillman, min. to Ecuador, April 4, 1896, For. Rel. 1896, 113.

[b] Mr. Tillman, min. to Ecuador, to Mr. Olney, Sec. of State, May 16, 1896, For. Rel. 1896, 114.

[c] For. Rel. 1899, 256.

[d] Mr. Hay, Sec. of State, to Mr. Sampson, min. to Ecuador, Feb. 27, 1899, For. Rel. 1899, 256.

sonal Instructions, and the Foreign Relations for 1895; that the former referred to " unsuccessful insurgents " and " offenders against the laws," and the latter to persons who had assumed office by revolution.   In the present instance, however, he had offered asylum to the regularly elected officers of government, so recognized for years, from possible outrage at the hands of " offenders against the laws," virtually " cutthroats " and " outlaws."   Had the latter succeeded, their success would have been temporary, since if they had not fled President Alfaro would have dislodged them and reestablished his Government, and the concession of asylum " would have saved from death the legitimate heads of the Government until such a time as they could again assume the functions of their respective offices." [a]

In its answer the Department of State, while quoting Mr. Olney's statement, in the case of General Savasti, the minister of war of the overthrown Ecuadorian Government, that " the case of a member of an overturned titular government " might be " different " from that of a revolutionist, " until the empire of law is restored, and the successful revolution establishes itself in turn as the rightful government, competent to administer law and justice in orderly process," said : "A general rule, in the abstract, can not be laid down for the inflexible guidance of the diplomatic representatives of this Government in according shelter to those requesting it.   But certain limitations to such grant are recognized.   It should not, in any case, take the form of a direct or indirect intervention in the internecine conflicts of a foreign country, with a view to the assistance of any of the contending factions, whether acting as insurgents or as representing the titular government.

" I therefore regret that I am unable to approve the promise of shelter made by you to the members of the titular government before the emergency had actually arisen for decision as to whether the circumstances then existing would justify or make it permissible; and especially am I unable to approve the apparent ground or motive of the promise, that you would have saved from death the legitimate heads of the Government ' until such a time as they would again assume the functions of their respective offices.'

" The Government of the United States remains a passive spectator of such conflicts, unless its own interests or the interests of its citizens are involved; and I conceive that it might lead to great abuses in the grant of such shelter, which is afforded only from motives of humanity, if assurances were given in advance to the leaders of either of the contending factions that they might carry the conflict to whatever extremes, with the knowledge that at last they should enjoy

---

[a] Mr. Sampson, min. to Ecuador, to Mr. Hay, Sec. of State, April 10, 1899, For Rel. 1899, 257.

immunity in the protection of this Government, yet such might be construed as the practical effect of the assurance given in this case. I am therefore constrained to withhold my approval of the assurances given at the time and under the circumstances stated in your dispatches and as understood by the Department."

> Mr. Hay, Sec. of State, to Mr. Sampson, min. to Ecuador, June 5, 1899, For. Rel. 1899, 257–259; MS. Inst. Ecuador, I. 571.

(6) HAYTI AND SANTO DOMINGO.

§ 300.

In Hayti and Santo Domingo both legations and consulates have been used as asylums for persons engaged in the disturbances that so often occur in those countries.

" 1. Consuls may harbor political refugees, but as the law of nations confers upon them no right to do this, and as the treaty between the United States and Hayti is silent upon the subject, no sufficient cause of complaint would arise if refugees so harbored were to be taken by the local authorities from the consular abode."

> Mr. Hunter, Act. Sec. of State, to Mr. Peck, Oct. 4, 1865, MS. Inst. Hayti, I. 62.

In a despatch of May 8, 1868, Mr. Hollister, then minister of the United States at Port au Prince, describes the disorders attending the return to that city of President Salnave at the head of his army, after an encounter with insurgents. The city, he said, was in a state of " consternation," and his dwelling was filled with " refugees—men, women, and children—to the number of one hundred and fifty." Mobs roamed the streets, as they had done for two weeks, firing their muskets promiscuously. In conclusion he said : " I beg instructions in relation to the receiving of refugees. It does more mischief here than it does good, and is really, as it is practised, little more than offering a premium for factious disturbances and a bid for sedition. The three chargés here are ready to recommend the discontinuance of this much-abused custom if our Government is ready to take the step."

On May 28 Mr. Seward replied as follows : " The right of a foreign legation to afford an asylum to political refugees is not recognized by the law of nations as applicable to civilized or constitutionally organized states. It is a practice, however, which, from the necessity of the case, is exercised to a greater or less extent by every civilized state in regard to barbarous or semibarbarous countries. The revolutionary condition seemed to become chronic in many of the South American nations after they had achieved their independence, and the United States, as well as the European nations, recognized and maintained the right of asylum in their intercourse with those republics,

We have, however, constantly employed our influence, for several years to meliorate and improve the political situation in these republics, with an earnest desire to relinquish the right of asylum there. In the year 1867 we formally relinquished and renounced that right in the Republic of Peru. This Government has also largely modified the exercise of that right among some of the oriental nations.

"Thus we are prepared to accept the opinion you have deliberately expressed that it is no longer expedient to practice the right of asylum in the Haytian Republic. Nevertheless, we should not be willing to relinquish the right abruptly, and in the midst of the anarchy which seems to be now prevailing in Hayti, in the absence of matured convictions on your part. Nor do we think it expedient that it should be renounced by the United States legation any sooner or in any greater degree than it is renounced by the legations of the other important neutral powers. With these reservations, the subject is confidently left to your own discreet judgment."

> Mr. Seward, Sec. of State, to Mr. Hollister, min. to Hayti, May 28, 1868, Dip. Cor. 1868, II. 358.
> Mr. Hollister's dispatch is in the same volume, p. 354.

On June 29 Mr. Hollister reported that, owing to the breaking out of disease in the legation, President Salnave had as a "sanitary measure" agreed to the safe departure of the women and children, and had permitted all the men to be put on board a merchant vessel for New York, except General Roman and six others, who with the consent of the President remained under the diplomatic roof. On this report Mr. Seward observed: "I see no reason to censure or disapprove of your proceedings mentioned, by which you obtained relief from the excessive incumbrance of refugees. The proceeding is in harmony with the instructions you have received from this Department, and with the settled policy of the United States. . . . In all cases the exercise of the right [of asylum] should be attended as far as possible with delicacy towards the state concerned, and with forbearance from all appearance of arrogance and dictation."

> Mr. Seward, Sec. of State, to Mr. Hollister, min. to Hayti, July 18, 1868, Dip. Cor. 1868, II. 360.

"Your dispatch No. 20, of the 20th ultimo, has been received. It represents that in consequence of the apprehended triumph of the armed opposition to the existing Government in Hayti, the foreign consulates, and even the legation of the United States, had been sought as asylums for persons and property. Occasions for this have of late years frequently arisen in the independent states of this hemisphere, but the proceeding has never been sanctioned by the Department, which, however, appreciates those impulses of humanity which make it difficult to reject such appeals for refuge. The expediency of granting an asylum in such cases, especially by consuls, is more than questionable, and the obligation to take that course has no foundation in public law, however in Hayti or elsewhere it may be tolerated and customary. While you are not required to expel those who may have sought refuge in the legation, you will give them to understand that your Government can not on that account assume any responsibility for them, and especially can not sanction any resistance by you to their arrest by the authorities for the time being."

> Mr. Fish, Sec. of State, to Mr. Bassett, min. to Hayti, Dec. 16, 1869, For. Rel. 1871, 695.
>
> A copy of this instruction was inclosed by Mr. Fish, May 18, 1871, to Mr. Torbert, minister to Salvador, ibid.
>
> See, also, Mr. Fish, Sec. of State, to Mr. Bassett, min. to Hayti, Feb. 4, 1870, MS. Inst. Hayti, I. 180.
>
> In March, 1875, the British minister in Hayti granted asylum to General Lamothe, whom the national constituent assembly had taken steps to prosecute for unfaithfulness in office as minister of the interior and of foreign affairs under the administration of President Saget. It was finally arranged that he should return to his home on giving security for any sums he might have misappropriated, the Government guaranteeing him against any irregular proceedings. Subsequently, on the receipt of a summons from a criminal tribunal not possessing jurisdiction of the case, General Lamothe returned to the British legation, but he again resumed his liberty on an assurance given by President Domingue to the British minister that the irregular proceedings would be discontinued. In this transaction the British minister had the cooperation of Mr. Bassett, the minister of the United States. (For. Rel. 1875, II. 682.)
>
> On receiving Mr. Bassett's report of the case, the Department of State said: "The Department regrets to notice that you have assented to doctrines on the subject [of asylum] which are believed to be in themselves untenable and which may be regarded as at variance with the instructions to you of the 16th of December, 1869." (Mr. Fish, Sec. of State, to Mr. Bassett, min. to Hayti, May 3, 1875, MS. Inst. Hayti, II. 48.)

In March, 1872, Mr. Jastram, vice commercial agent of the United States at St. Marc, Hayti, afforded asylum to General Batraville, who was pursued for proclaiming an insurrection. The chief of the department demanded that the fugitive be given up, and when the demand was refused, sent troops to arrest him. At the consular office a fracas ensued, and the troops not only searched the office and arrested the General, but they also seized Mr. Jastram and took him through the public streets with many demonstrations of violence. From this " undignified position," as he termed it, Mr. Jastram was rescued through the intervention of the French vice-consul. Mr. Bassett, in accordance with the instrutions of December 16 1869, declined to make any claim on account of the arrest of General Batraville, but he obtained an expression of regret from the Haytian Government for the indignity to the consul and a promise of future protection to consular officers. He also demanded the punishment of the officer at the head of the offending troops; but the Government met this demand to Mr. Bassett's entire satisfaction by assuring him that it would not fail to censure or punish that officer, if he had not "paid, in his own person, the last tribute to nature." Mr. Hale, Acting Secretary of State, congratulated Mr. Bassett that the case had been "adjusted upon a basis compatible with the honor of both Governments." [a]

In April, 1872, the British vice-consul at Cape Haytian caused great excitement by receiving political offenders and refusing to give them up. The British and American consular representatives at Gonaives pursued the same course, and the authorities stationed guards about their offices. Ultimately the refugees were delivered to Haytian agents, by whom they were embarked.[b] But in March, 1873, the authorities of Santo Domingo took from the British consulate at Puerto Plata, in that Republic, by force and against the consul's protest, three Dominicans who had sought asylum there after heading an armed demonstration against the cession of Samana Bay to the United States. Mr. St. John, British minister at Port au Prince and chargé d'affaires at Santo Domingo, immediately demanded their release and, with the intervention of a British man-of-war, compelled the Dominican authorities to give up the prisoners, censure the officers concerned in their arrest, and salute the British flag.[c] On the 1st of August Earl Granville, on learning the facts, instructed Mr. St. John to inform the Government of Santo Domingo, as well as all Her Majesty's consular officers there, that the British Government had determined to abandon the practice of receiving political refugees in its consulates in that Republic.[d]

"The immunities of an ambassador are not of a personal character. They belong to the government of which he is the representative. It is to be regretted, therefore, that you treated the invasion of your house and the arrest therein of your servants as a personal offense, to be atoned for by the simple release of the persons arrested, and a private note expressive of regret.

"This act, especially when regarded in connection with a recent invasion of the commercial agency at St. Marc, and other acts of disrespect, and of neglect of diplomatic and international courtesies, is significant of an intent which should have elicited from you a more

a For. Rel. 1872, 264–284.
b For. Rel. 1872, 270; 1873, I. 465–473.
c For. Rel. 1873, I. 460–463.
d For. Rel. 1874, 584.

emphatic protest than your unofficial communication to the Secretary of State, and a demand for more decided redress than that which you were content to accept."

> Mr. Fish, Sec. of State, to Mr. Bassett, min. to Hayti, March 26, 1873, For. Rel. 1873, I. 459.
>
> "It is preferred that there should be no stipulation [in a proposed consular convention] allowing the right of asylum to consular officers in Hayti. This is not a right conceded even to regular diplomatic agents by the law of nations and its exercise by consuls as a right is regarded as inadmissible. Serious inconvenience has heretofore been experienced by us from the granting of asylum by consular officers. The violation of such a right would be a grave offence which ought to be at once resented. To do this the President, under our system of government, would be powerless in the recess of Congress, and even if in session their certainty in promptly conferring the necessary authority should not be taken for granted." (Mr. Fish, Sec. of State, to Mr. Bassett, min. to Hayti, June 7, 1873, MS. Inst. Hayti, II. 1.)

"Your dispatches, numbered 364 and 365, of the 8th and 19th ultimo, respectively, have been received. They relate to the recent disturbances at Port au Prince, and to persons who have sought an asylum in the legation. It is regretted that you deemed yourself justified by an impulse of humanity to grant such an asylum. You have repeatedly been instructed that such a practice has no basis in public law, and, so far as this Government is concerned, is believed to be contrary to all sound policy. The course of the diplomatic representatives of other countries in receiving political refugees upon such occasions is not deemed sufficient to warrant this Government in sanctioning a similar step on the part of the representatives of the United States. Among other objections to granting such an asylum it may be remarked that that act obviously tends so far to incite conspiracies against governments, that if persons charged with offenses can be sure of being screened in a foreign legation from arrest they will be much more apt to attempt the overthrow of authority than if such a place of refuge were not open to them.

"Mr. Preston has been here by order of his Government to ask that you may be directed to set at large the refugees who have sought your protection. I answered him, however, that though it might have been preferable that you should not have received those persons, it was not deemed expedient to comply with his request. I added that if his Government would apply to you for them, in order that they might be tried, you would be authorized to give them up, provided the Government gives you its assurance that no punishment shall result from the trial, but that, if convicted, the parties will be allowed, without molestation, to leave the country. If, too, the persons who are with you should themselves or through you offer to surrender to the authorities on the same condition, and should it be acceptable, you will dismiss them."

> Mr. Fish, Sec. of State, to Mr. Bassett, min. to Hayti, June 4, 1875, For. Rel. 1875, II. 701.
>
> The case here referred to originated in a decree of May 1, 1875, by which President Domingue assumed extraordinary powers and ordered the banishment of forty-four persons whom he charged with conspiracy against the Government. In the execution of this decree he sent out squads of troops to make arrests. Many persons were seized and some were shot down in the streets. Ex-ministers Pierre and Brice, who forcibly resisted arrest, were besieged and killed in their houses, and in the fusilade of the soldiery the British and Spanish consulates were fired into. Simultaneously a company of troops was sent to take Boisrond Canal, charged with being the chief conspirator, who was at his home near La Coup. With four companions, two of whom were killed in the struggle, he fought his way to La Coup, and from thence escaped to the country house of Mr. Bassett, where he arrived with his surviving companions early in the morning of May 3. There were already at Mr. Bassett's house three persons, named Alerte, Iacinthe, and Modé, who were included in the decree of banishment. On the 2d of May President Domingue issued another decree, declaring that, as Boisrond Canal had answered a legal requisition by recourse to arms, he and "all his followers" were put outside the pale of the law. When Mr. Bassett went to his office in Port au Prince on the 3d of May he received a note from Mr. Excellent, secretary for foreign affairs, stating that the Government had been informed that there were certain rebels in his house and asking for a list of them. This was followed by another note specifically soliciting the surrender of Modé, Iacinthe, and Alerte. Mr. Bassett refused to comply with either of these requests, on the ground that it had been the uniform practice in Hayti to furnish a list of refugees only with a view to their release or embarkation.
>
> When Mr. Bassett returned to his home on the 3d he found it surrounded by large numbers of disorderly troops who stopped up the avenues of approach and prevented the free egress and ingress of himself and his family, besides creating apprehensions of personal violence. On the following morning, when setting out for his office, he was stopped by some of these men, who seized the bridle of his horse, drew their weapons, and used insolent language. One of his servants also was stopped and rudely treated while returning from market. Mr. Bassett asked that the troops be "at once retired from such near vicinity" to his house, and that those who had participated in the proceedings complained of be brought to a sense of responsibility. Mr. Excellent expressed regret at the disrespectful acts complained of, and assured Mr. Bassett that orders had been given to the agents of the Government to observe proper respect towards him, and to permit those attached to his suite to come and go with freedom and security. He did not refer to the request for the removal of the troops to a greater distance. Two weeks later Alerte, Iacinthe, and Modé, together with one of the companions of Boisrond Canal, were permitted to embark, and only the latter and his younger

brother remained in the legation. Two persons who were in the
house of the British minister were also allowed to depart.

In reporting these May incidents to his Government, Mr. Bassett defended
his concession of asylum on the ground that it was necessary to prevent the refugees from being shot down. Moreover, he said that the
Government of Hayti, besides uniformly countenancing the practice
of asylum, had once or twice refused to assent to its discontinuance,
and that lately it had arrested negotiations for a consular convention
with the United States by refusing to forbid the practice even in inferior consular offices. He also stated that in February, 1870, he had
been instructed by Mr. Fish that since the custom was tolerated in
Hayti by the other great powers, the Department of State was not
disposed " to place the representative of the United States in an
invidious position by positively forbidding him to continue the practice;" and in this relation Mr. Bassett said that the British minister
had received a communication from the Earl of Derby approving his
action in granting asylum to the persons under his roof. (For. Rel.
1875, II. 686–701. The instruction of 1870, to which Mr. Bassett
referred, was that of Feb. 4, 1870, MS. Inst. Hayti, I. 180. See Mr.
Hunter, Act. Sec. of State, to Mr. Bassett, min. to Hayti, Aug. 26,
1875, For. Rel. 1875, II. 726.)

Mr. Bassett subsequently reported that on June 23 his lordship again
wrote to the minister and, while approving his action in regard to
the refugees in question, said: " You should, however, endeavor to
arrange for their quitting Hayti." Mr. Bassett reported that the British minister, Major Stuart, when informing the minister for foreign
affairs of the contents of Lord Derby's first instructions, said: " Now,
Mr. Minister, I wish it distinctly understood that from this day forward I shall receive and protect, as I may judge best, in my legation
any and every person who may apply for my protection. This I wish
your Government to understand well." (For. Rel. 1875, II. 691, 724.)

See Mr. Fish, Sec. of State, to Mr. Preston, Haytian min., June 29, 1875,
For. Rel. 1875, II. 738; Mr. Fish, Sec. of State, to Mr. Bassett, min.
to Hayti, July 1, 1875, For. Rel. 1875, II. 708.

Before Mr. Bassett received Mr. Fish's instruction of the 4th of
June, a new device was adopted to obtain the dismissal of the refugees
whom he was sheltering. In order to worry him into compliance,
the bands of armed men who overran his grounds began to spend the
night in shouting, so that it was impossible for anyone in the house
to sleep. On the 26th of June Mr. Bassett addressed a note to the
minister of foreign affairs, Mr. Excellent, saying that while he did
not dispute the right of the Government " to exercise its own rightful
measures of police within its own jurisdiction," such measures ought
to be enforced " in such a way as not to become a marked trespass
upon the rights and immunities of foreign ministers." The complaint made by Mr. Bassett was brought to the attention of Mr.
Preston, the Haytian minister in Washington, by Mr. Cadwalader,
Acting Secretary of State, August 6, in the following terms: " It

can not be believed that these annoyances are instigated by the Haytian Government, and perhaps it may not be aware that they are practised. However this may be, it is expected that they will at once be discontinued. If this expectation should be disappointed, it will be regarded as an unfriendly proceeding on the part of the Haytian Government. Indeed, the demonstrations adverted to and all the circumstances make it advisable, in the opinion of the President, that a United States man-of-war should visit Port au Prince." [a]

It was not, however, till September 7 that Mr. Hunter, Acting Secretary of State, informed Mr. Bassett that it had been determined to send a man-of-war to Port au Prince with a view to his "protection from insult." [b] This determination was reached after the receipt on the 2d of the month of dispatches from Mr. Bassett saying that the annoyances of which he had complained were increasing. He also stated that the Government had resorted to the expedient of trying the refugees in the legations *par contumace* and had condemned several to death. [c]

Meanwhile negotiations were drawing to a close in Washington. Adhering to the proposition communicated by Mr. Fish to Mr. Bassett in the instructions of June 4, the Department of State, while acknowledging Hayti's right to try the fugitives, maintained that the asylum granted them should be inviolable "so long as it should generally be tolerated," and that, if convicted, they should be allowed of their own accord to leave the country. [d] When this proposition was made to Mr. Preston, coupled with a requirement that the fugitives should be furnished with passports, he declined to recommend it to this Government, insisting that they should be delivered to and embarked by agents of that Government, though Mr. Bassett might accompany them. [e] On September 27 the following agreement was concluded:

It is mutually agreed between Hamilton Fish, Secretary of State, and Stephen Preston, E. E. and M. P. of Hayti, that certain political refugees who, for some time past, have had an asylum in the residence of Mr. Bassett, the minister resident of the United States at Port au Prince, shall receive from the Haytian Government a full amnesty for all offences up to the time of their departure from the island; that Mr. Bassett shall give them up; that they shall be placed on board a vessel bound to some other country; that on their way to the vessel they shall be escorted by a Haytian military force, and that Mr. Bassett may also accompany them to the vessel. It is to be understood, however, that the

---

[a] Mr. Cadwalader, Acting Sec. of State, to Mr. Preston, Haytian min. Aug. 6, 1875, For. Rel. 1875, II. 739. See, also, same to same, Aug. 17, 1875, id. 741.

[b] For. Rel. 1875, II. 728.

[c] For. Rel. 1875, II. 715.

[d] Mr. Cadwalader, Act. Sec. of State, to Mr. Preston, Haytian min., Aug. 17, 1875, For. Rel. 1875, II. 741.

[e] Mr. Preston, Haytian min., to Mr. Cadwalader, Act. Sec. of State, Aug. 26, 1875, For. Rel. 1875, II. 742.

said refugees, or any of them, shall not return to Hayti without the permission of the Government of the Republic.

HAMILTON FISH,
Secretary of State.
STEPHEN PRESTON,
E. E. and M. P. of Hayti.[a]

On the 2d of October, President Domingue issued a decree commuting the sentence of the refugees to banishment for life, and on October 5 they were embarked by Haytian officers, accompanied by Mr. Bassett and the French *chargé d'affaires.* On the same day the guard was withdrawn from Mr. Bassett's grounds.[b] A few weeks later Mr. Preston submitted to Mr. Fish a series of propositions in relation to the practice of asylum in Hayti. These propositions were to the effect that asylum should never be granted to common criminals; that it should be accorded to "political offenders only in exceptional cases," and that in those cases the refugees should, if the Haytian Government insisted, at once be delivered up to justice, though "the minister who had granted the asylum might still use his influence to secure, should there be any reason to do so, an ultimate commutation of the penalty." Mr. Fish replied that while "some, at least," of these propositions appeared to be "fair enough," the Government of the United States was not "by itself, and independently of all others, disposed to absolutely prohibit" its representatives from granting asylum in every case in which an application for it might be made, and that until an understanding could be reached with other powers it would be better to treat each case on its merits than be "fettered in advance by rules which may be found not to be practically applicable or useful." [c]

In April, 1876, the Government of President Domingue was overthrown and he fled to the French legation, whence he escaped on a French man-of-war to St. Thomas. His unpopular minister, Rameau, was killed, by a mob in the street, while on his way with the French and Spanish ministers to the former's dwelling. Next day Boisrond Canal and other exiles, who had been directing the revolution from Jamaica, landed at Port au Prince, and a provi-

---

[a] For. Rel. 1875, II. 748. It is noticeable that in the representations of the Department of State there is no denial of the Haytian Government's right to prevent, by measures of police, the escape of the refugees, or communication with them, during their sojourn in the legation. This is clearly shown by Mr. Cadwalader's statement that it could not be supposed that the "annoyances" described by Mr. Bassett were instigated by the Haytian Government, which had caused the house to be guarded. Mr. Bassett had admitted the right of police.

[b] For. Rel. 1875, II. 682–748.

[c] Mr Fish, Sec. of State, to Mr. Preston, Haytian min., Dec. 11, 1875, For. Rel. 1876, 344. See, in the same volume, p. 338, Mr. Preston's note of Oct. 25, 1875.

sional government was set up with Boisrond Canal at the head.[a] In July he was duly installed as President, with every sign of great popularity.[b] Nevertheless, in the following year we find Mr. Bassett commenting upon the unpatriotic character of certain uprisings in the island;[c] and in March, 1878, his successor, Mr. Langston, announced that Port au Prince was in a state of revolution, stirred up during the absence of the president by General Tanis, his " special and trusted friend and adviser."[d] When the president returned and the insurrection was put down, General Tanis and some of his associates fled to the Liberian minister's; three took refuge in the American legation; others yet found asylum in the legations of France and Great Britain and in the Peruvian consulate. The diplomatic corps determined not to deliver up anyone in a legation or a consulate. Their action on this subject, said Mr. Langston, " was unanimous and emphatic." Under these circumstances the Government abandoned punitory proceedings against the refugees, and designated agents to receive them and convey them to their embarkation. On this incident Mr. Langston observes:

This seems to be the natural ending of Haytian revolutionary attempts. If they succeed, the administration of the Government is changed; if they fail, their leaders and a few of the more conspicuous followers are exiled. Occasionally some more unfortunate one is shot by the mob. It cannot be denied that asylum, as furnished in the legations and consulates located in this Republic, is in very important senses objectionable. It is surprising to witness the readiness and assurance with which a defeated revolutionst approaches the door of such places, demanding, as a matter of right, admission and protection. And before the revolutionary attempt is made, when the probabilities of success and defeat are being calculated, this protection in case of defeat is regarded and accounted as sure, and by this means, refuge and escape are sought and gained. Exile is regarded as the only possible infliction; and this, tempered by that sort of care which results from diplomatic and consular interest and assistance. Such interest and assistance always tend, too, to dignify while they encourage revolutionary efforts. Antagonisms, also, as between foreign governments and that whose overthrow is attempted, under such circumstances are quite inevitable, especially if the latter is earnest and decided in its purpose to deal vigorously and severely with the rebellious.[e]

In June, 1879, another insurrection broke out at Port au Prince. General François, secretary of war and marine, whom Mr. Langston described as " the most honorable and faithful man " in Hayti, was killed while charging the insurgents, who were put down only after considerable loss of life on both sides. Much property was destroyed, including several public buildings, with all their records. The defeated leaders of the insurrection fled by the dozen to the foreign legations and consulates, which emptied their revolutionary contents

---

[a] For. Rel. 1876, 325, 331.
[b] Id. 335.
[c] For. Rel. 1877, 317.
[d] For. Rel. 1878, 431.
[e] For. Rel. 1878, 431–444.

at night, and without Government military escort, chiefly into the British man-of-war *Boxer*.[a] On the 17th of July President Canal resigned and left the country, his course doubtless being influenced by insurrectionary movements in the north of the island.[b] Among the members of the provisional government then set up, we find General Lamothe, who was translated from the "central revolutionary committee," and who had been protected by the British minister in 1875, when prosecuted by the government of President Domingue. General Salomon, who was soon elected to the Presidency, enjoyed asylum in the Peruvian consulate after the insurrection of March, 1878.[c] Less fortunate, however, was General Bazelais. He was the leader of the unsuccessful outbreak at Port au Prince in June, 1879, and was among those who were granted asylum and who were subsequently embarked on the *Boxer*. When President Canal resigned, Bazelais proposed to come ashore and accept the Presidency, but his former associates were found to be resolutely opposed to him. On the 1st of August he was transferred from the *Boxer* to a German steamer, from which he landed at Gonaives, where he started another insurrection. Defeated by the forces of the provisional government, he fled to Jérémie and found refuge in the French consulate, from which he escaped to Jamaica.[d]

On August 6, 1879, Mr. Evarts, then Secretary of State, wrote to Mr. Langston as follows: "If the so-called 'right of asylum' (which this Government has never been tenacious in claiming for its officers abroad) is to continue to exist as a quasi rule of public law, in communities where the conspirators of to-day may be the government of to-morrow, it should at least be so exercised as to afford no ground of complaint on the score of aiding and comforting rebellion by conniving at communication between the refugees in asylum and their associates who are, it may be, engaged in hostilities against the existing government. It is evident that asylum would be as intolerable as reprehensible, were not the refugees supposed to be kept out of mischief as well as out of danger."[e]

President Salomon was driven from Hayti in 1888, and while he was escaping on a foreign man-of-war the places just occupied by his enemies in the legations and consulates were quickly filled by his partisans. His tenure of power had been unusually long and had been marked by remorseless determination in putting down insurrec-

---

a For. Rel. 1879, 564, 569.

b For. Rel. 1879, 572.

c For. Rel. 1878, 436.

d For. Rel. 1879, 564–582.

e Mr. Evarts, Sec. of State, to Mr. Langston, min. to Hayti, Aug. 6, 1879, For. Rel. 1879, 582.

tions which the exiles, *via diplomatica,* in Jamaica and other neighboring islands kept inciting. Most serious of all these outbreaks was that started at Jacmel in 1883 by the same General Bazelais whose career as a revolutionist protected by the legations has already been sketched. On that occasion President Salomon directly charged in the presence of the diplomatic corps that the responsibility for the insurrection rested with the British consul at Jacmel, who had permitted the conspirators to make his consulate their base of operations while enjoying asylum there.[a]

" This Government is well aware that the practice of extraterritorial asylum in Hayti has become so deeply established as to be practically recognized by whatever government may be in power, even to respecting the premises of a consulate, as well as a legation. This Government does not sanction the usage, and enjoins upon its representatives in Hayti the avoidance of all pretexts for its exercise. While indisposed from obvious motives of common humanity to direct its agents to deny temporary shelter to any unfortunates threatened with mob violence, it is proper to instruct them that it will not countenance them in any attempt to knowingly harbor offenders against the laws from the pursuit of the legitimate agents of justice."

> Mr. Frelinghuysen, Sec. of State, to Mr. Langston, min. to Hayti, Dec. 15, 1883, MS. Inst. Hayti, II. 367.
>
> See, also, Mr. Frelinghuysen, Sec. of State, to Mr. Langston, min. to Hayti, Feb. 15, 1884, MS. Inst. Hayti, II. 384.

" The Government of the United States does not *claim* for its legations abroad any extraterritorial privileges of aslyum, and consequently makes no such *claim* in respect of consular offices, or private residences of American citizens, or American merchant vessels in port. If, as a custom, in any country, the practice of asylum prevails, and is tacitly or explicitly recognized by the local authorities in respect of legations, consulates, private dwellings, or vessels of another nationality, the exercise of the consuetudinary privilege by Americans could not be deemed exceptional; and if, under any circumstances, refugees find their way to places of shelter under the American flag, or in the domicile of American citizens, we should certainly expect such privileges as would be accorded were the like shelter under the flag or domicile of another power. But we claim no right or privilege of asylum; on the contrary, we discountenance it, especially when it may tend to obstruct the direct operation of law and justice."

> Mr. Bayard, Sec. of State, to Mr. Thompson, min. to Hayti, Nov. 7, 1885, For. Rel. 1886, 530.
>
> In October, 1888, Mr. Goutier, consul of the United States at Cape Haytian, instructed his consular agents, that in the revolution then pend-

---

[a] For. Rel. 1883, 591.

ing they were not to receive political refugees, and that if they did, they "would in that case have forfeited all claims to the support" of their Government. Mr. Rives, Assistant Secretary of State, reaffirming the views expressed by Mr. Bayard, corrected Mr. Goutier's statement in the following language: "We do not regard extraterritorial asylum, either in a legation or a consulate, as a right to be claimed under international law. We do not sanction or invite the exercise of asylum in those countries where it actually exists as a usage, but in such cases we recognize and admit its existence, and should circumstances bring about the uninvited resort of a political refugee for shelter to a consulate or legation of the United States, we should expect equal toleration and privilege in this regard with that allowed by such local usage to any other consulate or legation. . . . Only the reported facts of an actual case arising could enable the Department to determine whether an abuse of the local usage had been committed." (Mr. Rives, Assist. Sec. of State, to Mr. Goutier, Oct. 31, 1888, For. Rel. 1888, I. 938.)

The instruction of Mr. Rives is quoted and affirmed in Mr. Blaine, Sec. of State, to Mr. Durham, min. to Hayti, Jan. 28, 1892, For. Rel. 1892, 347.

" So far as the general question of asylum is concerned, there appears to be no occasion to add to the Department's instructions on this subject heretofore. In the particular instance reported by your No. 45, it is considered fortunate that you found it convenient to answer Mr. Firmin's note as you did, assuring him that no refugees were with you, and that no one had applied to you for asylum. This negative reply in nowise prejudices your course under the Department's previous instructions. Your competency to furnish, at the request of the minister of foreign affairs, a list of fugitives under your protection charged with offenses against the common law during the last civil strife in the country, and not covered by the amnesty of November 15, 1889, is not apparent. It would involve the exercise on your part of a discrimination or judicial function not pertaining to your position as the representative of this Government; for it is not at all clear that, even if it were proper for you to furnish such a list, you would find it practicable to ascertain justly who might and who might not be excluded from benefits of the amnesty in question, or, for that matter, any other amnesty or discriminative provision of defense."

Mr. Blaine, Sec. of State, to Mr. Douglass, min. to Hayti, March 27, 1890, For. Rel. 1890, 523.

See, also, Mr. Blaine, Sec. of State, to Mr. Durham, min. to Hayti, Jan. 28, 1892, For. Rel. 1892, 347.

" This Government's uniform and emphatic discouragement of the practice of political asylum has been made known to your legation by repeated instructions. No right to protect such persons, by harboring them or withdrawing them from the territorial jurisdiction of their sovereign, is or can be claimed on behalf of the diplomatic agencies of this Government. It was proper for you to notify the foreign office of the fact of Mr. Dahlgren Lindor's uninvited resort to your legation, but your request for the 'usual courtesy' to permit you to place him on board some outgoing vessel is not understood. If the departure of this or any other Haytian subject is voluntarily permitted by his Government, no propriety in your intervention to put him on board an outgoing vessel is discernible. If the Haytian Government should exercise its evident right to refuse you such permission, you would be placed in a wholly indefensible position. The 'usual courtesy' of which you speak appears to be only another name for the practice of that form of alien protection of the citizens or subjects of the state which this Government condemns. Whatever the result of your request, you should at once notify Mr. Dahlgren Lindor that you can no longer extend to him your personal hospitality. You can most certainly, under your standing instructions, accord him nothing more."

> Mr. Olney, Sec. of State, to Mr. Smythe, min, to Haiti, Feb. 18, 1896, For. Rel. 1896, 381.

In 1899 one Duvivier, who was said to be implicated in a plot to overthrow the Haytian Government, was ordered to be arrested, and some soldiers were sent out to seize him. While fleeing from them he reached the United States legation and ran inside the door, where he was followed and taken by force. Mr. Powell, United States minister at Port au Prince, demanded his return to the legation, and this demand was complied with. Subsequently two other persons sought asylum in the legation, General Cicero François, a military officer under the previous Government, and Seneque Pierre, an ex-member of the senate.

In response to a telegram from Mr. Powell for instructions as to the Duvivier case, the Department of State said: " If newspaper telegrams correctly state Duvivier case, your remonstrance against violation and demand for refugee's return were rightly made. He should be sheltered against all but strictly regular legal process. Should he or any other refugee be demanded on regular warrant, you should decline judicial service upon legation, saying you can only recognize a request made through minister of foreign affairs. If such request be made, refer it to this Department for instructions."

> Mr. Adee, Act. Sec. of State, to Mr. Powell, min. to Haiti, tel., Aug. 3, 1899, For. Rel. 1899, 380 ; see, also, on the same page, a formal despatch of the same date from Mr. Adee to Mr. Powell, amplifying the foregoing views, id. 380.

In August, 1899, Mr. Powell, United States minister at Port au Prince, telegraphed that the Haytian Government had decreed that all refugees then in the legation at Port au Prince should leave the country by the first steamer. At that time there were three refugees, all citizens of Hayti, in the legation.

The Department of State on the 17th of August replied that if any Haytian sheltered in the legation was " amenable to regular justice on a charge of crime or offense," he should be notified that he could no longer be sheltered against the order of expulsion; that the Haytian Government had the right to expel its own citizens, and that they could not be shielded merely as guests; that shelter might be extended to persons under reasonable apprehension of lawless violence, but that the legation could not harbor an accused offender against Haytian law.

Mr. Powell subsequently stated that the Haytians in question were not charged with any crime, but were merely arrested as promoters of discontent, in order that the prevailing apprehensions of disorder might be quieted; and that those who had sought the protection of the legation would leave by the next German steamer on August 22 for St. Thomas and thence to Kingston. With reference to this statement Mr. Hay, on the 2d of September, said: " It is a right of sovereignty, more or less regulated by the constitution or law of the state, to expel from the national territory any citizens or subjects whose presence may be deemed to imperil the public good. The men in question appear from your statements to have been political suspects in this sense, and as such to have taken refuge in your dwelling to escape pursuit. On several occasions in the past your predecessors have exceeded their legitimate rights and functions in demanding and obtaining for this class of persons, natives of the country, permission to quit the territory unmolested—a practice which the Department has uniformly condemned. In this instance the Haytian Government seems to have anticipated some such demand on the part of the foreign representatives, and to have either ordered or permitted—it is not clear which—the departure of the refugees."

The refugees were retained awhile at the request of the Haytian Government, and arrangements were made by the legation for their departure by a French steamer for Cuba on the 6th of September. With reference to this arrangement the Department of State said: " The Department's previous instructions will show that it was here held that the order of expulsion was not executable by the minister of the United States. My telegram of the 17th of August was explicit in directing Mr. Powell to inform the refugees that he could not protect them against the order of expulsion. By this was meant that Mr. Powell should withdraw his protection and request the refugees to leave his premises. It was certainly not intended that he should see that they left the country by the first ship, or make arrangements for their departure, or become in any way responsible for their deportation. . . . It is hoped that Mr. Powell will be able to make the attitude of the United States in this regard clear to the Government of Hayti, and to remove any impression . . . that it was any part of the duty of the minister of the United States in that country to participate in the execution of the order of expulsion."

> Mr. Adee, Acting Sec. of State, to Mr. Powell, min. to Hayti, tel. Aug, 17, 1899, For. Rel. 1899, 386; Mr. Hay, Sec. of State, to Mr. Powell, Sept. 1, 1899, id. 388; same to same, No. 365, Sept. 2, 1899, id. 389; Mr. Adee, Acting Sec. of State, to Mr. Terres, chargé, Sept. 15, 1899, For. Rel. 1899, 392.

" I have received your dispatch No. 151, of the Santo Domingo series, dated August 14, in which you report your refusal of solicited asylum to a Dominican who thereby sought to escape proceedings in extradition upon the demand of the Government of Santo Domingo in virtue of a secret treaty with Hayti for the mutual surrender of political disturbers.

" The reasons leading to your decision appear to have rested mainly on the assumption that the applicant was in fact a conspirator against the peace of Santo Domingo, and might seek to conduct or consummate plots against that Government while enjoying immunity from arrest. You contrast his case with those of the Haytians recently sheltered by you, the latter having been so far as you know not conspirators, but innocent.

" The Department does not think it necessary to discuss the reasons assigned by you for your action in this incident further than to question your capacity to judge of the guilt or innocence of persons applying to you for shelter, and to make your individual impression on this point the basis of your action in your character as the representative of a friendly Government.

" Your course may, however, properly be approved, not for the reasons given by you, but because it is not shown there existed such circumstances of danger from lawless violence as makes it sometimes permissible to afford shelter."

> Mr. Hay, Sec. of State, to Mr. Powell, chargé d'affaires to Santo Domingo, No. 90, Sept. 2, 1899, For. Rel. 1899, 254; MS. Inst. Hayti, IV. 175.
> In his No. 655 of Nov. 11, 1899, Mr. Powell reported an invasion of the premises of Mr. Battiste, deputy United States consul at Port au Prince, by the chief of police and an armed force. It seems that the entire square on which the deputy consul's house was situated, was being searched for a thief, who was supposed to be hiding in that quarter. An application was made to the legation for leave to search the deputy consul's house, but, before an answer was received, the armed force in question arrived, broke down the yard fence, and " alarmingly invaded " the premises. The Department of State instructed Mr. Powell that the immunities of the office of deputy consul did " not include so-called asylum for persons charged with violating the law," and that " no objection could be seen to effecting

the proposed search after notification, and with the sanction and, if necessary, the full assistance of the officers of the legation; " but that he should impress upon the minister of foreign affairs " the obvious circumstance that no time was allowed to the legation to respond in the desired sense," and should express the hope that he might not again be called on to complain of " such offensive disregard of the consideration and official amenities due to the representative agents of the United States at Port au Prince or indeed anywhere else within Haytian jurisdiction." Mr. Powell was also to insist that, as Mr. Battiste's fence had been broken down, any injury done to his property should be made good. (Mr. Hay, Sec. of State, to Mr. Powell, min. to Hayti, Nov. 27, 1899, For. Rel. 1899, 407; MS. Inst. Hayti, IV. 195.)

February 1, 1904, Mr. Villain, American vice-commercial-agent at Samana, was requested by the delegate of the Dominican Government at that place to deliver up the former governor, who had taken refuge in Mr. Villain's office against the persecution of his political opponents. Mr. Villain refused to give him up on grounds of humanity, threats of shooting political prisoners being prevalent. The delegate of the Government then invaded Mr. Villain's house with an armed force, and took away the refugee against Mr. Villain's protest. The Italian consulate was also raided, and eleven refugees were taken out and sent to prison. President Morales, whose followers were in control at Samana, explained that he did not take the refugee from the commercial agency, but from Mr. Villain's country house, for the entry of which he took all legal measures. Mr. Villain stated, however, that he had temporarily established his office in his house. The Government of the United States instructed the legation at Santo Domingo City to say that under the custom prevailing in the Dominican Republic military authorities were not justified in invading consular offices and capturing refugees, and to make proper representations in the case.

For. Rel. 1904, 286–288.

Mr. Hay, Secretary of State, in an instruction to Mr. Powell, chargé d'affaires at Santo Domingo City, No 221, February 17, 1904, said: " While the vice-commercial-agent was perhaps overzealous he was probably justified, under the peculiar custom which prevails in the Dominican Republic, in extending shelter to the refugee." In this relation, Mr. Hay cited a similar case arising in Hayti, as reported in For. Rel. 1873, I. 473. (For. Rel. 1904, 288.)

When the government of President Wos y Gil in Santo Domingo fell in 1903, the ex-President took refuge in the house of Mr. Gosling, the British vice-consul at Santo Domingo City. On Mr. Gosling's request, a guard was furnished him from the U. S. S. *Newport*, and the American diplomatic representative assisted in arranging for General Gil's escort to the wharf on his departure for Porto Rico.

For. Rel. 1904, 327.

(7) MEXICO.

§ 301.

In January, 1877, during the revolution which resulted in the elevation of General Diaz to the Presidency of Mexico, Gen. F. O. Arce, an opponent of Diaz, upon the occupation of Mazatlan by the forces of the latter, took refuge in the American consulate. A few days afterwards, the consul informed the commander of the Diaz forces, Colonel Ramirez, that General Arce was under the protection of the consulate, whereupon the colonel gave assurance that the consulate would be respected. On February 20, Mr. J. W. Foster, then minister of the United States at the City of Mexico, learning that General Arce had taken refuge in the consulate and that there was a possibility of trouble with the military authorities growing out of the fact, wrote as follows: " It is to be borne in mind that the consulate does not possess the right of extraterritoriality, and that while it is an act of humanity to protect defenceless persons from mob violence and hasty revenge, during the transition of governments, it is advisable to avoid giving permanent protection to political refugees, and thus prevent conflicts with the local authorities."

It turned out that before these instructions were written a body of armed men had, in the absence of the consul and without his knowledge and consent, taken General Arce from the consulate, and that Colonel Ramirez, upon the complaint of the consul, had promised to restore General Arce and punish the officer making the arrest. But as the captive was not returned, and no steps were taken toward reparation, Mr. Foster presented the facts to the minister for foreign affairs, who subsequently informed him that instructions had been sent to the military commandant at Mazatlan to make a report of the affair, and assured him " that the Government would not fail to punish any officer who should be found wanting in courtesy to the consul or to his flag." The case does not appear again, and it is probable that nothing more was done; indeed, before the matter was presented to the minister for foreign affairs, General Arce called upon Mr. Foster, having arrived in the City of Mexico under his parole to report as a prisoner to President Diaz.[a]

(8) PARAGUAY.

§ 302.

Under the rule of F. S. Lopez in Paraguay, the years 1867 and 1868 present a scene of exceptional disorder, aggravated by a war waged against that country by the allied forces of Brazil, the Argentine

---

[a] Mr. Foster, min. to Mexico, to Mr. Evarts, Sec. of State, March 23, 1877, For. Rel. 1877, 398–400.

Republic, and Venancio Flores, the invader of Uruguay. On October 14, 1867, Mr. Washburn, then minister of the United States at Asuncion, apprehending that Lopez might order the city to be evacuated, said: "Should the evacuation of the town be ordered . . . , it is uncertain whether the foreigners will or will not be permitted to remain. If they are not, I apprehend that many will ask admission to my premises and request protection, which it would be hard to refuse and might be embarrassing to grant. As against the enemy, however, I have not hesitated to say that this legation will give whatever protection it can to whosoever, save notorious criminals, may resort to it in time of danger."

Replying on January 14, 1868, Mr. Seward, then Secretary of State, said: " Your intention to afford an asylum in the legation to those who may resort to it, save notorious criminals, as far as it can be done without compromising your neutral character or that of your country, is approved." [a]

On the approach of the Brazilian fleet in February the evacuation of the city was ordered. Mr. Washburn, however, refused to leave, and many persons applied to him for shelter. Numbers were turned away, but he received about thirty of various nationalities, among whom were two Americans named Manlove and Bliss and an Englishman named Masterman. On February 22 Mr. Washburn informed the minister of foreign relations that the critical condition of affairs in and near the capital had rendered it necessary for him to take into his " service " several persons in addition to those previously connected with the legation, at the same time transmitting a list of all those then " employed " by him.[b] On this list were Manlove and Bliss. To this communication the minister of foreign relations replied on the following day. Adverting to the fact that the city had been transformed into a military post, subject to the orders of its commander, he declined to recognize Manlove and Bliss as members of the legation. In order to " avoid unpleasant incidents " they might, he said, remain in the legation building; but they could not be allowed to go out, lest they might be arrested by the guards, who had " orders not to let any persons but public officials go about." [c] On the 24th of February Mr. Washburn wrote another note, saying that he had omitted to specify Masterman as one of the persons attached to the legation and including his name with those previously transmitted.[d] This note, however, was not delivered till the 4th of the ensuing April.[e] On the 3d of March Manlove, while riding on horseback

[a] Mr. Seward, Sec. of State, to Mr. Washburn, min. to Paraguay, Jan. 14, 1868, Dip. Cor. 1868, II. 652.

[b] Dip. Cor. 1868, II. 658.

[c] Dip. Cor. 1868, II. 659.

[d] Ibid.

[e] Dip. Cor. 1868, II. 665.

through the streets of Asuncion, was arrested for a breach of military regulations, but escaped after a violent colloquy with the authorities. A few days later he was again arrested on the street for another violation of military regulations and held as a prisoner. Mr. Washburn demanded his release, but when the authorities refused to grant it, discontinued the discussion and referred the correspondence to his Government, at the same time declaring that the arrest of Manlove appeared to be " a great affront " to the legation, " if not a direct violation of its rights." *a* No representations on the subject, however, appear to have been made by the Department of State.*b*

On the 20th of June the minister of foreign relations officially inquired of Mr. Washburn whether Senhor Leite Pereira, a Portuguese subject, was in the legation, and if so, why he remained there. He also requested a list of all persons who, without belonging to the legation, were sheltered in it.*c* Mr. Washburn, while disclaiming any " obligation, except as a matter of courtesy," to respond to inquiries pertaining " to the internal affairs " of the legation, stated that Leite Pereira, who had formerly acted as consul of the King of Portugal, came to the legation with his wife on the 16th of June " in the quality of guests," though he added: " Of his motives in coming here I am not further informed than that they are founded on the representations of Mr. Cuberville, at present in charge of the French consulate." Mr. Washburn also furnished a list of twenty-eight persons of various nationalities in the legation, not mentioned

---

a Dip. Cor. 1868, II. 657, 658, 659–666.

b The circumstances under which Manlove was admitted to the legation of the United States by a man of such high character as Mr. Washburn forcibly illustrate the liability of asylum to abuse. According to Mr. Washburn, Manlove was an adventurer who, after serving in the army of the Confederacy in the civil war in the United States, made his way to the scene of conflict in South America, where he succeeded by a ruse in getting through the lines of the allies and sought service under Lopez. His design, which was made known to Mr. Washburn before it was presented to Lopez, was to obtain from the latter blank commissions duly signed and executed, and, returning with them to the United States, to fit out cruisers to prey upon the commerce of Brazil as the *Alabama* and other Confederate cruisers obtained in England had preyed upon the commerce of the United States. As this projected violation of the neutrality laws of the United States was communicated to him in confidence, Mr. Washburn, while discouraging it as not likely to succeed, thought he should abstain from revealing it. Lopez, when the plan was presented to him, locked Manlove up as a spy and deliberated several weeks on having him shot; but in the end he was released and his expenses were paid to Asuncion. When the order was issued to evacuate the city, Manlove was, it would seem, without justifiable cause and most unfortunately, received into the legation of the United States, which Mr. Washburn declared to be " for the time United States territory." (Washburn's History of Paraguay, Vol. II. pp. 216–223.)

c Dip. Cor. 1868, II. 726.

in his note of February 24 as belonging to it.[a] On June 27 the minister of foreign relations wrote that Leite Pereira was " sheltered in the legation of the United States in contravention of all governmental regulations," and asked that, as he was " accused " and must " appear before the proper tribunal," he be delivered to the police officer who would present himself at the legation two hours after the delivery of the note.[b] When the officer appeared, Mr. Washburn refused to comply with the minister's request, but promised to answer his note on the following day. In his answer, dated June 28, Mr. Washburn, arguing upon the immunities of legations and citing the statement of Vattel that for persons charged with " ordinary transgressions," and often " rather unfortunate than criminal," the house of an ambassador might well serve as an asylum, said: " Under such circumstances I most respectfully request that the specific charges against Mr. Leite Pereira may be made known to me, when, if they shall be of the grave character that shall require it, he will be advised that this legation can no longer give him an asylum."[c]

On July 11 the minister of foreign relations addressed to Mr. Washburn an extended review of the correspondence and of the circumstances out of which it arose. In answer to Mr. Washburn's quotation from Vattel, he cites a subsequent passage of the same writer, in which it is declared that " it belongs to the sovereign to decide, on occasion, how far the right of asylum, which an ambassador claims as belonging to his house, is to be respected; and if the question relates to an offender whose arrest or punishment is of great importance to the state, the prince is not to be withheld by the consideration of a privilege which was never granted for the detriment and ruin of states." [d]

It was in view of this passage, the minister said, that he had requested that " Leite Pereira should be placed in the hands of justice." He also referred to the fact that the motive originally assigned for permitting the legation to be used as an asylum, was the approach of the Brazilian fleet, and that it was " nearly five months since the two hostile vessels appeared and were momentarily in the port of Asuncion." " Since that time," he continued, " disagreeable circumstances have occurred between this ministry and the legation of your excellency through the provocations given by your refugees, and, nevertheless, not one of them has left that residence in fulfilment of the orders of the Government, and on the contrary,

---

[a] Dip. Cor. 1868, II. 726–727.

[b] Dip. Cor. 1868, II. 727.

[c] Mr. Washburn, min. to Paraguay, to Señor Benitez, min. of for. aff., June 28 1868, Dip. Cor. 1868, II. 728, citing Vattel, book iv., c. 9, sec. 118.

[d] Señor Benitez, min. of for. aff., to Mr. Washburn, U. S. min., July 11, 1868, Dip. Cor. 1868, II. 730, citing Vattel, book iv., c. 9, sec. 118.

others are received, as is proved by your notes. . . . Laying aside, then, the question of the residence of your excellency in Asuncion, where there are no objects of diplomatic attention,[a] I proceed to state to you that the ostensible motive of the asylum given by the American legation having ceased, that asylum must also cease, especially since it has begun to seriously affect the military regulations of the post and the most precise orders of the Government. . . . In attention to what has been stated, I request you will please dismiss from your hotel to-morrow, before sunset, the said Leite Pereira, as well as all the other individuals who, not belonging to the legation, are at present in it, some as guests and others in other capacities, as your excellency expresses it."

When the demand of the minister of foreign relations was made known in the legation, all to whom it was intended to apply went away, except Bliss and Masterman. On July 13 the minister of foreign relations asked that they, too, be dismissed, since they were " accused of crimes not less grave than the others whose dismissal " had been required.[b] Mr. Washburn declined to dismiss them, on the ground that he would be abdicating his functions and rights as minister if he acknowledged that the Government might ask for the surrender of persons whom he considered as members of his legation. He said that Masterman had come to reside in the legation as a medical attendant in the preceding September, and that when the list of February 24 of persons belonging to the legation was transmitted to the Government on the 4th of the ensuing April, no objection was made to his inclusion in it. As to Bliss, who was included in the list of February 22 as well as in that of February 24, it was admitted that the Government had promptly refused, on the 23d of that month, to recognize him as belonging to the legation, and had announced that he must confine himself to the legation premises, since he would be liable to arrest if found outside of them. " For the last three months," said Mr. Washburn, Bliss had scrupulously observed this injunction, and, besides, had been of great assistance to him in his official duties.[c] It seems that Bliss, who possessed considerable knowledge of languages, was a roving literary hack, and that both he and Masterman had been to some extent in the employ of the Government before they took up their residence in the legation.[d] The minister of foreign relations, alleging that the two men were implicated in a conspiracy against the Government and were sheltered as criminals, refused to recognize Mr. Washburn's claims in regard to them, and demanded their expulsion or delivery.[e] Mr. Washburn still refused to yield,

---

[a] The note of the minister of foreign relations is dated at Luque, where the Government then was.

[b] Dip. Cor. 1868, II. 740.

[c] Dip. Cor. 1868, II. 741.

[d] Dip. Cor. 1868, II. 745, 831.

[e] Dip. Cor. 1868, II. 742–745.

though he promised, as they were charged with holding communication with persons outside, to keep them as close prisoners in the legation till he could send them out of the country, or till such time as the Government should not object to their being set at liberty. Under these circumstances they were not disturbed in the legation.[a] But they were seized while accompanying Mr. Washburn to the United States man-of-war *Wasp*, in order to depart with him out of the country.[b]

On September 26, 1868, Mr. Washburn, who had resigned and was then on his way to the United States, sent to the Department of State from Buenos Ayres a despatch in which, besides describing the deplorable condition of affairs in Paraguay, he said: " Lopez pretended, some three or four months ago, to have discovered some sort of a conspiracy, and after arresting almost all the foreigners, demanded of me that I should deliver up to the tribunals those who had sought asylum in my house at the time the Brazilian fleet went to Asuncion in February last. To defend these men and save them [c] from the clutches of Lopez, I had a correspondence with the Government long enough to make a volume of diplomatic despatches. It was all in vain, however. They all had to go; though none, except Bliss and Masterman, were taken by force."

Owing to the situation in Paraguay, this despatch of September 26 conveyed to the Department of State the first report from Mr. Washburn as to the affairs of his legation since the 17th of the preceding April. Apart from describing Bliss and Masterman as "members" of the legation, all the information it afforded as to their seizure and the abandonment of the legation by other individuals, was that contained in the passage above quoted. The correspondence to which it refers and from which the narrative of those incidents has been derived was transmitted with a despatch from Buenos Ayres, October 5, 1868. On the 18th of November, the despatch of September 26, but not that of October 5, having been received at Washington, Rear-Admiral Davis was ordered to Paraguay to take such measures as might be found necessary " to prevent violence to the lives and property of American citizens there, and, in the exercise of a sound discretion, to demand and obtain prompt redress for any extreme insult or violence that may have been arbitrarily committed against the flag of the United States or their citizens." [d]

---

[a] Dip. Cor. 1868, II. 745–815.

[b] Dip. Cor. 1868, II. 670, 826.

[c] In writing this account, Mr. Washburn evidently overlooked the case of Leite Pereira, who was received into the legation June 16, 1868.

[d] Dip. Cor. 1868, II. 689.

In a letter to the Secretary of the Navy, preceding the issuance of this order, Mr. Seward says: " Mr. Washburn's despatch conclusively shows that the situation of all foreigners, including United States citizens, at Asuncion, is greatly imperilled, and that, especially, Porter C. Bliss and George F. Masterman, United States citizens,[a] lately in some way connected with the United States legation, have suffered personal violence and have perhaps been murdered." At the same time Mr. Seward stated that the merits of the controversy could not be understood until the correspondence should have been received; and it was for this reason that the admiral was invested with such general discretion. [b]

When Admiral Davis sailed from Buenos Ayres for Asuncion he took with him General Martin T. McMahon, Mr. Washburn's successor, who had set out for his post in September. In a despatch dated on the United States flagship *Wasp*, off Angostura Batteries, Paraguay, December 11, 1868, General McMahon reports what had transpired. Immediately on arriving off the Batteries on the third of December, Admiral Davis addressed a note to President Lopez, stating that the American minister was on board, and saying: " As an indispensable preliminary step to the presentation by General McMahon to your excellency of his credential letter, I have to request that Messrs. Bliss and Masterman, the persons arrested and detained in Asuncion while under the protection and attached to the legation of the previous United States minister, be restored to the authority of the United States flag." In an interview with the admiral held on shore later in the day, President Lopez urged that Bliss and Masterman were guilty of serious crimes and were not members in good faith of the United States legation, and that they were then actually undergoing trial; nevertheless, confiding in the justice of the American Government, he said he would deliver them up, though he requested the admiral to withdraw his assertion that they were under the protection of and attached to the legation, lest it might seem that the point had been conceded. On the 4th of December the admiral withdrew his first note and substituted another, in which he omitted all reference to the American minister and merely requested the delivery of the prisoners as " individuals," without reference to their status. On these terms Bliss and Masterman were, after further correspondence intended by the Government of Paraguay to save all its contentions, surrendered with expressions of amity on both sides.[c]

It is remarkable, as affecting both the practice of asylum and the expediency of giving it countenance, that, while it was the principal source of Mr. Washburn's difficulties, neither the instructions of Mr.

a As has been seen, it turned out that Masterman was an Englishman.
b Dip. Cor. 1868, II. 687.
c Dip. Cor. 1868, II. 691–696.

Seward nor the subsequent correspondence complain of the refusal of
the Paraguayan Government to permit its continuance, though among
those who were forced to abandon the legation were several American
citizens.   It was only in behalf of Bliss and Masterman, the one an
American and the other an Englishman, who were not arrested in
the legation but outside of it, that redress was asked by Admiral
Davis; and in their case the claim of official connection with the legation, whether rightly or wrongly alleged, carried with it the assertion
of the personal immunity which the diplomatic character generally
confers.   It may also be observed that from the time Leite Pereira
came to the legation it was closely policed, probably fifty men, as Mr.
Washburn stated, being kept on guard day and night.[a]

(9) PERU.

§ 303.

" I have to acknowledge the receipt of your despatches to No. 180,
inclusive.   Those numbered 170, 177, and 180 refer particularly to
events of a serious character that had occurred within the precincts of
the consulate at Tumbez, involving, to a certain degree, as you have
presumed, the rights of the consul and the dignity of this Government.   From the despatch referred to, the following facts are
gathered:

"A Peruvian citizen, Don Domingo Elias (who had been imprisoned by his Government for incendiary publications against the President, but who was subsequently released), taking advantage of the
hostile relations with Bolivia, enlisted a party of followers in support
of his revolutionary schemes, and on the morning of the 21 October
approached Tumbez with the object of attacking the city.   Having
entered the town the party was passing in front of the United States
consulate, when it was attacked by the national guard and in a very
brief time defeated.   Don Domingo and nine others then took refuge
in the consulate, whither they were pursued by the soldiers of the
guard, and fired upon, with the effect of killing one of the followers
of Elias, and endangering the lives of the consul's family and of many
women and children who had taken refuge there.   At length the
firing ceased, and the house was surrounded by a guard, in spite of
which, however, Don Domingo escaped on the night of the 22d.

---

[a] Dip. Cor. 1868, II. 833, 834.   See Davis, Life of Charles Henry Davis, Rear-
Admiral, 321–330.

See, also, Mr. Seward, Sec. of State, to Mr. McMahon, min. to Paraguay, Jan.
23, 1869, MS. Inst. Paraguay, I. 136; Mr. Fish, Sec. of State, to Mr. McMahon,
min to Paraguay, Sept. 2, 1869, MS. Inst. Paraguay, I. 143.   Both these instructions express general approval of Mr. McMahon's course.

" It further appears that on the 26th October Señor Benavides, the governor of the province, arrived at Tumbez; that he sent for Consul Oakford, and during the interview which followed treated him in a most insulting manner; demanding the surrender of Don Domingo and threatening, in case of his refusing compliance, to send him to Lima in irons; declaring that the comandante of the town should have battered the consulate to the ground, with many other equally gross and violent remarks, uttered in the presence of a crowd, with the evident intention of making the insult as public as possible. Subsequently the governor moderated his tone, and reiterated his demand for the delivery of the refugees and their arms. The consul agreed to deliver the latter, but refused to surrender the former. Upon his return to his house, he was followed by the comandante, to whom were delivered the arms of the insurgents. At a second visit on the same day, the comandante demanded the men; this was refused. Within an hour or two the governor sent a written and peremptory demand for them, to which the consul replied as he had already done.

"After receiving this reply the comandante appeared at the consulate with a number of soldiers and said, in behalf of the governor, that he had come to take the men by force, and, the consul having stated that he could not resist as he had not the means of doing so, the refugees were taken by the officers and dragged from the consulate.

" In view of these outrageous proceedings you deemed it proper to demand, as you did by a note to the minister of foreign affairs of of the 5th December, in substance:

" 1. That the authorities at Tumbez should go officially to the house of the consul and publicly apologize to him for the attack on his residence of the 21st October, and

" 2. That Governor Benavides should also publicly apologize for his insult to the consul, and that he should be removed from office, and that such other satisfaction should be rendered as this Government might require. To these demands the minister has replied that Don Domingo and his followers fired from the consulate upon the authorities, and that the consul had allowed his house to be used as *a fort*, and these allegations are sustained by the testimony of Don Isadore Elias (a brother of Don Domingo) and Don Manuel Quintana, both of whom were of the party of refugees, and whose declarations were taken subsequently to their delivery to the Peruvian authorities. The minister's note closes by expressing the hope that the Government of the United States will disapprove of the conduct of the consul, and charge him to abstain from similar acts, while it will recommend to the governor that he should use less violent language in his interviews with the consul.

" You have determined not to accept this as a satisfactory arrangement of the differences at issue; and at the date of your last despatch intended to announce this determination to the minister.

" The Department does not concur in the view you have taken of this affair.

" Neither the law of nations nor the stipulations of our treaty with Peru recognizes the right of consuls to afford protection to those who have rendered themselves obnoxious to the authority of the government under which they dwell. And in a case so flagrant as that now under consideration it may be doubted whether even a high diplomatic functionary would be justified in casting the protection of his flag around those who were engaged in the commission of the highest crime recognized among civilized nations. It can not be questioned that the object of Don Domingo's band was rebellion and revolution. His character, as delineated in your 159, appears to be that of an active, ambitious and unscrupulous aspirant for power. To attain his end, it appears that in 1844 ' he seized upon the Government,' and his subsequent career seems to indicate a determination to subvert the existing order of affairs, with a view to his own elevation. But recently released from prison, to which he had been consigned for his incendiary publications, he endeavors to enlist an armed force to effect the accomplishment of his plans. There could be no doubt, therefore, as to the intention of himself and his followers. That their approach was expected and that it was regarded with terror by the helpless inhabitants of the town is proven by the fact stated by Consul Oakford, that his house was filled with women and children who had sought safety there. Had there been any doubt of the guilty intention of Don Domingo and his followers, the sympathies of the consul might with some reason have been enlisted in their behalf. Had they been unarmed men quietly traversing the streets and suddenly attacked by cruel and brutal soldiers, it would have been the dictate of a prompt and generous humanity to offer them an asylum, at all risks. But this Department sees no ground of the character adverted to to justify Consul Oakford's mistaken use of official prerogatives to screen the disturbers of peace from the necessary consequences of their acts.

" The defeated party, having sought protection in the consulate, were followed and fired upon by the soldiers of the town. At this point there is a marked discrepancy between Mr. Oakford's statement and that of Mr. James Houghton, whose affirmation before Consul Ringgold is the only account of the affair concurring generally in that of Mr. Oakford, with which the Department is furnished. The consul says that, as the party of Don Domingo entered his house, he took from every man his arms, which he noticed were loaded, and removed the caps from the locks; *therefore* it is impossible that any shots should have been fired from those in his house upon the soldiers in the street. This statement of the consul is directly at variance with the declaration of the Peruvian refugees to which the minister of foreign affairs has referred. It differs also from the testimony of Mr. Houghton, who, on the other hand, alleges that he was in the consulate on the morning of the 26th October, six days *after* the insurgents entered it, and he ' saw the consul enter his house followed by the governor of the town, and several Peruvian officers armed—that the governor demanded of the consul certain arms supposed to have belonged to several persons then under the protection of the United States consul. *The consul then requested these persons to deliver up their arms, which they did,* and the officers then left the house with said arms.'

" But, waiving for a moment the question as to the consul's right to afford protection to the defeated insurgents, after the heat of the engagement, it was his duty to deliver them to the Peruvian authorities upon demand. He was not the proper judge of their case; their offence was not against the laws of the United States, but against those of Peru, and to the properly recognized officers of that Republic they should have been surrendered. He says he feared they would be taken out and summarily shot. Such an apprehension on his part would have justified him in making every proper effort as an individual, in averting their fate; it would even have sanctioned his exertions to secure, if it had been possible, the pledge of the governor that they should not be harshly dealt with; but it did not justify him in stepping between the offended laws of Peru and the due administration of justice by the constituted authorities of a friendly government.

" The rudeness and insults addressed by Governor Benavides to the consul were inexcusable and ought to be atoned for; it is not surprising, however, that he should have been betrayed into an intemperate warmth of language by the interference of Consul Oakford in the discharge of duties with which he had been entrusted, and for which he and not the consul was accountable.

" The subsequent course of the governor, in sending to the consulate and arresting the insurgents, can not be condemned by this Government. The national flag was not insulted, nor the national dignity affected by this proceeding. The former had been unwarrantably used; under the treaty it would and should have protected the property of the consulate, and the persons and property of American citizens, but in this case no such plea for its use can be presented. The Government of the United States would not permit such an abuse of a foreign flag by a foreign consul to be made with impunity.

" The conduct of the consul is regarded by this Department as censurable in the highest degree, tending, if not disavowed by this Government, to impair our friendly relations with Peru, and establishing a precedent which would inevitably lead to consequences of a disastrous nature on the recurrence of similar events.

" You are instructed therefore to communicate to the minister of foreign relations the disapproval of this Government of Consul Oakford's course."

> Mr. Marcy, Sec. of State, to Mr. Clay, min. to Peru, Jan. 24, 1854, MS. Inst. Peru, XV. 126.

January 23, 1855, the Government of Peru, which had been installed by revolution on the 5th of the month, addressed to the diplomatic corps a circular containing a decree to the effect that " the ex-generals and all the refugees in the legations or on the foreign vessels " should " leave the Republic for the Isthmus of Panama, or go by that route." The minister of the United States replied that as foreign legations were " entirely extraterritorial," and as the Government of Peru had no jurisdiction either over them or over foreign vessels of war lying in her ports, he presumed that the object of the circular " was to notify the Peruvian citizens *in asylum* in this legation that they should prepare to leave the Republic," and was not intended " to affect or in any manner diminish the privileges secured to the undersigned by the law of nations." [a] The British minister, " as an act of pure courtesy," wrote that " the only refugee in the legation of Her Britannic Majesty was General Echenique, who left on yesterday's steamer; " but he also commented upon the " unbecoming tone of command " that pervaded the circular, and declared that he did " not admit that the provisional government of Peru " had " the right to issue orders on subjects which concern Her Britannic Majesty's legation, or the commanders of her war vessels." Of the same purport was the reply of the French minister, who, however, further informed his excellency that he should ask him " at the proper time," to give the refugees in the French legation a sum of money sufficient " to take them abroad " and a " passport without designation." The minister of Brazil, while deploring that " the necessity should exist in Peru of having recourse to the exercise of the right of asylum established in times when misfortune had need of every species of guarantees against the barbarity of the middle ages," declined, without consulting his Government, to enter into a discussion of the right in question, which had been " officially recognized and constantly respected by all the governments " in Peru since its independence. If the present Government, he continued, desired to introduce changes,

---

[a] Lawrence's Wheaton (1863), note 137.

he would communicate the fact to his Government; meanwhile, he was obliged to inform his excellency "that, whatever be these changes, they can not take effect without the previous accord of the whole diplomatic body, which enjoys them as an acquired right; as it does not seem conformable to the laws of equity that the present refugees should be treated with greater severity than their predecessors in misfortune." He therefore declined, as his colleagues had done, to give his refugees the directions contained in the decree.[a]

Ten years later the question of asylum arose again in Peru. In May, 1865, General Canseco, then engaged in an attempt to overthrow the government of General Pezet, was sheltered in the house of Mr. Robinson, the American minister. The Peruvian Government having protested against this act, the diplomatic corps agreed on the following points: (1) That apart from inhibitions in their instructions or in conventional stipulations, there were limits to the privilege of asylum which the prudence of diplomatic agents ought to counsel; (2) that the diplomatic corps adopted the instructions given by Brazil to its minister, according to which asylum was to be conceded with the greatest reserve, and only for such time as was necessary in order that the fugitive should secure his safety in another manner—an end which it was the duty of the diplomatic agent to do all in his power to accomplish. It was also agreed that these rules, which, in the absence of authoritative instructions, were adopted provisionally, should apply only to offences properly called political. The Peruvian Government declined to accept these conclusions, objecting with great force that, as they left everything to the discretion of the diplomatic agent, they afforded no solution of the difficulty then existing.[b]

In the following October a new minister of the United States, Mr. A. P. Hovey, set out for Peru, with instructions to recognize only the government of General Pezet, and if, when he arrived at the Peruvian capital, he found the revolutionary party in power there, to report the facts and await further directions.[c] On the 6th of November, a few days before Mr. Hovey's arrival at Lima, General Canseco, who seems to have had a safe deliverance from the American legation, captured the city and assumed control, only to be displaced in three weeks by Colonel Prado, who, at the instigation of certain officers of the army, was proclaimed dictator.[d] When defeated at Lima, General Pezet, with some of his ministers, fled to Callao and escaped on foreign men-of-war.[e] Four of his cabinet, however, sought asylum

[a] Bello, ed. 1883, II. Note HH, pp. 332, 381.

[b] Pradier-Fodéré, Cours de Droit Diplomatique, II. 79.

[c] Dip. Cor. 1866, part 2, p. 617.

[d] Id. 621.

[e] Id. 618.

in the French legation, where they remained unmolested till near the close of December. On the 19th of that month the central court decreed their arrest on charges of peculation, conspiracy, and treason, and the Government subsequently requested M. Vion, consul of France and *chargé d'affaires ad interim*, to deliver them up, which he refused to do. Admitting that the privilege of asylum had been abused, he declared that its benefits " amply compensated for a fault inspired by the sentiments of humanity." [a]

On December 20, 1865, Mr. Hovey informed his Government that several applications for asylum had been made to him by Peruvian citizens charged with crime against the Republic, and that he had refused to grant them.[b] He added: "A different practice has prevailed in Peru, and the houses of foreign ministers have become little less than the abode of criminals who flee from the vengeance of the law. It seems to me that this practice is highly censurable and leads to very evil consequences. . . . I have refused to recognize the doctrine of asylum as practised in this country, until I am otherwise directed by the Department of State."[c]

The receipt of Mr. Hovey's despatch was acknowledged without comment, and upon this implied approval he acted till his position was expressly sanctioned.[d]

In consequence of Peru's war with Spain, the discussion thus begun was interrupted for more than a year. But on January 15, 1867, a conference of the diplomatic corps was held, at the summons and under the presidency of the minister of foreign affairs, Señor Pacheco. All the members of the corps were present but Mr. Hovey, who, though unable to attend, on the same day communicated his views to Señor Pacheco in writing, as follows:

I believe that Peru is entitled to all the rights and privileges of a Christian nation, and as such should be placed precisely in the position of the United States, France, England, and other Christian countries, and that the doctrine of asylum can not be properly claimed or enforced here unless it be to shield persons from the violence of a mob. As soon as a legal charge of crime is made, whether political or not, I hold it to be the duty of the minister in whose legation the offending party has taken refuge to deliver him up to the legal authorities demanding his arrest. . . . Notwithstanding this view, if the Government of Peru should feel disposed to concede greater privileges to others, I, as the representative of my Government, would expect to be entitled to the same privileges granted them. In conclusion, I would briefly say, while I have the honor to represent my country, I shall claim no right here that my Government would not accord to the representative of Peru in Washington.[e]

---

[a] Pradier-Fodéré, Cours, II. 80 et seq.

[b] He cited as authority for his action: Wheaton, § 18, p. 416; Woolsey, Int. Law, § 92 b; Polson, Law of Nations, § 31.

[c] Dip. Cor. 1866, part 2, p. 624.

[d] Dip. Cor. 1866, part 2, 629; Id. 1867, part 2, 736.

[e] Dip. Cor. 1867, Part II, p. 738.

At the conference Señor Pacheco presented this communication and, arguing that " the right of asylum was introduced in Spanish America on the pretext of a pretended humanity," asked that it should be abolished. M. E. P. de Lesseps, chargé d'affaires of France, replied that the meeting was called to consider the regulation of the right, and that he was not empowered to discuss its abolition. The conference then broke up. The instructions of M. de Lesseps, which proceeded from M. Drouyn de Lhuys, French minister of foreign affairs, were to the effect that since the right of asylum only facilitated the departure from the country of men who could not remain in it without peril both to themselves and to the government, it was too conformable to the sentiments of humanity for France to forego it; especially as it appeared by the agreement of the diplomatic corps at Lima of May, 1865,[a] in which the European and a majority of the American representatives concurred, that the right was generally admitted in America, if exercised within the limits of prudence and good faith.[b]

On the 21st of January the diplomatic corps held a meeting to consider what further steps should be taken before conferring again with the Peruvian Government. At this meeting Mr. Hovey proposed the following resolutions:

1. The diplomatic body here assembled resolve that they, and each of them, jointly and severally, acknowledge and recognize Peru as a Christian nation.

2. As each Christian nation should, by international law, be entitled to all of the rights properly claimed by others, therefore—*Resolved:* That Peru is entitled to the same rights and privileges, through her diplomatic agents abroad, that we, as representatives near the Government of Peru, are respectively entitled to have, and that we can not in justice claim more than our respective Governments accord to the representatives of Peru.

3. *Resolved, therefore,* That we recognize the law of nations, as relating to the question of asylum, to be the same as practised in the United States, and in England, France, and other Christian nations of Europe.

The diplomatic corps did not accept these resolutions, but in reporting the fact to the Department of State Mr. Hovey made a statement which is so significant that it is worth while to quote the following passage:

I do not believe that the history of Peru can furnish a single example where the innocent have been shielded by asylum; nearly all the cases of which I have heard are those applying strictly to citizens of Peru charged with conspiracy or treason. One case, that of Captain Carwell, an Englishman, turned upon the point of his contempt of court in an order made for the delivery of property. Refusing to obey the warrant of the court, he fled for protection to the English legation, from whence, after eleven months, he made his escape, still refusing to obey the orders of the court, and taking with him the property

---

[a] Supra, p. 836.
[b] Pradier-Fodéré, Cours, II. 79–83.

in dispute. Another case, which transpired shortly before my arrival, was that of General Canseco, Vice-President of the Republic, charged with conspiracy against the Government; he remained in the legation of the United States some three or four months, where he was in daily communication with his coconspirators. At length he agreed with President Pezet to exile himself to Chile upon the payment of one year's salary; he received the pay, was permitted to depart, landed in two days upon the coast of Peru, and a few weeks afterwards returned with an invading army to the walls of Lima. The third case involves the question now pending between France and Peru. . . . As no person arrested by the Government upon any charge has as yet suffered the extreme penalty, it is apparent that the plea of cruelty or barbarity can not be sustained as the cause for giving asylum. Peruvians were dealing with Peruvians, and should, in my opinion, have been left to their own laws and courts. The practice of giving asylum has been and still is a prolific source of revolutions in and the instability of the South American republics. . . . If there should be a single unfriendly minister to the Government here (and there always is), his legation at once becomes the asylum and headquarters for the conspirators against the Government. . . . In my opinion, that man will prove a benefactor to South America who breaks down this ancient relic of barbarism and aids in bringing the guilty to the quick punishment of the laws against which they may have offended. . . . It need not be feared that the innocent would suffer; these people are peculiarly mild in their punishments, and crime is not as common in Lima (excepting conspiracy) as it is in Europe or in the United States. Since I have resided here not a single execution has taken place, although five or six several attempts have been made to revolutionize the Government or kill the President.[a]

" I observe that . . . you have taken these positions, viz,: That Peru is entitled to all the rights and privileges of a Christian nation, and as such should be placed precisely in the position of the United States, France, England and other Christian countries, and that the doctrine of asylum cannot be properly claimed or enforced in Peru, unless it be in exceptional cases recognized by the universal law of nations; that as soon as a legal charge of crime is made, whether political or not, you hold it to be the duty of the minister in whose legation an offending party has taken refuge to leave him without interference to the authorities demanding his arrest. Again, that you claim no diplomatic power or right in Peru that your Government does not accord to the representative of Peru at Washington.

" These positions are altogether approved."

> Mr. Seward, Sec. of State, to Mr. Hovey, min. to Peru, Feb. 25, 1867, Dip. Cor. 1867, II. 763, 764.
>
> On the 29th of January another conference with the Peruvian Government was held, Señor Pacheco presiding. There were also present

---

[a] Dip. Cor. 1867, part 2, pp. 736, 737. As an example of the "more than Christian charity" of the Peruvians in their political contests, Mr. Hovey transmitted to Mr. Seward, June 28, 1867, a law of the Congress ordering the remains of Grand Marshal Ramon Castilla, who died on the 30th of May while at the head of a rebellion against the Government, to be brought to Lima and deposited in a mausoleum of marble for which 16,000 soles were appropriated. (Id. 771.)

Mr. Hovey; Mr. Barton, acting chargé d'affaires of Great Britain; M. de Lesseps, chargé d'affaires of France; Signor Cavalchini, minister resident of Italy; Mr. Eldridge, chargé d'affaires of Hawaii; Señor Benavente, envoy of Bolivia; Señor Martinez, envoy of Chile; Senhor Varnhagen, minister resident of Brazil. Senhor Varnhagen said he would not contend that asylum was a right, nor would he discriminate between American and European nations. But as a diplomatic agent in Europe, he had observed that asylum had been granted in revolutionary periods in Spain, Italy, and Portugal, and even in France during the revolution of 1848, probably with the effect of preventing acts of inhumanity. A declaration abolishing it would destroy diplomatic inviolability, which would also be endangered by denying asylum in a special case. Serious questions might sometimes arise between foreign ministers and the secretary of foreign affairs, depending on the more or less conciliatory character of the latter. He thought, therefore, that asylum should be maintained as a practice in order to avoid greater difficulties.

Señor Martinez, acting under the instructions of his Government, abstained from discussing principles and limited himself to the consideration of asylum as a humane usage, which had its origin in political agitations that excited the passions. It had frequently happened that when those who had been in asylum were leaving it to occupy high stations, those who had been in power were obliged to seek shelter under the diplomatic roof. Nevertheless, the Government of Chile, though convinced that the practice of asylum had been abused and that it caused unpleasant discussions with foreign ministers, had deemed it advisable not to abolish the custom altogether, but to regulate it by fixed principles and confine it to certain cases, particularly to those in which the life of the refugee was endangered.

M. de Lesseps said that it was necessary before all things to save the principles of inviolability and extraterritoriality. If it was intended to deny the principle of inviolability and admit the possibility of violence against the house of a minister, he did not feel authorized to enter into the discussion.[a]

Señor Benavente was authorized to concur in the regulation of asylum, but not in its abolition. He said that, according to the assertions of MM. Varnhagen, Cavalchini, and de Lesseps, the practice was known in Spain, Portugal, and Italy, and that Signor Cavalchini knew of a case of temporary asylum in the United States during the civil war.

Mr. Hovey replied that the practice did not exist in the United States, and that if a case had occurred and the Government had demanded the delivery of the transgressor, he would have been given up. If a special custom had existed in Peru, it could be a subject of discussion between the Government of the country and the foreign ministers; but

---

[a] It is obvious that the argument presented by Senhor Varnhagen and M. de Lesseps involved a confusion of ideas. This is suggested later by Señor Pacheco, and has heretofore been demonstrated in the discussion of general principles. There is no logical connection between the exemption of the house of a minister from violence and the concession to him of a right to protect offenders against the demands of the lawful authorities. The confusion on this subject, as has heretofore been explained, arises from a misconception of the origin and nature of the immunities of diplomatic residences.

In order that a custom might acquire the force of law, it must have existed for a long time and without controversy. The diplomatic corps had no right to create new rules of international law.

Señor Pacheco did not regard the ideas expressed by Señor Martinez as incompatible with the position of the Peruvian Government, which admitted asylum in the case of danger of death, as a rule of international law. But if the Government demanded the delivery of a person indicted for a crime, he should be given up.

Mr. Barton suggested : "After sentence."

Señor Pacheco replied that the accused should be surrendered for trial. As to the argument that the abolition of asylum would impair the immunities of foreign ministers, Señor Pacheco observed that if this were so he would be forced to believe that in countries where there was no asylum diplomatic immunities did not exist. Repudiating also the alleged obligations of humanity, he invoked the testimony of all present that no act of violence had ever been committed in Peru to justify such an argument, and he referred besides to the penal legislation of the country, in which capital punishment was limited to certain cases of murder. He had been happy to hear the declaration of Senhor Varnhagen that asylum was not a right, but he could not accept his observation as to questions possibly arising from the lack of a conciliatory disposition on the part of the secretary of foreign affairs. A question of principle could not be solved by considering personal traits, and if there happened to be an obstinate foreign secretary there might be a foreign minister equally obstinate.

M. de Lesseps said he had not expected that the conference would result in placing the members in different positions, and he hoped that, without reference to principles, they would, in deference to public opinion, come to an agreement, For himself, he would accept a decision based on the instructions of the minister of Chile, the ideas of Senhor Varnhagen, his own instructions, or the ideas which Señor Pacheco himself might express in writing after mature consideration.

Señor Pacheco said that he had been studying the subject for more than a year. He was about to read a memorandum containing the conclusions of his Government, when, owing to the lateness of the hour, it was suggested that the document should be sent to the dean of the diplomatic corps. The conference was then adjourned.

In this memorandum, which was duly transmitted on the 1st of February, Señor Pacheco ably sustains, both by argument and the citation of authorities, the views presented by him in the conference. Moreover, he forcibly remarks that although the frequency of changes and commotions in South America has been alleged as an excuse for aslyum, those who have engaged in them, conscious that to-morrow they may be treated according to the measure of their own conduct, have generally abstained from acts of cruelty or ferocity which sometimes occur in lands where, because the government is more stable, the attempt to overthrow it generally lasts longer and excites greater vindictiveness. Nevertheless asylum had, said Señor Pacheco, been granted in Peru, not only to those in possible danger of losing their lives, but also to all classes of persons ; to those terrified by fancied persecutions ; to those against whom judgments had been pronounced by the legal authorities ; and to those who wished to rid themselves of obligations purely civil. ' Such a practice, which put a veto upon the administration of justice, constituted a refusal to recognize the sovereignty and independence of the nation and injured its highest rights. In conclusion Señor Pacheco made the following declarations:

" 1. That the Peruvian Government will not hereafter recognize diplomatic asylum as it has been practised up to the present time in Peru, but solely within the limits assigned to it by the law of nations, which are sufficient to solve the exceptional cases which might arise in this matter.

" 2. That, as diplomatic asylum exists in the states of South America, and therefore the legations of Peru in those states enjoy its exercise, Peru renounces on her part the right of her legation in such states to the said privileges, and denies the same to the legations of such states in Peru." [a]

Against these declarations there does not appear to have been any protest. The ministers of Chile and Brazil, while reserving any question that might be raised, referred the matter to their Governments; but the former stated that he was not aware of the existence in Chile of " anything extraordinary or exceptional" to affect " the modern law of nations in the matter of asylum." Mr. Hovey formally accepted the Peruvian declarations, and afterward communicated to the Government a general order of the admiral commanding the squadron of the United States in the Pacific, accepting the conclusions of the memorandum and applying them to his vessels.[b] On May 30, 1867, the Peruvian minister in London reported that Lord Stanley, then secretary of state for foreign affairs, having read the memorandum, had concurred in the views of the Peruvian Government. His lordship remarked that if any Fenians were to take refuge in an embassy in London, it would be ridiculous to suppose that the British Government would have no right to reclaim them. The right of aslyum had, he said, been greatly abused, and he hoped that it would be limited and finally done away with altogether.[c]

(10) VENEZUELA.

§ 304.

" That your mansion, as well as the house of other foreign legations in Caracas, should have been employed, during a period of popular excitement and alarm, as a temporary asylum for the weak or the timid who might have deemed their lives in jeopardy from lawless outrage, can nowhere be regarded either with surprise or regret,

---

[a] Dip. Cor. 1867, part ii, pp. 739–745.

[b] The text of this order is not given by Mr. Hovey. But he communicates to Mr. Seward, without dissent, the version of it given by the minister of foreign relations in his report to the Peruvian Congress, which is as follows: " The admiral says that asylum had not been granted to this time, except from motives of humanity; but as in his opinion that practice had only existed through the tolerance of the Peruvian Government, that Government formally repudiating it, the vessels of war of the United States ought to conform fully and in good faith to the wishes of the Peruvian Government in a matter which exclusively concerns it and its subjects." (Id. 759.)

[c] Dip. Cor. 1867, part ii, p. 773.

and it is gratifying to perceive that its employment for this purpose is not complained of in either of the notes addressed to you by the minister of foreign affairs for the Government of Venezuela, of which you have forwarded copies to this Department. The extent, however, to which this protection may be justly carried must be determined by the minister himself, under the exigencies of each particular case, and with reference to the established principles of the law of nations. A minister in a foreign country is regarded by the public law as independent of the local jurisdiction within which he resides, and responsible for any offenses he may commit only to his own Government. The same peculiar character belongs, also, to his suite, his family, and the members of his household, and in whatever relates to himself or to them is extended even to the mansion which he occupies. Whether its asylum can be violated under any circumstances, it is unnecessary, on this occasion, to inquire; but there is no doubt whatever that, if it can be rightfully entered at all without the consent of its occupant, it can only be so entered in consequence of an order emanating from the supreme authority of the country in which the minister resides, and for which it will be held responsible by his Government. For the established doctrine on this subject, I refer you to Vattel's Law of Nations, chapter 9, section 118; to Martens' Manuel Diplomatique, chapter 3, sect. 31; and to Wheaton's Elements of International Law, p. 174–184."

> Mr. Buchanan, Sec. of State, to Mr. Shields, min. to Venezuela, March 22, 1848, MS. Inst. Venezuela, I. 69.
>
> See Mr. Calhoun, Sec. of State, to Mr. Wise, min. to Brazil, July 18, 1844, MS. Inst. Brazil, XV. 106.

In 1858 a controversy arose in Venezuela with regard to the granting of asylum by the French chargé to General Monagas, who had then lately been forced to abandon the Presidency of Venezuela. In order to consider the situation thus created, Señor Urrutia, Venezuelan minister of foreign relations, invited the diplomatic corps to a conference, which was held on the 26th of March. Besides Señor Urrutia, there were present the diplomatic representatives of the United States, France, Great Britain, Spain, Brazil, and the Netherlands. Señor Urrutia proposed as a necessary basis of discussion that General Monagas should be placed at the disposal of the Government, and after some debate a protocol was drawn up and signed by all present. By this protocol it was agreed that General Monagas should, in writing, place himself at the disposal of the Government, at the same time promising that he would not oppose the progress of the revolution; that this declaration should be transmitted by the chargé d'affaires of France to the Venezuelan Government, whose members pledged their word that General Monagas should not be subjected to trial or in any way molested, but that he should be treated with decorum and respect; that he should be accompanied to his house by the governor of the province, and that the French minister or any other member of the diplomatic corps desiring so to do might go with them; that there should be in the house two respectable persons appointed by the Government to see that the General was well treated and not subjected to insult; that his wife and one of his sons should be allowed to accompany him, and that his other children, the members of the diplomatic corps, and all persons not inspiring the Government with distrust might come and go as they pleased; that the Venezuelan Government would be responsible for his safety while he remained in his dwelling, and that at the expiration of his stay, which was to be as brief as possible, he should be given a safe-conduct for himself and his family to go to a foreign country, where they were to remain as long as was necessary for the peace of Venezuela. The diplomatic corps individually and collectively pledged their word to make every effort within the sphere of their *moral action*, in order that the promises made by General Monagas in his letter of submission might be effective.

General Monagas wrote his submission, but the Government of Venezuela, while abstaining from any act of violence, repudiated the protocol and compelled Señor Urrutia to resign. On April 21, Señor Toro, his successor, informed the members of the diplomatic corps, (1) that the Government of Venezuela considered the cooperation of the foreign representatives in the case as merely an exercise of their good offices, and the signing of the protocol by them as only a solemn testimonial of the promise made to General Monagas by Señor Urrutia; (2) that the Government did not consider the foreign representatives as parties to that promise, or believe that they intended to interfere in the domestic affairs of Venezuela, which could not be tolerated. Mr. Eames, the minister of the United States, replied that this declaration contained an exact definition of the significance and character of the paper, which bound only the honor and good faith of the Government; and his opinion was concurred in by the representatives of Brazil and the Netherlands. The chargé d'affaires of Spain said that the diplomatic corps had been called in as " intercessor, mediator, witness, and then as a party in a certain manner and to a certain extent," though he disclaimed any purpose to intervene in Venezuelan affairs.

On the 10th and 15th of April, Mr. Levraud and Mr. Bingham, the representatives of France and Great Britain, who seem at the time to have lived in the same building, complained that their dwellings had been violated, and suspended diplomatic relations. It seems that the Venezuelan Government had required the delivery of two persons called Gutierrez and Giuseppe, whom the French representative was protecting, and had also, for reasons which it deemed sufficient, prevented the departure of General Monagas, though the promise in regard to his safety was kept.[a] Señor Toro defended the action of the Government. He claimed for Venezuela the same rights that were accorded to governments in Europe, and asserted the rule laid down by Baron C. F. de Martens, that if a minister grants asylum to persons prosecuted for crimes or offences, the Government may not only surrounded his hotel to prevent the escape of the culprits, but if the minister refuses to give them up on the solicitation of the competent authority, may also take them by force.[b] On the 5th of May the commanders of certain French and British ships of war assumed to demand reparation, which the Venezuelan Government refused to grant.[c] The difficulty was adjusted by negotiation.[d]

6. ASYLUM IN VESSELS.

(1) SHIPS OF WAR.

§ 305.

It is generally stated that a ship of war is not subject to the local jurisdiction in a foreign port.[e] This exemption is by some writers maintained to be so absolute as to amount to extraterrioriality.[f]

---

[a] Other grievances also were alleged. Mr. Bingham complained of having been burnt in effigy, an act which Señor Toro sought to explain by saying that it occurred on the day of the Feast of the Resurrection, when it was customary in Catholic countries as a pastime to hang up and burn something early in the morning in commemoration of the treacherous disciple.

[b] Guide Diplomatique, Geffcken's ed. § 29.

[c] Seijas, El Derecho Internacional Hispano-Americano, II. 78–94.

[d] In his message to the Congress, April 12, 1860, the Vice-President of Venezuela says: " This incident, the account of which will be presented by the minister for foreign affairs, happily terminated in a manner satisfactory to our national dignity, and gave rise to certain negotiations which will be duly made known to you in the report from that department. It is but justice to make honorable allusion here to the Licentiate José St. Jago Rodriguez, to whom was confided in Paris the special mission of explaining to the French Government the true character of the proceedings adopted by the executive power relative to M. Levraud. . . . Subsequently the friendly relations between both countries . . . have definitely recovered the genuine cordiality of former times." (51 Br. and For. St. Pap. 1305.) How long diplomatic relations between Great Britain and Venezuela remained in suspense, I am not informed. It appears, however, that a Postal Convention between the two countries was signed by the British minister at Caracas, May 1, 1861 (52 id. 944.) The message of the Vice-President of Venezuela refers to the disturbance of relations with France, but not with England.

[e] Levi, Int. Law, 114; Wheaton's Elements, part 2, ch. 2, § 95; Ferguson, Int. Law, § 112; Calvo, § 1550.

[f] Cauchy, Le Droit Maritime Int., 157; Halleck, Int. Law. Baker's ed., I. 176; Creasy's First Platform, 193.

Ortolan,[a] Maine,[b] and Testa [c] treat the surrender of refugees on a man-of-war as an act of extradition. Calvo, while saying that such a vessel is exempt from the civil and criminal jurisdiction, declares that the privilege can not be invoked to cover acts contrary to the law of nations, such as attacks against the safety of the state or violence against individuals.[d] Sir Travers Twiss and Bar, both of whom deny the extraterritoriality of a diplomatic residence, hold that if fugitives be admitted on board of a man-of-war they can not be taken out by the local authorities by force, against the will of the commander. In the case of a man-of-war, Bar maintains that extraterritoriality is inherent in the thing itself,[e] and the same view is expressed by Twiss.[f] In support of this contention the latter cites, among other things, the opinion of Chief Justice Marshall in the case of the schooner *Exchange*,[g] an American vessel which was seized and condemned by the French Government under the unlawful Rambouillet decree, and converted into a man-of-war called the *Balaou*. The vessel having subsequently come within the jurisdiction of the United States, the original owner brought suit to recover possession of his property. Marshall, delivering the opinion of the court, held that the action could not be maintained. He said that a public armed ship constituted a part of the military force of her nation, acted under the immediate command of her sovereign, and was employed by him in national objects. That sovereign had many and powerful motives for preventing those objects from being defeated by the interference of a foreign state, and such interference could not take place without affecting his power and dignity. The implied license, therefore, under which a man-of-war entered a friendly port might be construed as containing an exemption from the jurisdiction of the sovereign within whose territory she claimed the rights of hospitality; and nations had not in practice asserted their jurisdiction over the public armed ships of a foreign sovereign entering a port open for their reception. These statements seem to be most cogent as applied to the attempt to determine the title of the French Government to a man-of-war in a civil action, but they do not import the absolute extraterritoriality of a public vessel. In the case of the *Santissima Trinidad*,[h] Mr. Justice Story cited the case of the *Exchange* as authority for the proposition that the exemption of public ships from the local jurisdic-

[a] Dip. de la Mer, I. 267.

[b] Int. Law, 91.

[c] Le Droit Public Int. Maritime (Paris, 1886).

[d] § 1556.

[e] Int. Law, § 154.

[f] Law of Nations, I., § 165; Law Magazine and Review, 4th series, Vol. I., p. 201.

[g] 7 Cranch, 116.

[h] 7 Wheaton, 283, 352–353.

tion was not an absolute right, but a rule of comity and convenience, arising from the presumed consent or license of nations, "that foreign public ships coming into their ports, and demeaning themselves according to law, and in a friendly manner, shall be exempt from the local jurisdiction." Attorney-General Bradford in 1794 advised that a writ of *habeas corpus* might be awarded to bring up an American citizen unlawfully detained on a foreign ship of war.[a] In 1799 Attorney-General Lee held that criminal and civil process might be served on a British man-of-war, though he laid special stress on a treaty stipulation then in force between the United States and Great Britain, that " the ships of war of each of the contracting parties shall at all times be hospitably received in the ports of the other, *their officers and crews paying due respect* to the laws and government of the country." [b] Attorney-General Cushing accepted the doctrine of extraterritoriality.[c] On the other hand, Sir William Scott advised the British Government that the authorities of a foreign country would not be chargeable with illegal violence if they employed force to take a fugitive out of a British man-of-war; [d] and it was held by the Geneva Tribunal in 1872 that as the privilege of extraterritoriality accorded to vessels of war had been admitted into the law of nations, not as an absolute right, " but solely as a proceeding founded on the principle of courtesy and mutual deference between different nations," it could " never be appealed to for the protection of acts done in violation of neutrality." [e]

But, whatever may be said as to the extraterritoriality of ships of war, it is doubtless a universal custom to accord them a general exemption from the local jurisdiction; [f] and for the reason that such an exemption is accorded, it is held that considerations of propriety and good faith require the commanders of such ships to abstain from abusing the hospitality of the port in which they may be by making their vessels an asylum for offenders against the law. The question whether this rule should be applied to slaves has given rise to much discussion. On December 5, 1875, the British admirality issued to the commanders of Her Majesty's ships of war the following instructions:

Within the territorial waters of a foreign state, you are bound, by the comity of nations, while maintaining the proper exemption of your ship from local jurisdiction, not to allow her to become a shelter for those who would be chargeable with a violation of the law of the place. If, therefore, while your ship is within the territorial waters of a state where slavery exists, a person professing or appearing to be a fugitive slave seeks admission into your ship, you will not admit him, unless his life would be in manifest danger if he were not received on board. Should you, in order to save him from this danger,

a 1 Op. At. Gen. 47.

b 1 Id. 87, 89.

c 7 Id. 112 ; 8 id. 73.

d Halleck, note by Baker, I. 176.

e Moore, Int. Arbitrations, I. 655.

f Phillimore, Int. Law, Vol. I. cccxliv.

receive him, you ought not, after the danger is past, to permit him to continue on board; but you will not entertain any demand for his surrender, or enter into examination as to his status.[a]

The issuance of these instructions led to the appointment of a royal commission to consider whether the rules laid down abridged the rights of men-of-war. The commission differed as to the theory of extraterritoriality, which was maintained by Sir R. Phillimore, Mr. M. Bernard, and Sir Henry Maine, and denied by Lord Chief Justice Cockburn, Mr. Justice Archibald, Mr. Thesiger, Q. C., Sir H. T. Holland, Mr. Fitz-James Stephen, and Mr. Rothery. They all, however, concurred in a report that, whichever view prevailed, the fugitive should not be given up where the result of surrendering him would be to expose him to cruel usage.[b] By the treaty between the United States and Algiers of September 5, 1795, it was provided that if slaves of the regency should make their escape to ships of war of the United States, they should immediately be returned.[c] By the treaty between those countries of 1816 it was provided that if Christians, captives in Algiers, should escape or take refuge on such ships, they should not be required back again.[d] The treaty between the United States and Tunis of 1797 provided for the return of fugitive slaves by American men-of-war,[e] but the treaty of 1824 stipulated that slaves escaping or taking refuge on such vessels should be free. On the other hand, in the treaty with Madagascar of 1881, it is provided that Malagasy subjects shall not be permitted to embark on United States vessels without a passport from the native Government,[f] and the institution of slavery in that country is explicitly recognized.[g] By the general act of Brussels of July 2, 1890, for the suppression of the African slave trade, it is provided (Art. XXVIII.)

---

[a] 66 Brit. and For. State Papers, 892.

[b] Report of Royal Commission on Fugitive Slaves, 1876; Maine's Int. Law, 88; Journal of Jurisprudence, Vol. XX. pp. 188, 414. Mr. Justice Stephen states that he joined in the report because he regarded it "as a proposal that the British nation should deliberately take in this matter the course which it regards as just and expedient, although it is opposed to international law as it stands, and aims at its improvement." He maintains that the fundamental principles of international law, when consistently applied, require the commanding officers of ships of war in foreign territorial waters "to refuse protection in all cases whatever to those who break the local law, and to deliver up, on a lawful demand, political refugees, the victims of religious persecution, and slaves who have received or expect from their owners the treatment which a vicious brute would experience from a cruel master." (History of the Criminal Law, II. 57, 58.)

[c] Art. XI.

[d] Art. XIV.

[e] Art. VI.

[f] Art. VII. par. 2.

[g] Art. III. Stipulations specifically applicable to fugitive slaves are not infrequently found in treaties. (Report of Royal Commission on Fugitive Slaves, 1876.)

that any slave taking refuge on a ship of war of one of the signatory powers shall be " immediately and definitively set free," but that such freedom " shall not withdraw him from the competent jurisdiction if he has been guilty of any crime or offence at common law."

During the disorders at Naples in 1849, Lord Palmerston said that while it " would not be right to receive and harbor on board of a British ship-of-war any person flying from justice on a criminal charge or who was escaping from the sentence of a court of law," yet a British man-of-war had always been regarded as a safe place of refuge for persons fleeing " from persecution on account of their political conduct or opinions," whether the refugee " was escaping from the arbitrary acts of a monarchial government or from the lawless violence of a revolutionary committee." [a] In August of the preceding year the Duke of Parma, whose life was threatened, was embarked at Civita Vecchia on the British man-of-war *Hecate*,[b] and in the same month the British admiral ordered H. M. S. *Bulldog* to the same port to receive the Pope, should commotions render it desirable for His Holiness to seek refuge on board.[c] During the revolution in Greece in 1862, King Otho and his Queen were afforded protection on the British frigate *Scylla*,[d] while a member of the cabinet and his family were received on the *Queen*, and several persons were sheltered on the French man-of-war *Zénobie*. The instructions given by Vice-Admiral Sir William Martin on that occasion to the commanders of British ships of war declared that their duty was " limited to the protection of the lives and property of British subjects and to affording protection to any refugees whom you may be informed by Her Majesty's minister would be in danger of their lives without such protection." [e] Under these instructions the reception of refugees by the British commanders was carefully restricted.[f]

In April, 1831, Captain Sloat, of the United States man-of-war *St. Louis*, afforded temporary shelter from mob violence to the Vice-President of Peru and General Miller, with the concurrence of the Government of Peru and with the understanding that they should not remain on board longer than was necessary for their protection from such violence.[g] In 1862, while the city of New Orleans was occupied by the forces of the United States, three Spanish men-of-war then in that port received on board a large number of passengers for Cuba, among whom were many citizens of the United States who, under the orders then in force, were not permitted to leave the city

---

a 50 Br. and For. State Papers, 803.

b 41 Id. 1316.

c 41 Br. and For. State Papers, 1324.

d 58 Id. 1034.

e Id. 1057.

f Id. 1087.

g H. Ex. Doc. 272, 22 Cong. 1 sess.

without passes.   General Butler, the officer in command, claimed the right to search the vessels " for criminals other than rebels," and after much difficulty he obtained the privilege of searching two of the ships.   In consequence of this occurrence, he prohibited the entry of Spanish men-of-war above the forts till further orders from the War Department.   Mr. Seward, while recommending to the Secretary of War the suspension of the prohibition pending explanations from the Spanish Government, made urgent representations to the Spanish minister.   The Spanish Government, after considering the subject, defended the action of its naval officers, on the ground that asylum at least for political offenders might be granted on men-of-war.   Mr. Seward refused to concede this claim, saying that the United States adhered to its former declaration that no ship of war of any nation would be expected to carry into or out from any port of the United States which was either occupied by their forces or in the possession of the insurgents, any person who did not actually belong to the civil, military, or naval service of the country whose flag the vessel carried, and especially that ships of war should not, without express leave of the military authorities, carry into or out of such ports any citizen of the United States.   It was only, said Mr. Seward, on an expected compliance with these terms that any foreign ship of war could enter a port in military occupation during the civil war.[a]

During the war in Paraguay in 1866, Mr. Washburn, minister of the United States at Asuncion, suggested to Commander Crosby, of the United States man-of-war *Shamokin*, then in Paraguayan waters, that peace might sooner take place if " a certain distinguished person in Paraguay," meaning President Lopez, could find a safe means of escape from the country on that vessel.   Commander Crosby replied that he could exercise no discretion in the matter, since the Admiral had given him positive orders not to bring away President Lopez or any other Paraguayan.   When Mr. Washburn brought the subject to the attention of his Government, with an intimation that he himself should be invested with discretion in the case, Mr. Seward answered as follows:

The President sanctions the direction which was given by Admiral Godon to Commander Crosby. . . . This Government owes it to the belligerents, as well as to its own dignity, to abstain from everything which could be, or even appear to be, a departure from neutrality in the unhappy contest which is going on between Paraguay and her allied enemies.   You will be expected to conform your proceedings rigidly to the principles of noninterference.[a]

---

[a] Dip. Cor. 1863, II. 915.

[b] Dip. Cor. 1866, Part II. pp. 611–612; 1867, Part II. p. 705.   In November, 1865, a sailor belonging to the United States man-of-war *James Adger*, who was watching some stores belonging to the ship on one of the piers at Aspinwall (Colon), in Colombia, killed a British subject named Holmes, who was tres-

"This Department approves of the conduct of that officer in refusing to give up the men charged with larceny, to whom his dispatch refers. A man-of-war of one country in the port of another is, during her stay, to be regarded as a part of the country to which she belongs. As such, her commander may exercise his discretion as to whom he may admit on board. This right extends even to a refusal to see a ministerial officer of the law in the foreign port, or to recognize an application to give up a man on board who may have committed an offense on shore. Any person, however, attached to such a man-of-war, charged with an offense on shore, is liable to arrest therefor in the country where the offense may have been committed.

"In the event that a person on board the foreign ship should be charged with a crime for the commission of which he would be liable to be given up, pursuant to an extradition treaty, the commander of the vessel may give him up if such proof of the charge should be produced as the treaty may require. In such case, however, it would always be advisable to consult the nearest minister of the United States. This was done in this instance, and the decision of Mr. Marsh that the persons demanded were not liable to be given up pursuant to the treaty with Italy, is approved by the Department."

Mr. Fish, Sec. of State, to Mr. Case, Jan. 27, 1872, 92 MS. Dom. Let. 322,

During the civil war in Chili in 1891 the Secretary of the Navy of the United States gave, in respect to the reception of refugees, the following instructions:

In reference to the granting of asylum, your ships will not, of course, be made a refuge for criminals. In the case of persons other than criminals, they will afford shelter wherever it may be needed, to Americans first of all, and to others, including political refugees, as far as the claims of humanity may require and the service upon which you are engaged will permit.

The obligation to receive political refugees and to afford them an asylum is, in general, one of pure humanity. It should not be continued beyond the urgent necessities of the situation, and should in no case become the means whereby the plans of contending factions or their leaders are facilitated. You are not to invite or encourage such refugees to come on board your ship, but, should they apply to you, your action will be governed by considerations of humanity and the exigencies of the service upon which you are engaged. When, however, a political refugee has embarked, in the territory of a third power, on board an American ship as a passenger for purposes of innocent transit, and it appears

passing on the pier. The consul of the United States, to whom the local authorities applied to secure the surrender of the sailor, refused to intervene for that purpose, and he was carried away. Mr. Seward, replying to the representations of the Colombian minister, said that the United States did not sanction the omission to give the mariner up for trial, and that, if the case had been seasonably made known, an order for his delivery would have been issued, if it could have been done properly under the circumstances. (Dip. Cor. 1866, Part III. pp. 596–597; Part I. pp. 215–218; Dip. Cor. 1867, Part II. p. 818.)

upon the entry of such ship into the territorial waters that his life is in danger, it is your duty to extend to him an offer of asylum.[a]

During the disorders immediately following the downfall of Balmaceda the British ships refused to receive any refugees. The French ships, which lay far out from the shore, did not receive any. The Balmacedist President-elect, Señor Claudio Vicuña, and Admiral Viel, found refuge on the German man-of-war *Leipzig*. September 4 the United States man-of-war *Baltimore* sailed for Peru with nineteen refugees, part of whom had been sheltered by her and the rest by the flagship *San Francisco*. The new government was formally recognized by the United States September 5.[b] Admiral Brown sailed in the *San Francisco* from Valparaiso for Callao September 14, taking with him " two prominent Chilean refuges." [c]

The instructions given by the Secretary of the Navy in 1891, as above quoted, were substantially incorporated into the United States Navy Regulations of 1893.

" The Government of Salvador having been overthrown by an abrupt popular outbreak, certain of its military and civil officers, while hotly pursued by infuriated insurgents, sought refuge on board the United States war ship *Bennington*, then lying in a Salvadorean port. Although the practice of asylum is not favored by this Government, yet in view of the imminent peril which threatened the fugitives, and solely from considerations of humanity, they were afforded shelter by our naval commander, and when afterwards demanded under our treaty of extradition with Salvador for trial on charges of murder, arson, and robbery, I directed that such of them as had not voluntarily left the ship be conveyed to one of our nearest ports where a hearing could be had before a judicial officer in compliance with the terms of the treaty. On their arrival at San Francisco such a proceeding was promptly instituted before the United States district judge, who held that the acts constituting the alleged offenses were political, and discharged all the accused except one Cienfuegos, who was held for an attempt to murder. Thereupon I was constrained to direct his release, for the reason that an attempt to murder was not one of the crimes charged against him

---

[a] Mr. Tracy, Sec. of Navy, to Rear-Admiral Brown, March 26, 1891, H. Ex. Doc. 91, 52 Cong. 1 sess. 245. The last clause in these instructions obviously was suggested by the case of Barrundia, in the preceding year. In that case Mr. Tracy, as Secretary of the Navy, censured Commander Reiter, of the U. S. S. *Ranger*, for failing to offer Barrundia an asylum when he learned that the Guatemalan authorities would endeavor to arrest Barrundia on the Pacific Mail steamer on which he was a passenger.

[b] H. Ex. Doc. 91, 52 Cong. 1 sess. 71,

[c] H. Ex. Doc. 91, 52 Cong. 1 sess. 289.

and upon which his surrender to the Salvadorean authorities had
been demanded."

> President Cleveland, annual message, Dec. 3, 1894.
>
> In the case thus referred to, Commander Thomas of the U. S. S. *Ben-
> nington*, received on board his ship, which was then lying at La Liber-
> tad, in Salvador, seventeen refugees, among whom were General
> Antonio Ezeta and other military officers of the government of Carlos
> Ezeta, which had just been overthrown. See the case of the Salva-
> dorean Refugees, by J. B. Moore, the American Law Review, Jan.–
> Feb., 1895, p. 1.

One of the results of the case of the Salvadorean refugees was that
the Secretary of the Navy, August 15, 1894, substituted for article 287
of the Navy Regulations of 1893 (see art. 288 of Regulations of 1896)
the following paragraph:

> The right of asylum for political or other refugees has no foundation in inter-
> national law. In countries, however, where frequent insurrections occur, and
> constant instability of government exists, local usage sanctions the granting of
> asylum, but even in the waters of such countries officers should refuse all appli-
> cations for asylum except when required by the interests of humanity in extreme
> or exceptional cases, such as the pursuit of a refugee by a mob. Officers must
> not directly or indirectly invite refugees to accept asylum.

March 15, 1894, the Portuguese legation at Rio de Janeiro advised
the Brazilian Government that on the morning of the 13th "a
numerous group of insurgents" (apparently 493), who had for
months been in arms in Rio de Janeiro Bay, had gone aboard the
Portuguese men-of-war *Mindello* and *Alfonso de Albuquerque* and
begged for refuge and asylum, which was conceded to them, " according to the provisions of international law, and to the principles of
humanity generally recognized by civilized nations." [a] The Brazilian Government replied that it was acquainted with the circumstance, and, while recognizing the humane sentiments of the Portuguese officials, was obliged " to demand the delivery of those individuals, whom it considers as criminals, and who are not in circumstances to receive the protection extended to them." [b] The Portuguese officials having refused to comply with this demand, the
Brazilian Government caused it to be presented to the Government
of Portugal, at the same time declaring that the " rebels were declared
pirates by decree of October," that they did not represent any part of
political opinion, and that they should be surrendered for submission
to the competent tribunals for crimes, depredations and robbery.[b]

---

[a] For. Rel. 1894, 65–66. It seems that the Portuguese vice-admiral, Castilho,
was under instructions to act with regard to asylum only in concert with the
commanders of other foreign vessels; but the other foreign men-of-war received
no refugees.   (For. Rel. 1894, 513.)

[b] For. Rel. 1894, 66.

The decree referred to was issued October 10, 1893. The Portuguese minister of foreign affairs declined to comply with the demand and stated that he considered the refugees as political criminals; but he offered to act upon the same rule as the commanders of other ships which had given asylum to insurgents. The Brazilian Government answered that there were no rebels on the ships of other nations, and that it could not admit that another sovereignty could be opposed to its own in the port of the capital of the Republic. March 16, 1894, the Brazilian minister of foreign affairs, having heard that the *Alfonso de Albuquerque* had taken on board all the refugees and was about to sail, requested the Portuguese chargé d'affaires to order her departure to be delayed until the pending question should be decided. The Portuguese chargé d'affaires replied that the commander in chief of the *Mindello* was responsible for the guarding of the refugees and would not land them on foreign soil until the final decision of the diplomatic question, and, while affirming the right of the ships to proceed to any point as the convenience of the service might require, requested the commander of the *Mindello* temporarily to delay sailing.[a] It was subsequently agreed that the ships should for hygienic reasons leave the port for three or four days. The Portuguese ships, however, proceeded to Buenos Ayres, where questions arose with the Argentine Government, both because of the recapture of some of the refugees who had escaped, and because of the demand of the Argentine Government that all refugees should land in order to undergo quarantine. The Portuguese Government took the ground that it would not allow the landing of the refugees except on Portuguese soil, it being committed to this with the Brazilian Government. Subsequently the yellow fever broke out aboard, and the Argentine Government required the ships either to land the refugees or go to sea. The Portuguese Government thereupon ordered the ships to leave the port and await outside a ship which had been chartered to convey the refugees to the island of Assumption, whence they could be transported to Portugal. In reality large numbers of the refugees escaped at Buenos Ayres, including Admiral Saldanha da Gama, the head of the insurrection.[b] The Brazilian Government recalled its minister from Lisbon and sent the Portuguese chargé d'affaires at Rio his passports, thus suspending diplomatic relations. A misunderstanding seems to have occurred as to the terms on which the Portuguese ships left Rio, the Brazilian Government alleging that it was agreed that they should leave port for three or four days and that the Portuguese chargé d'affaires committed himself for their return. The Portuguese Government stated that this promise had been made without authority.[c]

---

[a] For. Rel. 1894, 67.   [b] For. Rel. 1894, 514, 515.   [c] For. Rel. 1894, 68–71.

While the controversy was pending, the British ambassador at Washington, under instructions from his Government, inquired whether the United States would join Great Britain in a friendly suggestion to the Government of Brazil to accept an offer of the Portuguese Government to land the refugees somewhere beyond the jurisdiction of Brazil, and there detain them till the fate of the insurrection should be known, when their right to asylum under the circumstances could be determined. The President, after full consideration, declined to join in the suggestion. A substantially similar request was received from the Government of Italy, through the American minister at Rio, and another from the Portuguese Government directly, through its minister at Washington. Both requests were declined.[a]

President Cleveland, in his annual message of Dec. 3, 1894, said: "Our firm attitude of neutrality was maintained to the end. The insurgents received no encouragement of eventual asylum from our commanders."

March 16, 1895, the Brazilian minister at Washington stated that diplomatic relations between Brazil and Portugal had been restored.[b]

(2) MERCHANT VESSELS.

§ 306.

Apart from acts affecting their internal order and discipline and not disturbing the peace of the port, merchant vessels, as a rule, enjoy no exemption from the local jurisdiction. It is therefore generally laid down that they can not grant asylum.[c]

It has been suggested by Ortolan that a fugitive offender who, merely as a passenger in transit from one country to another, enters

---

[a] Mr. Gresham, Sec. of State, to Mr. Bayard, amb. at London, April 6, 1894, For. Rel. 1894, 278. With reference to various reports that appeared in the press, Sir Edward Grey, parliamentary undersecretary of state for foreign affairs, May 4, 1894, said: "The action of Her Majesty's representative at Rio, and of the British naval officers, was directed solely to protect British commerce, and to preserve complete impartiality during the recent disturbances. Any statement that the British officials joined in any attempt to restore the monarchy, or in any way to change the political situation, is absolutely untrue." (For. Rel. 1894, 279.)

[b] It was stated in the press Oct. 21, 1900, that the Dutch war ship *Gelderland*, with President Krüger as a passenger, sailed from Lourenço Marquez on the preceding day. It seems that the ex-President was accompanied on board the ship by "the exalted Portuguese officials" of the place, and that before sailing he assured the governor on his honor that he would go direct to Holland, calling only at Marseilles. (N. Y. Sun, Oct. 22, 1900.)

[c] De Cussy, Phases et Causes Célèbres, I. 87; Journal du Droit Int. Privé, 1890, 643; Alex. Porter Morse, in 42 Albany Law Journal (Nov. 1, 1890), 345; Mr. Blaine, Sec. of State, to Mr. Mizner, min. to Cent. Am., Nov. 18 1890, For. Rel. 1890, 123; Wildenhus's case, 120 U. S. 1, 18.

the territorial limits of a third country, should not be seized in the latter country.[a] The exception thus suggested is discussed in cases in the next section. It would seem to be strictly confined to the circumstances stated, and not to have been intended to apply to a person merely because he is in transit in the physical sense, as where he enters another port of the country in which he embarked.

In 1840 the French packet boat *L'Océan*, which made regular voyages between Marseilles, the coast of Spain, and Gibraltar, received on board, at her anchorage at Valencia, M. Sotelo, a Spanish ex-minister, who was under prosecution for political offences. The vessel, having put to sea without knowledge of the number and personality of the passengers who had embarked, entered the port of Alicante. where, during the customs and police inspection, M. Sotelo was recognized, seized, taken ashore, and imprisoned. The captain of *L'Océan* protested against what he described as a violation of his flag, and in vain demanded that his passenger be set at liberty, invoking at the same time the right of asylum and the principle of extraterritoriality.

Diplomatic communications on the subject which were exchanged between the Governments of France and Spain established it in the clearest manner that the conduct of the authorities of Alicante was above reproach; that no injury was done to the flag, since the acts in question pertained to an ordinary merchant ship and to a high measure of police executed inside the port; that M. Sotelo, surreptitiously embarked at Valencia, a Spanish port, could have been regularly seized and arrested on *L'Océan* at another port of the same country; and, finally, that the fact that she had been on the high seas a certain time before entering Alicante could not alter the nature of the act done at the place of departure, and proved at the place of arrival, under the dominion of the same laws and of the same territorial legislation.

> Calvo, Droit International, 4th ed., I. 569.
> See, also, Snow, Cases on Int. Law, 147–150; Snow, Lectures on Int. Law, ed. by Stockton, 40–41.

Complaint was made of the arrest by the British authorities in Ireland of a Mr. McManus, on the American vessel *N. O. Chase*. As there was no allegation that the arrest took place on the high seas, it was presumed that it was made in British waters. If the arrest was made in British territorial waters, the United States, said the Department of State, had " no right to demand redress, either under the law of nations or by virtue of any treaty existing between the two countries. In case an American citizen charged with a crime in the city of New York should seek an asylum in a British merchant

---

[a] Diplomatie de la Mer, I. 304.

vessel, our authorities, I presume, would not hesitate to arrest him on board of such vessel whilst she remained within waters under our exclusive and absolute jurisdiction. In such a case the flag of Great Britain would afford no protection against the process of the law."

> Mr. Buchanan, Sec. of State, to Mr. Jordan, Jan. 23, 1849, 37 MS. Dom.
> Let. 98.

" Your despatch No. 446, of the 10th April last, in relation to an attempted arrest by the Government authorities of Hayti, of passengers on a French mail steamer, has been received.

" In reply I have to say it is the opinion of this Government that, without a special relinquishment of its rights by treaty, the Haytian Government has jurisdiction over all persons within its territorial limits, including passengers by mail steamers. A different doctrine, if carried into practice, would operate inconveniently to this Government."

> Mr. Fish, Sec. of State, to Mr. Bassett, min. to Hayti, May 27, 1876, MS.
> Inst. Hayti, II. 79.

" Your dispatch No. 44, of the 17th October last, in reference to the escape of a supposed revolutionist on board of a French bark, is received.

" It would be impossible to give you any instructions, as you request, with a view to the possibility of such a case happening on an American vessel. As you say that the case in point is without precedent, the probabilities of your being called upon to decide one of the same kind would seem to be remote. Without questioning the propriety of the action or judgment of the French minister in refusing to give up the refugee, I may say that international law does not recognize the right of asylum of foreign legations in any country, and that according to American principles of law a merchant vessel in port is under the authority of the local laws and officials, and that neither a consulate nor a legation would have anything to say in regard to a supposed criminal being taken from a ship. If the person claimed were a foreigner accused of a crime included in extradition treaties, the question as to rights and duties of consular or diplomatic officials would be different. The action of the local authorities and the foreign agents would seem to place this matter on a false extradition basis, which might lead to troublesome complications. It is hoped that no other unpleasant occurrence of the kind may occur, though, in case there should, the Department has no doubt that your good judgment will enable you to deal with the emergency prudently and wisely."

> Mr. Bayard, Sec. of State, to Mr. Thompson, min. to Hayti, Nov. 3, 1885,
> For. Rel. 1885, 542.

" Mr. Goutier [United States consul at Cape Haytian] next refers to the case of the insurgent who took refuge on the French bark *Panama*, and says that with the Department's instructions in view he would have been much perplexed had the vessel been American, for, says he, ' it would have been my duty to allow the authorities to go on board and arrest that Haytian insurgent.' And Mr. Goutier goes on to argue that if any other power claims the right of asylum in a given case, the United States could not forego a similar claim without loss of prestige.

"As we understand the case of the *Panama*, the local authorities applied to the consul for permission to go on board and take the fugitive. In a case which recently arose in Cuba, where application was made to a consul to order the delivery of a person then on board an American vessel in port, who was accused of common crimes, and where the consul, after examining the charge against the person, ordered the captain to deliver him up, this Department held that the consul had no authority to order such surrender.

" The application made to the consul converted a proceeding, which otherwise concerned only the domestic administration of justice, into a sort of proceeding in extradition, for which no authority is found in treaty or international law. The consul had no judicial function, and could not assume the character, for the nonce, of an examining magistrate, passing upon the evidence submitted and granting or withholding surrender in his discretion in territory not within the jurisdiction of the United States. He simply had no power, authority or discretion, either to decree a surrender, or to resist the ordinary operation of municipal justice within its own jurisdiction.

" Had Mr. Goutier's supposed case occurred, had the insurgent gone on board an American vessel in port and the like application been made to the American consul, it would have been his duty to decline to take upon himself the extraneous responsibility of ordering or aiding, in his official capacity, the surrender of the fugitive. His function in the premises would have been confined to watching that all due forms of arrest, on a judicial warrant, were observed, and that no arbitrary, unlawful or forcible invasion of the vessel occurred, especially in the case of political refugees.

" It does not seem pertinent to the present instruction to discuss the ethics of humanity, to which Mr. Goutier adverts. Section 48 of the Department's lately issued personal instructions to its diplomatic agents abroad is abundant evidence that the principles of common humanity, where arbitrary pursuit of merely political offenders is concerned, have not been overlooked in its ruling."

Mr. Bayard, Sec. of State, to Mr. Thompson, min. to Hayti, Nov. 7, 1885, MS. Inst. Hayti, II. 523 ; extracts printed in For. Rel. 1886, 530.

" It is laid down by the publicists, as a general rule, that the private vessels of a nation, as contradistinguished from its men-of-war, are, on entering the ports of another nation, not exempt from the local jurisdiction. At the same time it is stated that this rule is not absolute and unlimited, but that it is subject to important qualifications, both general and special. The vessels of a nation on the high seas are commonly spoken of as a part of its territory, and this character is not destroyed by their entrance into the port of another nation, although by such entrance they may, to a great extent, also become subject to another jurisdiction. [Here follows a citation of Mr. Webster's note to Lord Ashburton in the case of the *Creole*, Webster's Works, VI. 306, 307.]

" These principles were recently applied by the Supreme Court of the United States in the case of Wildenhus. In that case a murder was committed on board of a Belgian vessel in the port of Jersey City, in the State of New Jersey. The Belgian Government claimed exclusive jurisdiction of the offense under its treaty with the United States. The Supreme Court did not admit this claim, but, holding that the treaty was merely declaratory of the law of nations, said:

" The principle which governs the whole matter is this : Disorders which disturb only the peace of the ship or those on board are to be dealt with exclusively by the sovereignty of the home of the ship ; but those which disturb the public peace may be suppressed, and if need be the offenders punished by the proper authorities of the local jurisdiction. It may not be easy at all times to determine to which of the two jurisdictions a particular act of disorder belongs. Much will undoubtedly depend on the attending circumstances of the particular case, but all must concede that felonious homicide is a subject for the local jurisdiction, and that if the proper authorities are proceeding with the case in a regular way the consul has no right to interfere to prevent it. (Wildenhus's case, 120 U. S., 1, 18.) . . .

" Such, then, is the general rule and such are its general limitations. In this relation it may be observed that Calvo states the rule as follows:

" To sum up, as regards merchant vessels, for all crimes or offenses committed by seamen, either on board or ashore, against foreigners, or in such a way as to disturb public order or to affect the interests of the country in whose waters the vessel is at anchor, as well as for matters in which the parties interested ask of their own accord the aid and support of the local authorities, the police of the country have an absolute right to pursue the guilty party even on board of the vessel to which he belongs, if he has succeeded in taking refuge there, provided in this latter case they come to an understanding with the consul of the nation interested. (Calvo, Le Droit international, 4th ed., section 471.)

" In ordinary cases of arrest of criminals under legal process such concurrent action or permission has been the general practice among the Spanish-American countries, and there are many recent instances in which it has been observed. I am unaware of any reported case where the arrest was made or the demand enforced in

the event of a refusal on the part of a representative of the nation
to which the vessel belonged to act concurrently or to grant the permission sought.

" But the rule is also subject to special exceptions, resting upon
consent and secured either by express compacts or by custiom. This
principle is so clearly enunciated by Chief Justice Marshall that I
will quote that great jurist's statement of it, which is as follows:

" This consent may be either expressed or implied. In the latter case it is less
determinate, exposed more to the uncertainties of construction, but, if understood, not less obligatory. The world being composed of distinct sovereignities,
possessing equal rights and equal independence, whose mutual benefit is promoted by intercourse with each other and by an interchange of those good
offices which humanity dictates and its wants require, all sovereigns have consented to a relaxation in practice, in cases under peculiar circumstances, of
that absolute and complete jurisdiction within their respective territories
which sovereignty confers. This consent may, in some instances, be tested by
common usage and by common opinion growing out of that usage. (Case of
the schooner *Exchange*, 7 Cranch, 116.)

"As an illustration of the exceptions that prevail in some places, I
may cite the recent case of the British steamer *Charles Morand*, on
which the first officer was, in July, 1889, killed by a sailor, one Peter
Lynch, while the steamer was lying in the port of Manzanillo, in
the island of Cuba. Notwithstanding the gravity of the offense,
the local authorities declined to take jurisdiction of it, and the
offender was brought to the city of New York, where he was arrested
with a view to extradition. The case was duly examined by judicial
authority and the prisoner committed to wait the action of the Executive, upon whose warrant he was subsequently delivered up to be
tried in England for the murder charged to have been committed on
the British steamer in the port of Manzanillo.

" The general principles and the exceptions governing the subject
under consideration have so far been discussed in relation to common
crimes. ·. . .   Political offenses have been treated by publicists as constituting a separate class and as demanding a different consideration
and treatment from ordinary crimes; and, because of their special
character, they have also been the subject, in many instances and
in many places, of a very considerable abatement of jurisdictional
claims. In proof of this fact it is pertinent to consult the ' common
usage ' and the ' common opinion growing out of that usage,' to which
Chief Justice Marshall referred as evidence of that national consent
which may make the law for a particular place or for particular
countries, and which, as he declared in another part of his opinion,
can not be ' suddenly and without previous notice ' withdrawn by a
nation without a violation of its faith.

" The records of this Department afford several comparatively
recent instances of the arrest of alleged offenders on American ves-

sels in Spanish-American ports. In these cases the consular or diplomatic officer has invariably been applied to for his consent, and proof
has been furnished in authentic legal form of the crime alleged.
Where there has been ground for the suspicion that the application
bore a political complexion, ample proof has been adduced that the
offenses charged were ordinary in their character. This fact has
been made the basis of the request for the consent of the foreign
representative to the arrest, and the Department is not informed of
any case in which the arrest has been made when the representative
of the United States withheld his consent or the demand wore a political aspect.

"An illustration of the course pursued in respect to an ordinary
crime is found in the case of Leopoldo Olivella, who, being accused
of murder at Matanzas, in the island of Cuba, in 1880, fled to the
United States. Some months later he took passage at New York
under an assumed name on the American steamship *City of Alexandria*
for Vera Cruz, in Mexico, Havana being a regular port of call. The
Cuban authorities, learning of his departure from New York, applied
to the consul-general at Havana for a letter to the captain of the
steamer directing him to surrender Olivella to the chief of police.
The consul-general telegraphed to the Department, which, in replying, did not authorize the surrender, but confined itself to instructing
him to secure to the accused all the treaty rights to which he might be
found to be entitled. While the steamer lay in port the consul-
general went on board, followed by the chiefs of police of Havana and
Matanzas, who were provided with a regular warrant of arrest and
accompanied by witnesses to the fugitive's identity. After interrogation and complete identification, Olivella consented to go ashore, stipulating, however, that legal steps should be taken by the superior
authorities of the island ' to demand his extradition from the Government of the United States to the end that the said Government may
give its decision on this point.' A certificate of the proceeding, embracing this stipulation, was accordingly drawn up and signed by the
accused and by the several officers present, and the Spanish minister
subsequently presented it to the Department of State, with the evidence in the case, including the indictment and warrant of arrest, in
order that this Government might be ' fully satisfied with the formalities which have been observed in the matter of the arrest of
Olivella.'

" The course pursued in a case having a political aspect and the
recognition of that aspect as of substantial importance may be illustrated by the case of Emilio Nuñez during the late insurrection in the
island of Cuba. Nuñez, who is said to have taken part in an insurgent raid near Sagua, escaped to the United States, where he declared

his intention to become a citizen. In 1884 he returned to Sagua as one of the crew of an American vessel, remaining on board while in the port. The acting consul of the United States at Sagua was applied to by the chief of police for authority to take Nuñez from the vessel. The acting consul asked instructions of the consul-general at Havana, and General Badeau replied authorizing the surrender if the charge was criminal, not political. When information was sought on this point, evidence was produced by the acting consul that Nuñez was charged before the regular courts with various crimes, ' among others, assassination and robbery, as a bandit, of Don Amando Denis, at San Diego del Valle, and is therefore a criminal, and not a political offender.' Thereupon the acting consul gave his written consent to the surrender. It was afterwards disclosed that Nuñez had been amnestied by the governor of the province and permitted to leave the island after the process on account of murder had been instituted, and he was subsequently released without formal trial. In this instance it is clear that the instructions of the consul-general assumed to impose upon the acting consul at Sagua the function of ascertaining the charge and basing his consent on proof of its non-political character, and this condition was acquiesced in by the Cuban authorities."

> Mr. Blaine, Sec. of State, to Mr. Mizner, min. to Cent. Am., Nov. 18, 1890, For. Rel. 1890, 123, 133–136.

> "Your dispatch No. 2575, dated August 22, 1895, has been received. It encloses a letter from the captain of the port of Habana in the following language: 'The individual named Antolino Pujol y Moll, son of Peter and Antonia, having been commanded to appear before the department of Carthagena, and his kinsfolks having manifested that he is shipped on board of one of the steamers that run between this port and the United States, I beg you to order to have him stopped in case he is engaged in any of the steamers dispatched by that consulate of your worthy charge, and remitted to this commandancy; trusting you will advise me accordingly.'

> "You refer this request to the Department for instructions in view of the lack of authority in your office to comply with the captain of the port's request.

> "Your assumption that you have no authority to surrender a person on board of an American vessel in Cuban waters accused of an offence against the laws of Cuba is correct. If the local authorities proceed on board the vessel while it remains in the foreign port and take the man into custody, the consul should report the facts and leave the matter to the Department for such action as it may deem proper.

> "It has been the practice of the local authorities in Spanish-American ports to ask the consent of the consul or other representative of the United States at the port before making arrests in American vessels, and it is presumed that the letter of the captain of the port was written in deference to this practice. It is customary to accompany the application by a specification and proof of the charges upon which the arrest is sought. If the consul is satisfied that the person sought

is wanted to answer for an ordinary criminal offence as distinguished from a political offence, he may inform the authorities that he will not oppose the taking of the accused person from the vessel.

" You will find the precedents applicable to arrests of this character collected and discussed in an instruction of November 18, 1890, to Mr. Mizner, our minister to Guatemala, which is printed in the Foreign Relations for 1890 on pages 123 and following. . . .

" The arrest of offenders on American vessels in Cuban ports cannot be brought within the terms of our extradition treaty with Spain nor assimilated to extradition proceedings. The practice above described is one that has grown up and been acquiesced in as a matter of comity. The vessel is within Cuban jurisdiction, but the local authorities refrain from going on board to make an arrest without the consent of the consul. Where there is no reason to object, the consul informs the authorities that he will make no opposition to the arrest; where the offence is political or there is reason to object to the proceeding the consul informs the authorities that he will protest against their proposed action and report it to his Government. Neither the consul nor the master has authority to surrender the person sought. They can simply refrain from objecting.

" The facts are not given in the captain of the port's letter with any degree of fullness. Upon a full disclosure of the facts you will be able to act in accordance with these instructions. Your answer is not enclosed, but it is presumed that you informed the captain of the port that you had no authority to ' stop' the man as requested, if by stoppage, as is probable, arrest and surrender to the local authorities is meant." (Mr. Rockhill, Third Assist. Sec. of State, to Mr. Williams, consul-general at Havana, Sept. 5, 1895, 149 MS. Inst. Consuls, 433.)

In August, 1892, during a revolution in Venezuela, General Urdaneta forcibly removed from the American steamship *Caracas*, at Puerto Cabello, six Venezuelan passengers who had embarked at La Guayra for Curaçao. Mr. Scruggs, then minister of the United States at Caracas, requested the Government to interpose its authority, or, in default of authority, General Urdaneta being apparently a revolutionary leader, to employ its good offices to effect the prisoners' immediate release. Notes were afterwards exchanged in which Dr. Urbaneja, the Venezuelan minister of foreign affairs, besides intimating that it would be necessary to investigate the facts, observed that if the acts alleged had been committed " against individuals whom the Government of Venezuela considers as hostile," all ships, except foreign men-of-war and merchant vessels having on board " sovereigns or chiefs of foreign countries," entering Venezuelan waters became subject to the jurisdiction of the country so long as they remained there; while Mr. Scruggs replied that, although private vessels were " not exempt from local jurisdiction," the rule was subject to " important qualifications, both general and special," and that the jurisdiction of a nation over its vessels was not lost by their

entrance into the port of another nation, though it was not necessarily exclusive.

Mr. Scruggs, min. to Venezuela, to Mr. Foster, Sec. of State, Aug. 29, 1892,
For. Rel. 1892, 615–618. See, also, 619–620.

" Your action in the premises and your note of the 19th ultimo to
Dr. Urbaneja, then minister for foreign affairs, seem in the main
to have been discreet and proper. It is observed that your note
follows, in general outline, the precedents of the recent Barrundia
episode in Guatemala, so far as they appeared to you to be applicable
to the present case. There are, however, certain changed conditions
in the Puerto Cabello incident which should be borne in mind in any
future proceedings.

" The relation of Gen. Urdaneta to the party at the time in power,
at Caracas, is not clearly understood, but it is believed to have been
one of independent insurrection in the interest of the establishment
of a so-called western league of five Venezuelan States. Having
gained temporary possession of Puerto Cabello, he seems to have
made use of his arbitrary military power to invade a foreign mail
steamer in transit and to remove, by force, certain passengers who
had lawfully embarked at another port of Venezuela, and against
whom no lawful charge existed.

" It would be impossible for this Government to acquiesce in the
arbitrary and forcible violation of its flag by a merely military
power, without due and regular warrant of law and not in conformity
with the ordinary course of justice, even though such force were
exercised by the titular and responsible government of the country
with which this Government maintains friendly relations. The
defiance of international rights and the hostile violation of the flag
are more conspicuously indefensible, from every point of view,
when committed by an irresponsible military chief, representing no
recognized government and using brute force in furtherance of
an insurrectionary movement. . . .

" Should the six passengers still be held by Urdaneta, the commanders of the United States war ships would be fully warranted
in demanding their unconditional surrender, and, if refused, in back-
ing up the demand by all necessary force.

" Should they, however, in the shifting fortunes of war, fall into
the hands of any faction opposed to Urdaneta, and still be held
prisoners, it is probable that the right of this Government to have
them replaced under its flag would be promptly and cheerfully recognized upon request. This presumption would amount to full assurance should they be repossessed by a responsible national authority,
and in such case you will ask their return.

" The commanders of the United States naval vessels will be

furnished with a copy of this instruction, and will govern themselves accordingly."

> Mr. Foster, Sec. of State, to Mr. Scruggs, min. to Venezuela, Sept. 8, 1892, For. Rel. 1892, 623.
>
> The Venezuelan Government, Sept. 17, 1892, published a disavowal of the act of Gen. Urdaneta, stating that the passengers in question "had passports duly signed for Curaçao," and that "as the arrest was executed without orders from the National Executive, officials in all parts of the Republic are hereby directed to give to the above-mentioned citizens, wherever they may find them, every necessary facility to continue on their journey uninterrupted." (For. Rel. 1892, 627.) Oct. 18, 1892, Mr. Scruggs reported that the remnant of Gen. Urdaneta's forces had dispersed, and that Urdaneta himself had fled to Trinidad. (Id. 636.)

" Mr. Thompson reports that a Portuguese merchant vessel which was sailing out of the harbor on the previous day with 91 rebels on board was twice fired upon by the Government and stopped, the refugees being captured."

> Mr. Thompson, min. to Brazil, to Mr. Gresham, Sec. of State, March 17, 1894, For. Rel. 1893, 140. See, also, id. 139, 142.

(3) PASSENGERS IN TRANSIT.

§ 307.

" I have laid before the Earl of Aberdeen Sir J. Barrow's letter of the 9th instant, from which it appears that the Lords Commissioners of the Admiralty wish to know what line of conduct should be pursued by the commanders of the hired vessels which convey the mails between this country and the Peninsula, if it should happen that the authorities of Vigo should attempt to remove from any of these vessels a Spanish subject who may have embarked at Lisbon, being provided with a Portugese passport, countersigned by the British, French, and Belgian legations at Lisbon.

" In answer to the above inquiry, I am directed by Lord Aberdeen to acquaint you, for the information of the Lords Commissioners of the Admiralty, that there is no stipulation in the existing treaties between this country and Spain which can be deemed sufficient to debar the Spanish Government from exercising the right which, in his lordship's opinion, appertains to that Government of claiming its own subjects when they may be found in a Spanish port as passengers on board vessels hired to convey the mails between this country and the Peninsula."

> Opinion of Lord Aberdeen, communicated by Viscount Canning to the secretary of the Admiralty, March 20, 1844, Report of Royal Commission on Fugitive Slaves, 154; cited by Snow, Cases on Int. Law, 148.

In February, 1862, two American citizens, Henry Myers and J. F. Tunstall, members of the crew of the Confederate steamer *Sumter*, then lying at Gibraltar, embarked at that port on the French merchant steamer *Ville de Malaga* for the purpose of proceeding to Cadiz, in order to obtain a supply of coal for the *Sumter*. The *Ville de Malaga*, having called at Tangier, Morocco, Myers and Tunstall went ashore. The United States consul applied to the Moorish Government for a military guard and with its aid arrested the two sojourners while they were in the street and conveyed them to the consulate, where they were kept in irons till the arrival of the U. S. S. *Ino*, when, with the aid of another guard, furnished on application of the consul to the Moorish authorities, they were transferred in irons to that vessel. The commander of the *Ino* afterwards transshipped them to an American merchantman, on which they were brought to the United States. In April, 1862, they arrived at Boston, where they were committed to military custody at Fort Warren. The French Government, " in a very friendly and courteous manner," asked the Government of the United States to consider whether the prisoners while on shore at Tangier were not to be considered constructively as still on board the *Ville de Malaga*, and therefore entitled to the protection of the French flag. The Department of State answered this question in the negative.

Mr. Seward, Sec. of State, to Mr. McMath, consul at Tangier, April 28, 1862, Dip. Cor. 1862, 873–877.

On December 10, 1873, the Brazilian mail steamer *Cuyaba*, commanded by an honorary lieutenant in the Brazilian navy, and subsidized by the Imperial Government for the transportation of its correspondence from the province of Matto Grosso and its legation in Paraguay, arrived at Buenos Ayres, in the Argentine Republic, on a voyage from Asuncion to Rio. On board was one Rivarola, a native of the Argentine Republic and formerly in its military service, who had afterwards entered the army of Paraguay. He had embarked on the *Cuyaba* at Asuncion with his Paraguayan commission and a permit to leave the country, and his passage was paid to Montevideo by the Paraguayan Government. Shortly after the arrival of the steamer at Buenos Ayres an officer of the port went on board and demanded that he be allowed to arrest Rivarola as a political offender. In consequence of the refusal of the captain to acquiesce, the steamer was detained, and the Brazilian minister was informed that the *Cuyaba* could not leave the port unless Rivarola was surrendered. The Brazilian minister protested against the detention of the steamer, and the Argentine authorities " as a matter of courtesy " permitted her to proceed, laying special stress, just as the Brazilian minister had done, on the fact that Rivarola was in the service of the Paraguayan

Government and that the steamer was transporting correspondence of the Brazilian Government. The latter Government subsequently proposed that the treatment of vessels in transit should be regulated by agreement, in order to avoid the possibility of conflicts—a proposition in which the Argentine Government concurred.

> Mr. Shannon, min. to Brazil, to Mr. Fish, Sec. of State, No. 140, Dec. 24, 1873, 40 MS. Desp. from Brazil.
>
> Mr. Pitkin, min. to Arg. Rep., to Mr. Blaine, Sec. of State, March 16, 1891, enclosing a translation of the Brazilian-Argentine correspondence, made from the Argentine Memoria de Relaciones Exteriores, 1874, pp. 726–738. (29 MS. Desp. from Arg. Rep.)
>
> See the postal convention between France and Great Britain of September 24, 1856, by which it is provided that "vessels chartered or subsidized by government," when employed in the service regulated by the treaty, shall be "considered and treated as vessels of war," and that passengers admitted on board such vessels who do not think fit to land shall not under any pretext be removed from on board, be liable to any search, or be subjected to the formality of a visa of their passports. (Hertslet's Treaties, Vol. X. pp. 108, 110. A similar provision was in the earlier convention of April 3, 1843; id. Vol. VI. p. 349.)

"I have to acknowledge the receipt of your No. 316, of the 10th ultimo, in which you inclose copies of the correspond-

Case of Gámez.

ence between the legation at Guatemala and Mr. Leavitt, the United States consul at Managua, respecting the case of José Dolores Gomez [Gámez], and request more definite instructions for such cases.

"It appears that Mr. Gomez, who is said to be a political fugitive from Nicaragua, voluntarily took passage at San José de Guatemala for Punta Arenas, Costa Rica, on board the Pacific Mail steamship *Honduras*, with the knowledge that the vessel would enter *en route* the port of San Juan del Sur, Nicaragua.

"The Government of Nicaragua upon learnng this fact ordered the commandant of the port of San Juan del Sur to arrest Gomez upon the arrival of the *Honduras* at that port.

"The minister for foreign affairs of Nicaragua informed Mr. Leavitt, United States consul at Managua, of the action of the Government by a telegram. . . . It appears that before Mr. Leavitt had an opportunity to act upon this request [to telegraph the captain of the *Honduras* to support the commandant in executing the order], you telegraphed him as follows: ' Reported here arrest of a transit passenger bound to Panama on board steamer *Honduras* at San Juan del Sur. Say respectfully to Nicaraguan minister of foreign affairs that our Government never has consented and never will consent to the arrest and removal from an American vessel, in a foreign port, of any passenger in transit, much less if offence is political.'

" It appears that Mr. Leavitt declined to comply with the request of the minister of foreign affairs, and followed your instructions by submitting a copy in writing to the minister.

" From the brief outline given by the consul of the subsequent proceedings, it appears that the Government authorities at San Juan del Sur, upon the arrival of the *Honduras* at that port, requested the captain to deliver up Mr. Gomez. This he declined to do, and set sail without proper clearance papers.

" The consul reports that for these offenses the captain has been tried by the Nicaraguan Government and found guilty, and although he has not been able to learn the nature of the sentence, he is convinced, from the present attitude of the Government, that the sentence will be executed in case of the return of the captain or the vessel within the jurisdiction of the Government of Nicaragua.

"As the nature and character of the proceedings against the captain of the *Honduras* are not known to this Department, a full and detailed report should be made as early as practicable. It is clear that Mr. Gomez voluntarily entered the jurisdiction of a country whose laws he had violated.

" Under the circumstances it was plainly the duty of the captain of the *Honduras* to deliver him up to the local authorities upon their request.

" It may be safely affirmed that when a merchant vessel of one country visits the ports of another for the purposes of trade, it owes temporary allegiance and is amenable to the jurisdiction of that country, and is subject to the laws which govern the port it visits so long as it remains, unless it is otherwise provided by treaty.

"Any exemption or immunity from local jurisdiction must be derived from the consent of that country. No such exemption is made in the treaty of commerce and navigation concluded between this country and Nicaragua on the 21st day of June, 1867."

> Mr. Bayard, Sec. of State, to Mr. Hall, min. to Cent. Am., March 12, 1885, MS. Inst. Cent. Am. XVIII, 488. This instruction is also printed in For. Rel. 1885, 82, where, however, the following sentence is omitted: " Under the circumstances, it was plainly the duty of the captain of the *Honduras* to deliver him up to the local authorities upon their request." This sentence will be found in Mizner's report on the Barrundia case, For. Rel. 1890, 106, 107. The name of the fugitive was Gámez, not Gomez.

It appears that the foregoing case of Gámez was not judicially ended till 1892, and that the information received by Mr. Leavitt, United States consul at Managua, in February, 1885, as to the result of Captain McCrae's trial, was erroneous. A similar error appears in the special report of Señor Anguiano, minister for foreign affairs of Guatemala, bearing the date of March 31, 1890, on the Barrundia case, in which he states that Captain McCrae was "declared guilty by default."

The facts appear to be as follows:

By article 177 of the penal code of Nicaragua, the crime of " want of respect for the authorities " is committed by those who " openly resist or disobey " them.   An information was filed in the criminal court of first instance, at Rivas, charging Captain McCrae with this offence.   Sentence was rendered Feb. 9, 1885.   The court held (1) that the " open resistance or disobedience " to authority, which was essential to the crime in question, was not " clearly shown," because, while it was true that Captain McCrae did not comply with the command of the comandante, it was also true that the obligation to do so " did not exist, or at least is doubtful," and still more so in the form in which the demand was made, " since, although the ship from which such delivery was demanded is a merchant ship, and ships of this class, according to the general principles of international law, are subject to the local jurisdiction, this subjection is not absolute according to those same principles, but limited to crimes, as well as to offences falling within the jurisdiction of the police and committed on board of said ship;" (2) that the fact that Señor Gámez took passage on the steamer " from one of the ports of the other republics of Central America," rendered the obligation to deliver him up " still more doubtful . . . , because, when certain cases have arisen analogous to the one under consideration among nations more civilized than our own, it has been alleged, as a reason to justify the delivery, that both the embarking of the passenger, as well as his delivery, must be made in national waters; " (3) that Señor Gámez, as appeared by papers before the court, was accused, not of common crimes, but of political offences, under a decree of Sept. 9, 1884, and that " it is a doctrine universally accepted in the works of writers on international law that if indeed merchant vessels are subject to the local jurisdiction as regards persons accused of common crimes, they are always exempt from that jurisdiction as regards those accused of political offences, all of which relieves the captain from the obligation of making the delivery demanded of him; " (4) that, while governments have made little difficulty in stipulating " for the extradition, from places which enjoy extraterritoriality, of those accused of common crimes," yet something more is always required than " a simple verbal order," and, besides, Señor Gámez was " not a person accused of common crimes; " (5) that Captain McCrae's noncompliance with the comandante's order that he come ashore was excused by the fact that the object for which his presence was required was not expressed, no one being obliged to appear before the authorities except for a justifiable and stated cause; (6) that the departure of the *Honduras* before the lapse of the 24 hours did not constitute a crime, but fur-

nished, if anything, only a ground for a civil action; (7) that in
view of these considerations, and of the doctrines laid down by various writers, the charge of disrespect was not established. The court
so adjudged, at the same time sending the sentence for consultation
to the supreme court at Granada. The judgment of this court was
not pronounced till April, 1892, when the sentence below was
approved, without statement of reasons.

> Mr. Shannon, min. to Cent. Am., to Mr. Foster, Sec. of State, Oct. 13,
> 1892, For. Rel. 1892, 45–49.
>
> The court at Rivas cited, in its sentence, Bello, Principios de Derecho
> Internacional, Paris, 1882, Cap. IV., No. 8, pp. 72–73, to the effect
> that, while the local courts have general cognizance of offenses
> committed on merchant ships in territorial waters, yet they do not,
> in the case of a foreign ship, have jurisdiction of acts not prohibited
> by the local law, or of breaches of regulation and discipline committed
> on shipboard by members of the crew ; and Calvo, Derecho Interna-
> cional, Paris, 1868, part 1, Cap. V., sec. 200, pp. 316–317, where it is
> stated that the right of the local authorities to seize criminals who
> have sought refuge on merchant vessels does not exist unless such
> vessels are within the waters of the state, and where, with reference
> to the case of the Spanish political offender Señor Sotelo, who, hav-
> ing embarked on the French merchant vessel L'Océan, at Valencia,
> Spain, was arrested at Alicante, it is stated that " if the vessel had
> received Señor Sotelo at a point where there was no violation of the
> laws of any state, and where it could be considered as a part of
> French territory, the authorities of Alicante would not have been
> able rightfully to arrest the said Señor Sotelo."
>
> To the writers cited by the court, Mr. Shannon added, in his dispatch, a
> passage from Riquelme, Elementos de Derecho Publico Internacional,
> Madrid, 1849, Cap. X., pp. 249–251, where it is stated that if a refu-
> gee should enter a foreign merchant ship " while on the high seas or
> in the port of another state, although the vessel may be going to a
> port of the nation to which the refugee belongs, the extradition will
> not take place, because in granting such asylum there is no infringe-
> ment of the laws of the country in which the ship is."

A correspondent having inquired whether, if he should take passage at New York for Mexico in an American passenger boat, which
stopped for a " few hours " at Havana, he would receive " energetic
protection " from the Department of State in case his arrest should
be attempted by the authorities of that city during the stay of the
vessel in port, the Department replied: " While I am far from saying
that an arrest by Cuban authorities of an American citizen, in an
American passenger vessel, transiently in a Cuban port, the charge
being a political offense, would be looked upon with indifference by
this Department, yet I would advise you not to put yourself in a situation where you would be exposed to such an arrest."

> Mr. Bayard, Sec. of State, to Mr. Carrasco, July 16, 1886, 161 MS. Dom.
> Let. 9.

"The killing of General Barrundia on board the Pacific Mail
steamer *Acapulco*, while anchored in transit in the
Barrundia's case. port of San José de Guatemala, demanded careful
inquiry. Having failed in a revolutionary attempt to invade Guatemala from Mexican territory, General Barrundia took passage at
Acapulco for Panama. The consent of the representatives of the
United States was sought to effect his seizure, first at Champerico,
where the steamer touched, and afterwards at San José. The captain
of the steamer refused to give up his passenger without a written
order from the United States minister; the latter furnished the desired letter, stipulating, as the condition of his action, that General
Barrundia's life should be spared and that he should be tried only for
offenses growing out of his insurrectionary movements. This letter
was produced to the captain of the *Acapulco* by the military commander at San José, as his warrant to take the passenger from the
steamer. General Barrundia resisted capture and was killed. It
being evident that the minister, Mr. Mizner, had exceeded the bounds
of his authority in intervening, in compliance with the demands of
the Guatemalan authorities, to authorize and effect, in violation of
precedent, the seizure on a vessel of the United States of a passenger
in transit charged with political offenses, in order that he might be
tried for such offenses under what was described as martial law, I was
constrained to disavow Mr. Mizner's act and recall him from his post."

> President Harrison, annual message, Dec. 1, 1890. The case of Bar-
> rundia, referred to in the foregoing passage, has been much discussed.
> In these discussions the precise ground of Mr. Mizner's recall, as
> stated by President Harrison, has often been lost sight of. It seems
> to be assumed that Mr. Mizner was censured for his failure to assert
> a right of asylum, but this is hardly accurate. President Harrison,
> it is true, speaks of Barrundia's seizure as having been made "in
> violation of precedent," referring, of course, to what had been the
> practice in Central America. But he also states that when the
> Guatemalan authorities went on board the Acapulco to seize Bar-
> rundia, they read Mr. Mizner's letter authorizing that step as their
> warrant; and it was for "intervening" "to authorize and effect"
> the seizure that Mr. Mizner was recalled.
>
> When Mr. Mizner made his first report of the case by telegraph, the
> Department of State replied that "Barrundia entered the jurisdic-
> tion of Guatemala at his own risk, and it was for the Guatemalan
> authorities to assume jurisdiction at their own responsibility and
> risk; that the Department regretted his having advised or consented
> to the surrender, particularly as violation of the ordinary laws of
> Guatemala was not charged, and as the only allegation was that
> he was to be treated as an enemy under martial law." (Mr. Whar-
> ton, Act. Sec. of State, to Mr. Mizner, min. to Cent. Am., Sept. 2, 1890,
> For. Rel. 1890, 90.)
>
> As to General Barrundia's revolutionary movements in 1888–1890 and
> his reported efforts to raise an expedition in Mexico against the
> Government of Guatemala, see Mr. Bayard, Sec. of State, to Mr.

Bragg, min. to Mexico, Feb. 27, 1889, MS. Inst. Mexico, XXII. 363, referring to Mr. Bragg's No. 188 of Dec. 15, 1888; Mr. Bayard, Sec. of State, to Mr. Whitehouse, chargé, Dec. 15, 1888, MS. Inst. Mex. XXII. 325, referring to Mr. Whitehouse's No. 207, of Dec. 6, 1888; Mr. Blaine, Sec. of State, to Mr. Ryan, min. to Mexico, Feb. 10, 1890, MS. Inst. Mex. XXII. 526, enclosing copy of a dispatch from Mr. Mizner, No. 66, of Jan. 20, 1890; Mr. Wharton, Act. Sec. of State, to Mr. Ryan, min. to Mexico, tel., Aug. 7, 1890, MS. Inst. Mex. XXII. 601.

" In September, 1884, . . . an oral request was made by Señor Cruz, then minister for foreign affairs, of Mr. H. Remsen White-house, the consul-general of the United States, looking to his concurrence in the proposed detention of two men, Modesto Huerte and Francisco Ruiz Sandoval, who were alleged to have taken an active part in a then recent insurrection on the Mexican frontier, and who were passengers in transit on the Pacific Mail steamer *Clyde*, then lying in the port of San José. Mr. Whitehouse, with commendable discretion, answered Señor Cruz in writing that he did not consider himself authorized to act in the matter; and the arrest was not effected.

" A still later case is that of Gomez [Gámez], in Nicaragua, to which you advert as more than justifying your course in respect to General Barrundia. I have carefully examined that case, and am compelled to entertain a very different impression. . . .

" Mr. Bayard, then Secretary of State, in his instruction to Mr. Hall, No. 226 of March 12, 1885, after reviewing the facts so far as known and adverting to the incompleteness of the information as to the proceeding against the captain, said: ' Under the circumstances, it was plainly the duty of the captain of the *Honduras* to deliver him (Gomez) up to the local authorities upon their request.'

" By this, I take it, Mr. Bayard expressed his opinion that the captain, being within the local jurisdiction of a foreign state, might not resist the orderly application of its law to a passenger on board his ship. There is no suggestion that it was the duty of the United States minister to intervene by concurrence or express consent to effect the arrest, either with or without conditions as to the nature of the proceedings against the accused or the penalty to be inflicted. I have yet to find in the records of this Department the faintest trace of any instruction to that end or the slightest warrant for the assumption by any diplomatic or consular representative of authority so to act. It should also be noticed that Mr. Bayard discussed the situation simply from the point of view of the absolute jurisdiction of the country in which the port lies. . . . But between the general doctrine as broadly laid down by my predecessor in office and your action in respect to General Barrundia's seizure there is an impassable space. I am aware that it may be said that after all you merely advised the captain of his duty. But the captain did not simply seek *advice*. In his telegram from Champerico he says that on his arrival at San José he will place himself ' under the orders of the American minister.' He again telegraphed to you later from Champerico that he was ' awaiting your instructions,' and that at San José he expected ' your written orders.' In his last telegram to you, dispatched from San José on arriving at that port on the evening of August 27, he categorically inquires: ' Shall I deliver General Barrundia to the authorities here? If so, please send me a letter with your signature to that effect.'

" There is not here the slightest suggestion that Captain Pitts proposed to act otherwise than by your orders and under your responsibility. It was under these circumstances that you wrote the letter which became, in the hands of a Guatemalan official, the pretext of the attempted seizure of General Barrundia.

" I have adduced ample evidence to show that in respect to political offenders a very considerable and important exception has in practice been made in Spanish-American countries to the general rule as to the exercise of jurisdiction over foreign vessels. The same exception is also found to exist there in the case of asylum in foreign legations. . . . The causes that have operated to foster the maintenance of an asylum for political offenders in legations have contributed, perhaps even more powerfully, to secure a place of refuge for them on foreign vessels. In the first place, their presence on the latter, whether they are simply fleeing from pursuit or are in transit from one foreign country to another, being connected with the purpose of immediate departure, does not so directly tend to fan and perpetuate the popular frenzy as the spectacle of immunity without flight. In the second place, the principle means of communication between the countries of Spanish America is by water, and it has been a matter of common interest to permit such communication to be undisturbed by political events. These considerations peculiarly apply to the vessels of the Pacific Mail Steamship Company, which for many years have been the principal vehicles of transportation, especially for passengers, between several of those countries. Plying between San Francisco and Panama as terminal points, they call at various Central American ports, halting as long as may be necessary to unship and ship cargo, and lying at anchor for that purpose some distance from the shore. While it is true that, being in the ports of the country, the mere circumstance that they are not fastened to a wharf or brought close inshore does not exempt them from the local jurisdiction, yet it is proper to be taken into account as an explanation of the fact that considerations of convenience and interest have been more important and actual than the question of public order and tranquillity.

" It is not doubted that in the many years during which the vessels of the Pacific Mail Steamship Company have plied between San Francisco and Panama they have carried scores and hundreds of persons who have been concerned in political broils and insurrectionary movements in the countries at whose ports they call. Yet the Department is not informed of a single instance in which the peace of the vessel has been disturbed by the seizure of a person on board for any political cause. So far as the Department is able to ascertain, it is the common opinion that such a right of seizure is not asserted or supposed to exist. This is the ' common opinion ' of which Chief Justice Marshall spoke as evidence of that ' common usage ' which determines the law. No better evidence of that opinion could be adduced than the instances which have been disclosed, and with them we may include that of General Barrundia himself, of political fugitives who have gone on board of those vessels knowing that they would call at ports in which their lives would be sacrificed if they went on shore.

" I have said that no better evidence than this fact could be adduced. There is, however, one other circumstance that may be regarded as still more significant, and that is the conduct of the Guatemalan authorities on this particular occasion. To place this in its true light it is only necessary briefly to summarize the various steps taken by them up to the time of the attempted seizure, as follows :

"(1) The communication of the commandant at Champerico to the consular agent of the United States at that place, informing him that the Government of Guatemala intended to seize General Barrundia and requesting him to lend his aid so that the general might be delivered up.

"(2) The reference in this same communication to the extradition treaty, which was said to apply to the case.

"(3) The telegram of Mr. Hosmer to the consular agent at Champerico on the 25th of August, placing the right of seizure on the ground that the Government of Guatemala could search foreign vessels in her own waters for persons suspected of hostility ' in time of war.'

"(4) The repetition of this telegram to the captain of the *Acapulco* at the request of the President of Guatemala.

"(5) The refusal of the captain of the *Acapulco*, accustomed to ply in those waters, to surrender his passenger, and his notification that he placed himself under the orders of the United States minister.

"(6) The omission of the authorities at Champerico, in the face of this refusal, although they had the full sanction of the consul-general of the United States, to make the seizure at that place.

"(7) The assertion in the letter of the minister of foreign relations to Mr. Hosmer of a right to search foreign vessels in territorial waters *in time of war* and capture those suspected of being hostile.

"(8) The reference in the same letter to the contract with the company as the basis of a right to search and capture.

"(9) The guaranty given to you by the President and secretary of foreign relations on the night of the 26th of August that the life of General Barrundia should be spared and that his prosecution should be limited to certain offenses.

"(10) The reference in your telegram to Captain Pitts of the 27th of August, after your conference with the President and minister of foreign relations, to the right to arrest a person on a *neutral ship in time of war*.

"(11) Your letter of the same date to the minister of foreign relations affirming that position and asking guaranties for the treatment of General Barrundia.

"(12) The reply of the minister of foreign relations, who seems to shift his ground by an allusion to " common crimes," but still bases his assertion of the right to seize on the doctrines of contraband, which apply only to a state of war, and gives the guaranties which you requested.

" To these twelve evidences may be added the terms in which Señor Anguiano rejected Commander Reiter's proposition, referring again to a state of war and the exercise of belligerent rights, as well as to the alleged existence of ' martial law.'

" It is no exaggeration to say that these various and unquestionable facts are not compatible with any other theory than that the authorities of Guatemala knew that they were suddenly and without notice violating an established usage. If they had felt that they were acting within their acknowledged right, it would have been unnecessary to appeal to the doctrine of contraband, which was applicable solely to a state of war which had ceased to exist, and which would not, upon the facts then known, have been applicable to General Barrundia, even if war had been flagrant. It is proper to notice that you observed the incongruity of the Guatemalan position as to General Barrundia's status, but, unfortunately, you did not take a stand against it. You observed in your letter to Señor Anguiano of the 27th of August that the case was ' an unusual one, taken in connection with the peace which was practically concluded last night, and of which a general amnesty was a part.' The case was, indeed, most unusual; for if General Barrundia was in the service of the enemy, he came within the amnesty; if he was not in that service, he could not have been treated as contraband. So that on the one or the other horn of the dilemma the Guatemalan demand must fall.

" One other feature of the case yet remains to be considered, that
is, your communication to Commander Reiter, of the United States
steamship *Ranger*, and your failure to avail yourself of the presence
of that vessel. As has already been shown, you sent him two telegrams which you failed to report to this Department. The occasion
of your sending the first one does not appear; but it was sent before
the arrival of the *Acapulco*, and seems to have been intended to facilitate rather than discourage the design of Guatemala to seize General
Barrundia at San José. Upon the receipt of this telegram, Commander Reiter went ashore and telegraphed to you, suggesting that, as
peace was declared, you should ask the Government to permit the
United States steamship *Thetis* to take General Barrundia from the
steamer then in sight and carry him back to the port of Acapulco, in
Mexico. Your second telegram, which was in reply to this, informed
Commander Reiter of the rejection of this offer by the Government of
Guatemala and stated that you had ' advised ' Captain Pitts to
deliver his passenger to that Government. The naval force of the
United States in those waters thus became an acquiescent spectator
of events, although a merchant vessel of the United States was then
lying under the muzzle of guns manned by men who, as you state you
had every reason to believe, were prepared to resort to any act of violence, ' even,' as Señor Anguiano has since declared to you, ' to sinking
the ship, notwithstanding it might have involved a conflict with our
two war vessels then and there present.' "

> Mr. Blaine, Sec. of State, to Mr. Mizner, min. to Cent. Am., Nov. 18, 1890,
> For. Rel. 1890, 123, 136–141.
>
> Mr. Mizner's defense is published in For. Rel. 1890, 144. In the course of
> it, he said:
>
> " To the statement of the President that the attempted arrest was in vio-
> lation of precedent, permit me to say, with all due respect, that I con-
> sidered the law correctly laid down by your immediate predecessor,
> Mr. Bayard, when he said: ' It is clear that Mr. Gomez voluntarily
> entered the jurisdiction of the country whose laws he had violated.
> Under the circumstances, it was plainly the duty of the captain of
> the Honduras to deliver him up to the local authorities upon their
> request.'
>
> " Gomez was a citizen of and a political offender against the laws of
> Nicaragua. No charge of other crimes being made against him, the
> captain of the steamer on which he entered the local waters had
> made no request upon anyone concerning him, yet Mr. Bayard said
> ' it was plainly the duty of the captain to give him up to the local
> authorities.'
>
> " Barrundia was a citizen and a political offender against the laws
> of Guatemala. Besides being indicted for common crimes, he volun-
> tarily came into the jurisdiction of Guatemala on the merchant
> steamer *Acapulco*. The authorities sought to arrest him; the cap-
> tain of the ship asked me to instruct him; I advised him as follows:
> ' If your ship is within 1 league of the territory of Guatemala and

you have on board General Barrundia, it becomes your duty, under the law of nations, to deliver him to the authorities of Guatemala upon their demand.'

"If there is any difference between the two cases, it is in favor of the right of Guatemala to have made the arrest on the ground of his being both a political and common-crimes offender, and sustains me in giving the advice, as it was earnestly sought by the master of the *Acapulco;* while in the Gomez case the captain of the *Honduras* was silent.

"The details in both the Gomez and Barrundia cases were to have been left to the respective captains and local consuls, as it would be impossible for a minister, being hundreds of miles away, to give personal attention to such arrests.

"In the President's first annual message to Congress it was said that 'diplomacy should be frank and free from intrigue,' thereby implying it had not been so in the past; if, as must be conceded, Guatemala had the undoubted right to arrest Barrundia, would it have been 'frank' to have thrown any obstacles in the way of the exercise of that right? On the contrary, would it not have been 'intrigue' to have abetted the captain of the *Acapulco* in evading elementary international law, as we exercise the right to arrest all kinds of offenders on foreign merchant ships when in our ports?

"On the 4th of July last Captain Pitts permitted the authorities of Salvador to arrest Señor Delgado, the minister of foreign relations of that Republic, and take him against his will from the steamer *Acapulco*, as per affidavit sent you. It would seem that the same privilege should have been extended to Guatemala.

"These republics have in the most emphatic manner, in banquets and written communications, thanked me for our good offices in making peace, in which the people, almost en masse, have joined.

"The entire diplomatic corps in Central America, excepting the representative from Mexico, have in writing indorsed my course in the Barrundia case.

"Believing that under all the circumstances I acted in strict accordance with the law of nations, and being absolutely certain of the rectitude of my own intentions, I submit my action and unprecedented treatment to the considerate judgment of my countrymen."

Early in August, 1891, the authorities at La Union, Salvador, demanded the surrender, by the American steamer *City of Panama*, of General Letona, a passenger from Corinto, Nicaragua, to San José, Guatemala. The agent of the steamship company stated that he was demanded as a political criminal; the Salvadorian Government stated that he was demanded for common crimes. The officers of the ship declined to comply with the demand, and the authorities of the port refused to clear her. After waiting twenty-seven hours in port, she sailed without a clearance. On this ground she was, on her arrival at La Libertad, Salvador, detained by the authorities and declared to be confiscated. The Salvadorian Government complained, diplomatically, of the course of the officers of the ship. On the other hand, the minister of the United States in Salvador was instructed to

protest against any "arbitrary actions" of the authorities, and to
report all the facts. The steamer, although served with notice of confiscation, was after some delay permitted to proceed to San José,
Guatemala, where all her passengers were landed. It seems that the
master of the steamer omitted to call at Acajutla, having heard that
General Ezeta would be there, with an armed force, to arrest General
Letona and four other political refugees on board. The minister of
the United States at San Salvador was instructed that the President
of the United States desired an assurance that the steamer would not
be detained when she made her return trip; that it was expected that
the Government of Salvador would allow time for full inquiry, and
that "the sovereignty of Salvador will at the same time be shown due
respect." The Salvadorian Government replied that the steamer
would not be detained longer than usual, and that for any unlawful
detention indemnity would be made, but that the confiscation proceedings would continue to a termination, and that the United States
would be informed of the decision when it was reached. By the Salvadorian law the penalty of leaving port without a clearance is
confiscation.

> Mr. Wharton, Act. Sec. of State, to Mr. Pacheco, min. to Cent. Am., Aug.
> 10, Aug. 13, Aug. 28, Sept. 4, Sept. 14, 1891, For. Rel. 1891, 68, 69–74,
> 76–81.

In May, 1893, during a revolution in Nicaragua, a Krupp breech-
loading gun, carrying a 50-pound shell, was trained against the
Pacific Mail steamer *San José* when entering the port of Corinto,
Nicaragua, and the same thing occurred on the following day on the
entrance of the Pacific Mail steamer *City of New York*, although the
local government had been notified that the United States minister to
Nicaragua was on board. An officer held the firing lanyard in his
hand, so that an accident might have caused the discharge of the gun
and possibly the sinking of the ship, which was at close range. The
motive of the act seems to have been the supposed need of adopting
"extra precautions," owing to the fact that each vessel had called at
the port of San Juan del Sur, then occupied by revolutionists, who, it
was apprehended, might have sent an expedition against Corinto.
The minister of the United States in Nicaragua was instructed to intimate to the Government "that demonstrations of this character are
contrary to the precepts of international law and humanity,. and to
express the confident hope that they will not be permitted to recur in
a Nicaraguan port."

> Mr. Gresham, Sec. of State, to Mr. Baker, min. to Nicaragua, Aug. 18,
> 1893, For. Rel. 1893, 213.
> Assurances were given that the offence would not be repeated. (For.
> Rel. 1893, 214.)

Dr. Policarpo Bonilla, a native of Honduras, took passage on the
American steamer *Costa Rica* at Corinto, Nicaragua,
November 4, 1893, for San José, Guatemala. The
Costa Rica arrived at Amapala, Honduras, early in the morning on
the following day. During the afternoon an official in uniform
came on board and delivered to the master a letter, signed by the
captain of the port and demanding the surrender of Dr. Bonilla,
on the ground that he had been "sentenced by the courts of the
Republic." Coupled with the demand was an assurance that his
life would be guaranteed, and a statement that merchant vessels,
according to the laws of the United States and of Honduras, "do
not enjoy the immunities which they claim in waters of foreign
countries, they being wholly subject to the laws of the foreign
country in whose waters they happen to be."[a] The master replied
in writing: "After consultation with the minister of the United
States now on board my vessel, I beg to state that your demand
can not be complied with." The captain of the port protested,
"disclaiming all responsibilities for whatever may occur in consequence of such refusal;" but, later in the day, clearance papers
were issued to the steamer. At three o'clock on the morning of the
6th of November, a boat came alongside with an official bearing a
communication from the captain of the port, which renewed the
demand for Bonilla's surrender and stated that, if the steamer
weighed anchor without first delivering him up, she would be fired
on. The master orally replied that he would answer in half an hour,
and immediately proceeded to get underway. As he was getting
out of the harbor several cannon shots were fired at the steamer from
the shore, but none of them took effect, although one fell about 100
feet astern, between the *Costa Rica* and the *City of Panama*, another
American steamer which was anchored in the port. There were on
the *Costa Rica* at the time, besides 62 members of the crew, 74 passengers, including Mr. Baker, U. S. minister to Nicaragua, and his
family. Dr. Bonilla stated that he was engaged in a revolution in
Honduras two years previously, but that the Congress had since
granted an amnesty to the participants, and that he had become a
member of the Congress at Managua, Nicaragua. On being advised
by a telegram from Mr. Baker "that American steamer *Costa Rica*,
on which he was a passenger, was fired upon at Amapala after clearance because the captain refused, on demand, to give up Bonilla,
a Honduran, also a passenger," the Department of State, by direction
of the President, instructed the American minister to Honduras to
"protest against this wanton and illegal act;" and, it appearing that
he had inquired of the Honduran Government whether it had author-

Case of Bonilla.

---

[a] For. Rel. 1893, 161.

ized the firing, he was instructed to "protest without delay, . . . and demand disavowal and apology, whether President authorized firing or not." [a] These instructions were carried out. The minister of foreign affairs of Honduras, by instruction of the President of the Republic, answered: "This Government has already disavowed and does so now the acts referred to, not having caused them nor ever having had the least intention of causing any offence to the Government of the United States, with which the President always wishes to preserve the best relations. This Government became aware with great pain of such an unfortunate incident, whose details I hastened to transmit by telegraph to you on the 6th instant. As regards the satisfaction, it would be desirable before offering it to know the terms in which you ask it." The minister of the United States was instructed to reply: "The President accepts these frank expressions of disavowal and regret as sufficient and will waive further formal apology in the interest of friendly feeling." [b]

"I have given attention to your letter of the 13th instant, in which you refer to the recent firing upon your steamer *Costa Rica* in the Honduranian port of Amapala, and repeat the suggestion contained in your letter of November 11, 1893, that a definite policy in respect to surrendering accused criminals when claimed by the local authorities in a port of call be outlined for the guidance of your commanders.

"It is not practicable to lay down a general fixed rule applicable to the varying conditions in such cases. As a comprehensive principle, it is well established in international law that a merchant vessel in a foreign port is within the local jurisdiction of the country with respect to offenses or offenders against the laws thereof, and that an orderly demand for surrender of a person accused of crime by due process of law, with exhibition of a warrant of arrest in the hands of the regularly accredited officers of the law, may not be disregarded nor resisted by the master of the ship. On the same voyage when the Amapala incident occurred, Capt. Dow appears to have acted on this principle in allowing the arrest at other ports, on proper judicial warrant, of two or three other passengers accused of crime. That the passenger may have come on board at the port where the demand is

---

[a] Mr. Gresham, Sec. of State, to Mr. Young, min. to Honduras, Nov. 7 and Nov. 10, 1893, For. Rel. 1893, 154.

[b] Mr. Gresham, Sec. of State, to Mr. Young, min. to Honduras, tel., Nov. 12, 1893, For. Rel. 1893, 155. On the arrival of the *Costa Rica* at Acajutla, in Salvador, November 8, 1893, Commander Lyons, U. S. S. *Alliance*, appointed under article 1720, U. S. Naval Regulations of 1893, a board of three naval officers to proceed on board the *Costa Rica* and request her commanding officer, and, with his concurrence, others who had personal knowledge of the incident at Amapala, to make a statement under affirmation concerning it. The commission held the inquiry and made a report. (For. Rel. 1893, 158, 163.)

made, or at another port of the same country, is immaterial to the right of local jurisdiction.

"Arbitrary attempts to capture a passenger by force, without regular judicial process, in a port of call, may call for disavowal when, as in the present case at Amapala, the resort to violence endangers the lives of innocent men and the property of a friendly nation. Whether, if force be threatened, the master of the vessel is justified in putting in jeopardy, by his resistance, the interests committed to his care, must be largely a question for his discretion. It is readily conceivable that the consequences of futile resistance to overpowering force may be such as to make the resistance itself unwarrantable.

"The so-called doctrine of asylum having no recognized application to merchant vessels in port, it follows that a shipmaster can found no exercise of his discretion on the character of the offense charged. There can be no analogy to proceedings in extradition when he permits a passenger to be arrested by the arm of the law. He is not competent to determine whether the offense is one justifying surrender, or whether the evidence in the case is sufficient to warrant arrest and commitment for trial, or to impose conditions upon the arrest. His function is passive merely, being confined to permitting the regular agents of the law, on exhibition of lawful warrant, to make the arrest. The diplomatic and consular representatives of the United States in the country making the demand are as incompetent to order surrender by way of quasi-extradition as the shipmaster is to actively deliver the accused. This was established in the celebrated Barrundia case by the disavowal and rebuke of Minister Mizner's action, in giving to the Guatemalan authorities an order for the surrender of the accused.

" If it were generally understood that the masters of American merchantmen are to permit the orderly operation of the law in ports of call, as regards persons on board accused of crime committed in the country to which the port pertains, it is probable on the one hand that occasions of arrest would be less often invited by the act of the accused in taking passage with a view to securing supposed asylum, and on the other hand that the regular resort to justice would replace the reckless and offensive resort to arbitrary force against an unarmed ship which, when threatened or committed, has in more than one instance constrained urgent remonstrance on the part of this Government."

> Mr. Gresham, Sec. of State, to Mr. Huntington, Dec. 30, 1893, For. Rel. 1894, 296 ; 194 MS. Dom. Let. 678. Enclosed, Jan. 31, 1894, to Mr. Young, min. to Guatamala and Honduras, For. Rel. 1894, 297.
>
> This letter is quoted in an instruction to Mr. Dawson, vice-consul at San Salvador, in relation to the arrest of General Bustamente, on a Pacific Mail steamer, at Libertad, in 1895. On being requested to telegraph the facts, Mr. Dawson replied : " Bustamente arrested Libertad

waters. Captain Johnstone delivered him voluntarily, article 24, contract Government, Pacific Mail. Consul consented. No force employed.
No protest entered." Mr. Dawson was informed that this telegram
did not fully answer the Department's inquiry, the object of which
was to ascertain whether the arrest was made " by regular process of
law, under a judicial warrant . . . issued by a court of competent
jurisdiction," or whether the prisoner was " taken off the ship by military force, being surrendered by the captain of the ship with the
consent of the consul." (Mr. Rockhill, 3d Assist. Sec of State, to
Mr. Dawson, Sept. 21, 1895, 149 MS. Inst. Consuls, 573.)

The letter to Mr. Huntington was communicated by Mr. Gresham, Secretary of State, to Mr. Baker, United States minister to Nicaragua,
Jan. 31, 1894. March 22, 1898, Mr. Sherman, Secretary of State,
instructed Mr. Merry, Mr. Baker's successor, that he was to be
guided by it. (MS. Inst. Cent. Am. XXI. 290.)

As to the case of Moritz Stern, a citizen of the United States, taken from a
Chilean passenger steamer at Guayaquil, in Ecuador, see Mr. Uhl,
Act. Sec. of State, to Mr. Strobel, min. to Ecuador, May 23 and Sept.
14, 1894, MS. Inst. Ecuador, I. 432, 436, acknowledging the receipt
of dispatches. Stern was held in custody. The Department of
State expressed itself as " well satisfied " with Mr. Strobel's " efforts
to secure a speedy disposition of Stern's case in the court."

Nov. 9, 1892, the authorities at La Guayra, Venezuela, by order of
the minister of hacienda, demanded of the master of
Case of Mijares. the American steamer *Philadelphia* the surrender of
Pedro Vicente Mijares, a Venezuelan citizen, who had embarked at
the Dutch port of Curaçao for New York. No charge of violation by
Mijares of the ordinary law of the country was made; he was demanded simply as " an enemy of the Government," and the demand
was made orally. He was not a military man, nor did it appear that
he was in the service of any enemies of the Government. The civil
war had ended a month before, and there had since been no proclamation of martial law in any part of the Republic. The master declined
to surrender his passenger, and the customs authorities refused to
clear the vessel or to return her register. She was thereupon cleared
by the United States consul, acting under the instructions of Mr.
Scruggs (then American minister to Venezuela). When it became
known at Caracas that the steamer had been cleared by the consul and
would sail, Dr. Rojas, minister of foreign affairs, and Dr. Seijas, legal
adviser of the ministry, called on Mr. Scruggs and requested him to
order the master to deliver Mijares up. " I courteously but firmly
declined to do this," wrote Mr. Scruggs, " and before they left succeeded in convincing them that the captain had acted quite properly
in the premises. They denied the truth of the report (then current)
that an order had been issued to fire upon the *Philadelphia*, should
she attempt to leave with Mijares on board. . . . The *Philadelphia*
sailed next day (the 10th), but without her register, . . . I have

received the assurance of Dr. Rojas that the papers and other papers . . . will be delivered to the consul before the ship returns." [a]

Proceedings were then begun in the courts of Venezuela against the *Philadelphia*, under the revenue laws, for sailing without a clearance from the custom-house. They resulted, Dec. 2, 1892, in the imposition, by the national judge of finance, at La Guayra, of a fine of 10,000 bolivars (about $2,000) on the master. This judgment having come in the regular course before the high Federal court for revision, that tribunal, Jan. 12, 1893, reversed it for irregularities in procedure, and ordered a new trial. April 7, 1893, the judicial proceedings were ended by the chief of the executive power, who, "considering the peculiarity of the circumstances of the case and that the said [steamship] line has always shown itself strictly observant of its duties," granted, with the advice of his cabinet, a pardon to the steamship and her master. [b]

The case of thirty-three men who were expelled from Nicaraguan territory for being implicated in an insurrection, and who, it was apprehended, might attempt to reenter Nicaraguan jurisdiction, did not come within the principle of either the Barrundia case or the Gamez case; and if, when they were attempting to land, they were arrested by the judicial authority on a merchant ship in port, their release or delivery to an American naval commander could not be claimed, but he would be obliged to limit his action to the exercise of good offices so far as possible, in conjunction with the consular representative of the United States, to secure for them fair and open process of law with every opportunity of defence, and, if convicted, leniency of treatment.

> Mr. Hay, Sec. of State, to Sec. of Navy, July 15, 1899, 238 MS. Dom. Let. 487, enclosing a copy of an instruction to the United States consul at San Juan del Norte, No. 115, May 13, 1899.

---

[a] Mr. Scruggs, min. to Venezuela, to Mr. Foster, Sec. of State, Nov. 18, 1892, For. Rel. 1892, 637.

[b] Mr. Partridge, min. to Venezuela, to Mr. Gresham, Sec. of State, April 11, 1893, For. Rel. 1893, 722–724.

CHAPTER VIII.

THE HIGH SEAS.

I. *THE TERM "HIGH SEAS."*

§ 308.

" The term ' high seas,' as used by legislative bodies, the courts, and text writers, has been construed to express a widely different meaning. As used to define the jurisdiction of admiralty courts, it is held to mean the waters of the ocean exterior to low-water mark. As used in international law, to fix the limits of the open ocean, upon which all peoples possess common rights, the ' great highway of nations,' it has been held to mean only so much of the ocean as is exterior to a line running parallel with the shore and some distance therefrom, commonly such distance as can be defended by artillery upon the shore, and therefore a cannon shot o⁻ a marine league (three nautical or four statute miles)."

Second court of commissioners of Alabama claims, Stetson *v.* United States, No. 3993, class 1, Moore, Int. Arbitrations, IV. 4332, 4335. It was held in this case that section 5 of the act of June 5, 1882, which directed the examination of claims resulting from damage done on the " high seas " by Confederate cruisers, although the loss or damage occurred " within 4 miles of the shore," did not embrace claims for losses inflicted in the territorial waters of the United States, whether such waters lay within a line drawn 4 statute miles from the shore of the open sea, or within bays which, although more than 3 nautical or 4 statute miles in width, were to be considered as subject to the exclusive jurisdiction of the United States.

For a further discussion by the same tribunal of the meaning of the term " high seas " in the act of 1882, see the case of the ship *John H. Jarvis*, Moore, Int. Arbitrations, V. 4677.

As to what constituted a " Confederate cruiser " in the sense of the act, see Moore, Int. Arbitrations, V. 4673.

As to the extent of territorial waters, see, supra, §§ 144–153.

II. *FREEDOM OF THE SEAS.*

1. Prohibition of Visit and Search in Time of Peace.

§ 309.

Judicial decisions. " No nation can exercise a right of visitation and search upon the common and unappropriated parts of the sea, save only on the belligerent claim."

Lord Stowell, in the case of Le Louis, 2 Dodson, 210, 245, adopted by Mr. Cass, Sec. of State, in instructions to Mr. Dallas, min. to England, June 30, 1858, MS. Inst. Gr. Br. XVII. 115.

See, as to the fur-seal fisheries in Bering Sea, supra, §§ 172, 173.

As to the abandonment by Great Britain, as the result of the peace of Amiens, of the honor exacted from the Dutch to the British flag in the " narrow seas," including the British and St. George's Channel, see Hansard, XXXVI. (1802), 721.

For correspondence between the United States and Great Britain as to the protection of cattlemen on the ships of the two nations, see For. Rel. 1895, I. 728–736 ; 1896, 293–298.

For correspondence between the same countries as to fires on board cotton ships, see For. Rel. 1895, I. 736 ; 1896, 310–316.

The right of search is a strictly belligerent right.

The Antelope, 10 Wheat. 66 ; The Marianna Flora, 11 Wheat. 1.

See, in the same sense, Mr Fish, Sec. of State, to Mr. Borie, Sec. of Navy, May 18, 1869, 81 MS. Dom. Let. 124 ; supra, I. 193, § 67.

Ships of war sailing under the authority of their government, instructed to arrest pirates and other public offenders, may approach vessels at sea to ascertain their character.

A ship under such circumstances is not bound to lie by and await approach, but she has no right to fire at an approaching cruiser upon a mere conjecture that she is a pirate, especially if her own conduct has invited the approach ; and, if this be done, the cruiser may lawfully repel force by force and capture her.

The commander of a cruiser having fairly exercised his discretion, in judging whether an attack on him was piratical, can not be held responsible in damages for having come to a conclusion which subsequent judicial investigation shows to have been incorrect.

The Marianna Flora, 11 Wheat. 1.

On May 16, 1811, an encounter took place between the United States
frigate *President* and the British sloop of war *Little*
Incidents and dec- *Belt*, near Cape Charles. Only one person was
larations, 1811-
1872 : "Presi- wounded on the *President*, though her rigging was
dent" and "Lit- injured. On the *Little Belt* there were thirteen killed
tle Belt." and a number wounded. Courts of inquiry were held
in both countries, with conflicting results.

The British Government took the ground that the shot fired by the
President, for the purpose of hailing, was a hostile attack, and was to
be returned as such. On the other hand, it was maintained by Mr.
Monroe, Secretary of State, in a note to Mr. Foster, British minister,
October 11, 1811, " that Commodore Rodgers [of the *President*] pursued a vessel, which had at first pursued him, and hailed her as soon
as he approached within suitable distance, are circumstances which
can be of no avail to Captain Bingham [of the *Little Belt*]. The
United States have a right to know the national character of the
armed ships which hover on their coast, and whether they visit it
with friendly or illicit views; it is a right inseparable from the
sovereignty of every independent state, and intimately connected with
their tranquillity and peace. . . . For these reasons the conduct of
Commodore Rodgers, in approaching the *Little Belt*, to make the
necessary inquiries, and exchange a friendly salute, was strictly
correct."

A number of witnesses examined before the court of inquiry in the
United States concurred in testifying that the *Little Belt* did not
display her colors until it was too dark to distinguish them, and that
the first shot was fired by her and was returned by a single gun, and
that the general fire was commenced by the *Little Belt*. It was also
proved that when the fire of the *Little Belt* was silenced, Commodore
Rodgers exerted himself to save her from further injury. The findings of the court were in accordance with the evidence.

> Mr. Monroe, Sec. of State, to Mr. Foster, Brit. min., Oct. 11, 1811, Am.
> State Papers, For. Rel. III. 476.
> For the proceedings of the court of inquiry in the United States, see id.
> 477.

" The convention with Russia will, I presume, be very satisfactory
to the nation. It consists of six articles. By the first
Convention with it is stipulated that the citizens and subjects of the
Russia, 1824.
two parties shall not be disturbed in navigating the
great Pacific Ocean nor in landing on the coast (at points which are
not already occupied) for the purpose of commerce with the natives,
under the following restrictions: Article 2. That the citizens of the
United States shall not land at any point where there is a Russian
establishment without permission from the governor or comman-

dant, reciprocated as to Russians in our favor. 3. No establishment shall be formed by citizens of the United States, nor under their authority, on the northwest coast of America, nor in the adjacent islands, north of 54° 40′ north latitude; nor by Russians south of that latitude. 4. For ten years from the signature of the treaty the vessels of the two powers and of their citizens and subjects may reciprocally frequent, without impediment, the interior seas, gulfs, harbors, and creeks on the coast to fish and trade with the natives. 5. From this privilege of trade are excepted spirituous liquors, arms, swords, powder, and munitions of war of every kind. Both powers agree to give effect to this provision, it being stipulated that the vessels of neither shall visit or detain the vessels of the other, by the seizure of merchandise or any measure of force, which may be engaged in this commerce; the high contracting parties reserving to themselves the right to fix and inflict the penalties on any breaches of the article. The sixth requires that the ratifications be exchanged in ten months from its signature.

" By this convention the claim to the ' *mare clausum* ' is given up, a very high northern latitude is established for our boundary with Russia, and our trade with the Indians placed for ten years on a perfectly free footing, and after that term left open for negotiation. The British Government had, at our suggestion, agreed to treat in concert with us on both topics, the navigation and boundaries, including the trade with the Indians, but on seeing that passage in the message which discountenanced the idea of further colonization on this continent, declined it, on the presumption that it would give offense to Russia, a reason which was communicated by Mr. Bagot to the Russian Government and also to Mr. Middleton. By entering into the negotiation with us singly, and conceding to us these points, especially that relating to navigation, the Emperor has shown great respect for the United States. England will, of course, have a similar stipulation in favor of the free navigation of the Pacific, but we shall have the credit of having taken the lead in the affair. I think, also, that the event derives additional importance from the consideration that the treaty has been concluded since the receipt at Petersburg of the message at the opening of the last session of Congress, which expressed sentiments in regard to our principles and hemisphere adverse to those entertained by the Holy Alliance."

President Monroe to Mr. Madison, Aug. 2, 1824, Madison MSS. Library of Congress.

" The Governments of Great Britain and France have issued orders

British-French orders as to Cuba.

to their naval commanders on the West India station to prevent, by force if necessary, the landing of adventurers from any nation on the island of Cuba with hostile intent. The copy of a memorandum of a conversation on this subject between the chargé d'affaires of Her Britannic Majesty and the Acting Secretary of State and of a subsequent note of the former to the Department of State are herewith submitted, together with a copy of a note of the Acting Secretary of State to the minister of the French Republic and of the reply of the latter on the same subject. These papers will acquaint you with the grounds of this interposition of the two leading commercial powers of Europe, and with the apprehensions, which this Government could not fail to entertain, that such interposition, if carried into effect, might lead to abuses in derogation of the maritime rights of the United States. The maritime rights of the United States are founded on a firm, secure, and well-defined basis; they stand upon the ground of national independence and public law, and will be maintained in all their full and just extent. The principle which this Government has heretofore solemnly announced it still adheres to, and will maintain under all circumstances and at all hazards. That principle is that in every regularly documented merchant vessel the crew who navigate it and those on board of it will find their protection in the flag which is over them. No American ship can be allowed to be visited or searched for the purpose of ascertaining the character of individuals on board, nor can there be allowed any watch by the vessels of any foreign nation over American vessels on the coasts of the United States or the seas adjacent thereto. It will be seen by the last communication from the British chargé d'affaires to the Department of State, that he is authorized to assure the Secretary of State that every care will be taken that in executing the preventive measures against the expeditions which the United States Government itself has denounced as not being entitled to the protection of any government no interference shall take place with the lawful commerce of any nation.

" In addition to the correspondence on this subject herewith submitted, official information has been received at the Department of State of assurances by the French Government that in the orders given to the French naval forces they were expressly instructed, in any operations they might engage in, to respect the flag of the United States wherever it might appear, and to commit no act of hostility upon any vessel or armament under its protection."

> President Fillmore, second annual message, Dec. 2, 1851 (Mr. Webster, Sec. of State), Richardson's Messages and Papers of the Presidents, V. 117. See, in this relation, Mr. Dallas, min. to England, to Mr. Cass, Sec. of State, June 11, 1858, 2 Dallas' Letters from London, 28.

" There is no question in regard to our international relations which has within a recent period been more fully discussed than that respecting the limits to the right of visitation and search. This is a belligerent right, and no nation which is not engaged in hostilities can have any pretense to exercise it upon the open sea. The established doctrine upon this subject is " that the right of visitation and search of vessels, armed or unarmed, navigating the high seas in time of peace, does not belong to the public ships of any nation. This right is strictly a belligerent right, allowed by the general consent of nations in time of war, and limited to those occasions.' The undersigned avails himself of the authority and language of a distinguished writer on international law : ' We again repeat, that it is impossible to show a single passage of any institutional writer on public law, or the judgment of any court by which that law is administered, either in Europe or America, which will justify the exercise of such a right on the high seas in time of peace independent of special compact. The right of seizure for a breach of the revenue laws or laws of trade and navigation of a particular country, is quite different. The utmost length to which the exercise of this right on the high seas has ever been carried, in respect to the vessels of another nation, has been to justify seizing them within the territorial jurisdiction of the state against whose laws they offend, *and* pursuing them, in case of flight beyond that limit, arresting them on the ocean, and bringing them in for adjudication before the tribunals of that state. " This, however," suggests the Supreme Court of the United States, in the case before quoted of the *Marianna Flora*, " has never been supposed to draw after it any right of visitation *or* search. The party, in such case, seizes at his peril. If he establishes the forfeiture, he is justified." '

" This is not peculiarly an American doctrine; it has the sanction of the soundest expositors of international law. Upon the ocean, in time of peace, that is, among nations not in war, all are entirely equal. . . .

" The most distinguished judge that ever presided over the British high court of admiralty has expressed himself clearly and emphatically on the subject of the right of visit and search, and declared ' that no authority can be found which gives any right of *visitation or interruption* over the vessels or navigation of other states on the high seas, except what the right of war gives to belligerents against neutrals.' "

Mr. Marcy, Sec. of State, to Mr. Cueto, Span. min., March 28, 1855 : Report of Sec. of Navy, March 10, 1856, S. Ex. Doc. 1, 35 Cong. special sess. 4.

This note referred to the visitation and search by the Spanish cruiser *Ferrolona*, on the high seas, of the American mail steamer *El Dorado*, while the latter was on her regular route between Aspinwall and New Orleans.

With reference to this case, Mr. Dobbin issued the following instruction : " I . . . call your attention chiefly to the recent firing into the mail steamer *El Dorado*, and subjecting that vessel to delay, visitation, and search. This act is regarded as an exercise of power which the United States have ever firmly refused to recognize, and to which they will never submit. In the absence of a declaration of war, which alone belongs to Congress, our officers in command of ships of war would have no right to pursue and retaliate for such an act. But, if present when the offence is perpetrated upon a vessel rightfully bearing the flag of our country, the officer would be regarded as derelict in his duty if he did not promptly interpose, relieve the arrested American ships, prevent the exercise of this assumed right of visitation or search, and repel the interference by force," (Mr. Dobbin, Sec. of Navy, to Capt. Crabbe, U. S. S. *Jamestown*, April 3, 1855, S. Ex. Doc. 1, 35 Cong. special sess. 7–8.)

See, to the same effect, Mr. Dobbin to Commodore McCauley, April 10, 1855, id. 2–4.

" The Spanish Government claims the right to search or detain foreign vessels in its own territorial waters for the purpose of ascertaining their character, but it is not understood that it meets this case with a positive declaration that the *El Dorado* was within its territorial waters.

" The United States will never concede that, in the thoroughfares of commerce between Cape San Antonio and Yucatan, or between the Key of Florida and the Cuban coast, the territorial waters of Spain extend beyond cannon shot or a marine league. Considering the vast amount of property transported over those thoroughfares it is of the greatest importance to the interests of commerce that the extent of Spanish jurisdiction in these two straits should be accurately understood." (Mr. Marcy, Sec. of State, to Mr. Escalante, Span. min., Oct. 29, 1855, MS. Notes to Spain, VII. 67.)

"The course pursued by your Government in offering an adequate compensation for the interruption of the voyage of the *Dorcas C. Yeaton* [by the Peruvian armed vessel *Tumbes*], and its acceptance by the captain in satisfaction of the injury, has withdrawn the question of damages on account of that occurrence from the existing controversy; but the boarding of the *Dorcas C. Yeaton* by the Peruvian vessel of war presents very grave considerations for the interposition of this Government. The American vessel was sailing upon the high seas, under the flag of her country, when she was approached by the Peruvian vessel of war, which, to adopt the expression used by you, ' made the usual signal for her to heave to,' or, in other words, fired a gun to indicate to the unarmed ship that she must stop and await the pleasure of the armed one.

Case of the " Dorcas C. Yeaton." ·

" Before proceeding to examine the facts, it is necessary to lay down the principle of immunity which protects the vessels of every independent power upon the ocean from search or seizure by another power. In a recent correspondence with Lord Napier, the minister of Her Britannic Majesty to the United States, I had occasion to investigate this subject, and to make known the views of the United States in relation to it, and their determination not to submit to the detention and search of their vessels in time of peace under any pretext whatever. . . .

" While informing me that you deem it unnecessary '. to discuss or put forward the right of visitation,' you remark that in a conversation you had with me, I stated ' there were cases in which a national vessel might be justified in visiting a merchant vessel on the high seas, and that the Government of the United States would not in such cases make a formal reclamation,' and that I had put a case illustrative of this position applicable to the circumstances of the *Tumbes*. . . . By adverting to the extracts of the letter to Lord Napier, which accompany this communication, you will perceive at once that I do not occupy the position you assign to me. I claim a total immunity for the vessels of the United States ' upon the common and unappropriated parts of the ocean,' to use the expression of Lord Stowell, in time of peace, under all circumstances. There is no case in which a forcible entrance into them can be justified by another power. That is, there is no case in which such entry is a lawful act. It may be an excusable one under peculiar circumstances, of entrance and of conduct, which might well induce the aggrieved party to renounce all claim for reparation; as, for instance, if a piratical vessel were known to be cruising in certain latitudes, and a national armed ship should fall in with a vessel sailing in those regions, and answering the description given of the pirate, the visitation of a peaceable merchantman in such a case, with a view to ascertain her true character, would give no reasonable cause of offence to the nation to which she might belong, and whose flag she carried.

" But if I understand correctly the position you take in behalf of your Government respecting the detention of the *Dorcas C. Yeaton*, it is unnecessary for me to discuss the general question of the claim of visitation, except to express the dissent of the United States from the principles in relation to it which you have laid down. That being done, I have to observe that the question of private injury having been removed by the action of Peru, if the entrance into the American vessel were a peaceable one, without violence or menace, the United States have no demand to make of the Government of your country, either in satisfaction of the act or for the punishment of the officer by whose orders it was committed. There is conflicting testimony as to the precise circumstances which occurred, but there is no version of them which attributes any offensive character to the transaction. Assuming, therefore, that such are the views of your Government, and the use of force on this occasion being denied and disavowed on its behalf, the United States have no longer any cause of complaint against the Government of Peru for this detention of one of their vessels."

Mr. Cass, Sec. of State, to Mr. Osma, Peruvian min., May 22, 1858, 50 Br. & For. State Papers, 1146, 1147–1148, 1148–1149.

" In the despatch of Lord John Russell, I perceive he refers to the American flag as if it were contended that that national ensign afforded protection to the vessel bearing it. I beg you to assure his lordship that this country advances no such pretension. The immunity of a vessel upon the ocean depends upon her national character, to be ascertained, if contested, by her papers, and, if need be, by other circumstances, but not by the flag under which she sails. If a foreign cruiser boards a vessel with American colors, and she proves not to belong to this country, we have no right to complain of her examination or capture; but if the papers justify an assumption of the flag, and she is actually an American vessel, then a trespass has been committed by such cruiser, for which the government to which it belongs is responsible; and the act itself will be more or less condemnable as the circumstances leading to it are of a character to justify suspicion or to repel it, and as the conduct of the boarding party is more or less offensive or injurious." (Mr. Cass, Sec. of State, to Mr. Dallas, min. to England, Oct. 27, 1860, H. Ex. Doc. 7, 36 Cong. 2 sess. 505.)

July 27, 1858, Captain Jarvis, of the U. S. S. *Savannah*, was instructed to proceed to San Juan del Norte, in Nicaragua. He was directed at all times to afford protection to the citizens of the United States and their property, and, if occasion should arise, to " protect any vessel of the United States from search or detention on the high seas by the armed ships of any other power."

Mr. Toucey, Sec. of Navy, to Captain Jarvis, July 27, 1858, S. Ex. Doc. 29, 36 Cong. 1 sess. 2.

March 6, 1860, two vessels, apparently men-of-war, but without any colors flying, appeared at anchor off Antigua, a small place about 14 miles north of Vera Cruz. At that time the contest was still going on in Mexico between the constitutional government of President Jaurez at Vera Cruz and the Miramon government, which occupied the capital, and a number of American men-of-war lay off Vera Cruz under instructions to afford protection to the persons and property of American citizens. The two vessels above mentioned, after lying at anchor for some time, got under way and proceeded to the southward and eastward, paying no attention to the flags of the men-of-war nor to those of the castle, from which a gun was fired to attract their attention. Taking no notice of signals, they proceeded to Anton Lizardo, where they came to anchor. Under the circumstances Captain Jarvis, of the U. S. S. *Savannah*, in command of the American naval forces, deemed it to be his duty to ascertain who they were, and he instructed Commander Turner, U. S. S. *Saratoga*, to obtain the desired information. As the wind was ahead, Commander Turner made use of two small American steamers, called the *Indianola* and *Wave*, to take the *Saratoga* in tow, and, placing

Case of the "General Miramon."

on each of these vessels a detachment of men and marines, he proceeded to Anton Lizardo. On arriving there and after the tow was cast off the small steamers hailed and reported that the larger of the two vessels was under way and endeavoring to escape. Commander Turner ordered them to pursue and, if possible, to board it, so that he might communicate with the senior officer, and at the same time fired a shot ahead to bring the vessel to. When, however, the small steamers got close by, the vessel opened a fire of guns and musketry upon them, and it was reported that at the same time the other and smaller vessel was slipping her cable. Commander Turner believing the latter to be acting in complicity with and under the orders of the larger vessel, and being apprehensive that it might go to the latter's assistance and oblige him to recall the small steamers or to witness their capture and destruction, gave it a broadside. It then ran up the Spanish flag. Meanwhile the larger vessel was hotly engaged with the two small steamers, by which it was run aground and captured. It turned out that this vessel was the *General Miramon*, commanded by Captain Marin, and that the smaller vessel was the *Marquis of Havana*, a Spanish ship which was employed by Captain Marin as a tender to transport stores and munitions of war. Captain Marin subsequently stated to Commander Turner that when he observed the American ships entering the harbor he informed his crew that he believed them to be American men-of-war and forbade the men to fire, but that he had found it impossible to control the crew, which was composed of new and undisciplined men of various nationalities. Commander Turner stated, however, that during the action he heard Captain Marin calling on the men to board with him. Captain Jarvis in his report of the incident approved the action of Commander Turner, saying that he and the officers under him deserved " great credit for their promptness in defending their flag." Captain Jarvis stated that he should send the captured vessel to New Orleans as soon as possible, to be delivered to the United States marshal. The opinion of the Government of the United States was expressed by Mr. Toucey, Secretary of the Navy, as follows: " Upon the facts stated in these reports [of Captain Jarvis and Commander Turner] the Department approves of the conduct of both those gallant officers, and of the officers and men under their command."

> Special message of President Buchanan, March 29, 1860, transmitting to the Senate, in response to a resolution of the 21st of the same month, papers in relation to the capture of two Mexican war steamers by a naval force of the United States. (S. Ex. Doc. 29, 36 Cong. 1 sess.)

" The Captain-General of Cuba, about May last, issued a proclamation authorizing search to be made of vessels on the high seas.

Immediate remonstrance was made against this, whereupon the Captain-General issued a new proclamation limiting the right of search to vessels of the United States so far as authorized under the treaty of 1795. This proclamation, however, was immediately withdrawn."

> President Grant, annual message, Dec. 6, 1869, Richardson's Messages and Papers of the Presidents, VII. 32.
> See, as to these decrees, Moore, Int. Arbitrations, II. 1021–1022; S. Ex. Doc. 7, 41 Cong. 2 sess. 12.

In January, 1872, the " serious attention " of the Spanish minister at Washington was called to a report of the United States consul at Nassau, that the steamship *Florida*, a regularly documented vessel of the United States, while on her way to New York from Nassau, was followed by the Spanish gunboat *Descubridor*, and, when three miles at sea, was twice fired at, first with a blank shot and then with solid shot, and when brought to was boarded by an officer from the *Descubridor*, who, after an examination, allowed her to proceed. The Government of the United States, it was declared, " denies the right of the cruisers of any foreign power to search vessels of the United States on the high seas in time of peace." It was presumed, said the Department of State, that the proceedings of the *Descubridor* were not in accordance with orders, that the officer who committed the act would be made sensible of the displeasure of his Government, and that " a proper apology " would be made " for so flagrant a violation of the maritime rights of the United States." It was added that a similar act was not long previously committed by another Spanish man-of-war soon after the departure of the *Florida* from St. Thomas.

> Mr. Fish, Sec. of State, to Mr. Roberts, Spanish min., Jan. 13, 1872, MS. Notes to Span. Leg. IX. 62.

October 31, 1873, the steamer *Virginius*, flying the American flag and having an American register, was, after an eight hours' chase, overtaken and captured by the Spanish man-of-war *Tornado*. The pursuit began and ended on the high seas. The *Virginius* was taken to Santiago de Cuba, where, after a summary trial by court-martial, ostensibly on a charge of piracy, fifty-three of her officers, crew, and other persons on board, embracing Americans, British subjects, and Cubans, were condemned to death and shot. The rest were held as prisoners. The British man-of-war *Niobe*, which arrived at Santiago November 8, 1873, demanded that no further executions of British subjects should take place till the case should have been investigated by higher powers. The charge of piracy appears to have been based upon the fact that

Case of the "Virginius," 1873.

the vessel was engaged, in the service of Cuban insurgents, in conveying arms, ammunition, and men to aid the insurrection in Cuba.
November 14, 1873, Mr. Fish, who was then Secretary of State, telegraphed to General Sickles, United States minister at Madrid, as
follows: " Unless abundant reparation shall have been voluntarily
tendered, you will demand the restoration of the *Virginius*, and the
release and delivery to the United States of the persons captured
on her who have not already been massacred, and that the flag of the
United States be saluted in the port of Santiago, and the signal punishment of the officials who were concerned in the capture of the
vessel and the execution of the passengers and crew." In case satisfactory reparation was not assured within twelve days, General
Sickles was to close the legation and leave Madrid.[a]

November 18, 1873, Admiral Polo, then Spanish minister at Washington, communicated to Mr. Fish a telegram from the Spanish minister of state, declaring that the Spanish Government was " resolved
to abide by the principles of justice, to observe international law, to
punish all those who shall have made themselves liable to punishment, regardless of their station; to ask reparation for offences that
may have been done against us, and in our turn to make due reparation if right and our own conviction should so advise us." The
Spanish Government, however, asked for time to ascertain the facts,
alleging that a " conspiracy " had been " discovered in Cuba, which
was to have acted in concert with the arrival of the vessel, which
had already, on former occasions, landed supplies of war and filibus-
tering expeditions, and, on this very occasion, had not her papers in
order." [b]

" *Protocol of the conference held at the Department of State, at
Washington, on the 29th of November, 1873, between Hamilton
Fish, Secretary of State, and Rear-Admiral Don José Polo de
Bernabé, envoy extraordinary and minister plenipotentiary of
Spain.*

" The undersigned, having met for the purpose of entering into a
definitive agreement respecting the case of the steamer *Virginius*,
which, while under the flag of the United States, was on the 31st of
October last, captured on the high seas by the Spanish man-of-war
Tornado, have reached the following conclusions:

" Spain, on her part, stipulates to restore forthwith the vessel
referred to, and the survivors of her passengers and crew, and on the
25th day of December next to salute the flag of the United States.

[a] Mr. Fish, Sec. of State, to Gen. Sickles, min. to Spain, tel., Nov. 14, 1873,
H. Ex. Doc. 30, 43 Cong. 1 sess. 29. See, also, For. Rel. 1874, 923–1117.
[b] H. Ex. Doc. 30, 43 Cong. 1 sess. 73.

If, however, before that date Spain should prove to the satisfaction of the Government of the United States that the *Virginius* was not entitled to carry the flag of the United States, and was carrying it at the time of her capture without right and improperly, the salute will be spontaneously dispensed with, as in such case not being necessarily requirable; but the United States will expect, in such case, a disclaimer of intent of indignity to its flag in the act which was committed.

" Furthermore, if on or before the 25th day of December, 1873, it shall be made to appear to the satisfaction of the United States that the *Virginius* did not rightfully carry the American flag, and was not entitled to American papers, the United States will institute inquiry, and adopt legal proceedings against the vessel, if it be found that she has violated any law of the United States, and against any of the persons who may appear to have been guilty of illegal acts in connection therewith; it being understood that Spain will proceed, according to the second proposition made to General Sickles, and communicated in his telegram read to Admiral Polo on the 27th instant, to investigate the conduct of those of her authorities who have infringed Spanish laws or treaty obligations, and will arraign them before competent courts and inflict punishment on those who may have offended.

" Other reciprocal reclamations to be the subject of consideration and arrangement between the two Governments; and, in case of no agreement, to be the subject of arbitration, if the constitutional assent of the Senate of the United States be given thereto.

" It is further stipulated that the time, manner, and place for the surrender of the *Virginius*, and the survivors of those who were on board of her at the time of her capture, and also the time, manner, and place for the salute to the flag of the United States, if there should be occasion for such salute, shall be subject to arrangement between the undersigned within the next two days.

" HAMILTON FISH.

" JOSÉ POLO DE BERNABÉ."

The text of this protocol may be found in H. Ex. Doc. 30, 43 Cong. 1 sess. 81; 63 Br. & For. State Papers, 1872–73, 389.

For the agreement entered into, Dec. 8, 1873, as to the details mentioned in the last paragraph of the protocol, see H. Ex. Doc. 30, 43 Cong. 1 sess. 84.

As to the trial of General Burriel, see President's message, Jan. 21, 1876, H. Ex. Doc. 90, 44 Cong. 1 sess.

" It is a well-established principle, asserted by the United States from the beginning of their national independence, recognized by Great Britain and other maritime powers, and stated by the Senate in a resolution passed unanimously on the 16th of June, 1858, that

'American vessels on the high seas in time of peace, bearing the American flag, remain under the jurisdiction of the country to which they belong, and therefore any visitation, molestation, or detention of such vessels by force, or by the exhibition of force, on the part of a foreign power is in derogation of the sovereignty of the United States.'

" In accordance with this principle, the restoration of the *Virginius* and the surrender of the survivors of her passengers and crew, and a due reparation to the flag, and the punishment of the authorities who had been guilty of the illegal acts of violence, were demanded. The Spanish Government has recognized the justice of the demand, and has arranged for the immediate delivery of the vessel, and for the surrender of the survivors of the passengers and crew, and for a salute to the flag, and for proceedings looking to the punishment of those who may be proved to have been guilty of illegal acts of violence toward citizens of the United States, and also toward indemnifying those who may be shown to be entitled to indemnity."

President Grant, annual message, Dec. 1, 1873. (Richardson's Messages and Papers of the Presidents, VII. 241.) See infra, p. 946.

A copy of the protocol of Nov. 29 accompanied the message.

The Attorney-General, in an opinion mentioned in President Grant's special message of January 5, 1874, infra, found that the American citizen in whose name as owner the *Virginius* was registered made, as required by law, an oath that there was " no subject or citizen of any foreign prince or state, directly or indirectly, by way of trust, confidence, or otherwise, interested in such ship or vessel, or in the profits or issues thereof "; that this oath was false, as the vessel was then the property of certain Cuban residents of New York, who furnished the funds for her purchase; that the American citizen who commanded the vessel when she left New York was cognizant of the facts; that various other persons on board testified to the same effect, stating that one of the Cuban owners navigated and controlled the vessel and treated it in all respects as if it were his property; that there were no sureties on the bond given by the ostensible owner and commander, though the law required it; that there was no insurance on the vessel, and that, when it left New York, the principal Cubans who took passage did not embark at the wharf, but went on board by a tug after the vessel had left New York. The Attorney-General therefore held that the registration was " a fraud upon the navigation laws of the United States "; but he added:

" Assuming the question to be what appears to conform to the intent of the protocol, whether or not the *Virginius*, at the time of her capture, had a right, as against the United States, to carry the American flag, I am of the opinion that she had no such right, because she had not been registered according to law; but I am also of the opinion that she was as much exempt from interference on the high seas by another power, on that ground, as though she had been lawfully registered. Spain no doubt has a right to capture a vessel with an American register and carrying the American flag, found in her own waters, assisting, or endeavoring to assist the insurrection in Cuba, but she has no right to capture such a vessel on the high seas upon an apprehension that, in violation of the neutrality or navigation laws of the United States, she was on her way to assist said rebellion. Spain may defend her territory and people from the hostile attack of what is, or appears to be, an American vessel, but she has no jurisdiction whatever over the question as to whether or not such vessel is on the high seas in violation of any law of the United States. Spain cannot rightfully raise that question as to the *Virginius*, but the United States may, and, as I understand the protocol, they have agreed to do it; and, governed by that agreement, and without admitting that Spain would otherwise have any interest in the question, I decide that the *Virginius* at the time of her capture was without right and improperly carrying the American flag."

> Williams, At. Gen., Dec. 17, 1873, 14 Op. 340; For. Rel. 1874, 1113; H. Ex. Doc. 30, 43 Cong. 1 sess. 208.

" By direction of the President, I have the honor to inclose herewith a copy of this opinion and decision of the Attorney-General.

" The President directs me further to say that the conditions having thus been reached, on which, according to the protocol of the 29th of November last, the salute to the flag of the United States is to be spontaneously dispensed with, he desires that you will give the necessary orders and instruct the proper officers to notify the authorities of Santiago de Cuba of that fact, in time to carry out the intent and spirit of the agreement between the two Governments."

> Mr. Fish, Sec. of State, to Mr. Robeson, Sec. of Navy, Dec. 17, 1873, H. Ex. Doc. 30, 43 Cong. 1 sess. 210; For. Rel. 1874, 1115, 1116.

" Spain having admitted (as could not be seriously questioned) that a regularly documented vessel of the United States is subject on the high seas in time of peace only to the police jurisdiction of the power from which it receives its papers, it seemed to the President that the United States should not refuse to concede to her the right to adduce proof to show that the *Virginius* was not rightfully carrying our flag. When the question of national honor was adjusted, it also seemed that there was a peculiar propriety in our consenting to an arbitration on a question of pecuniary damages."

> Mr. Fish, Sec. of State, to Mr. Adee, chargé at Madrid, Dec. 31, 1873, H. Ex Doc. 30, 43 Cong. 1 sess. 69, 70; For. Rel. 1874, 976.

" On the 26th day of September, 1870, the *Virginius* was registered in the custom-house at New York as the property of a citizen of the United States, he having first made oath, as required by law, that he was ' the true and only owner of the said vessel, and that there was no subject or citizen of any foreign prince or state, directly or indirectly, by way of trust, confidence, or otherwise, interested therein.'

" Having complied with the requisites of the statute in that behalf, she cleared in the usual way for the port of Curaçao, and on or about the 4th day of October, 1870, sailed for that port. It is not disputed that she made the voyage according to her clearance, nor that, from that day to this, she has not returned within the territorial jurisdiction of the United States. It is also understood that she preserved her American papers, and that when within foreign ports she made the practice of putting forth a claim to American nationality, which was recognized by the authorities at such ports.

" When, therefore, she left the port of Kingston, in October last, under the flag of the United States, she would appear to have had, as against all powers except the United States, the right to fly that flag, and to claim its protection, as enjoyed by all regularly documented vessels registered as part of our commercial marine.

" No state of war existed, conferring upon a maritime power the right to molest and detain upon the high seas a documented vessel; and it can not be pretended that the *Virginius* had placed herself without the pale of all law by acts of piracy against the human race.

" If her papers were irregular or fraudulent, the offense was one against the laws of the United States, justiciable only in their tribunals.

" When, therefore, it became known that the *Virginius* had been captured on the high seas by a Spanish man-of-war; that the American flag had been hauled down by the captors; that the vessel had been carried to a Spanish port; and that Spanish tribunals were taking jurisdiction over the persons of those found on her, and exercising that jurisdiction upon American citizens, not only in violation of the rules of international law, but in contravention of the provisions of the treaty of 1795, I directed a demand to be made upon Spain for the restoration of the vessel, and for the return of the survivors to the protection of the United States, for a salute to the flag, and for the punishment of the offending parties.

" The principles upon which these demands rested could not be seriously questioned, but it was suggested by the Spanish Government that there were grave doubts whether the *Virginius* was entitled to the character given her by her papers; and that therefore it might be proper for the United States, after the surrender of the vessel and the survivors, to dispense with the salute to the flag, should such fact be established to their satisfaction.

and s
into
cludi
order
was o
but sl
of the
ance,
chara
ties h
tered
tional
vessel
even k
in wh
piracy
sion i
place
ously
is to
Britisl
famili
spond
the se
crew,
immin
duty o
form o
charge
that h
charge
under
Virgin

F

On

Incidents
18

search
the hig
the sch
voyage
obliged

" This seemed to be reasonable and just. I therefore assented to it, on the assurance that Spain would then declare that no insult to the flag of the United States had been intended.

" I also authorized an agreement to be made that, should it be shown to the satisfaction of this Government that the *Virginius* was improperly bearing the flag, proceedings should be instituted in our courts for the punishment of the offense committed against the United States. On her part Spain undertook to proceed against those who had offended the sovereignty of the United States, or who had violated their treaty rights.

" The surrender of the vessel and the survivors to the jurisdiction of the tribunals of the United States was an admission of the principles upon which our demands had been founded. I therefore had no hesitation in agreeing to the arrangement finally made between the two Governments—an arrangement which was moderate and just, and calculated to cement the good relations which have so long existed between Spain and the United States.

" Under this agreement the *Virginius*, with the American flag flying, was delivered to the Navy of the United States at Bahia Honda, in the island of Cuba, on the 16th ultimo. She was in an unseaworthy condition. In the passage to New York she encountered one of the most tempestuous of our winter storms. At the risk of their lives the officers and crew placed in charge of her attempted to keep her afloat. Their efforts were unavailing and she sank off Cape Fear. The prisoners who survived the massacres were surrendered at Santiago de Cuba on the 18th ultimo, and reached the port of New York in safety.

" The evidence submitted on the part of Spain to establish the fact that the *Virginius* at the time of her capture was improperly bearing the flag of the United States is transmitted herewith, together with the opinion of the Attorney-General thereon, and a copy of the note of the Spanish minister, expressing, on behalf of his Government, a disclaimer of an intent of indignity to the flag of the United States."

President Grant, special message, Jan. 5, 1874, H. Ex. Doc. 30, 43 Cong. 1 sess. 1.

As to the character and previous career of the *Virginius* see H. Ex. Doc. 30, 43 Cong. 1 sess. 85-145.

For the report of a United States naval board of inquiry on the sinking of the *Virginius*, see For. Rel. 1875, II. 1148.

"This Department has received despatches from the consuls of the United States at Puerto Cabello and Curaçao, relative to a regularly documented steamer of the United States, named the ' Virginius ' or ' Virgin,' whose proceedings in that quarter do not appear to be of an exclusively commercial character. That vessel is reported to have even been charged with piracy in the courts of Curaçao, although from the particulars of the charge contained in the des-

shot, sent a solid shot through her rigging. The schooner was boarded by a Spanish officer, who, after searching her, permitted her to proceed on her course. Her distance at the time from the Spanish coast was said to be between six and seven nautical miles.

The next case was that of the schooner *Eunice P. Newcomb*, of Wellfleet, Mass. The circumstances were altogether similar to those of the preceding case.

The third case was that of the American schooner *George Washington*. July 5, 1880, while on a voyage from the United States to Jamaica for fruit, she was boarded when about 15 miles distant from Cape Maysi by a boat's crew from a Spanish cruiser, supposed to be the *Blasco de Garay*. Her papers were examined, her hold searched, and her crew inspected; she was then permitted to proceed without explanation of the cause of her detention.

The fourth case was that of the schooner *Hattie Haskell*, of New York. July 6, 1880, while on a voyage from New York to Colombia with a general cargo, she was chased and compelled to heave to, when about 32 miles from Cape Maysi, by the Spanish cruiser *Blasco de Garay*. She was searched and her papers examined and was then permitted to proceed.

When the search of the *Ethel A. Merritt* was first reported through the press, the Spanish Government quickly disavowed the act and gave an assurance that, if the firing had taken place as reported, it was contrary to the express orders and wish of the Spanish Government; and, as the identity of the Spanish cruiser was uncertain, the United States, conjecturing that the proceeding might have been " the work of some piratical craft," sent the U. S. S. *Tennessee* to Cuban waters to make an investigation. The commander of the *Tennessee* learned that the search of the *Ethel A. Merritt* and *Eunice P. Newcomb* was admitted by the Spanish authorities at Santiago de Cuba, the explanation given by them being that the *guardia costas* were not permitted to cruise " at a greater distance than six miles from the Cuban shore," and that the schooners when boarded were not more than two or three miles from the Cuban coast. The reported search of the *George Washington* and *Hattie Haskell* was not admitted.

Mr. Evarts stated that the cases appeared to involve " an unwonted exercise of a right of search in time of peace, and to a greater extent than the existing treaty of 1795, between the two nations, in its eighteenth article, permits it to be exercised even in time of recognized public war, that article permitting visitation only, with inspection of the vessel's sea-letters, and not search." The interferences in question did not, he observed, even take the form of a revenue formality performed by the revenue vessels of Spain, but bore " most unequivocal features of belligerent searches made by the war vessels of Spain." He doubted whether, under color of revenue investigation, power could be invoked within the marine league " in time of peace to justify the interference of Spanish cruisers with the lawful commerce of nations passing along a public maritime highway, in a regular course of navigation which brings them near the Cuban coast, though not bound to its ports." The ships of a friendly nation were not, he declared, to be driven out of their proper course into adverse winds and currents " to avoid the offensive exercise of a right which is allowed only to the exigencies of a state of war, and to avert the imminent risk of armed attack and of discourtesy to the flag they bear. And it needs no argument to show that the exercise of any such asserted right upon commercial vessels, on the high seas, in time of peace, is inconsistent with the maintenance of even the most ordinary semblance of friendly relations between the nation which thus conducts itself and that whose merchant vessels are exposed to systematic detention and search by armed force.

" I have made use of the terms ' systematic detention and search ' advisedly, for although I am loath to believe that the Government of His Majesty has determined upon the adoption of a course towards the vessels of the United States, in or near the jurisdictional waters of Spain, which can only imply a standing menace to the integrity and honor of my country and its flag, yet the occurrence in quick succession of four such grave acts of offensive search of our peaceful traders, after so long an interval of repose since this question was last raised in the case of the American whalers on the southern coast of Cuba,[a] cannot but make me apprehensive that the Government of Spain, or the superior authority of Cuba, in pursuance of the discretionary power it is understood to possess, may have taken up a new line of action, and one wholly inconsistent with those relations between the two countries which both their reciprocal interests and duties require should be maintained unbroken.

" It is my profound hope that such apprehensions on my part may be found to be baseless. But in view of the length of time which has elapsed since the first of these occurrences was known to the public here and in Spain, of the anxiety which the minister of state expressed to you in the matter of the telegraphic inquiries made by him of the Cuban authorities, and of the immediate report of the early cases to the admiral at Havana, which is said to have been made, I cannot but express my surprise and regret that the Spanish Government should not of itself have hastened to make some explanation of the incidents calculated to allay the anxiety of a friendly power, whose just susceptibilities as respects the safety of its commerce and the honor of its flag are so well known to the Spanish Government.

---

[a] See the cases of the *Ellen Rizpah*, *Rising Sun*, and *Edward Lee*, infra, p. 913.

"I do not undertake, now, either a full exposition of the doctrine of this Government on the subject of the maritime jurisdiction of states over circumjacent waters, nor a particular inquiry, as to the diverse views, in some sense, which have been brought forward, heretofore, in the discussion between Spain and the United States on the subject of jurisdiction over Cuban waters.

"I desire, however, that the position heretofore more than once distinctly taken by this Government, in its diplomatic correspondence with Spain, shall be understood by you and firmly adhered to in any intercourse you may have in the pending situation with the Spanish minister of foreign affairs. This Government never has recognized and never will recognize any pretense or exercise of sovereignty on the part of Spain beyond the belt of a league from the Cuban coast over the commerce of this country in time of peace. This rule of the law of nations we consider too firmly established to be drawn into debate, and any dominion over the sea outside of this limit will be resisted with the same firmness as if such dominion were asserted in mid-ocean.

"The revenue regulations of a country framed and adopted under the motive and to the end of protecting trade with its ports against smuggling and other frauds which operate upon vessels bound to such ports have, without due consideration, been allowed to play a part in the discussions between Spain and the United States on the extent of maritime dominion accorded by the law of nations which does not belong to them. In this light are to be regarded the royal decrees which it has been claimed by the Spanish Government had for more than a hundred years established two leagues as the measure of maritime jurisdiction, asserted and exercised by the Spanish crown, both in peninsular and colonial waters. Of this character, obviously, are the regulations of our revenue system in force since 1799, which not only allow but enjoin visitation of vessels bound to our ports within four leagues from land, which, in her diplomatic correspondence with this Government, Spain has much insisted on as equivalent to its own dominion as asserted off its coasts, except that our authority was exerted at twice the distance from land.

"But the distinction between dominion over the sea, carrying a right of visit and search of all vessels found within such dominion, and fiscal or revenue regulations of commerce, vessels and cargoes engaged in trade as allowed with our ports to a reasonable range of approach to such ports, needs only to be pointed out to be fully appreciated. Every nation has full jurisdiction of commerce with itself, until by treaty stipulations it has parted with some portion of this full control. In this jurisdiction is easily included a requirement that vessels seeking our ports, in trade, shall be subject to such visitation and inspection as the exigencies of our revenue may demand, in the judgment of this Government, for the protection of the revenues and the adequate administration of the customs service. This is not dominion over the sea where these vessels are visited, but dominion over this commerce with us, its vehicles and cargoes, even while at sea. It carries no assertion of dominion, territorial and *in invitum*, but over voluntary trade in progress and by its own election, submissive to our regulations of it, even in its approaches to our coasts and while still outside of our territorial dominion.[a]

" You will observe, therefore, that the American vessels which have been interfered with thus unwarrantably were not engaged in trade with Cuba, and were in no degree subject to any surveillance or visitation of revenue regulation. The acts complained of, if, indeed, as our proofs seem to make clear, without the league accorded as territorial by the law of nations, have no support whatever from the principle of commercial regulation which I have explained. Spain had no jurisdiction over the waters in which our vessels were found, no jurisdiction over the trade in which they were engaged; and no warrant under the law of nations, to which alone these vessels in this commerce were subject, can be found for their arrest by the Spanish gunboats.

" As the offense against the rights of our commerce and the freedom of our flag, which we complain of in those four instances, is substantive, it is not necessary for me now to insist upon the form and manner of these visitations and searches as elements or aggravations of this offense. It cannot, however, escape notice that each transaction has unequivocal features of the exercise of direct sovereignty, and by mere force, as if by territorial and armed dominion over the sea which was the scene of the transactions. These were gunboats, a part of the naval power of Spain, under the threat of their armaments and by the presence of adequate armed force boarding these vessels, compelling submission; their action was neither more nor less than such as it would have been under a belligerent right on the high seas in time of war.

" In manner and form, then, as well as in substance, the power to which our commerce was obliged to succumb was not of commercial regulation or revenue inspection, or by any of the instruments employed in preventive or protective service with which commerce is familiar.

" Unless some face shall be put upon these disturbances of our peaceful and honest commerce in one of the most important thoroughfares which I can not anticipate, this Government will look to Spain for a prompt and ready apology for their occurrence, a distinct assurance against their repetition, and such an indemnity to the owners of

---

a See supra, § 151.

those several vessels as will satisfy them for the past and guarantee
our commerce against renewed interruption by engaging the interest
of Spain in restraint of rash or ignorant infractions, by subordinate
agents of its power, of our rights upon the seas."

> Mr. Evarts, Sec. of State, to Mr. Fairchild, min. to Spain, Aug. 11, 1880,
>   For. Rel. 1880, 922.
> In reply to an inquiry concerning the case of the *George Washington*, the
>   Department of State, in 1885, said:
> "The latest communication on the subject, appears to be an instruction
>   to Mr. Hamlin, then minister to Spain, dated January 14, 1882, in
>   which it was left to his discretion, whether to pursue the subject
>   further. This instruction alluded to the discrepancies above men-
>   tioned as seemingly hopeless; and the absence of further action in
>   the matter on Mr. Hamlin's part, seems to indicate that he could
>   not find a sufficiently stable basis on which to press the subject
>   upon the continued attention of His Catholic Majesty's Government.
> "On reviewing the correspondence it appears to me that while the state-
>   ments are doubtless honest, the element of discrepancy and the
>   diverse view respecting jurisdiction entertained on both parts leave
>   little ground to encourage further representation." (Mr. Bayard,
>   Sec. of State, to Mr. King, Oct. 12, 1885, 157 MS. Dom. Let. 342.)

The right of search can not be exercised in time of peace; nor is it
any excuse that the search was attempted in the port of a third
sovereign who makes no complaint of the outrage.

> Mr. Evarts, Sec. of State, to Mr. Asta-Buruaga, Mar. 3, 1881, MS. Notes
>   to Chili, VI. 259.

"This Department is informed that on the 8th instant the United
"Alliança" case,   States mail steamship *Alliança*, on her homeward
1895.   voyage from Colon to New York, when 6 miles from
                   the coast of Cuba, off Cape Maysi, was repeatedly
fired upon by a Spanish gunboat, with solid shot, which, fortunately,
fell short. The Windward Passage, where this occurred, is the
natural and usual highway for vessels plying between ports of the
United States and the Caribbean Sea. Through it several regular
lines of American mail and commercial steamers pass weekly within
sight of Cape Maysi. They are well known, and their voyage embraces no Cuban port of call. Forcible interference with them can
not be claimed as a belligerent act, whether they pass within 3 miles
of the Cuban coast or not, and can under no circumstances be tolerated when no state of war exists. This Government will expect
prompt disavowal of the unauthorized act and due expression of
regret on the part of Spain, and it must insist that immediate and
positive orders be given to Spanish naval commanders not to interfere
with legitimate American commerce passing through that channel,
and prohibiting all acts wantonly imperiling life and property law-

fully under the flag of the United States.   You will communicate this to the minister for foreign affairs, and urge importance of prompt and satisfactory response."

Mr. Gresham, Sec. of State, to Mr. Taylor, min. to Spain, tel., March 14, 1895, For. Rel. 1895, II. 1177.
This telegram was read by Mr. Taylor to the minister of foreign affairs. (For. Rel. 1895, II. 1178.)

" Sufficient information is still wanting to authorize a reply as precise and concrete as the Government of His Majesty sincerely desires, but I am pleased to assure you at once that it is not its purpose, and never has been, to put obstacles or obstructions of any kind in the way of the legitimate commerce of the United States.   With this feeling and without prejudice to the exercise of the right which belongs to us in our maritime zone, opportune instructions have been sent to the commanders of the ships of His Majesty, first by telegraph, and afterwards at greater length by mail.

" I shall have the honor to supplement this note as soon as I shall receive the report which has been ordered to be drawn up as rapidly as possible at Havana for the purpose of investigating the affair with the *Alliança*, and which my colleague the minister for the colonies expects to receive very soon.   The Cabinet at Washington may be sure that if the commander of the *Venadito*, believing to act within his rights, should have committed an error, His Majesty's Government shall regret it sincerely, and shall proceed respecting the said commander in the form and manner which the case requires."

Duke of Tetuan, min. of state, to Mr. Taylor, U. S. min., April 9, 1895, For. Rel. 1895, II. 1181.   At p. 1180 will be found a telegram of Mr. Taylor, communicating the contents of this note to the Department of State.

"A month having elapsed since you communicated to the Spanish Government the representations of this Government touching the firing upon the *Alliança* on the high sea off Cape Maysi while innocently sailing under the American flag, the President deprecates further delay in responding to our just expectations.   This Government has given due weight to the serious situation in Spain and Cuba, but the evidence appears to so clearly establish that the act complained of was indefensible, if not wanton, that delay is not understood."

Mr. Gresham, Sec. of State, to Mr. Taylor, min. to Spain, tel., April 16, 1895, For. Rel. 1895, II. 1182; communicated to minister of state, ibid.

"As I had the honor to tell you in my note of the 9th instant, I proposed to supplement it as soon as the report called for was received, which, having started from Havana by mail on the 30th ultimo, is expected at Madrid every day. The fact that my colleague of marine has transmitted to me a telegram from the commander-general of that station, which has been received in my department to-day, enables me, however, to recognize that when the *Venadito* fired upon the *Alliança* the latter was, in fact, outside of the jurisdictional zone of Spain, and that therefore, recognizing that fact, the official accidentally in charge of the command of the Spanish ship at that time committed an error undoubtedly involuntary.

" When His Majesty's Government shall be able to understand the event in all its details from the study of the report which will shortly arrive, as I have already said, it will examine the conduct of the official who then commanded the *Venadito*, in order to proceed as it shall be fit, as His Majesty's Government has promised. It can not but lament an occurrence so contrary to the sentiments which animate it—as it has said on various occasions—not to interfere with or hinder under any pretext the legitimate commerce of the United States."

> Duke of Tetuan, min. of state, to Mr. Taylor, United States min., April 18, 1895, For. Rel. 1895, II. 1183.

" The Government of His Majesty considers it its duty to inform your excellency, as another proof of its sincerity, that by the reports received in this ministry the fact is proven that when the official commanding the *Venadito*, during the absence of the commander, fired upon the *Alliança* with the sole purpose of stopping her, and having special care not to hit the American steamer, the latter was outside of the jurisdictional zone of Spain. There was, therefore, an error, though certainly involuntary, and no one laments it more than the Government of His Majesty, whose purpose never was to set obstacles or hindrances to the legitimate commerce of the United States and much less to give the slightest offense to the flag of a friendly power.

"As I have already told your excellency, instructions have been sent to the commanders of the ships of the navy in order to avoid the repetition of events similar to that now in question, which is disavowed by the Government of His Majesty.

" In order to remove any doubts which might arise if certain wholly unfounded rumors should be taken as true, I take pleasure in assuring you that when the incident of the *Alliança* took place the commander was not on board, but only the second chief, Señor Ibarra, who has been removed to another post of the same grade.

" I shall not conclude this note, Mr. Minister, without expressing my hope that the United States will find in the preceding spontaneous manifestations one more proof of the interest which Spain takes in all that relates to the great American Republic, and of the warm desire which animates the Government of His Majesty to contribute, for its part, to the definite and most satisfactory termination of this affair."

Duke of Tetuan, min. of state, to Mr. Taylor, U. S. min., May 16, 1895, For. Rel. 1895, II. 1184

" I have laid before the President the note of his excellency the minister of state, of the 16th ultimo, conveying the disavowal by His Majesty's Government of the act of the temporary commander of the *Venadito* in firing upon the *Alliança* and the assurance that instructions have been sent to Spanish naval commanders in order to avoid the repetition of any such occurrence.

" I am directed by the President to instruct you that, without conceding that the exact location of the *Alliança* at the time the shot was fired can be considered a controlling circumstance, this communication of His Majesty's Government is accepted as a sufficient and satisfactory explanation of the incident.

" You will add an expression of the President's high appreciation of the friendly tenor of the Duke of Tetuan's note."

Mr. Uhl, Act. Sec. of State, to Mr. Taylor, min. to Spain, June 5, 1895, For. Rel. 1895, II. 1185.

" Cuba is again gravely disturbed. . . One notable instance of interference by Spain with passing American ships has occurred. On March 8 last the *Alliança*, while bound from Colon to New York, and following the customary track for vessels near the Cuban shore, but outside the three-mile limit, was fired upon by a Spanish gunboat. Protest was promptly made by the United States against this act as not being justified by a state of war, nor permissible in respect of vessels on the usual paths of commerce, nor tolerable in view of the wanton peril occasioned to innocent life and property. The act was disavowed, with full expression of regret, and assurance of nonrecurrence of such just cause of complaint, while the offending officer was relieved of his command."

President Cleveland, annual message, Dec. 2, 1895. (For. Rel. 1895, I. xxxii, xxxiii.)

In April, 1896, a representation was made to the Spanish minister at Washington concerning the firing upon, detention, and search by two Spanish gunboats, on the 16th of the preceding month, of the American schooner *William Todd*, which was alleged to have been at the time off the Isle of Pines on the high seas, six or seven miles from land. A request was accordingly made for such a settlement of the case, " con-

Case of the "William Todd," 1896.

formably to the recent precedent of the *Alliança* incident, as the dignity of the United States and the rights of its citizens require."[a]

The Spanish Government, after investigating the case, replied that when the schooner was observed she was summoned by a blank shot to show her colors; that, as there was delay in hoisting the flag, the cannon was again loaded with powder only, which went off accidentally; that, as there was a suspicion that the flag then raised was not the true one, a boatswain and several seamen were sent on board to make an examination; and that the whole transaction took place within three miles of the shore. It was therefore maintained that the *Alliança* case was not in point. The Spanish Government, it was observed, " admitted in that case that the American vessel was outside of Spanish waters, and in view of that fact, and as was required by law, it disavowed the course pursued by the *Conde de Venadito*. The contrary is now the case. The American schooner *William Todd* was within those waters, and consequently the course pursued by the gunboat *Antonio Lopez* was strictly in harmony with the principles of international law. . . The instructions. . . issued to the commanders of Spanish vessels are so clear and explicit that if the commander of the *Antonio Lopez* had violated them he would have been called to account." The hope was expressed that these explanations would be accepted, and the correspondence was ended.[b]

The brig *Thomas of Havana*, flying the American flag, entered **Rights of cruiser of ship's own nation.** the port of Havana. Her papers were presented to the United States consul, who, perceiving them to be fraudulent, advised the commander of the U. S. S. *Ontario*, then in port, to seize and detain her. This advice having been acted upon, a correspondence ensued between the captain-general of Cuba and the consul concerning the violation of the jurisdictional rights of Spain. The correspondence ended in the captain-general's amicably consenting to the brig's continued detention. On the strength of this fact it was advised that the detention, so far as it concerned the brig and her master, was lawful. " Suppose," it was asked, " the Spanish authorities had given their consent to the seizure before it was made; then, what legal rights would have been violated? None, that I can perceive, more than if the seizure had been made on the high seas . . . That a public vessel of the United States has the

<hr/>

[a] Mr. Olney, Sec. of State, to Mr. Dupuy de Lôme, Span. min., April 11, 1896, and April 17, 1896, For. Rel. 1896, 696, 697, 698.

[b] Mr. Dupuy de Lôme, Span. min., to Mr. Olney, Sec. of State, June 24, 1896; Mr. Olney, Sec. of State, to Mr. Dupuy de Lôme, Span. min., July 18, 1896; Mr. Dupuy de Lôme, Span. min., to Mr. Olney, Sec. of State, July 24, 1896: For. Rel. 1896, 698–702.

right, on the high seas, to detain a merchant vessel of the United States, and to take possession of it, and retain that possession until the government can act upon the subject, where there is just cause to believe that such merchant vessel is engaged in an illicit trade forbidden by the laws of Congress, I presume no doubt can be entertained."

Grundy, At.-Gen., Jan. 12, 1839, 3 Op. 405.

In 1877, while the "Ten Years' War" was still going on in Cuba, the United States presented to Spain a complaint and claim for indemnity on account of the acts of Spanish officials in respect of the American whaling schooners *Ellen Rizpah* and *Rising Sun*. The *Ellen Rizpah*, while engaged in a whaling voyage, was overhauled when off the South Keys, which are uninhabited, and lie about 20 miles from the coast of Cuba, by a small Spanish armed vessel, and the master and mate were held prisoners for four days and subjected to ill treatment. The place apparently was considered as being within territorial waters. Not long afterwards the *Rising Sun* was fired upon and brought to near the same place. She was detained five days, till a Spanish gunboat arrived and searched her. Not long previously it was reported that the American whaling schooner *Edward Lee* was fired upon and chased near the same place by a Spanish gunboat. The United States asked that measures be at once adopted to put an end to such causes of complaint, and suggested to that end "an earnest and faithful observance of the stipulations of the eighteenth article of the treaty of 1795."

Mode of visit.

Mr. Evarts, Sec. of State, to Mr. Lowell, min. to Spain, Nov. 13, 1877, For. Rel. 1878, 769. See, also, For. Rel. 1877, 525–531.

In the case of the *Ellen Rizpah* and *Rising Sun*, Spain paid an indemnity of $10,000. (For. Rel. 1878, 779, 784, 786.) See, also, Mr. Evarts, Sec. of State, to Mr. Crapo, May 31, and June 3, 1879, 128 MS. Dom. Let. 303, 324.

The case of the *Edward Lee* seems to have been dropped for want of evidence. (Mr. Hunter, Act. Sec. of State, to Mr. Lowell, min. to Spain, Jan. 6, 1880, MS. Inst. Spain, XVIII. 419.)

Art. XVIII. of the treaty of 1795, referred to by Mr. Evarts, reads as follows :

"If the ships of the said subjects, people, or inhabitants, of either of the parties shall be met with, either sailing along the coasts [or] on the high seas, by any ship of war of the other, or by any privateer, the said ship of war or privateer, for the avoiding of any disorder, shall remain out of cannon-shot, and may send their boats aboard the merchant-ship, which they shall so meet with, and may enter her to the number of two or three men only, to whom the master or commander of such ship or vessel shall exhibit his passports, concerning the property of the ship, made out according to the form inserted in this present treaty; and the ship, when she shall have shewed such passports, shall be free and at liberty to pursue her voyage, so as it shall not be lawful to molest or give her chase in any manner, or force her to quit her intended course."

As to the firing upon the American schooner *Carrie A. Buckman* in Santo Domingo in 1889, see Mr. Adee, Act. Sec. of State, to Mr. Thompson, min. to Hayti, Sept. 9, 1889, MS. Inst. Hayti, III. 79; Mr. Blaine, Sec. of State, to Mr. Douglass, March 12, 1890, and Jan. 20, 1891, id. 120, 166.

" The usual mode of doing this [bringing to a vessel] is by hailing, if near enough; or by signaling; or, if too far away for the successful use of either the speaking trumpet or the flag signals, to fire a *semonce* or warning gun, not at the vessel, but with blank cartridge or in the air (*soit à poudre soit à boulet perdu*). It is only when these signals are disregarded that justification for the employment of force, or the semblance of force, may be claimed. In such a case it is usual to fire a second shot, across the vessel's bow, before firing directly at her."

Mr. Adee, Act. Sec. of State, to Mr. Thompson, Sept. 9, 1889, MS. Inst. Hayti, III. 79, in relation to the firing on the American schooner, *Carrie A. Buckman*, by the Dominican war vessel *El Presidente*, at San Domingo.

2. SLAVE TRADE.

§ 310.

The question of visit and search has been much discussed in connection with efforts to suppress the African slave trade. It was at first sought to found a right of visit and search in such cases on the theory that the trade constituted a violation of the law of nations, for which, as in the case of piracy, the offender might be seized on the high seas by the cruiser of any power. This theory was not accepted; but, while rejecting it, the British courts, in the early part of the nineteenth century, took the ground that, where a foreign vessel was captured on the high seas and was afterwards proceeded against in the British courts as a prize, the fact that she was engaged in the slave trade, if the act was forbidden by the laws of her own country as well as by those of Great Britain, would defeat a claim to restitution.

English prize doctrine, 1810–1813.

This doctrine was applied in the case of *The Amédie*, 1 Acton, 240, decided by the Lords Commissioners of Appeal, March 17, 1810. The case came up on an appeal from the sentence of the vice admiralty court of Tortolo, condemning the vessel, which was an American ship, and her cargo of slaves, as engaged in an illegal trade, from Bonny, on the coast of Africa, to Matanzas in Cuba. The United States had prohibited the slave trade after 1807, and it was alleged that the mas-

ter, under instructions from the owner of the vessel, proceeded to
Matanzas, being unable to reach Charleston, S. C., before Jan. 1,
1808. The first reason assigned by the captor for the condemnation
was that the ship was proceeding to a port of a colony belonging to
His Britannic Majesty's enemies, contrary to the order in council of
Nov. 11, 1807. The second reason was that the voyage was contrary
to the laws of the United States, and that, although this might not be
a substantive ground of condemnation, yet it ought to exclude the
claimant from any relaxation of the laws of war.

Sir W. Grant considered that the evidence showed that the vessel
was at the time of her capture " employed in carrying slaves from the
coast of Africa to a Spanish colony." The claimant was engaged, too,
in a traffic forbidden by the law of the United States and declared
by English law to be contrary to justice and humanity. "As the case
now stands, we think," said Sir W. Grant, " that no claimant can be
heard in an application to a court of prize for the restoration of the
human beings he carried unjustly to another country for the purpose
of disposing of them as slaves. . . . The claimant does not bring
himself within the protection of the law of his own country; he
appears to have been acting in direct violation of that law, which
admits of no right of property such as he claims. Ours is express and
satisfactory upon the subject. Where, therefore, there is no right
established to carry on this trade, no claim to restitution of this property can be admitted."

The sentence below was affirmed, condemning the ship and cargo as
lawful prize.

The next case was that of *The Fortuna*, 1 Dodson, 81, decided
March 12, 1811, in the high court of admiralty. This vessel also was
American, and was taken while on a voyage to Havana with slaves.
In deciding the case, Sir William Scott said:

" It has been established by recent decisions of the Supreme Court
that the Court of Prize, though properly a court purely of the law of
nations, has a right to notice the municipal law of this country in the
case of a British vessel which, in the course of a prize proceeding,
appears to have been trading in violation of that law, and to reject a
claim for her on that account. That principle has been incorporated
into the prize law of this country within the last twenty years, and
seems now fully incorporated. A late decision, in the case of the
Amedie, seems to have gone the length of establishing a principle,
that any trade contrary to the general law of nations, although not
tending to or accompanied with any infraction of the belligerent
rights of that country, whose tribunals are called upon to consider it,
may subject the vessel employed in that trade to confiscation. . . .
How far that judgment has been universally concurred in and ap-

proved, it is not for me to inquire, . . . because the decisions of that Court bind authoritatively the judicial conscience of this."

In the case of *The Diana*, 1 Dodson, 95, decided May 21, 1813, Sir W. Scott held, the vessel being Swedish, that the property of foreigners, engaged in the slave trade under the sanction of the laws of their own country, should be respected.

The foregoing cases all occurred during the Napoleonic wars, while the exercise, by Great Britain and the other parties to the conflict, of the belligerent right of visit and search was flagrant. Soon after the reestablishment of peace, however, there came before the court of admiralty the case of *Le Louis*, 2 Dodson, 210. The vessel was French, and she was captured at sea by a British cruiser early in 1816. The case was decided by Sir William Scott in the following year. He held that, as the " right of visitation " in the pending case had been " exercised in time of peace," it could be " legalized " only " upon the ground that the captured vessel is to be taken *legally* as a pirate," unless some " new ground " should be assumed for supporting a right which had been " distinctly admitted not to exist generally in time of peace." The right, however, wherever it had existed, had, he affirmed, " existed upon the ground of repelling injury, and as a measure of self-defense." No practice had carried it farther; and, although the slave trade was forbidden by the law of France as well as by that of England, he held that, as it did not constitute piracy by law of nations, the seizure was illegal.

Case of "Le Louis," 1817.

In the case of Madrazo *v.* Willes, 3 Barn. & Ald. 353, decided January 24, 1820, an action was brought by a Spaniard against a British officer for damages for the seizure of a ship and cargo of slaves. Abbott, C. J., declared that he was satisfied that the words of 58 Geo. III., c. 36, in relation to the slave trade, could " only be taken to be applicable to *British* subjects." He therefore held the verdict below right, which awarded the plaintiff £21,180, being £3,000 for deterioration of the ship's stores and goods, and £18,180 for the supposed profit of the cargo of slaves. Bayley, J., concurring, said : " It is true, that if this were a trade contrary to the law of nations, a foreigner could not maintain this action. But it is not; and as a Spaniard can not be considered as bound by the acts of the British legislature prohibiting this trade, it would be unjust to deprive him of a remedy for the wrong which he has sustained." Holroyd, J., likewise concurred. Best, J., also concurring, said : " If a ship be acting contrary to the general law of nations, she is thereby subject to confiscation; but it is impossible to say that the slave trade is contrary to what may be called the common law of nations. . . . Spain has reserved to her-

Case of Madrago v. Willes.

self a right of carrying it on in that part of the world where this transaction occurred. . . . These principles are confirmed by the decisions of the Court of Admiralty, and also by a judgment of Sir William Grant, pronounced at the Cock-pit. The cases to which I allude are, the *Fortuna*, the *Donna Marianna*, and the *Diana*, in the Court of Admiralty; and the *Amedie*, before the Privy Council. These cases establish this rule, that ships, which belong to countries that have prohibited the slave trade, are liable to capture and condemnation, if found employed in such trade; but that the subjects of countries which permit the prosecution of this trade, can not be interrupted while carrying it on. It is clear, from these authorities, that the slave trade is not condemned by the general law of nations.''

It may be observed that, in this citation of the cases of the *Amedie*, *Fortuna*, and *Diana*, which was not essential to the decision of the case before him, Mr. Justice Best does not advert to the distinction drawn by Sir W. Scott, in the case of *Le Louis*, between captures made in war, when the exercise of visitation and search by belligerents is lawful, and seizures in time of peace, when no such general right exists.

Referring to the cases of *The Amedie*, 1 Acton, 240; *The Fortuna*, 1
Case of the "Ante- Dodson, 81, and *The Diana*, 1 Dodson, 95, Chief Jus-
lope." tice Marshall observed that the principle common to these cases was, that the legality of the capture of a vessel engaged in the slave trade depended on the law of the country to which the vessel belonged. If that law gave its sanction to the trade, restitution would be decreed; if that law prohibited it, the vessel and cargo would be condemned as good prize. The whole subject, continued Chief Justice Marshall, came on afterwards to be considered in the *Louis*, 2 Dodson, 238, and the opinion of Sir William Scott in that case " demonstrates the attention he had bestowed upon it, and gives full assurance that it may be considered as settling the law in the case of the British Courts of Admiralty as far as it goes. . . . Sir William Scott, in explicit terms, lays down the broad principle that the right of search is confined to a state of war. It is a right strictly belligerent in its character, which can never be exercised by a nation at peace, except against professed pirates, who are the enemies of the human race. The act of trading in slaves, however detestable, was not, he said, . . . piracy. . . . No principle of general law is more universally acknowledged, than the perfect equality of nations. . . . Each legislates for itself, but its legislation can operate on itself alone. . . . As no nation can prescribe a rule for others, none can make a law of nations; and this traffic remains lawful to those whose governments have not forbidden it. . . . If it be neither repugnant to the law of

nations, nor piracy, it is almost superfluous to say in this Court, that the right of bringing in for adjudication in time of peace, even where the vessel belongs to a nation which has prohibited the trade, can not exist. The courts of no country execute the penal laws of another; and the course of the American government on the subject of visitation and search, would decide any case in which that right had been exercised by an American cruiser, on the vessel of a foreign nation, not violating our municipal laws, against the captors.

"It follows, that a foreign vessel engaged in the African slave trade, captured on the high seas in time of peace, by an American cruiser, and brought in for adjudication, would be restored."

    Marshall, C. J., The Antelope (1825), 10 Wheat. 66, 116–123.

By Article X. of the treaty of peace between the United States and Great Britain, signed at Ghent, December 24, 1814, it was declared that as the traffic in slaves was irreconcilable with the principles of humanity and justice, the contracting parties would use their best endeavors to promote its entire abolition.

Treaty of Ghent, and subsequent discussions.

The ministers of the United States in London, in 1818, were instructed to say to the British Government: "That the admission of a right in the officers of foreign ships of war to enter and search the vessels of the United States, in time of peace, under any circumstances whatever, would meet with universal repugnance in the public opinion of this country; that there would be no prospect of a ratification, by advice and consent of the Senate, to any stipulation of that nature; that the search by foreign officers, even in time of war, is so obnoxious to the feelings and recollections of this country, that nothing could reconcile them to the extension of it, however qualified or restricted, to a time of peace; and that it would be viewed in a still more aggravated light if, as in the treaty with the Netherlands, connected with a formal admission that even vessels under convoy of ships of war of their own nation should be liable to search by the ships of war of another."

    Mr. Adams, Sec of State, to Messrs. Gallatin and Rush, Nov. 2, 1818, Am. State Papers, For. Rel. V. 72, 73.

    The opponents of the slave trade "were introducing, and had already obtained the consent of Spain, Portugal, and the Netherlands to a new principle of the law of nations more formidable to human liberty than the slave trade itself—a right of the commanders of armed vessels of one nation to visit and search the merchant vessels of another in time of peace." (Mr. J. Q. Adams, April 29, 1819, as reported in 4 Memoirs of J. Q. Adams, 354.)

    As to seizure on suspicion of being concerned in the slave trade, "he (Lord Castlereagh) added, that no peculiar structure or previous appearances in the vessel searched, no presence of irons, or other presumptions of criminal intention—nothing but the actual finding of slaves on board was ever to authorize a seizure or detention." (Mr. Rush, minister at London, to Mr. Adams, Sec. of State, Apr. 15, 1818, 22 MS. Despatches, Gr. Brit. See to the same effect, Rush's Memoranda of a Residence at the Court of London, 212.)

The principles by which the United States was guided, in respect of measures for the abolition of the slave trade, were **Position of John Quincy Adams.** set forth by Mr. John Quincy Adams in reply to a proposal of the British Government, inviting the United States to accede to certain regulations which were exemplified by the treaties of Great Britain with Spain, Portugal, and the Netherlands. In accordance with this plan, it appeared, said Mr. Adams, that citizens of the United States would be liable " in time of peace to have their vessels searched and with their persons seized and carried away by the naval officers of a foreign power, subjected to the decision of a tribunal in a foreign land, without benefit of the intervention of a jury of accusation or of a jury of trial, by a court of judges and umpires half of whom would be foreigners and all irresponsible to the supreme authorities of the United States." The Government of the United States objected to this mode of procedure, as violative of the safeguards of individual liberty. With regard to the question of visitation and search, Mr. Adams said: " The United States had very recently issued from a war with Great Britain, principally waged in resistance to a practice of searching neutral merchant vessels for men in time of war, exercised by Great Britain, as the United States deem, in violation of the law of nations. A proposal involving the exercise in time of peace of this same practice of search, though for different purposes, could not be acceded to by the American Government consistently with their principles. Inadmissible as, under any circumstances whatever, they must have deemed this right of search to be, it was, in one of the treaties to the stipulation of which their accession was invited, presented under an aspect of peculiar import, authorizing its exercise in the case even of vessels under the convoy of a ship of war of their own nation. . . . There appeared to the American Government to be no conceivable combination of circumstances which could render the provision of this stipulation necessary or proper. . . . Of the right of mutual search it is clear that its efficiency depends altogether upon its universal adoption. So long as it shall be declined by any one maritime state, however inconsiderable, its adoption by all others would leave it altogether ineffectual. Without adverting to the strong repugnance which has been manifested to it by other maritime states of the first rank, it is scarcely to be expected that any principle so liable to misapplication and abuse can obtain, as an innovation upon the law of nations, the universal concurrence of all maritime powers. The expedient proposed on the part of the United States of keeping cruisers of their own constantly upon the coast where the traffic is carried on, with instructions to cooperate by good offices and by the mutual communication of information with the cruisers of other powers stationed and instructed to the attainment of the same end, appears in its own nature as well as to experience so far as it has abided that test, better adapted to the suppression of the traffic than that of the British Government, which makes the officers of one nation the executors of the laws of another."

Mr. Adams, Sec. of Sate, to Mr. Stratford Canning, British min., Aug. 15, 1821, MS. Notes to For. Leg. III. 22.

In May, 1821, Lieutenant Stockton, U. S. S. *Alligator*, captured off the coast of Africa four French vessels, *La Jeune Eugénie*, *La Matilde*, *La Julie*, and *L'Eliza*. The seizures were made on suspicion that the vessels, which were alleged to be engaged in the slave trade, were American and not French, and were committing an abuse of the American flag. They were brought to the United States and were libelled at Boston under the slave-trade acts. The French minister having demanded their restitution, and having presented proofs that they were really and exclusively the property of French subjects, the President directed the United States district attorney to suggest to the court that they should be delivered up, and the court, conformably to the suggestion, adjudged that they be delivered to the French consul, together with the evidence of participation in the slave trade, in order that they might be sent for trial to the tribunals of their own sovereign. In acquainting the French minister with this disposition of the cases, Mr. Adams, who was then Secretary of State, said: "The Government of the United States has never asserted, but has invariably disclaimed, the pretension of a right to authorize the search by the officers of the United States in time of peace of foreign vessels upon the high seas, without their jurisdiction. . . . Instructions have (since the restitution of the vessels in question) been issued from the Department of the Navy to the officers of the United States, charged with the duty of carrying into effect the laws for the suppresion of the slave trade, to forbear all examination or visitation of any vessel bearing a flag of any other nation than that of this Union. It is presumed that these measures will satisfy your Government . . . as to the disclaimer by the United States of all pretension to a right of search, in time of peace, of the vessels of any other nations, not having violated their laws."

Mr. Adams, Sec. of State, to Mr. Hyde de Neuville, French min., Feb. 22, 1822, MS. Notes to For. Leg. III. 50. See, also, Mr. Adams, Sec. of

State, to Mr. Blake, U. S. dist. atty. at Boston, Nov. 13, 1821, and
Jan. 22, 1822, 19 MS. Dom. Let. 196, 245.

Claims for indemnity were made by the French Government in behalf
of each of the four vessels. (H. Ex. Doc. 147, 22 Cong. 2 sess. 191,
196, 201, 206.) These claims were disposed of by Art. III. of the
convention between the United States and France of July 4, 1831,
under which the sum of 1,500,000 francs was paid to France in satisfaction of all claims, including those for unlawful seizures, captures,
and detentions of French vessels and cargoes.

" In the treaties of Great Britain with Spain, Portugal, and the
Netherlands for the suppression of the slave trade, heretofore communicated, with the invitation to the United States to enter into
similar engagements, three principles were involved, to neither of
which the Government of the United States felt itself at liberty to
accede. The first was the mutual concession of the right of search
and capture, in time of peace, over merchant vessels on the coast of
Africa. The second was the exercise of that right, even over vessels
under convoy of the public officers of their own nation; and the third
was the trial of the captured vessels by mixed commissions in colonial
settlements under no subordination to the ordinary judicial tribunals
of the country to which the party brought before them for trial
should belong. In the course of the correspondence relating to
these proposals it has been suggested that a substitute for the trial
by mixed commissions might be agreed to, and in your letter of the
8th of April an *expectation* is authorized that an arrangement for the
adjudication of the vessels detained might leave them to be disposed
of in the ordinary way by the sentence of a court of admiralty in the
country of the captor, or place them under the jurisdiction of a
similar court in the country to which they belonged; to the former
alternative of which you anticipate the unhesitating admission of
the United States in consideration of the aggravated nature of the
crime as acknowledged by their laws, which would be thus submitted
to a *foreign* jurisdiction. But it was precisely because the jurisdiction was *foreign* that the objection was taken to the trial by mixed
commissions; and if it transcended the constitutional authority of
the Government of the United States to subject the persons, property,
and reputation of their citizens to the decisions of a court partly
composed of their own countrymen, it might seem needless to remark
that the constitutional objection could not diminish in proportion as
its cause should increase, or that the power incompetent to make
American citizens amenable to a court consisting one-half of foreigners, should be adequate to place their liberty, their fortune, and
their fame at the disposal of tribunals entirely foreign. I would further remark that the sentence of a court of admiralty in the country

of the captor is not the *ordinary way* by which the merchant vessels of one nation, taken on the high seas by the officers of another, are tried in time of peace. There is, in the ordinary way, no right whatever existing to take, to search, or even to board them; and I take this occasion to express the great satisfaction with which we have seen this principle solemnly recognized by the recent decision of a British court of admiralty. . . .

" In the objections heretofore disclosed to the concession desired, of the mutual and qualified right of search, the principal stress was laid upon the repugnance which such a concession would meet in the public feeling of this country, and of those to whom its interests are intrusted in the department of its Government, the sanction of which is required for the ratification of treaties. The irritating tendency of the practice of search, and the inequalities of its probable operation, were slightly noticed and have been contested in argument or met by propositions of possible palliations or remedies for anticipated abuses in your letter. But the source and foundation of all these objections was, in our former correspondence, scarcely mentioned, and never discussed. They consist in the nature of the right of search at sea, which, as recognized or tolerated by the usage of nations, is a right exclusively of *war*, never exercised but by an outrage upon the rights of *peace*."

> Mr. Adams, Sec. of State, to Mr. Stratford Canning, Brit min. June 24, 1823, MS. Notes to For. Leg. III. 141. See, also, Mr. Adams, Sec. of State, to Mr. Rush, min. to England, June 24, 1823, Am. State Papers, For. Rel. V. 333.
>
> As to discussions of Mr. J. Q. Adams on right of search with Mr. Stratford Canning, see 5, J. Q. Adams's Mem. 181, 182, 192, 232.
>
> The correspondence from 1818 to 1825, in reference to the slave trade and the right of search, will be found in Am. State Papers, For. Rel. V. 69–80, 90–97, 108–127, 140, 315–359, 629, 782.

By the act of Congress of May 15, 1820, 3 Stat. 600, Rev. Stat. §§ 5375, 5376, slave trading was declared to be piracy and to be punishable with death. This act was general in its language, and was designed to enable the United States to join in the movement then on foot to assimilate the slave trade to piracy, both in the measure of its punishment and the method of its repression. This movement, however, did not succeed, owing to the opposition to opening the way to the establishment of the practice of visitation and search in time of peace.

Act of 1820 and subsequent negotiations.

"At the close of the last session of Congress a resolution was adopted, almost unanimously, by the House of Representatives, ' that the President of the United States be requested to enter upon, and to prosecute from time to time, such negotiations with the several maritime powers of Europe and America as he may deem expedient for the effectual abolition of the African slave trade, and its ultimate denunciation as piracy, under the laws of nations, by the consent of the civilized world.'

" In pursuance of this resolution, instructions for carrying it into effect have been given to the ministers of the United States destined to the Republics of Colombia and of Buenos Ayres, and to the several ministers of the United States in Europe.

"As a negotiation for cooperation to effect the suppression of the African slave trade had already been commenced with Great Britain, a special instruction upon the subject has been forwarded to Mr. Rush, together with a full power, and a draft of a convention, to be proposed, in substance, to the British Government, and which he is authorized to conclude.

"A necessary preliminary to the conclusion of this proposed convention, should it meet the assent of the British Government, will be the enactment of a statute declaring the crime of African slave trading piracy by the British law. In that event, it is proposed, by proper cooperation, that the influence of the two powers should be exerted to obtain the consent of other nations to the general outlawry of this traffic as piracy. In the meantime, to give at once effect to the concert of both nations, it is proposed that the armed vessels of both, duly authorized and *instructed*, shall have power to *capture* the slave-trading vessels which may assume the flag of *either*, and, if not of their own nation, to deliver over the captured slave trader to the officers or tribunals of his own country for trial and adjudication.

" This principle is essential, as connected with that of constituting the traffic piracy by the law of nations. So long as the offence was considered as of inferior magnitude, the Constitution of the United States forbade the submission of it, when charged upon their citizens, to any foreign tribunal; and when the crime and the punishment are aggravated to involve the life of the accused, it affords but a more imperative inducement for securing to him the benefit of a trial by his countrymen and his peers.

" It appears that, at the conferences of Verona, the proposition was made by the British Government that the slave trade should be recognized and proclaimed as piracy by the law of nations. We have, therefore, reason to hope that the proposal now made to them on the part of the United States will be favorably considered by them. In that case, further communications on the subject with other Governments will ensue.

"In the meantime, to fulfill the intentions of the House of Representatives in relation to the Netherlands, you will communicate to their Government a copy of the resolution, together with copies of the

laws of the United States prohibiting the slave trade, with particular
notice of the two sections of the act of 15th May, 1820, by which the
crime of being concerned in the African slave trade, when committed
by citizens of the United States, is declared to be and is made punishable as for piracy.   And you will announce the readiness of the American Government . . . to enter upon a negotiation for the purpose of
carrying into effect the object of the resolution of the House of Representatives, namely, the denunciation of the African slave trade as
piracy by the law of nations."

> Mr. Adams, Sec. of State, to Mr. A. H. Everett, chargé d'affaires to the
> Netherlands, Aug. 8, 1823, Am. State Pap. For. Rel. V. 338; MS. Inst.
> U. S. Min. X. 92.   See, to the same effect, Mr. Adams, Sec. of State,
> to Mr. Dearborn, min. to Portugal, Aug. 14, 1823, MS. Inst. U. States
> Min. X. 106; extract printed in Am. State Pap. For. Rel. V. 338.   See,
> also, for correspondence of the United States with Buenos Ayres,
> Colombia, France, Netherlands, Portugal, Russia, and Spain, 11 Br.
> & For. State Papers, 739–759.

March 13, 1824, after long negotiations, a convention was concluded
between the United States and Great Britain for the
suppression of the African slave trade.   The convention was signed at London by Mr. Rush on the part
of the United States, and by Messrs. Huskisson and Stratford Canning on the part of Great Britain.   By Article I. the cruisers of the
contracting parties were to have the right, in order to accomplish the
objects of the convention, to visit and search each other's vessels " on
the coasts of Africa, of America, and of the West Indies."   By Article VII. it was stipulated that the captain and crew of a captured
vessel should be proceeded against as pirates, except that they should
be sent for trial to the courts of their own country.   When the convention was submitted to the United States Senate, that body, on
May 21, 1824, by a vote of 36 to 2, amended it by providing that
either party should be free to denounce it at any time on six months'
notice.   May 22 the convention was further amended by striking out
of Article I. the words " of America," as well as in certain other particulars.

Failure of proposed arrangements.

> Am. St. Pap. For. Rel. V. 319–322, 361–362.   See, also, id. 344, 489, 585.

" The convention between the United States and Great Britain for
the suppression of the African slave trade is herewith transmitted to
you, with the ratification on the part of the United States, under certain modifications and exceptions, annexed as conditions to the advice
and consent of the Senate to its ratification.

" The participation of the Senate of the United States in the final
conclusion of all treaties, to which they are parties, is already well

known to the British Government; and the novelty of the principles established by the convention, as well as their importance, and the requisite assent of two-thirds of the Senators present to the final conclusion of every part of the ratified treaty, will explain the causes of its ratification under this form. It will be seen that the great and essential principles which form the basis of the compact are admitted, to their full extent, in the ratified part of the convention. The second article, and the portion of the seventh which it is proposed to expunge, are unessential to the plan, and were not included in the project of convention transmitted to you from hence. They appear, indeed, to be, so far as concerned the United States, altogether inoperative, since they could not confer the power of capturing slave traders under the flag of a third party—a power not claimed either by the United States or Great Britain, unless by treaty, and the United States having no such treaty with any other power. It is presumed that the bearing of those articles was exclusively upon the flags of those other nations with which Great Britain has already treaties for the suppression of the slave trade, and that, while they give an effective power to the officers of Great Britain, they conferred none upon those of the United States.

" The exception of the coast of America from the seas upon which the mutual power of capturing the vessels under the flag of either party may be exercised, had reference, in the views of the Senate, doubtless, to the coast of the United States. On no part of that coast, unless within the Gulf of Mexico, is there any probability that slave-trading vessels will ever be found. The necessity for the exercise of the authority to capture is, therefore, no greater than it would be upon the coast of Europe. In South America, the only coast to which slave traders may be hereafter expected to resort, is that of Brazil, from which it is to be hoped they will shortly be expelled by the laws of the country.

" The limitation by which each party is left at liberty to renounce the convention, by six months' notice to the other, may, perhaps, be useful in reconciling other nations to the adoption of its provisions. If the principles of the convention are to be permanently maintained, this limitation must undoubtedly be abandoned; and when the public mind shall have been familiarized to the practical operation of the system, it is not doubted that this reservation will, on all sides, be readily given up.

" In giving these explanations to the British Government, you will state that the President was fully prepared to have ratified the convention without alteration as it had been signed by you. He is aware that the conditional ratification leaves the British Government at liberty to concur therein or to decline the ratification altogether, but he will not disguise the wish that, such as it is, it may receive the sanction of Great Britain and be carried into effect. When the concurrence of both Governments has been at length obtained, by exertions so long and so anxiously continued, to principles so important and for purposes of so high and honorable a character, it would prove a severe disappointment to the friends of freedom and of humanity if all prospect of effective concert between the two nations for the extirpation of this disgrace to civilized man should be lost by differences of sentiment, in all probability transient, upon unessential details."

> Mr. Adams, Sec. of State, to Mr. Rush, min. to England, May 29, 1824, Am. St. Pap. For. Rel. V. 362.
>
> As to this proposed treaty, see the remarkable statement of Mr. Adams in the House, April 14, 1842, Schuyler's Am. Dip. 247; Cong. Globe, 27 Cong. 2 sess. 424. See Moore's American Diplomacy, 75–77.

" I have the honor to inform you that Mr. Secretary Canning has given me to understand, in an interview which I have this day had with him, that this Government finds itself unable to accede to the convention for the suppression of the slave trade, with the alterations and modifications that have been annexed to its ratification on the part of the United States. He said that none of these alterations or modifications would have formed insuperable bars to the consent of Great Britain, except that which had expunged the word America from the first article, but that this was considered insuperable. . . .

" The reasons which Mr. Canning assigned for this determination on the part of Great Britain I forbear to state, as he has promised to address a communication in writing to me upon the subject, where they will be seen more accurately and at large; but to guard against any delay in my receiving that communication, I have thought it right not to lose any time in thus apprising you, for the President's information, of the result."

> Mr. Rush, min. to England, to Mr. Adams, Sec. of State, Aug. 9, 1824, Am. State Pap. For. Rel. V. 364.
>
> Mr. Rush, Aug. 30, 1824, enclosed to Mr. Adams a copy of Canning's promised communication, which bore date Aug. 27. (Am. State Pap. For. Rel. V. 364.)

" The United States having on the 10th day of December, 1824, concluded a convention with the Republic of Colombia, for the same object of more effectually suppressing the slave trade, which was free from the objection of extending the qualified right of search to the American coasts, this latter convention was submitted, during the last session, to the consideration of the Senate. And that body, in the exercise of its constitutional participation of the treaty making power, has deemed it inexpedient to advise and consent to the ratification of the Colombian convention. From this decision the inference was irresistible, that even if the British and American Governments could come to an agreement to exclude from the operation of the proposed convention between them the American coasts, it would be still unacceptable to the Senate. Under these circumstances, the further continuation of the negotiation seems entirely useless; and I accordingly addressed a note to Mr. Addington, on the 6th day of April, 1825 (of which a copy, together with a copy of his answer to it, accompanies these instructions), informing him that the President declined treating any longer upon that subject."

> Mr. Clay, Sec. of State, to Mr. King, min. to England, May 10, 1825, MS. Inst. U. States Min. X. 314.
>
> For the text of the convention with Colombia, and a note of its rejection by the Senate on March 9, 1825, see Am. State Pap. For. Rel. V. 733–735.
>
> For correspondence and reports concerning the negotiations for the suppression of the slave trade, 1818–1825, see Am. State Pap. For. Rel. V. 69–80, 90–126, 140–141, 315–347, 353–355, 359–368, 629, 782.

In 1833 and 1834 the governments of France and Great Britain, through their ministers at Washington, sought the adhesion of the United States to the convention between those powers of November 30, 1831, and the supplementary convention of March 22, 1833, for the suppression of the African slave trade. The United States replied that the conventions in question were, in the opinion of the President, open to the objections which were on former occasions " deemed insuperable; " but that, if he had had any doubt on the subject, it would have been removed by the statement of the British minister, in a note of December 25, 1833, that in the act of accession it would be necessary "that the right of search should be extended to the coasts of the United States." This, it was declared, would have led the President, " under any circumstances, altogether to decline " the invitation.

Continued opposition to visit and search.

> Mr. McLane, Sec. of State, to Mr. Vaughan, Brit. min., March 24, 1834, MS. Notes to For. Leg. V. 191.
>
> See, in the same sense, Mr. Forsyth, Sec. of State, to Mr. Serurier, French min., Oct. 4, 1834, MS. Notes to French Leg. VI. 3.

" If, in the treaties concluded between Great Britain and other powers, the latter have thought fit, for the attainment of a particular object, to surrender to British cruisers certain rights and authority not recognized by maritime law, the officers charged with the execution of those treaties must bear in mind that their operation cannot give a right to interfere in any manner with the flag of nations not parties to them. The United States not being such a party, vessels legally sailing under their flag can in no case be called upon to submit to the operation of said treaties; and it behooves their Government to

protect and sustain its citizens in every justifiable effort to resist all
attempts to subject them to the rules therein established, or to any
consequent deductions therefrom. . . .

" The President has been advised that, on frequent occasions, the
flag of the United States, as well as those of other nations, has been
fraudulently used by subjects of other countries to cover illicit commerce, and elude the pursuit of British and other cruisers employed
in the suppression of the African slave trade; and that a pretext has
thereby been afforded for boarding, visiting, and interrupting vessels
bearing the American flag. The several complaints to which the subject has given rise should convince Her Majesty's Government of the
great abuse to which the practice is liable, and make it sensible of the
propriety of its immediate discontinuance. It is a matter of regret
that this practice has not already been abandoned. The President, on
learning the abuses which had grown out of it, and with a view to
do away with every cause for its longer continuance, having now
directed the establishment of a competent naval force to cruise along
those parts of the African coast which American vessels are in the
habit of visiting in the pursuit of their lawful commerce, and where
it is alleged that the slave trade has been carried on under an illegal
use of the flag of the United States, has a right to expect that positive
instructions will be given to all Her Majesty's officers to forbear from
boarding or visiting vessels under the American flag."

> Mr. Forsyth, Sec. of State, to Mr. Stevenson, min. to England, July 8,
> 1840, H. Ex. Doc. 115, 26 Cong. 2 sess. 39, 40.
> This document contains a large mass of papers and correspondence in
> relation to seizures and searches of American vessels on the coast of
> Africa.

In December, 1841, the representatives of England, France, Prussia,
Russia, and Austria signed at London a treaty for the
The Quintuple Treaty. suppression of the slave trade. The cruisers of each
nation were accorded the right to detain and search
vessels belonging to any of the others, should the vessel " on reasonable grounds be suspected of being engaged in the traffic in slaves."
February 1, 1842, General Cass, who was then minister to France,
published in Paris a pamphlet inveighing against the treaty on the
ground of its tendency towards the reestablishment of the practice of
visitation and search. The pamphlet was entitled " An Examination
of the Question, now in Discussion, between the American and British
Governments, concerning the Right of Search." February 13, 1842,
General Cass also addressed to M. Guizot, then minister of foreign
affairs, a protest against the quintuple treaty. The French Government refused to ratify the treaty, but in 1845 agreed to maintain an

effective fleet on the African coast, as the United States had done under the Webster-Ashburton treaty.

McLaughlin, Lewis Cass (American Statesmen Series), 176–184.

" The President directs me to say, that he approves your letter [to M. Guizot, of February 13, 1842], and warmly commends the motives which animated you in presenting it. The whole subject is now before us here, or will be shortly, as Lord Ashburton arrived last evening; and, without intending to intimate at present what modes of settling this point of difference with England will be proposed, you may receive two propositions as certain :

" 1st. That, in the absence of treaty stipulations, the United States will maintain the immunity of merchant vessels on the seas to the fullest extent which the law of nations authorizes.

" 2d. That, if the Government of the United States, animated by a sincere desire to put an end to the African slave trade, shall be induced to enter into treaty stipulations for that purpose with any foreign power, those stipulations will be such as shall be strictly limited to their true and single object, such as shall not be embarrassing to innocent commerce, and such, especially, as shall neither imply any inequality, nor can tend in any way to establish such inequality, in their practical operations."

Mr. Webster, Sec. of State, to Mr. Cass, min. to France, Apr. 5, 1842, 6
Webster's Works, 343, 345 ; MS. Inst. France, XIV. 272.

" Two essays, 'An Inquiry into the Validity of the British Claim to a Right of Visitation and Search, of American Vessels suspected to be engaged in the African Slave Trade,' by Mr. Wheaton, London, 1842; and ' Examen de la Question aujourd'hui pendante entre le Gouvernement des États Unis et celui de la Grande Bretagne, concernant le Droit de Visite ' (ascribed to Hon. Lewis Cass, then Minister to France), Paris, 1842, with the letter of General Cass to M. Guizot, dated 13th February, 1842, and which was in the nature of a protest against the Quintuple Treaty of 20th December, 1841, are understood to have had no little influence in preventing the ratification of that treaty by the Government of France.

" The publications referred to received, as it were, an official sanction from Mr. Legaré, on his assuming the seals of the State Department.   In his earliest instructions he said : ' I avail myself of the first opportunity afforded by our new official relations, to express to you my hearty satisfaction at the part you took, with General Cass, in the discussion of the " right of search," and the manner you acquitted yourself of it.   I read your pamphlet with entire assent.   It is due to the civilization of the age, and the power of opinion, even over the most arbitrary governments, that every encroachment on the rights of nations should become the subject of immediate censure and denunciation. One great object of permanent missions is to establish a censorship of this kind, and to render by means of it the appeals of the injured to the sympathies of mankind, through diplomatic organs, at once more easy, more direct, and more effective.' (Mr. Legaré to Mr. Wheaton, June 9, 1843. State Department MSS.) "

> Lawrence's Wheaton (1863), 262, 263.

By Article VIII. of the Webster-Ashburton treaty of August 9, 1842, the contracting parties agreed each to maintain on the African coast a sufficient squadron " to enforce, separately and respectively," their laws and obligations for the suppression of the slave trade. The two squadrons were to be " independent " of each other, but the two Governments were to give such instructions as would enable their forces effectually to act in concert and cooperation.

Webster - Ashburton treaty.

By article IX. of the same treaty, the contracting parties agreed to unite in representations to other powers with respect to the propriety and duty of closing all existing slave markets at once and forever.

> President Tyler's message of Aug. 11, 1842, as written by Mr. Webster, transmitting the treaty to the Senate, may be found, together with the text of the treaty and much correspondence, in 6 Webster's Works, 347 et seq.

" It is known that, in December last, a treaty was signed in London by the representatives of England, France, Russia, Prussia, and Austria, having for its professed object a strong and united effort of the five powers to put an end to the traffic [the slave trade]. This treaty was not officially communicated to the Government of the United States, but its provisions and stipulations are supposed to be accurately known to the public. It is understood to be not yet ratified on the part of France.

" No application or request has been made to this Government to become a party to this treaty; but the course it might take in regard to it has excited no small degree of attention and discussion in Europe, as the principle upon which it is founded, and the stipulations which it contains, have caused warm animadversions and great political excitement.

" In my message at the commencement of the present session of Congress, I endeavored to state the principles which this Government supports respecting the right of search and the immunity of flags. Desirous of maintaining those principles fully, at the same time that existing obligations should be fulfilled, I have thought it most consistent with the honor and dignity of the country, that it should execute its own laws, and perform its own obligations, by its own means and its own power. The examination or visitation of the merchant vessels of one nation by the cruisers of another, for any purpose except those known and acknowledged by the law of nations, under whatever restraints or regulations it may take place, may lead to dangerous results. It is far better, by other means, to supersede any supposed necessity, or any motive, for such examination or visit. Interference with a merchant vessel by an armed cruiser is always a delicate proceeding, apt to touch the point of national honor, as well as to affect the interests of individuals. It has been thought, therefore, expedient, not only in accordance with the stipulations of the treaty of Ghent, but at the same time as removing all pretext on the part of others for violating the immunities of the American flag upon the seas, as they exist and are defined by the law of nations, to enter into the articles now submitted to the Senate.

"The treaty which I now submit to you proposes no alteration, mitigation, or modification of the rules of the law of nations. It provides simply that each of the two Governments shall maintain on the coast of Africa a sufficient squadron to enforce, separately and respectively, the laws, rights, and obligations of the two countries for the suppression of the slave trade."

> President Tyler's message, Aug. 11, 1842, transmitting the Webster-Ashburton treaty of Aug. 9 to the Senate, 6 Webster's Works, 353.
>
> A copy of the treaty was sent by Mr. Webster to General Cass, with comments on the slave-trade stipulations, Aug. 29, 1842. (6 Webster's Works, 367; MS. Inst. France, XIV. 278.)

Mr. Cass having criticised the clauses of the Webster-Ashburton treaty in relation to the prevention of the slave trade, not because it admitted a right of search, but because the abandonment of that pretension was not made "a previous condition to any conventional arrangement upon the general subject," Mr. Webster replied:

"Inasmuch as the treaty gives no color or pretext whatever to any right of searching our ships, a declaration against such a right would have been no more suitable to this treaty than a declaration against the right of sacking our towns in time of peace, or any other outrage.

"The rights of merchant vessels of the United States on the high seas, as understood by this Government, have been clearly and fully asserted. As asserted, they will be maintained; nor would a declaration such as you propose have increased its resolution or its ability in this respect. The Government of the United States relies on its own power, and on the effective support of the people, to assert successfully all the rights of all its citizens on the sea as well as on the land; and it asks respect for these rights not as a boon or favor from any nation. The President's message, most certainly, is a clear declaration of what the country understands to be its rights, and his determination to maintain them, not a mere promise to negotiate for these rights, or to endeavor to bring other powers into an acknowledgment of them, either express or implied."

> Mr. Webster, Sec. of State, to Mr. Cass, late min. to France, Dec. 20, 1842, 6 Webster's Works, 381, 388.
> See, also, same to same, Nov. 14, 1842, id. 369.

"After the reception of the President's message [of December, 1842] in England, Lord Aberdeen, on the 18th of January, 1843, addressed a dispatch to Mr. Fox, still British minister here, and directed him to read it to Mr. Webster. . . . It took notice of that part of the President's message which related to the right of search, and denied that any concession on this point had been made by Great Britain in the late negotiations. . . . Mr. Fox was informed by Mr. Webster that an answer to this dispatch would be made in due time through Mr. Everett."

> 2 Curtis's Life of Webster, 149 et seq., where the debates in Parliament on this topic are given.

" In compliance with the resolution of the House of Representatives of the 22d instant, requesting me to communicate to the House ' whatever correspondence or communication may have been received from the British Government respecting the President's construction of the late British treaty concluded at Washington, as it concerns an alleged right to visit American vessels,' I herewith transmit a report made to me by the Secretary of State.

" I have also thought proper to communicate copies of Lord Aberdeen's letter of the 20th December, 1841, to Mr. Everett, Mr. Everett's letter of the 23d December in reply thereto, and extracts from several letters of Mr. Everett to the Secretary of State.

" I can not forego the expression of my regret at the apparent purport of a part of Lord Aberdeen's dispatch to Mr. Fox. I had cherished the hope that all possibility of misunderstanding as to the true construction of the 8th article of the treaty lately concluded between Great Britain and the United States was precluded by the plain and well-weighed language in which it is expressed. The desire of both Governments is to put an end as speedily as possible to the slave trade; and that desire, I need scarcely add, is as strongly and as sincerely felt by the United States as it can be by Great Britain. Yet it must not be forgotten that the trade, though now universally reprobated, was, up to a late period, prosecuted by all who chose to engage in it; and there were unfortunately but very few Christian powers whose subjects were not permitted and even encouraged to share in the profits of what was regarded as a perfectly legitimate commerce. It originated at a period long before the United States had become independent, and was carried on within our borders, in opposition to the most earnest remonstrances and expostulations of some of the colonies in which it was most actively prosecuted. Those engaged in it were as little liable to inquiry or interruption as any others. Its character, thus fixed by common consent and general practice, could only be changed by the positive assent of each and every nation, expressed either in the form of municipal law or conventional arrangement. The United States led the way in efforts to suppress it. They claimed no right to dictate to others, but they resolved, without waiting for the cooperation of other powers, to prohibit it to their own citizens, and to visit its perpetration by them with condign punishment. I may safely affirm that it never occurred to this Government that any new maritime right accrued to it from the position it had thus assumed in regard to the slave trade. If, before our laws for its suppression, the flag of every nation might traverse the ocean unquestioned by our cruisers, this freedom was not, in our opinion, in the least abridged by our municipal legislation.

"Any other doctrine, it is plain, would subject to an arbitrary and ever-varying system of maritime police, adopted at will by the great naval power for the time being, the trade of the world in any places or in any articles which such power might see fit to prohibit to its own subjects or citizens. A principle of this kind could scarcely be acknowledged, without subjecting commerce to the risk of constant and harassing vexations.

" The attempt to justify such a pretension from the right to visit and detain ships upon reasonable suspicion of piracy would deservedly be exposed to universal condemnation, since it would be an attempt to convert an established rule of maritime law, incorporated as a principle into the international code by the consent of all nations, into a rule and principle adopted by a single nation, and enforced only by its assumed authority. To seize and detain a ship upon suspicion of piracy, with probable cause and in good faith, affords no just ground either for complaint on the part of the nation whose flag she bears, or claim of indemnity on the part of the owner. The universal law sanctions, and the common good requires, the existence of such a rule. The right, under such circumstances, not only to visit and detain, but to search a ship, is a perfect right, and involves neither responsibility nor indemnity. But, with this single exception, no nation has, in time of peace, any authority to detain the ships of another upon the high seas, on any pretext whatever, beyond the limits of her territorial jurisdiction. And such, I am happy to find, is substantially the doctrine of Great Britain herself, in her most recent official declarations, and even in those now communicated to the House. These declarations may well lead us to doubt whether the apparent difference between the two Governments is not rather one of definition than of principle. Not only is the right of *search*, properly so called, disclaimed by Great Britain, but even that of mere visit and inquiry is asserted with qualifications inconsistent with the idea of a perfect right.

" In the dispatch of Lord Aberdeen to Mr. Everett of the 20th of December, 1841, as also in that just received by the British minister in this country, made to Mr. Fox, his lordship declares that if, in spite of all the precaution which shall be used to prevent such occurrences, an American ship, by reason of any visit or detention by a British cruiser, 'should suffer loss and injury, it would be followed by prompt and ample remuneration;' and in order to make more manifest her intentions in this respect, Lord Aberdeen, in the dispatch of the 20th December, makes known to Mr. Everett the nature of the instructions given to the British cruisers. These are such as, if faithfully observed, would enable the British Government to approximate the standard of a fair indemnity. That Government has in several cases fulfilled her promises in this particular, by making adequate reparation for damage done to our commerce. It seems obvious to remark, that a right which is only to be exercised under such restrictions and precautions, and risk, in case of any assignable damage, to be followed by the consequences of a trespass, can scarcely be considered anything more than a privilege asked for, and either conceded or withheld, on the usual principles of international comity.

" The principles laid down in Lord Aberdeen's dispatches, and the assurances of indemnity therein held out, although the utmost reliance was placed on the good faith of the British Government, were not regarded by the Executive as a sufficient security against the abuses which Lord Aberdeen admitted might arise in even the most cautious and moderate exercise of their new maritime police; and therefore, in my message at the opening of the last session, I set forth the views entertained by the Executive on this subject, and substantially affirmed both our inclination and ability to enforce our own laws, protect our flag from abuse, and acquit ourselves of all our duties and obligations on the high seas. In view of these assertions, the treaty of Washington was negotiated, and, upon consultation with the British negotiator as to the quantum of force necessary to be employed in order to attain these objects, the result to which the most deliberate estimate led was embodied in the eighth article of the treaty.

" Such were my views at the time of negotiating that treaty, and such, in my opinion, is its plain and fair interpretation. I regarded the eighth article as removing all possible pretext, on the ground of mere necessity, to visit and detain our ships upon the African coast because of any alleged abuse of our flag by slave traders of other nations. We had taken upon ourselves the burden of preventing any such abuse, by stipulating to furnish an armed force regarded by both the high contracting parties as sufficient to accomplish that object.

" Denying, as we did and do, all color of right to exercise any such general police over the flags of independent nations, we did not demand of Great Britain any formal renunciation of her pretension; still less had we the idea of yielding anything ourselves in that respect. We chose to make a practical settlement of the question. This we owed to what we had already done upon this subject. The honor of the country called for it; the honor of its flag demanded that it should not be used by others to cover an iniquitous traffic. This Government, I am very sure, has both the inclination and the ability to do this; and, if need be, it will not content itself with a fleet of eighty guns, but, sooner than any foreign Government shall exercise the province of executing its laws and fulfilling its obligations, the highest of which is to protect its flag alike from abuse or insult, it would, I doubt not, put in requisition for that purpose its whole naval power. The purpose of this Government is faithfully to fulfil the treaty on its part, and it will not permit itself to doubt that Great Britain will comply with it on hers. In this way, peace will best be preserved, and the most amicable relations maintained between the two countries."

> President Tyler, message of Feb. 27, 1843, House Ex. Doc. 192, 27 Cong.
> 3 sess.

" The eighth and ninth articles of the treaty of Washington constitute a mutual stipulation for concerted efforts to abolish the African slave trade. The stipulation, it may be admitted, has no other effects on the pretensions of either party than this: Great Britain had claimed as a *right* that which this Government could not admit to be a *right*, and, in the exercise of a just and proper spirit of amity, a mode was resorted to which might render unnecessary both the assertion and the denial of such claim.

" There probably are those who think that what Lord Aberdeen calls a right of visit, and which he attempts to distinguish from the right of search, ought to have been expressly acknowledged by the Government of the United States. At the same time, there are those on the other side who think that the formal surrender of such right of visit should have been demanded by the United States as a precedent condition to the negotiation for treaty stipulations on the subject of the African slave trade. But the treaty neither asserts the claim in terms, nor denies the claim in terms; it neither formally insists upon it, nor formally renounces it. . . .

"The British Government, then, supposes that the right of visit and the right of search are essentially distinct in their nature, and that this difference is well known and generally acknowledged; that the difference between them consists in their different objects and purposes: one, the visit, having for its object nothing but to ascertain the nationality of the vessel; the other, the search, by an inquisition, not only into the nationality of the vessel, but the nature and object of her voyage, and the true ownership of her cargo.

"The Government of the United States, on the other hand, maintains that there is no such well-known and acknowledged, nor, indeed, any broad and generic difference between what has been usually called visit, and what has been usually called search; that the right of visit, to be effectual, must come, in the end, to include search; and thus to exercise, in peace, an authority which the law of nations only allows in times of war. If such well-known distinction exists, where are the proofs of it? What writers of authority on public law, what adjudications in courts of admiralty, what public treaties, recognize it? No such recognition has presented itself to the Government of the United States; but, on the contrary, it understands that public writers, courts of law, and solemn treaties have, for two centuries, used the words 'visit' and 'search' in the same sense. What Great Britain and the United States mean by the 'right of search,' in its broadest sense, is called by continental writers and jurists by no other name than the 'right of visit.' Visit, therefore, as it has been understood, implies not only a right to inquire into the national character, but to detain the vessel, to stop the progress of the voyage, to examine papers, to decide on their regularity and authenticity, and to make inquisition on board for enemy's property, and into the business which the vessel is engaged in. In other words, it describes the entire right of belligerent visitation and search. Such a right is justly disclaimed by the British Government in time of peace. They, nevertheless, insist on a right which they denominate a right of visit, and by that word describe the claim which they assert. It is proper, and due to the importance and delicacy of the questions involved, to take care that, in discussing them, both governments understand the terms which may be used in the same sense. If, indeed, it should be manifest that the difference between the parties is only verbal, it might be hoped that no harm would be done; but the Government of the United States thinks itself not justly chargeable with excessive jealousy, or with too great scrupulosity in the use of words, in insisting on its opinion that there is no such distinction as the British Government maintains between visit and search; and that there is no right to visit in time of peace, except in the execution of revenue laws or other municipal regulations, in which cases the right is usually exercised near the coast, or within the marine league, or where the vessel is justly suspected of violating the law of nations by piratical aggression; but, wherever exercised, it is a right of search. . . .

"As we understand the general and settled rules of public law, in respect to ships of war sailing under the authority of their Government, 'to arrest pirates and other public offenders,' there is no reason why they may not approach any vessels descried at sea for the purpose of ascertaining their real characters. Such a right of approach seems indispensable for the fair and discreet exercise of their authority; and the use of it can not be justly deemed indicative of any design to insult or injure those they approach, or to impede them in their lawful commerce. On the other hand, it is as clear that no ship is, under such circumstances, bound to lie by or wait the approach of any other ship. She is at full liberty to pursue her voyage in her own way, and to use all necessary precautions to avoid any suspected sinister enterprise or hostile attack. Her right to the free use of the ocean is as perfect as that of any other ship. An entire equality is presumed to exist. She has a right to consult her own safety, but at the same time she must take care not to violate the rights of others. She may use any precautions dictated by the prudence or fears of her officers, either as to delay, or the progress or course of her voyage; but she is not at liberty to inflict injuries upon other innocent parties simply because of conjectural dangers.

" But if the vessel thus approached attempts to avoid the vessel approaching, or does not comply with her commander's order to send him her papers for his inspection, nor consent to be visited or detained, what is next to be done? Is force to be used? And if force be used, may that force be lawfully repelled? These questions lead at once to the elemental principle, the essence of the British claim. Suppose the merchant vessel be, in truth, an American vessel engaged in lawful commerce, and that she does not choose to be detained. Suppose she resists the visit. What is the consequence? In all cases in which the belligerent right of visit exists, resistance to the exercise of that right is regarded as just cause of condemnation, both of vessel and cargo. Is that penalty, or what other penalty, to be incurred by resistance to visit in time of peace? Or suppose that force be met by force, gun returned for gun, and the commander of the cruiser, or some of his seamen, be killed; what description of offense will have been committed? It would be said, in behalf of the commander of the cruiser, that he mistook the vessel for a vessel of England, Brazil, or Portugal; but does this mistake of his take away from the American vessel the right of self-defense? The writers of authority declare it to be a principle of natural law, that the privilege of self-defense exists against an assailant who mistakes the object of his attack for another whom he had a right to assail.

"Lord Aberdeen can not fail to see, therefore, what serious consequences might ensue, if it were to be admitted that this claim to visit, in time of peace, however limited or defined, should be permitted to exist as a strict matter of right; for if it exist as a right, it must be followed by corresponding duties and obligations, and the failure to fulfil those duties would naturally draw penal consequences after it, till ere long it would become, in truth, little less, or little other, than the belligerent right of search.

"If visit or visitation be not accompanied by search, it will be in most cases merely idle. A sight of papers may be demanded, and papers may be produced. But it is known that slave traders carry false papers and different sets of papers. A search for other papers, then, must be made where suspicion justifies it, or else the whole proceeding would be nugatory. In suspicious cases, the language and general appearance of the crew are among the means of ascertaining the national character of the vessel. The cargo on board, also, often indicates the country from which she comes. Her log-books, showing the previous course and events of her voyage, her internal fitting up and equipment, are all evidences for her, or against her, on her allegation of character. These matters, it is obvious, can only be ascertained by rigorous search. . . .

"On the whole, the Government of the United States, while it has not conceded a mutual right of visit or search, as has been done by the parties to the quintuple treaty of December, 1841, does not admit that, by the law and practice of nations, there is any such thing as a right of visit, distinguished by well-known rules and definitions from the right of search.

"It does not admit that visit of American merchant vessels by British cruisers is founded on any right, notwithstanding the cruiser may suppose such vessel to be British, Brazilian, or Portuguese. We can not but see that the detention and examination of American vessels by British cruisers has already led to consequences, and fear that, if continued, it would still lead to further consequences, highly injurious to the lawful commerce of the United States.

"At the same time, the Government of the United States fully admits that its flag can give no immunity to pirates, nor to any other than to regularly documented American vessels. It was upon this view of the whole case, and with a firm conviction of the truth of these sentiments, that it cheerfully assumed the duties contained in the treaty of Washington; in the hope that thereby causes of difficulty and difference might be altogether removed, and that the two powers might be enabled to act concurrently, cordially, and effectually for the suppression of a traffic which both regard as a reproach upon the civilization of the age, and at war with every principle of humanity and every Christian sentiment. , , ,

" Both houses of Congress, with a remarkable degree of unanimity, have made express provisions for carrying into effect the eighth article of the treaty. An American squadron will immediately proceed to the coast of Africa. Instructions for its commander are in the course of preparation, and copies will be furnished to the British Government; and the President confidently believes, that the cordial concurrence of the two governments in the mode agreed on will be more effectual than any efforts yet made for the suppresion of the slave trade."

Mr. Webster, Sec. of State, to Mr. Everett, min. to England, March 28, 1843, 6 Webster's Works, 331, 332, 335, 338, 341, 342.

On April 27, 1843, Mr. Everett wrote to Mr. Webster that he had read to Lord Aberdeen the instructions from which extracts are given above, and that Lord Aberdeen had said that " he did not know that he should wish to alter a word; that he concurred with you in the proposition that there is no such distinction as that between a right of search and a right of visit." (2 Curtis's Life of Webster, 165.)

" The views of Mr. Webster on this question are fully sustained by the best writers on public law in America and Europe. Chancellor Kent says most emphatically that the right of visitation and search ' is strictly and exclusively a war right, and does not rightfully exist in time of peace, unless conceded by treaty.' He, however, concedes the *right of approach* (as described by the Supreme Court of the United States in the *Marianna Flora*) for the sole purpose of ascertaining the real national character of the vessel sailing under suspicious circumstances. With respect to the right of *visit in time of peace*, claimed by the English Government, Mr. Wheaton defied the British admiralty lawyers ' to show a single passage of any institutional writer on public law, or the judgment of any court by which that law is administered, either in Europe or America, which will justify the exercise of such a right on the high seas in time of peace.' . . . ' The distinction now set up, between a right of *visitation* and a right of *search*, is nowhere alluded to by any public jurist, as being founded on the law of nations. The technical term of *visitation and search*, used by the English civilians, is exactly synonymous with the *droit de visite* of the continental civilians. The right of seizure for a breach of the revenue laws, or laws of trade and navigation, of a particular nation, is quite different. The utmost length to which the exercise of this right on the high seas has ever been carried, in respect to the vessels of another nation, has been to justify seizing them within the territorial jurisdiction of the state against whose laws they offend, *and* pursuing them, in case of flight, seizing them upon the ocean, and bringing them in for adjudication before the tribunals of that state. This, however, says the Supreme Court of the United States in the case, of the *Marianna Flora*, has never been supposed to draw after it any right of visitation or search. The party, in such case, seizes at his peril. If he establishes the forfeiture he is justified.' Mr. Justice Story, delivering the opinion of the Supreme Court, in the case of the *Marianna Flora*, says, that the right of visitation and search does not belong, in time of peace, to the public ships of any nation.

'This right is strictly a belligerent right, allowed by the general consent of nations in time of war, and limited to those occasions.' 'Upon the ocean, then, in time of peace, all possess an entire equality. It is the common highway of all, appropriated to the use of all, and no one can vindicate to himself a superior exclusive prerogative there. Every ship sails there with the unquestionable right of pursuing her own lawful business without interruption.'" (2 Halleck's Int. Law, Baker's ed., (1878) 270–271.)

Wharton, in a note in his International Law Digest, III. § 327, referring to the question of visit and search, said:

"It is said that this prerogative is essential to clear the seas of pirates. But the prerogative is an impertinent intrusion on the privacy of individuals as well as on the territory of the state whose domains are thus invaded; and the evil of sustaining such a prerogative is far greater than the evil of permitting a pirate for a few hours to carry a simulated flag. Pirates, in the present condition of the seas, have been very rarely arrested when setting up this simulation. They are now, in the few cases in which they appear, readily tracked by other means; and the fact that in some instances they are caught when carrying a false flag no more sustains the right of general search of merchant shipping than would the fact that conspirators sometimes carry false papers justify the police in seizing every business man whom they meet and searching his correspondence. In the very rare cases in which an apparent pirate is seized and searched on the high seas under a mistake, the vessel being a merchant ship, the defence must be, not prerogative, but necessity, only to be justified on the grounds on which is justified an assault made on apparent but unreal cause. (See to this effect Gessner, 12th ed., 303; Kaltenborn, Seerecht, II. 350; Wheat., Right of Visitation, London, 1842. See to the contrary Phill., III. 147, 148; Heffter, 164; Calvo, II. 656.) Ortolan holds that the function is to be exercised at the risk of the visiting cruiser as an extra-legal prerogative. (Ortolan, III. 258.)

"It may be added that basing the right to search a vessel on the assumption of piracy is a *petitio principii*, equivalent to saying that the vessel is to be searched because she is a pirate, when it is for the purpose of determining whether she is a pirate that she is searched. The searching, as is the case on issuing a search warrant in our ordinary criminal practice, should be at the risk of the party searching, and only on probable cause first shown, not for the purpose of inquiring whether there is probable cause. The right of British cruisers to search a foreign vessel for British sailors was claimed by the British Government prior to the war of 1812 between Great Britain and the United States. The right was not abandoned by Great Britain at Ghent, but it has never since been exercised. It is now virtually surrendered. (1 Wheat. Int. Law, 737.) 'I can not think,' says Sir R. Phillimore (3 Phill., 1879, 445), 'that the claim of Great Britain was founded on international law. In my opinion it was not.' The right to visit and search on certain conditions has frequently, it should be added, been given by treaty, in which case it is determined by the limitations imposed by the contracting states. (See specifications in Gessner, 12th ed., 305.) At the same time we must remember that independent of the right of search, a ship, whether public or private, has a right to approach another on the high seas, if it can, and to hail or speak it, and require it to show

Its colors, the approaching ship first showing its own. (Ortolan,
Rég. Int. et Dip. de la Mer, 233, &c.; Field's Int. Code, § 62.)"

" Our late treaty provides that each country shall keep a naval
force of a specified size on the coast of Africa, with the obvious view
to remove all occasion for any trespass by the one upon the other. We
have proceeded to execute our part of that stipulation, by sending to
that coast four vessels carrying more than eighty guns, a force altogether sufficient to watch over American commerce, and to enforce the
laws of the United States in relation to the slave trade. There can
not, therefore, be any pretense in future for any interference by the
cruisers of England with our flag. Of course, it is not probable that
there will be any further occasions for reclamations on that ground,
except in such flagrant cases as will leave no room for dispute or
doubts. With such a foundation for lasting harmony between the
two countries, at least so far as this dangerous and exciting subject is
concerned, it would seem to be an obvious dictate of prudence, as well
as of propriety, to remove, as speedily as possible, all existing causes
of complaint arising from the same source. Nothing would contribute more than this to a good understanding between the two Governments and their people."

> Mr. Upshur, Sec. of State, to Mr. Everett, Aug. 8, 1843, MS. Inst. Gr.
> Brit. XV. 106.
> In the Brit. and For. St. Pap. for 1843–'44, vol. 32, 433, 565, are given the
> following documents in respect to the right of search: Lord Aber-
> deen to Lord Ashburton, Feb. 8, 1842; Lord Ashburton to Lord Aber-
> deen, May 12, 1842, containing report of United States naval offi-
> cers as to slave trade; Mr. Fox to Lord Aberdeen, Mar. 4, 1843;
> message of the President of Feb. 28, 1843, as to right of search; Mr.
> Webster (Sec. of State) to the President, Feb., 1843; Mr. Everett
> (London) to Mr. Webster, Dec. 28, 1841; same to same, Dec. 31,
> 1841; Mr. Webster to Mr. Everett, Jan. 29, 1842.
> President Fillmore's message of July 30, 1850, as to cases of then recent
> stoppage and search of American vessels by British men-of-war is in
> Senate Ex. Doc. 66, 31 Cong. 1 sess.

" The forcible visitation of vessels upon the ocean is prohibited by
the law of nations, in time of peace, and this exemp-
British renuncia-
tion of visit and   tion from foreign jurisdiction is now recognized
search, 1858.   by Great Britain, and, it is believed, by all other
commercial powers, even if the exercise of a right of visit were
essential to the suppression of the slave trade. . . . But there is
just reason to believe that the value of a right of visitation, as a
means of putting an end to this traffic, has been greatly overrated.
The object of such visitation is to ascertain the national character of
the vessel. If found to belong to the same nation as the cruiser mak-

ing the visit, and violating its laws, she may be seized. If belonging to another nation she must be released, in whatever employment she may be engaged, unless indeed she has become a pirate, in which case she is liable to be captured by the naval force of any civilized power. If the United States maintained that by carrying their flag at her mast-head any vessel became thereby entitled to the immunity which belongs to American vessels, they might well be reproached with assuming a position which would go far toward shielding crimes upon the ocean from punishment. But they advance no such pretension, while they concede that if, in the honest examination of a vessel sailing under American colors, but accompanied by strongly marked suspicious circumstances, a mistake is made, and she is found to be entitled to the flag she bears, but no injury is committed and the conduct of the boarding party is irreproachable, no government would be likely to make a case thus exceptional in its character a subject of serious reclamation. . . .

" The police over their own vessels being a right inherent in all independent states, each of them is responsible to the public opinion of the world for its faithful preservation, as it is responsible for the execution of any other duty. The measures it will adopt, must depend upon its own judgment, and whether these are efficient or inefficient no other nation has a right of interference; and the same principles are applicable to territorial jurisdiction. Good laws it is the duty of every Government to provide, and also to make suitable provision for their just administration. But because offenders sometimes escape, nations are not therefore disposed to admit any participation in the execution of these laws, even though such a measure might insure their more faithful execution."

> Mr. Cass, Sec. of State, to Mr. Dallas, min. to England, Feb. 23, 1859, MS. Inst. Gr. Br. XVII. 150.
>
> See, also, same to same, March 31, 1860, H. Ex. Doc. 7, 36 Cong. 2 sess. 400; Mr. Cass, Sec. of State, to Lord Lyons, Br. min., April 3, 1860, H. Ex. Doc. 7, 36 Cong. 2 sess. 414; Mr. Cass, Sec. of State, to Count de Sartiges, French min., Jan. 25, 1859, MS. Notes to French Leg. VII. 8. The last-mentioned note relates to a memorandum with reference to the question of verifying the national character of merchant vessels on the high seas.

In a long note of April 10, 1858, addressed to Lord Napier, then British minister at Washington, in relation to measures for the suppression of the slave trade, Mr. Cass adverted to a statement of his lordship to the effect that the employment by a vessel of the American flag did " not protect the slaver from visit, but exonerates her from search." The distinction thus taken between " the right of visitation and the right of search, between an entry for

the purpose of examining into the national character of a vessel and
an entry for the purpose of examining into the objects of her
voyage," could not, said Mr. Cass, " be justly maintained upon
any recognized principle of the law of nations. . . . The United
States deny the right of the cruisers of any other power whatever,
for any purpose whatever, to enter their vessels by force in time of
peace. . . . No change of name can change the illegal character of
the assumption. Search, or visit, it is equally an assault upon the
independence of nations."

> Mr. Cass, Sec. of State, to Lord Napier, British min., April 10, 1858,
> S. Ex. Doc. 49, 35 Cong. 1 sess. 42, 47, 48. Concerning reports as
> to the detention and search of American vessels by British cruisers
> in the Gulf of Mexico and the adjacent seas, see Mr. Cass, Sec. of
> State, to Mr. Dallas, min. to England, May 18, 1858, MS. Inst.
> Great Britain, XVII. 105 ; same to same, July 1, 1858, id. 119.
> Mr. Cass's note to Lord Napier of April 10, 1858, may also be found in
> 50 Br. and For. State Papers, 707.

" Her Majesty's Government recognize as sound those principles
of international law which have been laid down by General Cass
in his note of the 10th of April to your lordship, principles which
he supports by the authority of Lord Stowell and the Duke of
Wellington, and Her Majesty's Government are also aware that
nothing in their treaty of 1842 with the United States supersedes that
law.

" Her Majesty's Government, however, think it most indispensable to civilization and the police of the high seas, that there should
exist, practically, a limited power of verifying the nationality of
vessels suspected, on good grounds, of carrying false colors. . . .

" General Cass observes, that ' a merchant vessel upon the high
seas is protected by her national character. He who forcibly enters
her, does so upon his own responsibility. Undoubtedly, if a vessel
assumes a national character to which she is not entitled, and is sailing under false colors, she can not be protected by this assumption
of a nationality to which she has no claim. As the identity of a person must be determined by the officer bearing a process for his
arrest, and determined at the risk of such officer, so must the
national identity of a vessel be determined, at the like hazard to
him who, doubting the flag she displays, searches her to ascertain
her true character. There, no doubt, may be circumstances which
would go far to modify the complaints a nation would have a right
to make for such a violation of its sovereignty. If the boarding officer
had just grounds for suspicion, and deported himself with propriety
in the performance of his task, doing no injury, and peaceably
retiring when satisfied of his error, no nation would make such an
act the subject of serious reclamation.'

" Her Majesty's Government agree entirely in this view of the case, and the question therefore becomes one solely of discretion on the part of the acting officer. It appears to Her Majesty's Government that it is one extremely dangerous to entrust, and onerous to bear; and that an exact definition of what each respective state would permit, for verifying nationality, and thereby securing general trade against piracy, should be agreed upon between Great Britain and the United States, and clearly embodied in their instructions of their naval commanders."

> Lord Malmesbury, British foreign secretary, to Lord Napier, British min. at Washington, June 11, 1858, 50 Brit. & For. State Papers (1859–1860), 737, 738–739.
>
> It should be observed, with reference to Lord Malmesbury's remark that the question became " one solely of discretion on the part of the acting officer," that the passage quoted by his lordship from General Cass's note of April 10, 1858, is qualified in that note by the following important statement: "*It is one thing to do a deed avowedly illegal, and excuse it by the attending circumstances; and it is another and quite a different thing to claim a right of action, and the right also of determining when, and how, and to what extent, it shall be exercised. And this is no barren distinction, so far as the interest of this country is involved, but it is closely connected with an object dear to the American people—the freedom of their citizens upon the great highway of the world.*" (50 Br. & For. State Papers, 716. The italics are the editor's.)

" In addition to the satisfactory assurances, which your correspondence contains, of the views of the British Government, it gives me pleasure to be able to inform you that this Department, by the directions of Lord Malmesbury, has been furnished by Lord Napier with the copy of a letter addressed to his lordship by Lord Malmesbury and dated the 11th instant, in which the same purposes are avowed and the same principles recognized as reported in your dispatch of the 8th instant. . . .

" The President desires you would express to Lord Malmesbury his gratification at this satisfactory termination of the controversy which has given so much trouble to our respective Governments, concerning the claim of a right in behalf of a British cruiser in time of peace to search or visit American merchant vessels upon the ocean. Her Britannic Majesty's Government has disclaimed that pretension and recognized the principles of international law laid down in the letter from this Department to Lord Napier of the 10th of April last, and which had been maintained by distinguished British statesmen and especially by that eminent jurist Lord Stowell, who said emphatically, while deciding a case judicially before him, that ' no nation can exercise a right of visitation and search upon the common and unappropriated parts of the ocean, except from the belligerent claim.' "

Mr. Cass, Sec. of State, to Mr. Dallas, min. to England, June 30, 1858, MS. Inst. Great Britain, XVII. 115.

Mr. Cass went on to say that the President was desirous to prevent the fraudulent assumption of the United States flag and that, while he entertained a strong conviction that the occasional abuse of the flag of any nation was an evil far less to be deprecated than would be the establishment of a pretension incompatible with the freedom of the seas, he was ready to receive any propositions which the British Government might feel disposed to make to prevent the false employment of national colors.

As reported in the London *Times* of June 18, 1858, Lord Malmesbury, referring in the House of Lords to measures adopted for the suppression of the slave trade, stated that the United States had " positively, categorically, and constantly " refused to admit any distinction between visit and search, and that the doctrine laid down by the United States was adopted by other countries. Lord Malmesbury added that " he had admitted the international law as laid down by the American minister for foreign affairs, though not, of course, without being fortified by the opinions of the law officers of the Crown." (H. Ex. Doc. 7, 36 Cong. 2 sess. 104, 105.)

July 4, 1858, Mr. Dallas, at a dinner of Americans in London, said: " Visit and search in regard to American vessels on the high seas in time of peace is finally ended." Referring to this statement, Lord Lyndhurst, July 26, 1858, speaking in the House of Lords, said: " Many persons . . . appear to think that . . . we have surrendered a most valuable and important right. The answer which I make to that is, that we have surrendered no right, for that, in point of fact, no right such as that which is contended for has ever existed. We have, my lords, abandoned the assumption of a right, and in doing so we have, I think, acted justly, prudently and wisely." Lord Malmesbury, referring to this statement, said: " It is with great pleasure that we have heard the views of my noble and learned friend on this important subject, because they conform precisely to the opinion of the law officers of the Crown, whom we thought it our duty to consult before we sent answer to the communications we received from the American Government. When we received General Cass' communication . . . , we immediately consulted the law officers of the Crown, and they unanimously asserted that the international law in relation to this question was precisely as it has been just described by my noble and learned friend. Upon that opinion Her Majesty's Government at once acted, and we frankly confessed that we have no legal claim to the right of visit and of search which has hitherto been assumed." (Fur Seal Arbitration, Vol. XIII. 326–329.)

President Buchanan, in his annual message of Dec. 6, 1858, said: " I am gratified to inform you that the long-pending controversy between the two Governments in relation to the question of visitation and search has been amicably adjusted." Richardson's Messages, V. 507. See also, President Buchanan's annual message of Dec. 3, 1860. Id. 640.

For a mass of correspondence with regard to the cases of vessels suspected of being engaged in the slave trade, see special message of President Buchanan, Dec. 5, 1860, H. Ex. Doc. 7, 36 Cong. 2 sess. See, also, H. Ex. Doc. 11, 35 Cong. 2 sess.

See Lawrence's Visitation and Search, Boston, 1858; Wharton's Com. on
Am. Law, § 194; 3 Phillimore's Int. Law (3d ed.), 522; 2 Halleck's
Int. Law, 3rd ed. by Baker, 246, 247, where it is shown that Sir R.
Phillimore's assertion that "the right of visit in time of peace, *for
the purpose of ascertaining the nationality of a vessel*, is a part, indeed, but a very small part, of the belligerent right of visit and
search," is founded on a misconception of the words of Bynkershoek
and Kent, to which it appeals. See, also, Edinburgh Rev. for Oct.,
1807, Vol. XI. 14.

June 16, 1858, the United States Senate, in consequence of reports

Senate resolution, 1858.
as to orders given to British and French cruisers to
visit and search vessels as suspected slavers in the
Gulf of Mexico and adjacent waters, unanimously
adopted a resolution declaring "that American vessels on the high
seas, in time of peace, bearing the American flag, remain under the
jurisdiction of the country to which they belong, and therefore any
visitation, molestation, or detention of such vessels by force, or by
the exhibition of force, on the part of a foreign power, is in derogation of the sovereignty of the United States." Mr. Cass, when
transmitting a copy of this resolution to the American legation in
London, declared that it expressed the universal sentiment of the
American people, and added: "The immunity of their merchant
vessels upon the high seas will be steadily maintained by the United
States under all circumstances, as an attribute of their sovereignty
never to be abandoned, whatever sacrifices its protection may require."

Mr. Cass, Sec. of State, to Mr. Dallas, min. to England, June 17, 1858,
H. Ex. Doc. 7, 36 Cong. 2 sess. 97.
For the text of the resolution, and Mr. Fish's comments thereon, see For.
Rel. 1874, 963. See, also, supra, pp. 897–898.

April 7, 1862, a treaty between the United States and Great Britain

Convention with Great Britain, 1862.
was concluded at Washington, by which the contracting parties agreed that their naval vessels, which
should be provided with special instructions for the
purpose, might visit such merchant vessels of the two nations as
should upon reasonable grounds be suspected of being engaged in the
African slave trade, or of having been fitted out for that purpose, or
of having during the voyage been engaged in such trade, and detain
and send them in for trial. For purposes of trial, it was agreed that
three mixed courts of justice, formed of an equal number of individuals of the two nations, should be established respectively at Sierra
Leone, Cape of Good Hope, and New York. On each of these courts
each Government was to appoint a judge and an arbitrator. It was
stipulated that the reciprocal right of search and detention should
be exercised only within the distance of 200 miles from the coast of
Africa, and to the southward of the 32nd parallel of north latitude,

and within 30 leagues from the coast of Cuba. By an additional article of February 17, 1863, this reciprocal right was extended to waters within 30 leagues of the islands of Madagascar, Porto Rico, and Santo Domingo. By an additional convention, concluded June 3, 1870, the mixed courts were abolished, and it was provided that the jurisdiction previously exercised by them should be committed to the courts of one or the other of the high contracting parties. American vessels detained by British cruisers were to be sent to New York or Key West, whichever should be the more accessible, or were to be handed over to a United States cruiser, while British vessels detained by United States cruisers were to be sent to the most accessible British colony, or handed over to a British cruiser.

Treaty Volume (1776–1887), 454, 466, 472.

For correspondence as to the treaty of April 7, 1862, see Dip. Cor. 1862, 65, 141, 158, 164, 181, 185, 289, 473, 509, 513; Dip. Cor. 1863, I. 413, 443; Dip. Cor. 1864, I. 733; II. 60, 638, 645; Dip. Cor. 1865, II. 173, 174, 190, 193; Dip. Cor. 1866, I. 31, 109; For. Rel. 1879, 415, 431.

September 16, 1870, Mr. Fish instructed Mr. Truman Smith, at Sierra Leone, if there was no unfinished business before the court, to close it up and send an inventory of the papers and other property belonging to the United States to the Department of State. Should there be any unfinished business, he was to report upon it to the Department, and, when it should have been disposed of, to close up the court, in conformity with the provisions of the treaty of June 3, 1870, and forward an inventory. (Mr. Fish, Sec. of State, to Mr. Smith, Sept. 16, 1870, 86 MS. Dom. Let. 326.)

A substantially similar letter was sent to Mr. Cephas Brainerd, one of the arbitrators at New York, and Mr. Benjamin Pringle, at Cape Town, Africa.

A parcel of papers relating to these mixed courts is in the custody of the Department of State.

See, in relation to the treaty of April 7, 1862, Schuyler's American Diplomacy, 263, 264; Moore's American Diplomacy, 78.

Wharton, in his International Law Digest (§ 327), says: "It is a serious objection to the treaty that it extends this right of search to our own coast, the Keys of Florida being within thirty leagues from Point Yeacos or Matanzas. It appears from a letter of Mr. Perry, minister at Madrid (U. S. Dip. Cor. 1862, 509), that the Spanish minister expressed surprise that the United States 'after combating the principle so long,' 'should have yielded now a right so exceedingly liable to be abused in practice'; and this surprise may still be expressed elsewhere than in Spain."

See, however, Mr. Seward's defense, Dip. Cor. 1862, 473.

The convention of April 7, 1862, is severely criticised in a pamphlet entitled "The Diplomatic Year: Being a Review of Mr. Seward's Foreign Correspondence of 1862. By a Northern Man. Philadelphia: 1863." The author of this pamphlet was Mr. William B. Reed.

As to overtures made by the United States to the Government of Egypt, looking to the conclusion of a convention between the two countries for the suppression of the African slave trade, see Mr. F. W. Seward, Acting Sec. of State, to Mr. Farman, agent and consul-general at Cairo, Aug. 19, 1879, MS. Inst. Egypt, XVI. 140, acknowledging receipt of Mr. Farman's No. 297, of May 1, 1879.

Persons trading to the west coast of Africa, on which coast two kinds of commerce are carried on—one (the regular trade) lawful, the other (the slave trade) criminal—should keep their operations so clear and distinct in their character as to repel the imputation of a purpose to engage in the latter. (The Slavers, 2 Wall. 350.)

" Mr. Machado's claim, as will be seen from this review, has two distinct relations. The first is for the affront to the flag of the United States which his two vessels bore. No foreign sovereign had then the right in time of peace to visit and search a vessel bearing that flag, unless in the single instance of piracy shown beyond reasonable doubt. At the very time Mr. Machado's vessels were thus arrested, Great Britain had been urging on us to give her this privilege in respect to American ships supposed to be slavers; but this proposition was peremptorily repelled. This very fact made the arrest in these particular cases an outrage which this Government was bound to resent. It is true that in 1862, under peculiar circumstances, a treaty with Great Britain granting this right on the basis of reciprocity was duly ratified and proclaimed; but this treaty has, in consequence of the cessation of the slave trade, practically ceased to operate; and visitation and search, in time of peace, of American vessels by British cruisers, except on the ground of piracy, was in 1854 and 1857, and still is, regarded by us as an offense requiring apology and indemnity. It is due to the British Government to say that, when called upon for an explanation, it expressed its regrets at the occurrences in question, tendered an apology, punished the offending officer, and agreed to pay such compensation to Mr. Machado as would, under the circumstances, be suitable. That Government then offered to arbitrate, as has been seen, in case of inability to agree upon the amount of damages."

> Mr. Bayard, Sec. of State, to Messrs. Sawyer and Spooner, Apr. 19, 1886, 159 MS. Dom. Let. 658.
>
> This letter refers to the cases of the vessels *Thomas Watson* and *Mary Varney*, concerning which more or less correspondence will be found in H. Ex. Doc. 7, 36 Cong. 2 sess. The claim was settled for $20,000.

By the General Act signed at Brussels July 2, 1890, to which the United States is a party, for the repression of the African slave trade, and the restriction of the importation and sale of firearms, ammunition, and spirituous liquors within a certain part of the African continent, the signatory powers recognize the desirableness of taking steps in common for the more effective repression of the slave trade in the maritime

General Act of Brussels, 1890.

zone in which it still exists. Article XXI. declares that "this zone extends, on the one hand, between the coasts of the Indian Ocean (those of the Persian Gulf and of the Red Sea included), from Beloochistan to Cape Tangalane (Quilimane); and, on the other hand, a conventional line which first follows the meridian from Tangalane till it intersects the 26th degree of South latitude; it is then merged in this parallel, then passes round the Island of Madagascar by the east, keeping 20 miles off the east and north shore, till it intersects the meridian at Cape Ambre. From this point the limit of the zone is determined by an oblique line, which extends to the coast of Beloochistan, passing 20 miles off Cape Ras-el-Had." Such of the signatory powers as shall have contracted among themselves conventions for the suppression of the slave trade agree to restrict the clauses of those conventions concerning the reciprocal right of visit, of search, and of seizure of vessels at sea to the above-mentioned zone, and to limit the right to vessels of less than 500 tons. All the signatory powers engage to adopt measures to prevent the unlawful use of their flag, as well as the transportation of slaves on vessels authorized to fly it. Information is to be exchanged, calculated to lead to the discovery of persons taking part in operations connected with the slave trade. The signatory powers also engage to exercise a strict surveillance over native vessels authorized to carry their flag, in the zone above mentioned, and over commercial operations carried on by such vessels.

By Articles XLII.–XLIX. rules are laid down with regard to the stopping of suspected vessels. The officers in command of war vessels of any of the signatory powers are authorized to examine the papers of any vessel of less than 500 tons, when it is found navigating in the above-mentioned zone, and when they have reason to believe that it is engaged in the slave trade or is guilty of the fraudulent use of a flag. It is stated, however, that this does not imply a change in the existing state of things as regards jurisdiction in territorial waters. In order that the ship's papers may be examined, she may be stopped and a naval officer in uniform sent on board, who is to act "with all possible consideration and moderation." The examination or search of the cargo can take place only in the case of vessels sailing under the flags of powers that have concluded special conventions, and in conformity with the stipulations of such conventions. The commander of the detaining man-of-war is required fully and promptly to report his action, and if he is convinced that an act connected with the slave trade has been committed on board during the voyage, or that irrefutable proofs exist against the captain, or fitterout, for accusing him of fraudulent use of the flag, or fraud, or participation in the slave trade, he is to conduct the arrested vessels to the nearest port of the zone where there is a competent magistrate of the power whose flag has been used. A suspected vessel may also be turned over to a cruiser of its own nation if the latter consents to take charge of it.

For purposes of investigation and trial, each signatory power engages to appoint in the zone in question territorial or consular authorities, or special delegates, competent to deal with the cases covered by the convention. Such a magistrate, when an arrested vessel is turned over to him, must proceed to make a full investigation according to the laws of his own country, in the presence of an officer belonging to the foreign cruiser. If it is proved that a flag has been fraudently used, the arrested vessel is to remain at the disposal of the captor. (Art. LI.) If the examination shows an act connected with the slave trade, proved by the presence on board of slaves destined for sale, or any other offense connected with the slave trade for which provision is made by special convention, the vessel and cargo are to remain sequestrated in charge of the magistrate. The captain and crew are then to be turned over for trial to the tribunal of the nation whose flag they used (Arts. LIV.–LVII.), and the slaves are to be set at liberty as soon as judgment has been pronounced. Damages are to be allowed where a vessel has been illegally arrested. (Arts. LIII., LVIII.)

> For the acceptance by the United States of the invitation of Belgium and Great Britain to attend the conference at Brussels, see Mr. Adee, Acting Sec. of State, to Mr. Le Ghait, Belg. min., Sept. 21, 1889, MS. notes to Belg. Leg. VII. 473. In expressing the acceptance of the invitation, Mr. Adee said: " This Government will always extend its moral aid in behalf of so philanthropic a cause and would, in the judgment of the President, gladly aid by the use of naval force to prevent the exportation of slaves from Africa. The invasion of Africa with a military force in conjunction with European powers who have territorial possessions or protectoral interests on that continent presents a different question, and the President is unwilling to commit the Government to such a course of action. In the judgment of the President, the United States should refrain from territorial acquisition in the Eastern Hemisphere, and from interference with the internal affairs thereof. With this explicit understanding, the Government of the United States will be represented by a delegate in the conference."
>
> As to the question of the exchange of ratifications of the General Act, and particularly as to a protocol assenting to the provisional reservation by France of her ratification of certain articles of the act relative to the right of search of vessels suspected of being slavers, see Mr. Blaine, Sec. of State, to Mr. Le Ghait, Belgian min., Dec. 31, 1891, MS. Notes to Belg. Leg. VII. 540.
>
> The United States embodied in its ratification a resolution of the Senate, comprising a declaration of the neutral and non-participant attitude of the United States with respect to any possible questions of territorial or protective rights in the African continent, within the effect-

ive sphere of operations of the General Act. (Mr. Blaine, Sec. of State, to Mr. Le Ghait, Belgian min., Jan. 20, 1892, MS. Notes to Belg. Leg. VII. 542.)

As to legislation to carry into effect certain provisions of the General Act, see Mr. Foster, Sec. of State, to Mr. Le Ghait, Belgian min., Nov. 12, 1892, and Feb. 6, 1893, MS. Notes to Belg. Leg. VII. 570, 578. See, also, in this relation, supra, §§ 228, 229.

As to the Philafrican Liberator's League, and its wish to cooperate with the parties to the General Act of Brussels, see Mr. Sherman, Sec. of State, to Mr. Caruth, min. to Portugal, May 3, 1897, MS. Inst. Portugal, XVI. 102.

" Having been invited by Belgium to participate in a congress, held at Brussels, to revise the provisions of the general act of July 2, 1890, for the repression of the African slave trade, to which the United States was a signatory party, this Government preferred not to be represented by a plenipotentiary, but reserved the right of accession to the result. Notable changes were made, those especially concerning this country being in the line of the increased restriction of the deleterious trade in spirituous liquors with the native tribes, which this Government has from the outset urgently advocated. The amended general act will be laid before the Senate, with a view to its advice and consent." (President McKinley, annual message, Dec. 5, 1899, For. Rel. p. xiv.)

The amended General Act was concluded June 8, 1890. The Senate advised and consented to the adhesion of the United States, Dec. 14, 1900, and it was proclaimed Feb. 6, 1901. See, in this relation, supra, §§ 228, 229.

3. PIRACY.

(1) NATURE OF THE OFFENCE.

§ 311.

In considering the subject of piracy, as affecting the exercise of authority or jurisdiction on the high seas, the distinc-
Definitions. tion should always be borne in mind between piracy by law of nations, to which the present discussion relates, and mere statutory piracy. For the punishment of piracy by law of nations, express provision is indeed usually made by statute; but municipal legislation sometimes also denounces as piracy acts which do not fall within that category, in the sense of international law. An example of such legislation is furnished by the statutes of the United States, passed for the suppression of the slave trade.[a] Municipal laws of this kind are enforceable only within the ordinary limits of national jurisdiction.[b] With regard to piracy by law of nations, the case is different. The offense, in its jurisdictional aspects, is *sui generis*. Though statutes may provide for its punishment, it is an

---

[a] Supra, § 310.

[b] Le Louis, 2 Dodson, 210; The Antelope, 10 Wheat. 66; supra, §§ 200–202.

offense against the law of nations; and as the scene of the pirate's operations is the high seas, which it is not the special right or duty of any nation to police, he is denied the protection of the flag which he may carry, and is treated as an outlaw, whom any nation may in the interest of all capture and punish.

" § 124. Pirates being the common enemies of all mankind, and all nations having an equal interest in their apprehension and punishment, they may be lawfully captured on the high seas by the armed vessel of any particular state, and brought within its territorial jurisdiction, for trial in its tribunals.

" This proposition, however, must be confined to piracy as defined by the law of nations, and can not be extended to offenses which are made piracy by municipal legislation. Piracy, under the law of nations, may be tried and punished in the courts of justice of any nation, by whomsoever and wheresoever committed; but piracy created by municipal statute can only be tried by that state within whose territorial jurisdiction, and on board of whose vessels, the offense thus created was committed. There are certain acts which are considered piracy by the internal laws of a state, to which the law of nations does not attach the same signification. It is not by force of the international law that those who commit these acts are tried and punished, but in consequence of special laws which assimilate them to pirates, and which can only be applied by the state which has enacted them, and then with reference to its own subjects, and in places within its own jurisdiction. The crimes of murder and robbery, committed by foreigners on board of a foreign vessel, on the high seas, are not justiciable in the tribunals of another country than that to which the vessel belongs; but if committed on board of a vessel not at the time belonging, in fact as well as right, to any foreign power or its subjects, but in possession of a crew acting in defiance of all law, and acknowledging obedience to no flag whatsoever, these crimes may be punished as piracy under the law of nations, in the courts of any nation having custody of the offenders."

Wheaton's Elements, Dana's ed., 193 et seq. Wheaton cites, as sustaining his views, the cases of United States v. Klintock, 5 Wheat. 144, and United States v. Pirates, 5 Wheat. 184.

Mr. Dana (Dana's Wheaton, 193, note 83) adds the following to Mr. Wheaton's definition of piracy:

" It must be admitted, that the attempted definitions of piracy are unsatisfactory; some being too wide, and some too narrow. The author's description, rather than definition, is perhaps the most adequate. Some writers, and even judges, seem to have treated the phrase *hostis humani generis* as if it were a definition of piracy. Dr. Tindal (Howell's State Trials, xii, 1271–1272, note), in the case of the privateers of James II., reports this point as made and overruled;

and says, 'It is neither a definition nor as much as a description of a pirate, but a rhetorical invective.' It is true, that a pirate *jure gentium* can be seized and tried by any nation, irrespective of his national character, or of that of the vessel on board which, against which, or from which, the act was done. The reason of that must be ; that the act is one over which all nations have equal jurisdiction. This can result only from the fact, that it is committed where all have a common, and no nation an exclusive, jurisdiction—*i. e.*, upon the high seas ; and, if on board ship, and by her own crew, then the ship must be one in which no national authority reigns. The criminal may have committed but one crime, and intended but one, and that against a vessel of a particular nation ; yet, if done on the high seas, under certain circumstances hereafter to be referred to, he may be seized and tried by any nation. In such case, it can not be necessary to satisfy the court affirmatively, as a fact, that he had a purpose to plunder vessels of all nations, or vessels irrespective of nationality ; nor would the court be driven to an artificial presumption of law, contrary to the facts in the case, that such general hostile purpose existed.

" On the other hand, that is too wide a definition which would embrace all acts of plunder and violence, in degree sufficient to constitute piracy, simply because done on the high seas. As every crime may be committed at sea, piracy might thus be extended to the whole criminal code. If an act of robbery or murder were committed upon one of the passengers or crew by another in a vessel at sea, the vessel being at the time and continuing under lawful authority, and the offender were secured and confined by the master of the vessel, to be taken home for trial,—this state of things would not authorize seizure and trial by any nation that chose to interfere, or within whose limits the offender might afterwards be found."

An exposition of the statutes of the United States in relation to piracy is given in the opinion of Mr. E. Peshine Smith, law officer of the Department, January 6, 1871, communicated by Mr. Fish, Sec of State, to Mr. Mazel, January 6, 1871. (MS. Notes to the Netherlands, VII. 186.)

A pirate is one who, without legal authority from any state, attacks a ship with intention to appropriate what belongs to it. The pirate is a sea brigand. He has no right to any flag and is justiciable by all. A ship which navigates without a flag or which, on being summoned to do so, does not show its flag, exposes itself to the suspicion of piracy.

Doubtful cases sometimes present themselves, in which the question arises whether a ship is a pirate. Some of these have acquired a certain notoriety. Thus in 1873 the *Virginius*, navigating without right under the Amercan flag, was engaged in transporting arms and munitions of war for the Cuban insurgents, but was not committing any acts of brigandage. The Spaniards arrested her on the high seas and executed some of the crew—wrongfully, for she was not a pirate. Yet again, in the same year occurred the case of the *Vittoria* and her tender *Vigilante*. Those vessels, which were seized by Spanish insurgents, sailed without a flag and committed depredations. The German rear-admiral was right in seizing them. He did not, however, punish the members of the crew as pirates, but confined himself to preventing them from plundering to the prejudice of German interests. Finally, another case is that of the *Huascar* (1878), which was on just grounds considered a pirate by the English admiral.

> Rivier, Principes du Droit des Gens, I. 249.
> For Mr. Jefferson's report of Dec. 30, 1790, as to the expediency of employing forcible measures for the suppression of Algerine piracy, see Am. State Papers, For. Rel. I. 104.
> As to piratical states, see supra, § 3; Phillimore, 3rd ed. I. 488.

The first legislation of the United States on the subject of piracy was that embraced in the Crimes Act of April 30, 1790. This legislation, as read in the text, has sometimes been supposed to have conferred on the courts of the United States a jurisdiction far more extensive than that which they have actually derived from it. Section 8 of the act provides " that if any person or persons shall commit upon the high seas, or in any river, haven, basin or bay, out of the jurisdiction of any particular State, murder or robbery, or any other offense, which, if committed within the body of a county, would by the laws of the United States be punishable with death; or if any captain or mariner of any ship or other vessel, shall piratically and feloniously run away with such ship or vessel, or any goods or merchandise to the value of fifty dollars, or yield up such ship or vessel voluntarily to any pirate; or if any seaman shall lay violent hands upon his commander, thereby to hinder and prevent his fighting in defense of his ship or goods committed to his trust, or shall make a revolt in the ship; every such offender shall be deemed, taken and adjudged to be a pirate and felon, and being thereof convicted, shall suffer death; and the trial of crimes committed on the high seas, or in any place out of the jurisdiction of any particular State, shall be in the district where the offender is apprehended, or into which he may first be brought." (1 Stat. 113–114.)

Legislation and decisions.

Under this section several cases have been adjudicated by the Supreme Court. The first was that of Palmer and others, decided in 1818. This case was certified from the circuit court of the United States for the district of Massachusetts, on a division of opinion between Mr. Justice Story and Judge Davis. The defendants were charged in the indictment with having committed a robbery on the high seas on a vessel belonging to persons unknown. There was no allegation that the defendants were citizens of the United States, two of them being described merely as " late of Boston," in the State of Massachusetts, and the other " as late of Newburyport," in the same State; and the goods were alleged to have been, at the time the

defendants boarded the vessel and seized them, in the custody of
" certain persons, being mariners, subjects of the King of Spain."
One of the questions certified from the circuit court was as follows:

" Whether the crime of robbery, committed by persons who are
not citizens of the United States, on the high seas, on board of any
ship or vessel, belonging exclusively to the subjects of any foreign
state or sovereignty, or upon the person of any subject of any foreign
state or sovereignty, not on board of any ship or vessel belonging
to any citizen or citizens of the United States, be a robbery or piracy,
within the true intent and meaning of the said eighth section of the act
of Congress aforesaid, and of which the circuit court of the United
States hath cognizance, to hear, try, determine, and punish the
same ? "

In response to this question, Chief Justice Marshall, who delivered
the opinion of the Supreme Court, said:

" The question, whether this act extends further than to American
citizens, or to persons on board American vessels, or to offenses committed against citizens of the United States, is not without its difficulties. . . . The words of the section are in terms of unlimited extent.
The words ' any person or persons,' are broad enough to comprehend
every human being. But general words must not only be limited to
cases within the jurisdiction of the state, but also to those objects to
which the legislature intended to apply them. . . . The court is of
opinion that the crime of robbery, committed by a person on the high
seas, on board of any ship or vessel belonging exclusively to subjects
of a foreign state, on persons within a vessel belonging exclusively
to subjects of a foreign state, is not a piracy within the true intent
and meaning of the act for the punishment of certain crimes against
the United States."

> United States *v.* Palmer (1818), 3 Wheat. 610.
> Although the offence charged in this case was robbery on the high
> seas, the Chief Justice, to sustain the limitation placed in the opinion
> on the words " any person or persons," as employed in the 8th sec-
> tion of the act of 1790, discussed the other provisions of the section
> as follows :
> " But these words [any person or persons] must be limited in some
> degree, and the intent of the legislature will determine the extent of
> this limitation. For this intent we must examine the law. The suc-
> ceeding member of the sentence commences with the words, ' if any
> captain or mariner of any ship or other vessel, shall piratically run
> away with such ship or vessel, or any goods or merchandise, to the
> value of fifty dollars, or yield up such ship or vessel voluntarily to
> any pirate.'
> " The words ' any captain, or mariner of any ship or other vessel,' compre-
> hend all captains and mariners, as entirely as the words ' any person
> or persons,' comprehend the whole human race. Yet it would be
> difficult to believe that the legislature intended to punish the captain

or mariner of a foreign ship, who should run away with such ship, and dispose of her in a foreign port, or who should steal any goods from such ship to the value of fifty dollars, or who should deliver her up to a pirate when he might have defended her, or even according to previous arrangement. The third member of the sentence also begins with the general words 'any seaman.' But it can not be supposed that the legislature intended to punish a seaman on board a ship sailing under a foreign flag, under the jurisdiction of a foreign government, who should lay violent hands upon his commander, or make a revolt in the ship. These are offenses against the nation, under whose flag the vessel sails, and within whose particular jurisdiction all on board the vessel are. Every nation provides for such offenses the punishment its own policy may dictate; and no general words of a statute ought to be construed to embrace them when committed by foreigners against a foreign government.

"That the general words of the two latter members of this sentence are to be restricted to offenses committed on board the vessels of the United States, furnishes strong reason for believing that the legislature intended to impose the same restriction on the general words used in the first member of that sentence."

The question of robbery on the high seas, under sec. 8 of the act of 1790, was again before the Supreme Court, in Klintock's case, in 1820. It was contended, in behalf of the defendant, that the section did not, under the ruling in Palmer's case, apply to an American citizen entering on board a foreign vessel exclusively owned by foreigners and committing piracy thereon. With reference to this contention, Chief Justice Marshall, reviewing the decision in Palmer's case, said:

"Upon the most deliberate reconsideration of that subject, the Court is satisfied, that general piracy, or murder, or robbery, committed in the places described in the 8th section, by persons on board of a vessel not at the time belonging to the subjects of any foreign power, but in possession of a crew acting in defiance of all law, and acknowledging obedience to no government whatever, is within the true meaning of this act, and is punishable in the Courts of the United States. Persons of this description are proper objects for the penal code of all nations; and we think that the general words of the act of Congress applying to all persons whatsoever, though they ought not to be so construed as to extend to persons under the acknowledged authority of a foreign state, ought to be so construed as to comprehend those who acknowledge the authority of no state. Those general terms ought not to be applied to offences committed against the particular sovereignty of a foreign power; but we think they ought to be applied to offenses committed against all nations, including the United States, by persons who by common consent are equally amenable to the laws of all nations."

United States v. Klintock (1820), 5 Wheat. 144, 152.

The result of these two cases—Palmer's and Klintock's—is that while general piracy was punishable under the 8th section of the act of 1790, and while in such case proof as to the nationality of the offender, or as to the origin of the vessel on which he sailed, was immaterial, a pirate being amenable to the jurisdiction of all nations alike, yet, where the offense charged under the section was not piratical in the general sense, but only by force of the statute, such averments must be made and such evidence produced as to the national character of the vessel on which the offense was committed, as would ordinarily give the courts of the United States jurisdiction. Such was the view announced by the Supreme Court in subsequent decisions. In United States v. Pirates, 5 Wheaton, 184, the court, while fully recognizing the decision in Palmer's case, said that "when embarked on a piratical cruise, every individual becomes equally punishable under the law of 1790, whatever may be his national character, or whatever may have been that of the vessel in which he sailed, or of the vessel attacked."

In the case of United States v. Holmes, 5 Wheaton, 412, decided, as was also that of the Pirates, in 1820, the Supreme Court, speaking through Mr. Justice Washington, laid down, as the result of the preceding cases, the following rules:

"If it [the offense] be committed on board of a foreign vessel by a citizen of the United States, or on board of a vessel of the United States by a foreigner, the offender is to be considered, *pro hac vice*, and in respect to this subject, as belonging to the nation under whose flag he sails. If it be committed either by a citizen or a foreigner, on board of a piratical vessel, the offense is equally cognizable by the courts of the United States, under the above-mentioned law."

It is to be observed that Mr. Justice Washington was a member of the Supreme Court at and prior to the time of the decision of Palmer's case, in February, 1818, as well as during the period intervening between that decision and the case of Holmes, his opinion in which has just been quoted; and in that intervening period, in April, 1818, just after the decision in Palmer's case, he had occasion to consider that decision, and the true construction of the 8th section of the act of 1790, in the circuit court of the United States for the State of Pennsylvania, in the case of United States v. Howard, 3 Wash. C. C., 340. Referring to Palmer's case, he said:

"It was, upon the whole, decided, that a robbery, committed by any person on the high seas, on board of a ship belonging exclusively to a foreign state, or to the subjects thereof, or upon the person of a subject of a foreign state, in a vessel belonging exclusively to subjects of a foreign state, is not piracy, within the true intent and meaning of the 8th section of that law. Although the offense of robbery is the only one stated in this decision; that being the only offense referred to in the question which was adjourned to the Supreme Court; yet there can be no doubt but that all the other acts of piracy, enumerated in that section, are included within the same principle."

It appears by this opinion, as well as by the opinion of Chief Justice Marshall in Klintock's case, as above quoted, that the Supreme Court when the judgment in Palmer's case was rendered, understood it to decide not only that the general words employed in the act of 1790 in reference to statutory piracy must be restricted so as to apply only to offenses committed on board of American vessels on the high seas, but also that the 8th section of the act did not include piracy by the law of nations, and therefore did not give the courts of the United States jurisdiction to punish it. We have seen that in Klintock's case, as well as in the other cases cited above from the decisions of the Supreme Court, it was subsequently held that that section did confer such jurisdiction; for, as it provided for the punishment of any person or persons for murder or robbery on the high seas, and as "the pirate is a man who satisfies his personal greed or his personal vengeance by robbery or murder in places beyond the jurisdiction of a state," [a] it was well held in the case of Klintock and of the Pirates, that piracy by the law of nations was punishable under the terms of the section. It is, however, worthy of notice that in March, 1819, after Palmer's case was decided, Congress passed a temporary act, which was subsequently renewed and made permanent, and is now substantially embodied in section 5368 Revised Statutes of the United States, expressly conferring on the courts of the United States jurisdiction of "piracy, as defined by the law of nations."

No attempt was made to remove or correct the limitation placed by the Supreme Court on the general words of the act of 1790, so far as they related to statutory piracy. And although, as has been seen, the court itself, in 1820, in the cases of Klintock, the Pirates, and Holmes, held that the 8th section of the act of 1790, under which the indictments in those cases were framed, covered piracy by the law of nations, and was not repealed by the act of 1819, yet it never was intimated that the previous decision respecting municipal piracy, under the act of 1790, was wrong. Indeed, in the case of Holmes, the latest of the cases cited, we observe in the opinion of the court a decided affirmation of the view expressed by the Chief Justice in Palmer's case, that the question of jurisdiction of acts of municipal piracy would be determined by the flag of the vessel on which the offense was committed. "If it [the offense] be committed," said the court in Holmes's case, "on board of a foreign vessel by a citizen of the United States, or on board of a vessel of the United States by a foreigner, the offender is to be considered *pro hac vice*, and in respect to this subject, as belonging to the nation under whose flag he sails." This principle was recognized by Congress in the act of the 3d of March, 1825, entitled, "An act more effectually to provide for the punishment of certain crimes against the United States, and for other purposes," by which many of the provisions of different sections of the act of 1790 were replaced, as well as in the act of March 3, 1835, which, in substituting provisions for the punishment of revolt on shipboard, in place of those contained in the 8th section of the act of 1790, expressly restricted the jurisdiction of the courts to acts committed by "one or more of the crew of any American ship or vessel."

Questions were raised whether the words " out of the jurisdiction of any particular State," in section 8 of the act of April 30, 1790, relat-

---

[a] Hall's Int. Law, 4th ed. 268 et seq. While piracy has been defined as robbery on the high seas, the more recent jurists hold that the depredation need not be *lucri causa.* Whart. Cr. L., § 1860; Heffter, Völkerrecht, § 104; Broglie, Sur la piraterie, III. 335; Wheaton's Int. Law, § 123, Dana's ed., p. 195.

ing to the punishment of piracy, included foreign as well as domestic
states, and whether a vessel at anchor in a road was not a vessel on the
high seas, as charged in the indictment. As to the first question, the
court held that the words quoted must be construed to mean " out of
any one of the United States," although it was remarked that the
reason was " not easy to imagine." On the second point, it was held
that a vessel in an open road might be found by a jury to be on the
high seas, even though it was within the jurisdictional limits of a
foreign state, since " those limits, though neutral to war, are not
neutral to crimes."

> United States v. Pirates (1820), 5 Wheat. 184, 200.

John Palmer, Thomas Wilson, and Barney Calloghan were indicted
in the circuit court of the United States at Boston, under section 8 of
the act of April 30, 1790, for piratically and feloniously taking certain
property from a Spanish vessel on the high seas. The facts in the
case are very imperfectly stated. It was brought before the Supreme
Court on a certificate of division of opinion between Mr. Justice
Story and Judge Davis. Some of the questions certified by the circuit
court related to the rights of a colony which had proclaimed its independence and was asserting it by force of arms. These questions the
Supreme Court did not decide, since it held that the crime of robbery,
committed by a person on the high seas, on a foreign vessel, and on the
persons therein, was not a piracy within the true intent and meaning
of the section under consideration.

> United States v. Palmer (1818), 3 Wheat. 610.

Ralph Klintock, a citizen of the United States, was indicted in the
United States circuit court at Richmond for piracy committed on a
Danish vessel called the *Norberg*. Klintock sailed as first lieutenant
on a vessel called the *Young Spartan*, which was owned outside the
United States and which cruised under a commission from Aury,
styling himself Brigadier of the Mexican Republic and Generalissimo
of the Floridas. The officers of the *Young Spartan* secreted Spanish
papers on board the *Norberg*, and then claimed her as a Spanish
vessel. They left her company on an island off the coast of Cuba,
and took the vessel herself to Savannah, Ga., where, personating the
Danish captain and crew, they entered her as a Danish vessel. The
Supreme Court, Chief Justice Marshall delivering the opinion,
stated that, so far as it could take any cognizance of the fact, Aury
could have no power either as Brigadier of the Mexican Republic,
of whose existence the court knew nothing, or as Generalissimo of the
Floridas, a province in the possession of Spain, to issue commissions
to authorize private or public vessels to make captures at sea, but
that, whether a person acting with good faith under such a commis-

sion might or might not be guilty of piracy, the judges were all of opinion that the commission could not justify what was done in the pending case. The whole transaction taken together demonstrated, said the court, that the *Norberg* "was not captured *jure belli*, but seized and carried into Savannah *animo furandi*. It was not a belligerent capture, but a robbery on the high seas. And although the fraud practiced on the Dane may not of itself constitute piracy, yet it is an ingredient in the transaction which has no tendency to mitigate the character of the offence."

> United States *v.* Klintock (1820), 5 Wheat. 144.
>
> Klintock was ultimately pardoned. (Mr. Adams, Sec. of State, to Mr. Morel, U. S. marshal at Savannah, April 5, April 10, June 9, 1820, 18 MS. Dom. Let. 20, 23, 72; to Mr. Meigs, M. C., April 29, 1820, id. 41; to Mrs. Klintock, June 29, 1820, 19 MS. Dom. Let. 63.)
>
> As to the circumstances under which the *Norberg* entered Savannah, and the disappearance of certain papers in the case, see Mr. Adams, Sec. of State, to Mr. Habersham, U. S. dist. attorney at Savannah, Oct. 31, 1820, 18 MS. Dom. Let. 166.

"I have received your letter of the 10th instant, and should take great satisfaction in furnishing you with any evidence in this Department, and any facility within its competency, for obtaining evidence from elsewhere which might tend to show the innocence or to extenuate the guilt of the prisoners with the defence of whose cause you have been charged.

"You are aware, I presume, that in December 1817 General Aury surrendered, to officers of the United States, Amelia Island, in the professed character of Commander in Chief of the Republic of the Floridas, and that on the 12th of December of that year he addressed a letter to the honorable assembly of representatives of that imaginary republic, stating to them that his authority for exercising belligerent powers was derived only from a minister plenipotentiary of a Congress of Mexico, not then existing. See Niles's Register, vol. 13, p. 350.

"In the 12th volume of Wait's State Papers, page 424, you will find all the authorities and commissions, under which the agent of General Aury at this place on the 7th of February 1818 alleged that he was authorized to act.

"In Niles's Register, vol. 15, p. 90, there is a proclamation by Louis Aury, 'commander-in-chief of the forces that have opened their campaign upon New Granada, *in the name* of the confederated Republics of Buenos Ayres and Chile.' It is dated at his headquarters in the Island of Providence and St. Catalina, the 10th day of July, 1818, 9th, which 9th, as I take it, means the 9th year of the independence of Venezuela dating from its first declaration.

"This was but a few days more than six months after he had surrendered Amelia Island to Col. Bankhead. But he had no commission or authority either from Buenos Ayres or Chile.

" I believe that he never had authority from any government to issue commissions; but that, from the revolutionary government of New Granada, while it lasted, he had a commission authorizing him to exercise belligerent rights. That he had no authority from the Governments of Buenos Ayres or of Chile, when at Amelia Island, was explicitly declared by the principal authorities of those republics to the commissioners of the United States nearly about the same time while he was issuing the above mentioned proclamation *in the name* of the confederated republics at Old Providence.

" Whether he has ever been commissioned by the Republic of Colombia I do not know, but I have no doubt that his commission to the *Snake, in the name* of the United Republics of Buenos Ayres and Chile, was unauthorized by them.

" I have thought it due as well in candor to you, as with reference to the United States in whose behalf your clients have been prosecuted, and to those unfortunate men themselves, to answer your enquiries explicitly, and to inform you of what is known to this Government concerning Aury and his proceedings. If Aury has ever had at any time authority from any of the South American governments, which could even color a commission issued by him to exercise belligerent rights, it can have been from no other than the Republic of Colombia. A minister from the United States to that republic will probably soon be dispatched; and any testimony which you may desire to obtain, which can serve the cause of the prisoners, may be without difficulty procured through him. Instructions to that effect will be given him, should you have the goodness to inform me that you wish it. In that case, I shall request you to transmit to me the inquiries to which you would propose that he should direct his attention."

> Mr. Adams, Sec. of State, to Messrs. Aylwin & Spooner, of Boston,
> March 19, 1823, 20 MS. Dom. Let. 139.

Thomas Smith was found guilty by special verdict in the United States circuit court for Virginia of the crime of piracy, on the following facts: In March, 1819, Smith and others, forming part of the crew of a privateer called the *Creollo*, commissioned by the government of Buenos Ayres, mutinied in the port of Margaritta, and leaving the vessel seized another privateer called the *Irresistible*, lying in that port, commissioned by the government of Artigas. They then proceeded to sea in the *Irresistible* without any documents or commission whatever, and in April, 1819, on the high seas, plundered and robbed a Spanish vessel. The circuit court certified the case to the

Supreme Court on a division of opinion as to whether the acts of which the defendants were found guilty were punishable as piracy under the act of Congress of March 3, 1819. The Supreme Court, Mr. Justice Story delivering the opinion, defined the offense of piracy as " robbery, or forcible depredations upon the sea, *animo furandi*," and held that as the defendant and his associates were at the time of committing the offense " freebooters upon the sea, not under the acknowledged authority, or deriving protection from the flag or commission of any government," they were undoubtedly guilty of piracy.

> United States *v.* Smith (1820), 5 Wheat. 153. See a note to this case by Mr. Justice Story, in which various definitions of piracy are collected from writers on the civil law, the law of nations, maritime law, and the common law.
>
> Thomas Smith, James Thomas (alias James West), Stephen Sidney, John Green, Isaac Sales (a man of color), Peter Johnson (a man of color), and Daniel Livingston were pardoned. (Mr. Adams, Sec. of State, to Mr. Pegram, U. S. marshal at Dinwiddie Court House, Va., Jan. 23, 1822, 19 MS. Dom. Let. 247.)

John Furlong, *alias* Hobson, a British subject, was indicted in the United States circuit court at Savannah for piracy. It appeared that the piratical vessel was American and was run away with by the master and crew, who committed depredations on an English vessel.

Benjamin Brailsford and James Griffin were indicted in the United States circuit court at Charleston for piracy. The question was raised whether an American citizen, fitting out a vessel in an American port to cruise against a power at peace with the United States, was protected by a commission from a belligerent from punishment for any offence committed against American vessels.

David Bowers and Henry Mathews were indicted in the United States circuit court at Savannah for a piratical robbery committed on an American ship. They were part of the crew of the privateer *Louise*, which was commissioned by Buenos Ayres and commanded by Captain Almeida. There was no proof that the *Louise* was American-owned. In October, 1818, her crew rose and, putting the officers out of the ship, proceeded on a piratical cruise in which they committed a robbery on the American vessel *Asia*, then at anchor in an open roadstead at the island of Bonavista. At that time the name *New York* had been painted on the stern of the *Louise*, and the person who was commanding her asserted himself and the vessel to be American.

The same persons, David Bowers and Henry Mathews, were also indicted for piracy, consisting in a robbery committed on board the British ship *Sir Thomas Hardy* on the high seas.

In the foregoing cases it was held that, so far as any question was involved of the national character of the prisoners or of the vessels, the moment the latter were taken from their officers " and proceeded on a piratical cruise, the crew lost all claim to national character, and whether citizens or foreigners," became equally punishable.

> United States *v.* Pirates (1820), 5 Wheat. 184.
>
> It appears that Bowers and Mathews were pardoned. (Mr. Adams, Sec. of State, to Mr. Habersham, U. S. dist. atty. at Savannah, April 4, 1820, and to Mr. Morel, U. S. marshal, April 5 and 10, and June 9, 1820, 18 MS. Dom. Let. 19, 20, 23, 72.)
>
> Benjamin Brailsford and James Griffin (alias John Jones) were reprieved, but, as to their associates, George Clarke and Henry Roberts, alias De Wolf, it was said that the President would allow them to be executed. (Mr. Adams, Sec. of State, to Mr. Waring, U. S. marshal at Charleston, April 3, 1820, 18 MS. Dom. Let. 16.) It was afterwards decided to pardon Brailsford and Griffin on the charge of piracy, on their being sentenced on certain indictments for misprision of felony, to which they had pleaded guilty. (Mr. Adams, Sec. of State, to Judge Drayton, April 15, 1820, 18 MS. Dom. Let. 25.)
>
> A pamphlet entitled " Particulars of the Piracies committed," etc., by the *Louise* and *Mary*, was published, apparently in the form of an appeal to Congress. (Mr. Adams, Sec. of State, to Mr. Parker, U. S. dist. attorney at Charleston, June 24, 1820, 18 MS. Dom. Let. 85. See. also, Mr. Bailey to Mr. Wheaton, June 24, 1820, ibid.)
>
> The following persons, convicted of piracy, were reprieved: John Jackson (alias Daniel Redding), Isaac Alister, William Murphey, Thomas O'Brien (Mr. Adams, Sec. of State, to Mr. Bentalou, U. S. marshal at Baltimore, April 1 and June 9, 1820, 18 MS. Dom. Let. 17, 73) ; Peter Morel, Charles Dickenson, Louis Pierre, Gervin Canchal, John McGee, Louis Philip, John Cousins, Ephraim Tompkins, Isaac Tillot, Thomas Tomson, Lawrence Pagas, Joseph Vallert, Juan Raynor, Julien Seddoner, William McClure. (Mr. Adams, Sec. of State, to Mr. Nicholson, U. S. marshal at New Orleans, April 3, 1820, and June 10, 1820, 18 MS. Dom. Let. 18, 73.)
>
> Pardons were issued in the following cases: John Trickhart (Mr.. Adams, Sec. of State, to Mr. Nicholas, U. S. marshal at New Orleans, June 10, 1820, 18 MS. Dom. Let. 74) ; Samuel Pool and Francis Ogilsbie (Mr. Adams, Sec. of State, to Mr. Stanard, U. S. dist. atty. at Richmond, and to Mr. Moore, U. S. marshal, June 10, 1820, 18 MS. Dom. Let. 74) ; Jacques Lacroix, Michael Lebrequet, James Louis Roney, Juan Raynor (Mr. Adams, Sec. of State, to Mr. Nicholson, Oct. 26, 1820, 18 MS. Dom. Let. 165) ; Luke Jackson, a man of color (Mr. Adams, Sec. of State, to Mr. Moore, U. S. marshal at Richmond, Oct. 26, 1820, 18 MS. Dom. Let. 164) ; Charles Waver. (Mr. Adams, Sec. of State, to Mr. Bentalou, U. S. marshal at Baltimore, Oct. 26, 1820, 18 MS. Dom. Let. 165.)
>
> Death warrants were issued in the following cases: John Desfarge and Robert Johnson (Mr. Adams, Sec. of State, to Mr. Nicholson, U. S. marshal at New Orleans, April 17 and June 10, 1820, 18 MS. Dom. Let. 27, 73) ; John F. Ferguson and Israel Denny. (Mr. Adams, Sec. of State, to Mr. Bentalou, April 1, 1820, 18 MS. Dom. Let. 17.)

William Holmes, Thomas Warrington, *alias* Warren Fawcett, and Edward Rosemaine were indicted in the United States circuit court at Boston for piracy. The facts appear to be that a vessel, apparently Spanish, was captured by two pretended Buenos Ayrean privateers. A prize crew was put on board the captured vessel, and among the crew were the prisoners, one of whom was a citizen of the United States, the rest being foreigners. They subsequently threw overboard the prize master and drowned him. It did not appear by any legal proof that the privateers had commissions from Buenos Ayres or any documents from that government, or were ever recognized as ships of that nation or of its subjects. The prisoners were convicted, and on motion for a new trial, the judges differing, certain questions were certified to the Supreme Court, one of which was whether the court had jurisdiction of the offence charged, if the vessel on which it was committed had at the time no real national character, but was possessed and held by pirates, or by persons not lawfully sailing under the flag or entitled to the protection of any government, and whether the burden of proof as to national character rested on the United States or on the prisoners. It was held that if the offence was committed on board of a piratical vessel it was cognizable by the United States, and that the burden of proof as to national character rested on the prisoners.

> United States *v.* Holmes et al. (1820), 5 Wheat. 412.
> In this case the President, after consulting the Attorney-General, declined to exercise clemency. (Mr. Adams, Sec. of State, to Mr. Prince, U. S. marshal at Boston, May 25, 1820, 18 MS. Dom. Let. 56.)

Under the 4th section of the act of March 3, 1819, any piratical aggression subjects the vessel to forfeiture, though not made *lucri causa*, and though the owners were entirely innocent and the vessel was armed for a lawful purpose and sailed on a lawful voyage.[a] But not every hostile attack in time of peace is piratical. It may be by mistake, or in necessary self-defence, or to repel a supposed meditated attack by pirates. If it is justifiable no blame attaches.[b] The aggression must be a *first* aggression, unprovoked by any previous act of hostility or menace from the other side.[c] Probable cause is a sufficient excuse for a capture for piratical aggression.[d]

The chargé d'affaires of Portugal having requested the immediate discharge of a Portuguese vessel which had been captured by Captain Stockton, U. S. S. *Allegator*, and sent in to Boston, on the ground that the capture was made in consequence of an attack by the Portuguese vessel under an erroneous impression that the *Allegator* was a South American privateer, the district attorney of the United

---

[a] United States *v.* Brig Malek Adhel, 2 How. 210.
[b] The Marianna Flora, 11 Wheat. 1.
[c] Black, At. Gen., 1860, 9 Op. 455.
[d] The Marianna Flora, 11 Wheat. 1; The Palmyra, 12 Wheat. 1.

States at Boston was instructed that it was the desire of the President, if the circumstances were found to be as stated, that the vessel should be restored to her captain, upon terms as easy and indulgent as might be compatible with the law.

> Mr. Adams, Sec. of State, to Mr. Blake, Jan. 4, 1822, 19 MS. Dom. Let. 231.

A merchant vessel whose subordinate crew rise in revolt, and, after killing the captain, make depredations on other shipping, is a pirate by the law of nations.

> Mr. Marcy, Sec. of State, to Mr. Starkweather, Sept. 18, 1854, MS. Inst. Chile, XV. 107.
>
> As to proceedings by United States consuls in foreign ports in cases of piracy, mutiny, or any other offense against the United States, see Mr. Buchanan, Sec. of State, to Committee on Claims, Mar. 4, 1846, 6 MS. Report Book, 172.

Where a portion of the crew of the steamer *Edgar Stewart* forcibly displaced the master from command and took possession of the vessel, it was advised that this did not constitute the offense of piracy, but of mutiny; that, for the latter offense, the parties charged are liable to be tried and punished under the laws of the United States, and that they may be tried therefor in any district into which they are first brought.

> Hill, Assistant At. Gen. (1872), 14 Op. 589.

It is not statutory piracy for the captain of a vessel, to whom the vessel and cargo have been consigned with instructions to proceed to the Pacific and there sell vessel and cargo and remit the proceeds to the owners, to fail to remit such proceeds after having made sale according to instructions; and his arrest on such a charge would be false imprisonment.

> Wirt, At. Gen. (1825), 2 Op. 19.

A mere intention or even preparation to commit piracy is not piracy.

> Mr. Clayton, Sec. of State, to Mr. Calderon de la Barca, July 9, 1850, MS. Notes to Spain, VI. 209.

A French vessel with kidnapped Africans on board was captured by pirates, and from them recaptured by an American **Kidnapped persons.** vessel and brought into port. A demand made by the French minister for the restoration of the Africans was held to be well founded.

> Wirt, At. Gen. (1822), 1 Op. 534.

Under the 9th article of the treaty of 1795, between the United States and Spain, providing for the restoration of property rescued from pirates and robbers on the high seas, it is necessary to show: (1) That what is claimed falls within the description of vessel or merchandise; (2) that it has been rescued on the high seas from pirates and robbers; (3) that the asserted proprietors are the true proprietors.

Under this article negroes lawfully held as slaves and subject to sale under the laws of Spain, on board a Spanish vessel, may be deemed merchandise; but native Africans, unlawfully kidnapped and imported into a Spanish colony contrary to the laws of Spain, as in this case, are not merchandise; nor can any person show that he is entitled to them as their proprietor, nor are they pirates and robbers, if they rise and kill the master and take possession of the vessel to regain their liberty.

United States *v.* The Amistad, 15 Pet. 518.

" I have to acknowledge the receipt of your despatches Nos. 129 and 132, dated respectively December 5th and 18th, both of which relate to the bark *Cayalte*, at Ḥakodadi. These documents tend to prove that the officers and crew of the vessel were Peruvians, and that, though the flag of the United States had been assumed with a view to protect the bark from belligerent capture during the war between Peru and Spain, the real owners were the captain, who is stated to have been a Portuguese, and Don Julian Zara Condigui (called by one of the witnesses Calandine), as to whom there is no proof or suggestion that they were citizens of the United States. The presumption is that the use of our flag was a fraud and abuse to which this Government can give no effect.

" In respect to the suggestion of Admiral Rowan, that ' there is reason to believe that these coolies are guilty of piracy under the law of nations,' I have to say that the evidence goes to show that their object in capturing the vessel was not robbery and plunder, nor did they manifest or appear to have contemplated that general hostility which enters into the definition of the crime. The motive, according to all the evidence, was to effect their return to their native land. We may adopt, I think, the language of the Supreme Court of the United States, when delivering its opinion upon a somewhat similar case: ' We may lament the dreadful acts by which they asserted their liberty and took possession of the *Amistad* and endeavored to regain their native country; but they can not be deemed pirates or robbers in the sense of the law of nations.' (15 Peters R. 594.) "

Mr. Seward, Sec. of State, to Mr. Van Valkenburg, min. to Japan, Feb. 19, 1869, MS. Inst. Japan, I. 316.
See Attorney-General *v.* Kwok-a-Sing (1873), L. R. 5 P. C. 179.

In October, 1873, the steamer *Virginius* cleared from Kingston, in
Hostile enter- Jamaica, for Port Limon, Costa Rica. After putting
prises—Case of to sea, she headed for the southeastern coast of Cuba.
the "Virginius." October 31, 1873, when about six miles from that coast,
she was sighted and chased by the Spanish man-of-war *Tornado.*
She turned and steamed back toward Jamaica, but, after an eight
hours' chase, was captured by the *Tornado* while still on the high seas.
The *Virginius* had on board a quantity of arms and ammunition and
a company of 155 persons, 53 of whom composed the crew, while the
rest were denominated passengers. Among those on board were four
officers in the Cuban insurgent army. The *Virginius* when captured
carried the American flag and had an American register, though it
was afterwards determined that she was not entitled to either. She
was taken by the *Tornado* to Santiago de Cuba, where, after summary
trial by a court-martial, 53 of the prisoners were shot. Further
executions were prevented by the appearance of foreign men-of-war.
Nineteen of the persons executed were British subjects. On account
of these the British Government demanded and obtained an indemnity. The United States also obtained a sum in settlement of the
claims which it had presented " in regard to the persons of the officers,
crew, and passengers," excluding the British subjects who had been
indemnified. The passengers included only six American citizens.

The ground on which the imprisonment and execution of the
persons on board was justified was that of piracy. The *Virginius*
was described in various Spanish documents as having a " piratical
character " and as being engaged in " piratical acts." The United
States, on the other hand, maintained that, while it was competent
for a state to apply the term " piracy," by its municipal laws, to
various offences other than those deemed piracy by law of nations, it
could not, by applying the epithet to such offences, subject them to
the penalties to which piracy by law of nations was liable. As to
what constituted piracy by law of nations, the United States said that
the definition given by Wheaton, as explained by his commentator,
Dana, would probably be recognized by the courts of all civilized
powers. In this relation the United States said : " Wheaton defines
this crime ' to be the offence of depredating on the seas without being
authorized by any sovereign state, or with commissions from different sovereigns at war with each other ; ' and Dana, in his note upon
this definition, says ' to constitute piracy *jure gentium*, it is necessary,
first, that the offence be adequate in degree—for instance, robbery,
destruction by fire, or other injury to persons or property—must be
committed on the high seas and not within the territorial jurisdiction
of any nation ; and, second, that the offenders, at the time of the commission of the act, should be in fact free from lawful authority, or

should have made themselves so by their deed, or, as Sir L Jenkins says, " out of the protection of all laws and privileges," or, in the words of the Duc de Broglie, " qui n 'a ni feu ni lieu; " in short, they must be in the predicament of outlaws.' "

> Mr. Fish, Sec. of State, to Admiral Polo, Spanish min., April 18, 1874, For. Rel. 1875, II. 1178, 1182. See supra, p. 895; infra, p. 980.
>
> See, also, Admiral Polo, Spanish min., to Mr. Fish, Sec. of State, Dec. 30, 1873; For. Rel. 1875, II. 1154.
>
> March 24, 1869, Captain-General Dulce issued a decree declaring that vessels captured in Spanish waters, or on the high seas near the island of Cuba, having on board men, arms and munitions of war, etc., should be considered as enemies and be treated as " pirates " in accordance with the ordinances of the navy, and that all persons captured in such vessels would, without regard to numbers, immediately be executed. The United States at the time protested against this decree as constituting a violation of public law and treaties and asked that it be recalled, or that such instructions be given as would prevent " its illegal application to citizens of the United States or their property." (Moore, Int. Arbitrations, II. 1022, citing Mr. Fish, Sec. of State, to Mr. Lopez Roberts, Spanish min., April 3, 1869, S. Ex. Doc. 7, 41 Cong. 2 sess. 12. See, also, For. Rel. 1875, II. 1181.)

By an agreement concluded at Madrid, February 27, 1875, the Spanish Government engaged to pay to the United States the sum of $80,000 in coin as an equitable and friendly settlement of " the reclamations presented by the Government of the United States, in consequence of what occurred at Santiago de Cuba, in regard to the persons of the officers, crew, and passengers of the steamer *Virginius*, it being understood that from these reclamations are to be excluded, in so far as respects the ship's company, all individuals indemnified as British subjects, and, with respect to passengers, including only six American citizens." The United States engaged to accept the money in satisfaction of all claims for personal indemnity which had been advanced against the Spanish Government and to distribute it among the families or parties interested, in the form and manner which it might judge most equitable, without being obliged to give any account of the distribution to the Spanish Government.

> For. Rel. 1875, II. 1250.
>
> The payment netted the sum of $77,797.44.

" It is not competent for Spain, by declaring that to be piracy which is not piracy under the definitions of international law, to extend the penalties of that crime, or the jurisdiction of its courts as to piracy, to the subjects of other nations, or to incorporate in any way its own municipal definition of the crime of piracy into the law of nations to any degree beyond the definition established by international law."

> Mr. Davis, Com. on For. Rel., July 14, 1897, Competitor case, S. Rep. 377, 55 Cong. 1 sess. 5,

(2) JUDICIAL PROSECUTION.

§ 312.

If the prize be a pirate, the officers and crew are to be prosecuted in the circuit court of the United States, without respect to the nation to which each individual may belong. If it be regularly commissioned as a ship of war, the officers and crew are to be detained as prisoners, except such as are citizens of the United States, who are to be tried for treason.[a] Prosecutions for piracy committed outside the jurisdiction of any particular State should take place in the district where the offender is apprehended, or into which he may be first brought.[b] The same rule applies to prosecutions under the act of March 3, 1819, for the punishment of piratical aggressions.[c]

The ship called *Sans Coulette*, otherwise called the *Unicorn*, equipped in the United States, manned chiefly by citizens thereof, and commanded by Capt. Peter Marshall, was proceeded against by the French authorities in the court of admiralty at Port de Paix, in San Domingo, as a pirate. Marshall and his crew were sentenced to imprisonment for their irregular and piratical conduct, and the ship was confiscated. " The goods and effects plundered by Marshall and his crew from the *America* and *Pallas*, American vessels, were ordered to be sold for the use of the Republic, saving and reserving the rights of the owners in case they should make any lawful claims." The American owners of the goods were advised that the proper way to recover their property would be to give a power of attorney to some person to demand and receive it of the administration at Port de Paix. The proceedings against the vessel and Captain Marshall were printed in a pamphlet.

Mr. Pickering, Sec. of State, to Capt. Shallcross, Nov. 9, 1795, 9 MS. Dom. Let. 13; Mr. Pickering, Sec. of State, to Mr. Caines, Nov. 16, 1795, 9 MS. Dom. Let. 15.

William Talbot and Edward Ballard, when tried for piracy at Charleston, S. C., were on trial by jury acquitted. (Mr. Randolph, Sec. of State, to Mr. Van Berckel, Dutch min., Jan. 5, 1795, 8 MS. Dom. Let. 35.)

On information from the French minister that 38 seamen, citizens of the United States, had been sent by the governor of Martinique to be delivered to the civil authorities of the United States on a charge of piracy, and that the vessel to which they were committed had arrived at Philadelphia, the district attorney of the United States in

---

[a] Lee, At. Gen., 1798, 1 Op. 85.

[b] Rush, At. Gen., 1815, 1 Op. 185.

[c] Taney, At. Gen., 1833, 2 Op. 559.

that city was instructed to take such measures as might be warranted
by law for having the men arrested and brought to trial.

> Mr. Adams, Sec. of State, to Mr. Ingersoll, May 7, 1821, 19 MS. Dom.
> Let. 7.
> As to the case of the French ship *Calypso*, captured Nov. 1, 1824, while on
> her way from St. Domingo, by pirates, from whom she was recap-
> tured on the Cuban coast by the English sloop *Lion* and the American
> corvette *Terrier*, see H. Ex. Doc. 147, 22 Cong. 2 sess. 191, 195, 201, 205.

(3) SALVAGE.

§ 313.

By the general maritime law, the recaptors of American vessels
from pirates are entitled to salvage, the rate resting in the discretion
of the court; and by the same law, as well as by the act of March 3,
1800, national vessels of the United States, rescuing the ships of
friendly powers, are entitled to salvage. By analogy to the act of
March 3, 1800, the rate of salvage to which the recaptors of an American vessel from pirates are entitled is one-sixth of the vessel and cargo,
or, if the vessel was armed after her capture, one-half of the vessel
and one-sixth of the cargo. But, if the vessel had been long in the
hands of pirates and used as their own, a higher rate of salvage
should be allowed than if she were recaptured in the moment of her
capture, having just struck, and the crew being still capable of
resistance.[a]

(4) CAPTURES BY PRIVATEERS

§ 314.

War having been recognized by the Government of the United
States to exist between Spain and her colonies, a
**Justified by bellig-
erent commission.** capture of a Spanish vessel and cargo by a privateer
commissioned by the province of Carthagena, while
it had an organized government and was at war with Spain, was held
not to be within the jurisdiction of the courts of the United States,
either by the general law of nations or by the treaty with Spain,
which stipulated for restitution in cases of piracy and captures in
violation of our neutrality, this being neither.

> The Neustra Señora de la Caridad, 4 Wheat. 497.
> See to the same effect, as to Buenos Ayres, The Santissima Trinidad,
> 7 Wheat. 283.
> The fact that a vessel cruising under the commission of a new govern-
> ment not acknowledged by the United States is employed by such
> government may be established by parol evidence, without proving
> the seal to such commission. (The Estrella, 4 Wheat. 298.)

---

[a] Wirt, At. Gen. (1822), 1 Op. 584.

Privateers of powers recognized as belligerents are not pirates by the law of nations.

> Clifford, J., Ford v. Surget, 97 U. S. 618, citing Dole and Another v. Merchants' Mutual Marine Ins. Co., 6 Allen, (Mass.) 373; Planters' Bank v. Union Bank, 16 Wall. 495; U. S. v. Baker, 5 Blatch. 6; Fifield v. Ins. Co. of Penn., 47 Pa. St. 166, and other cases.

Piracy is defined by the law of nations to be a forcible depredation upon property on the high seas, without lawful authority, done *animo furandi;* that is, as defined, in this relation, in a spirit and intention of universal hostility. A pirate is said to be one who roves the sea in an armed vessel, without any commission from any sovereign state, on his own authority, and for the purpose of seizing by force and appropriating to himself, without discrimination, every vessel he may meet.

In a state of war between two nations a commission to a private armed vessel from either of the belligerents affords a defense, according to the law of nations, in the courts of the enemy, against a charge of robbery or piracy on the high seas of which it might be guilty in the absence of such authority.

> United States v. Baker, 5 Blatch. 11–13.
> A non-commissioned cruiser may seize for the benefit of the government. (Carrington v. Merchants' Ins. Co., 8 Pet. 495.)

Where an American vessel commissioned with a letter of marque **Abuse, or invalidity, of commission.** and reprisal has been sold to foreigners, and the new owners are found cruising with the same commander, with the same letter and under the American flag, and there is good reason to suppose that the commission of the letter of marque has been intentionally transferred, it is such an abuse of the commission as will warrant a suit on the bond.

> Rush, At. Gen. (1814), 1 Op. 179.

During the civil war, the existence of which had been recognized by the United States, between Texas and Mexico, a Texan armed schooner captured an American merchantman on the ground that she was laden with provisions, stores, and munitions of war for the Mexican army. It was held that the capture could not be deemed an act of piracy unless it should appear that the principal actors in it were citizens of the United States, in which case they might be indicted for piracy under the 9th section of the crimes act of the 30th of April, 1790, which declares " that if any citizen shall commit any piracy or robbery, or any act of hostility, against the United States, or any citizen thereof, upon the high seas, under color of any commission from any foreign prince or state, or on pretense of authority from any person, such offender shall, notwithstanding the pretense of any such authority, be deemed, adjudged, and taken to be a pirate, felon, and robber, and, on being thereof convicted, shall suffer death."

> Butler, At. Gen., 1836, 3 Op. 120.
>
> In this opinion Mr. Butler laid down the following propositions:
>
> When a civil war breaks out in a foreign nation, and part of such nation erects a distinct and separate government, and the United States, though they do not acknowledge the independence of the new government, do yet recognize the existence of a civil war, our courts have uniformly regarded such party as a belligerent nation in regard to acts done *jure belli*.
>
> Such acts may be unlawful when measured by the laws of nations or by treaty stipulations; the individuals concerned in them may be treated as trespassers, and the nation to which they belong may be held responsible by the United States, but the parties concerned are not treated as pirates.
>
> Persons, however, acting under a commission from one of the belligerents, who make a capture, ostensibly in the right of war, but really with the design of robbery, are guilty of piracy.

" The issuing of letters of marque and reprisal is an act of high sovereign authority. Under the Constitution of the United States this power is intrusted alone to Congress. A declaration of war, without a special provision for the purpose, contained in the act, does not confer upon the President this authority. Whenever civilized governments resort to this expedient to annoy their enemies, they adopt the regulations and restrictions necessary to prevent or punish abuses almost necessarily arising from the grant to private individuals of the authority to make war upon the ocean. Responsible securities are required in such cases from the commanders of privateers, to prevent them from abusing their high trust. By means such as these the rights of the citizens and subjects of the power granting the commission, as well as those of neutrals, are maintained, and the rights of war, according to the practice of civilized nations, are secured even to the enemy. These precautions are necessary to prevent such commissions from falling into the hands of freebooters, slave traders, and pirates prepared to violate all laws, human and divine, in the pursuit of plunder.

" What, then, must be thought of a government, in the nineteenth century, which, disregarding all its high duties, sends its agents abroad with hundreds of blank commissions to privateers, to be sold to all the wretches upon earth, base enough to make the purchase? The high prerogatives of sovereign power are thus transferred to the lowest agent, who is authorized to fill up the blank in the commission, by inserting the name of the commander of the privateer.

Well did the President observe, in his last annual message to Congress, that, ' as the preliminaries required by the practice of civilized nations for commissioning privateers, and regulating their conduct, appear not to have been observed, and as these commissions are in blank, to be filled up with the names of citizens and subjects of all nations who may be willing to purchase them, the whole proceeding can only be construed as an invitation to all the freebooters upon earth, who are willing to pay for the privilege, to cruise against American commerce.' . . .

" This Government can not recognize the lawful existence of Mexican privateers in the Mediterranean. Those assuming this name have not received their commissions in Mexico, but in friendly countries, where to grant or to accept them was a violation of neutral rights; they do not belong to Mexican citizens, and their crews are composed chiefly of Spanish subjects, who, by the act of accepting such commissions, become pirates. These corsairs take to the seas, under color of commissions issued in blank and filled up in a Spanish port by some inferior agent, from whom they have purchased the privilege to plunder American vessels. Among their crews will be found pirates, slave traders, and freebooters of almost every country, except Mexico herself, ready to prey upon the commerce of all nations, when this can be done with impunity. The character and the interests of all Christendom require that they should not receive the countenance of any civilized nation.

" Our vessels of war in the Mediterranean will be ordered to seize and send home for trial as pirates, under the treaty of 1795 and the act of March 3, 1847, all Spanish subjects who have accepted and acted under such Mexican commissions."

> Mr. Buchanan, Sec. of State, to Mr. Saunders, June 13, 1847, MS. Inst. Spain, XIV. 224.

" The *Palmyra* was taken for acts of piratical aggression and depredation upon a vessel of the United States, and upon the property of their citizens. Acts of *piratical* aggression and depredation may be committed by vessels having lawful commissions as privateers, and many such had been committed by the *Palmyra*. The act of robbery from the *Coquette* was in every respect piratical; for it was committed while the privateer was under the Venezuelan flag, and under that flag she had fired upon the *Coquette* and brought her to. It was piratical therefore, not only as depredation of the property by the boat's crew, who took it away, but as aggression under the sanction of the captain of the privateer, who was exercising belligerent rights under false colors. To combat under any other flag than that of the nation by which she is commissioned by the laws of nations subjects a vessel though lawfully commissioned to seizure and condemnation as a pirate; (see Valin's Ordonnance de la Marine, vol. 2, p. 239) and although the decree of the district judge ordered the restitution of the vessel to her captain because it held him to have been lawfully commissioned, neither did the law of nations require, nor would the law of the United States permit, that men brought within the jurisdiction of the court and charged with piratical depredations upon citizens of the United States, should be discharged and turned over to a foreign tribunal for trial, as was demanded by Mr. Anduaga.   They had been brought within the jurisdiction of the court, not by the exercise of any right of search, but as part of the crew of a vessel which had committed piratical depredations and aggressions upon vessels and citizens of the United States. The district court, adjudging the commission of the privateers to have been lawful, and considering the gun fired under the Venezuelan flag to bring the *Coquette* to, though wrongful and unwarrantable, as not amounting rigorously to that conduct which would have been complete piracy, discharged the captain and portion of the crew which had not been guilty of the robbery of the *Coquette*, but reserved for trial the individuals charged with that act ".

> Mr. Adams, Sec. of State, to Mr. Nelson, min. to Spain, April 28, 1823, MS. Inst. U. States Ministers, IX. 183, 213–214.

The British position that American citizens employed on French privateers in the war with revolutionary France were pirates, is in conflict with settled principles of international law.

Question as to nationality of crew.

> Mr. Randolph, Sec. of State, to Mr. Hammond, Oct. 23, 1794, 7 MS. Dom. Let. 362.

The French decree of June 6, 1803, " importing that every privateer of which two-thirds of the crew should not be natives of England, or subjects of a power the enemy of France, shall be considered a pirate," is in contravention of the law of nations.

> Mr. Madison, Sec. of State, report of Jan. 25, 1806, 15 MS. Dom. Let. 70.

" The act of Congress of the last session to protect the commerce of the United States and punish the crime of piracy, referred to in your note of the 9th ult., has two objects—one to protect the property of the citizens of the United States from *piratical* aggressions, and the other to provide for the punishment of foreigners, guilty of the crime of piracy as defined by the law of nations, who may be taken on the high seas and brought within the jurisdiction of the United States. The question what aggression will in any individual case be deemed piratical is, by the nature of our institutions, to be determined by the judicial department of the Government. The executive government recognizes no commissions issued by foreign agents here, for any armed vessel, whether fitted out here or elsewhere, but if such commissions have been issued, whether any aggressions committed under color of them would or would not be piratical is a question in no wise affected by the above-mentioned act of Congress, and its decision is strictly within the province of the tribunals before whom it may be brought to issue. The same observation may be applied to all other questions suggested in your note. The act of Congress to which you refer has made no change in the laws, municipal or international, upon any of the points to which your queries are directed, neither can the executive administration consider it as having any bearing upon those questions. In these respects the law remains as it was before the passage of the act. It was not the intention of Congress to discriminate between the pretentions of the several provinces in South America asserting their independence by war or to determine which of them were competent and which were not to exercise the ordinary rights of belligerent powers. Of the several classes of commissions enumerated by you, some are not known by this Government to exist, the validity of others may depend upon the time when they were issued, or other circumstances on which no decision can be formed by anticipation. It is, however, distinctly to be observed, that no example is known of any nation that has ever classed among pirates an armed vessel, merely for not having a captain and two-thirds or even half its crew *natives* of the country or government granting the commission."

> Mr. Adams, Sec. of State, to the Chev. Onis, Span. min., April 7, 1819, MS. Notes to Foreign Legations, II. 355.

" With regard to the ideas suggested in your note of 22d of March of a common agreement to be adopted by all governments, or by several in amity with each other, to consider as a pirate every privateer with a commission delivered with blanks left for the names, unlimited in point of time, or whose captain, and at least half of its crew, should not be natives of the country under whose flag the privateer shall be navigated, I would submit to your enlightened consideration that, independently of the question whether all or any of the nations of Europe are prepared to agree upon such a mutual stipulation, there might be great difficulty to the admission of the principle in the code of the United States. By the laws of nations the punishment denounced against the crime of piracy is capital; a severity which, by the institutions of the United States, is confined to very few crimes of the most atrocious character. It would scarcely be compatible with the sentiments prevailing in this nation to extend that heaviest of all penalties to offenses the malignity of which might be so different in degree according to the various circumstances under which they might be perpetrated."

Mr. Adams, Sec. of State, to Mr. de Neuville, French min., Apr. 15, 1819,
MS. Notes, For. Leg. II. 356.

"THURSDAY, *March 16, 1854.*'

" Called at the Foreign Office by the invitation of Lord Clarendon. He presented me a printed treaty in blank, which he proposed should be executed by Great Britain, France and the United States. The chief object of it was that all captains of privateers and their crews should be considered and punished as pirates, who, being subjects or citizens of one of the three nations who were neutral, should cruise against either of the others when belligerent. The object undoubtedly was to prevent Americans from taking service in Russian privateers during the present war. We had much conversation on the subject, which I do not mean to repeat, this memorandum being merely intended to refresh my own memory. His lordship had before him a list of the different treaties between the United States and other nations on this subject.

" I was somewhat taken by surprise, though I stated my objections pretty clearly to such a treaty. Not having done justice to the subject in my own opinion, I requested and obtained an interview for the next day, when I stated them more fully and clearly. The heads were as follows:

" 1. It would be a violation of our neutrality in the war to agree with France and England that American citizens who served on board Russian privateers should be punished as pirates. To prevent this, Russia should become a party to the treaty, which, under existing circumstances, was impossible.

" 2. Our treaties only embraced a person of either nation who should take commissions as privateers, and *did not extend to the crew.* Sailors were a thoughtless race, and it would be cruel and unjust to punish them as pirates for taking such service, when they often might do it from want and necessity.

" 3. The British law claims all who are born as British subjects to be British subjects forever. We naturalize them and protect them as American citizens. If the treaty were concluded, and a British cruiser should capture a Russian privateer with a naturalized Irishman on board, what would be the consequence? The British law could not punish him as an American citizen under the treaty, because it would regard him as a British subject. It might hang him for high treason; and such an event would produce a collision between the two countries. The old and dangerous question would then be presented in one of its worst aspects.

" 4. Whilst such a treaty might be justly executed by such nations as Great Britain and the United States, would it be just, wise or humane to agree that their sailors who took service on board a privateer should be summarily tried and executed as pirates by several powers which could be named?

" 5. *Cui bono* should Great Britain make such a treaty with France during the existing war. If no neutral power should enter into it with them, it could have no effect during its continuance.

" 6. The time might possibly come when Great Britain, in a war with the despotisms of Europe, might find it to be exceedingly to her interest to employ American sailors on board her privateers, and such a treaty would render this impossible. Why should she unnecessarily bind her hands?

" 7. The objections of the United States to enter into entangling alliances with Europeans nations.

" 8. By the law of nations, as expounded both in British and American courts, a commission to a privateer, regularly issued by a belligerent nation, protects both the captain and the crew from punishment as pirates. Would the different commercial nations of the earth be willing to change this law as you propose, especially in regard to the crew? Would it be proper to do so in regard to the latter?

"After I had stated these objections at some length on Friday, the 17th of March, Lord Clarendon observed that when some of them were stated the day before, they had struck him with so much force after reflection, that he had come to the office from the House of Lords at night and written them down and sent them to Sir James Graham. In his own opinion the treaty ought not to be concluded, and if the cabinet came to this conclusion the affair should drop, and I agreed I would not write to the Department on the subject. If otherwise, and the treaty should be presented to the Government of the United States, then I was to report our conversation."

> Memorandum of Mr. Buchanan, minister at London, 2 Curtis' Buchanan, 128.

An American citizen, fitting out a vessel in a port of the United States to cruise against a power with which the United States are at peace, is not protected, by a commission from a belligerent, from punishment for any offense committed by him against vessels of the United States.

> United States *v.* Pirates, 5 Wheat. 184.
>
> Citizens of the United States are forbidden by statute to take part in the equipment or manning of privateers to act against nations at peace with the United States. (Act of June 14, 1797, 1 Stat. 520, and April 20, 1818, 3 Stat. 447, 448.) Treaties making privateering under such circumstances piracy have been negotiated with England, France, the Netherlands, Prussia, Spain, and Sweden.

It is no defense to an indictment against a citizen of the United States, for statutory piracy, for taking a privateer commission from foreign insurgents not recognized by us as belligerents, that the depredations charged were under the color of such commission.

> Wirt, At. Gen. (1818), 1 Op. 249, 251.

" The Government of the United States is prohibited by the laws of the Union from recognizing as a lawful Colombian privateer any vessel commanded, officered, and manned chiefly by citizens of this Union."

> Mr. Adams, Sec. of State, to Mr. Anderson, June 29, 1824, MS. Inst. U. States Ministers, X. 183.
>
> See the acts of June 14, 1797, and April 20, 1818, forbidding citizens of the United States from taking part in the equipment or manning of privateers to act against the property of citizens of countries with which the United States are at peace.

September 20, 1854, a treaty of amity and commerce, which was not afterwards ratified, was concluded between the United States and Venezuela, at Caracas. By art. 25 it was provided that, whenever one of the contracting parties should be engaged in war with another state, no citizen of the other contracting party should accept a commission or letter of marque for the purpose of hostilities against the former, under pain of being considered a pirate. Mr. Marcy, while approving the treaty in every other particular, expressed the opinion that this clause invaded the " constitutional prerogative " of Congress. " As the Constitution," said Mr. Marcy, " reserves to Congress the right to define piracy, this clause may be regarded as an assumption of power not granted to the Executive." He returned the treaty to the American minister at Caracas, and instructed him to explain to the Venezuelan Government this objection; and, if the Venezuelan Government adverted to the fact that a similar clause stood in several of the United States' existing treaties, he was to convey the assurance that the United States would endeavor to obtain a modification of them.

> Mr. Marcy, Sec. of State, to Mr. Eames, min. to Venezuela, Dec. 9, 1854, MS. Inst. Venez. I. 115.
>
> The Constitution of the United States provides that Congress shall have power to " define and punish piracies and felonies committed on the high seas." (Mr. Marcy, Sec. of State, to Mr. Aspuru, Venez. min., Nov. 15, 1854, MS. Notes to Venez. I. 35.)

" On the sea all the subjects of one belligerent are the enemies of all the subjects of the other, and entitled to do all such

Uncommissioned cruisers.

acts as war justifies between the belligerent powers themselves. Hence, whilst there may be impediments in the way of a private uncommissioned ship retaining the captures it may make, or disposing of them in any way it may please, those impediments arise from the enactments of municipal law, and are not imposed by international law, which in no way affects this question. But, secondly, if a private ship belonging to one of the belligerents attack and capture the vessel of a neutral power, without a commission of war, the case is widely different; here the attacking vessel may be treated as a pirate by the vessel attacked, or by any vessel coming to her aid."

> Abdy's Kent (1878), 227.
> That a non-commissioned cruiser may seize for the benefit of the Government, see Carrington v. Merchants' Ins. Co., 8 Pet. 495.

4. SELF-DEFENSE.

§ 315.

In June, 1873, the Spanish minister at London called the attention of the British Government to the steam yacht *Deer-*
Case of the "Deer-
hound."
hound, then at Plymouth, which was suspected of being engaged in an attempt to convey arms to Spain for the use of the Carlists. The *Deerhound* was registered in the name of Colonel Stuart, a British subject, who was said to be secretary of the Carlist committee in London. The British Government, after consulting the law officers of the Crown, declared that it could not interfere in the matter. Late in July, the British consul at Bayonne reported that the *Deerhound* had called at that port, and, after obtaining a supply of coal, had again put to sea, and that the Spanish consul there had stated that she had previously taken in a supply of arms and ammunition at Havre, and had delivered them to the Carlists on the coast of Spain. August 13 the *Deerhound* was seized off the French coast by the Spanish cruiser *Buena Ventura*, and, with her crew, was taken to San Sebastian. She had on board at the time a considerable quantity of muskets and cartridges. The British minister at Madrid was instructed by Earl Granville to press the Spanish Government to give orders for the surrender of the vessel and the release of her crew, and to say that the immediate release of the crew was indispensable. The Spanish Government at first refused to release the vessel unless she was acquitted by a prize court. The British Government, on the other hand, declined to recognize the competency of a prize court in the matter, declaring that it could not admit " that legal jurisdiction can be assumed by the Spanish Government over a British ship which, in time of peace, has been seized on the high seas by a public ship of Spain." The Spanish Government gave orders for the immediate release of the crew and the placing of the vessel at the disposal of her captain, but subsequently stated that the vessel was released " because of her having

been captured in neutral waters," and under the supposition that the British Government would impose on the owner the penalty he had incurred by his irregular proceedings. The British Government declined to present any claims for personal indemnity to the Spanish Government, on the ground, as Earl Granville declared, that persons who were engaged in such enterprises as that in question were "not entitled to the interference of Her Majesty's Government on their behalf in order to obtain compensation, either for personal loss or personal inconvenience to which they may have been subjected." On the other hand, Colonel Stuart was requested to pay without delay to the chief clerk of the British foreign office a sum of money advanced to him by the British vice-consul at Ferrol on account of Her Majesty's Government, in order to enable the *Deerhound* and her crew to proceed to a British port, which sum Colonel Stuart had undertaken to pay on demand.

> 65 Br. & For. State Papers (1873–1874), 508–527.
>
> For a reference to this case, see General Sickles, min. to Spain, to Mr. Fish, Sec. of State, Nov. 12, 1873, H. Ex. Doc. 30, 43 Cong. 1 sess. 24; For. Rel. 1874, 930. Also, Mr. Fish, Sec. of State, to Admiral Polo, Spanish min., April 18, 1874, For. Rel. 1875, II. 1191–1192.

In a note to Mr. Fish, February 2, 1874, Admiral Polo, in the course of an extended discussion of the various questions

Case of the "Virginius." involved in the case of the *Virginius*, cited Phillimore to the effect that international law considers the right of self-preservation paramount to that of territorial inviolability, and where they conflict justifies the maintenance of the former at the expense of the latter. Admiral Polo applied this doctrine to the case of a vessel transporting a hostile expedition or military supplies to insurgents. In reply, Mr. Fish said:

" The learned minister of Spain seeks to maintain, by a citation from an eminent English publicist, that this right of transportation may be subordinated by the necessities of self-preservation in the government which is contending with an insurrection. It is not necessary for the undersigned to assent to or to deny the justice of this proposition in the extreme case and with the great limitations stated by Sir R. Phillimore. But the acute intelligence of Admiral Polo can not fail to perceive that the supposed act of self-preservation is none the less an act of war because alleged to be done in self-defense; and the undersigned can not permit himself to assume that Spain maintains that such an invasion of the territory of another power as Phillimore refers to would confer upon the courts or military authorities of the invading nation the right to try and condemn, for alleged crimes, persons who might be captured on neutral soil. In the case of the *Virginius*, had Spain, after her capture by the

Tornado, restored her and her passengers and crew to the United States, to be dealt with according to their laws, the appropriateness of the citation from the British publicist would appear to be more manifest."

> Mr. Fish, Sec. of State, to Admiral Polo, Spanish min., April 18, 1874, For. Rel. 1875, II. 1178, 1192.
>
> The statement here made by Mr. Fish is highly significant. By the fuller account heretofore given (supra, §§ 309, 311) of the case of the *Virginius*, it appears that the demands of the United States for reparation were based chiefly upon the ground that the action of the Spanish authorities was unjustifiable in respect of (1) the charge of piracy and (2) the summary executions. See supra, pp. 895, 967.

" It may happen, as in a rebellion, that a hostile expedition may be surreptitiously fitted out in a friendly country, without the fault of the officials, and that a vessel is on its way to land troops and arms for aid in a civil war. In such a case self-defense authorizes search, and possibly seizure, whether such a vessel is found on the high seas or within the waters of the injured state. Of this the case of the *Virginius*, which is in some respects like that of the *Caroline*, is perhaps the most noticeable illustration in recent times. . . . The summary and informal process, the cruel execution of persons belonging to the crew, even of mariners and cabin boys, met with the just indignation of the world; but in addition to this, unless the *Virginius* can be shown to be a piratical vessel, the mode of trial was a violation of article 7 of our treaty of 1795 with Spain, which secures a regular trial, the use of solicitors, agents, etc., and their free access to the subjects or citizens of the one party arrested for offenses committed within the jurisdiction of the other. . . .

" The reasoning and opinion of the Attorney-General are examined by Mr. R. H. Dana, the editor of ' Wheaton,' in a Boston journal, of January 6, 1874. In brief, he takes the unassailable position that actual ownership by a person belonging to a state, places a ship on the high seas under the jurisdiction of that state. The *Virginius*, owned really by Spaniards, was really under Spanish jurisdiction; and ' the register of a foreign nation is not, and by the law of nations is not recognized as being, a national voucher and guaranty of national character to all the world.' ' Nations having cause to arrest a vessel, would go behind such a document to ascertain the jurisdictional fact which gives character to the document, and not the document to the fact.' ' Even a genuine passport, which is an assertion of national character, is not conclusive between nations on a question of right to arrest.' And if the Attorney-General thinks that Spain has no jurisdiction to inquire into violations of our laws, that the question, whether or not the register was fraudulently obtained, was a matter of our law and for our decision, it may be replied that, granting this

to be true, the fact does not touch the question of jurisdiction, which
depends on ownership. All that can fairly be said is, that while the
nation of the owners has a right to arrest, the *ostensible* ownership
appearing on the register fraudulently obtained, would suggest delay
and sequestration of the vessel until the facts could be established.
We add that the flag is no protection without a right to use it, and
that every nation—for purposes of jurisdiction over vessels of its subjects at sea, as well as for other reasons—has a right to decide by its
ships of war whether its own vessels are not wearing a foreign flag.

" But the Spanish captain who took the *Virginius* supposed it to be
a veritable American vessel, making an attempt to land men and instruments of war, in order to assist the insurrection in Cuba. What was
his duty in the premises? It was to defend the coasts of Cuba, to
the best of his ability, against a vessel which was known to be under
the control of the insurgents, for which he had been on the lookout,
and against which the only effectual security was capture on the high
seas. Of course such self-defense on the part of Spain involved a
risk, like that which was involved in the case of the *Caroline*, where,
as was mentioned in the text, Mr. Webster admitted that self-defense
was in extreme cases justifiable, although it might lie beyond the
ordinary course of international law. . . . An eminent lawyer, Mr.
George T. Curtis, examined the subject at large in ' The Case of the
Virginius, considered with Reference to the Law of Self-defense,'
and justifies the capture on the same ground."

Woolsey, International Law, § 214,

"A country the peace of which is threatened by persons on board
vessels sailing under the flag of another state may in an emergency
search and capture such vessels and arrest the persons on board, notwithstanding that as a general rule there is no right of visiting and
seizing vessels of a friendly power in time of peace upon the seas. . . .
Whether the danger was sufficient to justify the seizure of the vessel
[*Virginius*] at the moment when it was effected may, to say the least,
be doubtful; but assuming urgent danger to have existed, was its
capture in other respects permissible, and had the Spanish authorities
a right to punish insurgent subjects taken on board? The United
States maintained that the fact that the *Virginius* was prima facie
an American vessel was enough to protect her from interference of
any kind outside territorial waters. [Here the opinion of Attorney-
General Williams, supra, § 309, is quoted.] In taking up this position the United States in effect denied the right of doing any acts of
self-protection upon the high seas in time of peace in excess of ordinary peace rights. In the end, however, the question between it and
the Spanish Government was settled on the ground that the ship was
not duly invested with an American national character, according to

the requirements of the municipal law of the United States, so that much of what the latter country had contended for was surrendered. . . . The English Government . . . became mixed up in the affair through the presence of Englishmen on board the *Virginius* as part of the crew. In demanding reparation for the death of some of them who were executed it does ' not take the ground of complaining of the seizure of the *Virginius*, nor of the detention of the passengers and crew. . . . Much may be excused,' it was added with reference to their deaths, ' in acts done under the expectation of instant damage in self-defense by a nation as well as an individual. But after the capture of the *Virginius* and the detention of the crew was effected, no pretense of imminent necessity of self-defense could be alleged.' It is clear from this language that the mere capture of the vessel was an act which the British Government did not look upon as being improper, supposing an imminent necessity of self-defense to exist."

Hall, Int. Law, 4th ed., 287–290.

Early in 1869 the American brig *Mary Lowell* cleared from New York for Vera Cruz, Mexico, with a cargo of arms **Case of the "Mary Lowell."** and munitions of war. March 15, 1869, she was captured off Ragged Island, one of the Bahamas, by the Spanish man-of-war *Andeluza*. She was immediately taken to Havana, where with her cargo she was condemned as lawful prize. When her capture first became known the Government of the United States, acting upon information that it was effected in British waters, stated that it would look to Great Britain for indemnification for the losses of the owner and charterer in consequence of the illegal seizure. The British Government, however, did not find that the charge of seizure in British waters was made out; and a claim for damages was afterwards presented to the mixed commission under the arbitral agreement between the United States and Spain of February 11–12, 1871. The umpire, Baron Blanc, on June 9, 1879, dismissed the claims, on the ground that, even assuming that for the purposes of the controversy the capture of the brig and cargo by a Spanish force on the high seas was unauthorized by international law, yet, as the cargo consisted of arms and military supplies for the Cuban insurgents, and as the brig was either wilfully or negligently allowed to fall into the hands of persons actively interested in promoting the insurrection, " the claimants forfeited their right to the protection of the American flag, and are estopped from asserting any of the privileges of lawful intercourse in times of peace and any title to individual benefit of indemnity as against the acts of the Spanish authorities done in self-defense."

The advocate for the United States moved for a rehearing on the ground that the decision as to the right of self-defence was erroneous and destructive of the freedom of the seas, as well as on other grounds.

The umpire denied the motion, and in so doing elaborated his decision. He found, as matter of fact, that the cargo was shipped on the brig for delivery even by illegal means to the Cuban insurgents; that, even if her destination to Vera Cruz was not originally simulated, she was abandoned at the Bahamas by her captain and crew, who alleged unwillingness to participate in a descent on the Cuban coast; that she was then taken command of by one of a body of men organized as a military company, which had come from Florida with the owner of the brig himself in another one of his vessels; and that, at the time of her capture, the brig was in the possession and under the control of the insurgents.

On these facts the umpire found, as matter of law, that the brig and her cargo were at the time of their capture being used in an unlawful enterprise, outside the conditions of lawful intercourse in time of peace; that this illegality was of such a character " as to carry with it forfeiture of the protection of the United States flag and as to subject the property to such eventual action as might be deemed proper by the United States and by Spain according to the mutual rights and duties of the two governments; " that the abnormal situation of the owner and charterer, with reference to the United States as well as to Spain, could not be covered by the alleged infraction of international law in the capture of the brig and her cargo by the Spanish forces, and that they were therefore estopped from claiming indemnity for the consequences of their unlawful venture. The umpire declared, however, that he applied this rule of estoppel only to private claims, and that he did not deem it necessary to determine the respective rights of Spain and the United States with regard to the capture.

For a fuller account of this case, see Moore, International Arbitrations, III. 2772–2777. See, also, S. Ex. Doc. 108, 41 Cong. 2 sess.

This case was referred to in the discussions of the capture of the *Virginius.* With regard to it Mr. Fish said: " The undersigned would be at a loss to understand why reference is made to her [the *Mary Lowell*], were it not that Admiral Polo makes reference to the fact that a claim against Spain growing out of an illegal seizure of this vessel is now pending before a judicial tribunal in Washington, and attempts to prejudge the case. The United States having agreed to submit that question to arbitration, the undersigned declines to enter upon a diplomatic discussion of it." (Mr. Fish, Sec. of State, to Admiral Polo, Spanish min., April 18, 1874, For. Rel. 1875, II. 1193.)

The subsequent decision, which is given above, was treated as disposing of the case.

5. QUESTION OF HOT PURSUIT.

§ 316.

With regard to the question of hot pursuit, it may be observed that a vessel may bring herself constructively within territorial waters by carrying on operations there by means of boats. Thus in the case of the British Columbian sealing schooner *Araunah*, which was seized under Russian authority in 1888 in Bering Sea, the master alleged that she was at the time of her seizure six miles from the nearest land. The captors alleged that she was nearer. It appeared, however, that her crew were carrying on their operations in canoes between the schooner and the land, and it was affirmed that two of the canoes were within half a mile of the shore. With reference to these facts, Lord Salisbury said Her Majesty's Government were " of opinion that, even if the *Araunah* . . . was herself outside the three-mile territorial limit, the fact that she was, by means of her boats, carrying on fishing within Russian waters without the prescribed license warranted her seizure and confiscation."

> Blue Book " Russia No. 1 (1890)," cited in Moore, Int. Arbitrations, I. 824–825.
> The same principle was laid down by Lord Stowell with regard to a capture made in territorial waters by a vessel lying outside, by means of boats sent inside.

" For a crime committed in port a vessel may be chased into the high seas and there arrested, without a suspicion that territorial rights have been violated, while to chase a criminal across the borders and seize him on foreign soil is a gross offense against sovereignty."

> Woolsey, Int. Law, § 58.

In 1891, during the civil war in Chile, the leaders of the Congressional party, which had not been accorded belligerent rights, sent to the United States an armed transport, called the *Itata*, for the purpose of receiving and conveying to Iquique, where the insurgents had their headquarters, a cargo of arms and munitions of war. The *Itata* was subsequently seized at San Diego, California, under process of the United States courts, on a charge of violation of the neutrality laws. While in the custody of a person who had been left in charge of her by the United States marshal, the *Itata*, against the protest of the person in charge, got up steam and departed. The marshal's keeper was put ashore and the *Itata* then proceeded to San Clemente Island, within the jurisdiction of the United States, where, after receiving a cargo of arms and ammunition which had been sent by another vessel from San Francisco, she proceeded to Iquique, under the convoy of the Chilean cruiser *Esmeralda*, then in the service of the Congressional party. When information was received of the escape of the *Itata*, orders were given to the U. S. S. *Charleston* and the U. S. S. *Omaha* to go in search of her, and if she was found at sea to seize her and bring her into port. If she was convoyed by a Chilean war vessel, the circumstances of the escape were to be explained and a demand made for her restoration to the possession of the United States; if this demand was refused, it was to be enforced if practicable. The *Itata* arrived, however, at Iquique without being intercepted; but before her arrival there the Congressional authorities expressed disapproval of what had been done and voluntarily promised to restore her to the possession of the United States, together with the arms and ammunition taken on board " in San Diego." When it was ascertained that the arms and ammunition had been taken on board not at San Diego but at San Clemente Island, the Congressional authorities expressed a desire to retain them, but as they were taken on board within the jurisdiction of the United States, Rear-Admiral McCann, U. S. N., who was then in command of the United States naval forces in Chilean waters, declined to accept the suggestion, and the vessel, though no demand for her surrender had been made, was given up together with her cargo.

> For the orders to the *Charleston* and the *Omaha*, see Mr. Tracy, Sec. of Navy, to Capt. Remey, U. S. S. *Charleston*, May 8, 1891, H. Ex. Doc. 91, 52 Cong. 1 sess. 250.
>
> Other correspondence in relation to the case will be found in the same document, 250–270; and in For. Rel. 1891, 122, 132, 316, 317, 321, 322.
>
> As to the delivery of the *Itata* and her cargo, see Rear-Admiral McCann to Mr. Tracy, Sec. of Navy, June 13, 1891, H. Ex. Doc. 91, 52 Cong. 1 sess. 267–270; also the testimony of Rear-Admiral Brown, U. S. N., quoted in decision No. 21, The South American Steamship Co. *v.* The United States, No. 18, United States and Chilean Claims Commission under the convention of May 24, 1897. For the proceedings of the United States and Chilean Claims Commission in the case of the *Itata*, under convention of August 7, 1892, see Moore, Int. Arbitrations, III. 3067–3071.
>
> For the proceedings on the charge of violation of the neutrality laws of the United States, see United States *v.* Trumbull (1891), 48 Fed. Rep. 99.
>
> The case of the *Itata* is discussed in President Harrison's annual message of Dec. 9, 1891. It is stated in this message that it would have been " inconsistent with the dignity and self-respect of this Government not to have insisted that the *Itata* should be returned to San Diego to abide the judgment of the court;" but the question of pursuit on the high seas is not specially discussed.

III. CLAIM OF IMPRESSMENT.

1. ITS ASSERTION AND DENIAL.

§ 317.

Great Britain at one time claimed the right to impress into her navy British seamen found on board the vessels of other nations on the high seas. This claim was asserted, not as a peace-right, nor yet as an independent war-right, but as an incident of the admitted belligerent right of visit and search. While exercising this right, the British commander might, so it was claimed, take from the neutral vessel any persons on board who were recognized as British seamen. The fact that the claim was asserted in this form seems to have possessed no significance, except as a tacit acknowledgement that it did not itself rest on any text of the law of nations; nor did the question of form modify its practical operation. The ill-feeling engendered by the assertion of the claim was, besides, greatly intensified by the coincident enforcement of the rule of indelible allegiance, under which a person once a British subject might, although he had acquired the citizenship of another country, still be " recognized " as a British seaman and be impressed accordingly. The claim of impressment seems at the present day to possess, however, even if it has never been formally renounced, only an historic interest as a phase of the struggle for the establishment of the principle of the freedom of the seas. This great principle, Great Britain now fully recognizes and maintains; she also permits the expatriation of her subjects, and acknowledges the qualified nationality derived by seamen from their service; and, in the case of Mason and Slidell, she impliedly affirmed that the taking of persons from a neutral vessel, under cover of the belligerent right of visit and search, could not be justified by a claim to their allegiance.

" It will be remembered that it was never claimed that the officer of a British man-of-war could enter a neutral vessel for the purpose of searching for seamen. In the declaration of the Prince Regent in January, 1813, in reference to the causes of the American war, it is said: ' His Royal Highness can never admit, that, in the exercise of the undoubted and hitherto undisputed right of searching neutral merchant vessels in time of war, the impressment of British seamen, when found therein, can be deemed any violation of a neutral flag. Neither can he admit that the taking such seamen from on board such vessels can be considered by any neutral state as a hostile measure, or a justifiable cause of war.' "

Lawrence, Visitation and Search, 13; 1 Br. and For. State Papers, 1508, 1518.

"It will be expedient that you take proper opportunities, in the meantime, of conferring with the minister on this subject [impressment], in order to form some arrangement for the protection of our seamen on those occasions. We entirely reject the mode which was the subject of a conversation between Mr. Morris and him, which was that our seamen should always carry about them certificates of their citizenship; this is a condition never yet submitted to by any nation; one with which seamen would never have the precaution to comply. The casualties of their calling would expose them to the constant destruction or loss of this paper evidence, and thus the British Government would be armed with *legal authority* to impress the whole of our seamen. The simplest rule will be that the vessel being American shall be evidence that the seamen on board her are such. If they apprehend that our vessels might thus become asylums for the fugitives of their own nation from impress gangs, the number of men to be protected by a vessel may be limited by her tonnage, and one or two officers only be permitted to enter the vessel in order to examine the numbers aboard; but no press gang should be allowed ever to go on board an American vessel till after it shall be found that there are more than their stipulated number on board, nor till after the master shall have refused to deliver the supernumeraries (to be named by himself) to the press officer who has come on board for that purpose; and even then the American consul should be called in. In order to urge a settlement of this point before a new occasion may arise, it may not be amiss to draw their attention to the peculiar irritation excited on the last occasion, and the difficulty of avoiding our making immediate reprisals on their seamen here. You will be so good as to communicate to me what shall pass on this subject, and it may be made an article of convention to be entered into either there or here."

> Mr. Jefferson, Sec. of State, to Mr. Pinckney, min. to England, June 11, 1792, MS, Inst. U. States Ministers, I. 171.

"You are desired to persevere till you obtain a regulation to guard our vessels from having their hands impressed, and to inhibit the British navy officers from taking them under the pretext of their being British subjects. There appears but one practicable rule, that the vessel being American, shall be conclusive evidence that the hands are so, to a certain number proportioned to her tonnage."

> Mr. Jefferson, Sec. of State, to Mr. Pinckney, min. to England, May 7, 1793, MS. Inst. U. States Min. I. 278.

"Your information that we are not likely to obtain any protection for our seamen in British ports, or against British officers on the high seas, is of a serious nature indeed; it contrasts remarkably with the multiplied applications we are receiving from the British minister here for protection to their seamen, vessels, and property within our ports and bays, which we are complying with, with the most exact justice."

> Mr. Jefferson, Sec. of State, to Mr. Pinckney, min. to England, June 4, 1793, MS. Inst. U. States Ministers, I. 286.

" The insufferable practice of the British ships of war, in impressing American seamen from American ships, has constantly engaged my attention, as often as I have obtained any proofs. It still occupies the Government. Mr. Meade's note, though extremely defective in solemnity and explicitness, is the first piece of testimony in any shape, which I have been able to procure, relative to the seizure of passengers from our ships. The subject is under consideration, and what the law of nations will permit to be done, will not be omitted."

> Mr. Randolph, Sec. of State, to the Governor of Virginia, May 20, 1795, 8 MS. Dom. Let. 197.

" With regard to the insult on our flag, it will readily occur that the right of searching and stripping public vessels of war of their hands, if it exists at all, must be reciprocal; and it need not be asked whether a British naval commander would submit to it; neither will ours. But if such search for and taking away of seamen were at all admissible in practice, it should be in our favor; because American seamen are generally on board British ships only by *impressments;* whereas the British seamen to be found in the armed vessels of the United States are all *volunteers*. And you will recollect that the British Government have made a distinction between *volunteer* and *impressed* Americans, releasing the latter when their citizenship was proved, but detaining the former although they had entered and taken the bounty only in consequence of a *previous impressment*."

> Mr. Pickering, Sec. of State, to Mr. King, min. to England, Jan. 8, 1799, MS. Inst. U. States Ministers, V 49.
>
> See, also, same to same, June 14, 1799, ibid.
>
> For a report of Mr. Pickering, Sec. of State, Feb. 28, 1797, on impressments, see Am. State Papers, For. Rel. I. 761.

" The impressment of our seamen is an injury of very serious magnitude, which deeply affects the feelings and the honor of the nation.

" This valuable class of men is composed of natives and foreigners, who engage voluntarily in our service.

" No right has been asserted to impress the natives of America. Yet they are impressed, they are dragged on board British ships of war with the evidence of citizenship in their hands, and forced by violence there to serve until conclusive testimonials of their birth can be obtained. These must most generally be sought for on this side of the Atlantic. In the meantime, acknowledged violence is practiced on a free citizen of the United States, by compelling him to engage and to continue in foreign service. Although the Lords of the Admiralty uniformly direct their discharge on the production of this testimony, yet many must perish unrelieved, and all are detained a considerable time in lawless and injurious confinement. . . .

" The case of British subjects, whether naturalized or not, is more questionable; but the right even to impress them is denied. The practice of the British Government itself may certainly, in a controversy with that Government, be relied on. The privileges it claims and exercises ought to be conceded to others. To deny this, would be to deny the equality of nations, and to make it a question of power and not of right.

" If the practice of the British Government may be quoted, that practice is to maintain and defend in their sea service all those of any nation who have voluntarily engaged in it, or who, according to their laws, have become British subjects.

"Alien seamen, not British subjects, engaged in our merchant service, ought to be equally exempt with citizens from impressments: we have a right to engage them, and have a right to, and interest in, their persons, to the extent of the service contracted to be performed. Britain has no pretext of right to their persons or to their service. To tear them, then, from our possession, is at the same time an insult and an injury. It is an act of violence for which there exists no palliative."

> Mr. Marshall, Sec. of State, to Mr. King, min. to England, Sept. 20, 1800, Am. State Papers, For. Rel. II. 489, MS. Inst. U. States Ministers, V. 367.
>
> In an instruction of Mr. Madison, Sec. of State, to Mr. Monroe, min. to England, Jan. 5, 1804, the claim of impressment is fully discussed. (MS. Inst. U. States Ministers, VI. 161; Am. State Papers, For. Rel. II. 730; III. 81.)
>
> For lists of American seamen impressed into British ships, see Am. State Pap. For. Rel. II. 777; IV. 56.
>
> See, as to the practice of impressment, John Adams' Works, II. 226, 528; III. 503; VIII. 450, 451, 453, 455, 656; IX. 312, 330; X. 207.

Mr. King, at the close of his mission to England, in 1804, entered into an informal agreement with Lord St. Vincent, first lord of the admiralty, that neither nation should for the period of five years take seamen from the ships of the other on the high seas. When, however, this agreement was submitted to the ministry, it was returned with the qualification that it should not apply to the seas immediately washing Great Britain, which, it was alleged, had always been considered under British dominion. As this, in Mr. King's opinion, would be an admission of the right of impressment in those waters, he gave up the project entirely.

5 Hildreth's Hist. U. S., 535.   See Adams' Hist. of the U. S. II. 358.

By Gouverneur Morris the surrender to the British Government of impressment was urged, as his life by Sparks shows, with much per-
sistency.   But as to how far Gouverneur Morris, after his abandonment of his French mission, became a representative of the British
Government, see 1 J. Q. Adams's Mem. 149, 204, 215.

" On the impressment of our seamen our remonstrances have never been
intermitted.   A hope existed at one moment of an arrangement which
might have been submitted to, but it soon passed away, and the
practice, though relaxed at times in the distant seas, has been constantly pursued in those in our neighborhood.   The grounds on
which the reclamations on this subject have been urged will appear
in an extract from instructions to our minister at London now communicated."   (President Jefferson, Special Message, Jan. 17, 1806,
Richardson's Messages, I. 395.)

In 1806 Messrs. Monroe and Pinkney, the latter having been joined
with the former in the mission to London, were instructed to make
the express prohibition of the practice of impressment a condition
precedent not only to the conclusion of any treaty but also to the nonenforcement by the United States of the Non-importation Act against
Great Britain.   After a protracted negotiation the American negotiators wrote home that they had found it necessary, in order to make
a treaty, to abandon the subject of impressments and accept, instead
of a formal article on the subject, a note pledging the British Government to exercise the greatest care not to impress American citizens
and to afford redress should injury be inflicted while impressing
British seamen.   Under this arrangement a treaty was signed Dec. 1,
1806, containing no clause as to impressments.   President Jefferson
refused to submit the treaty to the Senate.

Adams' Hist. of the United States, III. 400, 408–411, 413, 431.

For the instructions to Monroe and Pinkney, signed by Mr. Madison as
Secretary of State, May 17, 1806, see Am. State Papers, For. Rel. III.
119.   See Mr. Madison to Messrs. Monroe and Pinkney, Feb. 3, 1807,
and other correspondence concerning the treaty, in the same volume ;
also, Jefferson's works (ed. 1854), V. 52, 63.

As to the reasons of Messrs. Monroe and Pinkney for signing the treaty,
see letter to Mr. Madison, April 22, 1807, and a draft of a private
letter to Mr. Jefferson, June, 1807 : Monroe MSS. Library of Congress.   See, also, Am. State Papers, For. Rel. III. 197, 200.

For returns of British impressments, reported by Mr. Madison, Sec. of
State, March 2, 1808, see Am. State Papers, For. Rel. III. 36.

2. CASE OF " CHESAPEAKE " AND " LEOPARD."

§ 318.

Early in 1807 a British squadron lay within the capes of the Chesapeake Bay watching for some French frigates which had taken
refuge at Annapolis.   One or more of the British ships lay occasion-

ally in Hampton Roads, or came to the navy-yard at Gosport for necessary repairs. Desertions were numerous—even the American ships of war had much difficulty from loss of men—and on March 7 a boat's crew of the British gun sloop *Halifax* made off and escaped to Norfolk. The commander of the *Halifax*, hearing that these men had enlisted on the American frigate *Chesapeake*, complained to the British consul and sought to recover them, but without success. One of them was named Jenkin Ratford, an Englishman. The British minister at Washington also made complaint that three deserters from the *Melampus* had enlisted on the *Chesapeake*. On inquiry it was ascertained that the three men in question, one of whom was a negro, were on board the *Chesapeake*, but that they were native Americans who had been impressed by the *Melampus*. Their nationality being admitted, the answer as to them was final; but the fact was overlooked that Ratford was on board the *Chesapeake*, under the name of Wilson.

The grievances of the British ships having been reported to Admiral Berkeley, at Halifax, he issued, June 1, 1807, without waiting for authority from England, a circular order to all the ships under his command, reciting the desertions from the British ships in the Chesapeake and the refusal of the authorities, civil and naval, to give the deserters up, and directing the commanders of the British ships, " in case of meeting with the American frigate *Chesapeake* at sea, and without the limits of the United States, to show the captain of her this order, and to require to search his ship for the deserters from the before-mentioned [British] ships, and to proceed and search for the same; and if a similar demand should be made by the American, he is to be permitted to search for any deserters from their service, according to the customs and usage of civilized nations on terms of peace and amity with each other."

This order was sent to the Chesapeake Bay by the frigate *Leopard*, commanded by Captain S. P. Humphreys. The *Leopard* arrived at Lynnhaven June 21. The frigate *Chesapeake*, commanded by Commodore Barron, was then lying in Hampton Roads, under orders for the Mediterranean. On the morning of June 22 she got under way. The *Leopard* also stood out to sea. About half-past three in the afternoon, both ships being eight or ten miles southeast by east of Cape Henry, the *Leopard* rounded to and hailed, saying that she had dispatches for the commodore. As British ships on distant stations not infrequently sent dispatches by the courtesy of American officers, the request implied no hostile purpose, and Commodore Barron answered the hail and heaved to. Shortly afterwards a lieutenant from the *Leopard* came on board. He was shown to the commodore's cabin, where he delivered to Commodore Barron a note from Captain

Humphreys, enclosing a copy of Admiral Berkeley's order, and expressing the hope that the matter might be "adjusted" in such a manner that "the harmony subsisting between the two countries may remain undisturbed." The *Melampus* was not mentioned in Admiral Berkeley's order as one of the British ships from which men had deserted, though other ships were specified. Commodore Barron, however, explained to the lieutenant the circumstances relating to the three men from the *Melampus*, and then wrote to Captain Humphreys a reply, stating that he had on board no such men as were described; that he had ordered the recruiting officers not to enter any deserters from British ships; that he was also instructed not to permit the crew of his ship to be mustered by any but their own officers; and that he was disposed to preserve harmony, and hoped this answer would prove satisfactory. The lieutenant immediately returned to the *Leopard*, and a few minutes later Captain Humphreys, edging nearer, hailed and cried: "Commodore Barron, you must be aware of the necessity I am under of complying with the orders of my commander in chief." The *Chesapeake* was not ready for action, but Commodore Barron gave orders to clear the guns and prepare for battle. Before the gunner got to his magazine he heard the first shot from the *Leopard*, and as he entered the magazine the *Leopard* fired a broadside. The crew of the *Chesapeake* were just beginning to clear the deck. In fifteen minutes the *Leopard* fired three broadsides without return. Commodore Barron, though wounded in the first broadside, kept the deck; but as his ship was badly damaged and practically helpless, after the third broadside he ordered the flag to be struck. As it touched the taffrail a gun, discharged by means of a live coal brought by a lieutenant in his fingers from the galley, sent a shot into the *Leopard*. Three men on the *Chesapeake* were killed, while eight were severely and ten slightly wounded.

Officers from the *Leopard* came on board the *Chesapeake* and mustered the ship's company. They selected the three Americans who had deserted from the *Melampus*, and were therefore not included in Admiral Berkeley's order. After a search they dragged Ratford out of a coal-hole. These four men were taken out and the two ships went their ways, Captain Humphreys declining to receive the *Chesapeake* as a prize. The four prisoners were carried to Halifax, where they were court-martialed. Ratford was sentenced to be hanged, and the sentence was executed. The three Americans were condemned each to receive, as deserters, five hundred lashes; but the sentence was not carried out, and they remained in prison.

The outbreak of popular feeling produced by the attack on the *Chesapeake* "made the month of July, 1807, a moment without a parallel in American history since the battle of Lexington." Its only result, however, in international law, was the establishment of the exemption of men-of-war from the claim of impressment. July 2, President Jefferson issued a proclamation requiring all armed British vessels to depart from American waters, and, in case they failed to do so, forbidding intercourse with them. Instructions were sent to Mr. Monroe, in London, to demand that the attack on the *Chesapeake* should be disavowed; that the men taken from her should be restored, and the offenders punished; that a special mission should be sent to America to announce the reparation, and that the practice of impressment from merchant vessels should be abandoned. Before these instructions arrived, Canning, on receiving news of the affair, disavowed " the pretension of a right to search ships of war in the national service of any state for deserters." He subsequently declined to consider, as part of the reparation, the abolition of impressment from merchant vessels; and when, in December, 1807, Mr. G. H. Rose was sent as minister to the United States to settle the case of the *Chesapeake*, he was instructed to require the revocation of the President's proclamation of July 2 as a condition of entering upon negotiations, Admiral Berkeley having already been disavowed and recalled. This demand was refused, and the case remained without formal adjustment.

> The foregoing account is condensed from Mr. Henry Adams' History of the United States, IV. 1–54, 178–199. See, also, Mahan's Sea Power in its Relations to the War of 1812, I. 155–168.
>
> For Canning's disavowal of a right of impressment from men-of-war, see Canning to Monroe, Aug. 3, 1807, Am. State Papers, For. Rel. III. 188.
>
> For the instructions to Monroe, see Madison to Monroe, July 6, 1807, Am. State Papers, For. Rel. III. 183.
>
> For Canning's instructions to Rose, Oct. 24, 1807, taken from the MS. British Archives, see Adams' History, IV. 178–188. See, also, the Declaration of the Prince Regent, Jan. 9, 1813, as to the war of 1812, 1 Br. and For. State Papers, 1519.
>
> For a report to the House of Representatives on the case of the *Chesapeake*, by a committee to whom it was referred, see Am. State Papers, For. Rel. III. 6.
>
> For the conclusions of the court of inquiry on the conduct of Commodore Barron, see Am. State Papers, For. Rel. III. 22. See, also, Adams' Hist. IV. 20–24.
>
> As to the case of the U. S. sloop of war *Baltimore*, see Life of Pickering, III. 339 et seq.

3. War of 1812.

§ 319.

In his message to Congress of June 1, 1812, recommending a declaration of war against England, President Madison mentioned as causes of complaint impressments, the violation of the American coasts, the practice of paper blockades, and the orders in council.

See Adams' Hist. of the United States, VI. 116–118, 134, 222.

As to the negotiations touching impressments, see Ingersoll's Hist. of the Late War, 1 series, I. 30.

On impressment as a cause of the war of 1812, see speech of T. Pickering, Life of Pickering, IV. 236, 242.

It was stated by Mr. Monroe, Sec. of State, July 16, 1811, to Mr. Foster, British minister at Washington, that "no order had been given by the Government for the recovery by force of any citizen so impressed [from American vessels] from any British ship of war." This statement was substantially repeated by Mr. Monroe in a note of Sept. 14, 1811. (Am. St. Papers, For. Rel. III. 472, 476.)

The claim of right by British men-of-war to search American vessels for British seamen, and to impress them when so found, though one of the causes of the war of 1812, was not formally surrendered by the treaty of Ghent. The Government of the United States did not insist on such surrender as a *sine qua non*. The instructions by the Secretary of State of October 4, 1814, when the fall of Napoleon left the United States the sole power with whom Great Britain was at war, gave the commissioners authority, " should you find it impracticable to make an arrangement more conformable to the instructions originally given, to agree to the *status quo ante bellum* as the basis of negotiation." It was added, however, after a clause guarding the fisheries, " nor is anything to be done which would give a sanction to the British claim of impressment on board our vessels." The treaty as executed contained no provision on the subject; but the claim was never afterwards asserted or exercised by Great Britain.

Mr. Bancroft Davis, Treaty Notes, Treaty Vol. (1776–1887), 1327–1328.

See Mr. Crawford to Mr. Clay, June 10, 1814, Colton's Cor. of Clay, 34 et seq.

" I see by several papers that a very unfair play is going on with respect to the unpublished residue of the dispatches from Ghent. It is given out that the suppression was the act of the Republicans in the Senate, and that an article prohibiting impressment was rejected by the British commissioners in a manner involving an abandonment of the American doctrine. The fact is, that the vote against publication was founded on the report of Mr. King, etc., and that the rejection of the American proposition as to impressment was followed by a protest, neutralizing at least the proceeding on that subject." (Mr. Madison, President, to Mr. Monroe, Sec. of State (unofficial), Apr. 4, 1815, Monroe Papers, Library of Congress.)

" I sincerely congratulate you on the peace, and more especially on the éclat with which the war was closed. The affair of New Orleans was fraught with useful lessons to ourselves, our enemies, and our friends, and will powerfully influence our future relations with the nations of Europe. It will show them we mean to take no part in their wars, and count no odds when engaged in our own. I presume that, having spared to the pride of England her formal acknowledgment of the atrocity of impressment in an article of the treaty, she will concur in a convention for relinquishing it. Without this she must understand that the present is but a truce, determinable on the first act of impressment of an American citizen committed by an officer of hers. Would it not be better that this convention should be a separate act, unconnected with any treaty of commerce, and made an indispensable preliminary to all other treaty. If blended with a treaty of commerce, she will make it the price of injurious concessions."

> Mr. Jefferson to President Madison, March 23, 1815, Jefferson's Works, VI. 453.
>
> " If they (the British Government) refuse to settle it (impressment), the first American impressed should be a declaration of war. The depredations on our merchants I would bear with great patience, as it is their desire. They make themselves whole by insurances, very much done in England. If the consequently increased price falls on the consumer, it still costs him less than a war, and still operates as a premium to our own manufactures. The other point, therefore, being settled, I should be slow to wrath on this." (Mr. Jefferson to Mr. Monroe, Sec. of State, July 15, 1815, Monroe Papers, Library of Congress.)

4. SUBSEQUENT CORRESPONDENCE.

§ 320.

" Peace having happily taken place between the United States and Great Britain, it is desirable to guard against incidents, which during periods of war in Europe, might tend to interrupt it: and, it is believed, in particular, that the navigation of American vessels exclusively by American seamen, either natives or such as are already naturalized, would not only conduce to the attainment of that object, but also to increase the number of our seamen, and consequently to render our commerce and navigation independent of the service of foreigners, who might be recalled by their governments under circumstances the most inconvenient to the United States. I recommend the subject, therefore, to the consideration of Congress; and, in deciding upon it, I am persuaded that they will sufficiently estimate the policy of manifesting to the world a desire on all occasions, to cultivate harmony with other nations by any reasonable accommodations, which do not impair the enjoyment of any of the essential rights of a free and independent people. The example on the part of the American government will merit, and may be expected to receive, a reciprocal attention from all the friendly powers of Europe."

> Message of President Madison, Feb. 25, 1815, 9 Wait's St. Pap. (3d ed.) 438.

" The permanency of peace between the two countries is utterly incompatible with the resumption of the practice of impressing men from our vessels on the high seas."

> Mr. Adams, Sec. of State, to Messrs. Gallatin and Rush, ministers to England, Nov. 2, 1818, Am. State Pap. For. Rel. IV. 399, MS. Inst. U. States Ministers, VIII. 251.
>
> See, also, Rush's Memoranda (2d ed.) 307, 383.
>
> For correspondence in 1826–27, see 14 Br. & For. State Papers, 831 et seq.

" Rush, according to his instruction, made two successive proposals to the British Government upon impressment—one the 18th of April and the other the 20th of June last. The first was to restrict reciprocally the naturalization of sailors, the other was totally to exclude each other's seamen from the respective services, whether in public or in merchant vessels, with a positive stipulation against the impressment of men in any case. The British Government, in the first instance, rejected both, but afterwards, on the 13th of August, Castlereagh intimated to Rush, as a suggestion of his own, upon which he had not consulted the other members of the cabinet, that the second proposition might be accepted with two modifications—one, that either party may withdraw from the engagement of the stipulation after three or six months' notice, as in the agreement concerning armaments on the Lakes; the other, that if a British officer, after entering an American vessel for purposes admitted to be lawful, should find a seaman there whom he should suspect to be English, he should be authorized to make a record or procès verbal of the fact, that it may be brought to the knowledge of the American Government, though not to take the man. The deliberation of this day was, whether Messrs. Gallatin and Rush should be instructed to agree to these modifications or not. Strong objections were urged against them both, particularly by Mr. Calhoun. Mr. Crawford inclined to accede to them both, and the President [Monroe] inclined to the same. Mr. Wirt, without expressing himself very decidedly, thought like the President. My own greatest objections were against the proposal as made by ourselves, to which I have always been utterly averse, thinking it an illiberal engagement. . . . As, however, we made the proposal, we must abide by it, if accepted; but its own character may justly make us scrupulous against accepting any modifications which render it still more exceptionable." . . . On the next day " the question upon Lord Castlereagh's proposed modifications to our proposal for abolishing impressment from our vessels on the high seas was again resumed, and argued with much earnestness—Crawford and Wirt adhering to their opinions, Calhoun and I to ours. The President ultimately found a middle term, upon which he concluded, after expressing his regret that he was obliged to decide between us, equally divided in opinion as we were. He determined to reject the second modification; first, because it implied that the boarding officer should have the power of mustering the crew of an American vessel and passing them individually under his inspection; and, secondly, because it implied a suspicion that we should not faithfully and sincerely carry our own laws into execution." . . . "He was convinced that if the British Government once brought themselves to contract the engagement not to take men from our ships, though it should be only for a year, they would never resort to the practice again".

4 J. Q. Adams's Memoirs, 146–149.

"As little foundation is there for the inference drawn by Mr. Anduaga from the decree of the district judge admiting the *Palmyra* to have been lawfully commissioned as a privateer, but detaining for trial the portion of her crew charged with the robbery from the *Coquette*, that it sanctions the right of search against which the United States have so long and so constantly protested. For in the first place the United States have never disputed the belligerent right of search, as recognized and universally practiced conformably to the laws of nations. They have disputed the right of belligerents, under colour of the right of search for contraband of war, to seize and carry away men, at the discretion of the boarding officer, without trial and without appeal; men, not as contraband of war or belonging to the enemy, but as subjects, real or pretended, of the belligerent himself, and to be used by him against his enemy. It is the fraudulent abuse of the right of search for purposes never recognized or admitted by the laws of nations; purposes in their practical operation of the deepest oppression and most crying injustice, that the United States have resisted and will resist, and which warns them against assenting to the extension in time of peace, of a right which experience has shown to be liable to such gross perversion in time of war."

Mr. Adams, Sec. of State, to Mr. Nelson, min. to Spain, April 28, 1823, MS. Inst. U. States Min. IX. 183, 212.

In reference to certain alleged instances of impressment in 1828, Mr. Clay, Secretary of State, in a letter of January 26, 1829, to Mr. Barbour, minister to England, said: "If these proceedings have had the sanction of the British Government, you will inform it that the American Government can not tolerate them; that, if persisted in, they will be opposed by the United States; and that the British Government must be answerable for all the consequences, whatever they may be, which may flow from perseverance in a practice utterly irreconcilable with the sovereign rights of the United States. If these proceedings have taken place without the sanction of the British Government, you will demand the punishment of the several British naval officers at whose instance they occurred, and the immediate adoption of efficacious measures to guard the navigation of the United States against the occurrence of similar irregularities."

> Mr. Clay, Sec. of State, to Mr. Barbour, min. to England, Jan. 26, 1829, MS. Inst. U. States Ministers, XII. 186.
>
> As to certain cases of impressment subsequent to the treaty of Ghent, see House Doc. 50, 19 Cong. 2 sess.; Am. St. Pap. For. Rel. VI. 368.

" The pretension set up by the British commander of his right to interfere " [in impressing from a United States vessel] " because the seamen claimed to be British is altogether inadmissible. It is understood that, in time of peace, British seamen are free, under their own laws, to engage in the foreign merchant service; but if it were otherwise, and if such service were forbidden by the laws of England, it can never be admitted that the commander of a British ship-of-war has authority to enforce the municipal law of Great Britain on board a foreign vessel, and within a foreign jurisdiction."

> Mr. Forsyth, Sec. of State, to Mr. Vail, July 31, 1834, MS. Inst. Gr. Brit. XIV. 170.
>
> Seamen on board vessels of the United States are protected by their flag from impressment, whether in foreign ports or on the high seas. (Mr. Forsyth, Sec. of State, to Mr. Stevenson, Jan. 20, 1837, MS. Inst. Gr. Br. XIV. 234.)

The question of impressment was the subject of an exchange of notes between Mr. Webster and Lord Ashburton, in the negotiations leading up to the conclusion of the treaty of August 9, 1842. In this correspondence Mr. Webster announced that the American Government was " prepared to say that the practice of impressing seamen from American vessels can not hereafter be allowed to take place; " that the practice was founded on principles which the United States did not recognize, and was " invariably attended by consequences so unjust, so injurious, and of such formidable magnitude, as can not be submitted to," and that " in future in every regularly documented American merchant ship the crew who navigate it will find their protection in the flag which is over them."

Lord Ashburton replied that he had " much reason to hope that a satisfactory arrangement " respecting the question might be made, " so as to set at rest all apprehension and anxiety."

> Mr. Webster, Sec. of State, to Lord Ashburton, Brit. min., Aug. 8, 1842; Lord Ashburton to Mr. Webster, Aug. 9, 1842, Webster's Works, VI. 318, 326.
>
> See, also, Curtis's Life of Webster, II. 124.

" Every merchant vessel on the seas is rightfully considered as part of the territory of the country to which it belongs. The entry, therefore, into such vessel, being neutral, by a belligerent, is an act of force, and is, *prima facie*, a wrong, a trespass, which can be justified only when done for some purpose allowed to form a sufficient justification by the law of nations. But a British cruiser enters an American merchant vessel in order to take therefrom supposed British subjects; offering no justification, therefor, under the law of nations, but claiming the right under the law of England respecting the King's prerogative. This can not be defended. English soil, English territory, English jurisdiction, is the appropriate sphere for the operation of English law. The ocean is the sphere of the law of nations; and any merchant vessel on the seas is by that law under the protection of the laws of her own nation, and may claim immunity, unless in cases in which that law allows her to be entered or visited."

Mr. Webster, Sec. of State, to Lord Ashburton, Aug. 8, 1842, 6 Webster's Works, 318, 320.

" The impressment of seamen from merchant vessels of this country by British cruisers, although not practiced in time of peace, and therefore not at present a productive cause of difference and irritation, has, nevertheless, hitherto been so prominent a topic of controversy, and is so likely to bring on renewed contentions at the first breaking out of a European war, that it has been thought the part of wisdom now to take it into serious and earnest consideration. The letter from the Secretary of State to the British minister explains the grounds which the government has assumed, and the principles which it means to uphold. For the defense of these grounds, and the maintenance of these principles, the most perfect reliance is placed on the intelligence of the American people, and on their firmness and patriotism, in whatever touches the honor of the country, or its great and essential interest."

President Tyler's message, transmitting the Treaty of Washington to the Senate, Aug. 11, 1842, 6 Webster's Works, 326.

"All that the Federal States Government can urge is that we did much the same thing ourselves before the war of 1812, when we stopped American ships and took out of them seamen whom we claimed as British. In point of fact it was not the same thing, for we merely asserted, on the part of the Crown, a right to the services of our own sailors; we imputed to the ships in which those sailors might be found no breach of neutrality, and consequently we had no right to take them before a Prize Court, and therefore, if the right was to be exercised at all, it was necessary that it should be exercised by our naval officers. But we do not undertake to justify all our acts half a century ago. The law of impressment has been abolished, and it is very certain that during the last fifty years nothing of the kind has been attempted or even imagined by England. The law of nations is deduced from the actual practice of nations, and as we during our last war (though sorely in need of sailors) did not revive our claim to take our sailors out of American ships, the claim must be held to have been conclusively abandoned."

> The Quarterly Review, Jan. 1862, art. 8, vol. 111, p. 269, in relation to the case of *The Trent.*

" The truth is that this practice [of impressment] never rested upon any principle of the law of nations at all, but upon a principle of municipal law at variance with the law of nations. That principle was the doctrine of the inalienable allegiance of subjects to their sovereign. . . . The inference was that the sovereign had a municipal right to claim the persons and services of his subjects wherever they could be found, and that, in particular, seamen were not protected by a neutral flag and had no right to serve a neutral power without the King's license. . . . He might therefore take them, under the old municipal theory of allegiance, wherever they could be found. But by the modern conceptions of the law of nations territorial independence is the more powerful principle of the two. Within the territorial limits or under the flag of another state, every foreign sovereignty becomes subject. . . . By the law of prize, a captor has no property in a captured vessel or her cargo until the rightfulness of the seizure has been decided by a court administering the law of nations; but as the seizure of British seamen in foreign ships on their allegiance to King George was a municipal right and not a right under the law of nations, it was never brought before the courts of admiralty at all. They had no jurisdiction in the matter."

> Edinburgh Review, Jan. 1862, art. 10, vol. 115, p. 271.

" But, though Earl Russell, in his note of the 3d of December, 1861, in making the demand for the liberation of the Commissioners, places it on no specific ground, Mr. Seward might be deemed fully justified by M. Thouvenel's reference, in his dispatch to the French minister at Washington, of the same date, to the previously declared sentiments of the American Government, and by the approbation with which the intervention based on that statement was received in London, to infer from the British demand not only an assimilation to the continental law of contraband, subsequently adopted by them in terms, but as a consequence thereof, an abandonment of any pretension to take persons, whether English subjects or others, from neutral vessels, on any pretext whatever, not within the conceded exception of military persons in the actual service of the enemy."

> Lawrence's Wheaton (1863), 217, 218, on the case of *The Trent.*

IV. *NATIONALITY OF VESSELS.*

1. EVIDENCE OF THE FLAG.

§ 321.

A national flag is *prima facie* evidence, on the high seas, that the nationality of the ship carrying it corresponds to that of the flag. It is true that when there is probable ground to believe that the flag is assumed for piratical purposes, this will excuse the arrest and search of the vessel. But unless there be such probable cause the vessel must be assumed by foreign cruisers to be entitled to carry the flag she flies.

" § 426. Maritime nations are free to fix the conditions on which they will recognize the nationality of foreign vessels in waters dependent upon their own territory; but the mutual interests of nations require that those conditions should not be of such a nature as to interfere with freedom of commerce and of navigation.

" In all cases the vessel should be furnished with proof of its nationality by means of authentic documents, or of certain distinctive signs which enable one to tell at first sight to what nation it belongs.

" § 427. The flag is the visible sign of the national character of a ship. Each state has its own colors, under which its nationals sail and which can not be used without its permission.

" The assumption of the flag of a foreign state without its authorization is considered as a violation of international law, as a device both fraudulent and injurious to the honor of such state. Both the state whose flag is wrongfully used and that in regard to which the use of the false flag is made have the right to demand the punishment of the guilty persons and, according to circumstances, to punish them themselves. . . .

" § 428. The flag alone does not suffice to prove the nationality of the ship; it offers too great facilities for abuse and usurpations. In order to have a more certain means of control, maritime nations have agreed that every merchant ship must be provided with papers or sea letters, which the captain is bound to produce whenever it is legitimately required. The ship's papers most usually consist of an act indicating the signal of the ship, its dimensions, its name, the details of its construction; the act authorizing the vessel to bear the national flag; a crew list mentioning the names and nationality of the sailors; and a bill of sale or of property and a passport or patent of navigation."

Calvo, Droit Int. (5th ed.), I. §§ 426–429.

" It is the province of each country to determine for itself the conditions for the use of its flag upon its vessels, and the United States' rule is that vessels *bona fide* owned by citizens of the United States are entitled, when abroad, to carry the flag of the United States irrespective of the question of the papers they may have on board."

> Mr. Bayard, Sec. of State, to Mr. Tree, min. to Belgium, Dec. 19, 1887, For. Rel. 1888, I. 27, 28.

" With reference to your note of the 14th ultimo, inquiring whether it would be possible for this Government to adopt any measures for preventing vessels sold to and owned by American citizens from continuing to sail under the British flag, I have the honor to inform you that the Secretary of the Treasury, to whom the matter was referred, reports that there does not seem to be any legislation of the United States bearing upon the subject, and that in the absence of such legislation it would not be practicable for the executive or judicial branch of this Government to intervene with a view to the prevention of transactions of the character mentioned in your note."

> Mr. Bayard, Sec. of State, to Sir L. S. S. West, Brit. min., March 6, 1888, For. Rel. I. 789–790.

It having been stated that the Norwegian steamship *Gyller*, chartered by an American company and engaged in the regular carrying trade between Galveston, Cuba, Porto Rico, and other West India Islands, was, in August, 1896, after leaving Cienfuegos, and at a point 10 miles from the Cuban coast, fired on with solid shot by a Spanish man-of-war, and afterwards boarded by armed forces, presumably in search of contraband of war, the Department of State said: " The vessel being under the Norwegian flag, this Government could not make the incident a subject of diplomatic complaint. In international law the flag covers the cargo, even if the vessel be under charter to citizens or subjects of another nation."

> Mr. Olney, Sec. of State, to Mr. Reymershoffer, Oct. 24, 1896, 213 MS. Dom. Let. 384.

2. REGISTRY.

§ 322.

" Registered vessels, which by sale (this is understood to mean a voluntary sale made by the American owner) become the property of foreigners, can never afterwards be registered, even tho' they should be again transferred to their former owners, or any other American citizen. This is expressly prohibited by the act of 27th of June, 1797. But registered vessels which, having been seized or captured and condemned, become the property of foreigners, are not in those cases absolutely disqualified from being registered anew, the . . . act declaring that if the owner or owners, at the time of seizure or capture, shall regain a property in such vessels, by purchase or otherwise, they shall not be debarred from claiming and receiving new registers for the same, as they might or could have done if that act had not been passed."

> Circular of the Comptroller of the Treasury, Sept. 10, 1803, transmitted by Mr. Madison, Sec. of State, to U. S. consuls and commercial agents, Oct. 1, 1803, 1 MS. Desp. to Consuls, 185, 186.

A contract in fraud of the positive laws and public policy of the United States, which exclude an alien from having any interest in an American registered vessel, by way of trust, confidence, or otherwise, will not be enforced.

> Duncanson v. McLure (1804), supreme court of Pennsylvania, 4 Dallas, 308; overruling Murgatroyd v. Crawford, 3 Dallas, 491.

It was held that an American-registered vessel partly sold while at sea by her American owners to other Americans did not forfeit her privileges as a registered vessel and become liable to alien dues, though the language of section 14 of the registry act might, if literally construed, work such a result. To require a new registration immediately after a sale under such circumstances would be to require an impossibility, since, under the registry act, it is necessary in order to obtain a new register to produce the old one, which the vessel is required to carry. It could not have been the intention of Congress to penalize the sale of a ship at sea.

> Willing v. United States (1804), 4 Dallas, 374, and appendix, xxxiv. See, to the same effect, United States v. Willings (1807), 4 Cranch, 48.

The benefit of the registry of an American vessel is lost to the owner during his residence in a foreign country, but upon his return to this country the disability ceases; nor does the fact that during the foreign residence of the owner the vessel carried a foreign flag work any divestiture of title, nor render the disability perpetual.

> Wirt, At. Gen. (1821), 1 Op. 523.

When an American vessel is sold abroad to an American citizen, not only the required bill of sale, reciting at length the certificate of registry, but also her register and other papers should accompany her, to be delivered up only upon her return to the United States, on application being made for her to be registered anew.

> Mr. Calhoun, Sec. of State, to Mr. Dorr, consul at Valparaiso, Feb. 26, 1845, 11 MS. Desp. to Consuls, 344.
>
> See, also, Mr. Upshur, Sec. of State, to Mr. Edwards, consul at Buenos Ayres, Dec. 19, 1843, 11 MS. Desp. to Consuls, 198.

Section 14 of the act of December 31, 1792, which provided that where a registered vessel was sold, in whole or in part, to a citizen of the United States, her former registry should be delivered up and a new registry obtained, seemed not to have contemplated the sale of American vessels beyond the limits of the United States. But, between the years 1792 and 1803, in consequence of the wars between European powers, growing out of the French Revolution, the United States had, to a considerable extent, become the carriers for the whole world. Under these circumstances, Congress deemed it necessary to provide expressly for the sale of American vessels to American citizens in all foreign countries; and by section 3 of the act of March 2, 1803, it was declared that where a registered vessel outside the United States was transferred, in whole or in part, to a citizen of the United States, such vessel, " on her first arrival in the United States thereafter," should be entitled to all the privileges of a vessel of the United States. This act did not require the vessel to return immediately after the sale, but recognized her, whenever she might return, as an American vessel. It was not intended to confer on consuls of the United States the power to decide whether an American citizen, who had lawfully purchased such a vessel in a foreign country, should or should not be compelled to send her immediately to the United States. The citizen, by such purchase, acquired rights which could not be divested by any officer of the Government, and the bill of sale, properly authenticated and reciting at length the original certificate of registry, became the substitute on board the vessel for that certificate until her " first arrival in the United States thereafter."

> Mr. Buchanan, Sec. of State, to Mr. Parks, consul at Rio de Janeiro, May 26, 1847, 13 MS. Desp. to Consuls, 1.
>
> Mr. Buchanan stated in the course of his instructions that, as the question from its nature partly belonged to the Treasury Department, he had consulted the head of that Department, who concurred with him in the opinions which he had expressed.
>
> See, to the same effect, circular of the Comptroller of the Treasury, Sept. 10, 1803, transmitted by Mr. Madison, Sec. of State, to United States consuls and commercial agents, Oct. 1, 1803, 1 MS. Desp. to Consuls, 185, cited supra.

" It is the opinion of this Department that by virtue of the act of Congress of June 17, 1864 (Stat. at Large, vol. 13, page 134), which, speaking of licensed and enrolled vessels, enacts that ' such boat, sloop or vessel shall be in every other respect liable to the rules, regulations and penalties now in force relating to registered and licensed vessels,' such vessels are placed on the same footing as registered vessels in the matter of their duties and liabilities to consular supervision and the payment of consular fees."

> Mr. J. C. B. Davis, Assistant Sec., to Mr. Dart, consul at Montreal, Oct. 22, 1869, 55 MS. Desp. to Consuls, 523.

A vessel constructed of materials bought and made abroad, though they are put together in the United States, is not " built " in the

United States in the sense of section 4132, Revised Statutes, as interpreted by the Treasury Department, and is not entitled to an American register.

Mr. Frelinghuysen, Sec. of State, to Mr. Stevens, min. to Sweden & Norway, Nov. 23, 1882, MS. Inst. Sw. & Nor. XV. 70.

The certificate of a vessel's registry and proof that she carried the American flag establish a prima facie case of proper registry under the laws of the United States and of the nationality of the vessel and her owners.

St. Clair *v.* United States (1894), 154 U. S. 134, 151.

The *Scipio*, a foreign-built steamship purchased by the Navy Department for use in the war with Spain, and subsequently sold to and owned by an American citizen, is not entitled to registry under the laws of the United States.

The regulation of commerce and navigation being entirely within the control of Congress, there is no authority for an Executive Department to make or enforce rules or regulations relative to the registry of vessels or kindred matters connected with such subjects.

Griggs, Atty. Gen., Aug. 11, 1899, 22 Op. 566.

The captain of the port of Manila had no authority to issue a provisional register to a foreign-built vessel owned by an American citizen.

Mr. Adee, Second Assistant Sec. of State, to Mr. Moseley, jr., No. 22, Oct. 21, 1899, 169 MS. Inst. Consuls, 520.

Under section 4132, Revised Statutes, a vessel lawfully condemned and sold as prize of war to an American citizen is entitled to an American registry, and this right is not lost by the subsequent reversal of the decree of condemnation by the Supreme Court of the United States.

Griggs, At. Gen. (Feb. 17, 1900), 23 Op. 29, distinguishing this case from that involved in the opinion of December 14, 1840, 3 Op. 606.

Section 9 of the act of April 12, 1900 (31 Stat. 79), providing for the nationalization of all vessels owned by the inhabitants of Porto Rico on April 11, 1899, places such vessels on the same footing as other American vessels and confers upon them the benefits of the act of June 26, 1884, in regard to consular services.

Griggs, At. Gen. (March 5, 1901), 23 Op. 414.

A British vessel going from San Francisco to Guam is not subject
to the penalties provided in section 4347, Revised Statutes, as amended.

> Decision No. 14, Department of Commerce and Labor, March 14, 1904,
> based on an opinion of Knox, At. Gen., March 10, 1904.

3. AMERICAN-OWNED FOREIGN-BUILT VESSELS.

(1) RIGHT OF PROTECTION.

§ 323.

" The persons and property of our citizens are entitled to the protection of our government in all places where they may lawfully go.
No laws forbid a merchant to buy, own, and use a *foreign-built* vessel.
She is, then, his lawful property, and entitled to the protection of his
nation whenever he is lawfully using her.

" The laws, indeed, for the encouragement of shipbuilding, have
given to home-built vessels the exclusive privilege of being registered
and paying lighter duties. To this privilege, therefore, the foreign-
built vessel, though owned at home, does not pretend. But the laws
have not said that they withdraw their protection from the foreign-
built vessel. To this protection, then, she retains her title, notwithstanding the preference given to the home-built vessel as to duties. It
would be hard, indeed, because the law has given one valuable right
to home-built vessels, to infer that it had taken away all rights from
those foreign built."

> Opinion of Mr. Jefferson, Sec. of State, May 3, 1793, 7 Jeff. Works, 624.

"As our citizens are free to purchase and use *foreign-built vessels*,
and these like all their other lawful property are entitled to the protection of their government, passports will be issued to them as freely
as to *home-built* vessels. This is strictly within our treaties, the letter
of which as well as their spirit authorizes passports to all vessels
belonging to citizens of the United States. Our laws, indeed, indulge
home-built vessels with the payment of lower tonnage, and to evidence
their right to this, permit them alone to take out registers from our
own offices; but they do not exclude foreign-built vessels owned by
our citizens from any other right."

> Mr. Jefferson, Sec. of State, to Mr. Pinckney, min to England, May 7, 1793,
> MS. Inst. U. States Ministers, I. 278.

" The laws do not authorize vessels engaged in a foreign voyage to
be navigated as vessels of the United States without a register, nor do
they recognize as such vessels which belong wholly or in part to
citizens of the United States who usually reside in a foreign country,

unless they be consuls, or agents for and partners in a house of trade consisting of citizens of and actually carrying on trade in the United States."

Mr. Forsyth, Sec. of State, to Mr. Shoemaker, consul at Matanzas, June 9, 1836, 8 MS. Desp. to Consuls, 106.

See, also, Mr. Upshur, Sec. of State, to Mr. Edwards, consul at Buenos Ayres, Dec. 19, 1843, 11 Desp. to Consuls, 198.

" The statutes of the United States recognize the following classes of sea-going vessels, namely:

" 1. Ships built in the United States, wholly owned by citizens thereof, employed in foreign commerce, which are entitled to be registered, and as such to enjoy all the rights and privileges conferred by any law on ships of the United States. (Act of December 31, 1792, 1 Stat. at L. 287.)

" Such a ship, of course, loses her privileges as a registered ship, in being sold to a foreigner, and is thereafter treated forever as foreign-built, even though she be purchased back by the original owner or any other citizen of the United States. (See Opinion of March 16, 1854, *ante*, 383.)

" 2. Vessels built in the United States, and wholly owned by citizens thereof, employed in the coasting trade or fisheries, which are entitled to be enrolled and licensed as such, and to enjoy all the privileges, in their particular employment, conferred by law on vessels of the United States. (Act of February 18, 1793, 1 Stat. at L. 305.)

" 3. Ships built in the United States, but owned wholly or in part by foreigners, which are entitled to be recorded, but not in general to be registered, or enrolled, and licensed. (Act of December 31, 1792, *ubi supra*.)

" 4. Ships not built in the United States, but owned by citizens thereof: of which more in the sequel.

" 5. Ships built out of the United States and not owned by citizens thereof.

" 6. Special provisions exist, in regard to the steamboats belonging to companies engaged in the transportation of ocean mails, as well as in regard to those navigating the bays and rivers of the country; which provisions relax the registry or enrollment laws, so as to admit ownership, under certain regulations, of persons not citizens of the United States.

" The registry and enrollment statutes of the United States are in imitation of those of Great Britain *in pari materia*, and for the same ob;ects, namely, to promote the construction and ownership of ships in the country, and to facilitate the execution of local or public law. They are classified with reference to the business they may pursue; their character is authenticated; and they enjoy various advantages, from which other vessels are wholly excluded, or to which these are partially admitted, according to the interests and policy of the Government. (Abbott on Shipping, p. 58.)

" It is with vessels of the fourth of the above classes, that we have more immediate concern.

" It is observable, in the first place, that there is nothing in the statutes to *require* a vessel to be registered or enrolled. She is entitled to registry or enrollment, under certain circumstances, and, receiving it, she thereupon is admitted to certain duties and obligations. But, if owned by a citizen of the United States, she is American property, and possessed of all the general rights of any property of an American.

" Secondly, the register or enrollment, or other custom-house document, such as sea-letter, is *prima facie* evidence only, as to the ownership of a ship, in some cases, but conclusive in none. The law even concedes the possibility of the register or enrollment existing in the name of one person, whilst the property is really in another. Property in a ship is a matter *in pais*, to be proved as fact by competent testimony like any other fact. (United States *v.* Pirates, 5 Wheaton, 187, 199; United States *v.* Amedy, 11 Wheaton, 409; United States *v.* Jones, 3 Wash. C. C. R. 209; Taggart *v.* Loring, 16 Mass. 336; Wendover *v.* Hogeboom, 7 Johnson, 308; Bass *v.* Steele, 3 Wash. C. C. R. 381; Leonard *v.* Huntington, 15 Johnson, 298; Ligon *v.* New Orleans Navigation Company, 7 Martin's R. (N. S.) 678; Brooks *v.* Bondsey, 17 Pickering, 441.) . . .

" This Government has not, as yet, followed the example of that of Great Britain, so far as to admit foreign-built vessels to registry; but such vessels may be lawfully owned by Americans.

" Upon full consideration, therefore, of all the relations of the subject, there remains no doubt, in my mind, as to the right of a citizen of the United States to purchase a foreign ship of a belligerent power, and this, anywhere, at home or abroad, in a belligerent port, or a neutral port, or even upon the high seas, provided the purchase be made *bona fide*, and the property be passed absolutely and without reserve; and the ship so purchased becomes entitled to bear the flag and receive the protection of the United States."

Mr. Cushing, At. Gen. (Aug. 7, 1854), 6 Op. 638, 647–652.

" In the opinion of this Department a foreign vessel, if purchased *in good faith* by a citizen of the United States, and by him taken into possession, becomes American property, and is entitled to protection as such, although a special act of Congress would be necessary to enable her to obtain a register.

"In the case of a fradulent sale, or fictitious transfer, no property, of course, can pass, and the sale might be disregarded or set aside should it ever become the subject of legal investigation. In every case the parties interested must assume the risk of such an investigation."

Mr. Cass, Sec. of State, to Mr. Cobb, Sec. of Treasury, June 13, 1859, 50 MS. Dom. Let. 387.

"I acknowledge the receipt of your despatch number 40, of January 20th, in relation to the transfer, actual or nominal, of Greek vessels to citizens of the United States, with an apparent view to the employment of such vessels under the American flag, in commerce with Turkish ports, which would be closed to them under the Greek flag. Your suggestions in respect to the cautious scrutiny with which the good faith of such transactions should be examined, and the impropriety of giving any sanction to transactions having for their object the contravening a public measure instituted by a government with which the United States are at peace, are approved.

"In reply to the application, for instructions, of our consul at the Piræus, my predecessor on the 20th ultimo directed his attention to the provisions of the act of Congress of June 28th, 1864 (13 Stat. 201, 202) 'that officers of vessels of the United States shall in all cases be citizens of the United States;' also to section 8 of the act of March 3, 1813 (2 Stat. 810), imposing upon the owner of a vessel a penalty of $500 for each person unlawfully employed in any one voyage. A compliance with the provisions in regard to officers appears to be essential to entitle the ship to the character of a vessel of the United States. Certainly the absence of such officers is a very significant indication not likely to be overlooked by belligerents exercising the right of visit and examination, or other parties interested in testing the *bona fides* of the ostensible character of the ship.

"It is proper that I should also direct your attention to the first and second sections of the act of December 31, 1792. (1 Stat. 285.) The first provides that registered vessels and *no other* (except those duly qualified for carrying on the coasting trade or fisheries) shall be denominated and deemed vessels of the United States, entitled to the benefit and privileges appertaining to such ships or vessels. The second denies a register to vessels of foreign build, 'if owned in whole or in part by any citizen of the United States who usually resides in a foreign country, during the continuance of such residence, unless such citizen be in the capacity of a consul of the United States or an agent for, and a partner in some house of trade consisting of citizens of the said States actually carrying on trade within the said States.' These provisions evince the jealous care of Congress to discriminate between vessels merely owned by citizens and those which are entitled to the national character of 'vessels of the United States.' Such property is entitled, in a certain sense, to the protection of this Government, as in case of arbitrary seizure; but this is something quite different from the vessels being entitled to the *privileges* which foreign nations have, by treaty or otherwise, accorded to vessels of the United States having the requisite documents to establish their national character.

"The regulations of the Treasury Department, in respect to the authentication of the ownership of foreign-built vessels in certain cases, by collectors of the customs, which have been followed by this Department in its instructions to consuls, have this distinction clearly in view. It concerns the good faith of this Government and its exemption from embarrassing complications that citizens applying for the authentication of their purchase of unregistered vessels should be made distinctly aware of the limited effect of such a document."

> Mr. Washburne, Sec. of State, to Mr. Tuckerman, min. to Greece, March 8, 1869, MS. Inst. Greece, I. 15.

"The provisions of the navigation laws are commercial in their character, and intended mainly for the protection of American commerce and property upon the high seas. The vessel in question is a British-built vessel, had a British register, and, upon the facts as they appear before me, has now been sold to an American citizen and is his property. By the sale to an American citizen she has forfeited her British registry, as I understand the British law upon that subject.

"The inquiry is, therefore: Is a foreign-built vessel, owned entirely by American citizens, and having no foreign registry, entitled to carry the American flag?

"I am of opinion that such vessel *is* entitled to carry the American flag, and in this way to assert her own nationality and her claim upon the American Government for protection.

"The haste in which I am required to answer this question prevents me from entering into any reasoning on the subject. I refer, however, to an opinion of Attorney-General Cushing upon the subject (6 Op. 638), and also to an opinion of Mr. Beaman, of this Department, approved by Attorney-General Akerman January 5, 1872."

> Devens, At. Gen., June 19, 1880, 16 Op. 533.
> The opinion of Mr. Beaman, approved by Attorney-General Akerman, Jan. 5, 1872, was given by Mr. Beaman in his official capacity as Examiner of Claims, or Solicitor, for the Department of State, a post which he then held. The opinion is as follows:

"I have the honor to state to you that I have carefully considered the questions presented for your opinion by Hon. Hamilton Fish, Secretary of State, in his letter to you of the 20th of November last, which letter was referred by you to me, with the direction that I should prepare an opinion on the same, and I beg to report the following as my opinion:

"The first question submitted by the Secretary of State is as follows:

"Is a foreign-built vessel, not a registered vessel of the United States, but wholly owned by citizens of the United States, entitled to bear the flag of the United States?'

"And to this question my answer is yes.

"I do not find that any statute law of the United States in any way declares what vessels shall or what vessels shall not carry the flag of the United States; but the so-called navigation laws declare, to speak generally, that only vessels built in the United States and owned by citizens of the United States can be registered as vessels of the United States, and further, that no other than registered vessels shall be denominated and deemed ships or vessels of the United States, entitled to the benefits and privileges appertaining to such ships or vessels. (See act of 31st Dec., 1792, 1 Stat. L. p. 287.)

"The benefits and privileges reserved by the act above cited to registered vessels of the United States do not, in my opinion, restrict the right to carry the flag of the United States, but refer particularly to certain commercial benefits and privileges which, by the various laws of the United States, are given to registered vessels of the United States; that is, to vessels built in the United States, in order that shipbuilding in the United States may be encouraged.

"While the navigation laws give such commercial privileges to vessels built in the United States, they in no way forbid citizens of the United States to own vessels built in other countries, nor is the protection of the United States in any way denied to such foreign-built vessels if they are owned by citizens of the United States.

"So held Mr. Cushing, in 1854 (6 Op. 638), and so held Mr. Talbot, Acting Attorney-General, on August 31, 1870. (See opinion, not printed.) The question submitted to Mr. Cushing by Mr. Marcy, referred directly to the right of a foreign-built vessel owned by citizens of the United States to carry the flag of the United States, and Mr. Cushing replied: 'Upon full consideration, therefore, of all the relations of the subject, there remains no doubt in my mind as to the right of a citizen of the United States to purchase a foreign ship of a belligerent power, and this anywhere, at home or abroad, in a belligerent port or a neutral port, or even upon the high seas, provided the purchase be made *bona fide*, and the property be passed absolutely and without reserve, and the ship so purchased becomes entitled to bear the flag and receive the protection of the United States.'

"Mr. Cushing's opinion is in terms limited to vessels purchased from belligerents, but if foreign-built vessels so purchased by citizens of the United States are entitled to the protection of the United States, still more are vessels purchased from foreign nations in time of peace entitled to such protection.

"You will notice that Mr. Cushing directly answers the first question of Mr. Fish, for he declares that the ship so purchased becomes entitled to bear the flag of the United States, and I should now simply refer to this opinion as an answer to the question submitted by Mr. Fish had not Mr. Talbot in a certain way dissented therefrom.

" In answer to questions submitted to him by Mr. Creswell, Postmaster-General, Mr. Talbot says : ' I have no hesitation in giving my opinion that this class of property, namely, vessels once foreign and now owned by citizens of the United States, are, in the words of your question, entitled to the protection of the Government of this country ; the word protection here being used in its primitive sense, and signifying protection from depredation or injury by foreign governments or powers.' So far he agrees with Mr. Cushing, but farther on he says : ' I refrain from expressing concurrence with Mr. Cushing's opinion that such vessels are entitled to bear the flag of the United States. While it might be true in a certain sense, yet I hesitate to assent to it as a truth having practical force. I doubt the propriety of declaring a vessel entitled to bear the flag of a nation when she can have on board no document known to international law as witnessing that title, and I apprehend belligerent cruisers upon the sea and prize courts upon the shore would give effect to this doubt.'

" Thus Mr. Talbot agrees with Mr. Cushing that any ship owned by citizens of the United States is entitled to the protection of the United States, but while Mr. Cushing would give to any such ship the right to carry the flag of the United States, Mr. Talbot hesitates to give the right to carry that flag to any ship not registered, that is, to speak generally, to any foreign-built ship. Mr. Cushing regards the bill of sale as the true evidence of American ownership, the one best known to international law, while Mr. Talbot regards the register as the only document recognized by prize courts.

" I can not think that Mr. Talbot was right. A flag is but the outward symbol which a ship carries to show her nationality, and this nationality is recognized by the law of nations as determined by the nationality of her owners. A ship's flag, therefore, should properly correspond with her actual ownership. Frequently in prize courts questions arise as to the ownership of a certain vessel, but when that question is determined the nationality of the ship is determined and the court practically say, this vessel is owned by citizens of a certain country, she is entitled to the protection of that country, she should carry the flag of that country, and must be condemned or released as the property of citizens of that country.

" The court may examine various papers and witnesses to ascertain the true ownership, and when there is a register that document may be among these papers, but in the words of Lord Stowell, ' a bill of sale is the proper title to which the maritime courts of all countries would look. It is the universal instrument of the transfer of ships in the usage of all maritime countries.' (The Sisters, 5 C. Rob. 155 ; see 3 Kent's Com. 130.)

" The flag, then, the outward symbol of ownership, should properly correspond with the bill of sale, the universal instrument of the actual ownership of a vessel.

" So has the flag come to be regarded as the outward symbol of nationality that even in solemn treaties it is spoken of as if it were the conclusive evidence of such nationality, and in this way the word flag is used in the rules laid down in the declaration of Paris, for example :

" The 2d article provides that the neutral flag (*le pavillon neutre*) covers enemy's goods, with the exception of contraband of war.

" And again, the third article provides that neutral goods, with the exception of contraband of war, are not liable to capture under the enemy's flag (*sous pavillon ennemi*).

"These rules release neutral goods in an enemy's ship in certain cases, but still the ship may be condemned because she carries the enemy's flag, that is, because she is owned by citizens of an enemy's country, and this irrespective of the fact that she was built in another country.

"If, then, vessels must be protected and may be condemned because they are owned by citizens of the United States, certainly they must not, except by express statute, be held as forbidden to carry the flag of the United States, which is but the sign they show to give notice that they are entitled to that protection. Without doubt Congress could have forbidden any foreign-built ship to carry the flag of the United States, but it has not done so. Previous to 1854, the registry laws of Great Britain were very similar to those of the United States, but the courts of Great Britain held that though a foreign-built ship could not be entitled to a British register, yet if wholly owned by British subjects such a ship was entitled to British protection. (See cases cited by Mr. Cushing.)

"By the act of 17 and 18 Victoria, ch. 104 (Aug. 10, 1854), all ships, wherever built, became entitled to receive a British register, provided they were owned by subjects of Great Britain. Formerly a British register was an evidence that a ship was built and owned in Great Britain; now a British register is simply evidence that a ship is owned in Great Britain and is, as it were, but confirmatory evidence of the bill of sale. Formerly a foreign-built ship could not be registered as a British ship, but was entitled to the protection of the British flag, provided she was owned by British subjects. Now every vessel owned by British subjects can have a British register, and the statute denies the right to use the British flag to any vessel which does not have a British register, that is, which does not have the official evidence that she is owned by British subjects.

"While the British registry law has changed, the United States law remains the same. The British law gives no exclusive privileges to vessels built in Great Britain, but denies the right to carry its flag to any vessel not having an official register as the evidence of her British ownership, while the United States does not deny its flag or protection to any vessel owned by citizens of the United States, but restricts the privileges and benefits of its commerce to those vessels which carry an official register as the evidence that they were built and owned in the United States. A British-built vessel, owned by citizens of the United States, can not be registered either in Great Britain or in the United States; she can not carry the British flag; she is entitled to the protection of the United States; the flag of the United States is but the outward sign that she is entitled to that protection; no statutes forbid her to carry that flag, and without such express statute I can not think that right should be denied her.

"Under the present laws, in my opinion, any vessel wholly owned by citizens of the United States is entitled to carry the flag of the United States.

"I am aware that this opinion might, under existing laws, if generally acted upon, be the source of some embarrassment, for the United States may be called upon to protect a vessel carrying its flag without possessing any official evidence that such vessel is entitled to that protection; but still more embarrassment would seem to me to result from the opinion of Mr. Talbot, should the United States be called upon to protect a vessel owned by citizens of the United States though sailing under a foreign flag.

" I pass on to consider the second question proposed by Mr. Fish, which is as follows:

" ' Which of the below-mentioned acts of Congress are applicable to foreign-built vessels which are not registered vessels of the United States, but which are wholly owned by citizens of the United States?

" 'Act of 28th February, 1803; 2 Stat. L., 203, particularly the 2d and 3d sections. (See Consular Regulations 1870, 212.)

" 'Act of 20th July, 1840; 5 Stat. L., 394. (See Consular Regulations 1870, 217.)

" 'Act of 29th July, 1850; 9 Stat. L., 140, section 6. (See Consular Regulations 1870, 222.)

" 'Act of August 18, 1856; 11 Stat. L., 52, particularly the sections 25 to 28, inclusive. (See Consular Regulations 1870, 239.'

" 'Act of August 5, 1861; 12 Stat. L., 315. (See Consular Regulations 1870, 254.)

" 'Act of February 19, 1862; 12 Stat. L., 340. (See Consular Regulations 1870, 255.)

" 'Act of April 29, 1864; 13 Stat. L., 61. (See Consular Regulations 1870, 262.)

" 'Act of June 28, 1864; 13 Stat. L., 201. (See Consular Regulations 1870, 264.)

" 'Act of June 29, 1870; 16 Stat. L., 169. (See Consular Regulations 1870, 271.)'

" This second inquiry of Mr. Fish refers in the first place to the 2d and 3d sections of the act of 28th February, 1803.

" The 1st section of this act provides what shall be done by the master of any vessel bound on a foreign voyage before a clearance be granted to her, and what he shall do on his arrival at the first port of the United States.

" The 2d section makes it the duty of every master or commander of a ship or vessel belonging to citizens of the United States, who shall sail from any port of the United States, on his arrival at a foreign port, to deposit his register, sea-letter, etc., with the consul, which register, sea-letter, etc., it shall be the duty of the consul to deliver to such master or commander on his producing to him a clearance from the proper officer of the port where the ship or vessel may be.

" The 3d section provides that whenever a ship or vessel belonging to a citizen of the United States shall be sold in a foreign country and her company discharged, or when a seaman or mariner, a citizen of the United States, shall, with his own consent, be discharged in a foreign country, three months' pay over and above the wages which may then be due to all mariners or seamen on board who may be designated as citizens of the United States shall be paid to the United States consul by the master or commander of that vessel.

" In 1831 some question arose as to whether the act of 1803 (particularly the first three sections thereof) was applicable to the mercantile marine of a foreign nation or people on which American seamen were employed or in which American citizens were interested as owners.

" The matter being referred to Mr. Berrien, he wrote to the Secretary of State (2 Op. 448), that in his opinion this act was confined ' to vessels owned by citizens of the United States and constituting a part of her mercantile marine by sailing under her flag.'

" In terms this opinion of Mr. Berrien would make these sections (quoting Mr. Fish) ' applicable to vessels which are not registered vessels of the United States,' but which are wholly owned by citizens of the United States, for, if my opinion before given is correct, such vessels may sail under the flag of the United States and so, in a certain sense, constitute part of her mercantile marine.

" It is not probable, however, that Mr. Berrien particularly considered the question as to whether any foreign-built vessel could carry the flag of the United States, but he evidently was of the opinion that the act of 1803 was confined to vessels that had a United States register, for he interpreted the same according to the terms of the 1st and 2d sections thereof, which sections are evidently confined to vessels that have a United States register. Therefore, while Mr. Berrien confined this act in terms to vessels constituting a part of the mercantile marine of the United States by sailing under her flag, it is evident from the argument he used that so far as he considered the question he regarded the words ' constituting a part of her mercantile marine by sailing under her flag,' as synonymous with the words ' having a United States register.'

" Mr. Berrien must therefore be held to have construed this act as not properly applicable to any vessels that did not have a United States register, and as therefore not applicable to the class of vessels described in the 2d question of Mr. Fish.

" Nor do the 2d and 3d sections of this act seem to me to be applicable to the class of vessels described by Mr. Fish, for although, in my opinion, such vessels are entitled to carry the flag of the United States, yet the 2d section clearly applies only to registered vessels, and though the 3d section, if standing alone, might be considered as applicable to vessels owned by citizens of the United States whether registered or not, yet when taken in connection with the first two sections of the act, I think this third section is more properly to be construed as applicable only to registered vessels of the United States, and therefore as not applicable to foreign-built vessels which are not registered vessels of the United States.

" The 2d inquiry of Mr. Fish refers, in the second place, to the act of 20th July, 1840, which act relates particularly to the shipping and discharge of seamen and to the duties of consuls in relation thereto. This act is in fact in extension of, and supplementary to, the act of 28th February, 1803, already considered, and must be construed like that act as not applicable to the class of vessels described by Mr. Fish, but only to registered vessels of the United States.

" The 2d inquiry of Mr. Fish refers, in the third place, to the 6th section of the act of 29th July, 1850, which section is but an amendment to the 12th section of the act of 20th July, 1840, already considered, and does not alter the construction I have already put upon that act.

" The 2d inquiry of Mr. Fish refers, in the fourth place, to sections 25 to 28, inclusive, of the act of 18th of August, 1856, which act is the general act of that date, to regulate the diplomatic and consular systems of the United States, and as far as sections 25 to 28, inclusive, are concerned is in amendment of the acts of 1803 and 1840, already considered, and like them must be construed as not applicable to the class of vessels described by Mr. Fish.

" The 2d inquiry of Mr. Fish, in the fifth place, refers to the act of 5th of August, 1861, which act declares that American vessels running regularly by weekly or monthy trips, or otherwise, to or between foreign ports shall not be required to pay fees to consuls for more than four trips in a year, anything in the law or regulations respecting consular fees to the contrary notwithstanding.

" In the several acts already considered vessels having a register of the United States are generally described as 'vessels of the United States,' and in this act of August, 1861, the words 'American vessels' are used in the same sense, as appears from the connection of this act with the earlier acts already considered.

" The words 'American vessels' and the words 'vessels of the United States' are in the statutes used interchangeably and perhaps somewhat loosely, and they were so used in the act submitted to Mr. Talbot for his opinion as above stated, but he was unable to give any meaning to the words 'American vessel' which did not imply that they meant a vessel having a United States register, and so the same words must be construed in the act of August 5, 1861.

" The 2d inquiry of Mr. Fish, in the sixth place, refers to the act of the 19th of February, 1862, which in exact terms is particularly applicable to vessels registered, enrolled, or licensed within the United States, the act being entitled 'An act to prohibit the coolie trade by American citizens in American vessels.'

" The 2d inquiry of Mr. Fish, in the seventh place, refers to the act of the 29th of April, 1864, which act is entitled 'An act to provide for the collection of hospital dues from vessels of the United States sold or transferred in foreign ports or waters,' and must be construed, like the acts of 1803 and 1840, relating to the same subject and already considered, as applicable only to registered vessels of the United States.

" The 2d inquiry of Mr. Fish refers, in the eighth place, to the act of 28th of June, 1864, which act repeals that portion of 'An act for the regulation of seamen on board the public and private vessels of the United States,' approved the 3d of March, 1813, which made it not lawful to employ on board any of the public or private vessels of the United States any person or persons, except citizens of the United States, etc. This act, under the construction already given to the words 'vessels of the United States,' is only applicable to registered vessels of the United States.

" The 2d inquiry of Mr. Fish, in the last place, refers to the act of June 29, 1870, which act provides that from the master or owners of every vessel of the United States arriving from a foreign port, or of registered vessels employed in the coasting trade, the sum of forty cents per ton shall be collected by the collectors of customs at the ports of the United States, and for each and every seaman who shall have been employed on said vessel since she last entered at any port of the United States, etc.

" This act in terms so distinctly relates to registered vessels of the United States that it seems to confirm all the constructions I have put upon the acts previously considered, viz, that like this act they are only applicable to 'vessels of the United States,' or 'American vessels;' that is, to registered vessels of the United States.

" I then arrive at this conclusion, that any vessel wholly owned by citizens of the United States is entitled to the protection of the United States, and can carry the flag of the United States, but that none of the acts, or parts of acts, referred to by Mr. Fish are applicable to any vessel that does not have a United States register.

"If this conclusion is right, a vessel owned by citizens of the United States, but not built in the United States, though entitled to its protection, would yet be under no relation thereto or to its consuls, from which that vessel, in a certain way, would be compelled to bear part of the cost of that protection by the payment of the fees due under existing statutes from registered vessels to the collectors, the consuls, and divers other officers of the United States, but she would sail the ocean flying the flag of the United States, entitled to demand protection from the Navy and the consuls of the United States, but yet without any official papers on board from officers of the United States which would present *prima facie* and official evidence that she was entitled to carry that flag and to receive that protection.

"While I have been unable to arrive at any other conclusion than above stated, I have not failed to see the difficulties that might arise, if under existing statutes the citizens of the United States should engage in foreign commerce in foreign-built ships, and I judge that the Secretary of State contemplated that the existing laws might be defective when he asked for your official opinion, so that, 'if necessary, Congress may at the coming session be called on to pass further legislation in the matter.'

"As I interpret the existing statutes, they seem to me to be defective. These defects, however, though existing for now many years, have only recently, by the great commercial changes that have taken place, come to be apparent and of considerable magnitude.

"The navigation act of 1792, on which all the acts hereinbefore considered are based, was enacted when United States citizens were engaged in no commerce which did not contemplate a voyage from and to a part of the United States. At that time England had practically closed her domestic and export commerce to vessels not built and owned in Great Britain. Under these circumstances Congress made laws which practically closed the domestic and export commerce of the United States to any but registered vessels of the United States, and generally enacted that no vessels should be registered as vessels of the United States except they were built in the United States.

"This legislation was doubtless intended to prevent, and did practically prevent, citizens of the United States from owning vessels not built in the United States, but it so prevented them, not by express enactment to that effect, but from the fact that in such vessels United States citizens could not in consequence of that act carry on any commerce with the United States, and no other commerce was open to them.

"To-day, however, the situation has changed, though the United States law remains the same.

"England opens her ports to the vessels of all nations, but of greater importance than this, China and Japan and other nations present a new field for commerce.

"Meanwhile the expense of building vessels in the United States has greatly increased; it is now possible, practicable, and profitable for citizens of the United States to carry on commerce particularly in the Pacific Ocean in vessels owned by them, but which vessels have no need to come to bring freight to or to export it from the ports of the United States.

" Under these circumstances the laws of the United States cease to be
effective to prevent citizens of the United States from owning vessels which are built out of the United States and are not registered in
the United States, and it does not seem to me strange, then, to find
that the laws of the United States have not as yet fixed any duties
upon the owners of these vessels which never come to the United
States, and so never have need of an American register to give them
the privileges of the domestic and export commerce of the United
States. If such vessels should come to the United States they must
bear all the burdens placed upon foreign vessels, and, knowing this,
they remain engaged in foreign commerce, entitled to the protection
of the United States, but under no special relations to the consuls of
the United States.

" Congress under these circumstances should, in my judgment, either
forbid any vessel to carry the flag of the United States which is not a
registered vessel of the United States, or should provide for the giving
of some official certificate to vessels wholly owned by citizens of the
United States wherever built, and should fix the status of such vessels in foreign ports and before the consuls of the United States.

" I quote from Mr. Cushing (6 Op. 653) : ' The question of what particular document, if any, shall be issued from the Treasury or State
Department to a foreign-built ship lawfully owned by a citizen of the
United States in the absence of any special legislation on the subject,
seems to me a proper one for the consideration of the Executive and
of Congress.'

" Commenting on these words of Mr. Cushing, Mr. Talbot, says : ' That
is, of the law-making power. Congress might undoubtedly authorize
the issuing of such papers, but as it was at the date of Mr. Cushing's opinion so is it now, Congress has not conferred the authority in
question.'

" Since Mr. Talbot's opinion Congress has passed no further legislation
on this matter, and the want of some legislation is still felt.

" What that legislation should be is to a great extent a question of policy.

" Should Congress think best to prevent the citizens of the United States
from engaging in commerce, even between foreign countries, except
in vessels built in the United States, it can practically do so by
enacting that no vessel shall be entitled to carry the flag of the United
States unless under existing laws she is a registered, enrolled, or
licensed vessel of the United States.

" On the other hand, should Congress while reserving the domestic
commerce of the United States to vessels built in the United States
think it wise to allow the citizens of the United States in any vessels
owned by them to compete for the profits of foreign commerce, it can
do so by some enactment which shall furnish the means by which
an official certificate of American ownership can be given to a vessel
wholly owned by citizens of the United States and by which a vessel
with such a certificate, her owners, charterers, officers, and crew
shall be declared subject to the same duties and entitled to the same
privileges in foreign countries and before a consul of the United
States that they would be subject or entitled to were they duly
registered vessels of the United States.

" In the same enactment Congress might also provide that no vessel
except a duly registered vessel of the United States, or a vessel
possessing a proper certificate that she was wholly owned by citizens

of the United States, should be entitled to carry the flag of the United States." (Enclosure with letter of Attorney General Akerman to Mr. Fish, Sec. of State, Jan. 8, 1872, Misc. Letters, November, 1872, Part I.)

February 22, 1875, the British minister at Washington presented a request that, with a view to prevent the use of unseaworthy ships, the consular officers of the United States in Great Britain should be instructed to communicate with the Board of Trade whenever a British vessel was about to be transferred to the flag of their country, in order that a survey of such vessel might be made by the government surveyor. The Department of State replied:

" The statutes of the United States have not given the privilege of carrying the American flag to any ships except those duly registered or enrolled. It is understood that foreign-built vessels (except under circumstances rarely occurring) are not entitled to registry or enrollment, and the consuls of the United States in Great Britain, as well as elsewhere, are already instructed that no register, enrollment, license, or any other marine document prescribed by the laws of the United States, can be lawfully issued by a consular officer to vessels which are sold and purchased at a foreign port, whether such vessels are American or foreign built. While this Government appreciates the importance of the prevention of the use of unseaworthy ships, the necessity of instructions such as are requested is not apparent."

> Mr. Fish, Sec. of State, to Sir Edward Thornton, British min., March 1, 1875, For. Rel. 1875, I. 653, 654.

May 26, 1875, Mr. J. L. Cadwalader, Assistant Secretary of State, by a circular instruction, in which it was said that there was understood to be " a considerable number of vessels in foreign contries, and especially in the East, regularly carry[ing] the American flag without being documented or registered in accordance with the laws of the United States," directed the United States consuls to communicate to the Department of State full information in regard to such vessels and their treatment.

> MS. Circulars, II. 67.

While the consular regulations state that foreign-built vessels purchased and wholly owned by citizens of the United States, whether purchased of belligerents or neutrals during a war to which the United States is not a party, or in peace of foreign owners, are entitled to the protection and flag of the United States as the property of American citizens, the same regulations require that the purchase " should have been in good faith. The purpose of the authority to consuls in the matter obviously was to enable citizens of the United States residing abroad to buy foreign-built vessels for lawful trade."

Mr. Fish, Sec. of State, to Mr. Marsh, min. to Italy, Jan. 29, 1877, MS. Inst. Italy, II. 11.

April 5, 1879, the Peruvian foreign office, in view of the outbreak of war with Chile, inquired (1) as to what conditions must be complied with in order that a merchant vessel might be considered as belonging to the United States, and (2) under what conditions a foreign vessel might in good faith legally use the United States flag. The United States legation at Lima, April 7, 1879, in reply to the first inquiry, quoted section 4131, Revised Statutes, by which registered vessels alone are " deemed vessels of the United States," entitled to all the benefits pertaining to such vessels. In response to the second inquiry, the legation quoted section 4132, Revised Statutes, which provides that " vessels built within the United States, and belonging wholly to citizens thereof, and vessels which may be captured in war by citizens of the United States, and lawfully condemned as prize, or which may be adjudged to be forfeited for a breach of the laws of the United States, being wholly owned by citizens, and no others, may be registered." On the strength of this section, the legation stated that there was " no law that permits foreign vessels to use the American flag." With regard to these responses, Mr. Evarts, who was then Secretary of State, observed that the first one appeared to be in conformity with the provisions of the Revised Statutes. As to the second, he said that it was correct as far as it went, but that the legation might have added " that there is no prohibition " of the use of the American flag by a foreign vessel beyond the jurisdiction of the United States, or any penalty provided therefor. Continuing, he said : " You are aware that the consular regulations provide for the purchase of foreign vessels abroad by citizens, and (section 220) that if such purchase is in good faith it entitles the vessel to protection as the lawful property of a citizen of the United States. The practice of making such purchases has advantageously been pursued from the origin of this government. There may have been instances in which it has been abused by collusion between a consul and the parties to the sale. If, however, circumstances justify on the part of that officer an opinion that the sale was honest, and that the vessel has really become the property of a citizen, she may properly fly the flag of the owner's country as an indication of her ownership, and as an emblem of his nationality."

Mr. Evarts, Sec. of State, to Mr. Christiancy, min. to Peru, May 8, 1879, For. Rel. 1879, 874.

For the dispatch to which this instruction was a reply, see For. Rel. 1879, 865–866.

In a further instruction to Mr. Christiancy, of June 20, 1879, Mr. Evarts somewhat elaborated the foregoing views. In this instruction he said:

"It may have been the intention of Congress when it prescribed the national flag, that it should be used only by vessels of the United States, as defined by law. No such intention, however, is expressed in any statute. As a citizen is not prohibited from purchasing and employing abroad a foreign-built ship, when such purchase is made in good faith, there is no reason why he should not fly the flag of his country as an indication of ownership. This is frequently and constantly done, especially in Chinese and other Eastern waters. It also appears from Mr. Osborn's letter to you that there are American vessels of foreign build frequenting Chilean ports, which were bought years ago. The right of these vessels to display the flag of the United States will not be questioned by this Department, and probably would be respected by any court of admiralty." (Mr. Evarts, Sec. of State, to Mr. Christiancy, min. to Peru, June 20, 1879, For. Rel. 1879, 884, 885.)

For a correspondence between Mr. Christiancy and Mr. Osborn, see For. Rel. 1879, 877–879.

See, also, for a further elaboration of the same views, Mr. Evarts, Sec. of State, to Mr. Christiancy, min. to Peru, Dec. 26, 1879. In this instruction Mr. Evarts said: "The duty of the consul, in reference to these transactions, is clearly enough indicated in Article XVII. of the Consular Regulations. He is forbidden by law to grant any marine document or certificate of ownership, but he may properly make record of the bill of sale in his office, authenticate its execution, and deliver to the purchaser a certificate to that effect, and also certify that the owner is a citizen of the United States. A considerable discretion and responsibility rest upon consuls in regard to determining the good faith of such transactions." (For. Rel. 1879, 895–896.)

An instruction similar to that sent to Mr. Christiancy, December 26, 1879, was sent to Mr. Osborn, minister to Chile. The substance of previous instructions was also sent to Mr. Osborn.

See Mr. Evarts, Sec. of State, to Mr. Osborn, min. to Chile, June 9, 1879, For. Rel. 1879, 177.

The action of the legation at Lima, in challenging the right of the *Itata*, a vessel said to have been bought by Henry L. Stevens, an American citizen resident in Chile, from a Chilean corporation, to fly the American flag, was approved under the circumstances of the case. (For. Rel. 1879, 861, 867, 896–897.)

"Inquiries have from time to time been addressed to the Department by consular officers in regard to the legal status, rights, and liabilities of foreign-built vessels purchased abroad and wholly owned by citizens of the United States. A recent instance of this kind, brought to the attention of the Department by the consul at Panama, in regard to the steamship *Honduras*, suggests the propriety of a general instruction on the questions involved in that case. The vessel in question was built at Liverpool in 1871, and upon her arrival in Panama, in September last (1879), was sold by her foreign owner to the Panama Railroad Company; soon after the railroad company sold the vessel to the Pacific Mail Steamship Company, both of these companies being American corporations. The Pacific Mail again sold the vessel to the Panama Railroad Company, which latter company now runs the steamer between Panama and the port of Champerico, Guatemala, in the common interest of both companies. Upon the facts the consul asked instruction upon two points:

" First. ' Is such a vessel required to pay tonnage dues, as required by law of registered American vessels? '

" Second. ' Is her crew to be shipped and discharged, in accordance with the law and regulations applicable to the crews of regularly registered or enrolled American vessels? '

" The existing regulations of the Treasury in regard to this class of vessels, and bearing especially upon the points under consideration, are found in Chapter IV. of the Regulations of 1874 of the Department. . . .

" The rulings and instructions of this Department have been in general accord with the . . . provisions of the Treasury Regulations. It is therefore concluded that foreign-built vessels purchased abroad and wholly owned by citizens of the United States, and plying in foreign waters, are to be considered subject to the exaction and payment of tonnage dues in the same manner as regularly registered or enrolled American vessels, and consuls are expected and required to collect such dues. In the case of vessels running regularly, by weekly or monthly trips, or otherwise, as is the case with the *Honduras*, the tonnage dues are required by law to be paid only for four trips a year, and this payment, in accordance with the former ruling of the Department, is to be made either at the principal port of departure or that of final destination of the vessel, and on the first four trips in the calendar year.

" In regard to the second question, namely, whether the crews are to be shipped and discharged before the consul, as in the case of registered or enrolled vessels, it is found that in many instances the crews of such vessels are made up largely of men who are not citizens of the United States, and who have not acquired the character of American seamen within the meaning of the law, by service on a registered vessel of the United States. As to these, when they ship at a foreign port, whether under contract to be discharged at another foreign port or not, extra wages are not to be demanded on their account, nor are they entitled to relief as destitute American seamen under the laws providing for such relief. Seamen of this character, therefore, serving on the vessels referred to, under a contract not made in the United States, are not considered to be within the jurisdictional cognizance of the consul as to their contracts of shipment and discharge. But seamen engaging on this class of vessels who are citizens of the

United States, and foreigners who have acquired the character of American seamen, within the meaning of the law, by service on registered or enrolled American vessels, and still claim and maintain that character, are to be shipped and discharged before the consul in the same manner as that provided by law and regulation for the shipment and discharge of American seamen of registered or enrolled American vessels. And this class of mariners, being entitled to relief as destitute American seamen, when found under the conditions essential to such relief, are entitled to have collected extra wages on their account when discharged at a foreign port under the conditions prescribed by law, for the demand and collection of the three months' extra wages."

> Mr. Evarts, Sec. of State, to U. S. consuls, circular, Feb. 18, 1880, For. Rel. 1880, 1; MS. Circulars, II. 455.

" I have received and read with care your number 501, of the 4th ultimo, detailing the transfer of the Chinese Merchants Steam Navigation Company's vessels to the American flag, July 31 last. The transaction appears to have been discreetly arranged, and the appropriateness of the vessels in question reverting under the flag which they first bore before the line passed under Chinese control is apparent."

> Mr. Frelinghuysen, Sec. of State, to Mr. Young, Oct. 23, 1884, MS. Inst. China, III. 662.
> This instruction refers to the sale, during the French-Chinese war then pending, of certain Chinese vessels to Russell & Co., citizens of the United States.
> An examination of Mr. Young's dispatch No. 501, and of the voluminous papers thereto attached, gives no indication that these vessels or any of them were built in the United States, or registered as such.

" The recent purchase by citizens of the United States of a large trading fleet heretofore under the Chinese flag has considerably enhanced our commercial importance in the East. In view of the large number of vessels built or purchased by American citizens in other countries and exclusively employed in legitimate traffic between foreign ports under the recognized protection of our flag, it might be well to provide a uniform rule for their registration and documentation, so that the *bona fide* property rights of our citizens therein shall be duly evidenced and properly guarded."

> President Arthur, Fourth Annual Message, Dec. 1, 1884. (For. Rel. 1884, iv.)
> In a dispatch from Mr. Smithers, then in charge of the American legation at Peking, to the Secretary of State, No. 58, dated August 28, 1885, it is stated that the vessels had been resold to a Chinese company. The closing paragraph of this dispatch is as follows: " In this connection, I may remark that Mr. Drummond, an English bar-

rister-at-law at Shanghai, who was the counsel of the Chinese company at the time the transfer took place to Russell & Co., has recently stated, over his own signature, that the sale of the ships was a perfectly honorable transaction, and that there was no obligation of any kind on the part of the Russells to return them to the Chinese. The fact is, as I have been credibly informed, after the refusal of the Chinese Government to continue the rice subsidy to the American firm, the property was not only unremunerative but would have proved disastrous to the holders." (MSS. Dept. of State.)

As to this resale, see Mr. Bayard, Sec. of State, to Mr. Smithers, Apr. 20, 1885, For. Rel. 1885, 170.

Foreign-built vessels owned by citizens of the United States are not within the provisions of the act of June 26, 1884, forbidding the collection of fees by consular officers from American vessels.

Garland, At. Gen., July 20, 1885, 18 Op. 234, following Brewster, At. Gen., Feb. 5, 1885, 18 Op. 111.

For an application of this opinion in the case of the steamship *Honduras*, at Panama, see Mr. Bayard, Sec. of State, to Mr. Lane, Sept. 24, 1885, 157 MS. Dom. Let. 206.

" I have no hesitation in saying that vessels owned by citizens of the United States, but foreign built, are entitled to carry the flag of the United States, and to obtain, in cases of vessels purchased abroad, the certificate specified in section 340 of the Consular Regulations [of 1881]. . . . Vessels of this class, it is true, can not enter our ports, not being duly registered under the navigation act. But there is no reason why they should not engage in foreign trade, and when in this trade carry the flag and enjoy the protection of the United States."

Opinion of Dr. Wharton, Solicitor of the Department of State, Nov. 30, 1885, MSS. Dept. of State. In printing this opinion in his Int. Law Digest Dr. Wharton substituted, for the words " can not enter our ports," the phrase " can not have in our ports the privileges given by statute to registered vessels."

" Was the *Arctic* such a vessel [a vessel of the United States, entitled to carry the flag]? It is conceded that she was not registered as such, and that she could not have been so registered, as her master was not a citizen of the United States and she was built abroad. On the other hand, she was owned by a citizen of the United States, and she belongs to a numerous class of vessels navigating the waters of Japan, China, and the North Pacific, which, carrying the flag of the United States, owned by citizens of the United States, and augmenting largely, if indirectly, the resources of the United States, are not registered as United States vessels. It has been ruled more than once by me, following in this a long line of precedents in this Department,

foreign nations nor to American vessels of foreign origin. (Act of December 31, 1792, Rev. Stat. §§ 4131, 4132.)

The distinction between "vessels of the United States" and vessels "owned by citizens of the United States" had not been observed in the wording of an act passed on 28th February, a few days previous to the passage of this supplement of March 2, 1803 (R. S. § 4309). It required "every master of a vessel belonging *to a citizen of the United States* who shall sail from any port of the United States, shall, on his arrival at a foreign port, deposit his register, sea-letter, and Mediterranean passport with the consul," whose duty it is, on the master producing a clearance from the proper officer of the port where he may be, to deliver to the master all of his papers, if such master has complied with the provisions of law relating to the discharge of seamen in a foreign country, and to the payment of the fees of consular officers. The same act imposed a penalty on the master for not doing so. But as the sea-letter and Mediterranean passport referred to in this act under the statute of 1796 could be obtained only by "vessels of the United States," and as the act of 28th February, 1803, recognized the right of vessels other than the vessels of the United States to obtain documents certifying to the nationality of their owners, so as to identify such vessels as American property, the act of March 2, 1803, was immediately passed requiring the collectors of the ports, on the request of the masters of "*unregistered vessels owned by a citizen of the United States and sailing with a sea-letter*," to furnish such vessel with a passport, "for which the master shall be subject to the rules and conditions prescribed for vessels of the United States." . . .

It therefore is certain that the Government has from an early period recognized that American property afloat in form of a ship was entitled, as well as cargo, to protection, without reference to the municipal law of the country which had put certain disabilities, in the foreign and coastwise trade, on this class of vessels, but which it is a mistake to suppose is wholly excluded from either the foreign or coastwise trade of the United States.

The views of Mr. Jefferson, Mr. Hamilton, Mr. Madison, and Mr. Dallas as to the national character of such vessels will be found in the . . . Digest of the International Law of the United States (supra, p. 1007; infra, pp. 1049–1053, 1059).

On the outbreak of the war between Russia and France and England, Mr. Cushing, then being the Attorney-General of the United States, at the request of the British minister, put in writing the view his Government had adopted (6 Op. 638; supra, p. 1008).

He took the ground which has since been followed by succeeding Attorneys-General, that citizens of the United States could lawfully purchase ships, the property of subjects of either of the belligerent powers; could lawfully employ and sail them under the flag of the United States; and that such vessels which had become in good faith the property of citizens of the United States, would lose their character as enemies' property and become neutral as regards either of the belligerents, and that the question as to the disabilities which the municipal rules of the government of the owners might impose on such vessels did not concern other nations nor affect their nationality.

He only expressed views previously adopted by his Government. He sustained them, however, with his usual consummate ability; they have never been departed from. His position has been reiterated by succeeding Secretaries of State, and similar opinions have been given by other Attorneys-General.

The transfer of the Chinese merchant fleet to American citizens, who placed the vessels under the flag of the United States during the late hostilities between China and France, was not questioned by the Government of France, nor do the vessels appear to have been molested, although the position taken by the United States was contested by France during the Russian war on the ground that enemy-built vessels can not be made neutral after hostilities break out. (3 Wharton's Dig. Int. Law, 522; infra, § 1188.)

So far as the international side of the question is concerned the position of such vessels is fixed.

Although the right of such vessels to carry the flag of the United States has been discussed in two late papers, there could hardly be occasion for such a question. A vessel's flag is only its signal to other vessels at sea.

The national bunting displayed is a communication to other vessels of the nationality of her owner, as her other signals are used to convey the name of the private owner, or of the line to which the vessel belongs.

There is no statute which authorizes " vessels of the United States " to carry a flag. The absence of a statute is unmeaning. There is no statute requiring any vessel to do so. Yet the right to carry a flag is recognized in the laws of war, and the abuse of the flag may procure the condemnation of a vessel.

The Treasury regulations, article 93, which declares such vessels entitled to the protection of the authorities and flag of the United States, recognizes the rights of these vessels to carry it.

The word " flag," when used either in public or private international law, in maritime subjects, designates the nationality of the vessel, arising from ownership, and the " law of the flag " is that which ascertains when a transaction is governed by the law of the country where the owner of the vessel resides, under which the master holds his authority to bind the vessel or its owner, or which governs the internal discipline of a ship or its liability to others. Expressions also have been used at times, with some looseness, in the maritime law, in which a vessel is spoken of as having a personality of its own, in reference to its liability *in rem*, independently of that of its owners. Such expressions are used by way of illustration, not of definition, and in this respect a vessel does not differ from other kinds of property; even real estate may in the same manner be considered as offending or guilty as well as indebted.

These expressions are used, however, with regard to an entirely different subject. A vessel as a subject of nationality is not considered a personality any more than any other chattel, and can not have any other nationality impressed on it except that arising from ownership. The place in which a vessel is built does not give it nationality any more than the place of origin affects that of its cargo. It is the residence of the owner which stamps alike the vessel and its cargo with its national character.

President Woolsey writes as follows:

" It is unsafe, then, to argue on the assumption that ships are altogether territory, as will appear, perhaps, when we come to consider the laws of maritime warfare. On the other hand, private ships have certain qualities resembling those of territory: (1) As against their crews on the high seas; for the territorial or municipal law accompanies them as long as they are beyond the reach of other law, or until they come within the bounds of some other jurisdiction. (2) As against foreigners who are excluded on the high seas from any act of sovereignty over them, just as if they were a part of the soil of their country. Public vessels stand on higher ground; they are not only public property, built or bought by the Government, but they are, as it were, floating barracks, a part of the public organism, and represent the national dignity, and on these accounts, even in foreign ports, are exempt from the local jurisdiction.

" In both cases, however, it is on account of the crew rather than of the ship itself that they have any territorial qualities. Take the crew away, let the

abandoned hulk be met at sea; it now becomes property and nothing more."
(Woolsey Int. Law, § 54.)

While these views of the distinguished author are not exact in making the national character of the vessel depend on that of its crew or inhabitants, it correctly illustrates the position that the nationality of the vessel is derived from the personal relation of the individuals who own it; because a member of the crew in this way becomes nationalized temporarily by inhabiting the vessel, in the same manner as a foreigner obtains or loses a qualified nationality by domicil or residence in the enemy's country. For this reason the right to registry is suspended by the residence abroad of the American owner of a vessel of the United States. (Rev. Stat. 4133.) Mr. Wirt, the Attorney-General, decided that the right to nationality of such vessels was not lost but only suspended, and that the vessel could be registered anew on the return of its owner to the United States, although the vessel had been placed, while the owner resided abroad, under the French flag. (1 Op. 393.)

The class of vessels owned by citizens of the United States which are called undocumented vessels is recognized in the regulations of the Treasury Department as a part of the mercantile marine of the United States, although not coming within the statutory definition of " vessels of the United States."

The provisions of these regulations are contained in articles 93, 94, 95, 96, 97 of the general regulations under the customs and navigation laws of the United States.

These articles recognize the right of such vessel to use the flag of the United States; authorize the collectors to record the bill of sale of such a vessel, to authenticate its validity, to certify to its authenticity and to the citizenship of the owners, and make such authentication *prima facie* proof of good faith.

A form of certificate is prepared authenticating the sale, and before granting such certificate the tonnage of the vessel is to be ascertained and inserted in the description of the vessel in the certificate.

A separate record is kept of these vessels, and in the tonnage returns they are reported in a separate column under the head, " Foreign-built vessels owned in the United States."

This review of the legislation in regard to undocumented vessels, and the action of the Departments in the construction of the navigation laws, is believed to be sufficient to establish not only the nationality of the vessels, but their recognition as a part of the mercantile marine of the United States. The construction of the laws by the proper Department, when long established and uniform, is binding upon the courts except in cases of very clear mistake. The same view of the national character of such vessels has been taken by the Department of State, the Treasury Department, and successive Attorneys-General.

These vessels are therefore a part of the mercantile marine of the United States under certain disabilities in regard to the trade of the United States. What these disabilities are and what law governs these vessels on the high seas has not been fully settled.

In construing the navigation laws of the United States in reference to a vessel's disabilities by reason of not being a " vessel of the United States," that is to say a vessel built in the United States, it is to be kept in mind that these laws in their inception were not a part of a protective system; they were intended to place foreign vessels, especially those of England, under the same disabilities as the laws of England placed our own.

As the Americans could build ships cheaper than the English, the American shipbuilders did not require the protection given to the British shipbuilder. (Reeves' Law of Shipping, 428, 429.)

The English, to preserve the carrying trade of the world to their own vessels, limited the trade to England by foreign vessels to the importation of wares the product or growth of the country of the vessel, the master and three-fourths of the crew being of the same country or place. It excluded such foreign vessels from carrying between England and her colonies, and to encourage shipbuilding against American competition it confined the trade carried on by British vessels, by its registry laws, to vessels of British origin. (Reeves' Law of Shipping, 244. See also Lecky's England in the 18th Century, vol. 2, p. 9.)

The navigation laws passed in 1792 were based upon the English laws then existing. The measures were retaliatory. We confined the benefits of registry for the foreign trade and enrollment for the coastwise trade of the United States to vessels of American origin, designating them by law as vessels of the United States.

In addition to this, in the early acts regulating importations into the United States, in imitation of the English act, discriminating duties were imposed in favor of importations in American vessels, and subsequently, in 1817, the right to *import* into the United States was confined to " vessels of the United States " and such foreign vessels as truly and wholly belonged to the citizens or subjects of that country of which the goods are the growth, production, or manufacture. (Rev. Stat. s. 2497.) The same act, as well as the previous acts discriminating in favor of vessels of the United States, provided that this restriction as to importation in foreign vessels should cease as to vessels of any nation which did not maintain a similar regulation against vessels of the United States.

This restrictive legislation as to importation in foreign vessels has been abrogated by treaties with the principal European nations.

But with the reason of the thing ceasing, the restriction still remains as to vessels owned by American citizens but not registered, including not only vessels of foreign origin but also vessels of American origin or construction which have become denationalized by a sale to a foreigner, and whose ownership has by a repurchase become again American. These last vessels still retain all the disabilities imposed by the original legislation and can not be again registered. (6 Op. 383.) These vessels are in the anomalous position that while when owned by foreigners they can import the merchandise and products of all countries into the United States, the same vessels if owned by Americans, and placed under the American flag, are excluded from the same trade they could enter into if owned by foreigners.

The denationalized vessel of American origin when owned by foreigners paid tonnage dues of 30 cents per ton, while the same vessel if owned by an American citizen paid 50 cents. (Rev. Stat. s. 4219.) On the other hand, this latter class of vessels had the advantage over foreign vessels of being exempted from the payment of light dues. (Rev. Stat. s. 4226.) Tonnage dues, however, are now payable at a uniform rate on all vessels entered from foreign ports, not to exceed 30 cents per annum. (23 Stat. L. 57.)

In reference to the foreign trade, the disability extends only to importation in such vessels. There is no statute which will prevent such vessels from coming in ballast to the United States, or with passengers, and it can obtain a clearance with cargo.

The statutes already quoted, especially the act of March 2, 1803, recognizes the right to clear for foreign countries with cargoes.

They are admitted also into the coasting trade of the United States from which foreign vessels are excluded (R. S. s. 4347) upon the payment of tonnage dues from which enrolled vessels are exempt. (Opinion of Nelson, Atty. Gen. 4 Op. 189.) By this opinion its privileges are confined to the trade in domestic merchandise and products other than distilled spirits, and it pays on each entry the same tonnage duties chargeable on foreign vessels. If found with foreign goods or distilled spirits on board the vessel is subject to forfeiture. (R. S. s. 4371.)

The construction of the Treasury Department as to the position of such vessels in relation to the foreign and coasting trade of the United States is found in a letter of the Treasury Department to the collector of Machias, Maine, dated May 2, 1872:

" I reply that if the Certificate Form No. 27, art. 96, part i, Rev. Reg., has been indorsed on the bill of sale of the vessel, you can clear her for St. John's, N. B., as desired. But she can not legally import goods, wares, or merchandise from foreign ports, and she would be subjected in the coasting trade to disabilities and exactions from which documented vessels of the United States are exempted."

The law governing vessels, the character of which we are now discussing in their relation to the laws of the United States, has been the subject of an opinion addressed by the examiner of claims to Mr. Fish, the Secretary of State (3 Wharton's Digest Int. Law, § 410, p. 679; supra, p. 1012), which was approved by the Attorney-General, Mr. Akerman. Possibly the attention of the latter was not attracted to the full extent to which that opinion went.

The question asked was as to the duties of American consuls in relation to this class of vessels, under the various acts of Congress relating to the deposit of papers with the consuls, and the shipment and discharge of seamen, and whether certain acts referred to applied to such vessels.

The result of the opinion was that none of the acts of Congress referred to by the Secretary of State applied to these undocumented vessels—in the following words:

" I then arrive at the conclusion that any vessel wholly owned by citizens of the United States is entitled to the protection of the United States, and can carry the flag of the United States, but that none of the acts, or parts of acts, referred to by Mr. Fish are applicable to any vessel that does not have a United States register.

" If this conclusion is right, a vessel owned by citizens of the United States, but not built in the United States, though entitled to its protection, would yet be under no relation thereto, or to its consuls, from which that vessel, in a certain way, would be compelled to bear part of the cost of that protection by the payment of the fees due under existing statutes from registered vessels to the collectors, the consuls, and divers other officers of the United States, but she would sail the ocean flying the flag of the United States, entitled to demand protection from the Navy and the consuls of the United States, but yet without any official papers on board from officers of the United States which would present *prima facie* and official evidence that she was entitled to carry that flag and to receive that protection."

It is to be regretted that such conclusions were approved by the law department of the Government, for if the same reasoning were followed in the construction of other statutes as is applied to those referred to for consideration, there would be no law governing the relation of crews nor means of enforcing the internal discipline of such ships; no power to punish desertion, or to protect the seamen from cruel treatment, or to release them on the fulfillment of their engagement. It is only in exceptional cases that courts will take cognizance of questions in relation to seamen and the internal discipline of foreign vessels. Of crimes committed on the high seas other than piracy there is no jurisdiction except in the tribunals of the country to which the vessel belongs, and a serious question would arise by what tribunals crimes could be punished on board of such ships, which happily, however, has been otherwise disposed of by adjudication.

As every ship carries with it the territorial law of the country of its owner-ship, no other nation can or will interfere with its internal affairs at sea, or even in port, unless the peace of the port is disturbed. It is generally only at the request of a consul of the vessel's nation that the authorities of another nation will take jurisdiction of disputes between the mariners. They are reluctant to do so. Seamen of any nationality are considered in the law as seamen of the nation to which the vessel belongs in the same way as a foreigner subjects him-self to the law of his domicil without regard to his actual citizenship.

It would seem to be indisputable that if the laws of the United States do not follow these vessels as a part of its territory the laws of no other nation can attach, and an anamoly is presented of property recognized as American without any law governing it except a guarantee of neutrality against belligerents.

Such a position is not supported by adjudications which will be referred to, nor by the opinion of Mr. Berrien, the Attorney-General, cited by the examiner of claims in his report to the Secretary of State, as to the construction of the pro-visions of the act of 28th February, 1803 (1 Op. 83), which were held to be inap-plicable " to the mercantile marine of a *foreign nation or people*, although American seamen may be employed on board their vessels and American citizens may be interested in them as owners. It belongs to such foreign nation or people to govern its own marine by regulations, which the master and mariners who sail under the flag of such nation or people are bound to observe, and *to which they must look for protection*."

The clause cited is inconsistent with the inference drawn by the examiner of the State Department, that protection was to be denied to American seamen sailing in a vessel carrying their own flag, as they could have none from any nation whose flag the vessel was not entitled to carry.

The comments of Mr. Berrien, Attorney-General, on the first three sections of the act under his consideration are not suggestive that he had in view their effect on any other class of vessels than foreign vessels.

The question to be answered was whether the first section of the act of 1803 " requiring a crew-list to be furnished by the master to the collector before clear-ance for a foreign port," could be construed to apply to foreign vessels as well as American vessels.

He refers to the other sections of the same act only to show that they could have no application to foreign vessels. They are as follows:

The second section of the act of 1803 which made it the duty of every master or commander of a ship or vessel belonging to citizens of the United States to deposit his register, sea-letter, and Mediterranean passport with the consul—in terms this section covers such undocumented vessels.

The third section of the same act under consideration relating to the consular protection of seamen on board of vessels sold abroad or discharged without their consent, refers in its words to those of " a ship or vessel belonging to a citizen of the United States."

The fourth section provides for the mariners or seamen of the United States who may be found destitute " within the consular districts," and requires all

NOTE.—The expressions used by Justice Nelson in delivering the opinion in White's Bank *v.* Smith, 7 Wallace, 655, 656, that vessels not brought within the registry and enrollment acts " are of no more value as American vessels than the wood and iron out of which they are constructed," and of Mr. Justice Miller in Badger *v.* Gutierez, 111 U. S. 736, 737, that a vessel of the United States with-out having the proper documents on board " in a foreign jurisdiction, or on the high seas, can claim no rights as an American vessel," were not involved or necessary to the decision of either case.

masters of vessels belonging to citizens of the United States and bound to some port of the same "to receive such mariners on board their vessels at the request of the consul."

There is nothing in these two last sections to suggest that the undocumented vessels and their crews are outside of consular supervision and protection, and none of them, except the first section, can have any bearing upon foreign vessels; or to intimate that Mr. Berrien, when using language which distinctly says that the sections of the act of 1803 were confined to vessels wholly owned by citizens of the United States and constituting a part of her mercantile marine by sailing under her flag, was not aware that foreign-built vessels had been allowed to sail under the flag of the United States, as a competent knowledge of the position of his Government in relation to such vessels and the legislation before referred to should be attributed to the highest law officer of the Government.

The conclusions that such undocumented vessels have the national character of American vessels, and yet are not regulated by the system of laws enacted to enforce discipline and to protect seamen on board of such vessels is not supported by his opinion and can not be accepted unless the legislation of the United States in positive terms excludes such vessels and their inhabitants from the operation of the laws governing other vessels of this nature. If these conclusions are correct these vessels are beyond the reach of all criminal process for offenses committed on the high seas. The judicial department, however, has not adopted this view. Judge Betts decided that an indictment for a revolt "by one or more of the crew of any American ship or vessel" under the second section of the act of March 3, 1835, Rev. Stat., § 5359, could be sustained by proof of American ownership, and that it was not in any way at issue whether the vessel was entitled to the privileges of an American bottom under our revenue laws. (U. S. v. Seagrist, 4 Blatch. 420.) Judge Woodbury held the same way in U. S. v. Peterson, 1 Wood & M. 305.

Judge Story's decision in U. S. v. Rogers, 3 Sumner, 342, "that the offense of revolt by one of the crew of an American vessel, on the high seas, was not punishable under the act of 1835 when committed on board of a registered vessel of the United States engaged in the whale fisheries, because the vessel had not been licensed and enrolled for that trade, and the voyage was unlawful," was followed by Thompson, Ch. J., in U. S. v. Jenkins, 1 N. Y. Leg. Obs., 344, without any approval, and for the sake of uniformity until reversed. It does not militate with the decision of Judge Betts or of Judge Woodbury, which applied to revolts on American vessels engaged in a lawful trade.

The system of laws called the navigation laws, like the criminal laws, must be interpreted as effective on all classes of vessels which come within the reason for enacting any laws at all on such subject. The use of particular words does not necessarily affect the construction of such statutes. Take the case of The Mohawk, reported in 3 Wallace, 556, where the provisions of the act of 1792, forfeiting a vessel "if any certificate of *registry* or record shall be fraudulently or knowingly used for any ship or vessel not then actually entitled to the benefit hereof," were held to apply to a vessel enrolled and not registered navigating the Lakes, although vessels enrolled in the coasting trade are not subject to forfeiture for such a cause, for the reason that an enrollment in the lake trade, in which the voyages are partly foreign and partly coastwise, is equivalent to a registry for the foreign trade to which the forfeiture applied.

It will be found that in some of the statutes referred to in the opinion given to the Department of State words are used which include these vessels as well as "registered vessels."

Thus in the act referred to, of 5th August, 1861 (12 Stat. L. 315), providing that "American vessels running regularly, &c., to or between foreign ports shall not be required to pay fees to consuls for more than four trips in a year," includes such vessels.

This statute naturally applies to this class of vessels whose trade is most generally between foreign ports, in which trade they are under no disabilities and it also must be read in connection with the statute of 1803 before referred to, requiring these vessels to deposit their passports with the American consuls and in terms to comply with the laws regulating the discharge of seamen and consular fees.

The words "American vessel" as a warranty of national character have been decided to be fulfilled by Kent, Ch. J., in Barker *v.* The Phœnix Ins. Co., 8 Johns R. 307, by a vessel wholly owned by American citizens, although not registered as a vessel of the United States, and the same decision was arrived at by Tilghman, Ch. J., in Griffith *v.* The Ins. Co., 5 Bin. 464; and the term American vessel, as used in the statute of March 3, 1835, applies to an offense committed on board of an American-owned vessel although not registered as a vessel of the United States.

So also the second section of the act of February 19, 1862, referred to, entitled "An act to prohibit the coolie trade by American citizens in American vessels," 12 Stat. L. 340, embraces such undocumented vessels under the terms "any ship or vessel, steamship or steam vessel belonging in whole or in part to citizens of the United States, or registered, enrolled, or licensed within the same or any port thereof"—the word *or* must be used in the disjunctive, because a vessel owned only in part by a citizen of the United States can not be registered or enrolled as a vessel of the United States.

For the same reason, in the fifth section of the same act extending the provisions of the passenger acts "to all vessels owned in whole or in part by citizens of the United States and registered, enrolled, or licensed within the same," the word "*and*" must also be read in the disjunctive.

In the laws referred to in the opinion, except the two last, it can be found according to the canons of construction that these vessels come within some of the provisions of the statutes.

One of the strongest arguments that can be urged against including these vessels in the mercantile marine of the United States is in the fact that the law does not require the officers of such vessels to be American citizens, as in the case of registered vessels. (Rev. Stat. § 4131.) Whether this has been from inadvertence, or because the exclusion of such vessels from some of the privileges of vessels of the United States was a reason sufficient for relaxing the policy of confining the command of such vessel to our own citizens, will not override the plain intent of legislation, if it can be discovered. Whether a master is a citizen or a foreigner, his nationality while his employment is in an American vessel necessarily subjects him, like a merchant domiciled in the United States, to the law of his vessel's flag. The reasons for excluding foreigners from the command of vessels of the United States is one of municipal policy, to encourage American citizens to enter into the merchant service, by retaining for them the command of vessels of the United States and exclude competition by foreigners in this calling, and are not founded on sentiment or national exclusiveness. Foreigners have served with distinction in high commands in the military service of the United States, and could equally well be trusted with that of merchant vessels but for the policy of reserving such position for American citizens.

In examining the various enactments relating to merchant seamen collected in the Revised Statutes it will be found that some of the sections apply only to " vessels of the United States," while in others they may be interpreted to apply equally to undocumented vessels, and in the latest legislation, section 4582 of the Revised Statutes, reading : " Whenever a vessel belonging to a citizen of the United States is sold in a foreign country, and her company discharged, or when a seaman or citizen of the United States is with his own consent discharged in a foreign country," has been amended by the act of June 26, 1884, section 5, so as to apply only to " a vessel of the United States sold in a foreign country and her company discharged." (23 Stat. L. 54.)

There seems to be a reason for amending this section in this manner, because the original section required payment of three months' extra wages to a seaman discharged with his own consent in a foreign port from such an undocumented vessel, the nature of whose employment requires generally the shipment and discharge of its seamen to be made in a foreign port. The extra wages to be paid on the sale of a vessel, and the discharge of her crew, is now only payable to the seamen of that class of vessels whose crews were originally shipped in the United States, and whose voyages habitually ended there.

By section 7 of the same act (23 Stat. L. 55), section 4578, Rev. Stats., which required masters of vessels belonging to citizens of the United States and bound to some port of the same, to take on board destitute seamen, is amended in certain particulars, and its provisions are confined to " masters of vessels of the United States bound to ports of the same." No reason can be assigned for this change unless, perhaps, as the voyages of such vessels seldom extend to ports of the United States it may not have been thought expedient to include them in its provisions. However this may be, this change in the description of vessels included in both these sections is noticeable in an act which, in the second, third, and fourth sections, relating to the discharge of seamen before consuls in foreign ports; in the sixth section, relating to the duty of consular officers; in the fourth section, relating to the slop chest; and in the twelfth section, abolishing consular fees, the same definition is not used, and the wording used applies equally to undocumented and registered vessels.

These views were prepared with regard to circumstances which might have occasioned a large number of foreign vessels to seek American ownership. If the views herein expressed are not correct, the evils attending belligerent character might be less than that of neutrality attached to the ownership of a class of vessels placed outside the regulation of the laws thought necessary for the protection of the crews and owners of all other vessels of the same nationality on the high seas and in foreign ports.

Such vessels might become free lances in case of war, being protected by the United States and under no subordination to its laws. If the opinion referred to is adopted as that of the Department of State it would give other nations, who must regard it as the official declaration of that Department of the Government, occasion for argument that protection as neutral property can not be claimed for such vessels, as the United States refuses to consider them a part of its territorial jurisdiction for the operation of its laws, as was mistakenly supposed to be the case by the English court in the case of Baring v. Claggett (33 B. & P. 201). A claim that such vessels are national for the purposes of neutrality, while in no respect a part of the commercial marine or controlled as to the acts of its owners and crew by the laws of the nation whose flag it carries, would be one very difficult to maintain as a part of the public law of the world.

Wharton's Int. Law Digest (2nd ed.) III. 993.

" Ships or vessels of the United States are the creations of the legislation of Congress. None can be denominated such,
Judicial decisions. or be entitled to the benefits or privileges thereof,
except those registered or enrolled according to the
act of September 1, 1789, and those which, after the last day of
March, 1793, shall be registered or enrolled in pursuance of the act
of 31st December, 1792, and must be wholly owned by a citizen, or
citizens of the United States, and to be commanded by a citizen of the
same. (1 Stat. 287.)

" And none can be registered or enrolled unless built within the
United States before or after the 4th of July, 1776, and belonging
wholly to a citizen, or citizens of the United States; or not built within
said States, but on the 16th of May, 1789, belonging, and thence continuing to belong, to a citizen or citizens thereof; or ships or vessels
captured from the enemy, in war, by a citizen, and lawfully condemned as prize, or adjudged to be forfeited for a breach of the laws
of the United States, and being wholly owned by a citizen or citizens
thereof. (1 Stat. § 2, 288.)

" Ships or vessels not brought within these provisions of the acts
of Congress, and not entitled to the benefits and privileges thereunto
belonging, are of no more value as American vessels than the wood
and iron out of which they are constructed. Their substantial if
not entire value consists in their right to the character of national
vessels, and to have the protection of the national flag floating at
their mast's head.

" Congress having created, as it were, this species of property, and
conferred upon it its chief value under the power given in the Constitution to regulate commerce, we perceive no reason for entertaining
any serious doubt but that this power may be extended to the security
and protection of the rights and title of all persons dealing therein.
The judicial mind seems to have generally taken this direction."

Nelson, J. White's Bank v. Smith, 7 Wall. 655–656. See supra, p. 1033,
note.
The point decided in this case was that under the act of July 29, 1850,
the recording of a mortgage in the office of a collector of the vessel's
home port has the effect, irrespective of State legislation, of giving
the mortgagee a preference over a subsequent purchaser or mortgagee. It was further held that the home port of the vessel is the
port in which the bill of sale, mortgage, etc., should be recorded.

By the act of March 1, 1817, 3 Stat. 351, the importation of goods
into the United States was prohibited, except (1) in vessels of the
United States, and (2) in vessels belonging wholly to citizens of the
country in which the goods were produced, or from which they were
most usually first shipped for transportation; but it was provided
that the prohibition should not extend to the vessels of any nation
which had not adopted a similar prohibition. It was held that a

vessel built in Canada, but owned by citizens of the United States and loaded with Canadian products, could not be regarded either as a vessel of the United States or as a foreign vessel belonging to citizens of the country of which the cargo was the product, and that she was therefore subject to forfeiture under the act. The owners sought to avail themselves of the proviso, on the ground that neither Great Britain nor Canada had adopted a similar prohibition; but the court answered that, as the vessel produced no register, or certificate, or document of any kind to show that she was a British ship, she was not entitled to that character. The fact that she was foreign built did not prove it; proof even that she was built in Great Britain would not establish it. The documents a vessel carried furnished, said the court, " the only evidence of her nationality." The vessel in question was " entirely destitute " of documents; and there was nothing therefore to bring her within the proviso.

> The Merritt, 17 Wall. 582, 585.

July 24, 1895, the Department of State enclosed to the Attorney-General a copy of a dispatch from the United States consul at Havre, No. 118, June 25, 1895, in which the consul reported his action in intervening, " by mutual consent of master and seamen," and on their invitation, and discharging certain dissatisfied members of the crew of the pleasure yacht *Barracouta*, a foreign-built vessel owned by a citizen of the United States. The Department, referring to a decision of the First Comptroller made August 29, 1894 (Decisions of the First Comptroller, 1893–1894, pp. 309–315), stated that it would have no hesitation in approving the action of the consul if the yacht were a registered American vessel, but that it was unwilling to assume the responsibility of determining the status of a foreign-built yacht. The Attorney-General declined to give an opinion on the question, on the ground that, as the consul had exercised no consular authority, but had, in effect, acted as arbitrator by consent of parties, no question arising out of his action was then pending in the administration of the Department of State.

> Mr. Adee, Act. Sec. of State, to Attorney-General, July 24, 1895, 203 MS. Dom. Let. 518; Harmon, At. Gen., July 26, 1895, 21 Op. 201–203.

" ARTICLE XX.—*American or foreign built vessels transferred abroad to citizens of the United States.*

" 341. *Right to acquire property in foreign ships.*—The right of citizens of the United States to acquire property in foreign ships has been held to be a natural right, independent of statutory law, and such property is as much entitled to protection by the United States as any other property of a citizen of the United States.

Consular Regulations, 1896.

"342. *Treasury regulations—sea letters.*—The existing general regulations of the Treasury Department under the customs and navigation laws (Customs Regulations, 1892) recognize the right of property in vessels of this character and declare them to be entitled to the protection of the authorities and to the flag of the United States, although no register, enrollment, license, or other marine document prescribed by the laws of the United States can lawfully be issued to such vessels whether they are American or foreign built. The former practice of issuing sea letters in the case of the purchase abroad of American or foreign vessels by citizens of the United States is no longer authorized. Nevertheless, though the issuing of sea letters to such ships is not now authorized, yet there would seem to be no good reason upon the face of our present legislation why the Department of State should not resume the practice, in case the United States should be a neutral in a war between maritime powers, if it should deem such letters more protective in their character than consular or customs certificates of sale.

"343. *Record of bill of sale, certificate, etc.*—In view of existing regulations, and to enable the owners of a vessel so situated to protect their rights, if molested or questioned, a consular officer, though forbidden by law to grant any marine document or certificate of ownership, may lawfully make record of the bill of sale in his office, authenticate its execution, and deliver to the purchaser a certificate to that effect; certifying, also, that the owner is a citizen of the United States. Before granting such a certificate the consular officer will require the tonnage of the vessel to be duly ascertained in pursuance of law and insert the same in the description of the vessel in his certificate. (Form No. 35.) These facts thus authenticated, if the transfer is in good faith, entitle the vessel to protection as the lawful property of a citizen of the United States; and the authentication of the bill of sale and of citizenship will be prima facie proof of such good faith.

"344. *Consul's responsibility.*—The authority of a consular officer to authenticate the transfer of a foreign vessel is wide in its effects and imposes great responsibility in making him, in the first instance at least, the sole judge of the good faith of the transaction. The question of the honesty and good faith of such a sale rises into the gravest importance in the event of a war between two or more powers in which the Government of the United States is a neutral. In such a war experience justifies the expectation that the citizens or subjects of one or more of the belligerents will seek to protect their shipping by a transfer to a neutral flag. In some instances this may honestly be done; but the sales of the vessels of belligerents in apprehension of or in time of war are always and properly liable to suspicion, and they justify the strictest inquiry on the part of the belligerent who may thereby have been defrauded of his right to capture the enemy's property. The acceptance of the pretended ownership of a vessel under these circumstances may be very profitable; and the temptation to abuse his trust in such a case to which a consular officer is subjected may be too great for persons of ordinary integrity, discernment, and firmness to withstand. Instances are not wanting in which citizens of the United States who were wholly incapable, from their previous well-known condition and pursuits, of making such a purchase have appeared as owners under sales of this character and have sought for them the protection of the Government.

" 345. *Careful investigation enjoined.*—It is the duty of a consular officer to use all available means, especially during the existence of a war to which this Government is not a party, to satisfy himself that the sale of a vessel is made in good faith and without a fraudulent intent. A considerable discretion and responsibility rest upon him in the determination of the good faith of such transactions. It is not to be concluded that all such sales, even in time of peace, are honest and free from collusion or fraud. It is the duty of the consular officer to notice all circumstances that throw doubt on the good faith of the transaction or point to its fictitious character, and, if he is satisfied in this respect, to refuse to grant his certificate. On the other hand, he is not permitted to regard the mere fact of the sale of a vessel to a citizen of the United States as any evidence of fraud. The presumption must be otherwise, and, in the absence of any indication of dishonesty, a sale in the regular way, with the usual business formalities, is to be regarded as made in good faith.

" 346. *Certificate, when to be issued.*—When a consular officer shall have satisfied himself, after the investigation with which he is charged, that the sale of a vessel is not fictitious and is made in good faith, and that the purchaser is a citizen of the United States, it is his duty, when requested, to record the bill of sale in the consulate, and to deliver the original to the purchaser, with his certificate annexed thereto, acording to Form No. 35. A copy of the bill of sale, together with any other papers belonging to the transfer, and of the consular certificate should be sent without delay to the Department of State, with a report of the facts and circumstances of the transaction.

" 347. *Right to fly the flag.*—The privilege of carrying the flag of the United States is under the regulation of Congress, and it may have been the intention of that body that it should be used only by regularly documented vessels. No such intention, however, is found in any statute. And as a citizen is not prohibited from purchasing and employing abroad a foreign ship, it is regarded as reasonable and

proper that he should be permitted to fly the flag of his country as
an indication of ownership and for the due protection of his property. The practice of carrying the flag by such vessels is now established. The right to do so will not be questioned, and it is probable
that it would be respected by the courts.

"348. *Disabilities of foreign-built vessels.*—It should be understood that foreign-built vessels not registered, enrolled, or licensed
under the laws of the United States, although wholly owned by citizens thereof, can not legally import goods, wares, or merchandise
from foreign ports, and are not allowed in the coasting trade.—*R. S.
secs. 2497, 4311.*

"349. *Forfeiture and tonnage duties.*—On arrival from a foreign
port undocumented foreign-built vessels, if laden with goods, wares,
or merchandise, may, with their cargoes, be subjected to forfeiture.—
R. S. sec. 2497; see Tariff act of 1894, sec. 15. If in ballast only, or
with passengers without cargo, they will be subject to a discriminating
tonnage duty.—*R. S., sec. 4219; 19 Stat. L., 250.* When in foreign
ports they are also subject to tonnage and other consular fees from
which regularly documented vessels are exempt. For instructions respecting the shipment and discharge and relief of seamen on vessels of
this character, and the collection of extra wages, consular officers are
referred to the several articles on these subjects."

Consular Regulations, 1896, §§ 341–349, pp. 132–136.

These sections are reprinted in the Report of the Commissioner of Navigation for 1901, p. 417.

In the Report of the Commissioner of Navigation for 1902, pp. 412–415,
may be found lists of (1) foreign-built steamers owned by Americans
and sailing under the American flag, (2) foreign-built steamships
owned by the War Department, (3) foreign-built steamships owned
by the Navy Department, and (4) foreign-built steam vessels admitted to American registration. The list of foreign-built steam vessels under the American flag by consular regulation contains 11
vessels, 6 of which were purchased at Shanghai in July and August,
1900, and 2 at Liverpool in December and January, 1901. Three were
steam yachts, 1 of which was bought in Scotland in December, 1900,
and 2 in England in January and May, 1901.

For vessels under the protection of the American flag in the Philippine
Islands, see Report of the Commissioner of Navigation for 1902, p. 219.

"No recent amendment has been made of the regulations embodied
in the Consular Regulations, 1896, relating to the rights of American-
owned foreign-built vessels. . . . For a short time it has been the
practice of this Bureau to award signal letters to such vessels on application when such action is considered to be for the material convenience of the private persons concerned."

H. Doc. 551—vol 2——66

Mr. Chamberlain, Commr. of Navigation, to Mr. Moore, April 17, 1903, MS. With the foregoing letter there was enclosed a copy of a letter of Mr. Chamberlain to Mr. Goodnow, United States consul-general at Shanghai, in relation to the application of A. E. Knights for signal letters and official numbers for the foreign-built and American-owned steam vessels *Chi Yuen, Too Nan, Taishun,* *Poochi,* and *Kwang Chi.* Mr. Chamberlain transmitted assignments of signal letters, but stated that official numbers could not be awarded under existing legislation. Mr Goodnow was requested to satisfy himself, at the time the letters were delivered, that " the owner or owners of the vessels shall be citizens of the United States, and that they and the vessels are duly recorded, as provided by the Consular Regulations."

Concerning vessels under the distinctive signal and coasting permit of Cuba, during the occupation of the island by the United States, see the following papers:

Circular of the Department of State, June 1, 1899, with an annexed circular of the War Department of May 23, 1899, regulating the clearance of such vessels for foreign ports or ports in the United States. (MS. Circulars, V.)

Circular of the Department State, July 11, 1899, with an annexed circular of the War Department of June 16, 1899, stating that such vessels were permitted to fly the American flag above the distinctive signal solely for the purpose of indicating that the Government of the United States, pursuant to treaty, had assumed and would discharge the obligations that might, under international law, result from the fact of the occupation of Cuba for the protection of life and property; and that the rights and privileges of such vessels as to entry, clearance, dues, and charges, in foreign ports and in ports of the United States, would be determined by the laws of the country in which the port might be situated. (MS. Circulars, V.)

As to the construction of the foregoing circulars in certain cases, see Mr. Hay, Sec. of State, to Sec. of War, July 22, 1899, 238 MS. Dom. Let. 613; Mr. Adee, Acting Sec. of State, to Sec. of War, Aug. 20, 1900, 247 MS. Dom. Let. 246.

As to pilotage dues of American and Cuban vessels, and of vessels of the French Trans-Atlantic Company at Havana, see Mr. Hay, Sec. of State, to Mr. Cambon, French amb., Feb. 9, 1900, MS. Notes to French Leg. XI. 14.

Seamen of Cuban vessels were not, because such vessels were permitted to fly the American flag under the order of June 16, 1899, entitled to relief as American seamen. (Mr. Cridler, Third. Assist. Sec. of State, to Mr. Maxwell, April 17, 1900, 172 MS. Inst. Consuls, 71).

By the act of February 10, 1900, Congress provided that Cuban vessels, documented by officers of the United States, should be entitled to the rights and privileges of vessels of the most favored nation. By section 4228, Revised Statutes, the President may by proclamation suspend discriminating duties on vessels of a foreign country whose government satisfies him that no discriminations are imposed by it on American vessels. The customs officers of Cuba, on the inauguration of their independent government, May 20, 1902, at once withdrew marine documents issued to Cuban vessels by American officers and substituted Cuban documents, but the necessary notice of the absence of any discrimination on American vessels was not simultaneously given to the United States. Notice was afterwards sent, but before it was received vessels arriving in the United States with Cuban marine documents were subjected to the discriminating tax of a dollar a ton, in addition to the usual rates. The imposition of this tax, though at the time required by the law, was considered a hardship, and Congress was asked to refund the amount collected. (Report of Mr. Chamberlain, Commr. of Navigation (1902), 20.)

(2) JURISDICTION.

§ 324.

In United States *v.* Rogers, 3 Sumner, 342 (1838), it may be inferred from Judge Story's opinion that a ship without proper municipal papers is not an "American vessel" under the statute of March 3, 1835, Rev. Stat., § 5359, making revolt indictable. (S. P., United States *v.* Jenkins, 1 N. Y. Leg. Obs., 344.) But in United States *v.* Peterson, 1 Wood. and M. 305 (1846), it was held by Judge Woodbury that an indictment in such case could be sustained on proof that the vessel was owned by American citizens and sailed from an American port. And in United States *v.* Seagrist, 4 Blatchf. 420 (1860), it was held that proof of American ownership alone was sufficient. "The objection that no documentary proof, such as a bill of sale or registry, was put in, establishing the national character of the vessel, can not avail the defendants. The master testified that she was owned in this city, by American citizens, and it was only necessary for the prosecution to prove that she was American property, to support the indictment. It was not, in any way, an issue, on the trial, whether she was entitled to the privileges of an American bottom, under our revenue laws. The only fact involved was whether she was American property, and of this there can be no doubt. (3 Kent's Com. 130, 132, 150.)"

Betts, J., United States *v.* Seagrist, 4 Blatchf. 421.

In May, 1886, Peter C. Fullert, a German subject, was convicted by the United States consul-general, at Yokohama, Japan, of aiding and assisting Paymaster Watkins to escape from the U. S. S. *Ossipee* at that port. At the time of the offense Fullert was serving as a seaman on board the *Arctic*, a foreign-built vessel owned by a citizen of the United States and flying the American flag, but not registered. Fullert having applied for a pardon, the Department of State submitted to the Attorney-General the question whether he was, at the time of the commission of the offense, subject as an American seaman to the jurisdiction of the United States consul. In its communication to the Attorney-General the Department stated that this question had been submitted to the Solicitor of the Department, and that he was of opinion that, while the vessel was entitled to fly the United States flag and to receive the protection of the United States, she was not, under the statutes establishing the consular courts, " a vessel of the United States in such a sense as to make foreign sailors in that vessel amenable to consular criminal jurisdiction." The Attorney-General advised that the proceedings against Fullert were unauthorized, and that he should be released. This opinion was broadly based upon the fact that " Fullert was, at the time the alleged offense was committed, a German subject," the Attorney-General declaring that the phrase " citizens of the United States " in section 4084, Revised Statutes, was to be understood " in its legal and ordinary signification, there being nothing in the context to show a different intention."

> Garland, At. Gen., Nov. 4, 1886, 18 Op. 498, in answer to Mr. Bayard, Sec. of State, to Mr. Garland, At. Gen., Oct. 20, 1886, 161 MS. Dom. Let. 670, 673.
>
> This opinion, in so far as it signifies that the question of jurisdiction was determined by the mere fact that Fullert was a German subject, is superseded by the decision of the Supreme Court in the case of Ross, the British subject, who, on the strength of his being a seaman on the American registered ship *Bullion*, was convicted by the United States consul-general at Kanagawa, Japan, of a murder on board that vessel in the harbor of Yokohama. (In re Ross, 140 U. S. 453.)

Should it be held that vessels, American owned but not registered, are not to be considered by the United States as " a part of its territorial jurisdiction for the operation of its laws, as was mistakenly supposed to be the case by the English court in the case of Baring *v.* Claggett (33 B. & P. 201)," ground might be given for the argument that such vessels are not entitled to protection as neutral American property. "A claim that such vessels are national for the purposes of neutrality, while in no respect a part of the commercial marine or controlled as to the acts of its owners and crew by the laws of the nation whose flag it carries, would be one very difficult to maintain as a part of the public law of the world."

> Opinion of Morton P. Henry, esq., author of a work on Admiralty Jurisdiction and Procedure, given to Dr. Francis Wharton, April, 1887, Wharton's Int. Law Digest, III. 1003, and supra, p. 1026 et seq.

" One of the first subjects that attracts attention in these regulations is the position assigned to foreign-built, but American-owned, vessels. Until the act of December 31, 1792 (Rev. Stat., § 4131), which defined what should be deemed vessels of the United States, all vessels carrying the flag and entitled to the protection of the United States were vessels of the United States. That act restricted the definition, and confined it to vessels only which should be registered pursuant to law, etc. Consequently, after the act of 1792, a class of vessels carrying the flag, and entitled to the protection of the United States, could no longer be deemed vessels of the United States, nor enjoy the benefits and privileges conferred on this latter class of vessels. Nevertheless, they were American-owned vessels, subject to many disabilities, and the objects, likewise, by subsequent legislation, of certain privileges.

" This was, and is, the *status* of foreign-built, but American-owned, vessels. The question is whether, when an act of Congress speaks of American vessels it means to include all vessels entitled to carry the flag and to receive the protection of the United States; or does it mean to exclude all but regularly documented vessels? The latter is the generally received construction of all such acts, and the construction adopted in the old edition of the Consular Regulations. But such construction at once encounters a serious practical difficulty. How can consuls exercise any jurisdiction over such vessels? How can the crimes act apply to the seamen on board of them? Obviously this difficulty has been overcome by the assumption that protection and amenability are correlative terms. And that when the protection is accorded, and the right to carry the flag is conceded, amenability to the law of the flag follows."

> Letter of Mr. Henry Flanders, of the Philadelphia bar, to Mr. Bayard, Sec. of State, April 30, 1887, transmitting the text of the revised Consular Regulations of 1888. (MS. Misc. Letters, April, 1887, Part II.)
>
> Offenses committed on British-owned, but unregistered, vessels on the high seas, are cognizable by the British courts, although such vessels are not entitled to clearance from British ports as British ships, or to any benefits, privileges, advantages, or protection usually enjoyed by British ships, or to use the British flag, or assume the British national character. Merchant Shipping Act, 17 & 18 Vict., c. 104, secs. 19, 106; R. *v.* Seberg, 11 Cox's C. C. 520.

4. PASSPORTS AND SEA-LETTERS.

§ 325.

" The title to a ship, acquired by purchase, passes by writing. A bill of sale is the true and proper muniment of title to a ship, and one which the maritime courts of all nations will look for, and, in their ordinary practice, require. In Scotland, a written conveyance of property in ships has, by custom, become essential; and, in England, it is made absolutely necessary by statute, with regard to British subjects. Possession of a ship, and acts of ownership, will, in this, as in other cases of property, be presumptive evidence of title, without the aid of documentary proof, and will stand good until that presumption be destroyed by contrary proof; and a sale and delivery of a ship, without any bill of sale, writing, or instrument, will be good at law, as between the parties."

3 Kent Com. 130, citing The Sisters, 5 C. Rob. 155; 1 Mason, 139; Weston v. Penniman, 1 id. 306; 2 id. 435; Ohl v. Eagle Ins. Co., 4 id. 390; Code de Commerce, art. 195; Robertson v. French, 4 East, 130; Sutton v. Buck, 2 Taunt. 302; Taggard v. Loring, 16 Mass. 336; Wendover v. Hogeboom, 7 Johns. 308; Bixby v. Franklin Ins. Co., 8 Pick. 86; Abbott on shipping, 5th Am. ed., 113; The Amelia, 6 Wall. 18, 30; Rice v. McLarren, 42 Me. 157, 166; McMahon v. Davidson, 12 Minn. 357, 369, 370; The Active, Olcott, 286; Fontaine v. Beers, 19 Ala. 722.

As to the policy of the navigation laws, see Reeve's Hist. of Law of Shipping; 3 Kent Com. 139; Bates's American Navigation (Houghton, Mifflin & Co.).

" No sea-letter or other document certifying or proving any vessel to be the property of a citizen of the United States shall be issued, except to vessels duly registered, or enrolled and licensed as vessels of the United States, or to vessels which shall be wholly owned by citizens of the United States, and furnished with or entitled to sea-letters or other custom-house documents." [Act Mar. 26, 1810.]

U. S. Rev. Stat., § 4190.

It is not competent for one sovereign to determine as to the municipal regularity or adequacy of the ship's papers issued by another sovereign. It is enough if such papers are in the shape of a protection or passport, and emanate from the sovereign of the owners of the ship, or from one of his subalterns.

Kaltenborn, Grundsätze des praktischen Europäischen Seerechts, Berlin, 1851, §§ 45 et seq.; Lewis Das Deutsche Seerecht, Leipsic, 1877, I. 14.

Wharton's Law Dict. (London, 1883), quoting 1 Marsh. on Ins., c. 9, s. 6, speaks of passports, sea briefs, and sea letters as papers " required by the law of nations to be on board neutral ships."

" The passport, sea brief, sea letter, or pass.—This is a certificate granted by authority of the neutral state, giving permission to the master of the ship to proceed on the voyage proposed, and declaring that while on such voyage the ship is under the protection of the neutral state. (The Vigilantia (1798), 1 C. Rob. 13; the Vreede Sholtys (1804), 5 C. Rob. 5, n.) It is indispensable to the safety of a neutral ship (1 Marshall Ins. 410, citing Hubner de la Saisie des Bâtiments neutres, pt. ii, chap. 3, s. 10, vol. i, 242); nor is any vessel permitted to disown the national character therein ascribed to her. The Vigilantia (1798), 1 C. Rob. 13. This does not apply to the goods; the Vrouw Elizabeth (1803), 5 C. Rob. 2; the Vreede Scholtys, ibid. 5 n."

Arnould's Marine Ins. (1901), II. § 661.

" On entend par lettre marine la passe de mer." (Ortolan, Régles de la Mer, I. 195.)

" If we look to the origin of the mercantile flag, it would appear to be a regulation of the municipal law of individual states, and not to be an institution of the general maritime law. The passport or sea-letter, as the case may be, is the formal voucher of the ship's national character. The passport purports to be a requisition on the part of the government of a state to suffer the vessel to pass freely with her company, passengers, goods, and merchandise, without any hindrance, seizure, or molestation, as being owned by citizens or subjects of such state. ' The first paper,' says Sir W. Scott, ' which we usually look for, as proof of property, is the pass.' The same learned judge elsewhere observes, ' It is a known and well-established rule with respect to a vessel, that if she is navigating under the pass of a foreign country, she is considered as bearing the national character of that nation under whose pass she sails. She makes a part of its navigation, and is in every respect liable to be considered as a vessel of that country.' The pass or sea-letter was, until very recent times, indispensable for the security of a neutral ship from molestation by belligerent cruisers, and it was the only paper to which any respect was paid by the corsairs of the Barbary States, as warranting the vessel to be within the protection of their respective treaty engagements with the European powers. If a vessel be furnished with a pass or sea-letter, it is immaterial whether she has any mercantile flag on board or not. The latter by itself is not a criterion of the national character of the owners of the vessel."

> Twiss, Law of Nations, as to war (2d ed.), 172.
>
> To this passage is appended the following note :
>
> " The best account of the passport is given by D'Abreu (part I, c. 2), who justly observes that it covers sometimes the cargo as well as the ship, but that it invariably names the ship, its build, the captain, and his residence. D'Abreu also gives an account of the sea-letter, which he describes as being in the same form as the pass. The difference between them would seem to consist in this, that whilst the pass is issued in the name of a sovereign power or state, the sea-letter is issued in the name of the civil authorities of the port from which the vessel is fitted out. The form of a sea-letter is annexed to the Treaty of the Pyrenees (A. D. 1659), under which it was provided that free ships should make free goods. It is termed ' literæ salvi conductus,' and the force and effect of it is thus described in the XVIIth article of the treaty itself : ' Ex quibus non solum de suis mercibus impositis, sed etiam de loco domicilii et habitationis, ut et de nomine tam Domini et magistri navis, quam navigii ipsius constare queat : quo per duo hæcce media cognoscatur, an merces vehant de *Contrebande*, et sufficienter tam de qualitate quam de Domino et magistro dicti navigii constet. His literis salvi conductus et certificationibus plena fides hebebitur.' In the Treaty of Copenhagen concluded 11 July, 1670, between Great Britain and Denmark, the sea-letter is termed a certificate ; and it is provided that the ships of either confederate shall carry letters of passport and a certificate, of which the forms are set forth in the body of the treaty. This sea-letter or certificate extended to the cargo."

D'Abreu (Tratado Juridico-Politico, sobre Pressas de Mar. 1st ed. 1746), to whom Twiss thus refers, enumerates (p. 18 et seq.) nine documents that ought to be found on board a merchant ship on the high seas, as follows:

1. El passaporte (the passport).
2. Las letras de mar (sea-letters).
3. El libro derrotero (the book of charts).
4. La certificacion ó patente de sanidad (the bill of health).
5. La pertenencia del navio (bill of sale or certificate of ownership).
6. El libro de sobordo (manifest).
7. La carta-partida (the charter-party).
8. El conocimiento (the bill of lading).
9. La factura (the invoice).

" El primer instrumento con que debe navegar todo navio mercantil, es el passaporte, y no es otra cosa, que una licencia de el soberano, del capitan, ó dueño del navio, para que este navegue, el qual se concede, unas veces por tiempo limitado, y otras sin limitacion: Se nombra en él el puerto á donde es el destino, y se refieren por mayor las mercadurias, que conduce; bien, que otras veces, ni se señala tiempo, ni lugar, ni carga; pero siempre el capitan, y navio, y la naturaleza, domicilio, ó residencia de aquel.

" Este instrumento es tan precisso y necessario para la navegacion, que el navio, que se halláre sin él, puede ser legitimamente apressado; como consta del Artículo 6 de la Ordinanza de Corso, en estas terminos: ' Han de ser de buena pressa todos los navios pertenecientes á enemigos, y los mandados por piratas cosarios, y otra gente, que corriere la mar sin Despacho de algun Principe, ni Estado Soberano.' Cuya disposicion conforma mucho con lo que observaban los Romanos en los passaportes de que usaban, para comerciar libre, y seguramente, y que registraban solamente los *agentes in rebus;* (2) porque sin los Despaches, que llamaban *'Evectiones ó Tractatorias,'* (3) no se podia conducir cosa alguna: y aunque algunos Interpretes al Codigo son de sentir, que estos Despachos eran con los que se assistia á los Correos, para que les diessen los Caballos necessarios á su viage; y otros los entienden de los que se libraban á los ministros, para el carruage, y utensilios, que se les mandaba dár en sus jornadas, no tenemos duda en que dichos Despachos, deben extenderse á los passaportes dados para el comercio de las mercaderias; (4) fuera de que en qualquiera inteligencia, que se les quiera dár, es constante, que quanto se comerciare, ha de ser ajustado á las ordenes, y Despachos, que previenen las Leyes; de suerte, que los efectos que se encontraren en navios mercantiles, que navagaran sin passaporte, han de ser de buena Pressa.

" El segundo instrumento es, las Letras de Mar, por las quales debe constár, no solamente de la carga del navio, sino tambien de el lugar de su habitacion, residencia, y nombre, assi del maestre, y patrón, como del navio mismo, para que de este modo se pueda reconocer, si lleva mercaderias de contravando, á cuyas Letras de Mar se debe dár entera fee y credito. Este instrumento lo creemos tambien absoluta, é indispensablemente necesario para la navegacion, pues el con Artículo 17 de Tratado de los Pirineos, despues de equipararlo con los passaportes, proviene que se lleye; y al fin de dicho Tratado, se encuentra su formulario, que es el siguiente:

" 'A todos los que las presentes vieren nuestros los regidores, consules, y magistrados de la villa de ———, hazémos saber á quien tocare, que N———, maestre del navio ———, pareció ante nos, y debaxo de juramento solemne declaró, que el navio, llamado N———, de porte de —— toneladas, poco mas, ó menos, del qual es maestre al presente, es navio francés: y deseando nosotros, que dicho maestre de navio sea ayudado en sus negocios, pedimos en general, y en particular á todas las personas, que encontraren dicho navio, y á todos los lugares donde llegare con sus mercaderías, tengan por agradable de admitirle favorablemente, tratarle bien, y recibirle en sus puertos, bahias, y dominios, ó permitirle fuera en sus riveras, mediante el pagamento de derechos de peage, y los demás acostumbrados, dexandole navegar, passar, frequentar, y negociar alli, ó en qualesquiera otras partes, que le pareciere á proposito, cosa que nosotros reconoceremos gratamente, en fee de lo qual havemos firmado las presentes, y selladolas con el sello de nuestra villa.' Aunque el Articulo de los Pirineos arriba citado, prescribe indispensablemente, que todo navio mercantil, que navegue, trayga las Letras de Mar, no creemos, sin embargo, que por la falta de este instrumento, deba reputarse el navio por de buena Pressa, siempre que trayga el passaporte de su Soberano, pues equivale este en substancia á las Letras de Mar."

By a resolution of Congress of Feb. 12, 1788, it was required, as a condition of the issuance of a sea letter, that it should be made to appear to the Secretary of Foreign Affairs, by oath or affirmation, or by such other evidence as should by him be deemed satisfactory, that the vessel was commanded by officers, citizens of the United States. An affidavit that one of the officers was an American, but without definite information as to the rest, was held to be insufficient.

> Mr. Jefferson, Sec. for For. Aff., to Mr. Joy, March 31, 1790, 4 MS. Am. Let. 121.

" The arrangement taken with respect to sea letters was, that they should be delivered to the collectors of the customs at every port of the United States as the persons who might the most conveniently countersign and deliver them out, and for this purpose, that they should be sent from my office to the commissioner of the revenue to be distributed, as being particularly within his department. Understanding that several vessels were waiting yesterday at this port, I took the liberty of troubling you with the passports directly without sending them through the commissioner of revenue. He is now supplied with a number and will hereafter be kept in a state of supply. With respect to the fee it is not within my province to decide anything. A moderate fee seems reasonable, and whether any law prohibits the taking it is a question which it belongs to the gentlemen of the law to decide, at least till the meeting of Congress, when this article may be placed regularly on the fee bill."

> Mr. Jefferson, Sec. of State, to Mr. Delaney, collector of the port of Philadelphia, April 30, 1793, 5 MS. Dom. Let. 97.

"It has been determined to issue passports to all vessels belonging wholly to American citizens, whether home or foreign built; to endeavor to give them only to those which are *bona fide* our own; to prevent all collusion, the prevalence of which might draw rigorous examinations and embarrassments on the vessels truly ours, and, as a means to prevent such collusion and its ill effects, to grant passports only to vessels within the ports of the United States, where they and their destinations will be under the eye of our own officers. Mr. Coxe will be pleased to give directions accordingly to the collectors of the customs in the different ports when he shall distribute the passports to them."

> Mr. Jefferson, Sec. of State, to Mr. Tench Coxe, Comr. of the Revenue, May 3, 1793, 5 MS. Dom. Let. 99.

"It being necessary, in the present state of war among the principal European powers, that all ships and vessels, belonging to citizens of the United States, should be furnished, as soon as possible, with sea-letters, for their more perfect identification and security, you will find within the inclosure, ten copies of two several documents of that kind, signed by the President of the United States, and countersigned by the Secretary of the Department of State, which have been received from that Department, for the purpose of being transmitted to the several custom-houses. One of each of these letters is to be delivered to every ship or vessel being actually and *bona fide* the property of one or more citizens of the United States, after the captain shall have duly made oath to the effect, and according to the tenor of the certificate, printed under that which is in Dutch and English, the substance and purport of which oath is comprised in the 10th, 11th, 12th, 13th, 14th and 15th lines of the said printed certificate. To this the captain is to be duly sworn, before some officer qualified to administer oaths. . . . The certificate is then to be signed by the magistrate; and the public seal (or if he has no public one, his private seal) is to be affixed. The blanks are to be filled up both in the English and Dutch copies of the sea-letter, by the collector, and in both the English and Dutch copies of the certificate, by the magistrate or judge. . . .

"You will acknowledge the receipt of all the sea-letters you shall receive from time to time, and you will keep a record thereof, and of your disposition of them, showing the names of the vessels (with their masters and owners) for which they were issued, the ports of the United States to which the vessels shall belong, the date at which you issue them, the officer before whom the captain shall be sworn, the burdens or tonnage of the vessels, and the ladings on board of them.

"Of these you will be pleased to make an abstract by way of return, up to the last day of every revenue quarter, and to transmit the same to this office, with a note of the sea-letters received and issued during such quarter, and of the quantity remaining on hand.

" These documents being of great importance to the United States, not only as they regard the benefits to be derived from the state of peace by the owners, navigators, and builders of ships, but also as they affect the importation of our supplies, and the exportation of our produce, at peace charges, you will execute the business in relation to them with proportionate circumspection and care."

> Mr. Hamilton, Sec. of Treasury, to Mr. Lamb, collector of customs for New York, May 13, 1793, cited in Sleght v. Hartshorne, 2 Johns. N. Y. 534.
> In the case of Sleght v. Hartshorne the court held that the sea-letter referred to in the United States statutes was a certificate of ownership, granted to unregistered vessels, belonging to citizens of the United States, and that a passport was to be granted to a vessel owned by a citizen and sailing under a sea letter.

" I send you the forms of the passports given here—the one in three columns is that now used, the other having been soon discontinued. It is determined that they shall be given in our own ports only, and to serve but for one voyage. It has also been determined that they shall be given to all vessels *bona fide* owned by American citizens *wholly*, whether built here or not. Our property, whether in the form of vessels, cargoes, or anything else, has a right to pass the seas untouched by any nation, by the law of nations; and no one has a right to ask where a vessel was built, but where is she owned ? To the security which the law of nations gives to such vessels against all nations are added particular stipulations with three of the belligerent powers. Had it not been in our power to enlarge our national stock of shipping suddenly in the present exigency, a great proportion of our produce must have remained on our hands for want of the means of transportation to market. At this time, indeed, a great proportion is in that predicament. The most rigorous measures will be taken to prevent any vessel not wholly and *bona fide* owned by American citizens from obtaining our passports. It is much our interest to prevent the competition of other nations from taking from us the benefits we have a right to expect from the neutrality of our flag; and I think we may be very sure that few, if any, will be fraudulently obtained within our ports."

> Mr. Jefferson, Sec. of State, to Mr. Morris, min. to France, June 13, 1793, MS. Int. U. States Ministers, I. 288.
> See, also, Mr. Jefferson, Sec. of State, to Mr. Pinckney, min. to England, May 7, 1793, MS. Inst. U. States Ministers, I. 278.

" Many objections lie to the issuing of passes by foreign agents to our vessels. In the case of a foreign consul at Boston, who officiously undertook to do it, the thing was forbidden. Were some of our vessels to have these passes, the want of them might subject others to doubts and obstacles in their voyages. The permission to grant these passes might lead to the most dangerous abuses, and the passports which we grant to our own vessels are perfectly sufficient. No instance has occurred, as far as we know, of our passports having been disrespected. The vessels of ours taken hitherto were such as had left our States before a knowledge of the war had reached us, and consequently before we had begun to issue passports."

> Mr. Jefferson, Sec. of State, to Mr. Bentalou, June 25, 1793, 5 MS. Dom. Let. 171.

" I have this day received your letter of the 22d ult. The case of the sloop *Hopestill*, Capt. Andrew Bent, of New York, arrived at New Orleans for the purpose of trade, ought not to have produced any difficulty on the part of the intendant. The object of the *sea letter* required by our treaty with Spain is to enable the armed vessels of Spain, now that she is at war, to distinguish American from other vessels, that the former, on the exhibition of the sea letter, may be suffered to pass. If destitute of a sea letter, an American vessel may be captured and carried into a Spanish port for examination, but then the American vessel has a right not only in reason, but by the very words of the treaty, to adduce other proof of the property. The words are ' legal satisfaction of their property by testimony entirely equivalent.' This testimony may be the register, the clearance, and any other documents under the signature and seal of the custom-house officer of the United States; and if required, the oral testimony of the master, mate and crew of the vessel may be given. But unless the official documents are justly suspected as being counterfeits, they ought to be admitted, as the *equivalent testimony*, without the aid of witnesses. Now the authenticity of the register and clearance of the sloop *Hopestill* may be readily ascertained by a comparison with the official papers from the same custom-house in the United States from which the *Hopestill* was cleared.

" The meaning of the treaty is so plain on this point, I can not but express some surprise that the intendant should appeal to the seventeenth article for the source and support of his doubt and objection. The question will probably be decided before this letter reaches you; but if a confiscation should ensue, the master of the vessel will doubtless appeal from so ill-founded a judgment."

> Mr. Pickering, Sec. of State, to Mr. Hulings, May 18, 1799, MS. Inst. U. States Ministers, V. 133.

" The multiplied abuses of the certificates which the consuls of the United States were, by the instructions of the 1st of August, 1801, authorized to give in the case of foreign vessels, purchased by a citizen of the United States, notwithstanding the precautions taken against them, have led to the conclusion that a discontinuance of the certificates altogether is the only effectual remedy. You will therefore forbear to grant any certificate whatever relative to such purchases, except to those who may satisfy you that the purchase was made without knowing this alteration in your instructions. Accordingly you will publicly advertise, that you are restrained from issuing certificates in such cases, with the sole exception just mentioned; and also from allowing the exception itself, after the expiration of two months from the date of the advertisement."

> Mr. Madison, Sec. of State, to U. S. consuls and commercial agents, circular, undated, MS. Circulars, I. 6.

" It is the usage for American vessels to take sea-letters, in voyages to Europe; but to the West Indies, and coastwise, they most generally sail with a certificate only."

> Radcliff and Hoffman, arguendo, in Sleght *v.* Rhinelander, 1 Johns. 198.

" In Marshall (p. 317) a distinction is made between a passport and a sea-letter. The former is defined to be a permission from a neutral state to a master of a ship, to proceed on the voyage proposed, and usually contains his name and residence, the name, description and destination of the ship, with such other matters as the practice of the place requires. This document he describes as essentially necessary for the safety of every ship. . . .

" It has been the policy of the United States, in common with other commercial nations, to encourage their own ships. Our navigation act enumerates and describes certain vessels, and emphatically denominates them *ships or vessels of the United States.* Their distinguishing characteristics are, that they are built, owned and commanded by citizens of this country. They are registered with the collector, and are entitled to a certificate, called a register. This register is of itself considered a competent document, to prove the ship American; and would, in most cases, serve as a sufficient protection against capture. But cases occur, wherein this register is not granted to vessels owned by citizens of the United States. The principal case is where the vessel is built out of the country. In such case, the collector can not grant a register; but it being proper and necessary, that the owner should have some document to protect his property against the rapacity of cruisers on the ocean, and to establish his neutrality, a formula has been devised and is granted, called a certificate of ownership. . . . Hence arises the division of vessels owned by citizens, into two classes, vessels of the United States, or registered vessels, and vessels belonging to the citizens of the United States, certificated but not registered. The owners of the latter description of vessels, considering this certificate of ownership as a sufficient shield for neutral property, denominated it a sea-letter; and it may have obtained that appellation at the time our first navigation act was passed, which was in the year 1789, some years before the letter from the Secretary of the Treasury, set forth in the bill of exceptions, was written. This term was, at a subsequent period, ingrafted into our statute book, as I shall presently show.

" In the year 1793, when a general war was kindled in Europe, the President of the United States, in order that our vessels might enjoy the benefits stipulated by treaties, and be generally protected against the depredations of the belligerents, ordered documents to be furnished from the custom-houses, *to all ships and vessels belonging to citizens of the United States.* This document is denominated, in the letter of the Secretary of the Treasury, a sea-letter, and is the formula of the passport adopted in the treaties, and was given to certificated, as well as registered, vessels. This was a mere executive regulation, unauthorized by any existing statute, and so it continued, until the 1st of June, 1796, when an act was passed, directing the Secretary of State to prepare a form which, when approved of by the President, should be deemed *the form of a passport for ships and vessels of the United States.* The form adopted was the same as described in the treaties. It was so constructed, in order that we might have the benefit of those treaties. The passports exhibited by the plaintiffs were issued subsequent to 1796; and, although conformable to the formulas prescribed in the treaties, they emanated from this statute. And here two remarkable circumstances occurred; the term sea-letter in the treaties was dropped in the statute, and the word passport adopted; and the passport was only authorized to be granted to registered vessels. This must have been considered as a negation of the right of the executive, heretofore exercised, of granting passports to certificated vessels. Hence the certificate of American ownership being their only guard, this certificate was, emphatically, denominated their sea-letter, or protection.

" The case before us occurred in the year 1798, two years after the passing of the statute, authorizing the granting of passports only to registered ships. Inconveniences having been sustained from this discrimination, and certificated ships being thus deprived of so important a document, a law was passed on the 2d day of March, 1803, and directing, that every unregistered ship or vessel, owned by a citizen or citizens of the United States, and sailing with a sea-letter, going to any foreign country, should be furnished with a passport, prescribed in the former act, for ships and vessels of the United States. This statute is one of the only two that contain the term sea-letter, and that it is used here in the sense of a certificate of ownership cannot be doubted. A passport is to be granted to a vessel owned by a citizen, sailing with a sea-letter. The passport authorized by a former statute is precisely the same with the sea-letter or passport of the treaties. If, then, by the term sea-letter in this statute, is intended the sea-letter or passport of the treaty, the provision is superfluous and idle, because it provides for what already exists; and changing the terms to the construction insisted on by the defendants, the statute would read thus: 'That every unregistered ship, sailing with a sea-letter, and owned by a citizen of the United States, shall be furnished with a sea-letter,' that is, provided with what it already possessed. The only way to escape from this absurdity, is to adopt a certificate of ownership as the true and legitimate sea-letter. But this is not all. Another statute was passed on the 14th day of April, 1802, where the word sea-letter is used precisely in the sense now contended for. This statute declares, that ' the second section of the act to retain a further sum or drawback, for the expenses incident to the allowance and payment thereof, and in lieu of stamp duties on debentures,' shall not be deemed to operate on unregistered ships or vessels, owned by citizens of the United States, at the time of passing the said act, in those cases where such ship or vessel, at that time, possessed a sea-letter, or other regular document, issued from a custom-house of the United States, proving such a ship or vessel to be American property. This provision is intended to operate in favor of unregistered vessels, owned by citizens. And the term sea-letter is used as synonymous with a regular document issued by a custom-house of the United States, to certificated vessels.

"I consider, therefore, the term sea-letter, although variously understood on former occasions, yet is now adopted, naturalized and legitimated in our statute book, and its meaning perfectly defined, in the sense contended for by the plaintiffs. Though mentioned in certain treaties as synonymous with passports; yet, by statutes subsequently created, the term passport is exclusively used, and the word sea-letter transferred and attached to a different idea. The court ought, therefore, to have decided, that the legal technical sea-letter, contemplated by the supreme legislature, and spoken of in our statutes, was the certificate of ownership, granted to unregistered vessels, belonging to citizens of the United States."

> Sleght v. Hartshorne, 2 Johns. (N. Y.), 531, 543, Clinton, Senator, giving opinion of majority of court.
> See Cushing, At. Gen., Aug. 7, 1854, 6 Op. 638, 647–649; supra, p. 1008.

"The insurance was upon 'The good American ship, called the *Rodman*.' These words amount to a warranty that the ship was American, according to the settled construction of the phrase, both in this and in the English courts. (1 Johns. Cas., 341; 2 *ibid.*, 168; 3 Bos. & Pull., 201, 506, 510, 514, 531; 6 East's Rep., 382.) A warranty that the property is American, undoubtedly means that it is not only so in fact, but that it shall be clothed with the requisite evidence of its American character, for the purpose of protection, and in reference to the law of nations, under the sanction of which the voyage in question was to be conducted. (1 Johns. Cas., 365; 2 *ibid.*, 148.) It was proved that the ship was owned by the plaintiff, and that he was an American citizen; and from the case we are to conclude, that the ship had all the papers requisite for an American vessel, except an American register. . . . Was the want of a register a breach of the warranty? At the time the policy was underwritten, there were two kinds of American vessels, the one registered, and the other unregistered and carrying a sea-letter, or an official certificate of ownership, and both kinds were recognized by law, as American vessels, though the former was entitled to higher privileges under the laws of Congress. (6 Laws U. S., 72.) But, in reference to the law of nations, and to security upon the high seas, both species of vessels were equally entitled to protection as American property. There was no use in requiring a register for any object within the purview of the warranty. The want of it did not enhance the risk. ' It is a known and established rule,' says Sir William Scott, in the case of the *Vigilantia* (1 Rob., 113), ' that if a vessel is navigating under the pass of a foreign country, she is considered as bearing the national character of that nation under whose pass she sails; she makes a part of its navigation, and is in every respect liable to be considered as a vessel of that country.' What was said by Lord Alvanley in Baring *v.* Claggett (3 Bos. & Pull., 201) is not applicable, nor does it affect this doctrine. He considered that the warranty of a ship to be American required an American register, under our navigation act and the French treaty, and that the privilege of carrying the American flag, as a safe-conduct among belligerent powers, was to be denied to all ships not sailing under a compliance with that act. The act he referred to was passed in 1792 (2 Laws U. S., 131), and declared that none but registered vessels should be deemed vessels of the United States entitled to the benefits and privileges appertaining to such vessels. He was not then apprised of the distinction between registered and unregistered vessels, and of the legislative recognition of the latter as American vessels, entitled to privileges in port, as such, under the act of 1802. The act of 1792, to which he referred, seems, by its terms, to have left unregistered vessels as alien vessels, and without the protection of the United States. Whether that was, or was not, the condition of such vessels at that time, is not now a material inquiry, since the vessel in question, at the time of the warranty, was not only American property in fact, but entitled, by her sea-letter, under our law, and under the law of nations, to the immunities of the American flag. This was equivalent to what was termed by Sir William Scott a national pass, and so it was considered in the Court of Errors, in the case of Sleght *v.* Hartshorne (2 Johns. Rep., 531)."

> Kent, Ch. J., Barker *v.* Phœnix Ins. Co., 8 Johns. Rep. 307, 319.
> See, to the same effect, Griffith *v.* Ins. Co. (1813), 5 Binney, 464, 466, et seq.; infra.

The construction of a warranty, in a policy of insurance on a vessel, turned upon the question whether an unregistered, but American-owned, vessel sailing under a sea letter was entitled to the protection of the United States. The court referred to the letter of Hamilton, supra, to the collectors of customs, May 13, 1793, in which he mentioned the necessity of furnishing " all ships and vessels belonging to *citizens of the United States,* with *sea-letters,* for their more perfect identification and security;" and, after quoting this passage, the court said:

" This letter was accompanied with sea letters according to the form prescribed by the government, and not materially different from that which had been used in the Revolutionary war. It is under the hand of the President, and seal of the United States, countersigned by the Secretary of State, and contains the name and burthen of the vessel, with the nature of her cargo, the name of her master and the voyage on which she is bound, with permission to depart and proceed on the voyage. It contains also a declaration that oath has been made by the master, proving the vessel to be the property of citizens of the United States only. Underneath the signature of the Secretary of State, is a certificate signed by the collector of the port from whence the vessel sails, that oath has been made before him by the master, that the said vessel is owned by citizens of the United States only. This certificate is addressed to all foreign kings and potentates, and prays that the said master may be received and treated with kindness and friendship, etc. This sea letter being furnished to all vessels, registered or unregistered, belonging to citizens of the United States, afforded the same protection to both. It was a passport within the meaning of our treaties with France, Spain, Holland, etc., nor have we any reason to suppose that its efficacy was called in question by either of them. Lord Alvanley appears, therefore, to have been mistaken, when he said in the case of Baring, etc., *v.* Claggett (3 Bos. & Pull., 213), that our unregistered vessels were not protected from capture by our treaty with France. It is true that by the registering act of the 31st of December, 1792, it is declared that none other than registered vessels ' should be denominated and deemed vessels of the United States, entitled to the benefits and privileges appertaining to such vessels.' But those benefits and privileges were of a municipal nature, with which foreign powers had no concern. On the 1st of June, 1796, an act was passed directing the Secretary of State, with the approbation of the President, to prepare a form of passport for ships and vessels of the United States going to foreign countries. And by a supplement to this act, passed the 2d of March, 1803, every unregistered ship or vessel, owned by citizens of the United States, and sailing with a sea letter, going to any foreign country, is entitled to one of the passports created by the original law. Hence it has been concluded by the counsel for the defendants, that unregistered vessels were unprovided with a passport during the interval between the passing of the acts of June, 1796, and March, 1803; that they carried in fact nothing but a certificate of ownership, which obtained in common parlance the name of a sea letter, but did not operate as a passport. But in this I think they are mistaken. During all that period, sea letters (which were passports) were granted to unregistered vessels, and the passports under the act of June, 1796, were what are commonly called Mediterranean passports, rendered necessary by our treaty with the Dey of Algiers, on the 5th of September, 1795, by the fourth article of which, eighteen months were allowed for furnishing the ships of the United States with passports. The sea letters which operated as passports among the European nations, are printed in the English, French, Spanish and Dutch languages. But the Mediterranean passports are in the English language only, ornamented with an engraving, and indented at the top, so that the Algerines might easily distinguish them by the eye, and by an examination of the indented part. Mr. Dallas's argument has thrown light upon the subject of passports and sea-letters."

Tilghman, C. J., in Griffith *v.* Ins. Co. of North America (1813), 5 Binn. (Pa.), 464, 466 et seq.

See, in a similar sense, Barker *v.* Phoenix Ins. Co., 8 Johns. Rep. 307, 319.

Form of Mediterranean passport in use in the Department of State when Mr. Jefferson was Secretary.

[Cut of full-rigged ship, and under it view of a harbor.]

BY THE PRESIDENT OF THE UNITED STATES OF AMERICA.

To all persons whom these may concern :

Suffer the ———, ——— master or commander, of the burthen of —— tons or thereabouts, mounted with ——— guns, navigated with —— men, to pass with her company, passengers, goods, and merchandise, without any hindrance, seizure, or molestation, the said —— appearing by good testimony to belong to one or more of the citizens of the United States, and to him or them only.

Given under my hand and the seal of the United States of America, the —— day of ——, in the year of our Lord —— thousand —— hundred and ——.

By the President:

Number —.

———— ————,
Secretary of State.

STATE OF ———,

District of ———.

Countersigned by

————. ————.

Mr. Dallas, as Secretary of the Treasury, February 25, 1815, in a circular to collectors of customs mentioned, as documents carried by American vessels, the following:

" 1. *The certificate of registry.*—This document is created by our own laws, and belongs, exclusively, to vessels *American* built and owned—or such particular vessels as are expressly adopted by the registering act. It is an instrument which the vessel must carry, in order to entitle her to the privileges of a vessel of the United States.

" 2. *The sea-letter.*—This document is an instrument of the maritime laws of nations, and under the denomination of a *passport*, as well as of a sea-letter, treaties sometimes require it to be carried by the merchant vessels belonging to the contracting parties. It is an instrument which gives no privilege as to duties of import; but simply declares the *American* ownership, and recommends the vessel to the comity of nations. Vessels are under no legal obligation to carry a sea-letter; and, indeed, it is only necessary for neutral vessels, in a time of war.

" 3. *The Mediterranean passport.*—This instrument, having been described under the general denomination of ' *passport*,' in some of the acts of Congress, has been occasionally confounded with the *sea-letter*, which has also been denominated a *passport*. The form was introduced soon after the treaty with Algiers, which called for the instrument; and it is intended as a protection for American vessels against the Barbary powers."

> This letter is quoted in Jacobson's Sea Laws, 68, in a note by the editor, William Frick.
>
> Mr. Frick, in the note in question, expresses the opinion that the passport and sea-letter were essentially the same, being intended to prove the nationality of the vessel and protect the cargo from belligerents, while the certificate of property differed from it in deriving its importance from the usage of the custom-house alone, not being prescribed by any law. He thinks that the confusion as to passports and sea-letters arose as follows: Under the treaties of the United States with France, Holland, Spain, the terms were used synonymously, and related solely to the vessel. Congress probably referred to the paper, thus indiscriminately called a passport or sea-letter, in directing the Secretary of State, by the act of 1796, to prepare a form of " passport " for American ships; and this supposition is confirmed by the fact that the Secretary, in transmitting the papers to the custom-houses, called them sea-letters. In the act of 1803, however, says Mr. Frick, " unregistered vessels sailing with a sea letter, are directed to be furnished on application with a passport. The word, when used in this statute, means, as we conceive, a Mediterranean pass, a paper entirely of domestic creation, and differing essentially from those papers required to be on board by the general law of nations. The object of the law of 1803, then, becomes manifest, viz, to extend to vessels foreign built, but owned in this country, the benefit of being protected under a Mediterranean passport. But the

use of the same word to express in the first act a sea-letter, and in
the second a Mediterranean pass has created the obscurity which
has prevailed upon this subject."

The records of the Department of State contain numerous refer-
ences to the Mediterranean passport. Aug. 1, 1797, Mr. Pickering,
as Secretary of State, sent to the President eighty such passports for
his signature.[a] May 14, 1802, Mr. Edward Savage was requested to
prepare and furnish a thousand Mediterranean passports, of which
two hundred were said to be " immediately requisite." They were all
to be of the " old impression." [b] A thousand more were soon ordered.[c]
Five hundred were ordered in 1808, and one thousand in 1811.[d] In
1811 a new plate was made, but, as it differed " in several particulars " from the old, "it was " thought that the immediate substitution of it might expose seamen and trade of the United States in the
Mediterranean to very material hazard; " and " a supply of a small
number, say two or three hundred," was ordered from the old plate.[e]
Subsequently, Col. Lear, the United States consul at Algiers, was instructed to notify the Regency of a change in the form of the
Mediterranean passport, and was furnished with " two or three hundred tops of the new passports, . . . to be distributed amongst the
Barbary States conformably with the projected alteration." But,
till it was known that those States had been duly advised of the
change, and that their cruisers had been furnished " with the tops "
of the new passports, it was deemed prudent to use the old.[f]

It having been reported that an American vessel had been seized
by the Spanish authorities at Valparaiso because she had no sea letter,
the matter was called to the attention of the Spanish minister at
Washington. It was stated that the vessel in question and numerous
other vessels which had gone on voyages to the Pacific had before
sailing applied to the Treasury Department for the sea letters specified
by Article XVII. of the treaty between the United States and Spain
of October 27, 1795. The applications were duly considered, and, a
general peace having taken place, it was concluded that such a document was not necessary, and the Treasury therefore declined to issue
any. Under these circumstances the Spanish minister was requested
to interpose his good offices for the discharge of the vessel in question

---

[a] 10 MS. Dom. Let. 102.

[b] Mr. Brent, chief clerk, to Mr. Savage, May 14, 1802, 14 MS. Dom, Let. 12;
same to same, Feb. 25, 1803, id. 131, states that Mr. Savage had then furnished
1,007 in all.

[c] Mr. Brent, chief clerk, to Mr. Savage, April 25, 1803, 14 MS. Dom. Let. 150.

[d] Mr. Brent, chief clerk, to Col. Wm. Duane, Aug. 9, 1808, and June 27, 1811,
15 MS. Dom. Let. 304, and 16 id. 28.

[e] Mr. Brent, chief clerk, to Col. Duane, July 30, 1811, 16 MS. Dom. Let. 29.

[f] Mr. Brent, chief clerk, to Col. Duane, June 12, 1812, 16 MS. Dom. Let. 60.

and of any other vessels which might have been seized for the same cause.

Mr. Monroe, Sec. of State, to the Chev. de Onis, Spanish min., July 2, 1816, MS. Notes to For. Leg. II. 153.

It was stated, in 1845, that a sea letter could legally be granted only to a registered vessel, and that sea letters were at that time " only granted to vessels trading beyond the Capes of Good Hope and Horn." Where, therefore, a vessel was found with a sea-letter but without a register, instructions were given to the consul at Valparaiso, if she should again visit that port, to take possession of her sea letter and cancel it.

Mr. Calhoun, Sec. of State, to Mr. Dorr, consul at Valparaiso, Feb. 26, 1845, 11 MS. Desp. to Consuls, 344.

" There is no authority in law warranting an American minister in China ' to grant sea letters or any documents of a like character to foreign vessels purchased by Americans residing in China, designed to be used in the coasting trade of that country.' "

Mr. Buchanan, Sec. of State, to Mr. Davis, Feb. 17, 1849, MS. Inst. China, I. 59.

" The law of nations does not require a register or any other particular paper as expressive of the ship's national character. Laws describing the kind of papers vessels must carry are considered as regulations purely local and municipal, for purposes of public policy, and vary in different countries. As evidence that the vessel has changed owners, the bill of sale is required by the practice of maritime courts, and is generally satisfactory. Sir William Scott says: 'A bill of sale is the proper title to which the maritime courts of all countries would look. It is the universal instrument of transfer of ships in the usage of all maritime countries.' "

Mr. Marcy, Sec. of State, to Mr. Mason, Feb. 19, 1856, MS. Inst. France, XV. 321.

How is the nationality of a foreign-built vessel, American owned, but unregistered, to be established?

"Ordinarily the nationality of sea-going vessels of the United States is shown by the possession of a register, enrolment or license, but neither of these documents can, under the laws of the United States, be issued to a vessel of the class under consideration. It had been the practice, however, from an early period in the history of the United States up to the year 1855, for collectors of customs to furnish to American owners of foreign-built vessels, on due proof of citizenship and of ownership, a *certificate of property*, so-called, by which the facts of such citizenship and ownership were formally recognized and authenticated.

" In common with sea-letters and other documents verifying the proprietary interest, they stood principally upon the provisions of treaties or the general law of nations (Abbott on Shipping, p. 347, note) ; were given by officers of the customs under a supposed general power to certify any facts made to appear to them in relation to ships and merchandise, and were practically regarded as equivalent to a sea-letter (2 Johns. R. 548). These certificates were in use as early as 1798, and received the formal sanction of this Department by circulars dated respectively February 25, 1815, and July 31, 1821.

" But in October, 1855, the Attorney-General, in reply to the question what document should be given to such vessels, communicated to the Secretary of the Treasury certain views which led to a modification of the *form* of certificate then in use (7 Op. 538).

" This modification consisted in certifying not the *fact* of ownership as before, but that the *evidence* of that fact had been examined and recorded in the office of the collector. The form of certificate as thus modified was embodied in the general Regulations of the Department issued in 1857 (article 76), has been in use ever since, and is retained in the Revised Regulations promulgated January 30, 1869, part first, article 96. It constitutes *prima facie* evidence of ownership, and as such indicates the nationality of the vessel, but is not *conclusive* any more than is a register, enrolment or license, all of which are documents resting upon local or municipal as distinguished from general or international law.

" If the purchase be made *bona fide* and the property be passed absolutely and without reserve, the ship so purchased becomes entitled ' *to bear the flag* and receive the protection of the United States ' (6 Op. 652) ; but this right may be questioned and must then be established by actual proof, not by presumptive evidence, the only character which can be claimed for the certificate here referred to."

> Open letter addressed by Mr. Boutwell, Sec. of Treasury, to Mr. Washburne, min. to France, May 23, 1871, and at the same time transmitted by copy to Mr. Fish, Sec. of State. (MS. Misc. Letters, May, 1871, Part II.)
>
> See, in this relation, circular of Mr. Evarts, Sec. of State, to U. S. Consuls, Feb. 18, 1880, For. Rel. 1880, 1 ; MS. Circulars, II. 455.
>
> See, also, a letter of Mr. Fish, Sec. of State, to Mr. Boutwell, Sec. of Treas., March 8, 1872, approving, with certain suggestions of amendment, a draft of " a bill to provide for the registration of foreign-built vessels owned by citizens of the United States." (93 MS. Dom. Let. 88.)

" Adverting to former correspondence upon the subject, I have the honor to inform you that, a supply of ' sea letters ' having now been received from the printer, one hundred copies have been forwarded to your address to-day in a separate package for the use of your Department."

Mr. Evarts, Sec. of State, to Mr. Sherman, Sec. of Treas., Nov. 8, 1880, 135 MS. Dom. Let. 141.

"Art. 14. Marine documents consist of certificates of registry and enrolment, and licenses.   R. S. 4312 and 4319.

"Art. 15. In addition to these, sea-letters and passports for vessels may be issued through collectors, on application, to registered vessels engaged in the foreign trade by sea, as an additional protection and evidence of nationality.   They are to be in all cases surrendered with the certificate of registry at the expiration of the voyage.   R. S., 4306 and 4307.

"Art 93. Foreign-built or denationalized vessels purchased and wholly owned by citizens of the United States, whether purchased of belligerents or neutrals during a war to which the United States are not a party, or in peace, of foreign owners, are entitled to the protection of the authorities and flag of the United States, as the property of American citizens, although no register, enrolment, license, or other marine document, prescribed by the laws of the United States, can be lawfully issued to such vessels.

"Art. 94. To enable, however, the owners of a vessel so circumstanced, to protect their rights, if molested or questioned, the collector of the customs, though forbidden by law to grant any marine document, may lawfully make record of the bill of sale in his office, authenticate its validity in form and substance, and deliver to the owner a certificate to that effect, certifying, also, that the owner is a citizen of the United States.

" These facts, thus authenticated, if the transfer was in good faith, entitle the vessel to protection as the lawful property of a citizen of the United States; and the authentication of the bill of sale and of citizenship will be *prima facie* proof of such good faith."

Treasury Regulations, 1884.

"As far as the records of the Department of State show, it was the usage of the Government to issue what were called ' Mediterranean letters,' a form of which is hereunto annexed. These letters were based, not on registry, but on alleged ownership by citizens of the United States, and authorized the vessels to which they were granted to sail under the flag of the United States. Subsequently, what were called ' sea letters ' were issued, a form of one of which is annexed.

" These letters, granted to vessels which are foreign built, and therefore not entitled to registry under our navigation laws, are well

1064 THE HIGH SEAS. [§ 325.

known in maritime practice. We find, for instance, in Bouvier's Law Dictionary, the following statement:

" ' Sea letter, or sea brief (mar. law), is a document which should be found on board of every neutral ship. It specifies the nature and quantity of the cargo, the place from whence it comes, and its destination. Chit. Law of Nat., 197.'

" Revised Statutes, section 4190, clearly leaves this practice undisturbed. This section, whose history is given by Mr. Cushing in an opinion to be presently quoted, is as follows:

" ' No sea letter or other document certifying or proving any vessel to be the property of a citizen of the United States shall be issued, except to vessels duly registered or enrolled and licensed as vessels of the United States, *or to vessels which shall be wholly owned by citizens of the United States*, and furnished with or entitled to sea letters or other custom-house documents.' . . .

" By a series of treaties the international authority of sea letters and of passports of the character in question is recognized. . . . It must be remembered that those treaties are not only, from their nature, declaratory of international law, but are as much a part of the supreme municipal law of the United States as are its statutes. And it also must be remembered that the term ' sea letter,' as used in these treaties, was accepted, so far as the United States was concerned, in the sense, which with us it always bore, of a passport to a vessel owned by citizens of the United States, irrespective of the question of registry. . . . I have no hesitation in saying that vessels owned by citizens of the United States, but foreign built, are entitled to carry the flag of the United States, and to obtain, in cases of vessels purchased abroad, the certificate specified in section 340 of the Consular Regulations above quoted. Vessels of this class, it is true, can not enter our ports, not being duly registered under the navigation act; [a] but there is no reason why they should not engage in foreign trade, and when in this trade carry the flag and enjoy the protection of the United States. It was under sea letters or similar letters, based not on our registration laws but on the principle of the law of nations, that ships owned by citizens of a country are entitled to 'the flag and protection of that country, that a large part of the carrying trade of the world was done, during the Napoleonic wars, under the flag of the United States, nor was the rightfulness of this title and this protection ever questioned by England during those bitter and terrible struggles, when she questioned almost every other maritime right we possessed. The English courts, as well as the courts of the continent of

---

[a] In printing this opinion in his Int. Law Digest, Dr. Wharton made this clause read " can not have in our ports the privileges given by statute to registered vessels,"

Europe, united in the principle, since then asserted by us on more than one important occasion, that while municipal laws expanding or contracting the law of nations, bind municipally, they do not bind internationally, and that while a nation may municipally impose peculiarly stringent rules on its own subjects, it does not, so far as concerns its own liability, bind its subjects to observe those rules in their dealings with foreigners or with foreign states. But it is not necessary to invoke this principle for the determination of the present issue. [I hold that even by our own legislation, documents of the character specified in section 340 of the Consular Regulations, and in section 94 of the Treasury Regulations, can be granted to vessels owned by citizens of the United States entitling them to fly the United States flag, and to receive the protection of the United States. And I see no reason, under our present legislation, why, in case of the United States being a neutral during a war between maritime powers, this Department should not resume the practice of issuing sea letters to foreign-built ships owned by citizens of the United States; though such sea letters might not confer on the vessels holding them any immunities beyond those conferred in similar cases at present by consular or customs certificates of sale."]

> Opinion of Dr. Wharton, Solicitor of Department of State and Examiner of Claims, Nov. 30, 1885, MS. Opinions of Solicitors, XIX. 22. This opinion is endorsed, " Not acted on."
>
> The last two sentences of the foregoing opinion, enclosed in brackets, are printed above, not as found in the MS. opinion, but as published by Dr. Wharton in his Int. Law Digest, evidently with modifications by himself. The concluding part of the opinion, as it is found in the record, reads as follows:
>
> " I hold that even by our own legislation sea letters, or in their place documents of the character specified in section 340 of the Consular Regulations, can be granted to vessels owned by citizens of the United States entitling them to fly the United States flag; and that this construction is confirmed, not only by the presumption in favor of freedom which prevails in cases of doubt, but by an almost unbroken line of rulings in this department, and in the Department of Justice. As, however, the question is one of great importance, I respectfully ask that copies of this opinion be sent to the Treasury Department and to the Department of Justice, and that the opinion of those Departments be asked on the question submitted.
>
> " In President Arthur's last message he made the following propositions to Congress in this connection :
>
> " ' The recent purchase by citizens of the United States of a large trading fleet heretofore under the Chinese flag has considerably enhanced our commercial importance in the east. In view of the large number of vessels built or purchased by American citizens in other countries and exclusively employed in legitimate traffic between ports under the recognized protection of our flag, it might be well to provide a uniform rule for their registration and documentation, so that the *bona fide* property rights of our citizens therein shall be duly evidenced and properly guarded.'

"This recommendation, assuming, as it does, the legality of sea letters, and of consular certificates of ownership, may well be repeated and could be safely carried out.

"Whether it is desirable to go further than this, and to define the authority to issue such letters and certificates, I beg leave with much submission to doubt. At present the whole matter is under the control of the Executive; and the best that legislation in this respect could do would be to confirm the practice now existing and constantly acted on by which consuls give certificates of ownership on due proof to citizens of the United States purchasing foreign built vessels in foreign ports. No legislation, also, is required to authorize the Department of State to issue sea letters in the form in which they were issued from the beginning of our government down to the present day. But one thing at least is clear. If we permit this prerogative of sovereignty, given to the Executive not only by our statutes but by the law of nations, to fall into disuse, we not only expose American ships on the high seas to depredations which we will be unable to check or punish, but we surrender the opportunity of absorbing, in case of a European war, the carrying trade of the belligerents, and we would subject by doing so, the commerce of the world, so far as concerns such belligerents, to almost total stoppage. In a war, at least, in which England is concerned, we are almost the only nation that could take up such carrying trade; and if we should take it up adequately so as to retain it, this must be by foreign-built vessels owned and manned by ourselves."

Sec. 340 of the Consular Regulations of 1881, above referred to, is the same as sec. 343 of the Cons. Regulations of 1896, supra.

The treaties referred to by Dr. Wharton in his opinion are those of the United States with the following countries: Algiers, 1795, Art. VIII.; 1815, Art. VII.; Argentine Confederation, 1853, Art. VII.; Belgium, 1858, Art. X., repeated in Art. IX. of the treaty of 1875; Bolivia, 1858, Arts. V., XXII.; Brazil, 1828, Arts. IV., XXI.; Chile, 1832, Art. XIX.; Colombia, 1824, Art. XIX.; Dominican Republic, 1867, Arts. VIII., XVI.; Ecuador, 1839, Art. V., XXII.; France, 1778, Art. XXX.; 1800, Art. XVII.; Guatemala, 1849, Art. XXI.; Hanover, 1840, Art. II.; 1846, Art. V.; Hanseatic Republics, 1827, Art. IV.; Hayti, 1864, Art. XXIII.; Italy, 1871. XVII.; Mecklenburg-Schwerin, 1847, Art. V.; Mexico, 1831, Art. XXIII.; Morocco, 1836, Art. IV.; Netherlands, 1782, Art. X.; 1839, Art. IV.; New Granada, 1846, Art. XXII.; Ottoman Empire, 1862, Art. X.; Paraguay, 1859, Art. VII.; Peru, 1851, Art. XXVIII.; Prussia, 1785, Art. XIV.; 1799, Art. XIV.; San Salvador, 1870, Art. XXII.; Spain, 1795, Art. XVII.; Sweden, 1783, Art. XI.; Two Sicilies, 1855, Art. IX.; Tripoli, 1796, Art. IV.; Tunis, 1797, Art. IV.; Venezuela, 1836, Arts. V., XXII.; 1860, Art. XVI.

" Although the act [of March 2, 1803] speaks of a sea letter and a passport, it is difficult to ascertain the difference between the two documents. In various treaties the words passport and sea letter are used as synonyms.

" The word *passport* appears to have been adopted with reference to the requirement of such a document for vessels bound to the Mediterranean, under the treaties with the Barbary Powers, certifying to the nationality of vessels owned by Americans. The Department of State, before the passage of this act, had adopted a certification of the American ownership of all American vessels, other than registered vessels, for the security of such vessels in the wars then pending in Europe, by reason of which the Americans, as neutrals, were enjoying a large part of the carrying trade.

" On May 13, 1793, Mr. Hamilton enclosed to the collector of the port of New York forms of *sea letters* to be furnished for the identification and security of all ships and vessels belonging to citizens of the United States, and Mr. Jefferson, the Secretary of State, in a letter to Mr. Morris, our minister in France, under date of June 13 in the same year, enclosed copies, which he terms *forms of passport*, in which he says: ' It is determined that they shall be given in our own ports only, and to serve but for one voyage. It has also been determined that they shall be given to all vessels bona fide owned by American citizens wholly, whether built here or not.'

" The vessels not registered furnished with such documents appear to have been called ' sea-letter vessels,' as distinguished from registered vessels of the United States. The ambiguity as to the meaning of the word passport arises from the statute of 1803 requiring passports to be issued to all vessels owned by American citizens sailing with a sea letter, and is not satisfactorily explained in the opinion in Sleght *v.* Hartshorne (2 Johns. R. 531–543). Chief Justice Tilghman, of Pennsylvania, however, in his opinion delivered in Griffith *v.* The Ins. Co. (5 Binn. 464), says that the *sea letter* issued under the authority of the President in 1793 was a *passport* within the meaning of our treaties with France, Spain, Holland, etc., and that the passport mentioned in the acts of 1796 and of 1803 was a document required by our treaty with the Dey of Algiers of the 5th of September, 1795, by the fourth article of which eighteen months were allowed for furnishing the ships of the United States with passports. The sea letters, which operated as passports among the European nations, he says, were printed in English, French, Spanish, and Dutch, while the Mediterranean passport was in the English language only, with an engraving, and indented at the top, so as to be easily distinguished by the eye by an examination of the indented part, of which a counterpart was furnished the Algerine cruisers. The chief justice accepted the view (as to the nature of these documents) of the Hon. A. J. Dallas, one of the counsel in the cause, who afterwards, as the Secretary of the Treasury, adopted this distinction between the sea-letter and the passport, in a circular to the collectors of the ports of the United States in 1815. The view that the word *passport* is to be confined to a Mediterranean pass under the treaties with the Barbary Powers is confirmed by Reeve's History of the Law of Shipping, 424, and the American document called a passport, of which the commencement is given in Baring *v.* Claggett (3 B. & P., 202), corresponds with that of the sea letter prepared during the administration of President Garfield. The sea letter would appear to be a certificate of nationality and distinct from the formal document called for by a treaty with that particular naval power.

" Congress also, in 1803 (Rev. Stat., § 4191), passed an act imposing a penalty on any person who should make, utter, or publish any false sea letter, Mediterranean passport, or certificate of registry, or who should avail himself of the same.

" This act recognizes the sea letter and Mediterranean passport as a certificate of national character similarly with the registry required by vessels of the United States, and later on, in 1825, an act was passed (Rev. Stat., § 5423) making it criminal to forge or alter as well such pass or passport and sea letter as a certificate of enrollment or registry.

" These acts sufficiently indicate that Congress has recognized the national character of undocumented vessels owned by American citizens, and has provided for their identification as vessels of the nationality of the owners.

" To what vessels sea letters should be issued, and the character of the document, was also defined by the subsequent act of 26th March, 1810. (Rev. Stat., § 4190.)

" It provides, ' No sea letter or other document certifying or proving any vessel to be the property of a citizen of the United States shall be issued except to vessels duly registered or enrolled and licensed as vessels of the United States or to vessels which shall be wholly owned by citizens of the United States, and furnished with or entitled to sea letters or other custom-house documents.' "

> Opinion of Morton P. Henry, esq. (of the Philadelphia bar, and author of a treatise on Admiralty Jurisdiction and Procedure), given to Dr. Francis Wharton, April, 1887, and printed in Wharton's Digest (2nd ed.) III. 994; also printed supra, p. 1026.

" In accordance with the request contained in your letter of the 28th ultimo, I enclose to you herewith a special passport for the American schooner *Sarah W. Hunt*, which it is hoped will be of use to her in her sealing and trading voyage to the South Seas."

> Mr. Blaine, Sec. of State, to Mr. Irsch, April 22, 1889, 172 MS. Dom. Let. 556.
>
> The passport was as follows:
>
> UNITED STATES OF AMERICA, DEPARTMENT OF STATE.
>
> To all whom it may concern: Know ye that the American schooner " Sarah W. Hunt," whereof James W. Budington, a citizen of the United States, is master, is bound from Stonington, one of the seaports of this country, to the South Seas on a sealing and trading voyage;

Whereof I request all whom it may concern not to give or to suffer to be given to her any hindrance or molestation, but on the contrary to afford her every aid and facility she may need in the prosecution of her voyage, and to permit said schooner, captain, and crew to pursue their calling unmolested within the law, and to aid and give them such privileges as are accorded to the vessels and citizens or subjects of the most favored nations.

In testimony whereof, I, James G. Blaine, Secretary of State of the United States of America, have hereunto set my hand and caused the seal of the Department of State to be affixed, at Washington, this 20th day of April, A. D. 1889, and of the Independence of the United States of America the one hundred and thirteenth.

[SEAL.] JAMES G. BLAINE.

In the case of the sale to an American company of the Corean schooner *Kyeng II.*, renamed *Janice*, the consular officer who acted in the matter was instructed that in giving in future the certificate (Form No. 35) referred to in § 343 of the Consular Regulations of 1896, he might, if for any reason he deemed it desirable, attach thereto a statement quoting §§ 341–347 of the Consular Regulations, as to the right to acquire property in foreign ships and to fly the United States flag on such vessels.

Mr. Cridler, Third Assist. Sec. of State, to Mr. Allen, consul-general at Seoul, May 1, 1900, 172 MS. Inst. Consuls, 230.

The commander in chief of the United States naval force on the Asiatic station was instructed to recall and cancel a provisional register which he had granted to the *Yiksang* and other foreign vessels. Mr. Cridler, Third Assist. Sec. of State, to Sec. of War, July 7, 1899, 238 MS. Dom. Let. 368.

" It is to be understood that every vessel of the United States, which is afloat, is bound to have with her from the officers of her home port, either a register or an enrolment. The former is used when she is engaged in a foreign voyage or trade, and the latter when she is engaged in domestic commerce, usually called the coasting trade. If found afloat, whether by steam or sail, without one or the other of these, and without the right one with reference to the trade she is engaged in, or the place where she is found, she is entitled to no protection under the laws of the United States, and is liable to seizure for such violation of the law, and in a foreign jurisdiction or on the high seas, can claim no rights as an American vessel."

Miller, J., Badger *v.* Gutierez, 111 U. S. 736, 737. See supra, p. 1033, note.

In this case it is held that a collector who detains a ship's papers, when the ship is not under seizure, and when her papers are not deposited with him for the purposes of entry and clearance, subjects himself to an action for damages.

5. Arming of Merchant Vessels.

§ 326.

" In answer to your request for an expression of opinion in regard to Mr. Ogden's question whether a vessel which he is said to be fitting out for a trading voyage to the South Sea Islands, can carry two guns and other arms for protection and defense against the natives, I am not aware of any international prohibition or of any treaty provision which would prevent a vessel trading amid the groups of islands of the South Sea from carrying a couple of guns and arms for the proper and necessary protection of the vessel against violence on the part of lawless or partially civilized communities, or of the piratical crews which are represented to occasionally frequent those waters, providing always that the vessel carrying such guns and arms itself be on a lawful voyage and be engaged in none other than peaceful commerce, and that such guns and arms be intended and be used solely for the purpose of defense and of self-protection."

> Mr. Fish, Sec. of State, to Mr. Morrill, Feb. 8, 1877, 117 Dom. Let. 54

" A copy of your No. 23, of the 10th instant, in regard to the case of the American schooner *Water Witch*, which arrived in Haytian waters with two cannon and sixty pounds of powder on board, having been transmitted to the Secretary of the Treasury, that official has replied to your enquiry whether sailing vessels of the United States are allowed to carry any armament as ship's stores, or otherwise, that the laws do not forbid the carrying of articles of the character mentioned, provided there shall be no violation of Chapter LXVII. of the Revised Statutes."

> Mr. Gresham, Sec. of State, to Mr. Smythe, min. to Hayti, Jan. 31, 1894, For. Rel. 1894, 337, MS. Inst. Hayti, III. 375.
>
> Chap. LXVII., R. S., embracing §§ 5281–5291, relates to neutrality. Sec. 5289 reads as follows:
>
> " Sec. 5289. The owners or consignees of every armed vessel sailing out of the ports of the United States, belonging wholly or in part to citizens thereof, shall, before clearing out the same, give bond to the United States, with sufficient sureties, in double the amount of the value of the vessel and cargo on board, including her armament, conditioned that the vessel shall not be employed by such owners to cruise or commit hostilities against the subjects, citizens, or property of any foreign prince or state, or of any colony, district, or people, with whom the United States are at peace."
>
> It should also be borne in mind that a merchant vessel using arms for acts of destruction on the high seas, unless duly commissioned for the purpose, may expose herself to a charge of piracy.

The law does not prohibit armed vessels belonging to citizens of the United States from sailing out of our ports; it only requires the owners to give security that such vessels shall not be employed by them to commit hostilities against foreign powers at peace with the United States.

United States *v.* Quincy, 6 Pet. 445.

The seizure by France of an American merchantman, and her condemnation, can not be justified by the fact that she was armed for defensive purposes.

Cushing *v.* United States, 22 Ct. Cl. 1; Hooper *v.* United States, 22 Ct. Cl. 408.

6. OFFICERS.

§ 327.

" In my opinion the command of American vessels should be confined to American citizens."

Mr. Jay, Sec. for For. Aff., to the Gov. of Virginia, Dec. 17, 1787, 3 MS. Am. Let. 308. See supra, pp. 1035, 1043–1044, 1049.

A tax on a vessel employing as mate an alien, imposed under section 4219, Revised Statutes, which provides that a vessel any officer of which shall not be " a citizen of the United States," shall pay a tax of 50 cents a ton, should not be remitted because such alien had duly declared his intention to become a citizen of the United States and had for more than three years continuously served on board American merchant vessels, if he had never actually been admitted to citizenship.

Harmon, At. Gen. (Sept. 15, 1896), 21 Op. 412.

7. LOSS OF RIGHT TO PROTECTION.

§ 328.

" I think it proper to meet cases which it appears from your dispatch are likely to arise, although you have not distinctly presented them. An American register of a vessel will not entitle its owner, even though he be [a] citizen resident here, to especial exemption from the operation of the laws of New Granada, if the vessel, instead of being employed in general commerce, is applied to the purposes of internal trade and navigation in New Granada for an indefinite period and without a purpose of returning her to our own waters or employing her in our own national commerce."

Mr. Seward, Sec. of State, to Mr. Burton, No. 12, Jan. 16, 1862, MS. Inst. Colombia, XVI. 20.

Referring to an application made by Mr. Henry Schuber, a citizen of the United States, to the Colombian Government for a license to run a steamboat coastwise on the Pacific coast of that country, Mr. Seward observed that it was solely within the competence of the Colombian Government to determine when and on what conditions a vessel of foreign build and foreign ownership should be allowed to engage in its coastwise trade, and that he was not aware of any law of the United States by which an American vessel, " in consequence of its employment in a foreign coasting trade forfeits the privileges attaching to its registry when it shall again resume a course of navigation under the laws of this country." Mr. Seward added, however, that Mr. Schuber should be informed " that, when a citizen of the United States, domiciled in a foreign country, engages in a regular coasting business generally forbidden to our vessels, in virtue of an exceptional license from the government of such country, he will be regarded, although such government may permit him to sail the vessel under our flag, as having elected to put it under the exclusive protection of the government whose license it bears and into whose commercial marine it is adopted, and to have waived any claim to the protection of this Government for his vessel while thus employed."

Mr. Seward, Sec. of State, to Mr. Sullivan, min. to Colombia, Dec. 4, 1867, MS. Inst. Colombia, XVI. 257.

It appears that Mr. Schuber obtained the license which he sought and placed in the Colombian coasting trade a steamer called the *Montijo*, which belonged to himself and his brother, who traded at Panama under the firm name of H. Schuber & Brother. In April, 1871, the steamer, while on a voyage from the port of David to the city of Panama, was seized by revolutionists, with whom the Colombian Government afterwards made an arrangement by which they were granted amnesty for their acts. The Government of the United States on becoming acquainted with the facts instructed the American minister at Bogotá to bring the case to the notice of the Colombian Government, and a claim for damages was afterwards presented through the American legation to that Government. This claim was referred to arbitration, and an award was made in favor of the claimants for $33,401. Among the defences made by Colombia were (1) that the Schubers were domiciled in that country, and (2) that the steamer when seized was sailing under a coasting license. With regard to the first point, the umpire found (*a*) that the claimants, though they had been engaged in business at Panama since 1849, were not domiciled in Colombia, and (*b*) that, even if they were so domiciled, the " United States would still have the right, under certain circumstances, to extend to them its protection." As to the second point, the umpire held that the coasting license, under which the vessel was permitted to sail under the flag of the United States, was legal, and that, even if it was legally defective, the Colombian Government

had impliedly waived the defect and could not set it up as an answer
to the claim for compensation.

> Case of the *Montijo*, agreement between the United States and Colombia,
> of August 17, 1874, Moore, Int. Arbitrations, II. 1421–1447.
>
> See, as to the case of the American steamer *Atrato*, Mr. Blaine, Sec. of
> State, to Sec. of Treas., June 7, 1889, 173 MS. Dom. Let. 313.

"I acknowledge the receipt of your despatch (No. 14) of the 18th
ultimo, enclosing the translation of a note from the secretary of state
for foreign affairs of Hayti, in which he states that the American
steamer *City of Port au Prince* was violently interdicted from entering the port of Gonaives by two war steamers in the service of rebels.
You add your own statement that the American vessel before named
is employed as a transport in the service of the Haytian Government,
and is often freighted with munitions of war [and] sent from port to
port under the control of that Government. The secretary for foreign affairs, in his note, mentions the fact that his colleague, the
secretary for war and marine, was on board the American vessel at
the time of its alleged exclusion from the port of Gonaives and furnished the information which is communicated by that note.

"The general views of this Government in respect to the vessels
in the service of the Haytian insurgents and to their operations were
communicated to you in my instructions (No. 11) of the 14th instant,
to which you are referred. It is only necessary to add that a vessel
of the United States entering into the service of a foreign power as
an auxiliary to military or naval operations must be regarded as
relying exclusively upon the protection of that power, and abjuring,
while such employment continues, any claim to the protection of this
Government. You will furnish Mr. Archier with a copy of this
despatch."

> Mr. Fish, Sec. of State, to Mr. Bassett, min. to Hayti, No. 12, Sept. 15,
> 1869, MS. Inst. Hayti, I. 154. See supra, pp. 1085–1086.

"I acknowledge the receipt of your despatch (No. 23) of November 1, 1869, enclosing copies of correspondence growing out of the
notice of Her Britannic Majesty's legation of an intention to hold
the American steam tug *Aspinwall*, and its owners, responsible for
any losses that may be incurred by the owners of the British schooner
Express, which had been captured by the Haytian Government, in
consequence of the schooner's being taken in tow by the tug while
the latter was in the employment of the Haytian Government.

"This occurrence confirms the propriety of my instruction to you
(No. 12) of September 15th, 1869, because it is a second exempli-
fication growing out of the same transaction of the embarrassments
to which this Government would subject itself, if it admitted that

an American vessel which has been voluntarily put into the service of a foreign government as an auxiliary to military or naval operations, could retain any right to our protection for the vessel, cargo, ship's company or passengers.

"The United States having in no wise directed or countenanced the entry of the tug *Aspinwall* into the service of the Haytian Government, will not concern themselves about any eventualities which may result from such service, but will leave the owners to such responsibility, if any, as the British Government may deem itself authorized to insist upon, and to such indemnification as the Haytian Government may feel itself bound to give."

> Mr. Fish, Sec. of State, to Mr. Bassett, min. to Hayti, No. 23, Dec. 7, 1869,
> MS. Inst. Hayti, I. 169.

March 3, 1885, the Colombian minister to the United States communicated to the Department of State a copy of a telegram from the authorities of Panama, reporting that the steam tug *Game Cock*, belonging to the Panama Railroad Company, had been captured by the insurgents. The Colombian minister requested that the naval commanders of the United States should be suitably instructed in the premises. A report was afterwards received from the commanding officer of the U. S. S. *Galena*, at Colon, to the effect that the *Game Cock* was not owned by citizens of the United States, but was French property, belonging to the Panama Canal Company; that at the time of her capture she was doing harbor duty temporarily for the railroad company; and that she was under the flag of Colombia. The Department of State held that such temporary employment in the service of an American corporation could not entail upon the United States any obligation such as might exist with respect to a vessel owned by citizens of the United States and sailing under the American flag.

> Mr. Bayard, Sec. of State, to Mr. Becerra, Colombian min., April 8, 1885,
> For. Rel. 1885, 249.
>
> It being subsequently ascertained that the *Game Cock* was the property of the Panama Railroad Company, Commander Willis, U. S. S. *Yantic*, seized her on August 6, 1885, and turned her over to the company. (Mr. Bayard, Sec. of State, to Messrs. Barlow et al., Aug. 22, 1885, 156 MS. Dom. Let. 611.)

The protection of the United States having been requested for certain vessels navigating the internal waters of Colombia, a report was subsequently received to the effect that they were for the moment in the service of insurgents against the titular government, under an agreement the terms of which seemed to repel the supposition of coercion, and that but little stock of the company by which the vessels were owned was held by citizens of the United States. Under these circumstances it was stated that, if the request for protection was further pressed, the Department of State would be pleased to learn:

" 1. Whether the stock is for the most part held by American citizens or aliens.

" 2. Whether the officers of the company are American citizens.

" 3. Whether the vessels fly the United States or the Colombian flag, and what registry they carry.

" 4. Does the Colombian concession to the company recognize or require the American nationality of the vessels."

> Mr. Bayard, Sec. of State, to Mr. Hood, July 6, 1885, 156 MS. Dom. Let. 184.

The steamship *Bolivar*, American owned and built, but undocumented, having finished a term of service under the Venezuelan Government and flag, desired to resume American colors and protection. The opinion was expressed that the vessel, being American owned, was entitled to claim protection as American property, provided that she was not " in the service of a foreign government; " but that, if it was desired to obtain for her all the privileges of a " vessel of the United States," documentation in the district including her home port was necessary, and would appear to be practicable, if her temporary service under the Venezuelan flag was not attended with loss of her American ownership.

> Mr. Bayard, Sec. of State, to Sec. of Treas., Sept. 14, 1888, 169 MS. Dom. Let. 671.

It having been stated that the American registered steamer *Pizatti* was chartered in Honduras by the President of the Republic for use against rebels who were in possession of the harbors of La Ceiba and Trujillo, and was granted for the time being permission to fly the Honduranean flag, the Treasury Department expressed the opinion that, as the case was not covered by section 4135, Revised Statutes, relating to vessels " authorized to sail under a foreign flag, and to have the protection of any foreign government during the existence of the rebellion," neither the vessel, nor her owners or master, had incurred any penalty or disability under the statutes of the United States. Nevertheless, it is very desirable that American vessels should avoid all interference in local conflicts in foreign countries, and rigidly preserve their neutral character.

> Mr. Foster, Sec. of State, to Mr. Scruggs, min. to Venezuela, Sept. 30, 1892, For. Rel. 1892, 627, 620–621 ; Mr. Foster, Sec. of State, to Mr. Pacheco, min. to Honduras, Sept. 27, 1892, For. Rel. 1893, 149–152.
> Information was subsequently received by the Department of State tending to show that preparation was made in the United States for

participation by the steamer and her officers in the struggle; and
the minister of the United States in Honduras was instructed to
inform the Government that such an allegation would "very materially modify" the opinion previously expressed. (Mr. Gresham,
Sec. of State, to Mr. Young, min. to Honduras, May 6, 1893, For. Rel.
1893, 151.) The *Pizatti* was afterwards libelled at New Orleans
under § 5283, R. S., for violation of the neutrality laws. (For. Rel.
1893, 152.)

V. *VESSELS CONTROLLED BY INSURGENTS.*

1. Cases and Opinions, 1776–1860.

§ 329.

By the British statute of 17 George III., ch. 9, in 1777, after reciting
that whereas a rebellion and war have been openly and traitorously
levied and carried on in certain of His Majesty's colonies and plantations in America, and "acts of treason and piracy have been committed on the high seas, and upon the ships and goods of his Majesty's
subjects, and many persons have been seized and taken, who are expressly charged or strongly suspected of such treasons and felonies,
and many more such persons may be hereafter so seized and taken;
and whereas such persons have been, or may be brought into this
kingdom, and into other parts of his Majesty's dominions, and it may
be inconvenient in many such cases to proceed forthwith to the trial
of such criminals, and at the same time of evil example to suffer them
to go at large;" it was enacted that all such persons (describing them)
may "be detained in safe custody, without bail or main-prize, until
the first day of January, one thousand seven hundred and seventy-
eight; and that no judge or justice of peace shall bail or try any such
person or persons without order from his Majesty's most honourable
privy council," before that time. (31 Pickering's Statutes, 312, continued annually by successive reenactments till the end of the war.
Id. vol. 32, 1, 175; vol. 33, 3, 183; vol. 34, 1.)

> Lawrence's Wheaton (1863), 249.
> The operation of this act was confined mainly to American privateers-
> men captured by British cruisers. None, however, were executed as
> pirates under this statute, and all were ultimately exchanged or
> released.

Three British vessels were captured in 1779 by the *Alliance*,
The Bergen Prizes. Captain Landais, of the squadron under John Paul
Jones, and carried into Bergen, in Norway, where, on
the demand of the British minister, they were seized by the Danish
Government and restored to their owners on the ground that, as
Denmark had not acknowledged the independence of the United
States, the prizes could not be considered as lawful. In a note to

M. Bernstorf, the Danish minister for foreign affairs, of December 22, 1779, Franklin asked that the order of restoration be repealed, or that if it had been executed the value of the prizes, which was estimated at £50,000, should be paid by Denmark to the United States. M. Bernstorf answered evasively, though in substance he pleaded duress as an excuse for the order, which had been carried into effect. In 1787 Congress instructed Jefferson, who was then minister of the United States at Paris, to make a representation on the subject to the King of Denmark; and Jefferson authorized Jones to pursue the claim at Copenhagen. Nothing, however, was accomplished, and in 1806 Congress passed an act appropriating $4,000 to Landais as prize money on account of the captures. In 1812 Mr. Monroe as Secretary of State addressed an inquiry in regard to the claim to Mr. Pedersen, then Danish chargé d'affaires at Washington, who replied that his government never had considered the claim as legal, and that it now regarded it as superannuated and abandoned. Subsequently the matter was several times brought to the attention of Congress. In 1848, however, the Secretary of the Treasury was authorized to pay to the legal representatives of Jones, and of the officers, seamen, and marines, their just proportions of the value of the prizes, adjusting their claims on principles of justice and equity, after deducting from Landais' share the sum he had received under the act of 1806.

With reference to this case, Mr. Wheaton, in 1843, after remarking that Denmark, during the war of the American Revolution, " remained passive," neither acknowledging the independence of the United States nor allying herself with either party, so that she was " bound to all the duties of impartial neutrality," except so far as they might have been modified by her treaty obligations to Great Britain, said: " This was not the case of an ordinary revolt in the bosom of a state, which has not yet assumed the character of a civil war, such as entitles both the contending parties to the rights of war in respect to each other, and to foreign nations. In the year 1779, the United States constituted a confederation of States, sovereign *de facto*, and engaged in war with Great Britain, in which the rights of war were acknowledged by the parent country. . . . The United States were associated, in the war against Great Britain, with two of the great powers of Europe—France and Spain; both of which had acknowledged their independence, whilst the former had concluded with them a treaty of intimate alliance. . . . The only reason said to have been alleged by the Danish Government for rescuing these prizes from the possession of the American captors in order to deliver them up to the original British owners, was, that Denmark had not yet acknowledged the independence of the United States. But the question is not whether she had acknowledged the independence of the United States, but whether such a state of war actually existed between the United

States and Great Britain as made it the duty of all nations professing to be neutral to respect the just exercise of the rights of war of both. Denmark must either have considered the United States as lawful belligerents, or as pirates incapable of acquiring any of the rights of just war."

> Mr. Wheaton, min. to Prussia, to Mr. Upshur, Sec. of State, Aug. 23, 1843, H. Ex. Doc. 264, 28 Cong. 1 sess. 4, 6.
>
> It may be remarked that Mr. Wheaton's assumption that the United States in 1779 were in enjoyment of belligerent rights is not invalidated by his inaccurate account of the situation as it then existed. Spain, whose entrance into war with Great Britain took place only in June, 1779, can not be classed with France as a power with which the United States were "associated" in the conflict, especially as Spain declined to recognize the independence of the United States. Her recognition was not given till after the close of the conflict, nor was her well-known repugnance to the idea of colonial independence inexplicable. See, in this relation, Count de Florida Blanca's official invitation to dinner, left at Mr. Jay's house, March 30, 1782, and the subsequent explanation that it was a "mistake," but that Mr. Jay might come "as a private gentleman." (Wharton, Dip. Cor. Am. Rev. V. 373–377.) See Moore's American Diplomacy, 17–19.
>
> For the act of March 21, 1848, appropriating money for the payment of the Bergen claims, see 9 Stat. 214.
>
> See, also, Lawrence's Wheaton, 3d ed., note 16, p. 41.
>
> See, further, as to the Bergen claims, Moore, Int. Arbitrations, V. 4572.

"I have been informed by Mr. Acosta, chargé d'affaires of New Granada, that General Belluche, who is a partisan of the party in arms against the constitutional Government of Venezuela, has two armed vessels, Baltimore clippers, cruising on the Venezuelan coast between Maracaibo and Cumana. As his party is on the eve of extinction, he may be disposed to prey upon the commerce of all nations, and as no government exists that will be responsible for his conduct it is proper that our naval force in that quarter should have an eye upon his movements."

> Mr. Forsyth, Sec. of State, to Sec. of Navy, Jan. 4, 1836, 28 MS. Dom. Let. 187.

Although it has been doubted whether a mere body of rebellious men can claim all the rights of a separate power on the high seas, without absolute or qualified recognition from foreign governments, there is no authority for a doubt that the parties to a civil war have the right to conduct it with all the incidents of lawful war within the territory to which they both belong.

> Black, At.-Gen. (1858), 9 Op. 140.

2. CIVIL WAR CASES.

§ 330.

" If it were necessary, on the part of the Government, to bring the crime charged in the present case, against the prison-
Baker's Case. ers within this definition of robbery and piracy, as known to the common law of nations, there would be great difficulty in so doing upon the evidence, and, perhaps, upon the counts in the indictment—certainly, upon the evidence. For that shows, if anything, an intent to depredate upon the vessels and property of one nation only—the United States—which falls far short of the spirit and intent, as we have seen, that are said to constitute essential elements of the crime."

Nelson, J., in United States v. Baker (1861), 5 Blatchf. 6, 12 ; Trial of the Officers of the Savannah, 371.

See Woolsey, Int. Law (ed. 1874), App. 3, p. 447.

A contrary view was taken by Judges Grier and Cadwalader in Smith's case, in Philadelphia in 1862, when a convic-
Smith's Case. tion took place, but there was no sentence, and the prisoners were transferred to military control as prisoners of war, and not as pirates.

The following statement as to the latter case is made by Mr. Ashton, one of the counsel for the prosecution :

WASHINGTON, *January 26, 1886.*
I think that there was no motion made for a new trial in the piracy cases— certainly none was ever argued. After the conviction of the prisoners a State question arose as to what should be done with them. The Confederate Government, it was understood, threatened retaliation if they were harmed. The Attorney-General, Mr. Bates, was in favor of their being duly sentenced, but Mr. Seward thought that they should be exchanged as prisoners of war, and his advice prevailed with the President; and my recollection is that the district attorney and marshal were instructed, in letters written by Mr. Seward, to turn the men over to the military custody of the Government. Mr. Seward was somewhat in the habit at that time of directing the marshals and district attorneys, a practice that Mr. Bates always resented when his attention was called to it, and afterwards succeeded in correcting. At any rate we were instructed to release the prisoners from civil custody, but how to do that was the question. Judge Cadwalader, in consultation with me on the subject, suggested—you know how fertile he was in suggestion—that the men be brought into court on a writ of *habeas corpus,* and that each should be asked to say whether he preferred to remain in his present civil custody or to be remanded to the military custody from whence he came. I adopted this suggestion, a writ was issued, the men were brought into court, and each was asked the above question by the court. It was, of course, answered as we supposed it would be ; and an order was made by the court for the delivery of the men, by the marshal of the district, to the military custody of the Government. In that way we got rid of our white elephants. My recollection is that Judge Grier was rather in favor of letting the law take its course in the cases, and

that he would have sentenced the men if I had asked for judgment. Judge Cadwalader, though believing the men had been rightly convicted, was satisfied to let them go in the way I have mentioned.

I believe that there is a report of Smith's case in the Law Library of Congress, but I suppose what I have mentioned is not contained in it.

November 16, 1863, the American merchant vessel *Joseph L. Gerrity* sailed from Matamoras, Mexico, for New York, with a cargo of cotton. On the following night, six persons, who had taken passage for New York, seized the ship in the name of the Confederate Government, and a few days afterwards they set the captain and a part of the crew adrift in a small boat. Four of the culprits having been found in Liverpool, Mr. Adams, United States minister at London, February 15, 1864, demanded their extradition on a charge of piracy. The case was finally disposed of May 24, 1864, by the court of Queen's Bench, on a writ of *habeas corpus*. The court agreed that, if their belligerent character could be established, the charge must fail, but no evidence was produced to show that the prisoners were acting under the authority of the Confederate Government. In the end, however, this question became unimportant, since the case went off on the point that the acts charged, if piracy at all, were piracy *jure gentium*, and not piracy under the treaty of August 9, 1842, which the court held to mean piracy by municipal statute.

Case of the "Joseph L. Gerrity."

In re Tivnan, 5 Best & S. 645; Dip. Cor. 1864, II. 30 et seq.

December 5, 1863, the United States merchant steamer *Chesapeake* sailed from New York for Portland, Me., with a general cargo and sixteen male passengers. December 7, at half-past one in the morning, when the steamer was off Cape Cod, the passengers surprised the watch, murdered the second mate, seized the captain and crew, and took possession of the steamer in the name of the Confederate Government, hoisting as a sign thereof the Confederate flag. The Government of the United States, on hearing of the seizure, sent gunboats in pursuit of the vessel, and on December 17 one of them found her in Sambro Harbor, Nova Scotia, about to be deserted by her captors and flying a signal of distress. The gunboat took possession of the vessel and of certain of the crew, and carried her into Halifax and delivered her over to the Canadian authorities. Mr. Seward demanded of the British Government the surrender of the *Chesapeake's* captors on charges of murder and piracy. The names of the persons included in the demand were Braine, Parr, Locke, Collins, Robinson, and Wade. Meanwhile, the United States consul at St. John, New Brunswick, hearing that three of the alleged

Case of the "Chesapeake."

pirates, Collins, McKealy, and Seeley, were in that province, obtained a warrant for their arrest. When brought before a magistrate for examination, they claimed that their acts were of a belligerent character, but that, if they constituted piracy, it was piracy *jure gentium*, and therefore not within the treaty of 1842. The magistrate committed them for surrender, and a writ of *habeas corpus* was obtained from Judge Ritchie of the Supreme Court of New Brunswick, who discharged the prisoners, on the ground among others that piracy *jure gentium* was justiciable by the courts of New Brunswick and was not within the treaty, thus avoiding the political aspects of the case. Efforts subsequently were made to secure either the surrender or the trial of the prisoners, but nothing appears to have come of the proceedings.

> Mr. Seward, Sec. of State, to Lord Lyons, British min., Dec. 20, 1863, Dip. Cor. 1864, II. 407.
>
> For a fuller and more minute history of the case, see Moore on Extradition, I. 316–319.

In November, 1864, the United States demanded the extradition from Canada of Bennet G. Burley on charges of piracy, robbery, and assault with intent to commit murder on the American merchant steamer *Philo Parsons*, on Lake Erie, September 19, 1864. It appeared that Burley had taken passage on the steamer, and that afterwards, when she was in American waters not far from the Ohio shore, he took forcible possession of her with the aid of certain persons for whom he had procured passage. Burley and his associates, when they took possession of the steamer, professed to act in behalf of the Confederate government, running up the Confederate flag and declaring their purpose to seize the United States war vessel *Michigan*, then in the lake, and to release some Confederate prisoners on Johnson's Island. Burley, though a British subject by birth, had been in the Confederate service, and on his examination he produced a commission as acting master in the Confederate navy, signed at Richmond, September 11, 1863, on which there was an endorsement, dated at Richmond, December 22, 1864, in the form of a proclamation of President Davis, declaring that the enterprise of Burley was a belligerent expedition, ordered and undertaken under the authority of the Confederate government and for which that government assumed responsibility. Burley was committed for surrender on the charge of robbery. He then obtained a writ of *habeas corpus*, and his case was argued before Chief Justice Draper and Mr. Justice Hagarty, of the Canadian Queen's Bench, and Chief Justice Richards and Mr. Justice Wilson, of the common pleas. Chief Justice Draper took the ground that, conceding that the prisoner was an officer in the Confederate

Burley's case.

service, the manifesto which had been put forward to shield him not only did not permit but even forbade any violation of neutral territory. Burley's associates were taken on board, by arrangement, at Canadian ports, and the expedition in which he was engaged was thus embarked from neutral territory and was deprived of the character of lawful hostility. Under these circumstances, Chief Justice Draper was of opinion that, as the acts taken by themselves established a prima facie case of robbery, the matters of defence which were alleged were proper to be submitted to a jury in the jurisdiction where the offence was committed. Chief Justice Richards took substantially the same ground, and cited the observation of Lord Chief Justice Cockburn in the case of Tivnan, that there must be an honest intention to assist a belligerent and that persons could not protect themselves from the consequences of acts really piratical merely by assuming the character of belligerents. Justices Hagarty and Wilson concurred in these opinions; and Burley was accordingly surrendered on the charge of robbery. He was tried before Judge Fitch, in Ohio. The court held that his acts were belligerent and not committed *animo furandi*. The jury disagreed, and Burley, who was released on small bail, left and did not reappear.

> Mr. Seward, Sec. of State, to Lord Lyons, British min., Nov. 29, 1864, Dip. Cor. 1864, II. 813 et seq.; The Extradition of Bennet G. Burley, Parliamentary Papers, North America, No. 3 (1876). For a fuller statement of the foregoing case, see Moore on Extradition, I. 319–321.
>
> In an opinion given in this case, Oct. 10, 1864, Attorney-General Bates intimated that Lake Erie was in the legal sense a "sea," so that piracy might be committed on it, although, in view of the opposite opinions held by many, he advised that the question be not raised. (11 Op. 114.)
>
> It has since been held that the Great Lakes are, in matters of criminal jurisdiction, to be considered as seas. (United States *v.* Rodgers (1893), 150 U. S. 249.)
>
> Although it has always been asserted in official records that Burley departed while out on bail, the statement has lately been made, on the authority of the sheriff who had him in custody, that he escaped from jail. It appears that Burley, who was a native of Scotland, afterwards became, under the name of "Burleigh," a famous war correspondent, on the staff of the London Daily Telegraph. See an interesting article entitled "Burleigh—and Johnson's Island," in the American Magazine of History, May and June, 1905, by Frederick J. Shepard, esq., of Buffalo, N. Y.

The question whether Captain Semmes, of the *Alabama*, should be prosecuted for piracy was discussed in the Atlantic Monthly for July and August, 1872, by Mr. Bolles, who was the Solicitor of the Navy Department, and to whom this question was referred. This article states at the outset that "By establishing a blockade of Confederate ports, our Government had recognized the Confederates as belligerents, if not as a belligerent state, and had thus confessed that Confederate officers and men, military or naval, could not be treated as pirates or guerrillas, so long as they obeyed the laws of war; that the same recognition was made when cartels for exchange of prisoners were established between the Federal and Confederate authorities; and, above all, when the Federal Executive, after the courts had declared Confederate privateersmen to be pirates, had deliberately set aside those judgments, and admitted the captured and condemned officers and men of the *Savannah* and the *Jeff Davis* to exchange as prisoners of war."

The conclusion is as follows:

" It is evident that, after it had been, as it soon was, resolved that neither treason nor piracy should be charged against Semmes before a military or naval tribunal, and that his methods of capturing, ' plundering,' and destroying vessels should not be treated as offenses against public law and duty, but that he should be dealt with as a belligerent naval officer, bound to obey the laws of war and entitled to their protection, it was needless to inquire where or by whom the *Alabama* was built, manned, armed, or commissioned; or whether a government without an open port can legitimately own or employ a naval force. These inquiries, however interesting or important they might be in other connections, were of no sort of interest or importance as elements of a trial for violating the laws of war in the conduct of a cruiser subject to those laws, and protected by them.

" In this way the field and the duty of inquiry were reduced to the two subjects of cruelty to prisoners and perfidy towards Captain Winslow and the power he represented."

These articles by Mr. Bolles are commented on by Sir A. Cockburn, in his opinion in the Geneva tribunal, and in 2 Bullock's Secret Service Conf. States, 116 et seq.

The " Confederate Government," owing to the disabilities to which its privateers were exposed in foreign ports, discontinued privateering, and its cruisers " claimed the rights of public ships of war, and were commanded by officers commissioned by the Confederate States."

> Mr. W. B. Lawrence, in N. Am. Rev., July, 1878, 21, 31, citing 22 Solicitor's Journal, 523.
>
> As to the status of Confederate cruisers in foreign ports, see report of Mr. Seward, Sec. of State, April 26, 1862, H. Ex. Doc. 104, 37 Cong. 2 sess.

3. Cases and Opinions, 1865-1884.

§ 331.

May 31, 1865, the steamer *Washington* was seized in Ecuador by
insurgents, who with her aid captured the Ecuadorian
Case of the "Washington." war vessel *Guayas.* The Government of Ecuador
by a decree declared the parties to be pirates, subject
to capture by any foreign man-of-war, even in Ecuadorian waters.
The American minister, on the request of the Ecuadorian Government, gave notice of the decree to the commander of the United
States naval forces on the Pacific station.

> See Mr. Seward, Sec. of State, to Mr. Hassaurek, min. to Ecuador, Sept.
> 15, 1865, MS. Inst. Ecuador, I. 175.

July 10, 1869, Mr. Robeson, Secretary of the Navy, instructed
Commander E. K. Owen, U. S. S. *Seminole,* to pro-
Case of the "Telegrafo." ceed without delay to Samana Bay in Santo Domingo
and ascertain whether a steamer was there named the
Telegraph (Telegrafo), under the command of one Luperon, or officers of his. Mr. Robeson said that the vessel had been " interfering
with American commerce, and sailing on the high seas without legal
authority." Commander Owen was directed to seize her and bring
her into the port of Baltimore. If he should not find the vessel in
Samana Bay, he was to search for her along the coast till he found
her.[a]

General Babcock stated before a committee of the Senate that the
Telegrafo was alleged to be a pirate and had overhauled a vessel
carrying the American flag; that she first sailed under the American
flag, and then hoisted the flag of Venezuela, under which she
appeared before the town of Puerto Plata and demanded its surrender; that the people refused to surrender and fired at her, whereupon she fired some shots into the town; that she then went around to
Samana Bay under the Dominican flag, and after remaining there
some days went to Barahona, where she landed her guns and munitions
of war.[b]

July 31, 1869, Commander Owen reported from St. Thomas his
arrival from Samana Bay. The *Telegrafo,* then called the *Restora-
cione,* was in the hands of the British Government and had been sold
to an English subject. No evidence had been gathered that the
vessel had interferred with American citizens or commerce. On the
4th of August Commander Owen reported that he had decided to
let the matter rest between the British and Dominican Governments.[c]

---

[a] S. Rep. 234, 41 Cong. 2 sess. 38. See, also, S. Ex. Doc. 34, 41 Cong. 3 sess. 5.
[b] S. Rep. 234, 41 Cong. 2 sess. 39.
[c] S. Ex. Doc. 34, 41 Cong. 3 sess. 6, 7.

" I acknowledge the receipt of your despatch (No. 13) of the 13th
ultimo, in which you enclose a copy of a note ad-

Vessels employed
by Haytian in-
surgents.

dressed by the secretary for foreign affairs of Hayti
to the several members of the diplomatic corps accredited to his Government, and relating to the armed steamers
formerly called the *Quaker City* and the *Florida* now in the service
of insurgents against the Government of Hayti. The secretary for
foreign affairs, after reciting the fact that those insurgents have not
been recognized by this or any other government as entitled to belligerent rights, declares that the vessels which form the subject of
his communication can not be considered according to the spirit of
international maritime law otherwise than real pirates, which it is
the duty of every regular navigator to pursue for the purpose of
sinking or capturing them. He further states it to be an object of
his communication to obtain from each one of the vessels of the respective nations, to whose representatives it was addressed, an adequate and efficacious cooperation in maintaining for the marine of the
civilized world the security of the seas and to guarantee the protection
of private property.

" The good understanding which this Government earnestly desires
to maintain with that of Hayti requires that this communication
should receive a frank and explicit reply.

" You will, therefore, say to the secretary for foreign affairs:

" 1. That we do not dispute the right of the Government of Hayti
to treat the officers and crew of the *Quaker City* and *Florida* [vessels
in the service of insurgents against Hayti] as pirates for all intents
and purposes. How they are to be regarded by their own legitimate
Government is a question of municipal law into which we have no
occasion, if we had the right, to enter.

" 2. That this Government is not aware of any reason which would
require or justify it in looking upon the vessels named in a different
light from any other vessels employed in the service of the insurgents.

" 3. That regarding them simply as armed cruisers of insurgents
not yet acknowledged by this Government to have attained belligerent
rights, it is competent to the United States to deny and resist the exercise by those vessels or any other agents of the rebellion of the privileges which attend maritime war, in respect to our citizens or their
property entitled to our protection. We may or may not, at our
option, as justice or policy may require, treat them as pirates in the
absolute and unqualified sense, or we may, as the circumstances of any
actual case shall suggest, waive the extreme right and recognize, where
facts warrant it, an actual intent on the part of the individual offenders, not to deprecate in a criminal sense and for private gain, but to
capture and destroy *jure belli*. It is sufficient for the present purpose
that the United States will not admit any commission or authority

proceeding from rebels as a justification or excuse for injury to persons or property entitled to the protection of this Government. They will not tolerate the search or stopping by cruisers in the rebel service of vessels of the United States, nor any other act which is only privileged by recognized belligerency.

"4. While asserting the right to capture and destroy the vessels in question, and others of similar character, if any aggression upon persons or property entitled to the protection of this Government shall recommend such action, we can not admit the existence of any obligation to do so in the interest of Hayti or of the general security of commerce.

"No facts have been presented to this Government to create a belief that the operations of the vessels in question have been with a view to plunder or had any other than a political object. That object is hostile to a government with which the United States have maintained a friendship that it requires no fresh manifestation to evince. We deem it most decorous to leave it to that Government to deal with the hostile vessels as it may find expedient, reserving the consideration of our action in respect to them till some offence, actual or apprehended, to the United States shall render it imperative.

"You may read this dispatch to the secretary of foreign affairs and leave a copy of it with him if he desires it."

> Mr. Fish, Sec. of State, to Mr. Bassett, min. to Hayti, No. 11, Sept. 14, 1869, MS. Inst. Hayti, I. 150. See supra, p. 1073.

The crew of a Peruvian monitor, the *Huascar*, anchored at Callao, revolted on May 6, 1877, and declared for the insur-

Case of the "Huascar."

gent Government of Pierola. The *Huascar* proceeded to sea without opposition from other Peruvian vessels in the harbor. On May 8 the titular Government of Peru issued a decree calling the *Huascar* crew "rebels," and authorizing her capture. The *Huascar* then stopped several British vessels, taking out of one of them two officers who were going to Peru to enter Government service. The British admiral on those coasts being advised of these proceedings, and also of the seizure of certain lighters of coal belonging to British subjects, sent the *Shah*, a British cruiser, to sea to seize the *Huascar*. An engagement took place, which was only partially successful, the *Huascar* ultimately eluding her assailant. The *Huascar* subsequently surrendered to Peru, and Peru claimed indemnity from Great Britain for the conduct of the British admiral. The law officers of the Crown, on the question being referred to them, held that as the *Huascar* was sailing under no national flag, and was an irresponsible depredating cruiser, approved the conduct of the admiral. When the question came up before the House of Commons, the attorney-general maintained that the

Huascar was a rover committing depredations on foreign shipping. It would have been otherwise, he conceded, if there had been an existing rebellion entitled to the rights of belligerency.

> 1 Halleck's Int. Law, note (3rd ed. by Baker), 447. See criticism in 1 Calvo, 5th ed., §504, p. 592.

"The expedient of declaring a revolted national vessel to be a 'pirate' has often been resorted to among the Spanish-American countries in times of civil tumult, and on late occasions in Europe. At the time of the Murcian rising, in 1873, the insurgents at Cartagena seized the Spanish ironclads in harbor and cruised with them along the coast, committing hostilities. The Spanish Government proclaimed the vessels pirates and invited their capture by any nation. A German naval commander then in the Mediterranean did in fact capture one of the revolted ships and claimed it as a German prize, but his act was disavowed. The rule is, simply, that a 'pirate' is the natural enemy of all men, to be repressed by any, and wherever found, while a revolted vessel is the enemy only of the power against which it acts. While it may be outlawed so far as the outlawing state is concerned, no foreign state is bound to respect or execute such outlawry to the extent of treating the vessel as a public enemy of mankind. Treason is not piracy, and the attitude of foreign governments toward the offender may be negative merely so far as demanded by a proper observance of the principle of neutrality."

> Mr. Frelinghuysen, Sec. of State, to Mr. Langston, min. to Hayti, Dec. 15, 1883, For. Rel. 1884, 297.

4. COLOMBIAN INSURRECTION, 1885.

§ 332.

Early in 1885 the tug *Game Cock* and certain other steam vessels belonging to the United Magdalena Steam Navigation Company, an American corporation, and plying on the Magdalena River, in Columbia, were taken possession of for hostile use by General Gaitan, one of the leaders in the insurrection then going on against the titular government of that country.

Case of the "Game Cock."

April 21, 1885, Dr. Francis Wharton, then Solicitor of the Department of State, made a report in which he said: "When vessels belonging to citizens of the United States have been seized and are now navigated on the high seas by persons not representing any government or belligerent power recognized by the United States, such vessels may be captured and rescued by their owners, or by United States cruisers acting for such owners; and all force which is necessary for such purpose may be used to make the capture effectual."

May 18, 1885, Doctor Wharton, on the submission of further facts, made an additional report, in which, after affirming the position he had previously taken, he advised that a suitable instruction be sent to the United States minister at Bogota, and that the papers be immediately forwarded to the Secretary of the Navy " with the request that the vessels thus unlawfully seized and now possessed by the insurgents be retaken when on the high seas by any force the United States may be able to use for that purpose. . . . The crews manning these vessels can not be regarded by this Government as pirates. But, while this is the case, and while it may be conceded that vessels seized by them on the high seas are seized under claim of right, yet, vessels belonging to citizens of the United States so seized by them may be rescued by our cruisers acting for the owners of such vessels in the same way that we could reclaim vessels derelict on the high seas."

These reports were approved, and a request was made to the Secretary of the Navy that " proper instructions be immediately issued to the commander of the naval authorities in Colombia for the recapture, when on the high seas, by any force the United States may be able to use for that purpose, of the vessels of the Magdalena Steam Navigation Company thus unlawfully seized and possessed by the insurgents."

> Mr. Bayard, Sec. of State, to Mr. Scruggs, May 19, 1885, For. Rel. 1885, 211–214. See, also, Mr. Bayard, Sec. of State, to Mr. Hood, May 16, 1885, 155 MS. Dom. Let. 403.
>
> For the request to the Secretary of the Navy for the issuance of the instructions above indicated, see Mr. Bayard, Sec. of State, to Mr. Whitney, Sec. of Navy, May 19, 1885, 155 MS. Dom. Let. 421.
>
> With reference to a statement subsequently made that the insurgents were using the steamers by agreement and giving compensation therefor, Mr. Bayard said: " If, as stated, the steamers are used in virtue of some understanding with the insurgents, they can not be regarded as stolen property liable to recovery. The Secretary of the Navy will, however, be requested to have this point carefully investigated by the Admiral before taking action." (Mr. Bayard, Sec. of State, to Mr. Hood, May 27, 1885, 155 MS. Dom. Let. 507.)
>
> As to the seizure of the *Game Cock* by the revolutionists, see a dispatch from the United States consul at Colon, No. 31, March 7, 1885, copy of which was enclosed by Mr. Bayard, Sec. of State, to Mr. Whitney, Sec. of Navy, March 21, 1885, 154 MS. Dom. Let. 546.
>
> Early in May, 1885, Mr. Becerra, Colombian minister at Washington, informed the Department of State that Prestan, the insurgent leader who had burned Colon, had with his forces escaped from that place and got possession of or stolen two or three vessels on which he had placed guns, and that he might seek to destroy Cartagena or might even return to harass the Isthmus anew. Mr. Becerra made no statement respecting the nationality of the vessels which Prestan was reported to have seized, but, in view of the possibility that they might be " the property of citizens of the United States and may have

been wrongfully taken by force," it was suggested that instructions be given to the United States naval officers on the coast "to ascertain the facts of the case, and act accordingly under existing instructions to the end of restoring such property to the lawful American owners from whom it may have been stolen if that fact positively appear." (Mr. Bayard, Sec. of State, to Mr. Whitney, Sec. of Navy, May 4, 1885, 155 MS. Dom. Let. 283.)

"There is reason, however, to believe that some of the vessels employed in the attack on Cartagena, and in patrolling that part of the coast now in the hands of the insurgents, are the property of citizens of the United States and were wronfully seized in the Magdalena River, and at Barranquilla by the insurgents. Our right in respect to any such vessels is wholly independent of the situation assumed to be created by the decree of the Colombian Government [declaring such vessels to be pirates], for such property, stolen from its lawful American owners by men whom we do not recognize as representing any government, and who are denounced as insurgents by the only government known to us there, could be recovered by force when on the high seas by its legitimate owners or by parties acting for them, without the intervention of any admiralty process. Such a rescue by or for the lawful owner of private property from an unlawful taker is permissible under any view." (Mr. Bayard, Sec. of State, to Mr. Whitney, Sec. of Navy, April 15, 1885, 155 MS. Dom. Let. 101.)

In February, 1899, Mr. Merry, the American minister in Nicaragua, declined to request the commander of the United States naval forces in Central American waters to seize the Nicaragua steamer *San Jacinto.* The Department of State, after remarking that sufficient facts were not shown to justify the intervention of the United States naval forces, added: "It does not appear that the *San Jacinto* is American property, unlawfully seized by the insurgents. If it were, it could be recaptured for the benefit of its lawful owners *on the high seas* by our naval force. See Mr. Bayard's instruction to Mr. Scruggs, May 19, 1885, Foreign Relations, 1885, page 211." (Mr. Hay, Sec. of State, to Mr. Merry, No. 197, March 3, 1899, MS. Inst. Cent. Am. XXI. 427.)

"The Government of the United States can not regard as piratical vessels manned by parties in arms against the Government of the United States of Colombia, when such vessels are passing to and from ports held by such insurgents, or even when attacking ports in the possession of the National Government. In the late civil war, the United States at an early period of the struggle surrendered the position that those manning the Confederate cruisers were pirates under international law. The United States of Colombia can not, sooner or later, do otherwise than accept the same view. But, however this may be, no neutral power can acquiesce in the position now taken by the Colombian Government. Whatever may be the demerits of the vessels in the power of the insurgents, or whatever may be the status of those manning them under the municipal law of Colombia, if

Discussions with Colombia, 1885.

they be brought by the act of the National Government within the operation of that law, there can be no question that such vessels, when engaged as above stated, are not, by the law of nations, *pirates;* nor can they be regarded as pirates by the United States.

"The status of *purpose* or of *employment*, which the Government of Colombia seeks to create against such vessels by decreeing them to be pirates, is, of course, wholly distinct from the inherent status as *floating property*. On this latter point we are not as yet adequately informed. The commanders of the naval vessels of the United States on the Colombian coast have, however, been told that if conclusive proof be shown that any vessels belonging to citizens of the United States have been unlawfully taken from them, the recovery of such property by the owners, or by others acting in their behalf, to the end of its restoration to their legitimate control, is warrantable. Such a right is inherent, depending wholly upon the circumstances of the case, and can not be derived from or limited by any municipal decree of the Colombian Government like that which you now bring to my notice."

> Mr. Bayard, Sec. of State, to Mr. Becerra, Colombian min., April 24, 1885, For. Rel. 1885, 254, 257.
>
> When the Colombian minister at Washington again advanced the claim, in 1900, that the vessels then controlled by insurgents against his Government were, " according to the provisions of international law, subject to the same conditions as piratical vessels," the Department of State replied by quoting the passage given above. (Mr. Hay, Sec. of State, to Señor Márquez, Colombian min., Aug. 1, 1900, For. Rel. 1900, 405.)

"I can assure you, Mr. Secretary of State, and I will even add that there is evidence of this at the Department of State, that all those vessels, with the single exception of the *General Cordova*, which is the property of the nation, have come into the possession of the insurgents through the commission of acts of robbery identical in their nature and the means whereby they were committed with those which are characterized as piracy by American law (section 5370 Revised Statutes of the United States), and for whose perpetrators the penalty of death is provided.

"The *Game Cock*, which is now known among the insurgents as the *General Gaitan*, belonged, for a time, at least, to the Panama Railway Company, and was forcibly removed from the Bay of Colon and taken to Cartagena by Benjamin Ruiz, one of the most active accomplices of the outlaw Pedro Prestan.

"The *Camacho Roldan*, another of the vessels in the service of the insurgents, belongs, if I am not mistaken, to an English company, the Atlas Line, which, in the prosecution of maritime trade, navigates the Cartagena channel. This vessel was likewise forcibly taken from the service in which it was engaged and from the control of its lawful owners by Ricardo Gaitan, one of the ringleaders of the insurgents, and is now in the mouth of the channel—that is to say, in one of the localities mentioned in the aforesaid section 5370 of the Revised Statutes.

" It is, moreover, a matter of public notoriety that the outlaw Prestan, after his flight from the city of Colon, which he had invaded, took forcible possession of Portobello, and of one or more large vessels, on board of which, together with many of his followers, he repaired to Cartagena, where he is now co-operating in the siege and perhaps in the ruin of that historic city.

" In view of these facts, and their nature being compared with the principles on which, in the present case, American law is based, I am unable to see how it could be maintained that a flotilla thus constituted (and whose officers and men are, if not all, at least in great part, the same who committed those acts of depredation and violence) deserves to be considered as a mere instrument of war of a political insurrection. If this opinion were to prevail, being supported by so high an authority as the American Government, it would be difficult to see to what a wretched extreme of insecurity and abandonment the interests of commerce and of civilization in general would be reduced on the coasts of those countries which, like Colombia, owing to their trusting, perhaps, too implicitly in peace and in the elements which are fostered by it, have no permanent forces sufficiently strong to prevent crime, because it is evident that then all that the captors of defenseless merchant vessels would have to do, in order to secure impunity, would be to cover the latter, when once in their hands, with the flag of the same country, and declare war against the constituted authorities.

" It will be urged that the repression and punishment of such outrages are matters to be attended to by the authorities of the country in which they are committed, to which it is easy to reply, first, that the state most directly injured thereby can with great difficulty prevent them, much less punish them in time.

" The powerlessness which occasioned them is equally great, or still greater, to effect their punishment.

" If the crime can be committed owing to the lack of vessels, it is evident that, owing to the same lack, the consequences of the depredation may be indefinitely delayed. And then the violation of international law, to the detriment of other nations, which, in such cases, is what constitutes the crime of piracy, naturally widens the jurisdiction of the judges who are to punish it. All civilized nations not only may, but ought, the case arising, to exercise that jurisdiction thus amplified, and with it their own right of self-preservation and self-defense.

" I am not aware that there is a single precedent in the history of the complicated enforcement of the rules of international law whereby the doctrine is established that merchant vessels which have been forcibly removed from the service in which they were engaged, by threats against the lives of their captains and crews, by surprise, and in bays, roadsteads, or mouths of rivers, ' or in any river where the sea ebbs and flows,' as the American statute says, can be made to constitute a regular force, worthy of the respect, not only of neutrals, but even of the very nations whose subjects or citizens have been the victims of such act of violence. In support of the opposite argument, I can cite many authoritative examples, among which the most pertinent is doubtless that of the Magellan pirates (see Phillimore), the law in which case was laid down by the English Judge Lushington. Certain individuals rose in arms, in the year 1851, against the authority of the regular Government of Chili, captured in the Strait of Magellan (which at that time had not been declared neutral by Chili) the *Eliza Cornish*, an English, and the *Florida*, an American vessel, and, after murdering one of the two captains, they placed both vessels in the service of their cause, hoisting the Chilian flag over them. The Government of that Republic (as does now that of Colombia) declared the said vessels to be pirates, and Admiral Moreby, who was then in command of the British naval station in those waters, ordered them to be pursued as such, and sent the *Virago*, a British man-of-war, for that purpose. The action of this vessel was so energetic that both vessels were speedily recaptured, and the leader of the band of insurgents and his accomplices, having been apprehended, were turned over to the Chilian courts, and were subsequently tried and punished as pirates.

" ' I am of opinion,' said Judge Lushington, in the final decision pronounced by him in this case, ' that the persons who did these acts were guilty of piracy. . . . It has been said that these acts were not committed on the high seas, and, therefore, this murder and robbery not properly or legally piratical. But in this case the ships were carried away and navigated by the very same persons who originally seized them [just as in the Colombian case]. I consider the possession at sea to have been a piratical possession, and the carrying away the ships on the high seas to have been piratical acts.'

" The agreement of the facts and the nature of the doctrine established could not be more striking; I mean the agreement of the facts with those of the origin of the vessels that are now making war upon the inhabitants of the Colombian coast, and the agreement of the doctrine above established with the fundamental principles of American law on the subject of piracy.

" The manner in which the aforesaid vessels were converted into instruments of war in the service of the insurgents having been sufficiently elucidated, it remains to examine the character subsequently assumed by the forces of those insurgents which are now operating against Cartagena.

" It is well known that the incendiary of Colon, at the head of about seventy of his accomplices, arrived in that port on board of the vessels captured by him at Portobello, and that a command was at once given to him among the forces of the insurgents, who, by this fact alone, lose any title that they otherwise might have had to consideration as representatives of an armed political movement. This is true, because, by associating with such men, and, what is even more serious, by giving a superior military command to their depraved leader, and with it the means of committing at Cartagena a crime equal to that committed at Colon, those insurgents declared by implication, though none the less positively, that they accepted the responsibility and consequently the disgrace of that act of vandalism, thereby pursuing a different course from that of the insurgent leader at Panama, who at least tried to extenuate his own guilt by stipulating (although unnecessarily and although he had no right to do so) for the punishment of his lieutenant.

" The territory which was partially laid waste by the torch of Prestan and his accomplices is, to a great extent, neutral territory, free to all nations, and open to their commerce and their people; in a word, it is the means possessed by those nations for communication between two hemispheres, and there the interests of the civilization of the present day have met, as it were, on common ground, in order that they may be mutually benefited and harmonized. For these numerous reasons it is proper to ask how those same nations and those same interests which were savagely attacked on the Isthmus of Panama by Prestan and his accomplices can respect that leader, his auxiliaries of yesterday and his upholders of to-day, now that the scene of his action has changed; how the United States Navy, which was, to a certain extent, a victim of the outrages and felonious acts of that outlaw, after having cooperated, in the name of its Government and in fulfillment of a treaty, in checking him at Colon, is now to respect him at Cartagena, considering him and his vessels as regular forces of an insurrectionary movement. The English admiral who recaptured the *Eliza Cornish* and the *Florida*, also took Cambiaso, the leader of the insurrection and the captor of those vessels, and it is certain that, if he had succeeded in escaping, and joined the partizans of his cause in any other part of the country, that mere change of locality would have affected neither the right by which the British officer so opportunely acted nor the principle on which he thus acted."

Mr. Becerra, Colombian min., to Mr. Bayard, Sec. of State, May 14, 1885, For. Rel. 1885, 264, 265.

" The principle upon which I based my note of April 24 was, generally, that there can not be *paper piracy* with international effects and obligations any more than there can be a *paper blockade* of effective character. In the one case as in the other no force or effect can be communicated by a municipal decree which is not inherent in the case itself, and I felt constrained to announce to you that this Government could not deem itself bound in any manner by such a decree, either as entailing any international obligation or as conferring upon it any derived jurisdiction in the premises. The position seemed so self-evident and is so abundantly supported by authority that I deemed it quite unnecessary to enter into argument or collation of precedents to sustain the simple announcement.

" It would seem, however, that you have misunderstood that announcement, and you now seek to controvert it on the assumption that it recognizes the vessels mentioned in the Colombian decree as legitimate belligerents, thereby divesting them of whatever inherent piratical character they may possess. Your argument, and the precedent of the Magellan pirates adduced by you, aim to show that vessels of this character, even though ostensibly in the service of a hostile insurrection, may be tainted with piracy to a degree to bring them within the jurisdiction of a foreign state whose forces may have captured them on the high seas.

" This position I am not disposed to deny, but I then did feel bound to deny, and do so still, that a municipal decree of a sovereign can communicate to a single vessel, or in comprehensive terms to a class of vessels, a character of piracy which they may not already possess under the circumstances surrounding each particular vessel, or that a foreign sovereign can derive or exercise any power, obligation, or jurisdiction in virtue of such a municipal decree which it does not already possess in the nature of the case under the law of nations. Were any foreign government to exercise such right or jurisdiction in the case of a vessel found committing acts in themselves piratical, a decree of this character could only, by the widest stretch, be deemed an acquiescence in and voluntary confirmation of the power and right so exercised by the law of nations. It could not be held to confer the right to capture and judge an actual pirate any more than, assuming the contrary position by way of hypothesis, it could deny or assume to annul that right in a given case.

" I find the general *dictum* of modern authority in this relation so well summed up by Calvo—whose impartiality as a jurist has never been questioned—that I cite his observations thereon in full :

" ' Has a government a fundamental right to declare pirates and to punish with death rebels who sail the seas in order to capture property belonging to subjects or citizens remaining faithful to the established power ? To solve this question, it is unnecessary to take into account the number and the situation of the rebels with respect to the government they attack, and the extent, organization and material forces of the insurrection.

" ' In principle, and so long as no more is proposed than the over-throw of the established power—the substitution of one government for another—rebellion is a political crime pertaining exclusively to the internal public law of each nation; its criminal character, and the civil or military jurisdiction under which it should be, depend, there-fore, on the special domestic laws governing the matter. The gov-ernment whose existence is set at stake by the rebellion is free and sovereign to proceed against and repress in its own way, by the forces at its command, attacks which may be leveled against it, *but it is not sufficient for it to attach to the act the qualification of piracy to cause such a rebellion to be transformed ipso facto, in the eyes of foreign states, into a crime against the law of nations, and to become punishable as such.* So true is this, that the country wherein has broken out a rebellion, which by its strength and duration assumes the character of a civil war, may from its own point of view, and to suit its own convenience, behold only acts of piracy in operations which other countries, aloof from the contest, may consider and respect as belligerent acts.' (Calvo, Droit International, 2d ed., 1870, I. 390.)

"A striking instance of the application of this principle occurred in Spain in 1873. An insurrection broke out in the province of Murcia, and the navy-yard at Cartagena was seized. The vessels found there, among them powerful ironclads, were manned and sent to cruise along the Mediterranean coast against the power of the established Government, to whom they belonged, and by whom they had been purchased or built. The president of the executive power by decree proclaimed those vessels to be *pirates*, and invited their capture as lawful prize, by any power, whereupon the commander of a German ironclad captured one of the revolted vessels in the Mediterranean. It was adjudged by the German admiralty court that the captured vessel was not good prize, because not a pirate under the law of nations, and that the German commander could derive no power or warrant from the municipal decree of the Spanish Government.

" The case of the Magellan pirates, to which you refer, was ad-judged on its merits to have been one of piracy *per se*, as is, indeed, abundantly evident from the facts narrated in Phillimore's summary, which you follow. Of the vessels seized by the mutinous convicts, one was British, the other American. The British admiral, Moresby, was not claimed to have acted in virtue of or in obedience to any decree of the Chilian Government, such as that to which you refer. He needed no such authority under the law of nations, nor could he have derived an iota of authority from such Chilian decree in the absence of international authority. In respect of the British vessel, the *Eliza Cornish*, he undoubtedly exercised the right of recovery of stolen property, which, as I explained to you in my note of April 24, is an inherent right, apart from the international-law right to capture an actual pirate, *hostis humani generis*. Had I deemed that the plain ground taken by the United States Government required elucidation or fortification by recorded precedent, I would have taken the case of the Magellan pirates as the nearest and aptest at hand, and I would have appended to it the following additional quotation from Calvo, which follows the passage above cited:

" 'As for isolated revolts, in a certain sense individual acts, and leading to predatory acts on the high seas committed under a flag which is not recognized as belonging to a constituted and sovereign state, it is evident that they fully involve assimilation with piracy and repression as a crime against the law of nations. (*Op. cit.* 1, 291.)'

" It is to the class of crimes thus described by Calvo that the fifty-three hundred and seventieth section of the Revised Statutes of the United States, cited by you, refers.

" It is evident, however, that the piratical character of such acts, and the consequent jurisdiction of any sovereign power in respect thereof, must depend on the circumstances of the individual case, and can not be derived from such a municipal enactment as the decree of the Colombian Government now under our consideration.

" That the Government of the United States fully comprehends its international-law duty in the premises is shown by the tenor of the instructions recently sent to its naval officers in the Caribbean Sea. Under those orders a vessel, the *Ambrose Light*, has been captured by one of our cruisers, and is now on its way to the United States for submission to the judgment of the courts. The responsibility accruing to our naval commanders under those instructions requires the reasonable ascertainment of the fact of piratical seizure or of the commission of piratical acts under the law of nations, in the case of each vessel. . . .

" Under all the circumstances, I am constrained to reaffirm the position heretofore announced on behalf of this Government, that the Colombian decree declaring certain vessels in the service of the insurgents to be pirates can not be recognized by the United States as importing international effects."

> Mr. Bayard, Sec. of State, to Mr. Becerra, Colombian min., June 15, 1885, For. Rel. 1885, 272, 273.
>
> In a letter to the Secretary of the Navy, April 15, 1885, it is stated that the incident of the Spanish iron-clads is related in despatches from Commodore C. H. Wells, U. S. S. *Shenandoah*, who was on the Mediterrean coast at the time. The letter contains the following state-

ment: "Certain Spanish iron-clads, then captured by the insurgents and sent out by them to hostilize the loyal towns on the coast, were declared pirates by the Government of the Republic, and their capture invited. A German iron-clad, the Friederich-Karl, took one of the revolted vessels. The German courts refused to declare the vessels lawful prize, and the Imperial Government disavowed the act of its commander and punished him. Under similar circumstances now, it is quite certain that no prize court of the United States could legitimatize the taking of one of the so-called piratical insurgent vessels of Colombia engaged in the attack on Cartagena; and any naval commander of the United States who might do such an act (except in self-defense if piratically attacked) would thereby directly intervene in the domestic strife in Colombia, which would be unauthorized." (Mr. Bayard, Sec. of State, to Mr. Whitney, Sec. of Navy, April 15, 1885, 155 MS. Dom. Let. 101.)

" In paragraph 18 of the twentieth chapter of the regulations for the government of the Navy, occurs the following clause:

" ' If any vessel shall be taken acting as a vessel of war or a privateer without having a proper commission so to act, the officers and crew shall be considered as pirates and treated accordingly.'

" It is stated that it was under this clause that the capture, by the United States vessel *Alliance*, of the *Ambrose Light*, a cruiser commissioned by the insurrectionary party now possessing the ports of the United States of Colombia was justified.

" It is proper for me to state that, in the view of this Department, two conditions are essential to constitute piracy.

" (1)· As piracy is ' robbery on the high seas ' there must, to constitute it, be the *animus furandi.*

(2) There must be hostility to seafaring vessels irrespective of nationality. This position was taken and, I believe, without dispute, by Judge Nelson, in the case of certain Confederate privateer's men, tried in New York, in 1861, where he told the jury that ' if it were necessary, on the part of the Government, to bring the crime charged ' ' against the prisoners within the definition of robbery and piracy, as known to the common law of nations, there would be great difficulty in so doing, perhaps upon the counts, certainly upon the evidence. For that shows, if anything, an intent to depredate upon the vessels and property of one nation only, the United States, which falls far short of the spirit and intent that are said to constitute essential elements of the crime.'

" I beg to submit to your consideration how far the article above quoted conflicts with the view as just expressed."

Mr. Bayard, Sec. of State, to Sec. of Navy, July 14, 1885, 156 MS. Dom. Let. 691.

" Pending these occurrences a question of much importance was presented by decrees of the Colombian Government, proclaiming the closure of certain ports then in the hands of the insurgents, and declaring vessels held by the revolutionists to be piratical and liable to capture by any power. To neither of these propositions could the United States assent. An effective closure of ports not in the possession of the government, but held by hostile partisans, could not be recognized; neither could the vessels of insurgents against the legitimate sovereignty be deemed *hostes humani generis* within the precepts of international law, whatever might be the definition and penalty of their acts under the municipal law of the state against whose authority they were in revolt. The denial by this Government of the Colombian propositions did not, however, imply the admission of a belligerent status on the part of the insurgents."

> President Cleveland, annual message, Dec. 8, 1885, For. Rel. 1885, v.
>
> That vessels sent from foreign ports by insurgents having no ports of their own are pirates is argued by Mr. Seward, Sec. of State, to Mr. Dayton, Nov. 21, 1863, Dip. Cor. 1863, II. 734, in relation to the cases of the Confederate cruisers *Florida* and *Georgia*.

April 24, 1885, Commander Clarke, of the U. S. S. *Alliance*, seized on the high seas, in the Caribbean Sea, about 20 miles

Case of the "Ambrose Light." westward of Cartagena, in Colombia, the brigantine *Ambrose Light*. The brigantine, when first sighted, was flying a strange flag, namely, a red cross on a white ground, but she afterwards exhibited the Colombian flag. On examination it was found that she had on board a number of armed soldiers, one cannon, and a considerable quantity of shot, shells and ammunition. She bore a commission from the governor of the province of Barranquilla, State of Bolivar, Colombia, where an insurrection then prevailed, purporting to authorize her to " navigate as a Colombian vessel-of-war in the waters touching the coast of this republic, in the Atlantic ocean." Commander Clarke, considering this commission to be irregular, sent the brigantine to New York for adjudication, and a libel was filed to procure her condemnation as a pirate. The proof showed that she was owned by one of the military leaders of the insurgents at Barranquilla, and that she was " engaged upon a hostile expedition against Cartagena, and designed to assist in the blockade and siege of that port by the rebels." It appears that she had left Sabanilla April 20, bound for Baru, near Cartagena, where the soldiers on board were disembarked, and that her instructions were " to fight any Colombian vessel " not showing the white flag with a red cross. It is stated that the proofs " did not show that any other depredations or hostilities were intended by the vessel than such as might be incident to the struggle between the insurgents and the government of Colombia, and to the so-called blockade and siege of Cartagena; " but the statement that the brigantine, when seized, was

engaged in conveying soldiers to Baru, near Cartagena, seems sufficiently to show that she was not then engaged in an actual attempt to
blockade the latter port. It was held that there was probable cause
for the seizure, but that the vessel should not be condemned, there
having been, as the court maintained, an implied recognition by the
United States of the belligerency of the Colombian insurgents.

With reference to the question of piracy, the court, Brown, J., took
the ground "that the liability of the vessel to seizure, as piratical,
turns wholly upon the question whether the insurgents had or had
not obtained any previous recognition of belligerent rights, either
from their own government or from the political or executive department of any other nation; and that, in the absence of recognition by
any government whatever, the tribunals of other nations must hold
such expeditions as this to be technically piratical; . . . that . . .
insurgents that send out vessels of war are, in legal contemplation, merely combinations of private persons engaged in unlawful
depredations on the high seas; that they are civilly and criminally
responsible in the tribunals for all their acts of violence; that in
blockading ports which all nations are entitled to enter, they attack
the rights of all mankind, and menace with destruction the lives and
property of all who resist their unlawful acts; that such acts are
therefore piratical, and entitle the ships and tribunals of every nation
whose interests are attacked or menaced, to suppress, at their discretion, such unauthorized warfare by the seizure and confiscation of
the vessels engaged in it." In conclusion, the court held that, in the
absence of any recognition of rebel belligerency or of an existing
state of war in Colombia, the commission of the *Ambrose Light* as a
vessel of war was, in international law, unauthorized and void; that
her seizure as a pirate was technically authorized by the law of
nations; but that the implied recognition which was held to have been
given of an existing state of war prevented condemnation, and that,
as the seizure was lawful at the time, the release of the vessel should
be ordered on payment of the disbursements of the proceeding.

　　The Ambrose Light (1885), 25 Fed. Rep. 408.
　　"He [Judge Brown] holds that the capture [of the *Ambrose Light*] at the
　　　time thereof was proper, but that by the letter of Mr. Bayard to Mr.
　　　Becerra of April 24, in which Mr. Bayard refused to admit that the
　　　ports held by the insurgents could be closed to commerce by a decree
　　　of the established government without an efficient blockade, and that
　　　this Government would not treat as pirates vessels and their crews
　　　engaged in operations against the established government, the United
　　　States had impliedly recognized a state of war and had given to the
　　　de facto government belligerent rights. . . . As the terms of the
　　　note . . . evidently do not justify the inference of Judge Brown that
　　　this Government had even impliedly recognized the *de facto* govern-
　　　ment named as possessed of belligerent rights, I have the honor to
　　　enclose herewith a copy of observations in the premises, made by

the law officer of the Department, the propriety of which appears to
me very clear." (Mr. Bayard, Sec. of State, to Mr. Garland, Atty.-
Gen., July 15, 1885, 156 MS. Dom. Let. 263. See, also, a subsequent
letter of Mr. Porter, Acting Sec. of State, to Mr. Garland, in the same
sense, Jan. 5, 1886, 158 MS. Dom. Let. 356; Mr. Bayard, Sec. of State,
to Mr. Garland, Feb. 25, 1886, 159 MS. Dom. Let. 163.)

" When we are notified, as we were in the present case, by a foreign
sovereign that an armed insurrection is in existence within his
domains, the fact is one of which we are bound to take notice. We
can not, it is true, give such insurgents hospitality in our ports; nor
do we release their titular sovereign, as we would do in case we
recognized their belligerency, from responsibility for their acts. But
while such is the case, we respond to such an announcement by applying to him and to them the rule of non-intervention in foreign disturbances on which our whole system of extraterritorial policy rests. . . .
We recognize foreign insurgency by refusing to send our military
and naval forces to attack its armies or its fleets, and by refusing
to deliver up those concerned in it when they take refuge on our
shores.

" We say in such cases to the titular government, whether it be
despotic or liberal, ' We can not intervene to fight your battles,
either on land or at sea; neither will we surrender political fugitives
who have escaped from you to our ships or our shores.' But a recognition of foreign belligerency is a very different thing. It is never
determined on until an insurrection has obtained permanency, and
stands on something like settled parity with the government it assails.
Such a recognition is announced by a proclamation of neutrality, and
is followed by placing insurgent and titular governments on the
same terms of access to the ports of the sovereign by whom the proclamation has been issued. Hence while in very many cases we have
recognized foreign insurgencies, we have never recognized such insurgencies as belligerent until they have shown themselves, by long and
enduring exhibition of strength, to be on something like a parity
with the state against which they revolt. The government of the
United States unquestionably recognized the *insurgency* of the forces
arrayed in April last against the Columbian titular government.
But it expressly declares that it did not recognize their *belligerency.* . . .

" I wish now to inquire what is the definition of piracy to be drawn
from those who may really be considered standard authors in international law. It so happens that I have before me letters on this topic
from Mr. Fiore, professor of international law at Naples; from Mr.
Westlake; from M. Martens, professor of international law at St.
Petersburg; from Baron de Neumann, professor of international law
at Vienna, and member of the Austrian House of Peers; and from

M. Calvo, Argentine minister at Berlin.   These gentlemen are all of
them authors of high standing in international law, and are leading
members of the Institute of International Law, in which I have the
honor to be one of their associates.   I sent them the note of Mr.
Bayard to Mr. Becerra shortly after it was made public, and as
is not unusual among the members of the institute, some of them
were good enough to favor me with replies, written, I need scarcely
say, some time before Judge Brown's decision was made known.   In
these replies the distinctions taken in Mr. Bayard's note are unequiv-
ocally sustained.   From M. Calvo's letter of June 5 last (and I
believe I could cite no higher authority) I quote the following:

" ' The government, the tranquillity and the existence of which are
imperilled by rebellion, is sovereign, as no one denies, in punishing
and repelling by all the forces it possesses the attacks directed against
it; but it does not suffice that it should attach to these attacks the
title of piracy, in order that the rebellion should be transformed, *ipso
facto*, as regards foreign states, into a crime against the law of
nations, punishable as such; these states can, at most, look on these
acts as those of belligerents, especially if the rebellion is prolonged,
assumes a serious form, and partakes clearly of the character of civil
war.   If the rebel ships do not limit themselves to attacking the
government or the forces of the government against which they have
rebelled, but commit acts of hostility or of damage against the ships
of other nations, these nations have then the right to obtain direct
satisfaction by seizing them and inflicting the customary punishment
on them, in conformity with the law of nations, or indirect, by hand-
ing them over to the government whose allegiance they have thrown
off by rebellion.   It is then from this government that the reparation
is to be expected, which we have the right to ask for the wrong done,
or the injury experienced.   The note of Mr. Bayard of April 24,
1885, is one precedent more in favor of the liberal doctrines which
are becoming more and more pronounced regarding the important
question of blockade, and the diminution of the rights of belligerents
in reference to those of neutrals, and to the liberty of intercourse and
of navigation; and a tribute is due to the Government of Washington that it has constantly and faithfully taken the side of progress
in this respect whenever it has found an opportunity.' . . .

" The works of the authors of which I speak are of the highest
rank among such standards, and . . . the letters of the authors are
the best interpreters of what their works say.   But I pass these to take
up two other authorities whom I select, because they undertake
rather to give the sense of international jurists as a body rather than
their own distinctive views.

"The first is Holzendorff in his Encyklopädie der Rechtswissenschaft, a work of singular accuracy and fullness. In this work we have the following:

"'*See-raub* (piraterie, piracy), ein Verbrechen, bestehend in dem räuberish gewaltsamen Angriff gegen Handelsschiffe auf hoher See.' Translating literally, this makes 'sea-robbery,' and the very title is significant, to consist in a forcible attack for purposes of robbery on merchant vessels on the high seas. He goes on to say that the offense is a crime by the law of nations; that the 'sea-robber' is *hostis humani generis,* who may be tried in any state into which he may be brought, and when caught in the act, may be forthwith killed by the captor.

"Among the admirable qualities of the late Sir R. Phillimore not the least distinguished was the patient impartiality with which he collected the sense of that branch of the profession of which for years he was the leading English representative. And Sir R. Phillimore (1 Int. Law, 411) gives the following definition: 'Piracy,' he says, 'is an assault upon vessels navigated on the high seas committed *animo furandi,* whether the robbery or forcible depredation be effected or not, and whether or not it be accompanied by murder or personal injury.' He proceeds to quote Judge Story's statement in U. S. *v.* Smith (5 Wheat. 163), that 'whatever may be the diversity of definitions in other respects, all writers concur in holding that robbery or forcible depredations upon the sea, *animo furandi,* is piracy.' He cites further a ruling of 'the judge of the vice-admiralty court at Charleston, S. C., in 1718, that piracy is a robbery committed on the sea, and a pirate is a sea-thief.' He shows also that the ruling of Dr. Lushington, in the case of the Magellan pirates (10 Jurist, 1165) was based, not on the position that the offenders in question were insurgents who had not been recognized as belligerents, but on the proof that their depredations were directed against others than their titular sovereign. '*I think it does not follow,*' he quotes Dr. Lushington, in giving his judgment in that case, as saying, that '*because persons who are rebels and insurgents may commit against the ruling powers of their country acts of violence, they may not be, as well as insurgents and rebels, pirates also; pirates for other acts committed against other persons.*'"

"The same view, it is held, is taken by Perels. (Seerecht, § 127.)

"President Woolsey . . . holds that the Confederate privateers, even from the standpoint of the United States, were not pirates (Int. Law App. 3, note 12 to 4th ed.) ; and in section 137 of the third edition President Woolsey defines piracy in such a way as expressly to exclude acts of war by insurgents against their parent state. The same position was maintained with great ability and learning by the late Mr. W. B. Lawrence, who was a master in this branch of jurisprudence. (Lawrence's Wheaton, 209, 246, 247, 248, 256, and note, furnished by Mr. Lawrence, to Whart. Cr. Law (8th and 9th ed.), § 1861.)

"The definitions of Mr. D. D. Field (Int. Code, 82) and of Sir J. F. Stephen (Dig. Cr. Law, art. 104) expressly exclude attacks by insurgent vessels on their titular sovereign.

"In Hall's International Law, page 223, the law is thus stated:

"'It is generally said that one of the conditions of the piratical character of an act is the absence of authority to do it derived from any sovereign state. Different language would no doubt have been employed if sufficient attention had been earlier given to societies actually independent, though not recognized as sovereign. Most acts which become piratical through being done without due authority are acts of war when done under the authority of a state; and as societies to which belligerent rights have been granted have equal rights with permanently established states for the purposes of war, it need scarcely be said that all acts authorized by them are done under due authority. Whether the same can be said of acts done under the authority of politically organized societies, which are not yet recognized as belligerent, may appear more open to argument, though the conclusion can hardly be different. Such societies being unknown to international law, they have no power to give a legal character to acts of any kind; at first sight, consequently, acts of war done under their authority must seem to be at least technically piratical. But it is by the performance of such acts that independence is established and its existence proved; when done with a certain amount of success, they justify the concession of belligerent privileges; when so done as to show that independence will be permanent, they compel recognition as a state. It is impossible to pretend that acts which are done for the purpose of setting up a legal state of things, and which may in fact have already succeeded in setting it up, are piratical for want of an external recognition of their validity, when the grant of that recognition is properly dependent in the main upon the existence of such a condition of affairs as can only be produced by the very acts in question. It would be absurd to require a claimant to justify his claim by doing acts for which he may be hanged. *Besides, though the absence of the competent authority is the test of piracy, its essence consists in the pursuit of private as contrasted with public ends. Primarily the pirate is a man who satisfies his personal greed or his personal vengeance by robbery or murder in places beyond the jurisdiction of a state. The man who acts with a public object may do like acts to a certain extent, but his moral attitude is different, and the acts themselves will be kept within well-marked bounds. He is not only not the enemy of the human race, but he is the enemy solely of a particular state. . . . The true view, then, would seem to be that acts, which are allowed in war when authorized by a politically organized society, are not piratical. Whether a particular society is or is not politically organized is a question of fact which must be decided upon the circumstances of the case.'* Hall Int. Law, 233 et seq.

" Under Mr. Wheaton's definition, to make cruisers of insurgent governments pirates, ' they must be " depredators." ' That this is all he meant by his ' definition,' is clear when we take in connection with it his reference to United States *v.* Klintock (5 Wheat. 153), where the court, according to Mr. Wheaton's own head-note, declined to decide whether the term ' piracy ' applies to ' a person acting with good faith under such a commission,' *i. e.,* a commission from ' a republic whose existence is unknown and unacknowledged.' Nor can we exclude from considering, as construing Mr. Wheaton's statement in his text-book, the note on piracy in 5 Wheat. 167, to which he refers us; a note which binds Mr. Wheaton, the ostensible author, none the less completely from the fact that it was written for him, as it is now known, by Judge Story. In this admirable note we have a long series of definitions, nearly thirty in number, in all of which the essential feature of piracy is declared to be robbery on the high seas. So, according to this note, speak Grotius, the old Roman jurists, Bynkershoek, Azuni, Bacon, Martens, Rutherforth, Woodeson, Burlamaqui, Calvinus, Bouchard, Bonnemant, Ferriere, the author of the Encyclopedie des Sciences (who define pirates as ' bandits ' of the sea), Valin, Straccha, Beawes, Molloy, Marshall, the author of Viner's Abridgment, Comyn, Coke, Targa, Blackstone, and Hawkins. The definition of Hawkins I here copy, not only because it is the most accurate, but because it has been virtually adopted by Sir J. F. Stephen :

" 'A pirate, at the common law, is a person who commits any of those acts of piracy, robbery, and depredation upon the high seas, which if committed upon land would have amounted to felony there.' And to this the note adds this comment : ' The intention of Hawkins must have been to use the phrase " at common law " in its most comprehensive sense; in which sense the law of nations itself is part of the common law.'

" The conclusions given are as follows :

" 1. We ought not, in cases of insurrections in foreign countries, to acknowledge insurgents as belligerents until the insurrection establishes itself on such a basis of apparent permanency as to put it, at least for a time, on an apparent parity with the parent State. When such a condition of things is manifest, then a proclamation of neutrality should be issued, and the insurgent vessels admitted to the same rights in our ports as are those of the government which they assail.

" 2. We ought not, in any case, to interfere to suppress insurrections in foreign states by attacking either the land or the maritime forces of the insurgents. To do so would be to cast aside that policy of non-interference in foreign systems which we have heretofore followed with scrupulous conscientiousness, would render us in most cases the supporters of despotisms as atrocious as those of Yturbide, of Francia, or of King Bomba, and would, when the interference was attempted on behalf of the weaker South American governments, throw such governments permanently on our hands, and thus subject us to burdens our system could not bear. To this policy of interference there should be but two exceptions. We should interfere to prevent any European power from effecting a new lodgment on this continent. We should interfere also on the isthmus when necessary to carry out our treaty guarantee of free transit. But beyond this our interference can not go. No matter how vehement may be the decrees of foreign governments declaring insurgents to be traitors and pirates, those decrees it should not be for us to execute."

> Dr. Francis Wharton, Solicitor of the Department of State, in the Albany Law Journal, Feb. 13, 1886, 125.

" Belligerency is recognized when a political struggle has attained a certain magnitude and affects the interests of the recognizing power; and in the instance of maritime operations, recognition may be compelled, or the vessels of the insugents, if molesting third parties, may be pursued as pirates. *The Ambrose Light*, 25 Fed. Rep. 408; 3 Whart. Dig. Int. Law, § 381; and authorities cited."

> The Three Friends (1897), 166 U. S. 1, 63.

Where a vessel was libelled for forfeiture under § 5283 R. S., which forbids the fitting out and arming of a vessel in the United States with intent that she shall be employed by any foreign state or people to cruise or commit hostilities against any state or people with which the United States are at peace, it was held that the vessel could not be condemned as piratical on the ground that she was in the employ of an insurgent party which had not been recognized by the United States as a belligerent.

> United States v. The Itata, 56 Fed. Rep. 505, 5 C. C. A. 608, citing United States v. Weed, 5 Wall. 62; The Watchful, 6 Wall. 91.

July 7, 1885, the Venezuelan Government issued a decree denouncing as pirates two steam vessels named *Justicia* **Venezuelan decree, 1885.** *Nacional* and *El Torito*, the latter having previously been called the *Annetta*. The decree stated that the vessels were not registered by any government nor manned in legal form, but were armed by persons in insurrection against the Venezuelan Government, and declared that they were a menace to commerce. In communicating this decree, the Venezuelan minister asked the United States to consider the vessels in question as "beyond the pale of the law," to refuse them fuel and provisions, and to subject them to criminal process if they should come into American jurisdiction. Replying to this request, the Department of State said that, while it was not the purpose of the United States to give aid and comfort to the enemies of Venezuela, the decree could not be admitted to have international force; and in this relation the Department enclosed to the Venezuelan minister a copy of the correspondence with Colombia, and cited Hall's International Law to the effect that "municipal laws extending piracy beyond the limits assigned to it by international custom affect only the subjects of the state enacting them and foreigners doing the forbidden acts within its jurisdiction." The Department of State added:

" It does not follow, however, that because this Government declines to regard the vessels to which you refer as pirates they will be received into the ports of the United States with the same privileges that are accorded to vessels bearing the flags of recognized Governments. Such vessels can not receive in our ports those immunities to which they would be entitled upon an exhibition of proper papers. While taking this position, however, I wish to be understood that it is here assumed with the usual qualification that gives to vessels coming to our ports in distress, even though they be without regular papers, such hospitality as is approved by the law of nations."

> Mr. Bayard, Sec. of State, to Mr. Soteldo, Venezuelan min., July 24, 1885, For. Rel. 1885, 935.

" I transmit herewith, for your information, a copy of a despatch from the United States representative at Port au **Haytian decree, 1889.** Prince, communicating the text of a decree of General Légitime, under date of the 25th ultimo, which purports to declare the steamer *Mercedes* a ' pirate ' and to authorize whom it may concern to seize her and deliver her to the Government of Port au Prince.

" Decrees of this nature, while frequently resorted to, are admitted by the consensus of good authority to be without international effect and incapable of communicating the character of piracy to a vessel which is not in fact a pirate according to the definitions of the law of nations by reason of committing acts of real piracy. An interesting examination of the status of such vessels under a municipal decree of piracy is printed in the volume of Foreign Relations for 1885, pages 272-275, being comprised in a note from Mr. Bayard to Mr. Becerra, then the Colombian minister at this capital.

"As the decree does not concern any American interest, so far as known, and imposes no obligation whatever upon this Government to recognize the status it assumes to create, or to treat the *Mercedes* on any other footing than is required by the rules of international law, there seems to be no occasion for instructing the representative of the United States at Port au Prince on the subject."

> Mr. Blaine, Sec. of State, to Sec. of Navy, May 17, 1889, 173 MS. Dom. Let. 115, enclosing copy of a dispatch of Mr. Thompson, min. to Hayti, No. 224, D. S., April 29, 1889.
>
> The substance of the foregoing letter was embodied in an instruction to Mr. Thompson. (Mr. Blaine, Sec. of State, to Mr. Thompson, min. to Hayti, May 17, 1889, MS. Inst. Hayti, III. 65.)

5. REVOLUTION IN CHILE, 1891.

§ 333.

In 1891 a revolution took place in Chile, growing out of a controversy between President Balmaceda and the Congress as to the power of the former to maintain in office a cabinet upon which Congressional censure had been pronounced. Under the Chilean constitution of 1833 the President possessed the power to appoint and remove public officials; but it had been the practice for the ministry, on a vote of censure by Congress, to resign. This custom President Balmaceda essayed to break. On the night of January 6, 1891, a number of the leaders of the opposition, including the vice-president of the Senate and the president of the Chamber of Deputies, went on board the national fleet lying at Valparaiso, and in the name of the Congress proclaimed a revolution. The ships taking part in the movement were the *Blanco Encalada*, *Almirante Cochrane*, *Esmeralda*, *Huascar*, *O'Higgins*, and *Magellanes*, the command of which when they revolted was assumed by Capt. Jorge Montt, of the Chilean navy.

In a report to the Secretary of the Navy, February 9, 1891, Rear-Admiral McCann, U. S. flagship *Pensacola*, stated that the insurgents had seized Chilean coast steamers for use as transports, but had not interfered with foreign steamers; that merchant vessels were asked for supplies, which were refused in order not to incur trouble with the shore authorities; that the insurgent ships were stationed off the port for observation rather than blockade, vessels being allowed to pass in and out freely; but that in some instances lighters loaded with supplies had been taken from alongside merchant steamers.

March 26, 1891, Mr. Tracy, Secretary of the Navy, gave to Rear-Admiral Brown, who had been sent out to relieve Rear-Admiral McCann, the following instructions:

" (1) To abstain from any proceedings which shall be in the nature of assistance to either party in the present disturbance, or from which sympathy with either party could be inferred.

"(2) In reference to the ships which have been declared outlawed by the Chilean Government, if such ships attempt to commit injuries or depredations upon the persons or property of Americans, you are authorized and directed to interfere in whatever way may be deemed necessary to prevent such acts; but you are not to interfere except for the protection of the lives or property of American citizens.

"(3) Vessels or other property belonging to our citizens which may have been seized by the insurgents upon the high seas and for which no just settlement or compensation has been made are liable to forcible recovery; but the facts should be ascertained before proceeding to extreme measures and all effort made to avoid such measures.

"(4) Should the bombardment of any place, by which the lives or property of Americans may be endangered, be attempted or threatened by such ships, you will, if and when your force is sufficient for the purpose, require them to refrain from bombarding the place until sufficient time has been allowed for placing American life and property in safety.

" You will enforce this demand if it is refused, and if it is granted, proceed to give effect to the measures necessary for the security of such life or property. . . .

" 6th. Referring to paragraph 18, page 137, of the Navy Regulations of 1876, which is as follows:

" 'If any vessel shall be taken acting as a vessel of war or a privateer without having proper commission so to act, the officers and crew shall be considered as pirates and treated accordingly.'

" You are informed that this paragraph does not refer to vessels acting in the interests of insurgents and directing their hostilities solely against the state whose authority they have disputed. It is only when such vessels commit piratical acts that they are to be treated as pirates, and unless their acts are of such a character or are directed against the persons or property of Americans you are not authorized to interfere with them.

" 7th. In all cases where it becomes necessary to take forcible measures, force will only be used as a last resort, and then only to the extent which is necessary to effect the object in view."

Mr. Tracy, Sec. of Navy, to Rear-Admiral Brown, U. S. N., March 26, 1891, H. Ex. Doc. 91, 52 Cong. 1 sess. 245–246.

As to the origin of the revolution, see H. Ex. Doc. 91, 52 Cong. 1 sess. 2–3.

For Rear-Admiral McCann's report of Feb. 9, 1891, see id. 234. A fuller report of the acts of the insurgent fleet may be found in the correspondence of the British Government, under whose supervision the commercial and shipping interests of the country, being largely in English hands, immediately fell. Questions were raised (1) as to blockade, (2) as to seizures of coal and other cargoes, and (3) as to the payment of duties.

Questions of blockade.—When the revolution was announced, the British naval forces in Chile were instructed by the Admiralty to "take no part except protection of British interests." [a] Early in the conflict, the Congressional deputation on the insurgent fleet notified the Government authorities and the foreign representatives that Iquique and Valparaiso would be blockaded on February 1, 1891. The Government declared that the blockade would be illegal, and urged the diplomatic corps to protest against it. At the request of the minister for foreign affairs, the diplomatic representatives of France, Germany, Great Britain, and the United States met at the foreign office to discuss the subject. On consulting they agreed that the blockade would be illegal, but that they could not directly protest against it, as this would involve a recognition of the insurgent fleet, which the Government had declared to be piratical. As a compromise they instructed the consuls to protest at their respective ports. A protest was made by the consular body at Iquique, January 18, 1891, to the captain of the *Almirante Cochrane* as follows: "The consular body being of opinion that the blockade notified to them will cause considerable damage to the persons and property of neutrals represented by them, protest against the act, and reserve the right to claim compensation for losses incurred." A similar protest was made by the consular corps at Valparaiso.[b]

At the same time Mr. Kennedy, then British minister at Santiago, telegraphed for instructions as to the course which should be pursued in the event of a blockade being established. The views of the foreign office on the subject may be found in a telegram to a firm in Glasgow, January 24, 1891, as follows: "Assuming effective blockade to exist, escort through it can not be given." [c]

In consequence of certain incidents the original notice was changed by the insurgents and it was announced that a blockade of Valparaiso would begin on the 18th of January, and of Iquique on the 20th of the same month. In reality neither blockade was actually established. Captain St. Clair, of H. B. M. S. *Champion*, expressed the belief that the nonenforcement of the blockade at Valparaiso was the

[a] Blue Book, Chile, No. 1 (1892), 2.

[b] Blue Book, 25–41. "These ships were formally commissioned by the Republic of Chile, but their officers and crews had, at the time they claimed to be a blockading force, thrown off their allegiance to that Republic, the Government of which was still in possession on land, and they had not been commissioned afresh by any state or recognized belligerent. It would appear, therefore, that the *status* of these armed vessels was simply that of pirates, and it is obvious that if such was the aspect which they presented to the diplomatic representatives accredited to the Chilean Government, those representatives could not possibly recognize the alleged blockade as having any validity in international law. This appears to us to be the probable ground of the action of the diplomatic body in Chile, and on the facts, as we understand them, quite independently of any possible question as to the sufficiency of the force for the alleged blockade, we do not see that any other course could consistently have been taken. And the action of the diplomatic body on this occasion would seem to have been both consonant with the principles of international law, and most favourable to the early restoration of peace to a disturbed country." (Law Mag. & Rev., Feb. 1891, 4th series, XVI. 174.)

[c] Blue Book, 8.

result of an interview which he held with Captain Montt, January
16, 1891, on board the *Blanco Encalada* at that port, and in which
he pointed out " the illegality of any captures he might make." [a]

It appears that when Captain St. Clair, on the 20th of January, delivered
to the commander of the *O'Higgins* the protest of the consular corps
against the proposed blockade of Valparaiso, he was assured that
only vessels carrying contraband of war would be interfered with.[b]

Rear-Admiral Hotham arrived at Iquique in H. B. M. S. *Warspite*, January 26, 1891. He found the *Almirante Cochrane* "blockading" the
port. She saluted his flag with 13 guns, "and," said Admiral
Hotham, " as it was a personal salute I returned it with the same
number." The blockade was merely nominal. The *Almirante Cochrane* permitted free access to the shore by British vessels, and also
allowed the mails, after examination, to be landed, and in some cases
passengers from English steamers.[c]

Admiral Hotham arrived at Valparaiso January 31. There were then no
Chilean men-of-war in the harbor, and vessels were going in and out
and loading as usual. On the night of February 1 a man-of-war was
seen in the " offing, showing a searchlight." Next day the *Esmeralda*
and two transports were observed some distance off the harbor and
later were seen by a British man-of-war 25 miles away standing to
the northward. The British steamer *Arica* arrived February 2, and
reported that she had been stopped off the port by an officer from the
Esmeralda, who took out of her some dispatches for the Government
authorities and searched the ship, but did not interfere with any
other mails.

Seizures of coal and other cargoes.—As to seizures of coal and other cargoes, it appears that early in January, 1891, Captain St. Clair
asked of the Congressionalists an assurance that neutral property
would not be interfered with in its transit from ship to shore or shore
to ship. Captain Montt replied that until the blockade should be
established free transit would be allowed to all foreign merchandise
not contraband of war.[b]

The British steamer *Arica*, on her arrival at Valparaiso on the 2d of
February, reported that on January 21 she was boarded 6 miles from
land by an officer from the insurgent transport *Cachapoal* and was
ordered not to go to certain ports to which she was bound, but to go
to Pisagua. The master protested, but had to go. On his arrival
there the captain of the insurgent ship *Magellanes* ordered him to
deliver up his cargo of bullocks. He protested, but, on the advice
of the British consul, delivered up the cattle and obtained a receipt
for them. He was then ordered to go to Coquimbo to get more
bullocks. He declined to comply with this demand and declared
that he would, on his arrival at Coquimbo, place himself under the
protection of H. B. M. S. *Acorn*. On hearing of the incident, Admiral Hotham dispatched Captain St. Clair in the *Champion* with
a letter to Captain Montt denouncing the act of the commander of
the *Magellanes* as " a piece of presumption " inconsistent with assurances given to Captain St. Clair, and requesting Captain Montt
to convey to his officers " the necessity of the discontinuance of such
proceedings." [d]

---

a Blue Book, 41.   *b* Blue Book, 47–50.   *c* Blue Book, 45.   *d* Blue Book, 45–47.

Early in February, 1891, the insurgent fleet sought to take coal from certain English and German ships and send it to Iquique. A guard from a British man-of-war was placed on board each of the British ships and a protest made to the commander of the Chilean squadron. The latter accepted the protest as to the British ships, but proceeded to coal from the German collier *Rajah*, which was towed out to sea. Admiral Hotham gave notice that he was charged with the protection of German, French, and Italian vessels as well as of British, and that he desired to impress upon the commander of the squadron " the absolute necessity of the ships of war under your orders refraining from any interference with the merchant vessels of the above-named nations trading with a friendly power. Cargoes of coal, provisions, etc., *bona fide* consigned to noncombatants, can not be considered as contraband of war ; and any seizure or detention of vessels carrying such cargoes is a gross breach of their neutral rights." It appears that besides the *Rajah*, a British collier, the *Kilmorey*, was seized by a Chinese transport under the orders of the *Esmeralda*. Admiral Hotham sent for the master of the *Kilmorey* and an arrangement was made with the insurgent fleet to purchase the coal on terms with which the master expressed himself as satisfied. Captain Montt offered in satisfaction of the seizure of the *Rajah* and *Kilmorey* (1) a salute of 21 guns to the English and German flags, and (2) a promise of indemnity for any damages which either the ships or the consignees of the cargoes might have sustained in consequence of the seizure. This offer was accepted by Admiral Hotham and the incident treated as closed. The ships on arriving at Iquique were fully compensated.[a]

February 17, 1891, Mr. Kennedy wrote to Lord Salisbury that the operations of the insurgent fleet up to that time had been limited to attempted landings on the coast, to the stoppage on the high seas of neutral ships chiefly for purposes of information, and to the seizure in various ports of launches laden with coal or provisions. For these articles payment had been made or promised and no serious complaint had reached him of violent acts committed against British shipping.[b]

April 10, 1891, the foreign office sent to the Admiralty a draft of a telegram to Admiral Hotham, drawn up in consultation with the law offices of the Crown, saying :

" Information has also been received that the Congressional party threaten that if steamers omit to call at the ports at which they usually touch such omission will be considered a hostile act, and will render them liable to be seized. You should state to the heads of the party that their right to dictate to British vessels which ports they shall visit can not be admitted by Her Majesty's Government, and that you have received instructions to protect such vessels from molestation on this account if necessary."[c]

Payment of duties.—Various questions arose as to the payment of duties, especially on the exportation of nitrates, in consequence of the claim of the Government to exercise authority over ports and places of which the insurgents, in the progress of the revolution, obtained possession. The British foreign office at first declined to take the responsibility of advising merchants as to the course they should

---

[a] Blue Book, 13, 59–62, 73, 113.   [b] Blue Book, 51–52.   [c] Blue Book, 70.

pursue, but suggested that if duties were exacted by insurgent authorities in actual possession, payment should be made on compulsion and under protest, and, better still, that a bond should be given for the amount if the insurgent authorities would accept it. On the other hand, it was declared that Her Majesty's Government did not admit the right of the Chilean Government to require the payment over again of duties when there was evidence that they had already been paid on compulsion and under protest to the authorities in actual and complete possession of the port of export. Should the claim be persisted in, a bond might be given for the amount pending a settlement between the two Governments.[a]

In June, 1891, a gunboat belonging to the Balmaceda Government entered the port of Tocopilla, then in possession of the insurgents, and exacted payment of duty on 1,600 tons of nitrate loading for a British company on the British steamship *Chepica*. The foreign office advised that if the Congressional authorities insisted on the payment of any further and separate duties, as a condition of the vessel's leaving the port, the best course would be to give a bond for the amount of such duties under protest. At the same time Mr. Kennedy was instructed that in the opinion of Her Majesty's Government the action of the gunboat in exacting duties was "altogether wrongful and irregular, such dues being ordinarily and properly payable to the Customs authorities at the port of clearance," and that the amount exacted would be claimed back from the Chilean Government. On arriving at the port Captain Parr, of H. B. M. S. *Melpomene*, found that the payment of the duties a second time was claimed by the revolutionary authorities, and that in default of their payment the shipment of the cargo had been stopped. Captain Parr remonstrated with the intendente and requested him to telegraph the provisional government at Iquique for instructions, which he did. The provisional government replied that "solely out of deference to the Comandante of the *Melpomene*, and as an act of respect to the British navy," they would accept payment of the duties in drafts on London, at ninety days' sight, thus giving the company four months and a half grace, as the term of the drafts would not begin to run till they were accepted. On receipt of this reply the manager of the nitrate firm agreed to sign the drafts as required.[b]

By this review it appears—

1. That the British Government admitted the right of the insurgents to establish a blockade on the usual condition of effectiveness.

2. That the British naval officers recognized the right of the insurgents to intercept contraband of war, and allowed them to a limited extent, but not as of right, to obtain coal and supplies for their fleet from neutral vessels.

3. That the right to collect duties was acknowledged to belong to the insurgents wherever they maintained complete and effective possession of the place.

---

[a] Blue Book, 69, 71, 75.   [b] Blue Book, 144, 157, 219–220.

6. NAVAL REVOLT IN BRAZIL, 1893-94.

§ 334.

" Under date of the 5th instant Captain Picking reports the effective fortification and armament of strategic positions within the limits of the city, adding that the naval commanders in conference had thereupon agreed that in view of this action they could no longer maintain their intention to prevent bombardment. The facts reported appear to justify this conclusion.

" An actual condition of hostilities existing, this Government has no desire to intervene to restrict the operations of either party at the expense of its effective conduct of systematic measures against the other. Our principal and obvious duty, apart from neutrality, is to guard against needless or illegitimate interference, by either hostile party, with the innocent and legitimate neutral interests of our citizens. Interruption of their commerce can be respected as a matter of right only when it takes one of two shapes—either by so conducting offensive and defensive operations as to make it impossible to carry on commerce in the line of regular fire, or by resort to the expedient of an announced and effective blockade.

" Vexatious interference with foreign merchant shipping, at a designated anchorage, or with the lighterage of neutral goods between such anchorage and a designated landing, by random firing not necessary to a regular plan of hostilities and having no other apparent object than the molestation of such commerce, is as illegitimate as it is intolerable. Hence, we have a right to expect and insist that safe anchorage and time and place for loading and unloading be designated, if practicable, to be interrupted only by notice of actual intention to bombard, or by notification and effective enforcement of blockade.

" The insurgents have not been recognized as belligerents, and should they announce a blockade of the port of Rio the sole test of its validity will be their ability to make it effective.

" Our naval commander at Rio has been instructed as above with regard to the protection of neutral commerce under our flag, which it would seem represents only a small part of the foreign commercial interests afloat in the harbor of Rio. The British ships there are said to outnumber those of the United States nine to one, but no substantial interference with our vessels, however few, will be acquiesced in, unless made effective with regard to all foreign shipping, and, moreover, so made effective in pursuance of some tangible plan of orderly military operations."

> Mr. Gresham, Sec. of State, to Mr. Thompson, min. to Brazil, Jan. 11, 1894, For. Rel. 1893, 99. The substance of these instructions may be stated thus:

1. That, an actual condition of hostilities existing, the right of the insurgents to carry on orderly military operations was admitted.

2. That the denial of this right by a foreign power would have constituted an act of intervention, incompatible with neutral duty.

3. That, in view of the creation of fortified and armed strategic positions within the limits of the city, the foreign naval forces would not be justified in forcibly preventing its bombardment.

4. That, while " an announced and effective " blockade, the enforcement of which would necessarily have involved the right to extend operations to the high seas, would be recognized, the insurgents would not be permitted, after they had allowed foreign commerce to enter the port, to seek to accomplish the objects of a blockade either by seizing particular vessels or by firing upon them when they were engaged in discharging or receiving cargo.

It may be superfluous to point out that, if the insurgents had established a blockade, the recognition of it would necessarily have involved the concession to them of belligerent rights. This is obviously what was meant by saying that, as the insurgents had " not been recognized as belligerents," the " sole test " of the " validity " of the blockade, should they announce one, would be " their ability to make it effective." This is precisely the rule that is applied in the case of recognized belligerents, effectiveness being the essential requisite and " sole test " of the validity of their blockades ; and it was intimated that the demonstration by the insurgents of their " ability " actually to enforce a blockade, involving, as the measure does, the assertion of one of the highest rights of public war, would be accepted as satisfactory proof of the justice and propriety of permitting them to exercise such rights.

The antecedents of the instruction of Jan. 11, 1894, and the events that followed, are of sufficient importance to justify a summary of them.

Beginning of the insurrection.—September 6, 1893, Mr. Thompson reported that the navy of Brazil had revolted, assumed complete control over the harbor, and seized all the war vessels, and that it threatened, unless the Vice-President resigned, to bombard the city. The revolted squadron, comprising the war ships *Aquidaban, Jupiter*, and *Republica*, together with a number of Brazilian merchant vessels which had been seized in the harbor, was under the command of Admiral José Custodio de Mello, of the Brazilian navy. The Government held possession of Fort Santa Cruz, which commands the entrance to the harbor, and retained the loyalty of the army. The squadron controlled the inner harbor to within a limited distance of the shore line, which was defended by artillery, infantry, and the police force. Oct. 10, 1893, the Government by proclamation declared the insurgent ships under Admiral Mello to have forfeited the protection of the national flag. (For. Rel. 1893, 45–60, 59–60, 147.)

Question of bombardment.—Toward the end of September much firing took place between the squadron and loyal forts and batteries on shore, and many shots from the ships fell in the city, causing much damage to property and some loss of life, while business houses remained closed because of rumors that the city would be bombarded. Under these circumstances, the commanders of the naval forces of the United States, Great Britain, France, Italy, and Portugal, then present in the harbor, informed Admiral Mello that they would oppose, by force if necessary, an attack upon the city; and the diplomatic representatives of those powers, "continuing in the line of conduct followed up to this time, not to interfere in the internal affairs of Brazil, but to assure the protection and safety of their fellow-countrymen and the higher interests of humanity," urgently requested the Brazilian Government, in view of the action of the foreign commanders, "to deprive Rear-Admiral de Mello of all pretext for hostile action" against the city. In the event of a refusal of this request, they stated that they would communicate the reply to their Governments and ask for instructions.

The Brazilian Government promised to deprive Admiral Mello of every pretext for hostilities against the city; but a misunderstanding immediately arose between the Government on the one hand and the foreign diplomatic and naval officers on the other as to whether this promise included the removal of cannon from some of the batteries and whether the work of strengthening the batteries was not actually continued; and in view of this misunderstanding the diplomatic representatives declared that they could not accept "any other responsibility than that which may result from the necessity of protecting the general interests of humanity and the lives and property of their countrymen."

Question of recognition.—On the 23d of October, 1893, Admiral Mello informed Mr. Thompson, through the officer in command of the United States naval forces, that the insurgents had established a provisional government at Desterro, the capital of the State of Santa Catharina, and asked that they be recognized as belligerents. This request the Government of the United States refused, on the ground that its concession "would be an unfriendly act toward Brazil and a gratuitous demonstration of moral support to the rebellion, the insurgents having not, apparently, up to date established and maintained a political organization which would justify such recognition;" but Mr. Thompson was instructed "to observe, until further advised, the attitude of an indifferent spectator."

Conduct of commercial operations.—On the 30th of October Mr. Thompson inquired by telegraph whether he was "authorized to protect American merchandise placed on Brazilian barges against the insurgents, using force if necessary." He explained that cargoes could not be landed in Rio de Janeiro unless barges were used.

Mr. Gresham, then Secretary of State, replied: "There having been no recognition by United States of the insurgents as belligerants, and there being no pretense that the port of Rio is blockaded, it is clear that if an American ship anchored in the harbor employs barges and lighters in transferring her cargo to the shore in the usual way and in doing so does not cross or otherwise interfere with Mello's line of fire and he seizes or attempts to seize the barges or lighters, he can and should be resisted. You will deliver or send a copy of this instruction to the commander of the insurgents."

December 1, 1893, Admiral Mello left Rio de Janeiro in his flagship, the *Aquidaban*, going south, and was succeeded in the command of the naval forces in the harbor by Rear-Admiral Luis Felippe de Saldanha dà Gama, who, after having maintained an apparent neutrality, announced in a proclamation his espousal of the cause of the revolution and of the restoration of the Empire, subject to ratification by the people.

December 25, 1893, threats of a bombardment having again been made, the commanders of the naval forces of the United States, France, Great Britain, Austria-Hungary, Italy, and Portugal replied that, in case such a measure should become inevitable, they would, while not committing themselves to any course of action, require a previous notice of at least two days to be given in order to insure the safety of the persons and property of their fellow-countrymen.

Meanwhile an effort was made by the foreign representatives to secure a safe place for the discharge of foreign shipping. This action was taken in consequence of an understanding that it was Admiral da Gama's intention to prevent all merchandise from reaching either the custom-house or the shore. November 6, 1893, the American, English, French, German, Italian, and Portuguese naval commanders, by a general communication, had informed Admiral Mello (1) that they did not recognize the right of the insurgent forces to interfere with commercial operations conducted anywhere "except in the actual lines of fire of the batteries of the land fortifications," and that they would protect merchandise not only on board vessels of their respective countries, but also on lighters, barges, and other transports, whatever might be their nationality, employed by those vessels in commercial operations, and (2) that such transports or their tugs would carry at their prow the flag of the country under whose protection they might at the time be. Difficulties and uncertainties, by reason of acts of the Government as well as of the insurgents, having arisen in the interpretation and enforcement of this plan, the question as to what constituted a "line of fire" being shifting and unsettled, Mr. Gresham, January 9, 1894, directed Mr. Thompson "to induce, by cooperation with the commanding officer of the forces of the United States, and if possible with others, the insurgents to designate a place, if such a place can be found, at which vessels of neutral nations may, without interfering with military operations, take and discharge cargoes in safety."

January 12, 1894, Mr. Thompson reported that the insurgents had taken possession of an island in the harbor, used as a coal depot, and with it had captured large quantities of coal belonging to the Royal Mail Steamship Company of England. It seems that Admiral da Gama issued orders to prevent the landing of coal, apparently with the object of preventing the Government from obtaining it for its ships. The subject was discussed by the diplomatic corps; and the British minister, with the concurrence of his Belgian, French, Italian, and Portuguese colleagues, declared that all other means would be exhausted, perhaps even that of recognition, before a resort to force to prevent the execution of the order.

January 12, 1894, Mr. Thompson reported that since the advent of Admiral da Gama several American vessels had gone to the docks on their own responsibility, and with the consent of the Government had discharged and taken in cargo without interference; that some German and other foreign ships had also proceeded with their operations without interruption; and that the Germans had maintained independently the position taken by all the powers in regard to commerce, in the communication to Admiral Mello.

On the 26th of January Mr. Thompson wrote that commercial operations in the harbor continued to be carried on "without any serious interference with American interests." Three days later, however, he telegraphed: "American vessels will be convoyed to the dock by the U. S. S. *Detroit*, and that a general engagement may follow if she is fired upon, as she is ready to return the fire." A telegram having also been received from Admiral Benham, who had succeeded Captain Picking in command of the United States naval force, indicating a serious situation, Mr. Gresham directed Mr. Thompson to make a full report, and particularly to state whether any, and if any what, change had taken place in the attitude of the United States naval force; whether Admiral Benham disagreed with the other naval commanders, and, if so, on what points; whether United States merchant vessels were enjoying any protection not previously given, and "whether a blockade is enforced by the insurgents or any attempt made by them to that end."

Mr. Thompson telegraphed January 31, 1894, the following reply:

"Mr. Thompson telegraphs that he is informed by Admiral Benham, with whom he had an interview on this day, that a full report of his action was sent on the preceding morning to the Navy Department. After notifying the insurgents and the city that he intended to protect by force, if necessary, and to place all American vessels who might wish to go to the docks alongside the wharves, the war vessels of the United States got under way and cleared for action. The *Detroit*, which was stationed in the best position for the ends of protection, had orders to fire back if the merchant vessels were fired upon. A shot from one of the insurgents' vessels was fired at, but missed, the boat of one of the American vessels that was making preparations for hauling in by means of a line running to the shore. The *Detroit* replied with a shot from a 6-pounder, which struck under the insurgent's bows. The latter then fired one shot to leeward from her broadside battery and subsequently another over the merchant vessel. The *Detroit* answered with a musket shot, which struck the sternpost of the insurgent vessel. The latter was hailed by the commander of the *Detroit*, as he passed by, who declared that he would return the fire and sink her, if necessary, in the event of her again firing. By this time one of the American vessels was moored near the dock in her new berth, and a tug came up offering to discharge without cost the cargoes of all the vessels. Notice was then given to the commander of the insurgent forces that the cargoes would be taken out of the vessels in the berths they then occupied, but that it was determined, as theretofore, that if American vessels wished to have berths in the docks they would be placed there and given full protection by the squadron of the United States. The *Detroit* was afterwards withdrawn and the war vessels anchored. He states that the naval or military operations of either side were not in the least interfered with by Admiral Benham, who entertains no such intention. What he proposes to do is to fulfill his duty of protecting the citizens and trade of the United States, and of this the insurgents have been notified by him. Admiral Benham declares that if American vessels get in the line of fire during the actual course of legitimate hostilities they must take the consequences, but their freedom of movement must be respected. The insurgents are denied the right to search neutral vessels or to seize any part of their cargoes, even though such cargoes should comprise such articles as would, in case of war between two independent governments, come within the class of merchandise defined as contraband of war. The insurgents, in their present status, would commit an act of piracy by forcibly seizing such merchandise.

"He adds that, to the best of his information, all the foreign commanders agree with Admiral Benham, and that the effective action of last Monday has restored complete tranquillity, broken the attempted blockade of commerce and trade, and placed everything in even motion."

Mr. Gresham, in acknowledging, on February 1, the receipt of this telegram, said "that Admiral Benham has acted within his instructions."[a]

On the 2nd of February Mr. Thompson telegraphed that the insurgents had "withdrawn their restrictive orders," that ships of all nationalities were "no longer kept from coming to the shore," and that a favorable progress was noticeable in commerce, all of which was due "to the influence of the war vessels of the United States having stopped the insurgents' fire against American merchant vessels."

When Admiral Benham took the action which has been narrated, Mr. Gresham's instructions to Mr. Thompson of the 11th of January had not reached Rio de Janeiro. Those instructions seem, however, to have been intended merely as an amplified and explanatory restatement of the position held by the United States from the beginning; and there is no reason to suppose that Mr. Gresham, when he telegraphed that the Admiral had "acted within his instructions," contemplated any departure from that position. On the contrary, his first inquiry, when advised of a serious situation, was whether any "change" had taken place in the attitude of the United States naval forces, and "whether a blockade is enforced by the insurgents or any attempt made by them to that end." As reported, Admiral Benham's action did not appear to have involved any question as to the right of the insurgents to prevent the supply of contraband of war to their antagonist; but it must be admitted that the intention to deny them such a right was declared in Mr. Thompson's telegram, and it was explicitly announced by Admiral Benham to Admiral da Gama in a letter of January 30, 1894, a copy of which could not, however, have reached Washington in the regular course till the insurrection was practically at an end. With regard to what had taken place, Admiral Benham in that letter said: "In no case have I interfered in the slightest way with the military operations of either side in the contest now going on, nor is it my intention to do so. . . . My duty is to protect Americans and American commerce and this I intend to do to the fullest extent. American vessels must not be interfered with in any way in their movements in going to the wharves or about the harbor, it being understood, however, that they must take the consequences of getting in the line of fire where legitimate hostilities are actually in progress."

[a] "In January last, during the Brazilian insurrection, a large fleet was concentrated in the harbor of Rio de Janeiro. The vigorous action of Rear-Admiral Benham in protecting the personal and commercial rights of our citizens during the disturbed conditions afforded results which will, it is believed, have a far-reaching and wholesome influence whenever in like circumstances it may become necessary for our naval commanders to interfere on behalf of our people in foreign ports." (President Cleveland, annual message, Dec. 3, 1894, For. Rel. xxvii.)

So much as to what had actually been done. Admiral Benham added, however, that there was "another point," of which it might be "well to speak." This was: "Until belligerent rights are accorded you, you have no right to exercise any authority whatever over American ships or property of any kind. You can not search neutral vessels or seize any portion of their cargoes, even though they be within the class which may be clearly defined as contraband of war, during hostilities between two independent Governments. The forcible seizure of any such articles by those under your command would be, in your present status, an act of piracy."

Mr. Thompson, in a telegram of February 1, 1894, stated that as the situation was understood by him Admiral Benham had maintained the same attitude as was from the first assumed by the United States forces, "except perhaps by refusing to recognize da Gama's authority." This statement, read in connection with Admiral Benham's letter to Admiral da Gama, seems to refer, at least inclusively, to the question of preventing the supply of contraband.

When the practical importance of this question is considered, not only from the point of view of the naval officer, but also from that of international relations, the position in which it was left by the record, especially in connection with the instructions to Mr. Thompson of Jan. 11, 1894, can hardly be considered satisfactory. It may be argued that, as the intention to prevent the insurgents from interfering with the supply of contraband articles to the government was clearly declared and not expressly disapproved, it was impliedly approved. On the other hand, it may be argued that, as the question was apparently not involved in the case that had arisen, the approval of what was done does not necessarily imply approval of all that was said; that the question of vexatiously interrupting commerce by firing upon or seizing innocent neutral ships, which is not permissible in any case, and that of preventing the supply of contraband are radically different; that by Mr. Gresham's instructions of January 11, 1894, the right of the insurgents, so far as foreign powers were concerned, to carry on hostilities was expressly recognized, and that this necessarily implied that they might prevent within the national theatre of hostilities the delivery of military supplies, such as arms and munitions of war, to their adversary.

The record being thus inconclusive, it is important to recur to certain elementary principles, which may be stated as follows:

1. The admission that insurgents may, without interference by foreign powers, carry on hostilities against the titular government, and the recognition of them as belligerents are different things and are not interdependent. When we speak of the "recognition" of belligerency, we necessarily imply to some extent the preexistence of the condition of things which we in that form acknowledge. It would not be difficult to cite instances in which insurgents have overthrown the titular government and established one of their own in its place without having received from any foreign power "recognition" as belligerents. Where such a contest exists foreign powers, if they profess to be neutral in the conflict, acknowledge, with or without recognition of belligerency, the duty of noninterference. So clearly is this the case that in recent times the word "insurgency" has found its way into the terminology of law and diplomacy, as a term denoting the existence of a state of domestic hostilities, without recognition of belligerency.

2. The existence of domestic hostilities does not in itself confer upon foreign powers any legal authority within the jurisdiction of the nation within which the insurrection prevails; nor is such authority gained either by conceding or withholding recognition of belligerency. As regards relations with foreign powers, the nonrecognition of belligerency has two results. The first is that the parties to the conflict are denied the right to interfere with neutral vessels on the high seas. There all nations are, in time of peace, equal, none possessing any authority over another; it is only in the abnormal condition of recognized belligerency that authority to interfere with such vessels on the high seas is conceded. The second result is, that the titular government remains presumptively responsible for the redress of injuries done to neutral aliens within the national jurisdiction. Should a foreign government recognize the insurgents as belligerents, it would thereby elect to look to the insurgent authorities for the redress of injuries which they may commit, and would to that extent relieve the titular government. But while responsibility may thus shift from one set of authorities to another, the national sovereignty remains supreme and the national jurisdiction inviolate. Within such jurisdiction foreign powers can set up no claim to equality with the titular sovereign as a ground on which to oppose the exercise by either party of the rights of war. Their right of interference is limited to acts of necessary self-defense, under circumstances such as justify a disregard of the rule of territorial sovereignty. Of these distinctions an apt illustration is afforded by the instructions given in the case of the insurrection in Colombia, in 1885, supra. In that case the assertion of the right of the United States naval forces to recapture the vessels was uniformly limited to the high seas. Although it by no means follows that the Government might not, under different circumstances, have gone further, this limitation is to be particularly noted, since the seizure of the vessels by the insurgents was assumed to have been an act of wrongful violence.

3. In estimating the quality of the act of supplying articles, such as arms and munitions of war, to the parties to an armed conflict, it is necessary to bear in mind what is meant by the statement so often made that the trade in contraband is lawful and not prohibited. This statement, when used with reference to the preventive duties of a neutral government, is quite correct, but if applied to the duties of individuals is quite incorrect. The acts which individuals are forbidden to commit and the acts which neutral governments are obliged to prevent are by no means the same; precisely as the acts which the neutral government is bound to prevent and the acts which it is forbidden itself to commit are by no means the same. The supply of materials of war, such as arms and ammunition, to either party to an armed conflict, although neutral governments are not obliged to prevent it, constitutes, on the part of the individuals who engage in it, a direct military aid to the party to whom the articles are delivered and as such is confessedly an unneutral act. The private citizen undertakes the venture at his own risk, and against this risk his government can not assure him without making itself a party to his unneutral act.

These elementary propositions are abundantly established by authority. (Infra, § 335.)

7. Cases and Opinions, 1899–1902.

§ 335.

February 14, 1899, Mr. Donaldson, United States consul at Managua, telegraphed to Mr. Merry, United States minister to Nicaragua: "The steamer *San Jacinto*, armed for war against the Government of Nicaragua, carries the flag of this Republic without authority, and in conseqeunce I have received an earnest intimation from the Government of Nicaragua that the American vessels of war should detain and disarm it as a vessel without a flag and a filibuster." [a] Mr. Merry replied: "Entirely beyond my control. Naval officer under control Secretary of the Navy for orders." [a] In reporting the case to his Government, Mr. Merry stated that the *San Jacinto* belonged to the Nicaraguan Government, and was stationed at Bluefields, where she was seized by General Reyes' insurgents and taken to San Juan del Norte, where she lay in their possession. Mr. Merry further said: "The suggestion that I shall countenance intervention by the United States naval force in the domestic disturbances of Nicaragua (except as necessary for the protection of the lives or property of our citizens) is inconsistent with the repeated instructions he [the consul] has received in regard to our neutrality obligations. Precisely the same question arose during the prospect of hostilities between Nicaragua and Costa Rica early in 1898. The Government of Salvador, under General Gutierrez, . . . fitted out its steamer *Cuscatlan* with men and war munitions to aid Costa Rica, although Salvador was then a member of the 'Greater Republic of Central America,' jointly with Nicaragua and Honduras. The *Cuscatlan* flew the flag of that 'political corporation,' now the flag of Nicaragua, . . . President Zelaya requested Commander Leutze of the U. S. S. *Alert* to seize the *Cuscatlan* for the same alleged reasons and met with a refusal." [b]

The Department of State replied: "There is not enough shown by your dispatch to justify the intervention of our naval forces. It does not appear that the *San Jacinto* is American property, unlawfully seized by the insurgents. If it were, it could be recaptured for the benefit of its lawful owners on the high seas by our naval force. See Mr. Bayard's instructions to Mr. Scruggs, May 19, 1885, Foreign Relations, 1885, page 211." [c]

---

[a] For. Rel. 1899, 553.

[b] For. Rel. 1899, 552–553.

[c] Mr. Hay, Sec. of State, to Mr. Merry, min. to Nicaragua, March 3, 1899, For. Rel. 1899, 554. See, also, Mr. Hay, Sec. of State, to Sec. of Navy, March 13, 1899, 235 MS. Dom. Let. 416.

September 26, 1899, while an insurrection was in progress in Venezuela, the commander of an American man-of-war, then in Venezuelan waters, addressed to the United States consul at Puerto Cabello a letter, in which he said:

"4. I further request that, in the event of the insurgent forces entering the town, you will immediately point out to the person in command of those forces that the undertaking in which he is engaged, is, in the eyes of international law, a mere act of lawlessness against the established authority of the Republic of Venezuela, and that any injury that he may bring upon the person or property of any foreign noncombatant will be looked upon as outlawry on mankind, and that for all such acts I shall hold him responsible; and it is my intention to employ the United States forces under my command to prevent such lawlessness."

With reference to this statement, the Department of State observed that it did "not appear clearly to discriminate between his unquestionable duty to protect American persons and property from wanton injury by whatever aggressor, as well as to hold responsible whatever party may appropriate or destroy American property for military purposes, and his supposed obligation to treat injury brought by the insurgents upon foreign noncombatant persons or property as 'outlawry on mankind.' It may also be remarked that his concluding declaration that it is his intention to employ the United States forces under his command 'to prevent such lawlessness' is ambiguous, inasmuch as 'such lawlessness' might be supposed to relate back to the initial phrase which defines the insurrectionary undertaking as, in the eyes of international law, 'a mere act of lawlessness against the established authority of the Republic of Venezuela,' and therefore to imply an intention to side with the titular authorities against the insurgents. This would of course be incompatible with the dictates of neutrality, and it is presumed that the commander's true intention was to protect American persons and property and the persons and property of alien neutrals placed under his protection, from any acts of wanton injury, to which end the forces of the United States could in extreme need be rightfully employed."

Mr. Hay, Sec. of State, to Sec. of Navy, Oct. 17, 1899, 240 MS. Dom. Let. 534.

"1. Insurgents not yet recognized as possessing the attributes of full belligerency can not establish a blockade according to the definition of international law.

"2. Insurgents actually having before the port of the state against which they are in insurrection a force sufficient, if belligerency had been recognized, to maintain an international law blockade, may not be materially able to enforce the conditions of a true blockade upon